The Porter Sargent Handbook Series

GUIDE TO
SUMMER PROGRAMS

PUBLISHER'S STATEMENT

Esteemed educational and social critic Porter Sargent established *The Handbook of Private Schools* in 1914, with the aim "to present a comprehensive and composite view of the private school situation as it is today. No attempt has been made at completeness. The effort on the contrary has been to include only the best, drawing the line somewhat above the average."

Today, **The Porter Sargent Handbook Series** continues its founder's mission: to serve parents, educators and others concerned with the independent and critical evaluation of primary and secondary educational options, leading to a suitable choice for each student.

The Handbook of Private Schools, Guide to Summer Programs (1924; formerly the *Guide to Summer Camps and Summer Schools*), *Schools Abroad of Interest to Americans* (1959) and *Guide to Private Special Education* (2011) provide the tools for objective comparison of programs in their respective fields.

GUIDE TO
SUMMER PROGRAMS

AN OBJECTIVE, COMPARATIVE REFERENCE SOURCE
FOR RESIDENTIAL SUMMER PROGRAMS

2012/2013
33rd Edition

PORTER SARGENT HANDBOOKS
A Division of Alloy Education

Editorial Office:
2 LAN Drive, Suite 100
Westford, Massachusetts 01886
Tel: 978-842-2812   Fax: 978-692-2304
info@portersargent.com   www.portersargent.com

PRINTED IN THE UNITED STATES OF AMERICA

ISBN: 978-0-87558-173-6 (cloth)
ISBN: 978-0-87558-174-3 (paper)
ISSN 0072-8705

All information as reported to Porter Sargent Handbooks as of 12/9/2011. Programs and organizations should be contacted for updated information.

Cost: US$27.00 (paper), US$45.00 (cloth) plus shipping and handling. Additional copies are available from booksellers or from the publisher's customer service center: 2 LAN Dr., Ste. 100, Westford, MA 01886. Tel: 978-692-9708. Fax: 978-692-2304. info@portersargent.com.   www.portersargent.com.

TABLE OF CONTENTS

6

SPECIAL-INTEREST PROGRAMS
INDEX BY FOCUS

TRAVEL PROGRAMS
INDEX BY DESTINATION

INSTRUCTIONAL SPORTS PROGRAMS
INDEX BY FOCUS

SPECIAL-NEEDS PROGRAMS
INDEX BY CONDITION ACCEPTED

PREFACE

Now in its 33rd edition, the *Guide to Summer Programs* traces its origin to 1915, when Porter Sargent's *Handbook of Private Schools* included a summer camp section. The popularity of this section led to the first publication of *A Handbook of Summer Camps* in 1924. The book's name changed to the *Guide to Summer Camps and Summer Schools* in the 1950s. Effective with this edition, the *Guide* assumed its current name to reflect the book's ever-increasing roster of academic and special-interest programs. While the breadth of summer options for young people has increased greatly since the publication of the first summer guide, the book's objective remains the same: to assist families, educators and advisors with the summer program selection process.

As is the case with all Porter Sargent Handbooks reference books, the *Guide* is characterized by its objectivity. Summer programs do not subscribe for space, but instead are listed free of charge as a service to both the programs involved and our readership. Our editors compose the listings based upon data provided by administrators on questionnaires. The resulting resource consists of formatted listings that allow for ready program comparison.

Although it does not purport to include every residential summer program in the US, the *Guide* is representative of programs throughout the United States and Canada, as well as travel, study and special-interest opportunities in other countries, and reveals a wealth of diverse and challenging options for boys and girls. Programs designed solely for individuals over age 19 do not appear.

Please note that each program listed in the *Guide* must accept boarders. Many camps and schools also accept day participants, however. In such instances, enrollment information and fees for day clients are detailed.

Please note that programs affiliated with a national organization (such as the Girl Scouts, the Boy Scouts, the YMCA or Camp Fire USA), which were once listed in the *Guide,* are no longer considered suitable for listing. We made this change for the 32nd edition, effectively reinstituting a policy observed in our book prior to the 28th edition, as we feel that these programs typically appeal strictly to local residents and thus are not of interest to the *Guide*'s national audience. Those seeking information on programs affiliated with the aforementioned organizations can find contact information for these and other groups under "Recreation" in the Associations and Organizations section.

The book's objective is to make available comparative facts on summer programs of varying types. Chapters are organized either alphabetically by state name (then by city and program name within each state) or alphabetically by program name, depending upon chapter focus. Please consult the Table of Contents or the individual chapter introductions for details.

Close editorial attention is paid to chapter placement. Program focus receives priority over program location; for example, a language immersion program conducted overseas would be listed in the Academic Programs—Specialized chapter, not in either Academic Programs Abroad (which describes general academic sessions) or Travel Programs. The goal is to lead readers more readily to suitable programs.

Cross-reference indexes precede certain chapters. These indexes make the book easy to use, thereby enabling families and advisors to match child or adolescent with the most appropriate program.

Over the past four editions, we have altered our method of reporting on camps that run concurrent boys' and girls' programs (as opposed to coeducational programs). These coordinate single-gender programs are now listed as "Coord" in the age range. When the boys' and girls' sections have different names, both names appear at the top of the listing.

Religious recreational camps occupy a distinct chapter, Camps with a Religious Focus.

The 33rd edition continues a trend toward more academic programs. These programs, which are usually quite competitive, serve able, academically motivated high school students. Listed in a distinct chapter, internships provide boys and girls with a unique opportunity to work on a project at an accelerated level, often alongside college students and field scholars. Unlike programs listed in other sections of the *Guide,* internships need not necessarily offer boarding. While program administrators generally assist interns with lodging, families may be required to arrange the student's accommodations. Most internships pay a salary or a stipend, however, which helps to defray student expense.

Programs that have been accredited by the American Camp Association (formerly known as the American Camping Association) include an accreditation reference in their editorial listings. The ACA is a community of camp professionals that accredits more than 2400 recreational camps that meet approximately 300 standards pertaining to health, safety and program quality.

Some programs with editorial listings also elect to reserve space in the optional Featured Programs section. Through display ads, schools and camps present what they consider to be their most significant features, unique distinctions and facilities.

Even more complete and meaningful representation is achieved through the objective reporting of facts in the editorial listing combined with a program's individual declaration of purpose contained in Featured Programs. These two accounts, both the listing of statistical and summary information and the attractive illustrated pages, prove to be the broadest basis for parent, advisor or camper to gain insight into the breadth and strength of the various programs.

The publisher does not intend for the *Guide* to be the sole tool of selection for those choosing a summer program; rather, the book should be used as a starting point and a method of narrowing one's search.

In closing, we are pleased to report that the *Guide*'s companion website, www.SummerProgramSearch.com, launched in early 2011. In addition to providing a search tool using the same categories as the *Guide,* the site also provides informative articles and lists educational consultants.

GUIDE TO SUMMER PROGRAMS

Senior Editor	Daniel P. McKeever
Production Manager	Leslie A. Weston
Editor	James S. Martinho

PORTER SARGENT HANDBOOKS
**A division of Alloy Education,
an Alloy Media + Marketing® company**

President & CEO	Joseph F. Moore
Vice President, Publishing	Meghan Dalesandro

Publishers	
1914-1950	Porter E. Sargent
1951-1975	F. Porter Sargent
1976-1999	J. Kathryn Sargent
2000-2007	Cornelia Sargent

HOW TO READ THE
PROGRAM DESCRIPTIONS

Listing arrangement varies by chapter; consult Table of Contents or chapter introductions for details.

1. **PORTER SARGENT SUMMER PROGRAM**
Res — Boys Ages 14-18; Day — Coed 12-18

2. **Downingtown, PA 88888. 1996 Victory Pl. Tel: 123-523-0945. Contact (Sept-May): 2 LAN Dr, Ste 100, Westford, MA 01886. Tel: 978-692-9708. Year-round Toll-free: 800-123-4567, Fax: 978-692-2304. www.portersargent.com E-mail: info@portersargent.com**

3. **Jack Curtin, Lew Bryson & Fred Eckhardt, Dirs. Student Contact: Bryan Antonio, E-mail: bam@portersargent.com.**

4. **Gr 7-PG (younger if qualified). Adm:** Selective. Admitted: 40%. Priority: URM. Prereqs: IQ 100. **Appl**—Fee $50. Due: Rolling. Transcript, rec.

5. **Enr:** 50. **Enr cap:** 50. Intl: 5%. Non-White 10%. **Fac 17.** Profs 12. Col/grad students 3. K-12 staff 1. Specialists 1. **Staff:** Admin 2. Res 5.

6. **Type of instruction:** Enrich SAT/ACT_Prep Study_Skills Undergrad. **Courses:** Eng Comp_Sci Hist Sci Dance Music Painting. **Avg class size:** 10. **Daily hours for:** Classes 4. Study 1. Rec 3. Homework. Tests. **Col Credit:** 3/crse, total 6.

7. **Conditions accepted:** ADD ADHD ED LD NLD. **Therapy:** Psych Speech.

8. **Intl program focus:** Lang Culture. Home stays avail. **Travel:** Europe.

9. **Features:** Eng ESL Expository_Writing Govt Creative_Writing Media Aquatics Farm Riding Rock_Climb Sail Basketball Equestrian Soccer Swim Tennis Track Watersports.

10. **Fees 2012: Res $11,500 (+$750), 5 wks. Day $8600 (+$525), 5 wks.** Aid 2011 (Merit & Need): $72,500.

11. **Housing:** Dorms. Avg per room/unit: 2. **Swimming:** Lake Pool. Campus facilities avail.

12. **Est 1914.** Nonprofit. Roman Catholic. **Spons:** GABF Foundation. **Ses:** 1. **Wks/ ses:** 5. Operates June-Aug. ACA.

13. PSSP provides a selection of review and credit courses six days per week. Pupils, who attend four courses per class day, have options in the disciplines of English, math, science, foreign languages and computer science. Special programs are available in SAT preparation, study skills, American history, computer science and public speaking. A well-balanced recreational schedule supplements academics.

14.

See Also Page 1500

1. PROGRAM NAME and TYPE. Following the program name is participant gender and age range information. "Coordinate" programs conduct concurrent single-gender boys' and girls' sessions.

2. CITY or TOWN, STATE, ZIP CODE, STREET ADDRESS, TELEPHONE, TTY (teletypewriter) and FAX NUMBERS, and WEB SITE and E-MAIL ADDRESSES. Program location and contact information is listed. In many cases, programs have both summer and winter coordinates. If so, summer information appears first, followed by winter data. Whenever possible, the winter address is prefaced parenthetically by the months for which it is in effect; if this information was not furnished by the program, "Winter" appears instead. If only one address, phone or fax number, or E-mail address is present, said contact point is valid year-round. Where available, toll-free phone numbers are listed; they begin with area codes 800, 855, 866, 877 and 888. Be advised that, although toll-free numbers often work throughout the US and Canada, the valid calling area may vary. For this reason, a toll number is listed whenever possible.

3. DIRECTOR. The name of the program head, who often serves as a contact person, is followed by the administrator's job title. Many programs, particularly family-run camps, will list more than one director. When programs have provided a contact for applicants aside from the director, this person's name and E-mail address follow.

4. GRADE RANGE, ADMISSIONS and APPLICATIONS. When applicant grade level is considered, this information follows. Note that grade listings refer to the applicant's grade level in the coming fall. Programs that accept qualified students in lower grades are so indicated. An appraisal of the program's admissions selectivity follows, with programs categorized as "Very selective," "Selective," "Somewhat selective" or "FCFS [first-come, first-served]." The final category is by far the most common, especially among recreational camps. Following are the percentage of applicants admitted, priority admissions policies (with "URM" used to designate enrollment priority for underrepresented minority groups) and prerequisites for admission. Listed next are application particulars: fee, deadline month (or "Rolling" if the application process continues until the session fills) and accompanying materials (e.g., transcript, recommendation).

5. ENROLLMENT, FACULTY and STAFF. The total number of participants enrolled in each session appears here, as does the capacity per session. When available, the percentages of international and non-White participants appear next. Teaching faculty (where appropriate) are listed as a total, then broken down into college professors, college/graduate school students, K-12 teachers and other specialists. Numbers of administrative staff, counselors, residential and special-needs staff follow.

6. TYPE OF INSTRUCTION and COURSES. For academic programs, the focus is indicated and primary courses are listed. If the program offers instruction for students with learning disabilities, either as its main focus or in addition to regular instruction, the services offered are detailed. Average class size and

average daily hours devoted to classes, study and recreation may also appear. Programs featuring homework, tests, grades or some combination are so noted. When credit is available, the number of college credits per course and the maximum available credits per session are shown; high school credit availability is also indicated, but the number of transferable credits granted depends upon the policies of the student's home school. Program accreditation by an outside institution is noted next.

7. CONDITIONS ACCEPTED and THERAPY. Listings of programs described in the chapters devoted to children with learning disabilities and other special needs indicate which conditions the program accommodates. (See Key to Conditions Accepted prior to the Special-Needs Programs chapter.) If the school or camp offers therapy, types of therapy are listed.

8. INTERNATIONAL PROGRAM FOCUS and TRAVEL. For programs that offer travel opportunities or study abroad, an emphasis on academics, language instruction or culture is noted, as is the availability of home stays. The program's destinations, both domestic and abroad, are listed next.

9. CENTRAL FOCUS and FEATURES. Specialized academic and special-interest programs have a focus listed. For all programs, offerings are listed alphabetically in the categories of academics, the arts, special-interest pursuits and sports.

10. FEES. Residential and day fees are provided, with grouped fee figures (for example, $1500-5000) generally indicating the fee span from the shortest to the longest session. The program's estimate of extra expenses incurred by the average participant follows in parentheses. Corresponding length of session appears next. Note that a reference year for listed tuition figure(s) precedes this data. Free sessions may be available to all or to state residents only. Programs that furnish data concerning need- or merit-based financial aid will often include a reference to total aid money provided over the course of a summer.

11. HOUSING and AMENITIES. This section provides information on the lodging option(s) that a program provides. Areas for swimming are listed next. School programs that make all of their campus facilities available to enrolled students are so indicated.

12. ESTABLISHMENT and CALENDAR. The establishment date, religious affiliation, sponsor, number of sessions and weeks per session (often expressed as a range) are cited. The program's months of operation follow. Note that a religious affiliation does not necessarily indicate a strong program emphasis on religion. Recreational camps that stress religion appear in the chapter entitled Camps with a Religious Focus. At the end of this section, programs that have been accredited by the American Camp Association include the designation "ACA."

13. PARAGRAPH DESCRIPTION. Significant aspects of the programs are objectively summarized at the end of the listing. Descriptions, which are written by Porter Sargent Handbooks editors, are based upon questionnaires and supplementary literature submitted by program officials.

14. PAGE CROSS-REFERENCE TO FEATURED PROGRAM. Some programs supply their own appraisals of ideals and objectives separately in the elective Featured Programs section. Page cross-references are appended to the paragraph descriptions of participating programs.

KEY TO ABBREVIATIONS

Commonly accepted abbreviations do not appear on this list. For further clarification, refer to How to Read the Program Descriptions.

ACA	American Camp Association
Accred	Accreditation
Actg	Acting
Adm	Admission(s)
Admin	Administration, Administrator
Adv	Advanced
Amer	American
Anat	Anatomy
Anthro	Anthropology
Appl	Applications
ASL	American Sign Language
Architect	Architecture
Avail	Available
Bio	Biology
Bus	Business
Canoe	Canoeing
Cap	Capacity
Climb	Climbing
Comp	Computer(s)
Coord	Coordinate
Couns	Counselors
Crse	Course
Dev	Development, Developmental
Ed, Educ	Education
Enr	Enrollment
Enrich	Enrichment
Environ	Environmental
ESL	English as a Second Language
FCFS	First-Come, First-Served
Fin	Finance
Geog	Geography
Gr	Grade(s)

Head	Head of Program, Headmaster, Headmistress
Impair	Impairments
Japan	Japanese
Journ	Journalism
JROTC	Junior Reserve Officers' Training Corps
Kayak	Kayaking
PG	Postgraduate
Philos	Philosophy
Phys	Physical
Pol	Political, Politics
Prgm	Program
Profs	Professors
PS	Preschool
Rec	Recreation, Recommendation
Rem	Remedial
Res	Residential, Residents
Sail	Sailing
SAT	Scholastic Aptitude Test
Sculpt	Sculpture
Sem	Semester
Ses	Session(s)
Sociol	Sociology
Speak	Speaking
Spons	Sponsor
Stud	Studies
Swim	Swimming
Tech	Technical, Technology
Theol	Theology
TOEFL	Test of English as a Foreign Language
Trng	Training
Tut	Tutorial, Tutoring
Undergrad	Undergraduates
URM	Underrepresented Minority

FEATURED PROGRAMS

This section is provided as a supplement to the editorial listings. Programs have paid for this space to portray—using their own words and images—their objectives and ideals. Please visit www.SummerProgramSearch.com for Email and Web links to these Featured Programs.

INDEX TO FEATURED PROGRAMS

ASTROCAMP
Guided Discoveries, Inc.
PO Box 1360
Claremont, CA 91711
Tel: 800-645-1423
Fax: 909-625-7305
www.guideddiscoveries.org

AstroCamp in Idyllwild, CA, is a hands-on science camp set in the beautiful surroundings of the San Jacinto Mountains. The facilities and labs are state-of-the-art, offering students (boys and girls ages 8-16) premier equipment for exploring science and the natural world. Students may choose from a wide array of program activities that include astronomy, Mars Expedition, rocketry, rock climbing, mountain biking, extreme science, hiking, robotics, astronaut training, and engineering. AstroCamp also offers students the opportunity to enjoy day and overnight camping trips, campfires, ice cream socials, carnival night, dances, a water slide, and the team-competition Astro-Olympics. AstroCamp's campus features rustic lodge-style buildings that offer students comfortable and spacious dormitory accommodations.

CATALINA SEA CAMP
Guided Discoveries, Inc.
PO Box 1360
Claremont, CA 91711
Tel: 800-645-1423   Fax: 909-625-7305
www.guideddiscoveries.org

Catalina Sea Camp, built around the extraordinary marine and land environments of Catalina Island, strives to provide outdoor education through unparalleled programs and activities, using the latest equipment and techniques in a supportive and fun setting. Located two and a half miles by water from the city of Avalon, CA, Toyon Bay on Catalina Island provides a campus that includes comfortable dormitories, indoor and outdoor dining facilities, aquaria, classrooms, and modern, state-of-the-art laboratories. Campers (boys and girls ages 8-17) choose from among such classes as SCUBA, board sailing, surfing, sailing, marine science, arts & crafts, snorkeling, climbing, leadership, kayaking, and extreme biking. Dive classes range from basic Open Water Certification to Master Diver, and our Toyon Bay Yacht Club can accommodate beginning to advanced sailors. In the evening, campers enjoy such activities as beach parties, outdoor movies, campfires, karaoke, games, and dances.

THE HUN SCHOOL OF PRINCETON
SUMMER ACADEMIC SESSION
176 Edgerstoune Rd., Princeton, NJ 08540
Tel: 609-921-7600   Fax: 609-921-0953
www.hunschool.org

The Summer Academic Session is an extension of our regular year academic program. The courses are designed to reinforce skills, preview work, or provide semester half or full credit in certain material. Small classes, traditional grading standards, and individual attention are hallmarks of the academic program. Courses begin for students entering sixth grade. Residents must be age 13.

A variety of credit and enrichment courses are available. Credit courses are for those wishing to accelerate through their curriculum at their own school. Students may also take credit courses to make up a failing grade. Each rigorous course covers a year's worth of work in five weeks.

A separate program, The American Culture and Language Institute (ACLI), is designed specifically for international students who wish to study English at an American school. Balancing academic classroom work with cultural enrichment, the program offers students an ideal environment to improve their English language skills while learning more about American customs and society.

For residential students, The Hun School is more than academic study in the summer. It is also about finding independence and experiencing new things. The summer resident faculty fosters a strong academic environment with a clear structure, while at the same time creating a sense of home. Living and learning with others enhances personal growth and sets a firm foundation for college and beyond.

Each weekday afternoon, resident students have the opportunity to participate in activities, including such off-campus pursuits as swimming, bowling, mini-golf, or "town permission." Our summer game room includes four large screen, flat-panel TVs, and Ping-Pong and foosball tables. Outside games and tournaments are organized based on student interest. Weekends may include trips to amusement parks, the movies, the New Jersey Shore, Hoagie Haven in Princeton, and sightseeing locations.

Residential 2012 tuition is $5275 for the Academic Session and $6800 for ACLI. For more information, contact Donna O'Sullivan, Director of Summer Programs, at donnaolsullivan@hunschool.org.

PHONE: 941-955-8869 or
800-255-7695 (toll free U.S. only)

WEB: www.ringling.edu/precollege

Prepare for your future
June 24-July 21

2012
PRECOLLEGE
PERSPECTIVE

RINGLING COLLEGE OF ART AND DESIGN

DAVIDSON

It's college, but you don't have to wait.

◆

Three weeks at a top liberal arts college
for rising high school juniors and seniors

June 30–July 21, 2012

**Davidson
July Experience**

www.davidson.edu/JulyExperience

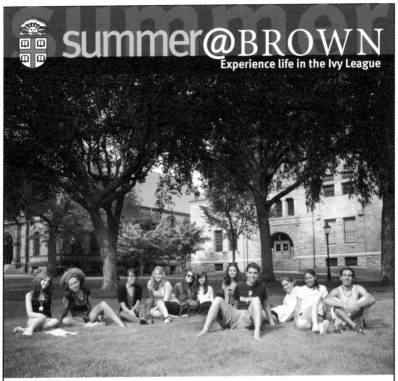

CAMP MI-A-KON-DA
RR # 2, Dunchurch, Ontario,
CANADA, P0A 1G0
Toll free: 877-642-5663   Fax: 905-648-1305
Web: www. miakonda.com   Email: plamont@miakonda.com

Established in 1955, Mi-A-Kon-Da is a summer camp for girls ages 7 to 16 who come from locations across Canada and around the world. Nestled amongst 200-year-old majestic pine trees in the heart of the Canadian Shield, Mi-A-Kon-Da is situated on beautiful Birch Island, near Parry Sound, Muskoka, and Algonquin Park, Ontario.

This private 24-acre island consists of secluded sandy beaches, calm bays, nature trails and granite rock outcroppings providing incredible views—all which serve as an outstanding backdrop for the wide range of activities that Mi-A-Kon-Da offers. Campers live in spacious tent cabins in groups of 4-5 campers of similar age.

Due to its unique camp size, the Mi-A-Kon-Da activity program has been designed to provide each camper with a wide selection of water and land-based activities—choices that campers make for themselves based on their interest level.

Providing rich overnight summer camping experiences for girls aged 7 - 16 since 1955, Camp Mi-A-Kon-Da is a fully accredited Ontario Camping Association residential summer camp for girls.

The caring, friendly and highly trained staff will make the Mi-A-Kon-Da experience unforgettable. Utilizing a high staff to camper ratio, Mi-A-Kon-Da will provide the safest and most enjoyable camping experience possible.

PORTSMOUTH ABBEY SUMMER PROGRAM

PORTSMOUTH, RI
Tel: 401-643-1225
Fax: 401-683-5888
E-mail: summer@portsmouthabbey.org

Mr. Tim Seeley, *Director*

Imagine yourself enjoying friends you've made from around the world; feeling a sense of real accomplishment from having studied things that interest you and will help you in your next year of school; remembering the fun times you had on trips to places like Boston and Martha's Vineyard; looking forward to improving your new-found skills in sports and other activities you had never tried before. Imagine, too, that you have been challenged to think about life, what it means to be a good person and how to become the person you want to be. And imagine that all these thoughts are enveloped in an experience that from start to finish was fun, challenging, exciting, and never dull for a moment.

That's what the Portsmouth Abbey Summer Program can do for you. Set on 500 beautiful acres on the shores of Narragansett Bay in Rhode Island, with full use of Portsmouth Abbey's magnificent facilities, the Summer Program is designed for students rising into grades 7-10 who want to get a look at important material for the coming year, take a class that their home school might not offer, and are seeking a little adventure that will introduce them to new people, activities and places.

If this sounds like you, whether you are interested in getting a sense of what boarding school is like or just want to have a fantastic summer experience, please contact me, and we can talk about what a month at the Portsmouth Abbey Summer Program can do for you.

Email summer@portsmouthabbey.org to receive more information.
Visit our website at www.portsmouthabbey.org/page/summerprogram and our Facebook page.

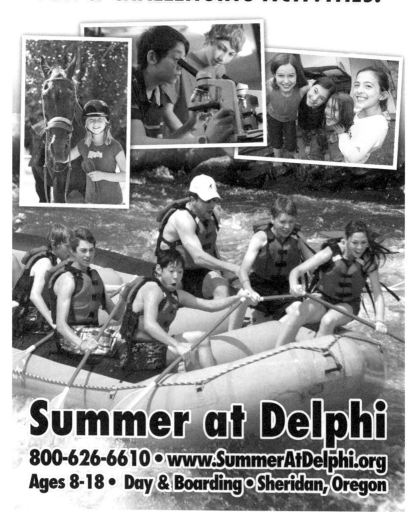

INDEXES BY FEATURE
FOR ACADEMIC CHAPTERS
AND INTERNSHIPS

Programs offering a family session are indicated by "FAM" at the end of the age range in the index, and programs granting high school credit [H], college credit [C] or both [CH] are denoted.

VERY SELECTIVE ADMISSIONS

VERY SELECTIVE *(CONT.)*

SCIENCE RESEARCH PROGRAMS

PROGRAMS FREE FOR IN-STATE RESIDENTS ONLY

PROGRAMS FREE FOR ALL PARTICIPANTS

PROGRAMS OFFERING ADVANCED CURRICULA FOR MIDDLE SCHOOL STUDENTS

DEVELOPMENTAL READING

DEVELOPMENTAL READING *(CONT.)*

REMEDIAL INSTRUCTION

REMEDIAL INSTRUCTION *(CONT.)*

Oak Hill Acad-VA *(Res & Day — Coed Ages 13-18)* **[H]**............ Mouth of Wilson, VA....126
(Eng Math)

Oakland *(Res — Coed Ages 8-14; Day — Coed 6-14)*...................................Keswick, VA....157
(Eng Read Math)

Randolph-Macon *(Res & Day — Coed Ages 11-18)* **[H]**....................... Front Royal, VA....126
(Eng Read Math)

Marquette Summer Sci *(Res — Coed Ages 15-17)* **[H]**.........................Milwaukee, WI....236
(Math)

Amer Intl Salzburg *(Res & Day — Coed Ages 10-19)* **[H]**.............Salzburg, AUSTRIA....177
(Eng Read)

Columbia Intl Coll *(Res — Coed Ages 9-19)*................. Hamilton, Ontario, CANADA....204
(Eng)

Schule Schloss Salem *(Res — Coed Ages 9-16)*..............................Salem, GERMANY....262
(Eng Read Math)

Institut Le Rosey *(Res — Coed Ages 9-18)* **[H]**....................... Rolle, SWITZERLAND....227
(Eng Read Math)

Institut Monte Rosa *(Res & Day — Coed Ages 6-19)*.......Montreux, SWITZERLAND....227
(Eng)

Leysin Amer *(Res — Coed Ages 8-18)* **[H]**...........................Leysin, SWITZERLAND....147
(Eng Read Math)

Surval Mont-Fleuri *(Res — Girls Ages 10-22)* **[CH]**.......Montreux, SWITZERLAND....272
(Eng Read Math)

College du Leman **[H]**.. Versoix, Geneva, SWITZERLAND....202
(Res — Coed Ages 8-18)   (Eng Read Math)

Le Chaperon Rouge ....Crans-sur-Sierre, Valais, SWITZERLAND ...232
(Res & Day — Coed Ages 6-16)   (Eng)

British Intl-Phuket *(Res — Coed Ages 8-15; Day — Coed 7-15)*... Phuket, THAILAND....190
(Eng Read)

SAT PREPARATION

Southwestern-AZ *(Res — Coed Ages 14-18)* **[H]**.. Rimrock, AZ......53

Abbey Road Summer *(Res — Coed Ages 14-19)* **[CH]**......................Los Angeles, CA....175

Ed Unlim-Prep Camps *(Res & Day — Coed Ages 14-17)*......................... Berkeley, CA....211

Ed Unlim-Berkeley *(Res — Coed Ages 16-18)* **[C]**.................................. Berkeley, CA......55

Summer Discovery-SB *(Res — Coed Ages 15-18)* **[C]**.................... Santa Barbara, CA......60

Summer Discovery-LA *(Res — Coed Ages 15-18)* **[C]**......................Los Angeles, CA......58

Summer Inst-UCLA *(Res & Day — Coed Ages 10-17)*........................Los Angeles, CA......58

Summer Inst-Berkeley *(Res & Day — Coed Ages 10-17)*......................... Berkeley, CA......55

Summerfuel-Berkeley *(Res — Coed Ages 15-18)* .... Berkeley, CA......56

SuperCamp *(Res — Coed Ages 11-24)*..Oceanside, CA....272

UCSD Acad Connection *(Res & Day — Coed Ages 14-18)* **[CH]**..............La Jolla, CA......57

Summer Study-CO *(Res — Coed Ages 15-18)* **[C]** .... Boulder, CO......62

Choate-Acad Enrich *(Res & Day — Coed Ages 12-18)* **[H]** .... Wallingford, CT......69

Exploration Senior *(Res & Day — Coed Ages 15-17)* ....New Haven, CT......65

SAT PREP *(CONT.)*

Hockaday *(Res — Coed Ages 12-17; Day — Coed 3-18)* **[H]** .... Dallas, TX.... 122

Summer Inst-TX *(Res & Day — Coed Ages 10-17)* .... Austin, TX.... 121

Wm & Mary Sci Trng *(Res — Coed Ages 16-17)* .... Williamsburg, VA.... 204

Fishburne Military *(Res — Boys Ages 12-17)* **[H]** .... Waynesboro, VA.... 127

Fork Union *(Res — Boys Ages 12-17)* **[H]** .... Fork Union, VA.... 125

4 Star Academics *(Res & Day — Coed Ages 12-18)* .... Charlottesville, VA.... 124

Hargrave *(Res & Day — Boys Ages 13-18)* **[H]** .... Chatham, VA.... 124

Massanutten *(Res & Day — Coed Ages 12-18)* **[H]** .... Woodstock, VA.... 127

Randolph-Macon *(Res & Day — Coed Ages 11-18)* **[H]** .... Front Royal, VA.... 126

U of WA U-DOC *(Res — Coed Ages 16-17)* .... Seattle, WA.... 300

Marquette Summer Sci *(Res — Coed Ages 15-17)* **[H]** .... Milwaukee, WI.... 236

Summerfuel-Oxford *(Res — Coed Ages 15-18)* **[H]** .... Oxford, ENGLAND.... 135

TASIS England **[H]** .... Thorpe, Surrey, ENGLAND.... 136
    (Res — Coed Ages 11-18; Day — Coed 5-11)

Summer Study-Paris *(Res — Coed Ages 15-17)* **[C]** .... Paris, FRANCE.... 138

Summer Discovery-Ita *(Res — Coed Ages 16-18)* **[C]** .... Florence, ITALY.... 142

Leysin Amer *(Res — Coed Ages 8-18)* **[H]** .... Leysin, SWITZERLAND.... 147

Surval Mont-Fleuri *(Res — Girls Ages 10-22)* **[CH]** .... Montreux, SWITZERLAND.... 272

ACADEMIC PROGRAMS

Academic programs are arranged in alphabetical state order, and within each state, programs are arranged alphabetically first by town and then name. An index beginning on page 41 lists programs by features, as shown in the Table of Contents.

For academic-year programs, see *The Handbook of Private Schools,* an annual descriptive survey of independent education, and *Schools Abroad of Interest to Americans,* a worldwide guide to elementary and secondary schools with English-speaking programs. For details, please visit www.portersargent.com or see page 880.

Academic Programs

ALABAMA

THE UNIVERSITY OF ALABAMA
CAPSTONE SUMMER HONORS PROGRAM
Res — Coed Ages 16-18

Tuscaloosa, AL 35487. Box 870169. Tel: 205-348-5599. Fax: 205-348-2247.
http://honors.cbhp.ua.edu   E-mail: klmerritt@ua.edu
Jacqueline Morgan, Dir.
Grade 12. Adm: Selective. Prereqs: ACT 28. **Appl**—Due: Apr. Transcript, essay, resume, 2 recs.
Type of instruction: Undergrad. **Courses:** Astron Comm Comp_Sci Econ Engineering Geol Intl_Relations Math Med/Healthcare Pol_Sci Relig_Stud Writing/Journ Fine_Arts Photog. **Daily hours for:** Classes 4. Homework. Tests. Grades. **College credit: 8.**
Features: Basketball Swim Tennis Volleyball.
Fees 2011: Res $1800, 4 wks.
Housing: Dorms. **Swimming:** Pool. Campus facilities avail.
Ses: 1. **Wks/ses:** 4. Operates June-July.

The program enables academically talented high schoolers to earn college credit and experience life on a university campus. Students enroll in two freshman-level courses alongside undergraduate students, in addition to an exploratory seminar class designed for the program.

ARIZONA

SOUTHWESTERN SUMMER ADVENTURES
Res — Coed Ages 14-18

Rimrock, AZ. Tel: 520-567-4581. Fax: 520-567-5036.
Contact: c/o Southwestern Academy Admissions Office, 2800 Monterey Rd, San Marino, CA 91108. Tel: 626-799-5010. Fax: 626-799-0407.
www.southwesternacademy.edu   E-mail: admissions@southwesternacademy.edu
Jack Leyden, Head. Student contact: Maia Moore.
Grades 9-12. Adm: FCFS. **Appl**—Fee $100. Due: Rolling.
Fac 5. Staff: Admin 3.
Type of instruction: Enrich Preview Rem_Eng Rem_Math Rem_Read Rev SAT/ACT_ Prep. **Courses:** Eng ESL Hist Math Sci Crafts Creative_Writing Fashion Fine_Arts Media Music. **Daily hours for:** Classes 6. Study 2. Rec 3. **High school credit.**
Features: Conservation Exploration Fishing Hiking Mtn_Biking Ranch Riding Wilderness_ Camp Basketball Soccer Softball Swim.
Fees 2012: Res $5500-13,920, 4-8½ wks.
Housing: Dorms. **Swimming:** Pool Stream.
Est 1963. Nonprofit. **Spons:** Southwestern Academy. **Ses:** 3. **Wks/ses:** 4-8½. Operates June-Aug.

The program offers high school credit for makeup or new courses in English, math, science and social studies, as well as remedial and enrichment work. Intensive, individualized morning classes are combined with informal, camp-style activities in the afternoon and evening. Various outdoor activities—as well as field trips to the Grand Canyon, Meteor Crater, the Petrified Forest and nearby Native American sites—round out the program.

FENSTER SCHOOL SUMMER SESSION
Res — Coed Ages 14-18

Tucson, AZ 85750. 8505 E Ocotillo Dr. Tel: 520-749-3340. Fax: 520-749-3349.
www.fensterschool.org   E-mail: registrar@fensterschool.org
Tony Tsang, Admin.
Grades 9-12. Adm: FCFS. **Appl**—Due: Rolling.
Enr: 85. Fac 10. Staff: Admin 5.
Type of instruction: Dev_Read Enrich Rem_Eng Rem_Math Rem_Read Tut. **Courses:**
Span Econ Eng ESL Govt Hist Sci Anat & Physiol. **Daily hours for:** Classes 6.
Features: Hiking Mtn_Trips Equestrian Golf Swim.
Fees 2012: Res $6000 (+$500), 6 wks. Day $4950 (+$500), 6 wks.
Housing: Dorms. **Swimming:** Pool.
Est 1944. Nonprofit. **Ses:** 1. **Wks/ses:** 6. Operates June-July.

Fenster offers makeup, remedial and advanced work in most academic areas: English, math, Spanish, science and social studies. Courses in developmental reading and English as a Second Language are also available, and capable underachievers may enroll. Fenster's daily structure includes regular monitoring of grades, attendance and homework. Recreation includes swimming and horseback riding, in addition to a variety of off-campus weekend activities.

UNIVERSITY OF ARIZONA
A SUMMER OF EXCELLENCE
Res — Coed Ages 16-18

Tucson, AZ 85716. PO Box 210006. Tel: 520-621-6901. Fax: 520-621-8655.
www.soe.honors.arizona.edu   E-mail: soe@email.arizona.edu
Rafael Meza, Dir.
Grades 11-PG. Adm: Selective. Prereqs: GPA 3.5. **Appl**—Fee $30. Due: Rolling. Transcript, 1-2 recs, essay.
Enr: 50-75.
Type of instruction: Adv Undergrad. **Courses:** Fr Ger Greek Ital Lat Russ Span Bus/Fin Comp_Sci Econ Eng Math Psych Sci Philos Sociol Dance Music Studio_Art Theater. Homework. Grades. **College credit:** 6.
Housing: Dorms.
Nonprofit. **Ses:** 2. **Wks/ses:** 5. Operates June-Aug.

High school students earn three to six units of transferable college credit during the five-week SOE session. Boys and girls take regular University of Arizona courses that are taught by university faculty. Pupils also learn strategies for a successful transition to college life, and peer advisors and counselors are on hand to offer support.

CALIFORNIA

ST. CATHERINE'S ACADEMY
SUMMER ENRICHMENT PROGRAM
Res and Day — Boys Ages 5-14

Anaheim, CA 92805. 215 N Harbor Blvd. Tel: 714-772-1363. Fax: 714-772-3004.
www.stcatherinesacademy.org   E-mail: admissions@stcatherinesacademy.org
Sr. Johnellen Turner, OP, Prin. Student contact: Graciela Salvador.
Grades K-8. Adm: FCFS. **Appl**—Fee $50. Due: Rolling. Transcript, standardized tests, rec.
Enr: 120. Fac 10. Staff: Admin 3. Couns 10.

Type of instruction: Adv Preview Rem_Eng Rem_Math Rem_Read Rev Study_Skills Tut. **Courses:** Environ_Sci ESL Expository_Writing Math Sci Creative_Writing Drawing Fine_Arts Music. **Avg class size:** 8. **Daily hours for:** Classes 4.
Features: Basketball Football Soccer Swim Volleyball.
Fees 2011: Res $2175-3175, 4 wks. Day $700-1250, 4 wks.
Housing: Dorms. **Swimming:** Pool.
Nonprofit. Roman Catholic. **Ses:** 1. **Wks/ses:** 4. Operates July.

St. Catherine's summer program includes new and review work in English, math, social studies and science. ESL and study skills courses are available, as are tutoring sessions. Students may register for beginning or intermediate instrumental music training. Recreational activities include sports and weekend trips.

EDUCATION UNLIMITED SUMMER FOCUS AT BERKELEY
Res — Coed Ages 16-18

Berkeley, CA. Univ of California.
Contact (Year-round): 1700 Shattuck Ave, Ste 305, Berkeley, CA 94709.
  Tel: 510-548-6612. Fax: 510-548-0212.
www.educationunlimited.com   E-mail: campinfo@educationunlimited.com
Matthew Fraser, Exec Dir.
Grades 11-12. Adm: Selective. Prereqs: GPA 3.0. **Appl**—Fee $0. Due: Rolling. Rec.
Enr cap: 15-35. **Fac 3. Staff:** Admin 8. Couns 2.
Type of instruction: Adv Enrich SAT/ACT_Prep Study_Skills Tut. **Courses:** Archaeol Astron Environ_Sci Expository_Writing Geol Govt Hist Pol_Sci Speech Writing/Journ Creative_Writing Fine_Arts Music. **Avg class size:** 30. **Daily hours for:** Classes 3. Study 4. Rec 5. **College credit:** 3-4/crse, total 4.
Features: Climbing_Wall Kayak Mtn_Trips White-water_Raft Badminton Baseball Basketball Martial_Arts Swim Tennis Volleyball Weight_Trng.
Fees 2012: Res $9750-10,550 (+$300-400), 6 wks. Aid avail.
Housing: Dorms. **Swimming:** Ocean Pool.
Est 1998. Inc. Ses: 4. **Wks/ses:** 6. Operates July-Aug.

Summer Focus enables rising high school juniors and seniors to take UC-Berkeley courses for university credit, while also previewing college life. Pupils attend class with continuing Berkeley students, visitors from other schools and countries, and members of the Bay Area community. In addition to taking core courses, program participants receive tutoring most evenings and have exclusive access to electives taught by Education Unlimited faculty. The program includes weekend excursions to San Francisco, Santa Cruz, nearby amusement parks, theatrical and musical productions, and professional baseball games.

SUMMER INSTITUTE FOR THE GIFTED
Res and Day — Coed Ages 10-17

Berkeley, CA. Univ of California.
Contact (Year-round): River Plz, 9 W Broad St, Stamford, CT 06902.
  Tel: 203-399-5188, 866-303-4744. Fax: 203-399-5455.
www.giftedstudy.org   E-mail: sig.info@giftedstudy.com
Barbara Swicord, Pres.
  Student contact: Christine Provencher, E-mail: cprovencher@giftedstudy.com.
Adm: Very selective. Admitted: 90%. **Appl**—Fee $95. Due: Rolling. Transcript, standardized test scores, classification as gifted/2 recs.
Intl: 25%.
Type of instruction: Adv Enrich SAT/ACT_Prep Study_Skills. **Courses:** Engineering Expository_Writing Forensic_Sci Math Sci Philos Photog Theater. **Avg class size:** 14.
  Daily hours for: Classes 6. Study 1. Rec 2.
Fees 2012: Res $4995, 3 wks. Day $2795, 3 wks.

Housing: Dorms.
Est 1984. Nonprofit. **Spons:** National Society for the Gifted & Talented. **Ses:** 2. **Wks/ses:** 3. Operates June-July.

SIG enrolls high-aptitude students at colleges across the country. The program combines introductory and college-level academics with cultural courses and traditional recreational summer camp activities. Pupils typically take either two or three academic classes, one or two arts/recreational courses, and one study/tutorial selection during each five-period weekday. Evening entertainment, Saturday field trips and weekend pursuits round out the program. See other SIG listings under Los Angeles; New Haven, CT; Atlanta, GA; Amherst, MA; Hanover, NH; Princeton, NJ; Poughkeepsie, NY; Bryn Mawr, PA; and Austin, TX.

SUMMERFUEL
THE COLLEGE EXPERIENCE
Res — Coed Ages 15-18

Berkeley, CA. Univ of California.
Contact (Year-round): c/o Academic Study Associates, 375 W Broadway, Ste 200, New York, NY 10012. **Tel:** 212-796-8340, 800-752-2250. **Fax:** 212-334-4934.
www.asaprograms.com/summerfuel   E-mail: summer@asaprograms.com
Willem Vroegh, Dir.
Grades 10-PG. Adm: FCFS. **Appl**—Fee $0. Due: Rolling. Transcript, rec.
Type of instruction: Enrich Preview SAT/ACT_Prep. **Courses:** Bus/Fin Expository_Writing Intl_Relations Law Math Psych Public_Speak Creative_Writing Film Music Painting Photog.
Features: Basketball Swim Volleyball.
Fees 2012: Res $6495, 4 wks.
Housing: Dorms. **Swimming:** Pool. Campus facilities avail.
Inc. **Spons:** Academic Study Associates. **Ses:** 1. **Wks/ses:** 4. Operates June-July.

This precollege program allows pupils who have completed grades 9-12 to take courses for university credit or enrichment while also sampling college life. In addition to morning and afternoon course work, students participate in various extracurricular activities. On weekends, participants may go on excursions around New England, some of which incur an additional fee. ASA conducts a similar program in Amherst, MA (see separate listing).

ACADEMY BY THE SEA ACADEMIC PROGRAM
Res — Coed Ages 12-16

Carlsbad, CA 92018. PO Box 3000. Tel: 760-434-7564. **Fax:** 760-729-1574.
www.abts.com   E-mail: summer@abts.com
Ken Weeks, Dir.
Grades 7-11. Adm: FCFS. **Appl**—Fee $0. Due: Rolling.
Enr cap: 180. **Fac 35. Staff:** Admin 13. Couns 18.
Type of instruction: Adv Enrich Preview Rem_Eng Rem_Math Rem_Read Rev Study_Skills Tut. **Courses:** Span ESL Hist Math Sci Writing/Journ Acting Crafts Dance Drama Filmmaking Music Studio_Art. **Avg class size:** 11. **Daily hours for:** Classes 4. Study 2. Rec 4. **High school credit:** 2.
Features: Aquatics Kayak Riflery Baseball Basketball Cricket Field_Hockey Football Lacrosse Rugby Soccer Softball Surfing Swim Tennis Ultimate_Frisbee Volleyball Watersports Weight_Trng Ping-Pong.
Fees 2012: Res $3895 (+$450), 4 wks. Day $750-1500 (+$450), 4 wks.
Housing: Cabins Dorms. Avg per room/unit: 2. **Swimming:** Ocean Pool.
Est 1943. Nonprofit. **Spons:** Army and Navy Academy. **Ses:** 2. **Wks/ses:** 4-5. Operates June-July.

Balancing academics and recreation, ABTS helps students prepare for the upcoming school year and for future educational endeavors. Pupils select four courses and learn in a small-class setting that enables faculty to address different learning styles and provide individual attention. Students choose either a four-week enrichment option or a five-week credit-bearing program that offers remediation only. Course work includes offerings in the traditional disciplines, ESL and various elective areas. A mandatory evening study hall operates five nights weekly. Afternoon activities and weekend excursions round out the program.

POMONA COLLEGE
ACADEMY FOR YOUNG SCHOLARS
Res — Coed Ages 15-16

Claremont, CA 91711. Office of Community & Multicultural Prgms, 170 E 6th St, Ste 231. Tel: 909-607-1810.
www.pomona.edu/ocmp/educationaloutreach.shtml E-mail: pays@pomona.edu
Sergio Marin, Dir.
Grades 10-11. Adm: Selective. Priority: Low-income. URM. **Appl**—Fee $0. Transcript, 2 recs, 2 essays.
Enr: 90. **Enr cap:** 90.
Type of instruction: Enrich. **Courses:** Japan Econ Math Sci. **Avg class size:** 15.
Features: Basketball Soccer.
Fees 2010: Free. Res 4 wks.
Housing: Dorms.
Nonprofit. **Ses:** 1. **Wks/ses:** 4.

This intensive academic program serves high schoolers from groups that are traditionally underrepresented in higher education, particularly those who are African-American or Latino or who come from low-income families. Students enroll in two faculty-taught core courses, math/problem solving and critical inquiry, as well as in two electives that are taught by Pomona College undergraduates. Rising seniors may apply for the program only if they attended PAYS during a previous summer. Boys and girls return home each weekend.

UNIVERSITY OF CALIFORNIA-SAN DIEGO
ACADEMIC CONNECTIONS
Res and Day — Coed Ages 14-18

La Jolla, CA 92093. MC 0176-S, 9500 Gilman Dr. Tel: 858-534-0804. Fax: 858-534-7385.
www.academicconnections.ucsd.edu E-mail: academicconnections@ucsd.edu
Edward Abeyta, Dir. Student contact: Robin Wittman, E-mail: rwittman@ucsd.edu.
Grades 10-12 (younger if qualified). Adm: Selective. Admitted: 80%. Prereqs: GPA 3.3. **Appl**—Fee $100. Due: June. Transcript, rec.
Enr: 309. **Enr cap:** 350. Intl: 5%. Non-White: 50%. **Fac 30.** Col/grad students 30. **Staff:** Admin 4. Res 25.
Type of instruction: Adv SAT/ACT_Prep Undergrad. **Courses:** Astron Comp_Sci Econ Engineering Environ_Sci Law Marine_Bio/Stud Oceanog Sci Writing/Journ Crafts Film-making Theater. **Avg class size:** 20. **Daily hours for:** Classes 5. Study 2. Rec 4. Homework. Tests. Grades. **High school & college credit:** 6/crse, total 6.
Travel: HI.
Features: Aquatics Exploration Hiking Rock_Climb Swim.
Fees 2012: Res $3450-3700, 1-3 wks. Day $2550, 3 wks.
Housing: Dorms. **Swimming:** Ocean Pool.
Est 2001. Nonprofit. **Ses:** 3. **Wks/ses:** 1-3. Operates July-Aug.

Academic Connections' curriculum consists of college-level course work in the physical and social sciences, engineering, and the arts and humanities. UCSD doctoral candidates generally teach the courses, which meet in five-hour blocks every weekday. Small classes (limited to 22 students each) emphasize active learning. An optional SAT test-taking workshop operates two nights per week, and students may meet with campus admissions representatives one evening a week. Offered for a slightly higher cost than the traditional three-week program, a weeklong, strictly residential session in Hawaii focuses on global environmental leadership and sustainability.

SUMMER DISCOVERY
Res — Coed Ages 15-18

Los Angeles, CA. Univ of California-Los Angeles.
Contact (Year-round): 1326 Old Northern Blvd, Roslyn, NY 11576. Tel: 516-621-3939.
   Fax: 516-625-3438.
www.summerdiscovery.com   E-mail: discovery@summerdiscovery.com
Bob Musiker, Exec Dir.
Grades 10-PG. Adm: FCFS. **Appl**—Due: Rolling.
Enr cap: 525.
Type of instruction: Enrich SAT/ACT_Prep Study_Skills. **Courses:** Archaeol Bus/Fin Debate ESL Expository_Writing Govt Speech Writing/Journ Crafts Creative_Writing Dance Filmmaking Fine_Arts Music Photog Theater. Tests. **College credit:** 8.
Features: Adventure_Travel Aquatics Canoe Community_Serv Hiking Kayak Mountaineering White-water_Raft Basketball Golf Lacrosse Soccer Swim Tennis Volleyball Watersports.
Fees 2011: Res $5499-8999, 3-6 wks.
Housing: Dorms. **Swimming:** Pool. Campus facilities avail.
Inc. **Ses:** 3. **Wks/ses:** 3-6. Operates June-Aug.

Precollege programs for high school students are held on university campuses throughout the US and abroad. Boys and girls take a college-credit course and an enrichment course during their stay. Other aspects of the program include community service, excursions, travel, sports and recreational activities. See other Summer Discovery listings under Santa Barbara; San Diego; Ann Arbor, MI; Washington, DC; Florence, Italy; and Valencia, Spain.

SUMMER INSTITUTE FOR THE GIFTED
Res and Day — Coed Ages 10-17

Los Angeles, CA. Univ of California-Los Angeles.
Contact (Year-round): River Plz, 9 W Broad St, Stamford, CT 06902.
   Tel: 203-399-5188, 866-303-4744. Fax: 203-399-5455.
www.giftedstudy.org   E-mail: sig.info@giftedstudy.org
Barbara Swicord, Pres.
   Student contact: Christine Provencher, E-mail: cprovencher@giftedstudy.com.
Adm: Selective. Admitted: 90%. **Appl**—Fee $95. Due: Rolling. Transcript, standardized test scores, gifted classification/2 recs.
Intl: 25%.
Type of instruction: Adv Enrich SAT/ACT_Prep Study_Skills. **Courses:** Expository_Writing Forensic_Sci Math Sci Dance Photog Theater. **Avg class size:** 14. **Daily hours for:** Classes 6. Study 1. Rec 2.
Fees 2012: Res $4995, 3 wks. Day $2795, 3 wks.
Housing: Dorms.
Est 1981. Nonprofit. **Spons:** National Society for the Gifted & Talented. **Ses:** 1. **Wks/ses:** 3. Operates July.

See program description under Berkeley, CA.

UNIVERSITY OF SOUTHERN CALIFORNIA
SUMMER SEMINARS
Res and Day — Coed Ages 15-18

Los Angeles, CA 90089. Office of Continuing Ed & Summer Prgms, 3415 S Figueroa St, Ste 107. Tel: 213-740-5679. Fax: 213-740-6417.
http://summer.usc.edu   **E-mail: summer@usc.edu**
Sonny Hayes, Dir.
Grades 10-PG. Adm: Selective. **Appl**—Fee $45. Due: May. Transcript, rec.
Type of instruction: Undergrad. **Courses:** Architect Bus/Fin Comm Engineering Environ_Sci Law Med/Healthcare Writing/Journ Neurosci Physiol Creative_Writing Photog Theater. **Daily hours for:** Classes 6½. Study 2. **College credit:** 3/crse, total 3.
Fees 2012: Res $7000, 4 wks. Day $4800, 4 wks. Aid (Need).
Housing: Dorms. Avg per room/unit: 2. Campus facilities avail.
Nonprofit. **Ses:** 2. **Wks/ses:** 2-4. Operates July-Aug.

Each participant in this USC program takes one college-level course during the session. Pupils enroll in either a two-week noncredit class or a four-week college-credit course. Students have full access to the university's library and computing facilities, while also taking part in daily study sessions, academic support groups and laboratory meetings. A workshop on the college application process is available at no additional cost. Boys and girls visit area tourist attractions on Saturdays.

OJAI VALLEY SCHOOL
SUMMER SCHOOL AND CAMP
Res — Coed Ages 8-18; Day — Coed 3-18

Ojai, CA 93023. 723 El Paseo Rd. Tel: 805-646-1423. Fax: 805-646-0362.
www.ovs.org   **E-mail: admission@ovs.org**
Eleanora Burright, Dir.
Grades PS-12. Adm: FCFS. **Appl**—Fee $50. Due: Rolling.
Type of instruction: Dev_Read Enrich Preview Rem_Eng Rem_Math Rem_Read Rev Study_Skills. **Courses:** Fr Span Bus/Fin Environ_Sci ESL Expository_Writing Writing/Journ Crafts Creative_Writing Fine_Arts Photog Theater. **Avg class size:** 9. **Daily hours for:** Classes 4. Rec 3½.
Features: Archery Climbing_Wall Cooking Hiking Riding Ropes_Crse Wilderness_Camp Woodcraft Equestrian Soccer Swim Tennis Volleyball.
Fees 2009: Res $2660-7580, 2-6 wks. Day $470-3930, 1-6 wks.
Housing: Dorms. **Swimming:** Pool.
Est 1943. Nonprofit. **Ses:** 4. **Wks/ses:** 1-6. Operates June-Aug.

OVS combines academic work with overnight camping, horseback riding and a variety of recreational activities. Enrichment courses include reading, math, study skills, ESL, computers, science and writing. Among afternoon activities are archery, sports, swimming, tennis, ceramics and pottery. Specialty camp sessions address the performing arts, environmental science and equitation.

ROBERT LOUIS STEVENSON SCHOOL SUMMER CAMP
Res and Day — Coed Ages 9-15

Pebble Beach, CA 93953. 3152 Forest Lake Rd. Tel: 831-625-8349. Fax: 831-625-5208.
www.stevensonschool.org/summer   **E-mail: summercamp@stevensonschool.org**
Tony Klevan, Dir. Student contact: Katie Klevan.
Grades 4-10. Adm: FCFS. Admitted: 100%. **Appl**—Fee $0. Due: May.
Enr: 144. **Enr cap:** 150. Intl: 30%. Non-White: 10%. **Fac 6.** K-12 staff 4. Specialists 2. **Staff:** Admin 6. Couns 24.
Type of instruction: Enrich Preview Rev Study_Skills. **Courses:** Span Eng Marine_Bio/

Stud Math Acting Ceramics Creative_Writing Dance Filmmaking Music Photog Studio_ Art. **Avg class size:** 9. **Daily hours for:** Classes 3. Rec 7.

Features: Aquatics Archery Hiking Mtn_Biking Mtn_Trips Wilderness_Camp Baseball Basketball Fencing Golf In-line_Skating Lacrosse Soccer Softball Swim Tennis Ultimate_ Frisbee Volleyball Watersports Weight_Trng.

Fees 2011: Res $5000 (+$225), 5 wks. Day $2400 (+$225), 5 wks. Aid 2009 (Merit & Need): $120,000.

Housing: Dorms. Avg per room/unit: 2. **Swimming:** Pool. Campus facilities avail.

Est 1972. Nonprofit. **Ses:** 1. **Wks/ses:** 5. Operates June-July.

Stevenson offers workshops in language skills, the sciences, math and the arts. Pupils attend morning workshops, then have time for socializing and relaxation after lunch. Each day concludes with afternoon sports. Resident campers participate in various evening activities and embark on weekend trips in the area.

SOUTHWESTERN SUMMER ADVENTURES
Res and Day — Coed Ages 12-18

San Marino, CA 91108. c/o Southwestern Academy, 2800 Monterey Rd.
   Tel: 626-799-5010. Fax: 626-799-0407.
www.southwesternacademy.edu/academics/summer.html
E-mail: admissions@southwesternacademy.edu
Kenneth R. Veronda, Head. Student contact: Maia Moore.
Grades 6-12. Adm: Selective. **Appl**—Fee $100. Due: Rolling. Transcript.
Enr: 39. **Enr cap:** 160. Intl: 90%. Non-White: 8%. **Fac 11.** K-12 staff 11. **Staff:** Admin 15. Res 6.

Type of instruction: Adv Enrich Rem_Eng Rem_Math Rev ESL/TOEFL_Prep. **Courses:** Span ESL Hist Marine_Bio/Stud Math Sci Creative_Writing Filmmaking Media. **Avg class size:** 5. **Daily hours for:** Classes 6. Study 3. Rec 4. Homework. Tests. Grades. **High school credit.**

Features: Exploration Mtn_Biking Baseball Basketball Soccer Swim Tennis Volleyball Ping-Pong.

Fees 2011: Res $7950-18,550 (+$200), 4-14 wks. Day $2640-9240, 4-14 wks. Aid 2010 (Need): $138,000.

Housing: Dorms Houses. **Swimming:** Ocean Pool. Campus facilities avail.

Est 1924. Nonprofit. **Spons:** Southwestern Academy. **Ses:** 3. **Wks/ses:** 4-14. Operates June-Sept.

Summer Adventures features morning academic class work in all subjects for enrichment, credit or review. English as a Second Language programming is available for international students seeking to prepare for American schools and colleges. Programs run for four or 14 weeks, depending upon the student's needs. On afternoons and weekends, boys and girls go on excursions to Los Angeles-area cultural sites, landmarks and beaches.

SUMMER DISCOVERY
Res — Coed Ages 15-18

Santa Barbara, CA. Univ of California-Santa Barbara.
Contact (Year-round): 1326 Old Northern Blvd, Roslyn, NY 11576. Tel: 516-621-3939.
   Fax: 516-625-3438.
www.summerdiscovery.com   E-mail: discovery@summerdiscovery.com
Bob Musiker, Exec Dir.
Grades 10-PG. Adm: Somewhat selective. **Appl**—Fee $95. Due: Rolling.
Enr cap: 200.
Type of instruction: Enrich SAT/ACT_Prep Study_Skills Undergrad. **Courses:** Archaeol Bus/Fin Debate ESL Expository_Writing Govt Speech Writing/Journ Crafts Creative_

Writing Dance Filmmaking Fine_Arts Music Photog Theater. Homework. Tests. **College credit:** 8.
Features: Adventure_Travel Aquatics Canoe Community_Serv Hiking Kayak Mountaineering White-water_Raft Basketball Golf Lacrosse Soccer Swim Tennis Volleyball Watersports.
Fees 2011: Res $6199-7699 (+$75), 4-6 wks. Aid (Need).
Housing: Dorms. **Swimming:** Ocean Pool. Campus facilities avail.
Inc. **Ses:** 2. **Wks/ses:** 4-6. Operates June-July.

See program description under Los Angeles, CA.

THOMAS AQUINAS COLLEGE
SUMMER GREAT BOOKS PROGRAM
Res — Coed Ages 17-18

Santa Paula, CA 93060. 10000 N Ojai Rd. Tel: 805-525-4417, 800-634-9797. Fax: 805-525-9342.
www.thomasaquinas.edu/admission/high-school-summer-program
E-mail: admissions@thomasaquinas.edu
Grades 12-PG. Adm: Selective. **Appl**—Fee $0. Due: Rolling. Transcript, rec, essay.
Type of instruction: Enrich. **Courses:** Eng Philos.
Fees 2009: Res $975, 2 wks.
Housing: Dorms.
Est 1997. Nonprofit. Roman Catholic. **Ses:** 1. **Wks/ses:** 2. Operates July-Aug.

Exceptionally talented students from around the country spend two weeks at Thomas Aquinas College reading and discussing works from such figures as Plato, Euclid, Sophocles, Pascal, Boethius and St. Thomas Aquinas with college faculty. During the first week of the program, boys and girls ponder questions of moral, political and religious authority, then consider the relationship between faith and reason. The second and final week begins with a Shakespearean examination of the imperfection and corruption of man, progresses to a discussion of Euclidean geometry and concludes with readings designed to spur further consideration of key issues of the session. Organized recreation and off-campus excursions balance academics.

EDUCATION PROGRAM FOR GIFTED YOUTH
SUMMER INSTITUTES
Res — Coed Ages 12-17

Stanford, CA 94305. Stanford Univ, 220 Panama St. Toll-free: 800-372-3749. Fax: 866-835-3312.
http://epgy.stanford.edu/summer   E-mail: epgysummer@epgy.stanford.edu
Grades 7-12. Adm: Selective. **Appl**—Fee $40. Due: Rolling. Transcript, teacher rec, standardized test results.
Type of instruction: Enrich. **Courses:** Bus/Fin Comp_Sci Econ Engineering Expository_ Writing Law Math Sci Humanities Philos Robotics Creative_Writing Playwriting.
Fees 2009: Res $3000-5600, 2-4 wks.
Housing: Dorms. Campus facilities avail.
Nonprofit. **Spons:** Stanford University. **Ses:** 6. **Wks/ses:** 2-4. Operates June-Aug.

Held at Stanford University, these residential programs serve motivated and academically talented middle school and high school pupils. Students enroll in intensive courses, taught by Stanford professors, on topics that are not typically available at the participant's grade level. Children in the Middle School Program (entering grades 7 and 8) study several related topics within a single subject area while getting an early exposure to college life. The more focused High School Program involves the intensive study of a single course.

STANFORD UNIVERSITY
HIGH SCHOOL SUMMER COLLEGE
Res and Day — Coed Ages 16-18

Stanford, CA 94305. Summer Session Office, 482 Galvez St. Tel: 650-723-3109. Fax: 650-725-6080.
http://summersession.stanford.edu   E-mail: summercollege@stanford.edu
Grades 12-PG (younger if qualified). Adm: Selective. **Appl**—Fee $50. Due: Rolling. Transcript, rec, standardized test scores, essay.
Type of instruction: Adv Tut Undergrad. **Courses:** Arabic Chin Fr Ger Japan Lat Span Astron Bus/Fin Col_Prep Comp_Sci Econ Eng Engineering Expository_Writing Hist Math Psych Relig_Stud Sci Anthro Genetics Philos Physiol Sociol Stats Drama Film Media Music Painting Photog Studio_Art. **College credit.**
Features: Yoga Basketball Golf Swim Tennis Ultimate_Frisbee.
Fees 2009: Res $9504-12,540 (+$682), 8 wks. Day $2902-9733 (+$630), 8 wks. Aid (Need).
Housing: Dorms. **Swimming:** Pool. Campus facilities avail.
Nonprofit. **Ses:** 1. **Wks/ses:** 8. Operates June-Aug.

This precollege program allows accomplished boys and girls who have completed grades 11 or 12 (or, in the case of particularly mature students, grade 10) to sample college life while taking undergraduate courses and earning Stanford University credit. Residential pupils register for at least eight units of course work during the eight-week session, commuters at least three units. In addition to the varied selection of college courses, boys and girls may participate in voluntary classes and seminars designed to prepare them for a successful transition to college; options address the college admission process, study skills and time management, and expository writing, among others. Field trips, intramural athletics, outreach projects, coastal excursions and informal discussions with Stanford faculty complement class work.

COLORADO

SUMMER STUDY IN COLORADO
Res — Coed Ages 15-18

Boulder, CO. Univ of Colorado.
Contact (Year-round): 900 Walt Whitman Rd, Melville, NY 11747. Tel: 631-424-1000, 800-666-2556. Fax: 631-424-0567.
www.summerstudy.com   E-mail: info@summerstudy.com
William Cooperman, Exec Dir.
Grades 10-PG. Adm: Selective. **Appl**—Fee $75. Due: Rolling. Transcript, standardized test scores.
Enr: 250. **Fac 25. Staff:** Admin 7. Couns 20.
Type of instruction: Adv Enrich Preview Rev ESL/TOEFL_Prep SAT/ACT_Prep Study_Skills Tut. **Courses:** Fr Architect Astron Bus/Fin Debate Econ Expository_Writing Hist Law Math Pol_Sci Relig_Stud Anthro Mythology Philos Sociol Women's_Stud Art Creative_Writing Dance Filmmaking Music Painting Photog Theater Pottery. **Daily hours for:** Classes 2½. Study 1. Rec 4. **College credit:** 3.
Features: Adventure_Travel Aquatics Bicycle_Tours Boating Caving Climbing_Wall Community_Serv Exploration Hiking Mountaineering Mtn_Biking Mtn_Trips Riding Rock_Climb White-water_Raft Wilderness_Camp Yoga Basketball Cross-country Football Ice_Hockey Lacrosse Roller_Hockey Soccer Softball Swim Tennis Track Ultimate_Frisbee Volleyball Watersports Weight_Trng Wrestling.
Fees 2012: Res $3995-5795, 3-5 wks. Aid (Need).
Housing: Dorms. **Swimming:** Pool.
Inc. **Spons:** Summer Study Programs. **Ses:** 2. **Wks/ses:** 3-5. Operates July-Aug.

High schoolers who have completed at least grade 10 and recent graduates earn two or three college credits over five weeks while taking freshman-level courses and previewing college life. Each student takes one or two courses for credit and one for enrichment. Pupils who have completed grades 9-11 may enroll in a three-week, noncredit enrichment session. The program's location lends itself to such outdoor pursuits as rock climbing, hiking, biking and white-water rafting; sports clinics and community service opportunities are among Summer Study's other activities. Weekends provide opportunities for travel to Vail, Breckenridge, Colorado Springs and Rocky Mountain National Park.

UNIVERSITY OF NORTHERN COLORADO
SUMMER ENRICHMENT PROGRAM
Res — Coed Ages 10-15

Greeley, CO 80639. 501 20th St, Campus Box 141. Tel: 970-351-2683.
  Fax: 970-351-1061.
www.unco.edu/sep   E-mail: sep@unco.edu
George T. Betts, Dir.
Grades 5-10. Adm: FCFS. **Appl**—Fee $0. Due: Rolling.
Enr: 300. **Enr cap:** 300. **Fac 32.**
Type of instruction: Adv Enrich. **Courses:** Comp_Sci Debate Hist Math Sci Creative_ Writing Dance Drama Fine_Arts Music Studio_Art. **Avg class size:** 14. **Daily hours for:** Classes 5.
Features: Swim.
Fees 2011: Res $1645 (+$50), 2 wks. Aid (Need).
Housing: Dorms. **Swimming:** Pool.
Est 1978. Nonprofit. **Ses:** 1. **Wks/ses:** 2. Operates July.

Gifted students enrolled in SEP take part in four 75-minute classes that they chose from dozens of offerings. The program also provides boys and girls with opportunities outside the classroom to express their creativity and develop their abilities; among these activities are library research, athletics and games, and arts and crafts. Pupils may participate in such pursuits as off-campus trips and quiz bowl during the weekend.

HIGH MOUNTAIN INSTITUTE SUMMER TERM
Res — Coed Ages 16-17

Leadville, CO 80461. PO Box 970. Tel: 719-486-8200, 888-464-9991.
  Fax: 719-486-8201.
www.hminet.org/summerterm   E-mail: admissions@hminet.org
Christina Reiff, Dir.
Grades 11-12. Adm: Selective. **Appl**—Fee $35. Due: Feb. Transcript, essays, 2 recs.
Enr: 17. **Enr cap:** 24. **Fac 3.**
Courses: Environ_Sci Leadership Humanities. **Avg class size:** 10. **Daily hours for:** Classes 4½. **High school credit.**
Features: Climbing_Wall Exploration Outdoor_Ed Rock_Climb White-water_Raft Wilderness_Camp.
Fees 2011: Res $7850 (+$400), 6 wks. Aid 2011 (Need): $30,000.
Housing: Cabins. Avg per room/unit: 10.
Est 2011. Nonprofit. **Ses:** 1. **Wks/ses:** 6. Operates June-Aug.

Rising high school juniors and seniors engage in a variety of academic, wilderness and community pursuits during a six-week session that represents a condensed version of HMI Semester. Students supplement a compulsory wilderness and leadership course with either an environmental science class or a multidisciplinary humanities offering that examines the manner in which Americans have viewed and interacted with the natural world. Seven- and nine-day backcountry expeditions develop wilderness skills and employ the mountains as an extended classroom.

UNITED STATES AIR FORCE ACADEMY
SUMMER SEMINAR
Res — Coed Ages 17-18

USAF Academy, CO 80840. 2304 Cadet Dr, Ste 200. Tel: 719-333-2236.
www.academyadmissions.com　E-mail: rr_webmail@usafa.edu
Grade 12. Adm: Selective. **Appl**—Due: Feb. Transcript, standardized test scores, resume.
Type of instruction: Enrich.
Fees 2009: Res $325, 1 wk.
Housing: Dorms. Campus facilities avail.
Nonprofit. **Ses:** 3. **Wks/ses:** 1.

Rising high school seniors enroll in this competitive program to sample college life at this service academy. Students choose from more than 30 course options in an array of subject areas.

CONNECTICUT

ACCESS CHESHIRE AT THE ACADEMY
Res and Day — Coed Ages 12-16

Cheshire, CT 06410. 10 Main St. Tel: 203-439-7400. Fax: 203-439-7442.
www.cheshireacademy.org　E-mail: summer@cheshireacademy.org
Diane K. Cook, Dir.
Grades 7-10. Adm: Selective. Admitted: 85%. **Appl**—Fee $65. Due: Rolling. Transcript, rec.
Enr: 100. **Enr cap:** 100. Intl: 33%. Non-White: 35%. **Fac 30.** Col/grad students 5. K-12 staff 25. **Staff:** Admin 5. Couns 25.
Type of instruction: Adv Enrich Rem_Eng Rem_Math Rem_Read ESL/TOEFL_Prep.
　Courses: Chin Architect Econ Eng ESL Forensic_Sci Sci Anat & Physiol Ceramics Film Media Photog. **Avg class size:** 8. **Daily hours for:** Classes 4. Study 3. Rec 3. Homework. Tests. Grades.
Features: Canoe Caving Climbing_Wall Community_Serv Conservation Exploration Fishing Hiking Kayak Mtn_Biking Mtn_Trips Outdoor_Ed Rappelling Rock_Climb Ropes_Crse White-water_Raft Wilderness_Camp Wilderness_Canoe Yoga Aerobics Basketball Fencing Golf Soccer Softball Swim Tennis Ultimate_Frisbee Volleyball Weight_Trng.
Fees 2012: Res $5295 (+$500), 4 wks. Day $3995 (+$500), 4 wks. Aid 2011 (Merit & Need): $30,000.
Housing: Dorms. Avg per room/unit: 2. **Swimming:** Ocean Pool. Campus facilities avail.
Est 2010. Nonprofit. **Spons:** Cheshire Academy. **Ses:** 1. **Wks/ses:** 4. Operates July-Aug.

Designed for students entering grades 7-10, ACCESS CHESHIRE provides four weeks of advanced study in the arts and sciences. All American participants enroll in one of five academic clusters; themes center around forensic science, Chinese language and culture, human endurance and strength, green engineering and sustainability, and media and society. A sixth option addressing American culture is open only to international students. Late afternoons provide time for sports and other recreation, and boys and girls may take part in various musical endeavors. Scheduled on Wednesday, Saturday and Sunday afternoons, off-campus activities take the form of museum and gallery visits, beach outings, mountain hikes, whale-watching voyages, amusement park trips, a weekend trip to Boston, and excursions to professional baseball games.

THE MARVELWOOD SCHOOL SUMMER PROGRAMS
Res and Day — Coed Ages 13-17

Kent, CT 06757. 476 Skiff Mountain Rd, PO Box 3001. Tel: 860-927-0047.
Fax: 860-927-2358.
www.marvelwood.org   E-mail: caitlin.lynch@marvelwood.org
Craig Ough, Dir.
Grades 8-11. Adm: Selective. **Appl**—Fee $50. Due: Rolling. Transcript, 3 recs.
Enr: 50. **Enr cap:** 60. **Fac 13.**
Type of instruction: Dev_Read Enrich Preview Rem_Eng Rem_Math Rev SAT/ACT_Prep
Study_Skills. **Courses:** Eng ESL Hist Math Sci Creative_Writing Drama Music Photog
Studio_Art. **Avg class size:** 6. **Daily hours for:** Classes 4. Study 3. Rec 2. **High school
credit.**
Features: Canoe Hiking Mtn_Biking Riding Sail Woodcraft Basketball Swim Tennis.
Fees 2011: Res $2700-5600 (+$600), 2-4 wks. Day $2000 (+$300), 4 wks.
Housing: Dorms. **Swimming:** Pond.
Est 1964. Nonprofit. **Ses:** 2. **Wks/ses:** 2-4. Operates July-Aug.

Marvelwood's four-week Academic and Leadership Program features core academic
enrichment classes, electives and study skills instruction, supplemented by afternoon leadership
seminars and art activities. Students are assigned an advisor and attend structured study hall
sessions six days each week. Afternoon leadership activities make use of nearby natural
resources and include whitewater canoeing, rock climbing and team-building challenges. The
two-week English Language Learners' Program immerses international students in American
culture and beginning or intermediate English.

EXPLORATION SENIOR PROGRAM
Res and Day — Coed Ages 15-17

New Haven, CT. Yale Univ.
Contact (Year-round): 932 Washington St, PO Box 368, Norwood, MA 02062.
Tel: 781-762-7400. Fax: 781-762-7425.
www.explo.org/senior   E-mail: summer@explo.org
Geoff Theobald, Head.
Grades 10-12. Adm: FCFS. **Appl**—Fee $0. Due: Rolling.
Enr: 650. **Enr cap:** 650. **Fac 70. Staff:** Admin 10.
Type of instruction: Enrich Preview SAT/ACT_Prep Study_Skills. **Courses:** Arabic
Archaeol Architect Bus/Fin Debate Ecol Engineering Environ_Sci ESL Expository_Writ-
ing Govt Law Marine_Bio/Stud Psych Public_Speak Relig_Stud Writing/Journ Anat &
Physiol Web_Design Acting Circus_Skills Crafts Creative_Writing Dance Drama Draw-
ing Fine_Arts Media Music Painting Photog Studio_Art Screenwriting. **Avg class size:**
15. **Daily hours for:** Classes 4.
Features: Canoe Chess Climbing_Wall Cooking Deep-sea Fishing Exploration Hiking
Kayak Mountaineering Sail Survival_Trng White-water_Raft Wilderness_Camp Wood-
craft Baseball Basketball Field_Hockey Football Golf Lacrosse Rugby Soccer Softball
Swim Tennis Track Ultimate_Frisbee Volleyball.
**Fees 2012: Res $5145-9515 (+$300-600), 3-6 wks. Day $2350-4295 (+$300-600), 3-6
wks.** Aid (Need).
Housing: Dorms. **Swimming:** Pool.
Est 1977. Nonprofit. **Spons:** Exploration School. **Ses:** 2. **Wks/ses:** 3. Operates June-Aug.

Previewing college life, the Senior Program allows students to learn on the Yale University
campus. The program includes ungraded courses, minicourses, college seminars, sports clinics
and SAT preparation; subject offerings include psychology, international law, architecture
and music theory, among others. Extracurricular activities, athletics, special events and
trips supplement academics. Exploration programs for younger students are available in
Southborough, MA, and Wellesley, MA (see separate listings).

SUMMER INSTITUTE FOR THE GIFTED
Res and Day — Coed Ages 13-17

New Haven, CT. Yale Univ.
Contact (Year-round): River Plz, 9 W Broad St, Stamford, CT 06902.
   Tel: 203-399-5188, 866-303-4744. Fax: 203-399-5455.
www.giftedstudy.org   E-mail: sig.info@giftedstudy.org
Barbara Swicord, Pres.
   Student contact: Christine Provencher, E-mail: cprovencher@giftedstudy.org.
Adm: Selective. Admitted: 90%. **Appl**—Fee $95. Due: Rolling. Transcript, standardized test
   scores, classification as gifted/2 recs.
Intl: 25%.
Type of instruction: Adv Enrich SAT/ACT_Prep Study_Skills. **Courses:** Engineering
   Expository_Writing Forensic_Sci Law Med/Healthcare Sci Writing/Journ Robotics Stats
   Creative_Writing Dance Photog Theater Screenwriting. **Avg class size:** 14.
Fees 2012: Res $5195, 3 wks. Day $2795, 3 wks.
Housing: Dorms. Campus facilities avail.
Nonprofit. **Spons:** National Society for the Gifted & Talented. **Ses:** 1. **Wks/ses:** 3. Operates
   June-July.

   See program description under Berkeley, CA.

YALE UNIVERSITY SUMMER SESSION
Res and Day — Coed Ages 16-21

New Haven, CT 06520. PO Box 208355. Tel: 203-432-2430. Fax: 203-432-2434.
www.yale.edu/summer   E-mail: summer.session@yale.edu
Kathryn Young, Dir.
Grades 12-Col. Adm: Very selective. **Appl**—Fee $55. Due: Rolling. Transcript, standard-
   ized test scores, 2 recs.
Enr: 1000. Intl: 20%. **Fac 200.** Prof 100. Col/grad students 20. Specialists 80. **Staff:** Admin
   10. Couns 40.
Type of instruction: Adv Undergrad. **Courses:** Arabic Chin Fr Ger Greek Ital Japan Lat
   Russ Span Nahuatl Portuguese Swahili Archaeol Astron Ecol Environ_Sci Writing/Journ
   Creative_Writing Drama Filmmaking Fine_Arts. **Avg class size:** 10. **Daily hours for:**
   Classes 2. Study 2. **College credit.**
Features: Swim.
Fees 2012: Res $8775, 5 wks. Day $6300, 5 wks.
Housing: Dorms. Avg per room/unit: 2. **Swimming:** Pool. Campus facilities avail.
Est 1975. Nonprofit. **Ses:** 2. **Wks/ses:** 5. Operates June-Aug.

   Qualified college students and high schoolers who have completed junior year may earn up
to 12 credit hours of college credit in such areas as humanities, the social and natural sciences,
languages and drama. Instructors cover the same amount of material in five weeks as they do
in a 13-week term during the academic year. Residential counselors (chosen from current Yale
students) organize an array of social and athletic events for boarding pupils.

SAINT THOMAS MORE SCHOOL SUMMER ACADEMIC CAMP
Res and Day — Boys Ages 12-17

Oakdale, CT 06370. 45 Cottage Rd. Tel: 860-823-3861. Fax: 860-823-3863.
www.stmct.org/summer-program.html   E-mail: triordan@stmct.org
Tim Viands, Dir.
Grades 7-12. Adm: FCFS. **Appl**—Fee $50. Due: Rolling.
Enr cap: 90.
Type of instruction: Dev_Read Enrich Rem_Eng Rem_Math Rem_Read Rev ESL/
   TOEFL_Prep SAT/ACT_Prep Study_Skills. **Courses:** Span Comp_Sci Eng ESL Hist

Math Sci Crafts Creative_Writing. **Avg class size:** 5. **Daily hours for:** Classes 4. Study 2. Rec 4. **High school credit:** 3.
Features: Boating Canoe Fishing Kayak Sail Baseball Basketball Cross-country Lacrosse Soccer Softball Swim Tennis Volleyball Watersports.
Fees 2010: Res $5495 (+$50-75), 5 wks. Day $3000 (+$50-75), 5 wks.
Housing: Dorms. **Swimming:** Lake. Campus facilities avail.
Est 1970. Nonprofit. Roman Catholic. **Ses:** 1. **Wks/ses:** 5. Operates July-Aug.

In addition to remedial and developmental reading, Saint Thomas More offers courses for makeup credit, enrichment or preview in various disciplines. A comprehensive English as a Second Language curriculum is available for international students. Recreational activities include a full waterfront program, water-skiing, sports and off-campus trips.

THE RECTORY SCHOOL
SUMMER@RECTORY
Res and Day — Coed Ages 10-14

Pomfret, CT 06258. 528 Pomfret St, PO Box 68. Tel: 860-928-1328. Fax: 860-928-4961.
www.rectoryschool.org   E-mail: summer@rectoryschool.org
Karl Koenigsbauer, Dir.
Grades 5-9. Adm: FCFS. **Appl**—Fee $0. Due: Rolling.
Enr: 85. Fac 15. Staff: Admin 3.
Type of instruction: Dev_Read Enrich Preview Rem_Eng Rem_Math Rem_Read Rev Study_Skills Tut. **LD Services:** Acad_Instruction Tut. **Courses:** Lat Span Environ_Sci ESL Expository_Writing Leadership Math SSAT_Prep Drama Media Music Photog. **Avg class size:** 8. **Daily hours for:** Classes 4. Study 1. Rec 3.
Conditions accepted: Dx LD.
Features: Canoe Chess Exploration Hiking Ropes_Crse Baseball Basketball Cross-country Golf Lacrosse Soccer Softball Swim Tennis Weight_Trng.
Fees 2011: Res $5725 (+$600), 4 wks. Day $1295 (+$300), 4 wks. Aid (Need).
Housing: Dorms. **Swimming:** Ocean Pool. Campus facilities avail.
Est 1950. Nonprofit. Episcopal. **Ses:** 1. **Wks/ses:** 4. Operates June-July.

Rectory's academic program stresses English, developmental and remedial reading, math and study skills. Each student receives tutoring for one period per day to address study skills or problems in a specific academic area. A supervised recreational program includes clubs, swimming and instructional sports clinics.

UNIVERSITY OF CONNECTICUT
UCONN MENTOR CONNECTION
Res — Coed Ages 15-17

Storrs, CT 06269. 2131 Hillside Rd, Unit 3007. Tel: 860-486-0283. Fax: 860-486-2900.
www.gifted.uconn.edu   E-mail: mentorconnection@uconn.edu
Joseph S. Renzulli, Dir. Student contact: Heather L. Spottiswoode.
Grades 11-12. Adm: Selective. Prereqs: GPA 3.0. **Appl**—Due: Apr. Transcript, 3 essays, 2 teacher recs.
Enr: 81. Enr cap: 85. Non-White: 50%. **Fac 30. Staff:** Admin 4. Couns 8.
Type of instruction: Adv. **Courses:** Archaeol Astron Engineering Expository_Writing Math Med/Healthcare Sci Web_Design Creative_Writing Fine_Arts Painting. **Avg class size:** 4. **Daily hours for:** Classes 7. Study 2. Rec 5. Grades. **College credit:** 3.
Features: Conservation Hiking Basketball Swim Volleyball.
Fees 2012: Res $3100 (+$75), 3 wks.
Housing: Dorms. Avg per room/unit: 2-4. **Swimming:** Pool.
Est 1996. Ses: 1. **Wks/ses:** 3. Operates July.

This program for rising high school juniors and seniors who are in the top quarter of their class allows students to participate in creative projects and research investigations in the arts and sciences under the supervision of university mentors. Research topics include archaeology, biology, chemistry, materials science, engineering, physics, psychology, Web design, education, nursing, pharmacy, arts and humanities. Special presentations address SAT preparation, college admissions and financial aid, and career planning. Recreation and weekend trips balance academic work.

THE SUMMER ACADEMY AT SUFFIELD
Res and Day — Coed Ages 12-18

**Suffield, CT 06078. 185 N Main St, PO Box 999. Tel: 860-386-4444. Fax: 860-668-2966.
www.suffieldacademy.org   E-mail: tony_oshaughnessy@suffieldacademy.org
Gregory Lynch, Dir.
Grades 7-12. Adm:** Selective. **Appl**—Fee $50. Due: Rolling. Rec, essay.
Enr: 130. **Fac 20. Staff:** Admin 2. Couns 35.
Type of instruction: Enrich SAT/ACT_Prep Study_Skills. **Courses:** Span ESL Expository_ Writing Math Sci Creative_Writing Fine_Arts Music Photog Theater. **Avg class size:** 10.
Daily hours for: Classes 6. Study 2, Rec 2. **High school credit.**
Features: Basketball Soccer Swim Tennis Weight_Trng.
Fees 2012: Res $6500 (+$900-1225), 5 wks. **Day $3750** (+$700), 5 wks. Aid (Need).
Housing: Dorms. **Swimming:** Pool.
Est 1995. Nonprofit. **Spons:** Suffield Academy. **Ses:** 1. **Wks/ses:** 5. Operates June-July.

Drawing its students from across the US and from other countries, Suffield provides a liberal arts curriculum that features intensive, 100-minute-long class and project periods. Course work is available in the arts, English, ESL, foreign language, science, math and the humanities. Pupils may also take part in a skills program that focuses on computer skills, study and research techniques, standardized test-taking strategies and planning for the college admission process. Recreational activities and trips supplement academics.

MARIANAPOLIS PREPARATORY SCHOOL SUMMER SESSION
Res and Day — Coed Ages 14-18

**Thompson, CT 06277. 26 Chase Rd, PO Box 304. Tel: 860-923-9565.
   Fax: 860-923-3730.
www.marianapolis.org/html/sumr_welcome.cfm
E-mail: esembor@marianapolis.org
Ed Sembor, Dir.
Grades 9-PG. Adm:** Selective. **Appl**—Fee $0. Due: Mar.
Type of instruction: Enrich. **Courses:** Comp_Sci Environ_Sci ESL Hist Marine_Bio/Stud Math Sci Film Photog Studio_Art. Homework. Tests. Grades.
Features: Aerobics Basketball Cross-country Lacrosse Soccer Softball Tennis Volleyball.
Fees 2009: Res $6000, 6 wks. **Day $2000,** 6 wks.
Housing: Dorms. Campus facilities avail.
Nonprofit. **Ses:** 1. **Wks/ses:** 6. Operates June-July.

In a small-class setting, Marianapolis enables boys and girls to choose two or three enrichment courses from a selection of offerings drawn from every major discipline. The school day incorporates time for athletics and study. Weekends provide opportunities for travel to nearby cities and recreational areas.

CHOATE ROSEMARY HALL
ACADEMIC ENRICHMENT PROGRAM
Res and Day — Coed Ages 12-18

Wallingford, CT 06492. 333 Christian St. Tel: 203-697-2365. Fax: 203-697-2519.
www.choate.edu/summerprograms   E-mail: choatesummer@choate.edu
J. Trent Nutting, Dir.
Grades 7-12. Adm: Selective. Admitted: 90%. **Appl**—Fee $60. Due: Rolling. Transcript, 3 recs.
Enr: 250. Intl: 25%. Non-White: 30%.
Type of instruction: Enrich SAT/ACT_Prep Study_Skills. **Courses:** Chin Fr Span Architect Bus/Fin Ecol Econ Expository_Writing Hist Math Pol_Sci Psych Public_Speak Sci Writing/Journ Ethics Forensic_Sci Robotics Dance Drama Fine_Arts Music. **Avg class size:** 12. **Daily hours for:** Classes 5½. Study 2. Rec 2. Homework. Tests. **High school credit.**
Features: Yoga Aerobics Baseball Basketball Rugby Soccer Softball Swim Tennis Volleyball.
Fees 2011: Res $6700 (+$500), 5 wks. Day $1040-2180/crse (+$500), 5 wks. Aid 2011 (Need): $300,000.
Housing: Dorms. Avg per room/unit: 2. **Swimming:** Pool. Campus facilities avail.
Est 1916. Nonprofit. Ses: 1. **Wks/ses:** 5. Operates June-July.

The Academic Enrichment Program allows students to develop skills and explore new subjects beyond the normal high school curriculum. Students select courses from offerings in the arts, English, history and social sciences, languages, math, science and interdisciplinary courses. Classes meet Monday through Saturday. Students engage in sports on weekday afternoons, with evening hours devoted to study. Choate schedules recreational trips on Wednesday and Saturday afternoons.

RUMSEY HALL SCHOOL SUMMER SESSION
Res and Day — Coed Ages 8-15

Washington Depot, CT 06794. 201 Romford Rd. Tel: 860-868-0535. Fax: 860-868-7907.
www.rumseyhall.org   E-mail: admiss@rumseyhall.org
Doug Kolpak, Dir.
Grades 3-9. Adm: FCFS. **Appl**—Fee $50-100. Due: Rolling. Transcript, standardized test scores, 1-2 recs.
Enr: 65. **Enr cap:** 65. **Fac 12. Staff:** Admin 1. Couns 2.
Type of instruction: Dev_Read Enrich Rev Study_Skills. **Courses:** Computers ESL Math Creative_Writing. **Avg class size:** 8. **Daily hours for:** Classes 4. Study 1. Rec 4.
Features: Canoe Fishing Hiking Riding Baseball Basketball Lacrosse Soccer Swim Tennis.
Fees 2011: Res $6800 (+$750), 5 wks. Day $1580-2430 (+$200), 5 wks. Aid (Need).
Housing: Dorms. Avg per room/unit: 2. **Swimming:** Lake. Campus facilities avail.
Est 1966. Nonprofit. Ses: 1. **Wks/ses:** 5. Operates June-July.

Rumsey Hall's summer program provides intensive academic review in English, mathematics, study skills and computers. Individual tutoring can be arranged, and instruction by trained reading specialists is available. Recreational and enrichment options include swimming, sports, daily hiking and horseback riding, and occasional off-campus trips.

TAFT SUMMER SCHOOL
Res and Day — Coed Ages 12-18

Watertown, CT 06795. 110 Woodbury Rd. Tel: 860-945-7961. Fax: 860-945-7859.
www.taftschool.org/summer   E-mail: summerschool@taftschool.org
Thomas W. Antonucci, Dir. Student contact: Kristina Kulikauskas.

Grades 7-12. Adm: Selective. **Appl**—Fee $50. Due: Rolling. Transcript, 2 teacher recs, guidance counselor rec.
Enr: 165. Intl: 45%. **Fac 35. Staff:** Admin 6. Res 41.
Type of instruction: Adv Enrich Preview Rev SAT/ACT_Prep Study_Skills. **Courses:** Fr Span Eng ESL Hist Math Public_Speak Sci Speech Ceramics Creative_Writing Drama Fine_Arts Photog Studio_Art. **Avg class size:** 10. **Daily hours for:** Classes 4½. Study 2. Rec 1½. Homework. Tests. Grades.
Features: Basketball Soccer Squash Tennis Track Ultimate_Frisbee Volleyball Weight_Trng.
Fees 2011: Res $5975 (+$450), 5 wks. Day $3500 (+$300), 5 wks. Aid 2010 (Merit & Need): $55,000.
Housing: Dorms. Avg per room/unit: 2. Campus facilities avail.
Est 1982. Nonprofit. **Ses:** 1. **Wks/ses:** 5. Operates June-Aug.

Taft's summer session, which comprises the Young Scholars Program (grades 7-9) and the Liberal Studies Program (grades 9-12), is designed for students who wish to improve their academic standing through a concentrated and rigorous program. Course work provides them with the opportunity to enrich their school experiences by taking classes not otherwise available to them or by concentrating on fundamental skills development. All pupils enroll in two major courses and two minor electives. Taft also conducts a full sports program, various on-campus activities and cultural weekend day trips.

OXFORD ACADEMY SUMMER PROGRAM
Res — Boys Ages 14-20

Westbrook, CT 06498. 1393 Boston Post Rd. Tel: 860-399-6247. Fax: 860-399-6805.
www.oxfordacademy.net   E-mail: admissions@oxfordacademy.net
Philip B. Cocchiola, Head. Student contact: Patricia Davis.
Grades 9-PG. Adm: FCFS. **Appl**—Due: Rolling.
Enr: 25. **Enr cap:** 25. **Fac 16. Staff:** Admin 4.
Type of instruction: Adv Enrich Rem_Eng Rem_Math Rem_Read Rev SAT/ACT_Prep. **Courses:** Fr Ger Span ESL Marine_Bio/Stud Art Photog. **Avg class size:** 1. **Daily hours for:** Classes 6. Study 2. Rec 4. **High school credit:** ½.
Focus: Study_Skills. **Features:** Deep-sea Fishing Hiking Kayak White-water_Raft Basketball Golf In-line_Skating Soccer Softball Swim Tennis Ultimate_Frisbee Volleyball Weight_Trng.
Fees 2011: Res $7298 (+$375), 5 wks.
Housing: Dorms. **Swimming:** Ocean.
Est 1906. Nonprofit. **Ses:** 1. **Wks/ses:** 5. Operates June-July.

Individualized education prepares both academically deficient and academically gifted students for college or further secondary work. Courses of study include remedial and advanced reading, English, math, history, foreign languages, science, art and English as a Second Language. A hands-on marine biology class takes advantage of the school's proximity to Long Island Sound and the Mystic Aquarium. White-water rafting, deep-sea fishing, kayaking and hiking excursions supplement course work, and boys and girls also go to concerts, amusement parks and cultural venues.

THE LOOMIS CHAFFEE SUMMER PROGRAM
Res and Day — Coed Ages 12-17

Windsor, CT 06095. 4 Batchelder Rd. Tel: 860-687-6355. Fax: 860-687-6859.
www.loomischaffee.org/summerprogram   E-mail: summer_program@loomis.org
Jeffrey Scanlon, Dir.
Grades 7-12. Adm: Selective. **Appl**—Fee $60. Due: Rolling. Transcript, 3 recs.
Enr cap: 100. **Fac 15.** Prof 1. K-12 staff 13. Specialists 1. **Staff:** Admin 2. Couns 20.
Type of instruction: Enrich SAT/ACT_Prep. **Courses:** Chin Environ_Sci Expository_Writ-

ing Hist Math Public_Speak Sci Robotics Creative_Writing Dance Drawing Painting Photog Studio_Art Theater Pottery. **Avg class size:** 10. **Daily hours for:** Classes 4. Study 2. Rec 2. Homework. **High school credit.**
Features: Aquatics Canoe Climbing_Wall Community_Serv Exploration Hiking Kayak Outdoor_Ed Ropes_Crse White-water_Raft Yoga Aerobics Basketball Soccer Swim Volleyball Weight_Trng.
Fees 2012: Res $6800 (+$500), 5 wks. Day $4700, 5 wks. Aid (Need).
Housing: Dorms. Avg per room/unit: 2. **Swimming:** Pool. Campus facilities avail.
Est 2011. Inc. **Ses:** 1. **Wks/ses:** 5. Operates July-Aug.

The cornerstone of the summer program at Loomis Chaffee is its emphasis on writing. Middle and upper school students choose from writing courses covering poetry, drama, fiction, nonfiction and public speaking. General studies course offerings are drawn from the areas of the humanities, mathematics, and the arts and sciences. SSAT and SAT exam preparation is also available.

DELAWARE

UNIVERSITY OF DELAWARE SUMMER COLLEGE
Res — Coed Ages 16-18

Newark, DE 19716. Honors Program, 186 S College Ave. Tel: 302-831-6560. Fax: 302-831-4194.
www.udel.edu/summercollege   E-mail: summercollege@udel.edu
Michael A. McCloskey, Coord.
Grades 11-12. Adm: Somewhat selective. **Appl**—Fee $50. Due: May. Transcript, essays, test scores, 2-3 recs.
Enr: 90. **Enr cap:** 135. **Fac 10. Prof 10. Staff:** Admin 1.
Type of instruction: Enrich Undergrad. **Courses:** Comm Econ Eng Intl_Relations Relig_ Stud Sci Dance Music Studio_Art. **Avg class size:** 25. **Daily hours for:** Classes 3. Study 6. Homework. Tests. Grades. **College credit:** 3-4/crse, total 7.
Features: Swim.
Fees 2009: Res $2495-5695 (+$500), 5 wks. Aid (Merit & Need).
Housing: Dorms. Avg per room/unit: 4. **Swimming:** Pool. Campus facilities avail.
Est 1983. Nonprofit. **Ses:** 1. **Wks/ses:** 5. Operates July-Aug.

Academically talented students entering grades 11 and 12 sample courses and earn up to seven college credits through this University of Delaware program. Core courses, composed entirely of Summer College students, vary by year. Qualified pupils may also enroll in Second Summer Session courses, introductory level classes offered to both Summer College students and current undergraduates.

DISTRICT OF COLUMBIA

THE GEORGE WASHINGTON UNIVERSITY
PRE-COLLEGE PROGRAM
Res — Coed Ages 15-17

Washington, DC 20052. 1922 F St NW, Ste 304. Tel: 202-994-6360. Fax: 202-994-9360.
www.precollege.gwu.edu   E-mail: gwsummer@gwu.edu
Yvonne Hood, Dir. Student contact: Andrea Binner, E-mail: abinner@gwu.edu.

Grades 10-12 (younger if qualified). Adm: Selective. **Appl**—Fee $50. Due: Apr. Transcript, rec, essay.
Enr: 100. **Intl:** 8%. **Fac 9.** Prof 8. Specialists 1. **Staff:** Admin 2. Couns 8.
Type of instruction: Adv Enrich Undergrad. **Courses:** Bus/Fin Environ_Sci Expository_ Writing Govt Law Pol_Sci Writing/Journ Creative_Writing Media Photog Theater. **Avg class size:** 20. **Daily hours for:** Classes 6. Study 4. Rec 3. Homework. Tests. Grades.
College credit: 3/crse, total 6.
Features: Hiking Ropes_Crse Swim Tennis.
Fees 2012: Res $2737-8575 (+$75), 1-6 wks. Day $1984-5269 (+$75), 1-6 wks.
Housing: Dorms. **Swimming:** Pool. Campus facilities avail.
Est 1968. Nonprofit. **Ses:** 5. **Wks/ses:** 1-6. Operates July-Aug.

The university offers one-, three- and six-week credit-bearing and noncredit courses for academically motivated high schoolers. Credit-bearing classes are limited to rising seniors, who attend class alongside George Washington undergraduates. Students enroll in a writing seminar and an elective course of their choosing. Weekly talks and demonstrations address academic exploration and college life. Noncredit courses are open to students entering grades 10-12. Participants in both programs make use of the cultural and intellectual resources of the city.

GEORGETOWN UNIVERSITY
SUMMER COLLEGE FOR HIGH SCHOOL STUDENTS
Res and Day — Coed Ages 15-18

Washington, DC 20007. School of Continuing Studies, 3307 M St NW, Ste 202.
Tel: 202-687-8600. Fax: 202-687-8954.
http://scs.georgetown.edu/hoyas   E-mail: highschool@georgetown.edu
Robert L. Manuel, Dir.
Grades 10-12. Adm: Selective. Prereqs: GPA 2.0. **Appl**—Fee $50. Due: Rolling. Transcript, essay, rec, standardized test results.
Enr: 41-87. **Staff:** Couns 12.
Type of instruction: Adv Undergrad. **Courses:** Arabic Fr Ger Span Bus/Fin Comp_Sci Econ Expository_Writing Forensic_Sci Hist Intl_Relations Law Math Pol_Sci Psych Public_Speak Sci Sociol Music Studio_Art Theater. **Daily hours for:** Classes 3. Study 3.
College credit: 3-6/crse, total 12.
Features: Basketball Cross-country Soccer Swim Tennis.
Fees 2011: Res $5536-7942, 5 wks. Day $3620-6842, 5 wks. Aid (Need).
Housing: Dorms. **Swimming:** Pool.
Nonprofit. **Ses:** 2. **Wks/ses:** 5. Operates June-Aug.

Boys and girls who have completed at least one year of high school enroll in one or two undergraduate courses suited to their interests, background and previous academic achievement. Alongside current Georgetown students, pupils choose from more than 100 offerings in the arts, foreign language, business, math, science, computers and the social sciences. Participants benefit from the services available through the university, take part in programs designed by the counseling staff, and learn the importance of time management. Activities include recreational options, trips to nearby theatrical performances and sporting events, and community service opportunities. Students may enroll in two sessions with the director's approval.

SUMMER DISCOVERY
Res — Coed Ages 15-18

Washington, DC. Georgetown Univ.
Contact (Year-round): 1326 Old Northern Blvd, Roslyn, NY 11576. Tel: 516-621-3939.
Fax: 516-625-3438.
www.summerdiscovery.com   E-mail: discovery@summerdiscovery.com

Bob Musiker, Exec Dir.
Grades 10-PG. Adm: FCFS. **Appl**—Fee $95. Due: Rolling.
Enr: 195. **Enr cap:** 225.
Type of instruction: Enrich SAT/ACT_Prep Study_Skills. **Courses:** Bus/Fin Debate ESL
Govt Speech Writing/Journ Crafts Creative_Writing Dance Drama Filmmaking Fine_
Arts Media Music Photog. Homework. Tests.
Features: Adventure_Travel Canoe Community_Serv Hiking Kayak Aerobics Basketball
Soccer Swim Tennis Weight_Trng.
Fees 2011: Res $6599, 4 wks. Aid (Need).
Housing: Dorms. **Swimming:** Pool River.
Inc. **Ses:** 1. **Wks/ses:** 4. Operates July.

See program description under Los Angeles, CA.

FLORIDA

FLORIDA AIR ACADEMY SUMMER SESSION
Res and Day — Coed Ages 11-18

Melbourne, FL 32901. 1950 S Academy Dr. Tel: 321-723-3211, 877-422-2338.
Fax: 321-676-0422.
www.flair.com   E-mail: admissions@flair.com
Col. James Dwight, Pres.
Grades 6-PG. Adm: Selective. **Appl**—Due: Rolling.
Enr: 150. **Fac 22.**
Type of instruction: Adv Dev_Read Enrich Preview Rem_Eng Rem_Math Rem_Read
Rev SAT/ACT_Prep Study_Skills Tut. **Courses:** Comp_Sci ESL Math. **Avg class size:**
8. **Daily hours for:** Classes 4. Study 2. Rec 5. **High school credit:** 1.
Features: Aviation/Aero Climbing_Wall Milit_Trng Rock_Climb Scuba Baseball Basketball
Cross-country Football Golf Martial_Arts Skateboarding Soccer Surfing Swim Tennis
Track Watersports.
Fees 2011: Res $6000 (+$1200), 6 wks. Day $2600 (+$600), 6 wks.
Housing: Dorms. **Swimming:** Ocean Pool. Campus facilities avail.
Est 1961. Inc. **Ses:** 1. **Wks/ses:** 6. Operates June-Aug.

Florida Air's summer session offers advanced, review and remedial courses. Instructional
courses include ESL, SAT Prep and tutoring and study skills sessions. The academy conducts
all levels of flight instruction, including Junior Wings for boys and girls in grades 6-8.

MONTVERDE ACADEMY SUMMER SCHOOL
Res and Day — Coed Ages 12-18

Montverde, FL 34756. 17235 7th St. Tel: 407-469-2561. Fax: 407-469-3711.
www.montverde.org   E-mail: admissions@montverde.org
Sue Tortora, Dir.
Grades 7-12. Adm: Selective. **Appl**—Due: Rolling.
Enr: 60. **Fac 10. Staff:** Admin 7.
Type of instruction: Enrich Rem_Read Rev SAT/ACT_Prep. **Courses:** Span Comp_Sci
Econ Eng ESL Govt Hist Math Sci Anat & Physiol. **Daily hours for:** Classes 5. Study 2.
Rec 4. **High school credit:** 1½.
Features: Aquatics Boating Canoe Weight_Loss Baseball Soccer Swim Tennis Track
Watersports.
Fees 2011: Res $2000-5000 (+$600), 2-4 wks. Day $1250-2500 (+$300), 2-4 wks.
Housing: Dorms. **Swimming:** Lake Pool. Campus facilities avail.
Nonprofit. **Ses:** 2. **Wks/ses:** 2-4. Operates June-July.

This summer session offers courses for review, preview and enrichment in English, math, civics, history, science and government. Activities include swimming, sports, and excursions to nearby theme parks and other local attractions.

GEORGIA

EMORY UNIVERSITY PRE-COLLEGE PROGRAM
Res — Coed Ages 15-18

Atlanta, GA 30322. Candler Library, Ste 200, MS 1580-002-2AA, 550 Asbury Cir.
Tel: 404-727-0671. Fax: 404-727-6724.
www.precollege.emory.edu   E-mail: precollege@emory.edu
Philip Wainwright, Dir. Student contact: Mollie Korski.
Grades 11-12. Adm: Selective. Prereqs: GPA 3.0. SAT: 1100. **Appl**—Fee $50. Due: Rolling. Transcript, standardized test scores, rec.
Enr: 80. **Enr cap:** 100. Intl: 5%. Non-White: 15%. **Fac 10.** Prof 10. **Staff:** Admin 6. Couns 9.
Type of instruction: Adv Undergrad. **Courses:** Fr Comp_Sci Econ Hist Math Med/Health-care Psych Philos Sociol Acting Drawing Film Photog Theater Poetry. **Avg class size:** 10. **Daily hours for:** Classes 3. Study 3. Rec 3. Homework. Tests. **College credit:** 4/crse, total 4.
Features: Swim.
Fees 2012: Res $3365-9009. Day $2385-5469.
Housing: Dorms. **Swimming:** Pool. Campus facilities avail.
Est 2009. Nonprofit. Methodist. **Ses:** 5. **Wks/ses:** 2-6. Operates June-Aug.

Rising high school juniors and seniors preview college life while enrolling in university-level courses along current Emory undergraduates in this program. Participants choose between two-week noncredit courses and six-week for-credit classes. Credit-bearing courses lead to transferable college credit. Boarding students live together in a campus dorm and participate in various programs, activities and excursions, many of which are designed to prepare boys and girls for college life.

SUMMER INSTITUTE FOR THE GIFTED
Res — Coed Ages 8-17; Day — Coed 10-17

Atlanta, GA. Emory Univ.
Contact (Year-round): River Plz, 9 W Broad St, Stamford, CT 06902.
Tel: 203-399-5188, 866-303-4744. Fax: 203-399-5455.
www.giftedstudy.org   E-mail: sig.info@giftedstudy.com
Barbara Swicord, Pres.
Student contact: Christine Provencher, E-mail: cprovencher@giftedstudy.com.
Grades 4-11. Adm: Very selective. Admitted: 90%. **Appl**—Fee $95. Due: Rolling. Transcript, standardized test scores, classification as gifted/2 recs.
Intl: 25%.
Type of instruction: Adv Enrich SAT/ACT_Prep Study_Skills. **Courses:** Engineering Expository_Writing Forensic_Sci Law Math Med/Healthcare Sci Writing/Journ Philos Robotics Creative_Writing Dance Photog Screenwriting. **Avg class size:** 14.
Fees 2012: Res $4395, 3 wks. Day $2495, 3 wks.
Housing: Dorms. Campus facilities avail.
Nonprofit. **Spons:** National Society for the Gifted & Talented. **Ses:** 1. **Wks/ses:** 3. Operates June-July.

See program description under Berkeley, CA.

ADVANCED ACADEMY OF GEORGIA
YOUNG SCHOLARS INSTITUTE
Res — Coed Ages 13-14

Carrollton, GA 30118. Univ of West Georgia. Tel: 678-839-6249. Fax: 678-839-0636.
www.advancedacademy.org/ysi.php   E-mail: scolgate@westga.edu
Susan Colgate, Dir.
Grades 8-9. Adm: Selective. **Appl**—Fee $0. Due: Rolling. Transcript, 2 teacher recs, standardized test scores.
Enr: 24. **Enr cap:** 24.
Type of instruction: Adv Enrich. **Courses:** Astron Debate Geol Math Sci Animation Creative_Writing Studio_Art.
Fees 2009: Res $500-900, 1-2 wks. Aid (Need).
Housing: Dorms.
Nonprofit. **Ses:** 2. **Wks/ses:** 1. Operates June.

On the University of West Georgia campus, YSI conducts two weeklong programs for highly able eighth and ninth graders. University professors teach daytime classes in which pupils explore various disciplines in depth, while evenings are devoted to social and recreational activities. The two sessions have different focuses—math and science for the first and arts and humanities for the second—and boys and girls may enroll in one or both weeks of the program.

RIVERSIDE MILITARY ACADEMY
SUMMER OPPORTUNITY AND ACADEMIC REVIEW
Res and Day — Boys Ages 12-17

Gainesville, GA 30501. 2001 Riverside Dr. Tel: 770-532-6251, 800-462-2338.
Fax: 678-291-3364.
www.riversidemilitary.com   E-mail: apply@riversidemilitary.com
Jim Robison, Dean.
Student contact: Lynne Henderson, E-mail: lhenderson@riversidemilitary.com.
Grades 7-11. Adm: FCFS. **Appl**—Fee $100. Due: Rolling.
Enr: 100. **Intl:** 10%.
Type of instruction: Adv Enrich Rem_Eng Rem_Math Rem_Read Rev SAT/ACT_Prep Study_Skills Tut. **Courses:** Span Comp_Sci Eng ESL Hist Math Sci Studio_Art. **Avg class size:** 14. **Daily hours for:** Classes 6. Study 2. Rec 3. Homework. Tests. Grades. **High school credit.**
Features: Canoe Climbing_Wall Community_Serv Rappelling Riflery Ropes_Crse Swim Tennis Volleyball.
Fees 2012: Res $4450-4725, 4 wks. Day $2075, 4 wks.
Housing: Dorms. Avg per room/unit: 2. **Swimming:** Lake Pool. Campus facilities avail.
Nonprofit. **Ses:** 1. **Wks/ses:** 4. Operates June-July.

SOAR helps students prepare for both the upcoming school year and future secondary school experiences. The program addresses study skills development, time-management and organizational skills, and note-taking skills. Boys choose either two repeat courses or one new course for credit. Students attend supervised study halls during the day and in the evening. Field trips and on-campus weekend activities round out the program.

GEORGIA DEPARTMENT OF EDUCATION
GOVERNOR'S HONORS PROGRAM
Res — Coed Ages 16-18

Valdosta, GA. Valdosta State Univ.
Contact (Year-round): 1852 Twin Towers E, Atlanta, GA 30334. Tel: 404-657-0183.
Fax: 678-605-6886.

www.valdosta.edu/ghp　E-mail: ghp@doe.k12.ga.us
Dale Lyles, Dir.
Grades 11-12. Adm: Very selective. **Appl**—Fee $0. Due: Dec.
Enr: 690. **Enr cap:** 690. **Fac 64. Staff:** Admin 4. Res 32.
Type of instruction: Adv Enrich. **Courses:** Fr Ger Lat Span Agriculture Comm Computers Eng Environ_Sci Math Sci Dance Music Studio_Art Theater. **Avg class size:** 15. **Daily hours for:** Classes 7. Homework.
Fees 2012: Free (in-state residents). Res 4 wks.
Housing: Dorms.
Est 1964. Nonprofit. **Ses:** 1. **Wks/ses:** 4. Operates June-July.

Hosted by Valdosta State University, GHP provides enriching educational opportunities not usually available during the school year for intellectually gifted and artistically talented Georgia high school students. Each student admitted into this free program chooses major and minor areas of study and engages in various extracurricular activities, among them educational seminars and arts performances. Interested pupils must be nominated by their schools.

HAWAII

HAWAII PREPARATORY ACADEMY SUMMER SESSION
Res and Day — Coed Ages 11-17

Kamuela, HI 96743. 65-1692 Kohala Mountain Rd. Tel: 808-881-4088.
Fax: 808-881-4071.
www.hpa.edu/summer　E-mail: summer@hpa.edu
Shirley Ann Fukumoto, Dir.
Grades 6-12. Adm: Selective. **Appl**—Fee $25-35. Due: Apr. Transcript, one rec, standardized testing.
Enr: 100. **Enr cap:** 100. **Fac 18.** K-12 staff 18. **Staff:** Admin 3.
Type of instruction: Adv Enrich Preview SAT/ACT_Prep Study_Skills. **Courses:** Japan Span Ecol Econ Environ_Sci ESL Marine_Bio/Stud Math Sci Writing/Journ Robotics Ceramics Crafts Creative_Writing Dance Filmmaking Fine_Arts Music Photog. **Avg class size:** 10. **Daily hours for:** Classes 6. Study 1. Rec 2.
Features: Aquatics Cooking Exploration Hiking Kayak Scuba Equestrian Swim Tennis.
Fees 2012: Res $4600 (+$500), 4 wks. Day $550/crse, 4 wks.
Housing: Dorms. Avg per room/unit: 2. **Swimming:** Ocean Pool.
Est 1974. Nonprofit. **Ses:** 1. **Wks/ses:** 4. Operates June-July.

HPA offers academic enrichment opportunities in science, math, English and other disciplines. Afternoon activities include intramural sports, an equestrian program, scuba certification, swimming, tennis lessons and driver education. In addition, students learn about the big island through excursions to Volcanoes National Park, ocean kayaking, snorkeling and hiking.

ILLINOIS

UNIVERSITY OF CHICAGO
INSIGHT SUMMER PROGRAMS FOR HIGH SCHOOL STUDENTS
Res and Day — Coed Ages 15-18

Chicago, IL 60637. Summer Session Office, 1427 E 60th St, 2nd Fl. Tel: 773-702-6033.
Fax: 773-834-0549.

https://summer.uchicago.edu/insight.cfm E-mail: summerhs@uchicago.edu
Student contact: Sarah Lopez.
Grades 10-12. Adm: Selective. Appl—Fee $40. Due: Rolling. Transcript, essay, 2 recs.
Enr: 15. Enr cap: 15. Intl: 8%. Staff: Admin 3. Couns 6.
Type of instruction: Adv Undergrad. Courses: Environ_Sci Expository_Writing Law
Psych Urban_Stud Creative_Writing. Homework. Tests. Grades. College credit: 3/crse,
total 3.
Features: Swim.
Fees 2012: Res $5210, 3 wks. Day $3295, 3 wks. Aid (Merit & Need).
Housing: Dorms. Swimming: Lake. Campus facilities avail.
Ses: 2. Wks/ses: 3. Operates June-July.

Insight's intensive three-week courses combine material taught in undergraduate-level courses with an experiential element that incorporates the city of Chicago. Subjects include American law and litigation, ancient Egypt, fiction writing, collegiate writing, developmental psychology, the science of sustainability and field studies in urban society. **See Also Page 32**

NORTHWESTERN UNIVERSITY
CENTER FOR TALENT DEVELOPMENT SUMMER PROGRAM
Res — Coed Ages 9-18; Day — Coed 4-18

Evanston, IL 60208. 617 Dartmouth Pl. Tel: 847-491-3782. Fax: 847-467-0880.
www.ctd.northwestern.edu/summer E-mail: summer@ctd.northwestern.edu
Andrea Steffan, Coord.
Grades PS-12. Adm: Selective. Appl—Fee $60. Due: Rolling. Transcript, standardized test
scores, essay, 2 recs, writing sample (certain courses).
Fac 60.
Type of instruction: Adv. Courses: Architect Astron Comp_Sci Debate Ecol Eng Exposi-
tory_Writing Forensic_Sci Hist Intl_Relations Psych Sci Writing/Journ Ethics Genetics
Philos Robotics Stats Web_Design Zoology Creative_Writing Drama. Avg class size:
18. Daily hours for: Classes 5. Study 3. Rec 4. Homework. Tests. High school credit:
1/crse, total 2.
Features: Swim.
Fees 2012: Res $1275-3330 (+$50-150), 1-3 wks. Day $770-1945 (+$50-150), 1-3 wks.
Aid (Need).
Housing: Dorms. Swimming: Lake.
Est 1982. Nonprofit. Ses: 8. Wks/ses: 1-3. Operates June-Aug.

CTD offers four academic programs for high-achieving students. Leapfrog (grades pre-K-3) is a weeklong enrichment curriculum offered in a language arts track and a math/science track. Apogee participants (grades 4-6) immerse themselves in a single intensive course. The Spectrum program (grades 7 and 8) enables pupils to complete a year- or semester-long honors-level course in three weeks. In Equinox (grades 9-12), a master teacher experienced with gifted adolescents teaches each course. The latter three programs meet for five hours each weekday and have homework requirements, while Leapfrog offers both half- and full-day enrollment options.

NORTHWESTERN UNIVERSITY
COLLEGE PREPARATION PROGRAM
Res and Day — Coed Ages 17-18

Evanston, IL 60208. 405 Church St. Tel: 847-467-6703. Fax: 847-491-3660.
www.northwestern.edu/collegeprep E-mail: cpp@northwestern.edu
Stephanie Teterycz, Dir.
Grade 12 (younger if qualified). Adm: Selective. Prereqs: GPA 3.0. Appl—Fee $50. Due:
Apr. Transcript, rec, personal statement.
Enr: 95. Fac 100. Staff: Admin 3. Couns 6.

Type of instruction: Adv Preview Undergrad. **Courses:** Arabic Fr Ger Ital Span Archaeol Astron Bus/Fin Ecol Environ_Sci Expository_Writing Govt Speech Writing/Journ Creative_Writing Fine_Arts Media Music Photog Theater. **Avg class size:** 15. **Daily hours for:** Classes 3. **College credit:** 9.
Features: Swim.
Fees 2012: Res $2800-4666 (+$500), 2-3 wks. Day $2000-4266 (+$500), 2-3 wks. Aid (Need).
Housing: Dorms. **Swimming:** Lake Pool.
Nonprofit. **Ses:** 1. **Wks/ses:** 2-9. Operates June-Aug.

CPP offers more than 350 college-level courses to rising high school seniors with at least a 3.0 grade point average; highly qualified rising juniors may also apply. Classes range in length from three to nine weeks. Participants may earn a full year of college credit in biology, chemistry, physics or a foreign language through an intensive, three-course sequence. The intensive session, for which pupils must receive prior CPP approval, covers a year's worth of material in an eight-week program that meets for approximately three hours each weekday (plus lab time). Two-week noncredit IN FOCUS seminars cover such topics as the legal professionion, global justice and environmental sustainabilitiy.

INDIANA

HOWE SCHOOL SUMMER CAMP
Res — Boys Ages 9-15

Howe, IN 46746. PO Box 240. Tel: 260-562-2131, 888-462-4693. Fax: 260-562-3678.
www.thehoweschool.org   E-mail: admissions@thehoweschool.org
George Douglass, Supt.
Grades 4-10. Adm: FCFS. Appl—Due: Rolling.
Enr: 122. Fac 10. Staff: Admin 4. Couns 18.
Courses: Crafts Theater.
Features: Aquatics Archery Canoe Hiking Milit_Trng Riding Ropes_Crse Sail Scuba Baseball Basketball Golf Swim Tennis Volleyball.
Fees 2012: Res $2200-3500 (+$50), 3-6 wks.
Housing: Cabins Houses. Swimming: Lake.
Est 1932. Nonprofit. Ses: 3. Wks/ses: 3-6. Operates June-July.

Howe combines academic work with a range of outdoor recreational activities and leadership training. Campers at all grade levels receive review instruction in science, mathematics, and English, while boys entering grades 9 and 10 take English or math courses for high school credit. In addition to traditional camping activities, boys may take part in less common pursuits, such as scuba, sailing, horsemanship and a ropes course, and instructors place emphasis on a different sport each week. Military training, designed to develop orderliness, self-discipline and social skills, is part of the daily program.

UNIVERSITY OF NOTRE DAME SUMMER SCHOLARS
Res — Coed Ages 16-18

Notre Dame, IN 46556. Office of Pre-College Prgms, 202 Brownson Hall.
Tel: 574-631-0990. Fax: 574-631-8964.
www.precollege.nd.edu/summer-scholars   E-mail: precoll@nd.edu
Alyssia J. Coates, Dir.
Grades 11-12. Adm: Selective. Appl—Fee $50. Due: Feb. Transcript, test scores, counselor report, rec.
Enr: 280. Enr cap: 280.

Type of instruction: Enrich. **Courses:** Bus/Fin Eng Law Psych Public_Speak Relig_Stud Sci Acting Film Music. **Avg class size:** 20.
Features: Community_Serv.
Fees 2012: Res $2800, 2 wks.
Housing: Dorms. Campus facilities avail.
Roman Catholic. **Ses:** 1. **Wks/ses:** 2. Operates July.

Summer Scholars preview college life and pursue intensive study in one of 14 academic tracks. Notre Dame faculty conduct all courses. The program schedule incorporates time for spiritual and personal development activities, and scholars have the opportunity to work with various service organizations. Among the available social and recreational activities are a talent show, sports, film screenings and campus lectures.

EARLHAM COLLEGE
EXPLORE-A-COLLEGE
Res — Coed Ages 15-17

Richmond, IN 47374. 801 National Rd W, Drawer 188. Tel: 765-983-1330, 800-327-5426. Fax: 765-983-1560.
www.earlham.edu/~eac   E-mail: exploreacollege@earlham.edu
Susan Hillmann de Castaneda, Dir.
Grades 10-12. Adm: Somewhat selective. Admitted: 98%. Prereqs: GPA 3.0. **Appl**—Fee $50. Due: Rolling. Transcript, 2 recs, essay.
Enr: 72. **Enr cap:** 100. Intl: 1%. Non-White: 45%. **Fac 10. Prof 10. Staff:** Admin 2. Couns 18.
Type of instruction: Adv Enrich Study_Skills. **Courses:** Japan Span Econ Expository_ Writing Psych Sci Creative_Writing Photog Studio_Art. **Avg class size:** 10. **Daily hours for:** Classes 5. Study 4. Rec 5. Homework. Tests. Grades. **College credit:** 2/crse, total 2.
Features: Climbing_Wall Community_Serv Peace/Cross-cultural Rock_Climb Swim.
Fees 2012: Res $1700 (+$150), 2 wks. Aid 2011 (Need): $28,000.
Housing: Dorms. Avg per room/unit: 2. **Swimming:** Pool. Campus facilities avail.
Est 1981. Nonprofit. Religious Society of Friends. **Ses:** 1. **Wks/ses:** 2. Operates July.

Conducted on its campus by Earlham College, the program provides high-ability high schoolers with the opportunity to develop college-level skills while sampling college life. College faculty teach courses in art, biology, English, philosophy, economics, Japanese, peace studies, psychology and Spanish. Students earn two semester hours of transferable college credit for each course completed. Current Earlham students serve as counselors and teaching assistants.

INDIANA STATE UNIVERSITY SUMMER HONORS PROGRAM
Res — Coed Ages 15-17

Terre Haute, IN 47809. Office of Adm, 218 N 6th St. Tel: 812-237-2121, 800-468-6478. Fax: 812-237-8023.
www.indstate.edu/experience   E-mail: admissions@indstate.edu
Grades 10-12. Adm: Selective. Prereqs: GPA 3.0. **Appl**—Due: Rolling. Transcript, rec.
Fac 23. Staff: Admin 1. Couns 6.
Type of instruction: Adv Undergrad. **Courses:** Astron Bus/Fin Education Engineering Med/Healthcare Fine_Arts Photog. **Daily hours for:** Classes 7. **College credit:** 2.
Features: Aviation/Aero Swim.
Housing: Dorms. **Swimming:** Pool.
Est 1969. Nonprofit. **Ses:** 1. **Wks/ses:** 1. Operates July.

High schoolers who have completed junior year may earn two college credits through a demanding weeklong seminar that covers a variety of liberal arts, science and business topics. Experienced ISU faculty guide all of the seminars. Recreational and cultural activities supplement academics.

PURDUE UNIVERSITY
GIFTED EDUCATION RESOURCE INSTITUTE
SUMMER YOUTH PROGRAMS
Res — Coed Ages 11-18; Day — Coed 4-10

West Lafayette, IN 47907. Beering Hall, Rm 5178, 100 N University St.
Tel: 765-494-7243. Fax: 765-496-2706.
www.purdue.edu/geri   E-mail: geri@purdue.edu
Matt Fugate, Coord. Student contact: Stacey L. Folyer, E-mail: sfolyer@purdue.edu.
Grades K-12. Adm: Selective. Admitted: 98%. Prereqs: IQ 120. **Appl**—Due: Rolling. Transcript, standardized test results, rec, essay.
Enr: 600. Intl: 10%. **Fac 25. Staff:** Admin 5. Res 15.
Type of instruction: Adv Enrich. **Courses:** Archaeol Bus/Fin Comp_Sci Debate Ecol Engineering Environ_Sci Expository_Writing Forensic_Sci Govt Marine_Bio/Stud Med/ Healthcare Speech Writing/Journ Crafts Creative_Writing Filmmaking Finc_Arts Media Painting Photog Studio_Art Theater. **Avg class size:** 15. **Daily hours for:** Classes 6. Study 1½. Rec 3.
Features: Adventure_Travel Aquatics Canoe Basketball Football Swim Tennis Volleyball.
Fees 2012: Res $975-1850 (+$50), 1-2 wks. Day $625, 1 wk. Aid 2010 (Need): $26,675.
Housing: Dorms. **Swimming:** Pool. Campus facilities avail.
Est 1977. Nonprofit. **Ses:** 4. **Wks/ses:** 1-2. Operates June-July.

GERI Super Summer day program provides enrichment opportunities for gifted young children. In GERI Summer Camps, students entering grades 5-12 pursue individual interests as they choose from course work in an array of subjects. Participants reside on campus and thus have access to the university's computers, labs, art studios, and athletic and recreational facilities.

IOWA

IOWA STATE UNIVERSITY
OFFICE OF PRECOLLEGIATE PROGRAMS
FOR TALENTED AND GIFTED SUMMER PROGRAMS
Res — Coed Ages 13-16; Day — Coed 8-16

Ames, IA 50011. 357 Carver Hall. Tel: 515-294-1772, 800-262-3810. Fax: 515-294-3505.
www.opptag.iastate.edu   E-mail: opptag@iastate.edu
Carmen P. Flagge, Coord.
Grades 3-11 (younger if qualified). Adm: Somewhat selective. Admitted: 97%. Prereqs: GPA 3.5. SAT M/CR 950; ACT 20. **Appl**—Fee $35-50. Due: May.
Enr: 100. **Enr cap:** 100. Intl: 5%. Non-White: 20%. **Fac 45.** Prof 5. Col/grad students 20. K-12 staff 20. **Staff:** Admin 4. Couns 9.
Type of instruction: Adv Enrich. **Courses:** Comp_Sci Math Sci Engineering Neurosci Robotics Web_Design Creative_Writing Drama Studio_Art. **Avg class size:** 15. **Daily hours for:** Classes 6. Study 1. Rec 3. Homework. Tests. **High school credit.**
Features: Canoe Swim Tennis.
Fees 2012: Res $700-2000 (+$50-600), 1-3 wks. Day $600-1500 (+$60-360), 1-3 wks. Aid 2011 (Need): $7000.
Housing: Dorms. **Swimming:** Pool.
Est 1986. Nonprofit. **Ses:** 3. **Wks/ses:** 1-3. Operates July-Aug.

OPPTAG conducts several precollege programs for gifted students. Adventures! allows day students who have completed grades 2-6 to choose from enrichment courses in various subjects. CY-TAG, enrolling pupils entering grades 8-11, combines three-week high school enrichment classes with social, recreational and cultural activities. A third program, Explorations!, provides rising eighth through tenth graders with one week of intensive instruction in a chosen subject. In lieu of a letter grade, students receive a written evaluation from the instructor upon completion of the course.

KANSAS

DUKE UNIVERSITY TALENT IDENTIFICATION PROGRAM
SUMMER STUDIES PROGRAMS
Res — Coed Ages 12-16

Lawrence, KS. Univ of Kansas.
Contact (Year-round): 1121 W Main St, Durham, NC 27701. Tel: 919-668-9100.
  Fax: 919-681-7921.
www.tip.duke.edu   E-mail: information@tip.duke.edu
Brian Cooper, Dir.
Grades 8-11. Adm: Selective. **Appl**—Fee $25. Due: Rolling. SAT/ACT requirement, personal statement.
Type of instruction: Adv Enrich. **Courses:** Architect Comp_Sci Engineering Expository_ Writing Med/Healthcare Writing/Journ Creative_Writing Filmmaking. **Avg class size:** 16. **Daily hours for:** Classes 7. Rec 3.
Fees 2011: Res $3550-3800, 3 wks.
Housing: Dorms.
Est 1980. Nonprofit. **Ses:** 2. **Wks/ses:** 3. Operates June-Aug.

Conducted on several college campuses, the Duke TIP Summer Studies Programs allow advanced students to intensively study a single subject. While previewing college life, boys and girls attend class for seven hours per day from Monday through Friday, then another three hours each Saturday morning. A residential staff supervises students during meals, recreational periods and free time. See other TIP listings under Boone, NC; Durham, NC; College Station, TX; and Davidson, NC.

KENTUCKY

WESTERN KENTUCKY UNIVERSITY
THE CENTER FOR GIFTED STUDIES
SUMMER CAMP FOR ACADEMICALLY TALENTED
MIDDLE SCHOOL STUDENTS
Res and Day — Coed Ages 12-14

Bowling Green, KY 42101. 1906 College Heights Blvd. Tel: 270-745-6323.
  Fax: 270-745-6279.
www.wku.edu/gifted   E-mail: gifted@wku.edu
Julia Roberts, Dir.
Grades 7-9. Adm: Selective. Prereqs: IQ 125. **Appl**—Fee $0. Due: Rolling.
Enr: 200. **Enr cap:** 200. **Fac 30. Staff:** Admin 5. Couns 18.
Type of instruction: Adv Enrich. **Courses:** Ger Expository_Writing Forensic_Sci Govt Hist

Leadership Math Sci Robotics Ceramics Dance Music Photog Studio_Art Theater. **Avg class size:** 16. **Daily hours for:** Classes 6. Rec 6.
Features: Community_Serv Yoga Baseball Basketball Cricket Soccer Softball Swim Volleyball.
Fees 2012: Res $1600 (+$20), 2 wks. Day $800, 2 wks. Aid (Need).
Housing: Dorms. **Swimming:** Pool.
Est 1982. Nonprofit. **Ses:** 1. **Wks/ses:** 2. Operates June.

SCATS offers boys and girls the opportunity to explore areas of academic interest in depth. Students enroll in four courses during the session. Evening recreational activities include movies, games, sports, dances and a talent show. Each applicant must be nominated by a teacher, a counselor or a principal.

WESTERN KENTUCKY UNIVERSITY
THE CENTER FOR GIFTED STUDIES
SUMMER PROGRAM FOR VERBALLY
AND MATHEMATICALLY PRECOCIOUS YOUTH
Res — Coed Ages 13-16

Bowling Green, KY 42101. 1906 College Heights Blvd, Rm 1031. Tel: 270-745-6323. Fax: 270-745-6279.
www.wku.edu/gifted   E-mail: gifted@wku.edu
Julia Roberts, Dir.
Grades 8-11. Adm: Selective. **Appl**—Fee $0. Due: Rolling. Standardized test results (SAT or ACT) through a talent search.
Enr: 200. **Enr cap:** 200. **Fac 14.** Prof 14. **Staff:** Admin 5. Couns 18.
Type of instruction: Adv Enrich. **Courses:** Chin Astron Comp_Sci Environ_Sci Forensic_Sci Math Pol_Sci Sci Writing/Journ Genetics Humanities. **Avg class size:** 16. **Daily hours for:** Classes 6. Study 2. Rec 6.
Features: Baseball Basketball Soccer Softball Swim.
Fees 2012: Res $2400 (+$30), 3 wks. Aid (Need).
Housing: Dorms. **Swimming:** Pool.
Est 1984. Nonprofit. **Ses:** 1. **Wks/ses:** 3. Operates June-July.

Students at VAMPY concentrate on one academic course for everyday study. Offered through a cooperative arrangement with the Talent Identification Program at Duke University, the program balances educational, cultural and recreational experiences. Boys and girls live in dormitories and participate in cookouts, sports, dances and a talent show.

KENTUCKY GOVERNOR'S SCHOLARS PROGRAM
Res — Coed Ages 16-18

Frankfort, KY 40601. 1024 Capital Center Dr, Ste 210. Tel: 502-573-1618. Fax: 502-573-1641.
www.kygsp.org   E-mail: gsp@ky.gov
Aristofanes Cedeno, Exec Dir.
Grade 12. Adm: Very selective. **Appl**—Due: Jan.
Enr: 1000.
Fees 2012: Free (in-state residents). Res 5 wks.
Housing: Dorms. Avg per room/unit: 2.
Est 1983. Nonprofit. **Ses:** 3. **Wks/ses:** 5. Operates June-Aug.

Conducted on three Kentucky college campuses, GSP encourages academic and personal growth by means of a strong liberal arts program. Rising high school seniors from Kentucky choose one major course from roughly two dozen subjects. Instruction follows a nontraditional, interdisciplinary approach. Guest speakers, student productions, publications, experiments and field trips enhance the curriculum. Faculty come from Kentucky colleges, universities and high schools. Interested pupils must be nominated by their schools.

MURRAY STATE UNIVERSITY
THE CENTER FOR GIFTED STUDIES
SUMMER CHALLENGE
Res and Day — Coed Ages 11-14

Murray, KY 42071. Office of Non-Credit & Youth Prgms, 211 Industry & Technology Ctr. Tel: 270-809-2539.
www.murraystate.edu/coe/centers/gifted   E-mail: joy.navan@coe.murraystate.edu
Joy L. Navan, Dir.
Grades 6-9. Adm: Very selective. Prereqs: IQ 125. **Appl**—Fee $0. Due: Mar. Rec.
Enr: 60. **Enr cap:** 75. **Fac 7. Staff:** Admin 3. Couns 6.
Type of instruction: Adv Enrich. **Courses:** Chin Span Architect Comp_Sci Photog. **Avg class size:** 10. **Daily hours for:** Classes 6. Rec 3.
Intl program focus: Acad Lang Culture.
Features: Martial_Arts Swim.
Fees 2012: Res $435 (+$20), 1 wk. Day $365 (+$10), 1 wk. Aid (Need).
Housing: Dorms. Avg per room/unit: 2. **Swimming:** Pool.
Est 1980. Ses: 2. **Wks/ses:** 1. Operates June-July.

Gifted students enrolled in Summer Challenge choose one class from a curriculum that includes such subjects as Chinese, computer science, architecture, photography and Spanish. Boarders reside in Murray State dormitories. Applicants should have an IQ of at least 125.

LOUISIANA

THE GOVERNOR'S PROGRAM FOR GIFTED CHILDREN
Res — Coed Ages 12-16

Lake Charles, LA 70609. McNeese State Univ, MSU Box 91490. Tel: 337-475-5446, 800-291-7840. Fax: 337-475-5447.
www.gpgc.org   E-mail: office@gpgc.org
Joshua Brown, Dir.
Grades 7-11. Adm: Selective. **Appl**—Fee $20. Due: Apr. Standardized test results, transcript.
Enr: 85. Non-White: 20%. **Fac 13.** Prof 3. K-12 staff 10. **Staff:** Admin 3. Couns 10.
Type of instruction: Adv Enrich. **Courses:** Debate Expository_Writing Creative_Writing Fine_Arts Music Theater. **Avg class size:** 10. **Daily hours for:** Classes 7. Study 2. Rec 2. **College credit:** 6.
Features: Swim.
Fees 2012: Res $2550-3550, 7 wks. Aid 2009 (Need): $35,000.
Housing: Dorms. **Swimming:** Pool.
Est 1959. Nonprofit. Ses: 1. **Wks/ses:** 7. Operates June-July.

Conducted on the McNeese State University campus for boys and girls whose score on an acceptable aptitude test is in the 96th percentile or higher, GPGC employs a project-based method in which students engage in independent individual and group projects. This approach enables pupils to maintain and stimulate their interest levels in areas ranging from the humanities to the fine arts to the social sciences. Information acquisition is secondary to the development of thinking and problem-solving skills. GPGC operates two divisions: Junior Division students follow the prescribed curriculum in science, humanities and composition, while Senior Division students (generally 15- and 16-year-olds) take college courses taught by McNeese State faculty. The program is not limited to Louisiana residents, although out-of-state students pay a higher tuition rate.

NORTHWESTERN STATE UNIVERSITY
ADVANCE PROGRAM FOR YOUNG SCHOLARS
Res — Coed Ages 13-17

Natchitoches, LA 71497. NSU Box 5671. Tel: 318-357-4500. Fax: 318-357-4547.
www.advanceprogram.org   E-mail: palmerh@nsula.edu
David Wood, Dir. Student contact: Harriette Palmer.
Grades 8-12. Adm: Somewhat selective. Admitted: 85%. **Appl**—Fee $130. Due: Apr. Test scores or teacher rec & 2 schoolwork examples, transcript.
Enr: 175-200. Non-White: 41%. **Fac 17. Staff:** Admin 6. Res 26.
Type of instruction: Adv. **Courses:** Comp_Sci Math Psych Sci Humanities Shakespeare Crafts Creative_Writing Film Fine_Arts. **Avg class size:** 15. **Daily hours for:** Classes 6. Study 1. Rec 3. **High school credit:** 1/crse, total 1.
Features: Chess Hiking Basketball Golf Soccer Swim Tennis Volleyball.
Fees 2011: Res $1970 (+$75-150), 3 wks. Aid 2006 (Need): $10,000.
Housing: Dorms. **Swimming:** Pool Stream.
Est 1989. Nonprofit. **Ses: 1. Wks/ses:** 3. Operates June.

Affiliated with and patterned after Duke University's Talent Identification Program, ADVANCE is an intensive educational summer program designed for academically gifted youth. Students enroll in one academic class and receive six hours of daily instruction in the chosen course of study. Evening study periods and recreational activities take place in the evening. Weekend activities include dances, movies, sports, arts and crafts, and a talent show.

MARYLAND

UNITED STATES NAVAL ACADEMY
SUMMER SEMINAR PROGRAM
Res — Coed Ages 17-18

Annapolis, MD 21402. Candidate Guidance Office, 117 Decatur Rd.
Tel: 410-293-4361.
www.usna.edu/admissions/nass.htm
Grade 12. Adm: Selective. **Appl**—Due: Apr. Transcript, standardized test scores.
Enr: 750. **Enr cap:** 750.
Type of instruction: Enrich. **Courses:** Architect Econ Eng Engineering Hist Math Pol_Sci Sci Ethics Meteorology.
Features: Seamanship Martial_Arts.
Fees 2009: Res $325, 1 wk.
Housing: Dorms. Campus facilities avail.
Nonprofit. **Ses: 3. Wks/ses: 1.** Operates May-June.

High-achieving students who have just completed their junior year of high school take part in a six-day program that balances academics, athletics and professional training. The Summer Seminar is designed especially for those boys and girls who are considering seeking an appointment the one of the US service academies. Each pupils attends eight 90-minute academic workshops during the session; while some course options have a nautical orientation, many others are in traditional subject areas.

JOHNS HOPKINS UNIVERSITY
CENTER FOR TALENTED YOUTH SUMMER PROGRAMS
Res — Coed Ages 11-18; Day — Coed 8-12

Baltimore, MD 21209. McAuley Hall, 5801 Smith Ave, Ste 400. Tel: 410-735-4100.
Fax: 410-735-6200.
www.cty.jhu.edu E-mail: ctyinfo@jhu.edu
Elizabeth Albert, Dir.
Grades 3-PG (younger if qualified). Adm: Selective. Admitted: 90%. Appl—Fee $50.
Due: Rolling. Standardized test results.
Intl: 7%.
Type of instruction: Adv Enrich. Courses: Chin Fr Greek Span Astron Comp_Sci Ecol
Engineering Environ_Sci Expository_Writing Forensic_Sci Hist Intl_Relations Law
Marine_Bio/Stud Math Oceanog Pol_Sci Sci Creative_Writing Drama Music. Avg class
size: 15. Daily hours for: Classes 5. Study 2. Rec 3. High school credit.
Locations: CA MA MD PA VA.
Features: Swim.
Fees 2011: Res $3650-4620 (+$75), 3 wks. Day $1930-2350, 3 wks.
Housing: Dorms. Swimming: Pool.
Est 1979. Nonprofit. Ses: 2. Wks/ses: 3. Operates June-Aug.

CTY conducts advanced programs in a range of disciplines for academically talented youth at colleges and preparatory schools in five states. Programs for young students include day-only courses for boys and girls who have completed grades 2-4 and residential programs for those who have completed grades 5 and 6; eligibility is based on School and College Abilities Test (SCAT) scores. CTY courses for students who have completed grade 7 or above require SAT, ACT or SCAT scores above the mean for college-bound high school seniors; the Academic Expressions program features courses with less selective eligibility requirements. A global issues program at Princeton University serves pupils who have completed grades 10-12.

UNIVERSITY OF MARYLAND YOUNG SCHOLARS PROGRAM
Res — Coed Ages 15-18; Day — Coed 16-17

College Park, MD 20742. Office of Extended Studies, 0132 Main Admin Bldg.
Tel: 301-405-7762. Fax: 301-314-4071.
www.ysp.umd.edu E-mail: ysp@umd.edu
Randy Tripp, Jr., Coord.
Grades 10-12. Adm: Selective. Prereqs: GPA 3.0. Appl—Fee $65. Due: Rolling. Transcript,
rec.
Enr: 560. Fac 30. Staff: Admin 2. Couns 30.
Type of instruction: Adv Undergrad. Courses: Architect Astron Bus/Fin Comp_Sci Engi-
neering Govt Pol_Sci Psych Sci Writing/Journ Kinesiology Philos Sociol Creative_Writ-
ing Dance Drawing Music Studio_Art. Avg class size: 25. Daily hours for: Classes 4.
Study 3. Rec 2. Homework. Tests. Grades. College credit: 3/crse, total 3.
Features: Ropes_Crse Yoga Aerobics Basketball Swim Ultimate_Frisbee.
Fees 2012: Res $2995 (+$40-90), 3 wks. Day $1850 (+$40-90), 3 wks.
Housing: Dorms. Swimming: Pool. Campus facilities avail.
Est 2001. Nonprofit. Ses: 1. Wks/ses: 3. Operates July.

High school upperclassmen preview college life while enrolling in one three-credit course. Students have the opportunity to pursue academic interests, explore potential career fields, and develop new skills and approaches to learning. Evening seminars and field trips enrich the program.

MASSACHUSETTS

EXCEL AT AMHERST COLLEGE
Res — Coed Ages 15-18

Amherst, MA. Amherst College.
Contact (Year-round): c/o Putney Student Travel, 345 Hickory Ridge Rd, Putney, VT
    05346. Tel: 802-387-5000. Fax: 802-387-4276.
www.goputney.com   E-mail: info@goputney.com
Peter Shumlin, Dir.
Grades 10-PG. **Adm:** FCFS. **Appl**—Due: Rolling.
Enr: 80-120.
Type of instruction: Adv Enrich Rem_Eng SAT/ACT_Prep Study_Skills. **Courses:** Fr Span
    Architect Bus/Fin Debate ESL Expository_Writing Hist Intl_Relations Law Public_Speak
    Relig_Stud Writing/Journ Philos Creative_Writing Dance Drawing Fashion Film Music
    Photog Theater Video_Production. **Avg class size:** 10. **Daily hours for:** Classes 4.
Features: Canoe Community_Serv Hiking Mountaineering Wilderness_Camp Baseball
    Basketball Golf Soccer Tennis Ultimate_Frisbee.
Fees 2012: Res $4990-8990, 3-6 wks.
Housing: Dorms.
Est 1950. Spons: Putney Student Travel. **Ses:** 3. **Wks/ses:** 3-6. Operates June-Aug.

Excel participants choose from courses in the arts, the humanities and contemporary issues, languages and SAT preparation in a collegiate learning environment. Each student enrolls in one major and one enrichment course. Community service opportunities; instructional sports clinics in tennis, soccer and golf; and evening activities supplement academics. See the other domestic Excel listing under Williamstown, MA.

SUMMER INSTITUTE FOR THE GIFTED
Res and Day — Coed Ages 10-17

Amherst, MA. Amherst College.
Contact (Year-round): River Plz, 9 W Broad St, Stamford, CT 06902.
    Tel: 203-399-5188, 866-303-4744. Fax: 203-399-5455.
www.giftedstudy.org   E-mail: sig.info@giftedstudy.org
Barbara Swicord, Pres.
    Student contact: Christine Provencher, E-mail: cprovencher@giftedstudy.com.
Adm: Very selective. Admitted: 90%. **Appl**—Fee $95. Due: Rolling. Transcript, standardized
    test scores, gifted classification/2 recs.
Intl: 25%.
Type of instruction: Adv Enrich SAT/ACT_Prep Study_Skills. **Courses:** Expository_Writ-
    ing Forensic_Sci Math Sci Dance Photog Theater. **Avg class size:** 14. **Daily hours for:**
    Classes 6. Study 1. Rec 2. **College credit.**
Features: Swim.
Fees 2012: Res $4495, 3 wks. Day $2495, 3 wks.
Housing: Dorms. **Swimming:** Pool.
Est 1984. Nonprofit. Spons: National Society for the Gifted & Talented. **Ses:** 1. **Wks/ses:**
    3. Operates July-Aug.

See program description under Berkeley, CA.

SUMMERFUEL
THE COLLEGE EXPERIENCE
Res — Coed Ages 15-18

Amherst, MA. Univ of Massachusetts.

Contact (Year-round): c/o **Academic Study Associates, 375 W Broadway, Ste 200, New York, NY 10012. Tel: 212-796-8340, 800-752-2250. Fax: 212-334-4934.**
www.asaprograms.com/summerfuel E-mail: summer@asaprograms.com
George Kinzel, Dir.
Grades 10-PG. Adm: FCFS. **Appl**—Fee $0. Due: Rolling. Transcript, rec.
Type of instruction: Enrich Preview SAT/ACT_Prep. **Courses:** Bus/Fin Econ ESL Expository_Writing Intl_Relations Psych Public_Speak Creative_Writing Film Fine_Arts Media Photog Theater Design.
Fees 2012: Res $3495-6495, 2-4 wks.
Housing: Dorms. Avg per room/unit: 4.
Est 1987. Inc. **Spons:** Academic Study Associates. **Ses:** 2. **Wks/ses:** 2-4. Operates June-July.

See program description under Berkeley, CA.

PHILLIPS ACADEMY SUMMER SESSION
Res and Day — Coed Ages 13-18

Andover, MA 01810. 180 Main St. Tel: 978-749-4400. Fax: 978-749-4414.
www.andover.edu/summer E-mail: summersession@andover.edu
Fernando Alonso, Dir.
Grades 8-12. Adm: Selective. **Appl**—Fee $60. Due: Rolling. Transcript, essay, 2 recs.
Enr: 659. Intl: 47%. **Fac 150. Staff:** Admin 16.
Type of instruction: Adv Enrich Preview Rev SAT/ACT_Prep Study_Skills Undergrad.
Courses: Chin Fr Lat Span Archaeol Astron Comp_Sci Debate Ecol Econ Engineering ESL Expository_Writing Intl_Relations Math Sci Speech Writing/Journ Acting Animation Ceramics Creative_Writing Dance Filmmaking Fine_Arts Media Music Painting Photog Theater Graphic_Design. **Avg class size:** 14. **Daily hours for:** Classes 3½. Study 4. Rec 2. Homework. Tests. Grades.
Features: Ropes_Crse Yoga Badminton Basketball Soccer Squash Swim Tennis Ultimate_ Frisbee Volleyball Weight_Trng Kickboxing.
Fees 2011: Res $7600 (+$700), 5 wks. Day $6000 (+$700), 5 wks. Aid 2010 (Need): $425,000.
Housing: Dorms. Avg per room/unit: 1-2. **Swimming:** Pool. Campus facilities avail.
Est 1942. Nonprofit. **Ses:** 1. **Wks/ses:** 5. Operates June-Aug.

Enrolling a diverse student body drawn from around the world, Andover maintains a selection of approximately 60 courses in all major disciplines. The individualized program features a low student-faculty ratio and small classes. As the Summer Session provides in-depth study of the material, pupils may take only two courses. In addition to class work, the program includes afternoon recreation, college counseling workshops and trips to nearby colleges, social and cultural opportunities, and a dormitory setting that approximates collegiate living. Rising eighth graders take part in the Lower School Institutes, in which boys and girls pursue an integrated curriculum in two areas of study: math/biology and literature/performance/film.

CUSHING ACADEMY SUMMER SESSION
Res and Day — Coed Ages 12-18

Ashburnham, MA 01430. 39 School St, PO Box 8000. Tel: 978-827-7700.
Fax: 978-827-6927.
www.cushing.org/summer E-mail: summersession@cushing.org
Margaret H. Lee, Dir.
Grades 7-12. Adm: Selective. **Appl**—Fee $60. Due: Rolling. Transcript, essay, recs.
Enr: 365.
Type of instruction: Adv Enrich Rev ESL/TOEFL_Prep SAT/ACT_Prep Study_Skills.
Courses: Chin Span Col_Prep ESL Creative_Writing Dance Filmmaking Painting

Photog Studio_Art Theater. **Avg class size:** 10. **Daily hours for:** Classes 4. Study 2. Rec 2. Homework. Tests. Grades. **High school credit:** 1.
Features: Chess Community_Serv Aerobics Basketball Martial_Arts Soccer Tennis Ultimate_Frisbee Volleyball Weight_Trng.
Fees 2012: Res $6675, 5 wks. Day $3195, 5 wks.
Housing: Dorms Houses.
Nonprofit. **Ses:** 1. **Wks/ses:** 5. Operates July-Aug.

Students from throughout the US and around the world enroll in one of five core programs. Prep for Success explores literature, writing, and math for students ages 12 and 13. Studio Art (ages 13-18) provides instruction in a variety of media. The ESL program places students ages 14-18 into appropriately leveled classes that increase proficiency in reading, writing, speaking and listening. College Prep courses offer Cushing Academy credit, and a college advising workshop admits rising juniors and seniors. Pupils choose from various performing/visual arts and athletic electives. Cushing schedules campus events and trips throughout New England.

See Also Page 39

BOSTON UNIVERSITY HIGH SCHOOL HONORS PROGRAM
Res and Day — Coed Ages 16-18

Boston, MA 02215. 755 Commonwealth Ave, Rm 105. Tel: 617-353-1378.
    Fax: 617-353-5532.
www.bu.edu/summer/high-school-programs/honors   E-mail: summerhs@bu.edu
Donna Shea, Dir. Student contact: Matthew Cobb, E-mail: mcobb@bu.edu.
Grades 11-12. Adm: Selective. **Appl**—Due: May. Transcript, personal statement, standardized test scores, 2 recs.
Enr: 86. Intl: 19%. Non-White: 36%. **Staff:** Admin 2. Couns 9.
Type of instruction: Adv Undergrad. **Courses:** Arabic Chin Fr Ger Greek Hebrew Ital Japan Span African-Amer_Stud Archaeol Astron Bus/Fin Comm Comp_Sci Econ Environ_Sci Expository_Writing Govt Hist Math Pol_Sci Sci Speech Writing/Journ Accounting Creative_Writing Filmmaking Fine_Arts Media Music Painting Photog Studio_Art Theater. **Avg class size:** 35. **Daily hours for:** Classes 3-5. Homework. Tests. Grades. **College credit:** 2-4/crse, total 8.
Features: Swim.
Fees 2011: Res $6700-7100, 6 wks. Day $4810, 6 wks. Aid (Merit & Need).
Housing: Dorms. Avg per room/unit: 2. **Swimming:** Pool. Campus facilities avail.
Est 1980. Ses: 1. **Wks/ses:** 6. Operates July-Aug.

Rising high school seniors and exceptional rising juniors enroll in two courses for credit alongside Boston University undergraduates. Course options vary each year and include more than 100 offerings in dozens of subject areas. Students participate in planned social and recreational activities, as well as workshops on the college application process.

BOSTON UNIVERSITY SUMMER CHALLENGE PROGRAM
Res — Coed Ages 15-17

Boston, MA 02215. 755 Commonwealth Ave, Rm 105. Tel: 617-353-1378.
    Fax: 617-353-5532.
www.bu.edu/summer/high-school-programs/summer-challenge
E-mail: summerhs@bu.edu
Donna Shea, Dir. Student contact: Matthew Cobb, E-mail: mcobb@bu.edu.
Grades 10-12. Adm: Selective. **Appl**—Due: Rolling. Transcript, personal statement.
Intl: 19%. **Fac 11. Staff:** Admin 2. Couns 14.
Type of instruction: Adv Enrich Preview. **Courses:** Chin Bus/Fin Engineering Expository_Writing Hist Law Pol_Sci Psych Writing/Journ Ethics Creative_Writing Visual_Arts.
    Avg class size: 20. **Daily hours for:** Classes 4. Study 2. Rec 3. Homework.
Features: Swim.

Fees 2011: Res $3260, 2 wks.
Housing: Dorms. **Swimming:** Pool.
Est 2002. Nonprofit. **Ses:** 3. **Wks/ses:** 2. Operates June-Aug.

Summer Challenge exposes high school students to the standards of college-level work. Participants enroll in two seminars during the two-week session, one that addresses an existing interest and another that leads to the exploration of a new subject. Seminars combine lectures, individual and group work, project-based assignments and field trips. Summer Challenge schedules various social activities for afternoons, evenings and weekends.

HARVARD UNIVERSITY SUMMER SCHOOL
SECONDARY SCHOOL PROGRAM
Res and Day — Coed Ages 16-18

Cambridge, MA 02138. 51 Brattle St. Tel: 617-495-3192. Fax: 617-496-4525.
www.ssp.harvard.edu   E-mail: ssp@dcemail.harvard.edu
William J. Holinger, Dir.
Grades 11-PG. Adm: Selective. **Appl**—Fee $50. Due: Rolling. Transcript, teacher & administrator recs, PSAT/SAT/ACT scores.
Enr: 1000. **Staff:** Admin 6.
Type of instruction: Adv Preview ESL/TOEFL_Prep Study_Skills Tut Undergrad. **Courses:** Arabic Chin Fr Ger Greek Ital Japan Lat Russ Span Hindi Korean Portuguese Sanskrit Archaeol Astron Comp_Sci Econ Education Engineering Environ_Sci ESL Expository_Writing Govt Math Psych Relig_Stud Writing/Journ Sociol Stats Creative_Writing Dance Drama Music Photog Studio_Art. **Daily hours for:** Classes 2. Homework. Tests. Grades. **College credit:** 4-8/crse, total 8.
Features: Boating Community_Serv Basketball Soccer Softball Swim Tennis Volleyball.
Fees 2011: Res $7230-9870, 7 wks. Day $2640-5280, 7 wks.
Housing: Dorms. **Swimming:** Pool. Campus facilities avail.
Est 1966. Nonprofit. **Ses:** 1. **Wks/ses:** 7. Operates June-Aug.

Highly qualified high schoolers who have completed their sophomore, junior or senior year may enroll for college credit in the full range of Harvard summer undergraduate courses. The college preparatory program includes study skills workshops, a college fair and trips to other colleges. Summer seminars, based on Harvard's freshman seminars, are limited to 15 students and allow for classroom discussions, close attention to writing and opportunities for independent research under a faculty member. Dances, trivia bowl, a talent show, musical groups, sports, and sightseeing excursions around Boston and New England are among the SSP's activities. SSP also offers distance-learning courses featuring online course materials, discussions and video lectures.

LIFE-TECH VENTURES
Res and Day — Coed Ages 8-16

Charlton, MA 01507. c/o Nature's Classroom, 19 Harrington Rd. Tel: 508-248-2741, 800-433-8375.
www.naturesclassroom.org   E-mail: info@naturesclassroom.org
John G. Santos, Dir.
Grades 3-10. Adm: FCFS.
Enr: 180. **Fac 12. Staff:** Admin 3.
Type of instruction: Enrich. **Courses:** Astron Ecol Environ_Sci Geol Fine_Arts Theater. **Avg class size:** 9.
Features: Aquatics Exploration Hiking Ropes_Crse Baseball Basketball Football Soccer Swim Volleyball.
Fees 2011: Res $690-1430 (+$80), 1-2 wks. Day $225, 1 wk.
Housing: Dorms. **Swimming:** Pond Pool.

Est 1972. Nonprofit. **Spons:** Nature's Classroom. **Ses:** 10. **Wks/ses:** 1-2. Operates July-Aug.

LTV offers specific core subjects to which children devote two and a half hours per day. Areas of study include natural science, physical science, computers, robotics, sports, the fine arts and the performing arts. In addition to core classes, each student participates in daily enrichment activities. Traditional recreational activities are also incorporated into the program.

BOSTON COLLEGE EXPERIENCE
Res and Day — Coed Ages 17-18

Chestnut Hill, MA 02467. McGuinn Hall, Rm 100. Tel: 617-552-3800.
Fax: 617-552-8404.
www.bc.edu/schools/summer/bce   E-mail: bce@bc.edu
Grade 12. Adm: Somewhat selective. Admitted: 90%. **Appl**—Fee $25. Due: Rolling. Transcript, standardized test scores, principal/counselor rec.
Type of instruction: Adv Undergrad. **Courses:** Fr Span Comp_Sci Econ Eng Geol Hist Math Psych Public_Speak Relig_Stud Sci Anat & Physiol Philos Sociol Film. **College credit.**
Features: Swim.
Fees 2012: Res $6000, 6 wks. Day $4161, 6 wks.
Housing: Dorms. Avg per room/unit: 1-2. **Swimming:** Pool.
Nonprofit. Roman Catholic. **Ses:** 1. **Wks/ses:** 6. Operates June-Aug.

This precollege program enrolls talented and motivated rising high school seniors who are interested in sampling college life. Alongside Boston College undergraduates, each student enrolls in two freshman-level courses for full college credit. Program participation leads to improved time-management skills and allows boys and girls to take classes not available in traditional high school settings. College visits and recreational and shopping excursions round out the program.

EAGLEBROOK SUMMER SEMESTER
Res — Coed Ages 11-13

Deerfield, MA 01342. 271 Pine Nook Rd, PO Box 7. Tel: 413-774-7411.
Fax: 413-774-9136.
www.eaglebrook.org   E-mail: kjk@eaglebrook.org
Karl J. Koenigsbauer, Dir.
Adm: Selective. **Appl**—Fee $40. Due: Rolling. Transcript, standardized test results, 2 recs.
Enr: 55. **Enr cap:** 55. **Fac** 20. **Staff:** Admin 5.
Type of instruction: Adv Dev_Read Enrich Preview Rem_Eng Rem_Math Rem_Read Rev Study_Skills Tut. **Courses:** Fr Span Computers Eng ESL Expository_Writing Math Sci Drama Studio_Art. **Avg class size:** 7. **Daily hours for:** Classes 4. Homework.
Features: Canoe Fishing Hiking Wilderness_Camp Baseball Basketball Field_Hockey Golf Lacrosse Soccer Softball Swim Tennis Ultimate_Frisbee.
Fees 2012: Res $6400 (+$375), 4 wks. Aid 2006 (Need): $5000.
Housing: Dorms. **Swimming:** Pool.
Est 1996. Nonprofit. **Spons:** Eaglebrook School. **Ses:** 1. **Wks/ses:** 4. Operates July.

Conducted by Eaglebrook School, Summer Semester enables young students to take four courses per day, two academic and two elective. Mornings and early afternoons consist of four hour-long learning blocks, while afternoons provide time for sports and leisure pursuits. Following an early evening activity period, pupils take part in a closely supervised study period five nights a week.

NORTHFIELD MOUNT HERMON SUMMER SESSION
Res and Day — Coed Ages 12-18

Northfield, MA 01354. 1 Lamplighter Way. Tel: 413-498-3290. Fax: 413-498-3112.
www.nmhschool.org/summer   E-mail: summer_school@nmhschool.org
Gregory T. Leeds, Dir.
Grades 7-12. Adm: FCFS. **Appl**—Fee $50. Due: Rolling. Transcript,2 recs.
Enr: 250. **Enr cap:** 250. **Fac 75.** Col/grad students 35. K-12 staff 40.
Type of instruction: Enrich SAT/ACT_Prep Study_Skills. **Courses:** Fr Span Econ ESL
  Expository_Writing Hist Math Psych Public_Speak Sci Writing/Journ Creative_Writing
  Dance Drama Drawing Music Photog Studio_Art. **Avg class size:** 11. **Daily hours for:**
  Classes 4. Study 2½. Rec 1½.
Features: Hiking Badminton Basketball Cross-country Lacrosse Soccer Swim Tennis Ulti-
  mate_Frisbee Volleyball Weight_Trng.
Fees 2012: Res $6700 (+$300-450), 5 wks.
Housing: Dorms. Avg per room/unit: 2. **Swimming:** Pool. Campus facilities avail.
Est 1961. Nonprofit. **Ses:** 1. **Wks/ses:** 5. Operates June-Aug.

NMH's Middle School Program (entering grades 7-9) provides a small-class environment in which motivated children take two major courses in the morning, along with a minor afternoon class. Boys and girls play sports in the afternoon. Students entering grades 10-12 may enroll in the College Prep Program, during which they pursue one intensive course three hours each morning (Monday through Saturday). In addition, a sport and an afternoon lab or a minor course convene four afternoons per week. College Prep pupils also spend a few days of the session participating in a community work program. Extracurricular activities typically include both on-campus events and optional trips to beaches, summer theater, an amusement park, classical music concerts, museums and professional baseball games.

EXPLORATION JUNIOR PROGRAM
Res and Day — Coed Ages 9-12

Southborough, MA 01772. c/o St Mark's School, 25 Marlborough Rd.
  Tel: 508-786-1350. Fax: 508-786-1360.
Contact (Sept-June): 932 Washington St, PO Box 368, Norwood, MA 02062.
  Tel: 781-762-7400. Fax: 781-762-7425.
www.explo.org   E-mail: summer@explo.org
David Torcoletti, Head.
Grades 4-7. Adm: FCFS. **Appl**—Fee $0. Due: Rolling.
Enr: 440. **Enr cap:** 440. **Fac 60. Staff:** Admin 8.
Type of instruction: Enrich. **Courses:** Fr Ital Archaeol Astron Bus/Fin Debate Ecol Engi-
  neering Environ_Sci ESL Govt Marine_Bio/Stud Sci Writing/Journ Circus_Skills Crafts
  Creative_Writing Dance Filmmaking Media Music Painting Photog Sculpt Theater. **Avg
  class size:** 14. **Daily hours for:** Classes 3.
Features: Aquatics Archery Canoe Chess Climbing_Wall Community_Serv Deep-sea
  Fishing Exploration Fishing Hiking Kayak Mtn_Trips Woodcraft Baseball Basketball
  Cross-country Field_Hockey Football Lacrosse Soccer Softball Swim Tennis Track Ulti-
  mate_Frisbee Volleyball.
**Fees 2011: Res $4865-9110 (+$300-600), 3-6 wks. Day $2220-4030 (+$300-600), 3-6
  wks.**
Housing: Dorms. **Swimming:** Pool. Campus facilities avail.
Est 1994. Nonprofit. **Spons:** Exploration School. **Ses:** 2. **Wks/ses:** 3. Operates June-Aug.

Conducted on the campus of St. Mark's School, the Junior Program allows children to explore academic, artistic and athletic interests in a relaxed setting. Programming combines intellectual inquiry and exploration with extracurricular activities, outdoor pursuits and adventure. Students choose from more than 60 hands-on courses in such areas as acting and directing, ceramics, forensic science, broadcast journalism, archaeology, business and swing dancing. Exploration programs for older students are available in Wellesley, MA, and New Haven, CT (see separate listings).

EXPLORATION INTERMEDIATE PROGRAM
Res and Day — Coed Ages 13-14

Wellesley, MA. Wellesley College.
Contact (Year-round): 932 Washington St, PO Box 368, Norwood, MA 02062.
   Tel: 781-762-7400. **Fax:** 781-762-7425.
www.explo.org/intermediate   E-mail: summer@explo.org
Elliot Targum, Head.
Grades 8-9. Adm: FCFS. **Appl**—Fee $0. Due: Rolling.
Enr: 630. **Enr cap:** 630. **Fac 70. Staff:** Admin 10. Couns 115.
Type of instruction: Enrich. **Courses:** Fr Ital Japan Astron Bus/Fin Comp_Sci Debate Ecol Engineering Environ_Sci ESL Forensic_Sci Govt Marine_Bio/Stud Sci Speech Writing/ Journ Acting Circus_Skills Crafts Creative_Writing Dance Drama Filmmaking Fine_Arts Media Music Painting Photog. **Avg class size:** 16. **Daily hours for:** Classes 3½.
Features: Aquatics Boating Canoe Chess Climbing_Wall Cooking Cruises Deep-sea Fishing Exploration Hiking Rock_Climb Ropes_Crse Sail Scuba Sea_Cruises Survival_ Trng White-water_Raft Wilderness_Camp Baseball Basketball Field_Hockey Football Lacrosse Martial_Arts Soccer Softball Street_Hockey Swim Tennis Track Ultimate_Frisbee Volleyball Watersports.
Fees 2012: Res $4945-9240 (+$300-600), 3-6 wks. Day $2270-4125 (+$300-600), 3-6 wks. Aid (Need).
Housing: Dorms. **Swimming:** Lake Pool.
Est 1984. Nonprofit. **Spons:** Exploration School. **Ses:** 2. **Wks/ses:** 3. Operates July-Aug.

The Intermediate Program prepares middle schoolers for high school life in an ungraded, noncompetitive environment on the campus of Wellesley College. Students participate in academic courses and minicourses as they study such subjects as African dance, physics, creative writing, sailing, Web design, painting, biology and theater. Activities, sports, and day trips to Boston and throughout New England complete the program. Exploration programs for younger and older students are available in Southborough and in New Haven, CT (see separate listings).

MICHIGAN

SUMMER DISCOVERY
Res — Coed Ages 15-18

Ann Arbor, MI. Univ of Michigan.
Contact (Year-round): 1326 Old Northern Blvd, Roslyn, NY 11576. **Tel:** 516-621-3939.
   Fax: 516-625-3438.
www.summerdiscovery.com   E-mail: discovery@summerdiscovery.com
Bob Musiker, Exec Dir.
Grades 10-PG. Adm: FCFS. **Appl**—Fee $95. Due: Rolling.
Type of instruction: Enrich SAT/ACT_Prep Study_Skills. **Courses:** Architect Bus/Fin Comm ESL Govt Law Med/Healthcare Speech Writing/Journ Sports_Management Creative_Writing Filmmaking Fine_Arts Music Photog Theater. Homework.
Features: Adventure_Travel Aquatics Canoe Community_Serv Hiking Kayak Aerobics Basketball Golf Lacrosse Soccer Softball Swim Tennis Track Weight_Trng.
Fees 2011: Res $3299-6899, 2-5 wks. Aid (Need).
Housing: Dorms. **Swimming:** Lake Pool.
Inc. **Ses:** 3. **Wks/ses:** 2-5. Operates June-July.

See program description under Los Angeles, CA.

TELLURIDE ASSOCIATION SUMMER PROGRAM
Res — Coed Ages 17-18

Ann Arbor, MI. Univ of Michigan.
Contact (Year-round): 217 West Ave, Ithaca, NY 14850. Tel: 607-273-5011.
Fax: 607-272-2667.
http://tasp.tellurideassociation.org   E-mail: telluride@tellurideassociation.org
Ellen Baer, Admin Dir.
Grade 12. Adm: Very selective. **Appl**—Fee $0. Due: Jan. Essays, transcript, standardized test scores.
Enr: 16-18.
Type of instruction: Adv Enrich. **Courses:** Eng Sci Philos.
Fees 2010: Free. Res 6 wks.
Housing: Dorms.
Nonprofit. **Ses:** 3. **Wks/ses:** 6. Operates June-Aug.

This free program for boys and girls who have completed junior year operates at several college sites around the country. At each location, TASP students attend an academic seminar that meets each weekday morning for about three hours. Two professors lead each seminar, which is organized around group discussions rather than lectures. Professors meet individually with pupils to discuss writing assignments; instructors do not grade these assignments, instead issuing written comments. Students also attend guest lectures and deliver speeches on topics that interest them.

MICHIGAN STATE UNIVERSITY
HIGH ACHIEVERS
Res and Day — Coed Ages 15-18

East Lansing, MI 48824. 186 Bessey Hall. Tel: 517-432-2129. Fax: 517-353-6464.
www.gifted.msu.edu   E-mail: mcdon288@msu.edu
Kathee McDonald, Dir.
Grades 10-PG. Adm: Somewhat selective. Admitted: 98%. Prereqs: SAT CR 530, CR/M 1040; PSAT CR 53, CR/M 104; ACT Eng 21, Comp 22; PLAN Eng 21, Comp 22. **Appl**— Fee $70. Due: Apr. Transcript, test scores, essay, rec.
Enr: 20. **Enr cap:** 20. **Staff:** Admin 3.
Type of instruction: Enrich Undergrad. **Courses:** Econ Global_Stud Sci Philos. **Daily hours for:** Classes 3. Study 2-3. Rec 3. Homework. Tests. Grades. **College credit:** 3½/crse, total 3.
Features: Swim.
Fees 2012: Res $3620-4688 (+$100-200), 4 wks. Day $1220-2288 (+$100-200), 4 wks.
Housing: Dorms. **Swimming:** Pool. Campus facilities avail.
Est 1986. Nonprofit. **Ses:** 2. **Wks/ses:** 4. Operates June-Aug.

High Achievers participants enroll in an honors-level college course and earn transferable credit. Courses are taught by MSU faculty on topics that vary by year. Boys and girls study a range of subjects through lectures or a combination of lectures and laboratory work.

LEELANAU SCHOOL SUMMER ACADEMY
Res — Coed Ages 14-18

Glen Arbor, MI 49636. 1 Old Homestead Rd. Tel: 231-334-5800, 800-533-5262.
Fax: 231-334-5898.
www.leelanau.org   E-mail: admissions@leelanau.org
Matt Ralston, Head. Student contact: Kate Auger-Campbell.
Grades 9-12. Adm: FCFS. **Appl**—Fee $50. Due: Rolling.
Enr: 40. **Fac 8. Staff:** Admin 4. Couns 1.
Type of instruction: Adv Enrich Preview Rev SAT/ACT_Prep Study_Skills. **Courses:** Eng

ESL Govt Hist Math. **Avg class size:** 6. **Daily hours for:** Classes 5. Study 2. Rec 2.
High school credit: 1/crse, total 2.
Features: Canoe Climbing_Wall Hiking Kayak Sail Wilderness_Camp Golf Soccer Softball
Swim Tennis.
Fees 2011: Res $6000 (+$650), 4 wks.
Housing: Dorms. **Swimming:** Lake.
Est 1929. Nonprofit. **Ses:** 1. **Wks/ses:** 4. Operates July-Aug.

Students taking part in this program, which is located on the Crystal River within the 65,000-acre Sleeping Bear Dunes National Park, hone their study habits while taking courses in both the traditional subjects and such areas as ESL and field biology. Boys and girls attend two classes per day, six days a week, during the course of the month-long program. Environmental awareness is an important aspect of the program, as pupils may engage in canoeing, kayaking, hiking, camping and visits to a local maritime museum.

CALVIN COLLEGE
ENTRADA SCHOLARS PROGRAM
Res — Coed Ages 16-18

Grand Rapids, MI 49546. Office of Pre-College Prgms, 3201 Burton St SE.
    Tel: 616-526-6749, 800-688-0122.
www.calvin.edu/academic/entrada/info.html   E-mail: precollege@calvin.edu
Grades 12-PG. Adm: Selective. Priority: URM. Prereqs: GPA 3.0. **Appl**—Fee $0. Due: Mar.
    Transcript, essay, test scores, 2 recs.
Type of instruction: Undergrad. Homework. Tests. Grades. **College credit:** 3-4/crse, total
    4.
Features: Community_Serv.
Fees 2012: Res $500, 4 wks.
Housing: Dorms. Campus facilities avail.
Ses: 1. **Wks/ses:** 4. Operates June-July.

Entrada Scholars enroll in summer-term classes alongside current Calvin students. Participants are assigned an academic coach, a trained teacher who attends classes with them in the morning and leads a study period after class. Worship services at local churches, Bible studies and daily devotions are also part of the program. While Entrada primarily serves African-American, Latino, Asian-American and Native American students entering grade 12, high school graduates may apply if they plan to matriculate at Calvin.

MICHIGAN TECHNOLOGICAL UNIVERSITY
SUMMER YOUTH PROGRAMS
Res and Day — Coed Ages 12-18

Houghton, MI 49931. 1400 Townsend Dr, 310 Administration Bldg. Tel: 906-487-2219,
    888-773-2655. Fax: 906-487-1136.
www.youthprograms.mtu.edu   E-mail: yp@mtu.edu
Steve Patchin, Dir.
Grades 7-12 (younger if qualified). Adm: FCFS. **Appl**—Fee $0. Due: Rolling.
Enr: 250. **Enr cap:** 250. Intl: 5%. Non-White: 40%. **Fac 150.** Prof 37. Col/grad students 90.
    K-12 staff 8. Specialists 15. **Staff:** Admin 7. Couns 75.
Type of instruction: Adv Enrich Preview. **Courses:** Bus/Fin Comp_Sci Engineering Foren-
    sic_Sci Web_Design Crafts Media Music Photog. **Avg class size:** 16. **Daily hours for:**
    Classes 7. Rec 3½. Homework. Tests. Grades.
Features: Adventure_Travel Aquatics Aviation/Aero Climbing_Wall Exploration Fishing
    Hiking Mountaineering Mtn_Biking Rappelling Rock_Climb Ropes_Crse Wilderness_
    Camp Swim.
Fees 2012: Res $795-920 (+$85-250), 1 wk. Day $450-500 (+$85-250), 1 wk. Aid (Merit
    & Need).

Housing: Dorms. Avg per room/unit: 2. **Swimming:** Lake Pool. Campus facilities avail. **Est 1973.** Nonprofit. **Ses:** 6. **Wks/ses:** 1. Operates June-Aug.

SYP enables students to explore careers and develop skills through hands-on laboratory, classroom and field experiences. Conducted by faculty members, graduate students and other specialists, each session explores one of six areas of study: engineering, science and technology, computers, business, environmental studies, or the arts and the human sciences. Evening and weekend activities facilitate student interaction.

MINNESOTA

CARLETON LIBERAL ARTS EXPERIENCE
Res — Coed Ages 15-16

Northfield, MN 55057. Carleton College, 100 S College St. Tel: 507-222-4190, 800-995-2275. Fax: 507-222-4526.
www.carleton.edu/summer/clae   E-mail: clae@carleton.edu
Brian Swann, Dir.
Grade 10. Adm: Very selective. Priority: URM. **Appl**—Fee $0. Due: Apr. Transcript, short essays, teacher recs.
Enr: 50. Enr cap: 50. Fac 4. Staff: Admin 2. Res 8.
Type of instruction: Enrich SAT/ACT_Prep Undergrad. **Courses:** Col_Prep Econ Expository_Writing Forensic_Sci Sci. **Daily hours for:** Classes 4. Study 2. Rec 1. Homework. Tests.
Features: Basketball Soccer Tennis Ultimate_Frisbee.
Fees 2012: Free. Res 1 wk.
Housing: Dorms. Avg per room/unit: 2. Campus facilities avail.
Est 2000. Nonprofit. **Spons:** Carleton College. **Ses:** 1. **Wks/ses:** 1. Operates July.

Current high school sophomores who are of African-American decent or who have an interest in African-American culture may apply to this free, weeklong program. CLAE introduces students to a college liberal arts setting through a varied curriculum that features courses in science, art, the social sciences and technology. In addition to academics, Carleton offers workshops designed to assist boys and girls with their high school and college careers; workshops address such topics as ACT/SAT preparation and the college application process. Various group activities, such as trips to sites of interest in Metropolitan Minneapolis-St. Paul, round out the program.

MINNESOTA INSTITUTE FOR TALENTED YOUTH
EXPAND YOUR MIND
Res and Day — Coed Ages 13-18

St Paul, MN 55105. c/o Macalester College, 1600 Grand Ave. Tel: 651-696-6590. Fax: 651-696-6592.
www.mity.org   E-mail: mity@macalester.edu
Roberta Seum, Dir.
Grades 8-12. Adm: Selective. **Appl**—Fee $0. Due: Apr. Transcript, teacher rec, essay.
Type of instruction: Adv Enrich. **Courses:** Architect Math Psych Sci Speech Writing/Journ Creative_Writing Studio_Art Theater Jazz. **Avg class size:** 13.
Features: Chess Soccer Ultimate_Frisbee.
Fees 2011: Res $1400, 2 wks. Day $560, 2 wks. Aid (Need).
Housing: Dorms. Campus facilities avail.
Est 1967. Nonprofit. **Ses:** 2. **Wks/ses:** 2. Operates June-July.

Held on the Macalester College campus, this two-week program allows able, intellectually curious teenagers to take a course in one of a variety of subject areas. EYM's enrichment classes employ a hands-on approach. Another program of the Minnesota Institute for Talented Youth, ExplorSchool, serves day pupils entering grades 5-7.

MISSISSIPPI

FRANCES A. KARNES CENTER FOR GIFTED STUDIES
SUMMER GIFTED STUDIES PROGRAM
Res — Coed Ages 10-14

Hattiesburg, MS 39406. Univ of Southern Mississippi, 118 College Dr, Box 8207. Tel: 601-266-5236. Fax: 601-266-4764.
www.usm.edu/gifted   E-mail: gifted.studies@usm.edu
Frances A. Karnes, Dir.
Grades 5-9. Adm: Somewhat selective. Admitted: 98%. Prereqs: IQ 120. **Appl**—Due: Mar.
Enr: 184. **Fac 9. Staff:** Admin 4 Couns 20.
Type of instruction: Adv. **Courses:** Bus/Fin Sci Studio_Art. **Avg class size:** 20. **Daily hours for:** Classes 6. Rec 1. Homework. Tests. Grades. **High school credit.**
Features: Peace/Cross-cultural Swim.
Fees 2009: Res $495, 1 wk.
Housing: Dorms. **Swimming:** Pool.
Est 1978. Nonprofit. **Spons:** University of Southern Mississippi. **Ses:** 1. **Wks/ses:** 1. Operates June.

The Summer Gifted Studies Program is designed to enhance cognitive, affective and psychomotor abilities of gifted students through planned enrichment and acceleration activities. Emphasis is placed on individual participation and in-depth analysis of specific topics of interest, including money, business, inventions, world cultures, design and writing. Boys and girls participate in leisure, recreational and cultural activities with other gifted youth. Applicants must score at the 90th percentile of a specified standardized test.

FRANCES A. KARNES CENTER FOR GIFTED STUDIES
SUMMER PROGRAM FOR ACADEMICALLY TALENTED YOUTH
Res — Coed Ages 13-16

Hattiesburg, MS 39406. Univ of Southern Mississippi, 118 College Dr, Box 8207. Tel: 601-266-5236. Fax: 601-266-4764.
www.usm.edu/gifted   E-mail: gifted.studies@usm.edu
Frances A. Karnes, Dir.
Grades 8-11. Adm: Somewhat selective. Admitted: 98%. **Appl**—Due: Apr.
Enr: 75. **Fac 8. Staff:** Admin 4. Couns 20.
Type of instruction: Adv. **Courses:** Debate Econ Forensic_Sci Marine_Bio/Stud Math Pol_Sci Sci Creative_Writing. **Avg class size:** 15. **Daily hours for:** Classes 6. Study 1. Rec 1. **High school credit.**
Features: Swim.
Fees 2009: Res $1700, 3 wks.
Housing: Dorms. **Swimming:** Pool.
Est 1988. Nonprofit. **Spons:** University of Southern Mississippi. **Ses:** 1. **Wks/ses:** 3. Operates July.

A cooperative effort between the University of Southern Mississippi and Duke University's Talent Identification Program, SPATY provides high-ability students with a balanced educational, cultural and recreational course of studies. Boys and girls spend roughly six hours daily in the classroom, with one hour per evening devoted to individual study. Students live in on-campus dormitories, and staff schedule cultural and recreational activities.

UNIVERSITY OF MISSISSIPPI
SUMMER COLLEGE FOR HIGH SCHOOL STUDENTS
Res — Coed Ages 16-17

University, MS 38677. PO Box 9. Tel: 662-915-7621. Fax: 662-915-1535.
www.outreach.olemiss.edu/schs   E-mail: umsummer@olemiss.edu
Jason E. Wilkins, Dir.
Grades 11-12. Adm: Selective. Prereqs: GPA 3.2. **Appl**—Fee $0. Transcript, 2 recs.
Type of instruction: ESL/TOEFL_Prep Undergrad. **Courses:** Span Bus/Fin Comp_Sci Engineering Law Med/Healthcare Writing/Journ Studio_Art. **Daily hours for:** Classes 4. **College credit:** 6.
Fees 2009: Res $1438-1885, 4 wks. Aid (Need).
Housing: Dorms. Campus facilities avail.
Est 1980. Nonprofit. **Ses:** 2. **Wks/ses:** 4. Operates May-July.

Academically gifted high school upperclassmen get a head start on their college careers by choosing two courses from a full complement of University of Mississippi offerings. In most cases, these courses, which are taught by university faculty and which result in an average of six hours of transferable college credit, also include current Ole Miss underclassmen. An accompanying noncredit class helps students explore their academic and career interests while also learning about the college selection process. Boys and girls devote some afternoon time to creative, academic and athletic activities, and weekends provide opportunities for various excursions and entertainment options.

MISSOURI

TRUMAN STATE UNIVERSITY
JOSEPH BALDWIN ACADEMY FOR EMINENT YOUNG SCHOLARS
Res — Coed Ages 13-15

Kirksville, MO 63501. 100 E Normal Ave, Baldwin Hall, Rm 110. Tel: 660-785-5406.
Fax: 660-785-7202.
http://jba.truman.edu   E-mail: jmorton@truman.edu
Kevin Minch, Dir. Student contact: Jana Morton.
Grades 8-10 (younger if qualified). Adm: Very selective. Admitted: 60%. **Appl**—Fee $0. Due: Nov. Transcript, teacher rec, ACT/SAT/PSAT scores, essays.
Enr: 179-200. **Enr cap:** 200. Non-White: 5%. **Fac 10.** Prof 10. **Staff:** Admin 3. Couns 32.
Type of instruction: Adv Enrich Undergrad. **Courses:** Ital Lat Russ Comm Comp_Sci Ecol Hist Math Pol_Sci Sci Drawing. **Avg class size:** 20. **Daily hours for:** Classes 7. Study 1½. Rec 3. Homework. Tests.
Features: Hiking Yoga Aerobics Basketball Softball Swim Tennis Ultimate_Frisbee Volleyball Watersports Weight_Trng.
Fees 2011: Res $1500 (+$60), 3 wks. Aid 2010 (Need): $18,000.
Housing: Dorms. Avg per room/unit: 2. **Swimming:** Lake Pool. Campus facilities avail.
Est 1985. Nonprofit. **Ses:** 2. **Wks/ses:** 3. Operates June-July.

The academy provides talented students entering grades 8-10 with an introduction to college life and a rigorous educational experience. Participants select one course from offerings in the humanities, the fine arts, the natural sciences and the social sciences. Course work emphasizes interdisciplinary studies and creative problem solving, and each accelerated class is the equivalent of a semester-long university course. Truman State faculty structure programming to suit the particular interests and abilities of the student. A selection of evening and weekend athletic, intellectual, creative and recreational activities balances academics. Suitable applicants should be nominated by a principal or counselor and should score in the 95th percentile or above on a standardized achievement test.

MISSOURI MILITARY ACADEMY
SUMMER SCHOOL
Res and Day — Coed Ages 12-17

Mexico, MO 65265. 204 N Grand St. Tel: 573-581-1776, 888-564-6662.
  Fax: 573-581-0081.
www.missourimilitaryacademy.org   E-mail: info@missourimilitaryacademy.org
Maj. Mark Vaughan, Dir.
Grades 7-12. Adm: FCFS. **Appl**—Due: Rolling.
Staff: Admin 3. Couns 15.
Courses: Span Eng ESL Hist Math Sci.
Features: Aquatics Archery Boating Canoe Exploration Fishing Hiking Milit_Trng Paintball Rappelling Riding Riflery Ropes_Crse Wilderness_Camp Wilderness_Canoe Basketball Equestrian Soccer Swim Tennis Watersports.
Fees 2012: Res $3750, 4 wks. Day $2500, 4 wks.
Housing: Dorms. **Swimming:** Pool.
Est 1999. Nonprofit. **Ses:** 1. **Wks/ses:** 4. Operates July.

This recovery and enrichment program allows students to repair poor past performances, expand scope of knowledge and sharpen study skills. Students may participate in a variety of recreational activities, and a sports camp is included in the cost of the boarding program. The academy also runs a two-week leadership camp for boys, ages 13-17.

WASHINGTON UNIVERSITY
HIGH SCHOOL SUMMER SCHOLARS PROGRAM
Res — Coed Ages 15-18

St Louis, MO 63130. Campus Box 1145, 1 Brookings Dr. Tel: 314-935-6834,
  866-209-0691. Fax: 314-935-4847.
http://summerexperiences.wustl.edu   E-mail: summerscholars@wustl.edu
Marsha Hussung, Dir.
Grades 11-12. Adm: Selective. Prereqs: GPA B+. PSAT M/CR/W 180; SAT M/CR/W 1800.
  Appl—Fee $35. Due: Rolling. Transcript, teacher & counselor recs.
Enr: 70. Intl: 12%. **Staff:** Admin 2. Couns 7.
Type of instruction: Undergrad. **Courses:** Fr Ger Ital Japan Span Archaeol Econ Environ_Sci Expository_Writing Geol Math Pol_Sci Psych Relig_Stud Sci Writing/Journ Anthro Creative_Writing Dance Drama Film Music. **Avg class size:** 12. **Daily hours for:** Classes 4. Study 6. Homework. Tests. Grades. **College credit:** 7.
Features: Swim.
Fees 2012: Res $6685 (+$500), 5 wks. Aid (Need).
Housing: Dorms. **Swimming:** Pool. Campus facilities avail.
Est 1988. Nonprofit. **Ses:** 2. **Wks/ses:** 5. Operates June-Aug.

The Summer Scholars Program enables rising high school juniors and seniors to enroll in college-level courses in various disciplines. Students spend 16 to 20 hours in class each week and take advantage of the cultural amenities and educational opportunities of the city and the university during their free time. Staff plan one large outing each weekend, as well as frequent social events on weekday evenings. Weekly seminars deliver information on college admission, financial assistance and career planning.

NEVADA

DAVIDSON INSTITUTE FOR TALENT DEVELOPMENT
THINK SUMMER INSTITUTE
Res — Coed Ages 13-16

Reno, NV. Univ of Nevada.
Contact (Year-round): 9665 Gateway Dr, Ste B, Reno, NV 89521. Tel: 775-852-3483.
Fax: 775-852-2184.
www.davidsongifted.org/think   E-mail: think@davidsongifted.org
Katie Anderson & Aimee Cummins, Prgm Mgrs.
Adm: Somewhat selective. Admitted: 90%. Prereqs: SAT M/CR 1130; ACT 26. **Appl**—Fee $50. Due: Jan. 2 recs, test scores, essay, resume.
Enr: 60. **Enr cap:** 60. Non-White: 30%. **Fac 6.** Prof 6. **Staff:** Admin 5. Res 15.
Type of instruction: Adv. **Courses:** Comp_Sci Math Pol_Sci Writing/Journ Anthro Geog. **Avg class size:** 18. **Daily hours for:** Classes 6. Study 3. Rec 2. Homework. Tests. Grades. **College credit:** 3/crse, total 6.
Features: Hiking.
Fees 2011: Res $3000, 3 wks. Aid (Need).
Housing: Dorms. Avg per room/unit: 2. Campus facilities avail.
Est 2004. Nonprofit. **Ses:** 1. **Wks/ses:** 3. Operates July-Aug.

Conducted on the campus of the University of Nevada-Reno, the THINK Summer Institute enables academically gifted students to choose two university-level courses from such options as political science, anthropology, journalism, geography, mathematics and computer science. Program participants live in dormitories and have access to university resources. Applicants must satisfy minimum SAT or ACT score requirements.

NEW HAMPSHIRE

CARDIGAN MOUNTAIN SCHOOL SUMMER SESSION
Res and Day — Coed Ages 8-15

Canaan, NH 03741. 62 Alumni Dr. Tel: 603-523-3526. Fax: 603-523-3565.
www.cardigan.org/summer   E-mail: mrinkin@cardigan.org
Matt Rinkin, Dir.
Grades 3-9 (younger if qualified). **Adm:** Selective. Admitted: 90%. **Appl**—Fee $50. Due: Rolling. Transcript, teacher rec, parent & student statements.
Enr: 146. **Enr cap:** 150. Intl: 40%. Non-White: 35%. **Fac 40.** Col/grad students 7. K-12 staff 33. **Staff:** Admin 7. Couns 40.
Type of instruction: Adv Dev_Read Enrich Rem_Eng Rem_Math Rem_Read Rev ESL/TOEFL_Prep SAT/ACT_Prep Study_Skills Tut. **Courses:** Fr Lat Span Ecol Environ_Sci ESL Expository_Writing Math Writing/Journ Crafts Creative_Writing Fine_Arts Music Photog Studio_Art Theater. **Avg class size:** 6. **Daily hours for:** Classes 4. Study 1. Rec 4. Homework. Grades.
Features: Canoe Hiking Riding Riflery Sail Wilderness_Camp Wilderness_Canoe Baseball Basketball Lacrosse Soccer Street_Hockey Swim Tennis Ultimate_Frisbee Weight_Trng.
Fees 2011: Res $5304-8840 (+$750), 3-6 wks. Day $2808-4680 (+$300), 3-6 wks. Aid 2011 (Need): $115,000.
Housing: Dorms Houses. Avg per room/unit: 2. **Swimming:** Lake. Campus facilities avail.
Est 1951. Nonprofit. **Ses:** 3. **Wks/ses:** 3-6. Operates June-Aug.

Cardigan Mountain offers individualized and intensive developmental, enrichment and remedial work in English, math, Spanish, Latin, French, environmental science, reading and study skills, computers and ESL. A language learning lab serves students who require significant remediation in reading or writing. Afternoons are devoted to such traditional camp activities as tennis, sailing, swimming and soccer.

PHILLIPS EXETER ACADEMY SUMMER SCHOOL
Res and Day — Coed Ages 13-18

Exeter, NH 03833. 20 Main St. Tel: 603-777-3488. Fax: 603-777-4385.
www.exeter.edu/summer   E-mail: summer@exeter.edu
Ethan Shapiro, Dir.
Grades 8-PG. Adm: Selective. **Appl**—Fee $65. Due: Rolling. Transcript, teacher & administrator recs, essay.
Enr cap: 750-780. **Fac 150.** K-12 staff 150. **Staff:** Admin 5.
Type of instruction: Adv Enrich SAT/ACT_Prep. **Courses:** Arabic Chin Fr Ger Ital Japan Lat Span Astron Bus/Fin Debate Environ_Sci Expository_Writing Govt Marine_Bio/Stud Speech Writing/Journ Creative_Writing Dance Fine_Arts Media Music Photog Theater. **Avg class size:** 12. **Daily hours for:** Classes 3. Study 3. Rec 2. Homework. Tests. Grades.
Features: Rowing/Sculling Basketball Cross-country Field_Hockey Golf Lacrosse Soccer Squash Swim Tennis Volleyball Watersports.
Fees 2012: Res $7350-7700 (+$400-600), 5 wks. Day $1150-4900 (+$300), 5 wks. Aid 2011 (Need): $1,000,000.
Housing: Dorms. Avg per room/unit: 2. **Swimming:** Ocean Pool. Campus facilities avail.
Est 1919. Nonprofit. **Ses:** 1. **Wks/ses:** 5. Operates July-Aug.

Academic work, physical education and recreational activities are balanced at this summer school, which comprises ACCESS EXETER (accelerated study in the arts and sciences for pupils who have completed grade 7 or 8) and UPPER SCHOOL (students who have completed grade 9, 10, 11 or 12). Course work includes English and writing skills, English for nonnative speakers, languages, math, science, history and social studies, psychology, computer studies, humanities, art, music and the performing arts. UPPER SCHOOL's selective Leadership Program welcomes students to enroll in two leadership seminars and a third course of their choosing. Extracurricular on-campus activities and a variety of trips (including college visits) supplement academics.   **See Also Page 25**

SUMMER INSTITUTE FOR THE GIFTED
Res and Day — Coed Ages 13-17

Hanover, NH. Dartmouth College.
Contact (Year-round): River Plz, 9 W Broad St, Stamford, CT 06902.
     Tel: 203-399-5188, 866-303-4744. Fax: 203-399-5455.
www.giftedstudy.com   E-mail: sig.info@giftedstudy.com
Barbara Swicord, Pres.
     Student contact: Christine Provencher, E-mail: cprovencher@giftedstudy.com.
Adm: Selective. Admitted: 90%. **Appl**—Fee $95. Due: Rolling. Transcript, standardized test scores, classification as gifted/2 recs.
Intl: 25%.
Type of instruction: Adv Enrich SAT/ACT_Prep Study_Skills. **Courses:** Engineering Expository_Writing Forensic_Sci Hist Law Med/Healthcare Sci Robotics Drawing Photog Theater Screenwriting. **Avg class size:** 14. **Daily hours for:** Classes 6. Study 1. Rec 2. **College credit.**
Fees 2012: Res $5195, 3 wks. Day $2795, 3 wks.
Housing: Dorms. Campus facilities avail.
Est 2010. Nonprofit. **Spons:** National Society for the Gifted & Talented. **Ses:** 1. **Wks/ses:** 3. Operates July-Aug.

See program description under Berkeley, CA.

OLIVERIAN SCHOOL SUMMER SESSION
Res — Coed Ages 14-17

Haverhill, NH 03765. Mt Moosilauke Hwy, PO Box 98. Tel: 603-989-5368.
Fax: 603-989-3055.
www.oliverianschool.org/summer_program
E-mail: bmackinnon@oliverianschool.org
Grades 9-12. Adm: FCFS. **Appl**—Due: Rolling.
Type of instruction: Enrich. **Courses:** Eng Math Dance Studio_Art Theater Pottery. **High school credit.**
Features: Hiking Kayak Paintball Riding Rock_Climb Martial_Arts Gardening.
Housing: Dorms.
Ses: 1. Wks/ses: 7. Operates June-Aug.

Oliverian combines academics with an experiential activities program. Courses, which lead to high school credit in English, math, art and the social sciences, convene in the morning on Monday through Thursday. Integrated learning and activities fill the afternoon hours, while Fridays are reserved for field trips and off-campus learning. Students spend one of the seven weeks of the session engaged in off-campus adventure instead of academics. Faculty schedule recreational and enrichment pursuits for evenings and weekends.

BREWSTER ACADEMY SUMMER SESSION
Res and Day — Coed Ages 13-17

Wolfeboro, NH 03894. 80 Academy Dr. Tel: 603-569-7155. Fax: 603-569-7050.
www.brewsteracademy.org   E-mail: summer@brewsteracademy.org
Raylene Davis, Dir.
Adm: Selective. **Appl**—Fee $35. Due: Rolling. Transcript, standardized test results, 2 teacher recs, writing samples (Eng/ESL core crses).
Enr: 60. Enr cap: 60. Fac 10. K-12 staff 10. **Staff:** Admin 8. Couns 10.
Type of instruction: Adv Enrich Study_Skills. **Courses:** Comp_Sci ESL Math Sci Comp_ Graphics Video_Production. **Avg class size:** 8. **Daily hours for:** Classes 4. Study 1½. Rec 3. Homework. Tests. Grades. **High school credit:** 1.
Features: Aquatics Canoe Climbing_Wall Hiking Kayak Mountaineering Rappelling Rock_ Climb Ropes_Crse Wilderness_Camp Basketball Soccer Softball Swim Volleyball.
Fees 2012: Res $7380-7850 (+$1000), 6 wks. Day $4200 (+$1000), 6 wks.
Housing: Dorms. **Swimming:** Lake. Campus facilities avail.
Est 1994. Nonprofit. **Ses: 1. Wks/ses: 6.** Operates June-Aug.

Brewster Summer Session offers a combination of classroom academics and outdoor education. Students take one core course in English, math or ESL, and choose two electives from computer graphics and design, experiential science, video production and instructional support. Afternoon outdoor activities include survival training, rock climbing, canoeing and kayaking. Recreational sports, games and social activities are popular evening pursuits.

WOLFEBORO
THE SUMMER BOARDING SCHOOL
Res — Coed Ages 10-18

Wolfeboro, NH 03894. 93 Camp School Rd, PO Box 390. Tel: 603-569-3451.
Fax: 603-569-4080.
www.wolfeboro.org   E-mail: school@wolfeboro.org
Edward A. Cooper, Head.
Grades 6-PG. Adm: Selective. Admitted: 25%. **Appl**—Fee $0. Due: Rolling.
Enr: 180. Enr cap: 180. Intl: 30%. Non-White: 20%. **Fac 35.** K-12 staff 35. **Staff:** Admin 6. Res 35.
Type of instruction: Adv Dev_Read Enrich Preview Rem_Eng Rem_Math Rem_Read Rev

SAT/ACT_Prep Study_Skills Tut. **Courses:** Fr Lat Span Eng Environ_Sci ESL Expository_Writing Hist Math Sci Fine_Arts. **Avg class size:** 5. **Daily hours for:** Classes 5. Study 4. Rec 4. Homework. Tests. Grades. **High school credit:** 3.
Features: Aquatics Boating Canoe Fishing Hiking Baseball Basketball Lacrosse Soccer Softball Swim Tennis Volleyball Watersports Weight_Trng.
Fees 2011: Res $12,500 (+$1500), 6 wks. Aid 2010 (Need): $190,000.
Housing: Tents. Avg per room/unit: 2. **Swimming:** Lake. Campus facilities avail.
Est 1910. Nonprofit. **Ses:** 1. **Wks/ses:** 6. Operates June-Aug.

Wolfeboro combines individualized academic instruction in the mornings with recreational activities in the afternoons and on weekends. Students may take courses for credit, or they may review or preview work, or strengthen skills in core subjects. Particularly noteworthy among extracurriculars is the school's strong intramural sports program. Boys and girls may go on weekend excursions to nearby events and areas of interest, including professional baseball games, water and amusement parks, and movies.

NEW JERSEY

NEW JERSEY SCHOLARS PROGRAM
Res — Coed Ages 16-18

Lawrenceville, NJ 08648. c/o Lawrenceville School, PO Box 6008. Tel: 609-620-6106. Fax: 609-620-6894.
www.lawrenceville.org/njsp　　E-mail: njsp@lawrenceville.org
John P. Sauerman, Dir.
Grade 12. Adm: Very selective. Priority: Low-income. **Appl—Fee $0. Due:** Jan. Essays, rec, group interview.
Enr: 39. Enr cap: 39.
Type of instruction: Adv Enrich. **Courses:** Expository_Writing Public_Speak Drama Music. **Daily hours for:** Classes 4½. Homework.
Features: Swim.
Fees 2012: Free (in-state residents). Res 5 wks.
Housing: Dorms. **Swimming:** Pool. Campus facilities avail.
Nonprofit. **Ses:** 1. **Wks/ses:** 5. Operates June-July.

Limited to New Jersey residents, NJSP brings highly motivated rising seniors from diverse socioeconomic, ethnic and racial backgrounds to the Lawrenceville School campus for five weeks of college-level study. Program topics, which rotate biennially, are interdisciplinary in nature. Each day begins with a whole-group lecture, after which boys and girls attend morning and afternoon group seminars and engage in extensive reading assignments and research at museums and libraries. Students work closely with college faculty to produce a 10- to 15-page research paper, and they also contribute to an arts festival that is thematically related to the academic curriculum. Each pupil must be nominated by his or her guidance counselor.

THE HUN SCHOOL OF PRINCETON
SUMMER ACADEMIC SESSION
Res — Coed Ages 13-17; Day — Coed 11-17

Princeton, NJ 08540. 176 Edgerstoune Rd. Tel: 609-921-7600. Fax: 609-921-0953.
www.hunschool.org　　E-mail: summer@hunschool.org
Donna O'Sullivan, Dir.
Grades 6-12. Adm: Somewhat selective. Admitted: 98%. **Appl—Fee $0. Due:** Rolling. Rec.
Enr: 120. Enr cap: 150. Intl: 20%. **Fac 25.** K-12 staff 25. **Staff:** Admin 5. Couns 12.

Type of instruction: Adv Enrich Preview Rev ESL/TOEFL_Prep SAT/ACT_Prep. **Courses:** Econ Eng Marine_Bio/Stud Math Sci Amer_Stud Human_Rights Creative_Writing. **Avg class size:** 12. **Daily hours for:** Classes 5. Study 2. Rec 6. Homework. Tests. Grades. **High school credit:** 1/crse, total 1.
Features: Basketball Soccer Ultimate_Frisbee Volleyball.
Fees 2012: Res $5275 (+$25-200), 5 wks. Day $1298-2250 (+$25-200), 5 wks.
Housing: Dorms. Campus facilities avail.
Est 1984. Nonprofit. **Ses:** 1. **Wks/ses:** 5. Operates June-July.

The Hun School offers summer classes for credit, preview, review and enrichment. Credit-bearing courses are available in chemistry, algebra, geometry and pre-calculus. Enrichment options include SAT critical reading and SAT math preparation, creative writing, literature, math and science. Fitness training, games and off-campus trips are popular activities.

See Also Page 27

SUMMER INSTITUTE FOR THE GIFTED
Res — Coed Ages 13-17

Princeton, NJ. Princeton Univ.
Contact (Year-round): River Plz, 9 W Broad St, Stamford, CT 06902.
   Tel: 203-399-5188, 866-303-4744. Fax: 203-399-5455.
www.giftedstudy.org   E-mail: sig.info@giftedstudy.com
Barbara Swicord, Pres.
   Student contact: Christine Provencher, E-mail: cprovencher@giftedstudy.com.
Adm: Very selective. Admitted: 90%. **Appl**—Fee $95. Due: Rolling. Transcript, standardized test scores, classification as gifted/2 recs.
Intl: 25%.
Type of instruction: Adv Enrich SAT/ACT_Prep Study_Skills. **Courses:** Expository_Writing Forensic_Sci Hist Math Sci Writing/Journ Philos Dance Photog Theater. **Avg class size:** 14. **Daily hours for:** Classes 6. Study 1. Rec 2.
Fees 2012: Res $5195, 3 wks.
Housing: Dorms.
Est 1984. Nonprofit. **Spons:** National Society for the Gifted & Talented. **Ses:** 1. **Wks/ses:** 3. Operates July-Aug.

See program description under Berkeley, CA.

NEW YORK

ALFRED UNIVERSITY
SUMMER PROGRAMS FOR TEENS
Res and Day — Coed Ages 12-17

Alfred, NY 14802. Office of Summer Prgms, 1 Saxon Dr. Tel: 607-871-2612.
   Fax: 607-871-2045.
www.alfred.edu/summer/hs.cfm   E-mail: summerpro@alfred.edu
Melody McLay, Dir.
Grades 7-12 (younger if qualified). Adm: Selective. Admitted: 85%. Prereqs: GPA 3.0.
   Appl—Fee $0. Due: Apr. Transcript, 2 recs, essay.
Enr: 20-25. **Enr cap:** 20-25. Intl: 1%. Non-White: 10%. **Fac 13.** Prof 12. Col/grad students 1. **Staff:** Admin 4. Couns 12.
Type of instruction: Adv Enrich. **Courses:** Chin Astron Bus/Fin Comp_Sci Engineering Sci Robotics Creative_Writing Studio_Art Theater. **Avg class size:** 15. **Daily hours for:** Classes 6. Study 2. Rec 3. Homework.
Features: Hiking Swim Bowling.

Fees 2011: Res $850-1995 (+$50-100), 1-2 wks. Day $595-995 (+$50-100), 1 wk.
Housing: Dorms. Avg per room/unit: 2. **Swimming:** Pool. Campus facilities avail.
Est 1998. Nonprofit. **Ses:** 10. **Wks/ses:** 1-2. Operates June-July.

Alfred University's high school programs enable students to learn more about a field of interest while sampling college life and meeting other pupils with similar interests and academic ability. Programs focus upon the following areas: computer science, engineering, astronomy, chemistry, robotics, entrepreneurship, art portfolio, creative writing and theater. Age range varies by program, and commuter options are frequently available.

NEW YORK MILITARY ACADEMY
SUMMER ACADEMIC PROGRAM
Res and Day — Coed Ages 13-17

Cornwall-on-Hudson, NY 12520. 78 Academy Ave. Tel: 845-534-3710, 888-275-6962.
Fax: 845-534-7699.
www.nyma.org   E-mail: admissions@nyma.org
Les McMillen, Dir. Student contact: Alisa Southweil, E-mail: asouthweil@nyma.org.
Grades 9-11. Adm: FCFS. **Appl**—Due: June.
Type of instruction: Enrich Rem_Eng Rem_Math Rem_Read ESL/TOEFL_Prep SAT/ACT_Prep Study_Skills. **Courses:** Eng Environ_Sci Sci. **Avg class size:** 8. **Daily hours for:** Classes 3. Study 1½. Rec 3. Homework. Tests. Grades. **High school credit:** 3/crse, total 3.
Features: Swim.
Fees 2011: Res $6000, 6 wks. Day $175/crse, 6 wks.
Housing: Dorms. **Swimming:** Pool. Campus facilities avail.
Est 1954. Nonprofit. **Ses:** 1. **Wks/ses:** 6. Operates July-Aug.

NYMA's summer program offers both credit-bearing and enrichment courses during the morning hours. Afternoon and evening activities include intramural sports, movies, music instruction and organized game nights.

CORNELL UNIVERSITY SUMMER COLLEGE
Res — Coed Ages 16-18

Ithaca, NY 14853. B20 Day Hall. Tel: 607-255-6203. Fax: 607-255-6665.
www.summercollege.cornell.edu   E-mail: summer_college@cornell.edu
Abby H. Eller, Dir.
Grades 11-PG. Adm: Selective. Admitted: 54%. **Appl**—Fee $55-65. Due: Rolling. Transcript, rec.
Enr: 800.
Type of instruction: Adv Undergrad. **Courses:** Architect Bus/Fin Col_Prep Comp_Sci Engineering Environ_Sci Law Med/Healthcare Sci Writing/Journ Film Media Studio_Art. Homework. Tests. Grades. **College credit:** 6-8.
Features: Rock_Climb Basketball Soccer Swim Ultimate_Frisbee Volleyball.
Fees 2012: Res $6020-9995, 3-6 wks. Aid (Need).
Housing: Dorms. **Swimming:** Pool. Campus facilities avail.
Est 1962. Nonprofit. **Ses:** 3. **Wks/ses:** 3-6. Operates June-Aug.

Summer College provides an opportunity for academically talented high school students to preview university life and earn college credit by taking regular Cornell summer session courses. In addition to taking classes, all pupils participate in a career exploration seminar that allows them to learn more about a particular field. Extracurricular activities include intramural sports, musical and dance groups, the Summer College newspaper and yearbook, community service projects and weekend dances.

ITHACA COLLEGE
SUMMER COLLEGE FOR HIGH SCHOOL STUDENTS
Res — Coed Ages 15-18

Ithaca, NY 14850. **Graduate & Professional Studies, 953 Danby Rd.**
  Tel: 607-274-3143. Fax: 866-924-6272.
  www.ithaca.edu/summercollege E-mail: gps@ithaca.edu
Warren Schlesinger, Dir.
Grades 10-12. Adm: Somewhat selective. Admitted: 85%. Prereqs: GPA 3.0. **Appl**—Fee $25. Due: Rolling. Transcript, essay.
Enr: 120. **Enr cap:** 120. Intl: 3%. Non-White: 22%. **Fac 21.** Prof 21. **Staff:** Admin 3. Couns 8.
Type of instruction: Adv Enrich Preview Undergrad. **Courses:** Bus/Fin Expository_Writing Med/Healthcare Psych Relig_Stud Sports_Management Acting Film Media Photog Sculpt Musical_Theater. **Avg class size:** 12. **Daily hours for:** Classes 3. Study 3. Rec 3. Homework. Tests. Grades. **College credit:** 2-4/crse, total 4.
Features: Basketball Golf Swim Tennis Volleyball.
Fees 2011: Res $1280-4280, 1-3 wks. Aid (Merit & Need).
Housing: Dorms. **Swimming:** Pool. Campus facilities avail.
Est 1997. Nonprofit. **Ses:** 2. **Wks/ses:** 1-3. Operates June-July.

High school students of above-average ability gain a preview of academic and residential college life through this program. Rising juniors and seniors enrolled in the three-week program choose one course for college credit; course tuition varies by the number of credits awarded. A weeklong session open to all high school students features a selection of ungraded, noncredit courses. In addition to academics, students take part in athletics, recreational activities, trips, volunteer opportunities and noncredit workshops.

TELLURIDE ASSOCIATION SUMMER PROGRAM
Res — Coed Ages 17-18

Ithaca, NY. **Cornell Univ.**
Contact (Year-round): 217 West Ave, Ithaca, NY 14850. Tel: 607-273-5011.
  Fax: 607-272-2667.
  http://tasp.tellurideassociation.org E-mail: telluride@tellurideassociation.org
Ellen Baer, Admin Dir.
Grade 12. Adm: Very selective. **Appl**—Fee $0. Due: Jan. Essays, transcript, standardized test scores.
Enr: 16-18.
Type of instruction: Adv Enrich. **Courses:** Eng Sci Philos.
Fees 2010: Free. Res 6 wks.
Housing: Dorms.
Nonprofit. **Ses:** 3. **Wks/ses:** 6. Operates June-Aug.

See program description under Ann Arbor, MI.

BARNARD COLLEGE
SUMMER IN THE CITY
Res and Day — Coed Ages 16-18

New York, NY 10027. **Office of Pre-College Prgms, 3009 Broadway, Milbank 235.**
  Tel: 212-854-8866. Fax: 212-854-8867.
  www.barnard.edu/precollege E-mail: pcp@barnard.edu
Ann Dachs, Dir.
Grades 11-12. Adm: Selective. **Appl**—Fee $50. Due: May. Transcript, essay, 2 recs.
Enr cap: 160. **Staff:** Admin 3. Res 22.
Type of instruction: Adv Enrich Undergrad. **Courses:** Architect Comp_Sci Hist Pol_Sci

Psych Sci Anthro Sociol Women's_Stud Acting Creative_Writing Dance Film Music Theater. **Avg class size:** 15. **Daily hours for:** Classes 4. Study 2. Rec 3. Homework.
Fees 2011: Res $1850-4950 (+$75-150), 1-4 wks. Day $1150-3100 (+$75-150), 1-4 wks. Aid (Need).
Housing: Dorms. Avg per room/unit: 2.
Est 1984. Nonprofit. **Ses:** 2. **Wks/ses:** 1-4. Operates June-July.

Barnard offers four-week courses and weeklong minicourses in the liberal arts and the humanities. Four-week program participants attend morning and afternoon classes four days each week, with Wednesdays spent visiting professional or community service organizations or attending on-campus seminars. Evening and weekend pursuits include dance classes, movie nights, and trips to New York City landmarks and festivals.

COLUMBIA UNIVERSITY
SUMMER PROGRAM FOR HIGH SCHOOL STUDENTS
Res and Day — Coed Ages 14-17

New York, NY 10027. 510 Lewisohn Hall, 2970 Broadway, Mail Code 4110.
Tel: 212-854-9699. Fax: 212-854-7077.
www.ce.columbia.edu/hs　E-mail: hsp-info@columbia.edu
Darlene Giraitis, Exec Dir.
Grades 9-12. Adm: Selective. Admitted: 75%. Prereqs: GPA 3.0. **Appl**—Fee $75-150. Due: Apr. Transcript, 2 recommendations, essay.
Enr: 1000. **Enr cap:** 1500. Intl: 33%. **Fac 80. Staff:** Admin 10. Res 150.
Type of instruction: Adv Enrich Study_Skills Undergrad. **Courses:** Bus/Fin Comp_Sci Debate Econ Engineering Expository_Writing Govt Law Creative_Writing Drawing Filmmaking Media Photog Theater. **Avg class size:** 25. **Daily hours for:** Classes 4. Homework.
Features: Swim.
Fees 2011: Res $6931 (+$985-1310), 3 wks. Day $3896 (+$285-1310), 3 wks.
Housing: Dorms. Avg per room/unit: 1. **Swimming:** Pool. Campus facilities avail.
Est 1987. Nonprofit. **Ses:** 2. **Wks/ses:** 3. Operates June-Aug.

The program enrolls high schoolers in two divisions, organized by grade level: one for students entering grades 9 and 10, the other for pupils entering grades 11 and 12. Participants in both sections follow a curriculum designed to meet the interests, talents and needs of college-bound students. The program includes time each day for independent study and tutorials, private meetings with instructors, extracurricular activities, and use of the university's libraries and other facilities. Although these noncredit courses do not culminate in letter grades, participants receive extensive performance evaluations throughout and at course's end.

HUMANITIES SPRING IN NEW YORK
Res and Day — Coed Ages 18 and up

New York, NY.
Contact (Year-round): Santa Maria di Lignano 2, Assisi, 06081 Italy.
Tel: 39-075-802400. Fax: 39-075-802400.
www.humanitiesspring.com　E-mail: info@humanitiesspring.com
Jane R. Oliensis, Dir. Student contact: Alessia Montanucci.
Adm: FCFS. **Appl**—Fee $50. Due: Rolling.
Enr: 15. **Enr cap:** 15. Intl: 80%. **Fac 4.** Prof 1. Col/grad students 1. K-12 staff 1. Specialists 1. **Staff:** Admin 1. Couns 2.
Type of instruction: Enrich. **Courses:** Architect NYC_Hist Poetry Creative_Writing Photog Studio_Art. **Daily hours for:** Classes 4. Study 1. Rec 7½.
Features: Cooking Swim.
Fees 2012: Res $4250 (+$500), 4½ wks. Day $3500 (+$100), 4½ wks. Aid 2011 (Merit & Need): $5000.

Swimming: Pool. Campus facilities avail.
Est 2006. Nonprofit. **Ses: 1. Wks/ses:** 4½. Operates July-Aug.

From their home base at the 92nd Street YMHA, HSNY students learn about New York City through a combination of academics and firsthand exploration of related works of art and architecture. During four hours of class work each morning, participants take courses that examine the history, architecture and art of the city. Pupils spend the afternoon hours visiting such sites as City Hall, the Chrysler Building and the Empire State Building in the company of New York architects. Applicants need not have any background knowledge of art or architecture.

CLARKSON UNIVERSITY YOUNG SCHOLARS
Res and Day — Coed Ages 16-17

Potsdam, NY 13699. 8 Clarkson Ave, PO Box 5650. Tel: 315-268-4425, 800-574-4425.
   Fax: 315-268-7991.
www.clarkson.edu/youngscholars   E-mail: bkozsan@clarkson.edu
Brenda R. Kozsan, Dir.
Grades 11-12 (younger if qualified). Adm: Selective. **Appl**—Fee $0. Due: Rolling. Transcript, essay, rec.
Enr: 25. **Enr cap:** 40. **Fac 4.** Prof 4. **Staff:** Admin 2. Res 4.
Type of instruction: Enrich. **Courses:** Bus/Fin Engineering Ethics. **Daily hours for:** Classes 5½. Rec 3. Homework.
Features: Swim Weight_Trng.
Fees 2012: Res $850 (+$20-50), 1 wk. **Day** $650 (+$20-50), 1 wk. Aid (Need).
Housing: Dorms. Avg per room/unit: 2. **Swimming:** Pool. Campus facilities avail.
Est 2004. Ses: 1. Wks/ses: 1. Operates July.

Conducted by The Clarkson School, a division of Clarkson University that serves talented high schoolers, Young Scholars takes an interdisciplinary approach to examining and solving a problem from three different perspectives: business, engineering and ethics/social values. The program topic changes each year. Students conduct research individually and in small groups, then prepare a final presentation for campus and community leaders. During the course of the week, boys and girls further develop their communicational and cooperative problem-solving skills. Families are welcome to attend the final presentation.

SUMMER INSTITUTE FOR THE GIFTED
Res and Day — Coed Ages 10-17

Poughkeepsie, NY. Vassar College.
Contact (Year-round): River Plz, 9 W Broad St, Stamford, CT 06902.
   Tel: 203-399-5188, 866-303-4744. Fax: 203-399-5455.
www.giftedstudy.org   E-mail: sig.info@giftedstudy.org
Barbara Swicord, Pres.
   Student contact: Christine Provencher, E-mail: cprovencher@giftedstudy.com.
Adm: Selective. Admitted: 90%. **Appl**—Fee $95. Due: Rolling. Transcript, standardized test scores, classification as gifted/2 recs.
Intl: 25%.
Type of instruction: Adv Enrich SAT/ACT_Prep Study_Skills. **Courses:** Expository_Writing Forensic_Sci Math Sci Dance Photog Theater. **Avg class size:** 14. **Daily hours for:** Classes 6. Study 1. Rec 2.
Fees 2012: Res $4495, 3 wks. **Day** $2495, 3 wks.
Housing: Dorms. Campus facilities avail.
Est 1984. Nonprofit. **Spons:** National Society for the Gifted & Talented. **Ses: 1. Wks/ses:** 3. Operates July.

See program description under Berkeley, CA.

SKIDMORE COLLEGE
PRE-COLLEGE PROGRAM IN THE LIBERAL AND STUDIO ARTS
Res — Coed Ages 16-18; Day — Coed 15-18

Saratoga Springs, NY 12866. 815 N Broadway. Tel: 518-580-5590. Fax: 518-580-5548.
www.skidmore.edu/precollege   E-mail: mcogan@skidmore.edu
Michelle Paquette, Dir. Student contact: Mary Cogan.
Grades 10-PG. Adm: Selective. **Appl**—Fee $40. Due: Rolling. Transcript, 2 recs, art samples.
Enr: 110. **Fac 20.** Prof 20. **Staff:** Admin 3.
Type of instruction: Adv Undergrad. **Courses:** Ecol Environ_Sci Expository_Writing Hist Sci Ceramics Creative_Writing Drama Filmmaking Music Painting Studio_Art. **Avg class size:** 10. **Daily hours for:** Classes 4. Study 4. **High school & college credit:** 8.
Features: Swim.
Fees 2011: Res $5375-6475, 5 wks. Day $1250-4400, 5 wks. Aid (Merit & Need).
Housing: Dorms. **Swimming:** Pool.
Est 1978. Nonprofit. **Ses:** 1. **Wks/ses:** 5. Operates July-Aug.

Students who have completed sophomore, junior or senior year may earn college credits in a variety of foundation-level Skidmore College courses in the liberal arts and sciences. In addition, rising sophomores may apply as commuter students to take noncredit studio arts classes that carry much of the same demands as for-credit courses. Extracurricular activities include poetry and fiction readings, films, art lectures, cultural field trips, and activities for recreation and relaxation.

SYRACUSE UNIVERSITY SUMMER COLLEGE
FOR HIGH SCHOOL STUDENTS
Res and Day — Coed Ages 15-18

Syracuse, NY 13244. 700 University Ave. Tel: 315-443-5000. Fax: 315-443-4410.
www.summercollege.syr.edu   E-mail: sumcoll@syr.edu
Binh Q. Huynh, Dir.
Grades 10-12. Adm: Somewhat selective. **Appl**—Fee $55. Due: May. Transcript, essay, rec.
Enr: 225. **Fac 35. Staff:** Admin 3. Couns 15.
Type of instruction: Adv Preview. **Courses:** Architect Bus/Fin Comm Comp_Sci Econ Engineering Forensic_Sci Govt Law Speech Writing/Journ Web_Design Acting Creative_Writing Dance Fashion Fine_Arts Media Painting. **Daily hours for:** Classes 6.
College credit: 7.
Features: Basketball Soccer Softball Swim Tennis.
Fees 2012: Res $2303-7952, 2-6 wks. Day $1543-5673, 2-6 wks. Aid (Need).
Housing: Dorms. Avg per room/unit: 2. **Swimming:** Pool.
Est 1961. Nonprofit. **Ses:** 4. **Wks/ses:** 2-6. Operates July-Aug.

Summer College's six-week programs enable high schoolers to explore academic and career interests while earning college credit. Students enrolling in the liberal arts program choose two courses from Syracuse's undergraduate humanities and social sciences offerings. Preprofessional programs in engineering and computer science, law and public communications require one specialized course plus one complementary elective, and studio/lab programs in acting and musical theater, architecture, fashion design, interior design and forensic science combine course work with substantial studio or laboratory time. Summer College also offers two-week noncredit programs in studio arts, interior design and management, as well as a two-week education program with both credit and noncredit options. Field trips and guest lecturers enrich the curriculum, and staff schedule various weekend activities.

RENSSELAER POLYTECHNIC INSTITUTE
SUMMER@RENSSELAER
Res — Coed Ages 15-18

Troy, NY 12180. Academic Outreach Programs Office, 110 8th St. Tel: 518-276-8351.
Fax: 518-276-8738.
http://summer.rpi.edu   E-mail: gunthm@rpi.edu
Student contact: Mike Gunther.
Grades 10-12. Adm: Somewhat selective. **Appl**—Fee $0. Due: Rolling.
Type of instruction: Enrich. **Courses:** Architect Bus/Fin Computers Engineering Med/
Healthcare Sci.
Fees 2011: Res $1400-3000, 1-2 wks.
Housing: Dorms.
Wks/ses: 1-2. Operates July.

Rensselaer conducts a range of residential, noncredit enrichment programs for high school students. Program sessions, which last for one or two weeks (depending upon the subject area), specialize in aerospace engineering, architecture, business, chemistry and medicine, computer game development and engineering. In addition to these high school residential options, RPI offers various commuter programs for elementary, middle school and high school pupils.

UNITED STATES MILITARY ACADEMY
SUMMER LEADERS SEMINAR
Res — Coed Ages 17-18

West Point, NY 10996. Office of Adm, 606 Thayer Rd. Tel: 845-938-4041.
www.admissions.usma.edu   E-mail: admissions@usma.edu
Grade 12. Adm: Selective. Admitted: 30%. **Appl**—Due: Apr. Transcript, standardized test
scores.
Enr: 400. **Enr cap:** 400.
Type of instruction: Enrich. **Courses:** Arabic Chin Leadership Math Sci.
Fees 2009: Res $325, 1 wk.
Housing: Dorms. Campus facilities avail.
Nonprofit. **Ses:** 2. **Wks/ses:** 1. Operates May-June.

Rising high school seniors from around the country preview college life during SLS. The selective weeklong program combines academic classes, military and physical fitness training, and intramural athletics.

NORTH CAROLINA

APPALACHIAN INSTITUTE FOR CREATIVE LEARNING
SUMMER ENRICHMENT CAMP
Res — Coed Ages 8-17; Day — Coed 8-12

Asheville, NC. Warren Wilson College.
Contact (Year-round): PO Box 9027, Knoxville, TN 37940. Toll-free: 800-951-7442.
www.appalachianinstitute.org   E-mail: info@appalachianinstitute.org
Chad Watson & Susan Goslee, Dirs.
Grades 3-12. Adm: FCFS. **Appl**—Due: Rolling.
Enr: 80. **Fac 20.**
Type of instruction: Adv Enrich Study_Skills. **Courses:** Japan Ecol Environ_Sci Math Sci
Circus_Skills Crafts Creative_Writing Dance Drawing Fine_Arts Media Music Photog
Theater. **Avg class size:** 7. **Daily hours for:** Classes 6. Study 1. Rec 2.
Features: Aquatics Cooking Hiking Cross-country Golf Swim Tennis Volleyball.

Fees 2012: Res $575-1100, 1-2 wks. Day $300-600, 1-2 wks.
Housing: Dorms. Avg per room/unit: 2. **Swimming:** Pool.
Est 1982. Nonprofit. **Ses:** 2. **Wks/ses:** 1. Operates July.

Held at Warren Wilson College, this academic program for gifted and talented children offers advanced courses in the sciences, social sciences and language arts. Workshops in the fine and performing arts enable pupils to explore personal areas of interest and receive individualized instruction.

APPALACHIAN STATE UNIVERSITY
CAMP BROADSTONE SUMMER ENRICHMENT PROGRAM
Res — Coed Ages 10-15; Day — Coed 8-11

Banner Elk, NC 28604. 1431 Broadstone Rd.
Contact (Sept-May): PO Box 32042, Boone, NC 28608.
Year-round Tel: 828-963-4640, Fax: 828-963-6588.
www.campbroadstone.com   E-mail: campbroadstone@appstate.edu
Judith Bevan, Dir. Student contact: Nancy Rogers, E-mail: rogersnm@appstate.edu.
Grades 4-10. Adm: Selective. Prereqs: IQ 120. **Appl**—Fee $0. Due: Rolling.
Enr: 84. **Enr cap:** 84. **Fac 6. Staff:** Admin 3. Res 10.
Type of instruction: Adv Enrich. **Courses:** Ecol Environ_Sci Expository_Writing Geol Writing/Journ Crafts Creative_Writing Dance Drama Filmmaking Media Music Photog. **Avg class size:** 12. **Daily hours for:** Classes 3.
Features: Adventure_Travel Canoe Climbing_Wall Community_Serv Hiking Mtn_Trips Rappelling Rock_Climb Ropes_Crse White-water_Raft Wilderness_Camp Swim.
Fees 2012: Res $975-1900, 1-2 wks. Day $250, 1 wk. Aid 2011 (Need): $4000.
Housing: Cabins Lodges Tents. Avg per room/unit: 18. **Swimming:** Pool.
Est 1975. Nonprofit. **Ses:** 6. **Wks/ses:** 1-2. Operates June-Aug.

Broadstone's program for academically gifted children combines morning enrichment classes with afternoon adventure programs. Prospective applicants should have at least a 120 IQ or they should be performing two years above grade level in math, language arts or both. Academic courses address environmental studies, arts and crafts, journalism, music, drama and cultural studies. Adventure pursuits include rock climbing, a ropes course, and activities involving rivers and trails. In the evening, campers participate in dances, swimming, games and skits.

DUKE UNIVERSITY TALENT IDENTIFICATION PROGRAM
SUMMER STUDIES PROGRAMS
Res — Coed Ages 12-16

Boone, NC. Appalachian State Univ.
Contact (Year-round): 1121 W Main St, Durham, NC 27701. Tel: 919-668-9100.
Fax: 919-681-7921.
www.tip.duke.edu   E-mail: information@tip.duke.edu
Brian Cooper, Dir.
Grades 8-11. Adm: Selective. **Appl**—Fee $25. Due: Rolling. SAT/ACT requirement, personal statement.
Type of instruction: Adv Enrich. **Courses:** Engineering Environ_Sci Expository_Writing Math Creative_Writing Filmmaking Theater. **Avg class size:** 16. **Daily hours for:** Classes 7. Rec 3.
Fees 2011: Res $3550-3800, 3 wks. Aid (Need).
Housing: Dorms.
Est 1980. Nonprofit. **Ses:** 2. **Wks/ses:** 3. Operates June-Aug.

See program description under Lawrence, KS.

DAVIDSON JULY EXPERIENCE
Res — Coed Ages 15-18

Davidson, NC 28035. c/o Davidson College, Box 7151. Tel: 704-894-2508.
www.davidson.edu/julyexperience   **E-mail: julyexp@davidson.edu**
Evelyn Gerdes, Dir.
Grades 11-12. Adm: Selective. **Appl**—Fee $0. Due: Apr. Transcript, PSAT/SAT results, essay, 2 recs.
Enr: 70-75. Intl: 15%. Non-White: 15%. **Fac 11.** Prof 11. **Staff:** Admin 1. Res 8.
Type of instruction: Adv Enrich Preview Undergrad. **Courses:** Eng Hist Math Pol_Sci Sci Anthro Music. **Avg class size:** 18. **Daily hours for:** Classes 3. Study 5. Rec 3. Homework. Tests. Grades.
Features: Boating Canoe Community_Serv Sail White-water_Raft Basketball Golf Soccer Swim Tennis Volleyball Water-skiing Watersports Weight_Trng.
Fees 2012: Res $3500 (+$175), 3 wks. Aid (Need).
Housing: Dorms. Avg per room/unit: 2. **Swimming:** Lake Pool. Campus facilities avail.
Est 1976. Nonprofit. **Spons:** Davidson College. Presbyterian. **Ses:** 1. **Wks/ses:** 3. Operates June-July.

Conducted by Davidson College, this enrichment program for rising high school juniors and seniors combines a preview of college life with an academic component featuring courses taught by Davidson professors. Boys and girls select two noncredit courses from several liberal arts disciplines. Class periods last 90 minutes, with additional laboratory sessions scheduled in certain subjects. Students take part in extracurricular activities and explore various area attractions, among them the college's private Lake Campus and the US National Whitewater Center.   **See Also Page 33**

DUKE UNIVERSITY TALENT IDENTIFICATION PROGRAM
SUMMER STUDIES PROGRAMS
Res — Coed Ages 12-16

Davidson, NC. Davidson College.
Contact (Year-round): 1121 W Main St, Durham, NC 27701. Tel: 919-668-9100.
   Fax: 919-681-7921.
www.tip.duke.edu   **E-mail: information@tip.duke.edu**
Brian Cooper, Dir.
Grades 8-11. Adm: Selective. **Appl**—Fee $25. Due: Rolling.
Type of instruction: Adv Enrich. **Courses:** Architect Bus/Fin Debate Engineering Math Med/Healthcare Sci Writing/Journ Creative_Writing. **Avg class size:** 16. **Daily hours for:** Classes 7. Rec 3.
Fees 2011: Res $3550-3800, 3 wks. Aid (Need).
Housing: Dorms.
Est 1980. Nonprofit. **Ses:** 2. **Wks/ses:** 3. Operates June-Aug.

See program description under Lawrence, KS.

DUKE UNIVERSITY TALENT IDENTIFICATION PROGRAM
SUMMER STUDIES PROGRAMS
Res — Coed Ages 12-16

Durham, NC 27701. 1121 W Main St. Tel: 919-668-9100. Fax: 919-681-7921.
www.tip.duke.edu   **E-mail: information@tip.duke.edu**
Brian Cooper, Dir.
Grades 8-11. Adm: Selective. **Appl**—Fee $25. Due: Rolling. SAT or ACT requirement, personal statement.
Type of instruction: Adv Enrich. **Courses:** Ecol Econ Environ_Sci Expository_Writing Forensic_Sci Intl_Relations Marine_Bio/Stud Sci Anat & Physiol Robotics Creative_

Writing Filmmaking Media Theater Music_Hist. **Avg class size:** 16. **Daily hours for:** Classes 7. Rec 3.
Fees 2011: Res $3550-3800, 3 wks. Aid (Need).
Housing: Dorms.
Est 1980. Nonprofit. **Ses:** 2. **Wks/ses:** 3. Operates June-Aug.

See program description under Lawrence, KS.

OAK RIDGE MILITARY ACADEMY
ACADEMIC SUMMER SCHOOL
Res and Day — Coed Ages 11-17

Oak Ridge, NC 27310. 2317 Oak Ridge Rd, PO Box 498. Tel: 336-643-4131.
Fax: 336-643-1797.
www.oakridgemilitary.com   E-mail: tsandiford@ormila.com
Student contact: Terrill M. Sandiford.
Grades 6-12. Adm: FCFS. **Appl**—Due: Rolling.
Fac 15.
Type of instruction: Adv Enrich Preview Rem_Eng Rem_Math Rem_Read Rev Study_ Skills. **Courses:** ESL. **Avg class size:** 11. **Daily hours for:** Classes 4. Study 2. Rec 4.
High school credit: 1.
Features: Canoe Hiking Leadership Milit_Trng Rappelling Scuba Survival_Trng Wilderness_Camp Baseball Basketball Soccer Swim Tennis Volleyball Watersports.
Fees 2009: Res $2100-4375, 2½-5 wks. Day $1000-1750, 2½-5 wks.
Housing: Dorms. **Swimming:** Lake Pool.
Nonprofit. **Ses:** 4. **Wks/ses:** 2½-5. Operates July-Aug.

This academic summer school enables students to develop academically while developing leadership and self-discipline skills. Pupils may earn high school credit in various subject areas. Three days per week and on weekends, participants take part in leadership training activities involving rappelling, confidence courses and athletics.

OHIO

OHIO UNIVERSITY
SUMMER HONORS ACADEMY
Res and Day — Coed Ages 15-17

Athens, OH 45701. Office of Summer Sessions/Honors, Haning Hall 219.
Tel: 740-593-1767, 888-551-6446. Fax: 740-593-2901.
www.outreach.ohio.edu/honorsacademy   E-mail: honorsacademy@ohio.edu
Patricia Davidson, Prgm Dir.
Grades 10-12. Adm: Selective. Admitted: 85%. Prereqs: GPA 3.25. **Appl**—Fee $0. Due: May. Transcript, teacher & counselor recs.
Enr: 14. **Enr cap:** 10-30. Intl: 7%. Non-White: 36%. **Staff:** Admin 1. Res 4.
Type of instruction: Preview SAT/ACT_Prep Study_Skills Undergrad. **Courses:** Col_Prep.
Daily hours for: Classes 4. Study 5. Rec 2. Homework. Tests. Grades. **College credit:** 1-4/crse, total 9.
Features: Bicycle_Tours Climbing_Wall Hiking Basketball Golf Skateboarding Swim Volleyball Bowling.
Fees 2011: Res $2848-3452 (+$200-300), 5 wks. Day $906-1812 (+$150-250), 5 wks. Aid 2010 (Need): $10,000.
Housing: Dorms. Avg per room/unit: 2. **Swimming:** Pool. Campus facilities avail.
Est 2001. Nonprofit. **Ses:** 1. **Wks/ses:** 5. Operates June-July.

Honors Academy students attend credit-bearing college classes and experience life on campus. The program begins with a one-day orientation session in which pupils and their parents tour the campus and select one or two Ohio University undergraduate courses. Faculty members and experienced professionals lead noncredit career exploration seminars offering guidance on the college application process, as well as on potential academic degrees and career paths. Optional math, writing and foreign language tutorials and a PSAT prep course are also part of the program. Undergraduate student mentors conduct social and cultural activities and provide advice and assistance. Tuition fees vary according to the number of credit hours pursued, and all participants receive a $1000 credit toward the comprehensive program cost.

THE GRAND RIVER SUMMER ACADEMY
Res — Coed Ages 14-17

Austinburg, OH 44010. 3042 College St. Tel: 440-275-2811. Fax: 440-275-1825.
www.grandriver.org   E-mail: admissions@grandriver.org
Grades 9-12. Adm: FCFS. **Appl**—Due: Rolling.
Enr: 100. **Fac 20. Staff:** Admin 6. Couns 1. Special needs 1.
Courses: Fr Span Eng ESL Expository_Writing Govt Hist Math Sci.
Features: Paintball Baseball Basketball Golf Swim Tennis Weight_Trng.
Fees 2012: Res $3500-3800 (+$60-150), 6 wks.
Housing: Dorms. **Swimming:** Lake.
Est 1990. Nonprofit. **Spons:** Grand River Academy. **Ses: 1. Wks/ses:** 6. Operates June-Aug.

Offering five- and seven-day boarding options, Grand River's summer program allows students to either work on an academic problem area or investigate a new subject. An ESL immersion program is available for international students. Study skills are an integral aspect of the program, and all pupils take part in a proctored study period for two hours daily. Students devote afternoons to activity blocks that include horseback riding, arts and crafts, recreational electives and a sports program, and Grand River also schedules excursions to area attractions.

WRIGHT STATE UNIVERSITY PRE-COLLEGE PROGRAMS
Res — Coed Ages 12-17; Day — Coed 5-14

Dayton, OH 45435. 3640 Colonel Glenn Hwy. Tel: 937-775-3135. Fax: 937-775-4883.
www.wright.edu/academics/precollege   E-mail: precollege@wright.edu
Brenda I. Dewberry, Dir.
Grades K-12. Adm: FCFS. **Appl**—Fee $0. Due: Rolling.
Fac 20. Staff: Admin 4.
Type of instruction: Adv Enrich Study_Skills. **Courses:** Comp_Sci Engineering Forensic_Sci Math Sci Speech Art Creative_Writing Music Photog Studio_Art Theater. **Avg class size:** 16. **Daily hours for:** Classes 6. Study 2. Rec 2. Homework.
Features: Swim.
Fees 2012: Res $600-625, 1 wk. Day $125, 1 wk.
Housing: Dorms. **Swimming:** Pool. Campus facilities avail.
Est 1988. Nonprofit. **Wks/ses:** 1. Operates June-Aug.

Wright State offers precollege enrichment programs in a rotating selection of subject areas. Residential Camps (for students entering grades 6-9) and Institutes (grades 10-12) are weeklong programs exploring engineering, law, leadership, math, science, technology, the arts, anatomy and physiology, forensic science and creative writing. Each program incorporates lectures, hands-on projects, small-group discussions and program-specific field trips. Nonresidential enrichment courses accommodate pupils entering grades K-9.

MIAMI UNIVERSITY JUNIOR SCHOLARS PROGRAM
Res — Coed Ages 16-18

Oxford, OH 45056. 202 Bachelor Hall. Tel: 513-529-5825. Fax: 513-529-1498.
www.muohio.edu/juniorscholars   E-mail: juniorscholars@muohio.edu
Robert Sefton Smith, Dir.
Grade 12. **Adm:** Very selective. Admitted: 18%. Prereqs: GPA 3.5. PSAT M/CR 110. **Appl—**
Fee $0. Due: Rolling. Transcript, test scores, rec.
Enr: 61. **Enr cap:** 85. Intl: 17%. Non-White: 10%. **Fac 40.** Prof 40. **Staff:** Admin 2. Couns
10.
Type of instruction: Adv Undergrad. **Courses:** Fr Ger Russ Span Architect Bus/Fin Comm
Comp_Sci Hist Math Pol_Sci Psych Relig_Stud Sci Studio_Art Theater. **Avg class size:**
15. **Daily hours for:** Classes 3. Study 6. Homework. Tests. Grades. **College credit:** 3-
4/crse, total 8.
Features: Chess Community_Serv Rock_Climb Basketball Golf Soccer Street_Hockey
Swim Team_Handball Tennis Volleyball Billiards Broomball.
Fees 2011: Res $2576-3822 (+$250), 6 wks.
Housing: Dorms. **Swimming:** Pool. Campus facilities avail.
Est 1982. Nonprofit. **Ses:** 1. **Wks/ses:** 6. Operates June-Aug.

Junior Scholars enables academically talented rising seniors to learn about college life
and earn six to eight hours of college credit, while also exploring an area of academic or
career interest. In addition to attending courses alongside MU students, participants take part
in seminars on such special topics as study skills, time management, interpersonal relations,
college admission and financial aid. Boys and girls choose from various social and recreational
activities on weekends and in the evening. Students who successfully complete the program
earn guaranteed admission to Miami University for undergraduate study.

OREGON

SOUTHERN OREGON UNIVERSITY
ACADEMIA LATINA
Res — Coed Ages 13-15

Ashland, OR 97520. 1250 Siskiyou Blvd. Tel: 541-552-6326. Fax: 541-552-6047.
www.sou.edu/youth/latino/index.html   E-mail: jensen@sou.edu
Carol Jensen, Dir.
Grades 8-10. **Adm:** FCFS. Priority: URM. **Appl—**Fee $0. Due: May. Transcript, 2 recs,
essay, signs of special interest.
Enr: 66.
Type of instruction: Enrich. **Courses:** Col_Prep Expository_Writing Forensic_Sci Math
Med/Healthcare Humanities Creative_Writing Dance Drama Music Photog Studio_Art.
Daily hours for: Classes 4½.
Fees 2009: Res $650, 1 wk.
Housing: Dorms.
Est 1999. Nonprofit. **Ses:** 1. **Wks/ses:** 1. Operates Aug.

This weeklong academic program exposes young Latino students to the learning and career
possibilities of college. Academia Latina integrates classes, field trips, cultural experiences
and recreational activities. The daily schedule on Monday through Friday includes three one-
and-a-half-hour classes, plus special presentations. Course work draws from the disciplines
of math, science, the humanities, social studies, cultural studies, and the fine and performing
arts.

SOUTHERN OREGON UNIVERSITY SUMMER ACADEMY
Res — Coed Ages 11-14

Ashland, OR 97520. 1250 Siskiyou Blvd. Tel: 541-552-6326. Fax: 541-552-6047.
www.sou.edu/youth/academy E-mail: jensen@sou.edu
Carol Jensen, Dir.
Grades 6-9. Adm: Selective. **Appl**—Fee $25. Due: Rolling. Transcript, achievement test scores, essay, 2 recs.
Enr: 100. **Enr cap:** 100. **Fac 25.** Prof 13. K-12 staff 12. **Staff:** Admin 7.
Type of instruction: Adv Enrich SAT/ACT_Prep Study_Skills. **Courses:** Comm Ecol Engineering Environ_Sci Forensic_Sci Writing/Journ Creative_Writing Filmmaking Fine_Arts Music Sculpt Theater. **Avg class size:** 15. **Daily hours for:** Classes 4. Study 1. Rec 3.
Features: Cooking Ropes_Crse Basketball Swim Volleyball.
Fees 2011: Res $675, 1 wk. Aid (Need).
Housing: Dorms. **Swimming:** Lake Pool. Campus facilities avail.
Est 1982. Nonprofit. **Ses:** 2. **Wks/ses:** 1. Operates June.

The academy offers talented students a balance of science, math, language, fine arts and social studies courses designed to provide stimulation and challenge. The daily schedule includes four one-hour classes, plus special presentations built around a theme. In addition to the boarding program for middle schoolers, the university conducts day sessions for elementary and high school students.

UNIVERSITY OF OREGON SUMMER ENRICHMENT PROGRAM
Res — Coed Ages 12-16

Eugene, OR 97403. 5259 Univ of Oregon Rd. Tel: 541-346-1405. Fax: 541-346-3594.
www.uoyouth.org E-mail: sep@uoregon.edu
James Engberg, Coord.
Grades 7-11. Adm: Selective. **Appl**—Due: Rolling.
Enr: 102. **Enr cap:** 110. **Fac 11. Staff:** Admin 7.
Type of instruction: Enrich. **Courses:** Chin Debate Eng Law Math Pol_Sci Dance Film Art_Hist Poetry. **Avg class size:** 10. **Daily hours for:** Classes 6. Rec 10.
Features: Aquatics Exploration Hiking Outdoor_Ed Peace/Cross-cultural Basketball Soccer Swim Ultimate_Frisbee Volleyball.
Fees 2010: Res $1345, 2 wks. Aid 2007 (Need): $16,800.
Housing: Dorms. **Swimming:** Lake Pool River.
Est 1978. Nonprofit. **Ses:** 2. **Wks/ses:** 2. Operates July-Aug.

Middle and high school students sample university course work and social life during SEP. Courses, which vary annually, feature a variety of topics in the arts and sciences, each taught at an introductory college level with no tests or assigned homework. Students live in residence halls in groups divided by age and gender, and evening activity options include sports, filmmaking, scavenger hunts, talent shows, dances and movie nights.

DELPHIAN SCHOOL
SUMMER AT DELPHI
Res — Coed Ages 8-18; Day — Coed 5-18

Sheridan, OR 97378. 20950 SW Rock Creek Rd. Tel: 503-843-3521, 800-626-6610.
Fax: 503-843-4158.
www.summeratdelphi.org E-mail: summer@delphian.org
Donetta Phelps, Dir.
Grades K-12 (younger if qualified). Adm: FCFS. **Appl**—Fee $50. Due: Rolling.
Enr: 300. **Enr cap:** 300. **Intl:** 42%. **Non-White:** 63%. **Fac 54.** K-12 staff 54. **Staff:** Admin 45.
Type of instruction: Enrich Rem_Eng Rem_Math Rem_Read Rev ESL/TOEFL_Prep

Study_Skills Tut. **Courses:** Fr Comm Computers Econ Eng Environ_Sci ESL Expository_Writing Hist Math Public_Speak Sci Ceramics Crafts Creative_Writing Drama Filmmaking Music Photog Studio_Art. **Avg class size:** 17. **Daily hours for:** Classes 5. Rec 5.
Features: Archery Hiking Riding Wilderness_Camp Yoga Basketball Soccer Softball Swim Tennis Volleyball.
Fees 2012: Res $4824 (+$1300), 4 wks. Day $2412 (+$990), 4 wks.
Housing: Dorms. Avg per room/unit: 3. **Swimming:** Lake Ocean Pool River Stream. Campus facilities avail.
Est 1976. Nonprofit. **Ses:** 2. **Wks/ses:** 4-6. Operates June-Aug.

Summer at Delphi blends academics, sports, challenging activities and weekend trips. Additionally, students may brush up on weak areas, get ahead in others, or take advantage of such curricular opportunities as computers, outdoor courses and special-interest projects. Delphi tailors each program to the individual pupil. One-on-one assistance is available, and individual progress speed is not related to that of the student's classmates. Those who have mastered the basics may proceed to advanced subjects or explore new areas. An ESL program serves boys and girls seeking to improve their English language skills. **See Also Page 40**

PENNSYLVANIA

SUMMER INSTITUTE FOR THE GIFTED
Res and Day — Coed Ages 10-17

Bryn Mawr, PA. Bryn Mawr College.
Contact (Year-round): River Plz, 9 W Broad St, Stamford, CT 06902.
Tel: 203-399-5188, 866-303-4744. Fax: 203-399-5455.
www.giftedstudy.org   E-mail: sig.info@giftedstudy.org
Barbara Swicord, Pres.
Student contact: Christine Provencher, E-mail: cprovencher@giftedstudy.com.
Adm: Selective. Admitted: 90%. **Appl**—Fee $95. Due: Rolling. Transcript, standardized test scores, gifted classification/2 recs.
Enr: 120. **Enr cap:** 150. Intl: 25%.
Type of instruction: Adv Enrich SAT/ACT_Prep Study_Skills. **Courses:** Expository_Writing Forensic_Sci Math Sci Dance Photog Theater. **Avg class size:** 14. **Daily hours for:** Classes 3. Study 1. Rec 2.
Fees 2012: Res $4395, 3 wks. Day $2495, 3 wks.
Housing: Dorms. Campus facilities avail.
Est 1984. Nonprofit. **Spons:** National Society for the Gifted & Talented. **Ses:** 1. **Wks/ses:** 3. Operates June-July.

See program description under Berkeley, CA.

INDIANA UNIVERSITY OF PENNSYLVANIA
ROBERT E. COOK HONORS COLLEGE
SUMMER HONORS PROGRAM FOR HIGH SCHOOL STUDENTS
Res — Coed Ages 16-18

Indiana, PA 15705. 290 Pratt Dr, 136 Whitmyre Hall. Tel: 724-357-4971, 800-487-9122.
Fax: 724-357-3906.
www.iup.edu/honors/summer   E-mail: honors@iup.edu
Janet Goebel, Dir.
Grades 11-12 (younger if qualified). Adm: Selective. **Appl**—Due: Rolling. Transcript, essays, 2 teacher recs.
Enr: 150. **Enr cap:** 200. **Fac 15. Staff:** Admin 4. Couns 18.

Type of instruction: Adv Enrich. **Courses:** Eng Forensic_Sci Law Psych Sci Writing/Journ Music. **Avg class size:** 18. **Daily hours for:** Classes 6. Study 2. Rec 2. **Fees 2012: Res $600-975 (+$100), 2 wks.** Aid (Need). **Housing:** Dorms. **Est 1995.** Nonprofit. **Ses:** 2. **Wks/ses:** 1-2. Operates July.

Conducted at the Honors College of the Indiana University of Pennsylvania, the Summer Honors Program enables rising high school juniors and seniors (and particularly able rising sophomores) to live and study in a university setting. In the morning, students attend a specialized course in a discipline such as physics, journalism or forensic science. Afternoons are devoted to a core course in which boys and girls develop critical thinking skills through group discussions, writing and presentations. In this interdisciplinary core course, pupils further develop their critical-thinking skills in the process of analyzing arguments and participating in group discussions, writing assignments and group presentations.

WYOMING SEMINARY COLLEGE PREP INSTITUTE
Res and Day — Coed Ages 14-18

Kingston, PA 18704. 201 N Sprague Ave. Tel: 570-270-2186, 877-996-7361. Fax: 570-270-2198.
www.wyomingseminary.org/summer
E-mail: summeratsem@wyomingseminary.org
Jason Thatcher, Dir.
Student contact: Gayle Sekel, E-mail: gsekel@wyomingseminary.org.
Grades 9-12. Adm: Somewhat selective. **Appl**—Fee $50. Due: Rolling. Transcript, 2 teacher recs.
Enr: 400. **Fac 16.** Prof 4. K-12 staff 12. **Staff:** Couns 20.
Type of instruction: Adv Dev_Read Enrich Preview Rem_Math Rev ESL/TOEFL_Prep. **Courses:** ESL Expository_Writing Math Med/Healthcare Public_Speak Speech Ceramics Crafts Creative_Writing Drama Fine_Arts Music Painting Photog Studio_Art. **Avg class size:** 15. **Daily hours for:** Classes 4. Study 2. Rec 1. Homework. Tests. Grades. **High school credit.**
Features: Aquatics Climbing_Wall Baseball Swim Tennis Weight_Trng.
Fees 2012: Res $2800, 4 wks. Day $650/crse, 4 wks. Aid (Need).
Housing: Dorms. **Swimming:** Pool. Campus facilities avail.
Est 1844. Nonprofit. **Ses:** 2. **Wks/ses:** 4. Operates June-July.

The College Prep Institute allows boys and girls to either explore academic interests in depth or preview upcoming courses. Boarding students attend morning and afternoon courses, and day students may enroll in one or both. Classes are available in the following areas: communications, the fine arts, history and government, and science and mathematics.

SAINT VINCENT COLLEGE CHALLENGE PROGRAM
Res and Day — Coed Ages 11-17

Latrobe, PA 15650. 300 Fraser Purchase Rd. Tel: 724-805-2363.
www.stvincent.edu/challenge_home   E-mail: challenge@email.stvincent.edu
Donna Hupe & Kathy Beining, Dirs.
Grades 6-12. Adm: Selective. **Appl**—Fee $0. Due: Rolling. Rec.
Enr: 125. **Fac 18. Staff:** Admin 4. Couns 12.
Type of instruction: Adv Enrich. **Courses:** Archaeol Comp_Sci Debate Hist Law Math Acting Dance Drama Media Music Painting Photog. **Avg class size:** 18. **Daily hours for:** Classes 6. Rec 6.
Features: Adventure_Travel Canoe Caving Chess Conservation Cooking Hiking Kayak Outdoor_Ed Ropes_Crse Survival_Trng Swim.
Fees 2011: Res $635, 1 wk. Day $535, 1 wk. Aid (Merit).
Housing: Dorms. Avg per room/unit: 2. **Swimming:** Pool. Campus facilities avail.

Est 1985. Nonprofit. Roman Catholic. **Ses:** 1. **Wks/ses:** 1. Operates July.

Saint Vincent conducts two programs for gifted, creative or talented pupils: one serving children entering grades 6-8, the other enrolling students entering grades 9-12. Challenge enables boys and girls to explore interests or develop skills through daytime classes in such areas as history, the humanities and computers. Course work content during the junior and senior high weeks differs to accommodate the varying age and ability levels of participating students. Evening activities include dinner parties, theater visits, swimming and dancing.

UNIVERSITY OF PENNSYLVANIA PRE-COLLEGE PROGRAM
Res — Coed Ages 16-18

Philadelphia, PA 19104. 3440 Market St, Ste 100. Tel: 215-749-6901.
   Fax: 215-573-2053.
www.upenn.edu/summer   E-mail: hsprogs@sas.upenn.edu
Grades 11-12 (younger if qualified). Adm: Selective. **Appl**—Fee $70. Due: Rolling. Transcript, test scores, personal statement, rec.
Enr: 96. Enr cap: 200. Intl: 39%. Staff: Couns 30.
Type of instruction: Adv Undergrad. **Courses:** Ital Archacol Bus/Fin Expository_Writing Govt Hist Intl_Relations Law Math Sci Writing/Journ. **Avg class size:** 18. Homework. Tests. Grades. **College credit:** 3/crse, total 6.
Fees 2011: Res $9799-12,599, 6 wks. Aid (Need).
Housing: Dorms. Campus facilities avail.
Nonprofit. **Ses:** 1. **Wks/ses:** 6. Operates July-Aug.

Rising high school juniors and seniors take either one or two University of Pennsylvania undergraduate courses for college credit through the Pre-College Program. Students enrolling in only one credit-bearing course also take a noncredit learning skills enrichment course; students taking two credit courses pay a higher tuition rate. Curricular offerings comprise introductory courses in the arts and sciences. Students are integrated into the university's regular summer courses and are subject to the same academic standards. Weekly workshops seek to bridge the gap between high school and college. Various social activities balance academics.

CARNEGIE MELLON UNIVERSITY
PRE-COLLEGE PROGRAMS
Res — Coed Ages 16-18; Day — Coed 15-18

Pittsburgh, PA 15213. 5000 Forbes Ave. Tel: 412-268-2082. Fax: 412-268-7838.
www.cmu.edu/enrollment/pre-college   E-mail: precollege@andrew.cmu.edu
Grades 10-PG (younger if qualified). Adm: Selective. **Appl**—Fee $40. Due: May. Transcript, test scores, 2 recs, essay, activities resume.
Enr: 35-117.
Type of instruction: Adv Enrich Preview. **Courses:** Russ Architect Comp_Sci Econ Engineering Hist Math Sci Creative_Writing Drama Drawing Music Painting Sculpt Studio_Art Design. **Avg class size:** 20. Homework. Tests. Grades. **College credit:** 6.
Features: Basketball Swim Tennis Weight_Trng.
Fees 2011: Res $6475-7700 (+$175-300), 6 wks. Day $4800-5700 (+$175-300), 6 wks.
Housing: Dorms. **Swimming:** Pool. Campus facilities avail.
Nonprofit. **Ses:** 1. **Wks/ses:** 6. Operates June-Aug.

Rising high school juniors and seniors may participate in precollege programming at CMU. Advanced Placement/Early Action (APEA) allows students to take two regular freshman-level courses for credit from offerings in math, science, engineering, humanities and social sciences. A series of noncredit fine arts programs in architecture, art, design, drama and music features instruction from faculty in Carnegie Mellon's graduate and undergraduate schools.

SUMMER STUDY AND SUMMER ENRICHMENT AT PENN STATE
Res — Coed Ages 14-18

University Park, PA. Pennsylvania State Univ.
Contact (Year-round): 900 Walt Whitman Rd, Melville, NY 11747. Tel: 631-424-1000, 800-666-2556. Fax: 631-424-0567.
www.summerstudy.com   E-mail: info@summerstudy.com
William Cooperman, Exec Dir.
Grades 9-PG. Adm: FCFS. **Appl**—Fee $95. Due: Apr. Transcript, test scores.
Enr: 900. **Fac** 70. **Staff:** Admin 7. Couns 80.
Type of instruction: Adv Enrich Preview Rem_Eng Rem_Math Rem_Read Rev SAT/ ACT_Prep Study_Skills Tut. **Courses:** Fr Ger Ital Russ Span Archaeol Astron Bus/Fin Debate Environ_Sci ESL Expository_Writing Geol Govt Crafts Creative_Writing Dance Filmmaking Fine_Arts Media Music Painting Photog Theater. **Daily hours for:** Classes 2½. Study 1. Rec 4. **College credit.**
Features: Adventure_Travel Aquatics Boating Canoe Chess Climbing_Wall Community_ Serv Hiking Kayak Mtn_Biking Sail Wilderness_Canoe Baseball Basketball Cross-country Field_Hockey Football Golf Gymnastics Ice_Hockey Lacrosse Roller_Hockey Soccer Softball Swim Tennis Track Volleyball Watersports Wrestling.
Fees 2012: Res $2595-7695, 2-6½ wks. Aid (Need).
Housing: Dorms. **Swimming:** Lake Pool.
Est 1989. Inc. **Spons:** Summer Study Programs. **Ses:** 8. **Wks/ses:** 2-6½. Operates June-Aug.

Summer Study allows students who have completed grade 10, 11 or 12 to take freshman-level courses for college credit while also experiencing university life. Each pupil enrolls in one or two college-credit classes, an enrichment offering and the Pathways to College guidance course. Shorter enrichment programs for pupils entering grades 10-12 enroll participants in two or three noncredit classes. Students in both programs may perform community service, enroll in SAT prep courses and visit nearby colleges on weekends. Two- and four-week enrichment programs serve students entering grade 9.

RHODE ISLAND

PORTSMOUTH ABBEY SUMMER SCHOOL PROGRAM
Res and Day — Coed Ages 12-16

Portsmouth, RI 02871. 285 Cory's Ln. Tel: 401-643-1225. Fax: 401-683-5888.
www.portsmouthabbey.org   E-mail: summer@portsmouthabbey.org
Tim Seeley, Dir.
    Student contact: Alex Fernandez, E-mail: afernandez@portsmouthabbey.org.
Grades 7-10. Adm: Somewhat selective. **Appl**—Fee $55. Due: Rolling. Transcript, rec.
Enr: 55. **Enr cap:** 75. **Fac** 16. **Staff:** Admin 2. Couns 6.
Type of instruction: Enrich Preview ESL/TOEFL_Prep Study_Skills. **Courses:** Fr Lat Span Debate Econ Eng Environ_Sci ESL Expository_Writing Geol Hist Marine_Bio/Stud Math Public_Speak Relig_Stud Speech Writing/Journ Creative_Writing Drama Film Media Studio_Art. **Avg class size:** 7. **Daily hours for:** Classes 3. Study 2. Rec 3. Homework. Tests. Grades.
Features: Aquatics Riding Sail Basketball Cross-country Equestrian Lacrosse Soccer Softball Squash Swim Tennis Track Volleyball Watersports.
Fees 2012: Res $6100 (+$300), 4 wks. Day $3500 (+$100), 4 wks. Aid 2011 (Merit & Need): $18,000.
Housing: Dorms Houses. **Swimming:** Ocean. Campus facilities avail.
Est 1943. Nonprofit. Roman Catholic. **Ses:** 1. **Wks/ses:** 4. Operates June-July.

    Portsmouth Abbey provides a variety of review and enrichment courses six days per week. Pupils, who attend three courses per class day, choose from options in history, politics and economics; English; faith and culture; and mathematics. Afternoon enrichment courses introduce students to landscape painting and environmental and marine sciences. A well-balanced recreational schedule supplements academics.   **See Also Page 37**

BROWN UNIVERSITY SCHOLAR ATHLETE PROGRAM
Res and Day — Coed Ages 15-17

Providence, RI 02912. Box T, 42 Charlesfield St. Fax: 401-863-3916.
www.brown.edu/scs/pre-college/scholar-athlete   E-mail: summer@brown.edu
Grades 10-12. Adm: Selective. Prereqs: GPA 3.0. **Appl**—Fee $45-90. Due: Rolling. Transcript, teacher rec.
Type of instruction: Enrich. **Courses:** Sci Writing/Journ Physiol. **Daily hours for:** Classes 3.
Features: Swim Tennis.
Fees 2011: Res $2505, 1 wk. Day $2002, 1 wk. Aid (Need).
Housing: Dorms. **Swimming:** Pool. Campus facilities avail.
Ses: 1. **Wks/ses:** 1. Operates July.

This unusual program combines enrollment in one course with athletic instruction in either tennis or swimming. Students spend three hours per day in one of the following classes: sportswriting, sport physiology, or biomechanics of sport and exercise. Boys and girls need not have advanced skills in the sport of choice. Planned cocurricular and social activities round out the program.   **See Also Page 35**

BROWN UNIVERSITY
SUMMER@BROWN
Res and Day — Coed Ages 15-18

Providence, RI 02912. Office of Continuing Ed, 42 Charlesfield St, Box T.
Tel: 401-863-7900. Fax: 401-863-3916.
www.brown.edu/summer   E-mail: summer@brown.edu
Karen H. Sibley, Dir.
Grades 10-PG. Adm: Selective. **Appl**—Due: Rolling.
Staff: Admin 21.
Type of instruction: Adv Enrich Undergrad. **Courses:** Arabic Chin Fr Ger Greek Ital Japan Span Architect Bus/Fin Comm Comp_Sci Econ Engineering ESL Expository_Writing Govt Math Med/Healthcare Pol_Sci Sci Speech Writing/Journ Creative_Writing Film Music Theater. Homework. Tests. Grades. **College credit:** 2.
Features: Fencing Swim Tennis.
Fees 2011: Res $2255-9697 (+$75), 1-7 wks. Day $1752-6213 (+$75), 1-7 wks.
Housing: Dorms. **Swimming:** Pool. Campus facilities avail.
Nonprofit. **Ses:** 7. **Wks/ses:** 1-7. Operates June-Aug.

The university provides two divisions of summer courses in the sciences, social sciences and humanities for qualified high school students. Seven-week Summer Session Credit Courses allow rising seniors and new high school graduates to earn college credit in two courses that they take alongside undergraduates; these classes are equivalent to first-year Brown courses. Separate one- to three-week, noncredit Pre-College Courses are offered on an ungraded basis to pupils entering grade 10 or higher. Students take one or two classes per session and may attend multiple sessions. Courses include daily assignments, group work, site visits, labs and hands-on projects. Participants in both programs attend events and social activities and have wide use of Brown's athletic, academic and recreational facilities.   **See Also Page 35**

TENNESSEE

VANDERBILT UNIVERSITY SUMMER ACADEMY
Res — Coed Ages 13-18

Nashville, TN 37203. Peabody 506, 230 Appleton Pl. Tel: 615-322-8261.
Fax: 615-322-3457.
www.pty.vanderbilt.edu/vsa.html   E-mail: pty.peabody@vanderbilt.edu
Tamra Stambaugh, Dir.
Grades 8-12. Adm: Selective. **Appl**—Fee $35. Transcript, essays, portfolio/qualifying test
scores.
Type of instruction: Adv Enrich. **Courses:** Astron Engineering Law Math Med/Healthcare
Relig_Stud Sci Creative_Writing Filmmaking. **Avg class size:** 14.
Fees 2012: Res $1250-3100 (+$30-90), 1-3 wks. Aid (Need).
Housing: Dorms. Avg per room/unit: 2.
Ses: 3. **Wks/ses:** 1-3. Operates June-July.

VSA offers advanced curricula in math, science and the humanities to gifted students. Taught
by Vanderbilt professors, lecturers and graduate students, courses integrate resources from
research centers and laboratories. Games, movies, sports and off-campus outings complement
academics. Weeklong programs accommodate rising eighth graders who have participated
in talent searches, two-week sessions serve pupils entering grades 9 and 10, and three-week
courses enroll students entering grades 11 and 12. Three-week Law School 101 and Med
School 101 programs operate in conjunction with Vanderbilt's professional schools; admission
to both is highly competitive and is distinct from admission into other VSA courses.

TEXAS

SUMMER INSTITUTE FOR THE GIFTED
Res and Day — Coed Ages 10-17

Austin, TX. Univ of Texas-Austin.
Contact (Year-round): River Plz, 9 Broad St, Stamford, CT 06902. Tel: 203-399-5188,
866-303-4744. Fax: 203-399-5455.
www.giftedstudy.org   E-mail: sig.info@giftedstudy.com
Barbara Swicord, Pres.
Student contact: Christine Provencher, E-mail: cprovencher@giftedstudy.com.
Adm: Very selective. Admitted: 90%. **Appl**—Fee $95. Due: Rolling. Transcript, standardized
test scores, classification as gifted/2 recs.
Type of instruction: Adv Enrich SAT/ACT_Prep Study_Skills. **Courses:** Expository_Writ-
ing Forensic_Sci Hist Math Sci Philos Dance Media Photog Theater. **Avg class size:** 14.
Daily hours for: Classes 6. Study 1. Rec 2.
Fees 2012: Res $4395, 3 wks. Day $2495, 3 wks.
Housing: Dorms. Campus facilities avail.
Est 1984. Nonprofit. Spons: National Society for the Gifted & Talented. **Ses:** 1. **Wks/ses:**
3. Operates June-July.

See program description under Berkeley, CA.

TELLURIDE ASSOCIATION SUMMER PROGRAM
Res — Coed Ages 17-18

Austin, TX. Univ of Texas.

Contact (Year-round): 217 West Ave, Ithaca, NY 14850. Tel: 607-273-5011.
Fax: 607-272-2667.
http://tasp.tellurideassociation.org   E-mail: telluride@tellurideassociation.org
Ellen Baer, Admin Dir.
Grade 12. Adm: Very selective. Appl—Fee $0. Due: Jan. Essays, transcript, standardized test scores.
Enr: 16-18.
Type of instruction: Adv Enrich. Courses: Eng Sci Philos.
Fees 2010: Free. Res 6 wks.
Housing: Dorms.
Nonprofit. Ses: 3. Wks/ses: 6. Operates June-Aug.

See program description under Ann Arbor, MI.

DUKE UNIVERSITY TALENT IDENTIFICATION PROGRAM SUMMER STUDIES PROGRAMS
Res — Coed Ages 12-16

College Station, TX. Texas A&M Univ.
Contact (Year-round): 1121 W Main St, Durham, NC 27701. Tel: 919-668-9100.
Fax: 919-681-7921.
www.tip.duke.edu   E-mail: information@tip.duke.edu
Brian Cooper, Dir.
Grades 8-11. Adm: Selective. Appl—Fee $25. Due: Rolling. Qualifying SAT/ACT scores, personal statement.
Type of instruction: Adv Enrich. Courses: Architect Debate Engineering Expository_Writing Law Pol_Sci SciVeterinary_Med Web_Design Creative_Writing. Avg class size: 16.
Daily hours for: Classes 7. Rec 3.
Fees 2011: Res $3550-3800, 3 wks. Aid (Need).
Housing: Dorms.
Est 1980. Nonprofit. Ses: 2. Wks/ses: 3. Operates June-Aug.

See program description under Lawrence, KS.

THE HOCKADAY SCHOOL COED SUMMER SESSION
Res — Coed Ages 12-17; Day — Coed 3-18

Dallas, TX 75229. 11600 Welch Rd. Tel: 214-360-6586. Fax: 214-739-8867.
www.hockaday.org   E-mail: ngale@mail.hockaday.org
Nancy Gale, Dir.
Grades PS-12. Adm: FCFS. Appl—Fee $25. Due: Rolling.
Enr: 750. Intl: 20%. Non-White: 20%. Fac 70. Col/grad students 10. K-12 staff 60. Staff: Admin 10. Res 10.
Type of instruction: Enrich Preview Rev ESL/TOEFL_Prep SAT/ACT_Prep Study_Skills.
Courses: Chin ESL Expository_Writing Govt Math Crafts Creative_Writing Dance Fine_Arts Music Painting Photog Theater. Avg class size: 10. Daily hours for: Classes 4. Study 2. Rec 4. Grades. High school credit: 6.
Features: Aquatics Archery Canoe Cooking Basketball Field_Hockey Lacrosse Martial_Arts Swim Tennis.
Fees 2009: Res $3450-6900, 3-6 wks. Day $295-1250, 3-6 wks.
Housing: Dorms. Swimming: Pool. Campus facilities avail.
Est 1978. Nonprofit. Ses: 2. Wks/ses: 3. Operates June-July.

Hockaday conducts a full range of academic courses, as well as arts and enrichment programs. These include standard offerings in English, math, history and science, in addition to a full range of fine arts, theater, study and reading skills, computer, sports, SAT prep and English as a Second Language programs. Hockaday also operates a creative arts camp for children in grades K-4. Field trips provide enrichment.

SOUTHERN METHODIST UNIVERSITY
GIFTED STUDENTS INSTITUTE SUMMER PROGRAMS
Res — Coed Ages 13-18

Dallas, TX 75275. PO Box 750383. Tel: 214-768-0123. Fax: 214-768-3147.
www.smu.edu/education/youth   E-mail: gifted@smu.edu
Grades 8-12. Adm: Selective. **Appl**—Fee $35. Due: Rolling. Transcript, essay, standardized test scores, 2 recs.
Type of instruction: Adv Enrich Undergrad. **Courses:** Comp_Sci Econ Eng Govt Law Math Pol_Sci Psych Sci Anthro Philos Rhetoric Film Theater. **Avg class size:** 14. **Daily hours for:** Classes 6. Study 2. Rec 4. **College credit:** 3/crse, total 6.
Features: Swim.
Fees 2011: Res $3365-4550 (+$100), 3-5 wks. Aid (Need).
Housing: Dorms. Avg per room/unit: 2. **Swimming:** Pool.
Est 1979. Nonprofit. **Ses:** 2. **Wks/ses:** 3-5. Operates June-Aug.

SMU's Gifted Studies Institute conducts two programs for able boys and girls. Students entering grades 8-10 may enroll in the Talented and Gifted (TAG) program, which allows them to take two classes: one in the morning and one in the afternoon. Particularly strong pupils may earn college credit for the morning course. Rising high school juniors and seniors take two college-level courses in the College Experience program. Each participant selects a morning course from the regular summer school credit offerings, then engages in an in-depth, interdisciplinary afternoon seminar.

CAMP KIOWA
Res — Coed Ages 7-16

Denton, TX 76204. PO Box 425286.
Contact (Aug-May): 1505 Kittyhawk Dr, Little Elm, TX 75068.
Year-round Tel: 940-239-5126, Fax: 940-239-5043.
www.campkiowa.com   E-mail: campinfo@campkiowa.com
Brian Manhart & Jennifer Manhart, Dirs.
Grades 3-8. Adm: FCFS. **Appl**—Fee $0. Due: May.
Enr: 100. **Fac 5. Staff:** Admin 4. Couns 16.
Type of instruction: Enrich. **Courses:** Writing/Journ Robotics Rocketry Creative_Writing Dance Drama Fashion Photog Sculpt Woodworking.
Features: Aquatics Archery Chess Community_Serv Cooking Kayak Rock_Climb Yoga Baseball Basketball Football Golf Martial_Arts Soccer Softball Swim Tennis Volleyball.
Fees 2012: Res $1289-4954, 1-4 wks. Aid (Need).
Housing: Dorms. **Swimming:** Pool.
Est 2004. Inc. **Ses:** 8. **Wks/ses:** 1. Operates June-July.

Held at Texas Woman's University, Kiowa combines academic enrichment with traditional summer recreation. Campers select two morning academic courses and two afternoon workshops in arts and sports. Evening activities include bingo, dance, karaoke, bowling, miniature golf and sports. Tennis and golf lessons are available for an additional fee.

TEXAS LUTHERAN UNIVERSITY
LONE STAR SCHOLARS ACADEMY
Res — Coed Ages 15-17

Seguin, TX 78155. 1000 W Court St. Tel: 830-372-8050, 800-771-8521.
Fax: 830-372-8096.
www.tlu.edu/admissions/lssa   E-mail: lssa@tlu.edu
Chris Bollinger, Dir.
Grades 10-12. Adm: Selective. Admitted: 95%. **Appl**—Fee $0. Due: Rolling. Transcript, rec, PSAT results.

Enr: 31. **Enr cap:** 60. **Fac 6.** Prof 6. **Staff:** Admin 2. Res 5.
Type of instruction: Adv Undergrad. **Courses:** ASL Astron Expository_Writing Forensic_
Sci Sci Creative_Writing Film. **Avg class size:** 12. **Daily hours for:** Classes 5. Study 2.
Homework. Tests. Grades. **College credit:** 2.
Features: Swim Tennis.
Fees 2011: Res $1825, 2 wks. Aid 2011 (Need): $900.
Housing: Dorms. Avg per room/unit: 2. **Swimming:** Pool. Campus facilities avail.
Est 1998. Nonprofit. **Ses:** 1. **Wks/ses:** 2. Operates July.

This two-week program allows academically advanced high schoolers to take two university-level courses for college credit. TLU faculty and area educators teach the courses in a small-class setting that provides boys and girls with a preview of the college experience. Field trips, a group service project and evening recreational activities round out LSSA's program. Applicants should rank in the top half of their class.

VIRGINIA

4 STAR ACADEMICS PROGRAMS
Res and Day — Coed Ages 12-18

Charlottesville, VA. Univ of Virginia.
Contact (Year-round): PO Box 3387, Falls Church, VA 22043. Tel: 703-866-4900,
800-334-7827. Fax: 703-866-7775.
www.4starcamps.com   E-mail: info@4starcamps.com
Mitch Popple & Lisa Popple, Exec Dirs.
Grades 7-12. Adm: FCFS. **Appl**—Due: Rolling.
Enr: 130. **Fac 20. Staff:** Admin 2.
Type of instruction: Adv Enrich SAT/ACT_Prep Study_Skills Tut. **Courses:** Architect
Astron Bus/Fin Econ Environ_Sci ESL Expository_Writing Math Psych Public_Speak
Writing/Journ Anat Civics Acting Creative_Writing Filmmaking Fine_Arts Photog
Studio_Art Theater. **Avg class size:** 8. **Daily hours for:** Classes 3. Study 1. Rec 5.
Features: Canoe Hiking Scuba Basketball Golf Soccer Swim Tennis Ultimate_Frisbee Volleyball.
Fees 2011: Res $1395-6495, 1-4 wks. Day $1095-5495, 1-4 wks.
Housing: Dorms. **Swimming:** Pool.
Est 1975. Inc. **Ses:** 10. **Wks/ses:** 2-4. Operates June-July.

Conducted on the University of Virginia campus, these programs combine morning academic course work with afternoon sports instruction and informal recreation. The Junior Program, serving rising seventh through ninth graders, allows children to choose two enrichment courses each weekday from a varied selection. Tutorials are available in math and writing for an additional fee. For students entering grades 10-12, the Senior Program blends enrichment courses with such offerings as reading comprehension and PSAT and SAT preparation. Other offerings include an ESL program and a fine arts program that features photography, studio art, cinematography and acting classes.

HARGRAVE MILITARY SCHOOL SUMMER SESSION
Res and Day — Boys Ages 13-18

Chatham, VA 24531. 200 Military Dr. Tel: 434-432-2481, 800-432-2480.
Fax: 434-432-3129.
www.hargrave.edu/summer-school   E-mail: admissions@hargrave.edu
Ryan Meyer von Bremen, Coord.
Grades 7-12. Adm: FCFS. **Appl**—Fee $75. Due: Rolling.

Fac 19. **Staff:** Couns 2.
Type of instruction: Adv Dev_Read Enrich Rem_Eng Rem_Math Rem_Read Rev SAT/ACT_Prep Study_Skills. **Courses:** Span Col_Prep Eng ESL Govt Hist Leadership Math Sci Robotics Art Creative_Writing Photog Studio_Art. **Avg class size:** 12. **Daily hours for:** Classes 5. Study 3. Rec 1½. **High school credit:** 2.
Features: Aquatics Canoe Climbing_Wall Exploration Hiking Mountaineering Mtn_Trips Rappelling Riflery Rock_Climb White-water_Raft Baseball Basketball Football Lacrosse Swim Tennis.
Fees 2012: Res $4000, 4 wks. Day $875-1750, 4 wks.
Housing: Dorms. **Swimming:** Pool.
Est 1926. Nonprofit. Baptist. **Ses:** 1. **Wks/ses:** 4. Operates July.

Hargrave offers remedial and advanced work in most academic subjects, including math, English and science. SAT Prep, leadership principles and art are available as electives. In the afternoon, students choose from a full complement of athletic activities led by the school's postgraduate and varsity coaches. Boys wear summer school uniforms and attend compulsory Christian services two times per week.

FERRUM COLLEGE SUMMER ENRICHMENT CAMP
Res — Coed Ages 11-13

Ferrum, VA 24088. PO Box 1000. Tel: 540-365-2121. Fax: 540-365-5589.
www.ferrum.edu/fcsec   E-mail: cphillips@ferrum.edu
Chip Phillips, Dir.
Grades 6-8. **Adm:** FCFS. **Appl**—Fee $0. Due: Rolling. Essay.
Enr: 120. **Enr cap:** 120. **Fac** 14. **Staff:** Admin 6.
Type of instruction: Enrich. **Courses:** Span Eng Forensic_Sci Sci Web_Design Creative_Writing Drama Drawing Media Photog. **Avg class size:** 14. **Daily hours for:** Classes 6½. Rec 1.
Features: Chess Climbing_Wall Cooking Farm Rappelling Ropes_Crse Basketball Soccer Softball Swim Tennis Volleyball.
Fees 2009: Res $585, 1 wk.
Housing: Dorms. **Swimming:** Pool.
Est 1990. Nonprofit. **Ses:** 2. **Wks/ses:** 1. Operates July.

Young students enrolled in FCSEC engage in four daily enrichment classes, as well as afternoon and evening activities. Applicants should have a successful school record and should be both academically motivated and well behaved in the classroom. Activities range from juggling to jazz and modern dance to yoga, and workshops are also available.

FORK UNION MILITARY ACADEMY SUMMER SCHOOL
Res — Boys Ages 12-17

Fork Union, VA 23055. PO Box 278. Tel: 434-842-4205, 800-462-3862.
Fax: 434-842-4300.
www.forkunion.com/summer   E-mail: admissions@fuma.org
Maj. John F. DeVault, Dir.
Grades 7-PG. **Adm:** FCFS. **Appl**—Fee $100. Due: Rolling. Transcript, 2 recs.
Enr: 200. **Fac** 25. **Staff:** Admin 10.
Type of instruction: Adv Rev SAT/ACT_Prep Study_Skills. **Courses:** Span Eng ESL Govt Hist Leadership Math Sci. **Avg class size:** 14. **Daily hours for:** Classes 6. Study 2. Rec 2. **High school credit:** 2.
Features: Aquatics Community_Serv Fishing Baseball Basketball Cross-country Football Lacrosse Soccer Swim Weight_Trng Wrestling.
Fees 2011: Res $3900 (+$60), 4 wks.
Housing: Dorms. **Swimming:** Pool. Campus facilities avail.
Nonprofit. Baptist. **Ses:** 1. **Wks/ses:** 4. Operates July.

Fork Union's nonmilitary summer program includes English composition and literature, math, history, SAT preparation and Spanish. With classes conducted six days per week, the session enables students to earn academic credit for new course work, correct deficiencies through repeat work and improve study habits. Enrichment field trips and athletic activities complement academics.

RANDOLPH-MACON ACADEMY SUMMER PROGRAM
Res and Day — Coed Ages 11-18

Front Royal, VA 22630. 200 Academy Dr. Tel: 540-636-5200, 800-272-1172. Fax: 540-636-5419.
www.rma.edu/summer-programs   E-mail: admission@rma.edu
Don Williams, Dir. Student contact: Paula Brady, E-mail: paulab@rma.edu.
Grades 6-12. Adm: Somewhat selective. Admitted: 88%. **Appl**—Fee $75. Due: Rolling. Transcript, rec.
Enr: 149. **Enr cap:** 200. **Fac 23.** K-12 staff 23. **Staff:** Admin 4. Couns 11.
Type of instruction: Adv Enrich Preview Rem_Eng Rem_Math Rem_Read Rev SAT/ACT_Prep Study_Skills. **Courses:** Span Computers ESL Govt Hist Sci Photog Studio_ Art. **Avg class size:** 12. **Daily hours for:** Classes 8. Study 1. Rec 3. Homework. Tests. Grades. **High school credit:** 1/crse, total 2.
Features: Aviation/Aero Swim.
Fees 2011: Res $2800 (+$975-1075), 4 wks. Day $500-900 (+$100-1000), 4 wks.
Housing: Dorms. Avg per room/unit: 2. **Swimming:** Pool. Campus facilities avail. Nonprofit. Methodist. **Ses:** 1. **Wks/ses:** 4. Operates June-July.

R-MA's nonmilitary summer school provides students with an opportunity to make up deficiencies in subjects previously studied, to earn credits and to generally improve their academic skills. Pupils may enroll in either one new class or two repeat courses. Supervised study periods and evening and weekend activities are also part of the program. For an additional fee, the academy offers a complete flight-training program that includes Cessna 172 flying lessons and ground school.

OAK HILL ACADEMY SUMMER SESSION
Res and Day — Coed Ages 13-18

Mouth of Wilson, VA 24363. 2635 Oak Hill Rd. Tel: 276-579-2619. Fax: 276-579-4722.
www.oak-hill.net/summersession.htm   E-mail: info@oak-hill.net
Michael D. Groves, Pres.
Grades 8-12. Adm: Selective. Admitted: 80%. **Appl**—Fee $50. Due: Rolling. Transcript, rec, interview.
Enr: 60. **Intl:** 20%. Non-White: 22%. **Fac 9.** K-12 staff 9.
Type of instruction: Rem_Eng Rem_Math Study_Skills. **Courses:** Span Bus/Fin Computers Eng Govt Hist Math Relig_Stud Sci Music Studio_Art. **Avg class size:** 10. **Daily hours for:** Classes 5. Study 2½. Rec 2½. Homework. Tests. Grades. **High school credit:** 2.
Features: Canoe Hiking Paintball Riding Swim.
Fees 2010: Res $3900, 5 wks.
Housing: Dorms. Avg per room/unit: 2. **Swimming:** Lake. Campus facilities avail. Nonprofit. Baptist. **Ses:** 1. **Wks/ses:** 5. Operates June-July.

Oak Hill's summer program offers courses for enrichment and credit in English, math, social studies and science. An intramural sports program includes basketball, volleyball, softball, tennis and soccer. Students take canoeing and hiking trips and may participate in horseback riding for an additional fee.

HOLLINS UNIVERSITY
HOLLINSUMMER
Res — Girls Ages 12-17

Roanoke, VA 24020. PO Box 9707. Tel: 540-362-6401, 800-456-9595. Fax: 540-362-6218.
www.hollins.edu/summerprograms E-mail: huadm@hollins.edu
Aimee Perkins, Dir.
Grades 7-12. Adm: Selective. **Appl**—Fee $0. Due: June. Rec.
Enr: 95. Fac 15. Staff: Admin 3. Couns 10.
Type of instruction: Adv Enrich Preview. **Courses:** Forensic_Sci Leadership Creative_ Writing Dance Fine_Arts Photog Studio_Art. **Avg class size:** 12. **Daily hours for:** Classes 6. Study 2. Rec 2.
Features: Aquatics Climbing_Wall Swim.
Fees 2011: Res $695-1375 (+$50-100), 1-2 wks.
Housing: Dorms. **Swimming:** Pool. Campus facilities avail.
Est 1990. Nonprofit. **Ses: 1. Wks/ses:** 1-2. Operates July.

Academic courses available to junior high and high school girls at Hollinsummer include creative writing, leadership, an array of arts offerings, psychology, navigation, forensic chemistry and politics in literature. Students meet with experienced guidance counselors to discuss the college search process. Hiking in the Blue Ridge Mountains and local trips are among the participants' recreational options.

FISHBURNE MILITARY SCHOOL SUMMER SCHOOL
Res — Boys Ages 12-17

Waynesboro, VA 22980. 225 S Wayne Ave, PO Box 988. Tel: 540-946-7700, 800-946-7773. Fax: 540-946-7738.
www.fishburne.org E-mail: admissions@fishburne.org
Col. Roy Zinser, USA (Ret), Supt.
Grades 7-12. Adm: FCFS. **Appl**—Fee $50. Due: Rolling.
Enr: 100. Fac 20.
Type of instruction: Adv Enrich Preview Rem_Eng Rem_Read Rev SAT/ACT_Prep Study_Skills Tut. **Courses:** Span Eng Govt Hist Leadership Sci. **Avg class size:** 12. **Daily hours for:** Classes 6. Study 3. Rec 4. **High school credit.**
Features: Milit_Trng Paintball Rappelling Ropes_Crse Basketball Football Golf Martial_ Arts Soccer Swim Tennis Weight_Trng.
Fees 2012: Res $3660-3890, 5 wks.
Housing: Dorms. Avg per room/unit: 2. **Swimming:** Pool.
Nonprofit. **Ses: 1. Wks/ses:** 5. Operates June-July.

Located in the Shenandoah Valley, this military program offers both new and repeat classes in English, math, science, social studies and leadership training (Army JROTC), as well as repeat courses in chemistry, Spanish and French. Afternoons are reserved for compulsory recreational activities, while weekends provide an opportunity for field trips to Busch Gardens, Kings Dominion and other nearby parks.

MASSANUTTEN MILITARY ACADEMY SUMMER SCHOOL
Res and Day — Coed Ages 12-18

Woodstock, VA 22664. 614 S Main St. Tel: 540-459-2167, 877-466-6222. Fax: 540-459-5421.
www.militaryschool.com E-mail: admissions@militaryschool.com
R. Craig Jones, Head.
Grades 7-12. Adm: Selective. Admitted: 60%. **Appl**—Fee $50. Due: Rolling. Transcript.
Enr cap: 200. Fac 15. Prof 3. K-12 staff 12. Staff: Admin 5. Couns 2.

Type of instruction: Rem_Eng Rem_Read SAT/ACT_Prep Study_Skills. **Courses:** Span Eng Govt Hist Math Sci Fine_Arts Music. **Avg class size:** 9. **Daily hours for:** Classes 6. Study 2. Rec 2. **High school credit:** 2.
Features: Canoe Fishing Hiking Milit_Trng Riflery Scuba Baseball Basketball Equestrian Football Soccer Tennis Wrestling.
Fees 2012: Res $3200 (+$750), 5 wks. Day $1145-1545 (+$750), 5 wks.
Housing: Dorms. Campus facilities avail.
Nonprofit. **Ses:** 1. **Wks/ses:** 5. Operates June-July.

Cadets in this program take at least two courses during the session; students may enroll in one new course or two repeat courses. SAT preparation and study skills classes are among the class offerings. A military structure characterizes the program.

WASHINGTON

WASHINGTON STATE UNIVERSITY
COUGAR QUEST
Res — Coed Ages 12-18

Pullman, WA 99164. 346 French Administration Bldg, PO Box 641035.
Tel: 509-335-1235. Fax: 509-335-4455.
www.cougarquest.wsu.edu   E-mail: cougarquest@wsu.edu
Linda Schoepflin, Dir. Student contact: Kim Mueller.
Grades 7-12. Adm: FCFS. **Appl**—Fee $0. Due: May.
Enr: 180. **Enr cap:** 260. Non-White: 25%. **Fac 36.** Prof 32. Col/grad students 4. **Staff:** Admin 4. Couns 28.
Type of instruction: Adv Enrich Study_Skills. **Courses:** Architect Astron Ecol Forensic_Sci SciVeterinary_Med Writing/Journ Crafts Dance Drama Fine_Arts Music Photog Printmaking. **Avg class size:** 20. **Daily hours for:** Classes 6. Rec 3.
Features: Climbing_Wall Cooking Fishing Rock_Climb Ropes_Crse Badminton Basketball Soccer Swim Track Volleyball.
Fees 2012: Res $605, 1 wk.
Housing: Dorms. **Swimming:** Pool. Campus facilities avail.
Est 2001. Nonprofit. **Ses:** 2. **Wks/ses:** 1. Operates July.

Cougar Quest comprises two programs: one for boys and girls entering grades 7-9 and another for those entering grades 9-12 (students entering grade 9 may attend either session). Pupils choose three workshops from a variety of subjects, all of which are taught by university faculty. Workshops incorporate interactive activities and new technologies whenever possible. Social and recreational activities complement academic work.

WEST VIRGINIA

WEST VIRGINIA WESLEYAN COLLEGE
SUMMER GIFTED PROGRAM
Res — Coed Ages 10-17

Buckhannon, WV 26201. 59 College Ave, Box 122. Tel: 304-473-8072.
Fax: 304-473-8704.
www.wvwc.edu/summergifted   E-mail: sgp@wvwc.edu
Nathaniel Sams, Dir.
Grades 5-12. Adm: Selective. Admitted: 95%. **Prereqs:** IQ 130. **Appl**—Fee $0. Due: June.

Enr: 50. **Enr cap:** 75. Intl: 3%. Non-White: 10%. **Fac 7.** Prof 7. **Staff:** Admin 1. Couns 2.
Type of instruction: Adv Enrich Preview. **Courses:** Comp_Sci Hist Math Sci Sociol Creative_Writing Music. **Avg class size:** 10. **Daily hours for:** Classes 6. Study 4. Rec 5. Homework. Tests. Grades. **College credit.**
Features: Soccer Swim Tennis.
Fees 2011: Res $1200 (+$20), 2 wks. Aid 2011 (Need): $10,000.
Housing: Dorms. **Swimming:** Pool. Campus facilities avail.
Est 1983. Nonprofit. **Ses:** 1. **Wks/ses:** 2. Operates June-July.

Gifted adolescents who have scored at the 97th percentile or above on the verbal or mathematics section on a standardized achievement test or have been accepted into another gifted program may enroll in SGP. Students receive instruction in mathematics, physics, computer programming, literature and creative writing. The goal of the various programs is to hasten development in the quantitative, verbal and social arenas.

WISCONSIN

WISCONSIN CENTER FOR ACADEMICALLY TALENTED YOUTH SUMMER PROGRAMS
Res and Day — Coed Ages 8-18

Madison, WI 53706. Teacher Education Bldg, Ste 264, 225 N Mills St.
Tel: 608-890-3260. Fax: 608-265-4309.
www.wcaty.org   E-mail: wcaty@education.wisc.edu
Carole Trone, Dir.
Grades 4-12 (younger if qualified). Adm: Selective. **Appl**—Fee $60. Due: May. Transcript, standardized test scores, writing sample, 2 recs.
Enr: 100-130. **Enr cap:** 140. **Fac 9.** Prof 2. Col/grad students 2. K-12 staff 5. **Staff:** Admin 4. Couns 9.
Type of instruction: Adv Enrich. **Courses:** Arabic Lat Russ Comp_Sci Eng Engineering Environ_Sci Writing/Journ Crafts Dance Filmmaking Fine_Arts Media Music Photog Studio_Art Theater. **Avg class size:** 12. **Daily hours for:** Classes 6. Study 1. Rec 5. Homework. Tests. Grades. **High school credit:** 1.
Features: Aquatics Community_Serv Conservation Cooking Exploration Hiking Outdoor_ Ed Peace/Cross-cultural Riding Badminton Basketball Football Golf Gymnastics Soccer Swim Tennis Ultimate_Frisbee Volleyball.
Fees 2011: Res $825-2400 (+$50-150), 1-3 wks. Day $500-1750 (+$50-150), 1-3 wks. Aid 2009 (Need): $75,000.
Housing: Dorms. Avg per room/unit: 2-3. **Swimming:** Lake Pool.
Est 1991. Nonprofit. **Ses:** 3. **Wks/ses:** 1-3. Operates June-Aug.

WCATY conducts summer programs for advanced students at the elementary, middle and high school levels. The weeklong Young Students Summer Program, held at Beloit College and serving children in grades 4-6, combines enrichment courses with an exposure to new disciplines. Students in grades 7 and 8 may enroll in the Summer Transitional Enrichment Program, which enables pupils to take one two-week course for enrichment or acceleration. The Accelerated Learning Program (grades 9-12) consists of an intensive three-week course for each student. ALP courses are equivalent to an honors-level high school class or a semester-long college course.

ACADEMIC PROGRAMS
ABROAD

Academic programs abroad are arranged alphabetically by country and name.

For academic-year programs, see *The Handbook of Private Schools*, an annual descriptive survey of independent education, and *Schools Abroad of Interest to Americans*, a worldwide guide to elementary and secondary schools with English-speaking programs. For details, please visit www.portersargent.com or see page 880.

Academic Programs Abroad

ENGLAND

THE CAMBRIDGE PREP EXPERIENCE
Res — Coed Ages 14-15

Cambridge, England.
Contact (Year-round): Oxbridge Academic Prgms, 601 Cathedral Pky, Ste 7R, New York, NY 10025. Tel: 212-932-3049, 800-828-8349. Fax: 212-663-8169.
www.oxbridgeprograms.com   E-mail: info@oxbridgeprograms.com
Rachel Powers, Dir.
Student contact: Doug Herman, E-mail: doug@oxbridgeprograms.com.
Grades 9-10 (younger if qualified). Adm: Selective. **Appl**—Fee $0. Due: Rolling. Transcript, essay.
Enr: 150. Intl: 20%.
Type of instruction: Adv Enrich. **Courses:** Debate Eng Expository_Writing Forensic_Sci Law Med/Healthcare Speech Philos Zoology Creative_Writing Drama Fine_Arts Studio_Art Art_Hist. **Avg class size:** 14. **Daily hours for:** Classes 4. Homework. Grades.
Fees 2012: Res $7720, 3½ wks. Aid (Merit & Need).
Housing: Dorms.
Est 1994. Spons: Oxbridge Academic Programs. **Ses:** 1. **Wks/ses:** 3½. Operates July.

Course work emphasizes writing and communicational skills and classes take a hands-on approach in this program, which operates at Peterhouse College. Each student takes two courses, one as a major and one as a minor. Major courses convene six mornings per week and entail both homework and project and preparation time; minor courses meet three afternoons a week, with all work contained within the class session. Cultural excursions to dramatic performances, art galleries, museums and historical sites enrich the program.

THE CAMBRIDGE TRADITION
Res — Coed Ages 15-18

Cambridge, England. Cambridge Univ.
Contact (Year-round): c/o Oxbridge Academic Prgms, 601 Cathedral Pky, Ste 7R, New York, NY 10025. Tel: 212-932-3049, 800-828-8349. Fax: 212-663-8169.
www.oxbridgeprograms.com   E-mail: info@oxbridgeprograms.com
Greg Gonzalez, Dir.
Grades 11-PG. Adm: Selective. **Appl**—Fee $0. Due: Rolling. Transcript, essay.
Enr: 250. Intl: 20%.
Type of instruction: Adv Enrich. **Courses:** Lat Architect Astron Bus/Fin Debate Eng Forensic_Sci Hist Med/Healthcare Psych Relig_Stud Speech Sports_Med Zoology Creative_Writing Drama Studio_Art Art_Hist. **Avg class size:** 12. **Daily hours for:** Classes 4. Homework.
Intl program focus: Acad.
Fees 2012: Res $7595, 4 wks. Aid (Merit & Need).
Housing: Dorms.
Est 1999. Spons: Oxbridge Academic Programs. **Ses:** 1. **Wks/ses:** 4. Operates July-Aug.

This precollege program, conducted at Cambridge University, enables students to engage in academic study while also taking advantage of the area's cultural resources. Pupils take two courses during the session, one as a major and one as a minor. Major courses, which meet six mornings per week, include homework and require additional project and preparation time.

Less intensive minor courses meet three afternoons weekly and demand no work outside the classroom.

OXFORD ADVANCED STUDIES PROGRAM SUMMER COURSE
Res — Coed Ages 16-18

Oxford, OX1 4HT England. 12 King Edward St. Tel: 44-1865-793333. Fax: 44-1865-793233.
www.oasp.ac.uk   E-mail: info@oasp.ac.uk
Ralph Dennison, Dir.
Student contact: Charles Duncan, E-mail: charles.duncan@otc.ac.uk.
Grades 11-PG. Adm: Selective. **Appl**—Fee $0. Due: May. Essay, rec, transcript.
Enr: 60. **Enr cap:** 80. Intl: 40%. **Fac 25. Staff:** Admin 4. Couns 8.
Type of instruction: Adv Tut. **Courses:** Fr Ger Ital Lat Russ Span Architect Bus/Fin Debate Econ Eng Expository_Writing Govt Hist Law Psych Writing/Journ Creative_Writing Film Fine_Arts Media Theater Poetry. **Avg class size:** 6. **Daily hours for:** Classes 2. Study 3. Rec 4. Homework. Grades. **High school credit:** 1/crse, total 3.
Intl program focus: Acad Lang.
Features: Baseball Basketball Gymnastics Soccer Swim Tennis Weight_Trng.
Fees 2012: Res $8750 (+$900), 3½ wks.
Housing: Dorms. **Swimming:** Pool.
Est 1982. Nonprofit. **Spons:** Oxford Tutorial College. **Ses: 1. Wks/ses:** 3½. Operates July-Aug.

OASP's summer program consists of four seminar hours plus one hourlong tutorial per week. Students choose two or three courses from a selection that includes art and architecture, literature, history, philosophy, economics, international relations, languages, sciences, mathematics and creative writing. While mornings are devoted to academic study, afternoons and evenings consist of cultural visits, social activities and sports. Optional workshops are offered in drama, creative writing, film production and debate.

OXFORD AND CAMBRIDGE SUMMER SCHOOL
Res — Coed Ages 16-18

London, E1 6LF England. 14 Bacon St, 1st Fl. Tel: 44-1-865-522-244.
www.oxfordandcambridgesummerschool.com
E-mail: info@oxfordandcambridgesummerschool.com
Sophie Frew, Leader.
Grade 11. Adm: Selective. Admitted: 25%. **Appl**—Fee $0. Due: Rolling. Transcript, personal statement.
Enr: 30. **Enr cap:** 30. Intl: 80%. **Fac 6.** Col/grad students 6. **Staff:** Admin 3. Couns 6.
Type of instruction: Adv Enrich Study_Skills Tut. **Courses:** Econ Eng Engineering Hist Law Med/Healthcare Psych Biochem Creative_Writing Media Theater. **Avg class size:** 5. **Daily hours for:** Classes 2. Study 4. Rec 2. Homework. Tests.
Intl program focus: Acad.
Features: Soccer.
Fees 2012: Res £2995 (+£100), 2 wks.
Housing: Houses. Avg per room/unit: 1. Campus facilities avail.
Est 2011. Nonprofit. **Ses: 2. Wks/ses:** 2. Operates July-Aug.

In a small-class and tutorial setting, students preview university life as they choose from courses that are modeled after the Oxford and Cambridge tutorial system. The program's Oxford- and Cambridge-educated instructors teach in classes limited to four to six pupils, and time is also allotted for one-on-one tutorials. In addition, students may attend academic skills workshops relating to such topics as college applications, interviewing skills, debating and lateral methods of thinking. Cultural and sightseeing trips complete the program.

THE OXFORD PREP EXPERIENCE
Res — Coed Ages 14-15

Oxford, England. Oxford Univ.
Contact (Year-round): c/o Oxbridge Academic Prgms, 601 Cathedral Pky, Ste 7R, New York, NY 10025. Tel: 212-932-3049, 800-828-8349. Fax: 212-663-8169.
www.oxbridgeprograms.com   E-mail: info@oxbridgeprograms.com
John Pendergast III, Dir.
Grades 9-10. Adm: Selective. **Appl**—Fee $0. Due: Rolling. Transcript, essay.
Enr: 150.
Type of instruction: Adv Enrich. **Courses:** Architect Debate Eng Expository_Writing Hist Intl_Relations Law Med/Healthcare Pol_Sci Psych Speech Writing/Journ Philos Shakespeare Creative_Writing Drama Studio_Art. Homework.
Intl program focus: Acad.
Features: Basketball.
Fees 2012: Res $7295, 3½ wks.
Housing: Dorms.
Est 2004. Spons: Oxbridge Academic Programs. **Ses:** 1. **Wks/ses:** 3½. Operates July.

This hands-on academic program takes place on the campus of Corpus Christi College at Oxford University. Students choose both a major and a minor course, with each class convening in a small group that is conducive to interactive learning. Cultural excursions to dramatic performances, art galleries, museums and historical sites enrich the program.

THE OXFORD TRADITION
Res — Coed Ages 15-18

Oxford, England.
Contact (Year-round): Oxbridge Academic Prgms, 601 Cathedral Pky, Ste 7R, New York, NY 10025. Tel: 212-932-3049, 800-828-8349. Fax: 212-663-8169.
www.oxbridgeprograms.com   E-mail: info@oxbridgeprograms.com
Michael McKinley, Dir.
    Student contact: Doug Herman, E-mail: doug@oxbridgeprograms.com.
Grades 11-PG. Adm: Selective. **Appl**—Fee $0. Due: Rolling. Transcript, essay.
Enr: 400. Intl: 20%.
Type of instruction: Adv. **Courses:** Archaeol Architect Debate Eng Engineering Hist Intl_Relations Law Med/Healthcare Speech Writing/Journ Bioethics Philos Creative_Writing Drama Film Music Photog Studio_Art Art_Hist. **Avg class size:** 14. **Daily hours for:** Classes 4.
Intl program focus: Acad.
Fees 2012: Res $7595, 4 wks.
Housing: Dorms.
Est 1985. Spons: Oxbridge Academic Programs. **Ses:** 1. **Wks/ses:** 4. Operates June-July.

Conducted at Oxford University, this precollege program provides a rigorous academic program in a small-class environment for students who have completed grades 10-12. Pupils take two courses during the session, one as a major and one as a minor. Major courses, which meet six mornings per week, include homework and require additional project and preparation time. Less intensive minor courses meet three afternoons weekly and demand no work outside the classroom. Faculty schedule frequent excursions to local cultural events.

SUMMERFUEL
THE OXFORD EXPERIENCE
Res — Coed Ages 15-18

Oxford, England. Oxford Univ.

Contact (Year-round): 375 W Broadway, Ste 200, New York, NY 10012.
Tel: 212-796-8340, 800-752-2250. Fax: 212-334-4934.
www.asaprograms.com   E-mail: oxford@asaprograms.com
Paul Saville & Sarah Gudis, Dirs.
Grades 10-PG. Adm: Selective. Appl—Due: Rolling. Transcript, rec.
Enr: 200. Staff: Admin 5. Couns 23.
Type of instruction: Adv Enrich Rev SAT/ACT_Prep. Courses: Chin Fr Architect Bus/
Fin Expository_Writing Hist Intl_Relations Psych Public_Speak Speech Writing/Journ
Anthro Ethics Shakespeare Acting Creative_Writing Film Fine_Arts Music Painting
Photog Studio_Art Theater. Avg class size: 10. Daily hours for: Classes 4½. Study 2.
Rec 4. High school credit.
Intl program focus: Acad.
Features: Soccer.
Fees 2012: Res $7695 (+airfare), 4 wks.
Housing: Dorms.
Est 1984. Inc. Spons: Academic Study Associates. Ses: 1. Wks/ses: 4. Operates June-
Aug.

Participants in the Oxford Experience pursue a range of courses in the following areas: humanities and the arts, the natural sciences, the social sciences and SAT preparation. Conducted at Oxford University, England, the program consists of three-hour seminars each morning and two-hour afternoon seminars four times weekly. Students incur additional fees for certain courses.

TASIS ENGLAND SUMMER SCHOOL
Res — Coed Ages 11-18; Day — Coed 5-11

Thorpe, TW20 8TE Surrey, England. Coldharbour Ln. Tel: 44-1932-565252.
Fax: 44-1932-564644.
Contact (Sept-May): c/o TASIS US Office, 112 S Royal St, Alexandria, VA 22314.
Tel: 703-299-8150. Fax: 703-299-8157.
www.tasisengland.org   E-mail: uksummer@tasisengland.org
Jeffrey Barton, Dir.
Grades K-12. Adm: FCFS. Appl—Fee $0. Due: Rolling.
Enr: 250. Enr cap: 250. Intl: 50%. Non-White: 50%. Fac 25. K-12 staff 25. Staff: Couns
10.
Type of instruction: Adv Enrich Rev SAT/ACT_Prep Study_Skills. Courses: Computers
Math Writing/Journ Crafts Dance Filmmaking Music Photog Studio_Art Theater. Avg
class size: 13. Daily hours for: Classes 4. Study 2. Rec 2. Homework. Grades. High
school credit: 1.
Intl program focus: Acad Lang Culture.
Features: Boating Caving Climbing_Wall Riding Aerobics Basketball Golf Soccer Softball
Swim Tennis Volleyball Water-skiing Watersports Weight_Trng.
Fees 2012: Res £3250-6300 (+airfare), 3-6 wks. Day £290 (+airfare), 1 wk. Aid (Need).
Housing: Dorms. Avg per room/unit: 4. Swimming: Pool. Campus facilities avail.
Est 1976. Nonprofit. Spons: TASIS Foundation. Ses: 10. Wks/ses: 1-6. Operates June-
Aug.

TASIS England provides an array of academic and enrichment courses for native or highly proficient English speakers. Students may take classes in traditional subjects and in such areas as SAT review, Shakespearean theater, movie animation, art in London, photography, dance and music. Each afternoon, pupils engage in arts and crafts and play various sports. On weekends, boarding boys and girls embark on day and overnight trips to the English cities of London, Bath, Windsor, Oxford and Cambridge, as well as to Paris, France; Brussels, Belgium; Wales; and Edinburgh, Scotland.

FRANCE

AMERICAN UNIVERSITY OF PARIS SUMMER SESSIONS
Res — Coed Ages 18 and up

Paris, France. 6 rue du Colonel Combes. Tel: 33-1-40-62-07-20. Fax: 33-1-47-05-34-32. www.aup.edu   E-mail: summer@aup.edu
Joumana Hassan, Dir.
Grades PG-Col (younger if qualified). Adm: Somewhat selective. Admitted: 98%. **Appl**— Fee 50. Due: Rolling. Transcript.
Enr: 220. **Enr cap:** 250. Intl: 50%. Non-White: 50%. **Fac 40.** Prof 30. Col/grad students 10. **Staff:** Admin 5.
Type of instruction: Adv Enrich Undergrad. **Courses:** Ital Architect Bus/Fin Comm Econ Eng Environ_Sci Expository_Writing Hist Math Pol_Sci Psych Art Film Painting Photog. **Avg class size:** 15. **Daily hours for:** Classes 3. Homework. Tests. Grades. **College credit:** 4-8/crse, total 8.
Intl program focus: Acad Lang Culture. Home stays avail.
Focus: Fr.
Fees 2011: Res €1774-7248, 3-7 wks. Aid (Merit).
Campus facilities avail.
Est 1962. Nonprofit. **Ses:** 3. **Wks/ses:** 3-7. Operates June-July.

AUP's programs are open to both college students and those just finishing secondary school. Participants take college courses in art history, fine arts, business administration, literature, math, economics, philosophy, French and international politics. A separate French immersion program offers a home stay residential option.

EXCEL PARIS/PROVENCE
Res — Coed Ages 15-18

Paris, France.
Contact (Year-round): 345 Hickory Ridge Rd, Putney, VT 05346. Tel: 802-387-5000. Fax: 802-387-4276.
www.goputney.com   E-mail: info@goputney.com
Bibba Walke, Dir.
Grades 10-PG. Adm: FCFS. **Appl**—Due: Rolling.
Courses: Fr Architect Hist Intl_Relations Creative_Writing Drawing Fashion Painting Photog Art_Hist.
Intl program focus: Acad.
Features: Cooking.
Fees 2010: Res $8190 (+$150-250), 4 wks.
Housing: Dorms.
Spons: Putney Student Travel. **Ses:** 1. **Wks/ses:** 4. Operates July.

Divided between central Paris and the university town of Aix-en-Provence, this Excel program provides students with field-based seminars that lead to an exploration of French history, art and culture. Pupils may choose either to refine their French language skills or to gain a deeper understanding of the country through course work that emphasizes France. Each student chooses one major course and one minor course; both meet throughout the program (three full days weekly for major classes and two full days per week for minor courses). Instructors make significant use of the cultural and historical opportunities presented by the two cities.

L'ACADEMIE DE PARIS
Res — Coed Ages 15-18

Paris, France.
Contact (Year-round): Oxbridge Academic Prgms, 601 Cathedral Pky, Ste 7R, New York, NY 10025. **Tel:** 212-932-3049, 800-828-8349. **Fax:** 212-663-8169.
www.oxbridgeprograms.com   E-mail: info@oxbridgeprograms.com
Richard W. J. Michaelis, Dir.
Grades 10-PG. Adm: Selective. **Appl**—Fee $0. Due: Rolling. Transcript, personal statement.
Enr: 190. **Fac 18.**
Type of instruction: Adv Enrich. **Courses:** Fr Architect Med/Healthcare Psych Existentialism Creative_Writing Film Photog Studio_Art Art_Hist. **Avg class size:** 14. **Daily hours for:** Classes 4. Homework.
Intl program focus: Acad.
Fees 2012: Res $7595, 4 wks.
Housing: Dorms.
Est 1990. Spons: Oxbridge Academic Programs. **Ses:** 1. **Wks/ses:** 4. Operates July-Aug.

Conducted in the heart of the city, this precollege program provides a curriculum that introduces pupils to French culture and Parisian life, regardless of the subjects selected. Offerings include art history, medicine, literature, international law and photography. Students who have taken French previously may participate in immersion classes taught by native French speakers; however, pupils need have no prior knowledge of French to attend. Each student takes both an in-depth major course and a less intensive minor class.

SUMMER STUDY IN PARIS
Res — Coed Ages 15-17

Paris, France. The Sorbonne.
Contact (Year-round): 900 Walt Whitman Rd, Ste 103, Melville, NY 11747.
Tel: 631-424-1000, 800-666-2556. **Fax:** 631-424-0567.
www.summerstudy.com/paris   E-mail: info@summerstudy.com
William Cooperman, Exec Dir.
Grades 10-12. Adm: Selective. **Appl**—Due: Rolling.
Enr: 300. **Fac 25. Staff:** Admin 7. Couns 20.
Type of instruction: Adv Enrich Preview Rev SAT/ACT_Prep. **Courses:** Fr Architect Bus/Fin Expository_Writing Hist Creative_Writing Drawing Fashion Film Photog Art_Hist. **Daily hours for:** Classes 2½. Study 1. Rec 4. **College credit:** 3/crse, total 3.
Intl program focus: Acad Lang Culture.
Features: Basketball Swim Tennis.
Fees 2012: Res $6395-8595 (+airfare), 3-5 wks. Aid (Need).
Housing: Dorms. Avg per room/unit: 3-4. **Swimming:** Pool.
Est 1989. Inc. Spons: Summer Study Programs. **Ses:** 2. **Wks/ses:** 3-5. Operates July-Aug.

Students interested in studying in France choose from two programs. During the five-week Summer Study program, pupils take either a college-credit French course or two noncredit enrichment classes. Boys and girls in the three-week program select two noncredit enrichment courses. Both programs provide an in-depth exploration of the city, athletic and other recreational activities, and weekend excursions. For an additional fee, students may embark on a weekend trip to London, England.

TUFTS UNIVERSITY EUROPEAN CENTER
TUFTS SUMMIT
Res — Coed Ages 15-18

Talloires, France.
Contact (Year-round): 108 Packard Ave, Medford, MA 02155. Tel: 617-627-3290.
  Fax: 617-627-3457.
www.ase.tufts.edu/europeancenter   **E-mail: france@tufts.edu**
Gabriella Goldstein, Dir. Student contact: David Baum.
Grades 11-12. Adm: Selective. **Appl**—Fee $75. Due: Mar. Transcript, short essay, 2 recs.
Enr: 30. **Enr cap:** 30. **Fac 3.** Prof 3. **Staff:** Admin 3. Couns 7.
Type of instruction: Enrich. **Courses:** Fr Intl_Relations. **Daily hours for:** Classes 4. Study
  2. Rec 3. Homework.
Intl program focus: Acad Lang Culture. Home stays avail.
Features: Hiking Swim Water-skiing.
Fees 2012: Res $5450 (+$1500), 4 wks. Aid 2011 (Merit & Need): $5000.
Housing: Apartments Houses. Avg per room/unit: 2. **Swimming:** Lake. Campus facilities
  avail.
Est 1993. Nonprofit. **Ses:** 1. **Wks/ses:** 4. Operates July.

While developing their French language skills, pupils enrolled in this Tufts University program also study international politics and diplomacy. Participants, who live with local host families, take two college-level courses that lead to a greater understanding of international relations. Daily French classes combine class exercises with exposure to aspects of French culture. Day trips to international organizations in Geneva, Switzerland, and historic sites in Lyon, France—in addition to various outdoor activities—round out the program.

GREECE

HYPHENOLOGY EDUCATIONAL SUMMER PROGRAMS
Res — Coed Ages 14-18

Mytilene, 81 100 Greece. 88 El Venizelou. Tel: 202-470-0922. Fax: 30-2251-027916.
www.hyphenology.com   **E-mail: director@hyphenology.com**
Cindy Camatsos, Dir.
Grades 9-PG. Adm: FCFS. **Appl**—Fee $0. Due: May.
Enr: 12. **Enr cap:** 25. **Intl:** 25%. Non-White: 10%. **Fac 6.** Prof 6. **Staff:** Admin 2. Couns 6.
Type of instruction: Adv Enrich Tut. **Courses:** Greek Astron Bus/Fin Environ_Sci Exposi-
  tory_Writing Writing/Journ Creative_Writing Dance Theater. **Avg class size:** 4. **Daily
  hours for:** Classes 3. Study 1. Rec 4. Homework. Tests. Grades.
Intl program focus: Acad Culture.
Features: Adventure_Travel Community_Serv Exploration Fishing Hiking Sea_Cruises
  Swim Volleyball Watersports.
Fees 2010: Res €1900 (+airfare), 2 wks. Aid 2008 (Merit & Need): 500.
Housing: Hotels. Avg per room/unit: 2. **Swimming:** Ocean Pool.
Est 2004. Inc. **Ses:** 1. **Wks/ses:** 2. Operates July.

Academically motivated students spend two weeks on the Greek island of Lesvos taking subjects outside the traditional high school curriculum. As a complement to class work, boys and girls perform community service in the area. Study of the Greek language is not a primary aim of the program (although Greek is available as a subject).

UNIVERSITY OF CHICAGO TRAVELING ACADEMY
Res — Coed Ages 14-18

Athens, Greece.

Contact (Year-round): Summer Session Office, 1427 E 60th St, 2nd Fl, Chicago, IL
60637. Tel: 773-834-3792. Fax: 773-834-0549.
http://summer.uchicago.edu/traveling-academy.cfm
E-mail: summerhs@uchicago.edu
Michaelangelo F. Allocca & Cynthia Rutz, Prgm Dirs.
Grades 10-12. Adm: Selective. Appl—Fee $40. Due: Apr. Transcript, essay, 2 recs.
Enr: 10. Enr cap: 15. Fac 2. Prof 2. Staff: Admin 3.
Type of instruction: Enrich. Courses: Greek Archaeol Drama. Homework. Tests. Grades.
College credit: 3/crse, total 3.
Intl program focus: Acad Culture. Travel: Europe.
Fees 2011: Res $7940, 3 wks. Aid (Merit & Need).
Housing: Dorms Hotels. Avg per room/unit: 2-3.
Ses: 1. Wks/ses: 3. Operates June-July.

This interdisciplinary humanities course takes high schoolers to Greece for the study of ancient Greek drama in its literary and social contexts and its place of origin. Excursions to archaeological sites and museums in and around Athens supplement the classroom portion of the program, which is conducted on the island of Spetses. Program directors guide students in close readings and critical analysis of selected works by Aeschylus, Sophocles, Euripides, and Aristophanes. Language instruction in modern Greek is part of the curriculum, and participants may attend dance classes, poetry readings and festivals.   See Also Page 32

IRELAND

THE IRISH WAY
SUMMER STUDY ABROAD FOR HIGH SCHOOL STUDENTS
Res — Coed Ages 14-18

Dublin, Ireland.
Contact (Year-round): Irish American Cultural Inst, 1 Lackawanna Pl, Morristown, NJ
07960. Tel: 973-605-1991.
www.iaci-usa.org/program_iw.htm   E-mail: irishway@iaci-usa.org
Grades 10-PG. Adm: FCFS. Appl—Due: Mar.
Enr: 100.
Type of instruction: Enrich. Courses: Irish_Hist Irish_Lit. Homework.
Intl program focus: Acad Culture. Travel: Europe.
Fees 2011: Res $4950, 3 wks. Aid (Need).
Housing: Dorms.
Est 1976. Nonprofit. Spons: Irish American Cultural Institute. Ses: 1. Wks/ses: 3. Operates
June-July.

The Irish Way provides an introduction to Ireland's history and traditions. Destinations include the cities of Dublin, Waterford, Killarney and Galway, where students live in traditional Irish boarding schools. Irish secondary school teachers conduct structured sessions in Irish language, literature, history and culture. Supplementary field trips and city excursions enrich the program. Students work on a group research project and have time to explore local host communities on their own. Participants tour the west coast of Ireland at the end of the session.

UNIVERSITY COLLEGE DUBLIN
SUMMER HIGH SCHOOL PROGRAM
Res — Coed Ages 16-18

Dublin, Ireland.
Contact (Year-round): North American Office, 345 Park Ave, 17th Fl, New York, NY

10154. Tel: 212-308-2877. Fax: 212-308-2899.
www.ucd.ie   E-mail: northamerica@ucd.ie
**Enda Carroll, Manager. Student contact: Molly Dineen, E-mail: molly.dineen@ucd.ie.
Grades 11-12. Adm:** Somewhat selective. Prereqs: GPA 2.5. **Appl**—Fee $0. Due: May.
Enr cap: 50. **Fac 5.** Prof 3. Col/grad students 2. **Staff:** Admin 4. Res 4.
Type of instruction: Enrich Preview Undergrad. **Courses:** Irish ArchitectCultural_Stud
  Eng Hist Pol_Sci Relig_Stud Dance Filmmaking Music Photog Theater Art_Hist. **Daily
  hours for:** Classes 3. Study 1½. Rec 6. Homework.
Features: Climbing_Wall Hiking Mtn_Trips Outdoor_Ed Lacrosse Soccer Softball Swim.
Fees 2012: Res €1900 (+airfare), 2½ wks.
Housing: Apartments. Avg per room/unit: 4. **Swimming:** Pool.
Est 2012. Nonprofit. **Ses:** 1. **Wks/ses:** 2½. Operates July.

Rising high school juniors and seniors sample university life abroad while studying various aspects of Ireland's culture and history in this UCD program. A four-part lecture series provides a thorough examination of Irish history. In addition, students explore an array of other topics related to Ireland, among them literature, religion, architecture, emigration, art, music and the Irish language. Interactive workshops and social activities include Ceili dancing, an introduction to Gaelic football and hurling, and a photography competition. Field trips to local sites of interest complete the program.

ITALY

CANADIAN COLLEGE ITALY
THE RENAISSANCE SCHOOL SUMMER ACADEMY
Res — Coed Ages 15-19

**Lanciano, Italy.
Contact (Year-round): 59 Macamo Ct, Maple, L6A 1G1 Ontario, Canada.
  Tel: 905-508-7108, 800-422-0548. Fax: 905-508-5480.**
www.ccilanciano.com   E-mail: cciren@rogers.com
**George Rutherford, Head.
Grades 10-12. Adm:** Selective. **Appl**—Fee $0. Due: Rolling. Transcript, 3 recs.
Enr: 70-120. **Fac 10.** K-12 staff 10. **Staff:** Admin 4.
Type of instruction: Adv. **Courses:** Ital Eng Hist Art. **Avg class size:** 12. **Daily hours for:**
  Classes 5½. Study 1. Rec 3. **High school credit:** 1.
Intl program focus: Acad Lang Culture.
Features: Hiking Swim.
Fees 2012: Res Can$5900, 4 wks.
Housing: Dorms. **Swimming:** Ocean.
Est 1995. Inc. **Ses:** 1. **Wks/ses:** 4. Operates June-July.

Students earn applicable North American high school credit while studying at this Canadian school in Lanciano. The academy provides free time for recreation and exploration of the area. Round-trip airfare to and from Toronto, Canada, is included in the tuition cost.

HUMANITIES SPRING IN ASSISI
Res — Coed Ages 15-19

Assisi, 06081 Italy. Santa Maria di Lignano 2. Tel: 39-075-802400. Fax: 39-075-802400.
www.humanitiesspring.com   E-mail: info@humanitiesspring.com
**Jane R. Oliensis, Dir. Student contact: Alessia Montanucci.
Grades 10-PG (younger if qualified). Adm:** FCFS. **Appl**—Fee $50. Due: Rolling.
Enr cap: 12. Intl: 20%. Non-White: 20%. **Fac 5.** Prof 1. K-12 staff 1. Specialists 3. **Staff:**
  Admin 2. Couns 4.
Type of instruction: Adv Preview. **Courses:** Greek Ital Archaeol Architect Relig_Stud

Crafts Creative_Writing Fine_Arts Painting Photog Art_Hist Poetry. **Avg class size:** 7. **Daily hours for:** Classes 4. Study 2. Rec 5½.
Intl program focus: Acad Lang Culture.
Features: Adventure_Travel Cooking Swim Gardening.
Fees 2012: Res $4250 (+$250), 4 wks. Aid 2011 (Merit & Need): $6000.
Housing: Houses. Avg per room/unit: 2. **Swimming:** Pool Stream. Campus facilities avail.
Est 1991. Nonprofit. **Ses:** 1. **Wks/ses:** 4. Operates June-July.

HSIA students take morning courses in Renaissance poetry, art, architecture and society; ancient Greek and Roman poetry, art and archaeology; and Italian language, literature and conversation. In the afternoon, boys and girls embark on study trips to view related works of art and architecture. HSIA schedules outings to the beach and to jazz and arts festivals; day trips to Florence, Ravenna and Tarquinia; and a three-day southern excursion to Pompeii, Paestum and the Amalfi Coast. Archaeology Boot Camp, which convenes right after the regular session and incurs an additional fee, enables students to join archaeologists for a week of intensive, in-depth study of Paestum and Pompeii.

ST. STEPHEN'S SCHOOL SUMMER PROGRAMS
Res and Day — Coed Ages 13-18

Rome, 00153 Italy. Via Aventina 3. Tel: 39-06-575-0605. Fax: 39-06-574-1941.
www.sssrome.it/summerprogram.php   E-mail: summer@ststephens-rome.com
Crispin Corrado, Dir.
Grades 8-PG (younger if qualified). Adm: FCFS. **Appl**—Fee $0. Due: Rolling.
Enr cap: 40.
Type of instruction: Enrich. **Courses:** Ital Lat Architect Creative_Writing Dance Film Music Photog Studio_Art. **Avg class size:** 13.
Intl program focus: Acad Culture.
Housing: Dorms.
Ses: 2. **Wks/ses:** 2-3. Operates July-Aug.

St. Stephen's conducts two summer programs for young English-speaking students each summer. Open to pupils ages 13-16, the Arts & Humanities Program employs St. Stephen's faculty and local teachers. The Brown University-St. Stephen's School Pre-College Summer Program, taught by instructors from both institutions, serves boys and girls ages 16-18. Participants in both programs enroll in a language course (either Italian or Latin); a core course that focuses on ancient Rome, Renaissance art or modern Italy; and an elective. Staff members schedule afternoon recreational activities and evening cultural events in the city. Weekends provide the opportunity for excursions to such locations as Pompeii, Sorrento, Siena and Florence.

SUMMER DISCOVERY
Res — Coed Ages 16-18

Florence, Italy.
Contact (Year-round): 1326 Old Northern Blvd, Roslyn, NY 11576. Tel: 516-621-3939.
    Fax: 516-625-3438.
www.summerdiscovery.com   E-mail: discovery@summerdiscovery.com
Bob Musiker, Exec Dir.
Grades 11-PG. Adm: FCFS. **Appl**—Fee $95. Due: Rolling.
Enr: 80. **Enr cap:** 100. **Staff:** Admin 3. Couns 5.
Type of instruction: Enrich SAT/ACT_Prep. **Courses:** Ital Hist Ceramics Crafts Dance Fashion Fine_Arts Media Painting Photog Sculpt Studio_Art. Grades. **College credit:** 4.
Intl program focus: Acad Lang Culture.
Features: Cooking Swim.

Fees 2010: Res $8299 (+airfare), 4 wks.
Housing: Hotels Lodges. **Swimming:** Pool.
Est 2006. Inc. **Ses:** 1. **Wks/ses:** 4. Operates July.

Precollege programs for high school students are held on university campuses throughout the US and abroad. Boys and girls take a college-credit course and an enrichment course during their stay. Other aspects of the program include community service, excursions, travel, sports and recreational activities. See other Summer Discovery listings under Los Angeles, CA; Santa Barbara, CA; San Diego, CA; Ann Arbor, MI; Washington, DC; and Valencia, Spain.

UNIVERSITY OF DALLAS
SUMMER PROGRAMS ABROAD
Res — Coed Ages 16-18

Rome, Italy.
Contact (Year-round): Rome & Summer Programs Office, 1845 E Northgate Dr, Irving, TX 75062. Tel: 972-721-5181. Fax: 972-721-5283.
www.udallas.edu/travel   E-mail: udsummer@udallas.edu
Rebecca Davies, Dir. Student contact: Jennifer Massicci.
Grades 11-PG (younger if qualified). Adm: Selective. **Appl**—Fee $0. Due: Rolling. Transcript, essay, test scores, 2 teacher recs.
Enr cap: 35-40. **Fac 4.** Prof 2. Col/grad students 2. **Staff:** Admin 2. Res 3.
Avg class size: 25.
Fees 2011: Res $5500-6500, 2-3 wks. Aid 2010 (Merit & Need): $750.
Housing: Dorms. Avg per room/unit: 2-3. **Swimming:** Pool.
Est 1993. Nonprofit. Roman Catholic. **Ses:** 2. **Wks/ses:** 2-3. Operates June-Aug.

Conducted on the University of Dallas' Rome campus, two summer programs for high school students combine classic and classical texts from the university's core curriculum with visits to historical sites. Shakespeare in Italy students read three complete plays in detail, as well as selections from plays and sonnets, examining how Italy's history, art, literature, philosophy and theology influenced the author. Latin in Rome participants study passages from Cicero, Pliny, Vergil and Horace relevant to their travels in Rome. Lectures, daily language tutorials and group discussions enhance site visits.

JORDAN

COLUMBIA UNIVERSITY
CULTURE AND HISTORY: UNDERSTANDING THE ARAB WORLD
Res — Coed Ages 16-18

Manja, Jordan. King's Academy.
Contact (Year-round): 203 Lewisohn Hall, 2970 Broadway, Mail Code 4119, New York, NY 10027. Tel: 212-854-9666.
www.ce.columbia.edu/high-school-programs-homepage
E-mail: hsp@columbia.edu
Anna Swank, Dir.
Grades 11-PG. Adm: Selective. **Appl**—Fee $75. Due: Mar. Transcript, personal statement, 2 recs.
Enr: 25.
Type of instruction: Enrich. **Courses:** Eng Hist Intl_Relations Pol_Sci Relig_Stud Anthro. Homework. Tests.
Intl program focus: Acad Lang.
Fees 2012: Res $13,750, 4 wks.
Housing: Dorms.
Est 2009. Ses: 1. **Wks/ses:** 4. Operates June-July.

Rising high school juniors and seniors engage in precollege study at both Columbia University and King's Academy in Jordan, in the process gaining exposure to the diverse cultures and history evident in the Arab world. After a week of study at Columbia, students spend two weeks living, studying and traveling in Jordan. Participants then return to New York to complete research projects for presentation. Visits to religious and cultural landmarks in Jordan are integral to the program. In lieu of grades, pupils receive written evaluations from their instructors upon successful completion of the program.

SCOTLAND

GORDONSTOUN INTERNATIONAL SUMMER SCHOOL
Res — Coed Ages 8-16

Elgin, IV30 5RF Moray, Scotland. Tel: 44-1343-837821. Fax: 44-1343-837825.
www.gordonstoun-int.com   E-mail: giss@gordonstoun.org.uk
Jenny Needham, Dir. Student contact: Alison Kellas.
Adm: FCFS. **Appl**—Due: Rolling.
Enr: 350. **Fac 150. Staff:** Admin 3.
Type of instruction: Enrich. **Courses:** Fr Computers Eng ESL Art Drama Music. **Avg class size:** 8. **Daily hours for:** Classes 2. Tests.
Intl program focus: Acad.
Features: Archery Boating Canoe Climbing_Wall Conservation Cooking Cruises Exploration Fishing Hiking Kayak Mountaineering Mtn_Trips Outdoor_Ed Rappelling Riding Riflery Rock_Climb Ropes_Crse Sail Sea_Cruises Seamanship Badminton Basketball Cross-country Equestrian Field_Hockey Football Golf Soccer Squash Swim Tennis Track Volleyball Watersports.
Fees 2012: Res £4900 (+airfare), 3½ wks.
Housing: Dorms Houses. **Swimming:** Ocean Pool. Campus facilities avail.
Est 1976. Nonprofit. **Ses:** 2. **Wks/ses:** 3½. Operates July-Aug.

Gordonstoun's academic program offers English as a Foreign Language or, for English speakers, French, computer studies or literature. Recreational activities include sports, sailing, creative arts and sightseeing trips. All participants go on a six-day mountaineering, canoeing and ocean sailing trip.

UNIVERSITY OF ST ANDREWS
SCOTTISH STUDIES SUMMER PROGRAMME
Res — Coed Ages 16-18

St Andrews, KY16 9AX Fife, Scotland. St Katherine's W, 16 The Scores.
Tel: 44-1334-462275. Fax: 44-1334-463330.
www.st-andrews.ac.uk/admissions/ug/int/summerschools
E-mail: rmd10@st-andrews.ac.uk
Ruth Harris, Head.
Grades 11-PG. Adm: Somewhat selective. Admitted: 95%. **Appl**—Fee £15. Due: Rolling. 2 recs, standardized test results, personal statement.
Enr: 24. Enr cap: 40. Intl: 20%. Non-White: 10%. **Fac 15.** Prof 7. Col/grad students 5. Specialists 3. **Staff:** Admin 2. Couns 2.
Type of instruction: Adv. **Courses:** Archaeol Ecol Eng Govt Hist Pol_Sci Film Music Photog Theater Art_Hist. **Daily hours for:** Classes 3. Study 3. Rec 4. Homework. Tests. Grades. **High school credit:** 12.
Intl program focus: Acad Culture.
Features: Conservation Exploration Hiking Mtn_Trips Swim.
Fees 2012: Res £2800, 4 wks.
Housing: Dorms. Avg per room/unit: 1. **Swimming:** Ocean Pool. Campus facilities avail.

Est 1999. Ses: 1. **Wks/ses:** 4. Operates June-July.

This academic program for North American students, taught by St Andrews faculty, focuses on Scottish studies. Employing an approach that includes seminars and tutorials, the program covers a millennium of Scottish history and also incorporates Scottish literature, archaeology, art history, film and traditional music. Frequent field trips and excursions—as well as cultural visits to art galleries, concerts and the theater—enrich the program.

SPAIN

COLUMBIA UNIVERSITY
THE BARCELONA EXPERIENCE
Res — Coed Ages 16-18

Barcelona, Spain. Univ of Barcelona.
Contact (Year-round): 203 Lewisohn Hall, 2970 Broadway, Mail Code 4119, New York, NY 10027. Tel: 212-854-9666.
www.ce.columbia.edu/the-barcelona-experience   E-mail: hsp@columbia.edu
Evelyn Tavarelli, Dir.
Grades 11-PG. Adm: Selective. **Appl**—Fee $75. Due: Mar. Transcript, 2 recs, personal statement.
Enr: 20.
Type of instruction: Enrich. **Courses:** Span Architect Hist Art. Homework. Tests.
Intl program focus: Acad Lang Culture.
Fees 2012: Res $12,500, 3 wks.
Housing: Dorms.
Ses: 1. **Wks/ses:** 3. Operates July.

A collaborative effort between Columbia and the University of Barcelona, this three-week enrichment program takes place at the Spanish university. Participants examine the history, the art and the urban development of Barcelona while also enriching their understanding of how European communities forge local, regional, national and international identities. A Spanish-language workshop (offered at all ability levels) supplements the three-course curriculum. Boys and girls devote two Fridays to enriching, program-related excursions. In lieu of grades, pupils receive written evaluations from their instructors upon successful completion of the program.

EXCEL MADRID/BARCELONA
Res — Coed Ages 14-18

Madrid, Spain.
Contact (Year-round): 345 Hickory Ridge Rd, Putney, VT 05346. Tel: 802-387-5000. Fax: 802-387-4276.
www.goputney.com   E-mail: info@goputney.com
Patrick Noyes, Dir.
Grades 9-12. Adm: FCFS. **Appl**—Due: Rolling.
Type of instruction: Enrich. **Courses:** Span Architect Creative_Writing Drawing Painting Photog Art_Hist.
Intl program focus: Acad.
Fees 2010: Res $8190 (+$150-250), 4 wks.
Housing: Dorms.
Spons: Putney Student Travel. **Ses:** 1. **Wks/ses:** 4. Operates July.

Participants in this Excel program split their time between Madrid and Barcelona while learning about the artistic, cultural and historical traditions of Spain. Students enroll in one major course and one minor course each; major courses convene three full days per week, while minor courses meet two full days weekly. Major course options are intermediate or advanced Spanish, creative writing, drawing and painting, Spanish art history and digital photography. All classes have a significant field component. Excel schedules frequent weekend excursions to areas of interest.

LA ACADEMIA DE ESPANA
Res — Coed Ages 15-18

Barcelona, Spain.
Contact (Year-round): c/o Oxbridge Academic Prgms, 601 Cathedral Pky, Ste 7R, New York, NY 10025. Tel: 212-932-3049, 800-828-8349. Fax: 212-663-8169.
www.oxbridgeprograms.com   **E-mail: info@oxbridgeprograms.com**
Jorge Rodriguez, Dir.
    Student contact: Doug Herman, E-mail: doug@oxbridgeprograms.com.
Grades 11-PG. Adm: Selective. **Appl**—Fee $0. Due: Rolling. Transcript, essay. Intl: 80%.
Type of instruction: Enrich. **Courses:** Span Architect Bus/Fin Hist Pol_Sci Creative_Writing Studio_Art Art_Hist. **Avg class size:** 14. **Daily hours for:** Classes 4. Homework. Grades.
Intl program focus: Acad.
Fees 2012: Res $7595, 4 wks.
Housing: Dorms.
Est 2006. Ses: 1. **Wks/ses:** 4. Operates July-Aug.

This academic program for students who have completed grades 10-12 features roughly 15 courses, with some employing English as the language of instruction and others using Spanish. Each pupil chooses a major and a minor class; the major course meets six times weekly, the minor three times. Certain offerings relate to Spanish culture, while others take a global perspective. Athletics, beach excursions, field trips to sites of historical interest, theater and concert outings, workshops and appearances by guest speakers complete the program.

LA ESCUELA PREPARATORIA DE BARCELONA
Res — Coed Ages 14-15

Barcelona, Spain.
Contact (Year-round): c/o Oxbridge Academic Prgms, 601 Cathedral Pky, Ste 7R, New York, NY 10025. Tel: 212-932-3049, 800-828-8349. Fax: 212-663-8169.
www.oxbridgeprograms.com   **E-mail: info@oxbridgeprograms.com**
Jorge Salas, Dir.
    Student contact: Doug Herman, E-mail: doug@oxbridgeprograms.com.
Grades 9-10. Adm: Selective. **Appl**—Fee $0. Due: Rolling. Transcript, essay.
Enr: 60. Intl: 20%.
Type of instruction: Enrich. **Courses:** Span Intl_Relations Marine_Bio/Stud Psych Creative_Writing Studio_Art Art_Hist. **Avg class size:** 14. **Daily hours for:** Classes 4. Homework. Grades.
Intl program focus: Acad.
Fees 2012: Res $7295, 4 wks.
Housing: Dorms.
Est 2008. Ses: 1. **Wks/ses:** 4. Operates July.

Held at the university residence Collegi Major Sant Jordi, this enrichment program for rising high school freshmen and sophomores combines English-medium courses in such areas as creative writing and marine biology with Spanish-medium culture and arts classes. Each student enrolls in a major course that meets six mornings a week and a minor subject that convenes three afternoons weekly. Athletics, beach excursions, field trips to sites of historical interest, theater and concert outings, workshops and appearances by guest speakers complete the program.

SUMMER DISCOVERY
Res — Coed Ages 16-18

Barcelona, Spain.
Contact (Year-round): 1326 Old Northern Blvd, Roslyn, NY 11576. Tel: 516-621-3939.
Fax: 516-625-3438.
www.summerdiscovery.com   E-mail: info@summerdiscovery.com
Bob Musiker, Exec Dir.
Grades 11-PG. Adm: FCFS. Appl—Fee $95. Due: Rolling.
Enr: 84. Enr cap: 100.
Courses: Span. **Daily hours for:** Classes 1½. **College credit.**
Intl program focus: Lang Culture.
Features: Boating Community_Serv Cooking Swim.
Fees 2011: Res $6899-7999 (+airfare), 3-4 wks.
Housing: Hotels. **Swimming:** Ocean Pool.
Inc. **Ses: 2. Wks/ses:** 3-4. Operates June-July.

See program description under Florence, Italy.

SWITZERLAND

LEYSIN AMERICAN SCHOOL
SUMMER IN SWITZERLAND
Res — Coed Ages 8-18

Leysin, 1854 Switzerland. Tel: 41-24-493-4723. Fax: 41-24-493-4889.
www.las.ch/summer   E-mail: sis@las.ch
Paul Magnuson & Mary Field Keenan, Dirs.
Grades 3-12. Adm: FCFS. Appl—Due: Rolling.
Enr: 250.
Type of instruction: Adv Enrich Rem_Eng Rem_Math Rem_Read ESL/TOEFL_Prep SAT/ACT_Prep. **Courses:** Fr Span Comp_Sci Eng Environ_Sci ESL Expository_Writing Math Writing/Journ Crafts Creative_Writing Dance Fine_Arts Music Photog Studio_Art Theater. **Avg class size:** 8. **Daily hours for:** Classes 4. Study 1. Rec 4. **High school credit:** 1.
Intl program focus: Acad Lang Culture. **Travel:** Europe.
Features: Adventure_Travel Bicycle_Tours Exploration Hiking Mountaineering Mtn_Biking Mtn_Trips Riding Rock_Climb Ropes_Crse Survival_Trng White-water_Raft Wilderness_Camp Basketball Equestrian Golf Martial_Arts Soccer Squash Swim Tennis Volleyball Winter_Sports.
Fees 2012: Res SwF4700-13,900, 2-7 wks.
Housing: Houses. **Swimming:** Lake Pond Pool.
Est 1962. Nonprofit. Ses: 7. Wks/ses: 2-7. Operates June-Aug.

Over the summer, LAS offers academic courses for enrichment and credit, recreational activities and cultural excursions. Serving children ages 8-12, SIS Alpine Adventure combines morning classes with group activities in the afternoon. The two-week sessions also include weekend half- and full-day excursions to cultural and recreational sites in nearby Swiss cities. Students in the three-week Alpine Exploration (ages 13-15) and Alpine Challenge (ages 16-18) programs follow a similar schedule of morning classes and afternoon activities; boys and girls may follow the core program or a specialized study of French immersion or ESL. Optional two-day hikes are conducted twice each session for interested students. A three-week theater program is also available for campers ages 13-18.

ST. GEORGE'S SCHOOL SUMMER CAMPS
Res and Day — Coed Ages 12-16

Clarens, 1815 Montreux, Switzerland. Chemin de St Georges 19.
Tel: 41-21-964-34-11. Fax: 41-21-964-49-32.
www.st-georges.ch   E-mail: summercamp@st-georges.ch
Ilya V. Eigenbrot, Prin.
Adm: FCFS. Appl—Fee $0. Due: Rolling.
Type of instruction: Enrich. Courses: Chin Fr ESL.
Intl program focus: Acad Lang.
Features: Tennis.
Fees 2009: Res SwF3750-3900, 2 wks. Day SwF2490, 2 wks.
Housing: Dorms.
Ses: 4. Wks/ses: 2. Operates June-Aug.

This academic program enables students to enroll in intensive French or English courses. International Baccalaureate preparation is a class option for those about to enter the two-year IB Diploma Program. Boys and girls ages 14 and up may receive introductory Mandarin instruction, while all pupils may take tennis lessons once or twice a week; both offerings incur an additional fee.

TASIS SUMMER PROGRAMS
Res and Day — Coed Ages 11-18

Montagnola-Lugano, Switzerland.
Contact (Year-round): c/o TASIS US Office, 112 S Royal St, Alexandria, VA 22314.
Tel: 703-299-8150, 800-442-6005. Fax: 703-299-8157.
www.tasis.com   E-mail: usadmissions@tasis.com
Jim Haley & Marc-Pierre Jansen, Dirs. Student contact: Gianna Kestenholtz.
Grades 6-12. Adm: Somewhat selective. Appl—Fee $0. Due: Rolling. Rec.
Enr: 120-160. Enr cap: 120-160. Intl: 80%. Fac 20. Col/grad students 20. Staff: Admin 6. Couns 15.
Type of instruction: Enrich ESL/TOEFL_Prep. Courses: Fr Ital ESL Expository_Writing Crafts Painting Photog Musical_Theater. Avg class size: 12. Daily hours for: Classes 4. Study 1. Rec 4. Homework. Grades.
Intl program focus: Lang Culture. Home stays avail.
Features: Hiking Mtn_Biking Rock_Climb Sail Basketball Soccer Swim Tennis Volleyball.
Fees 2012: Res SwF5900-7300 (+airfare), 3-4 wks. Day SwF3600-4400 (+airfare), 3-4 wks.
Housing: Dorms. Avg per room/unit: 3. Swimming: Lake Pool.
Est 1955. Nonprofit. Spons: TASIS Foundation. Ses: 2. Wks/ses: 3-4. Operates June-Aug.

TASIS Middle School Program (ages 11-13) and TASIS Summer Program (ages 14-18) balance academic subjects with intensive recreational and athletic activities. Students choose one course of study from a selection that comprises French, Italian, English as a Second Language, the performing and visual arts, and photography. Language instruction emphasizes spoken fluency and includes frequent practice time in the school's language lab. Courses in the performing and arts combine class work with off-campus enrichment trips. Regular homework assignments and compulsory evening study hall reinforce classroom learning. Younger children (ages 4-10) may enroll in Le Chateau des Enfants (see separate listing).

ACADEMIC PROGRAMS FOR STUDENTS WITH LEARNING DISABILITIES

Academic programs for students with learning disabilites are grouped by state, listed alphabetically. Within each state, programs are arranged alphabetically by town and then name. An index beginning on page 41 lists programs by features, as shown in the Table of Contents.

A more complete compilation of schools serving children or young adults with learning disabillities and special needs is available in Porter Sargent's *Guide to Private Special Education.* For details, please visit www.portersargent.com or see page 880.

Academic Programs for Students with Learning Disabilities

ARIZONA

OAK CREEK RANCH SCHOOL SUMMER SCHOOL
Res — Coed Ages 12-19

West Sedona, AZ 86340. PO Box 4329. Tel: 928-634-5571, 877-554-6277.
Fax: 928-634-4915.
www.ocrs.com   E-mail: dwick@ocrs.com
David Wick, Jr., Head.
Grades 7-12. Adm: FCFS. Appl—Due: Rolling.
Enr cap: 60.
Type of instruction: Dev_Read Rem_Read. Courses: Span Comp_Sci Eng Hist Math Sci Govt/Econ Theater. Avg class size: 10. High school credit.
Conditions accepted: ADD ADHD.
Features: Archery Fishing Riding Riflery White-water_Raft Golf Soccer Swim Volleyball Weight_Trng.
Fees 2012: Res $4750, 4 wks.
Housing: Dorms. Swimming: Pool.
Est 1972. Ses: 3. Wks/ses: 4-8. Operates June-Aug.

OCRS' summer session specializes in helping academic underachievers and students with attentional disorders. The program features developmental and remedial reading, English, computer, history, economics and government, math and science. Among OCRS' extracurricular activities are excursions to Fossil Creek, Sunset Crater, Meteor Crater and various Sedona hiking destinations.

GEORGIA

BRANDON HALL SCHOOL SUMMER PROGRAM
Res — Boys Ages 11-18; Day — Coed 10-18

Atlanta, GA 30350. 1701 Brandon Hall Dr. Tel: 770-394-8177. Fax: 770-804-8821.
www.brandonhall.org   E-mail: admissions@brandonhall.org
John Singleton, Pres.
Grades 5-12. Adm: FCFS. Admitted: 98%. Appl—Fee $25. Due: Rolling. Transcript.
Enr: 40. Fac 20. Staff: Admin 8.
Type of instruction: Dev_Read Preview Rem_Eng Rem_Math Rem_Read Rev ESL/TOEFL_Prep SAT/ACT_Prep Study_Skills Tut. LD Services: Mainstream Placement_Testing. Courses: Span Environ_Sci ESL Expository_Writing Govt. Avg class size: 4. Daily hours for: Classes 6. Study 2. Rec 4. High school credit: 1½.
Conditions accepted: ADD ADHD Dx LD.
Fees 2012: Res $2100-6300, 2-6 wks. Day $950-2850, 2-6 wks.
Housing: Dorms.
Est 1959. Nonprofit. Ses: 3. Wks/ses: 2-6. Operates June-July.

Brandon Hall primarily serves intelligent students who are not achieving to potential due to academic difficulties or a lack of motivation. The summer program offers remedial and enrichment courses for most academic subjects. Electives include ESL, SAT Prep and recreational sports. Girls may enroll in the day program only.

IOWA

ST. AMBROSE UNIVERSITY SUMMER TRANSITION PROGRAM
Res and Day — Coed Ages 16-18

Davenport, IA 52803. 518 W Locust St. Tel: 563-333-6275. Fax: 563-333-6243.
http://web.sau.edu/disabilityservices/transitionprogram.htm
E-mail: saddlerryanc@sau.edu
Ryan C. Saddler, Dir.
Grades 12-Col. Adm: FCFS. Admitted: 95%. Prereqs: GPA 1.9. SAT M/CR 600. Appl—Fee
$0. Due: Rolling.
Enr: 16. Enr cap: 16. Non-White: 1%. Fac 1. Prof 1. Staff: Admin 4. Couns 2. Res 1.
Type of instruction: Preview Rev Study_Skills Tut. LD Services: Mainstream. Courses:
Psych Sociol. Avg class size: 10. Daily hours for: Classes 2. Study 4. Rec 2. Home-
work. Tests. Grades. College credit: 3/crse, total 3.
Conditions accepted: ADHD Asp LD.
Features: Basketball Tennis Volleyball.
Fees 2011: Res $3339, 4 wks. Day $2699, 4 wks.
Housing: Dorms. Avg per room/unit: 1. Campus facilities avail.
Est 1990. Nonprofit. Ses: 1. Wks/ses: 4. Operates June-July.

The Summer Transition Program helps students with learning disabilities, attention deficit
disorder or Asperger's syndrome develop the skills necessary for a successful college career.
Depending on the year, students enroll in one three-credit introductory course in either
psychology or sociology. In small-group review sessions each morning, staff members assist
students with writing assignments and test preparation. Afternoon study skills and tutoring
sessions provide instruction in note taking, textbook reading, memorization and other study
skills. Academic orientation and self-advocacy seminars, held twice weekly, help students
access university and community resources and develop skills that will ease the transition to
college life. Students live in residence halls, play recreational sports on campus and visit local
attractions.

MASSACHUSETTS

RIVERVIEW SUMMER
Res — Coed Ages 12-18

East Sandwich, MA 02537. 551 Rte 6A. Tel: 508-888-0489. Fax: 508-833-7001.
www.riverviewschool.org   E-mail: admissions@riverviewschool.org
Grades 6-PG. Adm: FCFS. Prereqs: IQ 70-100. Appl—Due: Rolling.
Enr: 70. Fac 7. Staff: Admin 4. Couns 12.
Type of instruction: Dev_Read Rem_Math Rem_Read. Courses: Eng Math Crafts
Photog. Avg class size: 8. Daily hours for: Classes 4. Rec 5.
Conditions accepted: Dx LD Phys_Impair Speech & Lang TBI.
Features: Kayak Swim.
Fees 2011: Res $6984, 5 wks.
Housing: Dorms. Swimming: Pond Ocean Pool.
Est 1957. Nonprofit. Spons: Riverview School. Ses: 1. Wks/ses: 5. Operates July-Aug.

Riverview enrolls students with complex language, learning and cognitive disabilities and
an IQ between 70 and 100. Applicants should not have any primary emotional or behavioral
issues. Course work builds upon the student's individual skills while maintaining progress
achieved during the previous school year. The program seeks to develop pupil competence and
confidence in the academic, social and independent living areas.

EAGLE HILL SCHOOL SUMMER SESSION
Res — Coed Ages 10-18

Hardwick, MA 01037. 242 Old Petersham Rd, PO Box 116. Tel: 413-477-6000. Fax: 413-477-6837.
www.ehs1.org   E-mail: admission@ehs1.org
Peter J. McDonald, Head.
Adm: FCFS. Prereqs: IQ 90. **Appl**—Due: Rolling.
Enr: 70. **Enr cap:** 70. **Staff:** Admin 12.
Type of instruction: Dev_Read Enrich Rem_Eng Rem_Math Rem_Read Rev Study_Skills Tut. **LD Services:** Placement_Testing. **Courses:** Fr Lat Russ Span Astron Eng Expository_Writing Hist Psych Poetry Creative_Writing Film Fine_Arts Studio_Art Woodworking. **Avg class size:** 5. **Daily hours for:** Classes 4. Rec 6.
Conditions accepted: ADD ADHD Dx LD NLD.
Features: Bicycle_Tours Chess Climbing_Wall Cooking Deep-sea Fishing Fishing Hiking Kayak Mtn_Biking Paintball Ropes_Crse White-water_Raft Wilderness_Camp Woodcraft Basketball Equestrian Golf Soccer Swim Tennis Volleyball Weight_Trng.
Fees 2012: Res $8332 (+$750), 5 wks.
Housing: Dorms. **Swimming:** Pool.
Est 1967. Nonprofit. **Ses:** 1. **Wks/ses:** 5. Operates July-Aug.

Enrolling children with such learning differences as language-based learning disability, nonverbal learning disability and attentional disorders, this program offers a structured curriculum designed to build a basic foundation of academic competence. Various electives are available, and extracurricular and outdoor activities complement the educational program.

CURRY COLLEGE LEARNING ACADEMY
Res — Coed Ages 16-18

Milton, MA 02186. 1071 Blue Hill Ave. Tel: 617-333-2250. Fax: 617-333-2018.
www.curry.edu   E-mail: pal@curry.edu
Janis Peters, Coord.
Grade 12. Adm: Selective. **Appl**—Fee $0. Due: May. Interview, test results, rec.
Enr cap: 14. **Fac 3.** Prof 3. **Staff:** Admin 1. Couns 3.
Avg class size: 14. **Daily hours for:** Classes 6. Study 2. Rec 4. Homework. **College credit:** 1.
Conditions accepted: ADD ADHD Dx LD.
Features: Swim.
Fees 2012: Res $1600, 1 wk.
Housing: Dorms. **Swimming:** Pool.
Est 1996. Nonprofit. **Ses:** 2. **Wks/ses:** 1. Operates June-July.

This precollege program serves rising high school seniors diagnosed with a language-based learning disability or an attentional disorder. Students develop strategies for studying and taking tests, reading comprehension, written communication, time management, active listening and taking notes. Instructors also help familiarize students with the college search process, Web-based resources and assistive technologies. Students take part in various informal and planned activities, among them a tour of Boston. Applicants should possess average to above-average cognitive ability.

LINDEN HILL SCHOOL SUMMER PROGRAM
Res and Day — Coed Ages 7-17

Northfield, MA 01360. 154 S Mountain Rd. Tel: 413-498-2906. Fax: 413-498-2908.
www.lindenhs.org   E-mail: office@lindenhs.org
Jason Russell, Dir.
Student contact: Jennifer Russell, E-mail: jerussell@lindenhs.org.

Adm: Somewhat selective. **Appl**—Due: Rolling. Transcript, test scores, 3 teacher recs.
Enr: 44. **Enr cap:** 50. Intl: 11%. Non-White: 20%. **Fac 14. **K-12 staff 14. **Staff:** Admin 5. Couns 8.
Type of instruction: Dev_Read Enrich Rem_Eng Rem_Math Rem_Read Rev ESL/ TOEFL_Prep SAT/ACT_Prep Study_Skills. **Courses:** Environ_Sci ESL Expository_Writing Lang Speech Writing/Journ Crafts Creative_Writing Fine_Arts Music Theater. **Avg class size:** 3. **Daily hours for:** Classes 3. Rec 9. **High school credit.**
Conditions accepted: ADD ADHD Dx LD Speech & Lang.
Features: Aquatics Archery Bicycle_Tours Canoe Climbing_Wall Conservation Cooking Cruises Exploration Farm Fishing Hiking Mtn_Biking Riding Rock_Climb White-water_ Raft Basketball Cross-country Equestrian Golf Soccer Softball Swim Tennis.
Fees 2011: Res $6650-7880 (+$250), 4 wks. Day $4700 (+$100), 4 wks.
Housing: Dorms. **Swimming:** Lake Pool. Campus facilities avail.
Est 1998. Nonprofit. **Ses:** 1. **Wks/ses:** 4. Operates July-Aug.

Linden Hill's program consists of morning academics, afternoon and evening traditional camp activities, and weekend overnight trips. Focus courses provide review, preview, enrichment or, in some cases, academic credit. Each camper selects three such classes each morning from the following group: language training, organizational and study skills, mathematics, communication skills, ESL, creative arts, drama, penmanship, reading, videography, woodshop and driver education. Various activities and off-campus weekend trips round out the program.

LANDMARK SCHOOL SUMMER PROGRAMS
Res — Coed Ages 13-20; Day — Coed 7-20

Prides Crossing, MA 01965. 429 Hale St, PO Box 227. Tel: 978-236-3000.
Fax: 978-927-7268.
www.landmarkschool.org/summer-programs
E-mail: admission@landmarkschool.org
Carolyn J. Orsini Nelson, Dir.
Student contact: Emily Kahn, E-mail: ekahn@landmarkschool.org.
Grades 1-12. Adm: Selective. Prereqs: IQ 90. **Appl**—Fee $150. Due: Rolling.
Enr: 110. **Enr cap:** 110. **Staff:** Admin 8.
Type of instruction: Dev_Read Enrich Rem_Eng Rem_Math Rem_Read Rev Study_ Skills Tut. **LD Services:** Placement_Testing. **Courses:** Eng Math Photog AV_Production Visual_Arts. **Avg class size:** 6. **Daily hours for:** Classes 3. Study 1. Rec 3.
Conditions accepted: Dx LD.
Features: Kayak Ropes_Crse.
Fees 2012: Res $7775, 4-5 wks. Day $4625-5875, 4-5 wks.
Housing: Dorms.
Est 1971. Nonprofit. **Ses:** 2. **Wks/ses:** 4-5. Operates June-Aug.

Landmark's summer program, which combines academic skill development with recreational activities, serves students of average to above-average intelligence who have been diagnosed with a language-based learning disability. Instructors customize each pupil's program to improve reading, writing, spelling and study skills. Elementary and middle school boys and girls attend a five-week academic program that features two classes and a daily one-on-one tutorial; for an additional fee, students may take part in exploration or practical arts afternoon offerings. The four-week high school session includes four hourlong academic classes and a study hall. Residential life for those in grades 8-12 consists of after-school activities, weeknight events and weekend trips. For an extra charge, day pupils may join boarders in such after-school pursuits as marine science, visual arts, short-film production, and health and fitness training.

NEW YORK

DUNNABECK AT KILDONAN
Res and Day — Coed Ages 8-16

Amenia, NY 12501. 425 Morse Hill Rd. Tel: 845-373-8111. Fax: 845-373-9793.
www.kildonan.org   E-mail: admissions@kildonan.org
Benjamin N. Powers, Head. Student contact: David Tuttle.
Adm: FCFS. **Appl**—Fee $30. Due: Rolling.
Enr: 60. **Staff:** Admin 50.
Type of instruction: Rem_Eng Rem_Math Rem_Read Tut. **Courses:** Computers Expository_Writing Ceramics Crafts Media.
Conditions accepted: Dx.
Features: Aquatics Archery Boating Climbing_Wall Hiking Mountaineering Mtn_Biking Riding Rock_Climb Sail Woodcraft Equestrian Martial_Arts Swim Water-skiing Watersports.
Fees 2011: Res $9500 (+$500), 6 wks. Day $4800-7200 (+$250), 6 wks.
Housing: Dorms. **Swimming:** Pool. Campus facilities avail.
Est 1955. Nonprofit. **Spons:** Kildonan School. **Ses:** 1. **Wks/ses:** 6. Operates June-Aug.

Dunnabeck specializes in assisting intelligent children who are underachieving or failing in their academic work because of dyslexia. Teachers use the Orton-Gillingham approach while combining work in reading, writing and spelling. All tutoring is done individually, with each student receiving an hourlong daily lesson. Boys and girls engage in such extracurricular pursuits as horseback riding, mountain biking, watersports and arts offerings.

MAPLEBROOK SCHOOL SUMMER PROGRAM
Res — Coed Ages 10-18

Amenia, NY 12501. 5142 Rte 22. Tel: 845-373-9511. Fax: 845-373-7029.
www.maplebrookschool.org   E-mail: admissions@maplebrookschool.org
Student contact: Jennifer Scully.
Adm: Selective. Admitted: 40%. Prereqs: IQ 70-90. **Appl**—Fee $0. Due: Rolling.
Enr: 50. **Enr cap:** 50. Intl: 20%. Non-White: 40%.
Type of instruction: Dev_Read Enrich Rem_Eng Rem_Math Rem_Read Rev Study_Skills. **Courses:** Expository_Writing Speech Crafts Creative_Writing Fine_Arts Music Theater. **Avg class size:** 6. **Daily hours for:** Classes 3. Study 1. Rec 4. Grades.
Conditions accepted: ADD ADHD LD.
Features: Aquatics Cooking Hiking Wilderness_Camp Woodcraft Basketball Softball Swim Tennis Watersports.
Fees 2011: Res $8000, 6 wks.
Housing: Dorms. **Swimming:** Lake Pool. Campus facilities avail.
Est 1945. Nonprofit. **Ses:** 1. **Wks/ses:** 6. Operates July-Aug.

Maplebrook provides a structured academic environment for children with attentional disorders and other learning disabilities. Students attend classes and receive individualized tutoring in remedial English, reading and math, while also learning basic computer skills. Boys and girls attend enrichment classes in drama, dance, music and art during the afternoon. Cycling, horseback riding and swimming are among the evening activities. Off-campus trips include hiking and camping treks and day trips to local attractions and New York City.

THE GOW SCHOOL SUMMER PROGRAM
Res and Day — Coed Ages 8-16

South Wales, NY 14139. 2491 Emery Rd, PO Box 85. Tel: 716-652-3450.
  Fax: 716-687-2003.

www.gow.org **E-mail: summer@gow.org**
Eric Bray, Dir.
Adm: FCFS. **Appl**—Due: Rolling.
Enr: 125. **Enr cap:** 125. **Fac 37. Staff:** Admin 8. Couns 15.
Type of instruction: Adv Dev_Read Enrich Preview Rem_Eng Rem_Math Rem_Read Rev SAT/ACT_Prep Study_Skills Tut. **LD Services:** Acad_Instruction Placement_Testing Tut. **Courses:** Environ_Sci ESL Speech Writing/Journ Crafts Creative_Writing Dance Drama Filmmaking Fine_Arts Media Music Painting Studio_Art. **Avg class size:** 5. **Daily hours for:** Classes 4. Rec 5.
Conditions accepted: ADD ADHD Dx LD APD Dg.
Features: Archery Bicycle_Tours Canoe Chess Climbing_Wall Exploration Hiking Mountaineering Mtn_Biking Riding Rock_Climb Ropes_Crse Wilderness_Camp Wilderness_ Canoe Baseball Basketball Cross-country Equestrian Football Golf Lacrosse Roller_ Hockey Soccer Softball Swim Tennis Volleyball.
Fees 2012: Res $6950 (+$250), 5 wks. Day **$3600-4500, 5 wks.** Aid 2007 (Need): $60,000.
Housing: Dorms. **Swimming:** Pool Stream.
Est 1990. Nonprofit. **Ses:** 1. **Wks/ses:** 5. Operates June-July.

Developed for students who have experienced previous academic difficulties, Gow's program combines morning classes with traditional camp activities and weekend overnight trips. Each camper takes four courses for review, preview or enrichment in such areas as reconstructive language, organizational and study skills, computer literacy and communicational skills. Activities include various sports, arts and crafts, horseback riding, trail hiking, golf, soccer and a ropes course.

TEXAS

CHARIS HILLS SUMMER CAMP
Res — Coed Ages 6-18

Sunset, TX 76270. 498 Faulkner Rd. Tel: 940-964-2145, 888-681-2173.
Fax: 940-964-2147.
www.charishills.org **E-mail: info@charishills.org**
Rand Southard, Dir.
Student contact: Colleen Southard, E-mail: colleen@charishills.org.
Grades 1-12. Adm: FCFS. **Appl**—Fee $0. Due: Rolling.
Enr: 50. **Enr cap:** 60. Intl: 2%. Non-White: 6%. **Fac 4.** Col/grad students 4. **Staff:** Admin 5. Couns 40.
Type of instruction: Dev_Read Rem_Eng Rem_Math Rem_Read Rev Tut. **LD Services:** Tut. **Courses:** Astron Lang Sci Writing/Journ Crafts Creative_Writing Dance Music Photog Theater. **Avg class size:** 7. **Daily hours for:** Classes 1. Rec 7.
Conditions accepted: ADD ADHD Asp Au Dx LD.
Features: Aquatics Archery Boating Canoe Climbing_Wall Conservation Exploration Fishing Hiking Kayak Rappelling Riding Riflery Rock_Climb Wilderness_Camp Woodcraft Baseball Basketball Football Golf Soccer Softball Swim Volleyball Weight_Trng Snorkeling.
Fees 2012: Res $1190-2380, 1-2 wks. Aid 2009 (Need): $30,000.
Housing: Cabins Houses. Avg per room/unit: 9. **Swimming:** Lake. Campus facilities avail.
Est 2006. Nonprofit. Nondenom Christian. **Ses:** 7. **Wks/ses:** 1-2. Operates June-Aug.

Combining academics and recreation, Charis Hills seeks to promote social, emotional and physical growth in children with learning differences. In a Christian setting, students receive individualized instruction in reading, writing and language skills. Recreational activities emphasize self-esteem development and the acquisition of lifelong skills in a noncompetitive environment.

VIRGINIA

LITTLE KESWICK SCHOOL SUMMER PROGRAM
Res — Boys Ages 10-15

Keswick, VA 22947. Rte 731, PO Box 24. Tel: 434-295-0457. Fax: 434-977-1892.
www.littlekeswickschool.net   E-mail: lksinfo@littlekeswickschool.net
Marc J. Columbus, Head.
Adm: FCFS. **Appl**—Fee $350. Due: Rolling. Psychological evaluation.
Enr: 34. **Enr cap:** 34. **Fac 5. Staff:** Admin 5.
Type of instruction: Enrich Rem_Eng Rem_Math Rem_Read. **Courses:** Creative_Writing Fine_Arts. **Avg class size:** 7. Homework. Tests. Grades. **High school credit.**
Conditions accepted: ADD ADHD Dx ED LD. **Therapy:** Art Occup Psych Speech.
Features: Climbing_Wall Fishing Hiking Riding Woodcraft Basketball Equestrian Lacrosse Soccer Swim Watersports.
Fees 2012: Res $9850, 5 wks.
Housing: Dorms. **Swimming:** Pool. Campus facilities avail.
Est 1963. Inc. **Ses:** 1. **Wks/ses:** 5. Operates July-Aug.

Little Keswick serves boys of low-average to superior intelligence who have a history of learning, emotional or behavioral difficulties. The structured program features a selection of traditional recreational activities—among them woodcraft, riding, hiking, swimming and sports—in addition to a strong therapeutic component. While LKS gives admission preference to year-round students, boys may enroll for the summer program only.

OAKLAND SCHOOL AND CAMP
Res — Coed Ages 8-14; Day — Coed 6-14

Keswick, VA 22947. Boyd Tavern. Tel: 434-293-9059. Fax: 434-296-8930.
www.oaklandschool.net/summer-program   E-mail: information@oaklandschool.net
Carol Williams, Dir.
Grades 1-8. Adm: Selective. **Appl**—Due: Rolling. Transcript, achievement test scores, interview.
Enr: 125. **Enr cap:** 135. **Fac 20.** K-12 staff 20. **Staff:** Admin 4.
Type of instruction: Dev_Read Rem_Eng Rem_Math Rem_Read Rev Study_Skills.
Courses: Expository_Writing Crafts Music Photog. **Avg class size:** 5. **Daily hours for:** Classes 3½. Rec 9. Tests.
Conditions accepted: ADD ADHD Dx LD.
Features: Archery Cooking Fishing Hiking Riding Wilderness_Camp Basketball Equestrian Golf Lacrosse Soccer Softball Swim Tennis Volleyball.
Fees 2012: Res $8200, 6 wks. Day $4700, 6 wks.
Housing: Cabins Dorms. Avg per room/unit: 6. **Swimming:** Pool River Stream. Campus facilities avail.
Est 1950. Nonprofit. **Ses:** 1. **Wks/ses:** 6. Operates June-Aug.

Oakland's highly individualized program, which features one-on-one instruction, emphasizes the improvement of reading skills. Courses cover reading, English composition, phonics, word analysis, math and study skills. The summer session serves boys and girls with learning disabilities (including nonverbal learning disabilities), visual and auditory processing disorders, attentional disorders and organizational difficulties. Recreational activities on the 450-acre campus include swimming, sports, art and music instruction, and horseback riding.

ACADEMIC PROGRAMS—
SPECIALIZED

Specialized summer academic boarding programs are arranged alphabetically by name. The Table of Contents lists the subject areas presented, and an index beginning on page 160 lists the programs under each of those subjects.

For academic-year programs, see *The Handbook of Private Schools,* an annual descriptive survey of independent education, and *Schools Abroad of Interest to Americans,* a worldwide guide to elementary and secondary schools with English-speaking programs. For details, please visit www.portersargent.com or see page 880.

INDEX BY FOCUS

AFRICAN-AMERICAN STUDIES

AGRICULTURE

ARCHAEOLOGY

ARCHITECTURE

ASTRONOMY

BUSINESS & FINANCE

CAREER

COLLEGE PREPARATION

COMMUNICATIONS & JOURNALISM

COMPUTER SCIENCE

CULTURAL & GLOBAL STUDIES

DEBATE & PUBLIC SPEAKING

ECOLOGY & ENVIRONMENTAL

ECONOMICS

EDUCATION

ENGINEERING

ENGINEERING *(CONT.)*

ESL *(CONT.)*
College du Leman **[H]**...Versoix, Geneva, SWITZERLAND....202
   (Res — Coed Ages 8-18)
Le Chaperon Rouge ....Crans-sur-Sierre, Valais, SWITZERLAND....232
   (Res & Day — Coed Ages 6-16)
British Intl-Phuket *(Res — Coed Ages 8-15; Day — Coed 7-15)*... Phuket, THAILAND....190

EXPOSITORY WRITING
Carleton Writing *(Res — Coed Ages 16-17)* **[C]** ....Northfield, MN....194

FORENSIC SCIENCE
UMiami-Scholar-Acad *(Res — Coed Ages 16-17)* **[CH]** ....Coral Gables, FL....290
Natl Student Leader *(Res — Coed Ages 14-18)* **[C]**..................................... Chicago, IL....248
McDaniel-Forensic *(Res & Day — Coed Ages 16-18)* **[C]** .... Westminster, MD....238
MSU Forensic Sci *(Res — Coed Ages 12-15)*......................................East Lansing, MI....240

GOVERNMENT & POLITICAL SCIENCE
Junior State of Amer *(Res — Coed Ages 14-18)* **[H]** ....San Mateo, CA....229
Choate-JFK Inst *(Res & Day — Coed Ages 15-18)*................................. Wallingford, CT....199
Miss Porter's-Jr UN *(Res — Girls Ages 12-15)*.....................................Farmington, CT....245
Bill of Rights Inst *(Res — Coed Ages 16-17)* **[C]** .... Washington, DC....186
Georgetown-Intl Rel *(Res — Coed Ages 15-18)*................................. Washington, DC....221
St Albans-Publ Serv *(Res & Day — Coed Ages 16-18)* .... Washington, DC....260
Natl Student Leader *(Res — Coed Ages 14-18)* **[C]**.................................... Chicago, IL....248
U of MS-Lott Inst *(Res — Coed Ages 17-18)* **[C]** ....University, MS....292
Duke TIP-Field Stud *(Res — Coed Ages 15-18)* ....Durham, NC....210
UVA High Sch Leaders *(Res — Coed Ages 16-18)* **[C]**....................Charlottesville, VA....299

HISTORY
Wm & Mary Pre-Col *(Res — Coed Ages 16-18)* **[C]**...........................Williamsburg, VA....203

INTERNATIONAL RELATIONS
Auburn World Affairs *(Res — Coed Ages 15-18)*..Auburn, AL....182
Yale U Ivy Scholars *(Res — Coed Ages 15-18)*.....................................New Haven, CT....305
Georgetown-Intl Rel *(Res — Coed Ages 15-18)*.................................. Washington, DC....221
UMiami-Scholar-Acad *(Res — Coed Ages 16-17)* **[CH]** ....Coral Gables, FL....290
Natl Student Leader *(Res — Coed Ages 14-18)* **[C]**.................................... Chicago, IL....248
Carleton Reasoning *(Res — Coed Ages 15-18)* **[C]** ....Northfield, MN....195
Duke TIP-Field Stud *(Res — Coed Ages 15-18)* ....Durham, NC....210

LANGUAGE IMMERSION

LANGUAGE IMMERSION *(CONT.)*

LAW

LEADERSHIP

LEADERSHIP *(CONT.)*

MARINE SCIENCE & OCEANOGRAPHY

MATH

MEDICINE & HEALTHCARE

PALEONTOLOGY

RELIGIOUS STUDIES

SCIENCE

SPEECH

STUDY SKILLS

VETERINARY MEDICINE

Academic Programs—Specialized

ABBEY ROAD SUMMER PROGRAMS
Res — Coed Ages 14-19

Los Angeles, CA 90025. 1850 Camden Ave, Ste 12. Tel: 310-473-7300, 888-462-2239.
  Fax: 310-943-1592.
www.goabbeyroad.com   E-mail: info@goabbeyroad.com
Arthur Kian, Dir.
Grades 9-PG (younger if qualified). Adm: FCFS. Appl—Due: Rolling.
Type of instruction: ESL/TOEFL_Prep SAT/ACT_Prep Tut. Courses: Creative_Writing
  Fine_Arts Photog. Avg class size: 9. Daily hours for: Classes 3½. Homework. Tests.
  Grades. High school & college credit.
Intl program focus: Acad Lang Culture. Locations: CA MA Canada Europe. Home stays
  avail.
Focus: Col_Prep Environ_Sci Fr Ital Span. Features: Aquatics Boating Cooking Explora-
  tion Kayak Soccer Swim Tennis Volleyball Watersports.
Fees 2012: Res $3995-7895 (+airfare), 2-4 wks. Aid (Merit).
Housing: Dorms. Swimming: Pool.
Inc. Ses: 16. Wks/ses: 2-4. Operates June-Aug.

Abbey Road conducts a number of summer programs in Europe designed to facilitate cross-cultural understanding and enrichment through cultural immersion, intensive language study, exposure to new academic subjects, travel opportunities and recreational pursuits. Pupils may study French in Aix-en-Provence, Antibes, Beaulieu, Cannes (which also features precollege work), Cassis and St-Laurent, France; Italian in Amalfi, Bologna (which also includes precollege work) and Florence, Italy; and Spanish in Cadiz and Sanlucar, Spain. A separate program enables boys and girls to travel from the Italian cities of Athens, Rome and Florence to a final destination of Paris, France. This cultural immersion program serves as a hands-on study of Western civilization. In addition to the European sessions, Abbey Road conducts a French-immersion program in Quebec, Canada, as well as two programs in the US for American students: a precollege enrichment and SAT preparation session in Boston, MA, and an environmental studies program in Santa Barbara, CA.

ACADEMIC PROGRAMS INTERNATIONAL
Res — Coed Ages 18 and up

Austin, TX 78746. 301 Camp Craft Rd. Tel: 512-600-8900, 800-844-4124.
  Fax: 512-600-8999.
www.academicintl.com   E-mail: api@academicintl.com
Grade 12. Adm: FCFS.
Type of instruction: Preview. College credit.
Intl program focus: Lang Culture. Locations: Europe Mexico/Central_America.
Focus: Fr Ital Span.
Fees 2010: Res $3800-12,750, 3-14 wks.
Ses: 55. Wks/ses: 3-14. Operates May-Aug.

API provides travel, educational and cultural opportunities for American students in Argentina, Costa Rica, England, France, Ireland, Italy and Mexico. Certain language immersion programs bear college credit. In addition to language immersion, some programs enable students to choose from classes in the liberal and studio arts, the humanities, business, history and science.

ACADIA INSTITUTE OF OCEANOGRAPHY
MARINE SCIENCE CAMP
Res — Coed Ages 10-19

Seal Harbor, ME 04675. PO Box 285.
Contact (Sept-May): PO Box 8308, Ann Arbor, MI 48107.
Year-round Tel: 207-276-9825, 800-375-0058. Fax: 207-276-9825.
www.acadiainstitute.com   E-mail: info@acadiainstitute.com
Sheryl C. Gilmore, Exec Dir.
Adm: Somewhat selective. Admitted: 98%. **Appl**—Fee $0. Due: Rolling. Sci teacher rec.
Enr: 42. Enr cap: 35-44. Intl: 10%. **Fac 14.** Prof 3. Col/grad students 3. K-12 staff 8. **Staff:** Admin 2.
Type of instruction: Adv. **Courses:** Ecol Environ_Sci Geol Marine_Bio/Stud. **College credit:** 3/crse, total 3.
Focus: Oceanog. **Features:** Hiking Basketball Swim Tennis.
Fees 2012: Res $1100-2350 (+$60-80), 1-2 wks.
Housing: Dorms. Avg per room/unit: 10-18. **Swimming:** Lake Ocean. Campus facilities avail.
Est 1975. Inc. **Ses: 5. Wks/ses:** 1-2. Operates June-Aug.

Located on the southern end of Mount Desert Island, Marine Science Camp consists of an extensive program of marine studies. Student oceanographers work closely with their instructors in exploring the marine environment—from offshore dredging for invertebrates to whale and seal counts. AIO conducts introductory (ages 10-12), intermediate (ages 12-15) and advanced (ages 15-19) sessions.

AIGLON COLLEGE SUMMER SCHOOL
Res — Coed Ages 10-16

Chesieres-Villars, 1885 Switzerland. Ave Centrale. Tel: 41-24-496-6171.
Fax: 41-24-496-6162.
www.aiglon.ch/vacation-courses/summer-school
E-mail: vacationcourses@aiglon.ch
Adm: FCFS. **Appl**—Due: Rolling. Teacher rec.
Enr: 201. Enr cap: 204. Fac 22. Staff: Admin 2. Couns 68.
Type of instruction: Enrich. **Courses:** Circus_Skills Crafts Dance Music Painting. **Avg class size:** 10. **Daily hours for:** Classes 2½. Rec 5.
Intl program focus: Lang.
Focus: ESL Fr Ger Span. **Features:** Archery Bicycle_Tours Canoe Climbing_Wall Cooking Hiking Kayak Mountaineering Mtn_Biking Mtn_Trips Outdoor_Ed Rappelling Rock_Climb Ropes_Crse Sail White-water_Raft Badminton Baseball Basketball Field_Hockey Rugby Soccer Softball Swim Tennis Watersports.
Fees 2012: Res SwF7200 (+SwF300), 3 wks.
Housing: Dorms Lodges. **Swimming:** Lake Pool.
Est 1974. Nonprofit. **Ses: 1. Wks/ses:** 3. Operates July.

This British-style boarding school combines morning language instruction in English, French, German or Spanish with afternoon sports and other activities. Lessons, which are offered at introductory, intermediate and advanced levels, place emphasis on both conversational and written skills development. Each student receives approximately 48 hours of language instruction during the session. Often adventurous in nature, activities make significant use of the school's surroundings. Staff schedule a camping trip and several cultural excursions.

AMERICAN INTERNATIONAL SCHOOL-SALZBURG
SUMMER LANGUAGE PROGRAM
Res and Day — Coed Ages 10-19

Salzburg, 5020 Austria. c/o American International School-Salzburg, Moosstrasse 106. Tel: 43-662-824617. Fax: 43-662-824555.
www.ais-salzburg.at E-mail: office@ais-salzburg.at
Paul McLean, Head.
Adm: FCFS. **Appl**—Fee $0. Due: Rolling.
Enr: 90. **Fac** 7. **Staff:** Admin 4. Couns 4.
Type of instruction: Rem_Eng Rem_Read. **Avg class size:** 10. **Daily hours for:** Classes 5. Study 2. Rec 5. **High school credit.**
Intl program focus: Lang.
Focus: ESL Ger. **Features:** Bicycle_Tours Climbing_Wall Hiking Mtn_Trips Sail Whitewater_Raft Basketball Swim Tennis Ping-Pong.
Fees 2011: Res €1665-4160 (+€120), 2-6 wks. Day €985-2500, 2-6 wks.
Housing: Dorms. Avg per room/unit: 2-4. **Swimming:** Lake Pool.
Est 1977. Nonprofit. **Ses:** 3. **Wks/ses:** 2-6. Operates July-Aug.

Pupils from around the world enroll in intensive German or English language immersion courses at AIS-Salzburg. Participants attend classes for five hours daily, then engage in cultural and athletic activities each afternoon. Weekends provide time for excursions to historically and culturally significant sites in Munich, Innsbruck and the nearby Alps.

AMERISPAN STUDY ABROAD
TEENAGER STUDY ABROAD AND SUMMER CAMPS
Res — Coed Ages 13-18

Philadelphia, PA 19107. 1334 Walnut St, 6th Fl. Tel: 215-751-1100, 800-879-6640.
Fax: 215-751-1986.
www.amerispan.com E-mail: info@amerispan.com
John Slocum, Pres.
Adm: FCFS. **Appl**—Due: Rolling.
Type of instruction: Enrich. **Courses:** Fine_Arts Theater.
Intl program focus: Lang Culture. **Locations:** Africa Asia Canada Europe Mexico/Central_America South_America. Home stays avail.
Focus: Fr Ger Ital Span. **Features:** Cooking Badminton Basketball Soccer Volleyball.
Fees 2012: Res $415-6820 (+airfare), 1-4 wks.
Housing: Dorms Houses.
Est 1993. Inc. **Ses:** 31. **Wks/ses:** 1-4. Operates June-Aug.

AmeriSpan's immersion programs expose teenagers to foreign languages both in the classroom and the community. In addition to daily classroom study, students participate in organized sports and excursions or explore their surroundings independently. Three program options offer varying levels of schoolwork and supervision. Residential summer camps include dormitory living, structured activities and strict curfews. Students in the supervised programs live with host families with some supervision. Unsupervised programs allow mature 16- to 18-year-olds to participate in AmeriSpan's adult program with no curfews or organized activities.

ANDEO INTERNATIONAL HOMESTAYS
HIGH SCHOOL IMMERSION PROGRAMS
Res — Coed Ages 14-18

Portland, OR 97204. 620 SW 5th Ave, Ste 625. Tel: 503-274-1776, 800-274-6007.
Fax: 503-274-9004.
www.andeo.org E-mail: info@andeo.org

Melinda Samis, Dir. Student contact: Andrea Bailey, E-mail: andrea@andeo.org.
Adm: FCFS. **Appl**—Fee $0. Due: Rolling.
Staff: Admin 2.
Type of instruction: Enrich. **Courses:** Creative_Writing. **Avg class size:** 4. **Daily hours for:** Classes 4. Rec 4.
Intl program focus: Lang Culture. **Locations:** Europe Mexico/Central_America. Home stays avail.
Focus: Fr Ger Span. **Features:** Adventure_Travel.
Fees 2012: Res $1225-3000 (+airfare), 2-6 wks.
Housing: Houses.
Inc. **Ses:** 8. **Wks/ses:** 2-6. Operates June-Aug.

Andeo's Immersion Programs, which operate in France, Spain, Mexico and Germany, provide students with language-study opportunities and cultural connections. Course work takes place in an accredited university or a language institute whose curriculum conforms to university standards. Pupils study in one city to experience the local culture and live with a host family. The itinerary includes overnight excursions and day trips to sites of historical and cultural interest. Applicants must have two years of previous study in the target language.

ARIANA SUMMER COURSES
Res — Coed Ages 6-20

St Gallen, 9000 Switzerland. Hohenweg 60. Tel: 41-71-277-92-91.
Fax: 41-71-277-72-53.
www.ariana.ch   E-mail: info@ariana.ch
Monika A. Schmid, Dir.
Adm: FCFS. **Appl**—Due: Rolling.
Enr cap: 12.
Locations: Europe.
Focus: ESL Fr Ger. **Features:** Bicycle_Tours Hiking Riding Basketball Golf Soccer Swim Tennis Water-skiing.
Fees 2012: Res SwF1330-2100, 1 wk.
Housing: Dorms. **Swimming:** Lake Pool.
Est 1982. Ses: 4. **Wks/ses:** 4-7. Operates June-Aug.

Ariana offers summer language immersion programs in Seefeld, Austria, and at three Swiss locations: St. Gallen, Arosa and Lenk. Students participate in three lessons daily and two hours of conversation per week in either French, German or ESL. The programs include various recreational activities, and Ariana schedules organized excursions to sites of historical and cultural interest.

ARIZONA STATE UNIVERSITY
CRONKITE SUMMER JOURNALISM INSTITUTE
Res — Coed Ages 15-18

Phoenix, AZ 85004. 555 N Central Ave. Tel: 480-965-5251.
http://cronkite.asu.edu/beyond/hs_inst.php   E-mail: anita.luera@asu.edu
Anita F. Luera, Dir.
Grades 10-PG. **Adm:** Selective. **Appl**—Due: Mar. Transcript, rec, 3 writing samples (print prgm).
Type of instruction: Enrich.
Focus: Writing/Journ.
Fees 2010: Free. Res 2 wks.
Housing: Dorms.
Nonprofit. **Ses:** 1. **Wks/ses:** 2. Operates May-June.

Conducted by the Walter Cronkite School of Journalism and Mass Communication at

ASU's downtown campus, the Summer Journalism Institute comprises two tracks: the Broadcast Institute and the Print Journalism Institute. Both institutes seek to prepare high schoolers for college journalism studies while letting them explore future career options in a college setting. The Broadcast Institute features classes on writing, reporting, videography and editing; the opportunity to anchor, report, write, produce and direct a newscast; chances to meet and converse with broadcast professionals; and visits to local radio and television stations. The Print Journalism Institute includes classes on writing, editing, layout, design and photojournalism; discussions with professional journalists who provide advice on media careers; production of a newspaper; and visits to Phoenix media outlets.

ARIZONA STATE UNIVERSITY
JOAQUIN BUSTOZ MATH-SCIENCE HONORS PROGRAM
Res — Coed Ages 15-18

Tempe, AZ 85287. PO Box 871904. Tel: 480-965-1690. Fax: 480-965-0333.
www.asu.edu/mshp   E-mail: mshp@asu.edu
Cynthia Barragan Romero, Coord.
Grades 11-PG. Adm: Selective. Priority: URM. Prereqs: GPA 3.25. **Appl**—Fee $0. Due: Mar. Transcript, personal statement, rec.
Type of instruction: Adv Tut Undergrad. **Daily hours for:** Classes 6. Homework. Tests. Grades. **College credit:** 3-4/crse, total 6.
Focus: Math Sci.
Fees 2012: Free (in-state residents). Res 5-8 wks.
Housing: Dorms.
Est 1985. Nonprofit. **Ses:** 3. **Wks/ses:** 5-8. Operates May-Aug.

MSHP provides opportunities for Arizona residents from backgrounds traditionally underrepresented in the fields of math and science to begin university-level instruction while still in high school. Two five-week sessions offer three college credits, and an eight-week course yields four credits. Pupils complete daily homework, take quizzes twice a week and take weekly tests. Faculty provide tutoring and problem-solving sessions in the evening, and a variety of academic presentations and activities are scheduled during each session. High school graduates may enroll only if they are preparing for freshman year at Arizona State.

ASIAN AMERICAN JOURNALISTS ASSOCIATION
J CAMP
Res — Coed Ages 16-18

New Orleans, LA.
Contact (Year-round): 1182 Market St, Ste 320, San Francisco, CA 94102.
Tel: 415-346-2051. Fax: 415-346-6343.
www.aaja.org/programs/for_students/journalism_trainings/j_camp
E-mail: programs@aaja.org
Student contact: Nao Vang.
Grades 10-12. Adm: Very selective. Admitted: 10%. **Appl**—Fee $0. Due: Mar. Transcript, test scores, essays, rec.
Enr: 42.
Type of instruction: Enrich. **Courses:** Media Photog.
Focus: Writing/Journ.
Fees 2012: Free. Res 1 wk.
Housing: Dorms.
Est 2001. Ses: 1. **Wks/ses:** 1. Operates June.

Designed to confront the lack of diversity in journalism, J Camp assembles a multicultural group of high school students for six days of intensive journalism training. The curriculum consists of interactive workshops, hands-on projects, guest speakers and field trips. Students learn from experienced professional journalists and receive training in writing, photography, television broadcasting, online media and reporting. The program is not restricted to Asian-American students.

ASPIRE BY API
Res — Coed Ages 14-18

Austin, TX 78746. 301 Camp Craft Rd, Ste 100. Tel: 512-600-8977, 877-600-8977. Fax: 512-600-8999.
www.aspirebyapi.com **E-mail: hello@aspirebyapi.com**
Courtney Link, Dir.
Grades 9-PG (younger if qualified). Adm: Selective. Prereqs: GPA 3.0. **Appl**—Fee $0. Due: Rolling. Transcript, rec.
Enr: 25. Enr cap: 25.
Type of instruction: Enrich Undergrad. **Courses:** Fine_Arts Media Painting Photog Studio_Art Theater. **Daily hours for:** Classes 3½. Study 1. Rec 3½. Homework. Tests. Grades. **College credit:** 6.
Intl program focus: Acad Lang Culture. **Locations:** Europe Mexico/Central_America. Home stays avail.
Focus: Fr Ital Span. **Features:** Adventure_Travel Canoe Community_Serv Cooking Exploration Hiking Kayak Outdoor_Ed Ropes_Crse Swim Watersports.
Fees 2012: Res $1990-6690 (+airfare), 1-4 wks. Aid (Merit & Need).
Housing: Apartments Dorms Hotels Houses. **Swimming:** Lake Pool River.
Spons: Academic Programs International. **Ses:** 18. **Wks/ses:** 1-4. Operates June-July.

Aspire by API provides a variety of summer educational and cultural opportunities abroad for high school students. Language-immersion and cultural programs—some of which carry college credit—operate in Costa Rica, England, France, Ireland, Italy and Spain. In addition to language immersion in the classroom, certain programs feature home stay living accommodations that accelerate language learning. Cultural classes teach students about the host country's art and traditions.

ASTROCAMP
Res — Coed Ages 8-17

Idyllwild, CA 92549. 26800 Saunders Meadow Rd, PO Box 3399. Tel: 951-659-6062. Fax: 951-659-9843.
Contact (Sept-May): Tel: 909-625-6194, Fax: 909-625-7305.
Year-round Toll-free: 800-645-1423.
www.guideddiscoveries.org **E-mail: info@guideddiscoveries.org**
Allan Tiso, Dir.
Adm: FCFS. **Appl**—Fee $0. Due: Rolling.
Fac 20. Staff: Admin 5.
Type of instruction: Enrich. **Courses:** Geol Crafts.
Focus: Astron. **Features:** Hiking Mountaineering Mtn_Biking Rock_Climb Ropes_Crse Swim Volleyball.
Fees 2012: Res $995-1895, 1-2 wks.
Housing: Dorms. **Swimming:** Pool.
Est 1990. Nonprofit. **Spons:** Guided Discoveries. **Ses:** 5. **Wks/ses:** 1-2. Operates June-July.

At AstroCamp, boys and girls learn about astronomy and space exploration while also taking part in wilderness camping activities. Campers explore a mystery planetary surface, use telescopes and microscopes, launch rockets, go rock climbing and spend a week camping in the mountains. **See Also Page 25**

THE ATHENIAN SCHOOL
SUMMER ENGLISH LANGUAGE PROGRAM
Res — Coed Ages 12-17

Danville, CA 94506. 2100 Mt Diablo Scenic Blvd. Tel: 925-837-5375.
Fax: 925-362-7227.
www.athenian.org/esl   E-mail: debra.ataman@athenian.org
Nancy Glimme, Dir.
Adm: FCFS. **Appl**—Fee $0. Due: Rolling.
Fac 8. Staff: Admin 1. Couns 6.
Type of instruction: Enrich. **Courses:** Expository_Writing Lang Creative_Writing Music Theater. **Daily hours for:** Classes 3½. Study 1½. Rec 3½.
Focus: ESL. **Features:** Aquatics Basketball Swim Tennis.
Fees 2012: Res $6000 (+$300), 4 wks.
Housing: Dorms. Avg per room/unit: 1-2. **Swimming:** Pool.
Nonprofit. **Ses:** 1. **Wks/ses:** 4. Operates July-Aug.

Located on the school's 75-acre campus in the foothills of Mount Diablo, SELP aids international students with conversation, pronunciation, listening, reading, vocabulary, writing and grammar. Pupils with varying fluency levels may take part in this intensive session. The program incorporates field trips to cultural locations throughout the Bay Area. Athenian also schedules optional trips to Universal Studios and Magic Mountain.

AUBURN UNIVERSITY ARCHITECTURE CAMP
Res — Coed Ages 16-18

Auburn, AL 36849. Outreach Prgm Office, 301 O D Smith Hall. Tel: 334-844-5100.
Fax: 334-844-3101.
www.auburn.edu/outreach/opce/summercamps
E-mail: james.birdsong@auburn.edu
Carla Bell, Coord.
Grades 11-12. Adm: FCFS. **Appl**—Due: Rolling.
Type of instruction: Enrich.
Focus: Architect.
Fees 2012: Res $615, 1 wk.
Housing: Dorms.
Nonprofit. **Ses:** 2. **Wks/ses:** 1. Operates June-July.

This intensive workshop for rising high school upperclassmen interested in architecture begins with basic design concepts and ends with an architectural design project. Hands-on exercises, technical demonstrations and professional guest speakers round out the program. Students have studio space and access to computers and may engage in various social and recreational activities.

AUBURN UNIVERSITY BUILDING CONSTRUCTION CAMP
Res — Coed Ages 14-18

Auburn, AL 36849. OPCE Summer Experience, 301 O D Smith Hall.
Tel: 334-844-5100. Fax: 334-844-3101.
www.auburn.edu/outreach/opce   E-mail: james.birdsong@auburn.edu
James Birdsong, Coord.
Grades 9-12. Adm: FCFS. **Appl**—Fee $0. Due: Rolling.
Type of instruction: Enrich.
Focus: Architect.
Fees 2012: Res $615, 1 wk. Aid (Need).
Housing: Dorms.
Ses: 1. **Wks/ses:** 1. Operates June.

Students learn construction basics and how to integrate building design with site, climate, function and environmental considerations. Each day includes hands-on activities and instruction from Auburn faculty.

AUBURN UNIVERSITY
TEAMS AND INDIVIDUALS GUIDED
BY ENGINEERING RESOURCES
Res — Coed Ages 14-17

Auburn, AL 36849. OPCE Summer Experience, 301 O D Smith Hall.
Tel: 334-844-5100. Fax: 334-844-3101.
www.eng.auburn.edu/outreach/k-12/tigers.html
E-mail: james.birdsong@auburn.edu
James Birdsong, Coord.
Grades 9-12. Adm: FCFS. Appl—Due: Rolling.
Type of instruction: Enrich.
Focus: Engineering.
Fees 2012: Res $499-569, 1 wk.
Housing: Dorms.
Ses: 2. Wks/ses: 1. Operates June.

Auburn offers two sessions for students interested in engineering: one week for students entering grades 9 and 10, and another for those entering grades 11 and 12. The curriculum combines hands-on activities, workshops, tours and lectures. In addition, engineers and engineering students advise participants on the high school courses they should take before pursuing college study or a career in engineering.

AUBURN UNIVERSITY
WORLD AFFAIRS YOUTH SEMINAR
Res — Coed Ages 15-18

Auburn, AL 36849. Office of Professional & Continuing Ed, 301 O D Smith Hall.
Tel: 334-844-5100. Fax: 334-844-3101.
www.auburn.edu/outreach/opce   E-mail: opce@auburn.edu
James Birdsong, Coord.
Grades 10-12. Adm: FCFS. Appl—Fee $0. Due: Rolling.
Type of instruction: Enrich.
Focus: Intl_Relations.
Fees 2011: Res $549, 1 wk.
Housing: Dorms.
Est 1987. Ses: 1. Wks/ses: 1. Operates July.

World Affairs aims to develop the participant's global perspective of current events and world issues. Students attend classes, listen to guest speakers and conduct research in preparation for debates within the framework of Model United Nations sessions. Boys and girls preview college life through extracurricular activities.

AWESOMEMATH SUMMER PROGRAM
Res — Coed Ages 12-17

Plano, TX 75025. 3425 Neiman Rd. Tel: 214-549-6146.
www.awesomemath.org   E-mail: tandreescu@gmail.com
Titu Andreescu, Dir.
Grades 7-12 (younger if qualified). Adm: Selective. **Appl**—Fee $50. Due: May. Adm test, 2 recs, personal statement.

Enr: 120. **Fac 15.** Prof 10. K-12 staff 5. **Staff:** Admin 2.
Type of instruction: Adv Enrich. **Daily hours for:** Classes 6. Study 1½. Rec 3.
Locations: CA NY.
Focus: Math.
Fees 2012: Res $3885, 3 wks. Aid (Need).
Housing: Dorms. Campus facilities avail.
Ses: 2. **Wks/ses:** 3. Operates June-Aug.

Held on the campuses of Cornell University and the University of California-Santa Cruz, ASMP enables gifted math pupils to hone their problem-solving skills while exploring advanced topics in detail. Many participants seek to improve their performance in national math contests. Taught by distinguished faculty and Olympiad coaches from the US and abroad, lectures focus on number theory, Euclidean geometry, algebraic inequalities and techniques, modular arithmetic and computational geometry. A 90-minute problem-solving seminar (with active student participation) follows each teaching session.

BALL STATE UNIVERSITY
COLLEGE OF ARCHITECTURE AND PLANNING
SUMMER WORKSHOP
Res — Coed Ages 16-17

Muncie, IN 47306. AB 104. Tel: 765-285-5862.
www.bsu.edu/cap/workshop   E-mail: msmith@bsu.edu
Melanie Smith, Coord.
Grades 11-12. Adm: Selective. Prereqs: GPA 3.0. **Appl**—Fee $0. Due: Rolling.
Type of instruction: Enrich. **Daily hours for:** Classes 6.
Focus: Architect.
Fees 2009: Res $998, 2 wks. Aid (Need).
Housing: Dorms. Avg per room/unit: 2. Campus facilities avail.
Nonprofit. **Ses:** 1. **Wks/ses:** 2. Operates July.

Ball State's CAP Summer Workshop provides rising high school juniors and seniors with an intensive immersion into environmental design and problem solving. Faculty lead a series of exercises intended to both challenge students and encourage creative expression. Boys and girls engage in six hours of daily studio time, then have some unscheduled blocks in the evening to experience college life. A field trip study tour that includes bus travel to a major metropolitan city enriches classroom instruction. During the tour, participants analyze and document cultural aspects of the city's design and planning.

BARAT FOUNDATION
SUMMER PROGRAM IN PROVENCE
Res — Coed Ages 14-18

Provence, France.
Contact (Year-round): 765 Broad St, Newark, NJ 07102. Tel: 973-263-1013.
    Fax: 973-263-2287.
www.baratfoundation.org   E-mail: info@baratfoundation.org
Chandri Barat, Dir.
Grades 9-PG. Adm: FCFS. **Appl**—Fee $100. Due: Rolling. Transcript, teacher rec.
Type of instruction: Enrich. **Courses:** Hist Music Theater. **Daily hours for:** Classes 2.
Intl program focus: Lang.
Focus: Fr.
Fees 2009: Res $7295 (+airfare), 4 wks. Aid (Merit & Need).
Housing: Apartments.
Est 1997. Ses: 1. **Wks/ses:** 4. Operates June-July.

Accepting students at all levels of French proficiency, the Barat Foundation teaches the language through a combination of classes and workshops. Workshops address French conversation and literature, writing, art, cuisine, photography, cinema, dance and movement, and theater. Field trips—including visits to monuments, churches, nature preserves, museums, nearby cities, local businesses, vineyards and theatrical performances—reinforce classroom language learning.

BARNARD COLLEGE
YOUNG WOMEN'S LEADERSHIP INSTITUTE
Res — Girls Ages 16-18

New York, NY 10027. Office of Pre-College Prgms, 3009 Broadway, Milbank 235. Tel: 212-854-8866. Fax: 212-854-8867.
www.barnard.edu/precollege   E-mail: pcp@barnard.edu
Ann Dachs, Dir.
Grades 11-12. Adm: Selective. Appl—Fee $50. Due: Rolling. Essay, transcript, 2 recs.
Enr cap: 55. Fac 2. Staff: Admin 3. Couns 22.
Type of instruction: Enrich Undergrad. Courses: Career Women's_Stud. Avg class size: 18. Daily hours for: Classes 5. Study 2. Rec 3. Homework.
Focus: Leadership.
Fees 2011: Res $2400 (+$75-150), 1 wk. Aid (Need).
Housing: Dorms. Avg per room/unit: 2.
Est 1984. Nonprofit. Ses: 1. Wks/ses: 1. Operates July.

The Young Women's Leadership Institute focuses on the relationship between leadership and gender. Girls devote mornings to classes in gender studies and social issues, then spend their afternoons engaged in workshops, seminars and discussions. Students design and execute community service projects in small groups, and reading and writing assignments are also part of the program. In addition, Leadership Institute participants meet with Barnard alumnae in their workplaces to learn about different occupations and the educational or professional training they require.

BAYLOR UNIVERSITY
HIGH SCHOOL SUMMER SCIENCE RESEARCH PROGRAM
Res — Coed Ages 17-18

Waco, TX 76798. 1 Bear Pl, PO Box 97344. Tel: 254-710-4288. Fax: 254-710-3639.
www.baylor.edu/summerscience   E-mail: hsssrp@baylor.edu
Frank Mathis, Dir.
Grade 12. Adm: Very selective. Admitted: 10%. Appl—Due: Mar.
Enr: 10. Enr cap: 10. Fac 10. Staff: Admin 3.
Type of instruction: Adv. Courses: Astron Environ_Sci Geol Math. Avg class size: 1. Daily hours for: Classes 5½. Rec 2. College credit: 1.
Focus: Sci. Features: Swim.
Fees 2012: Res $500-700, 5 wks. Aid (Need).
Housing: Dorms. Swimming: Pool. Campus facilities avail.
Est 1991. Nonprofit. Baptist. Ses: 1. Wks/ses: 5. Operates June-July.

HSSSRP offers hands-on research experiences with Baylor University professors to rising high school seniors who are strong in science. Students use the latest research instruments, interpret data, participate in science and technology seminars, and engage in group recreational activities. Specific areas of study include astronomy, biochemistry, biology, chemistry, computer science, engineering, environmental studies, geology, mathematics, museum studies, neuroscience, nutrition, physics and psychology. Successful completion of the program results in one hour of college credit.

BELOIT COLLEGE
SUMMER INTENSIVE LANGUAGE PROGRAM
Res — Coed Ages 17 and up; Day — Coed 16 and up

Beloit, WI 53511. **Ctr for Language Studies, 700 College St. Tel: 608-363-2277, 800-356-0751. Fax: 608-363-7129.**
www.summerlanguages.com   E-mail: cls@beloit.edu
Thomas P. Kreiser, Dir.
Grades 12-Col. Adm: Selective. **Appl**—Fee $25. Due: Rolling. Transcript, 2 recs.
Type of instruction: Adv Undergrad. **Avg class size:** 10. **Daily hours for:** Classes 5½. Study 4½. Homework. Tests. Grades. **College credit.**
Focus: ESL Arabic Chin Japan Russ. **Features:** Swim.
Fees 2012: Res $3674-7248, 4-8 wks. Day $2666-5282, 4-8 wks. Aid (Merit).
Housing: Dorms. Avg per room/unit: 2. **Swimming:** Pool. Campus facilities avail.
Est 1983. Ses: 2. **Wks/ses:** 4-8. Operates June-Aug.

Advanced high school students complete course work in Arabic, Chinese, Japanese, Russian or English as a Second Language through Beloit's Center for Language Study. No prior experience is required in the target language. Students speak the language of instruction during all academic hours, and language groups eat lunch and dinner with program instructors. The four-week session is equivalent to one semester of language study; the eight-week session, a full year. Individualized tutorial sessions and weekly movie nights and cultural events round out the program.

THE BEMENT SCHOOL
ENGLISH LANGUAGE AND AMERICAN CULTURE PROGRAM
Res — Coed Ages 8-12

Deerfield, MA 01342. **94 Old Main St, PO Box 8. Tel: 413-475-3044. Fax: 413-774-7863.**
www.bement.org/elac   E-mail: jhayes@bement.org
Jennifer Hayes, Dir.
Adm: FCFS. **Appl**—Fee $50. Due: Rolling. Transcript, 1 Eng teacher rec, writing sample.
Enr cap: 20. Intl: 100%. Non-White: 90%. **Fac 4.** K-12 staff 4. **Staff:** Admin 3. Couns 4.
Type of instruction: Enrich Study_Skills. **Courses:** Lang Speech Writing/Journ Crafts Creative_Writing Dance Music Theater. **Avg class size:** 6. **Daily hours for:** Classes 4. Study 1½. Rec 4. Homework. Tests.
Focus: ESL. **Features:** Canoe Climbing_Wall Hiking Wilderness_Camp Basketball Soccer Softball Swim Ultimate_Frisbee.
Fees 2012: Res $4500 (+$250), 3½ wks.
Housing: Dorms. Avg per room/unit: 2. **Swimming:** Lake Pond Pool River. Campus facilities avail.
Nonprofit. **Ses:** 1. **Wks/ses:** 3½. Operates July-Aug.

Emphasizing speaking, listening, reading and writing proficiency, ELAC addresses speaking skills through interviewing, debate, oral presentation and group work. Students broaden vocabulary and analytical skills while reading various materials, and writing instruction focuses on sentence structure and paragraph construction. Teachers employ audio- and videotapes to improve listening abilities. Workshops assist children with SSAT and TOEFL preparation.

BENTLEY UNIVERSITY
WALL STREET 101
Res — Coed Ages 17-18

Waltham, MA 02452. **175 Forest St. Tel: 781-891-2598. Fax: 781-891-3414.**
www.bentley.edu/camp/wallst.cfm   E-mail: jehalt@bentley.edu
Jennifer Ehalt, Dir.

Grade 12. Adm: Selective. **Appl**—Fee $50. Due: Apr. Transcript, rec, standardized test scores, essay.
Type of instruction: Enrich.
Focus: Bus/Fin Econ.
Fees 2009: Res $1000, 1 wk.
Housing: Dorms.
Nonprofit. **Ses:** 1. **Wks/ses:** 1. Operates July.

This enrichment program employs hands-on exercises to teach students about the stock market and the process of investment. Course work addresses various aspects of the financial industry and other business fields. Boys and girls get to experience the trading-room environment through simulated trading sessions. Pupils work in groups of five to construct a diversified portfolio of equity securities, then prepare a formal presentation detailing the rationale of their selections. Wall Street 101 also features trips to Boston investment firms and other area attractions.

THE BILL OF RIGHTS INSTITUTE
CONSTITUTIONAL ACADEMY
Res — Coed Ages 16-17

Washington, DC.
Contact (Year-round): 200 N Glebe Rd, Ste 200, Arlington, VA 22203.
Tel: 703-894-1776, 800-838-7870. Fax: 703-894-1791.
www.constacademy.org   E-mail: info@billofrightsinstitute.org
John Croft, Dir.
Grades 11-12. Adm: Selective. Admitted: 90%. Prereqs: GPA 3.2. **Appl**—Fee $25. Due: Rolling.
Enr: 100. **Enr cap:** 100. Intl: 2%. Non-White: 15%. **Fac 6.** Prof 4. K-12 staff 2. **Staff:** Admin 5. Res 5.
Type of instruction: Undergrad. **Courses:** Hist. **Avg class size:** 40. **Daily hours for:** Classes 4. Study 1. Rec 3. Homework. Tests. Grades. **College credit:** 3/crse.
Focus: Pol_Sci.
Fees 2011: Res $3000. Aid (Merit & Need).
Housing: Dorms. Avg per room/unit: 2. Campus facilities avail.
Est 2007. Nonprofit. **Ses:** 2. **Wks/ses:** 1. Operates July.

Rising high school juniors and seniors who are capable of college-level work study the US Constitution and learn about the nation's founding in this precollege program. Students engage in five weeks of distance learning from home, then spend a week in a campus setting in Washington, DC, learning about and discussing constitutional principles. Field trips to the homes of several American founders, the US Capitol, the National Archives (to view the Constitution and the Declaration of Independence) and the Washington monuments complement class work. Program graduates earn three college credits from Ohio's Ashland University.

BISHOP'S COLLEGE SCHOOL SUMMER LANGUAGE CAMP
Res and Day — Coed Ages 11-16

Sherbrooke, J1M 1Z8 Quebec, Canada. 80 Moulton Hill, PO Box 5001, Lennoxville.
Tel: 819-566-0227. Fax: 819-822-8917.
www.bishopscollegeschool.com   E-mail: summer@bishopscollegeschool.com
Denise Addona, Coord.
Grades 6-11. Adm: FCFS. **Appl**—Fee $0. Due: Rolling.
Enr: 185. **Fac 20. Staff:** Admin 4.
Avg class size: 12. **Daily hours for:** Classes 4½. Study 1. Rec 2.
Intl program focus: Lang.

Focus: ESL Fr. **Features:** Canoe Climbing_Wall Riding Basketball Golf Soccer Softball Squash Swim Tennis Track Ultimate_Frisbee Volleyball.
Fees 2012: Res Can$3500 (+Can$100), 4 wks. Day Can$2075, 4 wks.
Housing: Dorms. **Swimming:** Lake Pool.
Est 1961. Ses: 1. **Wks/ses:** 4. Operates July.

BCS provides summer instruction for motivated students interested in gaining proficiency in French or English. Both programs offer instruction at beginning, intermediate and advanced levels. Each level includes oral and written work and offers a solid base for work in grammar and conversation. Supplementary study is required in the areas of reading, writing and comprehension. Pupils take placement exams at the beginning of the program, then frequent classroom tests thereafter.

BOSTON UNIVERSITY
PROGRAM IN MATHEMATICS FOR YOUNG SCIENTISTS
Res — Coed Ages 14-18

Boston, MA 02215. Dept of Mathematics, 111 Cummington St. Tel: 617-353-2563.
Fax: 617-353-8100.
www.promys.org   E-mail: promys@bu.edu
Glenn Stevens, Dir. Student contact: Kate Coughlin.
Grades 9-12. Adm: Selective. **Appl**—Fee $0. Due: May. Transcript, math teacher rec, problem set.
Enr: 70. **Enr cap:** 80. **Fac 4. Staff:** Admin 1. Couns 20.
Type of instruction: Adv Enrich. **Daily hours for:** Classes 2. Study 7.
Focus: Math.
Fees 2012: Res $2700 (+$100), 6 wks. Aid (Merit & Need).
Housing: Dorms.
Est 1989. Nonprofit. Ses: 1. **Wks/ses:** 6. Operates July-Aug.

A rigorous math program for motivated high schoolers, PROMYS exposes students to an assortment of difficult problems in number theory. The day begins with a morning lecture in number theory, with experienced students also attending seminars on other advanced topics. Pupils spend the rest of the day working on problem sets; some work in groups, others alone. Boys and girls are advised by resident college-age counselors who are working toward math careers. As an additional resource, senior mathematicians hold problem sessions thrice weekly for groups of 11 or 12 students.

BOSTON UNIVERSITY RESEARCH INTERNSHIP
IN SCIENCE AND ENGINEERING PROGRAM
Res and Day — Coed Ages 16-18

Boston, MA 02215. 755 Commonwealth Ave, Rm 105. Tel: 617-353-1378.
Fax: 617-353-5532.
www.bu.edu/summer/high-school-programs/research-internship
E-mail: rise@bu.edu
Donna Shea, Dir. Student contact: Matthew Cobb, E-mail: mcobb@bu.edu.
Grade 12 (younger if qualified). Adm: Very selective. Prereqs: GPA 3.89. SAT: 1470; PSAT: 142 (Math). **Appl**—Due: Apr. Transcripts, standardized test scores, 2 recs.
Enr: 50. **Non-White:** 54%. **Staff:** Admin 2. Couns 9.
Type of instruction: Adv Enrich. **Courses:** Astron Engineering Med/Healthcare Psych. **Daily hours for:** Classes 8.
Focus: Sci. **Features:** Swim.
Fees 2011: Res $6076-6246, 6 wks. Day $4050, 6 wks. Aid (Merit & Need).
Housing: Dorms. **Swimming:** Pool. Campus facilities avail.
Est 1978. Ses: 1. **Wks/ses:** 6. Operates July-Aug.

RISE allows academically motivated rising high school seniors to conduct university-level laboratory research, under the guidance of a Boston University faculty mentor, in one of the following areas: astronomy, biology, chemistry, engineering, medicine, physics or psychology. Pupils work on an ongoing research project in their chosen area, in the process developing technical and analytical skills and gaining insight into the scientific method. Each student prepares a poster for display at a session-closing scientific conference. Participants have been recognized by the Intel Science Talent Search and the Siemens Westinghouse Competition.

BRANDEIS UNIVERSITY GENESIS PROGRAM
Res — Coed Ages 15-17

Waltham, MA 02454. 415 South St, MS 085. Tel: 781-736-8416. Fax: 815-301-2874. www.brandeis.edu/genesis   E-mail: highschool@brandeis.edu
Dvora Goodman, Dir.
Grades 10-12 (younger if qualified). Adm: Selective. **Appl**—Fee $40. Due: Mar. Transcript, 2 essays, teacher & parent references.
Enr: 76. **Fac 10. Staff:** Admin 4. Couns 15.
Type of instruction: Adv. **Courses:** Law Writing/Journ Creative_Writing Dance Fine Arts Music. **Avg class size:** 13. **Daily hours for:** Classes 3.
Focus: Relig_Stud. **Features:** Community_Serv Cooking Peace/Cross-cultural Basketball Tennis.
Fees 2011: Res $4800 (+$160), 4½ wks. Aid (Need).
Housing: Dorms. Avg per room/unit: 2. Campus facilities avail.
Est 1997. Nonprofit. Jewish. **Ses:** 1. **Wks/ses:** 4½. Operates July-Aug.

Judaic studies, the arts and the humanities constitute this academic and religious program. Students with diverse educational experiences and varying degrees of experience with Judaism engage with scholars, artists, activists and experiential educators. Field trips and meetings with relevant professionals supplement hands-on seminars. Courses vary by year but include such subjects as journalism, law, technology and world religion. Afternoon and evening workshops provide direct experiences with Israeli foods, music, folk dancing and creative writing. Select participants may return to Genesis for a second summer to take a Brandeis undergraduate communications course for college credit.

BREBEUF CITY RESIDENTIAL PROGRAMME
Res — Coed Ages 9-17

Montreal, H34T 1W4 Quebec, Canada. 5625 Rue Decelle.
Contact (Sept-June): c/o CISS, 439 University Ave, Ste 2110, Toronto, M5G 1Y8 Ontario, Canada.
Year-round Tel: 416-646-5400, 866-258-4303. Fax: 416-646-5403.
www.brebeufsummer.com   E-mail: camps@cisscanada.com
Alexandre L'Archeveque, Dir.
Adm: FCFS. **Appl**—Due: Rolling.
Staff: Admin 4.
Courses: Art Crafts Dance Drawing Sculpt Visual_Arts. **Avg class size:** 15.
Intl program focus: Lang.
Focus: ESL Fr. **Features:** Basketball Figure_Skating Ice_Hockey Soccer Tennis Volleyball Ping-Pong Billiards.
Housing: Dorms.
Est 2000. Spons: Canadian International Student Services. **Ses:** 10. **Wks/ses:** 2-5. Operates July-Aug.

Located on Mount Royal, this French and English immersion program combines 15 hours of weekly instruction in the target language with afternoon excursions and recreational programming. Placement testing on the session's first day enables pupils to study with others of a similar aptitude level. Students choose either French or English—or both if the length of stay is four or five weeks. Staff converse with participants in the language of study outside of the classroom to enhance the immersion experience. Each week, Brebeuf organizes full-day, half-day and evening cultural excursions around Montreal and elsewhere in Quebec.

BRIARWOOD MARINE SCIENCE PROGRAM
Res — Coed Ages 10-15

Monument Beach, MA 02553. 586 Shore Rd. Tel: 508-759-7763. Fax: 508-759-4911.
Contact (Sept-May): 20 Newton St, Brookline, MA 02445. Tel: 617-454-2725.
 Fax: 617-522-8166.
www.dexter-southfield.org   E-mail: summer@dexter.org
Jason Cassista, Dir.
Grades 5-10. Adm: FCFS. **Appl**—Fee $0. Due: Rolling.
Enr: 40. **Enr cap:** 40. **Fac** 4. Col/grad students 2. K-12 staff 2. **Staff:** Admin 3. Couns 10.
Type of instruction: Enrich. **Courses:** Ecol Environ_Sci. **Avg class size:** 10.
Focus: Marine_Bio/Stud Oceanog. **Features:** Boating Fishing Hiking Kayak Sail Soccer Swim Volleyball.
Fees 2012: Res $895, 1 wk.
Housing: Cabins Lodges. Avg per room/unit: 8. **Swimming:** Ocean.
Est 2000. Nonprofit. **Spons:** Dexter School/Southfield School. **Ses:** 8. **Wks/ses:** 1. Operates June-Aug.

Participants in this program, operated jointly by Dexter School and Southfield School, learn about ecology, marine biology and weather through a noninvasive study of the habitats, niches and ecosystems of Cape Cod's animals and plants. Course work integrates life science, technology and math. Weekly sessions also include day and evening recreational activities, among them swimming, boating, informal games and nature hikes.

BRILLANTMONT INTERNATIONAL SCHOOL SUMMER COURSE
Res — Coed Ages 12-17

Lausanne, 1005 Switzerland. 16 Ave Secretan. Tel: 41-21-310-04-00.
 Fax: 41-21-320-84-17.
www.brillantmont.ch   E-mail: summercourse@brillantmont.ch
Philippe Pasche, Dir.
Grades 7-12. Adm: FCFS. **Appl**—Due: Rolling.
Enr: 90. **Fac 20. Staff:** Admin 3.
Type of instruction: Enrich. **Avg class size:** 15. **Daily hours for:** Classes 4. Study 1. Rec 3.
Intl program focus: Lang Culture.
Focus: ESL Fr. **Features:** Bicycle_Tours Hiking Mtn_Trips Rock_Climb Badminton Basketball Cross-country Field_Hockey Rugby Soccer Swim Tennis Volleyball Water-skiing Watersports.
Fees 2012: Res SwF1750, 1 wk.
Housing: Houses. Avg per room/unit: 2. **Swimming:** Lake Pool.
Est 1982. Ses: 6. **Wks/ses:** 1. Operates June-Aug.

Morning French or English language courses at Brillantmont emphasize oral communication, with attention also paid to grammar, written expression and vocabulary. In the afternoon, boys and girls engage in a sports program featuring such activities as tennis, basketball, windsurfing and water-skiing. Evening pursuits include bowling, ice skating, in-line skating and trips to the discotheque. Sundays are reserved for daylong excursions devoted to rock climbing, glacier walking, rafting or museum visitation, among other options.

BRITISH INTERNATIONAL SCHOOL-PHUKET
ENGLISH SUMMER SCHOOL
Res — Coed Ages 8-15; Day — Coed 7-15

Phuket, 83000 Thailand. 59 Moo 2, Thepkrasattri Rd, Tambon Koh Kaew, Amphur Muang. **Tel:** 66-7623-8711. **Fax:** 66-7623-8750.
www.bisphuket.ac.th   E-mail: summer@bisphuket.ac.th
Patrick du Preez, Dir.
Student contact: Christophe I. Espouy, **E-mail:** cespouy@bisphuket.ac.th.
Grades 3-9 (younger if qualified). Adm: FCFS. **Appl**—Fee $0. Due: Rolling.
Enr: 150. **Enr cap:** 180. Intl: 98%. **Fac 15. Staff:** Admin 6. Res 19.
Type of instruction: Enrich Rem_Eng Rem_Read Tut. **Courses:** Debate Expository_Writing Speech Crafts Creative_Writing Drama Music. **Avg class size:** 12. **Daily hours for:** Classes 3. Study 1½. Rec 3. Tests. Grades.
Intl program focus: Acad Lang Culture.
Focus: ESL. **Features:** Aquatics Boating Canoe Cruises Exploration Hiking Kayak Mtn_ Biking Paintball Rappelling Rock_Climb Sail Badminton Basketball Cricket Golf Rugby Soccer Softball Swim Tennis Volleyball Water-skiing Watersports Ping-Pong Snorkeling.
Fees 2011: Res Bt75,000 (+Bt5000), 4 wks. Day Bt59,000, 4 wks.
Housing: Dorms Hotels Houses Lodges. Avg per room/unit: 4. **Swimming:** Ocean Pool River Stream. Campus facilities avail.
Est 1996. Inc. Ses: 1. **Wks/ses:** 4. Operates July.

Students in this program receive small-group ESL instruction for 18 hours each week from native English speakers, and also learn English informally through participation in such activities as land sports and watersports, music, art and drama. Excursions off campus, which provide further exposure to English conversation, include trips to national parks and local beaches.

BROADREACH ACADEMIC TREKS
Res — Coed Ages 13-19

Raleigh, NC 27603. 806 McCulloch St, Ste 102. **Tel:** 919-256-8200, 888-833-1907. **Fax:** 919-833-2129.
www.academictreks.com   E-mail: info@academictreks.com
Carlton Goldthwaite, Dir.
Grades 8-Col. Adm: FCFS. **Appl**—Fee $0. Due: Rolling.
Enr: 10-12. **Enr cap:** 10-12. Intl: 10%. **Fac 3. Staff:** Admin 5. Couns 3.
Type of instruction: Adv. **Courses:** Ecol. **Avg class size:** 11. **Daily hours for:** Classes 4. Study 1. Rec 3. Homework. Tests. Grades. **High school & college credit:** 2-3/crse, total 3.
Intl program focus: Lang Culture. **Locations:** Africa Asia Canada Caribbean Europe Mexico/Central_America South_America. Home stays avail.
Focus: Environ_Sci Chin Fr Span Marine_Bio/Stud Community_Serv. **Features:** Adventure_Travel Caving Conservation Exploration Hiking Kayak Mountaineering Mtn_Trips Outdoor_Ed Peace/Cross-cultural Riding Sail Scuba Sea_Cruises Seamanship Whitewater_Raft Wilderness_Camp Wilderness_Canoe Swim.
Fees 2011: Res $3180-6280 (+airfare), 2-4 wks.
Housing: Dorms Hotels Tents. **Swimming:** Ocean River.
Est 1992. Inc. Ses: 3. **Wks/ses:** 2-4. Operates June-Aug.

This Broadreach program combines hands-on learning, adventure, service work, cultural immersion and international travel. Different Academic Treks focus on marine science, language immersion, cultural studies and community service. All trips include 10 to 55 hours of community service as a complement to students' academic work.

BROADREACH MARINE BIOLOGY ADVENTURE
Res — Coed Ages 15-18

San Salvadore, Bahamas.
Contact (Year-round): 806 McCulloch St, Ste 102, Raleigh, NC 27603.
Tel: 919-256-8200, 888-833-1907. Fax: 919-833-2129.
www.gobroadreach.com   E-mail: questions@gobroadreach.com
Carlton Goldwaithe, Dir.
Grades 10-PG. Adm: FCFS. **Appl**—Fee $0. Due: Rolling.
Enr: 10-14. **Enr cap:** 10-14. Intl: 10%. **Fac 5. Staff:** Admin 2. Couns 4.
Type of instruction: Adv. **Courses:** Ecol. **Avg class size:** 12. **Daily hours for:** Classes 4½. Study 1½. Rec 2. **High school & college credit:** 3/crse, total 3.
Intl program focus: Acad Culture.
Focus: Marine_Bio/Stud. **Features:** Community_Serv Conservation Exploration Hiking Kayak Peace/Cross-cultural Scuba Swim Water-skiing Watersports.
Fees 2011: Res $5480 (+airfare), 3 wks.
Housing: Dorms Lodges. **Swimming:** Ocean.
Est 1992. Inc. Ses: 2. Wks/ses: 3. Operates June-Aug.

Young people in this Broadreach program investigate the marine world through intensive field studies, research and diving. Students learn hands-on while diving alongside professional marine biologists on underwater reefs. Field research, labs, dive training and seminars qualify program participants for academic credit.

BROWN UNIVERSITY LEADERSHIP INSTITUTE
Res and Day — Coed Ages 14-18

Providence, RI 02912. Box T, 42 Charlesfield St. Tel: 401-863-7900. Fax: 401-863-3916.
www.brown.edu/scs/pre-college/leadership   E-mail: summer@brown.edu
Robin Rose, Dir.
Grades 9-PG. Adm: Selective. **Appl**—Fee $45-90. Due: Rolling. Transcript, teacher rec, essay.
Type of instruction: Enrich. **Courses:** Bus/Fin Film. **Daily hours for:** Classes 4½.
Focus: Leadership.
Fees 2011: Res $3446, 2 wks. Day $2422, 2 wks. Aid (Merit).
Housing: Dorms. Campus facilities avail.
Ses: 3. Wks/ses: 2. Operates June-Aug.

This program for high schoolers seeks to develop their leadership skills through enrollment in one course and participation in several evening programs in which current events and leadership issues are addressed. Class topics involve such issues as global engagement, the civil rights movement, conflict resolution, global health, social change, women and leadership, social entrepreneurship and documentary film for social change. During the session, boys and girls identify and analyze their personal learning styles, engage in group problem solving, and work on their public speaking and interpersonal communication skills.   **See Also Page 35**

BROWN UNIVERSITY SPARK PROGRAM
Res and Day — Coed Ages 12-14

Providence, RI 02912. 42 Charlesfield St, Box T. Tel: 401-863-7900. Fax: 401-863-7908.
www.brown.edu/scs/pre-college   E-mail: summer@brown.edu
Jennifer Aizenman, Dir.
Grades 8-9. Adm: Selective. **Appl**—Fee $45-90. Due: Rolling. Transcript, teacher rec, essay.
Type of instruction: Enrich. **Courses:** Anat Robotics. **Daily hours for:** Classes 4.
Focus: Ecol Environ_Sci Sci.
Fees 2011: Res $2255-3446 (+$40-90), 1-2 wks. Day $1999-2933 (+$40-90), 1-2 wks.

Housing: Dorms. Avg per room/unit: 1-2.
Nonprofit. **Ses:** 3. **Wks/ses:** 1-2. Operates July.

Designed for middle schoolers who have demonstrated noteworthy ability in science, SPARK provides students with an intellectual examination of concepts and familiar topics. Boys and girls attend class for four hours each morning, then take part in lab sessions or embark on field trips on Tuesday and Thursday afternoons. While the main program lasts for one week, a special two-week program focuses on the ecology of Narragansett Bay. This noncompetitive program features no tests or grades. Extracurricular activities and social events balance academics. **See Also Page 35**

BUCKSMORE SUMMER PROGRAMMES
Res — Coed Ages 7-17

London, SE10 8NB England. 259 Greenwich High Rd. Tel: 44-208-312-8060.
   Fax: 44-208-293-1199.
www.bucksmore.com   E-mail: info@bucksmore.com
Rory Wilkinson, Dir. Student contact: Matthew Tighe, E-mail: matt@bucksmore.com.
Adm: FCFS. **Appl**—Due: Rolling.
Enr: 700. **Fac** 50.
Courses: Drama. **Avg class size:** 12. **Daily hours for:** Classes 3. Rec 6. Homework. Tests. Grades.
Intl program focus: Acad Lang Culture.
Focus: ESL. **Features:** Kayak Sail Basketball Equestrian Soccer Swim Tennis Watersports.
Fees 2012: Res £790-1300, 1 wk.
Housing: Houses. **Swimming:** Pool.
Est 1978. Inc. **Ses:** 12. **Wks/ses:** 1. Operates June-Aug.

Operating residential programs at several centers in southeast England, Bucksmore combines morning English as a Second Language instruction with a recreational program consisting of activities, sports, sightseeing and excursions, and social events. Students may take part in specialized programs in tennis, adventure sports or drama.

C-TECH[2]
COMPUTERS AND TECHNOLOGY AT VIRGINIA TECH
Res — Girls Ages 16-18

Blacksburg, VA 24061. 215 Hancock Hall. Tel: 540-231-3973. Fax: 540-231-1831.
www.eng.vt.edu/ctech2   E-mail: ctech2@vt.edu
Susan Arnold Christian, Dir.
Grades 11-12. Adm: Somewhat selective. **Appl**—Due: Apr. Transcript, essay, 2 recs.
Type of instruction: Enrich. **Courses:** Comp_Sci.
Focus: Engineering Math. **Features:** Swim.
Fees 2011: Res $800, 2 wks. Aid (Need).
Housing: Dorms. **Swimming:** Pool. Campus facilities avail.
Nonprofit. **Spons:** Virginia Polytechnic Institute. **Ses:** 1. **Wks/ses:** 2. Operates June-July.

The program aims to develop and sustain the interests of young women in engineering and the sciences. Hands-on activities demonstrate the real-world applications of engineering, math and science. Seminars provided by Virginia Tech offices cover college admissions, scholarships, financial aid and career services, and presentations by each department of the College of Engineering explore academic and career possibilities within different engineering fields.

CALIFORNIA SCHOLASTIC PRESS ASSOCIATION
JOURNALISM WORKSHOP
Res — Coed Ages 16-18

San Luis Obispo, CA. California State Polytechnic Univ.
Contact (Year-round): 384 Mira Mar Ave, Long Beach, CA 90814. Tel: 714-834-3784.
www.cspaworkshop.org
Grades 10-PG. Adm: Selective. Appl—Fee $0. Due: Apr. Essay, 3 writing samples.
Enr: 25. Enr cap: 25. Fac 23. Specialists 23. Staff: Couns 3.
Type of instruction: Enrich. Courses: Photog.
Focus: Writing/Journ.
Fees 2012: Res $1200, 2 wks. Aid (Need).
Housing: Dorms.
Est 1951. Nonprofit. Ses: 1. Wks/ses: 2. Operates July.

Writing up to five stories each day, students enrolled in the Journalism Workshop gain in-depth knowledge of news, sports, feature and opinion writing; practice interviewing and learn research techniques; tour newspaper offices and television studios; and explore graphics, photography, blogging and social media. Instructors include reporters, editors, photographers, graphic designers and broadcasters from news outlets across California.

CANADA/USA MATHCAMP
Res — Coed Ages 13-18

Cambridge, MA 02139. 129 Hancock St. Toll-free: 888-371-4159. Fax: 888-371-4159.
www.mathcamp.org
Mira Bernstein, Exec Dir.
Adm: Selective. Admitted: 40%. Appl—Fee $20. Due: Apr. Qualifying quiz, 2 recs, personal statement.
Enr: 110. Enr cap: 110.
Type of instruction: Adv Enrich. Homework.
Focus: Math. Features: Hiking Basketball Soccer Swim Tennis Ultimate_Frisbee Volleyball.
Fees 2009: Res $3500, 5 wks. Aid (Need).
Housing: Dorms. Avg per room/unit: 1-2. Swimming: Pool. Campus facilities avail.
Spons: Mathematics Foundation of America. Ses: 1. Wks/ses: 5. Operates July-Aug.

Held on a different college campus each year, this program of the Mathematics Foundation of America is an intensive session of advanced math work for motivated high schoolers. An enrichment program, Mathcamp addresses advanced and unusual topics in pure and applied math through various formats: faculty-taught courses lasting anywhere from a few days to five weeks, lectures and seminars conducted by distinguished guests, math contests and problem-solving sessions, and hands-on workshops and individual projects. While students spend some time each evening completing homework, there is also time for recreational pursuits.

CANOE ISLAND FRENCH CAMP
Res — Coed Ages 9-16

Orcas, WA 98280. 278 Killebrew Lake Rd, PO Box 370. Tel: 360-468-2329.
Fax: 360-468-3027.
www.canoeisland.org   E-mail: info@canoeisland.org
Connie H. Jones, Dir.
Adm: FCFS. Appl—Fee $0. Due: Rolling.
Enr: 30-46. Intl: 10%. Non-White: 10%. Fac 10. Staff: Admin 2. Couns 10.
Type of instruction: Enrich Tut. Courses: Ecol Geol Marine_Bio/Stud Crafts Fine_Arts Music Painting Theater. Avg class size: 8. Daily hours for: Classes 1½. Rec 5.

Focus: Fr. **Features:** Aquatics Archery Boating Canoe Cooking Kayak Rappelling Rock_ Climb Sail Badminton Basketball Fencing Swim Tennis Volleyball Watersports.
Fees 2012: Res $1945-3295, 2-3 wks. Aid 2011 (Need): $36,000.
Housing: Tepees. Avg per room/unit: 4. **Swimming:** Pool. Campus facilities avail.
Est 1969. Nonprofit. **Ses:** 4. **Wks/ses:** 2-3. Operates June-Aug.

Campers learn French language, customs and traditions while taking part in an individualized activities program that includes watersports and land sports, theatricals and crafts, overnight hikes and trips to other islands in the San Juans. Canoe Island schedules family camps over the Memorial Day and Labor Day weekends each year. None of the camp's programs have language prerequisites.

CARLETON COLLEGE SUMMER SCIENCE INSTITUTE
Res — Coed Ages 15-18

Northfield, MN 55057. Office of Summer Academic Prgms, 1 N College St.
  Tel: 507-222-4038, 866-767-2275. Fax: 507-222-4540.
www.carleton.edu/summer   E-mail: cssi@carleton.edu
Cam Davidson, Dir.
  Student contact: Jeremy M. Updike, E-mail: jupdike@carleton.edu.
Grades 11-12. Adm: Very selective. Admitted: 27%. **Appl**—Fee $0. Due: Mar. Transcript, standardized test scores.
Enr: 48. Enr cap: 48. Non-White: 30%. **Fac 4.** Prof 4. **Staff:** Admin 1. Res 8.
Type of instruction: Adv Undergrad. **Avg class size:** 12. **Daily hours for:** Classes 8. Study 1. Rec 2. Homework. **College credit:** 3/crse, total 6.
Focus: Sci. **Features:** Climbing_Wall Swim.
Fees 2012: Res $3300, 3 wks. Aid 2011 (Merit & Need): $47,000.
Housing: Dorms. Avg per room/unit: 2. **Swimming:** Pool. Campus facilities avail.
Est 2009. Nonprofit. **Ses:** 1. **Wks/ses:** 3. Operates July-Aug.

CSSI enables rising high school juniors and seniors to engage in hands-on scientific research, in groups of 10 to 12 students each, alongside Carleton College faculty and undergraduate research assistants. During the three-week session, participants also rotate through three weeklong courses in such areas as neuroscience, geoscience, chemistry and animal behavior. The collaborative guided research project culminates in a presentation at the CSSI Research Symposium at program's end.

CARLETON COLLEGE SUMMER WRITING PROGRAM
Res — Coed Ages 16-17

Northfield, MN 55057. Office of Summer Academic Prgms, 1 N College St.
  Tel: 507-222-4038, 866-767-2275. Fax: 507-222-4540.
www.carleton.edu/summer/swp   E-mail: swp@carleton.edu
Deborah Appleman, Dir.
  Student contact: Jeremy M. Updike, E-mail: jupdike@carleton.edu.
Grade 12 (younger if qualified). Adm: Selective. **Appl**—Fee $0. Due: May. Transcript, expository writing sample, standardized test scores.
Enr: 65. Enr cap: 80. Non-White: 40%. **Fac 5.** Prof 5. **Staff:** Admin 1. Couns 6.
Type of instruction: Adv Undergrad. **Courses:** Creative_Writing. **Avg class size:** 17. **Daily hours for:** Classes 6. Study 2. Rec 2. Homework. **College credit:** 3/crse, total 6.
Focus: Expository_Writing. **Features:** Climbing_Wall Swim.
Fees 2011: Res $2495, 3 wks. Aid 2011 (Merit & Need): $23,500.
Housing: Dorms. **Swimming:** Pool. Campus facilities avail.
Est 1986. Nonprofit. **Ses:** 1. **Wks/ses:** 3. Operates July.

This intensive program, which follows a writing process approach, teaches students to compose college-style academic papers. In a small-class setting, pupils read contemporary and traditional literature, which then becomes the focus of their essays. Discussion sections led by current Carleton students and writing workshops meet daily. Faculty provide written evaluations of participants' three main papers. Successful program completion results in college credit.

CARLETON SUMMER QUANTITATIVE REASONING
Res — Coed Ages 15-18

Northfield, MN 55057. Office of Summer Prgms, 1 N College St. Tel: 507-222-4038, 866-767-2275. Fax: 507-222-4540.
www.carleton.edu/summer   E-mail: summer@carleton.edu
Al Montero, Dir. Student contact: Jeremy M. Updike, E-mail: jupdike@carleton.edu.
Grades 11-12. Adm: Selective. **Appl**—Fee $0. Due: Apr. Transcript, standardized test scores.
Enr cap: 36. **Fac 3.** Prof 3. **Staff:** Admin 1. Res 5.
Type of instruction: Adv Undergrad. **Courses:** Psych. **Avg class size:** 12. **Daily hours for:** Classes 6. Study 2. Rec 2. Homework. **College credit:** 3/crse, total 6.
Focus: Econ Intl_Relations. **Features:** Swim.
Fees 2012: Res $2500, 3 wks. Aid (Merit & Need).
Housing: Dorms. Avg per room/unit: 2. **Swimming:** Pool. Campus facilities avail.
Est 2012. Nonprofit. **Spons:** Carleton College. **Ses:** 1. **Wks/ses:** 3. Operates July-Aug.

CSQR provides rising high school juniors and seniors with a substantial college-level experience as they see how social scientists think about the world, measure important variables of study, prepare research and present their findings. Participants undertake hands-on examination of theories in three core disciplines—international relations, economics and psychology—as they collaborate on the design and the execution of an original research project with peers and a faculty advisor. The program's structure helps students to understand major theories and concepts in the three disciplines, as well as the manner in which social scientists study them. During the session, pupils use quantitative data to support written and oral arguments, learn to rigorously test hypotheses with statistical data, and gain experience in thinking through central problems and research questions while measuring relevant variables.

CDE NATIONAL DEBATE INSTITUTE SUMMER CAMPS
Res — Coed Ages 13-17

Albuquerque, NM. Univ of New Mexico.
Contact (Year-round): PO Box 1890, Taos, NM 87571. Tel: 575-751-0514, 866-247-3178. Fax: 575-751-9788.
www.cdedebate.com   E-mail: bennett@cdedebate.com
William H. Bennett, Chair.
Grades 8-12. Adm: FCFS. **Appl**—Fee $95. Due: May.
Enr: 70. **Fac 11. Staff:** Admin 4. Couns 9.
Type of instruction: Adv Enrich. **Avg class size:** 7. **Daily hours for:** Classes 8.
Focus: Debate Public_Speak. **Features:** Swim.
Housing: Dorms. **Swimming:** Pool.
Est 1979. Ses: 1. **Wks/ses:** 2. Operates July.

CDE operates several debate and public speaking camps on the campus of the University of New Mexico. Each camp features critiqued practice rounds, usually on three different topics. Some camp divisions are open to all age-eligible students; applicants to higher-level divisions must satisfy certain qualifications.

CENTER FOR AMERICAN ARCHEOLOGY
HIGH SCHOOL FIELD SCHOOL
Res — Coed Ages 13-17

Kampsville, IL 62053. PO Box 366. Tel: 618-653-4316. Fax: 618-653-4232.
www.caa-archeology.org   E-mail: caa@caa-archeology.org
Mary Pirkl, Dir.
Grades 8-12. Adm: FCFS. Appl—Fee $0. Due: Rolling.
Enr: 20. Enr cap: 20. Fac 4. Col/grad students 4. Staff: Admin 5. Couns 3.
Type of instruction: Adv Enrich. Courses: Ecol Geol. Avg class size: 15. High school
& college credit: 2.
Focus: Archaeol.
Fees 2012: Res $775-2500, 1-4 wks. Aid 2011 (Merit): $10,000.
Housing: Dorms. Avg per room/unit: 3.
Est 1955. Nonprofit. Ses: 1. Wks/ses: 1-4. Operates June-July.

The High School Field School allows students to work on an ongoing dig. Participants learn various excavation techniques and spend most days excavating. Boys and girls also assist in the lab and partake of educational activity sessions.

THE CENTER FOR CROSS-CULTURAL STUDY
HIGH SCHOOL SUMMER PROGRAM
Res — Coed Ages 16-18

Amherst, MA 01002. 446 Main St. Tel: 413-256-0011. Fax: 413-256-1968.
www.spanishstudies.org   E-mail: info@spanishstudies.org
Carmen Sales Delgado, Pepe Vives & Alfredo Brunori, Dirs.
Grades 11-12. Adm: Selective. Appl—Fee $0. Due: Rolling.
Enr: 30. Fac 11. Prof 11. Staff: Admin 4. Couns 2.
Type of instruction: Undergrad. Avg class size: 12. Daily hours for: Classes 4. Study 2.
Rec 3. Homework. Tests. Grades. High school & college credit: 4/crse, total 8.
Intl program focus: Acad Lang Culture. Locations: Europe South_America. Home stays
avail.
Focus: Span.
Fees 2011: Res $3438 (+$2000), 3½ wks.
Housing: Dorms Houses. Avg per room/unit: 2.
Est 1969. Inc. Ses: 2. Wks/ses: 3½. Operates June-July.

CC-CS summer terms in Cordoba, Argentina, and in the Spanish cities of Seville and Alicante combine language immersion with daily cultural activities and guided weekend excursions. Boys and girls live with local families, thereby facilitating more efficient language acquisition. CC-CS offers language instruction at beginning, intermediate and advanced levels, and students enroll in other academic courses related to the host country and its culture. High school students take courses alongside undergraduates.

CENTER FOR STUDY ABROAD
Res — Coed Ages 16 and up

Kent, WA 98032. 325 Washington Ave S, Ste 93. Tel: 206-583-8191.
www.centerforstudyabroad.com   E-mail: info@centerforstudyabroad.com
Alima K. Virtue, Prgm Mgr.
Grades 11-Col. Adm: FCFS. Appl—Fee $0. Due: Rolling.
Daily hours for: Classes 3½. College credit.
Intl program focus: Lang Culture. Locations: Asia Australia/New_Zealand Europe
Mexico/Central_America South_America. Home stays avail.
Focus: Chin Fr Ger Ital Japan Russ Span Vietnamese.
Fees 2009: Res $695-5795, 1-8 wks.

Est 1990. Nonprofit. **Wks/ses:** 1-8. Operates June-Aug.

CSA offers language immersion and culture study at overseas colleges, universities and language institutes in Germany, China, France, Austria, Japan, Spain, Mexico, Vietnam, Italy, Costa Rica, Russia, Australia, New Zealand, Brazil, Chile, England, Ireland, Peru, Portugal and Puerto Rico. Students of all ability levels may enroll, and transferable college credit is available. Participants live with host families, in hotels or at campus residences.
See Also Page 29

CENTRAL WISCONSIN ENVIRONMENTAL STATION SUMMER PROGRAMS
Res — Coed Ages 7-18

Amherst Junction, WI 54407. 10186 County Rd MM. Tel: 715-824-2428.
Fax: 715-824-3201.
www.uwsp.edu/cwes   E-mail: sjohnson@uwsp.edu
Scott D. Johnson, Dir.
Adm: FCFS. **Appl**—Due: Rolling.
Enr: 45. **Enr cap:** 55. **Fac** 3. **Staff:** Admin 4. Couns 9.
Type of instruction: Enrich. **Courses:** Ecol Sci Writing/Journ Crafts Music Studio_Art.
Focus: Environ_Sci. **Features:** Adventure_Travel Aquatics Archery Boating Canoe Climbing_Wall Conservation Exploration Fishing Hiking Kayak Outdoor_Ed Swim Volleyball.
Fees 2011: Res $260-430, 1 wk. Aid avail.
Housing: Cabins Lodges. **Swimming:** Lake.
Est 1975. Nonprofit. **Spons:** University of Wisconsin-Stevens Point. **Ses:** 10. **Wks/ses:** 1. Operates June-Aug.

A field station of the College of Natural Resources at the University of Wisconsin-Stevens Point, CWES offers nature exploration on 300 acres of forests, wetlands, lakes and fields. Programs for younger campers combine nature study and traditional camp activities, while those for older boys and girls focus on outdoor skill development. Natural Resource Careers Camp (for students ages 15-18) enables campers to explore career opportunities while gaining field experience in natural resource management and environmental protection.

CENTRE INTERNATIONAL D'ANTIBES
Res — Coed Ages 14-17

Antibes, 06600 France. 38 Blvd d'Aguillon. Tel: 202-470-6659. Fax: 33-811-035-167.
www.cia-france.com   E-mail: info@cia-france.com
Alexandre Garcia, Prgm Dir.
Adm: FCFS. **Appl**—Fee $0. Due: Rolling.
Staff: Admin 12.
Type of instruction: Enrich. **Avg class size:** 15. **Daily hours for:** Classes 3.
Intl program focus: Lang. Home stays avail.
Focus: Fr. **Features:** Sail Soccer Swim Tennis Volleyball.
Fees 2010: Res €645 (+airfare), 1 wk.
Housing: Dorms. Avg per room/unit: 2. **Swimming:** Ocean.
Est 1985. Ses: 6. **Wks/ses:** 1. Operates June-Sept.

Located between Nice and Cannes on the Cote d'Azur and conducted at Le Chateau Junior School, the Centre's Antibes program offers both standard and intensive French instruction. Pupils take 20 language courses per week, each of which lasts 45 minutes. Students often reside with host families and have access to the area's many beaches.

CENTRO KOINE
Res and Day — Coed Ages 14 and up

Florence, 50122 Italy. Via de Pandolfini 27. Tel: 39-055-213881. Fax: 39-055-216949.
www.koinecenter.com   E-mail: info@koinecenter.com
Adm: FCFS. **Appl**—Due: Rolling.
Enr: 70. **Enr cap:** 100. **Fac 10. Staff:** Admin 5. Couns 3.
Type of instruction: Adv Dev_Read Study_Skills Tut. **Courses:** Bus/Fin Comm Drama
Fine_Arts Photog Studio_Art. **Avg class size:** 8. **Daily hours for:** Classes 4. Study 2.
Rec 2. **College credit.**
Intl program focus: Lang. Home stays avail.
Focus: Ital. **Features:** Bicycle_Tours Cooking Hiking Mtn_Biking Outdoor_Ed Riding Sail
Scuba Cross-country Soccer Swim Tennis.
Fees 2009: Res €205-8182, 1-4 wks. Day €190-4780, 1-4 wks.
Housing: Hotels Houses Lodges. **Swimming:** Pool.
Est 1980. Nonprofit. **Wks/ses:** 1-4. Operates Year-round.

At locations in five Italian cities—Florence, Lucca, Cortona, Bologna and the Island of
Elba—the center offers Italian courses of varying lengths and ability levels. In addition to
language course work, pupils choose from a selection of Italian culture classes. Koine arranges
half or full boarding for each boy and girl with a host family or in a local hotel or hostel,
according to student preference.

CERAN LINGUA JUNIOR SUMMER PROGRAMS
Res — Coed Ages 10-18

Los Angeles, CA 90066. 3614 Wade St. Tel: 310-429-7406, 866-722-3726.
www.ceran.com/us   E-mail: info@ceran-us.com
Fabienne Carmanne, Dir.
    Student contact: Charlotte Neve, E-mail: charlotte@ceran-us.com.
Adm: FCFS. Admitted: 80%. **Appl**—Due: Rolling.
Enr: 250. **Enr cap:** 250. Intl: 90%. Non-White: 10%. **Fac 35. Staff:** Admin 19. Couns 30.
Type of instruction: Adv Study_Skills Tut. **Courses:** Crafts. **Avg class size:** 8. **Daily
hours for:** Classes 5. Study 2. Rec 5. Homework.
Intl program focus: Lang Culture. **Locations:** Europe.
Focus: ESL Fr Ger Span Dutch. **Features:** Bicycle_Tours Canoe Kayak Mtn_Biking Sail
Aerobics Badminton Basketball Cross-country Equestrian Soccer Swim Tennis Volley-
ball Ping-Pong.
Fees 2012: Res $1800 (+airfare), 1 wk.
Housing: Dorms. Avg per room/unit: 2. **Swimming:** Pool. Campus facilities avail.
Est 1975. Inc. **Ses:** 8. **Wks/ses:** 1. Operates June-Aug.

Ceran Lingua's summer programs offer intensive language immersion in five languages
and three countries. French, German, Dutch and English programs are available in Belgium,
English in the United Kingdom and Spanish in Spain. Students develop language skills through
participation in learning activities, sports, and cultural and social activities.

CHOATE ROSEMARY HALL ENGLISH LANGUAGE INSTITUTE
Res and Day — Coed Ages 12-18

Wallingford, CT 06492. 333 Christian St. Tel: 203-697-2365. Fax: 203-697-2519.
www.choate.edu/summerprograms   E-mail: choatesummer@choate.edu
J. Trent Nutting, Dir.
Grades 7-12. Adm: Selective. Admitted: 90%. **Appl**—Fee $60. Due: Rolling. Transcript, 3
recs, essay.
Enr: 50. Intl: 100%.
Type of instruction: Enrich ESL/TOEFL_Prep. **Courses:** Expository_Writing Public_Speak

Creative_Writing Dance Film Music. **Avg class size:** 11. **Daily hours for:** Classes 5½. Study 2. Rec 2. Homework. Tests.
Focus: ESL. **Features:** Yoga Aerobics Baseball Basketball Rugby Soccer Softball Swim Tennis Volleyball.
Fees 2011: Res $7365 (+$500), 5 wks. Day $6055 (+$500), 5 wks. Aid 2011 (Need): $300,000.
Housing: Dorms. **Swimming:** Pool. Campus facilities avail.
Nonprofit. **Ses:** 1. **Wks/ses:** 5. Operates June-July.

Serving nonnative speakers of English who have studied the language for at least three years in their home schools and who can converse in English, these intensive courses help students develop proficiency in standard English. Students develop ability in such language skills as writing, speaking, listening and reading, and they participate in minor courses, sports, meals, weekend dances and various social activities with students from the academic summer session. Integral components of this program are off-campus trips to various cities, museums and cultural events that supplement and relate to course work.

CHOATE ROSEMARY HALL
JOHN F. KENNEDY '35 INSTITUTE IN GOVERNMENT
Res and Day — Coed Ages 15-18

Wallingford, CT 06492. 333 Christian St. Tel: 203-697-2365. Fax: 203-697-2519.
www.choate.edu/summerprograms   E-mail: choatesummer@choate.edu
J. Trent Nutting, Dir.
Grades 10-12. Adm: Selective. Admitted: 90%. **Appl**—Fee $60. Due: Rolling. Transcript, essay, 3 recs, graded English paper.
Enr: 12. **Enr cap:** 12. Intl: 20%. Non-White: 20%.
Type of instruction: Enrich. **Courses:** Dance Drama Fine_Arts Music. **Avg class size:** 12.
Daily hours for: Classes 5½. Study 2. Rec 2. Homework. Tests.
Focus: Govt Pol_Sci. **Features:** Yoga Aerobics Baseball Basketball Rugby Soccer Softball Swim Tennis Volleyball.
Fees 2011: Res $7190 (+$500), 5 wks. Day $5635 (+$500), 5 wks. Aid 2011 (Need): $300,000.
Housing: Dorms. Avg per room/unit: 2. **Swimming:** Pool. Campus facilities avail.
Est 1985. Nonprofit. **Ses:** 1. **Wks/ses:** 5. Operates June-July.

Institute students take courses that focus on the formation of political ideas, the foundation and workings of the American government, and specific current domestic and foreign issues. Pupils spend the fourth week in Washington, DC, meeting with statesmen, interest groups, and organizations that work on the domestic and foreign issues that were discussed earlier in the session. Boys and girls engage in athletic, extracurricular and social activities with students from Choate's other summer programs.

CHOATE ROSEMARY HALL
MATH/SCIENCE INSTITUTE FOR GIRLS
Res and Day — Girls Ages 12-14

Wallingford, CT 06492. 333 Christian St. Tel: 203-697-2365. Fax: 203-697-2519.
www.choate.edu/summerprograms   E-mail: choatesummer@choate.edu
J. Trent Nutting, Dir.
Grades 7-9. Adm: Selective. Admitted: 90%. **Appl**—Fee $60. Due: Rolling.
Enr: 18. **Enr cap:** 24. Intl: 40%. Non-White: 10%.
Type of instruction: Enrich. **Courses:** Dance Drama Fine_Arts Music. **Avg class size:** 12.
Daily hours for: Classes 5½. Study 2. Rec 2. Homework. Tests.
Focus: Math Sci. **Features:** Yoga Aerobics Baseball Basketball Rugby Soccer Softball Swim Tennis Volleyball.

Fees 2011: Res $6700 (+$500), 5 wks. **Day** $5140 (+$500), 5 wks. Aid 2011 (Need): $300,000.
Housing: Dorms. Avg per room/unit: 2. **Swimming:** Pool. Campus facilities avail.
Nonprofit. **Ses:** 1. **Wks/ses:** 5. Operates June-July.

This intensive, five-week program enrolls middle school girls with a strong interest in math and science; advanced knowledge in these areas is not necessary. The institute seeks to build knowledge through hands-on projects, cooperative learning and team building; use of technology, including graphing calculators, computer spreadsheets, statistics software and word processors; research skill and technique instruction; and enriching field trips. The program culminates with an independent research project: Each student conducts library research on a topic of interest and formulates a scientific hypothesis, then designs and performs an experiment to test the hypothesis.

CHOATE ROSEMARY HALL
SUMMER STUDY ABROAD PROGRAMS
Res — Coed Ages 15-18

Wallingford, CT 06942. 333 Christian St. Tel: 203-697-2365. Fax: 203-697-2519.
www.choate.edu/summerstudyabroad   E-mail: choatesummer@choate.edu
J. Trent Nutting, Dir.
Grades 10-12. Adm: Selective. Admitted: 90%. **Appl**—Fee $60. Due: Rolling. Transcript, 2 recs.
Enr: 25. **Enr cap:** 25. **Intl:** 30%. **Non-White:** 25%.
Type of instruction: Enrich. **Avg class size:** 12. **Daily hours for:** Classes 4. Study 2. Rec 3. Homework. Tests.
Intl program focus: Acad Lang Culture. **Locations:** Asia Europe. Home stays avail.
Focus: Chin Fr Span.
Fees 2011: Res $7500, 5 wks.
Housing: Dorms Hotels.
Nonprofit. **Ses:** 3. **Wks/ses:** 5. Operates June-July.

Five-week programs in China, France and Spain, each beginning with a one- or two-day orientation at Choate, combine academic study with total immersion in the language and the culture. Each program features day trips and extended excursions to historical and cultural sites.

CHRISTCHURCH SCHOOL MARINE SCIENCE PROGRAMS
Res and Day — Coed Ages 8-15

Christchurch, VA 23031. 49 Seahorse Ln. Tel: 804-758-2306. Fax: 804-758-0721.
www.christchurchschool.org/marineadventurecamp
E-mail: aporter@christchurchschool.org
Amanda G. Porter, Dir.
Adm: FCFS. **Appl**—Fee $0. Due: Rolling.
Type of instruction: Enrich. **Courses:** Environ_Sci. **Avg class size:** 10.
Focus: Marine_Bio/Stud. **Features:** Boating Canoe Conservation Deep-sea Fishing Field_ Ecol Fishing Hiking Swim Watersports.
Fees 2011: Res $850, 1 wk. **Day** $550, 1 wk.
Housing: Dorms Tents. **Swimming:** River.
Est 1984. Nonprofit. **Ses:** 2. **Wks/ses:** 1. Operates June-July.

Christchurch offers two age-based marine science programs. For campers ages 8-11, Chesapeake Critter Camp involves the weeklong exploration of creatures dwelling in and around the Rappahannock River and Chesapeake Bay watersheds. Children search for insect and animal life while on foot or in a boat. Older boys and girls (ages 12-15) engage in a hands-on examination of the wetlands of the Chesapeake Bay Watersheds. Campers gain a better understanding of the wetlands and their importance by walking, crawling and swimming through swamps, bogs, and fresh- and saltwater marshes.

CIVIC LEADERSHIP INSTITUTE
Res — Coed Ages 15-18

Evanston, IL 60208. 617 Dartmouth Pl. Tel: 847-467-2572. Fax: 847-467-0880.
www.civiceducationproject.com; http://cty.jhu.edu/summer/leadership.html
E-mail: cep@northwestern.edu; ctyinfo@jhu.edu
Katrina Weimholt, Prgm Dir.
Grades 10-PG. Adm: Very selective. Prereqs: Gr 6-9: SAT CR 510; ACT R 24. **Appl**—Fee $50-60. Due: Rolling. Satisfy testing requirements or submit portfolio: test scores, transcript, 2 teacher recs.
Enr: 219. **Fac 15. Staff:** Admin 18. Couns 31.
Type of instruction: Adv. **Courses:** Govt. **Avg class size:** 15. **Daily hours for:** Classes 5. Study 2. Rec 4. **High school credit:** 1.
Locations: CA IL MD.
Focus: Leadership. **Features:** Community_Serv.
Fees 2011: Res $3175-3820 (+$110), 3 wks. Aid (Merit & Need).
Housing: Dorms. Avg per room/unit: 2.
Est 1997. Nonprofit. Spons: Northwestern University/Johns Hopkins University. **Ses:** 3.
Wks/ses: 3. Operates June-Aug.

A collaboration between the Civic Education Project at Northwestern University's Center for Talent Development and Johns Hopkins University's Center for Talented Youth, CLI integrates rigorous academics, community service and hands-on field experiences. This program for talented high schoolers emphasizes knowledge acquisition and leadership skills development. An introductory course in civic engagement and contemporary social issues explores challenges affecting communities through active discussions and group projects. Students engage in service-learning projects in urban neighborhoods, meet with community leaders, and attend special seminars and guest speaker presentations. Boys and girls apply through Northwestern CTD for the CLI program hosted by the University of Illinois-Chicago, or through Johns Hopkins CTY for sessions at John Hopkins University or San Francisco State University.

CLEMSON UNIVERSITY
SUMMER SCIENCE, ENGINEERING AND
ARCHITECTURE ENRICHMENT PROGRAM
Res — Coed Ages 12-18

Clemson, SC 29634. E-208 Martin Hall, Box 345136. Tel: 864-656-5849.
Fax: 864-656-1480.
www.clemson.edu/summerscience   E-mail: cnell@clemson.edu
Nell Coffey, Dir.
Grades 7-12. Adm: Selective. **Appl**—Fee $0. Due: May. Transcript, test scores, rec.
Type of instruction: Adv Enrich. **Courses:** Comp_Sci Forensic_Sci Math Psych.
Focus: Architect Engineering Environ_Sci Sci. **Features:** Swim Tennis.
Fees 2009: Res $850-1900, 1-2 wks.
Housing: Dorms. Avg per room/unit: 2. **Swimming:** Pool.
Ses: 8. **Wks/ses:** 1-2. Operates June-Aug.

Summer Science features weeklong introductions to college subjects for middle and high school students, as well as two-week specialized courses for advanced high school students. Classes, which vary by year, draw from the disciplines of the life sciences, math, engineering, computer science and architecture. Evening and weekend activities include nature study hikes, small-group discussions with Clemson faculty, and career and educational guidance.

COLLEGE DU LEMAN SUMMER CAMPUS
Res — Coed Ages 8-18

Versoix, 1290 Geneva, Switzerland. 74 Rte de Sauverny, PO Box 156.
Tel: 41-22-775-55-55. Fax: 41-22-775-55-59.
www.cdl.ch   E-mail: summercampus@cdl.ch
Francis A. Clivaz, Dir.
Grades 3-12. Adm: FCFS. **Appl**—Fee $0. Due: Rolling.
Enr: 300. **Fac 40. Staff:** Admin 20.
Type of instruction: Adv Dev_Read Enrich Preview Rem_Eng Rem_Math Rem_Read Rev. **Courses:** Circus_Skills. **Avg class size:** 12. **Daily hours for:** Classes 3. **High school credit:** 2.
Intl program focus: Lang.
Focus: ESL Fr. **Features:** Archery Bicycle_Tours Canoe Cooking Cruises Hiking Kayak Mtn_Trips Riding Sail Baseball Basketball Cross-country Equestrian Golf Gymnastics Lacrosse Martial_Arts Soccer Softball Swim Tennis Track Water-skiing Watersports.
Fees 2011: Res SwF6300, 3 wks. Day SwF3200, 3 wks.
Housing: Dorms. **Swimming:** Lake Pool.
Est 1960. Inc. **Spons:** Meritas. **Ses:** 2. **Wks/ses:** 3. Operates July-Aug.

College du Leman offers French and English language instruction at beginning through advanced levels. Pupils attend language courses each Monday through Saturday morning, with afternoons devoted to sports and arts-related activities. Summer Campus features excursions once a week to nearby places of interest.

COLLEGE OF THE ATLANTIC
ISLANDS THROUGH TIME
Res — Coed Ages 15-18

Bar Harbor, ME 04609. 105 Eden St. Tel: 207-288-5015, 800-597-9500.
Fax: 207-288-4126.
www.coa.edu/islandsthroughtime.htm   E-mail: mstivers@coa.edu
Marie Stivers, Dir.
Grades 11-12. Adm: Selective. **Appl**—Fee $0. Due: Apr. Rec, essays.
Enr: 16. **Enr cap:** 16. **Fac 5. Prof 5. Staff:** Admin 2. Couns 4.
Type of instruction: Adv Preview. **Courses:** Hist Marine_Bio/Stud Oceanog Writing/Journ Filmmaking Media Music Photog. **Avg class size:** 10. **Daily hours for:** Classes 7. Study 2½. Rec 1½. **College credit:** 3.
Focus: Ecol. **Features:** Conservation Exploration Hiking Kayak Outdoor_Ed Sea_Cruises Seamanship Swim.
Fees 2011: Res $3700, 2 wks. Aid (Need).
Housing: Dorms. Avg per room/unit: 1-2. **Swimming:** Ocean. Campus facilities avail.
Est 2007. Nonprofit. **Ses:** 1. **Wks/ses:** 2. Operates July-Aug.

Students enrolled in this intensive precollege program explore the relationship between humans and the environment. ITT begins with an introduction to the ecology, the history and the culture of the Maine coast, taught from an interdisciplinary perspective that incorporates marine biology, oceanography, anthropology and literature. Boys and girls conduct marine research at island field stations; learn the basics of navigation, steering and ship handling aboard a research vessel; examine the lives of coastal Maine residents; and work on their reading and writing skills with college faculty. At the conclusion of the program, pupils work in teams on multimedia presentations that detail their experiences.

COLLEGE OF THE ATLANTIC
RIVERS: A WILDERNESS ODYSSEY
Res — Coed Ages 16-18

Bar Harbor, ME 04609. 105 Eden St. Tel: 207-288-5015, 800-597-9500. Fax: 207-288-4126.
www.coa.edu/riversawildernessodyssey.htm   E-mail: mstivers@coa.edu
Marie Stivers, Dir.
Grades 11-12. Adm: Selective. **Appl**—Fee $0. Due: Apr. Rec, essays.
Enr: 8. **Enr cap:** 8. **Fac 3.** Prof 3. **Staff:** Admin 2. Couns 2.
Type of instruction: Adv Undergrad. **Courses:** Leadership Psych Creative_Writing Photog. **Daily hours for:** Classes 7. Study 2½. Rec 1½. **College credit:** 3.
Focus: Ecol. **Features:** Canoe Conservation Exploration Outdoor_Ed Wilderness_Camp Wilderness_Canoe Swim Watersports.
Fees 2011: Res $3700, 2 wks. Aid (Merit).
Housing: Dorms. Avg per room/unit: 1-2. **Swimming:** River. Campus facilities avail. Nonprofit. **Ses:** 1. **Wks/ses:** 2. Operates July-Aug.

This intensive program for rising high school juniors and seniors begins on the College of the Atlantic campus with an introduction to the history and policy of the northern Maine woods. Students learn about the natural history, literature, conservation and psychological aspects of wilderness and river systems through readings and discussion. Participants then explore Acadia National Park and canoe down the Allagash Wilderness Waterway. These expeditions serve as a laboratory to experience and investigate group dynamics in a wilderness setting while also examining leadership, authority and community. A group presentation at session's end enables students to share samples of their writings and photographs with program peers and professors and the public.

THE COLLEGE OF WILLIAM AND MARY
PRE-COLLEGIATE SUMMER PROGRAM
IN EARLY AMERICAN HISTORY
Res — Coed Ages 16-18

Williamsburg, VA 23187. c/o Natl Inst of American History & Democracy, PO Box 8795. Tel: 757-221-7652. Fax: 757-221-7655.
www.wm.edu/niahd/precollegiate.php   E-mail: precol@wm.edu
Carolyn S. Whittenburg, Dir.
Grades 11-PG. Adm: Selective. **Appl**—Fee $0. Due: Apr. Transcript, teacher rec, essay.
Enr cap: 60.
Type of instruction: Adv. **College credit:** 4.
Focus: Hist.
Fees 2010: Res $3490-3990, 3 wks. Aid (Need).
Housing: Dorms. Campus facilities avail.
Est 2002. Nonprofit. **Ses:** 2. **Wks/ses:** 3. Operates June-Aug.

In this program, rising high school juniors and seniors study the intertwined histories of Native Americans, Europeans, Africans and their descendants, while also gaining an introduction to college life. Lectures and performances by interpreters, tours with curators and archaeologists, and discussions with historians and other scholars complement classroom study. Students earn four hours of college credit upon successful completion of the program.

THE COLLEGE OF WILLIAM AND MARY
SCIENCE TRAINING AND RESEARCH PROGRAM
Res — Coed Ages 16-17

Williamsburg, VA 23187. Office of Multicultural Affairs, PO Box 8795.
Tel: 757-221-2300. Fax: 757-221-1105.
www.wm.edu/multiculturalaffairs/starprogram.php   E-mail: vjhurt@wm.edu
Vernon J. Hurte, Coord.
Grade 11. Adm: Very selective. Priority: Low-income. Prereqs: GPA 3.0. **Appl**—Fee $0.
  Due: May. Transcript, 2 recs.
Enr: 25. Enr cap: 25.
Type of instruction: Enrich SAT/ACT_Prep. **Courses:** Math. **Daily hours for:** Classes 6.
Focus: Sci.
Fees 2010: Free. Res 4 wks.
Housing: Dorms.
Nonprofit. **Ses: 1. Wks/ses: 4.** Operates June-July.

A free program for rising juniors from a disadvantaged background, the STAR Program is a precollege enrichment session that addresses the varied opportunities available in science, research and technology. Another aspect of the program enables boys and girls to engage in intensive SAT preparation workshops designed to improve their performance on the test. William and Mary assigns each pupil with a faculty mentor according to the student's individual interests; these relationships are an integral part of the program and they continue through the participant's high school years.

COLORADO SCHOOL OF MINES
SUMMER MINORITY ENGINEERING TRAINING PROGRAM
Res — Coed Ages 16-17

Golden, CO 80401. 1112 18th St. Tel: 303-273-3286, 800-446-9488. Fax: 303-273-3760.
http://mep.mines.edu   E-mail: mep@mines.edu
Lori Scheider, Dir.
Grades 11-12. Adm: Selective. Priority: URM. **Appl**—Fee $0. Due: Apr. Transcript, 2 recs,
  essays.
Enr: 24. Fac 8. Staff: Res 5.
Type of instruction: Enrich. **Courses:** Comp_Sci Geol Math Sci. **Avg class size:** 24.
  Homework. Tests. Grades.
Focus: Engineering. **Features:** Swim.
Fees 2011: Free (+$50), 3 wks.
Housing: Dorms. **Swimming:** Pool.
Est 1971. Nonprofit. **Ses: 1. Wks/ses: 3.** Operates June-July.

Designed for talented rising high school juniors and seniors with strong aptitude in math and science and a minority background, the SUMMET Program combines class work, hands-on projects, industry tours, athletic activities and social events. The curriculum, which consists of various math and science courses, addresses basic to advanced engineering concepts.

COLUMBIA INTERNATIONAL COLLEGE ESL SUMMER CAMP
Res — Coed Ages 9-19

Hamilton, L8S 4P3 Ontario, Canada. 1003 Main St W. Tel: 905-572-7883.
Fax: 905-572-9332.
www.cic-totalcare.com   E-mail: columbia@cic-totalcare.com
Clement Chan, Exec Dir.
Grades 4-12. Adm: FCFS. **Appl**—Due: Rolling.
Enr: 500. Intl: 100%. Non-White: 95%. Staff: Admin 8. Couns 35.
Type of instruction: Enrich Rem_Eng. **Courses:** Computers Debate Sci Speech Crafts

Creative_Writing Dance Music Painting Photog Theater. **Avg class size:** 18. **Daily hours for:** Classes 3.
Intl program focus: Lang Culture.
Focus: ESL. **Features:** Aquatics Archery Canoe Climbing_Wall Conservation Cooking Fishing Hiking Kayak Leadership Outdoor_Ed Peace/Cross-cultural Rock_Climb Ropes_Crse Survival_Trng White-water_Raft Wilderness_Camp Wilderness_Canoe Badminton Baseball Basketball Field_Hockey Football Golf Gymnastics Lacrosse Martial_Arts Soccer Swim Tennis Volleyball Watersports.
Fees 2012: Res Can$3050-4200 (+Can$245), 3-4 wks.
Housing: Dorms Houses. Avg per room/unit: 2-4. **Swimming:** Lake Pool.
Est 1995. Ses: 5. **Wks/ses:** 3-4. Operates June-Aug.

This English as a Second Language camp combines three hours of daily English lessons (at beginning through advanced levels) with recreational activities and cultural trips. Science and computers and technology courses, arts and crafts, and sports complement language instruction. CIC schedules cultural trips to historic and cultural sites on weekends. The four-week session, at Bark Lake, features leadership and team-building pursuits and outdoor recreational activities.

COLUMBIA SCHOLASTIC PRESS ASSOCIATION
SUMMER JOURNALISM WORKSHOP
Res and Day — Coed Ages 15-18

New York, NY 10027. Columbia Univ, MC 5711. Tel: 212-854-9400. Fax: 212-854-9401.
http://cspa.columbia.edu   E-mail: cspa@columbia.edu
Edmund J. Sullivan, Exec Dir.
Grades 10-12. Adm: FCFS. **Appl**—Fee $0. Due: Rolling.
Enr: 325. **Enr cap:** 325. Non-White: 15%. **Fac 13.** K-12 staff 13. **Staff:** Admin 4. Couns 4.
Type of instruction: Enrich. **Courses:** Media Photog Graphic_Design. **Avg class size:** 20.
Daily hours for: Classes 6. Study 5. Rec 4. Homework.
Focus: Writing/Journ.
Fees 2012: Res $1029 (+$200), 1 wk. Day $699, 1 wk.
Housing: Dorms. Avg per room/unit: 2.
Est 1982. Nonprofit. **Spons:** Columbia University. **Ses:** 1. **Wks/ses:** 1. Operates June.

This intensive, five-day program is open to high school newspaper and yearbook students and advisors. Enrolling as individuals or as part of a school group, participants choose a class sequence focusing on writing, editing, management or advanced design for either newspapers or yearbooks. Newspaper students also receive critiques of past issues of their schools' publications.

CONCORDIA LANGUAGE VILLAGES
Res — Coed Ages 7-18; Day — Coed 6-11

Moorhead, MN 56562. 901 S 8th St. Tel: 218-299-4544, 800-222-4750.
Fax: 218-299-3807.
www.concordialanguagevillages.org   E-mail: clv@cord.edu
Christine Schulze, Exec Dir.
Student contact: Carl-Martin Nelson, E-mail: cnelson@cord.edu.
Grades 1-12 (younger if qualified). Adm: FCFS. **Appl**—Fee $40. Due: Rolling.
Staff: Admin 50.
Type of instruction: Adv Enrich. **Courses:** Environ_Sci ESL Crafts Dance Filmmaking Media Music Theater. **Daily hours for:** Classes 3. Homework. Tests. Grades. **High school & college credit:** 4.
Focus: Arabic Chin Fr Ger Ital Japan Russ Span Danish Finnish Korean Norwegian Portuguese Swedish. **Features:** Bicycle_Tours Canoe Chess Conservation Cooking Fish-

ing Hiking Sail Wilderness_Camp Wilderness_Canoe Baseball Fencing Martial_Arts Soccer Swim Volleyball.
Fees 2011: Res $835-4225, 1-4 wks. Day $159-189, 1 wk. Aid (Merit & Need).
Housing: Cabins Tents. Avg per room/unit: 10. **Swimming:** Lake.
Est 1961. Nonprofit. **Spons:** Concordia College (MN). **Ses:** 124. **Wks/ses:** 1-4. Operates June-Aug.

Concordia provides immersion programs in more than a dozen languages. Students are immersed in the language and the culture of their village. In addition to one- and two-week sessions, Concordia offers an intensive four-week program that enables those entering grades 9-12 to earn high school credit or rising juniors or seniors to earn college credit. Twice each summer, the separate villages come together for International Day to share dance, arts and crafts, songs and languages from around the world.

COSMOS
CALIFORNIA STATE SUMMER SCHOOL
FOR MATHEMATICS AND SCIENCE
Res — Coed Ages 14-18

Oakland, CA 94612. 300 Lakeside Dr, 7th Fl. Tel: 510-987-9711. Fax: 510-763-4704.
www.ucop.edu/cosmos   E-mail: cosmos@ucop.edu
Melina Duarte, Dir.
Grades 9-PG. Adm: Selective. Prereqs: GPA 3.5. **Appl**—Fee $30. Due: Mar. Transcript, math & sci teacher recs.
Enr cap: 160.
Type of instruction: Adv Enrich.
Focus: Math Sci.
Fees 2011: Res $2675-6500, 4 wks. Aid (Need).
Housing: Dorms. Avg per room/unit: 2.
Nonprofit. **Ses:** 4. **Wks/ses:** 4. Operates June-Aug.

On University of California campuses in Davis, Irvine, San Diego and Santa Cruz, COSMOS enables advanced math and science students to engage themselves in an intensive academic experience that addresses topics not generally taught in high schools. Among these subject areas are astronomy, aerospace engineering, biomedical science, wetlands ecology, ocean science, robotics and game theory. Pupils enroll in two classes drawn from math and science, along with a science communication course. The program includes hands-on lab work, field activities, lectures and discussions, and students also complete a research project.

CROW CANYON ARCHAEOLOGICAL CENTER
SUMMER FIELD SCHOOL FOR TEENS
Res — Coed Ages 12-17

Cortez, CO 81321. 23390 Rd K. Tel: 970-565-8975, 800-422-8975. Fax: 970-565-4859.
www.crowcanyon.org   E-mail: summercamp@crowcanyon.org
Deborah Gangloff, Dir. Student contact: Debra K. Miller.
Grades 7-12. Adm: Somewhat selective. Admitted: 99%. Priority: URM.
Enr cap: 20-30. Intl: 5%. Non-White: 18%. **Fac 3.** K-12 staff 3. **Staff:** Admin 3. Couns 3.
Type of instruction: Adv. **Avg class size:** 25. **Daily hours for:** Classes 8. Rec 4. **High school & college credit:** 2.
Focus: Archaeol. **Features:** Conservation Exploration Hiking Outdoor_Ed White-water_ Raft.
Fees 2012: Res $1425-4325, 1-3 wks. Aid 2010 (Need): $8650.
Housing: Dorms. Avg per room/unit: 3-6.
Est 1983. Nonprofit. **Ses:** 3. **Wks/ses:** 1-3. Operates June-July.

Students in this hands-on introduction to archaeology spend up to three weeks exploring the

Mesa Verde region of southwestern Colorado. After studying the history of the Pueblo Indians, boys and girls join teams of professional archaeologists at a working excavation site and learn to sort and identify artifacts. Pupils gain knowledge about the culture and the lifestyles of the ancestral people through games, concerts, crafts and discussions. Scholarships are available to American Indian students, as well as to those from the Four Corners region.

CUB CREEK SCIENCE CAMP
Res — Coed Ages 7-17

Rolla, MO 65401. c/o Bear River Ranch, 16795 Hwy E. Tel: 573-458-2125. Fax: 573-458-2126.
www.bearriverranch.com   E-mail: director@bearriverranch.com
Lori Martin, Dir.
Grades 2-12. Adm: FCFS. **Appl**—Fee $0. Due: Apr.
Enr cap: 168. **Intl:** 5%. Non-White: 10%. **Fac 50. Staff:** Admin 5.
Type of instruction: Enrich. **Courses:** Forensic_Sci Geol Botany Entomology Crafts Photog Pottery. **Avg class size:** 8. **Daily hours for:** Classes 5. Rec 9.
Focus: Med/Healthcare Sci Veterinary_Med. **Features:** Aquatics Archery Caving Conservation Cooking Exploration Farm Fishing Hiking Outdoor_Ed Survival_Trng Swim.
Fees 2012: Res $795-4700 (+$40-160), 1-6 wks.
Housing: Cabins. Avg per room/unit: 14. **Swimming:** Pond Pool.
Est 1993. Inc. Ses: 10. **Wks/ses:** 1-6. Operates June-Aug.

At this science camp, children live on a working farm alongside some 200 animals representing more than 100 species. Campers enroll in two classes from a course list that combines animal courses with science and arts offerings. The hands-on junior veterinarian program prepares children to care for various mammals, birds and reptiles. Boys and girls gain experience in using the scientific method of inquiry.

CULTURAL EMBRACE JUNIOR SUMMER PROGRAMS
Res — Coed Ages 14-18

Austin, TX 78745. 7201 Bill Hughes Rd. Tel: 512-469-9089. Fax: 512-233-5140.
www.culturalembrace.com   E-mail: info@culturalembrace.com
Emlyn Lee, Pres.
Grades 9-12. Adm: FCFS. **Appl**—Fee $250. Due: Rolling.
Enr: 25. **Enr cap:** 25. **Staff:** Admin 3.
Type of instruction: Adv Rev. **Courses:** Crafts Dance Drama Fine_Arts Media Music Photog. **Daily hours for:** Classes 3. Rec 4. **High school & college credit:** 9.
Intl program focus: Lang Culture. **Locations:** Asia Australia/New_Zealand Europe Mexico/Central_America South_America. Home stays avail.
Focus: Chin Fr Ger Ital Span Thai. **Features:** Adventure_Travel Aquatics Bicycle_Tours Boating Canoe Community_Serv Conservation Cooking Exploration Fishing Hiking Kayak Mountaineering Mtn_Biking Mtn_Trips Outdoor_Ed Riding Rock_Climb Sail Scuba Swim.
Fees 2011: Res $2790-3385, 2-8 wks.
Housing: Cabins Dorms Houses. Avg per room/unit: 2. **Swimming:** Lake Pond Ocean Pool River Stream.
Est 2003. Inc. Wks/ses: 2-8.

Conducted in Mexico, China, Costa Rica, France, Germany, Italy, Spain, Thailand and Australia, the Junior Summer Programs combine intensive study in the host country's language with cultural immersion. Depending upon the country, students receive between 15 and 20 hours of language instruction per week; language courses are typically available at beginning, intermediate and advanced levels. Weekend excursions at all locations provide participants with opportunities for sightseeing and cultural exploration.

CULTURAL EXPERIENCES ABROAD SUMMER PROGRAMS
Res — Coed Ages 18 and up

**Tempe, AZ 85281. 2005 W 14th St, Ste 113. Tel: 480-557-7900, 800-266-4441.
Fax: 480-557-7926.
www.gowithcea.com   E-mail: info@gowithcea.com
Brian Boubek, Exec Dir.
Grades PG-Col. Adm:** FCFS. Prereqs: GPA 2.5. **Appl**—Fee $95. Due: Rolling.
Type of instruction: Enrich. **Courses:** Bus/Fin Econ Environ_Sci Art Theater.
Intl program focus: Lang Culture. **Locations:** Africa Asia Europe Mexico/Central_America South_America.
Focus: Chin Fr Ger Ital Russ Span Polish. **Features:** Community_Serv.
**Fees 2010: Res $2495-8495, 1-8 wks.
Ses: 117. Wks/ses:** 1-8. Operates June-Aug.

CEA offers study-abroad programs for recent high school graduates and college students in Argentina, China, Costa Rica, the Czech Republic, England, France, Germany, Ireland, Italy, Mexico, Poland, Russia, South Africa and Spain. While language and cultural immersion is the most common course emphasis, certain sessions address other subjects, including healthcare, the environment, history and business.

DAUPHIN ISLAND SEA LAB
RESIDENTIAL SUMMER OPPORTUNITIES
Res — Coed Ages 10-17

**Dauphin Island, AL 36528. 101 Bienville Blvd. Tel: 251-861-2141. Fax: 251-861-4646.
www.disl.org   E-mail: sejohnson@disl.org
Tina Miller-Way, Dir. Student contact: Sara E. Johnson.
Grades 5-12. Adm:** Somewhat selective. **Appl**—Fee $50. Due: Apr. HS: Transcript, 2 teacher recs, essay.
Enr: 15-30. **Enr cap:** 15-30. Non-White: 15%. **Fac 3.** K-12 staff 3. **Staff:** Admin 2. Couns 5.
Type of instruction: Enrich. **Courses:** Crafts. Tests. **High school credit.**
Focus: Marine_Bio/Stud Oceanog. **Features:** Fishing Basketball Soccer Swim Volleyball.
Fees 2011: Res $360-2050, 1-4 wks. Aid 2011 (Merit & Need): $7250.
Housing: Dorms. Avg per room/unit: 2. **Swimming:** Ocean Pool.
Ses: 4. Wks/ses: 1-4. Operates June-July.

Rising seventh through ninth graders may enroll in DISL's Gulf Island Journey, a weeklong enrichment program of hands-on marine science programming. Activities include a trawling expedition aboard Sea Lab's research vessel, exploration of the salt marshes of Dauphin Island, and beachcombing and bird watching on nearby Sand Island. A second program, High School Summer Course, is an accredited, four-week marine science class for rising 10th through 12th graders. During this four-week program, students conduct an intensive exploration of marine science through 150 hours of supervised academic activities in the form of lectures, laboratory work and field pursuits.

DILE CURSOS INTERNACIONALES DE ESPANOL
SPANISH COURSE FOR YOUNG PEOPLE
Res — Coed Ages 14-18

**Salamanca, 37007 Spain. Plaza del Oeste 3. Tel: 34-923-282-446.
Fax: 34-923-282-566.
www.dilecursos.com   E-mail: salamanca@dilecursos.com
Lourdes Prieto de los Mozos, Dir. Student contact: Susan Bernamont.
Adm:** FCFS. **Appl**—Fee $0. Due: Rolling.
Enr cap: 64. Fac 8. Prof 8. **Staff:** Admin 3.

Type of instruction: Enrich Tut. **Courses:** Dance Drama Music. **Avg class size:** 5. **Daily hours for:** Classes 4. Study 1. Rec 5. Homework. Tests. Grades.
Intl program focus: Lang. Home stays avail.
Focus: Span. **Features:** Boating Cooking Mtn_Biking Riding Basketball Equestrian Football Golf Soccer Swim Tennis Volleyball.
Fees 2012: Res €735-1845 (+€65), 2-6 wks.
Housing: Dorms Houses. **Swimming:** Pool.
Est 2000. Ses: 4. **Wks/ses:** 2. Operates July-Sept.

Students receive 20 lessons each week in this language immersion program. Classes ranging from beginning to advanced focus on listening and reading comprehension, as well as speaking and writing skills. Additional program elements are grammar structure, text analysis and composition, and various group activities. Outside class, pupils take part in dance, music, boating, equestrian, sports, cooking and weekend excursions.

DON QUIJOTE SUMMER CAMPS
Res and Day — Coed Ages 5-18

Madrid, 28015 Spain. Alberto Aguilera 26. Tel: 34-91-594-37-76. Fax: 34-91-594-51-59. www.donquijote.org E-mail: infocentral@donquijote.org
Antonio Anadon, Pres.
Adm: FCFS. **Appl**—Fee €65. Due: Rolling.
Enr cap: 50-220. Intl: 60%.
Type of instruction: Enrich. **Courses:** Crafts Dance Fine_Arts Theater. **Avg class size:** 14. **Daily hours for:** Classes 4½. Study 3. Rec 3. Homework. Tests. Grades.
Intl program focus: Lang Culture. **Locations:** Europe. Home stays avail.
Focus: Span. **Features:** Adventure_Travel Archery Cooking Riding Aerobics Badminton Basketball Equestrian Field_Hockey Golf Soccer Swim Tennis Ultimate_Frisbee Volleyball Watersports.
Fees 2012: Res €660-4500, 1-8 wks. Day €325-650, 1-2 wks.
Housing: Apartments Houses. **Swimming:** Pool.
Est 1986. Inc. **Wks/ses:** 1-8. Operates June-Aug.

With instruction for students of all ability levels, don Quijote offers Spanish immersion summer programs in seven Spanish locations: Barcelona, Salamanca, Marbella, Seville, Madrid, Granada and Valencia. At each location, boys and girls enroll in residential camp, day camp or language study only; those in the language course do not engage in any camp activities. Pupils attend four classes per weekday (each limited to 14 students) as they follow a syllabus that is compatible with the US academic credit system. Conversation and communication are the main points of emphasis.

DREXEL UNIVERSITY COLLEGE OF ENGINEERING SUMMER MENTORSHIP PROGRAM
Res and Day — Coed Ages 14-17

**Philadelphia, PA 19104. 3141 Chestnut St, CAT Rm 170. Tel: 215-895-2210. Fax: 215-895-4929.
www.drexel.edu/coe/special/summer/mentor E-mail: mentorship@coe.drexel.edu**
Grades 9-12. Adm: Selective. **Appl**—Due: Apr. Transcript, rec, essays, standardized test scores, interview.
Type of instruction: Adv Enrich.
Focus: Engineering.
Fees 2009: Res $300, 3 wks. Day $0, 3 wks.
Housing: Dorms.
Nonprofit. **Ses:** 1. **Wks/ses:** 3. Operates July-Aug.

This Drexel University program enables high school students to work in a university laboratory on an individualized engineering research project. Excursions to Atlantic City, NJ, and to cultural and sporting events in Philadelphia are popular extracurricular activities. Boarding costs represent the only program fees.

DREXEL UNIVERSITY
DISCOVERING ARCHITECTURE
Res — Coed Ages 16-18

Philadelphia, PA 19104. Dept of Architecture & Interiors, 3201 Arch St, Ste 110.
Tel: 215-895-2409. Fax: 215-895-4921.
www.drexel.edu/academics/comad/architecture   E-mail: architecture@drexel.edu
Grade 12. Adm: Selective. **Appl**—Fee $0. Due: Rolling. Transcript, essay.
Enr: 34. **Enr cap:** 34.
Type of instruction: Enrich Undergrad.
Focus: Architect. **Features:** Swim Volleyball.
Fees 2009: Res $2700, 2 wks.
Housing: Dorms. **Swimming:** Pool. Campus facilities avail.
Nonprofit. **Ses:** 1. **Wks/ses:** 2. Operates July.

Participants in this intensive two-week program attend architecture classes taught by Drexel faculty members in on-campus studios and computer labs. Students work closely with instructors on architectural design, attend lectures by distinguished speakers, embark on field trips to some of the city's noteworthy architectural sites and meet area architects at their offices. Pupils devote most afternoons in the studio developing design projects through drawings and models; some evening studio work is also likely. The session culminates in a formal presentation to faculty and invited professionals.

DUKE UNIVERSITY
ACTION SCIENCE CAMP FOR YOUNG WOMEN
Res and Day — Girls Ages 11-13

Durham, NC 27708. Continuing Stud, 201 Bishop's House, Box 90700.
Tel: 919-684-6259, 866-338-3853. Fax: 919-681-8235.
www.learnmore.duke.edu/youth/action   E-mail: youth@duke.edu
Randee Haven-O'Donnell, Dir. Student contact: Thomas Patterson.
Grades 6-8. Adm: FCFS. Admitted: 100%. **Appl**—Fee $0. Due: Rolling.
Enr cap: 30. **Fac 4.** Col/grad students 1. K-12 staff 3. **Staff:** Admin 6. Couns 3.
Type of instruction: Enrich. **Courses:** Ecol Environ_Sci Crafts. **Daily hours for:** Classes 4. Rec 3.
Focus: Sci.
Fees 2012: Res $1880 (+$75), 2 wks. Day $1005 (+$75), 2 wks. Aid (Need).
Housing: Dorms. Avg per room/unit: 2.
Est 1991. Ses: 1. **Wks/ses:** 2. Operates June.

Action Science Camp promotes scientific discovery through work in laboratories and at field sites in the Duke University forest. Girls examine ecological and biological principles through explorations of terrestrial and aquatic life, chemical and physical properties of the environment, and the impact of human activities on ecosystems.

DUKE UNIVERSITY TALENT IDENTIFICATION PROGRAM
FIELD STUDIES AND INSTITUTES
Res — Coed Ages 15-18

Durham, NC 27701. 1121 W Main St. Tel: 919-668-9100. Fax: 919-681-7921.
www.tip.duke.edu   E-mail: information@tip.duke.edu

Nicki Charles, Dir.
Grades 10-PG. Adm: Selective. **Appl**—Fee $35. Due: Mar. Transcript, test scores, rec, resume, essay.
Enr cap: 16-20.
Type of instruction: Adv Enrich. **Courses:** Psych Genetics Creative_Writing Filmmaking.
Locations: CA FL NM Asia Canada Europe Mexico/Central_America.
Focus: Architect Astron Ecol Intl_Relations Ger Law Leadership Marine_Bio/Stud Med/Healthcare Pol_Sci.
Fees 2011: Res $3450-4650 (+airfare), 2 wks. Aid (Need).
Housing: Dorms Hotels.
Est 1980. Nonprofit. **Ses:** 18. **Wks/ses:** 2. Operates June-Aug.

With content similar to a college field course, each Duke TIP field study combines an array of activities that may include discussions, research projects, field work and presentations. Program destinations, which vary each summer, consist of both domestic and international locations. Field courses incorporate the surroundings to enrich the learning experience. Institutes, held on the Duke campus, enable boys and girls to preview college life as they study university-level material and attend college admissions workshops. Each field study or institute explores a distinct program focus.

EARTHWATCH TEEN TEAMS
Res — Coed Ages 15-18

Allston, MA 02134. 114 Western Ave. Tel: 978-461-0081, 800-776-0188.
Fax: 978-461-2332.
www.earthwatch.org/teenteams   E-mail: info@earthwatch.org
Kate Quinn, Program Manager. Student contact: Colleen Spivey.
Grades 10-PG. Adm: FCFS. **Appl**—Fee $0. Due: Rolling.
Enr: 9-16. Intl: 44%. **Fac 3.** Prof 2. K-12 staff 1. **Staff:** Admin 100.
Type of instruction: Enrich. **Courses:** Ecol Geol Sci. **Avg class size:** 8.
Intl program focus: Acad Culture. **Locations:** NJ NY TX WY Africa Canada Caribbean Europe Mexico/Central_America South_America.
Focus: Archaeol Environ_Sci Marine_Bio/Stud. **Features:** Adventure_Travel Conservation Exploration Hiking Mtn_Trips Peace/Cross-cultural Scuba Wilderness_Camp Swim.
Fees 2012: Res $1995-3350 (+airfare), 1-2 wks. Aid (Need).
Housing: Cabins Dorms Houses Lodges Tents. Avg per room/unit: 2-4. **Swimming:** Lake Pond Ocean Pool River Stream.
Est 1970. Nonprofit. **Spons:** Earthwatch Institute. **Ses:** 15. **Wks/ses:** 1-2. Operates June-Aug.

Earthwatch recruits high school volunteers to assist scientists on field research and conservation expeditions in the US and around the world. The organization sponsors scholars in every field of study, from archaeology to marine biology and zoology. Projects include whale and dolphin surveys, archaeological excavations, rain forest mapping, animal behavior research and climate change studies, among others. Participants need not possess any special skills, as training is provided. Teen teams include additional organized group activities, as well as presentations on research and career development.

EDUCATION UNLIMITED
COLLEGE ADMISSION PREP CAMPS
Res and Day — Coed Ages 14-17

Berkeley, CA. Univ of California-Berkeley.
Contact (Year-round): 1700 Shattuck Ave, Ste 305, Berkeley, CA 94709.
Tel: 510-548-6612. Fax: 510-548-0212.
www.educationunlimited.com   E-mail: campinfo@educationunlimited.com
Matthew Fraser, Exec Dir.

Grades 9-12. Adm: FCFS. **Appl**—Due: Rolling.
Enr: 75. **Fac 8. Staff:** Admin 8. Couns 7.
Type of instruction: Adv Enrich Preview Rev SAT/ACT_Prep Tut. **Courses:** Expository_
   Writing. **Avg class size:** 11. **Daily hours for:** Classes 6. Study 3. Rec 5.
Locations: CA MA.
Focus: Col_Prep Study_Skills. **Features:** White-water_Raft Soccer Softball Swim Volley-
   ball.
Fees 2012: Res $2450-6995 (+$200), 1-3 wks. Day $2083-5946, 1-3 wks. Aid (Need).
Housing: Dorms. **Swimming:** Pool.
Est 1993. Inc. **Ses:** 2. **Wks/ses:** 1-3. Operates June-July.

Education Unlimited conducts similar college preparation programs at California and Massachusetts universities. Prep Camp Excel, enrolling pupils entering grades 9 and 10, focuses on PSAT preparation, essay writing and study skills training. College Admission Prep Camp Intensive, accepting rising juniors and seniors, provides SAT preparation, college counseling and information about college admissions procedures. Students in CAPC Intensive develop their time-management and interviewing skills, in addition to working one-on-one with writing instructors on application essays. Boys and girls also take part in recreational activities and go on a half-day excursion. CAPC Intensive also features a white-water rafting excursion and a daylong tour of nearby colleges.

EDUCATION UNLIMITED COMPUTER CAMP
Res and Day — Coed Ages 9-17

Berkeley, CA 94709. 1700 Shattuck Ave, Ste 305. Tel: 510-548-6612.
   Fax: 510-548-0212.
www.educationunlimited.com   E-mail: campinfo@educationunlimited.com
Matthew Fraser, Exec Dir.
Grades 4-12. Adm: FCFS. **Appl**—Fee $0. Due: Rolling.
Fac 1. Staff: Admin 8.
Type of instruction: Enrich. **Courses:** Filmmaking Media. **Avg class size:** 10. **Daily hours
   for:** Classes 6. Study 1. Rec 7.
Locations: CA.
Focus: Comp_Sci. **Features:** Baseball Basketball Soccer Swim Tennis Volleyball.
Fees 2012: Res $1895-2450 (+$50), 1 wk. Day $1395-2083, 1 wk. Aid (Need).
Housing: Dorms. **Swimming:** Pool.
Est 1995. Inc. **Ses:** 4. **Wks/ses:** 1. Operates June-Aug.

Appropriate for young people of all ability levels, Education Unlimited offers hands-on training in computer applications at Stanford and the University of California-Berkeley. The program addresses both creative and practical computer skills, and exposes boys and girls to emerging technologies and software. Students, each of whom has a dedicated computer, choose among camps focusing on video production, Java programming and Web design. Campers with multiple interests may enroll for more than one week to gain experience in different areas. Young students in grades 4-6 take a survey course that introduces them to desktop publishing and Web design.

EDUCATION UNLIMITED PUBLIC SPEAKING INSTITUTE
Res — Coed Ages 9-17

Berkeley, CA 94709. 1700 Shattuck Ave, Ste 305. Tel: 510-548-6612.
   Fax: 510-548-0212.
www.educationunlimited.com   E-mail: campinfo@educationunlimited.com
Matthew Fraser, Exec Dir.
Grades 4-12. Adm: FCFS. **Appl**—Fee $0. Due: Rolling.
Staff: Admin 8.

Type of instruction: Enrich. **Courses:** Expository_Writing Govt Creative_Writing Theater. **Avg class size:** 10. **Daily hours for:** Classes 7. Study 1. Rec 6. **Locations:** CA MA. **Focus:** Debate Public_Speak. **Features:** Baseball Basketball Soccer Swim. **Fees 2010: Res $1850-2150 (+$50), 1 wk. Day $1295-1828 (+$50), 1 wk.** Aid (Need). **Housing:** Dorms. **Swimming:** Pool. **Est 1995.** Inc. **Ses:** 9. **Wks/ses:** 1. Operates June-Aug.

Held at Stanford, UCLA, Tufts University and the University of California-Berkeley, PSI trains students in public speaking, rhetoric and logic through an interactive curriculum. A special weeklong program for high schoolers, the American Legal Experience, teaches speaking and communicational skills through a concentrated emphasis on the American judicial system. The institute's sizeable international enrollment lends itself to a rich cultural experience. Recreational activities and a half-day off-campus excursion complement class work.

EDUCATION UNLIMITED
SALLY RIDE SCIENCE CAMP
Res — Girls Ages 9-14; Day — Girls 4-9

Berkeley, CA 94709. 1700 Shattuck Ave, Ste 305. Tel: 510-548-6612.
Fax: 510-548-0212.
www.sallyridecamps.com   **E-mail:** campinfo@educationunlimited.com
Grades 4-9. Adm: FCFS. **Appl**—Due: Rolling.
Type of instruction: Enrich. **Courses:** Astron Engineering Marine_Bio/Stud Robotics.
Locations: CA MA.
Focus: Sci.
Housing: Dorms.
Wks/ses: ½-1½.

Conducted at five college campuses in California and one in Cambridge, MA, Sally Ride Science Camp enables girls to explore science, technology and engineering through such hands-on activities as the construction of rockets, robots and marine habitats. Each student chooses a science major that includes several small labs and a substantial culminating project. Four-day programs allow girls to choose between an introduction to marine science and an introduction to engineering; five- and seven-day sessions provide a choice between marine biology and astronomy; and the 10-day advanced program offers another two options: advanced marine science/marine ecology and robotics. Afternoon and evening enrichment activities take the form of workshops, experiments, guest speakers and recreational pursuits.

EF INTERNATIONAL LANGUAGE SCHOOLS
Res — Coed Ages 10 and up

Cambridge, MA 02141. 1 Education St. Tel: 617-619-1700, 800-992-1892.
Fax: 617-619-1701.
www.ef.com/ils   **E-mail:** ils@ef.com
Adm: FCFS. **Appl**—Fee $0. Due: Rolling.
Type of instruction: Adv Enrich Preview Rev. **Avg class size:** 11. **Daily hours for:** Classes 3½. Study 1½. Rec 2½. **College credit:** 11.
Intl program focus: Lang Culture. **Locations:** Asia Europe Mexico/Central_America South_America. Home stays avail.
Focus: Chin Fr Ger Ital Span.
Fees 2010: Res $840-7380 (+$150/wk), 2-10 wks.
Housing: Dorms.
Est 1965. Wks/ses: 2-10. Operates Year-round.

EF's year-round language immersion programs enable students to study French, Italian, Spanish, German or Chinese where it is natively spoken. Participants live either with a carefully chosen host family, on a university campus, or in an EF residence or apartment. In addition to language instruction, programming includes exam preparation, business classes and internships. Cultural activities and excursions round out the program.

EMAGINATION COMPUTER CAMPS
Res and Day — Coed Ages 8-17

Salem, NH 03079. 54 Stiles Rd, Ste 205. Tel: 781-933-8795, 877-248-0206.
  Fax: 781-497-9864.
www.computercamps.com   E-mail: camp@computercamps.com
Craig Whiting, Exec Dir. Student contact: Allison Fitzgerald.
Adm: FCFS. **Appl**—Fee $0. Due: Rolling.
Enr: 150-180. **Enr cap:** 200. Intl: 8%. Non-White: 15%. **Fac 20. Staff:** Admin 8. Res 20.
Courses: Drama. **Avg class size:** 8. **Daily hours for:** Classes 4½. Rec 1½.
Locations: GA IL MA PA.
Focus: Comp_Sci. **Features:** Basketball Soccer Swim Tennis.
Fees 2011: Res $1200-8500, 1-7 wks. Day $700-4900, 1-7 wks. Aid (Need).
Housing: Dorms. **Swimming:** Pool.
Est 1982. Ses: 4. **Wks/ses:** 1-2. Operates June-Aug.

Campers interested in computers and technology choose from various workshop options that allow them to further develop their skills, explore computer programming and think creatively; workshops accommodate beginners through advanced students. Each student is assigned a computer for the duration of the session. Leadership opportunities are available to boys and girls entering grade 10 or above. Emagination conducts on- and off-campus recreational activities—available to both boarders and day pupils—each Saturday. Camps operate on four college campuses: Bentley University (Waltham, MA), Mercer University (Atlanta, GA), Lake Forest College (Lake Forest, IL) and Rosemont College (Rosemont, PA).

EMORY UNIVERSITY
YOUTH THEOLOGICAL INITIATIVE SUMMER ACADEMY
Res — Coed Ages 16-18

Atlanta, GA 30322. Candler School of Theology, 1531 Dickey Dr. Tel: 404-712-9160.
  Fax: 404-727-2494.
www.yti.emory.edu   E-mail: yti@emory.edu
Elizabeth Corrie, Dir. Student contact: Brenda Bennefield.
Grades 11-12. Adm: Selective. Admitted: 60%. Priority: Low-income. URM. Prereqs: GPA 3.0. **Appl**—Fee $0. Due: Mar. Transcript, 2 recs, 4 essays.
Enr: 39. **Enr cap:** 39. Intl: 10%. Non-White: 50%. **Fac 11.** Prof 4. Col/grad students 5. Specialists 2. **Staff:** Admin 3. Couns 11.
Type of instruction: Enrich. **Courses:** Ethics Crafts Creative_Writing Dance Drama Music Painting. **Daily hours for:** Classes 4. Study 2. Rec 6. Homework.
Focus: Relig_Stud. **Features:** Climbing_Wall Community_Serv Conservation Cooking Peace/Cross-cultural Basketball Soccer Swim Ultimate_Frisbee.
Fees 2011: Res $1300 (+$50-100), 3 wks. Aid 2009 (Need): $6875.
Housing: Dorms. Avg per room/unit: 2. **Swimming:** Pool. Campus facilities avail.
Est 1993. Nonprofit. United Methodist. **Ses:** 1. **Wks/ses:** 3. Operates July.

With the goal of cultivating public theologians, YTI provides students with an intensive examination of theological issues. Faculty encourage boys and girls to ponder theological questions; explore theological literature (including the Bible); engage, analyze and address global issues from Christian theological perspectives; and experience various ways of worshiping together as an ecumenical group, such as attending services with Christian congregations and other religious communities. Students typically leave the program with more defined educational and vocational plans in theology.

ENFOREX
SUMMER LANGUAGE CAMPS IN SPAIN
Res and Day — Coed Ages 5-18

Madrid, 28015 Spain. Alberto Aguilera 26. Tel: 34-91-594-3776, 800-518-0412.
Fax: 34-91-594-5159.
www.enforex.com   E-mail: info@enforex.es
Antonio Anadon, Pres.
Grades 1-12. Adm: FCFS. Appl—Fee 65. Due: Rolling.
Intl: 40%. Staff: Admin 10.
Type of instruction: Adv Dev_Read Enrich Preview Rev. Courses: Crafts Dance Drama Fine_Arts Music Photog. Daily hours for: Classes 4½. Study 3. Rec 3. Tests. Grades.
Intl program focus: Lang Culture. Locations: Europe. Home stays avail.
Focus: Span. Features: Adventure_Travel Basketball Equestrian Fencing Golf Soccer Swim.
Fees 2011: Res €660-4100 (+€65), 1-8 wks. Day €305-610 (+€65), 2 wks.
Housing: Dorms Houses. Avg per room/unit: 1-5. Swimming: Ocean Pool.
Est 1989. Inc. Ses: 16. Wks/ses: 1-8. Operates July-Aug.

Offering language immersion summer programs in both Spanish and English, Enforex conducts programs in the Spanish cities of Barcelona, Granada, Madrid, Valencia, Salamanca, Seville and Marbella. Sixty percent of Spain program participants come from the host country, while the remainder of the students enroll from approximately 40 other countries. Culture and traditions are integral aspects of the program, and boys and girls may engage in various sports and cultural activities in their free time. Home stay programs at all Enforex locations serve those residential students who wish to live with a local family.

EPISCOPAL HIGH SCHOOL
FIELD EXPERIENCES IN ENVIRONMENTAL SCIENCE
Res and Day — Coed Ages 12-14

Alexandria, VA 22302. 1200 N Quaker Ln. Tel: 703-933-4043.
www.episcopalhighschool.org   E-mail: dcw@episcopalhighschool.org
Damian Walsh, Dir.
Grades 7-9. Adm: FCFS. Appl—Due: Rolling.
Type of instruction: Enrich.
Focus: Environ_Sci.
Fees 2011: Res $750, 1 wk. Day $600, 1 wk.
Housing: Dorms.
Nonprofit. Episcopal. Ses: 1. Wks/ses: 1. Operates June.

In this science program, rising seventh through ninth graders examine biological species and perform physical and chemical tests to determine the environmental quality of freshwater and terrestrial ecosystems. Campers collect data from streams, lakes, forests and mountains in the Washington, DC, area and the Blue Ridge Mountains, perform data analysis, and present their findings to classmates and families.

EXXONMOBIL BERNARD HARRIS SUMMER SCIENCE CAMP
Res — Coed Ages 11-14

Houston, TX 77056. 1330 Post Oak Blvd, Ste 2550. Tel: 713-877-1731.
Fax: 713-877-8669.
www.theharrisfoundation.org   E-mail: barbara@theharrisfoundation.org
Barbara Foots, Dir.
Grades 6-8. Adm: Selective. Priority: Low-income. URM. Appl—Fee $0. Transcript, essay, rec.
Enr: 48-54. Enr cap: 48-54.

Type of instruction: Adv Enrich. **Courses:** Environ_Sci.
Locations: AL AR CA DC FL LA MA NJ NM NY OH OK OR PA TX VA WY.
Focus: Engineering Math Sci.
Fees 2012: Free. Res 2 wks.
Housing: Dorms.
Est 2007. Spons: Harris Foundation. **Ses:** 25. **Wks/ses:** 2. Operates June-Aug.

Conducted on roughly two dozen college campuses across the US for members of traditionally underserved and underrepresented populations, these two-week residential camps seek to build students' mathematics and science skills, provide a preview of college life, and stimulate pupils' interest in science and engineering. Classes address problem solving, research, writing and communicational skills. The curriculum features biology, chemistry, physics, environmental, earth science, engineering and design concepts, and field excursions provide enrichment. Each college location designates the school districts and geographic areas from which students may apply.

FAY SCHOOL INTERNATIONAL STUDENT PROGRAM
SUMMER SESSION
Res — Coed Ages 10-15

Southborough, MA 01772. 48 Main St, PO Box 9106. Tel: 508-485-0100, 800-933-2925.
Fax: 508-481-5450.
www.fayschool.org   E-mail: ispsummer@fayschool.org
Scott LeBrun, Dir.
Grades 5-9. Adm: FCFS. **Appl**—Fee $100. Due: Rolling.
Enr: 60. **Enr cap:** 70. Intl: 100%. **Fac 14.** K-12 staff 14. **Staff:** Admin 4.
Type of instruction: Enrich Rem_Eng Rem_Math Rem_Read Study_Skills. **Courses:** Eng Hist Sci Crafts Dance Filmmaking Theater. **Avg class size:** 6. **Daily hours for:** Classes 3. Study 1½. Rec 4. Homework. Tests. Grades.
Focus: ESL. **Features:** Cooking Basketball Football Soccer Swim Tennis.
Fees 2012: Res $8225 (+$1200), 6 wks.
Housing: Dorms. **Swimming:** Pool. Campus facilities avail.
Est 1985. Nonprofit. Ses: 1. **Wks/ses:** 6. Operates July-Aug.

Fay's ISP Summer Session combines study of the language with opportunities for students to hone their skills during extracurricular activities. Beginners study English for three hours each morning, intermediate pupils for two hours and advanced boys and girls for one hour. Intermediate and advanced students fill out their mornings with elective course work in other subjects, for one hour and two hours, respectively. Participants gain an introduction to American culture as part of the curriculum.

THE FLORIDA FORENSIC INSTITUTE
Res and Day — Coed Ages 13-18

Cooper City, FL 33024. 10000 Stirling Rd, Ste 1.
www.ffi4n6.com
Howard S. Miller, Dir.
Adm: Somewhat selective. Admitted: 90%. **Appl**—Fee $0. Due: May.
Enr: 225. **Enr cap:** 250. Intl: 5%. Non-White: 40%. **Fac 40.** Prof 2. Col/grad students 10. K-12 staff 8. Specialists 20. **Staff:** Admin 6. Couns 4.
Type of instruction: Adv. **Daily hours for:** Classes 8.
Focus: Debate. **Features:** Swim.
Fees 2011: Res $1995, 2 wks. Day $1295, 2 wks. Aid 2011 (Merit & Need): $15,000.
Housing: Hotels. Avg per room/unit: 1-4. **Swimming:** Pool.
Est 1981. Inc. Ses: 1. **Wks/ses:** 2. Operates July-Aug.

FFI conducts a specialized summer program for young debaters of all ability levels. During the two-week session, boys and girls attend comprehensive courses in congressional debate, public forum debate, Lincoln-Douglas debate, extemporaneous speaking and original oratory. A four-day program extension at the conclusion of the regular session enables interested pupils to further develop their forensic skills through one-on-one tutorials with field experts.

FOUNDATION FOR ECONOMIC EDUCATION
SUMMER SEMINARS FOR HIGH SCHOOL STUDENTS
Res — Coed Ages 14-18

Irvington, NY 10533. 30 S Broadway. Tel: 914-591-7230, 800-960-4333.
Fax: 914-591-8910.
www.fee.org/seminars/high-school   E-mail: aensley@fee.org
Aaron Ensley, Dir.
Grades 9-12. Adm: Selective. Admitted: 70%. Prereqs: GPA 2.5. **Appl**—Fee $0. Due: Mar.
Enr: 100. **Enr cap:** 100. **Fac 6. Staff:** Admin 4. Res 5.
Type of instruction: Enrich. **Daily hours for:** Classes 8. Rec 1-2.
Locations: CO MI NY.
Focus: Bus/Fin Econ. **Features:** Swim.
Fees 2012: Free. Res 1 wk.
Housing: Dorms Lodges. Avg per room/unit: 2. **Swimming:** Pool.
Nonprofit. **Ses:** 2. **Wks/ses:** 1. Operates July.

These weeklong seminars introduce high school students to complex economic principles. Participants study the fundamentals of economics, as well as the early history and the growth of government in the United States. Topics of discussion include an introduction to free trade, money and inflation, and property rights. All successful applicants attend the session on full scholarship, with housing, meals, lectures and class materials covered.

FOUNDATION FOR TEACHING ECONOMICS
ECONOMICS FOR LEADERS
Res — Coed Ages 16-17

Davis, CA 95616. 260 Russell Blvd, Ste B. Tel: 530-757-4630, 800-383-4335.
Fax: 530-757-4636.
www.fte.org/student-programs   E-mail: information@fte.org
Debbie Henney, Dir.
Grade 12. Adm: Selective. Admitted: 32%. **Appl**—Fee $0. Due: Mar. Essay.
Enr: 30-50. **Enr cap:** 30-50. **Fac 3. Staff:** Admin 8.
Type of instruction: Enrich. **Daily hours for:** Classes 4. Study 2. Rec 3. Tests.
Locations: CA CO GA KS MA MI NY OH TN TX VA WA.
Focus: Econ Leadership. **Features:** Swim.
Fees 2011: Res $125-500, 1 wk.
Housing: Dorms. **Swimming:** Pool.
Ses: 13. **Wks/ses:** 1. Operates June-Aug.

Conducted on college campuses across the country, EFL teaches students about responsible leadership and economic analysis. Morning economics seminars introduce basic free-market concepts through simulations and discussions of current national and international issues. Outdoor leadership exercises in the afternoons challenge student teams with physical and mental problems. Among evening activities are a simulated political election and recreational and social events.

FOUNDATION GLOBAL EDUCATION
PERSPECTIVES OF CHINA
Res — Coed Ages 15-18

Shanghai, China. East China Normal Univ.
Contact (Year-round): 403-404 Chinachem Hollywood Ctr, 1 Hollywood Rd, Central, Hong Kong, Hong Kong. Tel: 852-8172-1072. Fax: 852-8169-1072.
www.foundationge.com   E-mail: perspectives@foundationge.com
Daniel Szeto, Dir.
Grades 10-PG. Adm: Selective. **Appl**—Fee $60. Due: Mar. Transcript, 2 recs.
Enr: 30. **Enr cap:** 40. Intl: 40%. **Staff:** Admin 10.
Type of instruction: Enrich. **Courses:** Econ Hist Intl_Relations Crafts Dance Fine_Arts Music Theater. **Avg class size:** 20. **Daily hours for:** Classes 6. Rec 2½.
Intl program focus: Lang Culture. Home stays avail.
Focus: Chin.
Fees 2011: Res $5490, 4 wks. Aid (Need).
Housing: Apartments Dorms Hotels. Avg per room/unit: 4.
Est 2001. Inc. **Ses:** 1. **Wks/ses:** 4. Operates July-Aug.

Participants in this program experience the distinctive culture and lifestyle of modern China through course work, investigative learning and interaction. Mandarin tutorials and classes on China's past and future are required of all students. Based in Shanghai, the program also examines the histories of other cities through overnight trips. Guest speakers and Chinese films complement class instruction.

FRANCES A. KARNES CENTER FOR GIFTED STUDIES
LEADERSHIP STUDIES PROGRAM
Res — Coed Ages 12-17

Hattiesburg, MS 39406. Univ of Southern Mississippi, 118 College Dr, Box 8207. Tel: 601-266-5236. Fax: 601-266-4764.
www.usm.edu/gifted   E-mail: gifted.studies@usm.edu
Frances A. Karnes, Dir.
Grades 7-12. Adm: FCFS. **Appl**—Fee $0. Due: Mar.
Enr: 126. **Staff:** Admin 4. Couns 20.
Type of instruction: Enrich. **Avg class size:** 20. **Daily hours for:** Classes 6. Rec 1.
Focus: Leadership.
Fees 2011: Res $520, 1 wk. Aid (Need).
Housing: Dorms.
Est 1989. Nonprofit. **Spons:** University of Southern Mississippi. **Ses:** 1. **Wks/ses:** 1. Operates June.

This University of Southern Mississippi program comprises three progressively advanced sessions. Leadership I stresses the fundamentals of leadership through instruction in written and oral communication, group dynamics, problem solving and decision making; Leadership II emphasizes the psychology of leadership; and Leadership III focuses on the legal aspects of leadership and features informal interaction with adult leaders.

THE GAIA SCHOOL SUMMER PROGRAM
Res — Coed Ages 14-17

Ancaster, L9G 1V3 Ontario, Canada. 10 Cumming Ct. Tel: 905-667-1228, 866-311-4242. Fax: 905-648-6437.
www.thegaiaschool.com   E-mail: info@thegaiaschool.com
Robert DiBacco, Dir.
Grades 9-12. Adm: FCFS. **Appl**—Fee $0. Due: Mar.
Fac 10. Staff: Admin 4.

Avg class size: 8. **Daily hours for:** Classes 3. Study 1. Rec 3.
Intl program focus: Lang Culture. **Locations:** South_America.
Focus: Span. **Features:** Adventure_Travel Bicycle_Tours Hiking Mtn_Biking Mtn_Trips Peace/Cross-cultural Wilderness_Camp Soccer Swim Tennis.
Fees 2012: Res $2325-4550 (+airfare), 2-4 wks.
Housing: Hotels. **Swimming:** Ocean Pool.
Est 2000. Ses: 3. **Wks/ses:** 2-4. Operates June-July.

The program combines two-week Spanish language immersion in either Chile or Argentina with cultural experiences and adventure treks. Instruction emphasizes four basics of language learning: reading, writing, speaking and listening. Beginning, intermediate and advanced pupils enroll in small classes of roughly seven or eight students. Participants learn about the host country by attending local workshops, touring nearby cities, and visiting important monuments and museums. A four-week option enables students to take part in both the Chilean and the Argentine programs.

THE GARCIA CENTER FOR POLYMERS AT ENGINEERED INTERFACES RESEARCH SCHOLAR PROGRAM FOR HIGH SCHOOL STUDENTS
Res and Day — Coed Ages 16-18

Stony Brook, NY 11794. State Univ of New York, 216 Engineering Bldg.
Tel: 631-632-6097. Fax: 631-632-5764.
http://polymer.matscieng.sunysb.edu/srprog.html
E-mail: lourdes.collazo@stonybrook.edu
Student contact: Lourdes Collazo, E-mail: lourdes.collazo@sunysb.edu.
Grades 11-12. Adm: Very selective. Prereqs: GPA 3.8. **Appl**—Due: Feb. Transcript, 3 recs.
Enr: 25.
Type of instruction: Adv Enrich.
Focus: Sci.
Fees 2009: Res $2150 (+$75), 7 wks. Day $950 (+$75), 7 wks.
Housing: Dorms.
Ses: 1. **Wks/ses:** 7. Operates June-Aug.

Funded by the National Science Foundation as part of its Materials Research Science and Engineering Center programs, the Garcia Center invites high school upperclassmen to work on focused polymer science and technology research teams. Participants create independent projects with the guidance of Garcia faculty and graduate students. In addition to entering national competitions, young men and women are encouraged to publish articles in scientific journals and to present their results at national conferences. Program dates are flexible, and students may continue their research during the following academic year. Participants have been recognized by the Intel Science Talent Search and the Siemens Competition in Math, Science & Technology.

GEORGE MASON UNIVERSITY WASHINGTON JOURNALISM AND MEDIA CONFERENCE
Res — Coed Ages 16-18

Fairfax, VA 22030. 4400 University Dr, MS 3A4. Tel: 703-993-5411. Fax: 703-993-4622.
www.wjmc.gmu.edu   **E-mail: wjmc@gmu.edu**
Caitlin Shear, Prgm Dir.
Grades 11-12. Adm: Selective. Prereqs: GPA 3.5. **Appl**—Due: Jan.
Enr cap: 250. **Fac 7.** K-12 staff 7. **Staff:** Admin 1. Couns 6.
Type of instruction: Undergrad. **Courses:** Media. **College credit:** 1.

Focus: Writing/Journ.
Fees 2012: Res $1885, 1 wk. Aid (Need).
Housing: Dorms. Avg per room/unit: 2.
Est 2009. Nonprofit. **Ses:** 1. **Wks/ses:** 1. Operates July.

Session attendees engage in hands-on learning through decision-making simulations that explore the creative, practical and ethical tensions in journalism and media. Students work in small groups that are led by faculty advisers with a background in journalism instruction. Guest speakers include professional journalists and media executives. A high school nomination must accompany each application.

GEORGETOWN PREPARATORY SCHOOL
ENGLISH AS A SECOND LANGUAGE PROGRAM
Res and Day — Coed Ages 14-17

North Bethesda, MD 20852. 10900 Rockville Pike. Tel: 301-214-1249.
 Fax: 301-214-8600.
www.gprep.org/esl   E-mail: rwhitman@gprep.org
Rosita A. Whitman, Dir.
Grades 9-12. Adm: FCFS. **Appl**—Fee $250. Due: Rolling.
Enr: 100. Intl: 90%. **Fac 8. Staff:** Admin 2. Couns 15.
Courses: Govt Speech Writing/Journ Creative_Writing Theater. **Avg class size:** 13. **Daily hours for:** Classes 4½. Study 2. Rec 3. Homework. Tests. Grades. **High school credit.**
Focus: ESL. **Features:** Baseball Basketball Golf Soccer Softball Swim Tennis Track.
Fees 2010: Res $6800, 6 wks. Day $4150, 6 wks. Aid (Merit & Need).
Housing: Dorms. **Swimming:** Pool. Campus facilities avail.
Nonprofit. Roman Catholic. **Ses:** 1. **Wks/ses:** 6. Operates June-Aug.

Georgetown Prep's ESL Program offers intensive audio-lingual training in English for young people of high school age with or without previous knowledge of English. Pupils receive four and a half hours of instruction each weekday, in addition to two hours of supervised homework daily. Supplementary course work is also available, as is a full schedule of recreational and social activities.

GEORGETOWN UNIVERSITY COLLEGE PREP PROGRAM
Res and Day — Coed Ages 15-18

Washington, DC 20057. Summer Prgms for High School Students, Box 571006.
 Tel: 202-687-8700. Fax: 202-687-8954.
http://summer.georgetown.edu   E-mail: scsspecialprograms@georgetown.edu
Susan Manion, Dir.
Grades 10-12. Adm: Selective. **Appl**—Fee $50. Due: Rolling. Transcript, rec, essay.
Enr: 49. **Staff:** Couns 12.
Type of instruction: Adv Rem_Eng Rem_Math SAT/ACT_Prep. **Courses:** Bus/Fin Computers Eng Expository_Writing Sci Speech Creative_Writing. **Daily hours for:** Classes 3. Study 3. Grades. **College credit.**
Focus: Col_Prep Study_Skills. **Features:** Basketball Cross-country Soccer Swim Tennis Track.
Fees 2012: Res $4780-5440 (+$548), 3 wks. Day $4300 (+$548), 3 wks. Aid (Need).
Housing: Dorms. **Swimming:** Pool River.
Ses: 1. **Wks/ses:** 3. Operates June-July.

Open to rising high school sophomores, juniors and seniors, this enrichment program helps improve students' English and math fundamentals while also preparing them for the SAT examinations and the college admissions process. Course work enables boys and girls to further develop their critical thinking, composition, writing, research and study skill, and SAT test-taking workshops and practice tests address all sections of the exams. Students also preview college life through shared meals, social events, and conversations with faculty and fellow pupils.

GEORGETOWN UNIVERSITY
FUNDAMENTALS OF BUSINESS
Res and Day — Coed Ages 15-18

Washington, DC 20007. Summer Programs for High School Students, 3307 M St NW, Ste 202. Tel: 202-687-8600. Fax: 202-687-8954.
http://scs.georgetown.edu/hoyas **E-mail:** highschool@georgetown.edu
Thomas Cooke, Dir.
Grades 10-12. Adm: Selective. **Appl**—Fee $50. Due: May. Transcript, test scores, rec, essay.
Enr: 53. **Enr cap:** 60. **Fac 2.** Prof 2.
Type of instruction: Adv. **Courses:** Comm Law. **Daily hours for:** Classes 3. Study 3. **College credit:** 3.
Focus: Bus/Fin. **Features:** Swim.
Fees 2011: Res $4532 (+$1100), 5 wks. Day $3716 (+$1100), 5 wks.
Housing: Dorms. **Swimming:** Pool River.
Ses: 2. **Wks/ses:** 5. Operates June-Aug.

During this five-week program, students examine various aspects of business, including finance, marketing, accounting, management, communications, strategy, planning, organizational behavior and business law. Course work also addresses basic business concepts, language and organization. Boys and girls, who are treated as college students, earn three college credits upon completion of the program. Participants take one field trip to a local company to learn firsthand about a working business.

GEORGETOWN UNIVERSITY
INTERNATIONAL RELATIONS PROGRAM
FOR HIGH SCHOOL STUDENTS
Res — Coed Ages 15-18

Washington, DC 20057. Summer Prgms for High School Students, Box 571006. Tel: 202-687-8700. Fax: 202-687-8954.
http://summer.georgetown.edu **E-mail:** scsspecialprograms@georgetown.edu
Anthony Clark Arend, Dir.
Grades 10-12. Adm: Selective. **Appl**—Fee $50. Due: Rolling. Transcript, rec, essay.
Enr: 233. **Fac 13.**
Type of instruction: Adv Enrich. **Courses:** Global_Stud. **Daily hours for:** Classes 3. Study 3.
Focus: Govt Intl_Relations Pol_Sci. **Features:** Swim.
Fees 2012: Res $2395, 1 wk. Aid (Need).
Housing: Dorms. **Swimming:** Pool River.
Nonprofit. **Ses:** 1. **Wks/ses:** 1. Operates July.

This eight-day program combines classroom lectures from Georgetown faculty and guest speakers with visits to organizations involved in foreign policy, small-group discussions of newsworthy topics and an international crisis simulation. Areas of study include diplomatic, economic and military instruments of foreign policy; international organizations; international law; competing ideologies in international order; self-determination; the environment; terrorism; civil war; weapons of mass destruction; problems in the developing world; and the future of the international system.

GLOBAL YOUNG LEADERS CONFERENCE
Res — Coed Ages 15-18

Washington, DC 20006. 1700 Pennsylvania Ave NW, Ste 400. Tel: 703-584-9373.
www.gylc.org/gylc   E-mail: gylc_adm@cylc.org
Marguerite C. Regan, Dir.
Adm: Selective. **Appl**—Due: Rolling.
Type of instruction: Enrich. **Courses:** Bus/Fin Econ Govt Law Pol_Sci.
Locations: DC NY Asia.
Focus: Leadership.
Fees 2010: Res $2995-5390, 1½-2 wks. Aid (Need).
Est 1985. Spons: Congressional Youth Leadership Council. **Ses:** 9. **Wks/ses:** 1½-2. Operates June-Aug.

This leadership development program allows high-achieving boys and girls to learn from successful businesspeople, policy officials, lobbyists, journalists, diplomats and academics in Washington, DC; New York City; or Beijing, Hangshou and Shanghai, China. Among concepts addressed on a broad scale during the GYLC sessions are communications, diplomacy, law, human rights, peace, security, economics and the role of the United Nations. All students are provided with written materials intended to promote self-directed, experiential learning. The Congressional Youth Leadership Council, which sponsors GYLC, identifies and nominates suitable candidates.

GLOBAL YOUTH VILLAGE
Res — Coed Ages 14-18

Bedford, VA 24523. 1020 Legacy Dr. Tel: 540-871-0882. Fax: 540-297-1860.
www.globalyouthvillage.org   E-mail: gyv@legacyintl.org
Mary Helmig, Dir.
Adm: Selective. Admitted: 75%. **Appl**—Fee $0. Due: May. Essays.
Enr: 65. **Enr cap:** 70. Intl: 40%. Non-White: 60%. **Fac 30.** Col/grad students 25. Specialists 5. **Staff:** Admin 5. Couns 10.
Type of instruction: Enrich. **Courses:** Debate Govt Crafts Fine_Arts Music Theater. **Avg class size:** 13. **Daily hours for:** Classes 2.
Focus: Environ_Sci Global_Stud. **Features:** Community_Serv Hiking Peace/Cross-cultural Rock_Climb Baseball Basketball Soccer Swim Volleyball.
Fees 2011: Res $1200-2600 (+$75), 1½-3 wks. Aid 2011 (Merit & Need): $24,000.
Housing: Cabins. Avg per room/unit: 9. **Swimming:** Pool.
Est 1979. Nonprofit. **Spons:** Legacy International. **Ses:** 3. **Wks/ses:** 1½-3. Operates July-Aug.

GYV emphasizes international understanding and comprises campers from many ethnic, racial and national backgrounds. Students participate in a dialogue that addresses such issues as prejudice reduction, conflict resolution, nonviolence, and leadership and communication. In addition, the program includes workshops pertaining to global issues, the environment and community service, and cross-cultural arts study. During each session, campers embark on a practical application field trip, and afternoon enrichment activities and sports round out the program.

GREAT BOOKS SUMMER PROGRAM
Res — Coed Ages 11-17

Fairfield, CT 06824. PO Box 743. Toll-free: 866-480-7323. Fax: 203-255-0675.
www.greatbookssummer.com   E-mail: info@greatbookssummer.com
Peter Temes, Dir.
Grades 6-12. Adm: Selective. **Appl**—Fee $0. Due: May. Nomination.
Type of instruction: Adv Enrich. **Courses:** Expository_Writing Art Music Theater.

Locations: CA MA.
Focus: Eng.
Fees 2009: Res $1650-5250 (+$125-600), 1-3 wks. Aid (Need).
Housing: Dorms.
Est 2002. Ses: 29. **Wks/ses:** 1-3. Operates June-July.

With locations at Amherst College and Stanford University, this intensive program features faculty from those two institutions and Columbia University. Participants learn how to read and analyze material at a college level; engage in active discussions; and develop their perceptual, critical-thinking and self-expression skills. Special guests, authors and educators join class discussions in each session. Sessions serve boys and girls in two age groups: the Intermediate Program (for children entering grades 6-8) and the Senior Program (for students entering grades 9-12).

GREEN RIVER PRESERVE
Res — Coed Ages 8-18

Cedar Mountain, NC 28718. 301 Green River Rd. Tel: 828-698-8828.
Fax: 828-698-9201.
www.greenriverpreserve.org   E-mail: info@greenriverpreserve.org
Case Kennedy, Dir.
Student contact: Missy Schenck, E-mail: missy@greenriverpreserve.org.
Grades 2-12. Adm: Somewhat selective. Admitted: 98%. **Appl**—Fee $0. Due: Rolling. Teacher rec.
Enr: 100. **Enr cap:** 102. Non-White: 2%. **Fac 15. Staff:** Admin 10. Couns 32.
Type of instruction: Enrich. **Courses:** Crafts Creative_Writing Drawing Music Painting Theater Pottery. **Avg class size:** 9.
Focus: Environ_Sci. **Features:** Archery Canoe Chess Climbing_Wall Conservation Cooking Exploration Farm Fishing Hiking Mtn_Trips Outdoor_Ed Riflery Rock_Climb Ropes_ Crse Survival_Trng Wilderness_Camp Woodcraft Fencing Swim Gardening.
Fees 2012: Res $1225-3450 (+$30-90), 1-3 wks. Aid (Need).
Housing: Cabins Lodges. Avg per room/unit: 7. **Swimming:** Lake Pond River Stream.
Est 1987. Nonprofit. **Ses:** 5. **Wks/ses:** 1-3. Operates June-Aug.

A wildlife preserve, GRP offers bright naturalists a recreational camp that combines the hands-on field study of natural science with work in the creative arts. Features include instruction in ecology and nature, as well as hiking and camping on the Preserve's 3400 acres in the Blue Ridge Mountains.

HAMPSHIRE COLLEGE SUMMER STUDIES IN MATHEMATICS
Res — Coed Ages 16-18

Amherst, MA 01002. Box NS, 893 West St. Tel: 413-559-5375. Fax: 413-559-5448.
www.hcssim.org   E-mail: dkelly@hampshire.edu
David C. Kelly, Dir.
Grades 11-12 (younger if qualified). Adm: Selective. **Appl**—Fee $0. Due: Rolling. Personal statement, rec, adm test.
Enr: 45. **Fac 10. Staff:** Admin 1.
Type of instruction: Adv Enrich. **Courses:** Comp_Sci. **Avg class size:** 17.
Focus: Math. **Features:** Basketball Soccer Softball Swim Tennis Volleyball.
Fees 2011: Res $2890, 6 wks. Aid (Need).
Housing: Dorms. **Swimming:** Pool. Campus facilities avail.
Est 1971. Nonprofit. **Ses:** 1. **Wks/ses:** 6. Operates July-Aug.

Intelligent, highly motivated high schoolers work both individually and in small groups during this rigorous program. HCSSiM participants investigate concrete problems, seek patterns and generalizations, formulate conjectures in the language of mathematics and apply insight and experience to the creation of proofs. For the first three weeks, college professors lead workshops covering undergraduate-level content in number theory, combinatorics/graph theory, modern algebra and other topics from outside the usual secondary school and early college curricula. Students then select one maxi-course (covering a semester-long elective's worth of material) and two minicourses. Most faculty live on campus and join students for meals and recreational activities.

HARVARD UNIVERSITY GRADUATE SCHOOL OF DESIGN
CAREER DISCOVERY PROGRAM
Res and Day — Coed Ages 18 and up

Cambridge, MA 02138. 48 Quincy St, 422 Gund Hall. Tel: 617-495-5453.
Fax: 617-495-8949.
www.gsd.harvard.edu/careerdiscovery   E-mail: discovery@gsd.harvard.edu
Jeffrey L. Klug, Dir.
Grades PG-Col. Adm: FCFS. Appl—Fee 40. Due: Apr. Transcript, essay, 2 recs.
Enr: 270. Enr cap: 300. Fac 40. Staff: Admin 4. Couns 3.
Type of instruction: Enrich Preview. Avg class size: 11. Daily hours for: Classes 7. Study 3. Rec 2.
Focus: Architect.
Fees 2012: Res $4060 (+$150), 6 wks. Day $2870 (+$150), 6 wks. Aid (Need).
Housing: Dorms.
Est 1973. Nonprofit. Ses: 1. Wks/ses: 6. Operates June-July.

Through Career Discovery, participants gain an introduction to the design professions by means of intense studio work, seminars and lectures, workshops and field trips. Students spend most of their time on short, intensive projects similar to first-year graduate school work in architecture, landscape architecture, urban planning or urban design concentrations. Other activities include career advising panel discusssions, field trips, office visits and drawing and computer workshops. Most participants are college students or professionals with no previous design training, although recent high school graduates make up a small percentage of attendees.

HELLO SPAIN
Res — Coed Ages 12-21

Madrid, 28036 Spain. 32 Alberto Alcocer. Tel: 34-91-457-9222. Fax: 34-91-457-8126.
www.hellospain.es   E-mail: info@english-systems.es
Leslie A. Freschet, Dir.
Adm: FCFS. Appl—Fee $0. Due: Rolling.
Staff: Admin 3.
Courses: Speech Dance Theater. Avg class size: 8.
Intl program focus: Lang Culture. Home stays avail.
Focus: Span. Features: Cooking.
Fees 2009: Res €1250-1875 (+airfare), 2-3 wks.
Housing: Houses. Avg per room/unit: 1.
Est 1993. Inc. Ses: 2. Wks/ses: 2-3. Operates July.

With locations in Madrid, Alicante and Malaga, this language immersion program teaches students Spanish in a small-class setting. Youth stay with Spanish families during the week and travel to cultural landmarks on weekends. Students take a three-day trip to Seville, as well as shorter excursions to Toledo and Segovia.

HOBART AND WILLIAM SMITH COLLEGES
ENVIRONMENTAL STUDIES SUMMER YOUTH INSTITUTE
Res — Coed Ages 16-18

Geneva, NY 14456. 300 Pulteney St. Tel: 315-781-4401. Fax: 315-781-3843.
http://academic.hws.edu/enviro   E-mail: essyi@hws.edu
Jim MaKinster, Dir.
Grades 11-12. Adm: Selective. **Appl**—Fee $25. Due: Rolling. Transcript, rec.
Enr cap: 34. **Fac 14.** Prof 14. **Staff:** Admin 4.
Type of instruction: Adv. **Courses:** Ecol Geol Marine_Bio/Stud Photog. **College credit.**
Focus: Environ_Sci. **Features:** Canoe Conservation Hiking Mtn_Trips Swim.
Fees 2012: Res $2400, 2 wks. Aid (Need).
Housing: Dorms. **Swimming:** Lake Pool.
Est 1992. Nonprofit. **Ses: 1. Wks/ses:** 2. Operates July.

Conducted by Hobart and William Smith faculty on the joint college campus in the Finger Lakes region, this college-level, interdisciplinary program serves as an introduction to various environmental issues and perspectives on nature and the environment for rising high school juniors and seniors. The program features work in the field, in laboratories and in classrooms as it directs students in the examination of scientific, social and humanistic perspectives in regard to environmental issues. Pupils also engage in studies on Seneca Lake aboard a 65-foot research vessel, and ESSYI schedules a four-day Adirondack camping and research trip.

HOTCHKISS SCHOOL
SUMMER ENVIRONMENTAL SCIENCE PROGRAM
Res — Coed Ages 12-15

Lakeville, CT 06039. 11 Interlaken Rd, PO Box 800. Tel: 860-435-3173.
Fax: 860-435-4413.
www.hotchkissportals.org   E-mail: summer@hotchkiss.org
Stephen C. McKibben, Dir. Student contact: Christiana Gurney Rawlings.
Grades 8-10 (younger if qualified). Adm: Selective. **Appl**—Fee $55. Due: Rolling. SSAT/ TOEFL scores.
Enr: 32. **Enr cap:** 36. Intl: 50%. **Fac 7.**
Type of instruction: Enrich. **Courses:** Ecol Fine_Arts. **Avg class size:** 12. **Daily hours for:** Classes 8. Study 1. Rec 2.
Focus: Environ_Sci. **Features:** Caving Farm Skateboarding Street_Hockey Swim Tennis Ultimate_Frisbee Volleyball.
Fees 2011: Res $4250 (+$50-100), 3 wks. Aid (Merit & Need).
Housing: Dorms. **Swimming:** Lake Pool.
Est 2004. Nonprofit. **Ses: 1. Wks/ses:** 3. Operates July.

The Hotchkiss SES program emphasizes hands-on field research, data collection and analysis techniques. Boys and girls begin by studying the basic aquatic and terrestrial ecology of the surrounding lakes, streams, woods, fields and farmland. They then connect with working environmental scientists on field projects that range from invasive species monitoring to global climate change modeling. Students who return for a second summer analyze data and formulate strategies for solving environmental problems; in their third summer, SES participants intern with local environmental organizations. Sports and other recreational activities round out the program.

ID TECH CAMPS
Res — Coed Ages 10-18; Day — Coed 7-18

Campbell, CA 95008. 42 W Campbell Ave, Ste 301. Tel: 408-871-2227, 888-709-8324.
Fax: 408-871-2228.

www.internaldrive.com E-mail: info@internaldrive.com
Pete Ingram-Cauchi, Pres.
Grades 2-12. Adm: FCFS. **Appl**—Fee $0. Due: Rolling.
Type of instruction: Adv Enrich Preview. **Courses:** Filmmaking Media Photog. **Avg class size:** 6. **Daily hours for:** Classes 5. Study 1. Rec 2.
Intl program focus: Acad. **Locations:** AZ CA CO CT DC FL GA IL IN MA MD MI MN MO NC NJ NY OH PA RI TN TX UT VA WA Canada.
Focus: Comp_Sci. **Features:** Golf Tennis.
Fees 2012: Res $1248-3499, 1-2 wks. Day $749-999, 1 wk.
Housing: Dorms.
Est 1998. Spons: internalDrive. **Wks/ses:** 1-2. Operates June-Aug.

Operated at more than 60 university campuses in the US and Canada, these one- and two-week computer camps provide the following courses: digital video and movie production, multimedia and game creation, software programming and robotics, and Web design and graphic arts. Programming platforms include iPhone and iPad, Google Android, and Xbox 360. Campers, who take one course per week, may enroll for additional weeks to further study one subject or to explore different topics. Many courses are available at the beginning through advanced levels, while some require prior experience in the subject area.

INDIANA UNIVERSITY HIGH SCHOOL JOURNALISM INSTITUTE
Res and Day — Coed Ages 14-17

Bloomington, IN 47405. Ernie Pyle Hall 212, 940 E 7th St. Tel: 812-855-0895.
  Fax: 812-855-1311.
www.journalism.indiana.edu/hsji E-mail: ljjohnso@indiana.edu
Teresa A. White, Dir.
Grades 9-12 (younger if qualified). Adm: FCFS. **Appl**—Fee $0. Due: Rolling.
Fac 19. Prof 3. K-12 staff 14. Specialists 2. **Staff:** Admin 1. Couns 8.
Type of instruction: Enrich. **Courses:** Media Photog. **Avg class size:** 18. **Daily hours for:**
  Classes 6. Study 3. Rec 2. Homework.
Focus: Writing/Journ. **Features:** Swim.
Fees 2012: Res $375 (+$80), 1 wk. Day $265, 1 wk. Aid (Need).
Housing: Dorms. Avg per room/unit: 2. **Swimming:** Pool. Campus facilities avail.
Est 1947. Nonprofit. Ses: 3. **Wks/ses:** 1. Operates July.

HSJI offers five-day, noncredit workshops for high school students wishing to explore journalism as an academic or career interest. Participants examine the role of media, analyze their own and other student publications, and work to develop their journalistic skills. Pupils choose among sections emphasizing television news, yearbook composition, newspaper/news magazine, business/advertising, photojournalism and online journalism.

INDIANA UNIVERSITY KELLEY SCHOOL OF BUSINESS
JUNIOR EXECUTIVE INSTITUTE
Res — Coed Ages 16-18

Bloomington, IN 47405. 1309 E 10th St, Rm 224. Tel: 812-855-0611.
  Fax: 812-856-0457.
www.kelley.iu.edu/ugrad/precollege/jei.cfm E-mail: ksbjei@indiana.edu
Jenny Olson, Coord.
Grades 11-12. Adm: Selective. Priority: URM. Prereqs: GPA 3.0. **Appl**—Fee $0. Due: Apr.
  Transcript, essay, rec.
Enr: 25-30. Intl: 5%. Non-White: 100%. **Fac 10.** Prof 10. **Staff:** Admin 3.
Type of instruction: Enrich Undergrad. **Courses:** Accounting Bus_Law Management Marketing. **Daily hours for:** Classes 5. Study 3½. Rec 2½.
Focus: Bus/Fin.
Fees 2012: Free. Res 1 wk.

Housing: Dorms. Avg per room/unit: 2.
Ses: 2. **Wks/ses:** 1. Operates June.

This free precollege program serving historically underrepresented populations is open to rising high school juniors and seniors identifying themselves as African-American, Latino or Native American. During the course of the week, students attend a series of presentations and engage in workshops on such topics as business strategy, entrepreneurship, finance and business operations. Participants also work together on a group project.

INSTITUT LE ROSEY SUMMER CAMP
Res — Coed Ages 9-18

Rolle, 1180 Switzerland. Chateau du Rosey. Tel: 41-21-822-55-00.
    Fax: 41-21-822-55-55.
www.roseysummercamps.ch   E-mail: summercamp@rosey.ch
Gregory Guinot, Dir. Student contact: Ingrid Kasnouar.
Adm: FCFS. **Appl**—Due: Rolling. Medical certificate, 2 passport photos.
Enr: 50-300. **Enr cap:** 80-300. Intl: 90%.
Type of instruction: Dev_Read Enrich Rem_Eng Rem_Math Rem_Read Rev. **Courses:** Web_Design Circus_Skills Dance Drawing Filmmaking Photog Theater Pottery. **Avg class size:** 12. **Daily hours for:** Classes 2. Tests. Grades. **High school credit.**
Intl program focus: Lang.
Focus: ESL Fr Span. **Features:** Adventure_Travel Archery Cooking Cruises Hiking Mountaineering Mtn_Trips Riding Rock_Climb Sail Wilderness_Camp Yoga Aerobics Badminton Baseball Basketball Equestrian Golf Martial_Arts Rugby Soccer Swim Tennis Volleyball Water-skiing Watersports.
Fees 2012: Res SwF11,500 (+$SwF500), 4 wks.
Housing: Cabins Dorms Houses Tents Tepees. Avg per room/unit: 2. **Swimming:** Lake Pool. Campus facilities avail.
Est 1975. Ses: 6. **Wks/ses:** 2-4. Operates June-Aug.

The program combines intensive morning language study with afternoon sports. Pupils study French, Spanish or English as a Second Language for two hours daily. Students choose from an array of sports and artistic pursuits in the afternoon.

INSTITUT MONTE ROSA SUMMER HOLIDAY PROGRAM
Res and Day — Coed Ages 6-19

Montreux, 1820 Switzerland. 57 ave de Chillon. Tel: 41-21-965-45-45.
    Fax: 41-21-965-45-46.
www.monterosa.ch   E-mail: info@monterosa.ch
Bernhard Gademann, Dir.
Adm: FCFS. **Appl**—Fee $0. Due: Rolling.
Enr: 90. **Enr cap:** 100. **Staff:** Admin 4.
Type of instruction: Adv Enrich Preview Rem_Eng Rev Tut. **Courses:** Crafts. **Avg class size:** 6. **Daily hours for:** Classes 3½. Rec 8.
Intl program focus: Lang.
Focus: ESL Fr Ger. **Features:** Aquatics Archery Bicycle_Tours Chess Cooking Hiking Kayak Mtn_Biking Mtn_Trips Riding Sail White-water_Raft Badminton Basketball Crosscountry Equestrian Gymnastics Soccer Swim Tennis Volleyball Water-skiing Watersports.
Fees 2011: Res SwF1900 (+SwF250), 1 wk. Day SwF1500 (+SwF100), 1 wk.
Housing: Cabins. Avg per room/unit: 2. **Swimming:** Lake Pool.
Ses: 9. **Wks/ses:** 1. Operates June-Aug.

Monte Rosa pupils take English, French or German immersion courses, receiving private tutoring if necessary. Students participate daily in one of three to five activity options, among them excursions and cultural visits to cities and areas of interest. Boys and girls complete an illustrated composition based on their work at session's end.

INTERN EXCHANGE INTERNATIONAL SUMMER INTERNSHIPS
Res — Coed Ages 16-18

London, England.
Contact (Year-round): 2606 Bridgewood Cir, Boca Raton, FL 33434.
Tel: 561-477-2434. Fax: 561-477-6532.
www.internexchange.com   E-mail: info@internexchange.com
Nina M. Glickman & Lynn A. Weinstein, Dirs.
Adm: FCFS. **Appl**—Fee $100. Due: Rolling. Transcript, teacher rec.
Enr: 200. **Enr cap:** 200. **Fac** 30. K-12 staff 30. **Staff:** Admin 6. Couns 12.
Courses: Archaeol Bus/Fin Computers Govt Law Med/HealthcareVeterinary_Med Writing/ Journ Genealogy Hotel_Management Public_Relations. **College credit:** 3/crse.
Intl program focus: Acad Culture.
Focus: Career.
Fees 2011: Res $7695 (+$1000), 4 wks.
Housing: Dorms.
Est 1987. Inc. Ses: 1. **Wks/ses:** 4. Operates June-July.

IEI's Summer Internships enable high school students to work alongside practicing professionals in such fields as archaeology, culinary arts, hotel management, information technology, law, medicine, public relations, publishing and veterinary medicine. Weekend activities include concerts, theater visits, excursions to London's tourist attractions and trips to historical sites outside of the city.

IXBALANQUE SPANISH SCHOOL
Res — Coed Ages 6 and up

Copan Ruinas, Honduras. Barrio el Centro. Tel: 504-651-4432. Fax: 504-651-4432.
www.ixbalanque.com   E-mail: ixbalanquehn@yahoo.com
Adm: FCFS. **Appl**—Fee $0. Due: Rolling.
Enr: 30.
Type of instruction: Enrich. **Daily hours for:** Classes 4.
Intl program focus: Lang Culture. Home stays avail.
Focus: Span.
Fees 2009: Res $210, 1 wk.
Ses: 4. **Wks/ses:** 1. Operates June-July.

Participants in this program take Spanish classes while learning about the local customs of Honduras and the Mayan culture. The school maintains a one-to-one student-teacher ratio, thereby ensuring individualized instruction. Ixbalanque's campus is proximate to the Mayan ruin of Copan and its archeological structures and sculptures. Students reside with a local family.

JOHN F. KENNEDY INTERNATIONAL SCHOOL
SUMMER CAMP
Res and Day — Coed Ages 6-14

Saanen, 3792 Switzerland. Tel: 41-33-744-13-72. Fax: 41-33-744-89-82.
www.jfk.ch   E-mail: lovell@jfk.ch
Catherine Lovell, Admin.
Adm: Somewhat selective. Admitted: 80%. **Appl**—Fee $0. Due: Rolling.
Enr: 100. **Enr cap:** 100. Intl: 100%. **Fac 25.** Prof 1. Col/grad students 24. **Staff:** Admin 6. Couns 23.

Courses: Crafts. **Avg class size:** 10. **Daily hours for:** Classes 1¼.
Focus: ESL Fr. **Features:** Archery Climbing_Wall Cooking Hiking Mtn_Biking Mtn_Trips Outdoor_Ed Riding Rock_Climb Badminton Basketball Soccer Swim Tennis.
Fees 2010: Res SwF5900 (+SwF500), 3 wks. Day SwF3400 (+SwF300), 3 wks.
Housing: Houses. **Swimming:** Pool. Campus facilities avail.
Est 1973. Ses: 2. Wks/ses: 3. Operates July-Aug.

The Kennedy School's summer program combines English or French immersion with sports, swimming, tennis, biking, music, outdoor education, camping, rock climbing, and arts and crafts. Most campers attend to learn English, but those already fluent in the language may study French instead. Each student participates in excursions to different parts of the country and in two overnight camping trips in the Swiss Alps.

JOHNS HOPKINS UNIVERSITY
ENGINEERING INNOVATION
Res — Coed Ages 16-18

Baltimore, MD 21218. 3400 N Charles St, Maryland Hall, Rm 221. Tel: 410-516-6224, 866-493-0517. Fax: 410-516-0264.
http://engineering-innovation.jhu.edu   E-mail: engineering-innovation@jhu.edu
Laura Marshallsay, Dir.
Grades 11-PG. Adm: Selective. **Appl**—Fee $50. Due: May. Transcript, standardized test scores, math/sci teacher rec.
Type of instruction: Undergrad. **Avg class size:** 21. **College credit:** 3.
Focus: Engineering.
Fees 2009: Res $3785, 4 wks. Day $1885, 4 wks.
Housing: Dorms.
Nonprofit. **Ses: 1. Wks/ses: 4.** Operates June-July.

Following a program developed by Johns Hopkins University, students apply their knowledge of math and science to hands-on projects and laboratory work pertaining to engineering. Boys and girls attend college-level lectures, test theories, solve problems and generate solutions. As a complement to classroom work, students also learn from practicing engineers about career possibilities, internships and educational opportunities within the field. In addition to the residential and day program at Johns Hopkins, Engineering Innovation operates comparable day sessions at locations across the country. Applicants should have spreadsheet knowledge, as well as experience with lab science, algebra II and trigonometry.

JUNIOR STATE OF AMERICA SUMMER SCHOOL
Res — Coed Ages 14-18

San Mateo, CA 94402. 800 S Claremont St, Ste 202. Tel: 650-347-1600, 800-334-5353. Fax: 650-347-7200.
www.jsa.org/summer-programs/summer-school
E-mail: summerprograms@jsa.org
Grades 9-12. Adm: Selective. **Appl**—Fee $0. Due: Rolling. Transcript, essay, rec.
Enr: 275. Fac 16. Prof 16. Staff: Admin 5.
Type of instruction: Adv Enrich. **Courses:** Comm Econ Intl_Relations Media. **Avg class size:** 30. **Daily hours for:** Classes 6. Homework. Grades. **High school credit.**
Locations: CA DC NJ.
Focus: Govt Pol_Sci. **Features:** Leadership.
Fees 2011: Res $4500, 3 wks. Aid 2011 (Merit & Need): $750,000.
Housing: Dorms.
Est 1941. Nonprofit. **Spons:** Junior Statesmen Foundation. **Ses: 4. Wks/ses: 3.** Operates July.

At Georgetown, Princeton and Stanford universities, high school students follow a curriculum that includes a systematic introduction to American government and politics, a speaker program and student debates on current issues. The collegiate academic environment stresses substantial reading, research and writing. Meeting six days each week, classes are equivalent to one-semester high school honors or Advanced Placement courses. AP exam preparation is offered in US government, comparative government, US history and macroeconomics. The Georgetown program includes a high-level speakers program that takes students around Washington, DC, to meet with political leaders.

KANSAS STATE UNIVERSITY
EXCITE! SUMMER WORKSHOP
Res — Girls Ages 13-15

Manhattan, KS 66502. Division of Continuing Ed, 1615 Anderson Ave. Tel: 785-532-3395. Fax: 785-532-2422.
www.k-state.edu/excite   E-mail: cregehr@k-state.edu
Carol Regehr, Coord.
Grades 9-10. Adm: FCFS. **Appl**—Due: Rolling.
Enr: 70. **Fac 2. Staff:** Admin 3. Couns 2.
Type of instruction: Enrich. **Courses:** Game_Design Nanotech Robotics. **Avg class size:** 11.
Focus: Engineering Math Sci.
Fees 2011: Res $350, ½ wk.
Housing: Dorms. Avg per room/unit: 2.
Est 2002. Nonprofit. **Ses:** 1. **Wks/ses:** ½. Operates June.

The three-day EXCITE! program guides young women through topics in mathematics, science, technology and engineering. The workshop emphasizes hands-on activities and team problem solving as students learn about the engineering design process. Girls work closely with KSU faculty and undergraduates in choosing a specific track from such fields as architecture, aeronautics, nanotechnology, robotics and game design.

KETTERING UNIVERSITY
LIVES IMPROVE THROUGH ENGINEERING
Res — Girls Ages 17-18

Flint, MI 48504. 1700 W 3rd Ave. Tel: 810-762-9679, 800-955-4464.
www.kettering.edu/futurestudents/precollege/lite   E-mail: lite@kettering.edu
Deborah Stewart, Prgm Dir.
Grade 12. Adm: Selective. Prereqs: GPA 3.0. **Appl**—Fee $0. Due: Apr. Transcript, essay, rec.
Enr: 36. **Enr cap:** 36. **Fac 6.** Prof 6.
Type of instruction: Enrich.
Focus: Engineering. **Features:** Swim.
Fees 2011: Res $600, 2 wks. Aid (Need).
Housing: Dorms. **Swimming:** Pool. Campus facilities avail.
Ses: 1. **Wks/ses:** 2. Operates July.

LITE shows young women how engineers use math, science and technology to solve human problems. Conducted by Kettering faculty, classes and labs address biomechanics, biochemistry, engineering for a sustainable society and vehicle collision analysis. Field trips to engineering sites, social activities and athletics round out the program.

LAKE FOREST ACADEMY
ENGLISH AS A SECOND LANGUAGE SUMMER PROGRAM
Res and Day — Coed Ages 13-18

Lake Forest, IL 60045. 1500 W Kennedy Rd. Tel: 847-615-3239. Fax: 847-295-8149.
www.lfanet.org/esl   E-mail: pdunlop@lfanet.org
Paul Dunlop, Dir.
Grades 8-12. Adm: Selective. Admitted: 70%. **Appl**—Fee $50. Due: Rolling. Transcript, TOEFL score (if taken).
Enr: 104. **Enr cap:** 120. Intl: 100%. Non-White: 60%. **Fac 10.** K-12 staff 10. **Staff:** Admin 1. Couns 10.
Type of instruction: Enrich. **Courses:** Eng Math. **Avg class size:** 12. **Daily hours for:** Classes 5. Study 2. Rec 2. Homework. Tests. Grades.
Focus: ESL. **Features:** Basketball Ice_Hockey Soccer Softball Swim Tennis Volleyball Weight_Trng.
Fees 2011: Res $6168 (+$600), 5 wks. Day $4825 (+$600), 5 wks. Aid 2009 (Need): $20,000.
Housing: Dorms. Avg per room/unit: 2. **Swimming:** Lake Pool. Campus facilities avail.
Est 1979. Nonprofit. **Ses:** 1. **Wks/ses:** 5. Operates July-Aug.

Conducted on the 100-acre LFA campus, this intensive ESL program prepares international boys and girls for academic and social life integration into independent boarding school. Each student takes an entry exam to determine class placement in one of five program levels (ranging from beginning to advanced). Courses in grammar, reading and writing, and speaking and listening are complemented by such afternoon and weekend activities as sports and field trips.

LANGUAGE LIAISON GLOBAL TEEN
Res — Coed Ages 13-17

Pacific Palisades, CA 90272. PO Box 1772. Tel: 310-454-1701, 800-284-4448.
Fax: 310-454-1706.
www.languageliaison.com   E-mail: learn@languageliaison.com
Nancy Forman, Dir.
Grades 8-12. Adm: FCFS. **Appl**—Due: Rolling.
Type of instruction: Enrich Study_Skills. **Avg class size:** 8. **Daily hours for:** Classes 3½. Rec 5.
Intl program focus: Lang. **Locations:** Canada Europe Mexico/Central_America Middle_East South_America. Home stays avail.
Focus: Fr Ger Ital Span. **Features:** Riding Sail Basketball Golf Surfing Swim Tennis Volleyball Water-skiing Watersports.
Fees 2011: Res $978-6526 (+$130-200), 1-4 wks.
Housing: Dorms Houses. **Swimming:** Lake Ocean Pool.
Est 1987. Inc. **Wks/ses:** 1-5. Operates June-Aug.

Designed specifically for high schoolers (although some courses accept younger pupils), Language Liaison offers language immersion in France, Ecuador, Germany, Canada, Austria, Italy, Costa Rica, Spain and Mexico. No prior study of the target language is required. Home stay with carefully selected families is an important element of the program.

THE LAWRENCE HALL OF SCIENCE
MARINE BIOLOGY RESEARCH CAMP
Res — Coed Ages 14-18

Berkeley, CA 94720. Univ of California-Berkeley, 1 Centennial Dr, Rm 5200.
Tel: 510-642-1334. Fax: 510-643-0994.
www.lawrencehallofscience.org/summercamp   E-mail: lhsweb@berkeley.edu

Grades 9-12. Adm: FCFS. **Appl**—Fee $0. Due: Rolling.
Type of instruction: Adv Enrich. **Courses:** Crafts. **Daily hours for:** Classes 7. Study 2. Rec 2.
Focus: Marine_Bio/Stud. **Features:** Archery Exploration Hiking Mtn_Trips Outdoor_Ed Wilderness_Camp Swim Volleyball.
Fees 2011: Res $1040, 1 wk. Aid (Need).
Housing: Dorms. **Swimming:** Lake Pool.
Est 1968. Nonprofit. **Spons:** University of California-Berkeley. **Ses:** 1. **Wks/ses:** 1. Operates Aug.

The Lawrence Hall of Science, the University of California-Berkeley's public science center, conducts a weeklong marine biology program at Bodega Marine Lab in Bodega Bay. High school students develop laboratory and field investigation skills as they examine the rocky tide pools, mudflats, estuaries, coastal dunes and sandy beaches surrounding the modern research station. Participants design their own research projects with guidance from LHS instructors and scientists. Boys and girls engage in supervised recreational activities each evening.

LE CHAPERON ROUGE
Res and Day — Coed Ages 6-16

Crans-sur-Sierre, 3963 Valais, Switzerland. Tel: 41-27-481-25-00.
   Fax: 41-27-481-25-02.
www.chaperonrouge.ch   E-mail: office@chaperonrouge.ch
Gabrielle Bagnoud, Dir.
Adm: FCFS. **Appl**—Fee $0. Due: Rolling.
Enr: 65. **Enr cap:** 65. **Staff:** Admin 2. Couns 2.
Type of instruction: Adv Enrich Rem_Eng Rev Study_Skills. **Courses:** Crafts Dance. **Avg class size:** 7. **Daily hours for:** Classes 3. Rec 7.
Intl program focus: Lang.
Focus: ESL Fr Ger Ital Span. **Features:** Archery Boating Climbing_Wall Fishing Hiking Mountaineering Mtn_Trips Paintball Riding Sail Badminton Basketball Equestrian Golf Gymnastics In-line_Skating Soccer Swim Tennis Volleyball Winter_Sports Ping-Pong.
Fees 2012: Res SwF3265-4570 (+SwF270-480), 2-3 wks. Day SwF2200-3000 (+SwF270-480), 2-3 wks.
Housing: Houses. Avg per room/unit: 8. **Swimming:** Pool.
Est 1954. Ses: 3. **Wks/ses:** 2-3. Operates June-Aug.

Students receive language lessons in French, German, Italian, Spanish or English for three to four hours each morning. Beginning, intermediate and advanced levels are available for all languages. Students may choose to study two languages during one session. Among afternoon and weekend recreational activities are crafts, horseback riding and sports.

LE CHATEAU DES ENFANTS
Res — Coed Ages 7-10; Day — Coed 4-10

Montagnola-Lugano, Switzerland.
Contact (Year-round): c/o TASIS US Office, 112 S Royal St, Alexandria, VA 22314.
   Tel: 703-299-8150. Fax: 703-299-8157.
www.tasis.com   E-mail: usadmissions@tasis.com
Betsy Newell, Dir.
Adm: FCFS. **Appl**—Due: Rolling.
Enr: 120. **Enr cap:** 120. **Fac 10. Staff:** Admin 3. Couns 15.
Type of instruction: Enrich. **Courses:** Crafts Drama. **Avg class size:** 8. **Daily hours for:** Classes 3. Rec 6.
Intl program focus: Lang.
Focus: ESL Fr Ital. **Features:** Basketball Soccer Swim.
Housing: Dorms Houses. **Swimming:** Lake Pool.

Est 1969. Nonprofit. **Spons:** TASIS Foundation. **Ses:** 2. **Wks/ses:** 3-4. Operates June-Aug.

This highly international camp combines French, Italian or English language instruction with an array of traditional recreational activities. Boys and girls take two daily lessons (in groups of four to six students) in the target language. Thematically designed lessons incorporate drama and singing periods as learning tools. Swimming, sports, and arts and crafts are all offered on a daily basis.

LEAD SUMMER BUSINESS INSTITUTE
Res — Coed Ages 17-18

Philadelphia, PA 19118. 14 E Hartwell Ln. Tel: 215-753-2490.
www.leadnational.org   E-mail: info@leadprogram.org
Grade 12. Adm: Selective. Prereqs: GPA 3.0. PSAT M/CR 100; SAT M/CR 1000; ACT 22.
Appl—Fee $35. Due: Feb. Transcript, essays, test scores, 2 recs.
Type of instruction: Enrich Undergrad. **Courses:** Comp_Sci Econ Ethics.
Locations: DC GA IL MI NC NH NY PA VA.
Focus: Bus/Fin.
Fees 2009: Res $900-1200, 3-4 wks. Aid (Need).
Housing: Dorms.
Est 1980. Wks/ses: 3-4.

Well-regarded American business schools throughout the country host rising high school seniors for a program that features interactive classes and one-on-one sessions led by university professors and corporate executives. SBI's curriculum addresses aspects of marketing, accounting, finance, economics, computer science and ethics. During the session, students employ case studies to work through business problems, analyze business issues and gain insight into difficulties faced by major corporations. Boys and girls develop a deeper understanding of business ownership through field trips to local businesses, meetings with entrepreneurs and the formulation of business plans.

LEAD SUMMER ENGINEERING INSTITUTE
Res — Coed Ages 16-18

Philadelphia, PA 19118. 14 E Hartwell Ln. Tel: 215-753-2490.
www.leadnational.org   E-mail: info@leadprogram.org
Grades 11-12. Adm: Selective. Priority: Low-income. URM. **Appl**—Fee $0. 2 recs, 2 essays.
Enr cap: 30.
Type of instruction: Adv Enrich. **Courses:** Comp_Sci Math.
Locations: CA GA MI VA.
Focus: Engineering.
Fees 2010: Free. Res 3 wks.
Housing: Dorms.
Est 2008. Ses: 4. **Wks/ses:** 3. Operates July-Aug.

SEI provides hands-on learning for mathematically inclined rising high school juniors and seniors from African-American, Latino, Native American, underrepresented Asian and economically disadvantaged populations. At multiple college locations, LEAD admits the same number of boys and girls into each of its sessions. Students gain an introduction to mechanical and chemical engineering, engineering design, and processes such as solar and wind power.

LEARNING PROGRAMS INTERNATIONAL
Res — Coed Ages 15-18

Austin, TX 78704. 1112 W Ben White Blvd. Tel: 512-474-1041, 800-259-4439. Fax: 512-275-0770.
www.lpiabroad.com E-mail: lpi@lpiabroad.com
Brian Pirttima, Exec Dir.
Grades 10-PG. Adm: Somewhat selective. Prereqs: GPA 2.0. **Appl**—Fee $0. Due: Rolling. Transcript, teacher rec.
Enr: 15-20. **Enr cap:** 45. **Fac 3.** Prof 3. **Staff:** Admin 10. Couns 3.
Type of instruction: Undergrad. **Courses:** Art. **Avg class size:** 15. **Daily hours for:** Classes 4½. Study 1. Rec 1½. Homework. Tests. Grades. **College credit:** 8.
Intl program focus: Lang Culture. **Locations:** Asia Europe. Home stays avail.
Focus: Chin Span. **Features:** Canoe Caving Hiking Mtn_Biking Riding Ropes_Crse Swim.
Fees 2012: Res $3300-6000 (+airfare), 2-6 wks. Aid 2011 (Merit & Need): $4500.
Housing: Dorms Houses. Avg per room/unit: 2-3. **Swimming:** Ocean Pool River. Campus facilities avail.
Est 1989. Inc. Ses: 3. **Wks/ses:** 2-6. Operates June-Aug.

Offering summer programs in Shanghai, China, and Malaga and Salamanca, Spain, LPI provides language instruction and cultural immersion for high school students at all levels of proficiency. Pupils take classes at accredited foreign universities while living in dorms or with host families. Staff at each location provide tutoring services and assistance with class and language performance. Students develop a working knowledge of either Spanish or Chinese, earn transferable college credit, experience another culture and explore the region through excursions.

LEE ACADEMY SUMMER ESL
Res — Coed Ages 14-19

Lee, ME 04455. 26 Winn Rd. Tel: 207-738-2252, 888-433-2852. Fax: 207-738-3257.
www.leeacademy.org E-mail: djacobs@leeacademy.org
Bruce Lindberg, Head. Student contact: Deborah Jacobs.
Grades 8-12 (younger if qualified). Adm: FCFS. **Appl**—Fee $0. Due: June.
Enr cap: 90. Intl: 100%. Non-White: 100%. **Fac 4.** K-12 staff 4. **Staff:** Admin 4. Res 9.
Avg class size: 10. **Daily hours for:** Classes 3. Study 2. Rec 4½. Homework. Tests.
Focus: ESL. **Features:** Boating Canoe Climbing_Wall Exploration Fishing Hiking Kayak Mtn_Trips Outdoor_Ed Paintball Rock_Climb Badminton Baseball Basketball Soccer Softball Swim Tennis Volleyball Weight_Trng.
Fees 2011: Res $3600 (+$100-200), 4 wks.
Housing: Dorms. Avg per room/unit: 2. **Swimming:** Lake Ocean. Campus facilities avail.
Est 2005. Nonprofit. Ses: 1. **Wks/ses:** 4. Operates July-Aug.

This month-long program serves international students interested in improving their English reading, writing and speaking skills. Ample daily recreational periods balance class and study time.

LES ELFES INTERNATIONAL SUMMER CAMP
Res — Coed Ages 8-18

Verbier, 1936 Switzerland. CP 174. Tel: 41-27-775-35-90. Fax: 41-27-775-35-99.
www.leselfesinternational.com E-mail: info@leselfes.com
Philippe Stettler & Nicole Stettler, Dirs.
    Student contact: Celine Lovey, E-mail: celine@leselfes.ch.
Adm: FCFS. **Appl**—Due: Rolling.
Enr: 140. **Enr cap:** 140. **Staff:** Res 25.

Daily hours for: Classes 1½. Rec 7. Tests.
Intl program focus: Lang.
Focus: ESL Fr Ger Span. **Features:** Aquatics Bicycle_Tours Climbing_Wall Hiking Mtn_ Biking Mtn_Trips Riding Rock_Climb Ropes_Crse Basketball Equestrian Golf Ice_ Hockey Soccer Swim Tennis Volleyball Water-skiing Watersports.
Fees 2012: Res SwF3965-6160, 2-3 wks.
Housing: Houses. Avg per room/unit: 3-4. **Swimming:** Lake Pool. Campus facilities avail.
Est 1987. Ses: 5. **Wks/ses:** 2-3. Operates June-Aug.

Les Elfes combines language instruction with traditional recreational pursuits. Students receive eight hours of instruction per week in French, German, Spanish or English for the standard tuition cost; those desiring more intensive instruction have two options for an extra fee: seven additional weekly hours of instruction or hourly private lessons. Other aspects of the program are cultural excursions and special events designed to help pupils expand their artistic skills. Boys and girls also choose from a wide selection of sports and outdoor activities.

LETRA HISPANICA INTENSIVE SUMMER PROGRAMS
Res — Coed Ages 13-18

Salamanca, 37002 Spain. Calle Pena Primera 18. Tel: 34-923-262-018.
 Fax: 34-923-262-018.
www.letrahispanica.com   E-mail: info@letrahispanica.com
Ada Calvo, Dir.
Adm: FCFS. **Appl**—Due: Rolling.
Enr: 50. **Enr cap:** 50. **Fac** 4. Col/grad students 4. **Staff:** Admin 3.
Type of instruction: Enrich Study_Skills. **Courses:** Dance Drama. **Avg class size:** 10.
 Daily hours for: Classes 3. Rec 2. Homework. Tests.
Intl program focus: Lang Culture. Home stays avail.
Focus: Span. **Features:** Gymnastics Swim.
Fees 2012: Res €2200-3900, 4-8 wks.
Housing: Apartments Houses. **Swimming:** Pool River.
Est 2000. Inc. Ses: 2. **Wks/ses:** 4-8. Operates July-Aug.

Each week, students take 15 hours of Spanish language classes (including communication practice) and participate in five hours of cultural activities or workshops. Boys and girls devote the rest of their time to such recreational activities as dance, drama, theater, nature, gymnastics and swimming. Enriching weekend excursions to historical sites and other areas emphasize Spanish culture.

LINGUA SERVICE WORLDWIDE
SUMMER LANGUAGE PROGRAMS FOR CHILDREN AND TEENAGERS
Res and Day — Coed Ages 5-18

West Redding, CT 06896. 14½ Long Ridge Rd. Tel: 203-938-7406, 800-394-5327.
 Fax: 203-938-7461.
www.linguaserviceworldwide.com   E-mail: info@linguaserviceworldwide.com
Leo Rodriguez, Dir.
Adm: FCFS. **Appl**—Fee $100. Due: Rolling.
Enr cap: 200. Intl: 65%. **Fac** 15. Prof 12. Col/grad students 3. **Staff:** Admin 8. Res 15.
 Avg class size: 12. **Daily hours for:** Classes 3½. Study 1. Rec 5. Homework. Tests. Grades. **High school credit.**
Intl program focus: Lang. **Locations:** Canada Europe Mexico/Central_America. Home stays avail.
Focus: Fr Ger Span. **Features:** Riding Sail Basketball Golf Soccer Swim Tennis Volleyball Handball.
Fees 2012: Res $940-6450, 1-6 wks. Day $504-4620, 1-6 wks.

Housing: Dorms Houses. Avg per room/unit: 3-5. **Swimming:** Ocean Pool. Campus facilities avail.
Est 1988. Inc. **Ses:** 33. **Wks/ses:** 1-6. Operates June-Aug.

These language immersion programs combine language learning with traditional summer camping activities. Pupils study Spanish, French and German language instruction where it is spoken; locations are Canada, France, Spain, Costa Rica, Germany and Austria. In each program, students receive at least 15 hours of weekly language instruction. A supervised activity program balances academics.

MARIST COLLEGE SUMMER INSTITUTES
Res — Coed Ages 16-18

Poughkeepsie, NY 12601. Office of Undergraduate Adm, 3399 North Rd.
Tel: 845-575-3226. Fax: 845-575-3215.
www.marist.edu/summerinstitutes   E-mail: precollege@marist.edu
Grades 11-12. Adm: Selective. **Appl**—Due: Rolling. Transcript, essay, rec.
Type of instruction: Undergrad. **College credit:** 3/crse, total 3.
Focus: Bus/Fin Comm Environ_Sci Span Law.
Fees 2012: Res $3095, 2 wks.
Housing: Dorms. Campus facilities avail.
Ses: 1. **Wks/ses:** 2. Operates July.

Students earn college credit and preview campus life through Marist's Summer Institutes in business, criminal justice, environmental studies, game design, Spanish and sports communications. Programming combines several class sessions each day with study time, local excursions, daylong field trips and recreational activities. Other institutes focus on areas in the arts: creative writing, digital moviemaking, fashion design, fashion marketing and merchandising, and theater (see separate listing).

MARQUETTE UNIVERSITY
SUMMER SCIENCE ENRICHMENT PROGRAM
Res — Coed Ages 15-17

Milwaukee, WI 53201. Walter Schroeder Complex, Rm 346, PO Box 1881.
Tel: 414-288-5505. Fax: 414-288-5987.
www.marquette.edu/programs/hcop_summer_enrichment.shtml
E-mail: manuel.santiago@marquette.edu
Manuel Santiago, Dir.
Grades 10-12. Adm: Selective. Admitted: 40%. Priority: Low-income. URM. Prereqs: GPA 3.0. **Appl**—Fee $0. Due: Apr. Transcript, 4 recs, essay.
Enr: 25. **Enr cap:** 25. **Staff:** Admin 2. Couns 4.
Type of instruction: Rem_Math SAT/ACT_Prep Undergrad. **Daily hours for:** Classes 6. Study 1. Homework. Tests. Grades. **High school credit.**
Focus: Med/Healthcare Sci. **Features:** Swim.
Fees 2012: Free (+$250), 6 wks.
Housing: Dorms. **Swimming:** Pool. Campus facilities avail.
Est 1998. Nonprofit. Roman Catholic. **Ses:** 1. **Wks/ses:** 6. Operates June-July.

This tuition-free program provides ethnic minorities and financially and educationally disadvantaged students with the opportunity to explore careers in healthcare. Advanced courses in biology, chemistry, ACT/SAT preparation and medical sciences complement seminars in test taking, time management and professional development. Boys and girls may focus on physical therapy, dentistry, speech pathology, clinical laboratory science or physician assistant studies.

MASSACHUSETTS INSTITUTE OF TECHNOLOGY
MINORITY INTRODUCTION TO ENGINEERING AND SCIENCE
Res — Coed Ages 16-18

Cambridge, MA 02139. 77 Massachusetts Ave, Rm 1-123. Tel: 617-253-3298.
Fax: 617-324-1120.
http://web.mit.edu/mites   E-mail: mites@mit.edu
Shawna Young, Dir.
Grade 12. Adm: Very selective. Priority: Low-income. URM. **Appl**—Fee $0. Due: Feb. Transcript, test scores, essays, 2 teacher recs.
Enr: 60-80.
Type of instruction: Adv Enrich Study_Skills Tut. **Courses:** Bus/Fin Comp_Sci Math Writing/Journ Humanities. Homework. Tests.
Focus: Engineering Sci.
Fees 2010: Free. Res 6 wks.
Housing: Dorms.
Est 1975. Nonprofit. **Ses:** 1. **Wks/ses:** 6. Operates June-Aug.

This rigorous, tuition-free program at MIT serves promising students from backgrounds traditionally underrepresented in science, engineering and technology. MITES participants choose five courses from offerings including calculus, physics, chemistry, biology, entrepreneurship, computer programming, humanities, genomics and robotics. Study skills workshops, tutoring sessions and guest speakers help students develop learning strategies, build confidence and plan their careers. At the program's conclusion, boys and girls deliver group presentations and receive faculty evaluations.

MASSACHUSETTS INSTITUTE OF TECHNOLOGY
WOMEN'S TECHNOLOGY PROGRAM
Res — Girls Ages 17-18

Cambridge, MA 02139. 77 Massachusetts Ave, Rm 38-491. Tel: 617-253-5580.
http://wtp.mit.edu   E-mail: wtp@mit.edu
Cynthia Skier, Dir.
Grade 12. Adm: Very selective. Admitted: 20%. **Appl**—Fee $0. Due: Jan. Transcript, standardized test scores, sci & math teacher recs.
Enr: 60. **Enr cap:** 60.
Type of instruction: Adv Enrich. **Avg class size:** 20.
Focus: Comp_Sci Engineering.
Fees 2009: Res $3000, 4 wks. Aid (Need).
Housing: Dorms.
Ses: 1. **Wks/ses:** 4. Operates June-July.

Taught by MIT students, this highly competitive enrichment program for girls serves rising high school seniors. Students enroll in one of two tracks: electrical engineering and computer science or mechanical engineering. The program is designed specifically for girls who have excelled in math and science but who have very little or no prior background in engineering or computer science. Both tracks feature intensive classroom sessions, projects, guest speakers, and lab tours and field trips.

MATHPATH
Res — Coed Ages 11-14

Swarthmore, PA 19081. c/o Swarthmore College, Math/Stat, 500 College Ave.
Tel: 415-830-3838.
www.mathpath.org   E-mail: smaurer1@swarthmore.edu
George R. Thomas, Exec Dir. Student contact: Stephen B. Maurer.
Adm: Very selective. **Appl**—Fee $0. Due: Apr. Math test, 2 recs.

Enr: 91. **Enr cap:** 95. Intl: 20%. Non-White: 2%. **Fac 10.** Prof 8. K-12 staff 2. **Staff:** Admin 3. Couns 9. Res 8.
Type of instruction: Adv Enrich. **Avg class size:** 18. **Daily hours for:** Classes 5½. Study 1. Rec 3. Homework.
Focus: Math. **Features:** Hiking Kayak Soccer Swim Tennis Ping-Pong.
Fees 2011: Res $4500, 4 wks. Aid 2010 (Merit & Need): $30,000.
Housing: Dorms. **Swimming:** Pool. Campus facilities avail.
Est 2002. Nonprofit. **Ses:** 1. **Wks/ses:** 4. Operates June-July.

Hosted on a different college campus each summer, this program for highly gifted math students balances foundation-building courses and problem-solving activities. University professors lead sessions on such enrichment topics as hyperbolic, spherical and analytical geometry; induction; number theory; and combinatorics. Also included are instruction on proofs, mathematical writing and the history of math, and problem-solving instruction prepares boys and girls for various math competitions. Guest lectures provide further enrichment. Evening field games and weekend trips to natural and local attractions round out the program.

MAUR HILL-MOUNT ACADEMY SUMMER ESL PROGRAM
Res — Coed Ages 11-19

Atchison, KS 66002. 1000 Green St. Tel: 913-367-5482. Fax: 913-367-5096.
www.mh-ma.com   E-mail: admissions@mh-ma.com
Student contact: Deke Nolan, E-mail: dnolan@mh-ma.com.
Grades 7-12 (younger if qualified). Adm: Somewhat selective. Admitted: 90%. **Appl—** Fee $100. Due: Rolling. SLEP/TOEFL score (if available).
Enr: 20. Intl: 100%. **Fac 3.** **Staff:** Admin 3. Couns 3.
Type of instruction: ESL/TOEFL_Prep. **Avg class size:** 8. **Daily hours for:** Classes 6. Study 1. Rec 1. Homework. Tests.
Focus: ESL. **Features:** Basketball Soccer Swim Volleyball.
Fees 2012: Res $4200 (+$250), 6 wks.
Housing: Dorms. Avg per room/unit: 2. **Swimming:** Pond Pool. Campus facilities avail.
Nonprofit. Roman Catholic. **Ses:** 1. **Wks/ses:** 6. Operates July-Aug.

This intensive English program serves foreign students who wish to learn English or improve proficiency. Classes are held six hours daily, five days a week. Each weekend, students take cultural trips to gain experience and utilize skills acquired in the classroom.

McDANIEL COLLEGE FORENSIC SCIENCE CAMP
Res and Day — Coed Ages 16-18

Westminster, MD 21157. 2 College Hill. Tel: 410-857-2458.
www.mcdaniel.edu/6801.htm
Brian Wladkowski, Dir.
Grades 12-PG. Adm: FCFS. **Appl**—Fee $0. Due: Rolling.
Type of instruction: Undergrad. **College credit:** 3.
Focus: Forensic_Sci.
Fees 2009: Res $675, 1 wk. Day $425, 1 wk.
Housing: Dorms.
Nonprofit. **Ses:** 2. **Wks/ses:** 1. Operates June-July.

This weeklong, college-level session addresses such topics as crime scene investigation, blood analysis, fingerprinting, analysis of hair and fibers, DNA analysis and ballistics analysis. Discussions and field trip complement class work. Successful completion of the program results in one semester of college credit.

MICHIGAN DEBATE INSTITUTES
Res — Coed Ages 14-17

Ann Arbor, MI 48109. 2205 Michigan Union, 530 S State St. Tel: 734-763-5903.
Fax: 734-763-5902.
www.michigandebate.com   E-mail: akall@umich.edu
Aaron Kall, Dir.
Grades 9-12. Adm: FCFS. **Appl**—Fee $60. Due: Rolling.
Type of instruction: Enrich.
Focus: Debate.
Fees 2009: Res $2000-5200, 3-7 wks.
Housing: Dorms.
Est 1985. Nonprofit. **Ses: 3. Wks/ses:** 3-7. Operates June-Aug.

With a faculty consisting of well-regarded high school and college coaches and top-tier intercollegiate debaters, these programs teach basic and advanced debating techniques to high schoolers. The three-week Michigan National Debate Institute emphasizes the development of well-organized arguments in national policy debate areas. The four-week Michigan Classic policy debate workshop provides communication skills and theory instruction for students wishing to debate at an advanced level in the coming school year. Finally, the exclusive Seven Week Program, which enrolls rising juniors and seniors, combines rigorous debate instruction with the university's extensive research facilities.

MICHIGAN STATE UNIVERSITY
CHINA ADVENTURE
Res — Coed Ages 16-18

East Lansing, MI 48824. 186 Bessey Hall. Tel: 517-432-2129. Fax: 517-353-6464.
www.gifted.msu.edu   E-mail: mcdon288@msu.edu
Kathee McDonald, Dir.
Grades 11-PG. Adm: Selective. Prereqs: GPA 3.5. **Appl**—Fee $55. Due: Mar. Standardized test results, 2 recs, essay.
Enr: 20. **Enr cap:** 20. **Staff:** Admin 3.
Type of instruction: Adv Enrich. **Daily hours for:** Classes 7. Rec 3. **College credit:** 4.
Intl program focus: Lang Culture. **Travel:** Asia.
Focus: Global_Stud Chin.
Fees 2010: Res $3850, 3 wks.
Housing: Dorms. Campus facilities avail.
Nonprofit. **Ses: 1. Wks/ses:** 3. Operates June-July.

After spending a week studying on the MSU campus, high-achieving students entering grades 11 and 12 spend two weeks touring and studying in Beijing, Hangzhou, Xi'an and Shanghai, China. Each day begins with a three-hour class on a topic such as the following: the physical and cultural geography of China; Chinese historical themes; the creation of a unified China; Confucianism and the Confucian state; Buddhism and the creation of the Daoist religion; poetry and literature; international trade; the establishment of the People's Republic of China; and contemporary China as viewed through its literature, music, politics and economics. In the afternoon, pupils will take a two-hour introductory Chinese language class (taught by an MSU instructor). Those wishing to earn four college credits may do so by successfully completing four equally weighted course elements: language study, analytical review of a selected book, an annotated journal of impressions and an analysis of time spent in China, and an individual project.

MICHIGAN STATE UNIVERSITY
CSI FORENSIC SCIENCE PROGRAM
Res — Coed Ages 12-15

East Lansing, MI 48824. 186 Bessey Hall. Tel: 517-432-2129. Fax: 517-353-6464.
www.gifted.msu.edu   E-mail: gifted@msu.edu
Kathee McDonald, Dir.
Grades 8-10. Adm: Somewhat selective. Admitted: 95%. Prereqs: GPA 3.5. **Appl**—Fee $50. Due: Apr. Test scores, rec.
Enr cap: 40. Intl: 5%. Non-White: 5%. **Fac 13.** Prof 4. Col/grad students 5. Specialists 4. **Staff:** Admin 3. Couns 2.
Type of instruction: Adv Enrich. **Daily hours for:** Classes 5. Study 2. Rec 3.
Focus: Forensic_Sci. **Features:** Aquatics Swim.
Fees 2012: Res $1250, 1 wk. Aid (Need).
Housing: Cabins. Avg per room/unit: 2. **Swimming:** Pool. Campus facilities avail.
Est 2006. Nonprofit. **Ses:** 1. **Wks/ses:** 1. Operates June.

Program participants learn about the field of forensic science through lectures and hands-on laboratory experiences conducted by experts in the field. Instructors include pathologists, anthropologists, entomologists, police experts, FBI agents, and volunteers who work with rescue and cadaver dogs.

MICHIGAN STATE UNIVERSITY
HIGH SCHOOL ENGINEERING INSTITUTE
Res — Coed Ages 15-18

East Lansing, MI 48824. College of Engineering. Tel: 517-353-7282.
www.egr.msu.edu/future-engineer/programs/hsei   E-mail: donadoto@msu.edu
Luis Donado, Dir.
Grades 10-12 (younger if qualified). Adm: Somewhat selective. Prereqs: GPA 3.0. **Appl**—Due: Rolling. Transcript, essay, math/sci teacher rec.
Enr: 100. **Enr cap:** 100.
Type of instruction: Enrich.
Focus: Engineering.
Fees 2011: Res $700, 1 wk.
Housing: Dorms. Avg per room/unit: 2.
Ses: 1. **Wks/ses:** 1. Operates June.

Conducted by MSU College of Engineering faculty with the assistance of graduate and undergraduate students, HSEI provides in-depth experience in engineering majors for rising high school sophomores and juniors who are seriously considering an engineering career. Each day, students learn about a major and take part in short lectures, demonstrations, hands-on experiments and team-based problem solving. Participants also tour engineering research facilities and attend presentations by the Honors College, the admissions office, the study abroad office, and the internship and undergraduate research opportunities center.

MICHIGAN STATE UNIVERSITY
HIGH SCHOOL HONORS SCIENCE, MATH
AND ENGINEERING PROGRAM
Res — Coed Ages 16-17

East Lansing, MI 48824. 319 Erickson Hall. Tel: 517-432-4854.
www.education.msu.edu/hshsp   E-mail: gailr@msu.edu
Gail Richmond, Dir.
Grade 12 (younger if qualified). Adm: Very selective. **Appl**—Due: Apr. Transcript, test scores, essay, 2 recs.
Enr: 24.

Type of instruction: Adv Enrich.
Focus: Engineering Math Sci.
Fees 2011: Res $3300, 7 wks.
Housing: Dorms.
Est 1958. Ses: 1. **Wks/ses:** 7. Operates June-Aug.

Conducted on Michigan State University's Arboretum campus, HSHSP allows rising high school seniors to research individually chosen areas of science, math or engineering using the university's laboratory and library facilities. Individual research is combined with group visits to university science facilities and guidance by faculty and doctoral candidates. Participants have been recognized by the Intel Science Talent Search and the Siemens Competition in Math, Science & Technology.

MICHIGAN STATE UNIVERSITY
MATH SCIENCE AND TECHNOLOGY AT MSU
Res — Coed Ages 13-15

East Lansing, MI 48824. 186 Bessey Hall. Tel: 517-432-2129. Fax: 517-353-6464.
www.gifted.msu.edu   E-mail: gifted@msu.edu
Kathee McDonald, Dir.
Grades 8-10. Adm: Selective. Prereqs: SAT M 530, CR 530, M/CR 1010; ACT 23. **Appl—** Fee $75. Due: May. Transcript, essay, rec, test results.
Enr cap: 135. **Fac 18.** Prof 9. K-12 staff 9. **Staff:** Admin 3.
Type of instruction: Adv Enrich. **Courses:** Astron Comp_Sci Genetics Nuclear_Astrophysics Physiol Creative_Writing Filmmaking Photog Visual_Arts. **Avg class size:** 17.
Daily hours for: Classes 4. Study 2. Rec 3. Homework.
Focus: Engineering Math Sci. **Features:** Basketball Soccer Swim.
Fees 2012: Res $1650, 2 wks. Aid (Need).
Housing: Dorms. Avg per room/unit: 2. **Swimming:** Pool. Campus facilities avail.
Nonprofit. **Ses:** 1. **Wks/ses:** 2. Operates July.

This two-week program for academically talented boys and girls emphasizes math, science and technology, as well as applications in those areas. MST at MSU attempts to challenge students without duplicating course work that is part of the traditional kindergarten through grade 12 curriculum. Pupils investigate problems that can be explored through a better understanding of math, science, engineering and technology; focus on an intensive area of study suited to interdisciplinary research in these subject areas; and become acquainted with possible career fields. In addition to meeting academic requirements, applicants must display evidence of potential in math, science or technology through past competition participation or involvement in extracurricular activities.

MICHIGAN STATE UNIVERSITY
PHYSICS OF ATOMIC NUCLEI PROGRAM
Res and Day — Coed Ages 15-18

East Lansing, MI 48824. 1 Cyclotron. Tel: 517-333-6363. Fax: 517-353-5967.
www.nscl.msu.edu/teachersstudents/programs/pan   E-mail: pan@nscl.msu.edu
Konrad Gelbke, Dir. Student contact: Zachary Constan.
Grades 10-PG. Adm: Selective. **Appl**—Fee $0. Due: Apr. 2 recs.
Enr: 24.
Type of instruction: Adv Enrich.
Focus: Astron Sci. **Features:** Swim.
Fees 2012: Free. Res 1 wk. Day 1 wk.
Housing: Dorms. Avg per room/unit: 2. **Swimming:** Pool. Campus facilities avail.
Ses: 1. **Wks/ses:** 1. Operates Aug.

Sponsored by the Joint Institute for Nuclear Astrophysics and the National Superconducting

Cyclotron Laboratory, PAN allows high school students to learn about research in a leading rare-isotope laboratory. NSCL scientists discuss their research in cosmic rays, nuclear astrophysics, detector technology and other fields. Young scientists form research teams to design and execute an experiment into the nature of cosmic rays. Evening activities include campus tours, movies and sports.

MICHIGAN STATE UNIVERSITY
SPARTAN DEBATE INSTITUTES
Res — Coed Ages 14-18

East Lansing, MI 48824. 10 Linton Hall. Tel: 517-432-9667. Fax: 517-432-9667.
www.debate.msu.edu/index_sdi.html   E-mail: debate@msu.edu
Greta Stahl, Dir.
Grades 9-12. Adm: Selective. **Appl**—Due: May.
Enr cap: 120-300. **Fac 19.**
Focus: Debate.
Fees 2009: Res $1100-4200, 2-5 wks. Aid (Need).
Housing: Dorms. Avg per room/unit: 2.
Est 1992. Ses: 4. **Wks/ses:** 2-5. Operates July-Aug.

The curriculum at SDI includes lectures, labs, library research and practice debates beginning as early as the second day of camp. Lab placements accommodate all skill levels, from a pre-novice section for pupils with no debate experience to one designed for those seeking to polish elite varsity skills. Two- and three-week sessions are first-come, first-served; admission is selective for the four-week session, which is followed by an optional, nine-day strategy forum.

MICHIGAN STATE UNIVERSITY
WIRELESS INTEGRATED MICROSYSTEMS FOR TEENS
Res — Coed Ages 12-14

East Lansing, MI 48824. 1408 Engineering Bldg. Tel: 517-353-7282.
Fax: 517-432-1356.
www.egr.msu.edu/future-engineer/programs   E-mail: kima@egr.msu.edu
Drew Kim, Dir.
Grades 7-9. Adm: Selective. **Appl**—Transcript, math/sci teacher rec.
Type of instruction: Enrich.
Focus: Engineering.
Fees 2009: Res $500, 1 wk.
Housing: Dorms.
Nonprofit. **Ses:** 1. **Wks/ses:** 1. Operates July.

Boys and girls wishing to explore the field of engineering who have at least a "B+" average in math and science may enroll in this experiential, research-based program. WIMS' students engage in precollege research in an environment that emphasizes the latest technology. Participants attend classes and workshops on relevant engineering topics while also developing a project for presentation at the end of the week.

MICHIGAN STATE UNIVERSITY
WOMEN IN ENGINEERING PROGRAM
Res — Girls Ages 15-17

East Lansing, MI 48824. 1340 Engineering Bldg. Tel: 517-355-6616.
Fax: 517-432-1356.
www.egr.msu.edu/wie   E-mail: cordes@msu.edu

Judy Cordes, Coord.
Grades 10-12. Adm: Selective. Prereqs: GPA 3.0. **Appl**—Due: Rolling. Transcript, math/sci teacher rec, essay.
Enr: 21.
Type of instruction: Adv Enrich.
Focus: Engineering.
Fees 2009: Res $500, 1 wk.
Housing: Dorms.
Nonprofit. **Ses:** 1. **Wks/ses:** 1. Operates July.

Young women entering grades 10-12 learn about different fields of engineering, alternative energy and wireless integrated microsystems during this weeklong program. Other components of the program include hands-on projects, demonstrations and lab tours. Each girl designs a poster on an area of engineering interest, then fields questions from parents and families about the poster at the closing ceremony. During the session, students also sample college life and learn about admission to MSU, in addition to experiential education and study abroad opportunities.

MICHIGAN TECHNOLOGICAL UNIVERSITY
YOUTH ENGINEERING PROGRAMS
Res — Coed Ages 15-17

Houghton, MI 49931. 1400 Townsend Dr, 310 Administration Bldg. Tel: 906-487-2219, 888-773-2655. Fax: 906-487-1136.
www.youthprograms.mtu.edu   E-mail: yp@mtu.edu
Jamie Lindquist, Coord.
Grades 10-12 (younger if qualified). Adm: Selective. Admitted: 80%. Priority: URM.
Appl—Fee $195. Due: May. Transcript, rec, essay.
Enr: 120-150. **Enr cap:** 150. Intl: 1%. Non-White: 60%. **Fac 20.** Prof 10. Col/grad students 10. **Staff:** Admin 7. Couns 50.
Type of instruction: Adv Enrich. **Courses:** Comp_Sci Math Sci Crafts. **Avg class size:** 12.
    Daily hours for: Classes 8. Rec 3.
Focus: Engineering. **Features:** Swim.
Fees 2012: Free (+$195), 1 wk.
Housing: Dorms. **Swimming:** Lake Pool. Campus facilities avail.
Est 1973. Nonprofit. **Ses:** 2. **Wks/ses:** 1. Operates June-July.

MTU offers two weeklong summer engineering programs for high school students. The Engineering Scholars Program enrolls boys and girls from minority or economically or educationally disadvantaged backgrounds, while Women in Engineering serves young women. Students explore careers in mechanical, environmental, electrical, chemical, civil, geological and material engineering, as well as such other disciplines as mathematics, technology, technical writing and computer science. The program features hands-on laboratory and field exercises, group projects, visits with engineering professionals, college and career planning advice, and recreational activities.

MIDDLEBURY COLLEGE LANGUAGE SCHOOLS
Res — Coed Ages 18 and up

Middlebury, VT 05753. Sunderland Language Ctr. Tel: 802-443-5510.
    Fax: 802-443-2075.
www.middlebury.edu/ls   E-mail: languages@middlebury.edu
Grades PG-Col (younger if qualified). Adm: Selective. Prereqs: GPA 3.0. **Appl**—Fee $65.
    Due: Rolling. Transcript, recs.
Enr: 1530. **Fac 320.**
College credit: 9-12/crse, total 12.

Locations: CA VT.
Focus: Arabic Chin Fr Ger Hebrew Ital Japan Russ Span Portuguese.
Fees 2011: Res $7303-9911, 6-8 wks. Aid (Merit & Need).
Housing: Dorms. Avg per room/unit: 2.
Est 1915. Ses: 3. **Wks/ses:** 6-8. Operates June-Aug.

Middlebury offers beginning through advanced intensive language courses in Arabic, Chinese, French, German, Hebrew, Italian, Japanese, Portuguese, Russian and Spanish. Students must be high school graduates at the time of registration, and at least one year of college-level study is recommended. Programs operate at Middlebury's campus in Vermont and at Mills College in Oakland, CA.

MIDDLEBURY-MONTEREY LANGUAGE ACADEMY
Res and Day — Coed Ages 10-18

Middlebury, VT 05753. 152 Maple St. Tel: 802-443-2900, 888-216-0135.
Fax: 802-443-3220.
www.mmla.middlebury.edu   E-mail: mmla.info@middlebury.edu
Cynthia Patterson, Dir.
Grades 5-PG. Adm: FCFS. **Appl**—Fee $65. Due: Rolling. Transcript, essay in target language.
Enr: 200-250.
Type of instruction: Adv Enrich Undergrad. **Courses:** Crafts Media Music Photog. **Avg class size:** 15.
Locations: CA OH PA VT.
Focus: Arabic Chin Fr Ger Span. **Features:** Aquatics Bicycle_Tours Canoe Hiking Soccer Swim.
Fees 2012: Res $5995, 4 wks. Day $1495-2495, 2-3 wks.
Housing: Dorms. **Swimming:** Pool.
Est 2008. Spons: Middlebury College/Monterey Institute of International Studies. **Ses:** 3.
Wks/ses: 4. Operates June-July.

A collaborative effort between Middlebury College and the Monterey Institute of International Studies, MMLA conducts four-week residential programs at Green Mountain College in Poultney, VT; Oberlin College in Oberlin, OH; Pomona College in Claremont, CA; and Swarthmore College in Swarthmore, PA. In addition, two- and three-week commuter sessions operate at other locations. Students work on fluency and comprehension skills in Arabic, Mandarin, French, German or Spanish each morning, then spend the rest of the day reinforcing their language skills during meals, field trips and recreational camp activities. MMLA groups pupils by ability level and houses them with others who are studying the same language. Weekend activities for boarders include field trips to local recreational and cultural attractions.

MILWAUKEE SCHOOL OF ENGINEERING
SUMMER PROGRAMS FOR HIGH SCHOOL STUDENTS
Res — Coed Ages 15-18

Milwaukee, WI 53202. 1025 N Broadway. Tel: 414-277-6763, 800-332-6763.
Fax: 414-277-7475.
www.msoe.edu/high_school_students/summer_programs/index.shtml
E-mail: summerprograms@msoe.edu
Student contact: Julie Schuster, E-mail: schuster@msoe.edu.
Grades 10-12 (younger if qualified). Adm: FCFS. **Appl**—Fee $0. Due: June.
Enr cap: 96. **Intl:** 1%. **Non-White:** 10%. **Fac 4. Prof 4. Staff:** Admin 4. Res 8.
Type of instruction: Preview. **Daily hours for:** Classes 8. Rec 4.
Focus: Bus/Fin Engineering Med/Healthcare. **Features:** Paintball Bowling.

Fees 2011: Res $700 (+$20), 1 wk. Aid 2010 (Need): $14,550.
Housing: Dorms. Avg per room/unit: 2. Campus facilities avail.
Est 1999. Nonprofit. **Ses:** 3. **Wks/ses:** 1. Operates July.

MSOE's summer programs enable students to experience college life as they explore career opportunities in engineering, business or nursing. Introductions to architectural, biomedical, computer, electrical, mechanical/industrial and software engineering include laboratory projects and tours of local industries. Business students learn about mission statements, leadership and teamwork, marketing strategies and presentation techniques. Nursing program participants tour a hospital facility and work closely with MSOE School of Nursing faculty on hands-on activities in a critical-care laboratory. Exceptional rising freshmen may apply to any of these programs.

MISS PORTER'S SCHOOL
JUNIOR MODEL UN
Res — Girls Ages 12-15

Farmington, CT 06032. 60 Main St. Tel: 860-409-3692, 800-447-2724.
   Fax: 860-409-3537.
www.porters.org/summerprograms   E-mail: summer_programs@missporters.org
Christine Neville-Smith & Michael Smith, Dirs.
Grades 7-10. Adm: Somewhat selective. Admitted: 90%. **Appl**—Due: Rolling.
Type of instruction: Enrich. **Daily hours for:** Classes 4.
Focus: Govt.
Fees 2011: Res $1000, 1 wk. Aid (Merit & Need).
Housing: Dorms. Avg per room/unit: 2.
Ses: 1. **Wks/ses:** 1. Operates July.

At Junior Model UN, girls learn about civics and current events while further developing their communicational skills and gaining a more global perspective. The program includes morning and afternoon sessions and guest speakers on the Miss Porter's campus. Participants enhance their research, public speaking, policy writing and collaborative skills as they prepare for a two-day, Model UN-style conference at the conclusion of the week. Girls also spend a day at the United Nations headquarters in New York City during the session.

MISSOURI UNIVERSITY OF SCIENCE & TECHNOLOGY
JACKLING INTRODUCTION TO ENGINEERING
Res and Day — Coed Ages 16-18

Rolla, MO 65409. Distance & Continuing Ed, 216 Centennial Hall, 300 W 12th St.
   Tel: 573-341-6222. Fax: 573-341-4992.
http://precollege.mst.edu/intro.html   E-mail: precollege@mst.edu
Will Perkins, Dir.
Grades 11-12. Adm: FCFS. **Appl**—Due: Rolling.
Type of instruction: Enrich.
Focus: Engineering.
Fees 2009: Res $475, 1 wk. Day $375, 1 wk.
Housing: Dorms.
Ses: 3. **Wks/ses:** 1. Operates June-July.

This five-day introductory course helps students understand the relationship that mathematics and the sciences have to engineering. Rising high school juniors and seniors learn about engineering disciplines and work on hands-on projects. Laboratory and industry visits and evening student competitions complete the program.

MISSOURI UNIVERSITY OF SCIENCE & TECHNOLOGY
MINORITY INTRODUCTION TO TECHNOLOGY & ENGINEERING
Res — Coed Ages 15-18

Rolla, MO 65409. Center for Pre-College Prgms, 500 W 16th St, 212 Engineering Research Lab. Tel: 573-341-4228. Fax: 573-341-4890.
http://precollege.mst.edu/MITE.html   E-mail: precollege@mst.edu
Frank Mack, Coord.
Grades 11-12 (younger if qualified). Adm: Somewhat selective. Admitted: 90%. Priority: URM. **Appl**—Fee $0. Due: Apr. Transcript, rec.
Enr: 30. **Enr cap:** 30. Non-White: 100%. **Fac 15.** Prof 11. Col/grad students 4. **Staff:** Admin 1. Couns 5.
Type of instruction: Enrich Preview.
Focus: Engineering.
Fees 2011: Res $150 (+$50), 1 wk. Aid 2009 (Merit & Need): $1800.
Housing: Dorms. Campus facilities avail.
Ses: 2. **Wks/ses:** 1. Operates June.

African-American, Hispanic and Native American students preview college life while learning about engineering careers and the demands faced by professional engineers. Participants devote mornings listening to lectures on various engineering disciplines, then gain practical engineering experience during afternoon lab and industry visits. Orientation sessions address admissions procedures and requirements, scholarships and financial aid. Recreational and social activities, which include sports, bowling, dances and picnics, enable boys and girls to interact with current Missouri S&T undergraduates.

MISSOURI UNIVERSITY OF SCIENCE & TECHNOLOGY
NUCLEAR ENGINEERING CAMP
Res — Coed Ages 16-19

Rolla, MO 65409. Nuclear Engineering Dept, 222 Fulton Hall, 301 W 14th St.
Tel: 573-341-4720. Fax: 573-341-4174.
http://precollege.mst.edu/nuce.html   E-mail: nuclear@mst.edu
Grades 11-PG. Adm: Selective. **Appl**—Fee $0. Due: Rolling. Transcript, ACT/SAT scores, rec.
Enr: 30. **Enr cap:** 30.
Type of instruction: Enrich.
Focus: Engineering.
Fees 2009: Res $600, 1 wk.
Housing: Dorms.
Ses: 1. **Wks/ses:** 1. Operates July.

This weeklong introduction to nuclear engineering careers features tours of a nuclear reactor and nuclear power plant; focus groups on the nuclear fuel cycle, reactor operations and radiation reality; and experiments on natural radioactivity, reactor operations and reactor shielding.

MONTE VISTA CHRISTIAN SCHOOL
ESL SUMMER INTENSIVE LANGUAGE INSTITUTE
Res — Coed Ages 12-18

Watsonville, CA 95076. 2 School Way. Tel: 831-722-8178. Fax: 831-722-6003.
www.mvcs.org   E-mail: admissions@mvcs.org
Carolyn Mariot, Dir.
   Student contact: Peter C. Gieseke, E-mail: petergieseke@mvcs.org.
Adm: FCFS. Admitted: 95%. **Appl**—Fee $0. Due: Rolling.
Enr: 24. **Enr cap:** 35. Intl: 100%. **Fac 4. Staff:** Admin 1. Couns 7.

Courses: Drama Fine_Arts Music. **Avg class size:** 8. **Daily hours for:** Classes 4½. Study 2. Rec 3. Homework. Tests.
Focus: ESL. **Features:** Cooking Swim.
Fees 2012: Res $6300 (+$200), 5 wks.
Housing: Dorms. **Swimming:** Pool. Campus facilities avail.
Est 1926. Nonprofit. Nondenom Christian. **Ses:** 1. **Wks/ses:** 5. Operates July-Aug.

Monte Vista helps students improve their English skills and learn more about American culture. Boys and girls receive language instruction at the beginning, intermediate and advanced levels. Evening and weekend leisure activities and trips provide further opportunities for pupils to develop their skills.

NASA/MORGAN STATE UNIVERSITY
SUMMER INSTITUTE OF ROBOTICS
Res — Coed Ages 15-18

Baltimore, MD 21251. School of Engineering, 1700 E Coldspring Ln.
Tel: 301-286-0904.
www.nasa.gov/offices/education/programs
Student contact: David Rosage, E-mail: david.j.rosage@nasa.gov.
Grades 10-12. Adm: Very selective. Admitted: 12%. Priority: URM.
Enr cap: 25. Intl: 12%.
Type of instruction: Adv Enrich. **Courses:** Public_Speak. **Daily hours for:** Classes 6½. Study 1½.
Focus: Comp_Sci Engineering.
Fees 2009: Free. Res 4 wks.
Housing: Dorms.
Est 2006. Ses: 1. **Wks/ses:** 4.

Developed as a collaboration between the NASA Robotics Academy at Goddard Space Flight Center and the School of Engineering at Morgan State University, SIR aims to increase the knowledge and understanding of the concepts and principles of robotics for urban high school students. Instruction covers robotic theory and design, computer programming and presentation skills. Lab work allows students to put skills to use in weekly competitions. The program also features visits to corporations that specialize in robotics, as well as trips to nearby engineering organizations and agencies.

NATIONAL COMPUTER CAMPS
Res and Day — Coed Ages 8-18

Milford, CT 06460. 102 Shorefront. Tel: 203-710-5771. Fax: 203-254-4277.
www.nccamp.com E-mail: info@nccamp.com
Michael Zabinski, Exec Dir.
Grades 2-12. Adm: FCFS. **Appl**—Fee $0. Due: Rolling.
Enr: 75. **Enr cap:** 75. **Fac** 12.
Type of instruction: Enrich.
Locations: CT GA NY OH.
Focus: Comp_Sci. **Features:** Basketball Soccer Swim Tennis.
Fees 2012: Res $985, 1 wk. Day $830, 1 wk.
Housing: Dorms. **Swimming:** Pool.
Est 1977. Inc. **Ses:** 15. **Wks/ses:** 1. Operates June-Aug.

These camps operate at Fairfield University (Fairfield, CT), Oglethorpe University (Atlanta, GA), Notre Dame College (Cleveland, OH) and Manhattanville College (Riverdale, NY). Small-group instruction is provided through workshops and lab sessions. NCC focuses on video game design, computer programming, digital video production, Web page design, and such software applications as animation, Flash and graphics. Campers may attend for one or more weeks; the continuous curriculum runs from beginning through highly advanced levels. An optional athletic program is available.

NATIONAL STUDENT LEADERSHIP CONFERENCE SUMMER PROGRAMS
Res — Coed Ages 14-18

Chicago, IL 60654. 320 W Ohio St, Ste 4W. **Tel: 312-322-9999, 800-994-6752. Fax: 312-765-0081.**
www.nslcleaders.org   E-mail: info@nslcleaders.org
Rick Duffy, Exec Dir.
Grades 10-12. Adm: Selective. Prereqs: GPA 3.0. **Appl**—Fee $0. Due: Rolling. Transcript.
Enr: 100. Enr cap: 100.
Type of instruction: Adv Preview. **Courses:** Fine_Arts. **Avg class size:** 16. **Daily hours for:** Classes 8. Rec 8. **College credit:** 3.
Locations: CA DC IL LA MD NY.
Focus: Bus/Fin Col_Prep Comm Education Engineering Forensic_Sci Intl_Relations Law Med/Healthcare Pol_Sci. **Features:** Community_Serv Peace/Cross-cultural Ropes_ Crse.
Fees 2012: Res $1895-2945, 1-2 wks. Aid 2011 (Need): $500,000.
Housing: Dorms.
Est 1989. Nonprofit. **Ses:** 47. **Wks/ses:** 2. Operates June-Aug.

NSLC helps high school students develop leadership skills and offers the opportunity to gain insight and experience in one of the following fields: education, business, engineering, forensic science, intelligence and national security, international business, international diplomacy, journalism and mass communication, sports and entertainment management, law or medicine. Meetings with national and world leaders and field trips are part of the program. Domestic programs operate at the University of Chicago, Northwestern University, Tulane University, Fordham University, the University of California-Berkeley, American University and the University of Maryland-College Park.

NATIONAL YOUTH SCIENCE CAMP
Res — Coed Ages 17-18

Bartow, WV.
Contact (Year-round): c/o Natl Youth Science Foundation, PO Box 3387, Charleston, WV 25333. **Tel: 304-342-3326. Fax: 866-833-0875.**
www.nysc.org   E-mail: andrew.blackwood@nysf.com
Andrew N. Blackwood, Dir.
Grade PG. Adm: Very selective.
Enr: 100. Enr cap: 100.
Type of instruction: Adv Enrich.
Focus: Sci. **Features:** Caving Hiking Kayak Mtn_Biking Rock_Climb Ultimate_Frisbee.
Fees 2010: Free. Res 3½ wks.
Housing: Cabins.
Est 1963. Nonprofit. **Spons:** National Youth Science Foundation. **Ses:** 1. **Wks/ses:** 3½. Operates July.

The governor of each state helps appoint two newly graduated delegates to this free science camp each year. A roster of educators and researchers leads NYSC, which has three main academic components: 60- to 90-minute lectures that are delivered to the entire camp community; directed study, three 90-minute sessions that consist of roughly 10 students and a presenter and typically involve a larger project or trips to a specific ecological area or scientific facility; and seminars, which are sometimes led by delegates and which may be nonscientific and informal. An unusual aspect of NYSC's session is the well-developed outdoor program:

Students engage in a variety of outdoor activities, including overnight backpacking and camping trips that range from short, nature-based hikes to more challenging backpacking treks along rough terrain.

NORTH CAROLINA STATE UNIVERSITY
ENGINEERING SUMMER PROGRAMS
Res — Coed Ages 16-18; Day — Coed 8-16

Raleigh, NC 27695. 118 Page Hall, Campus Box 7904. Tel: 919-515-3263.
www.engr.ncsu.edu/theengineeringplace/summerprograms
E-mail: engr.outreach@ncsu.edu
Laura Bottomley, Dir.
   Student contact: Kay Leager, E-mail: academicaffairs@ncsu.edu.
Grades 3-12. Adm: Selective. **Appl**—Fee $0. Due: Apr. Gr 3-10: Personal statement, rec; Gr 11 & 12: Transcript, personal statement, optional PSAT/SAT scores.
Type of instruction: Enrich. **Courses:** Comp_Sci. **Daily hours for:** Classes 6.
Focus: Engineering. **Features:** Swim.
Fees 2011: Res $700, 1 wk. Day $350, 1 wk. Aid (Need).
Housing: Dorms. **Swimming:** Pool. Campus facilities avail.
Nonprofit. **Ses:** 7. **Wks/ses:** 1. Operates June-July.

NC State's College of Engineering offers weeklong day camps for students entering grades 3-10, as well as residential workshops for rising high school juniors and seniors. Programming explores some of the following engineering disciplines: aerospace, electrical, biological, chemical and bio-molecular, civil and construction, computer science, industrial systems, materials science and mechanical. Students develop problem-solving techniques through hands-on, small-group experiences and field visits.

NORTH CAROLINA STATE UNIVERSITY
SUMMER COLLEGE IN BIOTECHNOLOGY AND LIFE SCIENCES
Res and Day — Coed Ages 16-18

Raleigh, NC 27695. Campus Box 7642. Tel: 919-515-2614. Fax: 919-515-5266.
www.cals.ncsu.edu   E-mail: summer_college@ncsu.edu
William Edwards, Dir.
Grades 11-12 (younger if qualified). Adm: Selective. Prereqs: GPA 3.5. **Appl**—Fee $0. Due: May.
Enr: 54. Fac 4. Staff: Admin 1. Couns 10.
Type of instruction: Adv. **Avg class size:** 18. **Daily hours for:** Classes 6½. Homework. Tests. Grades. **College credit:** 3/crse, total 3.
Focus: Sci. **Features:** Swim.
Fees 2011: Res $2076-3600 (+$400), 4 wks. Day $1076, 4 wks.
Housing: Dorms. **Swimming:** Pool.
Est 2003. Nonprofit. **Ses:** 1. **Wks/ses:** 4. Operates July.

Designed for college-bound students with a strong interest in science, SCIBLS offers rigorous course work, hands-on laboratory experiences and a preview of college life. Tours of nearby research facilities and visits with industry professionals complement course offerings, which include molecular biology, biotechnology, microbiology and biochemistry. Boarders participate in group activities on weekends and are responsible for their own meals. Applicants have completed high school biology and chemistry classes.

NORTH CAROLINA STATE UNIVERSITY
SUMMER TEXTILE EXPLORATION PROGRAM
Res — Coed Ages 17-18

Raleigh, NC 27695. **Office of Student Services, College of Textiles, Campus Box 8301. Tel: 919-515-3780.**
www.tx.ncsu.edu/step   E-mail: kent_hester@ncsu.edu
Grade 12. Adm: Selective. **Appl**—Fee $0. Due: May. Transcript, personal statement, rec.
Enr: 27. **Enr cap:** 28.
Type of instruction: Enrich. **Courses:** Bus/Fin Fashion.
Focus: Engineering.
Housing: Dorms. Campus facilities avail.
Ses: 4. **Wks/ses:** 1. Operates June-July.

Rising seniors with an interest in science-related fields spend their mornings engaged in textile-related presentations, T-shirt screen-printing, excursions to local businesses and tours of North Carolina State's campus. In the afternoon, participants dedicate their time to a project in one of the following fields: polymer and color chemistry, engineering, apparel design, fabric design or business management.

NORTH CAROLINA STATE UNIVERSITY
YOUNG INVESTIGATORS' SUMMER PROGRAM
IN NUCLEAR TECHNOLOGY
Res — Coed Ages 16-18

Raleigh, NC 27695. **Dept of Nuclear Engineering. Tel: 919-515-5876.**
Fax: 919-515-5115.
www.ne.ncsu.edu/outreach/young-investigators-program.html
E-mail: lisa.marshall@ncsu.edu
Lisa Marshall, Dir.
Grades 11-PG. Adm: Selective. Admitted: 80%. **Appl**—Fee $0. Due: Apr. Transcript, test scores, rec.
Enr: 20. **Enr cap:** 20. Intl: 1%. Non-White: 15%.
Type of instruction: Adv Enrich.
Focus: Engineering.
Fees 2012: Res $1200, 3 wks. Aid (Need).
Housing: Dorms. Campus facilities avail.
Est 1985. Nonprofit. **Ses:** 1. **Wks/ses:** 3. Operates July.

NCSU's Department of Nuclear Engineering conducts this precollege program, which enrolls high schoolers planning a college major in nuclear engineering. YISP explores nuclear energy sources, medical applications and environmental disposal issues. Topics covered by lectures, labs and guest speakers include fuel fabrication, radiation, plasma applications, fission power systems and nuclear waste management. Students work on group projects and make presentations at the conclusion of the program.

NORTHWESTERN COLLEGE NEUROSCIENCE CAMP
Res — Coed Ages 16-18

Orange City, IA 51041. **Department of Biology, 101 7th St SW. Tel: 712-707-7006.**
www.nwciowa.edu/biology/neuroscience/neuroscience-camp
E-mail: redavis@nwciowa.edu
Ralph Davis, Dir.
Grades 11-12. Adm: Selective. **Appl**—Due: Rolling. Rec.
Enr cap: 10.
Type of instruction: Enrich. **Daily hours for:** Classes 7.
Focus: Med/Healthcare Sci.

Fees 2009: Res $375, 1 wk.
Housing: Apartments.
Ses: 2. **Wks/ses:** 1. Operates June.

Lectures, demonstrations and hands-on experiments introduce NNC students to the study of the brain and nervous system. Participants conduct electrophysiology and neuropharmacology experiments, dissect a sheep brain, use computer simulation to dissect a human brain and learn to record electrical activity. The week includes visits to a local hospital's active neuroscience laboratories and imaging and scanning facilities.

NORTHWESTERN UNIVERSITY
NATIONAL HIGH SCHOOL INSTITUTE
Res — Coed Ages 15-18

Evanston, IL 60208. 617 Noyes St. Tel: 847-491-3026, 800-662-6474.
 Fax: 847-467-1057.
www.northwestern.edu/nhsi   E-mail: nhsi@northwestern.edu
Ruth Bistrow, Coord.
Grades 10-12. Adm: Selective. **Appl**—Fee $50. Transcript, PSAT scores, rec.
Enr cap: 30-80. **Fac 22.**
Type of instruction: Adv Enrich. **Courses:** Media Music. **Avg class size:** 15. **Daily hours for:** Classes 9. Study 2.
Focus: Debate Speech. **Features:** Swim.
Fees 2011: Res $4000-4500, 4 wks. Aid (Merit & Need).
Housing: Dorms. **Swimming:** Lake.
Est 1931. Nonprofit. **Ses:** 2. **Wks/ses:** 4. Operates July-Aug.

Serving academically talented high school students, NHSI programs in speech and debate comprise classes, workshops, field trips, projects and lectures. The Debate Institute offers rigorous four- and five-week programs for rising sophomores, juniors and seniors, with an emphasis on incoming seniors. Students attending the Speech Division's four-week session train for competition in debate, interpretation, oratory and extemporaneous speaking. Group outings and social events balance class work. Northwestern also conducts workshops in film and video production, musical theater and theater arts (see separate listing for details).

OCEAN EDUCATIONS
MARINE AND ENVIRONMENTAL SCIENCE PROGRAM
Res — Coed Ages 16-18

Victoria, British Columbia, Canada. Lester B Pearson College of the Pacific.
Contact (Year-round): 341 Price Rd, Salt Spring Island, V8K 2E9 British Columbia, Canada. Tel: 250-537-8464, 877-464-6059. Fax: 250-537-8465.
www.oceaned.com   E-mail: ian@oceaned.com
Ian Mitchell, Dir.
Grades 11-PG. Adm: FCFS. **Appl**—Fee $0. Due: Rolling.
Enr: 16. Fac 3. Staff: Admin 3. Couns 4.
Type of instruction: Adv Preview. **Courses:** Astron Ecol Environ_Sci Geol. **Avg class size:** 8. **Daily hours for:** Classes 4. Study 4. Rec 4. **High school credit.**
Focus: Marine_Bio/Stud. **Features:** Aquatics Canoe Conservation Exploration Scuba Basketball Soccer Swim Tennis.
Fees 2012: Res Can$4689 (+airfare), 3 wks.
Housing: Dorms. **Swimming:** Lake Ocean Pool.
Est 1996. Inc. **Ses:** 1. **Wks/ses:** 3. Operates July-Aug.

This marine science program is conducted at the Lester B. Pearson College of the Pacific in British Columbia. Pupils study the habitats and ecosystems of the animals and plants of the Pacific Coast. Selected field trips and excursions enrich class work: A salmon aquaculture farm, the Canadian Military's Fleet Diving Unit of the Pacific and the Cowichan Bay Marine Ecological Station are among the destinations. Boys and girls may earn scuba diving certification; those who are already certified may take part in specialty diving programs.

ODYSSEY EXPEDITIONS
TROPICAL MARINE BIOLOGY VOYAGES
Res — Coed Ages 13-24

Tarpon Springs, FL 34689. 418 Shaddock St. Tel: 352-400-4076, 800-929-7749. Fax: 815-642-1272.
www.odysseyexpeditions.com   E-mail: odyssey@usa.net
Jason Buchheim & Jon Buchheim, Dirs.
Grades 7-Col. Adm: FCFS. **Appl**—Fee $0. Due: Rolling.
Enr: 48. **Enr cap:** 48. Intl: 10%. Non-White: 5%. **Fac 14.** Col/grad students 6. Specialists 8. **Staff:** Admin 3. Res 15.
Type of instruction: Enrich. **Courses:** Ecol Environ_Sci Photog. **Avg class size:** 10. **Daily hours for:** Classes 3. Study 3. Rec 3. Homework. Tests. **College credit:** 5.
Intl program focus: Acad. **Locations:** Caribbean.
Focus: Marine_Bio/Stud. **Features:** Adventure_Travel Community_Serv Conservation Fishing Sail Scuba Seamanship Swim Water-skiing Watersports.
Fees 2011: Res $4990-6990, 2-4 wks.
Swimming: Ocean.
Est 1996. Inc. **Ses:** 14. **Wks/ses:** 2-4. Operates June-Aug.

Odyssey Expeditions conducts four marine biology voyages for capable swimmers. Discovery Voyages, which explores the British Virgin Islands, comprises scuba certification programs, sailing instruction, watersports, island exploration and more than 20 dives. The SEA program emphasizes marine biology research while also providing instruction in navigation and underwater photography. Advanced divers age 18 and up may enroll in Divemaster Challenge, which provides hands-on training for those considering a career in the field.

THE OHIO STATE UNIVERSITY
ROSS MATHEMATICS PROGRAM
Res — Coed Ages 14-18

Columbus, OH 43210. Dept of Mathematics, 231 W 18th Ave. Tel: 614-292-5101. Fax: 614-292-1479.
www.math.ohio-state.edu/ross   E-mail: ross@math.ohio-state.edu
Daniel Shapiro, Dir.
Grades 9-PG. Adm: Very selective. **Appl**—Due: Rolling. Transcript, teacher recs, essays.
Type of instruction: Adv Enrich Undergrad.
Focus: Math.
Fees 2009: Res $2500, 8 wks. Aid (Need).
Housing: Dorms.
Est 1957. Nonprofit. **Ses:** 1. **Wks/ses:** 8. Operates June-Aug.

A partnership between the university and the Clay Mathematics Institute, this intensive program enrolls precollege students who have displayed significant achievement in math. Participants explore concepts in number theory; work with mathematical ideas built from concrete observations and resulting in proofs of general patterns and abstract properties; and develop learning strategies for use in later scientific endeavors. On weekday mornings, students attend a number theory lecture and receive a problem set that leads to further exploration. Pupils also attend problem seminars given by experienced faculty members.

OPERATION ENTERPRISE
Res — Coed Ages 16-25

New York, NY 10019. c/o American Management Assoc, 1601 Broadway, 8th Fl.
Tel: 212-586-8100, 800-634-4262. Fax: 212-903-8509.
www.amanet.org/advantage/operation-enterprise.aspx
E-mail: operationenterprise@amanet.org
Marina Marmut, Dir.
Grades 11-Col. Adm: Selective. **Appl**—Due: Apr. Transcript, rec.
Enr: 25-30. **Enr cap:** 25-30. **Fac 10. Staff:** Admin 2. Couns 5.
Type of instruction: Adv Enrich. **Avg class size:** 25. **Daily hours for:** Classes 6. Study 1. Rec 3. **College credit:** 3.
Locations: GA NY TX.
Focus: Bus/Fin. **Features:** Leadership Swim.
Fees 2009: Res $1750, 1 wk. Aid (Need).
Housing: Dorms. **Swimming:** Pool.
Est 1963. Nonprofit. **Spons:** American Management Association. **Ses:** 4. **Wks/ses:** 1. Operates June-Aug.

This management and leadership development program consists of high school and college divisions. High school programs operate at Emory University (Atlanta, GA), Columbia University (New York, NY) and the University of Texas-Austin. Senior executives and American Management Association faculty conduct highly interactive, practical workshops that focus upon the skills necessary for success in business. The core curriculum in each program addresses leadership, management, business writing, presentation skills, strategic planning and negotiation. Practice presentations (given to a board of directors) and a full-day management simulation complete the program.

OREGON MUSEUM OF SCIENCE AND INDUSTRY
SCIENCE CAMPS AND ADVENTURES
Res — Coed Ages 7-18

Portland, OR 97214. 1945 SE Water Ave. Tel: 503-797-4661. Fax: 503-239-7800.
www.omsi.edu/camps-classes   E-mail: register@omsi.edu
Travis Neumeyer, Dir.
Grades 3-PG. Adm: FCFS. **Appl**—Fee $0. Due: Rolling.
Enr: 35. **Enr cap:** 40. **Fac 4.** Specialists 4. **Staff:** Admin 6. Couns 30.
Courses: Archaeol Astron Ecol Environ_Sci Geol Marine_Bio/Stud. **Avg class size:** 12. **Daily hours for:** Classes 6. Study 6. Rec 6.
Locations: CA ID OR UT WA.
Focus: Sci. **Features:** Canoe Climbing_Wall Conservation Exploration Hiking Mtn_Trips Survival_Trng White-water_Raft Wilderness_Camp Swim.
Fees 2009: Res $480-1200, 1-2 wks. Aid 2008 (Need): $90,000.
Housing: Cabins Houses Lodges Tents Tepees. Avg per room/unit: 8. **Swimming:** Lake Pond Ocean River.
Est 1951. Nonprofit. **Ses:** 86. **Wks/ses:** 1-3. Operates June-Aug.

Numerous science-oriented outdoor education courses—ranging from high-adventure backpacking trips to residential camp programs—are available in various locations throughout the West. Programs for young people, organized according to age, serve campers ages 7-10, 10-12, 12-14 and 14-18.

OREGON STATE UNIVERSITY
SUMMER EXPERIENCE IN SCIENCE
AND ENGINEERING FOR YOUTH
Res — Coed Ages 15-18

Corvallis, OR 97331. School of Chemical, Biological & Environmental Engineering, 103 Gleeson Hall. Tel: 541-737-4791. Fax: 541-737-4600.
http://cbee.oregonstate.edu/sesey   **E-mail:** skip.rochefort@oregonstate.edu
Willie E. Rochefort, Dir.
Grades 10-12. Adm: Selective. Priority: URM. **Appl**—Due: May. Transcript, essay.
Type of instruction: Enrich.
Focus: Engineering Sci.
Fees 2009: Res $150, 1 wk. Aid (Need).
Housing: Dorms.
Est 1997. Ses: 1. **Wks/ses:** 1. Operates July.

Targeting high school girls and minorities traditionally underrepresented in science and engineering, SESEY places students in research groups from Oregon State University's departments of chemical engineering or bioengineering. Each pupil works with a faculty member and college student mentors on such projects as plastics recycling, biomedical polymers, materials processing, biomedical technology and waste remediation. The program also includes a trip to the Hatfield Marine Science Center, computer instruction and evening recreational programs.

PICKERING COLLEGE ESL SUMMER CAMP
Res — Coed Ages 12-18

Newmarket, L3Y 4X2 Ontario, Canada. 16945 Bayview Ave. Tel: 905-895-1700, 877-895-1700. Fax: 905-895-9076.
www.pickeringcollege.on.ca   **E-mail:** eslsummer@pickeringcollege.on.ca
Claudia Chavez, Coord.
Grades 7-12. Adm: FCFS. **Appl**—Due: Apr.
Enr: 45. **Fac 3. Staff:** Admin 2. Couns 7.
Type of instruction: Enrich. **Courses:** Debate Expository_Writing Speech Crafts Creative_Writing Dance Drama. **Daily hours for:** Classes 5. Study ½. Rec 6.
Intl program focus: Acad Lang Culture.
Focus: ESL. **Features:** Aquatics Archery Canoe Climbing_Wall Rock_Climb Ropes_Crse Baseball Basketball Golf Soccer Softball Swim Ultimate_Frisbee Volleyball.
Fees 2012: Res Can$4900 (+Can$200-300), 4 wks.
Housing: Dorms. Avg per room/unit: 2. **Swimming:** Pool. Campus facilities avail.
Est 1990. Nonprofit. Ses: 2. **Wks/ses:** 4. Operates June-Aug.

Serving boys and girls planning to study in an English-speaking school or intending to take English as an academic subject in the home country, this college English as a Second Language program combines daytime academics with evening and weekend activities. Off-campus excursions serve to further improve English skills. Although the session length is four weeks, students may enroll for eight weeks.

PRINCETON UNIVERSITY SUMMER JOURNALISM PROGRAM
Res — Coed Ages 17-18

Princeton, NJ 08543. PO Box 5357. Tel: 609-258-8046.
www.princeton.edu/sjp   **E-mail:** sjp@princeton.edu
Richard Just, Michael Koike, Gregory Mancini & Rich Tucker, Dirs.
Grade 12. Adm: Very selective. Priority: Low-income. Prereqs: GPA 3.5. **Appl**—Fee $0.
Enr: 20. **Enr cap:** 20.
Type of instruction: Adv Enrich.

Focus: Writing/Journ.
Fees 2009: Free. Res 1½ wks.
Housing: Dorms.
Est 2002. Nonprofit. **Ses:** 1. **Wks/ses:** 1½. Operates July-Aug.

This intensive journalism program enrolls highly capable rising seniors from low-income homes. Reporters and editors representing newspapers, magazines and television networks from around the country conduct the session's classes. Students tour New York City media outlets; cover a professional sporting event; film and produce a television segment; cover a news event in Princeton; and perform reporting, writing, editing and designing duties for the SJP newspaper. Boys and girls also sample college life and attend seminars on every aspect of the college admissions process.

PURDUE UNIVERSITY
SEMINAR FOR TOP ENGINEERING PROSPECTS
Res — Coed Ages 17-18

West Lafayette, IN 47907. Neil Armstrong Hall of Engineering, Rm 1300, 701 W Stadium Ave. Tel: 765-494-3976. Fax: 765-494-5819.
www.engineering.purdue.edu/step   E-mail: rlhann3@purdue.edu
Grade 12. Adm: Selective. **Appl**—Due: Rolling.
Type of instruction: Enrich.
Focus: Engineering.
Fees 2010: Res $610-725, 1 wk. Aid (Need).
Housing: Dorms.
Ses: 3. **Wks/ses:** 1. Operates July.

STEP enables rising high school seniors to explore various engineering disciplines and job functions. Tours, demonstrations, classroom experiences and projects teach students about engineering and offer a preview of college life. Students work on engineering problems using software packages such as Microsoft Excel.

PURDUE UNIVERSITY
WOMEN IN ENGINEERING SUMMER CAMPS
Res — Girls Ages 13-16

West Lafayette, IN 47907. 701 W Stadium Ave. Tel: 765-494-3889. Fax: 765-496-1349.
www.engineering.purdue.edu/wiep/programs   E-mail: puwie@ecn.purdue.edu
Beth M. Holloway, Dir. Student contact: Jennifer Groh, E-mail: jgroh@purdue.edu.
Grades 8-11. Adm: Somewhat selective. Admitted: 90%. **Appl**—Fee $0. Due: Apr. Teacher rec.
Enr: 40. **Enr cap:** 40. Non-White: 30%. **Fac 8.** Prof 4. Col/grad students 4. **Staff:** Admin 3. Res 10.
Type of instruction: Preview. **Courses:** Crafts.
Focus: Engineering. **Features:** Swim.
Fees 2012: Res $400-450 (+$15-20), 1 wk. Aid 2010 (Need): $5000.
Housing: Dorms. Avg per room/unit: 2. **Swimming:** Pool.
Est 2000. Nonprofit. **Ses:** 3. **Wks/ses:** 1. Operates June-Aug.

Purdue offers two precollege programs for young women with an interest in engineering as a potential career choice: Engineering FYI, for girls entering grades 8 and 9, and Exciting Discoveries for Girls in Engineering (EDGE) for girls entering grades 10 and 11. Participants learn about various engineering disciplines while working with current Purdue engineering students on such hands-on activities as solar oven design or the construction of a robotic arm or an electronic device. Campers also tour engineering laboratories and production facilities and meet faculty and graduate pupils who are engaged in cutting-edge research.

THE PUTNEY SCHOOL
PROGRAM FOR INTERNATIONAL EDUCATION
Res — Coed Ages 14-17

Putney, VT 05346. Elm Lea Farm, 418 Houghton Brook Rd. Tel: 802-387-6297.
Fax: 802-387-6216.
www.putneyschoolsummer.org   E-mail: summer@putneyschool.org
Thomas D. Howe, Dir.
Grades 9-12. Adm: FCFS. Appl—Fee $50. Due: Rolling.
Enr: 20. Fac 40. Staff: Admin 7. Couns 18.
Type of instruction: Enrich. Courses: Dance Drawing Music Painting Sculpt Theater. Avg
class size: 10. Daily hours for: Classes 6. Rec 2.
Focus: ESL. Features: Farm Hiking Basketball Equestrian Soccer Swim Volleyball.
Fees 2011: Res $3900-7200, 3-6 wks. Aid (Need).
Housing: Dorms. Swimming: Pond.
Est 1987. Nonprofit. Ses: 2. Wks/ses: 3. Operates June-Aug.

PIE serves international students interested in improving their English language skills. Morning classes emphasize speaking and listening and incorporate work in writing, vocabulary and grammar. In the afternoon, students work on supervised group projects of their own design, embark on local trips or take part in outdoor activities with other Putney summer students. Regularly scheduled field trips to places of cultural interest are part of the program, as is a weekly full-day excursion to a larger city such as Montpelier, Burlington or Boston, MA.

PUTNEY STUDENT TRAVEL LANGUAGE LEARNING PROGRAMS
Res — Coed Ages 14-18

Putney, VT 05346. 345 Hickory Ridge Rd. Tel: 802-387-5885. Fax: 802-387-4276.
www.goputney.com   E-mail: info@goputney.com
Peter Shumlin & Jeffrey Shumlin, Dirs.
Grades 9-PG. Adm: FCFS. Appl—Fee $0. Due: Rolling.
Enr: 14-22.
Intl program focus: Lang. Locations: Europe Mexico/Central_America South_America.
Home stays avail.
Focus: Fr Span. Features: Adventure_Travel Bicycle_Tours Exploration Hiking Rock_
Climb Sail Watersports.
Fees 2012: Res $5690-9390, 4½-5½ wks.
Est 1952. Ses: 8. Wks/ses: 4½-5½. Operates June-Aug.

PST's overseas language programs allow pupils to study French in France and Spanish in Spain, Argentina or Costa Rica. Programs combine carefully planned itineraries with an active language learning approach. Students move toward fluency by communicating with local people during the course of everyday activities, and participants must agree to speak only the target language during the course of the program.

RASSIAS PROGRAMS
Res — Coed Ages 15-18

Hanover, NH 03755. PO Box 5456. Tel: 603-643-3007. Fax: 603-643-4249.
www.rassias.com   E-mail: rassias@rassias.com
William Miles, Pres.
Grades 10-12 (younger if qualified). Adm: Somewhat selective. Admitted: 80%. Appl—
Fee $0. Due: Rolling. Interview, 2 essays, 2 teacher recs.
Enr: 25. Enr cap: 25. Intl: 4%. Non-White: 4%. Fac 3. Prof 2. K-12 staff 1. Staff: Admin 1.
Type of instruction: Adv Enrich Rev. Avg class size: 7. Daily hours for: Classes 3. Rec
3.
Intl program focus: Lang. Locations: Asia Europe. Home stays avail.

Focus: Chin Fr Span. **Features:** Canoe Community_Serv Conservation Kayak Mtn_Trips Sail Soccer Swim Tennis.
Fees 2012: Res $8000-8200 (+$200-650), 4-6 wks. Aid 2011 (Need): $50,000.
Housing: Houses Lodges. **Swimming:** Lake Ocean Pool.
Est 1986. Inc. **Ses:** 6. **Wks/ses:** 4-6. Operates June-Aug.

Rassias enables older high schoolers to study French, Spanish or Chinese while traveling abroad. These immersion programs operate in Tours and Arles, France; Gijon, Segovia and Pontevedra, Spain; and Gyalthang, China. The French and Spanish programs enroll students with at least two years of previous study in the target language; Chinese program applicants need have no prior experience with the language. Community service in a school for poor mountain children and orphans is part of the Chinese program. Participants spend two and a half weeks of each session living with an area family.

RESEARCH SCIENCE INSTITUTE
Res — Coed Ages 13-18

Cambridge, MA. Massachusetts Inst of Technology.
Contact (Year-round): 8201 Greensboro Dr, Ste 215, McLean, VA 22102.
Tel: 703-448-9062. Fax: 703-448-9068.
www.cee.org/programs/rsi   E-mail: rsi@cee.org
Maite Ballestero, Dir.
Grade 12. Adm: Very selective. Prereqs: PSAT M/CR/W 220. **Appl**—Fee $50. Due: Jan. Transcript, standardized test results, 2 recs, essay.
Enr: 80. **Enr cap:** 80. **Fac 5. Staff:** Admin 9. Couns 6.
Type of instruction: Adv. **Avg class size:** 15. **Daily hours for:** Classes 6. Study 4. Rec 2. Homework.
Focus: Engineering Math Sci.
Fees 2012: Free. Res 6 wks.
Housing: Dorms.
Est 1984. Nonprofit. **Spons:** Center for Excellence in Education. **Ses:** 1. **Wks/ses:** 6. Operates June-Aug.

Held at the Massachusetts Institute of Technology, this tuition-free program combines on-campus course work with hands-on research experience. The first week of the program is dedicated to college-level classes in mathematics, science, engineering, computer skills and research techniques. Students spend the next four weeks conducting open-ended, relevant research projects at Boston-area colleges, universities, hospitals and corporate facilities, supervised by noted scientists and mathematicians. Students deliver their findings in conference-style oral and written presentations during the final week. Guest lectures, field trips around Boston and a weekend trip to the beach round out the program. Successful applicants should demonstrate superior achievement in math and science in the classroom and beyond. Exceptional students as young as 13 may apply if they have completed grade 11. Participants have been recognized by the Intel Science Talent Search; the Intel International Science and Engineering Fair; and the Siemens Competition in Math, Science & Technology.

RHODES COLLEGE SUMMER WRITING INSTITUTE
Res — Coed Ages 16-18

Memphis, TN 38112. 2000 N Pky. Tel: 901-843-3794. Fax: 901-843-3728.
www.rhodes.edu/writinginstitute   E-mail: writinginstitute@rhodes.edu
Rebecca Finlayson, Dir.
Grades 11-12. Adm: Selective. Admitted: 60%. **Appl**—Fee $0. Due: May. Transcript, writing sample, rec.
Enr: 64. Intl: 1%. Non-White: 25%. **Fac 7.** Prof 7. **Staff:** Admin 3.
Type of instruction: Adv. **Courses:** Expository_Writing Govt Hist Pol_Sci Creative_Writ-

ing. **Avg class size:** 13. **Daily hours for:** Classes 4. Study 4. Rec 4. Homework. Grades.
College credit: 2/crse, total 2.
Focus: Writing/Journ. **Features:** Swim.
Fees 2012: Res $1600, 2 wks. Aid (Need).
Housing: Dorms. **Swimming:** Pool. Campus facilities avail.
Est 1990. Nonprofit. **Ses:** 1. **Wks/ses:** 2. Operates June.

This intensive academic program for motivated high schoolers focuses on the development of critical-thinking and writing skills. Students improve their reading and analytical skills and, through course work in the humanities and the social sciences, also learn strategies for both expository and creative writing. At session's end, pupils receive a grade for both academic work and class participation, earn two transferable college credits and possess a portfolio of college-level writing.

ROBERT WOOD JOHNSON MEDICAL SCHOOL
SUMMER SCIENCE SCHOLARS ACADEMY
Res and Day — Coed Ages 17-18

**Piscataway, NJ 08854. Office of Special Academic Prgms, 675 Hoes Ln, Rm N-224.
Tel: 732-235-4558. Fax: 732-235-2121.**
www.rwjms.umdnj.edu/education/sap/s3a.html
E-mail: summerprogram@umdnj.edu
Grades 12-PG. Adm: Very selective. Prereqs: GPA 3.5. **Appl**—Due: Mar. Transcript, rec, essay.
Type of instruction: Adv Enrich SAT/ACT_Prep Study_Skills. **Courses:** Anat & Physiol.
Focus: Med/Healthcare Sci.
Fees 2011: Res $3886, 4 wks. Day $3000, 4 wks.
Housing: Dorms.
Ses: 1. **Wks/ses:** 4. Operates June-July.

This program for high-achieving students interested in medicine focuses on exploring the human body through a series of lectures, organ laboratories and clinical experiences. Core courses address anatomy, physiology, biopharmaceuticals and research methods in health. The academy also includes seminars on science and health career planning, clinical skills, public health and patient-centered care. Residential students live in Rutgers University dormitories adjacent to the medical school. SSSA enrolls only those pupils who have previously attended a health or science summer program.

ROGER WILLIAMS UNIVERSITY
MARINE BIOLOGY SUMMER CAMP
Res — Coed Ages 14-18

Bristol, RI 02809. 1 Old Ferry Rd. Tel: 401-254-3653. Fax: 401-254-3310.
http://departments.rwu.edu/biology/camp.html   **E-mail: pvinacco@rwu.edu**
Paul Webb, Dir.
Adm: FCFS. **Appl**—Fee $0. Due: Rolling.
Enr: 18. **Enr cap:** 18. **Staff:** Admin 1. Couns 4.
Courses: Career.
Focus: Marine_Bio/Stud. **Features:** Aquatics Boating Conservation Cruises Fishing Kayak Sea_Cruises Swim.
Fees 2012: Res $925 (+$50), 1 wk.
Housing: Dorms. Avg per room/unit: 2. **Swimming:** Ocean Pool.
Est 1990. Nonprofit. **Ses:** 2. **Wks/ses:** 1. Operates July-Aug.

This weeklong program serves as an introduction to the study of coastal ecosystems for high school students. Boys and girls utilize the marine environments of the southern New England coast as a classroom. Topics of study include coastal ecosystems, food webs, productivity of the sea, plants and animals in the coastal zone, and current events pertaining to marine biology. Students embark on hands-on field excursions in which they learn oceanographic sampling techniques, explore bay ecosystems by kayak, snorkel along barrier beaches and tidal pools, identify marine organisms and go whale watching. Lab demonstrations and guest presentations complete the program.

ROSE-HULMAN INSTITUTE OF TECHNOLOGY
OPERATION CATAPULT
Res — Coed Ages 16-18

Terre Haute, IN 47803. 5500 Wabash Ave. Tel: 812-877-8893, 800-248-7448. Fax: 812-877-8941.
www.rose-hulman.edu/catapult   E-mail: abby.croft@rose-hulman.edu
Patsy Brackin, Dir. Student contact: Abby Croft.
Grade 12. Adm: Selective. **Appl**—Fee $0. Due: Rolling. Counselor rec, standardized test scores.
Enr: 102-116. **Enr cap:** 125. **Fac 9.** Prof 9. **Staff:** Admin 4. Couns 11.
Type of instruction: Adv. **College credit:** 2.
Focus: Engineering Math Sci. **Features:** Caving Outdoor_Ed Basketball Soccer Swim Ultimate_Frisbee Volleyball.
Fees 2012: Res $2100 (+$100-150), 2½ wks.
Housing: Dorms. Avg per room/unit: 2. **Swimming:** Pond Pool. Campus facilities avail.
Est 1965. Nonprofit. **Ses:** 2. **Wks/ses:** 2½. Operates June-July.

Operation Catapult exposes students to principles of engineering and applied science through group project work. Groups design and conduct experiments, collect and analyze data, reach conclusions and make recommendations for further study. Lectures, demonstrations and tours of industrial plants round out the program. Applicants must have taken three years of high school mathematics and at least one year of chemistry or physics. College credit for program completion is available to those pupils who later matriculate at RHIT.

ROXBURY LATIN SCHOOL
ADVANCED BIOTECHNOLOGY INSTITUTE
Res and Day — Coed Ages 14-18

West Roxbury, MA 02132. 101 St Theresa Ave. Tel: 617-325-0547. Fax: 617-325-3585.
www.biotech-institute.org   E-mail: murphyl@mail.weston.org
Lawrence J. Murphy, Dir.
Grades 9-12 (younger if qualified). Adm: Selective. Admitted: 40%. **Appl**—Fee $0. Due: Apr. Transcript, sci teacher rec, essay.
Enr: 20. **Enr cap:** 20. Intl: 20%. Non-White: 20%. **Fac 3.** K-12 staff 3. **Staff:** Couns 3.
Type of instruction: Adv Enrich. **Daily hours for:** Classes 7½. Study ½. Rec ½. Homework.
Focus: Sci. **Features:** Swim Volleyball.
Fees 2012: Res $4765, 3 wks. Day $3400, 3 wks.
Housing: Dorms. Avg per room/unit: 1-2. **Swimming:** Pool.
Est 2002. Ses: 1. **Wks/ses:** 3. Operates June-July.

ABI conducts an advanced lab-based curriculum in DNA and protein science for top-tier high school science students. During the session, boys and girls apply the scientific method while exploring such topics as genetic engineering, DNA fingerprinting, immunology, genetically modified foods and gene silencing. Enhancing the rigorous program are visits to biotechnology and pharmaceutical companies and a lab-based excursion to the Woods Hole Oceanographic Institution on Cape Cod.

RUTGERS YOUNG SCHOLARS PROGRAM
IN DISCRETE MATHEMATICS
Res — Coed Ages 15-17

Piscataway, NJ 08854. SERC Bldg, Rm 225, 118 Frelinghuysen Rd. Tel: 732-445-2825.
www.dimacs.rutgers.edu/ysp   E-mail: toti@dimacs.rutgers.edu
Debby Toti, Dir.
Grades 10-12. Adm: Selective. **Appl**—Due: Rolling. Math problems, rec.
Enr: 30. **Enr cap:** 30.
Type of instruction: Adv Enrich.
Focus: Math.
Fees 2010: Res $3500, 4 wks. Aid (Need).
Housing: Dorms.
Est 1994. Nonprofit. **Spons:** Rutgers University. **Ses:** 1. **Wks/ses:** 4. Operates July.

This intensive program serves mathematically talented high schoolers who are considering careers in the mathematical sciences. Students gain an introduction to the growing area of discrete mathematics, in the process enhancing their problem-solving abilities by applying mathematical concepts to an array of problems. During the course of the four weeks, boys and girls also meet with professionals in the field who serve as mentors and help the student assess his or her suitability for a career in math. Instructional sessions, field trips, research projects, technology-based activities, career workshops, and informal evening and recreational activities are all part of the program.

ST. ALBANS SCHOOL
SCHOOL OF PUBLIC SERVICE
Res and Day — Coed Ages 16-18

Washington, DC 20016. Mount St Alban. Tel: 202-537-5286. Fax: 202-537-6464.
www.stalbansschool.org   E-mail: sps@cathedral.org
Suzanne Woods, Dir.
Grade 12. Adm: Selective. **Appl**—Due: Rolling. Transcript, standardized test results, essay, teacher rec.
Enr: 35. **Enr cap:** 35. **Fac 5. Staff:** Admin 3. Couns 4.
Type of instruction: Adv Enrich. **Courses:** Public_Speak Writing/Journ. **Avg class size:** 15. **Daily hours for:** Classes 3. Study 2. Rec 2.
Focus: Pol_Sci. **Features:** Swim.
Fees 2012: Res $5400 (+$120), 4 wks. Day $4400 (+$120), 4 wks. Aid (Need).
Housing: Dorms. **Swimming:** Pool.
Est 2001. Nonprofit. **Ses:** 1. **Wks/ses:** 4. Operates June-July.

Rising high school seniors who have demonstrated a high level of academic achievement, a strong interest in public policy issues, and a commitment to school involvement or community service learn about the nature of public service and the roles of government, private and nonprofit organizations, and citizens in the American democratic system. SPS course work combines in-depth discussions, research, case studies, guest speakers and field trips to institutions in the Washington area (including the White House, the Supreme Court and Congress). Students develop analytical and self-expression skills during the month-long course.

SAINT JOHN'S PREPARATORY SCHOOL GERMAN CAMP
Res — Coed Ages 8-16

Collegeville, MN 56321. 1857 Watertower Rd, PO Box 4000. Tel: 320-363-3315,
800-525-7737. Fax: 320-363-3513.
www.sjprep.net   E-mail: admitprep@csbsju.edu
Emmerich Sack, Dir.

Adm: FCFS. **Appl**—Fee $0. Due: Rolling.
Enr cap: 75. **Staff:** Admin 2. Couns 8.
Type of instruction: Enrich.
Focus: Ger. **Features:** Canoe Fishing Hiking Swim.
Fees 2012: Res $345 (+$20), 1 wk.
Housing: Dorms. **Swimming:** Lake Pool. Campus facilities avail.
Est 1979. Nonprofit. Roman Catholic. **Ses:** 1. **Wks/ses:** 1. Operates July.

German Camp enables children to study the German language and learn about German and Austrian culture. Campers receive individualized attention and work closely with counselors and other children in small groups. Native speakers of German and teachers and students who have studied in German-speaking countries constitute the staff. Applicants need not possess any previous knowledge of German.

ST. OLAF COLLEGE
ENGINEERING AND PHYSICS CAMP FOR GIRLS
Res and Day — Girls Ages 14-17

Northfield, MN 55057. 1520 St Olaf Ave. Tel: 507-786-3042. Fax: 507-786-3690.
www.stolaf.edu/camps   E-mail: summer@stolaf.edu
Teresa Lebens, Dir.
Grades 9-12. Adm: FCFS. **Appl**—Fee $0. Due: Rolling.
Enr: 40. **Enr cap:** 40-48. **Fac 10.** Prof 1. Col/grad students 8. K-12 staff 1. **Staff:** Admin 1.
Res 8.
Type of instruction: Enrich. **Avg class size:** 5.
Focus: Engineering Sci.
Fees 2011: Res $570, 1 wk. Day $520, 1 wk. Aid (Need).
Housing: Dorms.
Nonprofit. **Ses:** 1. **Wks/ses:** 1. Operates July.

High school girls learn physics and engineering principles and techniques as they construct their own Rube Goldberg machines during this weeklong camp. The hands-on building exercise forces students to account for various laws of physics to make their machines function as efficiently as possible. Girls put their completed machines on display for family, friends, faculty members and their fellow campers on the session's last day.

SALISBURY SUMMER SCHOOL
Res and Day — Coed Ages 12-18

Salisbury, CT 06068. 251 Canaan Rd. Tel: 860-435-5700. Fax: 860-435-5750.
www.salisburysummerschool.org   E-mail: admissions@salisburyschool.org
Ralph Menconi, Dir.
Grades 7-12. Adm: FCFS. **Appl**—Due: Rolling. Transcript, 2 recs, test scores.
Fac 33. Staff: Admin 1.
Type of instruction: Adv Dev_Read Enrich Preview Rem_Eng Rem_Math Rem_Read
Rev ESL/TOEFL_Prep SAT/ACT_Prep Tut. **Courses:** ESL Crafts Creative_Writing.
Daily hours for: Classes 5. Study 2. Rec 2.
Focus: Study_Skills. **Features:** Baseball Basketball Football Golf Lacrosse Soccer Softball
Swim Tennis.
Fees 2011: Res $7150 (+$250), 5 wks. Day $5150 (+$250), 5 wks.
Housing: Dorms. **Swimming:** Lake.
Est 1946. Nonprofit. **Spons:** Salisbury School. **Ses:** 1. **Wks/ses:** 5. Operates July-Aug.

Salisbury immerses students in a curriculum and an academic environment designed to improve organizational and reading and writing skills. The program addresses reading comprehension, composition, spelling, vocabulary, word attack, speed-reading and study methods. Maintaining a small-class environment, Salisbury utilizes assessments in place of letter grades. Math review, creative writing, ESL and SAT preparation courses are also available as electives.

SANTA CLARA UNIVERSITY SUMMER ENGINEERING SEMINAR
Res — Coed Ages 16-18

Santa Clara, CA 95053. 500 El Camino Real. Tel: 408-554-4728.
www.scu.edu/engineering/undergraduate/ses.cfm
E-mail: summerengineeringseminar@scu.edu
Grades 11-12. Adm: Selective. **Appl**—Due: Mar. 2 essays, rec.
Type of instruction: Enrich.
Focus: Engineering.
Fees 2010: Free. Res 1 wk.
Housing: Dorms.
Est 1990. Ses: 2. Wks/ses: 1. Operates Aug.

This tuition-free seminar introduces rising high school juniors and seniors to college life as they explore career possibilities in engineering. Taught by Santa Clara faculty, courses examine such engineering disciplines environmental engineering, robotics, nanotechnology and bioengineering. Students perform independent projects as part of the curriculum. SES particularly encourages young women and members of other groups lacking prominent representation in the field of engineering to apply.

THE SCHOOL FOR FIELD STUDIES
Res — Coed Ages 16-21

Salem, MA 01970. 10 Federal St, Ste 24. Tel: 978-741-3544, 800-989-4418.
Fax: 978-741-3551.
www.fieldstudies.org   E-mail: admissions@fieldstudies.org
Bonnie R. Clendenning, Pres.
Student contact: Leslie Granese, E-mail: sfs@fieldstudies.org.
Grades 12-Col. Adm: Selective. **Appl**—Fee $45. Due: Rolling.
Enr: 160.
Type of instruction: Adv. **Courses:** Ecol Marine_Bio/Stud. **Avg class size:** 23. **Daily hours for:** Classes 5. Study 3. Rec 2. **College credit:** 4.
Intl program focus: Acad. **Locations:** Africa Australia/New_Zealand Caribbean Mexico/ Central_America.
Focus: Environ_Sci. **Features:** Adventure_Travel Aquatics Community_Serv Conservation Farm Hiking Peace/Cross-cultural Scuba Wilderness_Camp Swim.
Fees 2011: Res $4350-8975 (+$870-1700), 5-6 wks. Aid (Need).
Housing: Cabins Dorms. Avg per room/unit: 5. **Swimming:** Lake Ocean Pool.
Est 1980. Nonprofit. Ses: 5. Wks/ses: 5-6. Operates June-Aug.

This alternative school develops and sponsors field experiences for rising high school seniors and college students in remote wilderness areas around the world. The program helps train students to address environmental issues through scientific research and fieldwork. Scuba diving, hiking, gardening and snorkeling present opportunities for learning and exploration. Programs operate in Mexico, Costa Rica, the Turks and Caicos Islands, Kenya, Tanzania, Bhutan and Australia.

SCHULE SCHLOSS SALEM
SALEM SUMMER SCHOOLS
Res — Coed Ages 9-16

Salem, 88682 Germany. Schlossbezirk. Tel: 49-7553-919-352. Fax: 49-7553-919-303.
www.salem-net.de   E-mail: anita.laleh@salem-net.de

Maike Haeusler, Dir. Student contact: Anita Laleh.
Adm: Somewhat selective. Admitted: 70%. **Appl**—Fee $0. Due: Apr.
Enr: 72. Intl: 90%. Non-White: 10%. **Fac 30. Staff:** Admin 7. Res 20.
Type of instruction: Enrich Preview Rem_Eng Rem_Math Rem_Read Rev Study_Skills.
  Courses: Creative_Writing Dance Fine_Arts Music Painting Photog Theater. **Avg class**
  size: 12. **Daily hours for:** Classes 3. Rec 4. Tests. Grades.
Intl program focus: Lang Culture.
Focus: ESL Ger. **Features:** Bicycle_Tours Canoe Climbing_Wall Hiking Kayak Mtn_Biking
  Mtn_Trips Rock_Climb Sail Basketball Soccer Swim Tennis Volleyball.
Fees 2012: Res €2200 (+€100), 2 wks. Aid (Merit).
Housing: Dorms. Avg per room/unit: 2-3. **Swimming:** Lake Pool. Campus facilities avail.
Est 1998. Nonprofit. **Ses:** 1. **Wks/ses:** 2. Operates July-Aug.

Situated on Lake Constance in southern Germany, the school combines intensive language courses in either English or German with such recreational pursuits as sailing, art and design, music, theater workshop and outdoor activities. Weekends feature trips to area historical sights.

SCIENCE CAMP WATONKA
Res — Boys Ages 7-15

Hawley, PA 18428. PO Box 127. Tel: 570-226-4779. Fax: 570-857-9653.
www.watonka.com   E-mail: mail@watonka.com
Donald Wacker, Dir.
Grades 1-11. Adm: FCFS.
Enr: 130. **Fac** 26. **Staff:** Admin 6. Couns 34.
Type of instruction: Adv Enrich Preview Rev. **Courses:** Astron Comp_Sci Ecol Environ_
  Sci Geol Marine_Bio/Stud Electronics Robotics Crafts Media Photog. **Avg class size:** 8.
  Daily hours for: Classes 3. Rec 6.
Focus: Sci. **Features:** Aquatics Archery Boating Canoe Chess Climbing_Wall Conserva-
  tion Fishing Hiking Kayak Mtn_Biking Riflery Ropes_Crse Sail Wilderness_Camp Wood-
  craft Basketball Field_Hockey Soccer Softball Swim Tennis Volleyball Watersports.
Fees 2011: Res $2500-6900, 2-8 wks.
Housing: Cabins. Avg per room/unit: 8. **Swimming:** Lake.
Est 1963. Inc. **Ses:** 10. **Wks/ses:** 2-8. Operates June-Aug.

Campers, who are grouped by age, interest and ability, spend half of each day receiving laboratory instruction in two of the following sciences: chemistry, electronics, robotics, computer science, biology, photography, rocketry, geology, astronomy, ecology, physics or earth science. The remainder of the day is devoted to free choice from a range of activities.

SEA EDUCATION ASSOCIATION
HIGH SCHOOL SUMMER SEMINARS
Res — Coed Ages 15-19

Woods Hole, MA 02543. PO Box 6. Tel: 508-540-3954, 800-552-3633.
  Fax: 800-977-8516.
www.sea.edu   E-mail: admission@sea.edu
John K. Bullard, Pres.
Grades 10-Col. Adm: Selective. **Appl**—Fee 25. Due: Rolling. Transcript, 2 essays, teacher
  rec.
Enr: 24. **Enr cap:** 24. **Fac 10.** Prof 10. **Staff:** Admin 6. Couns 5.
Type of instruction: Adv. **Courses:** Astron Ecol Environ_Sci Expository_Writing Geol.
  Daily hours for: Classes 8. Study 4. Rec 4. **College credit:** 3.
Locations: CA MA ME.
Focus: Marine_Bio/Stud Oceanog. **Features:** Adventure_Travel Fishing Sail Sea_Cruises
  Seamanship Swim.

Fees 2012: Res $4250-5200, 3 wks. Aid (Need).
Housing: Cabins Dorms. Avg per room/unit: 8. **Swimming:** Ocean. Campus facilities avail.
Est 1971. Nonprofit. **Ses: 3. Wks/ses: 3.** Operates July-Aug.

SEA conducts three distinct high school seminars for motivated high schoolers and recent graduates interested in science, the sea and learning to sail: Science at SEA (Woods Hole), Oceanography of the Gulf of Maine (Appledore Island, ME) and Oceanography of the Southern California Bight (Catalina Island, CA). Students commence each program with academic course work during a shore component in which they live in a community setting and develop team-building and leadership skills. The second half of each program takes place at sea, where boys and girls gain hands-on experience on a modern sailing research vessel. While at sea, students collect scientific data, set and strike sails, operate sophisticated equipment and help out in the ship's galley.

SEACAMP
Res — Coed Ages 12-18

San Diego, CA 92109. 1380 Garnet Ave, PMB E6. Tel: 858-268-0919, 800-732-2267.
Fax: 858-268-0229.
www.seacamp.com   E-mail: seacamp@seacamp.com
Phil Zerofski, Exec Dir.
Grades 7-12. Adm: FCFS. **Appl**—Fee $0. Due: Rolling.
Enr cap: 28-56. **Fac 11. Staff:** Admin 5.
Courses: Ecol Environ_Sci Sci Speech Photog.
Focus: Marine_Bio/Stud. **Features:** Adventure_Travel Aquatics Boating Kayak Scuba Sea_Cruises Swim.
Fees 2012: Res $815-1700 (+$75), 1 wk.
Housing: Dorms. **Swimming:** Ocean.
Est 1986. Inc. **Ses: 9. Wks/ses: 1.** Operates June-Aug.

SEACAMP provides marine science education in San Diego. Combining traditional classroom and laboratory teaching with hands-on experience, the program allows students to participate in a core curriculum of marine biology, marine mammals and behavior, marine ecology and physical oceanography. Students also explore career opportunities and educational programs in the marine sciences.

SEACAMP
Res — Coed Ages 12-17

Big Pine Key, FL 33043. 1300 Big Pine Ave. Tel: 305-872-2331, 877-732-2267.
Fax: 305-872-2555.
www.seacamp.org   E-mail: info@seacamp.org
Grace Upshaw, Dir.
Grades 7-12. Adm: FCFS. **Appl**—Due: Rolling.
Enr: 160. **Enr cap:** 160. Intl: 20%. **Fac 18.** Col/grad students 18. **Staff:** Couns 30.
Type of instruction: Adv Enrich. **Courses:** Archaeol Astron Ecol Environ_Sci Expository_ Writing Geol Writing/Journ Crafts Creative_Writing Music. **Avg class size:** 10. **Daily hours for:** Classes 6.
Focus: Marine_Bio/Stud Scuba. **Features:** Aquatics Boating Canoe Exploration Fishing Kayak Sail Woodcraft Swim Volleyball Watersports.
Fees 2011: Res $3775 (+$425), 2½ wks.
Swimming: Ocean.
Est 1966. Nonprofit. **Ses: 3. Wks/ses: 2½.** Operates June-Aug.

This comprehensive marine science program offers teenagers an opportunity to explore the waters of the Florida Keys, both in the Atlantic Ocean and in the Gulf of Mexico.

Seacamp offers certification courses in scuba diving to qualified campers. Snorkeling, sailing, windsurfing, kayaking, a camp newspaper, music and arts, and crafts are among the camp's other daily offerings.

SEATTLE UNIVERSITY
ALBERS SCHOOL OF BUSINESS AND ECONOMICS
SUMMER BUSINESS INSTITUTE
Res — Coed Ages 16-17

Seattle, WA 98122. 901 12th Ave, PO Box 222000. Tel: 206-296-5700.
Fax: 206-296-5795.
www.seattleu.edu/albers/sbi.aspx   E-mail: cmarino@seattleu.edu
Carl Marino, Prgm Dir.
Grade 12. Adm: Selective. Admitted: 60%. Priority: URM. Prereqs: GPA 3.0. Appl—Fee $0.
Due: Apr. Personal statement, teacher/counselor rec.
Enr: 25. Enr cap: 26. Non-White: 100%. Fac 8. Staff: Admin 2. Couns 6.
Type of instruction: Enrich Preview. Courses: Econ Accounting Bus_Law Ethics Marketing. Daily hours for: Classes 6. Study 3. Rec 3. Homework.
Focus: Bus/Fin. Features: Badminton Basketball Swim Bowling.
Fees 2011: Res $50, 1 wk.
Housing: Dorms. Avg per room/unit: 2. Swimming: Pool.
Est 2003. Nonprofit. Ses: 1. Wks/ses: 1. Operates June.

SBI provides a preview of university life for African-American, Latino and Native American pupils with an interest in business. Hands-on seminars acquaint students with college course work in such business areas as economics, accounting, business law, ethics, finance, business administration, international business, management and marketing. Participants visit the corporate headquarters of program sponsors and meet with executives. The program also addresses the college selection and financial aid processes, and current Seattle University undergraduates are available for guidance.

SEATTLE UNIVERSITY JOURNALISM SUMMER WORKSHOP
Res — Coed Ages 15-18

Seattle, WA 98122. Communication Dept, Lynn Bldg, 901 12th Ave. Tel: 206-296-5300.
www.seattleu.edu/artsci/jsw   E-mail: tomasg@seattleu.edu
Tomas Guillen, Dir.
Grades 10-12. Adm: Selective. Appl—Due: Apr.
Enr: 15. Enr cap: 15.
Type of instruction: Enrich.
Focus: Writing/Journ.
Fees 2010: Free. Res 1 wk.
Housing: Dorms.
Ses: 1. Wks/ses: 1. Operates June.

This weeklong workshop enrolls talented high schoolers with an interest in journalism. Pupils receive intensive instruction and mentoring from professional journalists and college professors. Student work is published by major Seattle news organizations. Each year, the university awards two college scholarships to particularly strong workshop participants.

SHEDD AQUARIUM
HIGH SCHOOL MARINE BIOLOGY SUMMER PROGRAM
Res — Coed Ages 14-17

Chicago, IL 60605. 1200 S Lake Shore Dr. Tel: 312-692-3158.

www.sheddaquarium.org   E-mail: sbohr@sheddaquarium.org
Stephanie Bohr, Coord.
Grades 9-12. Adm: Selective. **Appl**—Due: Dec. Transcript, rec, swim test.
Enr: 30. **Enr cap:** 30. **Fac 4.**
Courses: Ecol Environ_Sci Sci.
Travel: Caribbean.
Focus: Marine_Bio/Stud. **Features:** Adventure_Travel Aquatics Boating Conservation Exploration Outdoor_Ed Sea_Cruises Seamanship Swim Snorkeling.
Swimming: Ocean Pool.
Est 1973. Nonprofit. **Ses:** 1. **Wks/ses:** 3. Operates July-Aug.

The aquarium's program offers students the opportunity to learn the fundamentals of marine biology and island ecology through lectures, field study and experimentation. Following an introduction at the Shedd Aquarium, participants spend six days living on a research vessel off the coast of the Bimini, Bahamas. Pupils spend the final week at the aquarium analyzing the data from the field. Students must make housing arrangements for their time in Chicago.

SILC INTERNATIONAL SUMMER CENTRES
Res — Coed Ages 13-17

Angouleme Cedex, 16022 France. 32 rempart de l'Est. Tel: 33-5-45-97-41-25.
    Fax: 33-5-45-94-20-63.
www.silc-in-france.com   E-mail: volodia.m@silc.fr
Adm: FCFS. **Appl**—Due: Rolling.
Enr cap: 8-15. Intl: 85%. Non-White: 30%. **Staff:** Admin 3. Couns 2.
Type of instruction: Enrich. **Courses:** Music Theater. **Avg class size:** 13. **Daily hours for:** Classes 3. Homework. Tests. Grades.
Intl program focus: Lang Culture. Home stays avail.
Focus: Fr. **Features:** Soccer.
Fees 2010: Res €314-1253 (+airfare), 1-4 wks.
Est 1965. Inc. **Ses:** 4. **Wks/ses:** 1-4. Operates June-Aug.

With locations in suburban Paris (Bretigny-sur-Orge) and the French Riviera (Biarritz), the Summer Centres feature 15 hours of weekly French language study. SILC accepts students at beginning, elementary, intermediate and advanced levels. Boys and girls reside with a host family, thereby hastening the pupil's language development.

SMITH COLLEGE
SUMMER SCIENCE AND ENGINEERING PROGRAM
Res — Girls Ages 13-18

Northampton, MA 01063. Center for Community Collaboration, Wright Hall.
    Tel: 413-585-3060. Fax: 413-585-3068.
www.smith.edu/ssep   E-mail: ccc@smith.edu
Gail E. Norskey, Dir.
Grades 9-12. Adm: Selective. **Appl**—Fee $0. Due: Rolling. Transcript, essay, teacher rec.
Enr: 100. Non-White: 50%. **Fac 14.** Prof 14. **Staff:** Admin 4.
Type of instruction: Adv Enrich. **Courses:** Astron Ecol Environ_Sci Expository_Writing Crafts Creative_Writing Dance Music Theater. **Avg class size:** 14. **Daily hours for:** Classes 5. Rec 5.
Focus: Engineering Med/Healthcare Sci. **Features:** Basketball Equestrian Swim Tennis Track Volleyball.
Fees 2011: Res $4850, 4 wks. Aid (Need).
Housing: Dorms. **Swimming:** Pool. Campus facilities avail.
Est 1990. Nonprofit. **Ses:** 1. **Wks/ses:** 4. Operates July.

Conducted by Smith College faculty, SSEP is a month-long enrichment program for talented high school girls with interests in science, engineering and medicine. During their stay, girls select two two-week research courses in such subjects as astronomy, biochemistry, biology, chemistry, engineering, women's health and writing. The program offers cooperative, hands-on investigations in engineering and the life and physical sciences. In their free time, students participate in organized sports, as well as in various recreational and cultural activities.

SOCIETY OF AMERICAN MILITARY ENGINEERS ENGINEERING & CONSTRUCTION CAMPS
Res — Coed Ages 15-18

Bothell, WA 98012. 18421 38th Dr SE.
http://posts.same.org/camps   E-mail: camp.info@same.org
Student contact: Erin Ingersoll, E-mail: erini@meetingvisions.net.
Grades 10-12. Adm: Selective. Prereqs: GPA 3.0. **Appl**—Due: Mar.
Type of instruction: Enrich.
Locations: CA CO MI.
Focus: Engineering. **Features:** Basketball Volleyball.
Fees 2009: Res $275, 1 wk.
Housing: Dorms.
Est 1999. Nonprofit. **Ses:** 3. **Wks/ses:** 1. Operates June-July.

Weeklong SAME camps provide students who excel in math, science and technical courses with opportunities to learn from professional engineers from the military and private sectors, develop practical skills and gain exposure to the service academies. Camps take place at three locations annually: the US Army Camp in Vicksburg, MS; the US Air Force Academy Camp in Colorado Springs, CO; and the US Navy Seabees Camp in Port Hueneme, CA.

SOTOGRANDE CAMPS
Res — Coed Ages 7-14; Day — Coed 3-14

Sotogrande, 11310 Cadiz, Spain. Apartado 15. Tel: 34-956-795-902.
Fax: 34-956-794-816.
www.sotograndecamps.com   E-mail: info@sotograndecamps.com
Adm: FCFS. **Appl**—Fee $0. Due: Rolling.
Enr cap: 200. **Staff:** Admin 4.
Intl program focus: Lang.
Focus: ESL Span. **Features:** Golf Soccer Swim Tennis.
Fees 2012: Res €1675-2995, 2-4 wks. Day €1080-1970, 2-4 wks.
Housing: Dorms. **Swimming:** Ocean Pool.
Est 1978. Spons: Sotogrande International School. **Ses:** 3. **Wks/ses:** 2-4. Operates June-July.

Conducted on the campus of Sotogrande International School, the camp combines intensive Spanish or English language instruction with professionally taught sports. During the session, campers concentrate on one of the following sports: tennis, soccer, golf or paddle tennis.

SOUTH CAROLINA STATE UNIVERSITY SUMMER TRANSPORTATION INSTITUTE
Res — Coed Ages 14-17

Orangeburg, SC 29117. PO Box 8144. Tel: 803-516-4781.
www.nrc.scsu.edu   E-mail: lbutler@scsu.edu
Larrie B. Butler, Dir.
Grades 9-11. Adm: Selective. Prereqs: GPA 2.5. **Appl**—Fee $0. Due: May. Transcript, essays, standardized test scores, 2 recs.
Enr: 16. Non-White: 100%. **Fac 6. Staff:** Admin 2. Couns 2.

Type of instruction: Enrich SAT/ACT_Prep.
Focus: Engineering.
Fees 2012: Free (in-state residents). Res 4 wks.
Housing: Dorms.
Est 1993. Nonprofit. **Ses:** 1. **Wks/ses:** 4. Operates July.

STI exposes South Carolina high schoolers to career opportunities in transportation industries. Program topics include highway design, transportation of people and cargo, laws, regulations, safety and environmentalism. Among other activities are SAT prep courses, computer training, reading and writing enhancement skills and field trips.

STANFORD NATIONAL FORENSIC INSTITUTE
Res and Day — Coed Ages 14-18

Palo Alto, CA 94301. 555 Bryant St, Ste 599. Tel: 650-723-9086. Fax: 510-548-0212.
www.snfi.org　　E-mail: info@snfi.org
Matthew Fraser, Exec Dir.
Grades 9-12. Adm: FCFS. **Appl**—Fee $0. Due: May.
Type of instruction: Enrich.
Focus: Debate.
Fees 2009: Res $1150-4670, 1-4 wks. Day $950-3670, 1-4 wks.
Housing: Dorms. Avg per room/unit: 2.
Spons: Stanford University. **Ses:** 5. **Wks/ses:** 1-4. Operates July-Aug.

High school students choose from the following camps at SNFI: individual events, Lincoln-Douglas debate, parliamentary debate, policy debate and public forum debate. Those choosing the policy debate program have an accelerated camp option, and boys and girls in the policy, public forum and Lincoln-Douglas programs may enroll in a fourth week (other programs last one to three weeks). Programming balances lab time, practice rounds, mandatory lectures and electives.

STANFORD UNIVERSITY MATHEMATICS CAMP
Res — Coed Ages 15-17

Stanford, CA 94305. Math Dept, Bldg 380, 450 Serra Mall. Tel: 650-725-6284.
http://math.stanford.edu/sumac　　E-mail: sommer@math.stanford.edu
Rick Sommer, Dir.
Grades 11-12. Adm: Selective. Admitted: 33%. **Appl**—Transcript, standardized math tests, teacher recs.
Type of instruction: Enrich.
Focus: Math.
Fees 2009: Res $4500, 4 wks. Aid (Need).
Housing: Dorms. Campus facilities avail.
Est 1995. Nonprofit. **Ses:** 1. **Wks/ses:** 4. Operates July-Aug.

SUMaC enrolls motivated and mathematically motivated high school upperclassmen who are interested in exploring advanced math topics over the summer. The program includes the following: an intensive course in higher math, a guided research project allowing pupils to pursue a focused and course-related area of interest, a series of guest lectures, group problem solving and one-on-one tutoring, and social events and outings. Boys and girls have access to Stanford's athletic and library facilities.

STANSTEAD COLLEGE SUMMER LANGUAGE ADVENTURE
Res — Coed Ages 11-16

Stanstead, J0B 3E0 Quebec, Canada. 450 Dufferin St. Tel: 819-876-7891.
Fax: 819-876-5891.
www.stansteadcollege.com/scla **E-mail: summer.school@stansteadcollege.com**
Marc Ghilarducci, Dir.
   Student contact: Joanne Carruthers, E-mail: admissions@stansteadcollege.com.
Grades 6-11. Adm: FCFS. **Appl**—Fee $0. Due: Rolling.
Enr: 120. **Enr cap:** 150. Non-White: 35%. **Fac 30. Staff:** Admin 2.
Type of instruction: Enrich. **Avg class size:** 12. **Daily hours for:** Classes 4½. Rec 4½.
   Tests. Grades.
Intl program focus: Lang. Home stays avail.
Focus: ESL Fr Span. **Features:** Wilderness_Camp Swim.
Fees 2012: Res Can$2275, 3 wks.
Swimming: Lake. Campus facilities avail.
Est 1986. Nonprofit. **Ses:** 1. **Wks/ses:** 3. Operates July.

Participants take four and a half hours of foreign language classes per day in French or English at beginning, intermediate or advanced levels. Outdoor experiences such as recreational sports and weekend camping complement class instruction and further reinforce language learning.

CAMP START-UP
Res and Day — Coed Ages 14-18

Wilbraham, MA. Wilbraham & Monson Acad.
Contact (Year-round): 1209½ De La Vina St, Santa Barbara, CA 93103.
   Tel: 805-965-0475. Fax: 805-965-3148.
www.independentmeans.com **E-mail: info@independentmeans.com**
Melinda L. Little, Dir.
Adm: FCFS. **Appl**—Fee $0. Due: Rolling.
Enr cap: 30. Intl: 8%. Non-White: 45%. **Fac 7. Staff:** Admin 2. Res 7.
Type of instruction: Enrich. **Courses:** Leadership.
Focus: Bus/Fin. **Features:** Basketball Swim Tennis.
Fees 2012: Res $2400, 1½ wks. Day $1600, 1½ wks. Aid (Merit & Need).
Housing: Dorms. Avg per room/unit: 2. **Swimming:** Pool. Campus facilities avail.
Est 1994. Inc. **Spons:** Independent Means. **Ses:** 1. **Wks/ses:** 1½. Operates July-Aug.

Conducted at Wilbraham & Monson Academy, Camp Start-Up enables teenagers from around the world to learn about entrepreneurship, budgeting, saving and investing. Students work in groups to form mock start-ups, build business plans and create investment portfolios. They also meet local business leaders from successful companies on class field trips. Leadership skills training is an important aspect of each session. Boys and girls may engage in various recreational and athletic pursuits during their free time.

STERLING COLLEGE
SUMMER SUSTAINABLE AGRICULTURE PROGRAM
Res — Coed Ages 16 and up

Craftsbury Common, VT 05827. PO Box 72. Tel: 802-586-7711, 800-648-3591.
   Fax: 802-586-2596.
www.sterlingcollege.edu/summer-ag.html
E-mail: admissions@sterlingcollege.edu
Adm: Selective. **Appl**—Fee $35. Due: May. Transcript, 2 recs, essay.
Enr: 6. **Enr cap:** 12. **Fac 4. Staff:** Admin 3. Couns 2.
Type of instruction: Adv. **Courses:** Eng Environ_Sci Crafts Music. **College credit:** 8.

Focus: Agriculture. **Features:** Canoe Climbing_Wall Community_Serv Conservation Cooking Exploration Farm Hiking Riding Work Soccer Swim Ultimate_Frisbee.
Fees 2012: Res $8811, 5 wks. Aid (Need).
Housing: Tents. Avg per room/unit: 2. **Swimming:** Lake River Stream.
Nonprofit. **Ses:** 2. **Wks/ses:** 5. Operates May-Aug.

SAS serves academically advanced high school students, college students and adults who have an interest in ecological management. Participants live in a tent village and acquire hands-on experience with the daily rhythms and realities of farming. Students attend core courses in livestock management, organic crop production and agricultural power systems, and enroll in an additional elective course. In addition to classroom instructed, pupils receive training on farm equipment and work 20 hours per week. Participants learn to prepare nutritious meals and also partake of recreational activities in northern Vermont.

STEVENS INSTITUTE OF TECHNOLOGY
EXPLORING CAREER OPTIONS IN ENGINEERING AND SCIENCE
Res — Coed Ages 16-18

Hoboken, NJ 07030. 1 Castle Point on Hudson. Tel: 201-216-8076.
www.stevens.edu/sit/admissions/highschool/ecoes.cfm
E-mail: maia.hadidi@stevens.edu
Maia Hadidi, Coord.
Grades 11-12. Adm: Selective. **Appl**—Due: June. Transcript, test scores, rec.
Type of instruction: Enrich.
Focus: Engineering Sci. **Features:** Swim.
Fees 2011: Res $1800, 2 wks.
Housing: Dorms. Avg per room/unit: 2. **Swimming:** Pool. Campus facilities avail.
Ses: 2. **Wks/ses:** 2. Operates July-Aug.

ECOES explores a range of fields in science and engineering through academic modules and laboratory experiences. Students work in teams on hands-on engineering design or science projects, visit local Fortune 500 companies and sample college life.

STONELEIGH-BURNHAM SCHOOL
A VOICE OF HER OWN
Res — Girls Ages 11-17

Greenfield, MA 01301. 574 Bernardston Rd. Tel: 413-774-2711. Fax: 413-772-2602.
www.sbschool.org   E-mail: summerprograms@sbschool.org
Paul Bassett, Dir.
Adm: FCFS. **Appl**—Fee $0. Due: Rolling.
Enr: 40. **Enr cap:** 40. **Fac** 5. **Staff:** Admin 3. Couns 5.
Type of instruction: Adv.
Focus: Debate Public_Speak. **Features:** Aquatics Swim.
Fees 2012: Res $450, 1 wk.
Housing: Dorms. **Swimming:** Pool.
Est 1982. Nonprofit. **Ses:** 1. **Wks/ses:** 1. Operates July.

A Voice of Her Own teaches lifetime speaking and debating skills to young women. Instruction includes interpretive reading, dramatic interpretation, impromptu speaking, persuasive speaking and various forms of debate. Girls devote mornings to preparing speeches or debate briefs, then spend afternoons polishing their delivery of the material. Participants deliver presentations to the assembled camp each evening.

STUDY CENTRE C & L SUMMER PROGRAMME
Res and Day — Coed Ages 18 and up

**Montreux, 1820 Switzerland. Ave de Naye 15, PO Box 77. Tel: 41-21-963-08-80.
Fax: 41-21-963-73-34.
www.studycentre.ch   E-mail: studycl@studycentrecl.ch
Hermann Schusterbauer, Dir.
Adm:** FCFS. **Appl**—Fee $0. Due: Rolling.
Enr: 40. **Fac 9. Staff:** Admin 3.
Type of instruction: Enrich. **Avg class size:** 6. **Daily hours for:** Classes 4. Study 2.
Intl program focus: Lang.
Focus: ESL Fr Ger. **Features:** Bicycle_Tours Hiking Mtn_Biking Mtn_Trips Riding Swim
Tennis Watersports.
Fees 2011: Res $1583-4750 (+$300), 2-6 wks. Day $767-2300 (+$84), 2-6 wks.
Housing: Apartments Lodges. **Swimming:** Lake Pool.
Est 1968. Inc. **Ses:** 5. **Wks/ses:** 2-6. Operates July-Aug.

Students take 20 lessons per week in either French and German, French and ESL, German and ESL, or French only. The program includes weekly day trips around Switzerland, as well as sports and visits to entertainment and cultural facilities.

SUMMER INSTITUTE FOR MATHEMATICS AT THE UNIVERSITY OF WASHINGTON
Res — Coed Ages 17-18

**Seattle, WA 98195. Dept of Math, Box 354350. Tel: 206-543-1150. Fax: 206-543-0397.
www.math.washington.edu/~simuw   E-mail: simuw@math.washington.edu
Ron Irving, Exec Dir.
Grade 12 (younger if qualified). Adm:** Selective. **Appl**—Fee $0. Due: Mar. Transcript,
math problems, math teacher rec.
Enr: 24. **Enr cap:** 24.
Type of instruction: Adv Enrich.
Focus: Math.
Fees 2010: Free. Res 6 wks.
Housing: Dorms.
Nonprofit. **Ses:** 1. **Wks/ses:** 6. Operates June-Aug.

A select group of high school upperclassmen from Washington State, Oregon, Idaho, Alaska and British Columbia, Canada, who have completed at least three years of high school math may apply for this intensive program. Two instructors lead each of the three two-week blocks; during four of the five weekdays of the week, participants meet with one instructor in the morning, the other in the afternoon. These sessions combine work on math problems with some limited lecture time. On the fifth weekday, SIMUW schedules a special program in which a morning speaker discusses math's role in his or her line of work; in the afternoon, students will either listen to a second speaker or engage in a special activity or field trip related to math. Boys and girls embark on trips to local places of interest on Saturdays, then have Sundays available for group or individual activities.

SUMMER SCIENCE PROGRAM
Res — Coed Ages 15-17

**Cary, NC 27519. 108 Whiteberry Dr. Toll-free: 866-728-0999.
www.ssp.org   E-mail: info@ssp.org
Richard Bowdon, Exec Dir.
Grades 11-12. Adm:** Very selective. Admitted: 15%. **Appl**—Fee $0. Due: Feb. Transcript,
test scores, essays, 2-3 recs.
Enr: 36. **Enr cap:** 36. Intl: 10%. Non-White: 65%. **Fac 2.** Prof 2. **Staff:** Admin 1. Couns 5.

Type of instruction: Adv Enrich. **Courses:** Comp_Sci Math. **Avg class size:** 36. **Daily hours for:** Classes 6. Homework.
Locations: CA NM.
Focus: Astron Sci. **Features:** Hiking Basketball Cross-country Golf Soccer Swim Tennis Ultimate_Frisbee Weight_Trng.
Fees 2012: Res $3950 (+$100), 5½ wks. Aid 2011 (Need): $80,000.
Housing: Dorms. **Swimming:** Ocean Pool. Campus facilities avail.
Est 1959. Nonprofit. **Ses:** 2. **Wks/ses:** 5½. Operates June-Aug.

This precollege enrichment program features college-level instruction in astronomy, math, physics and computer programming for able science students. Working in teams of three, students perform a research project in celestial mechanics from start to finish, in the process determining the orbit of an asteroid using their own observations, measurements and software. Educational and recreational field trips and guest speakers supplement lectures and project work. Although most participants are rising seniors, a handful of academically accelerated rising juniors gain admission each year. SSP operates at two locations: Westmont College in Santa Barbara, CA, and the New Mexico Institute of Mining and Technology in Socorro, NM.

SUPERCAMP
Res — Coed Ages 11-24

Oceanside, CA 92056. 1938 Avenida del Oro. Tel: 760-722-0072, 800-285-3276.
Fax: 760-305-7770.
www.supercamp.com　　**E-mail: info@supercamp.com**
Bobbi DePorter, Pres. Student contact: Ruth Everett, E-mail: reverett@qln.com.
Grades 6-Col. Adm: FCFS. **Appl**—Fee $0. Due: Rolling.
Enr: 100. **Enr cap:** 100. Intl: 5%. **Fac 4. Staff:** Admin 28.
Type of instruction: Dev_Read Enrich Preview Rev SAT/ACT_Prep. **Daily hours for:** Classes 10. Rec 2.
Locations: CA FL NC OH RI.
Focus: Study_Skills. **Features:** Rock_Climb Swim.
Fees 2012: Res $2195-3095, 1-1½ wks.
Housing: Dorms. **Swimming:** Pool.
Est 1982. Inc. **Ses:** 26. **Wks/ses:** 1-1½. Operates June-Aug.

SuperCamp's academic program focuses on improving learning skills. Middle school, high school and college-age programs are held on university campuses throughout the US. The curriculum addresses power reading, memory mastering, writing, problem solving, note taking and test taking. Students also take part in a life skills program.

SURVAL MONT-FLEURI SUMMER HOLIDAY COURSE
Res — Girls Ages 10-22

Montreux, 1820 Switzerland. Rte de Glion 56. Tel: 41-21-966-16-16.
Fax: 41-21-966-16-17.
www.surval.ch　　**E-mail: info@surval.ch**
Jean-Pierre Fauquez, Dir.
Adm: Somewhat selective. Admitted: 90%. **Appl**—Fee SwF450. Due: Rolling.
Enr: 75. **Enr cap:** 85. Intl: 75%. Non-White: 30%. **Fac 36. Staff:** Admin 7.
Type of instruction: Adv Rem_Eng Rem_Math Rem_Read SAT/ACT_Prep Tut. **Courses:** Ger Ital Span Bus/Fin Ceramics Crafts Dance Fine_Arts Music Painting Photog. **Avg class size:** 10. **Daily hours for:** Classes 6. Homework. Tests. Grades. **High school & college credit.**
Intl program focus: Lang.
Focus: ESL Fr. **Features:** Bicycle_Tours Cooking Cruises Riding Aerobics Gymnastics Swim Tennis Water-skiing Watersports.

Fees 2011: Res SwF6300 (+SwF1500), 3 wks.
Housing: Dorms. Avg per room/unit: 3. **Swimming:** Lake Pool. Campus facilities avail.
Est 1961. Ses: 3. **Wks/ses:** 3. Operates June-Aug.

Girls enrolled at Surval Mont-Fleuri study French or English intensively for four hours each weekday morning. A full- or half-day excursion is scheduled every Saturday. For an additional fee, students may enroll in cooking, pastry, ceramics, photography and etiquette classes, among others.

SUSQUEHANNA UNIVERSITY
LEADERSHIP INSTITUTE FOR ENTREPRENEURSHIP
Res — Coed Ages 15-17

Selinsgrove, PA 17870. c/o Office of Continuing Ed, 530 University Ave.
Tel: 570-372-4235. Fax: 570-372-4021.
www.susqu.edu/life   E-mail: mischel@susqu.edu
Leann Mischel, Coord.
Grades 10-12. Adm: Selective. **Appl**—Due: Rolling. Transcript, recs.
Type of instruction: Enrich. **Courses:** Leadership.
Focus: Bus/Fin.
Fees 2010: Res $995, 1 wk.
Housing: Dorms.
Nonprofit. **Ses:** 1. **Wks/ses:** 1. Operates July.

This hands-on introduction to entrepreneurship enables students in grades 10-12 to engage in a simulated experience as a business owner. Pupils learn about finance, banking, stocks and bonds, sales, advertising, global trade issues and the importance of effective collaboration. As owner of a theoretical business, each student acquires seed money, hires personnel, pays expenses, manages inventory, and sells his or her company. Faculty and staff from the university's Sigmund Weis School of Business conduct the program.

TASIS MIDDLE SCHOOL PROGRAM
Res and Day — Coed Ages 11-13

Montagnola-Lugano, Switzerland.
Contact (Year-round): 112 S Royal St, Alexandria, VA 22314. Tel: 703-299-8150.
Fax: 703-299-8157.
www.tasis.com   E-mail: usadmissions@tasis.com
Chris Tragas, Dir.
Adm: FCFS. **Appl**—Fee $0. Due: Rolling. Rec.
Enr: 130. **Enr cap:** 130. **Fac** 15. **Staff:** Admin 4.
Type of instruction: Enrich. **Courses:** Art Theater. **Avg class size:** 12. **Daily hours for:** Classes 3. Study 1. Rec 4.
Intl program focus: Lang Culture.
Focus: ESL Fr Ital. **Features:** Archery Hiking Mtn_Biking Riding Rock_Climb Basketball Soccer Swim Tennis Volleyball Water-skiing.
Fees 2012: Res SwF7300 (+airfare), 3-4 wks. **Day** SwF4400 (+airfare), 3-4 wks.
Housing: Dorms. **Swimming:** Lake Pool.
Est 1976. Nonprofit. **Spons:** TASIS Foundation. **Ses:** 2. **Wks/ses:** 3-4. Operates June-Aug.

Accepting students of all ability levels, MSP provides three hours each morning of intensive French or English instruction. While fluency is the primary goal, classes also emphasize grammar, vocabulary and written work; advanced pupils also study literature. Boys and girls devote two afternoons per week to artistic workshops or specialized sports, then choose from various activities on other class days. In addition, MSP schedules full-day excursions and special events on Sundays and Mondays.

TASIS SPANISH SUMMER PROGRAM
Res — Coed Ages 11-17

Salamanca, Spain.
Contact (Year-round): 112 S Royal St, Alexandria, VA 22314. **Tel:** 703-299-8150.
Fax: 703-299-8150.
www.tasis.com   E-mail: usadmissions@tasis.com
Chris Tragas, Dir.
Grades 6-11. Adm: Somewhat selective. Admitted: 99%. **Appl**—Fee $0. Due: Rolling.
Rec.
Enr: 52. **Enr cap:** 52. **Fac 10. Staff:** Admin 4. Couns 7.
Avg class size: 12. **Daily hours for:** Classes 4. Homework. Tests. Grades. **High school credit:** 1/crse, total 1.
Intl program focus: Lang Culture.
Focus: Span. **Features:** Soccer Swim Tennis Track.
Fees 2011: Res €3700-4850, 3-4 wks.
Housing: Dorms. **Swimming:** Pool. Campus facilities avail.
Est 1991. Nonprofit. **Spons:** TASIS Foundation. **Ses:** 2. **Wks/ses:** 3-4. Operates July.

This language immersion program enables students who pass a final examination and fulfill all session requirements to earn high school credit in Spanish. Pupils receive extensive practice in listening, speaking, reading and writing, and they also learn about Spanish culture. TASIS accommodates Spanish speakers of all fluency levels.

TELLURIDE ASSOCIATION SOPHOMORE SEMINARS
Res — Coed Ages 16-17

Ithaca, NY 14850. 217 West Ave. Tel: 607-273-5011. **Fax:** 607-272-2667.
www.tass.tellurideassociation.org   E-mail: telluride@tellurideassociation.org
Ellen Baer, Admin Dir.
Grade 11. Adm: Very selective. Priority: URM. **Appl**—Fee $0. Due: Jan. Essays, transcript, rec, interview.
Enr: 36. **Enr cap:** 36. **Fac 8.** Prof 4. Col/grad students 4.
Type of instruction: Adv Enrich. **Courses:** Expository_Writing Public_Speak. **Daily hours for:** Classes 3. Homework.
Locations: IN MI.
Focus: African-Amer_Stud.
Fees 2012: Free. Res 6 wks.
Housing: Dorms.
Est 1993. Nonprofit. **Ses:** 2. **Wks/ses:** 6. Operates June-Aug.

TASS, held on two college campuses, is a free, six-week program in which rising juniors interested in African-American studies explore this area and other topics that address diversity in society. After convening for a three-hour seminar each weekday morning with two college professors, students spend the remainder of the day completing reading, writing and oral-presentation assignments with the assistance of college-age tutors; watching films related to their seminar topic; and attending guest lectures. Undergraduate student-tutors live in residence halls with TASS pupils, working with them on critical reading and writing skills. Outside the classroom, boys and girls have opportunities to attend cultural events and explore the host institution.

TERRA LINGUA USA SUMMER OUTBOUND PROGRAMS
Res — Coed Ages 13-18

Terryville, CT 06786. 3 Helen Rd. Tel: 203-525-1231. **Fax:** 860-583-4002.
www.terralinguausa.org   E-mail: kellie@terralinguausa.com
Kelly Iacovella, Exec Dir.

Adm: FCFS. Admitted: 98%. **Appl**—Due: Rolling.
Fac 2. K-12 staff 2. **Staff:** Admin 1. Res 2.
Type of instruction: Enrich. **Courses:** Global_Stud. **Daily hours for:** Classes 4. Study 2. Rec 2. Homework. Tests. Grades.
Intl program focus: Lang Culture. **Locations:** Asia Europe Mexico/Central_America. Home stays avail.
Focus: Ger Span. **Features:** Swim Tennis.
Housing: Dorms Houses Lodges. Avg per room/unit: 1. **Swimming:** Lake Pond Ocean Pool River Stream.
Est 1997. Nonprofit. **Wks/ses:** 1-2. Operates June-Aug.

Terra Lingua USA matches its summer students with host families for a language-immersion experience. Summer Outbound Programs operate in China, Spain, Germany and Costa Rica. The German program combines language study with professional tennis instruction. Pupils have access to staff representatives in both the US and the host country.

TETON SCIENCE SCHOOLS SUMMER YOUTH ADVENTURES
Res — Coed Ages 12-18; Day — Coed 3-18

Jackson, WY 83001. 700 Coyote Canyon Rd. Tel: 307-733-1313. Fax: 307-733-7560.
www.tetonscience.org   E-mail: info@tetonscience.org
April Landale, Dir.
Grades PS-12. Adm: FCFS. **Appl**—Due: Mar.
Enr cap: 24. **Staff:** Couns 3.
Courses: Environ_Sci Geol. **High school credit.**
Focus: Ecol Sci. **Features:** Canoe Conservation Exploration Fishing Hiking Mtn_Trips Wilderness_Camp.
Fees 2011: Res $898-3780, 1-4 wks. Day $225-710, 1-1½ wks. Aid (Need).
Housing: Cabins Lodges Tents. Avg per room/unit: 3.
Est 1967. Nonprofit. **Ses:** 25. **Wks/ses:** 1-4. Operates June-Sept.

Utilizing the Grand Teton National Park as an outdoor classroom, Teton Science Schools offers summer programming in the natural sciences, natural history and conservation. Students entering grades 11 and 12 and high school graduates enroll in a four-week course that leads to high school credit in field ecology. Participants identify and investigate plants and animals, study natural communities and learn about the foundations of geology. A three-week course in natural field history serves boys and girls entering grades 9-11. For junior high schoolers entering grades 7-9, TSS conducts a 10-day field ecology course. Backpacking and canoeing are elements of all programs.

TEXAS A&M UNIVERSITY-GALVESTON SEA CAMP
Res — Coed Ages 10-18

Galveston, TX 77553. PO Box 1675. Tel: 409-740-4525. Fax: 409-740-4894.
www.tamug.edu/seacamp   E-mail: seacamp@tamug.edu
Grades 5-12. Adm: FCFS. **Appl**—Due: Rolling.
Staff: Admin 4.
Type of instruction: Adv Enrich. **Courses:** Environ_Sci Photog.
Intl program focus: Culture. **Locations:** Canada.
Focus: Ecol Marine_Bio/Stud Oceanog. **Features:** Adventure_Travel Fishing Swim.
Fees 2012: Res $850-915, 1 wk.
Housing: Dorms. **Swimming:** Ocean Pool.
Est 1986. Nonprofit. **Ses:** 16. **Wks/ses:** 1. Operates June-Aug.

This weeklong, hands-on camp enables boys and girls to study marine and estuarine environments. Students have access to research vessels, oceanographic equipment and lab facilities as they learn about various aspects of marine science and ecology. While most sessions take place at the university, Sea Camp conducts a marine science expedition to Vancouver, Canada, for pupils ages 15-18.

TEXAS A&M UNIVERSITY-GALVESTON
TALENTED AND GIFTED DISTINGUISHED ACHIEVEMENT
SUMMER PROGRAMS
Res — Coed Ages 13-17

Galveston, TX 77553. PO Box 1675. Tel: 409-740-4525, 877-322-4443.
Fax: 409-740-4894.
www.tamug.edu   E-mail: duersond@tamug.edu
Daisy Duerson, Dir.
Grades 8-12. Adm: Selective. Appl—Due: Rolling.
Enr: 20. Staff: Admin 2. Couns 2.
Type of instruction: Adv Enrich.
Focus: Career Marine_Bio/Stud Med/Healthcare Veterinary_Med. Features: Swim.
Fees 2012: Res $950, 1 wk.
Housing: Dorms. Swimming: Ocean Pool.
Nonprofit. Ses: 8. Wks/ses: 1. Operates June-Aug.

A precollege program for high-ability students, TAG offers career-oriented courses that enable boys and girls to explore an area of interest. Veterinary medicine, marine biology research, marine engineering, premedical studies and marine science research are the class options. Students reside on campus and have access to the university's athletic and academic facilities. Classes meet in the morning and early afternoon, leaving late afternoons and evenings open for organized recreational activities.

TEXAS A&M UNIVERSITY
SUMMER MATHEMATICS RESEARCH TRAINING
Res — Coed Ages 14-18

College Station, TX 77843. Math Dept. Tel: 979-862-3257. Fax: 979-862-4190.
www.math.tamu.edu/outreach/Camp   E-mail: camp@math.tamu.edu
Peter Kuchment, Dir.
Adm: Selective. Appl—Fee $0. Due: Apr. Transcript, math teacher rec.
Enr: 20. Enr cap: 20.
Type of instruction: Adv Enrich.
Focus: Math.
Fees 2009: Free. Res 2 wks.
Housing: Dorms.
Est 2009. Ses: 1. Wks/ses: 2. Operates June.

The main topics addressed at this advanced math program for high schoolers are number theory, combinatorial mathematics and algebra. Morning lectures deal with these areas and their applications, and problem sessions and guest lectures occupy the afternoon hours. Under the guidance of counselors, boys and girls undertake most of the technical work involved in problem solving. Each student group participates in evening meetings. Texas A&M faculty deliver various guest lectures.

TEXAS ACADEMY OF MATHEMATICS AND SCIENCE
SUMMER MATH INSTITUTE
Res — Coed Ages 12-16

Denton, TX 76203. c/o Univ of North Texas, PO Box 305309. Tel: 940-565-4369.
Fax: 940-369-8796.

www.tams.unt.edu
Wendy Boyd-Brown, Dir.
Grades 7-11. Adm: Selective. **Appl**—Due: Rolling.
Staff: Res 5.
Daily hours for: Classes 6. Study 1.
Focus: Math.
Fees 2009: Res $2200, 3 wks. Aid (Need).
Housing: Dorms. Avg per room/unit: 2.
Ses: 1. **Wks/ses:** 3. Operates July.

SMI participants cover the equivalent of a year's worth of math material in one class during their three weeks at the academy. Students attend class for six hours on weekdays and three hours on Saturdays, and they must also attend a supervised study/tutorial session for an hour each Monday through Friday evening. At the end of the program, faculty formulate a final performance report for the pupil's school and his or her parents.

TEXAS STATE UNIVERSITY
AQUATIC SCIENCES ADVENTURE CAMP
Res and Day — Coed Ages 9-15

San Marcos, TX 78666. 248 Freeman Bldg. Tel: 512-245-2329. Fax: 512-245-2669.
www.eardc.txstate.edu/camp.html   E-mail: lg16@txstate.edu
Lendon Gilpin, Dir.
Grades 4-10. Adm: FCFS. **Appl**—Due: Rolling.
Enr: 26. **Enr cap:** 26. **Fac** 5. Prof 1. K-12 staff 4. **Staff:** Res 4.
Type of instruction: Adv Enrich. **Courses:** Environ_Sci. **Daily hours for:** Classes 4. Rec 4.
Focus: Marine_Bio/Stud. **Features:** Aquatics Fishing Scuba White-water_Raft Swim.
Fees 2012: Res $680, 1 wk. Day $130, ½ wk.
Housing: Dorms. Avg per room/unit: 2. **Swimming:** Pool River.
Est 1988. Ses: 10. **Wks/ses:** ½-1. Operates June-Aug.

TSU's Edwards Aquifer Research and Data Center guides this program, in which boys and girls study freshwater ecosystems in the Central Texas Hill Country. Mornings at the camp are devoted to educational activities related to water resources, aquatic biology and water chemistry, while afternoons include aquatic activities (such as tubing, scuba/snorkeling, rafting, fishing and swimming) that are intended to increase campers' appreciation of aquatic resources. Although two two-day commuter options are available, most sessions accommodate boarders only.

TEXAS STATE UNIVERSITY
MATHWORKS HONORS SUMMER MATH CAMP
Res — Coed Ages 15-18

San Marcos, TX 78666. ASB South 110, 601 University Dr. Tel: 512-245-3439.
Fax: 512-245-1469.
www.txstate.edu/mathworks   E-mail: mathworks@txstate.edu
Max L. Warshauer, Dir.
Grades 10-12 (younger if qualified). Adm: Very selective. Admitted: 30%. **Appl**—Fee $0. Due: Apr. Transcript, math teacher rec.
Enr: 100. **Enr cap:** 100. Intl: 7%. Non-White: 90%. **Fac 4.** Prof 4. **Staff:** Admin 2.
Type of instruction: Adv Enrich. **Daily hours for:** Classes 6. Study 4. Rec 4. Homework.
Focus: Math. **Features:** Aquatics Fishing Hiking Aerobics Basketball Swim Volleyball.
Fees 2012: Res $2700 (+$20), 6 wks. Aid (Need).
Housing: Dorms. **Swimming:** Pool River.
Est 1989. Ses: 1. **Wks/ses:** 6. Operates June-July.

Courses and problem-solving sessions provide a solid foundation in such mathematical areas as number theory, combinatorics, abstract algebra, analysis and topology. Students use computer software to model real-world problems and attend an honors seminar designed to familiarize them with the opportunities available at a university. Recreational activities include athletics, hiking, shopping and a weekend trip to Bamberger Ranch.

TEXAS STATE UNIVERSITY
MATHWORKS JUNIOR SUMMER MATH CAMP
Res — Coed Ages 11-13; Day — Coed 8-13

San Marcos, TX 78666. ASB South 110, 601 University Dr. Tel: 512-245-3439.
Fax: 512-245-1469.
www.txstate.edu/mathworks   E-mail: mathworks@txstate.edu
Max L. Warshauer, Dir.
Grades 4-8 (younger if qualified). Adm: FCFS. **Appl**—Fee $0. Due: Apr. Math teacher rec.
Enr: 180-200. **Enr cap:** 200.
Type of instruction: Enrich. **Daily hours for:** Classes 4. Rec 1.
Focus: Math. **Features:** Basketball.
Fees 2012: Res $995, 2 wks. Day $295, 2 wks.
Housing: Dorms.
Est 1995. Ses: 1. **Wks/ses:** 2. Operates June.

Offered at five levels of instruction, the Junior Summer Math Camp ranges from a first-year program that introduces students to beginning concepts in algebra through play-acting and drama to a more advanced program in problem solving and discrete math. Residential accommodations at the most advanced level are limited to 32 students entering grades 6-8. The boarding program includes recreation in the afternoon, supervised problem sessions in the evening and special guest lectures.

360° STUDENT TRAVEL LANGUAGE PROGRAMS
Res — Coed Ages 14-18

Mamaroneck, NY 10543. 154 E Boston Post Rd. Tel: 914-835-0699, 800-767-0227.
Fax: 914-835-0798.
www.360studenttravel.com   E-mail: info@360studenttravel.com
Ira Solomon, Prgm Dir.
Grades 9-PG. Adm: FCFS. **Appl**—Fee $0. Due: Rolling.
Enr: 18-50. **Enr cap:** 18-50.
Type of instruction: ESL/TOEFL_Prep Undergrad. **Courses:** ESL. **Daily hours for:** Classes 4. **College credit:** 3/crse, total 3.
Intl program focus: Lang Culture. **Locations:** Europe Mexico/Central_America South_America.
Focus: Span. **Features:** Swim.
Fees 2011: Res $3999-7199 (+airfare), 2-4 wks. Aid 2007 (Need): $6999.
Housing: Dorms Hotels. **Swimming:** Pool.
Est 1982. Inc. Ses: 9. **Wks/ses:** 2-4. Operates June-Aug.

The program combines Spanish immersion with travel in Spain, Costa Rica or Peru. Language study takes place in the morning, leaving afternoons for cultural outings or trips to the beach. Boys and girls may earn three credits of college language credit in certain programs. Students devote significant periods of time to travel within the host country.

TUFTS UNIVERSITY
ADVENTURES IN VETERINARY MEDICINE
Res — Coed Ages 15-18; Day — Coed 13-21

North Grafton, MA 01536. Cummings School of Veterinary Med, 200 Westboro Rd.
Tel: 508-839-7962. Fax: 508-839-7952.
www.tufts.edu/vet/avm   E-mail: avm@tufts.edu
Grades 8-Col. Adm: Selective. **Appl**—Fee $40. Due: Rolling. Transcript, essay, 2 recs.
Enr: 20-40. **Enr cap:** 20-40. **Staff:** Admin 2. Couns 5.
Type of instruction: Enrich.
Focus: Veterinary_Med. **Features:** Swim.
Fees 2012: Res $2990 (+$100), 2 wks. Day $700-1920, 1-2 wks. Aid 2006 (Need):
$12,000.
Housing: Dorms. **Swimming:** Pool.
Est 1991. Nonprofit. **Ses:** 9. **Wks/ses:** 1-2. Operates Apr-Aug.

This academic career exploration program allows boys and girls to learn about veterinary school and consider alternatives within the veterinary profession. Students spend about half the day attending lecture-style classes, the other half involved in hands-on activities. AVM offers separate middle school (entering grades 8 and 9; day only), high school (entering grades 10-PG; boarding and day), and college (rising sophomores, juniors and seniors; day only) programs.

UNITED STATES COAST GUARD ACADEMY
ACADEMY INTRODUCTION MISSION
Res — Coed Ages 17-18

New London, CT 06320. 31 Mohegan Ave. Tel: 860-444-8500, 800-883-8724.
Fax: 860-701-6700.
www.uscga.edu   E-mail: aim@uscga.edu
Grade 12. Adm: Selective. Admitted: 37%. Priority: URM. **Appl**—Fee $0. Due: Apr. Transcript, essay, teacher rec.
Enr: 167. **Enr cap:** 167. Non-White: 16%. **Fac 12.** Prof 12. **Staff:** Admin 23. Couns 65.
Type of instruction: Enrich. **Daily hours for:** Classes 4.
Focus: Col_Prep Engineering Leadership. **Features:** Boating Milit_Trng Sail Seamanship Work Aerobics Baseball Basketball Cross-country Soccer Softball Swim Ultimate_Frisbee Volleyball.
Fees 2012: Res $400, 1 wk. Aid 2009 (Need): $8750.
Housing: Dorms. Avg per room/unit: 2. **Swimming:** Pool.
Est 1955. Nonprofit. **Ses:** 3. **Wks/ses:** 1. Operates July.

AIM allows rising high school seniors to sample life at the US Coast Guard Academy while also completing an engineering project and engaging in military training. The physically demanding weeklong session approximates the undergraduate experience at the academy. Applicants must be in good health and physical condition and must not be colorblind, have asthma or have vision that is not correctable to 20/20. Roughly half of AIM graduates earn appointments to the academy.

UNITED STATES DEPARTMENT OF AGRICULTURE
AGDISCOVERY PROGRAM
Res — Coed Ages 12-17

Riverdale, MD 20737. APHIS, Office of the Admin, 4700 River Rd, Unit 92.
Tel: 301-734-6312. Fax: 301-734-3698.
www.aphis.usda.gov/agdiscovery   E-mail: terry.a.henson@aphis.usda.gov
Terry Henson, Coord.
Adm: Selective. **Appl**—Due: Apr. Essay, 3 recs.

Type of instruction: Enrich.
Locations: AL AR AZ DE FL GA HI IO KY MD MI NC SC.
Focus: Agriculture Environ_Sci Sci Veterinary_Med.
Fees 2012: Free. Res 2-3 wks.
Housing: Dorms.
Est 2002. Ses: 13. **Wks/ses:** 2-3. Operates June-July.

Hosted on approximately a dozen college campuses, AgDiscovery allows participants to preview college life while learning about careers in animal science, veterinary medicine, agribusiness and plant pathology from university professors, practicing veterinarians and government professionals. Students gain experience through hands-on labs, workshops, field trips, and other group and team-building activities. While one program enrolls boys and girls ages 12-16, all other programs accept applicants ages 14-17.

UNIVERSITY OF ALASKA-ANCHORAGE
DELLA KEATS HEALTH SCIENCES SUMMER PROGRAM
Res — Coed Ages 17-18

Anchorage, AK 99508. UAA WWAMI School of Medical Ed, 3211 Providence Dr, HSB 301. Tel: 907-786-1019. Fax: 907-786-4700.
www.uaa.alaska.edu/wwami/programs   E-mail: della-keats@uaa.alaska.edu
Ian van Tets, Dir.
Grades 12-PG (younger if qualified). Adm: Selective. Priority: Low-income. **Appl**—Fee $0. Due: Apr. Transcript, 2 recs, standardized test scores.
Enr: 20. **Enr cap:** 20.
Type of instruction: Enrich.
Focus: Med/Healthcare.
Fees 2012: Free (in-state residents). Res 6 wks.
Housing: Dorms.
Nonprofit. **Ses:** 1. **Wks/ses:** 6. Operates June-July.

Students who have recently completed grades 11 and 12 may apply to this free program if they meet one or more of the following qualifications: are economically disadvantaged or come from an ethnic minority background, live in a rural area of Alaska, are a first-generation American or speak English as a second language. The six-week program encourages students to pursue their interest in a career in medicine or another healthcare field through educational enrichment activities and job shadowing. Boys and girls also gain an introduction to college life. During the session, students complete a public health research project; rising seniors will share these projects with their home communities during the following school year.

UNIVERSITY OF ALASKA-FAIRBANKS
ALASKA SUMMER RESEARCH ACADEMY
Res — Coed Ages 13-18; Day — Coed 14-18

Fairbanks, AK 99775. College of Natural Sci & Math, PO Box 755940.
Tel: 907-474-7077. Fax: 907-474-5101.
www.uaf.edu/asra   E-mail: jdrake@gi.alaska.edu
Jeff Drake, Dir. Student contact: Kate Pendleton, E-mail: fnkp@uaf.edu.
Grades 8-12. Adm: Selective. **Appl**—Fee $50. Due: Rolling. Essay, 2 references.
Enr cap: 120.
College credit: 1.
Focus: Archaeol Astron Comp_Sci Engineering Marine_Bio/Stud Math Med/Healthcare Sci Creative_Writing Photog.
Fees 2009: Res $1200-1600, 2 wks. Day $800, 2 wks. Aid (Need).
Housing: Dorms.
Ses: 1. **Wks/ses:** 2. Operates July.

Emphasizing exploration and creativity, ASRA immerses students in a single subject for two weeks of intensive, hands-on research. Topics vary by year; past subjects have included archaeology, biomedicine, creative writing, earth and space science, earthquakes, engineering design, photography, fisheries, energy and climate change, physiology, marine biology, marine mammals, programming and robotics. Certain remote modules require participants to travel off-campus and stay at camp sites or research facilities.

UNIVERSITY OF ARIZONA ASTRONOMY CAMP
Res — Coed Ages 13-18

Tucson, AZ 85721. 933 N Cherry Ave. Tel: 520-621-4079, 800-232-8278. Fax: 520-621-9843.
www.astronomycamp.org   E-mail: dmccarthy@as.arizona.edu
Don McCarthy, Dir.
Grades 7-12 (younger if qualified). Adm: Somewhat selective. Admitted: 95%. **Appl—** Fee $0. Due: Rolling. Essay, teacher rec.
Enr: 30. **Enr cap:** 30. Intl: 90%. Non-White: 10%. **Fac 9.** Prof 2. Col/grad students 7. **Staff:** Admin 2. Couns 10.
Type of instruction: Adv Enrich. **Courses:** Environ_Sci Geol Crafts. **Avg class size:** 30.
Focus: Astron. **Features:** Aviation/Aero Hiking Volleyball.
Fees 2012: Res $950-975, 1 wk. Aid 2006 (Need): $4000.
Housing: Dorms.
Est 1988. Nonprofit. **Ses:** 2. **Wks/ses:** 1. Operates June.

An astronomy program that emphasizes hands-on learning, the camp has students operate research telescopes, keep nighttime hours, interact with scientists and interpret their own observations. Facilities at the Mount Lemmon site include several telescopes and direct imaging, solar imaging and spectroscopy equipment. Applicants need not possess any prior knowledge of astronomy.

UNIVERSITY OF ARIZONA
BUSINESS CAREERS AWARENESS PROGRAM
Res — Coed Ages 16-18

Tucson, AZ 85721. McClelland Hall 301, PO Box 210108. Tel: 520-621-3713. Fax: 520-621-3742.
www.accounting.eller.arizona.edu/bcap   E-mail: bcap@eller.arizona.edu
Leslie Eldenburg, Dir.
Student contact: Katie Cordova Maxwell, E-mail: maxwellk@email.arizona.edu.
Grade 12 (younger if qualified). Adm: Somewhat selective. Priority: URM. **Appl—**Fee $0. Due: Mar. Transcript, 2 recs.
Enr cap: 30. **Fac 6.** Prof 6. **Staff:** Couns 7.
Type of instruction: Enrich.
Focus: Bus/Fin.
Fees 2012: Free. Res 1 wk.
Housing: Dorms. Avg per room/unit: 2.
Ses: 1. **Wks/ses:** 1. Operates June.

Sponsored by the University of Arizona and the accounting firm Ernst & Young, BCAP provides students from populations that are underrepresented in college accounting classes with an opportunity to explore the field. The program features introductory accounting, finance and economics classes; a case study competition; visits to local nonprofit organizations and corporations; and etiquette training for formal dining.

UNIVERSITY OF ARIZONA SUMMER ENGINEERING ACADEMY
Res — Coed Ages 14-18

Tucson, AZ 85721. Engineering Bldg, Rm 200, PO Box 210020. Tel: 520-621-6032.
Fax: 520-621-9995.
www.engineering.arizona.edu/future   E-mail: gaxiola@engr.arizona.edu
Grades 9-12. Adm: Selective. **Appl**—Fee $10. Due: Apr. Transcript, rec.
Type of instruction: Enrich.
Focus: Engineering.
Fees 2009: Res $485, 1 wk.
Housing: Dorms.
Ses: 3. **Wks/ses:** 1. Operates June.

SEA serves as a weeklong investigation into engineering careers. Classroom sessions with university professors address topics ranging from the fundamentals of aerodynamics to materials used in engineering. Working in teams, students design aerodynamic cars and devices, then test their models in a specially built wind tunnel. During the program, participants learn to use three-dimensional computer-aided design software. The first session hosts rising freshmen and sophomores, while the second and third sessions enroll rising juniors and seniors.

UNIVERSITY OF CALIFORNIA-DAVIS YOUNG SCHOLARS PROGRAM
Res — Coed Ages 16-17

Davis, CA 95616. School of Ed, 1 Shields Ave. Tel: 530-574-0289.
http://ysp.ucdavis.edu
J. Richard Pomeroy, Dir.
Grades 11-12. Adm: Selective. **Appl**—Due: Mar. Transcript, sci teacher rec, another rec.
Enr: 40. **Enr cap:** 40.
Type of instruction: Adv. Grades. **College credit:** 5.
Focus: Environ_Sci Sci.
Fees 2009: Res $5000, 6 wks. Aid (Need).
Housing: Dorms.
Ses: 1. **Wks/ses:** 6. Operates June-Aug.

This apprentice-level research opportunity for rising high school juniors and seniors involves extensive laboratory experience (85 percent of the session time). The program focuses on original research that includes experimental design, data collection, statistical analysis, and the communication of results through both written and oral means. YSP's six-week session features morning lectures, group study, educational excursions, seminars, and individual and group instruction time. Students complete research notebooks, write an article describing the research project and its conclusions, make a presentation of the individual project at a research symposium and present their research to pupils at the home high school.

UNIVERSITY OF CALIFORNIA-IRVINE AMERICAN INDIAN SUMMER ACADEMY
Res — Coed Ages 14-18

Irvine, CA 92697. Center for Educational Partnerships, 407 Social Science Tower.
Tel: 949-824-0291. Fax: 949-824-8219.
www.airp.uci.edu/aisa.php   E-mail: yleon@uci.edu
Yolanda Leon, Coord.
Grades 9-12. Adm: Selective. Prereqs: GPA 2.5. **Appl**—Fee $0. Due: Apr. Transcript, essay.
Type of instruction: Enrich.
Focus: Cultural_Stud.
Fees 2012: Free (in-state residents). Res 2 wks.

Housing: Dorms.
Ses: 1. **Wks/ses:** 1. Operates July.

Students interested in contributing to the American Indian community participate in interactive presentations from various UC-Irvine departments, cultural workshops and activities, field trips and social events. Group projects identify and address an important issue pertaining to the American Indian community, and boys and girls present their work at a closing symposium. AISA participants receive follow-up mentorship from university staff and students throughout their remaining high school years.

UNIVERSITY OF CALIFORNIA-IRVINE
AMERICAN INDIAN SUMMER INSTITUTE
IN COMPUTER SCIENCES
Res — Coed Ages 14-18

Irvine, CA 92697. Center for Educational Partnerships, 407 Social Science Tower.
Tel: 949-824-0291. Fax: 949-824-8219.
www.airp.uci.edu/aisics.php   E-mail: yleon@uci.edu
Yolanda Leon, Coord.
Grades 9-12. Adm: Selective. Prereqs: GPA 2.5. **Appl**—Fee $0. Due: Apr. Transcript, personal statement, rec.
Type of instruction: Enrich. **Courses:** Comm.
Focus: Comp_Sci Cultural_Stud.
Fees 2012: Free. Res 2 wks.
Housing: Dorms.
Ses: 1. **Wks/ses:** 2. Operates June-July.

AISICS participants work with professors, college students and invited community members to develop interactive story projects that combine computer game technology with traditional American Indian culture. Computer science courses, interactive presentations, field trips and social activities are part of the program. Scholarships address transportation expenses for those accepted into this nationwide program. AISICS pupils receive follow-up mentorship from UC-Irvine staff and students throughout their remaining high school years.

UNIVERSITY OF CALIFORNIA-LOS ANGELES
SCI/ART NANOLAB SUMMER INSTITUTE
Res and Day — Coed Ages 16-18

Los Angeles, CA 90095. California NanoSystems Inst, 570 Westwood Plaza, Rm 5419. Tel: 310-983-1026. Fax: 310-825-9233.
http://artsci.ucla.edu/summer   E-mail: sciart@cnsi.ucla.edu
Adam Stieg, Dir.
Grades 11-12 (younger if qualified). Adm: Selective. Admitted: 75%. **Appl**—Fee $0. Due: May. Essay, teacher/counselor rec.
Enr: 45. **Enr cap:** 45. Intl: 17%. Non-White: 40%. **Fac 6.** Col/grad students 6. **Staff:** Admin 3. Res 4.
Type of instruction: Adv Undergrad. **Courses:** Biotech Nanotech Web_Design Fine_Arts Media Photog. **Avg class size:** 15. **Daily hours for:** Classes 8. Study 2. Rec 2. Homework. Grades. **College credit:** 4/crse, total 4.
Focus: Sci. **Features:** Swim.
Fees 2011: Res $2810 (+$200), 2 wks. Day $1900 (+$200), 2 wks.
Housing: Dorms. Avg per room/unit: 2. **Swimming:** Pool. Campus facilities avail.
Est 2008. Nonprofit. **Ses:** 1. **Wks/ses:** 2. Operates June-July.

Conducted at UCLA's California NanoSystems Institute, this rigorous precollege program is a joint venture between the institute and Design Media Arts at UCLA that enables high school juniors and seniors to examine the impact of new sciences (such as bio- and nanotechnology) on contemporary art and popular culture through the completion of a credit-bearing, pass-fail course. The two-week program comprises 80 hours of required lab time, lectures and discussions; 40 hours of field trip time; and daily written compositions that reflect upon lectures and the daily science topic. During the session, boys and girls further benefit from their interactions with undergraduate science students in two different programs: one dealing with design and media, the other with cutting-edge scientific research.

UNIVERSITY OF CHICAGO
RESEARCH IN THE BIOLOGICAL SCIENCES
Res — Coed Ages 14-18

Chicago, IL 60637. Summer Session Office, 1427 E 60th St, 2nd Fl. Tel: 773-834-3792. Fax: 773-834-0549.
http://summer.uchicago.edu/ribs.cfm   E-mail: summerhs@uchicago.edu
Christopher Schonbaum & Rosemary Zaragoza, Prgm Dirs.
Grades 11-12. Adm: Very selective. **Appl**—Fee $40. Due: May. Transcript, essay, 2 recs.
Enr: 30. **Enr cap:** 36. Intl: 6%. **Fac** 2. Prof 2. **Staff:** Admin 3. Couns 6.
Type of instruction: Adv Undergrad. **Daily hours for:** Classes 7. Homework. Tests. Grades. **College credit:** 6.
Focus: Sci. **Features:** Swim.
Fees 2011: Res $8541 (+$740), 4 wks. Aid (Merit & Need).
Housing: Dorms. Avg per room/unit: 2. **Swimming:** Lake. Campus facilities avail.
Ses: 1. **Wks/ses:** 4. Operates June-July.

This intensive training program exposes students to a broad range of biological research laboratory techniques. Using a project-based approach, the course progresses from a survey of basic lab procedures to the application of current molecular techniques in developmental biology and microbiology. Lectures provide background and introduce new concepts, but pupils spend most of their time in labs working on two main projects: mechanisms of antibiotic resistance in bacteria and genetic regulation of development. Students keep lab notebooks, make group presentations and participate in a research forum. Participants earn college credit equivalent to two undergraduate courses.   **See Also Page 32**

UNIVERSITY OF CHICAGO STONES AND BONES PROGRAM
Res — Coed Ages 15-18

Chicago, IL 60637. Summer Session Office, 1427 E 60th St, 2nd Fl. Tel: 773-834-3792. Fax: 773-834-0549.
http://summer.uchicago.edu/stones-and-bones.cfm
E-mail: summerhs@uchicago.edu
Lance Grande, Dir.
Grades 10-12. Adm: Selective. **Appl**—Fee $40. Due: May. Transcript, essay, 2 recs.
Enr: 7. **Enr cap:** 20. **Fac** 1. Prof 1. **Staff:** Admin 3. Couns 1.
Courses: Geol. **Daily hours for:** Classes 7. Homework. Tests. Grades. **College credit:** 6.
Travel: WY.
Focus: Paleontol. **Features:** Swim.
Fees 2011: Res $9526 (+$740), 4 wks.
Housing: Dorms Tents. **Swimming:** Lake. Campus facilities avail.
Ses: 1. **Wks/ses:** 4. Operates June-July.

Stones and Bones begins with a weeklong introduction to basic geology, paleontological method, stratigraphy and fossil preparation at the Field Museum in Chicago. Students then join an ongoing expedition at the Green River Project in Wyoming, spending two weeks prospecting and evaluating fossils from the Cenozoic Period. Upon their return to Chicago, pupils catalog and analyze their discoveries in the Field Museum's preparation labs. Participants earn college credit equivalent to two undergraduate courses.   **See Also Page 32**

UNIVERSITY OF DAYTON
WOMEN IN ENGINEERING SUMMER CAMP
Res — Girls Ages 15-18

Dayton, OH 45469. 300 College Park. Tel: 937-229-3296. Fax: 937-229-2756.
www.udayton.edu/engineering/wie.php   E-mail: wie@udayton.edu
Annette Packard, Coord.
Grades 10-12. Adm: Somewhat selective. Admitted: 99%. Prereqs: GPA 2.5. **Appl**—Fee $0. Due: June.
Enr: 78. **Enr cap:** 80. **Fac 10.** Prof 10. **Staff:** Res 10.
Type of instruction: Preview.
Focus: Engineering. **Features:** Climbing_Wall Swim.
Fees 2011: Res $600, 1 wk. Aid 2010 (Need): $1425.
Housing: Dorms. Avg per room/unit: 2. **Swimming:** Pool. Campus facilities avail.
Est 1974. Nonprofit. Roman Catholic. **Ses:** 1. **Wks/ses:** 1. Operates July.

WIE enables young women to explore careers in engineering through hands-on activities. Guided by faculty from the University of Dayton School of Engineering, girls conduct experiments in engineering. Participants visit an industry job site, meet women working professionally as engineers and receive one-on-one advice from female engineering students at the University of Dayton, who serve as camp counselors. Residence hall living offers a preview of college life.

UNIVERSITY OF DELAWARE
FAME/UNITE/MERIT/UD SUMMER RESIDENTIAL PROGRAM
Res — Coed Ages 16-18

Newark, DE 19716. College of Engineering, 141 Dupont Hall. Tel: 302-831-6315.
Fax: 302-831-7399.
www.engr.udel.edu/rise/fame   E-mail: mlbrown@udel.edu
Marianne T. Johnson, Dir. Student contact: Michele L. Brown.
Grades 11-12. Adm: Selective. Admitted: 65%. Priority: URM. Prereqs: GPA 3.0. **Appl**— Fee $0. Due: Apr. Transcript, essay, 2 recs.
Enr: 40. **Enr cap:** 40. Non-White: 98%. **Fac 9.** Prof 3. Col/grad students 2. K-12 staff 4.
Staff: Admin 2. Couns 8.
Type of instruction: Enrich Undergrad. **Courses:** Eng. **Avg class size:** 11. **Daily hours for:** Classes 3½. Study 4½. Rec 3. Homework. Tests. Grades.
Focus: Engineering Math Sci.
Fees 2011: Res $100 (+$40-60), 4 wks.
Housing: Dorms. Avg per room/unit: 2.
Est 1980. Nonprofit. **Ses:** 1. **Wks/ses:** 4. Operates June-July.

Although students of all backgrounds may apply, this program for high school upperclassmen seeks to facilitate increased participation of African-American, Latino and Native American youth in engineering and other science professions. Course work, which is conducted in a demanding academic setting, consists of accelerated enrichment classes in math, science, English and engineering. Personal/professional development workshops, college selection advice, and information on engineering and other science professions complement academics. Participants should plan on attending all four weeks of the program; students go home each weekend.

UNIVERSITY OF EVANSVILLE OPTIONS
Res — Girls Ages 12-17

Evansville, IN 47722. 1800 Lincoln Ave. Tel: 812-488-2651, 800-423-8633.
Fax: 812-488-2780.
http://options.evansville.edu   E-mail: tn2@evansville.edu

Phil Gerhart, Dir. Student contact: Tina Newman.
Grades 7-12. Adm: Somewhat selective. Admitted: 95%. **Appl**—Fee $0. Due: Rolling. Transcript, essay.
Enr: 20. **Enr cap:** 20. Non-White: 30%. **Fac 11.** Prof 7. Col/grad students 4. **Staff:** Admin 3. Res 4.
Type of instruction: Enrich. **Courses:** Comp_Sci. **Daily hours for:** Classes 8. Rec 6.
Focus: Engineering. **Features:** Rock_Climb Swim Volleyball.
Fees 2012: Res $250-500, 1 wk. Aid (Need).
Housing: Dorms. **Swimming:** Pool. Campus facilities avail.
Est 1992. Nonprofit. Methodist. **Ses:** 2. **Wks/ses:** 1. Operates June.

Conducted by University of Evansville faculty and staff, UE Options consists of two sessions for girls interested in learning more about engineering as an area of potential future study. Middle school sessions enroll pupils about to enter grades 7-9, while the high school Options program accepts girls preparing for grades 9-12. Course work comprises short classes, plant tours to observe engineers and computer scientists at work, and recreational pursuits with participants and college student counselors. Options also acquaints students with career possibilities for individuals with a degree in engineering or computer science.

UNIVERSITY OF FLORIDA
STUDENT SCIENCE TRAINING PROGRAM
Res — Coed Ages 16-18

Gainesville, FL 32611. 334 Yon Hall, PO Box 112010. Tel: 352-392-2310.
Fax: 352-392-2344.
www.cpet.ufl.edu/sstp   E-mail: sstp@cpet.ufl.edu
Deborah Paulin, Admin.
Grades 11-12. Adm: Selective. **Appl**—Due: Mar. Transcript, rec.
Enr: 88. **Enr cap:** 100. **Fac 80. Staff:** Admin 5. Couns 10.
Type of instruction: Adv. **Courses:** Archaeol Astron Computers Ecol Engineering Environ_Sci Geol Marine_Bio/Stud Med/Healthcare Speech. **High school & college credit:** 6.
Focus: Sci. **Features:** Social_Servs Work Basketball Swim Tennis Volleyball Racquetball.
Fees 2011: Res $3500 (+$100-200), 7 wks. Aid (Need).
Housing: Dorms. Avg per room/unit: 2. **Swimming:** Pool. Campus facilities avail.
Est 1959. Nonprofit. **Ses:** 1. **Wks/ses:** 7. Operates June-July.

SSTP introduces students to various disciplines of science, medicine and engineering to aid them in choosing career fields. Students spend more than two dozen hours a week participating in active projects with research professors in on-campus laboratories. Lectures, field trips and seminars supplement laboratory participation and class instruction. Topics assigned cover a broad area of scientific study; some students will do field research, some bench research and some computer research. Weekend activities include sports and social activities. Students may earn up to six college credits, and high school credit may be available to Florida students.

UNIVERSITY OF FLORIDA SUMMER JOURNALISM INSTITUTE
Res — Coed Ages 15-18

Gainesville, FL 32611. 2070 Weimer Hall, College of Journ & Communications, PO Box 118400. Tel: 941-661-0021.
www.jou.ufl.edu/sji   E-mail: sji@jou.ufl.edu
Meredith Cochie, Dir.
Grades 10-12. Adm: Selective. **Appl**—Due: Rolling. Advisor/prin rec.
Type of instruction: Enrich. **Courses:** Photog.
Focus: Writing/Journ.
Fees 2011: Res $500, 1 wk.
Housing: Dorms.

Nonprofit. **Ses:** 1. **Wks/ses:** 1. Operates June.

This six-day program offers specialized classes in writing, editing, photography, broadcasting and Web design. Guest speakers address such topics as communications law and the role of journalism in society. University of Florida faculty members, high school publications advisers and journalism graduate students serve as course instructors.

UNIVERSITY OF HOUSTON
MENTORING AND ENRICHMENT SEMINAR
IN ENGINEERING TRAINING
Res — Coed Ages 17-18

Houston, TX 77204. E301 Engineering Bldg 2. Tel: 713-743-4222. Fax: 713-743-4228.
www.egr.uh.edu/promes/camps   E-mail: promes@egr.uh.edu
Grade 12. Adm: Selective. **Appl**—Fee $0. Due: Apr. Transcript, test scores, essay, rec.
Enr: 100.
Type of instruction: Enrich.
Focus: Engineering.
Fees 2009: Res $200, 1 wk. Aid (Need).
Housing: Dorms.
Ses: 2. **Wks/ses:** 1. Operates June-July.

MESET introduces students to various disciplines of engineering. The project-based curriculum features a team competition in engineering design. Site visits to Houston-area engineering firms, panel discussions by working engineers and current engineering students, and activities at the campus sports and recreation center round out the program. Texas residents receive admissions priority, and MESET actively encourages young women and underrepresented minorities to apply.

UNIVERSITY OF IDAHO
JUNIOR ENGINEERING MATH AND SCIENCE
SUMMER WORKSHOP
Res — Coed Ages 16-19

Moscow, ID 83844. PO Box 441011. Tel: 208-885-6479, 888-884-3246.
    Fax: 208-885-6645.
www.uidaho.edu/engr/jems   E-mail: jems@uidaho.edu
Richard J. Nielsen, Dir. Student contact: Sue Branting.
Grades 12-PG. Adm: Selective. Prereqs: GPA 3.0. **Appl**—Fee $0. Due: May. Transcript,
    resume, essay.
Enr: 37. **Enr cap:** 60. Intl: 1%. Non-White: 31%. **Fac 3. Staff:** Admin 5.
Type of instruction: Adv. **Courses:** Comp_Sci. **Avg class size:** 30. **Daily hours for:**
    Classes 7. Study 4. Rec 1. Homework. Tests. Grades. **College credit:** 2.
Focus: Engineering.
Fees 2010: Res $750, 2 wks. Aid 2009 (Need): $12,000.
Housing: Apartments Dorms.
Nonprofit. **Ses:** 1. **Wks/ses:** 2. Operates July.

JEMS introduces high school upperclassmen to engineering through the study of real-world problems within their technical and social contexts. The curriculum includes lectures and hands-on activities in leadership, engineering design, modeling and computer-aided drawing. Classes specific to an annual design project, such as environmental engineering, computer programming, robotics and computer graphics, are also offered. Laboratory work, computer exercises, guest speakers, field trips and recreational activities round out the program.

UNIVERSITY OF ILLINOIS
COLLEGE OF AGRICULTURAL, CONSUMER
AND ENVIRONMENTAL SCIENCES
RESEARCH APPRENTICE PROGRAM
Res — Coed Ages 14-18

Urbana, IL 61801. 123 Mumford Hall, 1301 W Gregory Dr. Tel: 217-333-3380. Fax: 217-244-6537.
www.summerprograms.aces.illinois.edu   E-mail: jthomps5@illinois.edu
Jesse Thompson, Coord.
Grades 10-12. Adm: Selective. Priority: Low-income. URM. Prereqs: GPA 3.0. **Appl**—Fee $25. Due: Mar. Transcript, 2 recs.
Enr: 85. Enr cap: 85. Fac 5. Staff: Admin 2.
Type of instruction: Adv Enrich Rev SAT/ACT_Prep. **Courses:** Engineering MathVeterinary_Med. **Avg class size:** 20. **Daily hours for:** Classes 4. Study 4. Rec 2. Homework.
Focus: Environ_Sci Sci. **Features:** Swim.
Fees 2011: Free. Res 2-7 wks.
Housing: Dorms. **Swimming:** Pool.
Est 1989. Nonprofit. **Ses:** 2. **Wks/ses:** 4-7. Operates June-Aug.

The tuition-free Research Apprentice Program provides career exploration opportunities for students in the top quarter of their class who represent underserved or economically disadvantaged groups. RAP I, a four-week session for students entering grades 10-11, explores career pathways in either food; human and environmental sciences; or children, families and education. Participants visit corporate facilities, attend seminars and minicourses and work in teams to solve problems. RAP II is an intensive, seven-week laboratory and academic program for previous RAP I students and others entering grade 12 who have an interest in food, agricultural and environmental sciences. Laboratory research topics include plant genetics, animal physiology, nutritional sciences, food chemistry and engineering, veterinary medicine, computer imaging and environmental studies.

UNIVERSITY OF ILLINOIS
GIRLS' ADVENTURES IN MATHEMATICS,
ENGINEERING AND SCIENCE
Res — Girls Ages 14-17

Urbana, IL 61801. 210A Engineering Hall, MC 272, 1308 W Green St.
Tel: 217-244-3817. Fax: 217-244-4974.
www.engineering.illinois.edu/wie/games   E-mail: wie@illinois.edu
Kris Ackerman, Dir.
Grades 9-11. Adm: Selective. **Appl**—Fee $0. Due: Apr. Transcript, teacher rec, personal statement.
Enr: 235. Enr cap: 250. Non-White: 40%. Staff: Admin 3.
Type of instruction: Adv. **Courses:** Math Robotics Crafts Dance Music. **Avg class size:** 18. **Daily hours for:** Classes 7. Rec 3.
Focus: Comp_Sci Engineering Sci. **Features:** Swim.
Fees 2011: Res $850-1150, 1 wk. Aid (Need).
Housing: Dorms. **Swimming:** Pool.
Est 1998. Nonprofit. **Ses:** 1. **Wks/ses:** 1. Operates July.

Conducted at the University of Illinois-Urbana, GAMES enables high school girls to explore science and engineering through demonstrations, classroom presentations, hands-on activities and meetings with professional women in relevant fields. The Structures program introduces girls entering grades 9 and 10 to civil engineering basics, and campers design and construct bridges, water towers or boats. Also serving girls entering grades 9 and 10, the robotics camp explores computer technology and hands-on robotic development. The bio-imaging program for girls entering grades 9-11 explores biomedical imaging, optics and image analysis. In the chemical engineering program, girls entering grades 9-11 learn about developing medical advances and alternative energy sources in University of Illinois laboratories. Three programs serve students entering grades 10-12: one focusing on aerospace engineering; another on electrical engineering; and a third on energy generation, conversion and efficiency.

UNIVERSITY OF IOWA LIFE SCIENCE SUMMER PROGRAM
Res — Coed Ages 14-15

Iowa City, IA 52242. 24 Phillips Hall. Tel: 319-335-3555. Fax: 319-353-2537.
http://cde.uiowa.edu/index.php/lssp-summer-residential-program.html
E-mail: cde@uiowa.edu
Grades 9-10. Adm: Very selective. **Appl**—Fee $0. Due: Apr. Transcript, essay, rec.
Type of instruction: Enrich. **Daily hours for:** Classes 6.
Focus: Sci.
Fees 2011: Res $50, 2 wks.
Housing: Dorms.
Nonprofit. **Ses:** 1. **Wks/ses:** 2. Operates July.

Motivated high schoolers who have demonstrated significant achievement in science may take part in this low-cost, intensive program, which provides hands-on laboratory instruction and classroom study of a wide range of topics in the area of developmental biology. The curriculum also integrates health issues and current events. After spending mornings and afternoons in class or on field trips, students participate in mandatory academic activities (including career panels, faculty seminars and ethics discussions) or required social activities.

UNIVERSITY OF KANSAS
JAYHAWK DEBATE INSTITUTE
Res — Coed Ages 15-18

Lawrence, KS 66045. Dept of Communication Stud, 1440 Jayhawk Blvd, 102 Bailey Hall. Tel: 785-864-9893. Fax: 785-864-5203.
www.ku.edu/~coms3/camp   E-mail: jayhawkdebateinstitute@gmail.com
Grades 10-12. Adm: Selective. **Appl**—Due: Rolling.
Enr cap: 64-96. **Fac 7.**
Type of instruction: Enrich.
Focus: Debate.
Fees 2009: Res $1100-1350, 2-3 wks. Day $650-850, 2-3 wks.
Housing: Dorms.
Ses: 2. **Wks/ses:** 2-3. Operates June-July.

JDI offers two-week intermediate and advanced and three-week advanced policy debate workshops. Programming includes topic lectures; classes in debate theory, case construction, strategy and refutation; research at the University of Kansas libraries; and practice debates and tournaments.

UNIVERSITY OF MARYLAND
DISCOVERING ENGINEERING
Res — Coed Ages 16-17

College Park, MD 20742. 1131 Glenn L Martin Hall. Tel: 301-405-0287. Fax: 301-314-9867.
www.ursp.umd.edu/summer/discovering-engineering.html
E-mail: summerengr@umd.edu
Bruk Berhane, Dir.

Grades 11-12. Adm: Selective. **Appl**—Due: Apr. Transcript, rec, personal statement.
Enr: 30. **Enr cap:** 30.
Type of instruction: Enrich.
Focus: Engineering.
Fees 2011: Res $1000, 1 wk.
Housing: Dorms. Campus facilities avail.
Nonprofit. **Ses:** 2. **Wks/ses:** 1. Operates July-Aug.

Rising high school juniors and seniors with a strong interest in engineering, math, science or a combination thereof sample college living as they explore different engineering disciplines during this weeklong session. Programming consists of lab work and demonstrations, lectures, discussions, computer instruction and a team design project. Students visit each of the engineering majors to learn more about specific departments and their projects.

UNIVERSITY OF MASSACHUSETTS MEDICAL SCHOOL HIGH SCHOOL HEALTH CAREERS PROGRAM
Res — Coed Ages 16-18

Worcester, MA 01655. Office of Outreach Prgms, S3-104, 55 Lake Ave N.
Tel: 508-856-2707, 877-395-3149. Fax: 508-856-6540.
www.umassmed.edu/outreach/hshcp.aspx
E-mail: outreach.programs@umassmed.edu
Robert E. Layne, Dir.
Grades 11-12. Adm: Very selective. Priority: Low-income. URM. **Appl**—Fee $0. Due: Mar. Transcript, essay, 3 recs, interview.
Type of instruction: Enrich Study_Skills. **Courses:** Comp_Sci Eng Math Sci.
Focus: Med/Healthcare.
Fees 2012: Free (in-state residents). Res 4 wks.
Housing: Dorms.
Ses: 1. **Wks/ses:** 4. Operates July.

HSHCP exposes Massachusetts high schoolers from backgrounds lacking strong representation in medicine to healthcare professions and biomedical and biotechnology careers. Classroom sessions address language arts skills, math, science/biology and information technology. Students also take part in internships with physicians and other healthcare professionals. Seminars provide information about college application and financial aid procedures.

UNIVERSITY OF MIAMI SUMMER SCHOLAR PROGRAMS
Res — Coed Ages 16-17

Coral Gables, FL 33124. PO Box 248005. Tel: 305-284-4000. Fax: 305-284-6629.
www.miami.edu/ssp   E-mail: ssp.cstudies@miami.edu
Grades 11-12. Adm: Selective. Prereqs: GPA 3.0. **Appl**—Fee $35. Due: May. Transcript, essay, rec.
Enr: 196. **Fac 25. Staff:** Admin 1.
Type of instruction: Adv. **Courses:** Sports_Admin Sports_Med. **Avg class size:** 18. **Daily hours for:** Classes 6. Study 3. Rec 2. **High school & college credit:** 3/crse, total 6.
Focus: Bus/Fin Engineering Forensic_Sci Intl_Relations Marine_Bio/Stud Med/Healthcare Writing/Journ. **Features:** Community_Serv Swim.
Fees 2011: Res $5730, 3 wks.
Housing: Dorms. **Swimming:** Ocean Pool.
Est 1991. Nonprofit. **Ses:** 1. **Wks/ses:** 3. Operates June-July.

The programs, taught by university faculty, allow highly motivated rising high school juniors and seniors to pursue course work in the following areas: broadcast journalism, business, engineering, forensic investigation, health and medicine, international relations, marine science, sports administration and sports medicine. Guest speakers and visits to local sites relevant to the field of study supplement in-class work. Students earn three to six college credits, which are also accepted at many high schools. In addition to the disciplines mentioned above, the university conducts a program focusing on filmmaking (see separate listing for details).

UNIVERSITY OF MICHIGAN MEDICAL SCHOOL
SUMMER SCIENCE ACADEMY
Res — Coed Ages 16-17

Ann Arbor, MI 48109. 2919C Taubman Medical Library, 1135 Catherine St. Tel: 734-734-8185. Fax: 734-615-4828.
www.med.umich.edu/medschool/ssa   E-mail: umms.ssa@umich.edu
Yolanda Campbell, Dir.
Grades 11-12. Adm: Selective. **Appl**—Fee $0. Due: Mar. Transcript, 2 recs, personal statement.
Enr: 50.
Type of instruction: Enrich. **Courses:** Expository_Writing Sci.
Focus: Med/Healthcare.
Fees 2009: Res $1500 (+$50), 2 wks. Aid (Need).
Housing: Dorms.
Nonprofit. **Ses:** 1. **Wks/ses:** 2. Operates June.

Sponsored by the university's Diversity and Career Development Office, this enrichment program enables rising high school juniors and seniors from Michigan to preview medical school and college life. Current medical school and program alumni live in the dorms with SSA participants as they provide classroom tutoring, intellectual and social stimulation, one-on-one and small-group mentoring, and insight into college and medical school. During the day, pupils attend classes taught by experts in the field. Evening recreational pursuits include activities in the arts.

UNIVERSITY OF MICHIGAN
MICHIGAN MATH AND SCIENCE SCHOLARS
Res and Day — Coed Ages 15-17

Ann Arbor, MI 48109. 2082 East Hall, 530 Church St. Tel: 734-647-4466. Fax: 734-763-0937.
www.math.lsa.umich.edu/mmss   E-mail: mmss@umich.edu
Stephen DeBacker, Dir.
Grades 10-12. Adm: Selective. **Appl**—Fee $100. Due: Rolling. Transcript, rec, personal statement.
Type of instruction: Adv Enrich. **Courses:** Astron Ecol Environ_Sci Geol. **Avg class size:** 15.
Focus: Math Sci.
Fees 2009: Res $1700-3400 (+$100), 2-4 wks. Day $1000-2000 (+$100), 2-4 wks.
Housing: Dorms. Campus facilities avail.
Nonprofit. **Spons:** University of Michigan. **Ses:** 2. **Wks/ses:** 2. Operates June-July.

In classes of 15 students, MMSS exposes high schoolers to current developments and research in the sciences in a college setting. Each session features such course selections as astronomy; chemistry; ecology and evolutionary biology; geology; math, molecular, cellular and developmental biology; physics; environmental studies; and statistics. Students conduct research, work in computer labs and engage in fieldwork with their professors. Boys and girls take one course per session and may attend one or both two-week sessions.

UNIVERSITY OF MICHIGAN SUMMER ENGINEERING ACADEMY
Res — Coed Ages 15-18; Day — Coed 12-14

Ann Arbor, MI 48109. Center for Engineering Diversity & Outreach, 2121 Bonisteel Blvd, 153 Chrysler Ctr. **Tel:** 734-647-7120. **Fax:** 734-647-7011.
www.engin.umich.edu/diversity   E-mail: lucieh@umich.edu
Lucie Howell, Dir.
Grades 8-12. Adm: Selective. **Appl**—Fee $0. Due: Mar. Transcript, essay, 2 recs.
Enr: 30-60.
Type of instruction: Enrich Study_Skills. **Courses:** Math Sci.
Focus: Engineering.
Fees 2012: Res $100-300, 2 wks. Aid (Need).
Housing: Dorms. Avg per room/unit: 2.
Ses: 3. **Wks/ses:** 2. Operates June-Aug.

The university's summer precollege engineering offerings include the Summer Enrichment Program at the Michigan Engineering Zone, Michigan Introduction to Technology and Engineering (for rising sophomores and juniors) and the Summer College Engineering Exposure Program (for rising seniors). SEP at MEZ is a commuter program educating rising eighth and ninth graders about applied engineering. MITE classes address math, engineering concepts, communication skills and study skills, while guidance workshops focus on college admissions and financial aid. SCEEP exposes students to various engineering departments and covers the skills required as one transitions from high school to college.

UNIVERSITY OF MISSISSIPPI
LOTT LEADERSHIP INSTITUTE FOR HIGH SCHOOL STUDENTS
Res — Coed Ages 17-18

University, MS 38677. PO Box 9. **Tel:** 662-915-6614. **Fax:** 662-915-5138.
www.lottinst.olemiss.edu/Outreach/Summer_Inst.html
E-mail: jewilkin@olemiss.edu
Jason E. Wilkins, Dir.
Grade 12. Adm: Selective. Prereqs: GPA 3.2. **Appl**—Fee $0. Due: Jan. Transcript, 2 recs.
Enr: 20. **Enr cap:** 20.
Type of instruction: Adv. **Courses:** Leadership Public_Speak. **College credit:** 6.
Focus: Pol_Sci Leadership.
Fees 2009: Res $600, 5 wks.
Housing: Dorms.
Est 1990. Nonprofit. **Ses:** 2. **Wks/ses:** 5. Operates May-July.

Rising high school seniors who have been nominated by their high school principals. The program combines college course work in political science (for transferable college credit) with general college preparation. Participants have opportunities to meet college administrators, student leaders and community figures while engaged in current event debates, discussions and decision-making activities. The program concludes with a weeklong trip to Washington, DC, during which students observe the Federal Government, hear from national politicians and tour the Capitol.

UNIVERSITY OF NEW HAMPSHIRE PROJECT SMART
Res — Coed Ages 16-18

Durham, NH 03824. Rudman Hall, Rm 108. **Tel:** 603-862-3840. **Fax:** 603-862-4013.
www.smart.unh.edu   E-mail: sminocha@unh.edu
Subhash C. Minocha, Dir.
Grades 11-12. Adm: Selective. Priority: Low-income. **Appl**—Fee $0. Due: Rolling. Two recs.
Enr: 42. **Enr cap:** 60. **Intl:** 30%. **Fac 21.** Prof 21. **Staff:** Admin 5.

Type of instruction: Adv Enrich. **Courses:** Biotech Nanotech. **Avg class size:** 24. **Daily hours for:** Classes 7. Rec 3½. Homework. Grades. **College credit:** 4/crse, total 4. **Travel:** MA ME NH.
Focus: Environ_Sci Marine_Bio/Stud Sci. **Features:** Swim.
Fees 2012: Res $2700-3200 (+$100), 4 wks. Aid 2010 (Need): $25,000.
Housing: Dorms. Avg per room/unit: 2. **Swimming:** Pool. Campus facilities avail.
Est 1991. Nonprofit. Ses: 1. Wks/ses: 4. Operates July.

Students enrolled in the Science and Mathematics Achievement through Research Training summer institute take part in an interdisciplinary program that includes modules in biotechnology and nanotechnology, space science, and marine and environmental science. Boys and girls engage in advanced study through lectures, demonstrations, hands-on laboratory experiences, and field trips to museums and private laboratories, while also acquiring research skills through work with faculty and graduate students. During the session, pupils apply math and computer principles to science.

UNIVERSITY OF NEW ORLEANS
THE GLORIES OF FRANCE
Res — Coed Ages 16-17

Montpellier, France.
Contact (Year-round): International Ed, 2000 Lakeshore Dr, New Orleans, LA 70148.
   Tel: 504-280-7455. Fax: 504-280-7317.
www.inst.uno.edu/france   E-mail: gofmc@uno.edu
Marie Kaposchyn, Dir.
Grades 11-12. Adm: Selective. **Appl**—Fee $150. Due: Mar.
Enr: 50. Fac 10. Staff: Admin 8. Couns 8.
College credit.
Travel: Europe.
Focus: Fr. **Features:** Swim.
Fees 2012: Res $4395 (+airfare), 5 wks.
Housing: Dorms. Avg per room/unit: 1. **Swimming:** Pool.
Est 1973. Ses: 1. Wks/ses: 5. Operates July-Aug.

Four days per week, students spend mornings at this academic program taking college-level French courses or other classes (taught in English) relevant to their college studies. Ten proficiency tracks are available for French study. Leisure time and weekend activities include trips to Mediterranean beaches, an optional excursion to Barcelona, Spain, and recreational activities.

THE UNIVERSITY OF NORTHERN COLORADO
FRONTIERS OF SCIENCE INSTITUTE
Res — Coed Ages 15-18

Greeley, CO 80639. Campus Box 123. Tel: 970-351-2976. Fax: 970-351-1269.
www.mast.unco.edu/fsi   E-mail: lori.ball@unco.edu
Lori K. Ball, Prgm Admin.
Grades 11-12 (younger if qualified). Adm: Selective. Admitted: 62%. Prereqs: GPA 3.0.
Appl—Fee $0. Due: Apr. Transcript, 3 recs.
Enr: 23. Enr cap: 30. Intl: 10%. Non-White: 26%. **Fac 7.** Prof 2. Col/grad students 2. K-12 staff 2. Specialists 1. **Staff:** Admin 1. Couns 2.
Type of instruction: Adv. **Courses:** Astron Comp_Sci Engineering Environ_Sci Geol. **Avg class size:** 13. **Daily hours for:** Classes 4. Rec 4. Grades. **College credit:** 4/crse, total 4.
Focus: Sci. **Features:** Caving Hiking Ropes_Crse Wilderness_Camp Basketball Swim Volleyball.
Fees 2011: Res $800-3000, 6 wks. Aid 2009 (Merit & Need): $61,600.

Housing: Dorms. Avg per room/unit: 2. **Swimming:** Pool. Campus facilities avail. **Est 1959.** Nonprofit. **Ses:** 1. **Wks/ses:** 6. Operates June-July.

Selected for their overall academic acheivement and their interest in science, FSI participants engage in various aspects of science, technology, engineering and math through classroom and lab activity, field trips and industrial visits, and seminars conducted by academic and industry professionals. Although the curriculum varies year to year, instructors place particular emphasis on the relationships and interdependence among such math and science disciplines as biology, chemistry, physics, earth and space science, computer science and engineering. Most boys and girls work with a mentor on an in-depth scientific research project.

UNIVERSITY OF NOTRE DAME
INTRODUCTION TO ENGINEERING
Res — Coed Ages 17-18

Notre Dame, IN 46556. 384 Fitzpatrick Hall of Engineering. Tel: 574-631-6092. Fax: 574-631-9260.
http://iep.nd.edu   E-mail: iep@nd.edu
Ramzi K. Bualuan, Dir.
Grade 12 (younger if qualified). Adm: Selective. Admitted: 60%. **Appl**—Fee $0. Due: Apr.
Enr: 65. **Enr cap:** 65. **Fac 18.** Prof 18. **Staff:** Admin 2. Res 15.
Type of instruction: Enrich Undergrad. Homework.
Focus: Engineering.
Fees 2012: Res $1750, 2 wks. Aid (Need).
Housing: Dorms. Campus facilities avail.
Nonprofit. **Ses:** 2. **Wks/ses:** 2. Operates June-July.

Designed for rising high school seniors, IEP provides students with an overview of the elements of engineering design and computer programming, a discussion of career opportunities in engineering, a chance to meet professional engineers and a preview of college life. In the morning, boys and girls attend two hourlong lectures, while afternoons provide time for hands-on computer sessions and work in the engineering learning center. Pupils write a report on each talk, learn concepts of design and implement them by building systems, and team up with fellow students to compose and deliver a presentation during the program's final week. Two plant trips to nearby engineering facilities complete the curriculum.

UNIVERSITY OF NOTRE DAME
SCHOOL OF ARCHITECTURE
CAREER DISCOVERY
Res — Coed Ages 16-18

Notre Dame, IN 46556. 110 Bond Hall. Tel: 574-631-2322. Fax: 574-631-8486.
www.architecture.nd.edu/programs/career_discovery.aspx   E-mail: arch@nd.edu
Grades 11-12. Adm: FCFS. **Appl**—Due: Apr.
Type of instruction: Enrich.
Focus: Architect.
Fees 2009: Res $1650, 2 wks.
Housing: Dorms.
Ses: 1. **Wks/ses:** 2. Operates June.

Young men and women considering careers in architecture learn about both college-level study and the steps they can take in grades 11 and 12 to prepare themselves for a future in the field. Notre Dame professors and advanced university pupils teach architectural history, as well as the skills and responsibilities required in contemporary architectural practice. Design studios, architecture seminars and field trips to notable architectural sites enrich the program.

UNIVERSITY OF PENNSYLVANIA
LEADERSHIP IN THE BUSINESS WORLD
Res — Coed Ages 17-18

Philadelphia, PA 19104. G95 Jon M Huntsman Hall, 3730 Walnut St.
Tel: 215-746-8765.
http://undergrad.wharton.upenn.edu/precollege/lbw
E-mail: leadership@wharton.upenn.edu
Helene Elting, Dir.
Grade 12. Adm: Selective. **Appl**—Fee $75. Due: Mar. Transcript, 2 recs, standardized test results, essay.
Enr: 60. **Enr cap:** 60.
Type of instruction: Enrich.
Focus: Bus/Fin.
Fees 2009: Res $5400, 4 wks. Aid (Need).
Housing: Dorms.
Est 1999. Ses: 1. **Wks/ses:** 4. Operates June-July.

Sponsored by Penn's Wharton School of Business, LBW enrolls a select group of rising high school seniors who have an interest in the business world. Students engage in classroom discussions about leadership, business ethics, entrepreneurship, accounting, management and economics; attend lectures and presentations by Wharton faculty and guest speakers; visit business enterprises and converse with businesspeople in the areas of finance, entrepreneurship, entertainment, real estate and retail; work in teams to design, prepare and formulate a business plan for evaluation by a panel of venture capitalists; receive coaching on communicational and team-building skills from six upper-level Wharton undergraduates; and improve their leadership skills through collaborative teamwork.

UNIVERSITY OF PENNSYLVANIA
MANAGEMENT AND TECHNOLOGY SUMMER INSTITUTE
Res — Coed Ages 17-18

Philadelphia, PA 19104. 3537 Locust Walk, Ste 100. Tel: 215-898-4145.
www.upenn.edu/fisher/summer   E-mail: mgtech@seas.upenn.edu
Jaime Davis, Coord.
Grade 12 (younger if qualified). Adm: Selective. **Appl**—Fee $75. Due: Apr. Transcript, 2 recs, standardized test results, essay.
Enr: 50. **Enr cap:** 50.
Type of instruction: Adv. **College credit.**
Focus: Bus/Fin Engineering.
Fees 2009: Res $5400 (+$225-375), 3 wks.
Housing: Dorms.
Ses: 1. **Wks/ses:** 3. Operates July-Aug.

This unusual credit-bearing program for rising high seniors (and a limited number of particularly capable rising juniors) addresses both technological concepts and management principles. College professors and successful entrepreneurs teach M&TSI's classes. Other aspects of the program are intensive team projects, activities focusing upon the principles and the practice of technological innovation, and field trips to companies and research and development facilities. In addition to gaining an introduction to core engineering and business disciplines, participants also learn about academic and career opportunities available in these two fields.

UNIVERSITY OF PENNSYLVANIA
PENN SUMMER SCIENCE ACADEMIES
Res and Day — Coed Ages 15-18

Philadelphia, PA 19104. 3440 Market St, Ste 100. Tel: 516-621-3939.
Fax: 215-573-2053.
www.upenn.edu/summer/highschool E-mail: hsprogs@sas.upenn.edu
Grades 10-12. Adm: Selective. Admitted: 57%. Appl—Fee $70. Due: May. Transcript, rec, essay, resume, standardized test scores.
Enr: 100. Fac 3. Staff: Couns 30.
Type of instruction: Adv Enrich. Courses: Physics. Daily hours for: Classes 7. Study 2. Rec 3.
Focus: Med/Healthcare Sci. Features: Swim.
Fees 2012: Res $7599, 4 wks. Day $6599, 4 wks. Aid (Need).
Housing: Dorms. Swimming: Pool.
Est 1987. Nonprofit. Ses: 1. Wks/ses: 4. Operates July.

This intensive, noncredit science program comprises guided laboratory projects, seminars, faculty lectures, discussion groups, problem-solving sessions and field trips. University of Pennsylvania scientists and students provide all instruction. Participants choose a concentration in experimental physics or biomedical research, and the Monday through Friday programming varies according to the pupil's chosen concentration. Although some local day students attend PSSA, most boys and girls elect to board at the university.

UNIVERSITY OF ST ANDREWS
INTERNATIONAL SCIENCE SUMMER PROGRAMME
Res — Coed Ages 16-18

St Andrews, KY16 9AX Fife, Scotland. St Katharine's W, 16 The Scores.
Tel: 44-1334-462275. Fax: 44-1334-463330.
www.st-andrews.ac.uk/admissions/ug/int/summerschools
E-mail: rmd10@st-andrews.ac.uk
Ruth Harris, Head.
Grades 11-PG. Adm: Somewhat selective. Prereqs: GPA 3.0. Appl—Fee £15. Due: Rolling. 2 recs, standardized test results, personal statement.
Enr cap: 20. Intl: 20%. Non-White: 10%. Fac 16. Prof 8. Col/grad students 8. Staff: Admin 2. Couns 2.
Type of instruction: Adv. Courses: Ecol Math Geosci Music Photog Theater. Daily hours for: Classes 3. Study 3. Rec 4. Homework. Tests. Grades. College credit: 12.
Intl program focus: Acad.
Focus: Sci. Features: Conservation Exploration Hiking Mtn_Trips Swim.
Fees 2012: Res £3000 (+£200), 4 wks.
Housing: Dorms. Avg per room/unit: 1. Swimming: Ocean Pool. Campus facilities avail.
Est 2012. Ses: 1. Wks/ses: 4. Operates June-July.

This precollege program provides students with a college-level academic experience that focuses on various science disciplines, including biology, chemistry, ecology, physics and geoscience. Graduate students and full-time professors from the University of St Andrews serve as course instructors. Extensive field trips to sites of scientific interest enrich the curriculum. Cultural excursions and activities round out the program.

UNIVERSITY OF ST. THOMAS
THREESIXTY JOURNALISM SUMMER WORKSHOP
Res and Day — Coed Ages 15-20

St Paul, MN 55105. 2115 Summit Ave, Mail 5057. Tel: 651-962-5282.
www.threesixtyjournalism.org E-mail: info@threesixtyjournalism.org

Lynda McDonnell, Exec Dir.
Grades 10-PG. Adm: Selective. Priority: Low-income. URM. **Appl**—Due: Apr. Transcript, rec, writing sample, essay.
Enr: 15. **Enr cap:** 15. **Fac** 4. **Staff:** Admin 3. Couns 3.
Type of instruction: Enrich. **Courses:** Media.
Focus: Writing/Journ. **Features:** Swim.
Fees 2010: Free. Res 2 wks. Day 2 wks.
Housing: Dorms. **Swimming:** Pool.
Est 2001. Nonprofit. **Ses:** 2. **Wks/ses:** 2. Operates June-July.

Designed primarily for minority students with an interest in writing and reporting—especially those who work on high school newspapers or television production—this tuition-free program consists of writing and reporting courses, layout and design classes, visits to Twin Cities' newspapers and television stations, team production of special newspaper pages for publication in two area newspapers, and assignment of a professional reporter/writer as a mentor for each student. Writers, photographers, artists and editors employed by the Minneapolis *Star Tribune* and the St. Paul *Pioneer Press;* reporters, producers and photographers from local TV stations; and members of the St. Thomas journalism staff serve as faculty for the program. Particularly able pupils may earn a four-year scholarship to study journalism at the University of St. Thomas.

UNIVERSITY OF SOUTHERN CALIFORNIA
FRONTIERS OF ENERGY RESOURCES SUMMER CAMP
Res — Coed Ages 16-18

Los Angeles, CA 90089. Ctr for Interactive Smart Oilfield Technologies, 3710 S McClintock Ave, RTH 311. Tel: 213-740-1076. Fax: 213-740-1077.
http://cisoft.usc.edu/uscchevron-frontiers-of-energy-resources-summer-camp
E-mail: cisoft@vsoe.usc.edu
Student contact: Juli Legat.
Grade 12. Adm: Selective. **Appl**—Due: Apr. Transcript, teacher rec.
Enr: 23.
Type of instruction: Adv Enrich.
Focus: Sci. **Features:** Swim.
Fees 2012: Free. Res 1 wk.
Housing: Dorms. **Swimming:** Pool.
Est 2009. Ses: 1. **Wks/ses:** 1. Operates June-July.

This USC program offers a preparatory, interactive training program that focuses on various energy resources, among them fossil fuels, solar power, bio-fuels, wind power, nuclear energy and information technologies for energy-efficient operations. Students develop problem-solving techniques and team-building skills while living in residence halls and previewing the college experience.

UNIVERSITY OF TEXAS-ARLINGTON
ENGINEERING AND COMPUTER SCIENCE SUMMER CAMPS
Res — Coed Ages 12-15; Day — Coed 11-16

Arlington, TX 76019. College of Engineering, PO Box 19014. Tel: 817-272-1295.
Fax: 817-272-1296.
www.uta.edu/engineering/summercamps   E-mail: engineeringoutreach@uta.edu
J. Carter M. Tiernan, Dir. Student contact: Ashley Bigley, E-mail: ashleyb@uta.edu.
Grades 6-11. Adm: Selective. Admitted: 90%. **Appl**—Fee $0. Due: Apr. Transcript, teacher rec.
Enr: 50. **Enr cap:** 50. Intl: 5%. Non-White: 45%. **Fac 15.** Prof 12. Col/grad students 3. **Staff:** Admin 3. Couns 2.

Type of instruction: Enrich. **Courses:** Math Sci.
Focus: Comp_Sci Engineering. **Features:** Aviation/Aero Basketball Soccer.
Fees 2012: Res $375, 1 wk. Day $225, 1 wk. Aid 2009 (Need): $7600.
Housing: Dorms. Avg per room/unit: 2.
Est 1994. Nonprofit. **Ses:** 5. **Wks/ses:** 1. Operates June-July.

Weeklong day and residential camps expose middle and high school students to various engineering disciplines (aerospace, biomedical, civil and environmental, computer science, electrical, materials science and mechanical), as well as related topics in chemistry and physics. Professors and graduate and undergraduate students lead lectures, hands-on exercises and special presentations. Field trips to local businesses introduce students to engineering careers.

UNIVERSITY OF THE SOUTH
BRIDGE PROGRAM IN MATH AND SCIENCE
Res — Coed Ages 17-18

Sewanee, TN 37383. 735 University Ave. Tel: 931-598-1997. Fax: 931-598-1864.
www.sewanee.edu/bridgeprogram   E-mail: bridgeprogram@sewanee.edu
Tina Nader, Dir.
Grade 12. Adm: Selective. Admitted: 40%. Priority: URM. **Appl**—Fee $0. Due: Mar. Transcript, standardized test scores, 2 recs.
Enr: 20. Enr cap: 20. Non-White: 90%. **Fac 3.** Prof 3. **Staff:** Admin 2. Couns 5.
Type of instruction: Adv Enrich Undergrad. **Courses:** Astron Comp_Sci. **Daily hours for:** Classes 5. Study 2. Rec 5. Homework.
Focus: Math Sci. **Features:** Canoe Caving Climbing_Wall Hiking Mtn_Trips Ropes_Crse Basketball Golf Soccer Swim Tennis Track Ultimate_Frisbee Weight_Trng.
Fees 2012: Free. Res 3 wks.
Housing: Dorms. Avg per room/unit: 2. **Swimming:** Lake Pool. Campus facilities avail.
Est 1999. Nonprofit. **Ses:** 1. **Wks/ses:** 3. Operates June-July.

This intensive precollege program enrolls rising seniors who have displayed high achievement in math and science, particularly those students of ethnic groups lacking prominent representation in these fields of study. University faculty members teach calculus and research-based science classes in astronomy and computer science. Current Sewanee undergraduates assist the professors and serve as mentors to Bridge Program participants. Students need pay only for their trip to campus, as the university covers all program expenses.

UNIVERSITY OF UTAH
SUMMER MATHEMATICS PROGRAM
FOR HIGH SCHOOL STUDENTS
Res and Day — Coed Ages 17-18

Salt Lake City, UT 84112. Math Dept, 155 S 1400 E, JWB 223. Tel: 801-585-9478.
Fax: 801-581-4148.
www.math.utah.edu/hsp   E-mail: gardiner@math.utah.edu
Grade 12 (younger if qualified). Adm: Selective. **Appl**—Due: Mar. Transcript, standardized test scores, rec, personal statement.
Type of instruction: Adv. **College credit:** 3.
Focus: Math.
Fees 2010: Free. Res 3 wks. Day 3 wks.
Housing: Dorms.
Nonprofit. **Ses:** 1. **Wks/ses:** 3. Operates June-July.

This precollege program comprises four parts: a three-week class on number theory, a lunch period that provides opportunities for informal math discussions, an afternoon colloquium lecture series and a computer lab in which students explore questions relating to number theory using the Python language. (Pupils need have no previous experience with Python.) Problem sessions are integrated into morning classes, and participants work on problems both individually and in groups. The program runs Monday through Thursday each week. Nonlocal students may be assessed a nominal boarding fee.

UNIVERSITY OF VERMONT
GOVERNOR'S INSTITUTES OF VERMONT
ENGINEERING SUMMER INSTITUTE
Res — Coed Ages 15-18

Burlington, VT 05405. College of Engineering & Mathematical Sciences, 113 Votey Hall. Tel: 802-656-8748. Fax: 802-656-8802.
www.cems.uvm.edu/summer   E-mail: densmore@cems.uvm.edu
Dawn Densmore, Exec Dir.
Grades 10-12. Adm: Selective. **Appl**—Due: Rolling.
Enr: 100.
Type of instruction: Enrich. **Courses:** Robotics.
Focus: Engineering.
Fees 2012: Res $1200, 1 wk. Aid (Need).
Housing: Dorms. Avg per room/unit: 2.
Ses: 1. **Wks/ses:** 1. Operates July.

The institute introduces students to sustainable engineering practices through hands-on projects, laboratory experiences, faculty presentations and off-campus industry tours. Students work in groups on projects in the areas of renewable/sustainable engineering, robotics systems, aerospace engineering and engineering design.

UNIVERSITY OF VIRGINIA INTRODUCTION TO ENGINEERING
Res — Coed Ages 16-18

Charlottesville, VA 22904. 351 McCormick Rd, PO Box 400255. Tel: 434-924-0614.
www.seas.virginia.edu/diversity/pre_college/ite.php   E-mail: eng-cde@virginia.edu
Carolyn Vallas, Dir.
Grades 11-12. Adm: Selective. Prereqs: GPA 3.0. **Appl**—Due: Apr. Essay, transcript, standardized test scores.
Staff: Couns 4.
Type of instruction: Enrich.
Focus: Engineering.
Fees 2010: Res $400, 1 wk. Aid (Need).
Housing: Dorms.
Est 1987. Nonprofit. **Ses:** 1. **Wks/ses:** 1. Operates June.

ITE features daily introductory engineering classes, seminars on college admissions and financial aid, demonstrations, hands-on experiments, and departmental and university tours. Instructors devote special attention to the concerns of groups typically underrepresented in engineering fields.

UNIVERSITY OF VIRGINIA
SORENSEN INSTITUTE FOR POLITICAL LEADERSHIP
HIGH SCHOOL LEADERS PROGRAM
Res — Coed Ages 16-18

Charlottesville, VA 22904. PO Box 400206. Tel: 434-243-2470. Fax: 434-982-5536.
www.sorenseninstitute.org/programs/hslp   E-mail: april.auger@virginia.edu
April Auger, Dir.

Grades 11-PG (younger if qualified). Adm: Selective. Admitted: 50%. **Appl**—Fee $0. Due: Mar. Transcript, reference, essay, interview.
Enr: 32. Enr cap: 35. Fac 2. Prof 2. **Staff: Admin 5.** Couns 3.
Type of instruction: Enrich. **Daily hours for:** Classes 7. Study 2. Rec 1. Homework. Grades. **College credit: 3.**
Focus: Govt Leadership Pol_Sci. **Features:** Ropes_Crse.
Fees 2011: Res $1625, 2 wks. Aid (Need).
Housing: Dorms. Avg per room/unit: 4.
Est 2003. Nonprofit. **Ses: 1. Wks/ses:** 2. Operates July.

HSLP participants, who must be either state residents or out-of-state pupils studying in Virginia, engage in substantive public policy debates and interact with political and business leaders. Classroom instruction focuses on local- and state-government structures and processes, major policy issues and advocacy tools. Students work in groups on a culminating project in which they develop policy proposals and reports for presentation to a group of government and business professionals. Guest speakers include a range of elected officials, business and nonprofit leaders, academics, lobbyists and government employees.

UNIVERSITY OF WASHINGTON SCHOOL OF MEDICINE
U-DOC HIGH SCHOOL SUMMER PROGRAM
Res — Coed Ages 16-17

Seattle, WA 98195. Office of Multicultural Affairs, 1959 NE Pacific St, HSC T545 Box 357430. Tel: 206-685-2489. Fax: 206-685-9063.
www.myomca.org   E-mail: fabeyta@uw.edu
Felicity Abeyta-Hendrix, Coord.
Grades 11-12. Adm: Very selective. Priority: Low-income. **Appl**—Fee $0. Due: Mar. Transcript, 2 recs.
Enr: 16.
Type of instruction: Enrich SAT/ACT_Prep Study_Skills. **Courses:** Sci. **Daily hours for:** Classes 3. Study 3. Rec 4. Homework. Tests. Grades.
Focus: Med/Healthcare. **Features:** Hiking Ropes_Crse Swim Gardening.
Fees 2012: Free (in-state residents). Res 3-5 wks.
Housing: Dorms. **Swimming:** River. Campus facilities avail.
Nonprofit. **Ses: 1. Wks/ses:** 4. Operates June-July.

Designed for residents of Washington State who come from a disadvantaged background, U-DOC provides able students with an exposure to the fields of medicine and dentistry. The program includes an overview of premedical and pre-dental college curricula; work on research, writing and study skills; test-taking instruction; college application tips; and hands-on research experience.

UNIVERSITY OF WISCONSIN-MADISON
ENGINEERING SUMMER PROGRAM
Res — Coed Ages 16-17

Madison, WI 53706. 1150 Engineering Hall, 1415 Engineering Dr. Tel: 608-263-5367. Fax: 608-262-6400.
http://studentservices.engr.wisc.edu/diversity/esp
E-mail: mpdavis@engr.wisc.edu
Grades 11-12. Adm: Very selective. Priority: URM. Prereqs: GPA 3.0. **Appl**—Fee $0. Due: Apr. Transcript, math & sci teacher recs, essay.
Type of instruction: Enrich Undergrad. **Courses:** Math Sci.
Focus: Engineering.
Fees 2010: Free. Res 6 wks.
Housing: Dorms.
Nonprofit. **Ses: 1. Wks/ses:** 6. Operates June-July.

Designed for rising high school juniors and seniors from groups traditionally underrepresented in science, technology, math and engineering (including females), ESP addresses math, engineering, science and technical communications. This free, structured program promotes further understanding of the field of engineering and its disciplines through industry site visits, cultural enrichment activities and faculty mentoring. Students sample a university environment and learn the importance of early college preparation.

UTAH BUSINESS WEEK
Res — Coed Ages 16-17

Logan, UT. Utah State Univ.
Contact (Year-round): c/o Workers Compensation Fund, 392 E 6400 S, Salt Lake City, UT 84107. Tel: 801-288-8340, 800-446-2667. Fax: 801-284-8984.
www.utahbusinessweek.org   E-mail: ubw@utahbusinessweek.org
Grades 11-12. Adm: Selective. **Appl**—Due: May. Rec, essay.
Type of instruction: Enrich.
Focus: Bus/Fin.
Fees 2009: Res $80, 1 wk. Aid (Need).
Housing: Dorms. Avg per room/unit: 2.
Nonprofit. **Ses:** 1. **Wks/ses:** 1. Operates Aug.

Conducted at Utah State University, UBW gives rising high school juniors and seniors a taste of college life while educating them about all aspects of business and preparing them for a future business career. Students develop leadership and teamwork skills through a program that includes speakers, tours of local companies, simulations and team-building exercises. Volunteers from the Utah business community organize and completely run the program.

VANDERBILT UNIVERSITY PRE-COLLEGE PAVE
Res and Day — Coed Ages 16-18

Nashville, TN 37235. 2301 Vanderbilt Pl, VU Sta B 351736. Tel: 615-322-7827. Fax: 615-322-3297.
http://pave.vanderbilt.edu   E-mail: pave@vanderbilt.edu
John Veillette, Dir.
Grades 12-PG. Adm: Selective. **Appl**—Due: Apr. Transcript, recs, standardized test scores.
Enr: 175. **Enr cap:** 175. Intl: 30%.
Type of instruction: Adv Enrich Undergrad. **Daily hours for:** Classes 6. Study 2½.
Focus: Engineering Med/Healthcare Sci.
Fees 2012: Res $6270, 6 wks. Day $4350, 6 wks.
Housing: Dorms.
Est 1990. Nonprofit. **Ses:** 1. **Wks/ses:** 6. Operates June-Aug.

PAVE seeks to strengthen the academic skills of students planning to enter a college engineering, pre-medicine, science or technology program. Rising high school seniors expecting to take Advanced Placement or honors math or science courses stand to benefit, and the six-week session may also help pupils improve their ACT, AP, SAT or TOEFL scores. The program addresses problem-solving, technical writing, computer application and laboratory skills through experimentation. Participants also gain an introduction to college life.

VICTORY BRIEFS INSTITUTE
Res and Day — Coed Ages 13-18

Los Angeles, CA 90049. 925 N Norman Pl. Tel: 310-472-6364. Fax: 208-248-9801.
http://victorybriefs.com   E-mail: help@victorybriefs.com

Mike Bietz, Dir.
Grades 8-12. Adm: FCFS. **Appl**—Due: Rolling.
Type of instruction: Enrich.
Focus: Debate.
Fees 2009: Res $1800-2500, 2-3 wks. Day $1300-1800, 2-3 wks. Aid (Need).
Housing: Dorms. Avg per room/unit: 2.
Est 2003. Ses: 2. **Wks/ses:** 2-3. Operates July-Aug.

VBI offers two- and three-week sessions on the campuses of the University of California-Los Angeles and Loyola Marymount University. The curriculum includes lectures, smaller seminars, demonstration and practice rounds, informal discussions and one-on-one sessions with coaches. The institute places students in lab groups of 12 to 15 based upon area of focus and experience level. A novice lab serves boys and girls with no previous Lincoln-Douglas experience. High school debate coaches and former invitational and national tournament champions serve as VBI instructors.

WASHINGTON UNIVERSITY
ARCHITECTURE DISCOVERY PROGRAM
Res — Coed Ages 17-18

St Louis, MO 63130. Campus Box 1031, 1 Brookings Dr. Tel: 314-935-8652.
    Fax: 314-935-6462.
www.samfoxschool.wustl.edu/summer/adp
E-mail: wardenburg@samfox.wustl.edu
Student contact: Kim Wardenburg.
Grade 12. Adm: Selective. **Appl**—Fee $35. Due: May.
Enr: 60. **Enr cap:** 60. **Fac 4.** Col/grad students 4. **Staff:** Admin 2. Res 4.
Type of instruction: Undergrad. **Avg class size:** 12. **College credit:** 1/crse, total 3.
Focus: Architect.
Fees 2012: Res $2325 (+$250), 2 wks.
Housing: Dorms. Campus facilities avail.
Ses: 1. **Wks/ses:** 2. Operates July.

Conducted by Washington University's Sam Fox School of Design & Visual Arts, this introduction to architecture for rising seniors focuses on creative design and environmental sustainability. Morning activities include field trips to construction sites, visits to architecture firms, lectures and drawing sessions. Afternoons provide time for work in the studio, where students initiate and develop an architectural design for a final review.

WESTERN WASHINGTON UNIVERSITY COLLEGE QUEST
Res — Coed Ages 15-18

Bellingham, WA 98225. 516 High St, MS 5293. Tel: 360-650-6820. Fax: 360-650-6858.
www.wwu.edu/collegequest   E-mail: youth@wwu.edu
Debbie Gibbons, Prgm Mgr.
Grades 10-12. Adm: FCFS. **Appl**—Fee $0. Due: Rolling. Transcript, essay.
Enr: 70. **Enr cap:** 100. **Fac 9. Prof 9. Staff:** Admin 2. Couns 35.
Type of instruction: Preview Undergrad. **Courses:** Environ_Sci Law Psych Sci Creative_
    Writing Filmmaking. **Avg class size:** 15. **Daily hours for:** Classes 4. Study 4. Rec 2.
    Homework. Grades. **College credit:** 1/crse, total 2.
Focus: Col_Prep. **Features:** Hiking Swim.
Fees 2012: Res $800 (+$140), 1 wk.
Housing: Dorms. **Swimming:** Lake Pool.
Est 2001. Nonprofit. Ses: 1. **Wks/ses:** 1. Operates July.

This precollege program enables high schoolers to live in a campus residence hall, take a course for academic credit and participate in group activities that showcase college life.

Students participate in class lectures, labs and field trips while researching and preparing assignments and projects. Course offerings include environmental studies and filmmaking, psychology, criminal law and chemistry/renewable energy.

WESTMINSTER COLLEGE ROBOTICS CAMP
Res — Coed Ages 14-18; Day — Coed 10-13

Salt Lake City, UT 84105. 1840 S 1300 E. Tel: 801-832-2562.
www.westminstercollege.edu/camps
E-mail: summercamps@westminstercollege.edu
Emily Hadfield, Coord.
Grades 5-12. Adm: FCFS. **Appl**—Due: Rolling.
Type of instruction: Enrich.
Focus: Comp_Sci Engineering.
Fees 2009: Res $370, 1 wk. Day $175, 1 wk.
Housing: Dorms.
Ses: 1. **Wks/ses:** 1. Operates July.

Participants in this precollege program work in groups of two to four to create, design and build a robot with programming capabilities. Computer programming faculty provide instruction and guidance. Students also learn about robotics competitions and career options.

WHALE CAMP
Res — Coed Ages 10-17

Grand Manan Island, New Brunswick, Canada.
Contact (Year-round): PO Box 63, Cheney, PA 19319. Tel: 610-399-1463,
888-549-4253. Fax: 610-399-4482.
www.whalecamp.com   E-mail: info@whalecamp.com
Dennis Bowen, Dir.
Grades 5-12. Adm: FCFS. **Appl**—Fee $0. Due: Rolling.
Enr cap: 36-38. **Fac 11. Staff:** Admin 3. Couns 9.
Type of instruction: Enrich. **Courses:** Ecol Geol Creative_Writing Fine_Arts Photog.
Focus: Environ_Sci Marine_Bio/Stud Oceanog. **Features:** Adventure_Travel Aquatics Boating Conservation Exploration Hiking Kayak Outdoor_Ed Sail Sea_Cruises Seamanship Field_Hockey Roller_Hockey Soccer Swim Ultimate_Frisbee Volleyball Watersports.
Fees 2012: Res $1395-5085, 1-3 wks.
Housing: Dorms. **Swimming:** Lake Ocean.
Est 1983. Inc. **Ses:** 22. **Wks/ses:** 1-3. Operates June-Aug.

Students in this marine science program sail aboard the program's schooner while learning about the geology of Canada's Bay of Fundy region, the bay's marine life and the land-based life of Grand Manan Island. Aspects of the program include whale tracking, whale research, study of marine mammals and birds, ocean life photography, sailing, sea kayaking, hiking and sea navigation. Students utilize professional marine science and oceanography equipment.

WHITMAN NATIONAL DEBATE INSTITUTE
Res — Coed Ages 13-19

Walla Walla, WA 99362. Whitman College, Dept of Rhetoric. Tel: 509-527-5499.
Fax: 509-527-4959.
www.whitman.edu/debate/camp   E-mail: hansonjb@whitman.edu
Jim Hanson, Dir.
Grades 8-12 (younger if qualified). Adm: FCFS. **Appl**—Fee $0. Due: May.
Enr: 126. Non-White: 20%. **Fac 30.** Col/grad students 30. **Staff:** Admin 4. Couns 3.

Type of instruction: Adv Enrich. **Avg class size:** 8. **Daily hours for:** Classes 10. Rec 3. Homework.
Focus: Debate. **Features:** Basketball.
Fees 2012: Res $1145-2245, 1-3 wks. Aid 2011 (Merit & Need): $14,000.
Housing: Dorms. Avg per room/unit: 2.
Est 2000. Nonprofit. **Spons:** Whitman College. **Ses:** 5. **Wks/ses:** 1-3. Operates July-Aug.

WNDI conducts two- and three-week policy and Lincoln-Douglas debate camps, as well as a weeklong public forum debate session. The first part of the policy debate camp consists of lectures, examples, drills and lab work for affirmative cases, disadvantages, counterplans, kritiks and topicality arguments; the second part features independent research projects, practice and tournament debates, and advanced theory lectures. During the first part of the Lincoln-Douglas camp, the focus is on case construction and value argumentation in both traditional and mainly contemporary styles, along with lab work and practice debates and drills on current Lincoln-Douglas topics. The final week provides time for in-depth topic exploration, extensive work on delivery and presentation, discussion of additional philosophies and value conflict issues, and a round-robin competition. The public forum camp begins with an emphasis on core argument and delivery skills and the development of case and argument preparation. Public forum students engage in frequent practice debates and attend lectures on domestic and international policy.

WINCHENDON SCHOOL SUMMER SEMESTER
ENGLISH IMMERSION PROGRAM
Res — Coed Ages 13-18

Winchendon, MA 01475. 172 Ash St. Tel: 978-297-4476, 800-622-1119.
Fax: 978-297-0911.
www.winchendon.org   E-mail: admissions@winchendon.org
Elliot Harvey, Dir.
Grades 8-12. Adm: FCFS. **Appl**—Fee $0. Due: June.
Type of instruction: Study_Skills. **Courses:** Drawing Painting. **Avg class size:** 7. **High school credit.**
Focus: ESL. **Features:** Badminton Baseball Basketball Golf Soccer Swim Tennis.
Fees 2011: Res $6500 (+$330), 6 wks.
Housing: Dorms. **Swimming:** Pool. Campus facilities avail.
Est 1973. Nonprofit. **Ses:** 1. **Wks/ses:** 6. Operates July-Aug.

Featuring intensive, structured instruction in and out of the classroom, Summer Semester helps students wishing to improve their English proficiency through a combination of English immersion, classroom study and experiential learning. Boys and girls choose from four levels of ESL instruction: beginning, intermediate, advanced and transition (a bridge course to mainstream English). Faculty devote the entire school day to English instruction in a variety of contexts. Classes seek to develop vocabulary, reading comprehension, oral and written communication skills, and subject-specific terminology. Experiential education takes the form of afternoon excursions, lectures and student interviews of local citizens.

WYOMING SEMINARY
ENGLISH AS A SECOND LANGUAGE INSTITUTE
Res — Coed Ages 13-18

Kingston, PA 18704. 201 N Sprague Ave. Tel: 570-270-2186. Fax: 570-270-2198.
www.wyomingseminary.org/summer
E-mail: summeratsem@wyomingseminary.org
John R. Eidam, Dir.
   Student contact: Gayle Sekel, E-mail: gsekel@wyomingseminary.org.
Grades 9-12. Adm: FCFS. **Appl**—Fee $100. Due: Rolling. Transcript, 2 recs.

Intl: 100%. **Fac 12.** K-12 staff 12. **Staff: Couns** 20.
Type of instruction: Preview Rev. **Courses:** Crafts Drama Painting. **Daily hours for:**
Classes 4. Study 2. Rec 1. Homework. Tests. Grades. **High school credit.**
Travel: ME.
Focus: ESL. **Features:** Climbing_Wall Basketball Swim Weight_Trng.
Fees 2012: Res $4100-10,750 (+$290), 4-9 wks.
Housing: Dorms. **Swimming:** Pool. Campus facilities avail.
Est 1988. Nonprofit. **Ses: 3. Wks/ses:** 4-5. Operates June-Aug.

The ESL Institute provides an introduction to boarding school life for students who have had some exposure to the English language. Wyoming Seminary groups boys and girls by ability level in a program that addresses listening, speaking, reading and writing skills. Advanced students read short stories and novels, then write objective, critical essays. Activities include sports, fine arts courses and performing arts ensembles. Dances, movies, and day trips to historic and metropolitan areas enrich the weekend schedule. Participants enrolled in the second session may continue on for a fifth week in August that features a four-night experiential camping trip through Maine.

YALE UNIVERSITY IVY SCHOLARS PROGRAM
Res — Coed Ages 15-18

New Haven, CT 06520. PO Box 208353. Tel: 203-436-4097. Fax: 203-432-6250.
www.yale.edu/ivyscholars   E-mail: ivy.scholars@yale.edu
Minh A. Luong, Dir.
Grades 10-PG. Adm: Very selective. **Appl**—Fee $50. Due: May. Transcript, essay, 2 recs.
Enr: 46. **Enr cap:** 60. **Fac 11. Staff:** Admin 5.
Type of instruction: Adv Enrich. **Courses:** Bus/Fin Econ Hist Public_Speak.
Focus: Intl_Relations Leadership.
Fees 2012: Res $4488, 3 wks. Aid (Need).
Housing: Dorms. Campus facilities avail.
Nonprofit. **Ses: 3. Wks/ses:** 2. Operates July-Aug.

Ivy Scholars combines college-level academic study in applied ethics, business, economics, history, international relations, law, politics and public policy with strategic leadership and advocacy skills instruction. The program features morning lectures by Yale faculty, afternoon seminars on grand strategy, and mentoring sessions with distinguished alumni and rising professionals. Evening training sessions address the areas of public speaking and debate, writing, networking, social and professional etiquette, study skills and time management.

YOSEMITE INSTITUTE SUMMER FIELD RESEARCH
Res — Coed Ages 15-18

Yosemite National Park, CA 95389. PO Box 487. Tel: 209-379-9511.
Fax: 209-379-9510.
www.naturebridge.org/yosemite/summer-field-research
E-mail: yi@naturebridge.org
Michael Bilodeau, Educ Dir.
Grades 11-12 (younger if qualified). Adm: Somewhat selective. Admitted: 90%. **Appl**—Fee $0. Due: Rolling.
Enr: 12. **Enr cap:** 12. **Fac 5. Staff:** Admin 15. Couns 35.
Courses: Environ_Sci Geol Photog. **Daily hours for:** Classes 6. Study 2. Rec 2. Grades.
College credit: 3.
Focus: Ecol Field_Ecol. **Features:** Exploration Fishing Hiking Mountaineering Mtn_Trips Outdoor_Ed Rock_Climb Survival_Trng White-water_Raft Wilderness_Camp Woodcraft Swim.
Fees 2012: Res $1800-2300, 2 wks. Aid 2011 (Need): $9000.
Housing: Cabins Tents. Avg per room/unit: 3. **Swimming:** River.

Est 1999. Nonprofit. **Ses:** 1. **Wks/ses:** 2. Operates July-Aug.

Summer Field Research students conduct original ecological research projects and earn college credit on 25-mile backpacking trips through the Sierra Nevada Mountains. The program begins at Yosemite Institute's Crane Flat campus, where students learn basic concepts of ecology and natural history as they pertain to the region. Two field researchers lead teams of 12 students, in the process using modern research equipment, recording field observations and identifying patterns, collecting data and presenting their findings to other scientists. Campers also learn and apply lessons in route finding, map and compass use, outdoor leadership, cooking and conservation.

INTERNSHIP PROGRAMS

Internships, which are usually quite competitive, serve able, academically motivated high school students. Participants have a unique opportunity to work on a project at an accelerated level, often alongside college students and field scholars. Unlike programs listed in other sections of the *Guide,* internships need not necessarily offer boarding. While program administrators generally assist interns with lodging, families may be required to arrange the student's accommodations. Most internships pay a salary or a stipend, however, which helps to defray student expense.

Internship programs are arranged alphabetically by name.

Internship Programs

BANK OF AMERICA STUDENT LEADERS
Res — Coed Ages 17-18

Charlotte, NC 28202. Office of Corporate Philanthropy, 100 N Tryon St.
Toll-free: 800-218-9946.
http://ahead.bankofamerica.com/supporting-communities
Grades 12-PG. Adm: Very selective. Admitted: 6%. **Appl**—Due: Feb. **Enr:** 230.
Locations: AZ CA CT DC DE FL GA IL MA MD MI MO NC NJ NV NY OR PA RI TN TX
VA WA Europe.
Focus: Bus/Fin.
9 wks: 35 hrs/wk. **Salary:** $10 (per hour).
Housing: Housing provided.
Est 2004. Operates June-July.

Participants each complete an eight-week paid internship with a nonprofit or charitable organization, then attend a weeklong leadership summit in Washington, DC. Five positions are available in each of 45 markets across the US and in London, England. Student Leaders arranges travel and accommodations for the leadership summit, which provides various perspectives on civic, social and business partnerships.

CITY OF HOPE CANCER CENTER
EUGENE AND RUTH ROBERTS SUMMER STUDENT ACADEMY
Res and Day — Coed Ages 16-18

Duarte, CA 91010. 1500 E Duarte Rd. Tel: 626-256-4673.
www.cityofhope.org/education/summer-student-academy
E-mail: robertsacademy@coh.org
Michelle Navarro, Coord.
Grades 11-Col. Adm: Very selective. Admitted: 18%. **Appl**—Due: Mar. Interview. **Enr:** 50.
Focus: Med/Healthcare Sci.
10 wks. Salary: $4000 (lump sum).
Housing: Nonlocal interns must arrange housing independently.
Est 1975. Operates June-Sept.

At City of Hope, high school and college students work with faculty mentors on a research project of their choosing. Individual investigators select applicants whose background and interests are best suited to each lab. In addition to lab work, young men and women attend weekly seminars in which they share their research findings with their peers, and they also participate in workshops on such topics as biomedical ethics. While program dates are flexible, all students must complete a 10-week internship.

CORIELL INSTITUTE FOR MEDICAL RESEARCH
SUMMER EXPERIENCE PROGRAM
Res and Day — Coed Ages 17-18

Camden, NJ 08103. 403 Haddon Ave. Tel: 856-966-7377. Fax: 856-964-0254.
www.coriell.org/education/summer-experience-for-students
E-mail: croyds@coriell.org
Grades 12-Col. Adm: Selective. **Appl**—Due: Feb. Resume.
Type of instruction: Adv Enrich.
Focus: Med/Healthcare Sci.
8 wks: 40 hrs/wk. **Salary:** $8 (per hour).
Housing: Nonlocal interns must arrange housing independently.

Students who excel in science may apply for a limited number of internships at Coriell Institute laboratories and offices researching tissue cultures, nucleic acids biochemistry, molecular biology, differentiated cells, cryogenics, cytogenetics and other topics. The principal investigator/supervisor of the laboratory designs projects for each intern.

IOWA STATE UNIVERSITY
GEORGE WASHINGTON CARVER INTERNSHIP PROGRAM
Res — Coed Ages 16-18

Ames, IA 50011. Agriculture Minority Prgms, 23 Curtiss Hall. Tel: 515-294-1701. www.ag.iastate.edu/diversity/gwc   E-mail: acurbelo@iastate.edu Student contact: Aurelio Curbelo. Grades 11-12. Adm: Selective. Prereqs: GPA 3.0. **Appl**—Due: Feb. Transcript, 2 references. **Enr:** 15.
Focus: Sci.
6 wks: 40 hrs/wk. **Salary:** $1500 (lump sum).
Housing: Dorms.
Est 1993. Operates June-Aug.

Designed for high school and undergraduate students from minority backgrounds, GWC internships match participants with faculty mentors from the College of Agriculture and Life Sciences and other ISU departments. Interns live in residence halls, attend weekly seminars, complete an original research project, prepare an abstract and a written report, and present their findings at a program-ending research symposium. In addition, students receive advice and guidance about undergraduate and graduate admissions and prospective career opportunities.

J. CRAIG VENTER INSTITUTE INTERNSHIP PROGRAM
Res and Day — Coed Ages 16-18

Rockville, MD 20850. 9704 Medical Center Dr. Tel: 301-795-7394. Fax: 301-795-7055. www.jcvi.org/cms/education/internship-program   E-mail: internships@jcvi.org Grades 12-Col. Adm: Very selective. Admitted: 30%. Prereqs: GPA 3.0. **Appl**—Due: Feb. Transcript, resume, essay, 2 recs. **Enr:** 32.
Locations: CA.
Focus: Sci.
8 wks: 40 hrs/wk. **Salary:** $9.90 (per hour).
Housing: Nonlocal interns must arrange housing independently.
Nonprofit. Operates June-Aug.

A genomics research institute with facilities in both Rockville, MD, and San Diego, CA, JCV assigns interns to a mentor who serves on the institute's faculty or senior staff. The research program/work experience takes into account the participant's education level and capabilities. Interns present a compulsory summary of their research/work experience to the institute's staff at the conclusion of the internship. In addition to genomics research, internships are available in informatics, human resources, policy, safety, education, legal and other administrative departments.

JACKSON LABORATORY SUMMER STUDENT PROGRAM
Res — Coed Ages 16-18

Bar Harbor, ME 04609. Educ Office, 600 Main St. Tel: 207-288-6250. http://education.jax.org/summerstudent/index.html   E-mail: jon.geiger@jax.org Student contact: Jon Geiger. Grades 12-Col. Adm: Very selective. Admitted: 7%. **Appl**—Due: Jan. Transcript, essay, 2 recs. **Enr:** 12.

Type of instruction: Adv Enrich.
Focus: Med/Healthcare Sci.
9 wks. Salary: $3600 (lump sum).
Housing: Houses.
Est 1924. Nonprofit. Operates June-Aug.

Rising seniors, high school graduates and college undergraduates may apply for summer positions conducting biomedical research. Under the guidance of a mentor, students develop an independent research project, implement their plan, analyze data and report on their results. Possible research areas include science writing, bio-informatics and computational biology, cancer, developmental biology and aging, genomics, hematology/immunology, metabolic diseases, and neurobiology and sensory deficits. Students also attend short courses and seminars on current genetics research. Participants reside at a 40-room seaside mansion on the outskirts of Acadia National Park.

MAGEE WOMEN'S RESEARCH INSTITUTE
HIGH SCHOOL STUDENT SUMMER INTERNSHIP PROGRAM
Res — Coed Ages 17-18

Pittsburgh, PA 15213. 204 Craft Ave, Rm B408. Tel: 412-641-6003.
www.mwrif.org/29/high-school-interns
Janet Hahalyak, Coord.
Grades 12-PG. Adm: Very selective. Admitted: 20%. **Appl**—Due: Mar. Personal statement, 2 recs.
Focus: Sci.
4 wks: 40 hrs/wk. **Salary:** $400 (lump sum).
Housing: Nonlocal interns must arrange housing independently.

Designed to promote careers in biomedical research, this program allows rising seniors and high school graduates to participate in research projects of either basic science or clinical orientation. Students attend weekly scientific seminars to enhance their knowledge of the different aspects of research, particularly as they relate to women's and infants' health. Starting and ending internship dates are flexible.

MOUNT DESERT ISLAND BIOLOGICAL LABORATORY
HIGH SCHOOL RESEARCH FELLOWSHIP
Res and Day — Coed Ages 16-18

Salisbury Cove, ME 04672. Old Bar Harbor Rd, PO Box 35. Tel: 207-288-9880.
www.mdibl.org/high_school_students.php   E-mail: internships@mdibl.org
Michael McKernan, Dir.
Grades 11-PG. Adm: Selective. **Appl**—Due: Feb. Transcript, rec. **Enr:** 12.
Focus: Sci.
8 wks.
Housing: Dorms. Avg per room/unit: 2.
Operates June-Aug.

This laboratory experience enables qualified high school upperclassmen to engage in biological research. Students meet with mentors to plan their projects, then spend the rest of the fellowship conducting experiments, collecting data, analyzing results, and updating their lab notebooks and research portfolios. Participants meet weekly to discuss their projects and listen to guest speakers. Schools must nominate interested applicants. Fellowships cover all travel and housing expenses and pay a weekly stipend.

NASA GODDARD SPACE FLIGHT CENTER
SCIENTIFIC AND ENGINEERING STUDENT INTERNSHIP PROGRAM
Res and Day — Coed Ages 17-23

Greenbelt, MD 20771. Public Inquiries, Mail Code 130. Tel: 301-286-3011.
http://hesperia.gsfc.nasa.gov/~interns E-mail: interns@helio.gsfc.nasa.gov
Student contact: Cori Quirk.
Grades 12-Col. Adm: Very selective. **Appl**—Fee $0. Due: Apr. Resume, interview. **Enr:**
25.
Focus: Engineering Sci.
12 wks: 40 hrs/wk.
Housing: Some assistance is provided in securing housing.
Operates June-Aug.

Rising high school seniors, as well as college undergraduates, are eligible for 12-week paid internships in this program. Jointly operated by the Goddard Space Flight Center and the Catholic University of America, the session provides research opportunities in the areas of high-energy astrophysics, astrochemistry, geophysics, solar and planetary sciences, and applied engineering.

NATIONAL INSTITUTE ON DRUG ABUSE
SUMMER RESEARCH WITH NIDA
FOR UNDERREPRESENTED STUDENTS
Res — Coed Ages 15-18

Bethesda, MD 20892. Special Populations Office, 6001 Executive Blvd, Rm 4216,
MSC 9567. Tel: 301-443-0441. Fax: 301-480-8179.
www.drugabuse.gov/pdf/sposummer.pdf E-mail: flindsey@nida.nih.gov
Student contact: Flair Lindsey.
Grades 10-Col. Adm: Very selective. Priority for: URM. **Appl**—Due: Mar. Transcript, essay,
2 recs.
Locations: CA CO CT GA IO IL MA MD MI MN NJ NY TN TX.
Focus: Sci.
8 wks: 40 hrs/wk. **Salary:** $8 (per hour).
Housing: Interns must live within commuting distance.
Est 1997.

This program encourages students from groups lacking strong representation in the sciences to pursue careers in biomedical and behavioral research. Students work with distinguished scientists at hospitals, universities and research centers across the country. Duties may include formal courses, participation in meetings, data collection, data analysis, interviewing, laboratory experiments, manuscript preparation and library research, among others. Applicants under age 18 must apply to sites within commuting distance.

NATIONAL INSTITUTES OF HEALTH
SUMMER INTERNSHIP PROGRAM IN BIOMEDICAL RESEARCH
Res — Coed Ages 16-8; Day — Coed 16-18

Bethesda, MD 20892. 10 Center Dr, Bldg 10, Rm 2N242. Tel: 301-451-9440.
Fax: 301-594-8133.
http://dir.nhlbi.nih.gov/oe/summerprogs.asp E-mail: direducation@nhlbi.nih.gov
Debbie Cohen, Dir.
Grades 11-Col. Adm: Very selective. Admitted: 20%. Prereqs: GPA 3.0. **Appl**—Due: Mar.
Transcript, resume, 2 recs.
Locations: AZ MD MI MT NC.
Focus: Med/Healthcare Sci.
8 wks: 40 hrs/wk. **Salary:** $1300 (lump sum).

Housing: Nonlocal interns must arrange housing independently. Operates June-Aug.

This competitive program enables talented high school, college, graduate, medical and dental students to work together on biomedical research. Most internships take place on the main NIH campus in Bethesda, MD, although opportunities are also available at specialized laboratories and institutes in Baltimore and Frederick, MD; Detroit, MI; Research Triangle Park, NC; Phoenix, AZ; and Hamilton, MT. Interns on the main campus may engage in various summer activities, among them a lecture series featuring NIH investigators, informal lunchtime talks on training for research careers and a trainee poster day.

OFFICE OF NAVAL RESEARCH
SCIENCE & ENGINEERING APPRENTICE PROGRAM
Res and Day — Coed Ages 16-18

Washington, DC 20036. 1818 N St NW, Ste T-50.
http://seap.asee.org   E-mail: seap@asee.org
Grades 10-PG. Adm: Very selective. **Appl**—Due: Jan. **Enr:** 250.
Locations: AZ CA DC FL MD MI PA RI VA.
Focus: Engineering Sci.
8 wks. Salary: $1500 (lump sum).
Housing: Nonlocal interns must arrange housing independently.
Operates June-Aug.

Talented high school students gain an exposure to careers in science and engineering through SEAP's eight-week apprenticeships at 16 Department of Defense research centers, laboratories, observatories and warfare centers. Projects range from radiobiology and medical research to aircraft and weapons systems engineering. SEAP encourages students to apply to centers close to home. Some laboratories may accept 15-year-olds.

SATURDAY ACADEMY
APPRENTICESHIPS IN SCIENCE AND ENGINEERING PROGRAM
Res — Coed Ages 15-18

Portland, OR 97205. 830 SW 10th Ave, Ste 200. Tel: 503-200-5861. Fax: 503-200-5899.
www.saturdayacademy.org/ase   E-mail: ase@saturdayacademy.org
Grades 10-12. Adm: Selective. **Appl**—Fee $25. Due: Mar. Transcript, essays, 2 recs. **Enr:** 120.
Locations: OR WA Canada.
Focus: Engineering Sci.
8 wks. Salary: $0-1000 (lump sum).
Housing: Nonlocal interns must arrange housing independently.
Operates June-Aug.

The ASE program matches students from Oregon and Washington with professional scientists and engineers who act as mentors. Participating organizations in Oregon, southwest Washington and Vancouver, British Columbia, include IBM, Intel, Nike and the National Weather Service. Research topics include archaeology, biology, biomedical, chemistry, computer science, earth science, environmental science, engineering, mathematics, physics and social sciences. Students attend a two-day conference of seminars and workshops and present research findings at a symposium. Participants in certain programs receive a stipend.

SIMONS SUMMER RESEARCH FELLOWSHIP PROGRAM
Res and Day — Coed Ages 17-18

Stony Brook, NY 11794. State Univ of New York, Melville Library N-3070.
Tel: 631-632-7114. Fax: 631-632-4525.
www.sunysb.edu/simons   E-mail: karen.kernan@stonybrook.edu
Karen Kernan, Dir.
Grade 12. Adm: Very selective. Admitted: 15%. **Appl**—Due: Jan. Transcript, 3 recs. **Enr:** 31.
Focus: Engineering Sci.
7 wks: 40 hrs/wk. **Salary:** $1000 (lump sum).
Housing: Dorms. Avg per room/unit: 2. Housing available for $1200 fee.
Est 1984. Operates June-Aug.

Simons fellows participate in ongoing research projects, learn laboratory techniques and tools, write a research abstract and experience life at a research university. Students, who are paired with faculty researchers, conduct ongoing studies in physics, marine science, chemistry, life science, engineering and other fields. In addition to full-time laboratory work, fellows also participate in weekly brown-bag lunches and workshops and visit other laboratories and research groups. Participants have been recognized by the Intel Science Talent Search and the Siemens Competition in Math, Science & Technology.

STANFORD INSTITUTES OF MEDICINE
SUMMER RESEARCH PROGRAM
Res — Coed Ages 17-18

Stanford, CA 94305. Stanford School of Med, 300 Pasteur Dr. Tel: 650-723-4000.
http://simr.stanford.edu   E-mail: simr-program@stanford.edu
Grades 12-PG. Adm: Very selective. **Appl**—Due: Feb. Transcript, test scores, 2 essays, rec. **Enr:** 45.
Focus: Med/Healthcare Sci.
8 wks: 40 hrs/wk. **Salary:** $1500 (lump sum).
Housing: Nonlocal interns must arrange housing independently.
Est 1998. Operates June-Aug.

High school upperclassmen from diverse backgrounds perform basic research with Stanford faculty, postdoctoral fellows, undergraduates and researchers on a medically oriented project. Students work with a mentor from one of five institutes: cancer biology, stem cell biology, neuroscience, immunology or cardiovascular medicine. In addition to full-time lab work, interns attend institute-specific lectures, safety training sessions and field trips to biotech firms. A poster session at the conclusion of the program enables participants to present their findings. Participants have been recognized by the Intel Science Talent Search and the Siemens Competition in Math, Science & Technology.

TEXAS TECH UNIVERSITY
CLARK SCHOLARS PROGRAM
Res — Coed Ages 16-18

Lubbock, TX 79409. Box 43131. Fax: 806-742-2963.
www.clarkscholars.ttu.edu   E-mail: lynda.durham@ttu.edu
Michael San Francisco, Dir. Student contact: Lynda Durham.
Grades 12-PG. Adm: Very selective. Admitted: 9%. **Appl**—Fee $0. Due: Feb. Transcript, 3 recs, standardized test scores. **Enr:** 12.
Focus: Engineering Hist Math Sci Veterinary_Med Music Theater.
7 wks. Salary: $750 (lump sum).
Housing: Dorms. Provided for all interns.

Operates June-Aug.

Clark Scholars Program allows gifted students to work hand-in-hand with faculty in intensive research settings. The seven-week program also includes weekly seminars, discussions and field trips designed to develop students' critical thinking abilities and career interests. Students choose from research areas in not only the natural sciences and mathematics but the humanities and fine arts as well. Participants have gained recognition through the Intel Science Talent Search; the American Academy of Neurology's Neuroscience Research Prize; and the Siemens Competition in Math, Science & Technology.

UNIVERSITY OF COLORADO CANCER CENTER
STUDENT CANCER RESEARCH FELLOWSHIP PROGRAM
Res — Coed Ages 17 and up; Day — Coed 16 and up

**Aurora, CO 80045. Mailstop F434, 13001 E 17th Pl. Tel: 303-724-3174.
Fax: 303-724-3163.
www.ucdenver.edu/academics/colleges/medicalschool/centers/cancercenter
E-mail: jill.penafiel@ucdenver.edu
Jill Penafiel, Coord.
Grades 12-Col. Adm:** Very selective. Admitted: 5%. Prereqs: GPA 3.5. **Appl**—Fee $0. Due: Feb. **Enr:** 45.
Focus: Sci.
9 wks: 40 hrs/wk. **Salary:** $250 (per week).
Housing: Nonlocal interns must arrange housing independently.
Operates June-Aug.

Open to undergraduate, graduate and medical students, this rigorous program also offers a few positions to the most advanced rising high school seniors. Full-time, eight- or nine-week fellowships pair students with preceptors from a variety of laboratories and clinics at the University of Colorado-Denver, University of Colorado-Boulder, University of Colorado Hospital and other Denver-area healthcare institutions. Intern duties, which vary according to the needs of the preceptor, may include data collection, cell cultures, data analysis and testing. Fellows attend twice-weekly lectures and present their research findings at a concluding poster session. Applicants should have prior experience with advanced high school science classes, preferably those carrying an Advanced Placement or International Baccalaureate designation.

UNIVERSITY OF WASHINGTON GENOM PROJECT
ALVA SUMMER RESEARCH PROGRAM
Res — Coed Ages 17-18

**Seattle, WA 98195. Univ of Washington, Box 352180.
http://depts.washington.edu/genomics/precoll/p-high.htm
Student contact: Allison Kang, E-mail: allikang@u.washington.edu.
Grades 12-PG. Adm:** Selective. Priority for: URM. **Appl**—Due: Mar. Transcript, resume, essay, 2 recs. **Enr:** 12.
Focus: Sci.
9 wks: 40 hrs/wk.
Housing: Dorms.
Operates June-Aug.

This program is open to rising high school seniors and incoming University of Washington freshmen interested in genomics, life sciences, ecogenetics and bioengineering research. During the first two weeks, students participate in intensive laboratory training. Through interactive learning, students learn pipetting skills, DNA extractions, and various biological processes and lab techniques such as PCR and gel electrophoresis. Students then work collectively on a research project with a lab mentor. Dormitory housing is provided and students earn an hourly wage for lab work.

VANDERBILT UNIVERSITY RESEARCH INTERNSHIP PROGRAM
Res and Day — Coed Ages 16-18

Nashville, TN 37232. 806 Light Hall. Tel: 615-322-7140. Fax: 615-322-7169.
www.scienceoutreach.org/research.php   E-mail: cso@vanderbilt.edu
Grade 12. Adm: Very selective. **Appl**—Due: Mar.
Focus: Engineering Sci.
6 wks.
Housing: Nonlocal interns must arrange housing independently.
Operates June-July.

This intense immersion program takes place in a research lab at Vanderbilt University or Vanderbilt University Medical Center. Rising high school seniors engage in an independent project under the mentorship of a research faculty member and present their findings in a poster session. Weekly sessions led by faculty, postdoctoral researchers and graduate students provide information on college studies and scientific careers. Some stipends may be available.

MUSIC AND ARTS
PROGRAMS

Music and arts programs are arranged alphabetically by name. The Table of Contents lists the subject areas presented, and an index beginning on page 318 lists the programs under each of those subjects.

INDEX BY FOCUS

DANCE

DANCE *(CONT.)*

FILMMAKING (CONT.)

FINE ARTS

MEDIA

MUSIC

MUSIC *(CONT.)*

PHOTOGRAPHY *(CONT.)*

SCULPTURE

THEATER *(CONT.)*

Music and Arts Programs

ACADEMY OF ART UNIVERSITY
PRE-COLLEGE SUMMER ART EXPERIENCE
Res and Day — Coed Ages 15-18

San Francisco, CA 94105. 79 New Montgomery St. Tel: 415-274-2200, 800-544-2787.
www.academyart.edu/degrees/summer_artexperience.html
E-mail: experience@academyart.edu
Grades 10-PG. **Adm:** FCFS. **Appl**—Fee $525. Due: Rolling.
Type of instruction: Enrich. **Courses:** Animation Fashion Filmmaking Photog Sculpt.
Focus: Studio_Art.
Housing: Dorms.
Ses: 1. **Wks/ses:** 6½. Operates June-Aug.

Students in this intensive precollege program take up to four arts classes during the course of the session. Courses, which meet twice a week for two hours and 50 minutes per class, provide boys and girls with an exposure to college life and also help them determine if art and design is a suitable area for future study. Chaperoned recreational, cultural and community-oriented activities supplement course work.

THE AILEY SCHOOL SUMMER INTENSIVE PROGRAMS
Res — Coed Ages 15-25; Day — Coed 12-15

New York, NY 10019. 405 W 55th St. Tel: 212-405-9000. Fax: 212-405-9001.
www.theaileyschool.edu   E-mail: admissions@alvinailey.org
Student contact: JoAnne Ruggeri.
Adm: Selective. **Appl**—Due: Rolling. Live audition or DVD recording & photos.
Type of instruction: Enrich.
Focus: Dance.
Fees 2009: Res $4200-4700, 5-6 wks. Day $1850-2200, 5-6 wks.
Housing: Dorms.
Ses: 2. **Wks/ses:** 5-6. Operates June-July.

The Ailey School offers a six-week Professional Division Summer Intensive for dancers ages 16-25 and a five-week Junior Division program for those ages 12-15 (only 15-year-olds may attend as boarding students). Students take 12 to 15 technique classes weekly from the school's core curriculum, including daily ballet classes and Horton- or Graham-based modern classes five to six times a week. Additional instruction addresses jazz, tap, hip-hop, Dunham, barre a terre, yoga, body conditioning and two levels of pointe. Guest choreographers conduct repertory workshops. Boarding students live in Fordham University housing. Three years of prior ballet training is a prerequisite.

ALFRED UNIVERSITY
SUMMER INSTITUTES IN CREATIVE WRITING
Res — Coed Ages 15-17

Alfred, NY 14802. Office of Summer Prgms, Carnegie Hall, 1 Saxon Dr.
Tel: 607-871-2612. Fax: 607-871-2045.
www.alfred.edu/summer/hs.cfm   E-mail: summerpro@alfred.edu
Susan Morehouse, Dir. Student contact: Melody McLay, E-mail: mclaym@alfred.edu.
Grades 10-12. Adm: Selective. Admitted: 85%. Prereqs: GPA 3.0. **Appl**—Fee $0. Due: Apr.
Transcript, 2 recs, essay, 2 creative writing samples.
Enr: 25. **Enr cap:** 25. Intl: 1%. Non-White: 10%. **Fac 2.** Prof 2. **Staff:** Admin 4. Couns 12.

Type of instruction: Adv Enrich Undergrad. **Avg class size:** 15. **Daily hours for:** Classes 6. Study 2. Rec 3. Homework.
Focus: Creative_Writing. **Features:** Swim Bowling.
Fees 2011: Res $850 (+$50), 1 wk. Day $595 (+$50), 1 wk.
Housing: Dorms. Avg per room/unit: 2. **Swimming:** Pool. Campus facilities avail.
Est 1999. Nonprofit. **Ses:** 2. **Wks/ses:** 1. Operates July.

While sampling college life, high schoolers enrolled in the program gain an introduction to several genres of creative writing: poetry, short fiction, creative nonfiction and drama. During morning and afternoon sessions, students complete writing-intensive exercises that address voice, character, metaphor, persona and narrative. Workshop sessions employ a seminar-like model that enables writers to critique and revise their work. In addition, staff conduct reading-intensive classes and roundtables designed to facilitate discussion of writers and their strategies.

ALFRED UNIVERSITY SUMMER THEATER INSTITUTE
Res and Day — Coed Ages 15-17

Alfred, NY 14802. Office of Summer Prgms, 1 Saxon Dr. Tel: 607-871-2612.
Fax: 607-871-2045.
www.alfred.edu/summer/hs.cfm   E-mail: summerpro@alfred.edu
Melody McLay, Dir.
Grades 10-12. Adm: Selective. Admitted: 85%. Prereqs: GPA 3.0. **Appl**—Fee $0. Due: Apr. Transcript, 2 recs, essay.
Enr: 15. **Enr cap:** 15-20. Intl: 1%. Non-White: 10%. **Fac 3.** Prof 3. **Staff:** Admin 4. Couns 12.
Type of instruction: Adv Undergrad. **Avg class size:** 15. **Daily hours for:** Classes 6. Rec 5. **College credit:** 2/crse, total 2.
Focus: Acting Theater. **Features:** Swim.
Fees 2011: Res $1995 (+$100), 2 wks. Day $995 (+$100), 2 wks.
Housing: Dorms. **Swimming:** Pool. Campus facilities avail.
Est 2007. Nonprofit. **Ses:** 1. **Wks/ses:** 2. Operates July.

The AU Theater Institute provides high schoolers with training in acting, voice, movement, design, technical theater and stage management. Students work on improving their skills and developing new levels of expertise in two or three of these areas. Included in the schedule is an outing to a professional theater. The two-week program culminates in a group performance. Rising juniors and seniors may earn two hours of college credit by completing extra assignments and paying an additional fee.

ALPHA SCIENCE FICTION/FANTASY/HORROR WORKSHOP FOR YOUNG WRITERS
Res — Coed Ages 14-19

Greensburg, PA. Univ of Pittsburgh-Greensburg.
Contact (Year-round): PO Box 3681, Pittsburgh, PA 15230. Tel: 412-344-0456.
www.alpha.spellcaster.org
Diane Turnshek, Dir.
Adm: Very selective. Admitted: 25%. **Appl**—Fee $10. Due: Mar. 2000- to 6000-word genre piece.
Enr: 20. **Enr cap:** 20. **Fac 4.** Specialists 4. **Staff:** Admin 2. Couns 10.
Type of instruction: Enrich. **Daily hours for:** Classes 4. Study 4. Homework.
Focus: Creative_Writing.
Fees 2012: Res $995, 1½ wks. Aid (Merit & Need).
Housing: Dorms. Avg per room/unit: 1. Campus facilities avail.
Est 2002. Nonprofit. **Ses:** 1. **Wks/ses:** 1½. Operates July.

Alpha seeks talented young writers who have a strong interest in one of the following genres: science fiction, fantasy or horror. Topics covered in lectures and writing studios include character creation, plot, conflict and tension, dialogue, pace and structure. Working with professional authors, participants brainstorm on story ideas, compose first drafts, receive feedback and rewrite their pieces. Students also deliver public readings and learn about submitting manuscripts for publication.

AMERICAN BOYCHOIR SCHOOL
CAMP ALBEMARLE
Res — Coed Ages 9-14; Day — Coed 7-14

Princeton, NJ 08540. 19 Lambert Dr. Tel: 609-924-5858. Fax: 609-924-5812.
www.americanboychoir.org   E-mail: rellsworth@americanboychoir.org
Carl Nelson, Dir. Student contact: Roberta Griffith Ellsworth.
Grades 2-9. Adm: FCFS. **Appl**—Due: Rolling.
Enr: 75-100. Non-White: 20%. **Fac 4.** K-12 staff 4. **Staff:** Admin 3. Couns 8.
Courses: Crafts. **Avg class size:** 10. **Daily hours for:** Classes 3. Rec 7.
Focus: Music. **Features:** Basketball Soccer Softball Swim Volleyball.
Fees 2011: Res $1420 (+$35), 2 wks. Day $1115, 2 wks.
Housing: Dorms. **Swimming:** Pool. Campus facilities avail.
Est 1941. Inc. **Ses: 2. Wks/ses: 2.** Operates July.

This American Boychoir School music camp accepts any child, with or without previous training. Choral singing and musicianship training classes are at the core of the program. Albemarle balances its musical curriculum with an active, compulsory recreational sports program designed to address both social and motor skills. Daily supervised swimming is a noteworthy aspect of the recreational program.

AMERICAN BOYCHOIR SCHOOL EXPERIENCE CAMP
Res and Day — Boys Ages 8-12

Princeton, NJ 08540. 19 Lambert Dr. Tel: 609-924-5858. Fax: 609-924-5812.
www.americanboychoir.org   E-mail: rellsworth@americanboychoir.org
Carl Nelson, Dir. Student contact: Roberta Griffith Ellsworth.
Grades 3-6. Adm: Selective. **Appl**—Fee $0. Due: Rolling. Audition.
Enr: 29. **Enr cap:** 40. **Fac 6.** Prof 1. Col/grad students 3. K-12 staff 2. **Staff:** Admin 3.
Type of instruction: Enrich. **Courses:** Crafts Music_Theory. **Daily hours for:** Classes 4. Rec 4.
Focus: Music. **Features:** Aquatics Swim.
Fees 2011: Res $800, 1 wk. Day $650, 1 wk.
Housing: Dorms. **Swimming:** Pool. Campus facilities avail.
Est 2009. Nonprofit. **Ses: 1. Wks/ses: 1.** Operates July.

This choral music camp enrolls young boys with or without previous training. Boys further develop their vocal skills in small-group instruction classes, while also improving their music theory skills in sight reading and ear training by following the Kodaly Method. Traditional recreational activities round out the program. Candidates for admission should have unchanged voices and must also pass an audition.

AMERICAN DANCE FESTIVAL
Res and Day — Coed Ages 12 and up

Durham, NC 27708. Box 90772. Tel: 919-684-6402. Fax: 919-684-5459.
www.americandancefestival.org   E-mail: adf@americandancefestival.org

James Frazier & Gerri Houlihan, Deans.
Student contact: Nicolle Wasserman, **E-mail:** school@americandancefestival.org.
Adm: FCFS. **Appl**—Fee $40. Due: Rolling.
Enr: 42-310. **Fac 70.** Prof 70. **Staff:** Admin 50. Couns 11.
Avg class size: 30. **Daily hours for:** Classes 6. Grades. **College credit:** ½/crse, total 2.
Focus: Dance. **Features:** Swim.
Fees 2012: Res $1135-4515, 1-6 wks. Day $875-1990, 1-6 wks. Aid (Merit & Need).
Housing: Apartments Dorms. Avg per room/unit: 2. **Swimming:** Pool. Campus facilities avail.
Est 1934. Nonprofit. **Ses:** 3. **Wks/ses:** 1-6. Operates June-July.

ADF offers classes in modern, ballet, hip-hop and African dance technique; composition, improvisation and repertory; performance technique and music for dancers; and anatomy and kinesiology. Also featured are performances and workshops for young dancers, dance professionals, critics and teachers. Students choose from six-week (for dancers 16 and older only), three-week and weeklong sessions.

AMERICAN UNIVERSITY
DISCOVER THE WORLD OF COMMUNICATION
Res — Coed Ages 15-18; Day — Coed 13-18

Washington, DC 20016. School of Communication, 4400 Massachusetts Ave NW.
Tel: 202-885-2098. Fax: 202-885-2019.
www.audiscover.org E-mail: audiscover@gmail.com
Sarah Menke-Fish, Dir.
Grades 9-PG. Adm: FCFS. **Appl**—Fee $0. Due: Rolling.
Enr: 250. **Enr cap:** 250. Intl: 10%. Non-White: 20%. **Fac 20.** Prof 15. Col/grad students 2. Specialists 3. **Staff:** Admin 3. Couns 15.
Type of instruction: Adv Enrich Undergrad. **Courses:** Speech Writing/Journ Sportswriting Web_Design Screenwriting. **Avg class size:** 12. **Daily hours for:** Classes 6. Study 1. Rec 3. Homework. **College credit:** 1-2/crse.
Intl program focus: Acad Culture. **Locations:** Mexico/Central_America.
Focus: Comm Acting Animation Film Filmmaking Media Photog. **Features:** Aquatics Baseball Basketball Soccer Swim.
Fees 2012: Res $1500-3000, 2-4 wks. Day $650-2200, 2-4 wks. Aid 2011 (Need): $5000.
Housing: Dorms. **Swimming:** Pool. Campus facilities avail.
Nonprofit. **Ses:** 2. **Wks/ses:** 2. Operates June-July.

High schoolers taking part in this program have access to the resources of American University and its school of communication. Students focus upon fiction or documentary filmmaking, acting and directing, public speaking, photography, broadcast journalism or animation. In addition to the Washington, DC, program, the program includes a Costa Rica option that incorporates environmental filmmaking, Spanish-language immersion and community service. **See Also Page 38**

APPEL FARM ARTS CAMP
Res — Coed Ages 9-17

Elmer, NJ 08318. 457 Shirley Rd, PO Box 888. Tel: 856-358-2472, 800-394-8478.
Fax: 856-358-6513.
www.appelfarmartscamp.org E-mail: camp@appelfarm.org
Jennie Quinn & Cori Solomon, Dirs.
Grades 4-12. Adm: FCFS. **Appl**—Fee $0. Due: Rolling.
Enr: 224. **Enr cap:** 224. Intl: 5%. Non-White: 25%. **Fac 85.** Prof 5. Col/grad students 60. K-12 staff 15. Specialists 5. **Staff:** Admin 18. Res 85.

Courses: Environ_Sci Writing/Journ Crafts Filmmaking Fine_Arts. **Avg class size:** 9. **Daily hours for:** Classes 5. Rec 5.
Focus: Creative_Writing Dance Media Music Painting Photog Sculpt Theater. **Features:** Aquatics Community_Serv Farm Swim Tennis.
Fees 2011: Res $3000-8300 (+$50), 2-8 wks. Aid 2008 (Need): $282,300.
Housing: Cabins. Avg per room/unit: 10. **Swimming:** Pool.
Est 1960. Nonprofit. **Ses:** 5. **Wks/ses:** 2-8. Operates June-Aug.

The program features music, fine arts, crafts, drama, dance, theater, creative writing, video production and photography. Appel Farm conducts no auditions, accepting campers from beginner through highly advanced levels. Aside from structured instructional time, the program consists of workshops, ensembles, performances, noncompetitive sports, short trips, campwide activities and free time.

APPLE HILL CENTER FOR CHAMBER MUSIC
SUMMER CHAMBER MUSIC WORKSHOP
Res — Coed Ages 12 and up

Sullivan, NH 03445. PO Box 217. Tel: 603-847-3371. Fax: 603-847-9734.
www.applehill.org E-mail: music@applehill.org
Amelia Perron, Coord.
Adm: FCFS. **Appl**—Fee $75. Due: Apr. CD/DVD/digital placement recording.
Enr: 60. **Enr cap:** 60. Intl: 20%. **Fac 10.** Specialists 10. **Staff:** Admin 2. Couns 11. Res 10.
Courses: Dance. **Daily hours for:** Classes 3. Study 1-2. Rec 3.
Focus: Music. **Features:** Hiking Soccer Swim Bowling Ping-Pong.
Fees 2012: Res $1500-2800 (+$10-40), 1½-3 wks. Aid (Need).
Housing: Cabins. Avg per room/unit: 4-6. **Swimming:** Pond. Campus facilities avail.
Est 1971. Nonprofit. **Ses:** 5. **Wks/ses:** 1½. Operates June-Aug.

Apple Hill conducts short sessions for musicians at many different skill levels who are placed in two ensembles, according to ability. Each ensemble rehearses daily. Both informal and structured sight-reading sessions of chamber works are offered. In the student concerts that close each session, all groups perform for an audience of fellow participants, faculty, family and friends.

ARROWBEAR MUSIC CAMP
Res — Coed Ages 9-18

Running Springs, CA 92382. PO Box 180. Tel: 909-867-2782. Fax: 909-867-2794.
www.arrowbear.com E-mail: info@arrowbear.com
Grades 4-PG. Adm: FCFS. **Appl**—Fee $0. Due: Rolling.
Courses: Crafts.
Focus: Music. **Features:** Hiking Swim.
Fees 2011: Res $460-1260 (+$20-40), 1-3 wks. Aid (Need).
Housing: Cabins. **Swimming:** Pool.
Est 1942. Inc. **Ses:** 6. **Wks/ses:** 1-3. Operates June-Aug.

Arrowbear's emphasis is on music in the areas of large-group band, orchestra and choral performance. The camp combines lessons and rehearsals with social activities and recreation. Campers are divided into three age groups, with choral and jazz improvisation sessions available to high school students. Recitals and concerts are part of the program.

ASPEN MUSIC FESTIVAL AND SCHOOL
Res — Coed Ages 15 and up; Day — Coed 8 and up

Aspen, CO 81611. 2 Music School Rd. Tel: 970-925-3254. Fax: 970-925-3802.

www.aspenmusicfestival.com   E-mail: school@aspenmusic.org
Robert Spano, Dir.
Adm: Selective. **Appl**—Fee $25-100. Due: Jan. CD/DVD recordings.
Enr: 625. **Fac 140.**
Focus: Music.
Fees 2011: Res $4000-6300 (+$600), 4-8 wks.
Housing: Dorms. Avg per room/unit: 2-3.
Est 1949. Nonprofit. **Ses:** 3. **Wks/ses:** 4-8. Operates June-Aug.

Aspen Music School, designed for students of college age or older, enrolls a limited number of exceptionally talented younger students who possess outstanding maturity, strong musical talent and serious professional intent. The students, in conjunction with members of the artist/ faculty and guests, present the Aspen Music Festival concurrent with the school term. Younger students generally participate in orchestras and chamber ensembles.

ATHENS CENTRE SUMMER WORKSHOPS
Res — Coed Ages 16 and up

Athens, 116 36 Greece. 48 Archimidous St. Tel: 30-210-7012-268.
    Fax: 30-210-7018-603.
www.athenscentre.gr   E-mail: athenscr@ath.forthnet.gr
Rosemary C. Donnelly, Dir.
Grades 12-Col. Adm: FCFS. **Appl**—Fee 250. Due: Rolling.
Enr: 40. **Enr cap:** 50. Intl: 70%. Non-White: 2%. **Fac 5.** Prof 5. **Staff:** Admin 7. Couns 2.
Type of instruction: Adv. **Courses:** Greek Poetry. **Avg class size:** 10. **Daily hours for:** Classes 4. Grades. **College credit:** 6.
Intl program focus: Acad.
Focus: Fine_Arts. **Features:** Bicycle_Tours Hiking Swim.
Fees 2012: Res €1670-2060 (+€500), 3 wks.
Housing: Apartments. Avg per room/unit: 2. **Swimming:** Ocean.
Est 1969. Nonprofit. **Ses:** 2. **Wks/ses:** 3. Operates June-July.

The Centre operates separate arts and poetry summer workshops in Athens. The poetry seminar focuses on the writing and appreciation of poetry. Students read and discuss Homer's Odyssey and an array of poems from contemporary and modern Greek and Anglophone authors. The arts workshop concentrates on creating images of island life through drawing, painting and mixed media.

AUBURN UNIVERSITY MUSICAL THEATRE CAMP
Res — Coed Ages 14-18

Auburn, AL 36849. Office of Professional & Continuing Ed, 301 O D Smith Hall.
    Tel: 334-844-5100. Fax: 334-844-3101.
www.auburn.edu/outreach/opce/summercamps
E-mail: james.birdsong@auburn.edu
James Birdsong, Coord.
Grades 9-12. Adm: FCFS. **Appl**—Fee $0. Due: Rolling.
Type of instruction: Enrich. **Courses:** Dance Music.
Focus: Theater.
Fees 2011: Res $600, 1 wk.
Housing: Dorms.
Ses: 1. **Wks/ses:** 1. Operates June-July.

This weeklong workshop features classes in acting, dance, singing and musical theater history. Instructors include music and theater professionals from Auburn's faculty.

CAMP BALLIBAY
Res — Coed Ages 6-16

Camptown, PA 18815. 1 Ballibay Rd. Tel: 570-746-3223, 877-746-2667.
Fax: 570-746-3691.
www.ballibay.com E-mail: camp@ballibay.com
John J. A. Jannone, Dir.
Adm: FCFS. Admitted: 100%. **Appl**—Due: Rolling.
Enr: 150. Intl: 20%. Non-White: 5%. **Fac 40.** Prof 5. Col/grad students 25. K-12 staff 10.
Staff: Admin 7.
Courses: Creative_Writing Fine_Arts Painting Studio_Art. **Daily hours for:** Classes 4. Rec 1½.
Focus: Ceramics Dance Media Music Photog Theater. **Features:** Aquatics Riding Equestrian Swim Tennis.
Fees 2012: Res $3775-7400, 3-6 wks.
Housing: Cabins. Avg per room/unit: 10. **Swimming:** Pool. Campus facilities avail.
Est 1964. Inc. **Ses:** 7. **Wks/ses:** 2-7. Operates June-Aug.

Ballibay offers extensive programs in theater, music (including rock music), dance, video and art. Other opportunities include an active waterfront program, daily riding and overnight camp outs, as well as various team and individual sports.

BARD COLLEGE AT SIMON'S ROCK YOUNG WRITERS WORKSHOP
Res — Coed Ages 15-18

Great Barrington, MA 01230. 84 Alford Rd. Tel: 413-528-7231. Fax: 413-644-4280.
www.simons-rock.edu/young_writers E-mail: jamieh@simons-rock.edu
Jamie Hutchinson, Dir.
Grades 10-12. Adm: Selective. Admitted: 65%. **Appl**—Fee $0. Due: Rolling. Essay, teacher rec.
Enr: 84. **Enr cap:** 84. Intl: 2%. Non-White: 9%. **Fac 7.** Prof 7. **Staff:** Admin 2. Res 10.
Type of instruction: Adv Enrich. **Avg class size:** 12. **Daily hours for:** Classes 4½. Study 2.
Focus: Creative_Writing. **Features:** Climbing_Wall Basketball Soccer Softball Swim Tennis Ultimate_Frisbee Volleyball Watersports Weight_Trng.
Fees 2012: Res $2525 (+$200), 3 wks. Aid 2007 (Need): $15,000.
Housing: Dorms. Avg per room/unit: 2. **Swimming:** Lake Pool.
Est 1983. Nonprofit. **Ses:** 1. **Wks/ses:** 3. Operates July-Aug.

The Young Writers Workshop is part of the National Writing and Thinking Network, the largest consortium of summer writing programs in the country. Unlike conventional workshops in creative or expository writing, Simon's Rock's program focuses on using informal, playful expressive writing as a way to strengthen skills of language and thinking. Subject matter ranges from stories and poems to personal experiences, natural phenomena and works of art. More polished pieces—such as personal narratives, stories, poems and exploratory essays—arise from the informal writing activities.

BATES DANCE FESTIVAL YOUNG DANCERS WORKSHOP
Res — Coed Ages 14-18

Lewiston, ME 04240. Pettigrew Hall, 305 College St. Tel: 207-786-6381.
Fax: 207-786-8282.
www.bates.edu/dancefest E-mail: dancefest@bates.edu
Laura Faure, Dir. Student contact: Nancy Salmon.
Adm: Selective. **Appl**—Fee $0. Due: Rolling.
Enr: 100. **Enr cap:** 100. **Fac 8. Staff:** Admin 2. Couns 9.
Avg class size: 20. **Daily hours for:** Classes 5½.

Focus: Dance. **Features:** Swim.
Fees 2011: Res $2340-2400, 3 wks. Aid (Merit & Need).
Housing: Dorms. Avg per room/unit: 1-2. **Swimming:** Pool.
Est 1992. Nonprofit. **Spons:** Bates College. **Ses:** 1. **Wks/ses:** 3. Operates June-July.

Serving serious dance students with a minimum of three years of current and continuous dance training in modern technique and at least one year of ballet, the Young Dancers Workshop provides highly structured and closely supervised instruction. Students take 90-minute morning classes in modern dance and ballet, then select two 75-minute courses from the following options—jazz, hip-hop, African or repertory—during the afternoon session. In addition, boys and girls develop material in their classes for a final performance. Placement classes determine the appropriate level of study for each dancer.

BELVOIR TERRACE
Res — Girls Ages 8-17

Lenox, MA 01240. Tel: 413-637-0555. Fax: 413-637-4651.
Contact (Oct-May): 101 W 79th St, New York, NY 10024. Tel: 212-580-3398.
 Fax: 212-579-7282.
www.belvoirterrace.com   E-mail: info@belvoirterrace.com
Nancy Goldberg & Diane Goldberg Marcus, Dirs.
Grades 2-11 (younger if qualified). Adm: FCFS. **Appl**—Due: Rolling.
Enr: 200. Intl: 10%. **Fac 95.** Prof 10. Col/grad students 75. Specialists 10. **Staff:** Admin 10. Res 30.
Type of instruction: Adv Enrich SAT/ACT_Prep. **Courses:** Creative_Writing. **Avg class size:** 8. **Daily hours for:** Classes 5. **High school credit.**
Focus: Ceramics Dance Media Music Painting Photog Theater. **Features:** Aquatics Archery Riding Basketball Cross-country Swim Tennis Volleyball.
Fees 2012: Res $10,700 (+$500), 6½ wks. Aid (Merit & Need).
Housing: Dorms. Avg per room/unit: 7. **Swimming:** Pool. Campus facilities avail.
Est 1954. Inc. **Ses:** 1. **Wks/ses:** 6½. Operates June-Aug.

This individually structured arts program emphasizes professional instruction in art, dance, theater and music. Students may also take lessons in tennis, swimming and horseback riding.

BERKLEE SUMMER PERFORMANCE PROGRAM
Res and Day — Coed Ages 15 and up

Boston, MA 02215. Office of Summer Prgms, 1140 Boylston St, MS-155 SP.
 Tel: 617-747-2245, 877-237-5533. Fax: 617-262-5419.
www.berklee.edu/summer/5week.html   E-mail: summer@berklee.edu
Dana Acker, Dir. Student contact: Shelly Booth, E-mail: sbooth@berklee.edu.
Adm: FCFS. **Appl**—Fee $50. Due: Rolling.
Enr: 1100. Intl: 27%. Non-White: 54%. **Fac 60.** Prof 60. **Staff:** Admin 4.
Type of instruction: Enrich. **Courses:** Bus/Fin. **Avg class size:** 15. **Daily hours for:** Classes 7. Homework. Tests. Grades.
Focus: Music.
Fees 2011: Res $7495 (+$100), 5 wks. Day $4420 (+$185), 5 wks. Aid 2011 (Merit): $3,500,000.
Housing: Dorms. Campus facilities avail.
Est 1987. Nonprofit. **Spons:** Berklee College of Music. **Ses:** 1. **Wks/ses:** 5. Operates July-Aug.

High school and college students with at least six months of playing or singing experience may enroll in this immersion program. Participants, who are placed with other musicians of similar training and ability, play in ensembles, develop improvisational and reading skills, work on technique during weekly private lessons, and attend lectures and demonstrations conducted by both faculty and visiting artists. The following tracks are available: jazz, pop/rock, funk/fusion (instrumental only) and pop/R&B (vocalists only).   **See Also Page 31**

BLUE LAKE FINE ARTS CAMP
Res — Coed Ages 10-17

Twin Lake, MI 49457. 300 E Crystal Lake Rd. Tel: 231-894-1966, 800-221-3796.
Fax: 231-893-5120.
www.bluelake.org
Heidi Stansell, Dir.
Grades 5-12. Adm: FCFS. **Appl**—Fee $0. Due: Rolling.
Enr: 1325. **Intl:** 2%. Non-White: 20%. **Fac 250. Staff:** Admin 30. Couns 200.
Type of instruction: Enrich. **Avg class size:** 15. **Daily hours for:** Classes 5. Study 2. Rec 2.
Intl program focus: Culture. **Travel:** Europe. Home stays avail.
Focus: Dance Music Studio_Art Theater. **Features:** Soccer Swim Ultimate_Frisbee Volleyball.
Fees 2011: Res $1178 (+$75), 2 wks. Aid 2011 (Merit & Need): $2,200,000.
Housing: Cabins. Avg per room/unit: 11. **Swimming:** Pool.
Est 1966. Nonprofit. **Ses:** 4. **Wks/ses:** 2. Operates June-Aug.

Students at Blue Lake choose from four major study areas: dance, art, drama and music. Musical concerts, drama and dance presentations, and art exhibits enrich the program. An international exchange program offers participants an opportunity to combine musical performance with educational travel to Europe. Elective activities include recreational opportunities, choir, art, theater, dance and jazz.

BOSTON UNIVERSITY ACADEMY OF MEDIA PRODUCTION
Res — Coed Ages 16-18

Boston, MA 02215. College of Communication, 640 Commonwealth Ave.
Tel: 617-353-5015. Fax: 617-353-3405.
www.academyofmediaproduction.com   E-mail: leglaser@bu.edu
Lauren Glaser, Coord.
Grades 11-12. Adm: Selective. **Appl**—Fee $25. Due: May. Transcript, essay, rec.
Enr: 60. **Fac 17. Staff:** Admin 2. Couns 2.
Type of instruction: Enrich. **Avg class size:** 15. **Daily hours for:** Classes 6.
Focus: Filmmaking Media. **Features:** Swim.
Fees 2011: Res $4879 (+$400), 4 wks.
Housing: Dorms. **Swimming:** Pond Ocean Pool.
Est 1987. Nonprofit. **Ses:** 1. **Wks/ses:** 4. Operates July-Aug.

Students interested in television, film, and radio production and programming choose three AMP workshops from the following options: film, field video production, studio television, editing, and radio for broadcast and the Web. Each workshop consists of eight classes. Participants create and deliver original programs and attend weekly seminars in directing, producing or screenwriting that include group discussion, role playing, project work and critiques. Guest lectures and site visits round out the program.

BOSTON UNIVERSITY TANGLEWOOD INSTITUTE
Res — Coed Ages 14-19

Lenox, MA 01240. 45 West St. Tel: 413-637-1430. Fax: 413-637-2792.
Contact (Sept-May): 855 Commonwealth Ave, Boston, MA 02215. Tel: 617-353-3386.
Fax: 617-353-7455.
www.bu.edu/tanglewood   E-mail: tanglewd@bu.edu

Shirley A. Leiphon, Admin Dir.
Grades 9-PG (younger if qualified). Adm: Selective. Admitted: 38%. **Appl**—Fee $75. Due: Feb. Live or recorded audition, teacher rec.
Enr: 350. Intl: 8%. Non-White: 15%. **Fac 85. Staff:** Admin 15. Couns 17.
Type of instruction: Adv. **Courses:** Fine_Arts. **Daily hours for:** Classes 8. Grades. **College credit:** 8.
Focus: Music. **Features:** Hiking Yoga Basketball Swim Tennis.
Fees 2011: Res $2585-6975, 2-8 wks. Aid 2010 (Merit & Need): $450,000.
Housing: Dorms. Avg per room/unit: 2. **Swimming:** Lake. Campus facilities avail.
Est 1966. Nonprofit. **Ses:** 8. **Wks/ses:** 2-8. Operates June-Aug.

Musicians at the institute choose from a range of programs that includes orchestral and chamber music, vocal technique, composition, wind ensemble, piano and harp, as well as two-week workshops in a variety of instruments. Except for the workshops, all programs include private lessons as part of the curriculum.

BOSTON UNIVERSITY THEATRE INSTITUTE
Res and Day — Coed Ages 16-18

Boston, MA 02215. 855 Commonwealth Ave, Rm 470. Tel: 617-353-3390.
Fax: 617-353-4363.
www.bu.edu/cfa/theatre/sti   E-mail: pdifabio@bu.edu
Emma Dassori, Dir.
Grades 11-12. Adm: Selective. **Appl**—Fee 65. Due: Apr. Resume, essay, 2 recs.
Enr: 70. **Enr cap:** 70. **Fac 6. Staff:** Admin 3. Res 6.
Type of instruction: Adv. **Avg class size:** 15. **Daily hours for:** Classes 10. Study 1. Rec 2. **College credit:** 4.
Focus: Acting Theater.
Fees 2011: Res $5264-5406, 5 wks. Day $3575, 5 wks.
Housing: Dorms.
Est 1980. Nonprofit. **Ses:** 1. **Wks/ses:** 5. Operates June-Aug.

The institute features intensive professional training in acting (improvisation, monologue work and scene study), dramatic literature, movement for actors and singing with a faculty of working artists. Instruction also addresses script analysis, character development and playwriting. A master class in Shakespeare performance is also offered. Workshops offered throughout the summer introduce students to an array of subjects. Each student is cast in a performance project that rehearses throughout the five weeks.

BOSTON UNIVERSITY VISUAL ARTS SUMMER INSTITUTE
Res and Day — Coed Ages 14-17

Boston, MA 02215. College of Fine Arts, 855 Commonwealth Ave, Rm 552.
Tel: 617-353-3371. Fax: 617-353-7217.
www.bu.edu/cfa/visual-arts/summer   E-mail: visuarts@bu.edu
Jeanette Guillemin & Alana Silva, Dirs.
Grades 9-12 (younger if qualified). Adm: Selective. Admitted: 75%. **Appl**—Fee $75. Due: Apr. Art samples, essay, rec.
Enr cap: 25. Intl: 20%. Non-White: 10%. **Fac 8.** Prof 4. Col/grad students 4. **Staff:** Admin 2. Couns 3.
Type of instruction: Undergrad. **Courses:** Photog Bookmaking Printmaking Silkscreen. **Daily hours for:** Classes 6. Study 4. Rec 4. Homework. Grades. **College credit:** 3/crse, total 3.
Focus: Drawing Painting Sculpt Studio_Art. **Features:** Climbing_Wall Swim.
Fees 2011: Res $4225-4339 (+$150), 4 wks. Day $2875 (+$150), 4 wks. Aid 2011 (Merit & Need): $1000.
Housing: Dorms. Avg per room/unit: 2. **Swimming:** Pool. Campus facilities avail.

Est 2005. Nonprofit. **Ses:** 1. **Wks/ses:** 4. Operates June-July.

The institute enables high school students interested in art to gain skills in drawing, painting, printmaking and sculpture while living on the campus of Boston University. Boys and girls also learn about art through museum trips and attendance at master classes taught by professional artists. Successful completion of the four-week program results in the credit equivalent of one college course.

BRANDEIS UNIVERSITY BIMA PROGRAM
Res — Coed Ages 15-18

Waltham, MA 02454. 415 South St, MS 065. Tel: 781-736-8416. Fax: 815-301-2874.
www.brandeis.edu/highschool   E-mail: highschool@brandeis.edu
Rachel Happel, Dir.
Grades 10-12. Adm: Selective. **Appl**—Fee $40. Due: Mar. Arts sample, essays, 2 recs.
Enr: 95. Fac 10. Specialists 10. **Staff:** Admin 6. Couns 12.
Type of instruction: Enrich. **Courses:** Relig_Stud. **Avg class size:** 13.
Focus: Creative_Writing Dance Filmmaking Music Studio_Art Theater.
Fees 2012: Res $5400, 4 wks. Aid (Need).
Housing: Dorms. Avg per room/unit: 2. Campus facilities avail.
Est 2004. Nonprofit. Jewish. **Ses:** 1. **Wks/ses:** 4. Operates July-Aug.

BIMA participants hone their artistic skills while exploring Jewish traditions and Jewish identity. The program addresses six core areas of artistic study: filmmaking, music (instrumental or vocal), visual arts, creative writing, theater and dance. Boys and girls develop techniques and collaborate artistically with other participants. In addition, students choose from a range of workshops pertaining to various media. Other activities include concerts, performances and exhibitions at cultural institutions. The community celebrates Shabbat, and Kosher dining is observed at all meals.

BRANT LAKE DANCE CENTRE
Res — Girls Ages 12-16

Brant Lake, NY 12815. 7586 State Rte 8. Tel: 518-494-2406. Fax: 518-494-7372.
www.blcdance.com   E-mail: dance@brantlake.com
Lynn Brown, Dir.
Grades 7-11. Adm: FCFS. **Appl**—Fee $0. Due: Apr.
Enr: 60. Fac 4. Staff: Admin 10. Couns 12.
Type of instruction: Enrich. **Courses:** Crafts Drama Drawing Painting Photog Sculpt.
   Daily hours for: Classes 5.
Focus: Dance. **Features:** Aquatics Canoe Climbing_Wall Sail Golf Swim Tennis Water-skiing Watersports.
Fees 2012: Res $6675, 4½ wks.
Housing: Cabins. **Swimming:** Lake.
Ses: 1. **Wks/ses:** 4½. Operates June-July.

Located in the Adirondack Mountains, Brant Lake provides professional instruction at all levels of dance. Advanced dancers may take up to five hourlong classes daily, while others round out their schedules with various recreational camping pursuits. One evening each week, the group attends a ballet performance, a rock concert or a play, while other evenings are usually spent in shared social activities with the affiliated Brant Lake Camp for boys.

BREVARD MUSIC CENTER
Res — Coed Ages 14-28

Brevard, NC 28712. 349 Andante Ln, PO Box 312. Tel: 828-862-2100.
   Fax: 828-884-2036.
www.brevardmusic.org   E-mail: bmcadmissions@brevardmusic.org
Keith Lockhart, Dir.
   Student contact: Dorothy Knowles, E-mail: dknowles@brevardmusic.org.
Grades 9-Col. Adm: Very selective. Admitted: 23%. **Appl**—Fee $65. Due: Mar. Recorded audition.
Enr: 410. **Enr cap:** 410. Intl: 3%. Non-White: 10%. **Fac 65.** Prof 63. Specialists 2. **Staff:** Admin 15.
Type of instruction: Adv.
Focus: Music. **Features:** Soccer Swim.
Fees 2012: Res $5100 (+$200), 6 wks. Aid 2011 (Merit & Need): $1,020,000.
Housing: Cabins. Avg per room/unit: 16. **Swimming:** Lake.
Est 1936. Nonprofit. **Ses: 1. Wks/ses:** 6. Operates June-Aug.

Conducting high school and college divisions, BMC provides an intensive program in music study and practice. Brevard offers five courses of study: orchestral studies, piano, composition, voice for high schoolers and opera for college students. During the course of the session, young musicians participate in more than 80 public performances, many of which feature renowned guest artists. While most students attend for six or seven weeks, pianists and high school singers may enroll for either three or six weeks.

BRIANSKY BALLET CENTER
Res and Day — Coed Ages 10-18

South Hadley, MA 01075. c/o Mount Holyoke College, 50 College St.
   Tel: 413-538-3472. Fax: 413-538-3473.
Contact (Aug-June): 220 W 93rd St, New York, NY 10025. Tel: 212-799-0341.
   Fax: 212-799-0341.
www.briansky.org   E-mail: olegbriansky@msn.com
Oleg Briansky, Dir.
Adm: Selective. **Appl**—Fee $25. Due: May. Audition by video or DVD.
Enr: 100. **Enr cap:** 100. Intl: 40%. **Fac 5.** Specialists 5. **Staff:** Admin 2. Couns 6.
Courses: Fine_Arts Music Photog Theater. **Avg class size:** 20. **Daily hours for:** Classes 3.
Focus: Dance. **Features:** Swim.
Fees 2012: Res $2307-4315, 2-4 wks. Day $430, 1 wk. Aid (Need).
Housing: Dorms. **Swimming:** Pool. Campus facilities avail.
Est 1965. Nonprofit. **Ses: 3. Wks/ses:** 2-4. Operates July.

Operating on the campus of Mount Holyoke College, BSBC is a serious ballet academy and cultural summer camp that provides intensive technique and performance training. Students are placed in intermediate or advanced levels and receive instruction in pointe, variations and repertory, as well as jazz and Broadway dance and choreography workshops. Guest teachers, lecturers and films enrich the program. Prospective day students should arrive with at least two years of prior ballet study.

BROADWAY THEATRE PROJECT
Res — Coed Ages 16 and up

Tampa, FL. Univ of South Florida.
Contact (Year-round): 2780 E Fowler Ave, Ste 106, Tampa, FL 33612.
   Toll-free: 888-874-1764.
www.broadwaytheatreproject.com   E-mail: broadwaytp@aol.com

Merrick Wolfe, Exec Dir.
Grades 10-Col. Adm: Selective. **Appl**—Fee $35. Due: Mar. Live/DVD audition, rec.
Enr cap: 200. **Fac 50. Staff:** Admin 12. Couns 7.
Courses: Dance Fine_Arts Music.
Focus: Theater. **Features:** Swim.
Fees 2012: Res $3500 (+$50), 3 wks. Aid (Need).
Housing: Hotels. **Swimming:** Pool.
Est 1991. Nonprofit. **Ses:** 1. **Wks/ses:** 3. Operates July.

Conducted at the University of South Florida, BTP enables high school and college students who have prior musical theater training to study intensively with professional artists and educators in theater, film and television. Pupils attend classes in acting, dance, voice and writing, with emphasis placed on the collaborative process and the collective creation of art. The program also includes specialty classes in stage combat, Broadway repertory and auditioning, as well as private vocal and acting lessons. Participants spend evenings rehearsing for a final performance at the Tampa Bay Performing Arts Center.

BROWN UNIVERSITY THEATREBRIDGE
Res — Coed Ages 16-18

Providence, RI 02912. Box T, 42 Charlesfield St. Tel: 401-863-7900. Fax: 401-863-3916.
www.brown.edu/scs/pre-college/theatrebridge   E-mail: summer@brown.edu
Mark Cohen, Dir.
Grades 11-PG. Adm: Selective. **Appl**—Fee $45-90. Due: Rolling. Transcript, teacher rec, video interview.
Type of instruction: Enrich. **Courses:** Creative_Writing.
Focus: Acting Theater.
Fees 2011: Res $7100, 6 wks. Aid (Need).
Housing: Dorms. Campus facilities avail.
Ses: 1. **Wks/ses:** 6. Operates June-July.

This intensive precollege theater program provides promising actors and actresses with an opportunity to hone their acting, directing and writing skills as they work under the guidance of established theater professionals. Classes, which meet six days a week, address text, improvisation and movement. Students spend the majority of their evening and weekend hours rehearsing and preparing for class. TheatreBridge culminates in a free public performance on the final afternoon. **See Also Page 35**

BUCK'S ROCK PERFORMING AND CREATIVE ARTS CAMP
Res — Coed Ages 9-16

New Milford, CT 06776. 59 Buck's Rock Rd. Tel: 860-354-5030, 800-636-5218.
Fax: 860-354-1355.
www.bucksrockcamp.com   E-mail: bucksrock@bucksrockcamp.com
Mickey Morris & Laura Morris, Dirs.
Grades 5-12 (younger if qualified). Adm: FCFS. **Appl**—Fee $0. Due: Rolling.
Enr: 350. **Enr cap:** 350. **Fac 160. Staff:** Admin 6.
Courses: Writing/Journ Crafts Creative_Writing Filmmaking Fine_Arts Media Culinary_ Arts Fiber_Arts Glassblowing Metalsmithing Printmaking.
Focus: Ceramics Dance Music Painting Photog Sculpt Theater. **Features:** Aquatics Archery Caving Farm Hiking Badminton Basketball Fencing Martial_Arts Soccer Softball Swim Tennis Ultimate_Frisbee Volleyball.
Fees 2012: Res $3090-9490 (+$200-300), 2-7½ wks. Aid (Need).
Housing: Cabins Houses. Avg per room/unit: 4-6. **Swimming:** Pool.
Est 1942. Inc. **Ses:** 5. **Wks/ses:** 2-7½. Operates June-Aug.

Buck's Rock features a comprehensive free-choice curriculum in the creative and performing arts. Options include theater, clowning and improvisation, dance, orchestra, chorus, chamber music, jazz band, guitar, weaving, silk-screening, sculpture, ceramics, painting and drawing, woodworking, printing, publications, photography, batik, sewing, computer science, radio broadcasting and farming. Campers select their activities on a daily basis and work in a noncompetitive environment that enables them to explore their interests. Boys and girls also take part in a noncompetitive sports program. A two-week session serves nine- and 10-year-olds only.

BURKLYN BALLET THEATRE
Res and Day — Coed Ages 10-25

Johnson, VT 05656. c/o Johnson State College, 337 College Hill. Tel: 802-635-0438.
Contact (Sept-May): PO Box 923, Denville, NJ 07834. Tel: 973-625-9300.
Year-round Toll-free: 877-287-5596, Fax: 973-625-9304.
www.burklynballet.com   E-mail: burklyn@gmail.com
Joanne E. Whitehill, Dir.
Adm: Selective. Admitted: 80%. **Appl**—Fee $25. Due: Rolling. Live/video audition.
Enr: 85. **Enr cap:** 85. Intl: 1%. **Fac 12. Staff:** Admin 3. Couns 20.
Type of instruction: Adv Enrich. **Avg class size:** 28. **Daily hours for:** Classes 8.
Travel: Europe.
Focus: Dance. **Features:** Swim.
Fees 2011: Res $2731-5853 (+$30/wk), 2-6 wks. Day $309-670 (+$90), 1 wk. Aid (Merit).
Housing: Dorms. **Swimming:** Pool. Campus facilities avail.
Est 1976. Inc. **Ses:** 7. **Wks/ses:** 2-6. Operates June-Aug.

Conducted at Johnson State College and designed for the serious ballet student at an intermediate or advanced level, the program includes weekly performances and study with some of the country's finest master teachers. Pupils also learn basic backstage procedures and makeup techniques, as well as character and variations, in order to prepare for professional careers. All dancers perform weekly at the campus theater. Twenty students may participate in the Edinburgh Connection, a two-week program that features travel to Scotland with the director following four weeks of study at Burklyn.

CALIFORNIA COLLEGE OF THE ARTS PRE-COLLEGE PROGRAM
Res and Day — Coed Ages 15-18

Oakland, CA 94618. Office of Extended Ed, 5212 Broadway. Tel: 510-594-3638.
Fax: 510-594-3771.
www.cca.edu/precollege   E-mail: precollege@cca.edu
Corisa Cobden, Coord.
Grades 10-PG. Adm: Selective. **Appl**—Fee $75. Due: Mar.
Enr: 250. Intl: 3%. **Fac 25. Prof 25. Staff:** Admin 6.
Type of instruction: Adv Enrich Undergrad. **Courses:** Architect. **Avg class size:** 12. **Daily hours for:** Classes 6. Homework. Grades. **College credit:** 3/crse, total 3.
Focus: Animation Creative_Writing Drawing Fashion Filmmaking Painting Photog Sculpt Studio_Art.
Fees 2012: Res $3575 (+$130-275), 4 wks. Day $2700, 4 wks. Aid 2007 (Merit & Need): $95,000.
Housing: Dorms. Avg per room/unit: 2-3. Campus facilities avail.
Est 1986. Nonprofit. **Ses:** 1. **Wks/ses:** 4. Operates June-July.

CCA's Pre-College Program enables high schoolers to earn three college credits while studying creative writing or one of 17 studio options: animation, architecture, community arts and drawing, drawing/painting and sculpture, fashion design, digital cinema, graphic design, illustration and printmaking, industrial design, jewelry/metal arts, painting and drawing, black and white photography, color photography, digital photography, textiles or printmaking and drawing. As an immersion program, Pre-College requires students to attend class each morning and afternoon, then develop work outside of class time.

CAZADERO MUSIC CAMP
Res — Coed Ages 10-18

Cazadero, CA.
Contact (Year-round): PO Box 7908, Berkeley, CA 94707. Tel: 510-527-7500.
  Fax: 510-527-2790.
www.cazadero.org   **E-mail: execdir@cazadero.org**
Jim Mazzaferro, Dir. Student contact: Emily Brockman, E-mail: emily@cazadero.org.
Grades 5-12. Adm: Selective. **Appl**—Fee $40. Due: Rolling. Music teacher rec.
Enr: 120. **Enr cap:** 160. **Fac 40. Staff:** Admin 4.
Courses: Crafts Dance Theater.
Focus: Music. **Features:** Hiking Basketball Swim Volleyball.
Fees 2012: Res $795-1500 (+$40), 1-2 wks. Aid (Merit & Need).
Housing: Cabins Dorms Tents. **Swimming:** Pool.
Est 1957. Nonprofit. **Ses:** 6. **Wks/ses:** 1-2. Operates June-Aug.

Located in an old-growth redwood grove in the Russian River Valley of Sonoma County, Cazadero provides music instruction for young people and families. Students in grades 5-8 who have at least a year of prior musical training may enroll in the Young Musicians session; campers take classes in technique and music theory while also playing in an ensemble. The middle school session (grades 6-8), for which two years of primary instrument instruction is a prerequisite, encourages further development of ensemble skills through participation in chamber groups, orchestra, symphonic band and campwide chorus. A more challenging program is in place for junior high students (grades 7-9), while accomplished players with at least four years of musical training refine their skills during the high school session (grades 9-12).

CENTAURI SUMMER ARTS CAMP
Res and Day — Coed Ages 8-18

Wellandport, L0R 2J0 Ontario, Canada. RR 3.
Contact (Sept-June): 85 Humbercrest Blvd, Toronto, M6S 4L2 Ontario, Canada.
Year-round Tel: 416-766-7124, Fax: 416-766-7655.
www.centauriartscamp.com   **E-mail: info@centauriartscamp.com**
Julie Hartley & Craig Hartley, Dirs.
Adm: FCFS. **Appl**—Fee $0. Due: Rolling.
Enr: 145. **Enr cap:** 145. **Fac 10. Prof 10. Staff:** Admin 5. Couns 26.
Type of instruction: Adv Enrich. **Courses:** Crafts Drama Filmmaking Music Studio_Art.
  Avg class size: 16. **Daily hours for:** Classes 4.
Focus: Creative_Writing Dance Film Fine_Arts Media Painting Photog Sculpt Theater.
  Features: Baseball Basketball Football Soccer Swim Volleyball.
Fees 2011: Res Can$1100-1428, 1-2 wks. Day Can$460-1039, 1-2 wks. Aid 2006 (Need): Can$2500.
Housing: Dorms. **Swimming:** Pool.
Est 1994. Inc. **Ses:** 4. **Wks/ses:** 1-2. Operates July-Aug.

Trained professionals instruct campers in theater, dance, art, photography, musical theater, film and writing. Campers receive instruction in the art form of their choice in the morning, then take part in recreational activities each afternoon.

CENTER FOR CREATIVE YOUTH
Res — Coed Ages 14-18

Middletown, CT 06459. c/o Wesleyan Univ. Tel: 860-685-3307. Fax: 860-685-3311.
Contact (Aug-May): 15 Vernon St, Hartford, CT 06106. Tel: 860-757-6391.
Fax: 860-757-6377.
www.crec.org/ccy   E-mail: ccy@wesleyan.edu
Nancy Wolfe, Dir.
Grades 10-12. Adm: Somewhat selective. Admitted: 85%. Appl—Fee $35. Due: Mar. Personal statement, 2 recs.
Enr: 170. Fac 10. Staff: Admin 2. Couns 23.
Courses: Musical_Theater. Daily hours for: Classes 5½. High school credit: 1½.
Focus: Creative_Writing Dance Filmmaking Music Photog Studio_Art Theater. Features: Swim.
Fees 2011: Res $4100 (+$100), 5 wks. Aid (Merit & Need).
Housing: Dorms. Swimming: Pool.
Est 1977. Nonprofit. Ses: 1. Wks/ses: 5. Operates June-July.

Conducted at Wesleyan University, CCY enrolls students who are talented in music, creative writing, theater, visual arts, dance, photography, filmmaking and technical theater. Students participate in intensive daily sessions in areas of interest and attend interdisciplinary classes. The program also includes leadership training opportunities.

CHAUTAUQUA SUMMER SCHOOLS OF FINE & PERFORMING ARTS
Res — Coed Ages 16-28

Chautauqua, NY 14722. 1 Ames Ave, PO Box 1098. Tel: 716-357-6233.
Fax: 716-357-9014.
www.ciweb.org/school-of-art   E-mail: art@ciweb.org
Don Kimes, Dir.
Student contact: Sarah R. Malinoski-Umberger, E-mail: smalinoski@ciweb.org.
Adm: Very selective. Admitted: 10%. Appl—Fee $30-40. Live audition or CD/DVD recording.
Enr: 285. Enr cap: 285. Fac 50. Staff: Admin 100. Couns 10.
Type of instruction: Adv. College credit: 3.
Focus: Dance Fine_Arts Music Theater. Features: Golf Swim Tennis Weight_Trng.
Fees 2012: Res $2200-4400, 7 wks. Aid 2009 (Merit & Need): $500,000.
Housing: Dorms. Avg per room/unit: 2. Swimming: Lake Pool. Campus facilities avail.
Nonprofit. Spons: Chautauqua Institution. Ses: 1. Wks/ses: 7. Operates June-Aug.

Chautauqua's summer programs offer serious preprofessional study in the fine and performing arts. Various formal and informal courses, particularly in music, the arts, theater and dance, are offered. In addition, the school conducts special studies courses and workshops, as well as courses carrying university credit. Recreational activities supplement class work.

CHOATE ROSEMARY HALL
DOCUMENTARY FILMMAKING
Res — Coed Ages 14-18

Wallingford, CT 06492. 333 Christian St. Tel: 203-697-2365. Fax: 203-697-2519.
www.choate.edu/summerprograms   E-mail: choatesummer@choate.edu
Peter B. Kaufman, Dir.
Grades 9-12. Adm: Selective. Admitted: 90%. Appl—Fee $60. Due: Rolling. Transcript, 3 recs, optional CD/DVD of work.
Enr: 12. Intl: 5%. Non-White: 5%.
Type of instruction: Enrich. Courses: Dance Drama Fine_Arts Music. Avg class size: 12.
Daily hours for: Classes 5½. Study 2. Rec 2. Homework.

Focus: Filmmaking. **Features:** Yoga Aerobics Baseball Basketball Rugby Soccer Softball Swim Track Volleyball.
Fees 2011: Res $2830 (+$200), 2 wks. Aid 2011 (Need): $300,000.
Housing: Dorms. Avg per room/unit: 2. **Swimming:** Pool. Campus facilities avail.
Nonprofit. **Ses:** 1. **Wks/ses:** 2. Operates June-July.

During the first week of this introductory documentary filmmaking program, high schoolers attend screenings of landmark films and iconic moving images. Students develop critical skills for reading and appreciating screen-based communication during the week. The second week, which includes a shooting and editing practicum, culminates in the creation of a documentary short film or a personal video essay. Guest presenters enrich the program during both weeks.

CHOATE ROSEMARY HALL THEATER ARTS INSTITUTE
Res — Coed Ages 12-18

Wallingford, CT 06492. 333 Christian St. Tel: 203-697-2365. Fax: 203-697-2519.
www.choate.edu/summerprograms   E-mail: choatesummer@choate.edu
James Balmer & Mary C. Nelson, Dirs.
Grades 7-12. Adm: Selective. Admitted: 90%. **Appl**—Fee $60. Due: Rolling. Transcript, 3 recs, performance CD/DVD, personal statement.
Enr: 24. Intl: 10%. Non-White: 10%.
Type of instruction: Enrich. **Courses:** Dance Fine_Arts Music. **Avg class size:** 12. **Daily hours for:** Classes 5. Rec 2.
Focus: Theater. **Features:** Yoga Aerobics Baseball Basketball Rugby Soccer Swim Tennis Volleyball.
Fees 2011: Res $4985 (+$400), 4 wks. Aid 2011 (Need): $300,000.
Housing: Dorms. Avg per room/unit: 2. **Swimming:** Pool. Campus facilities avail.
Nonprofit. **Ses:** 1. **Wks/ses:** 4. Operates June-July.

In this immersive, four-week theater program, boys and girls of all ability levels study vocal performance; develop dance skills in tap, ballet, modern and jazz styles; and learn classical and modern acting techniques. A New York City trip during the second full weekend of the institute enables students and faculty to attend Broadway and off-Broadway shows, museums and other cultural venues. Field trips to evening performances are also part of the program. Participants collaborate on an original theater piece and musical revue.

CHOATE ROSEMARY HALL WRITING WORKSHOPS
Res — Coed Ages 12-18; Day — Coed 11-18

Wallingford, CT 06492. 333 Christian St. Tel: 203-697-2365. Fax: 203-697-2519.
www.choate.edu/summerprograms   E-mail: choatesummer@choate.edu
J. Trent Nutting, Dir.
Grades 6-12. Adm: Selective. Admitted: 90%. **Appl**—Fee $60. Due: Rolling. Transcript, essay, 3 recs, 2 graded English papers.
Enr: 50. Intl: 30%. Non-White: 25%.
Type of instruction: Enrich. **Courses:** Expository_Writing Dance Drama Fine_Arts Music. **Avg class size:** 12. **Daily hours for:** Classes 5½. Study 2. Rec 2. Homework.
Focus: Creative_Writing. **Features:** Yoga Aerobics Baseball Basketball Rugby Soccer Softball Swim Tennis Volleyball.
Fees 2011: Res $2830 (+$200), 2 wks. Day $2145 (+$200), 2 wks. Aid 2011 (Need): $300,000.
Housing: Dorms. Avg per room/unit: 2. **Swimming:** Pool. Campus facilities avail.
Nonprofit. **Ses:** 2. **Wks/ses:** 2. Operates June-July.

This intensive writing course serves students interested in exploring, improving and gaining confidence in their writing skills. Working with the teacher either individually or in small groups, pupils learn the importance of including detail and description in their creative writing and evidence and support in their analytical pieces. Boys and girls experiment with different kinds of writing, such as personal narrative, dialogue, poetry, short stories and thesis papers. Students play sports on weekday afternoons and engage in on- and off-campus social activities on weekends. Rising sixth graders attend as day pupils.

COLORADO COLLEGE SUMMER DANCE FESTIVAL
Res — Coed Ages 16 and up; Day — Coed 14 and up

Colorado Springs, CO 80903. 14 E Cache La Poudre St. Tel: 719-389-6353, 877-894-8727. Fax: 719-389-6145.
www.coloradocollege.edu/summerprograms/summerfestivalofthearts
E-mail: dancefestival@coloradocollege.edu
Patrizia Herminjard, Dir.
    Student contact: Karin Henriksen, E-mail: precollege@coloradocollege.edu.
Adm: Selective. Appl—Fee $40-50. Due: Rolling. Live audition.
Fac 12.
Daily hours for: Classes 6. Grades. College credit: 4.
Focus: Dance.
Fees 2011: Res $2760-3835, 3 wks. Day $1600-2675, 3 wks. Aid (Need).
Housing: Dorms.
Est 2001. Ses: 1. Wks/ses: 3. Operates June-July.

This intensive program features six hours of daily technique work, with an emphasis on modern dance. Other techniques covered include flamenco, capoeira, ballet, contact improvisation, yoga and repertory. Evening activities consist of lectures, performances, movies and open rehearsal space for participants wishing to choreograph their own work. Boys and girls should arrive with at least two years of prior dance experience.

CRANE YOUTH MUSIC
Res and Day — Coed Ages 12-18

Potsdam, NY 13676. c/o State Univ of New York-Potsdam, 389 Van Housen Ext, 44 Pierrepont Ave. Tel: 315-267-2167. Fax: 315-267-3350.
www.potsdam.edu/academics/crane/cym   E-mail: cym@potsdam.edu
Julianne Kirk Doyle, Dir.
Adm: FCFS. Appl—Fee $0. Due: Rolling.
Enr: 370. Enr cap: 370. Fac 40. Staff: Admin 3. Couns 49.
Type of instruction: Enrich. Daily hours for: Classes 1½. Rec 1½.
Focus: Music. Features: Swim.
Fees 2012: Res $975, 2 wks. Day $650, 2 wks. Aid 2011 (Merit & Need): $1200.
Housing: Dorms. Avg per room/unit: 2. Swimming: Pool. Campus facilities avail.
Est 1972. Ses: 1. Wks/ses: 2. Operates July.

Located on the SUNY-Potsdam campus, CYM addresses all aspects of music for young students. Classes are offered in piano, instrumental and orchestral music, and vocal performance. Boys and girls engage in planned recreational activities in the afternoon, and evening concerts include performances by student groups, visiting artists and performers, and faculty.

CAMP CURTAIN CALL
Res — Coed Ages 8-18

Dugspur, VA 24325. 849 River Rd. Tel: 276-730-0233. Fax: 276-728-4217.
Contact (Aug-May): PO Box 366, Seymour, TN 37865. Tel: 865-573-7002.
    Fax: 865-573-7002.
www.campcurtaincall.com   E-mail: info@campcurtaincall.com
Eddie Armbrister, Dir.

Adm: FCFS. **Appl**—Fee $0. Due: Rolling.
Enr: 30-45. **Enr cap:** 54. **Fac 15.** Prof 2. Col/grad students 9. K-12 staff 2. Specialists 2.
  Staff: Admin 3. Couns 16. Res 15.
Type of instruction: Enrich. **Courses:** Crafts Filmmaking Fine_Arts Media. **Daily hours**
  for: Classes 7. Study 2. Rec 3.
Focus: Circus_Skills Dance Music Painting Photog Theater. **Features:** Adventure_Travel
  Archery Bicycle_Tours Chess Hiking Kayak Mtn_Biking Aerobics Baseball Football Golf
  Gymnastics Soccer Softball Swim Tennis Volleyball Watersports Weight_Trng Wres-
  tling.
Fees 2010: Res $1195-6395 (+$179), 1-7 wks. Aid 2009 (Merit & Need): $9000.
Housing: Cabins. Avg per room/unit: 8. **Swimming:** Lake Pool River.
Est 2001. Inc. **Ses:** 7. **Wks/ses:** 1-7. Operates June-Aug.

Offering instruction in music, theater, fine arts, dance, magic and circus arts, Curtain Call provides a flexible schedule that enables campers to sample each of its programs. Professional staff lead classes, individual lessons, recitals and performance groups. Campers choose among recreational activities in the areas of sports, aquatics, crafts, nature and trips. Older campers typically attend for at least three weeks, although those ages 10-18 may enroll in an intensive, weeklong session in which they focus on theater, magic or dance. Another one-week session serves boys and girls ages 7-13.

DENISON UNIVERSITY
JONATHAN R. REYNOLDS YOUNG WRITERS WORKSHOP
Res — Coed Ages 16-18

Granville, OH 43023. English Dept, Box 810. Tel: 740-587-6207, 800-336-4766.
  Fax: 740-587-5680.
http://reynolds.denison.edu   E-mail: reynoldswriting@denison.edu
Margot Singer, Dir.
Grades 11-PG. Adm: Selective. Admitted: 50%. **Appl**—Fee $25. Due: Apr. Rec, creative
  writing sample.
Enr: 30. **Enr cap:** 36. Intl: 1%. Non-White: 16%. **Fac 3.** Prof 3. **Staff:** Admin 1. Couns 5.
Type of instruction: Enrich Undergrad. **Courses:** Creative_Nonfiction Fiction Poetry.
Focus: Creative_Writing. **Features:** Swim.
Fees 2012: Res $1200, 1 wk. Aid 2010 (Need): $18,100.
Housing: Dorms. **Swimming:** Lake Pool. Campus facilities avail.
Est 1994. Nonprofit. **Ses:** 1. **Wks/ses:** 1. Operates June.

Workshop participants choose a primary area of focus—poetry, fiction or creative nonfiction—for the duration of the eight-day session. Small, intensive groups of 10 or fewer students meet daily, and boys and girls also engage in one-on-one conferences with faculty members. Structured writing time is built into the program. In addition, pupils attend workshops with visiting writers and gain exposure to other genres through cross-writing sessions.

DUKE UNIVERSITY CREATIVE WRITERS' WORKSHOP
Res — Coed Ages 16-17

Durham, NC 27708. Continuing Stud, 201 Bishop's House, Box 90700.
  Tel: 919-684-6259. Fax: 919-681-8235.
www.learnmore.duke.edu/youth/creativewriter   E-mail: youth@duke.edu
Grades 11-12. Adm: Selective. **Appl**—Due: Rolling.
Type of instruction: Enrich.
Focus: Creative_Writing.
Fees 2010: Res $1655, 2 wks. Day $1065, 2 wks.
Housing: Dorms.
Ses: 1. **Wks/ses:** 2. Operates June-July.

Similar to a college creative writing course, the CWW has each student design and pursue a writing project with advisory help from a primary instructor. Course faculty are practicing writers with advanced degrees in their craft. Writing time takes up most of the day, with feedback and constructive criticism being important aspects of the program. Prospective applicants should have significant creative writing experience and should be interested in developing and refining their writing for a particular genre.

DUKE UNIVERSITY
EXPRESSIONS! PERFORMING ARTS CAMP
Res and Day — Coed Ages 11-14

Durham, NC 27708. Continuing Stud, 201 Bishop's House, Box 90700.
  Tel: 919-684-6259, 866-338-3853. Fax: 919-681-8235.
www.learnmore.duke.edu/youth/expressions   E-mail: youth@duke.edu
Karen Wade, Dir. Student contact: Thomas Patterson.
Grades 6-9 (younger if qualified). Adm: FCFS. Admitted: 100%. **Appl**—Fee $0. Due:
  May.
Enr: 36. **Enr cap:** 36. **Fac 4.** K-12 staff 4. **Staff:** Admin 6. Couns 3.
Type of instruction: Enrich. **Courses:** Fine_Arts. **Daily hours for:** Classes 3.
Focus: Dance Music Theater.
Fees 2011: Res $1810 (+$75), 2 wks. Day $945 (+$75), 2 wks. Aid (Need).
Housing: Dorms.
Est 1995. Ses: 1. **Wks/ses:** 2. Operates June-July.

This intensive, two-week arts program for middle school children consists of class work in drama, vocal training, dance and musical theater. Boys and girls focus upon three of the four strands. After developing their skills, students work on individual and group projects that emphasize one or more areas of concentration. A gallery and a final performance showcase campers' work.

DUKE UNIVERSITY YOUNG WRITERS' CAMP
Res and Day — Coed Ages 12-17

Durham, NC 27708. Continuing Stud, 201 Bishop's House, Box 90700.
  Tel: 919-684-6259. Fax: 919-681-8235.
www.learnmore.duke.edu/youth/youngwriter   E-mail: youth@duke.edu
Thomas Patterson, Dir.
Grades 7-12. Adm: Selective. **Appl**—Due: Rolling.
Type of instruction: Enrich.
Focus: Creative_Writing.
Fees 2010: Res $1655, 2 wks. Day $825-1065, 2 wks.
Housing: Dorms.
Ses: 3. **Wks/ses:** 2. Operates June-July.

Middle school and high school students enrolled in this Duke program explore different creative writing genres, among them short fiction, poetry, journalism and playwriting. Professional writers and educators lead the program, and local guest speakers are also featured. A daily readers' forum enables pupils to share their work with peers.

EASTERN MUSIC FESTIVAL
Res — Coed Ages 14-22

Greensboro, NC 27420. PO Box 22026. Tel: 336-333-7450, 877-833-6753.
  Fax: 336-333-7454.
www.easternmusicfestival.org   E-mail: admissions@easternmusicfestival.org
Stephanie Cordick, Exec Dir. Student contact: Melissa M. Edwards.

Adm: Very selective. **Appl**—Fee $60. Due: Mar. Live/recorded audition.
Enr: 200. Intl: 5%. **Fac 80. Staff:** Admin 6. Couns 10.
Type of instruction: Adv. **Courses:** Fine_Arts.
Focus: Music.
Fees 2012: Res $4825 (+$375), 5 wks. Aid (Merit & Need).
Housing: Dorms.
Est 1961. Nonprofit. **Ses:** 1. **Wks/ses:** 5. Operates June-Aug.

EMF provides gifted young musicians with opportunities to participate in a performance-oriented program and to present a series of classical music programs for concertgoers in the Southeast. Students may engage in orchestral, chamber music and piano studies.

EASTERN U.S. MUSIC CAMP AT COLGATE UNIVERSITY
Res and Day — Coed Ages 10-18

Hamilton, NY. c/o Colgate Univ, Dana Arts Ctr. Tel: 315-228-7041. Fax: 315-228-7557.
Contact (Aug-June): 7 Brook Hollow Rd, Ballston Lake, NY 12019. Tel: 518-877-5121.
  Fax: 518-877-4943.
Year-round Toll-free: 866-777-7841.
www.easternusmusiccamp.com   E-mail: summer@easternusmusiccamp.com
Thomas A. Brown & Grace R. Brown, Dirs.
Grades 5-12. Adm: FCFS. **Appl**—Fee $0. Due: Rolling.
Enr: 195. **Enr cap:** 200. **Fac 42. Staff:** Admin 18.
Type of instruction: Enrich. **Courses:** Fine_Arts. **Avg class size:** 12. **High school credit.**
Focus: Music. **Features:** Climbing_Wall Basketball Golf Softball Swim Tennis Track Volleyball.
Fees 2011: Res $2214-4428, 2-4 wks. Day $995-1990, 2-4 wks.
Housing: Dorms. Avg per room/unit: 2. **Swimming:** Pool.
Est 1976. Nonprofit. **Ses:** 6. **Wks/ses:** 2-4. Operates June-July.

Conducted at Colgate University, the camp offers a well-balanced program in instrumental and choral music that features group and one-on-one instruction. Students choose from daily rehearsals in symphonic band, symphony orchestra, jazz ensembles, jazz combos, studio orchestra, concert choir, chamber orchestra, madrigal choir, boys' choir, girls' choir and all instruments (including piano, harp and guitar). Classes in beginning and advanced theory, harmony, composition and arranging, improvisation and conducting are also available, and participants may earn high school credit. Activities include supervised sports, swimming, tennis, gymnastics, track, golf, crafts, movies, wall climbing, informal recreational offerings and a day trip to Cooperstown.

EDUCATION UNLIMITED CALIFORNIA ACTORS WORKSHOP
Res — Coed Ages 14-17

Palo Alto, CA. Stanford Univ.
Contact (Year-round): 1700 Shattuck Ave, Ste 305, Berkeley, CA 94709.
  Tel: 510-548-6612. Fax: 510-548-0212.
www.educationunlimited.com   E-mail: campinfo@educationunlimited.com
Matthew Fraser, Exec Dir.
Grades 9-12. Adm: FCFS. **Appl**—Fee $0. Due: Rolling. Personal statement.
Enr cap: 15-40. **Fac 3. Staff:** Admin 8.
Type of instruction: Enrich. **Avg class size:** 10. **Daily hours for:** Classes 6. Rec 5.
Focus: Acting Theater. **Features:** Swim.
Fees 2012: Res $4095 (+$50-150), 2 wks. Day $3481 (+$50-150), 2 wks. Aid (Need).
Housing: Dorms. **Swimming:** Pool.
Est 1999. Inc. **Ses:** 1. **Wks/ses:** 2. Operates July.

This studio theater program, held on the campus of Stanford University, focuses on developing various skills integral to a young actor's success. Students enroll in morning core courses and choose from a variety of specialized afternoon electives. The core curriculum focuses on combining creative intuition with concrete technical skills, and electives may include solo performance, musical theater and stand-up comedy.

EDUCATION UNLIMITED EMERGING WRITERS INSTITUTE
Res and Day — Coed Ages 15-18

Berkeley, CA 94709. 1700 Shattuck Ave, Ste 305. Tel: 510-548-6612.
   Fax: 510-548-0212.
www.educationunlimited.com   E-mail: campinfo@educationunlimited.com
Matthew Fraser, Exec Dir.
Grades 10-12. Adm: Selective. **Appl**—Due: Rolling.
Staff: Admin 8.
Type of instruction: Adv Enrich. **Avg class size:** 10. **Daily hours for:** Classes 7. Study 1. Rec 6.
Locations: CA.
Focus: Creative_Writing. **Features:** Swim.
Fees 2012: Res $4045 (+$50), 2 wks. Day $3481, 2 wks. Aid (Need).
Housing: Dorms. **Swimming:** Pool.
Est 2007. Inc. Ses: 2. **Wks/ses:** 2. Operates July-Aug.

Held at Stanford University and the University of California-Berkeley, the Emerging Writers Institute seeks to develop students' imaginative writing across the literary genres of fiction, nonfiction, playwriting and poetry. Daily writing workshops, one-on-one instructor evaluations, group editing sessions and creative presentations of student work focus upon both the technical and the artistic aspects of writing. Participants benefit from the literary culture of Berkeley and the Bay Area.

EMERSON COLLEGE
ARTS & COMMUNICATION PRE-COLLEGE PROGRAM
Res and Day — Coed Ages 14-18

Boston, MA 02116. Dept of Professional Stud & Special Prgms, 120 Boylston St.
   Tel: 617-824-8280. Fax: 617-824-8158.
www.emerson.edu/academics/professional-studies/programs-high-school-students
E-mail: continuing@emerson.edu
Tori Weston, Dir.
Grades 10-12. Adm: Somewhat selective. Admitted: 90%. **Appl**—Fee $0. Due: Rolling. Essay, resume, writing samples.
Non-White: 10%. **Fac 20.** Prof 16. Col/grad students 4. **Staff:** Admin 6. Couns 3.
Type of instruction: Enrich Undergrad. **Courses:** Media. **Daily hours for:** Classes 8. Homework. **College credit:** 4.
Focus: Writing/Journ Acting Creative_Writing Filmmaking Theater. **Features:** Ultimate_ Frisbee.
Fees 2012: Res $5490-7990, 5 wks. Day $2495-4895, 5 wks.
Housing: Dorms. Campus facilities avail.
Ses: 1. **Wks/ses:** 5. Operates July-Aug.

Rising seniors and exceptional rising juniors may earn college credit through courses in college writing, film production and film writing. Emerson also offers noncredit summer programs in creative writing, studio television and filmmaking (open to boys and girls entering grades 9-12); stage design (entering grades 10-12) and acting and musical theater (entering grades 11 and 12). Hands-on workshops and projects help students develop skills knowledge, and professors provide feedback on participants' work.

ENCORE! BAND CAMP
Res — Coed Ages 11-15

Milledgeville, GA. Georgia College & State Univ.
Contact (Year-round): 1240 Lakehaven Pky, McDonough, GA 30253.
  Tel: 770-914-8866. Fax: 770-914-2161.
www.encoremusiccamps.com E-mail: lvolman@bellsouth.net
Larry Volman, Dir.
Grades 6-10 (younger if qualified). Adm: FCFS. **Appl**—Fee $50. Due: June.
Enr: 150-220. **Enr cap:** 250. **Fac** 20. K-12 staff 20. **Staff:** Couns 20.
Type of instruction: Enrich. **Daily hours for:** Classes 6. Rec 4.
Focus: Music. **Features:** Swim.
Fees 2012: Res $475-495, 1 wk.
Housing: Dorms. Avg per room/unit: 2. **Swimming:** Pool. Campus facilities avail.
Est 1984. **Inc. Ses:** 1. **Wks/ses:** 1. Operates July.

Conducted at Georgia College and State University, Band Camp features rehearsals, master classes and performances. During the course of the weeklong session, students develop their technique for future auditioning success. Various social and recreational activities round out the program.

CAMP ENCORE/CODA
Res and Day — Coed Ages 9-18

Sweden, ME 04040. 50 Encore/Coda Ln. Tel: 207-647-3947.
Contact (Sept-May): 32 Grassmere Rd, Brookline, MA 02167. Tel: 617-325-1541.
Year-round Fax: 207-647-3259.
www.encore-coda.com E-mail: jamie@encore-coda.com
Jamie Saltman & Ellen Donohue-Saltman, Dirs.
Grades 4-12. Adm: FCFS. **Appl**—Fee $0. Due: Rolling.
Enr: 140. **Enr cap:** 140. **Fac** 60. **Staff:** Admin 5.
Courses: Crafts Theater.
Focus: Music. **Features:** Aquatics Canoe Kayak Sail Badminton Basketball Soccer Softball Swim Tennis Volleyball.
Fees 2012: Res $3950-7300, 3-6½ wks. Day $1975-3650, 3-6½ wks. Aid (Need).
Housing: Cabins. **Swimming:** Lake.
Est 1950. **Ses:** 3. **Wks/ses:** 3-6½. Operates June-Aug.

Encore/Coda offers a summer of music and sports. Musical instruction includes symphony orchestra, jazz band, chamber groups, private instrumental lessons, musical theater, voice and guitar. Waterfront activities and team sports complete the program.

ENDLESS MOUNTAINS DANCE CAMP
Res — Coed Ages 8-16

Camptown, PA 18815. 1 Ballibay Rd. Tel: 570-746-3223, 877-746-2667.
  Fax: 570-746-3691.
www.endlessmountainsdancecamp.com
E-mail: office@endlessmountainsdancecamp.com
Kristin A. Fieseler, Dir.
Adm: FCFS. **Appl**—Due: Rolling.
Focus: Dance.
Fees 2012: Res $2690, 2 wks.
Housing: Cabins.
Spons: Ballibay Camps. **Ses:** 2. **Wks/ses:** 2. Operates July.

EMDC's two-week program revolves around daily classes in modern, jazz and ballet dance technique, as well as in improvisation and composition. Technique classes accommodate varying ability levels, and individual and class goal setting is part of the session. All classes emphasize proper placement and alignment. Improvisation and composition classes feature improvisational exercises and choreographic tools. These classes culminate in a camper-choreographed group dance at session's end. When not engaged in dance classes or rehearsals, boys and girls may engage in traditional recreational activities at EMDC's sister camp, Camp Ballibay.

ENSEMBLE THEATRE COMMUNITY SCHOOL
Res — Coed Ages 14-18

Eagles Mere, PA 17731. PO Box 188. Tel: 570-525-3043.
Contact (Sept-June): 43 Lyman Cir, Shaker Heights, OH 44122. Tel: 216-378-2188.
Year-round Fax: 216-378-2188.
www.etcschool.org   E-mail: info@etcschool.org
Seth Orbach, Dir.
Grades 9-12. Adm: FCFS. **Appl**—Due: Rolling. Personal statement.
Enr: 20. **Fac** 11. **Staff:** Couns 6.
Courses: Dance Music.
Focus: Acting Theater. **Features:** Swim.
Fees 2011: Res $3000 (+$100), 3 wks. Aid (Need).
Housing: Houses. **Swimming:** Lake.
Est 1984. Nonprofit. **Ses:** 1. **Wks/ses:** 3. Operates June-July.

ETC School focuses on teaching and performing the dramatic arts in a small community atmosphere. Each student takes acting, movement and music, in addition to workshops in the performing arts. Study, rehearsals, relaxation and shared household duties round out the daily schedule.

EPISCOPAL HIGH SCHOOL YOUNG WRITERS WORKSHOP
Res and Day — Coed Ages 13-15

Alexandria, VA 22302. 1200 N Quaker Ln. Tel: 703-933-4043.
www.episcopalhighschool.org   E-mail: dcw@episcopalhighschool.org
Damian Walsh, Dir.
Grades 7-9. Adm: FCFS. **Appl**—Due: Rolling.
Type of instruction: Enrich. **Courses:** Public_Speak. Homework.
Focus: Expository_Writing Creative_Writing.
Fees 2011: Res $750, 1 wk. **Day** $600, 1 wk.
Housing: Dorms.
Nonprofit. Episcopal. **Ses:** 2. **Wks/ses:** 1. Operates June.

The Young Writers Workshop offers intensive instruction in written communication skills while providing multiple opportunities for students to practice public speaking. The course focuses on three major types of writing—creative, persuasive and analytical—by devoting a full day to the specific techniques of each genre. Participants present their work to peers in a concluding poetry reading/storytelling event. Activities outside the classroom include guest speakers and a field writing experience at the Botanical Gardens in Washington, DC.

THE FARM ARTS CAMP
Res — Coed Ages 6-16

Camptown, PA 18815. 1 Ballibay Rd. Tel: 570-746-3223, 877-746-2667.
  Fax: 570-746-3691.
www.thefarmartscamp.com   E-mail: directors@thefarmartscamp.com
Suzanne Goldenberg, Dir.
Adm: FCFS. **Appl**—Fee $0. Due: Rolling.

Courses: Printmaking.
Focus: Ceramics Drawing Music Painting Photog. **Features:** Canoe Cooking Riding Martial_Arts Swim.
Fees 2012: Res $2490-2690, 2 wks.
Housing: Cabins. **Swimming:** Lake Pool.
Est 1964. Spons: Ballibay Camps. **Ses:** 4. **Wks/ses:** 2. Operates July-Aug.

Campers at the farm either pursue a single art form intensively or sample a range of artistic experiences. Areas of specialization are painting and drawing, photography and printmaking, ceramics, and music and radio. Other activities, some of which are conducted in conjunction with the affiliated Camp Ballibay, include swimming, riding, nature pursuits, martial arts, gardening and cooking.

FRENCH WOODS FESTIVAL OF THE PERFORMING ARTS
Res — Coed Ages 7-17

Hancock, NY 13783. PO Box 609. Tel: 845-887-5600. Fax: 845-887-5075.
Contact (Sept-May): PO Box 770100, Coral Springs, FL 33077. Tel: 954-346-7455.
Fax: 954-346-7564.
Year-round Toll-free: 800-634-1703.
www.frenchwoods.com   E-mail: admin@frenchwoods.com
Ron Schaefer & Isaac Baumfield, Dirs.
Grades 2-12. Adm: FCFS. **Appl**—Fee $0. Due: Rolling.
Enr: 600. **Enr cap:** 600. **Intl:** 15%. Non-White: 15%. **Fac 150. Staff:** Admin 25. Couns 300.
Type of instruction: Dev_Read Preview Rem_Eng Rem_Math Rev SAT/ACT_Prep Study_Skills Tut. **Courses:** Computers ESL Writing/Journ Circus_Skills Crafts Filmmaking Media Painting Photog.
Focus: Dance Fine_Arts Music Theater. **Features:** Aquatics Boating Canoe Climbing_Wall Kayak Mountaineering Mtn_Biking Riding Ropes_Crse Sail Woodcraft Baseball Basketball Cross-country Equestrian Field_Hockey Football Golf Gymnastics Lacrosse Martial_Arts Roller_Hockey Skateboarding Soccer Softball Swim Tennis Volleyball Waterskiing Watersports Weight_Trng.
Fees 2012: Res $3950-10,700 (+$150), 3-11 wk.
Housing: Cabins. Avg per room/unit: 12. **Swimming:** Lake Pool.
Est 1970. Inc. **Ses:** 4. **Wks/ses:** 3. Operates June-Aug.

Major activities at French Woods include music, art, theater, magic, dance, nature, circus skills, skateboarding, fitness, a sports clinic (basketball, soccer and gymnastics), tennis, riding and waterfront offerings. Minor activities are offered in various artistic and athletic areas, including martial arts and circus skills. French Woods occupies a lakeside site in the western Catskill Mountains. **See Also Page 34**

FRIENDS MUSIC CAMP
Res — Coed Ages 10-18

Barnesville, OH 43713. c/o Olney Friends School, 61830 Sandy Ridge Rd.
Tel: 740-425-3655.
Contact (Aug-June): PO Box 59311, Chicago, IL 60659. Tel: 773-573-9181.
Year-round Fax: 937-767-2254.
www.friendsmusiccamp.org   E-mail: musicfmc@yahoo.com
Drea Gallaga & Nicholas Hutchinson, Dirs.
Grades 5-12. Adm: FCFS. **Appl**—Fee $100. Due: Rolling. 2 recs.
Enr: 75. **Intl:** 2%. Non-White: 3%. **Fac 20. Staff:** Admin 3. Couns 6.
Courses: Dance Theater. **Daily hours for:** Classes 6. Study 1. Rec 2.
Focus: Music. **Features:** Swim.
Fees 2012: Res $1375-2000 (+$30-50), 2-4 wks. Aid 2009 (Need): $22,000.
Housing: Dorms. **Swimming:** Pool.

Est 1980. Nonprofit. Religious Society of Friends. **Ses:** 2. **Wks/ses:** 2-4. Operates July-Aug.

Held at Olney Friends School, FMC conducts a varied music program in a Quaker setting. Each camper receives instruction on the instrument of his or her choice and participates in ensemble lessons, chorus, swimming and sports. While older boys and girls attend for four weeks, 10- and 11-year-olds enroll in a two-week session. Participants should arrive at the camp with at least one year of previous study.

GLICKMAN-POPKIN BASSOON CAMP
Res — Coed Ages 18 and up

Little Switzerland, NC.
Contact (Year-round): 717 S Marshall St, Ste 103, Winston-Salem, NC 27101.
  Tel: 336-602-5159. Fax: 336-777-8254.
www.bassooncamp.com   E-mail: amber@bassooncamp.com
Loren Glickman, Dir.
Adm: FCFS.
Enr: 100. **Fac 5. Staff:** Admin 2.
Focus: Music.
Fees 2011: Res $750, 1½ wks.
Housing: Lodges. Avg per room/unit: 2.
Est 1977. Nonprofit. **Ses:** 1. **Wks/ses:** 1½. Operates May-June.

The camp offers master classes in performance practices, reed making and repertoire. Performers of all skill levels are welcome to attend. Guest artists, lectures and instrument repair complement instruction.

HARAND CAMP
Res — Coed Ages 8-18

Kenosha, WI 53140. c/o Carthage College, 2001 Alford Park Dr. Tel: 262-551-2140.
  Fax: 262-551-2142.
Contact (Aug-May): 1569 Sherman Ave, Ste 201A, Evanston, IL 60201.
  Tel: 847-864-1500. Fax: 847-864-1588.
www.harandcamp.com   E-mail: harandcamp@aol.com
Sulie Harand, Janice Gaffin Lovell, Nora Gaffin Shore & Judy Friedman Mooney,
  Dirs.
Grades 3-12. Adm: FCFS. **Appl**—Fee $0. Due: Mar.
Enr: 200. **Fac 15. Staff:** Admin 9. Couns 33.
Courses: Speech Acting Circus_Skills Crafts Creative_Writing Dance Fine_Arts Media Music.
Focus: Theater. **Features:** Baseball Basketball Gymnastics Soccer Swim Tennis Track Volleyball.
Fees 2012: Res $950-5100 (+$50), 1-6 wks. Aid (Need).
Housing: Dorms. **Swimming:** Pool.
Est 1955. Inc. **Ses:** 4. **Wks/ses:** 1-6. Operates June-Aug.

Integral to this musical theater/performing arts program, which is conducted on the campus of Carthage College, are daily acting, singing and dance classes. Classes are coordinated with musical theater productions that boys and girls deliver at the end of each session. Sports, electives and other activities round out the program.

HARDING UNIVERSITY SUMMER HONOR CHOIR
Res — Coed Ages 15-18

Searcy, AR 72149. Box 10877. Tel: 501-279-4311. Fax: 501-279-4086.

www.harding.edu/honorchoir   E-mail: ganus@harding.edu
Cliff Ganus, Dir.
Grades 10-PG (younger if qualified). Adm: FCFS. **Appl**—Fee $0. Due: Rolling. Choral director's rec.
Enr: 62. **Enr cap:** 70. Non-White: 5%. **Fac 7.** Prof 5. K-12 staff 2. **Staff:** Admin 1. Couns 4.
Avg class size: 14. **Daily hours for:** Classes 7. Rec 1. Grades. **College credit:** 1/crse, total 1.
Focus: Music.
Fees 2010: Res $395, 1 wk. Aid 2009 (Merit): $6000.
Housing: Dorms. Avg per room/unit: 2.
Est 2003. Nondenom Christian. **Ses:** 1. **Wks/ses:** 1. Operates July.

Students have a college-level music experience at a Christian liberal arts university through Summer Choir. In daily classes, choristers develop their music-reading and vocal skills and presentation, then rehearse in preparation for a final concert. Special performances, events, devotionals and recreational activities are also part of the program. Boys and girls earn one hour of college credit upon completion of the program.

HEIFETZ INTERNATIONAL MUSIC INSTITUTE
Res — Coed Ages 14-25

Staunton, VA. Mary Baldwin College.
Contact (Year-round): PO Box 6443, Ellicott City, MD 21042. Tel: 410-480-8007.
   Fax: 410-480-8010.
www.heifetzinstitute.org   E-mail: office@heifetzinstitute.org
Daniel Heifetz, Pres.
   Student contact: Patrick Locklin, E-mail: patrick@heifetzinstitute.org.
Adm: Very selective. Admitted: 35%. **Appl**—Fee $95. Due: Feb. Live or recorded audition.
Enr: 62. **Enr cap:** 75. Intl: 40%. **Fac 40.** Prof 40. **Staff:** Admin 14. Couns 5.
Type of instruction: Adv. **Courses:** Public_Speak Dance Drama. **Avg class size:** 8. **Daily hours for:** Classes 2. Study 5.
Focus: Music. **Features:** Boating Hiking Swim.
Fees 2012: Res $5600, 6 wks. Aid 2011 (Merit & Need): $150,000.
Housing: Dorms. **Swimming:** Pool River.
Est 1996. Nonprofit. **Ses:** 1. **Wks/ses:** 6. Operates June-Aug.

Serving advanced students of violin, viola, cello and piano, Heifetz seeks to develop the expressive potential of every performer while encouraging technical growth. In addition to twice-weekly private lessons and five hours of daily practice time, participants take a series of afternoon classes in public speaking, voice, drama, movement and freedom of expression. The schedule incorporates three weekly performance opportunities, a celebrity concert series and guest artists.

HOTCHKISS SCHOOL CHAMBER MUSIC PROGRAM
Res — Coed Ages 12-18

Lakeville, CT 06039. 11 Interlaken Rd, PO Box 800. Tel: 860-435-3173.
   Fax: 860-435-4413.
www.hotchkissportals.org   E-mail: summer@hotchkiss.org
Stephen C. McKibben, Dir. Student contact: Christiana Gurney Rawlings.
Grades 8-12. Adm: Selective. **Appl**—Fee $55. Due: Apr. Transcript, recorded audition, 2 recs.
Enr: 35. **Fac 7.**
Type of instruction: Adv. **Daily hours for:** Classes 8. Study 2. Rec 2.
Focus: Music. **Features:** Climbing_Wall Basketball Skateboarding Street_Hockey Swim Ultimate_Frisbee.
Fees 2012: Res $4250 (+$50-100), 3 wks.

Housing: Dorms. **Swimming:** Lake Pool.
Est 2004. Nonprofit. **Ses:** 1. **Wks/ses:** 3. Operates June-July.

Students enrolled in this intensive chamber music program participate in an ensemble, learn music history and appreciation, and receive coaching and lessons from resident and visiting musicians. In the instrumental program, talented string players and pianists ages 12-15 receive daily instruction from faculty artists, attend private lessons, participate in weekly master classes and perform in public concerts. The vocal program joins high school students with other classical vocalists to form small ensembles and learn one-per-part vocal chamber music. Concerts by guest artists enrich both programs.

IDYLLWILD ARTS SUMMER PROGRAM
Res — Coed Ages 9-18; Day — Coed 5-18

Idyllwild, CA 92549. 52500 Temecula Rd, PO Box 38. Tel: 951-659-2171.
    Fax: 951-659-4552.
www.idyllwildarts.org   E-mail: summer@idyllwildarts.org
Steven Fraider, Dir. Student contact: Diane Dennis.
Adm: Selective. **Appl**—Fee $25. Due: Rolling. Audition.
Enr: 450-500. **Enr cap:** 500. Intl: 5%. **Fac 80.** Prof 8. K-12 staff 32. Specialists 40. **Staff:** Admin 5. Couns 35.
Type of instruction: Adv Enrich. **Courses:** Ceramics Crafts Media Painting Photog Band Choir Jazz Musical_Theater Orchestra Poetry Screenwriting. **Daily hours for:** Classes 8. Rec 2.
Focus: Animation Creative_Writing Dance Filmmaking Fine_Arts Music Theater. **Features:** Swim.
Fees 2012: Res $2550-4195 (+$70), 2-3 wks. **Day** $335 (+$20), 1 wk. Aid 2010 (Need): $500,000.
Housing: Dorms. Avg per room/unit: 4-5. **Swimming:** Pool. Campus facilities avail.
Est 1950. Nonprofit. **Spons:** Idyllwild Arts Foundation. **Ses:** 3. **Wks/ses:** 2-3. Operates July-Aug.

Idyllwild's summer program offers intensive, hands-on workshops in dance, film, music, theater, visual arts and creative writing to students of all ages and ability levels. Programs include the Children's Art Center (day and boarding programs for children ages 5-12), Junior Arts Center (ages 11-13) and Youth Art Center (13-18). All workshops are taught by professional artist-teachers. Weeklong festivals and special programs add dimension and depth to specific artistic pursuits. Idyllwild schedules one family camp week each summer. Some programs are first-come, first-served, while others have selective admissions and require an audition.

INNERSPARK
CALIFORNIA STATE SUMMER SCHOOL FOR THE ARTS
Res — Coed Ages 14-18

Valencia, CA 91355. c/o California Inst of the Arts, 24700 McBean Pky.
    Tel: 661-255-1050.
Contact (Winter): PO Box 1077, Sacramento, CA 95812. Tel: 916-274-5815.
Year-round Fax: 916-274-5814.
www.innerspark.us   E-mail: application@innerspark.us
Student contact: Neil Brilliante.
Grades 9-12. Adm: Very selective. Admitted: 45%. **Appl**—Fee $20. Due: Feb. Recorded audition, portfolio, screening, 2 teacher recs.
Enr: 520. **Enr cap:** 520. Intl: 1%. Non-White: 49%. **Fac 129.** Prof 58. Col/grad students 20. Specialists 51. **Staff:** Admin 10. Couns 18.

Courses: Digital_Arts. **Avg class size:** 16. **Daily hours for:** Classes 7. Study 4. **College credit:** 3.
Focus: Animation Creative_Writing Dance Film Music Painting Photog Sculpt Theater.
Features: Basketball Swim Tennis.
Fees 2012: Res $1550-5000 (+$60-325), 4 wks. Aid 2008 (Need): $218,000.
Housing: Dorms. **Swimming:** Pool. Campus facilities avail.
Est 1985. Nonprofit. **Ses:** 1. **Wks/ses:** 4. Operates July-Aug.

A rigorous preprofessional training program for talented high schoolers interested in a career in the arts or entertainment, InnerSpark offers course work in seven disciplines: animation, dance, theater, music, creative writing, the visual arts and film/video. Admission is highly competitive, with all boys and girls having to audition, complete specific artistic assignments and submit teacher recommendations; priority is given to California residents, although a limited number of out-of-state and international students enroll each year. Participants may earn three units of California State University elective credit upon completion of the program. Scholarships are available to California residents only.

INTERLOCHEN SUMMER ARTS CAMP
Res — Coed Ages 8-18

Interlochen, MI 49643. PO Box 199. Tel: 231-276-7472, 800-681-5912.
Fax: 231-276-7464.
www.camp.interlochen.org   E-mail: admission@interlochen.org
Jeffrey S. Kimpton, Pres.
Grades 4-PG. Adm: Selective. Admitted: 85%. **Appl**—Due: Feb. Varying audition/portfolio requirements.
Enr: 2500. **Fac 247. Staff:** Admin 205. Couns 208.
Type of instruction: Enrich. **Courses:** Ceramics Crafts Media Painting Photog Sculpt.
Daily hours for: Classes 6. Study 4. Rec 2.
Focus: Creative_Writing Dance Filmmaking Music Theater. **Features:** Aquatics Boating Canoe Exploration Fishing Hiking Outdoor_Ed Ropes_Crse Sail Swim Watersports.
Fees 2012: Res $1000-7970, 1-6 wks. Aid (Merit & Need).
Housing: Cabins Lodges. **Swimming:** Lake. Campus facilities avail.
Est 1928. Nonprofit. **Ses:** 7. **Wks/ses:** 1-6. Operates June-Aug.

Interlochen offers intensive study of the arts—music, visual arts, dance, creative writing, motion picture arts and theater—from beginning through advanced levels. Students choose from junior (entering grades 4-7), intermediate (entering grades 7-10) and high school (entering grade 10 through recent high school graduates) divisions. Many of the programs for younger children do not require an audition, but the more challenging and competitive intermediate and high school programs often necessitate an audition. Private lessons are available at an additional fee in all band and orchestral instruments, piano, organ, voice and classical guitar. A diverse recreational program, including watersports, is available.

INTERNATIONAL MUSIC CAMP SUMMER SCHOOL OF FINE ARTS
Res — Coed Ages 12-18

Dunseith, ND 58329. 10834 Peace Garden Dr. Tel: 701-263-4211. Fax: 701-263-4212.
Contact (Aug-May): 111 11th Ave SW, Ste 3, Minot, ND 58701. Tel: 701-838-8472.
Fax: 701-838-1351.
www.internationalmusiccamp.com   E-mail: info@internationalmusiccamp.com
Timothy Wollenzien, Dir.
Grades 5-12. Adm: FCFS. Admitted: 100%. **Appl**—Due: Rolling.
Enr: 300. **Enr cap:** 500. Intl: 37%. Non-White: 2%. **Fac 150.** Prof 100. K-12 staff 50. **Staff:** Admin 4. Couns 50.

Courses: Speech. **Avg class size:** 23. **Daily hours for:** Classes 6. Study 2. Rec 2. **College credit.**
Focus: Creative_Writing Dance Music Photog Studio_Art Theater. **Features:** Basketball Soccer Volleyball.
Fees 2011: Res $370-400 (+$35), 1 wk.
Housing: Dorms.
Est 1956. Nonprofit. **Ses:** 7. **Wks/ses:** 1. Operates June-July.

Students may attend one or more of seven weeklong sessions. Courses include band, orchestra, chorus, ballet, modern dance, dramatic arts, chamber music, piano, jazz ensembles, a cappella choir, creative writing, art, vocal jazz, digital photography, garage band, sound technology, world percussion, speech, and piping and drumming.

JACOB'S PILLOW DANCE FESTIVAL AND SCHOOL
Res — Coed Ages 16 and up

Becket, MA 01223. 358 George Carter Rd. Tel: 413-243-9919. Fax: 413-243-4744.
www.jacobspillow.org   E-mail: info@jacobspillow.org
J. R. Glover, Dir.
Adm: Selective. **Appl**—Fee $25-50. Due: Mar. Audition, personal statement, resume.
Enr: 25. **Enr cap:** 25. **Fac 30.**
Type of instruction: Adv. **College credit.**
Focus: Dance. **Features:** Swim.
Fees 2012: Res $1400-1800, 2-3 wks. Aid (Merit & Need).
Housing: Cabins. Avg per room/unit: 20. **Swimming:** Lake.
Est 1933. Nonprofit. **Ses:** 4. **Wks/ses:** 2-3. Operates June-Aug.

Advanced students, professionals and teachers may enroll in this school of dance. Ballet, modern, culturally specific, choreographic, jazz/musical theater and community dance courses are offered. An intern/apprentice program provides on-the-job training in arts management and technical production. Pupils may earn undergraduate college credit.

JUILLIARD SCHOOL SUMMER DANCE INTENSIVE
Res — Coed Ages 15-17

New York, NY 10023. Office of Adm, 60 Lincoln Center Plz. Tel: 212-799-5000.
Fax: 212-769-6420.
www.juilliard.edu/summer/dance.html   E-mail: danceadmissions@juilliard.edu
Grades 10-12. Adm: Selective. **Appl**—Fee $40. Due: Jan. Video/DVD/live audition, ballet teacher rec.
Enr: 44. **Enr cap:** 44.
Type of instruction: Adv Enrich.
Focus: Dance.
Fees 2009: Res $2040, 3 wks. Day $1100, 3 wks. Aid (Merit & Need).
Housing: Dorms.
Ses: 1. **Wks/ses:** 3. Operates July-Aug.

Rising high school sophomores, juniors and seniors who are advanced ballet dancers may apply to this precollege program; females should be en pointe. Each day begins in one of Juilliard's studios with a ballet technique class, followed by pointe, men's or classical partnering classes. After lunch, students take a modern dance class, then contemporary partnering, ballroom and music. Dancers supplement daily technique classes with evening rehearsals of new choreography and repertoire. Students perform the resulting pieces on the session's final day as part of a production that includes ballroom and music class presentations.

JUILLIARD SCHOOL SUMMER PERCUSSION SEMINAR
Res — Coed Ages 15-17

New York, NY 10023. Office of Adm, 60 Lincoln Center Plz. Tel: 212-799-5000.
  Fax: 212-769-6420.
www.juilliard.edu/youth-adult/summer   E-mail: jgramley@umich.edu
Joseph Gramley, Dir.
Grades 10-12. Adm: Selective. Appl—Fee $45. Due: Mar. Audition recording, resume.
Type of instruction: Enrich.
Focus: Music.
Fees 2009: Res $1290, 2 wks.
Housing: Dorms.
Ses: 1. Wks/ses: 2. Operates July.

Advanced high school percussionists entering grades 10-12 may enroll in this intensive program. Students engage in hands-on study of all major percussive instruments: two- and four-mallet keyboard, snare drum, timpani and orchestral accessories. In addition, participants gain an introduction to world hand drums, percussion chamber music, and both solo- and multi-percussion repertoire. Programming combines master classes, clinics, lectures, rehearsals and performances. Private lessons are also part of the program.

KANSAS CITY ART INSTITUTE PRE-COLLEGE ARTLAB
Res — Coed Ages 15-18

Kansas City, MO 64111. Special Prgms Office, 4415 Warwick Blvd. Tel: 816-802-3505.
www.kcai.edu/spce/highschool/precollege   E-mail: rkartman@kcai.edu
Ruth Kartman, Dir.
Grades 10-PG. Adm: Selective. Appl—Fee $0. Due: Apr. Porfolio, transcript, rec.
Enr: 65.
Type of instruction: Adv. Courses: Printmaking. Daily hours for: Classes 6. College
  credit: 3.
Focus: Animation Fashion Painting Photog Sculpt.
Fees 2009: Res $2599, 3 wks. Aid (Merit).
Housing: Dorms.
Ses: 1. Wks/ses: 3. Operates June-July.

Participants in this residency program for high schoolers choose a studio major (photography, animation, sculpture, painting, kiln-fired glass, fashion design or printmaking) and a liberal arts course. Along with an intensive life drawing course, these programmatic elements teach students about the level of commitment and creativity required to become an artist. Within a college-like environment, boys and girls spend nine days each weekday working in the arts. Students exhibit their work in a public show, and each participant receives a portfolio review at the conclusion of the session.

THE KENYON REVIEW YOUNG WRITERS WORKSHOP
Res — Coed Ages 16-18

Gambier, OH 43022. Finn House, 102 W Wiggin St. Tel: 740-427-5207.
  Fax: 740-427-5417.
www.kenyonreview.org/workshops-ywinfo.php
E-mail: youngwriters@kenyonreview.org
Anna Duke Reach, Dir.
Grades 11-12. Adm: Very selective. Appl—Fee $0. Due: Mar. Transcript, teacher rec,
  essay.
Enr cap: 90. Intl: 5%. Non-White: 40%. Fac 8. Prof 6. K-12 staff 2. Staff: Admin 5. Couns
  9.
Type of instruction: Enrich. Avg class size: 13. Daily hours for: Classes 6. Homework.

Focus: Creative_Writing. **Features:** Hiking Swim.
Fees 2012: Res $2275, 2 wks. Aid (Need).
Housing: Dorms. **Swimming:** Pool. Campus facilities avail.
Est 1989. Nonprofit. **Ses:** 2. **Wks/ses:** 2. Operates June-July.

Young Writers helps students explore ideas through writing and develop their creative and critical abilities with respect to language. Three 90-minute workshops each day balance class discussions of assigned readings with frequent work in small writing or inquiry groups and time for individual writing. In addition to free-writing exercises and responses to prompts, pupils compose stories, poetry, personal narratives, dialogues, reflective passages and experimental pieces. Participants regularly share works-in-progress both in class and in smaller peer review groups. Students each read pieces aloud as part of a series of public readings by visiting poets, fiction writers and essayists. Weekend activities include social events and field trips.

LEBANON VALLEY COLLEGE SUMMER MUSIC CAMP
Res and Day — Coed Ages 14-17

Annville, PA 17003. 101 N College Ave. Tel: 717-867-6293. Fax: 717-867-6390.
www.lvc.edu/music-camp   E-mail: mixon@lvc.edu
Joe Mixon, Dir.
Grades 9-12 (younger if qualified). Adm: FCFS. Admitted: 100%. **Appl**—Fee $0. Due: Rolling.
Enr: 100. **Enr cap:** 100. Intl: 2%. **Fac 12.** Prof 12. **Staff:** Admin 1. Couns 10.
Type of instruction: Enrich. **Daily hours for:** Classes 6. Study 1. Rec 1.
Focus: Music. **Features:** Baseball Basketball Swim Tennis.
Fees 2011: Res $585 (+$22), 1 wk. Day $395 (+$22), 1 wk.
Housing: Dorms. **Swimming:** Pool. Campus facilities avail.
Est 1987. Nonprofit. **Ses:** 1. **Wks/ses:** 1. Operates July.

Students choose their own programs from a selection of seminars, ensembles and private instruction. Academic electives such as music theory, jazz improvisation and music technology, as well as performance opportunities, are available. Pupils may take half-hour private lessons for an additional fee.

LIM COLLEGE SUMMER FASHION LAB
Res — Coed Ages 15-17

New York, NY 10022. 12 E 53rd St. Tel: 646-388-8421. Fax: 212-750-3479.
www.limcollege.edu   E-mail: fashionlab@limcollege.edu
Jennifer Bullis, Coord.
Grades 10-12. Adm: FCFS. **Appl**—Fee $25. Due: Rolling.
Enr: 260. Intl: 8%.
Type of instruction: Undergrad. **Avg class size:** 20. **Daily hours for:** Classes 7½. **College credit:** 1/crse, total 3.
Focus: Fashion.
Fees 2011: Res $625-3400 (+$10-35/crse), 1-4 wks. Day $225-1800 (+$10-35/crse), 1-4 wks.
Housing: Dorms. Avg per room/unit: 2-3. Campus facilities avail.
Ses: 1. **Wks/ses:** 1-4. Operates July-Aug.

Summer Fashion Lab's series of weeklong courses allows participants to explore various career opportunities in the fashion business. Students may enroll in one course in the morning session, one course in the afternoon session or both, for a total of up to eight courses over four weeks. Course offerings cover fashion buying, event planning, photography, fashion magazines, fashion show production, styling, marketing, Photoshop, social media and visual merchandising. Boarders live in a LIM College dormitory and participate in organized evening activities.

LITCHFIELD JAZZ CAMP
Res and Day — Coed Ages 13 and up

Litchfield, CT 06759. PO Box 69. Tel: 860-361-6285. Fax: 860-361-6288.
www.litchfieldjazzcamp.com E-mail: info@litchfieldjazzfest.com
Don Braden, Dir.
   Student contact: Karen Hussey, E-mail: karenh@litchfieldjazzfest.com.
Adm: FCFS. **Appl**—Fee $50. Due: Rolling.
Enr: 100-150. **Enr cap:** 150. Intl: 2%. Non-White: 33%. **Fac 30.** Specialists 30. **Staff:** Admin 4.
Avg class size: 10. **Daily hours for:** Classes 8. Rec 2.
Focus: Music.
Fees 2012: Res $1370-5510, 1-5 wks. Day $960-4140, 1-4 wks. Aid 2011 (Need): $100,000.
Housing: Dorms.
Est 1996. Nonprofit. **Spons:** Litchfield Performing Arts. **Ses:** 5. **Wks/ses:** 1. Operates July-Aug.

Boys and girls of all ability levels study with an internationally recognized faculty of jazz musicians at the camp. Students perform in combos at the appropriate skill level, both at the school and on the Jazz Festival stage. Faculty guide students through classes in performance, improvisation, jazz history, rhythm and percussion, music theory, composition, recording and the business of music, among others. Instructors teach voice, piano, guitar, bass, drums, Latin rhythms, saxophones, clarinet, flute, trumpet, trombone and violin. Private instruction is available for an additional fee.

LONG LAKE CAMP FOR THE ARTS
Res — Coed Ages 10-16

Long Lake, NY 12847. 83 Long Lake Camp Way. Tel: 518-624-4831.
   Fax: 518-624-6003.
Contact (Sept-June): 199 Washington Ave, Dobbs Ferry, NY 10522.
   Tel: 914-693-7111. Fax: 914-693-7684.
Year-round Toll-free: 800-767-7111.
www.longlakecamp.com E-mail: marc@longlakecamp.com
Marc Katz, Susan Katz & Geoffrey Burnett, Dirs.
Grades 5-11. Adm: FCFS. Admitted: 100%. **Appl**—Fee $0. Due: Rolling.
Enr: 235. **Enr cap:** 250. Intl: 10%. Non-White: 12%. **Fac 140. Staff:** Admin 4.
Courses: Ecol Environ_Sci Expository_Writing Speech Writing/Journ Ceramics Crafts Creative_Writing Photog Sculpt.
Focus: Circus_Skills Dance Filmmaking Fine_Arts Music Painting Theater. **Features:** Archery Canoe Hiking Mountaineering Mtn_Trips Riding Sail Seamanship Wilderness_ Camp Woodcraft Baseball Basketball Equestrian Field_Hockey Football Golf Gymnastics Martial_Arts Soccer Swim Tennis Volleyball Water-skiing Watersports.
Fees 2012: Res $5450-8795 (+$20-375), 3-6 wks. Aid 2009 (Need): $100,000.
Housing: Cabins Houses. Avg per room/unit: 10. **Swimming:** Lake.
Est 1969. Inc. **Ses:** 5. **Wks/ses:** 3-6. Operates June-Aug.

Long Lake's activities include theater; orchestra; chorus; ballet, modern and folk dance; jazz ensembles; rock 'n' roll bands; guitar and folk singing; and choreography. Participants deliver full-scale performances on campus and in surrounding communities. An arts and crafts program includes painting, silver, sculpture, ceramics, photography, weaving, printing, computer science and creative writing. Horseback riding, waterfront activities, an overnight canoe trip and sports complete the camp's offerings.

LUZERNE MUSIC CENTER
Res — Coed Ages 11-18

Lake Luzerne, NY 12846. PO Box 35.
Contact (Oct-May): 899 S College Mall Rd, Ste 353, Bloomington, IN 47401.
Year-round Tel: 518-696-2771, Fax: 518-615-1226.
www.luzernemusic.org   E-mail: info@luzernemusic.org
William Schulman, Dir.
Grades 6-12 (younger if qualified). Adm: Selective. Admitted: 75%. **Appl**—Fee $50. Due: Rolling. Teacher rec, performance recording/audition.
Enr: 85. **Enr cap:** 100. Intl: 5%. Non-White: 25%. **Fac 30.** Prof 10. Col/grad students 5. Specialists 15. **Staff:** Admin 3. Couns 18.
Type of instruction: Adv. **Avg class size:** 6. **Daily hours for:** Classes 5. Study 2. Rec 2.
Focus: Music. **Features:** Boating Canoe Chess Hiking Peace/Cross-cultural Sail White-water_Raft Wilderness_Canoe Baseball Basketball Cross-country Soccer Softball Swim Tennis Ultimate_Frisbee.
Fees 2012: Res $1950-3750, 2-4 wks. Aid 2011 (Merit & Need): $120,000.
Housing: Cabins Lodges. Avg per room/unit: 5. **Swimming:** Lake.
Est 1980. Nonprofit. **Ses:** 4. **Wks/ses:** 2-4. Operates June-Aug.

Luzerne offers instruction in orchestra, chamber music, piano, woodwinds, brass, percussion, jazz, conducting, vocal studies, and theory and composition, and students perform in concerts each week. Recreational and waterfront programs include tennis, baseball, hiking, swimming, sailing and canoeing. The program is divided into a junior session (ages 11-14) and a senior session (ages 15-18).

MAINE ARTS CAMP
Res — Coed Ages 8-15

Unity, ME 04988. c/o Unity College, 90 Quaker Hill Rd.
Contact (Sept-June): PO Box 812076, Boca Raton, FL 33481.
Year-round Tel: 561-865-4330, Fax: 561-865-0855.
www.maineartscamp.com   E-mail: info@maineartscamp.com
Rick Mades, Dir.
Grades 3-10. Adm: FCFS. **Appl**—Fee $0. Due: Rolling.
Enr: 100. **Enr cap:** 130. Intl: 5%. Non-White: 5%. **Fac 35.** Col/grad students 20. K-12 staff 15. **Staff:** Admin 2. Couns 30.
Type of instruction: Enrich. **Courses:** Comp_Sci Robotics Creative_Writing Music. **Avg class size:** 8. **Daily hours for:** Classes 3. Rec 5.
Focus: Ceramics Crafts Dance Drawing Fine_Arts Painting Photog Sculpt Studio_Art Theater. **Features:** Archery Canoe Chess Climbing_Wall Cooking Farm Hiking Kayak Mtn_Biking Rock_Climb Yoga Golf Martial_Arts Tennis Ultimate_Frisbee Gardening Rocketry.
Fees 2012: Res $3000-5150 (+$50-100), 2-4 wks.
Housing: Dorms. Campus facilities avail.
Est 2005. Inc. **Ses:** 3. **Wks/ses:** 2-4. Operates July-Aug.

Conducted at Unity College, this general arts camp allows each student to create an individual program of activities. Individual sports, robotics, Web design, and kayaking and canoeing supplement instruction in the visual and performing arts. Trips to Sebago Lake and the Big Adventure Center complete the program.

MAINE COLLEGE OF ART PRE-COLLEGE
Res and Day — Coed Ages 16-18

Portland, ME 04101. 522 Congress St. Tel: 207-699-5062, 800-699-1509.
Fax: 207-879-5748.

www.meca.edu   E-mail: precollege@meca.edu
Ian Anderson, Dir.
Grades 11-PG. Adm: FCFS. **Appl**—Fee $40. Due: Apr. Rec, essay.
Enr: 40. **Enr cap:** 40. **Fac 9.**
Type of instruction: Adv Undergrad. **Courses:** Art_Hist. **Avg class size:** 20. **Daily hours for:** Classes 7. Study 2. Rec 1. Grades. **College credit:** 4.
Focus: Ceramics Drawing Fine_Arts Painting Sculpt.
Fees 2011: Res $3880, 4 wks. Day $2230, 4 wks. Aid (Merit & Need).
Housing: Dorms. Avg per room/unit: 2.
Nonprofit. **Ses:** 1. **Wks/ses:** 4. Operates July-Aug.

Pre-College at MECA provides an opportunity for students who have completed sophomore, junior or senior year to earn college credit for intensive studio arts study. Pupils choose one of four majors for in-depth pursuit: painting, sculpture, ceramics or graphic design. All participants enroll in foundation classes in drawing, art history and two-dimensional and three-dimensional design. The teaching staff comprises professional artists and college instructors from MECA and art schools around the country. Lectures, field trips and visiting artist workshops enrich the program.

MAINE SUMMER YOUTH MUSIC
Res and Day — Coed Ages 11-18

Orono, ME 04469. c/o Univ of Maine, 5788 Class of 1944 Hall, Rm 208.
Tel: 207-581-4703. Fax: 207-581-4701.
www.umaine.edu/spa   E-mail: cathy.brown@umit.maine.edu
Christopher G. White, Dir.
Grades 6-12. Adm: FCFS. **Appl**—Fee $0. Due: Rolling.
Fac 35. Staff: Admin 5.
Courses: Theater.
Focus: Music. **Features:** Swim.
Fees 2012: Res $545-760, 1 wk. Day $215-325, 1 wk. Aid (Merit).
Housing: Dorms. **Swimming:** Pool.
Est 1963. Nonprofit. **Spons:** University of Maine-Orono. **Ses:** 2. **Wks/ses:** 1. Operates July.

Conducted by the University of Maine's School of Performing Arts, MSYM is primarily a large-ensemble camp that provides opportunities in symphonic band, concert band, jazz band, orchestra, chorus and musical theater. Other classes address improvisation, music history, theory, music literature, opera, chamber music and careers in music. The junior camp accepts children entering grades 6-8, while the senior camp serves boys and girls entering grades 9-12. Recreation and evening activities round out the program.

THE MARIE WALSH SHARPE ART FOUNDATION
SUMMER SEMINAR
Res — Coed Ages 17-18

Colorado Springs, CO. Colorado College.
Contact (Year-round): 830 N Tejon St, Ste 120, Colorado Springs, CO 80903.
Tel: 719-635-3220. Fax: 719-635-3018.
www.sharpeartfdn.org   E-mail: kim@sharpeartfdn.org
Kimberly M. Taylor, Dir.
Grade 12. Adm: Selective. **Appl**—Fee $0. Due: Apr. Art teacher rec, artwork, personal statement.
Enr: 20. **Enr cap:** 20. **Fac 2. Staff:** Admin 3. Couns 5.
Type of instruction: Adv Enrich. **Avg class size:** 20.
Focus: Drawing Fine_Arts Painting.
Fees 2011: Free. Res 2 wks.

Housing: Dorms. Avg per room/unit: 1-2. Campus facilities avail.
Est 1987. Nonprofit. **Ses:** 3. **Wks/ses:** 2. Operates June-July.

Held on the campus of Colorado College, this art institute offers intensive visual arts instruction for rising high school juniors who are artistically gifted. Students experience college-level drawing and painting courses in a group setting, with artists-in-residence serving as instructors. The development of a portfolio, small-group discussions with artists and sessions concerning careers in art are other program features. Scholarship funding covers full tuition, room and board, and related expenses.

MARIST COLLEGE SUMMER INSTITUTES
Res — Coed Ages 16-18

Poughkeepsie, NY 12601. Office of Undergraduate Adm, 3399 North Rd.
Tel: 845-575-3226. Fax: 845-575-3215.
www.marist.edu/summerinstitutes   E-mail: precollege@marist.edu
Grades 11-12. Adm: Selective. **Appl**—Due: Rolling. Transcript, essay, rec.
Type of instruction: Undergrad. **College credit:** 3/crse, total 3.
Focus: Creative_Writing Fashion Filmmaking Theater.
Fees 2012: Res $3095, 2 wks.
Housing: Dorms. Campus facilities avail.
Ses: 1. **Wks/ses:** 2. Operates July.

Students earn college credit and preview campus life through Marist's Summer Institutes in creative writing, digital moviemaking, fashion design, fashion marketing and merchandising, and theater. Programming combines several class sessions each day with study time, local excursions, daylong field trips and recreational activities. Other institutes focus on academic areas: business, criminal justice, environmental studies, game design, Spanish and sports communications (see separate listing).

MARROWSTONE MUSIC FESTIVAL
Res and Day — Coed Ages 13-25

Bellingham, WA. Western Washington Univ.
Contact (Year-round): c/o Seattle Youth Symphony Orchestras, 11065 5th Ave NE,
Ste A, Seattle, WA 98125. Tel: 206-362-2300. Fax: 206-361-9254.
www.marrowstone.org   E-mail: marrowstone@syso.org
Dan Petersen, Exec Dir.
Adm: Selective. **Appl**—Fee $55-80. Due: May. Audition CD, teacher rec.
Enr: 200. **Fac 20. Staff:** Admin 7. Couns 12.
Type of instruction: Adv. **College credit.**
Focus: Music. **Features:** Swim.
Fees 2011: Res $2275, 2 wks. Day $1875, 2 wks. Aid (Merit & Need).
Housing: Dorms. **Swimming:** Lake Pool.
Est 1943. Nonprofit. **Spons:** Seattle Youth Symphony Orchestras. **Ses:** 1. **Wks/ses:** 2.
Operates July-Aug.

Marrowstone offers students a program of intense musical study. A diverse group of artist faculty guide students in a curriculum that includes master classes, chamber music coaching, orchestra and section rehearsals. These elements culminate in orchestral and chamber performances. Students may apply for college credit for chamber music, orchestra and elective course work.

MARYLAND INSTITUTE COLLEGE OF ART
BALTIMORE PRE-COLLEGE STUDIO RESIDENCY PROGRAM
Res — Coed Ages 16-17

Baltimore, MD 21217. 1300 W Mt Royal Ave. Tel: 410-225-2219. Fax: 410-225-2229.
www.mica.edu/programs/cs/precollege E-mail: precollege@mica.edu
Grades 11-12. Adm: Selective. **Appl**—Fee $50. Due: Apr. Transcript, portfolio, rec, personal statement.
Enr: 250. Enr cap: 250.
Type of instruction: Undergrad. **Courses:** Architect Animation Painting Photog Sculpt Video. **College credit:** 3.
Focus: Studio_Art.
Fees 2009: Res $3900-4100, 4 wks.
Housing: Dorms. Avg per room/unit: 1-2.
Est 1994. Ses: 1. Wks/ses: 4. Operates June-July.

Participants in MICA's intensive, four-week program earn three college credits for completion of a core class and a workshop. Students choose from 11 core classes and 12 workshops in such disciplines as figure painting, graphic design, sculpture, black and white photography, digital photography, 3-D gaming and animation, illustration, fiber, architecture and video. Enrollment in a class entitled critical methods of studying art completed the academic experience. Field trips to Washington, DC, and New York City to explore contemporary art and noteworthy historical pieces at galleries and museums enrich the program.

MASSACHUSETTS COLLEGE OF ART SUMMER STUDIOS
Res and Day — Coed Ages 16-18

Boston, MA 02115. 621 Huntington Ave. Tel: 617-879-7170. Fax: 617-879-7171.
www.massart.edu/ce E-mail: k12@massart.edu
Liz Rudnick, Dir.
Grades 11-12. Adm: FCFS. **Appl**—Fee $0. Due: Rolling. 2 recs.
Enr: 90. Enr cap: 96. Intl: 1%. Non-White: 37%. **Fac 25.** Prof 2. Col/grad students 6. K-12 staff 17. **Staff:** Admin 2. Couns 5.
Type of instruction: Enrich Undergrad. **Courses:** Crafts Fine_Arts Graphic_Design Jewelry Printmaking. **Avg class size:** 16. **Daily hours for:** Classes 7. Homework.
Focus: Animation Ceramics Fashion Filmmaking Painting Photog. **Features:** Ultimate_ Frisbee.
Fees 2011: Res $4530 (+$200), 4 wks. Day $2100 (+$200), 4 wks. Aid 2009 (Need): $48,150.
Housing: Dorms. Avg per room/unit: 4. Campus facilities avail.
Nonprofit. **Ses: 1. Wks/ses: 4.** Operates July-Aug.

This intensive experience in art creation and viewing enables high school juniors and seniors to work with professional artists. Participants develop their portfolios while improving their work habits. In the morning, students attend 2D & 3D Fundamentals and Issues & Images, then choose two (out of 12) studio electives in the afternoon.

MEXART SUMMER TEEN PROGRAM
Res — Coed Ages 14-18

San Miguel de Allende, Mexico.
Contact (Year-round): 9902 Crystal Ct, Ste 107, BC-2323, Laredo, TX 78045.
Tel: 202-391-0004. Fax: 52-415-152-8900.
www.gomexart.com E-mail: carly@gomexart.com
Carly Cross, Dir.
Grades 9-PG. Adm: FCFS. **Appl**—Fee $0. Due: Rolling. Essay.
Enr: 20. Enr cap: 20. **Fac 16. Staff:** Admin 2. Couns 4.

Type of instruction: Adv Enrich Preview Rev Tut. **Courses:** Span Crafts Fine_Arts Photog. **Daily hours for:** Classes 7. Study 1½. Rec 3. **Intl program focus:** Acad Lang Culture. Home stays avail. **Focus:** Dance Studio_Art. **Features:** Community_Serv Peace/Cross-cultural. **Fees 2010: Res $3800 (+$200), 4 wks. Housing:** Dorms. **Est 1999.** Inc. **Ses:** 3. **Wks/ses:** 4. Operates June-Aug.

MexArt participants take daily Spanish classes with either art or dance courses. Art students choose one focus area and one or two electives from the following selections: painting, drawing, ceramics, photography, printmaking, color and design, welding and silver jewelry. Those in the dance program choose from jazz, hip-hop, modern and ballet in the morning session, and salsa, flamenco and improvisation in the afternoon. Dance students also teach dance to local children as a community service project.

MINNEAPOLIS COLLEGE OF ART AND DESIGN
PRE-COLLEGE SUMMER SESSIONS
Res — Coed Ages 16-18

Minneapolis, MN 55404. Continuing Stud Office, Morrison Bldg, Rm M105, 2501 Stevens Ave. Tel: 612-874-3765. Fax: 612-874-3695.
www.mcad.edu/ses   E-mail: continuing_studies@mcad.edu
Lara Roy, Dir.
Grades 11-PG. Adm: Selective. **Appl**—Fee $25. Due: Rolling. Transcript, portfolio, rec, personal statement.
Type of instruction: Undergrad. **Courses:** Animation Media Music Painting Photog. Homework. Grades. **College credit:** 2/crse.
Focus: Studio_Art.
Fees 2012: Res $2275, 2 wks. Aid (Merit).
Housing: Dorms. Avg per room/unit: 4.
Ses: 2. **Wks/ses:** 2. Operates June-July.

Designed to replicate the first year at an art college, MCAD Summer Expressions allows high schoolers to earn college credits, produce art and build a portfolio, and participate in social activities. Two distinct two-week sessions operate each summer, one focused upon music and media and the other on singular and sequential images. Students enrolled in the music session major in digital photography, documentary video, graphic design and multimedia, music video, or sound design and recording. Major options during the second session are animation, comic art, game design and painting.

NATIONAL GUITAR WORKSHOP
Res and Day — Coed Ages 14 and up

Lakeside, CT 06758. PO Box 222. Tel: 860-567-3736, 800-234-6479. Fax: 860-567-0374.
www.guitarworkshop.com   E-mail: julreich@guitarworkshop.com
Tom Dempsey, Pres.
Adm: FCFS. **Appl**—Fee $0. Due: Rolling.
Fac 200.
Type of instruction: Enrich. **Daily hours for:** Classes 7. **College credit:** 1.
Locations: CA CT MT TX.
Focus: Music.
Fees 2012: Res $1520 (+$75), 1 wk. Day $995 (+$75), 1 wk. Aid avail.
Housing: Dorms.
Est 1983. Inc. **Ses:** 7. **Wks/ses:** 1. Operates July-Aug.

Designed for students who are beginning, intermediate or advanced guitarists, bassists, keyboardists, drummers, singers or songwriters, the program provides classes, workshops and performances in an environment of concentrated study. Pupils attend intensive classes in a major area such as rock, jazz, blues, classical or acoustic, while also enrolling in specialized clinics in such areas as music theory, alternate tunings, complex rhythms and practicing. The program also features master classes taught by guest artists. Programs operate in New Milford, CT; Bigfork, MT; Austin, TX; Norwich, CT; and Los Angeles, CA.

NEW ENGLAND MUSIC CAMP
Res — Coed Ages 12-18

Sidney, ME 04330. 8 Golden Rod Rd. Tel: 207-465-3025. Fax: 207-465-9831.
Contact (Sept-May): 47 Cedar Grove Ter, Essex, CT 06426. Tel: 860-767-6530.
  Fax: 860-767-6548.
www.nemusiccamp.com   E-mail: playatnemc@aol.com
John Wiggin & Kim Wiggin, Dirs.
Grades 6-12. Adm: Somewhat selective. Admitted: 98%. **Appl**—Due: Rolling. Audition recording.
Enr: 195. **Fac 40. Staff:** Admin 10.
Type of instruction: Adv. **Courses:** Dance Theater. **Daily hours for:** Classes 4. Study 1. Rec 2.
Focus: Music. **Features:** Aquatics Archery Boating Canoe Fishing Hiking Mountaineering Sail Basketball Cross-country Golf Martial_Arts Soccer Softball Swim Tennis Volleyball.
Fees 2012: Res $3750-7450 (+$120-240), 3-7 wks.
Housing: Cabins Dorms. **Swimming:** Lake.
Est 1937. Nonprofit. **Ses:** 3. **Wks/ses:** 3-7. Operates June-Aug.

  NEMC offers a program of music and recreation on Lake Messalonskee. Musical activities include bands, choirs, orchestras, stage and jazz bands, a brass choir and ensembles. Class work and two private lessons are conducted weekly. A full range of social and recreational activities rounds out the program. Campers must be able to read music.

NEW ENGLAND SCHOOL OF COMMUNICATIONS
MAINE MEDIA CAMP
Res and Day — Coed Ages 15-17

Bangor, ME 04401. 1 College Cir. Tel: 207-941-7176, 888-877-1876. Fax: 207-947-3987.
www.nescom.edu   E-mail: info@nescom.edu
Mark F. Nason, Dir.
Grades 10-12. Adm: FCFS. **Appl**—Fee $25. Due: Rolling.
Enr cap: 40. **Fac 8. Staff:** Couns 3.
Type of instruction: Enrich.
Focus: Comm Writing/Journ Media Music_Tech. **Features:** Swim.
Fees 2011: Res $625, 1 wk. Day $400, 1 wk. Aid 2007 (Need): $1500.
Housing: Dorms. **Swimming:** Pool. Campus facilities avail.
Est 1989. Ses: 1. **Wks/ses:** 1. Operates Aug.

  Maine Media Camp introduces participants to career opportunities in such media fields as audio engineering, digital photography, journalism, marketing communications, radio broadcasting, video production and Web media. The curriculum comprises lectures, labs, hands-on instruction, professional speakers, and tours of local television and radio stations.

NEW YORK FILM ACADEMY
Res — Coed Ages 14-17; Day — Coed 10-17

New York, NY 10003. 100 E 17th St. Tel: 212-674-4300, 800-611-3456.
  Fax: 212-477-1414.

www.nyfa.com   E-mail: film@nyfa.com
Jerry Sherlock, Pres.
Adm: FCFS. Admitted: 98%. **Appl**—Fee $25. Due: Rolling.
Intl: 40%. Non-White: 30%.
Type of instruction: Enrich. **Courses:** Animation Screenwriting. **Avg class size:** 16. **Daily hours for:** Classes 8. Grades. **College credit:** 1-6/crse, total 6.
Locations: CA FL NY Europe.
Focus: Acting Filmmaking.
Fees 2010: Res $1500-12,900, 1-6 wks. Day $1000-2000, 1-2 wks.
Housing: Apartments Dorms Lodges. Campus facilities avail.
Est 1996. Wks/ses: 1-6. Operates May-Aug.

NFYA's summer programming for high schoolers is designed for those with little or no previous filmmaking, acting or animation experience. Conducted at two locations—in Union Square, New York City, and at Universal Studios in California—introductory day camps for boys and girls ages 10-13 focus on introductory filmmaking, introductory acting for film, intermediate filmmaking and intermediate acting for film. Intermediate programs serve only those students who have previously completed the appropriate introductory program at NYFA. Offering boarding and day programs at two Manhattan locations, Universal Studios, Harvard University (MA) and Disney-MGM Studios (FL), as well as in London, England, Paris, France, Rome, Italy, Cartagena, Colombia, Shanghai and Beijing, China, Seoul, Korea, and Tokyo, Japan, NYFA enables pupils ages 14-17 to study 16 mm and digital filmmaking, acting for film, 3-D animation, screenwriting and digital journalism.

NEW YORK MILITARY ACADEMY
NEW TRADITIONS JAZZ PROGRAM
Res and Day — Coed Ages 13-18

Cornwall-on-Hudson, NY 12520. 78 Academy Ave. Tel: 845-534-3710, 888-275-6962.
Fax: 845-534-7699.
www.nyma.org   E-mail: jfurman@nyma.org
Jason Furman, Dir. Student contact: Alisa Southwell, E-mail: asouthwell@nyma.org.
Grades 8-12. Adm: Very selective. **Appl**—Fee $200. Due: June.
Enr cap: 20.
Avg class size: 5.
Focus: Music. **Features:** Swim.
Fees 2011: Res $2500, 2 wks. Day $1500-2000, 2 wks.
Housing: Dorms. **Swimming:** Pool.
Est 2011. Ses: 1. **Wks/ses:** 1. Operates July.

Advanced middle school instrumentalists join high school musicians of all ability levels in this two-week program that focuses on jazz study and performance (in solo and small-group settings). The curriculum addresses three main areas: bebop and post bop, modal music, and avant-garde and ethereal styles. Private lessons and classes on improvisation, music theory and listening reinforce small-group playing. Ensembles perform weekly in a forum setting, and the program culminates in a final performance. Students may also participate in master classes and attend concerts with faculty and guest artists.

NEW YORK UNIVERSITY
SUMMER INSTITUTE OF MUSIC TECHNOLOGY
Res — Coed Ages 16-18

New York, NY 10012. 35 W 4th St, Ste 777. Tel: 212-998-5141. Fax: 212-995-4043.
www.steinhardt.nyu.edu/music/technology   E-mail: roginska@nyu.edu
Kenneth J. Peacock, Dir. Student contact: Agnieszka Roginska.

Grades 11-12 (younger if qualified). Adm: Very selective. Admitted: 30%. Priority: URM.
Appl—Fee $50. Due: Apr. Short essays, optional work samples.
Enr cap: 24. Intl: 10%. Non-White: 15%. **Fac 8.** Prof 8. **Staff:** Admin 2. Couns 2.
Type of instruction: Enrich Undergrad. **Courses:** Media. **Daily hours for:** Classes 7. Rec 4.
Focus: Music_Tech.
Fees 2012: Res $3530, 2 wks. Aid 2009 (Need): $4000.
Housing: Dorms. Avg per room/unit: 2-3.
Nonprofit. **Ses:** 1. **Wks/ses:** 2. Operates July.

Through class lectures, labs and individualized studio time, students learn the fundamentals of music technology and audio engineering. The curriculum covers music studio formation; signal representation and synthesis; MIDI and sequencing; sound recording in analog and digital, single and multitrack; and editing, mixing and postproduction. Participants learn to use ProTools and Reason software and work in small groups on a project of their choice, with assistance from graduate students. Other activities include trips to recording and postproduction studios, concerts and audio installations, Broadway shows, tours of New York City and evenings with experts in the music technology field.

NEW YORK UNIVERSITY
TISCH SCHOOL OF THE ARTS SUMMER HIGH SCHOOL
Res — Coed Ages 16-17

New York, NY 10003. 721 Broadway, 12th Fl. Tel: 212-998-1517. Fax: 212-995-4578.
www.specialprograms.tisch.nyu.edu   E-mail: tisch.special.info@nyu.edu
Pari Shirazi, Dir.
Grade 12 (younger if qualified). Adm: Selective. Prereqs: GPA 3.0. **Appl**—Fee $75. Due: Feb. Transcript, 2 teacher recs, statement, arts resume.
Enr cap: 280. **Fac 25.**
Type of instruction: Adv Undergrad. **Avg class size:** 16. **Daily hours for:** Classes 8. Rec 6. **College credit:** 6.
Intl program focus: Acad Culture. **Locations:** NY Europe.
Focus: Acting Creative_Writing Drama Film Filmmaking Photog.
Fees 2012: Res $8678-10,920 (+$245-515), 4 wks. Aid (Need).
Housing: Dorms.
Est 1988. Nonprofit. **Ses:** 1. **Wks/ses:** 4. Operates July-Aug.

Students earn college credit by completing specialized acting, dramatic writing, filmmaking, drama and photography course work. Participants receive eight hours of classroom instruction daily and take advantage of New York City's cultural events through outings to museums, screenings, concerts and theatrical productions. International programs enable pupils to study acting and filmmaking in Dublin, Ireland, or Paris, France.

NORTHWESTERN UNIVERSITY
NATIONAL HIGH SCHOOL INSTITUTE
Res — Coed Ages 17-18

Evanston, IL 60208. 617 Noyes St. Tel: 847-491-3026, 800-662-6474.
Fax: 847-467-1057.
www.northwestern.edu/nhsi   E-mail: nhsi@northwestern.edu
Ruth Bistrow, Coord.
Grade 12. Adm: Selective. **Appl**—Fee $50. Due: Apr. Transcript, PSAT scores.
Enr: 850. **Enr cap:** 850. **Fac 100.**
Type of instruction: Adv Enrich. **Courses:** Music. **Avg class size:** 15. **Daily hours for:** Classes 9. Study 2.
Focus: Acting Filmmaking Theater. **Features:** Swim.

Fees 2011: Res $4000-6900, 4-7 wks. Aid (Need).
Housing: Dorms. **Swimming:** Lake.
Est 1931. Nonprofit. **Ses:** 4. **Wks/ses:** 4-7. Operates June-Aug.

Serving artistically inclined rising high school seniors, the institute offers college-level study and experience in film and video production (including concentrations in acting, production, animation and screenwriting), musical theater and theater arts. NHSI's academic program comprises classes, workshops, field trips, projects and lectures. Group outings and social events balance class work. Workshops are also available in speech and debate (see separate listing for details).

OBERLIN CONSERVATORY OF MUSIC SUMMER PROGRAMS
Res — Coed Ages 16-18

Oberlin, OH 44074. Oberlin Univ, 77 W College St. Tel: 440-775-8044.
Fax: 440-775-8942.
http://new.oberlin.edu/conservatory/summer
E-mail: anna.hoffmann@oberlin.edu
Anna Hoffmann, Admin.
Grades 10-12. Adm: Selective. **Appl**—Fee $50. Due: Apr. DVD audition, repertoire list, rec.
Type of instruction: Enrich.
Focus: Music.
Fees 2012: Res $730-1175, 1-2 wks. Aid (Need).
Housing: Dorms Hotels.
Spons: Oberlin University. **Ses:** 3. **Wks/ses:** 1-2. Operates June-July.

Oberlin offers three programs to high school pupils considering a college major in music. Students in the Summer Academy for High School Organists attend five days of private lessons and master classes and have access to 17 practice organs. The weeklong Sonic Arts Workshop, which focuses on the composition of original electroacoustic music, addresses digital-audio editing and manipulation, real-time performance techniques, sampling and production using Macintosh-based software. The nine-day Vocal Academy for High School Students features master classes on performance practice, diction, style, phrasing and textual communication, in addition to private lessons and evening workshops on audition techniques. Each participant performs at a final concert.

OKLAHOMA SUMMER ARTS INSTITUTE
Res — Coed Ages 14-19

Norman, OK 73072. 2600 Van Buren St, Ste 2606. Tel: 405-321-9000.
Fax: 405-321-9001.
www.oaiquartz.org   E-mail: oai@oaiquartz.org
Emily Clinton, Dir.
Grades 9-PG. Adm: Very selective. Admitted: 19%. **Appl**—Fee $20-50. Due: Feb. Audition, 2 recs.
Enr: 270. **Enr cap:** 270. **Fac 35.**
Type of instruction: Enrich. **Daily hours for:** Classes 6.
Focus: Acting Creative_Writing Dance Drawing Filmmaking Music Painting Photog Studio_Art. **Features:** Hiking.
Fees 2010: Free (+$250; in-state residents), 2 wks.
Housing: Cabins Dorms.
Ses: 1. **Wks/ses:** 2. Operates June.

Hosted by Quartz Mountain Arts and Conference Center at a state park, this highly competitive, intensive academy serves motivated Oklahoma high schoolers. Students receive professional training in such disciplines as acting, creative writing, ballet, modern dance, orchestra, chorus, drawing and painting, photography, and film and video. Boys and girls gain exposure to various art forms and learning experiences and attend or participate in performances, gallery openings, poetry readings and ballroom dance classes. All participants attend on full scholarship, aside from a processing fee.

OTIS COLLEGE OF ART AND DESIGN
SUMMER OF ART
Res and Day — Coed Ages 15 and up

Los Angeles, CA 90045. 9045 Lincoln Blvd. Tel: 310-665-6864, 800-527-6847. Fax: 310-665-6821.
www.otis.edu/soa E-mail: soa@otis.edu
Kathleen Masselink, Prgm Mgr.
Adm: FCFS. **Appl**—Fee $0. Due: Rolling.
Enr cap: 20. Fac 30. Staff: Admin 2.
Type of instruction: Adv Enrich Preview. **Courses:** Architect Anime Graphic_Design Product_Design Toy_Design. **Daily hours for:** Classes 6. Homework. Grades. **College credit:** 3.
Focus: Animation Drawing Fashion Media Painting Photog Sculpt.
Fees 2011: Res $4080 (+$200-400), 4 wks. Day $2811 (+$200-400), 4 wks. Aid (Merit & Need).
Housing: Apartments Dorms. Avg per room/unit: 3.
Est 1918. Nonprofit. **Ses: 1. Wks/ses: 4.** Operates July.

During this four-week precollege program, students engage in both foundation courses and hands-on studio classes in a chosen area of concentration. Concentration courses meet three times a week for six hours, while the one participant's one selected foundation class convenes twice a week for six hours. Areas of concentration are as follows: architecture/landscape/interiors, animation, fashion design, graphic design, illustration, product design, life drawing, digital media, painting, traditional black-and-white photography, digital photography and toy design. The three foundation choices are beginning drawing, advanced drawing and life drawing.

OX-BOW PRE-COLLEGE PROGRAM
Res — Coed Ages 16-18

Saugatuck, MI 49453. 3435 Rupprecht Way, PO Box 216. Fax: 269-857-5636.
Contact (Sept-May): 36 S Wabash Ave, 12th Fl, Chicago, IL 60603. Fax: 312-629-6156.
Year-round Tel: 269-857-5811, 800-318-3019.
www.ox-bow.org E-mail: program@ox-bow.org
Jason Kalajainen, Exec Dir.
Grades 11-12. Adm: FCFS. **Appl**—Fee $0. Due: Mar.
Enr: 300-400. **Fac 50.** Prof 50. **Staff:** Admin 5. Couns 25.
Type of instruction: Adv Enrich. **Daily hours for:** Classes 6. **College credit:** 1/crse, total 1.
Focus: Drawing. **Features:** Canoe Hiking Swim Volleyball.
Fees 2012: Res $1781, 1 wk. Aid 2011 (Merit & Need): $15,000.
Housing: Cabins Dorms. Avg per room/unit: 1-2. **Swimming:** Lake Pond. Campus facilities avail.
Est 1910. Nonprofit. **Spons:** School of the Art Institute of Chicago. **Ses: 1. Wks/ses: 1.** Operates July.

Ox-Bow's Pre-College Program in landscape drawing enables rising high school juniors and seniors to receive college-level instruction while exploring drawing, design and composition. Students draw upon the terrain of Ox-Bow's campus and employ a wide variety of drawing materials. Slide lectures, critiques and meetings with visiting artists are a part of evening programming. High school pupils interact with college and graduate student-artists enrolled in concurrently operating Ox-Bow summer courses.

OXBOW SUMMER ART CAMP
Res — Coed Ages 14-16

Napa, CA 94559. Oxbow School, 530 3rd St. Tel: 707-255-6000. Fax: 707-255-6006.
www.oxbowschool.org/summercamp   E-mail: summercamp@oxbowschool.org
Susan Lynn Smith, Dir.
Adm: FCFS. **Appl**—Fee $0. Due: Rolling.
Enr: 50. **Enr cap:** 50. **Fac 5. Staff:** Admin 1. Couns 6.
Type of instruction: Enrich. **Courses:** Drawing Painting. **Daily hours for:** Classes 4½. Study 1½. Rec 4½.
Focus: Media Photog Studio_Art.
Fees 2012: Res $3200, 2 wks.
Housing: Dorms. Avg per room/unit: 2-4.
Spons: Oxbow School. **Ses:** 2. **Wks/ses:** 2. Operates July-Aug.

Similar in content to Oxbow School's semester program, sessions focus on creating project-based art in various media. Professional artists and teachers teach all courses. Campers explore the fundamentals in drawing, painting, sculpture, fabrication and photography in the first week, then propose and develop a studio project in the medium of their choice. Students exhibit their work in a session-concluding show.

PACIFIC MUSIC CAMP
Res and Day — Coed Ages 12-18

Stockton, CA 95211. Univ of the Pacific, Conservatory of Music, 3601 Pacific Ave.
Tel: 209-946-2416.
www.pacific.edu/conservatory   E-mail: musiccamp@pacific.edu
Steve Perdicaris, Dir.
Grades 5-PG. Adm: FCFS. **Appl**—Fee $0. Due: Rolling. Audition (piano camp).
Enr: 450. **Fac 60. Staff:** Admin 6. Couns 16.
Focus: Music. **Features:** Swim.
Fees 2011: Res $625-650, 1 wk. Day $525-550, 1 wk.
Housing: Dorms. Avg per room/unit: 2. **Swimming:** Pool.
Est 1946. Nonprofit. **Spons:** University of the Pacific. **Ses:** 3. **Wks/ses:** 1. Operates June-July.

In addition to separate camps for junior high and high school students interested in joining a band, orchestra or choir, Pacific offers a jazz camp for pupils entering grades 8-12 and a piano camp for those entering grades 9-12. Two years of prior study of the subject instrument are compulsory, and piano camp applicants must submit an audition tape. Private lessons are available for an additional fee.

PACIFIC NORTHWEST COLLEGE OF ART
PRE-COLLEGE SUMMER STUDIOS
Res and Day — Coed Ages 14-18

Portland, OR 97209. 1241 NW Johnson St. Tel: 503-821-8967. Fax: 503-226-3587.
www.pnca.edu/programs/ce/c/precollege   E-mail: precollege@pnca.edu
Sara Kaltwasser, Coord.
Adm: FCFS. **Appl**—Fee $0. Due: Rolling. Transcript, personal statement, rec, portfolio.
Fac 4. Prof 3. Specialists 1. **Staff:** Couns 1.
Type of instruction: Undergrad. **Courses:** Art_Hist Illustration. **Daily hours for:** Classes 6. **College credit:** 3.

Focus: Fine_Arts Painting.
Fees 2012: Res $3185-5127, 3 wks. Day $1790-3732, 3 wks. Aid (Merit).
Housing: Dorms.
Ses: 1. **Wks/ses:** 3. Operates July-Aug.

Pre-College Studios begins with a week of foundation courses in figure drawing and modeling, perspective drawing and composition, surface and color design, space design and time-based arts. Students then focus on one specialized studio in either three-dimensional design, design and illustration, or painting. As a complement to studio work, boys and girls participate in group discussions, visit working artists in their studios, take trips to museums and galleries, and view films and slide shows. The program concludes with a public gallery exhibition. Participants reside at Concordia University.

THE PERFORMING ARTS INSTITUTE OF WYOMING SEMINARY
Res and Day — Coed Ages 12-18

Kingston, PA 18704. 201 N Sprague Ave. Tel: 570-270-2186. Fax: 570-270-2198.
www.wyomingseminary.org/pai   E-mail: onstage@wyomingseminary.org
Nancy Sanderson, Dir.
Adm: Selective. Admitted: 50%. **Appl**—Fee $35-50. Due: Rolling. 2 recs, live/recorded audition.
Enr: 185. **Enr cap:** 235. Intl: 14%. Non-White: 8%. **Fac 40.** Prof 34. K-12 staff 3. Specialists 3. **Staff:** Admin 5. Couns 18.
Type of instruction: Adv Enrich. **Courses:** Music_Theory. **Avg class size:** 12. **Daily hours for:** Classes 8. Study 2. Rec 1.
Focus: Dance Music Theater. **Features:** Swim.
Fees 2012: Res $2950-5600, 3-6 wks. Day $1125-2225, 3-6 wks. Aid 2010 (Merit & Need): $185,000.
Housing: Dorms. **Swimming:** Pool. Campus facilities avail.
Est 1998. Nonprofit. **Ses:** 2. **Wks/ses:** 3. Operates June-Aug.

Comprising distinct programs in music, dance and musical theater, PAI enrolls students with a keen interest in the performing arts. Elements of the programs include two orchestras, a wind ensemble, two choirs, a jazz band, chamber music, music classes, a jazz track, and full dance and theater productions.

PERRY-MANSFIELD PERFORMING ARTS CAMP
Res — Coed Ages 10-24; Day — Coed 8-24

Steamboat Springs, CO 80487. 40755 Routt County Rd 36. Tel: 970-879-7125,
800-430-2787. Fax: 970-879-5823.
www.perry-mansfield.org   E-mail: p-m@perry-mansfield.org
Sophie Aikman, Dir.
Grades 3-Col. Adm: Selective. **Appl**—Fee $0-50. Due: Apr. Video audition/writing sample, 3 recs (certain programs).
Enr: 450.
Courses: Fine_Arts Musical_Theater. **Avg class size:** 12. **Daily hours for:** Classes 5. **College credit.**
Focus: Creative_Writing Dance Music Theater. **Features:** Equestrian.
Fees 2012: Res $2700-4995, 2-6 wks. Day $500-1995, 1-6 wks.
Housing: Cabins Dorms.
Est 1913. Nonprofit. **Ses:** 7. **Wks/ses:** 1-6. Operates June-Aug.

Boys and girls at Perry-Mansfield's various performing arts camps receive daily instruction in the areas of dance, theater, musical theater, music, art and creative writing. Older students take a minimum of four classes daily and participate in evening rehearsals six days a week. These rehearsals conclude with theater, dance and musical productions. Younger campers gain an introduction to the performing arts while also participating in such activities as hiking, swimming, horseback riding and field trips.

PORTSMOUTH ACADEMY OF PERFORMING ARTS CAMP
Res — Coed Ages 8-16

Raymond, ME.
Contact (Year-round): c/o Seacoast Repertory Theatre, 125 Bow St, Portsmouth, NH 03801. Tel: 603-433-4793. Fax: 603-431-7818.
www.papacamp.org   E-mail: lnelson@seacoastrep.org
Lindsey Nelson, Dir.
Adm: Selective. **Appl**—Fee $0. Due: June.
Enr: 100.
Focus: Acting Dance Music Theater. **Features:** Hiking Swim.
Fees 2011: Res $1295, 2 wks.
Housing: Cabins. **Swimming:** Lake.
Est 1989. Nonprofit. **Spons:** Seacoast Repertory Theatre. **Ses: 1. Wks/ses: 2.** Operates Aug.

A program of the Seacoast Repertory Theatre, PAPA Camp allows boys and girls to choose their own programs of study from a curriculum that includes acting, singing, dance, poetry and storytelling. All campers participate in the following core classes: drama workshop, choral singing and dance. Traditional camp activities such as swimming, boating, canoeing, tennis and hiking are also available.

PRATT INSTITUTE PRECOLLEGE PROGRAM
Res and Day — Coed Ages 16-18

Brooklyn, NY 11205. Ctr for Continuing & Professional Stud, 200 Willoughby Ave. Tel: 718-636-3453. Fax: 718-399-4410.
www.pratt.edu/prostudies   E-mail: precollege@pratt.edu
Elizabeth Kisseleff, Coord.
Grades 11-PG. Adm: FCFS. **Appl**—Fee $35. Due: Apr. Rec.
Enr cap: 400. **Fac 60. Staff:** Admin 6.
Type of instruction: Undergrad. **Courses:** Architect Art_Hist. **Avg class size:** 15. **Daily hours for:** Classes 7. Homework. Grades. **College credit:** 4.
Focus: Creative_Writing Drawing Fashion Fine_Arts Media Painting Photog Sculpt Studio_ Art.
Fees 2012: Res $4516 (+$300), 4 wks. Day $2895 (+$300), 4 wks. Aid (Merit & Need).
Housing: Dorms. Avg per room/unit: 2. Campus facilities avail.
Nonprofit. **Ses: 1. Wks/ses: 4.** Operates July-Aug.

This intensive, college-level program covers the fine arts, design, architecture, fashion, creative writing, sculpture and photography. The structured curriculum includes a credit-bearing foundation course that explores drawing, color and design, or writing; a second credit-bearing course in a elective area of choice; and noncredit, pass-fail art history and portfolio development courses. Most courses are taught by Pratt's faculty architects, artists and designers, with the assistance of guest lecturers and critics.

PRINCETON BALLET SCHOOL SUMMER INTENSIVE WORKSHOP
Res — Coed Ages 14-21; Day — Coed 13-21

Princeton, NJ 08540. 301 N Harrison St. Tel: 609-921-7758. Fax: 609-921-3249.
www.arballet.org   E-mail: pbsandarb@aol.com
Mary Pat Robertson, Dir. Student contact: Carol Bellis, E-mail: cbellis@arballet.org.
Adm: Very selective. Admitted: 60%. **Appl**—Fee $25-35. Due: Rolling. Live/DVD audition.

Enr: 100. **Enr cap:** 100. Intl: 15%. Non-White: 15%. **Fac 10.** Specialists 10. **Staff:** Admin 7. Couns 5.
Type of instruction: Adv. **Avg class size:** 20. **Daily hours for:** Classes 8. Rec 5.
Focus: Dance. **Features:** Swim.
Fees 2009: Res $4250 (+$100), 5 wks. Day $1950 (+$100), 5 wks. Aid 2009 (Merit): $15,000.
Housing: Dorms. Avg per room/unit: 2. **Swimming:** Pool.
Est 1980. Nonprofit. **Spons:** American Repertory Ballet. **Ses: 1. Wks/ses: 5.** Operates June-July.

Students enrolled in this preprofessional program receive three hours of ballet instruction daily. Additional classes are offered in pointe and partnering as well as in modern and jazz dance. PBS also schedules choreography workshops, lectures and rehearsals for a final performance. Faculty are former professional dancers with major US companies. The program is open to advanced and advanced intermediate students by in-person or recorded audition.

THE PUTNEY SCHOOL CREATIVE WRITING WORKSHOPS
Res and Day — Coed Ages 14-17

Putney, VT 05346. Elm Lea Farm, 418 Houghton Brook Rd. Tel: 802-387-6297. Fax: 802-387-6216.
www.putneyschool.org/summer   E-mail: summer@putneyschool.org
Thomas D. Howe, Dir.
Grades 9-12. Adm: Selective. **Appl**—Fee $50. Due: Rolling. Rec, 2-3 writing samples.
Enr: 15. **Fac** 4. **Staff:** Admin 3. Couns 17.
Type of instruction: Enrich. **Courses:** Dance Filmmaking Fine_Arts Music Photog Theater Playwriting. **Avg class size:** 15. **Daily hours for:** Classes 6. Rec 2.
Focus: Creative_Writing. **Features:** Farm Hiking Riding Soccer Swim Volleyball.
Fees 2012: Res $3800-7400 (+$100-150), 3-6 wks. Day $1450-2500, 3-6 wks. Aid (Merit & Need).
Housing: Dorms. **Swimming:** Pond.
Est 1987. Nonprofit. **Ses: 3. Wks/ses:** 3-6. Operates June-Aug.

This enrichment program enables participants to explore all aspects of writing. Types of writing addressed include essay composition, nature writing, poetry, journal writing, fiction, memoir writing and creative nonfiction. Roundtable seminars, free writing time, one-on-one instruction, group editing, and presentations and class readings by guest writers help pupils further develop their writing skills. Boys and girls may read selections from new work each week during programwide open-reading sessions, and students produce a literary magazine at program's end.

THE PUTNEY SCHOOL
VISUAL AND PERFORMING ARTS WORKSHOPS
Res and Day — Coed Ages 14-17

Putney, VT 05346. Elm Lea Farm, 418 Houghton Brook Rd. Tel: 802-387-6297. Fax: 802-387-6216.
www.putneyschool.org/summer   E-mail: summer@putneyschool.org
Thomas D. Howe, Dir.
Grades 9-12. Adm: Selective. **Appl**—Fee $50. Due: Rolling. Rec.
Enr: 120. **Enr cap:** 130. Intl: 12%. Non-White: 20%. **Fac 40. Staff:** Admin 4. Couns 21.
Type of instruction: Enrich. **Courses:** Filmmaking Media Painting Sculpt. **Avg class size:** 8. **Daily hours for:** Classes 6. Rec 2.
Focus: Ceramics Creative_Writing Dance Fine_Arts Music Photog Theater. **Features:** Canoe Farm Hiking Riding Woodcraft Basketball Equestrian Soccer Swim Ultimate_ Frisbee Volleyball.

Fees 2011: Res $3700-6875 (+$50), 3-6 **wks. Day** $1375-2350 (+$45), 3-6 **wks.** Aid (Need).
Housing: Dorms. **Swimming:** Pond.
Est 1987. Nonprofit. **Ses:** 2. **Wks/ses:** 3. Operates June-Aug.

Designed for students displaying serious interest in the visual or performing arts, these workshops encompass the following: animation, audio art, ceramics, chamber music, dance, drawing, filmmaking, glass arts, metalwork and jewelry, music composition, painting, photography, printmaking, sculpture, songwriting, theater, vocal ensemble, wearable art, and weaving and fiber arts. Pupils choose two workshops during the session, one in the morning and one in the afternoon. The program features meetings with local artists and field trips to galleries and museums, and Putney schedules student exhibits and performances on closing day.

RHODE ISLAND SCHOOL OF DESIGN PRE-COLLEGE PROGRAM
Res and Day — Coed Ages 16-18

Providence, RI 02903. Continuing Ed, 2 College St. Tel: 401-454-6200, 800-364-7473.
Fax: 401-454-6218.
www.risd.edu/precollege   **E-mail: cemail@risd.edu**
Joy McLaughlin, Coord.
Grades 10-12. Adm: Somewhat selective. **Appl**—Fee $0. Due: Apr. Essay, rec.
Enr: 420. Intl: 20%. Non-White: 35%. **Fac 75. Staff:** Admin 8. Couns 25.
Type of instruction: Adv Enrich. **Courses:** Furniture_Design Game_Design Illustration Interior_Design Jewelry Printmaking Web_Design. **Avg class size:** 15. **Daily hours for:** Classes 6. Study 2. Rec 2. Homework. Grades.
Focus: Animation Ceramics Drawing Fashion Filmmaking Painting Photog Sculpt Studio_ Art.
Fees 2012: Res $7477 (+$800), 6 **wks. Day** $5025 (+$800), 6 **wks.** Aid (Merit & Need).
Housing: Dorms.
Est 1970. Nonprofit. **Ses:** 1. **Wks/ses:** 6. Operates June-Aug.

The program provides a preprofessional introduction to the visual arts for rising high school sophomores, juniors and seniors. Students choose from 20 major course offerings (meeting for two full days each week) in addition to foundation courses in drawing, design and critical studies. Studio work, evening workshops and extracurricular activities complement classroom instruction.

RINGLING COLLEGE OF ART AND DESIGN
PRECOLLEGE PERSPECTIVE
Res — Coed Ages 16-18

Sarasota, FL 34234. 2700 N Tamiami Trail. Tel: 941-955-8866, 800-255-7695.
Fax: 941-955-8801.
www.ringling.edu/precollege   **E-mail: cssp@ringling.edu**
Student contact: Nancy Godfrey, E-mail: precollege@ringling.edu.
Grades 11-PG. Adm: FCFS. **Appl**—Fee $50. Due: Rolling. Recommendation, essay.
Enr: 147. **Enr cap:** 150. Intl: 10%. **Fac 20.** Prof 18. Col/grad students 2. **Staff:** Admin 5. Couns 24.
Type of instruction: Preview Undergrad. **Courses:** Animation Drawing Fine_Arts Media Painting Photog. **Avg class size:** 17. **Daily hours for:** Classes 5. Study 5. Rec 2. Homework. **College credit:** 3/crse, total 3.
Focus: Studio_Art. **Features:** Community_Serv Sea_Cruises Basketball Swim Weight_ Trng.
Fees 2012: Res $4644 (+$300), 4 **wks.** Aid 2010 (Need): $20,000.
Housing: Dorms. Avg per room/unit: 2. **Swimming:** Ocean Pool. Campus facilities avail.
Est 1986. Nonprofit. **Ses:** 1. **Wks/ses:** 4. Operates June-July.

Ringling's PreCollege Perspective enables students interested in art and design to sample a challenging curriculum that is based upon that followed by a first-year pupil in the college's Bachelor of Fine Arts degree program. All participants live on campus in freshman residence halls while enrolling in five courses in art and design fundamentals, as well as two immersive workshops based on the college's BFA majors. Guest speakers, campus art festivals, museum visits and beach trips complete the program. **See Also Page 30**

THE ROCK FARM
Res — Coed Ages 8-16

Camptown, PA 18815. 1 Ballibay Rd. Tel: 570-746-3223, 877-746-2667.
 Fax: 570-746-3691.
www.rock-farm-music-camp.com   E-mail: directors@rock-farm-music-camp.com
John J. A. Jannone, Exec Dir.
Adm: FCFS. **Appl**—Fee $0. Due: Rolling.
Courses: Ceramics Dance Drawing Painting Photog Theater.
Focus: Music. **Features:** Riding Swim Gardening.
Fees 2012: Res $2490-2690, 2 wks.
Housing: Cabins. **Swimming:** Lake Pool.
Est 1988. Spons: Ballibay Camps. **Ses:** 4. **Wks/ses:** 2. Operates June-Aug.

Campers gain experience playing guitar, drums or electric bass at this rock music camp. The program features band rehearsals each morning, lessons on the player's primary instrument and another rock instrument of his or her choice, daily time periods for practice and jamming, master classes conducted by teachers and visiting artists, and frequent shows (including a session-ending group performance). Various elective activities are available through the affiliated Camp Ballibay.

RUTGERS UNIVERSITY SUMMER ACTING CONSERVATORY
Res — Coed Ages 15-18

New Brunswick, NJ 08901. Theater Arts Dept, 2 Chapel Dr, Douglass College.
 Tel: 732-932-9891. Fax: 732-932-1409.
www.rsac-hs.org   E-mail: mjones3@rci.rutgers.edu
Marshall Jones III, Dir.
Grades 10-12. Adm: Very selective. **Appl**—Fee $50. Due: Rolling. Essay, resume, rec, video/live audition.
Enr: 36.
Type of instruction: Adv. **Courses:** Musical_Theater. **College credit:** 3.
Focus: Acting.
Fees 2009: Res $4250, 4 wks. Aid (Need).
Housing: Dorms.
Est 2003. Ses: 1. **Wks/ses:** 4. Operates June-July.

Working theater professionals teach RSAC's daily classes in acting, movement and voice/speech. Evenings feature master classes, special seminars and workshops conducted by visiting actors, producers, writers and other professionals. Field trips to three Broadway shows and other cultural institutions round out the program. A musical theater track, limited to about 12 students, places equal emphasis on acting, singing and dancing.

ST. OLAF COLLEGE MUSIC CAMP
Res and Day — Coed Ages 15-18

Northfield, MN 55057. 1520 St Olaf Ave. Tel: 507-786-3042, 800-726-6523.
 Fax: 507-786-3690.

www.stolaf.edu/camps   E-mail: summer@stolaf.edu
Teresa Lebens, Dir.
Grades 10-PG (younger if qualified). Adm: FCFS. **Appl**—Fee $0. Due: Rolling.
Enr: 200. **Enr cap:** 200. **Fac 35.** Prof 25. Col/grad students 10.
Focus: Music.
Fees 2011: Res $565, 1 wk. Day $515, 1 wk.
Housing: Dorms.
Est 1970. Nonprofit. **Ses:** 1. **Wks/ses:** 1. Operates June.

All campers at St. Olaf participate in a band, choir or orchestra, and involvement in a second large ensemble is possible. In addition, there are opportunities for solo and small-ensemble performance. Tuition includes two private lessons on an instrument or in voice.

ST. OLAF COLLEGE SUMMER PIANO ACADEMY
Res and Day — Coed Ages 14-18

Northfield, MN 55057. 1520 St Olaf Ave. Tel: 507-786-3042, 800-726-6523.
   Fax: 507-786-3690.
www.stolaf.edu/camps   E-mail: summer@stolaf.edu
Kent McWilliams, Dir. Student contact: Teresa Lebens, E-mail: lebens@stolaf.edu.
Grades 9-PG (younger if qualified). Adm: Selective. Admitted: 75%. **Appl**—Fee $0. Due:
   Apr. Audition tape: 2 pieces of contrasting styles.
Enr: 20. **Enr cap:** 20. **Fac 5.** Prof 3. Col/grad students 2. **Staff:** Admin 3. Res 2.
Type of instruction: Adv. **Avg class size:** 10.
Focus: Music.
Fees 2011: Res $665, 1 wk. Day $615, 1 wk.
Housing: Dorms.
Nonprofit. **Ses:** 1. **Wks/ses:** 1. Operates June.

Accomplished high school piano players work closely with St. Olaf's piano faculty in private lessons, master classes, chamber ensembles and enrichment classes. The daily schedule includes classes and rehearsals, elective recreation, and performances by St. Olaf faculty and student counselors. Applicants must furnish a 10-minute audition tape that comprises two pieces of contrasting styles.

ST. OLAF COLLEGE THEATRE CAMP
Res — Coed Ages 13-17

Northfield, MN 55057. 1520 St Olaf Ave. Tel: 507-786-3042, 800-726-6523.
   Fax: 507-786-3690.
www.stolaf.edu/camps   E-mail: summer@stolaf.edu
Todd Edwards & Mishia B. Edwards, Dirs.
   Student contact: Teresa Lebens, E-mail: lebens@stolaf.edu.
Adm: FCFS. **Appl**—Fee $0. Due: Rolling.
Enr cap: 55. **Fac 6.** Prof 2. Col/grad students 4. **Staff:** Admin 1. Couns 6.
Focus: Theater.
Fees 2011: Res $505-595, 1 wk.
Housing: Dorms.
Nonprofit. **Ses:** 1. **Wks/ses:** 1. Operates June.

Serving aspiring thespians who may or may not have prior acting experience, the camp addresses all facets of theater through classes and rehearsals. Program topics include movement, vocal expression, playwriting, character development, basic stage combat, auditioning techniques, theater production and musical theater. A master class option enrolls students who have attended at least one previous session of the program. All participants take part in a session-closing theatrical production.

SAN FRANCISCO ART INSTITUTE PRECOLLEGE PROGRAM
Res and Day — Coed Ages 16-18

San Francisco, CA 94133. 800 Chestnut St. Tel: 415-749-4554. Fax: 415-351-3516.
www.sfai.edu/precollege   E-mail: precollege@sfai.edu
Tammy Ko Robinson, Dir.
Grades 11-PG. Adm: Selective. **Appl**—Fee $65. Due: May. Portfolio (5-8 samples), rec, essay.
Type of instruction: Adv. **Courses:** Animation Creative_Writing Drawing Film Painting Photog Art_Hist. **Daily hours for:** Classes 6. Grades. **College credit:** 1-2/crse, total 5.
Focus: Studio_Art.
Fees 2009: Res $4300 (+$50), 5 wks. Day $2750 (+$50-300), 5 wks. Aid (Need).
Housing: Dorms. Avg per room/unit: 2.
Nonprofit. **Ses:** 1. **Wks/ses:** 5. Operates July-Aug.

Designed for aspiring artists who have completed grade 10 but have not yet started college, this credit-bearing program provides a preview of art school life as it exposes students to the broad range of techniques, concepts and debates that constitute the contemporary art scene. Programming combines interdisciplinary thinking with studio practice. In addition to a required art history seminary, boys and girls select two core studio courses (each of which meets for three hours per day) that replicate an introductory course of study and offer an experience comparable to that of first-year bachelor of fine arts pupils at SFAI.

SARAH LAWRENCE COLLEGE
SUMMER HIGH SCHOOL PROGRAMS
Res and Day — Coed Ages 15-18

Bronxville, NY 10708. Office of Special Prgms, 1 Mead Way. Tel: 914-395-2693.
Fax: 914-395-2694.
www.slc.edu/high-school   E-mail: specialprograms@sarahlawrence.edu
Grades 10-12. Adm: FCFS. **Appl**—Fee $25. Due: Rolling.
Type of instruction: Enrich. **Courses:** Hist. Homework.
Focus: Creative_Writing Dance Filmmaking.
Fees 2011: Res $2875-6425, 3-5 wks. Day $1300-4050, 3-5 wks.
Housing: Dorms. Avg per room/unit: 1.
Ses: 4. **Wks/ses:** 3-5. Operates June-July.

Sarah Lawrence's noncredit summer offerings include a three-week creative writing program; a five-week course in filmmaking (in partnership with the International Film Institute of New York); a three-week musical theater program; and a three-week session that examines the literature, history, filmmaking and science of New York City. Students in all courses meet at least twice with faculty in one-on-one conferences to discuss their personal motivations and interests. Evening and weekend pursuits include film viewings; karaoke nights and other social events; and visits to New York City museums, parks and concerts.

SAVANNAH COLLEGE OF ART AND DESIGN
PROGRAMS FOR HIGH SCHOOL STUDENTS
Res — Coed Ages 15-18

Savannah, GA 31402. PO Box 3146. Tel: 912-525-5100, 800-869-7223.
Fax: 912-525-5986.
www.scad.edu/admission/summer_programs   E-mail: admission@scad.edu
Grades 10-12. Adm: FCFS. **Appl**—Due: Rolling.
Type of instruction: Adv Undergrad. **College credit.**
Focus: Fashion Studio_Art.
Housing: Dorms.
Nonprofit. **Wks/ses:** 1-5.

SCAD conducts two residential arts programs for high schoolers. Rising Star, which serves rising seniors, enables students to enroll in two college-level classes while also building or enhancing their visual arts portfolios. Successful completion of the session results in college credit for use at SCAD or another institution. Field trips and excursions to area parks and attractions enrich the program. For pupils entering grades 10-12, the Summer Seminars program consists of weeklong educational workshops in Savannah and Atlanta.

THE SCHOOL OF AMERICAN BALLET SUMMER COURSE
Res and Day — Coed Ages 12-18

New York, NY 10023. 70 Lincoln Center Plz. Tel: 212-769-6600. Fax: 212-769-4897.
www.sab.org/summercourse
Peter Martins, Dir.
Adm: Selective. **Appl**—Fee $35. Due: Feb. Live audition.
Enr cap: 200. **Fac 13.**
Focus: Dance.
Fees 2009: Res $5105 (+$225), 5 wks. Day $2455 (+$225), 5 wks.
Housing: Dorms. Avg per room/unit: 2-3.
Ses: 1. **Wks/ses:** 5. Operates July-Aug.

Conducted on SAB's self-contained campus in Lincoln Center, Summer Course has dancers of all ability levels take two daily classes in ballet technique, variations, pointe, character or adagio. Pilates instruction, weight training and other seminars are also part of the program. Participants view performances by the New York City Ballet and other major companies. Recreational and social activities include games, movies, and visits to New York City landmarks, museums and Broadway shows. SAB sometimes invites a few particularly talented dancers to continue their studies at the school's winter term.

SCHOOL OF CINEMA AND PERFORMING ARTS SUMMER CAMPS
Res and Day — Coed Ages 13-18

New York, NY 10013. Tribeca Film Ctr, 375 Greenwich St. Tel: 212-941-4057,
800-718-2787. Fax: 646-536-8725.
www.socapa.org   E-mail: info@socapa.org
Jamie Yerkes, Dir.
Adm: FCFS. **Appl**—Fee $0. Due: Rolling. Transcript.
Enr: 80. Intl: 30%. **Fac 10.** Prof 8. Col/grad students 2. **Staff:** Admin 10. Couns 15.
Type of instruction: Undergrad. **Avg class size:** 16. **Daily hours for:** Classes 7. Grades.
    College credit: 3/crse, total 3.
Locations: CA NY VT.
Focus: Acting Dance Filmmaking Media Photog Theater. **Features:** Hiking Kayak Swim.
Fees 2012: Res $2350-4785 (+$400-750), 2-3 wks. Day $1600-3000 (+$400-750), 2-3
    wks. Aid 2011 (Need): $20,000.
Housing: Dorms. Avg per room/unit: 2. **Swimming:** Lake Pool River.
Est 1998. Inc. Ses: 22. **Wks/ses:** 2-3. Operates June-Aug.

With locations on five college and prep school campuses—Polytechnic University in Brooklyn, NY; the New School in New York, NY; Occidental College in Hollywood, CA; Champlain College in Burlington, VT; and St. Johnsbury Academy in St. Johnsbury, VT— SOCAPA conducts distinct programs in filmmaking and advanced filmmaking, film acting, photography and dance. Schedules for all programs include in-class instruction on Mondays, Tuesdays and Wednesdays, then on-location direction, photography or performance on Thursdays and Fridays. Saturdays are devoted to organized off-campus excursions and group dinners.

SCHOOL OF THE MUSEUM OF FINE ARTS
PRE-COLLEGE SUMMER STUDIO
Res and Day — Coed Ages 16-18

Boston, MA 02115. Continuing Ed, 230 The Fenway. Tel: 617-369-3644, 800-591-1474. Fax: 617-369-3679.
www.smfa.edu/precollege **E-mail: precollege@smfa.edu**
Katherine Mitchell, Coord.
Grades 11-12 (younger if qualified). Adm: Selective. **Appl**—Fee $50. Due: Rolling. Portfolio, rec, essay.
Enr: 88. Enr cap: 90. **Fac 9. Staff:** Admin 5. Couns 6.
Avg class size: 13. **Daily hours for:** Classes 6. **College credit:** 5.
Focus: Drawing Fine_Arts Media Painting Photog Sculpt Studio_Art.
Fees 2012: Res $4000-6500 (+$200), 3-5 wks. Day $2400-3800 (+$200), 3-5 wks. Aid (Merit & Need).
Housing: Dorms.
Nonprofit. **Ses:** 2. **Wks/ses:** 3-5. Operates June-July.

This rigorous precollege program serves high school upperclassmen with an interest in the visual arts. Summer Studio's interdisciplinary curriculum addresses painting, drawing, printmaking, sculpture, installation, video, digital photography, sound art and performance. Faculty, teaching assistants and graduate student mentors help participants advance their technical skills in all subjects, learn to work independently and collaboratively, and participate in an artists' community. During the final week of the program, SMFA admissions officers and professional artists provide insights on portfolio building, the college application process and potential career paths in the arts. Visits to Boston museums and galleries are integral to the program. Each session culminates in a final exhibition of student work.

SCHOOL OF VISUAL ARTS SUMMER PRE-COLLEGE PROGRAM
Res and Day — Coed Ages 16-18

New York, NY 10010. 209 E 23rd St. Tel: 212-592-2100, 800-436-4204. Fax: 212-592-2116.
www.schoolofvisualarts.edu **E-mail: admissions@sva.edu**
Grades 11-12. Adm: FCFS. **Appl**—Due: Rolling.
Enr: 400.
Type of instruction: Undergrad. **Courses:** Advertising Graphic_Design Interior_Design Screenwriting. **Avg class size:** 20. **Daily hours for:** Classes 6. Rec 3. **College credit:** 3/crse, total 3.
Focus: Animation Drawing Filmmaking Painting Photog Sculpt.
Fees 2012: Res $3375-3900 (+$75-300), 3 wks. Day $2100 (+$75-300), 3 wks. Aid (Merit & Need).
Housing: Dorms. Avg per room/unit: 2.
Ses: 1. **Wks/ses:** 3. Operates July.

SVA's summer program allows rising high school juniors and seniors to enhance their creative skills, learn more about a particular field, develop a portfolio and earn college credit. Taught by SVA faculty, courses explore a range of general topics within a chosen field of study. Pupils attend classes during the day, with evenings reserved for optional supervised social and cultural activities, open studio sessions or free time for students to explore the city. Students display their work in a final exhibit.

CAMP SHAKESPEARE
Res and Day — Coed Ages 16 and up

Cedar City, UT 84720. c/o Utah Shakespearean Festival, 351 W Center St.
Contact (Winter): c/o California State Univ, Dept of English, 9001 Stockdale Hwy,

Bakersfield, CA 93311.
Year-round Tel: 661-654-2121, Fax: 661-654-2063.
www.csub.edu/campshakespeare　E-mail: mflachmann@csub.edu
Michael Flachmann, Dir.
Grades 11-Col. Adm: FCFS. Appl—Due: Rolling.
Enr: 90. Fac 20. Staff: Admin 2.
Type of instruction: Preview. College credit: 3.
Focus: Theater. Features: Swim.
Fees 2012: Res $1330-1570, ½-1 wk. Day $1180-1370, ½-1 wk.
Housing: Dorms. Swimming: Pool.
Ses: 3. Wks/ses: ½-1. Operates July-Aug.

Participants in this theater program may earn three semesters of college credit. Daily classes feature lectures and discussions led by actors, directors, designers, stage technicians and scholars. Tuition includes tickets to each play performed at the Utah Shakespearean Festival.

SHERBORNE SUMMER SCHOOL OF MUSIC
Res and Day — Coed Ages 18 and up

Sherborne, Dorset, England.
Contact (Year-round): PO Box 629, Godstone, RH9 8WG Surrey, England.
　Tel: 44-1342-893963. Fax: 44-1342-893977.
www.sherbornesummerschoolofmusic.co.uk
E-mail: summermusicschool@btinternet.com
Malcolm Binney, Dir.
Adm: FCFS. Appl—Fee £100. Due: Rolling.
Enr: 750. Fac 50.
Type of instruction: Adv Dev_Read Preview Rev Tut. Courses: Dance. Daily hours for:
　Classes 5.
Intl program focus: Culture.
Focus: Music. Features: Swim.
Fees 2012: Res £500 (+£53-68), 1 wk. Day £393, 1 wk.
Housing: Dorms Houses. Swimming: Pool.
Est 1952. Inc. Ses: 3. Wks/ses: 1. Operates Aug.

Sherborne offers courses in the Alexander technique; vocal technique; choral music; wind chamber music, band and orchestra; jazz music; brass band; string chamber and orchestra; piano accompaniment; chamber orchestra; percussion; opera; composition; and conducting. Sports and planned social activities complete the program.

SIGNATURE MUSIC CAMP
Res — Coed Ages 12-17

Ithaca, NY. Ithaca College.
Contact (Year-round): 118 Julian Pl, Ste 229, Syracuse, NY 13210. Tel: 315-478-7840.
　Fax: 315-478-0962.
www.signaturemusic.org　E-mail: contact@signaturemusic.org
Richard W. Ford, Exec Dir.
Grades 7-12. Adm: Somewhat selective. Admitted: 95%. Priority: Low-income. URM.
　Appl—Fee $0. Due: Rolling. 2 teacher recs.
Enr: 85. Enr cap: 100. Intl: 3%. Non-White: 10%. Fac 16. Prof 3. Col/grad students 8. K-12
　staff 5. Staff: Admin 4. Res 30.
Type of instruction: Adv Enrich. Avg class size: 10. Daily hours for: Classes 6. Rec 4.
Focus: Music. Features: Swim.
Fees 2012: Res $2100, 2 wks. Aid 2009 (Need): $20,000.
Housing: Dorms. Avg per room/unit: 2. Swimming: Pool.
Est 1993. Nonprofit. Ses: 1. Wks/ses: 2. Operates June-July.

Students in this instructional program at Ithaca College choose from jazz, vocal/piano, and band/choir programs. Sight singing, jazz ensemble, show choir, concert band, jazz and film music history, improvisation and master classes are offered to all students. Swimming, game nights and other recreational activities are part of the program, as are recitals and cabaret.

SOUTH CAROLINA GOVERNOR'S SCHOOL FOR THE ARTS AND HUMANITIES SUMMER PROGRAMS
Res — Coed Ages 12-18

Greenville, SC 29601. 15 University St. Tel: 864-282-3713. Fax: 864-282-3712.
www.scgsah.org   E-mail: admissions@scgsah.state.sc.us
Anna King, Dir.
Grades 7-12. Adm: Selective. Prereqs: GPA 2.5. **Appl**—Fee $25. Due: Jan. Work samples/ audition, interview, transcript, 2 teacher recs.
Type of instruction: Enrich. **Daily hours for:** Classes 6. Rec 2. Homework.
Focus: Creative_Writing Drama Music Studio_Art.
Fees 2012: Res $850-2000 (+$50), 2-5 wks. Aid (Need).
Housing: Dorms. Avg per room/unit: 2. Campus facilities avail.
Ses: 3. **Wks/ses:** 2-5. Operates June-July.

Governor's School summer students receive intensive arts training from practicing artists. Limited to South Carolina residents, the two-week Discovery (for rising ninth graders) and Academy (for rising 10th graders) programs focus upon creative writing, drama, visual arts, and vocal or instrumental music. The curriculum incorporates studio work, self-directed studies, performances, field trips, lectures and presentations by faculty and guest artists. The five-week Summer Dance program, open to students around the world entering grades 7-12, offers complex exercise training in both classical ballet and modern dance. Participants in all programs may showcase their work in end-of-session recitals, readings and presentations.

SOUTHERN ILLINOIS UNIVERSITY YOUNG WRITERS WORKSHOP
Res and Day — Coed Ages 15-18

Carbondale, IL 62901. Div of Continuing Ed, MC 6705, Washington Sq C.
Tel: 618-453-2121.
www.angelfire.com/il/yww   E-mail: aljoseph@siu.edu
Allison Joseph, Dir.
Grades 10-12. Adm: FCFS. **Appl**—Due: Rolling. Writing sample.
Enr: 30. **Enr cap:** 30.
Type of instruction: Enrich.
Focus: Creative_Writing.
Fees 2010: Res $300, 1 wk. Day $275, 1 wk.
Housing: Dorms.
Est 1999. Ses: 1. **Wks/ses:** 1. Operates June.

This five-day program consists of daily poetry and prose classes, readings shared by faculty and participants, and panels on special writing topics. Workshops help students generate new story and poem ideas, and hourlong minisessions offer an introduction to various creative writing topics. Graduate students and creative writing faculty at SIU constitute YWW's faculty.

SPOLETO STUDY ABROAD SUMMER SESSION
Res — Coed Ages 15-19

Spoleto, Umbria, Italy.

Contact (Year-round): c/o Ashley Hall, 172 Rutledge Ave, Charleston, SC 29403. Tel: 843-822-1248.
www.spoletostudyabroad.com   E-mail: spoletoabroad@gmail.com
Lorenzo Muti & Jill Muti, Dirs.
Student contact: Nancy Langston, E-mail: spoleto@mindspring.com.
Grades 10-12 (younger if qualified). Adm: Selective. Appl—Fee $75. Due: Feb. 2 essays, 2 teacher recs, portfolio/audition CD.
Enr: 50. Enr cap: 50. Fac 10. Prof 4. K-12 staff 6. Staff: Admin 2.
Type of instruction: Enrich. Courses: Ital. Avg class size: 10. Daily hours for: Classes 6.
Intl program focus: Acad Lang Culture.
Focus: Creative_Writing Fine_Arts Music Painting Photog Studio_Art Theater. Features: Aquatics Soccer Swim.
Fees 2012: Res $5650 (+airfare), 3 wks. Aid 2010 (Merit): $6000.
Housing: Dorms. Swimming: Pool.
Est 1997. Nonprofit. Ses: 1. Wks/ses: 3. Operates July.

This intensive, interdisciplinary summer session for high schoolers focuses on the arts and the humanities. The program, which takes place in central Italy, enables students to explore their academic and artistic interests in a European setting. Pupils study the visual arts, photography, vocal music, creative writing and drama while also learning about the cultural and artistic heritage of the Italian Renaissance. Twice-weekly day trips to historically and artistically noteworthy Italian cities complement class work. A consortium of highly regarded US independent schools cosponsors the program.

STAGEDOOR MANOR
Res — Coed Ages 10-18

Loch Sheldrake, NY 12759. 116 Karmel Rd. Tel: 845-434-4290.
Contact (Sept-May): 8 Wingate Rd, Lexington, MA 02421. Tel: 540-337-7619.
Year-round Toll-free: 888-782-4388, Fax: 845-434-3779.
www.stagedoormanor.com   E-mail: info2012@stagedoormanor.com
Cynthia Samuelson, Dir.
Adm: FCFS. Appl—Fee $0. Due: Rolling.
Enr: 240. Fac 150. Staff: Admin 10.
Courses: Dance Media Music.
Focus: Acting Theater. Features: Soccer Swim Tennis Volleyball.
Fees 2012: Res $5395-9895 (+$150), 3-6 wks.
Housing: Dorms. Swimming: Pool.
Est 1976. Inc. Ses: 5. Wks/ses: 3-6. Operates June-Aug.

Stagedoor's program consists of daily class work in acting, musical comedy, dance, modeling, television acting, voice, directing, stagecraft and costuming. Stagedoor provides specialized programs for younger campers and college-level courses for high school students. Boys and girls perform at the camp's theaters and at major resort hotels.

STANFORD JAZZ WORKSHOP JAZZ CAMP
Res and Day — Coed Ages 12-17

Stanford, CA 94309. PO Box 20454. Tel: 650-736-0324. Fax: 650-856-4155.
www.stanfordjazz.org   E-mail: info@stanfordjazz.org
Jim Nadel, Dir. Student contact: Janel Thysen, E-mail: registrar@stanfordjazz.org.
Adm: FCFS. Appl—Fee $0. Due: Rolling.
Enr: 200. Enr cap: 200. Fac 55. Staff: Admin 6. Couns 12.
Type of instruction: Enrich. Avg class size: 6. Daily hours for: Classes 8. Study 1½. Rec 1½.
Focus: Music. Features: Swim.

Fees 2011: Res $1790-3675 (+$100), 1-2 wks. **Day** $995 (+$100), 1 wk. Aid 2011 (Need): $110,000.
Housing: Dorms. Avg per room/unit: 2. **Swimming:** Pool.
Est 1972. Nonprofit. **Spons:** Stanford University. **Ses:** 2. **Wks/ses:** 1. Operates July.

Serving students from beginning to advanced skill levels, Jazz Camp is open to players of all instruments (including violin, viola and cello), and to vocalists as well. Campers play with other young people while learning from a faculty composed of well-known professional jazz musicians and educators. The curriculum comprises jazz ensemble playing, master classes, private lessons and performances, as well as theory, musicianship and jazz history courses. In addition to daily class sessions and rehearsals, participants attend jam sessions and Stanford Jazz Festival evening concerts to enhance their training and experience.

STONELEIGH-BURNHAM SCHOOL
SORVINO DANCE INTENSIVE
Res — Girls Ages 11-17

Greenfield, MA 01301. 574 Bernardston Rd. Tel: 413-774-2711. Fax: 413-772-2602.
www.sbschool.org   E-mail: summerprograms@sbschool.org
Ann Sorvino, Dir.
Adm: FCFS. **Appl**—Due: Rolling.
Enr: 24. **Enr cap:** 24. **Staff:** Admin 3. Couns 3.
Focus: Dance. **Features:** Aquatics Swim.
Fees 2012: Res $575, 1 wk.
Housing: Dorms. **Swimming:** Pool.
Est 1997. Nonprofit. **Ses:** 2. **Wks/ses:** 1. Operates July.

Girls enrolled in the program work on their dancing skills in an intensive and noncompetitive environment. Experienced teachers offer instruction in modern dance, ballet and jazz techniques. Special repertory, improvisation and choreography sessions are also available. Applicants must display a serious interest in dance but need not audition.

STUDIO ART CENTERS INTERNATIONAL SUMMER TERM
Res — Coed Ages 18 and up

Florence, Italy.
Contact (Year-round): 50 Broad St, Ste 1617, New York, NY 10004. Tel: 212-248-7225, 877-257-7225. Fax: 212-248-7222.
www.saci-florence.org   E-mail: admissions@saci-florence.org
Mary Beckinsale, Pres.
Grades PG-Col. **Adm:** FCFS. **Appl**—Fee $60. Due: Rolling. Transcript.
Enr: 150. **Enr cap:** 150. **Intl:** 20%. **Fac 13. Staff:** Admin 18.
Type of instruction: Adv. **Courses:** Archaeol Lang Filmmaking Media. **Daily hours for:** Classes 8. **College credit:** 6.
Intl program focus: Acad Culture.
Focus: Ceramics Creative_Writing Fine_Arts Painting Photog Sculpt Studio_Art. **Features:** Conservation.
Fees 2012: Res $6500 (+airfare), 4 wks.
Housing: Apartments. Avg per room/unit: 6.
Est 1975. Nonprofit. **Ses:** 1. **Wks/ses:** 4. Operates July.

Open to those who have completed high school with an interest in art, art history, art conservation or the Italian language, SACI's Summer Studies Program operates in the heart of Florence. Students may earn up to six college credits while taking one studio and one academic course from the following options: drawing, painting, printmaking, ceramics, sculpture, photography, computer art, design, batik, jewelry, Renaissance art history, beginning painting conservation, Italian, serigraphy and creative writing. The program's location lends itself to frequent field trips to relevant locations, performances and events.

SUMMER SONATINA INTERNATIONAL PIANO CAMP
Res — Coed Ages 7-16

Bennington, VT 05201. 5 Catamount Ln. Tel: 802-442-9197. Fax: 802-447-3175.
www.sonatina.com   E-mail: piano@sonatina.com
Polly van der Linde, Dir.
   Student contact: Andrea Lindhardt, E-mail: andrea@sonatina.com.
Adm: FCFS. **Appl**—Fee $0. Due: Rolling.
Enr: 150. **Enr cap:** 170. **Intl:** 10%. **Non-White:** 10%. **Fac 6.** Prof 4. Col/grad students 2. **Staff:** Admin 2. Couns 10.
Type of instruction: Adv Enrich Rev Study_Skills Tut. **Courses:** Crafts. **Avg class size:** 42. **Daily hours for:** Classes 1. Study 3. Rec 2½.
Focus: Music. **Features:** Cooking Hiking Kayak Soccer Swim Volleyball Croquet.
Fees 2012: Res $975, 1 wk.
Housing: Houses. **Swimming:** Lake Pool. Campus facilities avail.
Est 1969. Inc. **Ses:** 5. **Wks/ses:** 1. Operates June-July.

Summer Sonatina, located in the historic Vermont mansion of the van der Linde family, offers a piano program for beginning through advanced performers. Students live with the family and share in household duties while receiving three to five private lessons weekly and classes in sight-reading, chorus, music theory and composition. Pupils attend performances at Tanglewood and the Saratoga Performing Arts Center once a week.

TENNESSEE GOVERNOR'S SCHOOL FOR THE ARTS
Res — Coed Ages 16-18

Murfreesboro, TN 37132. Middle Tennessee State Univ, 1301 E Main St, Box 38.
   Tel: 615-898-2223. Fax: 615-898-2326.
www.gsfta.com   E-mail: gjrobins@mtsu.edu
Raphael B. Bundage, Dir. Student contact: Glenna Robinson.
Grades 11-12. Adm: Very selective. **Appl**—Fee $0. Due: Nov. Transcript, 2 recs, audition.
Enr: 230. **Enr cap:** 230.
Type of instruction: Enrich. **Courses:** Ceramics Drawing Painting Sculpt. **College credit:** 3.
Focus: Dance Filmmaking Music Studio_Art Theater.
Fees 2011: Free (in-state residents). Res 4 wks.
Housing: Dorms.
Ses: 1. **Wks/ses:** 4. Operates June-July.

Professional visual and performing artists lead these intensive programs for Tennessee residents in visual arts, dance, filmmaking, theater and music. Visual arts media include clay, drawing, painting, sculpture, printmaking, computer imagery, photography and video. The dance program covers ballet and pointe technique, modern and jazz. Filmmakers produce a five- to 10-minute narrative. Music students choose from orchestra, wind, chorale, piano and guitar ensembles. The theater program develops both technical and performance skills. All boys and girls attend nightly demonstrations, slide shows, films and lectures.

TEXAS ARTS PROJECT
Res — Coed Ages 9-18

Austin, TX 78746. c/o St Stephen's Episcopal School, 6500 St Stephen's Dr.
   Tel: 512-553-6276. Fax: 512-327-1311.
www.texasartsproject.com   E-mail: info@texasartsproject.com

Ginger Morris, Dir.
Grades 1-12. Adm: Somewhat selective. Admitted: 90%. **Appl**—Fee $0. Due: Rolling. Video/portfolio submission for advanced program.
Enr: 58. **Enr cap:** 75. Intl: 2%. Non-White: 15%. **Fac 30.** Prof 3. Col/grad students 10. K-12 staff 5. Specialists 12. **Staff:** Admin 2. Couns 10.
Courses: Classical_Guitar Musical_Theater. **Avg class size:** 10. **Daily hours for:** Classes 8. Study 2. Rec 2.
Focus: Acting Dance Filmmaking Music Theater. **Features:** Swim.
Fees 2011: Res $1050-2875, 1-4 wks. Aid 2010 (Merit & Need): $20,000.
Housing: Dorms. Avg per room/unit: 4. **Swimming:** Lake Pool. Campus facilities avail.
Est 2001. Nonprofit. **Spons:** St. Stephen's Episcopal School. **Ses:** 3. **Wks/ses:** 1-4. Operates June-July.

Conducted at St. Stephen's Episcopal School, TAP is a summer training program for young artists interested in developing their skills in musical theater, dance, acting, filmmaking and technical theater. The program consists of classes, private lessons, master classes with visiting artists, theater outings and seminars. The junior session (for children ages 9-12) lasts for one week, while the main session (ages 13-18) runs for three weeks. All sessions culminate in a production on the final day that enables campers to display their talents.

UNIVERSITY OF CALIFORNIA-LOS ANGELES
ACTING AND PERFORMANCE INSTITUTE
Res and Day — Coed Ages 15-18

Los Angeles, CA 90095. Summer Sessions & Special Prgms, 1332 Murphy Hall.
Tel: 310-267-4836. Fax: 310-825-3383.
www.summer.ucla.edu/institutes/acting&performance/overview.htm
E-mail: institutes@summer.ucla.edu
Patricia Harter, Dir.
Grades 10-PG. Adm: Selective. **Appl**—Due: Rolling. Rec.
Type of instruction: Adv. **College credit:** 2.
Focus: Acting Theater.
Housing: Dorms. Avg per room/unit: 2.
Nonprofit. **Ses:** 1. **Wks/ses:** 6. Operates June-July.

High school students with a serious interest in theater gain exposure at UCLA to the training and discipline required for participation in a university theater program or a career in the performing arts. Boys and girls attend morning performance classes addressing acting fundamentals, movement and improvisation, and scene. A performance workshop in the afternoon offers practical experience in the rehearsal and performance process. Under the guidance of an instructor, students take part in all aspects of the creative process: conceptualizing, writing and transforming ideas into dramatic action. A collaborative project leads to a session-closing performance for invited guests.

UNIVERSITY OF CALIFORNIA-LOS ANGELES
SUMMER DANCE-THEATER INTENSIVE
Res — Coed Ages 16-18

Los Angeles, CA 90095. Summer Sessions & Special Prgms, 1332 Murphy Hall.
Tel: 310-267-4836.
www.summer.ucla.edu/institutes/dance/overview.htm
E-mail: institutes@summer.ucla.edu
Kevin Kane, Dir.
Grades 11-PG. Adm: Selective. **Appl**—Due: Rolling. Rec.
Type of instruction: Adv. **Courses:** Music. **College credit:** 2.
Focus: Dance Theater.

Fees 2009: Res $1350, 1 wk.
Housing: Dorms. Avg per room/unit: 2.
Nonprofit. **Ses:** 1. **Wks/ses:** 1. Operates June.

This eight-day program for advanced high schoolers combines the disciplines of dance, theater, music and social activism. The program is particularly suited to those interested in exploring the ways in which art can raise awareness and consciousness pertaining to various socially relevant themes. Students engage in daily movement classes, ensemble physical theater, and improvisation and composition. The Dance-Theatre Intensive is noncompetitive and does not involve any conservatory-style dancing. Parents and friends may attend the session-closing collaborative performance.

UNIVERSITY OF IOWA YOUNG WRITERS' STUDIO
Res — Coed Ages 16-18

Iowa City, IA 52242. C215 Seashore Hall. Tel: 319-335-4209. Fax: 319-335-4743.
www.uiowa.edu/youngwriters   E-mail: iyws@uiowa.edu
Stephen Lovely, Dir.
Grades 11-PG (younger if qualified). Adm: Very selective. **Appl**—Fee $0. Due: Feb. Creative writing sample, transcript, teacher rec, essay.
Enr: 60. **Enr cap:** 60.
Type of instruction: Enrich. **Avg class size:** 12.
Focus: Creative_Writing.
Fees 2010: Res $1600, 2 wks. Aid (Need).
Housing: Dorms.
Nonprofit. **Ses:** 2. **Wks/ses:** 2. Operates June-July.

Participants in this college program for high school students focus upon a single course of study for the duration of this two-week program. Options are poetry, fiction and creative writing (a survey course that comprises fiction, poetry and creative nonfiction). Each course includes both a seminar and a workshop; the same instructor teaches both. Seminars provide participants with a broad range of readings, while workshops enable boys and girls to work on their writing with the benefit of constructive criticism from fellow students and the instructor.

UNIVERSITY OF KANSAS
MIDWESTERN MUSIC ACADEMY
Res and Day — Coed Ages 11-18

Lawrence, KS 66045. 460 Murphy Hall, 1530 Naismith Dr. Tel: 785-864-9751.
Fax: 785-864-5866.
www.musicacademy.ku.edu   E-mail: musicacademy@ku.edu
Dan Gailey, Dir.
Grades 6-PG. Adm: FCFS. **Appl**—Fee $0.
Enr: 400. **Staff:** Admin 30. Couns 23.
Courses: Computers.
Focus: Music.
Fees 2011: Res $540-595, 1 wk. Day $315-370, 1 wk. Aid (Merit).
Est 1936. Nonprofit. **Ses:** 7. **Wks/ses:** 1. Operates June-July.

Midwestern Music Academy's offers four weeklong summer programs, all taught by University of Kansas faculty and guest artists. Junior High Music Camp, open to band and choir students entering grades 6-9 and orchestra students entering grades 6-8, offers instruction through master classes, rehearsals and electives. Programs for students completing grades 8-12 include the String Institute; the Wind, Brass and Percussion Institute; and the Jazz Workshop.

UNIVERSITY OF MASSACHUSETTS-AMHERST
JUNIPER INSTITUTE FOR YOUNG WRITERS
Res and Day — Coed Ages 15-18

Amherst, MA 01003. c/o University Conference Services, 918 Campus Ctr, 1 Campus Center Way. Tel: 413-545-5503. Fax: 413-545-3880.
www.umass.edu/juniperyoungwriters
E-mail: juniperyoungwriters@hfa.umass.edu
Betsy Wheeler, Dir.
Grades 11-PG (younger if qualified). Adm: Selective. Admitted: 50%. **Appl**—Fee $25. Due: Rolling. Creative writing sample, rec, personal statement.
Enr: 72. Enr cap: 72. Intl: 2%. Non-White: 20%. **Fac 10.** Col/grad students 10. **Staff:** Admin 3. Couns 7.
Courses: Crafts Theater. **Avg class size:** 12. **Daily hours for:** Classes 4½. Study 1½. Rec 3½. Homework. **College credit:** 2/crse, total 2.
Focus: Creative_Writing.
Fees 2012: Res $1250, 1 wk. Day $1050, 1 wk. Aid 2011 (Merit & Need): $2775.
Housing: Dorms. Avg per room/unit: 2.
Est 2005. Nonprofit. **Ses: 1. Wks/ses: 1.** Operates June.

Hosted by the University of Massachusetts' MFA Program for Poets and Writers, this intensive, weeklong program combines creative writing workshops, studio courses and readings. Daily workshops in poetry and fiction form the core of the session. Participants work with Juniper faculty and a core group of their peers to generate new work, revise work in progress and form a community of writers designed to foster shared feedback. Question and answer sessions with faculty and writers-in-residence enable students to explore the creative process and the writing life. Noted authors and poets deliver evening readings.

UNIVERSITY OF MIAMI SUMMER SCHOLAR PROGRAMS
Res — Coed Ages 16-17

Coral Gables, FL 33124. PO Box 248005. Tel: 305-284-4000. Fax: 305-284-6629.
www.miami.edu/ssp   E-mail: ssp.cstudies@miami.edu
Grades 11-12. Adm: Selective. Prereqs: GPA 3.0. **Appl**—Fee $35. Due: May. Transcript, rec, essay.
Enr: 196. Fac 25. Staff: Admin 1.
Avg class size: 18. **Daily hours for:** Classes 6. Study 3. Rec 2. **High school & college credit:** 3/crse, total 6.
Focus: Filmmaking. **Features:** Community_Serv Swim.
Fees 2011: Res $5730, 3 wks.
Housing: Dorms. **Swimming:** Ocean Pool.
Est 1991. Nonprofit. **Ses: 1. Wks/ses: 3.** Operates June-July.

SSP, taught by university faculty, allows highly motivated rising high school juniors and seniors to pursue course work in filmmaking. Guest speakers and visits to local sites relevant to the field of study supplement in-class work. Students earn three to six college credits, which are also accepted at many high schools. In addition to filmmaking, the university conducts programs focusing on broadcast journalism, business, engineering, forensic investigation, health and medicine, international relations, marine science, sports medicine and sports administration (see separate listing for details).

UNIVERSITY OF MICHIGAN
MPULSE SUMMER PERFORMING ARTS INSTITUTE
Res — Coed Ages 13-18

Anne Arbor, MI 48109. 1281 Moore Bldg, 1100 Baits Dr. Tel: 734-936-2660, 866-936-2660. Fax: 734-647-0140.

www.music.umich.edu/mpulse   E-mail: mpulse@umich.edu
Mary Simoni, Prgm Dir. Student contact: Sarah J. Rau.
Grades 10-PG. Adm: Selective. Admitted: 50%. **Appl**—Fee $60. Audition.
Enr: 200. **Enr cap:** 200. Intl: 2%. Non-White: 15%. **Fac 65.** Prof 50. Col/grad students 15.
Staff: Admin 3. Res 12.
Type of instruction: Adv. **Courses:** Fine_Arts. **Daily hours for:** Classes 8. Study 2½. Rec
2. Homework. Tests.
Focus: Dance Music Theater. **Features:** Swim.
Fees 2012: Res $1750-3390, 2-3 wks. Aid 2011 (Merit & Need): $20,000.
Housing: Dorms. Avg per room/unit: 2. **Swimming:** Pool.
Ses: 14. **Wks/ses:** 2-3. Operates July.

MPulse enables high school musicians and performing arts to develop their skills in the areas of music performance, music technology, theater, musical theater and dance under the guidance of University of Michigan professors and alumni. Programming is designed for students who are considering college majors in these areas. Participants tour the campus and have the opportunity to meet with admissions counselors from the university's School of Music, Theatre & Dance. Information about the university's undergraduate application and audition process is also available during MPulse.

UNIVERSITY OF NORTH CAROLINA SCHOOL OF THE ARTS
SUMMER SESSION
Res — Coed Ages 12-21

Winston-Salem, NC 27127. 1533 S Main St. Tel: 336-770-1432. Fax: 336-770-1497.
www.uncsa.edu/summersession   E-mail: rhotona@uncsa.edu
Grades 7-Col. Adm: Somewhat selective. **Appl**—Fee $60. Due: Rolling. 2 recs, live/
recorded audition.
Enr: 370. **Enr cap:** 500. **Staff:** Admin 2.
Type of instruction: Adv Enrich. **Courses:** Filmmaking Fine_Arts. **Avg class size:** 20.
Daily hours for: Classes 7. Rec 3.
Focus: Dance Drama Film Music Painting Sculpt. **Features:** White-water_Raft Basketball
Volleyball.
Fees 2012: Res $1014-3915, 1-5 wks.
Housing: Dorms. Avg per room/unit: 2. Campus facilities avail.
Est 1965. Nonprofit. **Ses:** 6. **Wks/ses:** 1-5. Operates June-July.

UNCSA combines workshops and rehearsals for its programs in dance, drama, filmmaking, music and the visual arts. Performance opportunities and private lessons are part of some programs. Extracurricular activities and off-campus trips supplement departmental programming.

UNIVERSITY OF ST ANDREWS
CREATIVE WRITING SUMMER PROGRAMME
Res — Coed Ages 16-18

St Andrews, KY16 9AX Fife, Scotland. St Katharine's W, 16 The Scores.
Tel: 44-1334-462275. Fax: 44-1334-463330.
www.st-andrews.ac.uk/admissions/ug/int/summerschools
E-mail: rmd10@st-andrews.ac.uk
Ruth Harris, Head.
Grades 11-PG. Adm: Selective. Admitted: 90%. Prereqs: GPA 3.0. **Appl**—Fee £15. Due:
May. Creative writing sample (4 poems or piece of short fiction), 2 recs, standardized
test results, personal statement.
Enr: 24. **Enr cap:** 30. Intl: 20%. Non-White: 10%. **Fac 12.** Prof 1. Col/grad students 4. Spe-
cialists 7. **Staff:** Admin 2. Couns 2.

Type of instruction: Adv. **Courses:** Fine_Arts Music Photog Theater. **Daily hours for:** Classes 4. Study 3. Rec 3. Homework. Grades. **College credit:** 12.
Intl program focus: Acad Culture.
Focus: Creative_Writing. **Features:** Conservation Exploration Hiking Mtn_Trips Swim.
Fees 2012: Res £2800 (+£200), 4 wks.
Housing: Dorms. Avg per room/unit: 1. **Swimming:** Ocean Pool. Campus facilities avail.
Est 2003. Ses: 1. **Wks/ses:** 4. Operates June-July.

Aspiring young fiction writers and poets who have completed grades 10-12 take a series of master classes and workshops with noted Scottish writers and poets. Skills addressed include editing, analysis and oral presentation. Frequent field trips and excursions—in addition to cultural visits to art galleries, concerts and the theater—enrich the program.

THE UNIVERSITY OF THE ARTS
PRE-COLLEGE SUMMER INSTITUTE
Res and Day — Coed Ages 16-18

Philadelphia, PA 19102. 320 S Broad St. Tel: 215-717-6430, 800-616-2787.
   Fax: 215-717-6538.
http://cs.uarts.edu/precollege   E-mail: precollege@uarts.edu
Heather Jo Wingate, Coord.
Grades 11-12 (younger if qualified). Adm: Selective. Admitted: 85%. Prereqs: GPA 2.0.
   Appl—Fee 50. Due: May. Transcript, teacher rec, portfolio/audition, essay.
Enr: 250. **Enr cap:** 350. **Fac** 150. **Staff:** Admin 8.
Type of instruction: Undergrad. **Avg class size:** 12. **Daily hours for:** Classes 8. **College credit:** 3/crse, total 3.
Focus: Acting Dance Media Music Photog Studio_Art Theater.
Fees 2012: Res $2225-4350 (+$150-600), 2-4 wks. Day $1450-1600 (+$150-600), 2 wks. Aid (Need).
Housing: Apartments Dorms. Avg per room/unit: 2-4.
Est 1900. Nonprofit. Ses: 2. **Wks/ses:** 2-4. Operates July-Aug.

The Pre-College Summer Institute offers talented high school students the opportunity to study the visual and performing arts. Course offerings in performing arts include acting, musical theater, dance and jazz performance, while art and media offerings include animation, Web design, photography, painting, printmaking, sculpture, graphic design, film, industrial design, illustration, mixed media, jewelry, fibers and ceramics.

UNIVERSITY OF THE SOUTH
SEWANEE SUMMER MUSIC FESTIVAL
Res — Coed Ages 13-25

Sewanee, TN 37383. 735 University Ave. Tel: 931-598-1225. Fax: 931-598-1706.
www.sewaneemusicfestival.org   E-mail: ssmf@sewanee.edu
Katherine Lehman, Dir.
Adm: Selective. **Appl**—Fee $60. Due: Apr. Live/recorded audition, 2 recs.
Enr: 165. **Staff:** Admin 8.
Focus: Music. **Features:** Swim.
Fees 2011: Res $3500, 4 wks.
Housing: Dorms. **Swimming:** Lake Pond Pool Stream.
Est 1957. Nonprofit. Ses: 1. **Wks/ses:** 4. Operates June-July.

All students at SSMF participate in an orchestra and in chamber ensembles, take private lessons, practice daily and attend classes such as theory, composition and conducting. Emphasis is placed on performance. Rehearsals, master classes, concerts, special events and recreational activities round out the program. Qualified high school graduates may earn five hours of college credit.

UNIVERSITY OF VIRGINIA YOUNG WRITERS WORKSHOP
Res — Coed Ages 14-17

Charlottesville, VA 22904. c/o The Curry School, PO Box 400273. Tel: 434-924-0836.
www.uvawriters.com   E-mail: writers@virginia.edu
Margo Figgins, Dir.
Grades 9-12. Adm: Selective. **Appl**—Due: Mar. Writing samples, rec.
Type of instruction: Enrich.
Focus: Creative_Writing.
Fees 2009: Res $1300-1975, 2-3 wks. Aid (Need).
Housing: Dorms.
Est 1982. Ses: 2. Wks/ses: 2-3. Operates June-July.

UVA conducts two annual sessions for aspiring writers: a two-week program for those new to study within a specific genre, and a three-week program for writers who wish to deepen their understanding and mastery of a specific genre. Both sessions feature intensive workshops, labs, readings, conferences with instructors, independent writing time, and opportunities for publication and performance. Intensive workshops employed in the three-week program focus upon songwriting, poetry, screen- and playwriting, fiction and creative nonfiction.

THE WALDEN SCHOOL YOUNG MUSICIANS PROGRAM
Res — Coed Ages 9-18

Dublin, NH 03444. PO Box 432. Tel: 603-563-8212.
Contact (Sept-May): 31A 29th St, San Francisco, CA 94110. Tel: 415-648-4710.
Year-round Fax: 415-648-1561.
www.waldenschool.org   E-mail: students@waldenschool.org
Seth Brenzel, Exec Dir.
Adm: Somewhat selective. Admitted: 80%. **Appl**—Fee $50. Due: Apr. Essay, teacher rec, recording/portfolio.
Enr: 50. Intl: 8%. Non-White: 16%. **Fac 12. Staff:** Admin 6.
Courses: Dance. **Avg class size:** 4. **Daily hours for:** Classes 4. Study 4. Rec 2.
Focus: Music. **Features:** Hiking Soccer Swim.
Fees 2012: Res $6750 (+$150-250), 5 wks. Aid 2011 (Need): $70,000.
Housing: Dorms. **Swimming:** Lake.
Est 1972. Nonprofit. **Ses:** 1. **Wks/ses:** 5. Operates June-July.

Walden students follow a comprehensive curriculum that includes musicianship, improvisation, composition and chorus. A concert series, collaborative artist and ensemble residencies, and weekly student composer forums enrich the program. Course work varies slightly each summer based upon the needs of the pupils, and instruction is available at all levels of musical accomplishment.

WALNUT HILL SCHOOL SUMMER DANCE PROGRAMS
Res — Coed Ages 10-17; Day — Coed 5-13

Natick, MA 01760. 12 Highland St. Tel: 508-653-4312. Fax: 508-655-3726.
http://why.walnuthillarts.org/ballet/summer-programs
E-mail: admissions@walnuthillarts.org
Michael Owen, Dir.
Adm: Selective. **Appl**—Fee $30. Due: Rolling. Live/recorded audition, rec.
Avg class size: 20.
Focus: Dance. **Features:** Swim.
Fees 2012: Res $2550-5000, 3-5 wks. Day $160-1500, 1-3 wks.
Housing: Dorms. **Swimming:** Pool.
Nonprofit. **Ses:** 4. **Wks/ses:** 1-5. Operates June-Aug.

Offering intensive preprofessional training grounded in pure classical technique, Walnut

Hill's five-week Summer Dance (ages 13-17) places a strong emphasis on ballet, with supplementary classes provided in pointe; variation; men's work; and jazz, modern and character dance. All classes are graded according to age, technical ability and physical strength. Dancers take a minimum of three classes each day, in addition to participating in evening rehearsals or workshops and one Saturday class. A weekly lecture or a short workshop and planned recreational events are important aspects of the program. Other options include the three-week-long Summer Youth Dance (residential and day, ages 10-13) and two weeklong junior workshops for commuting children ages 5-11.

WALNUT HILL SUMMER WRITING PROGRAM
Res — Coed Ages 13-17

Natick, MA 01760. 12 Highland St. Tel: 508-650-5020. Fax: 508-653-9593.
www.walnuthillarts.org   E-mail: admissions@walnuthillarts.org
Margaret Funkhouser, Dir.
Adm: Selective. **Appl**—Fee $30. Due: May. Essay, Eng teacher/guidance counselor rec.
Fac 6. Staff: Admin 1.
Type of instruction: Enrich. **Courses:** Poetry.
Focus: Creative_Writing. **Features:** Swim.
Fees 2012: Res $3000, 3 wks. Aid (Need).
Housing: Dorms. **Swimming:** Pool.
Inc. **Ses:** 1. **Wks/ses:** 3. Operates July.

Students enrolled in this intensive, multigenre writing program develop their skills through workshops in poetry and fiction. Students work individually in collaborative projects and meet with faculty one-on-one. Published authors visit campus to teach master classes and give readings of their work. Excursions to local museums and literary landmarks

WARTBURG COLLEGE SUMMER BROADCASTING WORKSHOP
Res — Coed Ages 14-18

Waverly, IA 50677. 100 Wartburg Blvd, PO Box 1003. Tel: 319-352-8534.
www.wartburg.edu/news/iba
Grades 9-PG. Adm: Selective. **Appl**—Due: Rolling. Rec, essay.
Enr: 20. **Enr cap:** 20.
Type of instruction: Enrich.
Focus: Media.
Fees 2011: Res $225, 1 wk.
Housing: Dorms.
Est 1989. Nonprofit. **Ses:** 2. **Wks/ses:** 1. Operates July.

This weeklong workshop teaches high schoolers and recent graduates about television, radio and the business of broadcasting. Students use Wartburg's digital equipment and facilities as they prepare live broadcasts for local radio and television stations. Other aspects of the program are tours of professional radio and TV facilities, meetings with area media professionals, and activities designed to help pupils develop relevant skills.

WASHINGTON UNIVERSITY
PORTFOLIO PLUS
Res and Day — Coed Ages 16-18

St Louis, MO 63130. 1 Brookings Dr, Campus Box 1031. Tel: 314-935-8652.
Fax: 314-935-6462.
www.samfoxschool.wustl.edu/summer/portplus   E-mail: lee@samfox.wustl.edu
Belinda Lee, Dir.

Grades 11-12. **Adm:** Somewhat selective. Admitted: 80%. **Appl**—Fee $35. Due: May. Transcript, rec, personal statement.
Enr cap: 45. **Fac 9.** Prof 6. Col/grad students 3. **Staff:** Admin 2. Res 3.
Type of instruction: Undergrad. **Courses:** Drawing Fashion Painting Printmaking. **Avg class size:** 15. **Daily hours for:** Classes 6. **College credit:** 6.
Focus: Studio_Art. **Features:** Swim.
Fees 2012: Res $5390 (+$350), 5 wks. Day $3900 (+$350), 5 wks.
Housing: Dorms. Avg per room/unit: 2. **Swimming:** Pool. Campus facilities avail.
Est 2004. Ses: 1. Wks/ses: 5. Operates June-July.

This five-week introduction to the study and practice of making art is open to rising high school juniors and seniors. All participants take a morning art foundations course, then choose from afternoon electives in digital photography, fashion design, painting and printmaking/book arts. Outside of class, students embark on organized trips to museums and visit artist studios. Successful completion of the program yields six college credits.

WESTMINSTER CHOIR COLLEGE SUMMER PROGRAMS
Res and Day — Coed Ages 11-18

Princeton, NJ 08540. 101 Walnut Ln. Tel: 609-924-7416. Fax: 609-921-6187.
www.rider.edu/woce   E-mail: woce@rider.edu
Scott R. Hoerl, Exec Dir.
Grades 6-PG. Adm: Somewhat selective. **Appl**—Fee $50. Due: Rolling. DVD audition for certain programs.
Type of instruction: Adv Enrich. **Courses:** Theater.
Focus: Music.
Fees 2012: Res $850-1700, 1-2 wks. Aid (Need).
Housing: Dorms. Avg per room/unit: 2.
Est 1926. Nonprofit. Spons: Rider University. **Ses:** 14. **Wks/ses:** 1-2. Operates June-Aug.

Part of Rider University, Westminster Choir College conducts summer music programs for middle school and high school students. Classes are available in choral studies, piano, organ, voice, music education, composition and musical theater, among others. The program includes private and group lessons, concerts, recitals and on-campus recreational activities.

CAMP WINNARAINBOW
Res — Coed Ages 7-14

Laytonville, CA 95454. PO Box 1359. Tel: 707-984-6507. Fax: 707-984-8087.
Contact (Sept-May): 1301 Henry St, Berkeley, CA 94709. Tel: 510-525-4304.
Fax: 510-528-8775.
www.campwinnarainbow.org   E-mail: arainbow@mcn.org
Jahanara Romney & Wavy Gravy, Dirs.
Adm: FCFS. **Appl**—Due: Rolling.
Enr: 150. **Enr cap:** 150. **Fac 10. Staff:** Admin 4. Couns 34.
Courses: Crafts. **Daily hours for:** Classes 2. Rec 3.
Focus: Circus_Skills Dance Music Theater. **Features:** Peace/Cross-cultural Basketball Gymnastics Swim.
Fees 2012: Res $800-6700 (+$20), 1-9 wks. Aid 2008 (Need): $154,000.
Housing: Tepees. Avg per room/unit: 9. **Swimming:** Lake.
Est 1972. Nonprofit. Ses: 5. Wks/ses: 1-9. Operates June-Aug.

The camp focuses on performing arts and circus skills. Activities and classes include acting and play production; clowning, mime, juggling, falling and stilt walking; unicycling; tightrope; trapeze; cloud swing and Spanish web; gymnastics; music; dance; arts and crafts; mask making; magic; martial arts; swimming; team sports; nature walks; poetry; songwriting; capoeira; and hip-hop and salsa dancing.

WRITERS WORKSHOP AT SUSQUEHANNA UNIVERSITY
Res — Coed Ages 16-18

Selinsgrove, PA 17870. 514 University Ave. Tel: 570-372-4164. Fax: 570-372-2741.
www.susqu.edu/writers   E-mail: gfincke@susqu.edu
Gary Fincke, Dir.
Grades 11-12. Adm: Selective. **Appl**—Due: May. Rec, 5-6 poems/6-8 pages of fiction/creative nonfiction.
Enr: 60. **Fac 6.** Prof 6. **Staff:** Admin 2. Couns 6.
Type of instruction: Enrich. **Avg class size:** 15. **Daily hours for:** Classes 7.
Focus: Creative_Writing. **Features:** Swim.
Fees 2012: Res $730 (+$50), 1 wk.
Housing: Dorms. **Swimming:** Pool.
Est 1988. Ses: 1. **Wks/ses:** 1. Operates June-July.

Serving experienced writers about to enter grade 11 or 12, the program features workshops in fiction, creative nonfiction and poetry. Each day, the Writers Workshop offers such activities as group workshops; individual conferences; and readings by students, faculty and guest writers.

YOUNG ACTORS CAMP
Res — Coed Ages 7-17

Azusa, CA. Azusa Pacific Univ.
Contact (Year-round): 689 W Foothill Blvd, Ste A, Claremont, CA 91711.
Tel: 909-982-8059. Fax: 909-482-2011.
www.youngactorscamp.com   E-mail: request@youngactorscamp.com
Nichelle Rodriguez, Dir.
Adm: Selective. Admitted: 25%. **Appl**—Fee $0. Due: Apr. Phone interview, nomination (Casting Call prgm).
Enr: 200. Intl: 60%. Non-White: 20%. **Fac 20.** Prof 4. Col/grad students 12. Specialists 4.
Staff: Admin 4. Couns 20.
Type of instruction: Undergrad. **Courses:** Media Theater. **Avg class size:** 12. **Daily hours for:** Classes 6. Study 1. Rec 4. **College credit:** 4/crse, total 4.
Focus: Acting.
Fees 2012: Res $990-7620, 1-5 wks.
Housing: Dorms. Campus facilities avail.
Est 2000. Inc. Spons: Inspire Me Corporation. **Ses:** 4. **Wks/ses:** 1-5. Operates June-July.

Children and adolescents who wish to improve their acting skills attend sessions at Azusa Pacific University. The Acting Camp enrolls boys and girls ages 7-17 with or without acting experience into a program that features an on-camera commercial workshop, an exploration of acting terms and techniques, on-camera screen study, improvisational games and memory skills training. Campers of the same age with at least a year of acting experience may enroll in the Pre-Professional Program, where they learn extensively about the film and television industries. Boys and girls ages 12-17 who are serious about pursuing a career in film or television—and who can furnish a referral from an acting teacher, director or out-of-state agent—may apply for the Casting Call program; this is an invitation-only session, and a phone interview is required.

YOUNG ARTISTS' WORKSHOPS
Res — Coed Ages 14-18

Rockport, ME 04856. 70 Camden St. Tel: 207-236-8581, 877-577-7700.
Fax: 207-236-2558.
www.mainemedia.edu   E-mail: info@mainemedia.edu
Charles Altschul, Exec Dir.

Adm: Somewhat selective. Admitted: 95%. **Appl**—Fee $55. Due: Rolling. Portfolio required for advanced classes.
Enr: 16. **Enr cap:** 16. **Fac 1.** Specialists 1. **Staff:** Couns 4.
Courses: Animation.
Focus: Acting Filmmaking Media Photog. **Features:** Hiking Swim.
Fees 2012: Res $1395-2595, 1-2 wks. Aid (Merit & Need).
Housing: Dorms. **Swimming:** Lake Ocean.
Est 1973. Nonprofit. **Spons:** Maine Media Workshops/Maine Media College. **Ses:** 33. **Wks/ses:** 1-2. Operates June-Aug.

Artistically talented high schoolers enrolled in this Maine Media Workshops summer program spend their time studying and exploring a potential career field in one of the following areas: photography, filmmaking and video, multimedia, documentary, acting or digital media. Instructors, who are drawn from industry professionals and experienced educators, each receive classroom support from a teaching assistant. Students spend weekends on class field trips, at work in labs or editing suites, or engaged in recreational pursuits along the coast of Maine.

YOUNG MUSICIANS & ARTISTS
Res — Coed Ages 10-18

Salem, OR. Willamette Univ.
Contact (Year-round): PO Box 13277, Portland, OR 97213. Tel: 503-281-9528.
Fax: 888-793-2583.
www.ymainc.org   E-mail: info@ymainc.org
Quinland D. Porter, Exec Dir.
Grades 5-PG. Adm: FCFS. **Appl**—Fee $0. Due: Apr.
Enr: 110. **Enr cap:** 140. Non-White: 18%. **Fac 30. Staff:** Admin 10. Couns 20.
Type of instruction: Adv Enrich. **Avg class size:** 8. **Daily hours for:** Classes 5. Study 1. Rec 3.
Focus: Creative_Writing Dance Music Painting Photog Studio_Art Theater. **Features:** Badminton Soccer Softball Tennis Volleyball.
Fees 2012: Res $1550 (+$25), 2 wks. Aid 2011 (Need): $58,000.
Housing: Dorms. Avg per room/unit: 2.
Est 1965. Nonprofit. **Ses:** 2. **Wks/ses:** 2. Operates June-July.

Held at Willamette University, YMA offers a range of arts programs that encompasses instrumental music, theater, musical theater, choir, piano, dance, digital photography, creative writing and the visual arts. Students select a major area of study, then also enroll in an elective class. Classes meet Monday through Saturday, with boys and girls spending four hours daily attending class in their majors, 45 minutes in the elective class and 30 minutes in an orientation class. Supervised recreational activities round out the day.

YOUTH THEATRE OF NEW JERSEY
SUMMER THEATRE INSTITUTE-NEW YORK CITY
Res — Coed Ages 14-19

New York, NY. Juilliard School.
Contact (Year-round): 23 Tomahawk Trl, Sparta, NJ 07871. Tel: 201-415-5329.
www.youththeatreinstitutes.org   E-mail: youththeatreallyn@yahoo.com
Allyn Sitjar, Dir.
Grades 9-PG (younger if qualified). Adm: Selective. **Appl**—Fee $75. Due: Rolling. Live/DVD audition.
Enr: 30. Intl: 10%. Non-White: 25%. **Fac 10.** Prof 5. Specialists 5. **Staff:** Admin 3. Couns 3.
Courses: Dance Music Directing Mime Musical_Theater Playwriting. **Avg class size:** 15. **Daily hours for:** Classes 10.
Focus: Acting Theater.
Fees 2012: Res $6075, 4 wks. Aid 2009 (Merit): $800.

Housing: Dorms. Avg per room/unit: 2.
Est 1989. Nonprofit. **Ses:** 1. **Wks/ses:** 4. Operates June-July.

Summer Theatre Institute-NYC offers intensive training with professional artists in a variety of theater techniques. Instruction combines core classes with specialized training in acting, musical theater, playwriting and directing. The session culminates in an original production that is a result of work at the institute. Professional theater teaching artists—many of whom teach at area colleges—serve as program instructors. Students live in Juilliard School dormitories and train at studios in the city's theater district.

SPECIAL-INTEREST
PROGRAMS

Special-interest programs are arranged alphabetically by name. The Table of Contents lists the subject areas presented, and an index beginning on page 400 lists the programs under each of those subjects. Programs offering a family session are indicated by "FAM" at the end of the age range in the index.

INDEX BY FOCUS

CONSERVATION & FIELD ECOLOGY

COOKING

FARM

LEADERSHIP

PEACE AND CROSS-CULTURAL

RANCH

RAPPELLING

RIDING

RIDING *(CONT.)*

ROCK CLIMBING

SAILING

SCUBA-DIVING

SEA CRUISES

SEAMANSHIP

SECULARISM

SURVIVAL TRAINING

WILDERNESS CAMP

WILDERNESS CAMP *(CONT.)*

WILDERNESS CANOEING

WILDLIFE STUDIES

SeaWorld Camps-TX *(Res — Coed Ages 10-22; Day — Coed 5-12)* ....San Antonio, TX....443
Burgundy Wildlife *(Res — Coed Ages 8-15)* .... Capon Bridge, WV....415

WORK CAMPS

Hidden Villa Camp *(Res — Coed Ages 9-17; Day — Coed 6-9)* ..... Los Altos Hills, CA....424
Circle Pines Ctr *(Res — Coed Ages 7-17; FAM)* ....Delton, MI....417
VISIONS Adventures *(Res — Coed Ages 11-18)* ....Bozeman, MT....450
Camp Celo *(Res — Coed Ages 7-12)* ....Burnsville, NC....415
X-Cultural Solutions *(Res — Coed Ages 15+)* ....New Rochelle, NY....418
Longacre Farm *(Res — Coed Ages 12-18)* ....Newport, PA....428
Tamarack Farm *(Res — Coed Ages 15-17)*... Plymouth, VT....446
Volunteers for Peace *(Res — Coed Ages 15+; FAM)*............................. Burlington, VT....450

Special-Interest Programs

ACTIONQUEST
Res — Coed Ages 13-19

Sarasota, FL 34277. PO Box 5517. Tel: 941-924-6789, 800-317-6789.
Fax: 941-924-6075.
www.actionquest.com   E-mail: info@actionquest.com
Mike Meighan & James M. Stoll, Dirs.
Adm: FCFS. **Appl due:** Rolling. **Staff:** Admin 8. Couns 40.
High school credit.
Travel: Asia Australia/New_Zealand Caribbean Europe South_America.
Focus: Adventure_Travel Sail Seamanship. **Features:** Marine_Bio/Stud Boating Community_Serv Exploration Hiking Outdoor_Ed Scuba White-water_Raft Swim Water-skiing Watersports.
Fees 2012: Res $4570-6570 (+airfare), 2-3 wks.
Swimming: Ocean.
Est 1986. Ses: 3. Wks/ses: 2-3. Operates June-Aug.

ActionQuest offers programs for both beginners and more experienced students in the Caribbean, the Mediterranean, Australia, the Galapagos and the South Pacific. These experiential, expedition-based programs focus on sailing, scuba diving, cultural immersion, marine biology and exploration. Participants live aboard 50-foot sailing yachts while cruising from island to island. Shipmates are part of the crew-in-training and rotate on-board responsibilities daily. Advanced certification programs are available for shipmates with previous experience.

ADVENTURE TREKS
Res — Coed Ages 12-18

Flat Rock, NC 28731. PO Box 1321. Tel: 828-698-0399, 888-954-5555.
Fax: 828-698-0339.
www.adventuretreks.com   E-mail: info@adventuretreks.com
Niki Gaeta, Dir.
Grades 7-12. Adm: Somewhat selective. Admitted: 95%. **Appl due:** Rolling. **Enr:** 24. **Enr cap:** 24. **Staff:** Admin 5.
Travel: AK CA CO ME NC NH OR TN UT VT WA Canada.
Focus: Mountaineering Outdoor_Ed Wilderness_Camp. **Features:** Adventure_Travel Boating Canoe Caving Cooking Deep-sea Fishing Hiking Kayak Mtn_Biking Mtn_Trips Rappelling Rock_Climb Sail Survival_Trng White-water_Raft Wilderness_Canoe Swim.
Fees 2012: Res $2995-4995 (+airfare), 2-4 wks. Aid 2011 (Merit & Need): $50,000.
Housing: Tents. **Swimming:** Lake Pond Ocean River Stream.
Est 1994. Inc. Ses: 24. Wks/ses: 2-4. Operates June-Aug.

Adventure Treks offers wilderness adventure programs for teenagers in mountain regions around the US and in British Columbia, Canada. Program activities include white-water rafting, backpacking, mountaineering, rock climbing, canoeing, sailing, sea kayaking and mountain biking.

ALPENGIRL
Res — Girls Ages 11-17

Manhattan, MT 59741. PO Box 1138. Tel: 406-570-6312, 800-425-1841.
www.alpengirlcamp.com   E-mail: info@alpengirlcamp.com
Alissa Farley, Dir.

Grades 6-12. Adm: FCFS. **Appl due:** Rolling. **Enr:** 12. **Enr cap:** 12. **Staff:** Admin 2. Couns 6.
Locations: AK HI MT WA Europe.
Focus: Wilderness_Camp. **Features:** Ecol Environ_Sci Writing/Journ Creative_Writing Photog Adventure_Travel Canoe Cooking Hiking Kayak Mountaineering Mtn_Trips Outdoor_Ed Rappelling Riding Rock_Climb Weight_Loss White-water_Raft Wilderness_ Canoe Yoga Equestrian Surfing Swim.
Fees 2011: Res $775-3255 (+$150), 1-3 wks. Aid (Need).
Housing: Tents. Avg per room/unit: 3-4. **Swimming:** Lake Pond Ocean Pool River Stream.
Est 1997. Inc. **Ses:** 11. **Wks/ses:** 1-3. Operates June-Aug. ACA.

Alpengirl offers mountain adventures for teenage girls in wilderness areas and national parks of the western US, Hawaii and Scandinavia. Primary activities are rock climbing, rafting, canoeing, horseback riding, surfing, backpacking, sea kayaking, hiking, yoga and outdoor cooking.

AMERICAN FARM SCHOOL GREEK SUMMER
Res — Coed Ages 15-18

Thessaloniki, Greece. 12 Marinou Antipa St, PO Box 23. Tel: 212-463-8434.
Fax: 30-2310-492-727.
www.afs.edu.gr/greeksummer   E-mail: rkaryp@afs.edu.gr
Grades 10-PG. Adm: FCFS. **Appl due:** Rolling. **Enr:** 35. **Enr cap:** 35. **Staff:** Admin 4. Couns 3.
Intl program focus: Culture. **Travel:** Europe. Home stays avail.
Focus: Community_Serv Peace/Cross-cultural. **Features:** Lang Ceramics Dance Music Adventure_Travel Farm Mountaineering Social_Servs Swim.
Fees 2012: Res $6000 (+airfare), 6 wks.
Housing: Dorms Hotels Houses. Avg per room/unit: 2. **Swimming:** Ocean Pool.
Est 1970. Nonprofit. **Ses:** 1. **Wks/ses:** 6. Operates June-Aug.

Held on the campus of American Farm School, Greek Summer combines community service with instruction about Greek folk music, Greek cooking, beekeeping and ecological issues. Students complete a service project for the benefit of the local community while living with a host family in a small Greek village. During their time on campus, boys and girls assist with the daily operation of the school's dairy, poultry unit, vineyard, olive groves, greenhouses and vegetable gardens. Another aspect of the session enables participants to spend 1o days traveling and visiting historical sites throughout Greece.

AMIGOS DE LAS AMERICAS
Res — Coed Ages 16-21

Houston, TX 77057. 5618 Star Ln. Tel: 713-782-5290, 800-231-7796.
Fax: 713-782-9267.
www.amigoslink.org   E-mail: info@amigoslink.org
Emily Untermeyer, Exec Dir.
Grades 11-Col. Adm: FCFS. **Appl due:** Mar. **Staff:** Admin 19. Res 100.
High school & college credit.
Intl program focus: Lang Culture. **Locations:** Mexico/Central_America South_America. Home stays avail.
Focus: Community_Serv. **Features:** Lang Crafts Photog Theater Adventure_Travel Peace/ Cross-cultural Social_Servs Work Soccer Swim.
Fees 2009: Res $4400 (+$800), 6-8 wks. Aid 2009 (Merit & Need): $70,000.
Housing: Houses. Avg per room/unit: 1-3. **Swimming:** Lake Pond Ocean River Stream.
Est 1965. Nonprofit. **Ses:** 11. **Wks/ses:** 6-8. Operates June-Aug.

Program volunteers spend up to eight weeks living with host families and working in rural areas or underserved semi-urban neighborhoods in one of six Latin American countries: the Dominican Republic, Honduras, Mexico, Nicaragua, Panama or Paraguay. Participants live and work in teams of two or three, collaborating with local families and youth and Latin American sponsoring agencies to address community public health and development issues.

ANDERSON HIGH ADVENTURES
Res — Coed Ages 13-17

Gypsum, CO 81637. c/o Anderson Western Colorado Camps, 7177 Colorado River Rd. Tel: 970-524-7766, 800-832-4851. Fax: 970-524-7107.
www.andersoncamps.com   E-mail: andecamp@andersoncamps.com
Christopher Porter, Dir.
Adm: FCFS. **Appl due:** Rolling. **Enr:** 12. **Staff:** Admin 4. Couns 18.
Travel: CO UT.
Focus: Wilderness_Camp. **Features:** Adventure_Travel Archery Caving Climbing_Wall Conservation Exploration Fishing Hiking Kayak Mountaineering Mtn_Biking Mtn_Trips Outdoor_Ed Rappelling Riding Riflery Rock_Climb Ropes_Crse White-water_Raft Basketball Soccer Softball Swim Ultimate_Frisbee Volleyball Watersports.
Fees 2011: Res $2475-3715 (+$100), 2-3 wks.
Housing: Cabins Tents. Avg per room/unit: 7. **Swimming:** Pond Pool.
Est 1968. Inc. **Spons:** Anderson Western Colorado Camps. **Ses:** 3. **Wks/ses:** 2-3. Operates July-Aug.

At Anderson High Adventures, participants further develop their skills in such specialty areas as rock climbing, rappelling and kayaking. Campers spend much of their time on various out-of-camp trips, including white-water rafting, backpacking, rock climbing and mountain climbing excursions.

ANDERSON WESTERN COLORADO CAMPS
Res — Coed Ages 7-17

Gypsum, CO 81637. 7177 Colorado River Rd. Tel: 970-524-7766, 800-832-4851. Fax: 970-524-7107.
www.andersoncamps.com   E-mail: andecamp@andersoncamps.com
Christopher Porter, Dir.
Grades 1-12. Adm: FCFS. **Appl due:** Rolling. **Enr cap:** 130. **Staff:** Admin 4. Couns 18.
Focus: Outdoor_Ed Wilderness_Camp. **Features:** Adventure_Travel Aquatics Boating Caving Climbing_Wall Fishing Hiking Mountaineering Mtn_Biking Mtn_Trips Rappelling Riding Riflery Rock_Climb Ropes_Crse White-water_Raft Equestrian Swim Ultimate_Frisbee.
Fees 2011: Res $2150-3715 (+$225-300), 2-3 wks.
Housing: Cabins. Avg per room/unit: 7. **Swimming:** Pond Pool.
Est 1962. Inc. **Ses:** 4. **Wks/ses:** 2-3. Operates June-Aug.

Among the daily options at this Rocky Mountains adventure camp are white-water rafting, kayaking, riding, mountain biking, mountain climbing, a climbing wall, rappelling, a low ropes course, trapshooting, riflery, archery and swimming. Campers also engage in camp outs and embark on a four- to five-day rafting, caving, riding or mountain climbing trip.

APPALACHIAN MOUNTAIN CLUB
TEEN WILDERNESS ADVENTURES
Res — Coed Ages 12-18

Gorham, NH 03581. PO Box 298. Tel: 603-466-2727. Fax: 603-466-3871.
www.outdoors.org/education/twa   E-mail: information@outdoors.org
Andrew J. Falender, Exec Dir.

Adm: FCFS. **Appl due:** Rolling. **Enr:** 8. **Staff:** Admin 5. Couns 12.
Travel: ME NH.
Focus: Outdoor_Ed Wilderness_Camp Wilderness_Canoe. **Features:** Canoe Conserva-
tion Exploration Hiking Kayak Mtn_Biking Mtn_Trips Rock_Climb Survival_Trng Swim.
Fees 2009: Res $770-4395, 1-4 wks.
Housing: Lodges Tents. Avg per room/unit: 8. **Swimming:** River.
Est 1992. Nonprofit. **Ses:** 35. **Wks/ses:** 1-4. Operates June-Aug.

Through excursions lasting five to 23 days, TWA provides summer outdoor adventure education in the White Mountains of northern New Hampshire and Maine. Trips typically include such elements as backpacking, canoeing, kayaking, mountain biking and rock climbing. A minimum of two instructors leads each group of six to eight campers. Participants in each session may take part in a service project to help maintain the trail systems in the White Mountains. Specialty camps in mountain biking, white-water kayaking and leadership are available to boys and girls who wish to concentrate on a specific skill.

BATES BAR J RANCH
Res — Coed Ages 8-15

Cochrane, T4C 1A8 Alberta, Canada. PO Box 700. Tel: 403-637-2199.
www.batesbarj.com   E-mail: bates@batesbarj.com
Kristina Bates & Randy Bates, Dirs.
Adm: FCFS. **Appl due:** Rolling. **Enr:** 70. **Staff:** Admin 7. Couns 14.
Focus: Outdoor_Ed Ranch Riding. **Features:** Hiking Swim.
Fees 2011: Res Can$775, 1 wk.
Housing: Dorms Lodges. **Swimming:** River.
Est 1962. Ses: 6. **Wks/ses:** 1. Operates July-Aug.

Bates Bar J features riding while also addressing the grooming, the feeding and the care of horses. The program also includes swimming, fishing, games, campfires, crafts, wagon rides, trampolining and dances. A nature awareness program offers hiking and wilderness survival.

BEAVER CAMP WILDERNESS ADVENTURE
Res — Coed Ages 11-18

Lowville, NY 13367. 8884 Buck Point Rd. Tel: 315-376-2640. Fax: 315-376-7011.
www.beavercamp.org   E-mail: info@beavercamp.org
Christa Scott, Dir.
Adm: FCFS. **Appl due:** Rolling. **Staff:** Admin 5. Couns 20.
Focus: Canoe Fishing Rock_Climb Wilderness_Camp. **Features:** Aquatics Boating Caving
Climbing_Wall Hiking Kayak Mtn_Biking Mtn_Trips Rappelling Ropes_Crse Sail Wilder-
ness_Canoe Basketball Soccer Swim.
Fees 2012: Res $325-360, 1 wk. Aid (Need).
Housing: Cabins Lodges Tents. **Swimming:** Lake.
Est 1969. Nonprofit. Mennonite. **Ses:** 5. **Wks/ses:** 1. Operates July-Aug. ACA.

Campers at this Christian camp take part in various wilderness activities through this Beaver Camp program. Specialized, weeklong wilderness adventures focus upon rock climbing, mountain biking, river canoeing and fishing.

BIKING X
Res — Coed Ages 11-17

Asheville, NC 28816. PO Box 17227. Toll-free: 800-654-5957. Fax: 408-676-0998.
www.bikingx.com   E-mail: info@bikingx.com
Fiona McColley, Dir.

Adm: FCFS. **Appl due:** Rolling.
Intl program focus: Culture. **Travel:** CO IL KS KY MA ME MO NC NH NV OR UT VA VT WA Canada South_America.
Focus: Bicycle_Tours Mtn_Biking. **Features:** Adventure_Travel Rock_Climb Swim.
Fees 2011: Res $1495-4895, 1-8½ wks.
Swimming: Lake River.
Ses: 24. **Wks/ses:** 1-8½. Operates June-Aug.

The program offers mountain biking and road touring adventures throughout the US, Canada and Ecuador. Trips serve beginning, intermediate and advanced riders, and boys and girls on each tour also engage in other activities, among them hiking, swimming and sightseeing. Participants raise money for charity during a 60-day biking trek that progresses from California to Virginia.

CAMP BIRCHWOOD FOR BOYS
Res — Boys Ages 7-17

Grand Marais, MN 55604. 12586 Gunflint Trail, Slip 85. Tel: 218-388-4402, 800-451-5270. Fax: 218-388-0311.
www.birchwoodforboys.com   E-mail: info@birchwoodforboys.com
Dan Bredemus & Melissa Bredemus, Dirs.
Grades 2-11. Adm: FCFS. **Appl due:** May.
Focus: Wilderness_Camp. **Features:** Painting Archery Canoe Fishing Hiking Kayak Mtn_ Biking Outdoor_Ed Riflery Rock_Climb Sail Woodcraft Swim Watersports.
Fees 2012: Res $1450-3942, 1-4 wks.
Housing: Cabins. Avg per room/unit: 6-7. **Swimming:** Lake.
Est 1968. Ses: 10. **Wks/ses:** 1-4. Operates June-Aug. ACA.

Boys at Birchwood receive instruction in wilderness skills such as canoeing, fishing, rappelling, backpacking, biking, orienteering and rock climbing. Recreational activities and wilderness adventure trips complement the program. The camp maintains an affiliation with Camp Birchwood in LaPorte.

BIRMINGHAM-SOUTHERN COLLEGE
STUDENT LEADERS IN SERVICE
Res — Coed Ages 16-18

Birmingham, AL 35254. 900 Arkadelphia Rd, Box 549008. Tel: 205-226-4673. Fax: 205-226-3074.
www.bsc.edu/academics/hess/leadership/slis.cfm   E-mail: shawk@bsc.edu
James Randolph, Dir.
Grades 11-12. Adm: Selective. **Appl due:** Apr. **Enr cap:** 25.
Focus: Community_Serv Leadership. **Features:** Hiking Ropes_Crse.
Fees 2012: Res $500, 1 wk.
Housing: Dorms.
Nonprofit. **Ses:** 1. **Wks/ses:** 1. Operates June.

SLIS exposes rising high school seniors to different leadership styles and provides opportunities for students to develop leadership skills through community service. Participants study leadership and ethics during lectures and simulations, then join in service projects across Birmingham, working with children, the environment, the working poor and others in need. Students also sample college life during the session.

BLACK RIVER FARM AND RANCH SUMMER HORSE RANCH
Res — Girls Ages 6-15

Croswell, MI 48422. 5040 Sheridan Line Rd. Tel: 810-679-2505. Fax: 810-679-3188.
www.blackriverfarmandranch.com   E-mail: info@blackriverfarmandranch.com
Michael F. Ciferri, Exec Dir.
Adm: FCFS. **Appl due:** Rolling. **Enr:** 136. **Staff:** Admin 5. Couns 25.
Focus: Riding. **Features:** Crafts Aquatics Boating Farm Ropes_Crse Equestrian Gymnastics Swim Tennis Volleyball Watersports.
Fees 2012: Res $625-3625, ½-4 wks.
Housing: Cabins. Avg per room/unit: 10. **Swimming:** Pool.
Est 1962. Inc. **Ses:** 6. **Wks/ses:** ½-4. Operates June-Aug. ACA.

Western riding is featured at this dude ranch, which occupies a 360-acre site. Instructors address the basics of walking, trotting, cantering and horse care, as well as advanced saddle, bareback, drill team, Western games and vaulting. Other camp activities include swimming, boating, hayrides, tennis, sports, dramatics, crafts and a low ropes course. A four-day minisession serves first-time campers and children age 9 or younger.

BROADREACH SUMMER ADVENTURES FOR TEENAGERS
Res — Coed Ages 13-19

Raleigh, NC 27603. 806 McCulloch St, Ste 102. Tel: 919-256-8200, 888-833-1907.
Fax: 919-833-2129.
www.gobroadreach.com   E-mail: questions@gobroadreach.com
Carlton Goldthwaite, Dir.
Grades 8-PG. Adm: FCFS. **Appl due:** Rolling. **Enr:** 10-12. **Enr cap:** 10-12. **Staff:** Admin 12. Couns 70.
Intl program focus: Culture. **Locations:** Asia Australia/New_Zealand Caribbean Mexico/Central_America Middle_East South_America.
Focus: Sail Scuba Seamanship Wilderness_Camp. **Features:** Ecol Photog Adventure_Travel Boating Community_Serv Conservation Cruises Exploration Hiking Kayak Mountaineering Mtn_Trips Outdoor_Ed Peace/Cross-cultural Rappelling Riding Rock_Climb Sea_Cruises White-water_Raft Wilderness_Canoe Yoga Swim Water-skiing Watersports.
Fees 2011: Res $3180-5980 (+airfare), 2-4 wks.
Housing: Dorms Hotels Tents. **Swimming:** Ocean River.
Est 1992. Inc. **Ses:** 60. **Wks/ses:** 2-4. Operates June-Aug.

Broadreach conducts experiential summer adventure programs in the Caribbean, Central America, South America, Egypt, Australia, Fiji and the Solomon Islands. Programs address sailing, scuba diving and wilderness activities. Characteristics of all programs are small groups (each offering has a limit of 10 to 12 participants), hands-on instruction, cultural appreciation and skill building. Scuba certification is a prerequisite for certain programs.

BUFFALO COVE OUTDOOR EDUCATION CENTER
EARTH CAMP
Res — Coed Ages 12-17

Deep Gap, NC 28618. 664 Buckskin Hollow. Tel: 828-964-1473.
www.buffalocove.com   E-mail: charleecamp@aol.com
Nathan Roark, Dir.
Adm: FCFS. **Appl due:** Mar. **Enr:** 20. **Enr cap:** 20.
Focus: Outdoor_Ed. **Features:** Archery Fishing Survival_Trng Wilderness_Camp.
Fees 2009: Res $1400, 2 wks.
Nonprofit. **Ses:** 1. **Wks/ses:** 2. Operates July.

Earth Camp teaches children to connect with the environment through outdoor skills instruction and a range of activities. Returning campers may leave base camp to participate in a more intense program of woodland adventure.

BURGUNDY CENTER FOR WILDLIFE STUDIES
Res — Coed Ages 8-15

Capon Bridge, WV 26711. HC 83, Box 38DD. Tel: 304-856-3758. Fax: 304-856-3758.
Contact (Sept-May): 3700 Burgundy Rd, Alexandria, VA 22303. Tel: 703-960-3431.
  Fax: 703-960-5056.
www.burgundycenter.org   E-mail: bcws2@earthlink.net
Lavinia Schoene, Dir.
Adm: FCFS. Appl due: Rolling.
Focus: Wildlife_Stud. Features: Crafts Hiking Swim.
Fees 2011: Res $795-1375, 1-2 wks.
Housing: Dorms. Swimming: Pond.
Est 1963. Ses: 4. Wks/ses: 1-2. Operates June-Aug. ACA.

Burgundy Center is situated on a 500-acre mountain sanctuary in the Appalachians. The field study program features introductions to ornithology, botany, freshwater biology, herpetology, geology and related subjects. Older students may engage in independent projects. Extracurricular pursuits include photography, swimming, day and overnight hikes, and optional backpacking trips.

CAMP CELO
Res — Coed Ages 7-12

Burnsville, NC 28714. 775 Hannah Branch Rd. Tel: 828-675-4323.
www.campcelo.com   E-mail: info@campcelo.com
Gib Barrus & Barbara Barrus Perrin, Dirs.
Adm: FCFS. Appl due: Rolling. Enr: 62. Enr cap: 62. Staff: Admin 3. Couns 17.
Focus: Farm Work. Features: Crafts Drama Climbing_Wall Community_Serv Cooking Hiking Mountaineering Mtn_Trips Riding Wilderness_Camp Woodcraft Soccer Swim.
Fees 2012: Res $875-1825, 1-3 wks. Aid (Need).
Housing: Tents. Avg per room/unit: 5. Swimming: River.
Est 1948. Inc. Religious Society of Friends. Ses: 5. Wks/ses: 1-3. Operates June-Aug.

This farm program centers around the Quaker values of nonviolence, simplicity and environmental awareness. Campers gain an appreciation for nature and learn to minimize their impact on the environment. In addition to completing chores throughout the day, boys and girls engage in various crafts and recreational pursuits. Eleven- and 12-year-old campers take part in a separate, more independent farm session that includes two-, three- and four-day backpacking hikes.

CHELEY COLORADO CAMPS
Res — Coed Ages 9-17

Estes Park, CO 80517. 3960 Fish Creek Rd, PO Box 1170. Tel: 970-586-4244.
  Fax: 970-586-3020.
Contact (Oct-May): 601 Steele St, PO Box 6525, Denver, CO 80206. Tel: 303-377-3616.
  Fax: 303-377-3605.
Year-round Toll-free: 800-226-7386.
www.cheley.com   E-mail: office@cheley.com
Brooke Cheley Klebe & Jeff Cheley, Dirs.
Adm: FCFS. Appl due: Rolling. Enr: 430. Enr cap: 500. Staff: Admin 11. Couns 200.
Focus: Wilderness_Camp. Features: Crafts Archery Bicycle_Tours Climbing_Wall Fish-

ing Hiking Mountaineering Mtn_Biking Mtn_Trips Pack_Train Rappelling Riding Riflery Rock_Climb Ropes_Crse White-water_Raft Woodcraft Equestrian.
Fees 2012: Res $4700-9250 (+$150), 4-8 wks. Aid 2010 (Need): $160,000.
Housing: Cabins. Avg per room/unit: 18.
Est 1921. Inc. **Ses:** 2. **Wks/ses:** 4. Operates June-Aug. ACA.

Conducted on three separate properties encompassing 1300 acres of high-country land bordering the Rocky Mountain National Park and the Roosevelt National Forest, Cheley Camps provides separate adventure programs for boys and girls. The age-appropriate camps allow participants to choose their own adventures each week, with options ranging from half-day to five-day trips. Each summer, Cheley offers four camps for boys and four for girls; coeducational activities are interspersed throughout the term.

CHEWONKI WILDERNESS TRIPS
Res — Coed Ages 13-18

Wiscasset, ME 04578. c/o Chewonki Foundation, 485 Chewonki Neck Rd.
Tel: 207-882-7323. Fax: 207-882-4074.
www.chewonki.org   E-mail: camp@chewonki.org
Ryan Linehan, Dir.
Adm: FCFS. **Appl due:** Rolling. **Enr:** 100. **Staff:** Admin 5. Couns 45.
Travel: ME NH NY VT Canada.
Focus: Wilderness_Camp. **Features:** Ecol Environ_Sci Marine_Bio/Stud Crafts Drama Fine_Arts Adventure_Travel Aquatics Archery Canoe Conservation Exploration Farm Hiking Kayak Mtn_Trips Outdoor_Ed Ropes_Crse Sail Seamanship Wilderness_Canoe Woodcraft Baseball Basketball Soccer Swim Tennis Ultimate_Frisbee.
Fees 2012: Res $4700-7200, 3-7 wks. Aid (Need).
Housing: Cabins Tents. Avg per room/unit: 8. **Swimming:** Lake Ocean River Stream.
Est 1915. Nonprofit. **Spons:** Chewonki Foundation. **Ses:** 19. **Wks/ses:** 3-7. Operates June-Aug. ACA.

Single-gender and coeducational wilderness expeditions for teenagers range along the Maine coast, as well as into several other northeastern states and Quebec, Canada. Features include canoeing, hiking, sea and white-water kayaking, sailing and rowing, and camping. One program combines the building of wooden sea kayaks at camp with a subsequent expedition.

CHRISTCHURCH SCHOOL SAILING CAMP
Res and Day — Coed Ages 8-15

Christchurch, VA 23031. 49 Seahorse Ln. Tel: 804-758-2306. Fax: 804-758-0721.
www.christchurchschool.org/summersailingcamp
E-mail: admission@christchurchschool.org
Amanda G. Porter, Dir.
Adm: FCFS. **Appl due:** Rolling. **Enr:** 40. **Enr cap:** 40.
Focus: Sail. **Features:** Boating Canoe Fishing Swim Watersports.
Fees 2011: Res $850, 1 wk. Day $550, 1 wk.
Housing: Dorms. **Swimming:** River.
Est 1993. Nonprofit. **Ses:** 3. **Wks/ses:** 1. Operates June-July.

One of the Summer Camps on the River, Christchurch's sailing camp covers techniques, rigging, points of sail, terminology and safety training for sailors at various experience levels. In addition to lectures and onshore instruction, the program features practical sailing experience on the Rappahannock River. Christchurch conducts beginning, intermediate, adventure and racing sessions, the latter two of which have prior sailing experience or previous attendance at a CCS sailing camp as a prerequisite.

CIRCLE PINES CENTER COOPERATIVE SUMMER CAMP
Res — Coed Ages 7-17

Delton, MI 49046. 8650 Mullen Rd. Tel: 269-623-5555. Fax: 269-623-9054.
www.circlepinescenter.org E-mail: info@circlepinescenter.net
Tom VanHammen, Dir.
Grades 2-12. Adm: FCFS. **Appl due:** Rolling. **Enr:** 35-70. **Enr cap:** 70. **Staff:** Admin 4. Couns 16. Res 4.
Avg class size: 8.
Focus: Community_Serv Peace/Cross-cultural Work. **Features:** Ecol Crafts Creative_Writing Dance Drama Music Aquatics Canoe Chess Conservation Cooking Exploration Farm Hiking Outdoor_Ed Yoga Basketball Soccer Softball Swim Ultimate_Frisbee Volleyball.
Fees 2012: Res $500-1000, 1-2 wks. Aid 2011 (Need): $23,000.
Housing: Cabins Lodges. Avg per room/unit: 7. **Swimming:** Lake.
Est 1938. Nonprofit. **Ses:** 3. **Wks/ses:** 1-2. Operates June-Sept. ACA.

CPC's summer program emphasizes cooperation, community building and peace while taking an ecological approach to rural living. Participants take part in daily work projects and meal chores. Campers work on individual projects in the areas of the arts, nature study, swimming and gardening, as well as in groups for work projects, singing, drama, cooperative games, storytelling, folk dancing and the operation of a cooperative store.

CIRCLE R RANCH
Res — Coed Ages 7-17

Long Prairie, MN 56347. 32549 State 27. Tel: 320-547-2176. Fax: 320-732-2176.
www.circlerranch.com E-mail: crranch@circlerranch.com
Jack McCoy, Dir.
Adm: FCFS. **Appl due:** Rolling. **Enr cap:** 125. **Staff:** Admin 4.
Focus: Ranch Riding. **Features:** Crafts Drama Aquatics Archery Canoe Farm Hiking Baseball Basketball Equestrian Soccer Softball Swim Tennis Volleyball.
Fees 2011: Res $535-1070, 1-2 wks.
Housing: Cabins Dorms. **Swimming:** Lake Pond Pool.
Est 1969. Inc. **Ses:** 10. **Wks/ses:** 1-2. Operates June-Aug.

Horseback riding is the main focus at this working ranch. Instructors give basic instruction on horsemanship, and each child learns to groom, saddle and bridle a horse. Circle R conducts trail rides, overnights and a horse show. Other activities include swimming, tennis, paddleboat riding, pony-cart riding, team sports and canoeing.

COTTONWOOD GULCH EXPEDITIONS
Res — Coed Ages 10-18

Thoreau, NM 87323. HC 62, Box 2200. Tel: 505-862-7503. Fax: 505-862-7324.
Contact (Sept-May): PO Box 25106, Albuquerque, NM 87125. Tel: 505-248-0563.
   Fax: 505-248-3319.
Year-round Toll-free: 800-246-8735.
www.cottonwoodgulch.org E-mail: info@cottonwoodgulch.org
Mike Sullivan, Exec Dir.
Adm: FCFS. **Appl due:** Rolling. **Enr:** 10-20. **Enr cap:** 10-20. **Fac** 4. **Staff:** Admin 3. Couns 20.
Travel: AZ CO NM UT.
Focus: Archaeol Field_Ecol Wilderness_Camp Wildlife_Stud. **Features:** Environ_Sci Geol Sci Art Crafts Photog Adventure_Travel Canoe Community_Serv Conservation Exploration Hiking Mountaineering Mtn_Trips Rappelling Rock_Climb Ropes_Crse Wilderness_Canoe Swim.
Fees 2012: Res $1375-4575 (+$100-500), 1-6 wks. Aid 2009 (Merit & Need): $35,000.

Housing: Cabins Tents. Avg per room/unit: 4-8. **Swimming:** Pool Stream. **Est 1926.** Nonprofit. **Ses:** 9. **Wks/ses:** 1-6. Operates June-Aug.

This outdoor education program allows campers to pursue interests in archaeology, animal tracking, mapping, forestry, ornithology, geology, archeology, and Native American crafts and history. Wilderness expeditions include mountain climbing, exploration and investigation of ancient Native American dwellings.

THE COUNTRY SCHOOL FARM SUMMER CAMP
Res — Coed Ages 6-12

Millersburg, OH 44654. 3516 Township Rd 124. Tel: 330-231-2963.
www.tcsfarm.com   E-mail: barkers@tcsfarm.com
Richard Barker, Dir.
Adm: FCFS. **Appl due:** Rolling. **Enr:** 30. **Enr cap:** 30. **Staff:** Admin 1. Couns 5.
Focus: Farm Wildlife_Stud.
Fees 2012: Res $760 (+$40), 1 wk.
Housing: Houses.
Est 1976. Ses: 12. **Wks/ses:** 1. Operates June-Aug.

Children with a love of animals participate fully in the life of a working family farm in this program. Farm work includes livestock care, garden and orchard maintenance, food preparation and preservation, and farm repairs and improvements. Campers learn through experience about sensible approaches to land, water and waste management, as well as about other farming techniques and activities.

CROSS-CULTURAL SOLUTIONS
Res — Coed Ages 15 and up

New Rochelle, NY 10801. 2 Clinton Pl. Tel: 914-632-0022, 800-380-4777.
    Fax: 914-632-8494.
www.crossculturalsolutions.org   E-mail: info@crossculturalsolutions.org
Steven C. Rosenthal, Exec Dir.
Adm: FCFS. **Appl due:** Rolling. **Staff:** Admin 33. Res 100.
Intl program focus: Culture. **Locations:** Africa Asia Europe Mexico/Central_America South_America.
Focus: Community_Serv Peace/Cross-cultural Work. **Features:** Crafts Dance Music Painting Adventure_Travel Canoe Caving Conservation Exploration Hiking Mtn_Trips Outdoor_Ed Riding Yoga Aerobics.
Fees 2011: Res $1946-7735, 1-12 wks. Aid (Need).
Housing: Houses.
Est 1995. Nonprofit. **Wks/ses:** 1-12. Operates Year-round.

These year-round programs, which range in duration from one to 12 weeks, combine volunteer work, cultural and learning activities, and leisure-time pursuits. Insight Abroad involves project-based work that can be completed in one week. The most popular program, Volunteer Abroad, offers the greatest flexibility of locations and start dates, allowing participants to tailor their program to their skills and interests. A third program, Intern Abroad, serves students interested in earning academic credit, securing international work experience or conducting field research. Specially designed for teenagers, Teen Volunteer Abroad (ages 15-17) enables boys and girls to volunteer in China, Costa Rica, Ghana, Guatemala or South Africa. Program fees are tax deductible for US residents.

CULINARY INSTITUTE OF AMERICA
CAREER DISCOVERY FOR HIGH SCHOOL STUDENTS
Res — Coed Ages 16-18

Hyde Park, NY 12538. 1946 Campus Dr. Tel: 845-452-9430, 800-285-4627.
Fax: 845-905-4058.
www.ciachef.edu/admissions/experience/cdhs.asp
E-mail: careerdiscovery@culinary.edu
Grades 11-12. Adm: Somewhat selective. **Appl due:** Mar. **Enr cap:** 18.
Type of instruction: Enrich.
Focus: Cooking.
Fees 2011: Res $650, 1 wk.
Housing: Hotels.
Ses: 6. **Wks/ses:** 1. Operates June-Aug.

Career Discovery provides a four-day preview of life as a CIA student. Participants attend and participate in lectures and cooking demonstrations, learn about career opportunities in the food-service and hospitality industries, and work in CIA kitchens under the guidance of chef instructors.

DARROW WILDERNESS TRIP CAMP
Res — Coed Ages 11-18

Grand Lake Stream, ME 04637. PO Box 9.
Contact (Sept-May): PO Box 11, Hanover, ME 04237.
Year-round Toll-free: 888-854-0810.
www.darrowcamp.org   E-mail: info@darrowcamp.org
Andrew Buckman, Exec Dir.
Adm: FCFS. **Appl due:** Rolling. **Enr:** 100. **Staff:** Admin 3. Couns 14.
Focus: Wilderness_Camp Wilderness_Canoe. **Features:** Adventure_Travel Exploration Hiking Mtn_Trips Swim.
Fees 2012: Res $2495-6495, 2-6 wks.
Swimming: Lake.
Est 1957. Nonprofit. **Ses:** 11. **Wks/ses:** 2-6. Operates June-Aug. ACA.

Utilizing wilderness areas, Darrow features a series of lake and white-water canoeing trips in Maine and northern Quebec, as well as backpacking excursions on the Appalachian Trail in Maine. Base camp training before all trips emphasizes low-impact camping, cooking and canoeing.

DEEP WOODS CAMP
Res — Boys Ages 10-14

Brevard, NC 28712. 848 Deep Woods Rd. Tel: 828-885-2268.
www.deepwoodscamp.com   E-mail: deepwoods@citcom.net
Kells Hogan, Dir.
Grades 4-9. Adm: FCFS. **Appl due:** Rolling. **Enr:** 28. **Enr cap:** 28. **Staff:** Admin 1. Couns 7. Res 1.
Focus: Wilderness_Camp. **Features:** Canoe Hiking Mtn_Biking Mtn_Trips Rock_Climb White-water_Raft Swim.
Fees 2012: Res $2000-5000, 4-10 wks.
Housing: Cabins. Avg per room/unit: 7. **Swimming:** Lake Pond.
Est 1970. Inc. **Ses:** 6. **Wks/ses:** 4-10. Operates June-Aug.

Deep Woods emphasizes hiking and backpacking trips, while also offering white-water canoeing, white-water rafting and rock climbing. Other activities include swimming and mountain biking. The camp maintains a small enrollment of campers and rangers for each session.

DEER CROSSING CAMP
Res — Coed Ages 9-17

Pollock Pines, CA.
Contact (Year-round): 1919 Ridge Rd, Mokelumne Hill, CA 95245. **Tel:** 209-293-2328.
Fax: 209-293-2328.
www.deercrossingcamp.com   **E-mail:** mail@deercrossingcamp.com
James Wiltens, Dir.
Adm: FCFS. **Appl due:** Rolling. **Enr cap:** 50. **Staff:** Admin 2. Couns 12.
Focus: Wilderness_Camp. **Features:** Crafts Drama Music Aquatics Archery Canoe Kayak Rock_Climb Sail Survival_Trng White-water_Raft Swim Volleyball Watersports.
Fees 2012: Res $1100-3500 (+$250), 1-4 wks.
Housing: Tents. Avg per room/unit: 3-5. **Swimming:** Lake.
Est 1983. Inc. Ses: 11. Wks/ses: 1-4. Operates June-Aug. ACA.

Backpacking, canoeing, kayaking, sailing, white-water rafting, windsurfing and fishing are among the main pursuits at this wilderness camp, while archery, arts and crafts, rock climbing, orienteering and environmental awareness are other popular activities. A three-day llama backpacking trip and an overnight white-water rafting trip are among Deer Crossing's excursions. Campers ages 14-17 have leadership program opportunities.

EDUCO ADVENTURE SCHOOL SUMMER PROGRAMS
Res — Coed Ages 10-19

100 Mile House, V0K 2E0 British Columbia, Canada. PO Box 1978. Tel: 250-395-3388, 877-245-9191. **Fax:** 888-769-0054.
www.educo.ca   **E-mail:** info@educo.ca
Stuart Clark, Exec Dir.
Adm: FCFS. **Appl due:** Rolling. **Enr:** 80. **Staff:** Admin 1. Couns 22.
Focus: Wilderness_Camp. **Features:** Adventure_Travel Canoe Climbing_Wall Exploration Hiking Kayak Mountaineering Mtn_Trips Rock_Climb Ropes_Crse Survival_Trng Wilderness_Canoe Swim.
Fees 2012: Res Can$870-2415 (+$40), 1-2 wks.
Housing: Cabins Houses Lodges. **Swimming:** Lake.
Est 1969. Nonprofit. Ses: 8. Wks/ses: 1. Operates July-Aug.

Educo emphasizes personal growth and discovery through wilderness challenges. Trips may include canoeing, kayaking, mountaineering, backpacking, rock climbing, rappelling or spelunking. Participants are expected to contribute to discussions and must work well in a group.

ELK CREEK RANCH AND TREK PROGRAMS
Res — Coed Ages 13-18

Cody, WY 82414. PO Box 1476. Tel: 307-587-3902. **Fax:** 307-587-8828.
www.elkcreekranch.com   **E-mail:** info@elkcreekranch.com
Tina Moore & Rob Plakke, Dirs.
Adm: Somewhat selective. Admitted: 95%. **Appl due:** Rolling. **Enr cap:** 35. **Staff:** Admin 4. Couns 18. Res 20.
Travel: MT WY.
Focus: Ranch Wilderness_Camp. **Features:** Fishing Hiking Mountaineering Mtn_Trips Outdoor_Ed Pack_Train Riding Riflery Rock_Climb White-water_Raft Work Working_Cattle_Ranch Swim.
Fees 2012: Res $4350-7300 (+$100), 4-8 wks.
Housing: Cabins. Avg per room/unit: 8. **Swimming:** Lake River Stream.
Est 1957. Inc. Ses: 4. Wks/ses: 4-8. Operates June-Aug.

Elk Creek's ranch program (serving ages 13-17), which emphasizes Western riding and ranch work, includes backpacking, fishing, glacier skiing and horse pack trips, as well as 25-day backpacking excursions for boys and girls ages 15-18. The trek program (ages 15-18) features four-week backpacking expeditions in the Absaroka and Beartooth wilderness areas of northwestern Wyoming and southwestern Montana. Participants receive training in such basic wilderness skills as packing, low-impact camping, cooking and high-altitude dietary requirements, map and compass reading, first aid and evacuation, physical health and group dynamics.

EMBRY-RIDDLE AERONAUTICAL UNIVERSITY SUMMER ACADEMY
Res and Day — Coed Ages 12-18

Daytona Beach, FL 32114. 600 S Clyde Morris Blvd. Tel: 386-226-7945, 800-359-4550. Fax: 386-226-7630.
www.erau.edu/summeracademy   E-mail: summer@erau.edu
Pamela Peer, Coord.
Adm: FCFS. Admitted: 80%. **Appl due:** Rolling. **Fac 20. Staff:** Admin 3. Couns 15.
Type of instruction: Adv. **Daily hours for:** Classes 6. Study 3. Rec 3. **College credit:** 3/crse, total 6.
Focus: Bus/Fin Aviation/Aero.
Fees 2012: Res $450-18,500 (+$50-400), 1-7 wks. Day $900, 1 wk.
Housing: Dorms.
Est 1926. Nonprofit. **Ses:** 12. **Wks/ses:** 1-7. Operates June-Aug.

The Summer Academy hosts various commuter and residential summer camps designed to introduce the latest technology to aspiring aviators, astronauts, engineers and scientists. High school students earn college credit and gain insight into developments in space technology through three-week Aerospace I and II courses. Executive Training Academy introduces girls ages 14-17 to the world of business. Aviation Career Exploration programs allow middle and high school students to explore fields such as space technology, flight, air traffic control, meteorology, and engineering through the use of state-of-the-art simulation devices plus labs, field trips, classroom interaction, and guest speakers. Boys and girls interested in flight training choose from a flight exploration program (ages 12-18) and several precollege SunFlight offerings that serve beginners and serious pilots alike.

FAITH RANCH HIGH ADVENTURE HORSE CAMP
Res — Coed Ages 7-18

Jewett, OH 43986. PO Box 355. Tel: 740-946-2255. Fax: 740-946-7661.
www.faithranch.org   E-mail: reservations@faithranch.org
William D. Wiley, Dir.
Grades 2-12. Adm: FCFS. **Appl due:** Rolling. **Enr cap:** 200. **Staff:** Admin 8. Couns 18.
Focus: Ranch Riding. **Features:** Crafts Dance Drama Archery Boating Canoe Climbing_Wall Exploration Farm Fishing Hiking Outdoor_Ed Rappelling Ropes_Crse Wilderness_Camp Working_Cattle_Ranch Equestrian Swim Watersports.
Fees 2012: Res $350, 1 wk.
Housing: Cabins Dorms Houses Tents Tepees. **Swimming:** Lake Stream.
Est 1972. Nonprofit. Nondenom Christian. **Ses:** 5. **Wks/ses:** 1. Operates June-Aug.

At Faith Ranch, campers receive their own horse to groom, saddle and care for while at camp. Riding instruction accommodates boys and girls of all skill levels, with strong riders eligible to participate in drama drill team riding. Teenagers may lead cattle drives and play pony polo. Other activities include pony races, camp craft, archery, rappelling, nature walks, fishing, boating, swimming and an obstacle course.

FLYING CLOUD
Res — Boys Ages 11-14

Plymouth, VT 05056. c/o Farm & Wilderness Foundation, 263 Farm & Wilderness Rd. Tel: 802-422-3761. Fax: 802-422-8660.
www.farmandwilderness.org   E-mail: info@farmandwilderness.org
Zachary Podhorzer, Dir.
Adm: FCFS. **Appl due:** Rolling. **Enr:** 35.
Focus: Outdoor_Ed Wilderness_Camp. **Features:** Crafts Cooking Hiking Survival_Trng Woodcraft Work Swim.
Fees 2011: Res $4300-7100, 3½-7 wks. Aid (Merit & Need).
Housing: Tepees. Avg per room/unit: 4. **Swimming:** Pond.
Est 1964. Nonprofit. **Spons:** Farm and Wilderness Foundation. **Ses: 3. Wks/ses:** 3½-7. Operates June-Aug. ACA.

Boys at Flying Cloud take part in various wilderness living activities. Campers learn craft and wood skills that are useful in the natural environment. Areas addressed include bow drill fire making, buckskin hide tanning, animal tracking, woodcarving and consumption of wild edibles. At night, boys gather for celebratory dancing, games, singing or storytelling around a campfire.

FORT SMITH MOUNTAIN MEN BOYS SUMMER CAMPS
Res — Boys Ages 11-17

Georgetown, TX 78628. 107 River Wood Dr. Tel: 512-869-8929, 800-296-1906.
www.fortsmithmountainmen.com   E-mail: ron@fortsmithmountainmen.com
Ronald J. Smith, Pres.
Grades 6-12. Adm: FCFS. **Appl due:** Apr. **Enr:** 30. **Enr cap:** 30. **Staff:** Admin 2. Couns 6.
Intl program focus: Culture. **Travel:** AK AZ CA CO HI ID MT NM NV OR TX UT WA WY Canada.
Focus: Leadership Outdoor_Ed Wilderness_Camp. **Features:** Astron Ecol Environ_Sci Geol Hist Crafts Creative_Writing Filmmaking Photog Adventure_Travel Aquatics Canoe Caving Community_Serv Conservation Cooking Cruises Deep-sea Fishing Exploration Fishing Hiking Mtn_Biking Mtn_Trips Peace/Cross-cultural Ranch Rappelling Rock_ Climb Social_Servs White-water_Raft Wilderness_Canoe Basketball Football Softball Swim.
Fees 2012: Res $3646 (+$250), 3 wks. Aid (Need).
Housing: Cabins Tents. Avg per room/unit: 6. **Swimming:** Lake Pond Pool River Stream.
Est 2001. Inc. Nondenom Christian. **Ses: 2. Wks/ses:** 3. Operates June-July.

Fort Smith provides adventure travel camping and science/engineering career awareness programs for boys with a strong interest in the outdoors. Destinations and program content vary from year to year. All activities—including cooking and sleeping—are conducted outside. Although none of the pursuits are overly strenuous, much of the boys' time is spent walking and hiking at elevations between 5000 and 12,000 feet. Science career exploration features visits to several US national research laboratories, as well as to certain universities that are conducting research in the areas of energy, water and the environment. Campers also study the history of the American westward expansion.

FUTURE LEADER OF AMERICA
Res — Coed Ages 12-17

Manchester, NH 03103. 105 S Gray St. Tel: 603-232-6023.
www.futureleadersofamerica.com
Bernard Hillard, Dir.
Adm: FCFS. **Appl due:** Rolling. **Enr:** 30. **Staff:** Admin 4. Couns 4.

Focus: Leadership Milit_Trng. **Features:** Debate Conservation Hiking Ropes_Crse Martial_Arts.
Housing: Tents.
Est 2002. Ses: 1. **Wks/ses:** 2. Operates Aug.

Designed for typical adolescents, this military training camp emphasizes leadership, discipline and confidence development. Among the session activities are hiking, self-defense training, first-aid instruction, light physical workouts and marching drills.

GLOBAL ROUTES HIGH SCHOOL PROGRAMS
Res — Coed Ages 14-17

Northampton, MA 01060. 1 Short St. Tel: 413-585-8895. Fax: 413-585-8810.
www.globalroutes.org   E-mail: mail@globalroutes.org
Kenneth Hahn, Exec Dir.
Grades 9-12. Adm: FCFS. **Appl due:** Rolling. **Enr:** 18. **Enr cap:** 18. **Staff:** Admin 4. Couns 2.
Intl program focus: Lang Culture. **Locations:** Africa Asia Caribbean Mexico/Central_ America South_America. Home stays avail.
Focus: Adventure_Travel Community_Serv. **Features:** Yoga.
Fees 2011: Res $3525-6225 (+airfare), 2½-5 wks.
Est 1986. Nonprofit. **Ses:** 17. **Wks/ses:** 2½-5. Operates June-Aug.

Global Routes enables students to immerse themselves in the daily life and rituals of a host community while working with locals on projects chosen by community leaders. For instance, boys and girls may teach English in Asia, build a community center in South America or construct a school in Africa. The program begins with a five- to eight-day orientation to the culture, language, religion and government of the host country. Course work culminates with a six- to 10-day exploration of the country's environment. One year of prior Spanish study is a prerequisite for certain programs.

GLOBAL WORKS
Res — Coed Ages 14-18

Boulder, CO 80304. 2342 Broadway. Tel: 303-545-2202. Fax: 303-545-2425.
www.globalworkstravel.com   E-mail: info@globalworkstravel.com
Erik Werner, Dir.
Grades 9-12. Adm: FCFS. **Appl due:** Rolling. **Fac 3. Staff:** Admin 8.
Type of instruction: Enrich. **Daily hours for:** Classes 4. High school credit.
Intl program focus: Lang Culture. **Travel:** Africa Asia Australia/New_Zealand Caribbean Europe Mexico/Central_America South_America. Home stays avail.
Focus: Community_Serv. **Features:** Crafts Creative_Writing Dance Music Painting Photog Adventure_Travel Aquatics Bicycle_Tours Boating Caving Exploration Farm Hiking Kayak Mtn_Biking Mtn_Trips Outdoor_Ed Peace/Cross-cultural Rock_Climb Ropes_ Crse Sail Scuba Sea_Cruises White-water_Raft Yoga Basketball Rugby Soccer Swim Ultimate_Frisbee Volleyball Watersports.
Fees 2012: Res $3395-6895 (+airfare), 2-5 wks.
Housing: Cabins Dorms Hotels Houses Lodges Tents. **Swimming:** Lake Ocean Pool River.
Est 1989. Inc. **Ses:** 31. **Wks/ses:** 2-5. Operates June-Aug.

Global Works offers environmental and service-based travel programs that include language learning and home stay options. Programs operate in Peru, Ecuador, Thailand, Costa Rica, Puerto Rico, Spain, Australia, New Zealand, the Fiji Islands, France, Panama, Nicaragua, Zambia, China and Argentina. Service projects include construction of community centers and playgrounds, reforestation, habitat restoration and conservation work. When not working on projects, participants take part in adventure activities and make visits to cultural and historical sites.

HIDDEN VILLA SUMMER CAMP
Res — Coed Ages 9-17; Day — Coed 6-9

Los Altos Hills, CA 94022. 26870 Moody Rd. Tel: 650-949-8641. Fax: 650-948-1916.
www.hiddenvilla.org   E-mail: camp@hiddenvilla.org
Nikki Bryant, Dir.
Grades 1-12. Adm: FCFS. **Appl due:** May. **Staff:** Admin 3. Couns 60.
Focus: Farm Work. **Features:** Ecol Crafts Creative_Writing Dance Fine_Arts Music Climbing_Wall Hiking Mountaineering Mtn_Trips Rock_Climb Ropes_Crse Wilderness_Camp Basketball Soccer Softball Swim.
Fees 2012: Res $550-1025, 1-2 wks. Day $405-430, 1 wk. Aid (Need).
Housing: Cabins. **Swimming:** Pool.
Est 1960. Nonprofit. **Ses:** 19. **Wks/ses:** 1-2. Operates June-Aug.

Campers at Hidden Villa take part in hands-on agriculture and farming, including cow milking, harvesting of organic vegetables, and care and feeding of farm animals. Daily chores integrate community responsibility and teach boys and girls environmental awareness. Crafts, pottery, archery, swimming and hiking are recreational options. Campers ages 14-16 may take a backpacking trip to the Santa Cruz Mountains.

HIGH MOUNTAIN INSTITUTE HIGH PEAKS ADVENTURE
Res — Coed Ages 13-14

Leadville, CO 80461. PO Box 970. Tel: 719-486-8200, 888-464-9991.
   Fax: 719-486-8201.
www.hminet.org/shortandsummerprograms   E-mail: admissions@hminet.org
Christina Reiff, Dir.
Grades 8-9. Adm: Somewhat selective. **Appl due:** Rolling. **Enr:** 9. **Enr cap:** 12. **Staff:** Admin 2. Couns 4.
Focus: Community_Serv Mountaineering Outdoor_Ed Wilderness_Camp. **Features:** Climbing_Wall Mtn_Biking Rock_Climb White-water_Raft.
Fees 2011: Res $2995 (+$150), 2 wks. Aid 2011 (Need): $4000.
Housing: Cabins. Avg per room/unit: 6.
Est 2004. Nonprofit. **Ses:** 1. **Wks/ses:** 2. Operates July.

This wilderness instruction program begins with an extended backpacking trip in the mountains of central Colorado. While in the backcountry, campers devote two days to service work on trails on one of the state's 14,000-foot peaks. The group then returns to base camp for a day of rock climbing, another day of mountain biking on local trails and a session-concluding white-water rafting trip.

HORIZON ADVENTURES
Res — Coed Ages 13-17

Denver, CO 80220. 1370 Birch St. Tel: 303-393-7297. Fax: 303-393-7296.
www.horizonadventures.com   E-mail: woody@horizonadventures.com
Paul Woodward, Dir.
Adm: FCFS. **Appl due:** Rolling. **Enr:** 10. **Enr cap:** 10. **Staff:** Admin 1. Couns 13.
Travel: CO UT.
Focus: Wilderness_Camp. **Features:** Adventure_Travel Exploration Hiking Mountaineering Mtn_Biking Mtn_Trips Rock_Climb White-water_Raft.
Fees 2011: Res $795-1395, 1-2 wks.
Housing: Tents.

Est 1985. Nonprofit. **Ses:** 8. **Wks/ses:** 1-2. Operates June-Aug.

Trips through Colorado and Utah include such activities as technical rock climbing, backpacking, mountain biking, white-water rafting and mountaineering. Courses serve both beginners and those with previous experience.

HYDE SCHOOL TEEN LEADERSHIP PREP
Res — Coed Ages 12-14

Bath, ME 04530. 616 High St. Tel: 207-443-7101. Fax: 207-443-1450.
www.hyde.edu   E-mail: rsanner@hyde.edu
Adm: FCFS. Appl due: Rolling.
Focus: Leadership. **Features:** Public_Speak Creative_Writing Dance Music Theater Canoe Climbing_Wall Community_Serv Exploration Hiking Ropes_Crse Survival_Trng White-water_Raft Wilderness_Camp Wilderness_Canoe Swim.
Fees 2011: Res $1500 (+$500), 1½ wks.
Housing: Dorms Tents. **Swimming:** Lake Ocean Pool.
Nonprofit. **Ses:** 1. **Wks/ses:** 1½. Operates July.

Conducted on Hyde School's Bath campus, TLP combines outdoor education with leadership training. During the 10-day sessions, students engage in various seacoast and wilderness adventures in Maine, including hiking and canoeing trips. Individual peer mentoring is part of the curriculum. Athletics, performing arts, ropes course and climbing wall activities, public speaking and community service are also integral to the program.

INTERNATIONAL SEMINAR SERIES
SERVICE LEARNING IN PARIS AND BARCELONA
Res — Coed Ages 16-18

Manchester, VT 05254. PO Box 1212. Tel: 802-362-5855. Fax: 802-362-5855.
www.study-serve.org   E-mail: iss@study-serve.org
John H. Nissen, Dir.
Adm: Selective. **Appl due:** Apr. **Enr:** 35. **Enr cap:** 35. **Fac 12.**
Type of instruction: Enrich. **Avg class size:** 10. **Daily hours for:** Classes 3. Rec 3.
Intl program focus: Acad Lang Culture. **Locations:** Europe.
Focus: Fr Span Community_Serv. **Features:** Govt Creative_Writing Peace/Cross-cultural Swim.
Fees 2012: Res $6950 (+$1200), 4 wks. Aid 2009 (Need): $30,000.
Housing: Dorms. **Swimming:** Pool.
Est 1998. Inc. **Ses:** 2. **Wks/ses:** 4. Operates July.

Conducted at sites in Paris, France, and Barcelona, Spain, this cultural immersion program combines community service with language study. In addition to the core program, ISS includes a required seminar on contemporary issues that is supplemented by an art and architecture course. Language instruction in the host country's language, which takes place five mornings each week, ranges from beginning through advanced ability levels.

ISLAND ESCAPADES ADVENTURE CAMPS
Res — Coed Ages 12-18; Day — Coed 8-12

Salt Spring Island, V8K 2T9 British Columbia, Canada. 163 Fulford-Ganges Rd.
Tel: 250-537-2553, 888-529-2567. Fax: 250-537-2532.
www.islandescapades.com   E-mail: escapades@saltspring.com
Jack Rosen & Candace Snow, Dirs.
Adm: FCFS. Admitted: 90%. **Appl due:** Rolling. **Enr:** 10-12. **Enr cap:** 10-12. **Fac 2. Staff:** Admin 3. Couns 3. Res 4.

Focus: Kayak Leadership Mountaineering Outdoor_Ed Rappelling Rock_Climb Wilderness_Camp. **Features:** Ecol Environ_Sci Geol Marine_Bio/Stud Crafts Adventure_Travel Aquatics Climbing_Wall Conservation Cooking Exploration Fishing Hiking Mtn_Trips Seamanship Survival_Trng Woodcraft Surfing Swim Ultimate_Frisbee Watersports.
Fees 2012: Res Can$750-1675 (+Can$25), 1-2 wks. Day Can$490-495, 1 wk.
Housing: Cabins Tents. **Swimming:** Lake Ocean.
Est 1993. Inc. Ses: 9. Wks/ses: 1-2. Operates July-Sept.

Day camps at Island Escapades teach the essentials of ocean kayaking, while also featuring hiking, orienteering, swimming and climbing. Overnight camps address similar skills in a more intensive setting, with different programs focusing on ocean kayaking, mountaineering, wilderness skills or a combination of the three. Campers ages 15-18 who possess strong outdoor skills may enroll in a leadership program that provides early training for boys and girls interested in summer or year-round employment in outdoor education or recreation.

JAMESON RANCH CAMP
Res — Coed Ages 6-14

Glennville, CA 93226. PO Box 459. Tel: 661-536-8888. Fax: 661-536-8896.
www.jamesonranchcamp.com   E-mail: thejamesons@jamesonranchcamp.com
Ross Jameson & Debby Jameson, Dirs.
Grades 1-9. Adm: FCFS. **Appl due:** Rolling. **Enr:** 80. **Staff:** Admin 4. Couns 20.
Focus: Outdoor_Ed Ranch Riding. **Features:** Crafts Dance Photog Theater Aquatics Archery Boating Canoe Conservation Farm Fishing Hiking Kayak Mtn_Biking Rappelling Riflery Rock_Climb Ropes_Crse Sail Woodcraft Working_Cattle_Ranch Equestrian Swim.
Fees 2012: Res $2200-2350, 2 wks. Aid (Need).
Housing: Tents. **Swimming:** Lake Pool.
Est 1936. Ses: 4. **Wks/ses:** 2. Operates June-Aug. ACA.

Campers help produce some of their food, take care of farm animals and share assorted tasks at this self-sufficient mountain ranch. A well-developed horsemanship program features lessons in western and bareback riding, trail riding, recreational riding and, for experienced riders, cattle herding. Campers may also develop rock-climbing skills and engage in an active waterfront program. Boys and girls select their daily activities.

KIMBALL UNION ACADEMY GIRLS' LEADERSHIP CAMP
Res — Girls Ages 11-13

Meriden, NH 03770. PO Box 188. Tel: 603-469-2115. Fax: 603-469-2040.
www.kua.org/girlsleadership   E-mail: bwheeler@kua.org
Brooklyn Wheeler, Dir.
Grades 6-8. Adm: Selective. **Appl due:** May. **Staff:** Admin 5. Couns 4. Res 4.
Focus: Leadership. **Features:** Dance Music Theater Canoe Community_Serv Hiking Yoga Softball Swim Ultimate_Frisbee.
Fees 2012: Res $1175, 1 wk.
Housing: Dorms. Avg per room/unit: 2. **Swimming:** Pool.
Nonprofit. **Ses:** 1. **Wks/ses:** 1. Operates Aug.

This pre-high school program enables girls to develop their leadership skills in a variety of settings. Students examine pertinent topics through a series of hands-on workshops that teach girls how to maintain a positive self-image, resolve conflict, become positive digital citizens, communicate effectively, build healthy relationships, lead others and themselves, define personal values, identify negative and positive peer pressure, and set and reach achievable goals. Morning wellness activities, team competitions, sports, an overnight camping trip and community service opportunities complete the program.

CAMP KOOCH-I-CHING
Res — Boys Ages 8-18

International Falls, MN 56649. PO Box 271. Tel: 218-286-3141. Fax: 218-286-3255.
Contact (Sept-May): 3515 Michigan Ave, Cincinnati, OH 45208. Tel: 513-772-7479.
Fax: 513-772-5673.
www.koochiching.org   E-mail: office@koochiching.org
Stephen M. Heinle, Dir.
Grades 3-12. Adm: FCFS. **Appl due:** Rolling. **Enr:** 150. **Staff:** Admin 8. Couns 50. Res 2.
Travel: MN MT Canada.
Focus: Wilderness_Camp. **Features:** Crafts Dance Media Archery Canoe Climbing_Wall
Fishing Hiking Kayak Mountaineering Mtn_Trips Rappelling Riflery Rock_Climb Ropes_
Crse Sail Wilderness_Canoe Woodcraft Swim Tennis Water-skiing Weight_Trng.
Fees 2012: Res $3300-7450 (+$100-400), 3-8 wks. Aid (Need).
Housing: Cabins. Avg per room/unit: 7. **Swimming:** Lake.
Est 1924. Nonprofit. **Spons:** Camping and Education Foundation. **Ses:** 3. **Wks/ses:** 3-8.
Operates June-Aug. ACA.

Kooch-i-ching features canoeing, backpacking and climbing trips. A base camp program offers many sports, including swimming, sailing and riflery, plus activities unique to the Northwoods, such as Native American dancing and ecology. A three-week program enrolls boys ages 8-10, while four- and eight-week sessions serve those ages 8-18.

KROKA EXPEDITIONS SUMMER PROGRAMS
Res — Coed Ages 9-18

Marlow, NH 03456. 767 Forest Rd. Tel: 603-835-9087. Fax: 866-795-4973.
www.kroka.org   E-mail: summer@kroka.org
Lynne Boudreau, Coord.
Grades 3-12. Adm: FCFS. **Appl due:** Rolling. **Enr:** 12. **Enr cap:** 12. **Staff:** Admin 5. Couns
25. Res 10.
Intl program focus: Culture. **Travel:** MA ME NH NY VT Canada Mexico/Central_America
South_America.
Focus: Outdoor_Ed Wilderness_Camp. **Features:** Ecol Environ_Sci Crafts Creative_Writ-
ing Drama Adventure_Travel Bicycle_Tours Boating Canoe Caving Community_Serv
Conservation Cooking Exploration Farm Hiking Kayak Mountaineering Mtn_Biking
Peace/Cross-cultural Rock_Climb Survival_Trng White-water_Raft Wilderness_Canoe
Woodcraft Swim.
Fees 2012: Res $780-2500, 1-2 wks. Aid 2010 (Need): $50,574.
Housing: Tents Tepees. Avg per room/unit: 4-12. **Swimming:** Lake Pond Ocean River
Stream.
Est 1996. Nonprofit. **Ses:** 22. **Wks/ses:** 1-3. Operates June-Aug.

Kroka offers a variety of outdoor education and wilderness adventure programs at beginning, intermediate and advanced levels. Elements common to all programs include the following: use of wood, leather and plants to meet daily necessities; use of solar power and alternative energy sources; consumption of locally produced, organically grown food whenever possible; adherence to a simple lifestyle; work on community service projects; and outdoor sleeping arrangements. In addition to its sessions in five American states, Kroka conducts programs in Ecuador, Mexico and northern Canada.

LIFEWORKS
Res — Coed Ages 14-19

Sarasota, FL 34277. PO Box 5517. Tel: 941-924-2115, 800-808-2115.
Fax: 941-924-6075.
www.lifeworks-international.com   E-mail: info@lifeworks-international.com

James M. Stoll, Dir.
Adm: FCFS. **Appl due:** Rolling. **Staff:** Admin 4.
Intl program focus: Culture. **Locations:** Asia Caribbean Mexico/Central_America South_America. Home stays avail.
Focus: Community_Serv. **Features:** Environ_Sci Lang Marine_Bio/Stud Crafts Adventure_Travel Conservation Exploration Hiking Outdoor_Ed Sail Seamanship Whitewater_Raft Swim.
Fees 2012: Res $4470-5870, 2½-3 wks.
Housing: Dorms Houses Lodges. **Swimming:** Ocean.
Est 2003. Nonprofit. **Ses:** 17. **Wks/ses:** 2½-3. Operates June-Aug.

With destinations in the British Virgin Islands, the Galapagos Islands, Costa Rica, China, Thailand, Ecuador, India and Peru, this service-learning travel program combines community service projects with cultural immersion and outdoor adventure activities. Participants work in collaboration with established local, national and international service organizations. Each Lifeworks program maintains a distinct focus.

LONGACRE EXPEDITIONS
Res — Coed Ages 11-19

Fort Collins, CO 80527. PO Box 273385. Tel: 970-568-8795, 800-433-0127.
Fax: 800-433-0127.
www.longacreexpeditions.com   E-mail: longacre@longacreexpeditions.com
Jason Eckman & Nicole Eckman, Dirs.
Grades 5-PG. Adm: FCFS. **Appl due:** Rolling. **Enr:** 10-16. **Enr cap:** 10-16. **Staff:** Admin 4. Couns 100.
Intl program focus: Culture. **Travel:** CO HI ME NH NY OR PA VT WA Canada Europe Mexico/Central_America South_America. Home stays avail.
Focus: Adventure_Travel Outdoor_Ed Wilderness_Camp. **Features:** Photog Aquatics Bicycle_Tours Boating Canoe Climbing_Wall Community_Serv Conservation Exploration Hiking Kayak Mountaineering Mtn_Biking Mtn_Trips Peace/Cross-cultural Riding Rock_Climb Ropes_Crse Sail Scuba Seamanship Weight_Loss White-water_Raft Surfing Swim Winter_Sports.
Fees 2011: Res $500-6900 (+$50-100), 1-4½ wks.
Housing: Cabins Dorms Lodges Tents. **Swimming:** Lake Pond Ocean Pool.
Est 1981. Inc. **Ses:** 15. **Wks/ses:** 1-4½. Operates June-Aug. ACA.

Longacre offers outdoor adventure education programs throughout New England, the western US and Hawaii, Canada, Europe, and Central and South America. Most trips feature backpacking, bicycle tours and white-water rafting, and specialized programs incorporate leadership opportunities and wellness training. Spanish language immersion is available in certain programs.

LONGACRE FARM
Res — Coed Ages 12-18

Newport, PA 17074. 1001 Markelsville Rd. Tel: 717-567-3349. Fax: 717-567-3955.
www.longacre.com   E-mail: connect@longacre.com
Susan Smith, Megan Gantt & Louise Warner, Dirs.
Grades 7-PG. Adm: Somewhat selective. Admitted: 83%. **Appl due:** Rolling. **Enr:** 72. **Enr cap:** 72. **Staff:** Admin 3. Couns 21. Res 20.
Focus: Farm Leadership Work. **Features:** Crafts Dance Drama Fine_Arts Music Bicycle_Tours Caving Chess Climbing_Wall Community_Serv Conservation Exploration Hiking Mountaineering Mtn_Biking Outdoor_Ed Riding Rock_Climb White-water_Raft Wilderness_Camp Woodcraft Basketball Equestrian Soccer Swim Tennis Ultimate_Frisbee Volleyball.
Fees 2012: Res $4590-5950 (+$120-180), 4-6 wks. Aid 2011 (Need): $40,000.

Housing: Tents. Avg per room/unit: 6. **Swimming:** Pond Pool. **Est 1975.** Inc. **Ses:** 2. **Wks/ses:** 4-6. Operates June-Aug. ACA.

Campers develop leadership and communicational skills through their participation in the daily life and the operation of a 200-acre working farm. Boys and girls choose daily activities from a variety of work and recreational options. Experiential education is the program's focus.

MARINE MILITARY ACADEMY SUMMER CAMP
Res — Boys Ages 12-17

Harlingen, TX 78550. 320 Iwo Jima Blvd. Tel: 956-423-6006. Fax: 956-421-9273.
www.summer-camp-mma.com   E-mail: admissions@mma-tx.org
Col. R. Glenn Hill, USMC (Ret), Supt.
Adm: FCFS. **Appl due:** Rolling. **Enr cap:** 300.
Focus: Leadership Milit_Trng. **Features:** Adventure_Travel Archery Canoe Climbing_Wall Hiking Paintball Rappelling Riflery Ropes_Crse Basketball Soccer Softball Swim Volleyball Boxing.
Fees 2011: Res $3300 (+$500), 4 wks.
Housing: Dorms. **Swimming:** Pool.
Est 1965. Nonprofit. **Ses:** 1. **Wks/ses:** 4. Operates June-July.

MMA's program of physical fitness and military-style training follows a structured daily schedule. Campers begin each morning with a physical fitness routine, then take part in various military activities. After playing team sports in the afternoon, boys gain an introduction to military customs and courtesies in the evening.

MISS PORTER'S SCHOOL
SARAH PORTER LEADERSHIP INSTITUTE
Res — Girls Ages 12-15

Farmington, CT 06032. 60 Main St. Tel: 860-409-3692, 800-447-2724.
Fax: 860-409-3537.
www.porters.org/summerprograms   E-mail: summer_programs@missporters.org
Christine Neville-Smith & Michael Smith, Dirs.
Grades 7-10. Adm: Somewhat selective. Admitted: 90%. **Appl due:** Rolling. **Enr:** 25-30.
Staff: Admin 3. Couns 8. Res 11.
Focus: Leadership. **Features:** Community_Serv Ropes_Crse White-water_Raft Wilderness_Camp Swim.
Fees 2011: Res $1000, 1 wk. Aid (Merit & Need).
Housing: Dorms. Avg per room/unit: 2. **Swimming:** Pool.
Est 2003. Nonprofit. **Ses:** 2. **Wks/ses:** 1. Operates June-July.

While working closely with female high schoolers and college students who have demonstrated leadership skills and have held leadership positions, girls in the institute learn about the knowledge, skills and resources required for effective leadership. The program features a panel on civic leadership, guest speakers, a self-defense class and community service. Topics addressed include leadership ethics, leadership styles, communication skills and public speaking, mediation skills and conflict resolution, management techniques, assertiveness, goal setting, and group dynamics and roles. Girls who have completed Level 1 of the institute may return the following summer for Level 2, where they further develop their leadership skills through service work in Greater Hartford.

MOUNTAIN ADVENTURE GUIDES SUMMER ADVENTURE CAMP
Res — Coed Ages 12-16

Erwin, TN 37650. 2 Jones Branch Rd. Tel: 423-743-7111, 866-813-5210.
Fax: 423-370-1357.
www.mtnadventureguides.com   E-mail: camp@mtnadventureguides.com
Richard Dulworth, Dir.
Grades 4-12. Adm: FCFS. **Appl due:** Feb.
Locations: NC TN.
Focus: Outdoor_Ed. **Features:** Mtn_Biking Rock_Climb White-water_Raft Wilderness_ Camp.
Fees 2010: Res $725-1500 (+$35-70), 1-2 wks.
Housing: Tents.
Est 1999. Ses: 12. **Wks/ses:** 1-2. Operates June-Aug.

These adventure treks through North Carolina's Blue Ridge Mountains emphasize the development of outdoor skills, independence and self-confidence. Age-appropriate activities include white-water rafting, backpacking, rock climbing, caving and mountain biking. Campers sleep in tents or on tarps.

THE MOUNTAIN INSTITUTE
MOUNTAIN ADVENTURES SUMMER CAMP
Res — Coed Ages 12-17

Circleville, WV 26804. HC 75, Box 24. Tel: 304-567-2632. Fax: 304-567-2666.
www.mountain.org/summercamp   E-mail: cking@mountain.org
Andrew Taber, Exec Dir.
Adm: FCFS. **Appl due:** Rolling. **Enr:** 12. **Fac 2. Staff:** Admin 3.
Focus: Field_Ecol Mountaineering Outdoor_Ed Wilderness_Camp. **Features:** Astron Ecol Environ_Sci Geol Sci Creative_Writing Photog Adventure_Travel Canoe Caving Conservation Exploration Hiking Mtn_Biking Rappelling Rock_Climb Survival_Trng White-water_Raft Wilderness_Canoe Woodcraft Swim.
Fees 2012: Res $850-2950 (+$40), 1-4 wks.
Swimming: River Stream.
Est 1972. Nonprofit. Ses: 4. **Wks/ses:** 1. Operates June-July.

TMI leads hands-on explorations through the peaks and river valleys of the Appalachian Mountains. Campers study the area's diverse ecology and learn about Appalachia's natural history and cultural heritage. Wilderness camping activities include canoeing, caving, rock climbing, survival training and white-water rafting.

MOUNTAIN LAKE CHESS CAMP
Res and Day — Coed Ages 6-17

Chula Vista, CA 91910. 155 G St. Toll-free: 800-675-1227. Fax: 619-863-5484.
www.chesscamp.net   E-mail: larry@chesscamp.net
Larry D. Evans, Dir.
Adm: FCFS. **Admitted:** 100%. **Appl due:** Rolling. **Enr:** 56. **Enr cap:** 150. **Fac 13. Staff:** Admin 2.
Focus: Chess. **Features:** Crafts Archery Climbing_Wall Exploration Riding Ropes_Crse Sail Baseball Basketball Equestrian Swim Volleyball.
Fees 2012: Res $589, 1 wk. Day $110, 1 wk. Aid 2006 (Need): $1000.
Housing: Cabins Dorms Houses Lodges. **Swimming:** Pool.
Est 1993. Ses: 12. **Wks/ses:** 1. Operates June-Aug.

Players ranging in ability from beginners to tournament veterans may develop their skills in Mountain Lake's chess programs. Socratic-style seminars, exhibition matches, speed chess and regulation tournaments utilize the camp's teaching method. Day camps held at the San

Diego Chess Club feature instruction in the morning and museum trips in the afternoon. Residential campers at Lake Arrowhead may participate in swimming, crafts, archery, sailing and horseback riding.

THE MOUNTAIN WORKSHOP
Res — Coed Ages 11-17

Danbury, CT 06810. 35 Miry Brook Rd. Tel: 203-797-1435, 800-831-1273.
Fax: 203-797-1436.
www.mountainworkshop.com   E-mail: info@mountainworkshop.com
Susan Friedrich, Exec Dir.
Adm: FCFS. **Appl due:** Rolling. **Enr:** 6-13. **Enr cap:** 6-13.
Travel: MA ME NY Canada.
Focus: Community_Serv Wilderness_Camp. **Features:** Adventure_Travel Canoe Exploration Hiking Kayak Mountaineering Mtn_Biking Rappelling Riding Sail White-water_Raft Wilderness_Canoe Swim.
Fees 2011: Res $1550-2850, 1-2 wks. Aid (Need).
Housing: Tents. **Swimming:** Lake Pond Ocean Pool River Stream.
Est 1979. Inc. **Ses:** 7. **Wks/ses:** 1-2. Operates June-Aug.

These adventure programs operate in various locations in the eastern United States and Quebec, Canada. Wilderness activities include river rafting, mountain biking, backpacking, canoeing, sea kayaking, rock and snow climbing, in-line skating, horseback riding and white-water kayaking.

MYSTIC SEAPORT MUSEUM
JOSEPH CONRAD SUMMER CAMP
Res — Coed Ages 10-15

Mystic, CT 06355. 75 Greenmanville Ave, PO Box 6000. Tel: 860-572-5322.
Fax: 860-572-5398.
www.mysticseaport.org/conradcamp   E-mail: education@mysticseaport.org
Hallie Payne, Dir.
Adm: FCFS. **Enr cap:** 45. **Staff:** Admin 3. Couns 4. Res 7.
Focus: Sail Seamanship.
Fees 2012: Res $635-690, 1 wk. Aid (Need).
Est 1949. Ses: 5. **Wks/ses:** 1. Operates June-Aug.

Joseph Conrad Summer Camp combines maritime history with basic sailing and seamanship skills. Students live on board the permanently berthed, square-rigged *Joseph Conrad* for a week. Programming includes sailing instruction in nine-foot Dyer Dhows, rowing in seine boats, dead reckoning and piloting, splicing and knot tying.

NATIONAL OUTDOOR LEADERSHIP SCHOOL
Res — Coed Ages 14 and up

Lander, WY 82520. 284 Lincoln St. Tel: 307-332-5300, 800-710-6657.
Fax: 307-332-1220.
www.nols.edu   E-mail: admissions@nols.edu
John Gans, Exec Dir.
Grades 8-Col. Adm: FCFS. **Appl due:** Rolling. **Staff:** Admin 125. Couns 500.
Type of instruction: ESL/TOEFL_Prep.
Travel: AK AZ ID NY WA WY Africa Australia/New_Zealand Canada Europe Mexico/Central_America South_America.
Focus: Leadership Mountaineering Outdoor_Ed Wilderness_Camp. **Features:** Ecol Environ_Sci Geol Adventure_Travel Canoe Caving Conservation Fishing Hiking Kayak

Mtn_Trips Pack_Train Peace/Cross-cultural Ranch Rock_Climb Sail White-water_Raft Wilderness_Canoe.
Fees 2011: Res $3120-11,220 (+$250), 2-11 wk.
Housing: Tents.
Est 1965. Nonprofit. **Wks/ses:** 2-11. Operates Year-round.

NOLS provides extended wilderness, water and mountaineering expeditions, along with semester-long courses. Each course emphasizes a core curriculum of risk management and judgment, leadership and teamwork, outdoor skills and environmental studies. International programs serve students age 18 and up. Participants may earn college credit through certain programs.

NAVAJO TRAILS
Res — Coed Ages 7-17

Bicknell, UT 84715. PO Box 88. Tel: 435-425-3469. Fax: 435-425-3215.
Contact (Sept-May): PO Box 55, Draper, UT 84020. Tel: 801-571-0804.
   Fax: 801-576-0759.
Year-round Toll-free: 800-200-2267.
www.navajotrails.com   E-mail: amyh@navajotrails.com
Amy Hugh & K'Leena Mellor, Dirs.
Adm: FCFS. **Appl due:** June. **Enr:** 120. **Staff:** Admin 3. Couns 13.
Focus: Wilderness_Camp. **Features:** Environ_Sci Theater Aquatics Bicycle_Tours Hiking Kayak Mountaineering Mtn_Biking Mtn_Trips Pack_Train Ranch Riding Rock_Climb Survival_Trng Swim Water-skiing Watersports.
Fees 2011: Res $495-4125, 1-5 wks.
Housing: Cabins Lodges. **Swimming:** Pond River.
Est 1965. Inc. **Ses:** 8. **Wks/ses:** 1-5. Operates June-Aug. ACA.

Campers at Navajo Trails spend each week concentrating on a wilderness skill such as backpacking, hiking, rock climbing, horseback riding, survival training, kayaking, water-skiing or wakeboarding. Participants take part in traditional camp activities on weekends.

NAWA SUMMER PROGRAMS
Res — Coed Ages 10-18

French Gulch, CA 96033. 17351 Trinity Mountain Rd. Tel: 530-359-2215,
   800-358-6292. Fax: 530-359-2229.
www.nawa-summer-programs.com   E-mail: info@nawa-summer-programs.com
Grades 5-12. Adm: FCFS. **Appl due:** Rolling. **Fac 2. Staff:** Admin 7. Couns 12.
Type of instruction: Dev_Read Rem_Eng Rem_Math Rem_Read Study_Skills Tut. **LD Services:** Acad_Instruction Tut. **Avg class size:** 12. **Daily hours for:** Classes 3. **High school credit:** 15.
Conditions accepted: ADD ADHD Dx LD.
Focus: Outdoor_Ed Wilderness_Camp. **Features:** Ecol Environ_Sci Govt Lang Crafts Creative_Writing Adventure_Travel Aquatics Canoe Caving Climbing_Wall Conservation Cooking Exploration Fishing Hiking Leadership Mountaineering Mtn_Trips Paintball Rappelling Rock_Climb Survival_Trng White-water_Raft Basketball Skateboarding Swim Ultimate_Frisbee Volleyball Watersports Weight_Trng.
Fees 2011: Res $5100-5500, 4 wks. Aid (Need).
Housing: Tents. **Swimming:** Lake River Stream.
Est 1988. Inc. **Spons:** Nawa Academy. **Ses:** 1. **Wks/ses:** 4. Operates June-Aug.

Emphasizing outdoor and rescue training, group activities and experiential education, Nawa operates four summer programs that offer a variety of backpacking, caving, climbing and rafting opportunities. Three of the programs span grades 7-12, while all of them are able to accommodate campers with learning differences, attentional disorders and time-management difficulties. Great Challenge, Lassen Expedition and Girls on the Go are adventure programs that allow students to combine wilderness training with the chance to earn up to 15 high school credits. Trinity Challenge offers the same opportunities on a noncredit basis for younger boys and girls ages 10-13.

NEW YORK MILITARY ACADEMY
SUMMER ADVENTURE PROGRAM
Res — Coed Ages 13-17

Cornwall-on-Hudson, NY 12520. 78 Academy Ave. Tel: 845-534-3710, 888-275-6962. Fax: 845-534-7699.
www.nyma.org   E-mail: admissions@nyma.org
Les McMillen, Dir.
Grades 8-12. Adm: FCFS. **Appl due:** June. **Enr cap:** 10. **Staff:** Admin 3.
Focus: Outdoor_Ed. **Features:** Aquatics Archery Canoe Hiking Kayak Milit_Trng Rappelling Riflery Ropes_Crse Survival_Trng Swim.
Fees 2011: Res $2000-5000, 2-6 wks.
Housing: Dorms. Avg per room/unit: 2. **Swimming:** Pool.
Ses: 3. **Wks/ses:** 2-6. Operates July-Aug.

NYMA's Adventure Program consists of adventure learning, guided outdoor activities and challenge opportunities. The curriculum typically includes an obstacle course, orientation and navigation, marksmanship training at an indoor rifle range, field engineering projects, wilderness survival, military drill team, rappelling, kayaking and canoeing, and technical tree climbing.

NORTHWATERS & LANGSKIB WILDERNESS PROGRAMS
Res — Boys Ages 10-19, Girls 11-19

Temagami, P0H 2H0 Ontario, Canada. PO Box 358. Fax: 705-237-8663.
Contact (Sept-June): PO Box 205, Westport, NY 12993. Fax: 518-962-8768.
Year-round Tel: 518-962-4869, 866-458-9974.
www.northwaters.com   E-mail: canoe@northwaters.com
C. G. Stephens, Dir.
Adm: FCFS. **Appl due:** Rolling. **Enr:** 125. **Enr cap:** 125. **Staff:** Admin 6. Couns 40.
Locations: Canada.
Focus: Wilderness_Camp Wilderness_Canoe. **Features:** Adventure_Travel Canoe Conservation Exploration Fishing Hiking Kayak Outdoor_Ed Survival_Trng Swim.
Fees 2012: Res $1950-6100 (+$110), 2-7 wks.
Housing: Cabins Lodges Tepees. **Swimming:** Lake River.
Est 1971. Inc. Ses: 12. **Wks/ses:** 2-7. Operates June-Aug.

Located in Ontario's Temagami Forest Reserve, these programs consist of two distinct wilderness programs: Langskib provides boys-only trips, while Northwaters offers both coeducational and girls-only experiences. Canoe trips are the backbone of the program, and campers also develop outdoor skills. Boys and girls, who enter Langskib and Northwaters with varying skill and experience levels, embark on canoeing excursions that last from two to seven weeks.

NORWICH UNIVERSITY FUTURE LEADER CAMP
Res — Coed Ages 15-18

Northfield, VT 05663. 27 I D White Ave. Tel: 802-485-2531, 800-468-6679. Fax: 802-485-2739.
www.norwich.edu/admissions/futureleader   E-mail: flc@norwich.edu
Lt. Col. Skip Davison, Dir.

Grades 10-PG. Adm: Selective. **Appl due:** Rolling. **Enr:** 80. **Staff:** Admin 5. Couns 8.
Focus: Leadership Milit_Trng. **Features:** Adventure_Travel Archery Canoe Climbing_ Wall Hiking Kayak Mountaineering Mtn_Trips Paintball Rappelling Riflery Rock_Climb Ropes_Crse Survival_Trng Wilderness_Camp Swim.
Fees 2012: Res $1775, 2 wks.
Housing: Dorms. **Swimming:** Lake Pool River.
Est 1998. Nonprofit. **Ses:** 2. **Wks/ses:** 2. Operates July-Aug.

FLC combines adventure training, group discussions, teamwork, physical fitness and assigned leadership opportunities. Morning and afternoon training focuses on individual and team skill development and features a ropes course, climbing wall, a rappelling tower, map reading and orienteering, and rifle marksmanship; evenings include interactive classroom instruction and group discussions. FLC is not designed for students with disciplinary problems and instead serves boys and girls with at least a 2.5 GPA with prior experience in leadership-driven organizations.

OAK RIDGE MILITARY ACADEMY LEADERSHIP ADVENTURE CAMP
Res — Coed Ages 11-18

Oak Ridge, NC 27310. 2317 Oak Ridge Rd, PO Box 498. Tel: 336-643-4131.
Fax: 336-643-1797.
www.oakridgemilitary.com   E-mail: blipke@ormila.com
Grades 6-12. Adm: FCFS. **Appl due:** Rolling. **Enr:** 150. **Staff:** Couns 15.
Focus: Leadership Milit_Trng. **Features:** Environ_Sci Sci Canoe Exploration Hiking Rappelling Riflery Ropes_Crse Survival_Trng Wilderness_Camp Baseball Basketball Golf Swim.
Fees 2009: Res $1950 (+$15-20), 2 wks.
Housing: Dorms. **Swimming:** Pool.
Est 1980. Nonprofit. **Ses:** 3. **Wks/ses:** 2. Operates June-Aug.

The camp combines leadership training with recreational activities and adventure training. Programming emphasizes drills and physical fitness, and campers attend classes in survival techniques, camouflage skills, and paintball safety and tactics. Other aspects of training include introductory courses on rappelling and marksmanship safety.

OCEAN CLASSROOM FOUNDATION SEAFARING CAMPS
Res — Coed Ages 12-18

Boothbay Harbor, ME 04538. 1 Oak St. Tel: 207-633-2750, 800-724-7245.
Fax: 207-633-4337.
www.oceanclassroom.org   E-mail: mail@oceanclassroom.org
Susan Hodder, Dir.
Grades 7-PG. Adm: FCFS. **Appl due:** Rolling. **Enr:** 20. **Enr cap:** 22. **Fac 3. Staff:** Admin 6. Couns 10. Res 10.
Type of instruction: Enrich. **Avg class size:** 12. **Daily hours for:** Classes 3. Rec 8.
Travel: CT MA ME RI Canada.
Focus: Sail Sea_Cruises Seamanship. **Features:** Ecol Environ_Sci Marine_Bio/Stud Adventure_Travel Swim.
Fees 2011: Res $1350-2750, 1-2 wks. Aid 2011 (Need): $10,000.
Swimming: Ocean.
Est 1994. Nonprofit. **Ses:** 2. **Wks/ses:** 1-2. Operates July-Aug.

Ocean Classroom conducts introductory (ages 12-16) and advanced (ages 14-18) programs on its three schooners that focus on seamanship and maritime studies. Boys and girls fully explore marine ecosystems, including whales, seals, seabirds, fish and invertebrates. While sailing, participants learn such seafaring skills as line and sail handling, compass navigation, knot tying, splices and rope work, and log keeping. During port visits, the SEAfaring Camps explore museums, lighthouses and archaeological sites of maritime significance.

OUTPOST WILDERNESS ADVENTURE
Res — Coed Ages 11-17

Lake George, CO 80827. 20859 County Rd 77. Tel: 719-748-3080.
**Contact (Sept-May): 1208 Deer Creek Cir, Dripping Springs, TX 78620.
Tel: 512-731-7596.**
Year-round Fax: 719-213-2703.
www.owa.com   E-mail: chelsea@owa.com
Chelsea Faerber & James Faerber, Dirs.
Adm: FCFS. **Enr:** 100. **Staff:** Admin 1. Couns 15.
Travel: CO WY.
Focus: Mountaineering Mtn_Biking Rock_Climb Wilderness_Camp. **Features:** Adventure_Travel Bicycle_Tours Conservation Exploration Fishing Hiking Mtn_Trips.
Fees 2010: Res $975-1950, 1-2 wks.
Housing: Cabins Dorms Lodges Tents.
Est 1979. Ses: 10. **Wks/ses:** 1-2. Operates June-Aug.

OWA offers specialty camps in rock and alpine climbing, fly-fishing and mountain biking. The organization conducts backcountry expeditions into Colorado and Wyoming, as well as a residential adventure program in Colorado.

OUTWARD BOUND
Res — Coed Ages 12 and up

Golden, CO 80401. 910 Jackson St. Tel: 720-497-2340, 866-467-7651.
Fax: 720-497-2341.
www.outwardboundwilderness.com   E-mail: info@outwardbound.org
Adm: FCFS. **Appl due:** Rolling.
Locations: AK CA CO FL MA MD ME MN MT NC OR TX UT WA WY Caribbean.
Focus: Outdoor_Ed. **Features:** Adventure_Travel Canoe Climbing_Wall Community_Serv Exploration Hiking Kayak Mountaineering Mtn_Biking Mtn_Trips Rappelling Rock_Climb Ropes_Crse Sail White-water_Raft Wilderness_Camp Wilderness_Canoe Swim Watersports.
Fees 2012: Res $1425-5295 (+$500), 1-4 wks. Aid 2007 (Need): $2,000,000.
Swimming: Lake Pond Ocean River Stream.
Est 1962. Nonprofit. Wks/ses: 1-4. Operates Year-round.

Outward Bound conducts year-round wilderness adventures throughout the country. Program instructors make use of wilderness areas to expose young people to a strenuous environment, while also challenging them mentally and physically. Pursuits include mountaineering/ backpacking, mountain biking, and white-water rafting and canoeing, among others.

OUTWARD BOUND CANADA
Res — Coed Ages 15 and up

Toronto, M4W 3X8 Ontario, Canada. 550 Bayview Ave, Ste 404. Tel: 705-382-5454, 888-688-9273. **Fax:** 705-382-5959.
www.outwardbound.ca   E-mail: info@outwardbound.ca
Sarah Wiley, Exec Dir.
Adm: FCFS. **Appl due:** Rolling.
High school credit.
Intl program focus: Culture. **Travel:** Canada.
Focus: Mountaineering Wilderness_Camp Wilderness_Canoe. **Features:** Creative_Writ-

ing Aquatics Canoe Climbing_Wall Community_Serv Hiking Kayak Mtn_Trips Rappel-
ling Rock_Climb Ropes_Crse Survival_Trng Swim.
Fees 2012: Res Can$1700-4450, 1-4½ wks. Aid (Need).
Housing: Tents. Avg per room/unit: 10. **Swimming:** Lake River.
Est 1976. Nonprofit. **Ses:** 18. **Wks/ses:** 1-4½. Operates July-Aug.

Stressing adventure and personal growth through challenging wilderness activities,
Outward Bound Canada's programs center around extended canoe expeditions, tracing the
remote Indian and trapper routes of northwestern Ontario. Critical-thinking skills, map and
compass navigation, environmental awareness and first-aid experience are integrated into
the overall Outward Bound educational philosophy. A mountaineering program explores the
Rocky Mountains of Alberta. Participants in some programs may earn high school credit in
certain programs.

PANIMWORKS
IMPACT: DC
Res — Coed Ages 16-18

Washington, DC. George Washington Univ.
Contact (Year-round): c/o PANIM, 6163 Executive Blvd, Rockville, MD 20852.
Tel: 301-770-5070. Fax: 301-770-6365.
www.bbyo.org/teens/experiences/impact_dc   E-mail: impact@bbyo.org
Natalie Sukienik, Prgm Dir.
Grades 11-PG. Adm: FCFS. **Appl due:** Rolling. **Enr:** 56. **Enr cap:** 60. **Fac 4. Staff:** Admin
2. Couns 5.
Avg class size: 15. **Daily hours for:** Classes 2½. Rec 2.
Focus: Community_Serv Leadership. **Features:** Econ Environ_Sci Crafts Music Bicycle_
Tours Hiking White-water_Raft Baseball Basketball Soccer Softball Ultimate_Frisbee.
Fees 2012: Res $2300-4500, 2-4 wks. Aid (Need).
Housing: Dorms.
Est 2003. Nonprofit. **Spons:** PANIM. Jewish. **Ses:** 3. **Wks/ses:** 2-4. Operates June-July.

DC JAM serves high school students interested in Judaism, politics and community
service. Participants work on service projects, learn about advocacy from guest activists and
policymakers, and attend courses in such subjects as economics, ethics, climate study and
education policy. Boys and girls, who board at George Washington University, take advantage
of the local and national institutions of Washington, DC. The four-week Internship Bridge
enables participants to shadow a professional at a city advocacy organization. Each student
may earn credit towards his or her high school's community service requirement.

POULTER COLORADO CAMPS
Res — Coed Ages 9-17

Steamboat Springs, CO 80477. PO Box 770969. Tel: 970-879-4816, 888-879-4816.
Fax: 970-879-4816.
www.poultercamps.com   E-mail: info@poultercamps.com
Andrew Stoller, Dir.
Grades 4-12. Adm: FCFS. **Appl due:** Rolling. **Enr cap:** 40. **Staff:** Admin 5. Couns 17.
Travel: CO UT Mexico/Central_America.
Focus: Wilderness_Camp. **Features:** Ecol Environ_Sci Geol Crafts Filmmaking Music
Painting Adventure_Travel Aquatics Archery Caving Conservation Exploration Fishing
Hiking Kayak Mountaineering Mtn_Trips Outdoor_Ed Riding Rock_Climb Survival_Trng
White-water_Raft Badminton Basketball Equestrian Soccer Swim Ultimate_Frisbee Vol-
leyball.
Fees 2010: Res $1550-3300, 1½-4 wks. Aid (Need).
Housing: Cabins Tents. Avg per room/unit: 5. **Swimming:** Lake Pool.
Est 1966. Inc. **Ses:** 3. **Wks/ses:** 1½-4. Operates June-Aug. ACA.

Campers ages 11-17 are introduced to the wilderness through such activities as hiking, white-water rafting, kayaking, caving, technical climbing, backpacking, team building, orienteering and snow travel. Trips made to locations in Colorado and Utah last between four and 14 days. Younger campers (ages 9-11), who also participate in wilderness adventures and shorter excursions, spend more time on traditional activities at base camp.

PUTNEY STUDENT TRAVEL COMMUNITY SERVICE PROGRAMS
Res — Coed Ages 15-18

Putney, VT 05346. 345 Hickory Ridge Rd. Tel: 802-387-5000. Fax: 802-387-4276.
www.goputney.com   E-mail: info@goputney.com
Peter Shumlin & Jeffrey Shumlin, Dirs.
Grades 10-PG. Adm: FCFS. **Appl due:** Rolling.
Intl program focus: Culture. **Locations:** HI Africa Asia Australia/New_Zealand Caribbean Mexico/Central_America South_America. Home stays avail.
Focus: Community_Serv. **Features:** Adventure_Travel.
Fees 2012: Res $4690-6790, 3-4½ wks.
Est 1952. Ses: 21. **Wks/ses:** 3-4½. Operates June-Aug.

Participants in these service programs work within a group to assist individuals in developing countries and disadvantaged communities. Service involves such activities as work at hospitals and schools, housing construction and repair, and operation of enrichment programs. Putney selects community service locations—after receiving invitations from host governments—based upon the area's safety, stability and demonstrated need. Programs operate in Ecuador, Tanzania, Costa Rica, Senegal, Nicaragua, Nusa Penida, the Dominican Republic, Vietnam, Argentina, Ghana, Peru, India, Dominica and Hawaii.

CAMP QUEST
Res — Coed Ages 8-17

Columbus, OH 43216. PO Box 2552. Tel: 614-441-9534.
www.camp-quest.org   E-mail: camp@camp-quest.org
Amanda K. Metskas, Exec Dir.
Adm: FCFS. **Appl due:** Rolling. **Enr:** 48. **Enr cap:** 60. **Staff:** Admin 5. Couns 20.
Locations: CA MI MN MT OH SC TN TX VA WA Canada Europe.
Focus: Secularism. **Features:** Crafts Drama Aquatics Archery Canoe Chess Climbing_ Wall Riding Ropes_Crse Woodcraft Badminton Swim.
Fees 2011: Res $400-600, 1 wk. Aid 2007 (Need): $4500.
Housing: Cabins. **Swimming:** Pool.
Est 1996. Nonprofit. Wks/ses: 1. Operates June-Aug.

The first residential summer camp for children of atheists, agnostics, freethinkers, secular humanists and others who hold a naturalistic worldview, Camp Quest holds camps at nine locations in the US, as well as in Canada, England, Ireland and Norway. Programming emphasizes rational inquiry, critical thinking, the scientific method, ethics, free speech, and the separation of religion and government. Campers participate in games and skits, learn about noteworthy freethinkers throughout history, and engage in open dialogue about science, religion and morality.

RAWHIDE RANCH
Res — Coed Ages 7-15

Bonsall, CA 92003. 6987 W Lilac Rd, PO Box 216. Tel: 760-758-0083.
Fax: 760-758-0440.
www.rawhideranch.com   E-mail: info@rawhideranch.com

Tom Ewan & Val Ewan, Dirs.
Adm: FCFS. **Appl due:** Rolling.
Focus: Ranch Riding Equestrian. **Features:** Crafts Creative_Writing Drama Archery
Riflery Swim.
Fees 2012: Res $895, 1 wk.
Housing: Cabins Tepees. Avg per room/unit: 10. **Swimming:** Pool.
Est 1963. Inc. **Ses:** 9. **Wks/ses:** 1. Operates June-Aug. ACA.

Riding is a particular point of evidence at this ranch camp: Campers may ride under the
guidance of trainers every day if they so choose. Animal science and animal care are also
part of the program. Other popular activities include swimming, Western crafts, country and
western dancing, and creative writing.

REALITY RANCH MILITARY CAMP
Res — Boys Ages 10-15

Mesa, AZ 85209. PO Box 51791. Tel: 480-278-5981, 877-273-7427. Fax: 480-371-1179.
www.realityranchcamp.com   E-mail: realityranchmilitarycamp@yahoo.com
Jeremy M. Denton, Sr., Prgm Dir.
Adm: FCFS. **Appl due:** Rolling. **Enr cap:** 80.
Focus: Milit_Trng. **Features:** Climbing_Wall Community_Serv Conservation Cooking Deep-
sea Fishing Hiking Mountaineering Mtn_Trips Paintball Ranch Riflery Social_Servs Sur-
vival_Trng Wilderness_Camp Aerobics Football Skateboarding Track Ultimate_Frisbee.
Housing: Tents.
Est 1999. Inc. Nondenom Christian. **Ses:** 2. **Wks/ses:** 2-4. Operates June-Aug.

Reality Ranch's outdoor educational experience for boys emphasizes life skills instruction,
emotional growth, and the development of healthy nutrition, hygiene and exercise habits.
During the session, campers experience all that a soldier in basic training undergoes. Boys
enroll from various backgrounds and religious denominations; some have attentional disorders,
while others may simply be lacking in motivation or self-discipline.

THE ROAD LESS TRAVELED
Res — Coed Ages 13-19

Chicago, IL 60614. 2331 N Elston Ave. Tel: 773-342-5200, 800-939-9839.
Fax: 480-247-5433.
www.theroadlesstraveled.com   E-mail: info@theroadlesstraveled.com
Jim Stein & Donna Stein, Dirs.
Grades 7-12. **Adm:** FCFS. **Appl due:** Rolling. **Enr:** 13-18. **Enr cap:** 13-18. **Staff:** Admin
7. Couns 30.
Intl program focus: Lang Culture. **Travel:** AK AZ CO FL HI ID LA MT NM SD UT WA WY
Africa Asia Canada Caribbean Europe Mexico/Central_America South_America.
Focus: Adventure_Travel Community_Serv Wilderness_Camp. **Features:** Canoe Con-
servation Exploration Hiking Kayak Mountaineering Mtn_Biking Mtn_Trips Outdoor_Ed
Ranch Rappelling Rock_Climb Sail White-water_Raft Wilderness_Canoe Swim.
Fees 2010: Res $1695-7450 (+airfare), 1-5½ wks. Aid 2009 (Need): $80,000.
Housing: Apartments Cabins Hotels Tents. **Swimming:** Lake Ocean.
Est 1991. Inc. **Ses:** 35. **Wks/ses:** 1-5½. Operates June-Aug. ACA.

RLT participants choose from a range of community service, wilderness adventure and
language immersion programs. Adventure Expeditions campers explore wilderness areas in
the western United States, Alaska and Norway. Leadership Training programs in Washington
State and British Columbia or Costa Rica and Nicaragua offer Wilderness First Responder
certification. Global Perspectives Programs immerse students in remote cultures in Bhutan and
Costa Rica. Service Learning program destinations include Colorado, South Dakota, Florida,
Louisiana (for Hurricane Katrina relief), Hawaii, India, Tanzania and Namibia. Language

and Service programs combine formal language instruction with service work and adventure activities in Costa Rica, Panama, Ecuador, Peru and Guatemala.

ROAD'S END FARM HORSEMANSHIP CAMP
Res — Girls Ages 8-16

Chesterfield, NH 03443. 149 Jackson Hill Rd, PO Box 197. Tel: 603-363-4900.
Fax: 603-363-4949.
www.roadsendfarm.com
Thomas E. Woodman, Dir.
Grades 3-11. Adm: FCFS. **Appl due:** Rolling. **Enr:** 65. **Enr cap:** 65. **Staff:** Admin 2. Couns 13. Res 19.
Focus: Riding. **Features:** Crafts Canoe Farm Hiking Equestrian Swim.
Fees 2012: Res $2230-9785 (+$112), 2-9 wks.
Housing: Cabins Houses. Avg per room/unit: 9. **Swimming:** Lake River.
Est 1958. Ses: 28. **Wks/ses:** 2-9. Operates June-Aug.

Located on a 360-acre horse farm, this camp teaches English pleasure riding and horse care on a daily basis. Riding is noncompetitive and enjoyed on three riding rings and 20 miles of bridle paths. Road's End Farm also encourages girls to participate in other farm activities. Daily lake swimming and weekly canoeing trips on the Connecticut River are other aspects of the program.

ROARING BROOK CAMP FOR BOYS
Res — Boys Ages 9-16

Bradford, VT 05033. 480 Roaring Brook Rd. Tel: 802-222-5702.
Contact (Sept-May): 300 Grove St, Unit 4, Rutland, VT 05701. Tel: 802-747-0282.
Year-round Toll-free: 800-832-4295, Fax: 802-786-0653.
www.roaringbrookcamp.com E-mail: rainest@sover.net
Candice L. Raines & J. Thayer Raines, Dirs.
Adm: FCFS. **Appl due:** Rolling. **Enr:** 45. **Enr cap:** 45. **Staff:** Admin 2. Couns 10.
Travel: ME NH VT.
Focus: Mountaineering Outdoor_Ed Wilderness_Camp. **Features:** Crafts Adventure_ Travel Archery Canoe Conservation Cooking Fishing Hiking Kayak Mtn_Biking Mtn_ Trips Rappelling Riflery Rock_Climb Ropes_Crse Survival_Trng White-water_Raft Wilderness_Canoe Woodcraft Swim.
Fees 2012: Res $2200-5500 (+$80), 2-6 wks.
Housing: Lodges. Avg per room/unit: 6. **Swimming:** Lake.
Est 1965. Inc. **Ses:** 4. **Wks/ses:** 2-6. Operates June-Aug. ACA.

Canoeing and backpacking trips offered at Roaring Brook vary, allowing boys to return in future years without repeating the route taken. The backpacking trip program traverses mountains in Vermont, New Hampshire and Maine, with boys assisting with route and campsite selection in groupings that are organized by age and hiking ability. The mountaineering program, conducted on the camp's 35-foot cliff, features instruction in rock climbing, rappelling and Tyrolean traverse safety procedures, equipment use and movement techniques. A ropes program enables campers to attempt 16 interconnected low and high ropes courses.

ROCK CLIMBING NEW ENGLAND
Res — Coed Ages 14-17

Rutland, VT 05701. 223 Woodstock Ave. Tel: 802-773-3343. Fax: 802-773-4509.
www.vermontclimbing.com E-mail: dave@vermontclimbing.com
Dave Muller, Prgm Mgr.
Adm: FCFS. **Appl due:** Rolling.

Locations: NH VT.
Focus: Mountaineering Rock_Climb.
Fees 2009: Res $800, 1 wk.
Spons: Green Mountain Rock Climbing Center. **Ses:** 1. **Wks/ses:** 1. Operates July.

Boys and girls develop rock climbing skills as they journey through northern New Hampshire and Vermont with professional guides. Participants learn the intricate details of rock climbing during a five-day program that addresses technique, movement and safety precautions.

SAIL CARIBBEAN
Res — Coed Ages 13-19

Northport, NY 11768. 256 Main St, Ste 1203. Tel: 631-754-2202, 800-321-0994.
  Fax: 631-754-3362.
www.sailcaribbean.com   **E-mail: info@sailcaribbean.com**
Mike Liese, Dir.
Grades 7-Col. Adm: FCFS. **Appl due:** Rolling. **Enr:** 20-60. **Staff:** Admin 12. Couns 50.
Type of instruction: Adv Enrich. **High school & college credit:** 4.
Travel: Caribbean.
Focus: Community_Serv Sail Scuba Seamanship. **Features:** Environ_Sci Marine_Bio/ Stud Adventure_Travel Boating Conservation Cooking Exploration Hiking Kayak Outdoor_Ed Peace/Cross-cultural Sea_Cruises Swim Volleyball Water-skiing Watersports.
Fees 2012: Res $3795-5595 (+airfare), 2-3 wks. Aid (Need).
Housing: Cabins. Avg per room/unit: 2. **Swimming:** Ocean.
Est 1979. Inc. **Ses:** 24. **Wks/ses:** 2-3. Operates June-Aug.

Students learn sailing, racing and seamanship aboard 50-foot yachts while cruising the waters of the British Virgin and Leeward islands. Activities include snorkeling, scuba diving, water-skiing, windsurfing, kayaking and island exploration. Boys and girls assist with the maintenance and the operation of the vessel. Students live in single-gender cabins while participating in marine biology and outdoor adventure education. Boys and girls in all Sail Caribbean programs may undertake community service projects of five to 30 hours' duration. Projects include mentoring of local youth and environmental conservation. No prior experience is necessary for enrollment in any program.

ST. GEORGE'S SCHOOL GERONIMO PROGRAM
Res — Coed Ages 14 and up

Newport, RI 02840. PO Box 1910. Tel: 401-842-6747.
www.sailgeronimo.org   **E-mail: geronimo@stgeorges.edu**
Deborah Hayes, Prgm Dir.
Grades 10-Col. Adm: FCFS. **Appl due:** Rolling. **Enr:** 8.
Focus: Sail Seamanship.
Fees 2009: Res $2700, 2 wks.
Est 1974. Ses: 2. **Wks/ses:** 2. Operates June-July.

Participants in the program learn sailing and navigation skills aboard a 70-foot vessel in the Atlantic Ocean. Students stand watch, navigate, perform sail maneuvers, steer, cook and clean as responsibilities progress over the course of the voyage. Affiliations with research organizations provide opportunities for marine science research. Voyages depart from or arrive in Newport, RI, and itineraries vary from year to year. No prior sailing experience is necessary.

CAMP ST. JOHN'S NORTHWESTERN
Res and Day — Boys Ages 11-16

Delafield, WI 53018. 1101 N Genesee St. Tel: 262-646-7199, 800-752-2338.
Fax: 262-646-7128.
www.sjnma.org   E-mail: admissions@sjnma.org
Lt. Mark D. Weigel, Dir.
Grades 6-11. Adm: Selective. **Appl due:** Rolling. **Enr:** 150. **Fac 3. Staff:** Admin 8. Couns 20.
Type of instruction: Rev. **Avg class size:** 8. High school credit.
Focus: Leadership. **Features:** Aquatics Archery Canoe Climbing_Wall Fishing Hiking Kayak Milit_Trng Paintball Rappelling Riflery Ropes_Crse Sail Scuba Survival_Trng Golf Martial_Arts Swim.
Fees 2012: Res $1175, 1 wk. Day $700, 1 wk.
Housing: Dorms. **Swimming:** Lake Pool.
Est 1995. Nonprofit. **Spons:** St. John's Northwestern Military Academy. Episcopal. **Ses:** 4. **Wks/ses:** 1. Operates July-Aug. ACA.

This structured semi-military camp combines adventure training and physical challenges to encourage leadership development and team building. Activities offered include archery, orienteering, marksmanship, paintball and rappelling, in addition to many typical outdoor sports and pursuits. Campers may also develop basic self-defense skills.

CAMP ST. MICHAEL
Res — Coed Ages 11-18

Leggett, CA 95585. PO Box 237. Tel: 707-984-6877.
Contact (Sept-May): PO Box 9447, Santa Rosa, CA 95405. Tel: 707-703-9171.
Year-round Fax: 707-984-8582.
www.campstmichael.org   E-mail: office@campstmichael.org
Michelle Campbell, Dir.
Grades 6-12. Adm: FCFS. **Appl due:** Rolling. **Enr:** 50. **Staff:** Admin 5. Couns 30.
Focus: Outdoor_Ed. **Features:** Astron Ecol Environ_Sci Geol Crafts Aquatics Archery Conservation Cooking Exploration Fishing Hiking Mtn_Trips Rappelling Riding Riflery Rock_Climb Ropes_Crse Survival_Trng Wilderness_Camp Baseball Equestrian Field_ Hockey Swim.
Fees 2011: Res $415-835, 1-2 wks. Aid (Need).
Housing: Tents. **Swimming:** River.
Est 1963. Nonprofit. Roman Catholic. **Ses:** 6. **Wks/ses:** 1-2. Operates June-Aug. ACA.

Separate boys' and girls' programs at St. Michael focus on outdoor education and adventure activities. The Core and Challenge programs concentrate on the fundamentals of outdoor living and include backpacking, nature, crafts, a ropes course, swimming, horseback riding, archery and riflery. The Advanced Program (grades 9-11) features a three-day backpacking trip and introductory training in survival skills. Designed for a challenging physical experience, the Adventure/Survival Program includes advanced camp craft and outdoor skills, two separate three-day backpacking trips, training in survival skills, rock climbing, rappelling, and a 24-hour solo without sleeping bags or food.

ST. OLAF COLLEGE
OLECHESS
Res and Day — Coed Ages 9 and up

Northfield, MN 55057. 1520 St Olaf Ave. Tel: 507-786-3042, 800-726-6523.
Fax: 507-786-3690.
www.stolaf.edu/camps   E-mail: summer@stolaf.edu
Kevin Bachler, Dir.

Adm: FCFS. **Appl due:** Rolling. **Enr:** 50. **Staff:** Admin 2. Couns 4. Res 5.
Focus: Chess.
Fees 2011: Res $640, 1 wk. Day $590, 1 wk.
Housing: Dorms. Avg per room/unit: 2.
Nonprofit. **Ses:** 1. **Wks/ses:** 1. Operates July.

Participants in this weeklong program, which accepts players of differing skill levels, receive instruction from premier players and grandmasters. Various camp activities reinforce the player's new skills, and boys and girls have ample opportunities to play matches. Many of the instructors take a historical approach to teaching, helping campers to understand the game's tactical progression over time. OleChess' rotating schedule enables campers to study with several teachers during the course of the session. An intensive study option features lectures and other events in the evening. An adult chaperone may join young boarders; chaperones must accompany nine-year-old residents.

SALTASH MOUNTAIN CAMP
Res — Coed Ages 11-14

Plymouth, VT 05056. c/o Farm & Wilderness Foundation, 263 Farm & Wilderness Rd. Tel: 802-422-3761. Fax: 802-422-8660.
www.farmandwilderness.org   E-mail: info@farmandwilderness.org
Jeff Bounds, Dir.
Adm: FCFS. **Appl due:** Rolling. **Enr:** 40. **Enr cap:** 40.
Focus: Wilderness_Camp. **Features:** Crafts Drama Music Boating Canoe Conservation Exploration Hiking Mtn_Trips Outdoor_Ed Peace/Cross-cultural Rock_Climb Wilderness_Canoe Swim Ultimate_Frisbee.
Fees 2011: Res $4300-7100, 3½-7 wks. Aid (Merit & Need).
Housing: Cabins. Avg per room/unit: 8. **Swimming:** Lake.
Est 1962. Nonprofit. **Spons:** Farm and Wilderness Foundation. **Ses:** 3. **Wks/ses:** 3½-7. Operates June-Aug. ACA.

This wilderness tripping camp adheres to Quaker values. Six to eight campers, led by two counselors, go on each trip. Participants may rock climb on Deer's Leap; reroute a part of the Appalachian Trail; canoe on Maine's Flagstaff Lake; hike a 5000-foot peak in the White Mountains; or scale Camel's Hump on Vermont's Long Trail to see the sunset, then return for sunrise a few hours later. While on these trips, campers develop such outdoor living skills as fire building, cooking, knot making, and facility with a map and compass.

SARGENT CENTER ADVENTURE CAMP
Res — Coed Ages 10-17

Hancock, NH 03449. 36 Sargent Camp Rd. Tel: 603-525-3311. Fax: 603-525-4151.
www.naturesclassroom.org   E-mail: dougsuth@naturesclassroom.org
Doug Sutherland, Dir.
Adm: FCFS. **Appl due:** Apr. **Enr cap:** 8-12. **Staff:** Admin 6. Couns 40.
Focus: Kayak Outdoor_Ed Rock_Climb Wilderness_Camp Wilderness_Canoe. **Features:** Crafts Aquatics Archery Canoe Climbing_Wall Community_Serv Conservation Cooking Hiking Mtn_Biking Mtn_Trips Ropes_Crse Woodcraft Swim Watersports.
Fees 2011: Res $735-2145, 1-3 wks. Aid 2007 (Need): $3000.
Housing: Cabins Dorms Tents. **Swimming:** Pond.
Est 1912. Nonprofit. **Spons:** Nature's Classroom. **Ses:** 37. **Wks/ses:** 1-3. Operates June-Aug. ACA.

Operated by Nature's Classroom, Sargent Center occupies 700 acres of woodland in the Monadnock region of southern New Hampshire. All campers participate in core activities, which include team building, high ropes courses, swimming and crafts. Each camper may also select either backpacking, canoeing, rock climbing, sea kayaking or mountain biking as his or her trek activity.

SEATREK
Res — Coed Ages 12-23

Flushing, MI 48433. 549 Oakbrook Cir. Tel: 810-487-1616, 877-467-2454.
Fax: 810-487-1633.
www.seatrekbvi.com   E-mail: monk@seatrekbvi.com
R. Monk Daniel, Dir.
Adm: FCFS. **Appl due:** Rolling. **Enr:** 36. **Enr cap:** 36. **Staff:** Admin 2. Couns 12.
High school & college credit.
Travel: Caribbean.
Focus: Marine_Bio/Stud Sail Scuba Seamanship. **Features:** Photog Adventure_Travel Aquatics Boating Community_Serv Exploration Hiking Kayak Sea_Cruises Swim Volleyball Water-skiing Watersports.
Fees 2012: Res $4250-5990 (+airfare), 2-3 wks.
Housing: Cabins. Avg per room/unit: 10. **Swimming:** Ocean.
Est 2000. Inc. **Ses:** 21. **Wks/ses:** 2-3. Operates June-Aug.

SeaTrek's two- and three-week voyages combine marine science, sail training, scuba instruction and watersports. Cruises take place aboard yachts in the waters of the British Virgin Islands. Boys and girls select a trek based upon their interests, and no prior knowledge of marine science or sailing experience is necessary. Campers spend some time hiking and exploring the islands themselves.

SEAWORLD AND BUSCH GARDENS ADVENTURE CAMPS
Res — Coed Ages 10-18; Day — Coed 5-12

Orlando, FL 32821. 7007 SeaWorld Dr. Toll-free: 866-968-6226.
www.seaworld.com
Grades 5-PG. Adm: FCFS. **Appl due:** Rolling.
Focus: Wildlife_Stud. **Features:** Marine_Bio/StudVeterinary_Med Zoology Outdoor_Ed.
Fees 2011: Res $995-1495, 1 wk. Day $240-245, 1 wk.
Housing: Dorms Hotels.
Ses: 25. **Wks/ses:** 1. Operates June-Aug. ACA.

Residential and day Adventure Camps operate at Busch Gardens in Tampa Bay and SeaWorld in Orlando. Boys and girls with an interest in pursuing a science career care for, interact with and study various animals during the course of the session. Alongside veterinarians, trainers and other animal-care experts, campers engage in hands-on interactions with such animals as dolphins, giraffes, penguins and great apes. Similar programs run at SeaWorld locations in San Antonio, TX (see separate listing), and San Diego, CA.

SEAWORLD SAN ANTONIO ADVENTURE CAMPS
Res — Coed Ages 10-22; Day — Coed 5-12

San Antonio, TX 78251. 10500 Sea World Dr. Toll-free: 800-700-7786.
Fax: 210-523-3898.
www.seaworld.org/camps   E-mail: swsaeducation@seaworld.com
Brittany Gandin, Dir.
Grades 5-Col. Adm: FCFS. **Appl due:** Rolling. **Enr cap:** 100. **Staff:** Couns 11. Res 14.
Type of instruction: Enrich.
Focus: Wildlife_Stud. **Features:** Marine_Bio/Stud Swim.
Fees 2011: Res $850-1100, 1 wk. Day $185-225, 1 wk.
Housing: Dorms. **Swimming:** Lake Pool.

Est 1992. Inc. **Ses:** 11. **Wks/ses:** 1. Operates June-Aug.

SeaWorld San Antonio conducts various residential and day camps that offer a hands-on look at the park's killer whales, penguins and sharks. Working alongside zoological team members, participants in Career Camp and Advanced Career Camp monitor animal behavior, prepare food, and learn about the fields of veterinary science, animal training and conservation. Similar programs run at SeaWorld locations in Orlando, FL (see separate listing), and San Diego, CA.

SHP SUMMER BICYCLING ADVENTURES
Res — Coed Ages 12-18

Conway, MA 01341. 1356 Ashfield Rd, PO Box 419. Tel: 413-369-4275.
Contact (Winter): 305 Hulmeville Ave, Langhorne, PA 19047. Tel: 215-757-2427.
Year-round Toll-free: 800-343-6132, Fax: 215-891-9917.
www.bicycletrips.com   E-mail: shpbike@gmail.com
Steve Galazin & Nadra Galazin, Dirs.
Grades 7-12. Adm: FCFS. **Appl due:** Rolling. **Enr:** 8-12. **Staff:** Admin 4. Couns 50.
Intl program focus: Culture. **Travel:** CA DC KY MA ME NH NY OH OR PA VT WA Canada Europe.
Focus: Bicycle_Tours. **Features:** Adventure_Travel Canoe Exploration Hiking Kayak Mtn_ Biking White-water_Raft Swim.
Fees 2011: Res $1255-5495 (+$70-435), 2-7 wks.
Housing: Tents. **Swimming:** Lake Pond Ocean Pool.
Est 1970. Inc. **Spons:** Student Hosteling Program. **Ses:** 40. **Wks/ses:** 2-7. Operates June-Aug.

Bicycling groups travel through the countryside of Europe, Canada and the Continental US. Campers choose from easy, moderate and challenging cycling tours and mountain biking trips. Participants spend overnights at campgrounds and hostels.

SMOKY MOUNTAIN ADVENTURE CAMP
Res — Coed Ages 8-18

Cosby, TN 37722. 246 Incline Way. Tel: 770-427-6054, 866-876-2267.
www.smacamp.com   E-mail: info@smacamp.com
George Spier, Dir.
Adm: FCFS. **Admitted:** 100%. **Appl due:** Rolling. **Enr:** 40. **Enr cap:** 40. **Staff:** Admin 3. Couns 5. Res 2.
Focus: Wilderness_Camp. **Features:** Aquatics Archery Canoe Caving Climbing_Wall Hiking Kayak Mtn_Biking Outdoor_Ed Rappelling Riding Rock_Climb Ropes_Crse White-water_Raft Swim.
Fees 2012: Res $695-2495, 1-4 wks.
Housing: Cabins Tents. Avg per room/unit: 8. **Swimming:** River.
Est 2002. Ses: 8. **Wks/ses:** 1-4. Operates June-July.

Smoky Mountain offers a variety of adventure activities for those with a strong interest in the outdoors. Backcountry hiking, rafting, biking, challenge courses, horseback riding and rock climbing are among the available pursuits. Campers may also embark upon one- to four-night canoeing and backpacking trips.

SPACE CAMP AND AVIATION CHALLENGE
Res — Coed Ages 9-18; Day — Coed 7-11

Huntsville, AL 35805. US Space & Rocket Ctr, 1 Tranquility Base. Tel: 256-837-3400, 800-637-7223. Fax: 256-837-6137.

www.spacecamp.com   E-mail: info@spacecamp.com
Grades 4-12. Adm: FCFS. **Appl due:** Rolling. **Enr:** 1100.
Avg class size: 16. College credit.
Focus: Aviation/Aero. **Features:** Archery Canoe Climbing_Wall Kayak Rappelling Ropes_ Crse Scuba Survival_Trng Swim.
Fees 2009: Res $799-1299, 1 wk. Day $275-1125, 1-5 wks. Aid 2007: $55,000.
Housing: Dorms. **Swimming:** Lake.
Est 1982. Nonprofit. **Ses:** 52. **Wks/ses:** 1. Operates Year-round.

Space Camp programs emphasize astronaut training, simulated space shuttle missions and space lab experiments, while Aviation Challenge programs focus on simulated fighter pilot training and land and water survival training. Youngsters tour the US Space & Rocket Center Museum.

SPACE FLIGHT ADVENTURE CAMP
Res — Coed Ages 11-15

Wallops Island, VA 23337. 7290 Enterprise St. Tel: 757-824-3800, 866-757-7223.
Fax: 757-824-6207.
www.vaspaceflightacademy.org   E-mail: ed@vaspaceflightacademy.org
Robert W. Marshall, Exec Dir.
Grades 6-10. Adm: FCFS. **Appl due:** Rolling. **Enr:** 28. **Enr cap:** 34. **Staff:** Admin 2. Couns 10.
Focus: Aviation/Aero.
Fees 2012: Res $795 (+$40), 1 wk.
Housing: Lodges. Avg per room/unit: 12.
Est 1998. Nonprofit. **Spons:** Virginia Space Flight Academy. **Ses:** 7. **Wks/ses:** 1. Operates June-Aug.

Located at a working NASA flight facility, this camp offers firsthand experience for students interested in the science and the engineering of rockets and space flight. Campers build model rockets, use computer flight simulators and engineer a simulated rocket launch, while also touring all of the NASA, NOAA and US Navy facilities.

TALL SHIP ADVENTURES SUMMER PROGRAM
Res — Coed Ages 13-18

Toronto, M5T 2C7 Ontario, Canada. 215 Spadina Ave, Ste 413. Tel: 416-596-7117.
Fax: 416-596-7117.
www.torontobrigantine.org   E-mail: office@torontobrigantine.org
Adm: FCFS.
Focus: Sail Seamanship.
Fees 2011: Res Can$650-1680, 1-2 wks.
Est 1962. **Spons:** Toronto Brigantine. **Ses:** 7. **Wks/ses:** 1-2. Operates June-Sept.

Participants in this nonprofit program learn sailing procedures and operations aboard two brigantines (tall ships) and two sloops on the Great Lakes. Each crew learns about knots, safety procedures and rigging; shares in watch duties; and partakes of activities, contests, evening entertainment and shore leaves. No prior sailing experience is necessary, but applicants should be physically fit and competent swimmers.

TALL SHIP SUMMER SAILING
Res — Coed Ages 10-18

Claremont, CA 91711. PO Box 1360. Tel: 909-625-6194. Fax: 909-625-7305.

www.guideddiscoveries.org/tallshipsummersailing.html
E-mail: registrar@guideddiscoveries.org
Adm: FCFS. **Appl due:** Rolling.
Focus: Sail.
Fees 2012: Res $1495-3900, 1-3 wks.
Spons: Ballibay Camps. **Ses:** 5. **Wks/ses:** 1-3. Operates June-Aug.

Program participants choose from seven-, 13- and 20-day sailing sessions that focus on sail training, marine science and island exploration. Aboard a large sailing vessel, campers receive instruction in sailing from a professional crew that gradually shifts responsibility for running the ship to the young sailors. Such activities as climbing aloft, steering, standing watch and cleaning the ship are integral to the program. Other pursuits include marine science lessons, snorkeling and diving in kelp forests, boogie boarding at remote beaches and kayaking in the Channel Islands.   **See Also Page 26**

TAMARACK FARM
Res — Coed Ages 15-17

Plymouth, VT 05056. c/o Farm & Wilderness Foundation, 263 Farm & Wilderness Rd.
   Tel: 802-422-3761. Fax: 802-422-8660.
www.farmandwilderness.org   E-mail: info@farmandwilderness.org
Tom Barrup, Dir.
Adm: FCFS. **Appl due:** Rolling. **Enr cap:** 68.
Focus: Community_Serv Farm Work. **Features:** Crafts Drama Music Canoe Climbing_ Wall Conservation Cooking Exploration Hiking Outdoor_Ed Rock_Climb Ropes_Crse Wilderness_Camp Wilderness_Canoe Woodcraft Swim Ultimate_Frisbee.
Fees 2011: Res $7100, 7 wks. Aid (Merit & Need).
Housing: Cabins. Avg per room/unit: 8. **Swimming:** Lake.
Est 1951. Nonprofit. **Spons:** Farm and Wilderness Foundation. **Ses:** 1. **Wks/ses:** 7. Operates June-Aug. ACA.

Guided by an experienced staff and centering around community building, cooperative work projects and community service, the program delegates responsibilities to campers within the community. Participants learn to build cabins, milk cows, pick scarlet runner beans, lay a stone walk, shingle a roof and pour a concrete floor. Work projects are often service oriented: Boys and girls may build a play structure for a local women's shelter or help preserve wildlife habitats. Many leisure-time recreational activities are available.

TANAGER LODGE
Res — Coed Ages 7-14

Merrill, NY 12955. 85 Youngs Rd. Tel: 518-425-3386.
Contact (Oct-May): 602 Park Ave, Greensboro, NC 27405. Tel: 336-389-9716.
www.tanagerlodge.com   E-mail: tanagerlodge@yahoo.com
Ali Schultheis & Tad Welch, Dirs.
Grades 2-8. Adm: FCFS. **Appl due:** Rolling. **Enr:** 48. **Staff:** Admin 2. Couns 10. Res 20.
Focus: Wilderness_Camp. **Features:** Crafts Archery Boating Canoe Conservation Fishing Hiking Kayak Mtn_Trips Rock_Climb Sail Wilderness_Canoe Woodcraft Swim.
Fees 2011: Res $4400 (+$50), 6 wks.
Housing: Tents. Avg per room/unit: 4. **Swimming:** Lake.
Est 1925. Inc. **Ses:** 1. **Wks/ses:** 6. Operates July-Aug.

Located on Upper Chateaugay Lake in the Adirondacks, Tanager Lodge is a small, noncompetitive wilderness camp that emphasizes individual growth and appreciation of the natural world. Activities include canoeing, swimming, hiking and camping trips. In addition to weekly day trips, campers embark on one three- or four-day trek during their stay.

TASC CANADIAN WILDERNESS FISHING CAMPS
Res — Boys Ages 10-17

Gogama, Ontario, Canada.
Contact (Year-round): 5439 Countryside Cir, Jeffersonton, VA 22724.
Tel: 540-937-8272, 800-296-8272. Fax: 540-937-8272.
www.tascforteens.com E-mail: tasc@peoplepc.com
Paul Oesterriecher, Dir.
Grades 5-12. Adm: Somewhat selective. Admitted: 90%. **Appl due:** Rolling. **Enr:** 16. **Enr cap:** 2010. **Staff:** Admin 2. Couns 8.
Focus: Fishing. **Features:** Adventure_Travel Boating Outdoor_Ed.
Fees 2011: Res $2995 (+$100), 2 wks.
Housing: Cabins. Avg per room/unit: 16.
Est 1976. Inc. Ses: 2. Wks/ses: 2. Operates June-Aug.

Campers fish onboard motorboats for northern pike, perch and walleye on Mattagami Lake in northern Ontario. A relaxed schedule allows campers to choose their fishing time. Boys of all ability levels may enroll, and personal instruction is readily available. Staff members also instruct campers in basic survival skills and wilderness appreciation.

TETON VALLEY RANCH CAMP
Res — Coord Ages 11-15

Jackson, WY 83001. PO Box 3968. Tel: 307-733-2958. Fax: 307-733-0258.
www.tvrcamp.org E-mail: mailbag@tvrcamp.org
Tom Holland, Exec Dir.
Adm: FCFS. **Appl due:** Rolling. **Enr:** 130. **Enr cap:** 130. **Staff:** Admin 6.
Focus: Riding Wilderness_Camp. **Features:** Crafts Painting Photog Adventure_Travel Archery Community_Serv Conservation Exploration Fishing Hiking Mtn_Trips Outdoor_ Ed Pack_Train Ranch Riflery Survival_Trng Swim.
Fees 2012: Res $5400 (+$150), 4 wks. Aid (Need).
Housing: Cabins Tents. Avg per room/unit: 11. **Swimming:** Pond River.
Est 1939. Nonprofit. Ses: 2. Wks/ses: 4. Operates June-Aug. ACA.

TVRC combines riding and ranch activities with various in-camp pursuits. Campers select a morning activity and an afternoon activity each day, or sign up for a half- or full-day ride or hike. Multi-day trips and pack trips, typically lasting from three to five days, enable boys and girls to further develop their outdoor skills. Boys and girls attend separate sessions.

360° STUDENT TRAVEL COMMUNITY SERVICE
Res — Coed Ages 14-18

Mamaroneck, NY 10543. 154 E Boston Post Rd. Tel: 914-835-0699, 800-767-0227.
Fax: 914-835-0798.
www.360studenttravel.com E-mail: info@360studenttravel.com
Ira Solomon, Dir.
Grades 9-12. Adm: FCFS. **Enr:** 12-21. **Enr cap:** 12-21.
Intl program focus: Culture. **Locations:** AK CA HI Africa Mexico/Central_America South_ America.
Focus: Community_Serv. **Features:** Adventure_Travel Canoe Caving Exploration Hiking Kayak Mtn_Biking Outdoor_Ed Peace/Cross-cultural Riding Rock_Climb Ropes_Crse Sail Scuba White-water_Raft Swim Water-skiing.
Fees 2011: Res $2899-6799 (+airfare), 1½-4 wks.
Housing: Cabins Dorms Houses. **Swimming:** Ocean Pool River.
Est 1982. Inc. Ses: 19. Wks/ses: 1½-4. Operates June-Aug.

Participants in this service and travel program perform six to eight hours daily of physical labor on service days. Program administrators partner with such service organizations as

Habitat for Humanity, Boys and Girls Club, and the Food Bank of Alaska in developing the program. Boys and girls choose from domestic programs in several states and international options in Costa Rica, Ecuador, Africa and Peru.

360° STUDENT TRAVEL GLOBAL ADVENTURES
Res — Coed Ages 13-19

Mamaroneck, NY 10543. 154 E Boston Post Rd. Tel: 914-835-0699, 800-767-0227. Fax: 914-835-0798.
www.360studenttravel.com   E-mail: info@360studenttravel.com
Mark Segal, Dir.
Grades 8-PG. Adm: FCFS. **Appl due:** Rolling. **Enr:** 10-20.
Intl program focus: Culture. **Travel:** Asia Canada Europe Mexico/Central_America.
Focus: Adventure_Travel Outdoor_Ed. **Features:** Boating Canoe Caving Climbing_Wall Community_Serv Cruises Exploration Hiking Kayak Mountaineering Mtn_Biking Mtn_ Trips Rappelling Riding Rock_Climb Ropes_Crse Sail Scuba Survival_Trng Whitewater_Raft Baseball Basketball Soccer Softball Surfing Swim Ultimate_Frisbee Volleyball Water-skiing Winter_Sports.
Fees 2011: Res $2899-7699 (+airfare), 1½-4 wks.
Housing: Dorms Hotels Lodges Tents. **Swimming:** Lake Ocean Pool.
Est 1982. Inc. **Spons:** Westcoast Connection. **Ses:** 15. **Wks/ses:** 1½-4. Operates June-Aug.

This adventure program allows participants to develop new outdoor skills under the supervision of professional guides. During the tour of western Canada, young people engage in such activities as white-water rafting, snow skiing, rock climbing, kayaking, snowboarding, mountain biking, hiking, canoeing, riding, sailing and caving. Other programs include two- and four-week backpacking treks around Europe, and a 10-day rainforest adventure in Costa Rica. No prior outdoor experience is necessary.

CAMP TRINITY ON THE BAR 717 RANCH
Res — Coed Ages 8-16

Hayfork, CA 96041. Star Rte, Box 150. Tel: 530-628-5992. Fax: 530-628-9392.
www.bar717.com   E-mail: camptrinity@bar717.com
Kent Collard & Gretchen Collard, Dirs.
Grades 3-11. Adm: FCFS. **Appl due:** Rolling. **Enr:** 120. **Staff:** Admin 3. Couns 30.
Focus: Wilderness_Camp. **Features:** Crafts Music Theater Aquatics Archery Conservation Farm Hiking Mountaineering Mtn_Trips Pack_Train Riding Ropes_Crse Work Working_Cattle_Ranch Swim.
Fees 2012: Res $2420-3510 (+$125-300), 2-3 wks.
Housing: Cabins. **Swimming:** River.
Est 1930. Inc. **Ses:** 3. **Wks/ses:** 2-3. Operates June-Aug.

At Camp Trinity, children engage in horsemanship, mountain ranch living, camping and backpacking, homesteading and animal husbandry. Other offerings include cooking and baking, practical arts, gardening, ranch projects, a nature program, music and dance, arts and crafts, pottery and swimming.

CAMP UNALAYEE
Res — Coed Ages 10-17

Trinity Alps Wilderness, CA.
Contact (Year-round): 3921 E Bayshore Rd, Palo Alto, CA 94303. Tel: 650-969-6313, 866-805-6901. Fax: 650-962-8234.
www.unalayee.org   E-mail: gocampu@gmail.com

Lowell Fitch II, Dir.
Adm: FCFS. **Appl due:** Rolling. **Enr:** 75. **Staff:** Admin 8. Couns 25.
Focus: Mountaineering Wilderness_Camp. **Features:** Crafts Drama Music Archery Canoe Climbing_Wall Cooking Fishing Hiking Rappelling Rock_Climb Survival_Trng Basketball Swim Volleyball.
Fees 2012: Res $1100-1775, 1-2 wks. Aid avail.
Housing: Tents. Avg per room/unit: 10. **Swimming:** Lake.
Est 1949. Nonprofit. **Ses:** 3. **Wks/ses:** 1-2. Operates June-Aug. ACA.

All campers at Unalayee, which is located in the Trinity Alps Wilderness Area of northern California, participate in two backpacking excursions. An additional program allows interested boys and girls to hike trails and learn wilderness skills. Counselors and campers alike take part in meal preparation, shelter building and other activities designed to encourage responsibility and cooperation. A CIT program enrolls 16- and 17-year-olds.

UNIVERSITY OF MAINE
4-H CAMP AND LEARNING CENTER AT BRYANT POND
SUMMER CAMP PROGRAMS
Res — Coed Ages 8-18; Day — Coed 10-13

Bryant Pond, ME 04219. PO Box 188. Tel: 207-665-2068. Fax: 207-665-2768.
http://umaine.edu/bryantpond/summer-camp/ E-mail: bp@umext.maine.edu
Ryder Scott, Prgm Dir.
Adm: FCFS. **Appl due:** Rolling. **Staff:** Admin 5. Couns 30.
Focus: Conservation Outdoor_Ed Wilderness_Camp. **Features:** Environ_Sci Crafts Film-making Media Painting Photog Aquatics Archery Boating Canoe Community_Serv Exploration Farm Fishing Hiking Kayak Mountaineering Mtn_Trips Riflery Ropes_Crse Survival_Trng Wilderness_Canoe Woodcraft Swim.
Fees 2011: Res $595-2875, 1-4 wks. Day $175, 1 wk.
Housing: Cabins Dorms Tents. **Swimming:** Lake.
Est 1956. Nonprofit. **Ses:** 10. **Wks/ses:** 1-4. Operates June-Aug.

Bryant Pond summer programs follow three paths—woodcraft skills, naturalist skills and primitive skills—as students progress from introductory through advanced skill levels. Each path provides a different manner of demonstrating and reinforcing one's connection to the natural world. Boys and girls also may select from various special-interest youth development and outdoor adventure offerings.

UNIVERSITY OF NORTH DAKOTA
INTERNATIONAL AEROSPACE CAMP
Res — Coed Ages 16-17

Grand Forks, ND 58202. UND Aerospace, Student Services, 3980 Campus Rd, Stop 9007. Tel: 701-777-4934, 800-258-1525. Fax: 701-777-6165.
www.aero.und.edu E-mail: polovitz@aero.und.edu
Ken Polovitz, Dir.
Grades 11-12. Adm: FCFS. Admitted: 100%. **Appl due:** Jan. **Enr:** 30. **Enr cap:** 30. **Fac 5. Staff:** Admin 10. Couns 3.
Type of instruction: Adv.
Focus: Aviation/Aero.
Fees 2012: Res $1150, 1 wk.
Housing: Dorms. Avg per room/unit: 2.
Est 1983. Nonprofit. **Ses:** 2. **Wks/ses:** 1. Operates June-July.

The program offers participants hands-on experience in flying, aerobatics aircraft, trainer aircraft and simulators. During the weeklong session, UND also provides a comprehensive look at career opportunities in the aerospace industry.

VISIONS SERVICE ADVENTURES
Res — Coed Ages 11-18

Bozeman, MT 59715. 321 E Main St, Ste 426. Tel: 406-551-4423, 800-813-9283.
Fax: 406-551-1525.
www.visionsserviceadventures.com   E-mail: info@visionsserviceadventures.com
Katherine Dayton, Exec Dir.
Grades 6-PG. Adm: FCFS. Appl due: Rolling. Enr: 16-25. Enr cap: 25. Staff: Admin 6.
Couns 70.
Intl program focus: Lang Culture. Locations: AK MI MT Africa Asia Caribbean Mexico/
Central_America South_America.
Focus: Fr Span Community_Serv Work. Features: Adventure_Travel Aquatics Boating
Climbing_Wall Conservation Cooking Exploration Fishing Hiking Kayak Mountaineer-
ing Mtn_Trips Peace/Cross-cultural Rappelling Riding Rock_Climb Sail Scuba Wilder-
ness_Camp Swim.
Fees 2012: Res $4000-5500 (+airfare), 3-4 wks. Aid 2010 (Need): $62,500.
Housing: Dorms. Swimming: Lake Ocean Pool River.
Est 1989. Inc. Ses: 18. Wks/ses: 3-4. Operates June-Aug.

VISIONS combines construction-based and other community service, cross-cultural living
and learning, and outdoor exploration; certain programs also feature language immersion in
French or Spanish. Small service groups (with a maximum of 25 students and six staff) live
and work together in communities in native villages of Alaska and Montana, the Mississippi
Gulf Coast, Peru, Ecuador, Costa Rica, Nicaragua, the British Virgin Islands, Dominica, the
Dominican Republic, Guadeloupe, Vietnam and Ghana. Participants in language immersion
programs must have completed two years of foreign language study.

VOLUNTEERS FOR PEACE
Res — Coed Ages 15 and up

Burlington, VT 05401. 7 Kilburn St, Ste 316. Tel: 802-540-3060. Fax: 802-540-3061.
www.vfp.org   E-mail: info@vfp.org
Meg Brook, Dir.
Adm: FCFS. Appl due: Rolling. Staff: Admin 3.
Intl program focus: Lang Culture. Locations: AK CA DC HI IL IN MD ME MI MO ND NH
NY OH PA TX VT WI WV Africa Asia Australia/New_Zealand Canada Caribbean Europe
Mexico/Central_America Middle_East South_America. Home stays avail.
Focus: Community_Serv Work. Features: Archaeol Ecol Environ_Sci Govt Marine_Bio/
Stud Crafts Dance Filmmaking Fine_Arts Media Music Photog Theater Adventure_
Travel Bicycle_Tours Conservation Cooking Exploration Hiking Peace/Cross-cultural
Social_Servs Wilderness_Camp Wilderness_Canoe Yoga Soccer.
Fees 2011: Res $300-500, 2-3 wks. Aid 2010 (Need): $4000.
Housing: Cabins Dorms Houses Lodges Tents Tepees.
Est 1981. Nonprofit. Ses: 2500. Wks/ses: 2-3. Operates Year-round.

VFP places volunteers in more than 2500 programs in approximately 90 countries.
Participants work with inhabitants of the host country on service projects. Roughly 50 domestic
programs are also available.

W. ALTON JONES ENVIRONMENTAL EDUCATION CENTER
Res — Coed Ages 9-17; Day — Coed 5-15

West Greenwich, RI 02817. Univ of Rhode Island, 401 Victory Hwy. Tel: 401-397-3304.
Fax: 401-397-3293.
www.altonjonescamp.org   E-mail: altonjones@uri.edu
John Jacques, Mgr.

Grades K-12. Adm: FCFS. **Appl due:** Rolling. **Enr:** 200. **Enr cap:** 200. **Staff:** Admin 4. Couns 70.
Focus: Field_Ecol Outdoor_Ed Wildlife_Stud. **Features:** Astron Ecol Environ_Sci Marine_ Bio/Stud Sci Adventure_Travel Aquatics Canoe Conservation Exploration Farm Hiking Kayak Mountaineering Mtn_Trips Rappelling Rock_Climb Survival_Trng Wilderness_ Camp Wilderness_Canoe Swim.
Fees 2011: Res $650-1625, 1-2 wks. Day $270-355 (+$35), 1 wk. Aid (Need).
Housing: Cabins. Avg per room/unit: 16. **Swimming:** Lake Ocean.
Est 1964. Nonprofit. **Spons:** University of Rhode Island. **Ses:** 7. **Wks/ses:** 1-2. Operates June-Aug.

W. Alton Jones' programs for children include farming, forest ecology, marine ecology, outdoor skills and wetland ecology camps. Canoeing, kayaking, rock climbing and backpacking expeditions for teens provide ecology instruction and adventure education.

CAMP WABUN
Res — Coed Ages 10-18

Temagami, P0H 1C0 Ontario, Canada. Bear Island PO. Tel: 705-237-8910.
Contact (Sept-May): 460 Jewett Rd, Hopkinton, NH 03229. Tel: 603-369-3677.
Year-round Fax: 888-287-9214.
www.wabun.com   E-mail: rpl@wabun.com
Richard P. Lewis III, Dir.
Adm: FCFS.
Focus: Wilderness_Camp Wilderness_Canoe. **Features:** Outdoor_Ed.
Housing: Cabins.
Est 1933. Ses: 3. **Wks/ses:** 3-6. Operates June-Aug.

Canadian canoe trips at the camp include fishing, swimming and running rapids. Wabun's program accommodates both novice campers and experienced canoeists with participants divided into sections based on age, grade, size and experience. Time at the base camp between trips is limited to two nights. While most campers attend for six weeks, a three-week option is available to boys and girls ages 10-12.

CAMP WAHOO
Res — Coed Ages 9-16

Cle Elum, WA 98922. 1780 Nelson Siding Rd. Tel: 509-674-9554, 888-235-0111.
Fax: 509-674-6852.
www.campwahoo.com   E-mail: info@highcountry-outfitters.com
Stacy Sutton, Dir.
Adm: FCFS. **Appl due:** Rolling. **Enr cap:** 21. **Staff:** Admin 4. Couns 10. Res 4.
Focus: Riding. **Features:** Archery Outdoor_Ed Wilderness_Camp Equestrian Swim.
Fees 2011: Res $850-1025, 1 wk.
Housing: Cabins Tents. **Swimming:** Stream.
Est 1982. Inc. **Ses:** 10. **Wks/ses:** 1. Operates June-Sept.

This wilderness horse camp offers sessions according to age and experience with such features as daily riding and handling, overnight trail rides and pack trips, outdoor camping and survival skills.

CAMP WANAPITEI
Res — Coed Ages 7-18

Temagami, P0H 2H0 Ontario, Canada. Sandy Inlet. Tel: 705-237-8830.
Fax: 705-944-5840.
Contact (Sept-June): 5 Wyndham St N, Apt 303, Guelph, N1H 4E2 Ontario, Canada.

Tel: 519-767-9714. Fax: 519-827-1701.
Year-round Toll-free: 888-637-5557.
www.wanapitei.net   E-mail: campinfo@wanapitei.net
Eoin Wood, Dir.
Grades 2-12. Adm: FCFS. Appl due: Rolling. Enr: 100. Staff: Admin 4. Couns 30.
Focus: Outdoor_Ed Wilderness_Camp. Features: Crafts Music Adventure_Travel Aquat-
ics Archery Canoe Conservation Hiking Kayak Ropes_Crse Sail Survival_Trng Wilder-
ness_Canoe Soccer Swim.
Fees 2012: Res Can$750-7755 (+Can$150), 1-4 wks.
Housing: Cabins Tents. Avg per room/unit: 8. Swimming: Lake River.
Est 1931. Inc. Ses: 29. Wks/ses: 1-8. Operates July-Aug.

This canoeing camp teaches self-reliance and leadership skills through adventure treks.
Trips range from six-day excursions through the Temagami lakes to two-month journeys along
Canada's Arctic rivers. In addition to canoeing and wilderness camping instruction, in-camp
activities include swimming, games, arts and crafts, kayaking, hiking, archery, sailing and a
low ropes course.

WILDERNESS ADVENTURE AT EAGLE LANDING
Res — Coed Ages 9-18

New Castle, VA 24127. PO Box 760. Tel: 540-864-6792, 800-782-0779.
    Fax: 540-864-6800.
www.wilderness-adventure.com   E-mail: info@wilderness-adventure.com
Patrick Boas, Dir.
Adm: FCFS. Appl due: Rolling. Enr: 200. Staff: Admin 25. Couns 20.
Intl program focus: Culture. Locations: AK PR VA WV Asia Mexico/Central_America
South_America.
Focus: Wilderness_Camp. Features: Adventure_Travel Archery Bicycle_Tours Boating
Canoe Caving Climbing_Wall Community_Serv Exploration Fishing Hiking Kayak Moun-
taineering Mtn_Biking Mtn_Trips Outdoor_Ed Peace/Cross-cultural Rappelling Rock_
Climb Ropes_Crse Sail Scuba Survival_Trng White-water_Raft Wilderness_Canoe.
Fees 2012: Res $895-3250, 1-4 wks.
Housing: Cabins Lodges Tents Tepees. Avg per room/unit: 12.
Est 1990. Ses: 15. Wks/ses: 1-4. Operates June-Aug.

With various age-appropriate programs, Wilderness Adventure operates a base camp in the
Blue Ridge Mountains and also offers adventure and travel programs in Puerto Rico, Ecuador,
Alaska and Vietnam. Boys and girls develop leadership skills and confidence as they take
part in an array of outdoor pursuits. Sessions increase in duration and level of challenge as
campers age. All programs are under the direction of trained and certified leaders and activity
specialists.

WILDERNESS EXPERIENCES UNLIMITED
Res — Coed Ages 10-17; Day — Coed 6-13

Southwick, MA 01077. 526 College Hwy. Tel: 413-569-1287. Fax: 413-569-6445.
www.weu.com   E-mail: campweu@gmail.com
T. Scott Cook, Dir.
Adm: FCFS. Appl due: Rolling. Enr: 60. Staff: Admin 2. Couns 17.
Focus: Wilderness_Camp. Features: Adventure_Travel Aquatics Bicycle_Tours Canoe
Caving Climbing_Wall Conservation Hiking Kayak Mountaineering Mtn_Biking Mtn_
Trips Outdoor_Ed Rock_Climb Ropes_Crse Scuba Swim.
Fees 2012: Res $479-989, 1-2 wks. Day $279, 1 wk.
Housing: Cabins Lodges Tents. Swimming: Lake Pool River Stream.
Est 1981. Inc. Ses: 8. Wks/ses: 1-2. Operates June-Aug.

WEU conducts various summer adventure programs. Counselors stress ecology and environmental awareness in all programs. Trips emphasize such wilderness skills as rafting, caving, backpacking, kayaking and rock climbing. Outdoor activities include hiking, canoeing, orienteering, camp craft, mountain biking and scuba diving.

WILDERNESS VENTURES
Res — Coed Ages 12-20

Jackson Hole, WY 83001. PO Box 2768. Tel: 307-733-2122, 800-533-2281. Fax: 307-739-1934.
www.wildernessventures.com   E-mail: info@wildernessventures.com
Mike Cottingham & Helen Cottingham, Dirs.
Grades 7-Col. Adm: FCFS. **Appl due:** Rolling. **Staff:** Admin 8.
Intl program focus: Culture. **Travel:** AK CA CO HI ID MA OR WA WY Australia/New_Zealand Canada Europe Mexico/Central_America South_America.
Focus: Wilderness_Camp. **Features:** Adventure_Travel Bicycle_Tours Canoe Community_Serv Hiking Kayak Mountaineering Mtn_Biking Mtn_Trips Rock_Climb Sail Scuba Wilderness_Canoe.
Fees 2009: Res $2890-7290, 2-6 wks. Aid 2011 (Need): $75,000.
Est 1973. Inc. **Wks/ses:** 2-6. Operates June-Aug.

Wilderness Ventures conducts wilderness travel expeditions to the Pacific Northwest, the northern Rockies, Alaska and several international locations. Activities include backpacking, rock climbing, white-water rafting, kayaking, mountaineering, canoeing and mountain biking.

WILDWOOD
Res — Coed Ages 9-17

Rindge, NH. Tel: 603-899-5589.
Contact (Sept-May): 208 S Great Rd, Lincoln, MA 01773. Tel: 781-259-2183.
Year-round Toll-free: 866-627-2267.
www.wildwoodcamp.org   E-mail: wildwood@massaudobon.org
Bob Speare, Dir.
Grades 4-12. Adm: FCFS. **Appl due:** Rolling. **Enr:** 100. **Enr cap:** 108. **Staff:** Admin 4. Couns 24.
Focus: Outdoor_Ed. **Features:** Crafts Drama Adventure_Travel Aquatics Archery Canoe Community_Serv Conservation Exploration Fishing Hiking Kayak Mtn_Biking Mtn_Trips Ropes_Crse Sail Wilderness_Camp Wilderness_Canoe Swim.
Fees 2011: Res $920-1890 (+$25-50), 1-2 wks. Aid (Need).
Housing: Cabins Tents. Avg per room/unit: 12-24. **Swimming:** Pond.
Est 1949. Nonprofit. **Spons:** Massachusetts Audubon Society. **Ses:** 10. **Wks/ses:** 1-2. Operates July-Aug. ACA.

Operated by Mass Audubon on a 153-acre tract alongside Hubbard Pond, Wildwood conducts multidimensional programs focusing on active exploration of the natural world. Campers ages 9-14 examine stars and planets, plot courses and build shelters, fish, track animals, plant seeds and paint pictures. Each week, campers choose an activity and spend the week exploring one topic in depth. Teen adventure trips (ages 14-17) include brief service projects and meetings with environmental professionals. Campers entering grades 10-12 may enroll in the Leaders-In-Training Program, which consists of workshops, directed group activities, personal reflection, or participation in one- to two-week adventure trips.

WILLIWAW ADVENTURES
Res — Coed Ages 13-17

Bristol, RI 02809. 51 Greylock Rd. Toll-free: 800-585-2523.

www.williwawadventures.com   E-mail: info@williwawadventures.com
Mike Dawson, Dir.
Grades 7-12. Adm: FCFS. **Appl due:** Rolling. **Enr:** 10-12. **Staff:** Admin 1. Couns 5.
Intl program focus: Culture. **Travel:** MA ME NH OR WA Caribbean.
Focus: Outdoor_Ed Wilderness_Camp. **Features:** Adventure_Travel Aquatics Boating Canoe Community_Serv Conservation Exploration Hiking Kayak Mountaineering Mtn_Trips Sail Sea_Cruises Seamanship White-water_Raft Wilderness_Canoe Swim Watersports.
Fees 2011: Res $1150-3450, 1-4 wks. Aid (Need).
Housing: Tents. Avg per room/unit: 3. **Swimming:** Lake Pond Ocean River.
Est 1999. Inc. Ses: 9. **Wks/ses:** 1-4. Operates June-Aug.

Williwaw operates wilderness excursions to the Maine coast, the mountains and the forests of the Pacific Northwest, and the Bahamas. Experienced guides lead groups of 10 to 12 campers, all of whom share in planning and decision making. Each expedition begins with wilderness backpacking as campers hone their outdoor skills and explore the area. Depending on the session, groups then travel to various sites for kayaking, rafting, sailing or alpine hiking.

WOLF CAMP
Res — Coed Ages 9-17; Day — Coed 6-12

Snohomish, WA 98290. 1313 2nd St, Ste A. Tel: 425-248-0253.
www.wolfcamp.com   E-mail: chris@wolfcamp.com
Chris Chisholm, Dir.
Grades 1-12. Adm: FCFS. Admitted: 90%. **Appl due:** Rolling. **Enr:** 40. **Enr cap:** 40. **Staff:** Admin 2. Couns 20.
Focus: Outdoor_Ed Survival_Trng Wilderness_Camp. **Features:** Archaeol Astron Ecol Environ_Sci Geol Govt Marine_Bio/Stud Crafts Creative_Writing Fine_Arts Music Photog Adventure_Travel Aquatics Archery Bicycle_Tours Boating Canoe Caving Community_Serv Conservation Cooking Cruises Deep-sea Fishing Exploration Farm Fishing Hiking Kayak Mountaineering Mtn_Biking Mtn_Trips Paintball Peace/Cross-cultural Ranch Riding Rock_Climb Sail Sea_Cruises Seamanship Social_Servs Woodcraft Work Swim Hunting.
Fees 2012: Res $695, 1 wk. Day $300, 1 wk. Aid 2008 (Merit & Need): $3000.
Housing: Houses Tents Tepees. Avg per room/unit: 5. **Swimming:** Lake Ocean River Stream.
Est 1997. Inc. Ses: 12. **Wks/ses:** 1. Operates June-Aug.

Each weeklong session of Wolf Camp focuses on one aspect of earth skills education. Wildlife tracking, geology, anthropology, oceanography, herbal studies, primitive living skills, permaculture, pioneering, wilderness survival and skills of the ancient scout are points of program emphasis. Applicants for certain sessions must have previous experience in the subject area.

WORLD HORIZONS INTERNATIONAL
Res — Coed Ages 14-18

Bethlehem, CT 06751. PO Box 662. Tel: 203-707-0565. **Fax:** 888-241-5328.
www.worldhorizons.com   E-mail: worldhorizons01@gmail.com
Stuart L. Rabinowitz, Dir.
Grades 9-12. Adm: FCFS. **Appl due:** Rolling. **Enr cap:** 12. **Staff:** Admin 3. Couns 2.
Intl program focus: Lang Culture. **Travel:** LA UT Asia Caribbean Europe Mexico/Central_America Middle_East South_America.
Focus: Community_Serv Peace/Cross-cultural. **Features:** Lang Photog Adventure_Travel Conservation Hiking Social_Servs Yoga Snorkeling.
Fees 2011: Res $2650-5750 (+$300), 2-4 wks. Aid 2011 (Need): $12,000.
Housing: Apartments Dorms Hotels Houses.

Est 1987. Inc. Ses: 11. **Wks/ses:** 2-4. Operates June-Aug.

Students choose from international locations in Fiji, Central America, South America, Iceland, Israel, Italy, England and Dominica—as well as the domestic destinations of New Orleans, LA, and Utah—where they work in groups of eight to 12 with local residents to perform group community projects. At some locations, participants spend part of each day on an individual internship. Boys and girls assist with evening meal preparation on a rotating basis. Participants decide as a group which recreational activities they will pursue during weekends. World Horizons also offers a photography tour of England and Iceland that incorporates some community service.

Y O RANCH ADVENTURE CAMP
Res — Coed Ages 9-17

Mountain Home, TX 78058. 1736 Y O Ranch Rd NW. Tel: 830-640-3220, 866-439-2527. Fax: 830-640-3348.
www.yoadventurecamp.com   **E-mail:** info@yoadventurecamp.com
Matthew Krueger, Dir.
Grades 4-11. Adm: FCFS. **Appl due:** Rolling. **Enr:** 20. **Enr cap:** 25. **Staff:** Admin 3. Couns 10.
Focus: Outdoor_Ed Wilderness_Camp. **Features:** Crafts Archery Climbing_Wall Conservation Hiking Ranch Riding Riflery Ropes_Crse Survival_Trng Working_Cattle_Ranch Equestrian Swim.
Fees 2011: Res $945-3500 (+$45), 1-2 wks.
Housing: Cabins. **Swimming:** Pool.
Est 1977. Inc. Ses: 10. **Wks/ses:** 1-2. Operates June-Aug.

Campers choose from an array of programs conducted on the 40,000-acre ranch. Cowboy camp teaches participants grooming, saddling and horse safety. Campers learn basic pole patterns and engage in roping, riding and cattle work; they also ride out on the ranch for an overnight. Hunting camp teaches fundamental outdoor skills such as archery and shotgunning, and campers also learn the importance of hunting, conservation and wildlife management. Other aspects of the program include survival skills training, camp outs and wildlife projects. Advanced sessions accommodate experienced campers.

TRAVEL
PROGRAMS

Travel programs are arranged alphabetically by name. An index beginning on page 458 lists the world regions to which participants travel. Programs offering a family session are indicated by "FAM" at the end of the age range in the index.

INDEX BY DESTINATION

INTERNATIONAL REGIONS

CANADA

CARIBBEAN ISLANDS

EUROPE

MIDDLE EAST

MIDDLE EAST *(CONT.)*

SOUTH AMERICA

USA

Travel Programs

ADVENTURE IRELAND
Res — Coed Ages 12-17

Bundoran, Donegal, Ireland. c/o Donegal Adventure Centre, Bayview Ave. Tel: 353-71-98-42418. Fax: 353-71-98-42429.
www.adventure-ireland.com   E-mail: info@adventure-ireland.com
Niamh Hamill, Dir.
Adm: FCFS. **Appl due:** Rolling. **Staff:** Admin 8. Couns 18.
Intl program focus: Culture. **Travel:** Europe.
Focus: Surfing. **Features:** Adventure_Travel Aquatics Boating Canoe Climbing_Wall Cruises Fishing Hiking Kayak Mountaineering Mtn_Trips Rappelling Riding Rock_Climb Ropes_Crse Sea_Cruises Basketball Equestrian Golf Soccer Swim Tennis Volleyball Watersports.
Fees 2012: Res €1400-2500 (+airfare), 2-3 wks.
Housing: Dorms Houses. **Swimming:** Ocean Pool.
Est 1996. Inc. **Ses:** 2. **Wks/ses:** 2-3. Operates July.

Enrolling predominantly Americans and Canadians, Adventure Ireland offers programs combines cultural immersion with adventure pursuits. Campers learn about Irish culture (including traditional and modern Irish music), embark on sightseeing trips throughout the northwestern part of the country, visit nearby historical sites and engage in an active sports program. Surf and activities camps offer surfing instruction and cultural activities.

ADVENTURES CROSS-COUNTRY
Res — Coed Ages 13-18

Mill Valley, CA 94941. 242 Redwood Hwy. Tel: 415-332-5075, 800-767-2722. Fax: 415-332-2130.
www.adventurescrosscountry.com   E-mail: info@adventurescrosscountry.com
Ellery Fink, Prgm Dir.
Grades 7-12. Adm: FCFS. **Appl due:** Rolling. **Staff:** Admin 10. Couns 90.
Intl program focus: Lang Culture. **Travel:** AK CA CO HI UT Africa Asia Australia/New_Zealand Canada Caribbean Europe Mexico/Central_America Middle_East South_America. Home stays avail.
Focus: Adventure_Travel Community_Serv. **Features:** Aquatics Boating Conservation Exploration Hiking Kayak Mountaineering Mtn_Trips Outdoor_Ed Peace/Cross-cultural Rappelling Rock_Climb Ropes_Crse Sail Scuba White-water_Raft Wilderness_Camp Surfing Swim Watersports.
Fees 2012: Res $2795-6295 (+$100-250), 2-5 wks. Aid (Need).
Housing: Cabins Dorms Hotels Lodges Tents. Avg per room/unit: 3. **Swimming:** Lake Ocean Pool River Stream.
Est 1983. Inc. **Ses:** 25. **Wks/ses:** 2-5. Operates June-Aug.

ARCC offers domestic and international programs in a variety of outdoor settings throughout the world. Participants choose from programs focusing on community service, languages (French or Spanish) or multi-sport activities. Programs typically combine cultural immersion, leadership opportunities and adventure.

AMERICAN TRAILS WEST
Res — Coed Ages 12-17

Great Neck, NY 11021. 92 Middle Neck Rd. Tel: 516-487-2800, 800-645-6260. Fax: 516-487-2855.

www.atwteentours.com   E-mail: info@atwteentours.com
Howard Fox, Pres.
Grades 7-12. Adm: FCFS. **Appl due:** Rolling. **Enr:** 43.
Intl program focus: Culture. **Travel:** AK AZ CA CO FL GA HI MA MT NM NY PA SC SD UT VA WA WY Canada Europe.
Features: Hiking Mtn_Biking White-water_Raft Swim Water-skiing.
Fees 2012: Res $2595-10,495, 2-5 wks.
Housing: Dorms Hotels Tents. **Swimming:** Lake Ocean Pool.
Est 1965. Inc. **Ses:** 22. **Wks/ses:** 2-5. Operates June-Aug.

Diversified itineraries give participants a comprehensive view of the Continental US, Canada, Alaska, Hawaii and Europe. Trips offer accommodations of camping, college dorms, hotels or a combination thereof. Participants are grouped by age, and ATW maintains a favorable camper-staff ratio.

BOLD EARTH TEEN ADVENTURES
Res — Coed Ages 11-18

Golden, CO 80401. 2308 Fossil Trace Dr. Tel: 303-526-0806. **Fax:** 303-531-2717.
www.boldearth.com   E-mail: info@boldearth.com
Sean Kuprevich, Dir.
Grades 7-12. Adm: FCFS. **Appl due:** Rolling. **Enr:** 12-16. **Staff:** Admin 5. Couns 70.
Avg class size: 5. **Daily hours for:** Classes 4. Rec 7.
Intl program focus: Lang Culture. **Travel:** AK AZ CA CO HI OR UT WA Africa Asia Europe Mexico/Central_America South_America. Home stays avail.
Features: Environ_Sci Crafts Adventure_Travel Bicycle_Tours Boating Canoe Caving Community_Serv Conservation Cooking Exploration Hiking Kayak Mountaineering Mtn_Biking Mtn_Trips Outdoor_Ed Rappelling Riding Rock_Climb Ropes_Crse Sail Scuba Seamanship White-water_Raft Wilderness_Camp Yoga Equestrian Surfing Swim Water-skiing Watersports Winter_Sports.
Fees 2012: Res $3088-6888 (+airfare), 2-4 wks. Aid 2011 (Need): $25,000.
Housing: Cabins Hotels Lodges Tents. Avg per room/unit: 2-4. **Swimming:** Lake Pond Ocean Pool River Stream.
Est 1976. Inc. **Ses:** 24. **Wks/ses:** 2-4. Operates June-Aug. ACA.

Offering roughly two dozen programs around the world, Bold Earth conducts adventure travel camps that focus on travel, outdoor activities, service learning and Spanish-language immersion. Domestic programs operate in Alaska, Hawaii, and the American West, Northwest and Southwest, while international destinations include Europe, Central and South America, Asia and Africa.

CLASSICAL PURSUITS
A GRAND TOUR OF ITALY
Res — Coed Ages 10-16

Toronto, M6G 2N5 Ontario, Canada. 349 Palmerston Blvd. Tel: 416-892-3580, 877-633-2555. **Fax:** 416-323-3576.
www.classicalpursuits.com   E-mail: info@classicalpursuits.com
Ann Kirkland, Pres.
Adm: FCFS. **Appl due:** Rolling. **Staff:** Admin 3. Couns 2. Res 3.
Intl program focus: Culture. **Travel:** Europe.
Features: Adventure_Travel.
Fees 2012: Res $3900 (+$1000), 1½ wks.
Housing: Hotels. Avg per room/unit: 2-4.
Est 1999. Inc. **Ses:** 1. **Wks/ses:** 1½. Operates June-July.

This unusual intergenerational program takes children and their grandparents on an experiential learning trip around Italy. After spending three days in Rome, participants tour Castellamare, Pompeii, the Amalfi Coast, Umbria, Florence and Venice. Along the way, families stay at heritage properties (many of which are run by religious orders) located in the historic center of each city. Children must be accompanied by at least one grandparent to attend.

COSTA RICA RAINFOREST OUTWARD BOUND SCHOOL SUMMER ADVENTURES
Res — Coed Ages 17 and up

San Jose, 02050 Costa Rica. PO Box 1817-2050, San Pedro. Toll-free: 800-676-2018. Fax: 866-374-2483.
www.crrobs.org   E-mail: enrollment@crrobs.org
James Rowe, Exec Dir.
Adm: FCFS. **Appl due:** Rolling. **Fac 2. Staff:** Admin 10.
Avg class size: 10. **Daily hours for:** Classes 2. Rec 6. **High school & college credit:** 3/crse, total 9.
Intl program focus: Acad Lang Culture. **Travel:** Mexico/Central_America. Home stays avail.
Focus: Adventure_Travel. **Features:** Ecol Environ_Sci Crafts Canoe Climbing_Wall Community_Serv Conservation Exploration Hiking Kayak Mountaineering Mtn_Trips Rappelling Rock_Climb Sail Scuba White-water_Raft Wilderness_Camp Wilderness_Canoe Surfing Swim Water-skiing.
Fees 2012: Res $1415-4599, 1½-4 wks.
Housing: Cabins Dorms Lodges Tents. Avg per room/unit: 2. **Swimming:** Ocean River.
Est 1997. Nonprofit. **Ses:** 18. **Wks/ses:** 1½-4. Operates June-Aug.

CRROBS offers various adventure-oriented summer programs, some of which integrate Spanish language immersion. Students learn through an interactive teaching style focusing on language supplements, verbal communication and cultural immersion. Adventure options include rainforest hikes, white-water rafting and sea kayaking, surfing at various beaches and exploration of the country's volcano region.

THE EXPERIMENT IN INTERNATIONAL LIVING
Res — Coed Ages 14-18

Brattleboro, VT 05302. 1 Kipling Rd, PO Box 676. Tel: 802-257-7751, 800-345-2929. TTY: 802-258-3388. Fax: 802-258-3428.
www.experimentinternational.org   E-mail: experiment@worldlearning.org
Tony Allen, Dir.
Grades 9-12. Adm: FCFS. **Appl due:** Rolling.
Intl program focus: Lang Culture. **Travel:** AZ NM Africa Asia Australia/New_Zealand Europe Mexico/Central_America Middle_East South_America. Home stays avail.
Features: Ecol Lang Dance Filmmaking Fine_Arts Music Painting Photog Theater Adventure_Travel Bicycle_Tours Community_Serv Conservation Cooking Exploration Hiking Mtn_Trips Peace/Cross-cultural Riding White-water_Raft Wilderness_Camp Soccer.
Fees 2012: Res $4000-7900, 3-5 wks. Aid (Need).
Housing: Dorms Hotels Houses Lodges Tents. Avg per room/unit: 2.
Est 1932. Nonprofit. **Ses:** 45. **Wks/ses:** 3-5. Operates June-Aug.

EIL conducts summer abroad programs in Africa, Asia, Australia, Europe and the Americas. All programs include home stay with a local host family and a cross-cultural orientation component. Depending on the program chosen, travel, language study, community service, peace studies, the arts or ecology may be featured. Emphasis throughout is on in-depth immersion into a foreign culture. Prior language training is a prerequisite for certain programs.

INTERNATIONAL SUMMER CAMP MONTANA
Res — Coed Ages 8-17

Crans-Montana, 3963 Switzerland. 43 Rte de La Moubra, CP 369. Tel: 41-27-486-86-86. Fax: 41-27-486-86-87.
www.campmontana.ch   E-mail: info@campmontana.ch
Philippe Studer & Erwin Mathieu, Dirs.
Adm: FCFS. **Appl due:** Apr. **Enr cap:** 380. **Staff:** Admin 6. Couns 100.
Type of instruction: Enrich. **Avg class size:** 8. **Daily hours for:** Classes 1. Rec 7.
Intl program focus: Lang Culture. **Travel:** Europe.
Features: ESL Circus_Skills Crafts Creative_Writing Dance Music Theater Aquatics Archery Bicycle_Tours Climbing_Wall Conservation Hiking Mountaineering Mtn_Biking Mtn_Trips Riding Rock_Climb Sail White-water_Raft Wilderness_Camp Aerobics Baseball Basketball Cross-country Equestrian Fencing Field_Hockey Golf Gymnastics Martial_Arts Soccer Softball Swim Tennis Track Volleyball Watersports.
Fees 2012: Res SwF6400 (+SwF200-500), 3 wks.
Housing: Dorms. **Swimming:** Pool.
Est 1961. Ses: 3. **Wks/ses:** 3. Operates July-Sept.

Located in the Swiss Alps, this program is an American-style recreational camp with European traditions in sports and education. Excursions, hikes, swimming, lifesaving, tennis, horseback riding, summer skiing, gymnastics and crafts are among the camp's activities. An optional language program enables boys and girls to study English, French or Spanish as a foreign language. Native speakers conduct these lessons, which occur five times a week.

INTRAX STUDY ABROAD HIGH SCHOOL SUMMER PROGRAMS
Res — Coed Ages 15-18

San Francisco, CA 94108. 600 California St, 10th Fl. Toll-free: 800-579-1709. Fax: 415-434-5470.
www.intraxstudyabroad.com   E-mail: info@intraxstudyabroad.com
Grades 10-PG. **Adm:** FCFS. **Appl due:** Mar. **Staff:** Admin 3.
Intl program focus: Lang Culture. **Travel:** Asia Europe Mexico/Central_America. Home stays avail.
Fees 2012: Res $6295-7895, 2-4 wks. Aid (Merit & Need).
Housing: Houses.
Est 1980. Nonprofit. **Ses:** 6. **Wks/ses:** 2-4. Operates June-Aug.

Intrax' summer programs allow pupils to immerse themselves in the culture of one of the following locations: Berlin, Germany; Florence, Italy; Alajuela, Costa Rica; Geneva, Switzerland; Tokyo, Japan; or Amboise, France. Depending upon the program selected, students may have language-study options. Participants board with host families.

MACHANEH BONIM IN ISRAEL
Res — Coed Ages 15-16

New York, NY 10011. 114 W 26th St, Ste 1004. Tel: 212-255-1796. Fax: 212-929-3459.
www.habonimdror.org   E-mail: programs@habonimdror.org
Ari Brian Schwartz, Prgm Dir.
Grade 11. **Adm:** FCFS. **Appl due:** Feb. **Staff:** Admin 9. Couns 12.
Intl program focus: Culture. **Travel:** Middle_East.
Features: Ecol Govt Lang Relig_Stud Dance Media Theater Exploration Hiking Kayak Peace/Cross-cultural Rappelling Swim.
Fees 2012: Res $6450 (+$200), 5 wks.
Swimming: Lake Pond Ocean Pool.
Est 1935. Nonprofit. Orthodox Jewish. **Ses:** 1. **Wks/ses:** 5. Operates July-Aug.

Habonim Dror, the progressive Labor Zionist Youth Movement, emphasizes peer-led activities that foster Zionist identities through education about Zionism, Judaism and cooperative community building. The MBI program, for those who have completed grade 10, provides the opportunity for participants to tour the sites and cities of Israel and experience a kibbutz. The program focuses on peace building, coexistence and current events and may include such activities as hiking, kayaking and rappelling.

NFTY IN ISRAEL
Res — Coed Ages 15-18

New York, NY 10017. c/o Union for Reform Judaism, 633 3rd Ave, 7th Fl. Tel: 212-452-6517. Fax: 212-650-4199.
www.nftyisrael.org E-mail: nftytravel@urj.org
Laurence Jacobs, Coord.
Grades 10-12. Adm: FCFS. **Appl due:** Rolling. **Enr:** 500. **Staff:** Admin 5. Couns 60.
High school credit: 3. Accred: Middle States Association of Colleges and Schools.
Intl program focus: Lang Culture. **Travel:** Europe Middle_East.
Features: Archaeol Ecol Environ_Sci Geol Govt Lang Dance Music Photog Theater Adventure_Travel Aquatics Bicycle_Tours Boating Canoe Caving Climbing_Wall Community_Serv Conservation Cooking Cruises Exploration Hiking Kayak Milit_Trng Mountaineering Mtn_Biking Mtn_Trips Outdoor_Ed Peace/Cross-cultural Rappelling Rock_Climb Ropes_Crse Survival_Trng Wilderness_Camp Swim Watersports.
Fees 2012: Res $7275-9175 (+$400), 4-6 wks.
Housing: Hotels Tents. **Swimming:** Lake Ocean Pool.
Est 1964. Nonprofit. **Spons:** Union for Reform Judaism. Jewish. **Ses:** 4. **Wks/ses:** 4-6. Operates June-Aug.

NFTY conducts high school summer programs in Israel that combine touring with a special activity: camping and hiking, taking part in an archaeological dig, performing social service work or studying Hebrew. The L'Dor V'Dor program option begins with a week spent exploring European Jewish heritage in Prague, Czech Republic, and Krakow, Poland, before students arrive in Israel.

OVERLAND
Res — Coed Ages 10-18

Williamstown, MA 01267. 63 Spring St, PO Box 31. Tel: 413-458-9672. Fax: 413-458-5208.
www.overlandprograms.com E-mail: info@overlandprograms.com
Tom Costley, Dir.
Grades 5-PG. Adm: FCFS. **Appl due:** Rolling. **Enr:** 12. **Enr cap:** 12. **Fac** 3. **Staff:** Admin 15. Couns 150.
Type of instruction: Enrich. **Daily hours for:** Classes 4.
Intl program focus: Lang Culture. **Travel:** AK AL AR AZ CA CO GA HI KS MA ME MI NH NM OK OR VT WA Africa Canada Caribbean Europe Mexico/Central_America South_America. Home stays avail.
Features: Expository_Writing Creative_Writing Adventure_Travel Bicycle_Tours Boating Community_Serv Conservation Exploration Farm Hiking Kayak Mountaineering Mtn_Trips Outdoor_Ed Peace/Cross-cultural Rappelling Rock_Climb Ropes_Crse Scuba White-water_Raft Wilderness_Camp Swim.
Fees 2012: Res $1495-6995, 1-6 wks. Aid 2010 (Merit & Need): $65,000.
Housing: Apartments Dorms Tents. **Swimming:** Lake Pond Ocean Pool River.
Est 1984. Inc. **Ses:** 150. **Wks/ses:** 1-6. Operates June-Aug.

Overland provides small-group travel throughout the United States, Europe, Central and South America, and Africa. Points of emphasis for the tours include hiking, bicycling, community service work, writing and language study abroad.

PEOPLE TO PEOPLE STUDENT AMBASSADOR PROGRAM
Res — Coed Ages 11-19

Spokane, WA 99224. Dwight D Eisenhower Bldg, 1956 Ambassador Way.
Tel: 509-568-7000, 866-794-8309. Fax: 509-568-7050.
www.studentambassadors.org   E-mail: info@peopletopeople.com
Mary Eisenhower, Pres.
Grades 6-PG. Adm: Selective.
College credit: 12.
Intl program focus: Culture. **Travel:** CA CO DC FL MT Africa Asia Australia/New_Zealand Canada Europe. Home stays avail.
Features: Bus/Fin Govt Fine_Arts Canoe Climbing_Wall Community_Serv Conservation Cruises Hiking Peace/Cross-cultural Rappelling Baseball Basketball Golf Soccer Softball Swim Tennis Volleyball.
Swimming: Lake Ocean River.
Est 1963. Inc. Wks/ses: 1-3.

Student delegations gain balanced exposure to a variety of nations in a specific region and a comprehensive overview of economic, political and cultural factors through such activities as special briefings, visits to factories and schools, meetings at international organizations, attendance at cultural performances and home stays with selected families.

PROJECTS ABROAD HIGH SCHOOL SPECIALS
Res — Coed Ages 15-19

New York, NY 10018. 347 W 36th St, Ste 903. Tel: 212-244-7234, 888-839-3535.
Fax: 212-244-7236.
www.projects-abroad.org/projects/2-week-high-school-specials
E-mail: info@projects-abroad.org
Peter M. Slowe, Dir.
Grades 10-PG. Adm: FCFS. **Appl due:** Rolling. **Enr:** 5-60.
Type of instruction: Tut.
Intl program focus: Acad Lang Culture. **Travel:** Africa Asia Caribbean Europe Mexico/ Central_America South_America. Home stays avail.
Features: Archaeol Bus/Fin Environ_Sci Law Med/Healthcare Writing/Journ Music Photog Adventure_Travel Community_Serv Conservation Peace/Cross-cultural Scuba Work Soccer.
Fees 2012: Res $2045-3595 (+airfare), 2 wks.
Housing: Dorms Houses. Avg per room/unit: 2.
Est 1992. Inc. Ses: 50. **Wks/ses:** 2. Operates June-Aug.

During the summer months, Projects Abroad offers two-week programs designed to combine travel abroad with work experience or skill development. Programming blends instruction, hands-on and observational work, and weekend excursions as students immerse themselves in another culture. Each placement has a distinct focus: Topics addressed in a typical summer include childcare and community work, journalism, medicine, photography, language instruction, sports, conservation issues and veterinary medicine.

REIN TEEN TOURS
Res — Coed Ages 12-18

Wayne, NJ 07470. 30 Galesi Dr. Tel: 973-785-1113, 800-831-1313. Fax: 973-785-4268.
www.reinteentours.com   E-mail: summer@reinteentours.com
Norman Rein, Dir.
Adm: FCFS. **Appl due:** Rolling. **Staff:** Admin 20. Couns 100.
Intl program focus: Culture. **Travel:** AK AZ CA CO DC FL HI MA ME MI MN MT NC NH NV NY OH OR PA SC SD UT VA WA WI WY Canada Europe.

Features: Circus_Skills Adventure_Travel Canoe Community_Serv Cruises Exploration Ropes_Crse White-water_Raft Wilderness_Camp Basketball Swim Tennis Volleyball Watersports.
Fees 2012: Res $2495-9799, 2-6 wks.
Housing: Dorms Tents. **Swimming:** Ocean Pool.
Est 1985. Inc. Ses: 40. **Wks/ses:** 2-6. Operates June-Aug.

Rein conducts tours of varying lengths in the United States, Canada and Europe. Teens stay in hotels, campgrounds and university dorms in cities and national parks. Activities include hiking in national parks, summer snow skiing, surfing, jet boating, jeep tours and sand buggy trips and theme park visits. Boys and girls may also engage in sports and other traditional recreational camping pursuits. Two California tours focus on community service.

RUSTIC PATHWAYS SUMMER PROGRAMS
Res — Coed Ages 12 and up

Willoughby, OH 44096. PO Box 1150. Tel: 440-975-9691, 800-321-4353.
   Fax: 440-975-9694.
www.rusticpathways.com   E-mail: rustic@rusticpathways.com
David Venning, Chrm.
Grades 10-12. Adm: FCFS. **Appl due:** Rolling.
Intl program focus: Culture. **Travel:** LA Africa Asia Australia/New_Zealand Europe Mexico/Central_America South_America.
Features: Adventure_Travel Community_Serv.
Fees 2010: Res $995-4995 (+airfare), 1-3½ wks.
Est 1983. Ses: 98. **Wks/ses:** 1-3½. Operates June-Aug.

Rustic Pathways conducts summer programs focusing on language immersion, community service, adventure and life skills in the following locations: Costa Rica, Thailand, the Fiji Islands, Australia, India, New Zealand, Vietnam, China, Cambodia, Africa, Laos, Mexico and Peru. In addition, a domestic program focuses upon rebuilding in New Orleans, LA.

TRAVEL FOR TEENS
Res — Coed Ages 13-18

Wayne, PA 19087. 900 W Valley Rd, Ste 300. Tel: 484-654-1032, 888-457-4534.
   Fax: 484-654-1041.
www.travelforteens.com   E-mail: info@travelforteens.com
Patricia Maloney, Pres.
Grades 8-PG. Adm: FCFS. **Appl due:** Rolling.
Intl program focus: Lang Culture. **Travel:** Africa Asia Australia/New_Zealand Europe Mexico/Central_America.
Features: Fine_Arts Photog Adventure_Travel Bicycle_Tours Community_Serv Cooking Exploration Hiking Peace/Cross-cultural Scuba Swim.
Fees 2012: Res $2685-5685 (+airfare), 1½-3 wks.
Housing: Hotels. **Swimming:** Ocean Pool.
Est 2003. Ses: 29. **Wks/ses:** 1½-3. Operates June-Aug.

Travel for Teens offers language study, community service and cultural exploration trips at a variety of destinations. Participants in language programs attend French or Spanish classes in the morning and apply their lessons in afternoon and evening activities. Nonlanguage programs typically emphasize community service, backpacking, photography or adventure. In all programs, boys and girls immerse themselves in the host culture.

WEISSMAN TEEN TOURS
Res — Coed Ages 13-17

Ardsley, NY 10502. 517 Almena Ave. Tel: 914-693-7575, 800-942-8005. Fax: 914-693-4807.
www.weissmantours.com   E-mail: wtt@cloud9.net
Eugene Weissman & Ronee Weissman, Dirs.
Grades 8-12. Adm: Somewhat selective. Admitted: 90%. **Appl due:** Rolling. **Enr cap:** 120. **Staff:** Couns 16.
Intl program focus: Culture. **Travel:** AZ CA CO HI MT NV UT WA WY Canada Europe Mexico/Central_America.
Features: Adventure_Travel Aquatics Boating Climbing_Wall Community_Serv Cruises Hiking Kayak Mountaineering Mtn_Biking Rock_Climb Scuba Sea_Cruises White-water_Raft Aerobics Golf Swim Tennis Volleyball Water-skiing Watersports Winter_Sports Parasailing.
Fees 2012: Res $5399-11,899 (+airfare), 2-6 wks.
Housing: Hotels Lodges. Avg per room/unit: 3. **Swimming:** Lake Ocean Pool.
Est 1974. Inc. **Ses:** 9. **Wks/ses:** 3-5. Operates June-Aug.

Teen tours enable participants to explore the natural beauty of the western US (including Hawaii), Canada and Europe, while also learning more about a region's history, culture and people. Planned activities include sightseeing, a full social and athletic program, theater excursions and concerts. Domestic and Canadian tours serve students ages 13-17, while European tours accommodate those ages 14-17.

WESTCOAST CONNECTION ACTIVE TEEN TOURS
Res — Coed Ages 13-19

Mamaroneck, NY 10543. 154 E Boston Post Rd. Tel: 914-835-0699, 800-767-0227. Fax: 914-835-0798.
www.westcoastconnection.com   E-mail: info@westcoastconnection.com
Mark Segal, Dir.
Grades 8-Col. Adm: FCFS. **Appl due:** Rolling.
Intl program focus: Culture. **Travel:** AK AZ CA CO DC FL HI IL ME MI MN MI NH NV NY OR UT VA WA Asia Australia/New_Zealand Canada Europe Mexico/Central_America Middle_East South_America.
Features: Adventure_Travel Bicycle_Tours Boating Canoe Caving Community_Serv Cruises Exploration Hiking Kayak Mtn_Biking Mtn_Trips Outdoor_Ed Rappelling Riding Rock_Climb Ropes_Crse Sail Scuba Sea_Cruises White-water_Raft Baseball Basket-ball Soccer Softball Swim Tennis Ultimate_Frisbee Volleyball Water-skiing Watersports.
Fees 2011: Res $3999-9299 (+airfare), 2-6 wks.
Housing: Dorms Hotels Tents. **Swimming:** Lake Ocean Pool.
Est 1982. Inc. **Ses:** 60. **Wks/ses:** 2-6. Operates June-Aug.

Combining recreational activities, nightlife and sightseeing, this Westcoast Connection program allows participants to explore major cities and the outdoors in the US and abroad. Tours focus on California, Alaska, Hawaii, western Canada, the US East Coast and eastern Canada, North American national parks and canyon areas major European cities and Australia. Participants stay in hotels, resorts or dormitories, and some tours feature outdoor camping trips.

WHERE THERE BE DRAGONS SUMMER YOUTH PROGRAMS
Res — Coed Ages 15 and up

Boulder, CO 80301. 3200 Carbon Pl, Ste 102. Tel: 303-413-0822, 800-982-9203. Fax: 303-413-0857.
www.wheretherebedragons.com   E-mail: info@wheretherebedragons.com

Simon Hart, Dir.
Adm: FCFS. **Appl due:** Rolling. **Enr:** 12. **Enr cap:** 12. **Staff:** Admin 12. Couns 60.
Intl program focus: Lang Culture. **Travel:** Africa Asia Mexico/Central_America Middle_ East South_America. Home stays avail.
Features: Bus/Fin Expository_Writing Govt Fine_Arts Adventure_Travel Community_Serv Conservation Exploration Hiking Mountaineering Mtn_Trips Outdoor_Ed Pack_Train Peace/Cross-cultural Social_Servs Wilderness_Camp.
Fees 2011: Res $5950-7400 (+airfare), 4-6 wks. Aid (Need).
Housing: Houses Lodges Tents.
Est 1993. Inc. **Ses:** 23. **Wks/ses:** 4-6. Operates June-Aug.

Dragons offers small-group learning adventures throughout the developing world. Programs involve one or more of the following: community service, language learning, the study of religion philosophy, and home stays. Summer sessions operate in China, Tibet, North India, Laos, Thailand, Cambodia, Burma, Indonesia, Brazil, Guatemala, Peru, Bolivia, Senegal, Morocco, Rwanda and Jordan/Syria. In addition to its summer options, Dragons conducts gap-year semester programs.

WINDSOR MOUNTAIN STUDENT TRAVEL
Res — Coed Ages 13-18

Windsor, NH 03244. 1 World Way. Tel: 603-478-3166, 800-862-7760. Fax: 603-478-5260.
www.windsormountain.org   E-mail: mail@windsormountain.org
Jake Labovitz, Dir.
Grades 8-PG. Adm: FCFS. **Appl due:** Rolling. **Enr:** 103. **Fac 8. Staff:** Admin 10. Couns 75.
Type of instruction: Adv Rem_Eng Tut. **Daily hours for:** Classes 3. Rec 2. **High school & college credit:** 1.
Intl program focus: Lang Culture. **Travel:** MA ME NH PR VT Africa Asia Caribbean Mexico/Central_America. Home stays avail.
Focus: Fr Span. **Features:** ESL Writing/Journ Circus_Skills Crafts Creative_Writing Dance Filmmaking Fine_Arts Music Painting Photog Theater Adventure_Travel Aquatics Archery Boating Canoe Caving Climbing_Wall Community_Serv Conservation Cooking Exploration Fishing Hiking Kayak Mountaineering Mtn_Biking Mtn_Trips Outdoor_Ed Pack_Train Peace/Cross-cultural Ranch Rappelling Riding Rock_Climb Ropes_Crse Sail Scuba Social_Servs White-water_Raft Wilderness_Camp Wilderness_Canoe Woodcraft Work Yoga Basketball Cricket Football Gymnastics Martial_Arts Rugby Soccer Softball Swim Tennis Ultimate_Frisbee Volleyball Watersports.
Fees 2012: Res $1995-5195, 2-4 wks. Aid (Need).
Housing: Cabins Dorms Houses Lodges Tents. Avg per room/unit: 6. **Swimming:** Lake Pond River.
Est 1961. Inc. **Ses:** 12. **Wks/ses:** 2-4. Operates June-Oct.

Windsor Mountain conducts small-group educational travel adventures for students having completed grades 7-12. Destinations include the Caribbean, Peru, Puerto Rico, Ecuador, France, Puerto Rico, southern Africa, Montana, New Orleans and the West Coast. Programs focus on adventure and wilderness, language and culture, the environment, world change, community service and traveling theater.

YOUTH FOR UNDERSTANDING
INTERNATIONAL EXCHANGE SUMMER PROGRAMS
Res — Coed Ages 15-18

Bethesda, MD 20817. 6400 Goldsboro Rd, Ste 100. Tel: 240-235-2100, 800-833-6243. Fax: 240-235-2104.
www.yfu-usa.org   E-mail: admissions@yfu.org
Grades 9-PG. Adm: Somewhat selective. **Appl due:** Apr. **Staff:** Admin 2. Couns 3.

High school & college credit.
Intl program focus: Acad Lang Culture. **Travel:** Africa Asia Australia/New_Zealand Europe Middle_East South_America. Home stays avail.
Focus: Chin Fr Japan Span Adventure_Travel. **Features:** Community_Serv Peace/Cross-cultural.
Fees 2012: Res $6495-10,995 (+$250-375), 4-6 wks. Aid (Merit & Need).
Est 1951. Nonprofit. **Ses:** 25. **Wks/ses:** 4-6. Operates June-Aug.

YFU's summer sessions allow students to live in and experience another culture while participating in intensive language study, journey or discovery programs. Not all programs are academic in nature, but many of them have a significant classroom component. Students at all locations embark on trips and engage in recreational activities while living with a host family.

INSTRUCTIONAL SPORTS PROGRAMS

Instructional sports programs are arranged alphabetically by name. The Table of Contents lists the subject areas presented, and an index beginning on page 474 lists the programs under each of those subjects. Programs offering a family session are indicated by "FAM" at the end of the age range in the index.

INDEX BY FOCUS

CHEERLEADING

CRICKET

CROSS COUNTRY

DIVING

EQUESTRIAN

EQUESTRIAN *(CONT.)*

EXTREME SPORTS

FENCING

FIELD HOCKEY

FOOTBALL

GENERAL SPORTS

GOLF

GYMNASTICS

U of IL Sport Camps *(Res & Day — Coed Ages 8-18; FAM)* ....Champaign, IL....521
Kutsher's Sports *(Res — Coed Ages 7-17)*...................................Great Barrington, MA....502
Woodward Camp *(Res — Coed Ages 7-18)* ....Woodward, PA....526
Dunkley's Gymnastics *(Res — Coed Ages 7-17)* ....South Hero, VT....492
Lake Owen Camp *(Res — Coed Ages 7-17)* ....Cable, WI....502
Olympia Sports Camp *(Res — Coed Ages 8-19)*......... Huntsville, Ontario, CANADA....511

ICE HOCKEY

Pro Ambitions Hockey *(Res — Coed Ages 10-17; Day — Coed 6-17)* .... Dover, MA....513
Camp All-Star *(Res — Coed Ages 8-15)*.. Kents Hill, ME....485
Maine Golf & Tennis *(Res — Coed Ages 8-17; FAM)*.................... North Belgrade, ME....504
U of Maine Sports *(Res — Coed Ages 8-18; Day — Coed 6-18)* ....Orono, ME....521
Heartland Hockey ....Deerwood, MN....497
   (Res & Day — Coed Ages 4+ (Coord — 4-18); FAM)
Minnesota Hockey *(Res — Coed Ages 8+; Day — Coed 5-8; FAM)* ....Nisswa, MN....508
Top Dog Hockey Camps *(Res & Day — Coed Ages 5-18)* ....Minneapolis, MN....521
Princeton U Sports *(Res — Coed Ages 10-18; Day — Coed 5-18)* .... Princeton, NJ....512
Okanagan Hockey Sch .... Penticton, British Columbia, CANADA....511
   (Res — Coed Ages 10-18; Day — Coed 5+)
Hockey Opportunity ....Sundridge, Ontario, CANADA....498
   (Res & Day — Coed Ages 7-16)
Olympia Sports Camp *(Res — Coed Ages 8-19)*......... Huntsville, Ontario, CANADA....511
Christian Hockey *(Res & Day — Coed Ages 9-17)*.........Montreal, Quebec, CANADA....489

IN-LINE SKATING

Woodward Camp *(Res — Coed Ages 7-18)* ....Woodward, PA....526

LACROSSE

Camp Greylock *(Res — Boys Ages 6-16; FAM)* ....Becket, MA....496
Kutsher's Sports *(Res — Coed Ages 7-17)*...................................Great Barrington, MA....502
Camp All-Star *(Res — Coed Ages 8-15)*.. Kents Hill, ME....485
Camp Skylemar *(Res — Boys Ages 7-15; FAM)*... Naples, ME....517
Princeton U Sports *(Res — Coed Ages 10-18; Day — Coed 5-18)* .... Princeton, NJ....512
McCallie Lacrosse *(Res — Boys Ages 11-15; Day — Boys 8-15)* ....Chattanooga, TN....506
McCallie Sports Camp *(Res — Boys Ages 9-15)*................................Chattanooga, TN....506
Merestead Sport Camp *(Res & Day — Girls Ages 10-17)* ....Richmond, VA....507
Camp Chikopi *(Res — Boys Ages 7-17)* ....Magnetawan, Ontario, CANADA....489
Olympia Sports Camp *(Res — Coed Ages 8-19)*......... Huntsville, Ontario, CANADA....511

ROLLER HOCKEY

ROWING/SCULLING

RUGBY

SKATEBOARDING

SOCCER

SOCCER *(CONT.)*

SOFTBALL

SQUASH

SURFING

SWIMMING

TEAM HANDBALL

TENNIS

TRACK

TRACK *(CONT.)*

Kutsher's Sports *(Res — Coed Ages 7-17)* .... Great Barrington, MA....502
U of Maine Sports *(Res — Coed Ages 8-18; Day — Coed 6-18)* .... Orono, ME....521
Princeton U Sports *(Res — Coed Ages 10-18; Day — Coed 5-18)* .... Princeton, NJ....512
McCallie Sports Camp *(Res — Boys Ages 9-15)*.................................Chattanooga, TN....506
Camp Chikopi *(Res — Boys Ages 7-17)* .... Magnetawan, Ontario, CANADA....489

ULTIMATE FRISBEE

Camp Chikopi *(Res — Boys Ages 7-17)* .... Magnetawan, Ontario, CANADA....489

VOLLEYBALL

Big Bear Sports *(Res — Coed Ages 7-17)* ....Big Bear City, CA....486
Dunphy Volleyball *(Res — Coord Ages 14-18)* .... Malibu, CA....493
U of SD Sports Camps *(Res & Day — Coed Ages 6-18)* ....San Diego, CA....522
U of IL Sport Camps *(Res & Day — Coed Ages 8-18; FAM)* ....Champaign, IL....521
Kutsher's Sports *(Res — Coed Ages 7-17)* .... Great Barrington, MA....502
Hartwick Col-Sports .... Oneonta, NY....497
   (Res — Coed Ages 8-18; Day — Boys 10-16, Girls 8-18)
Camp Chikopi *(Res — Boys Ages 7-17)* .... Magnetawan, Ontario, CANADA....489
Madawaska Sports *(Res — Coed Ages 9-18)*........ Palmer Rapids, Ontario, CANADA....503
Olympia Sports Camp *(Res — Coed Ages 8-19)* .... Huntsville, Ontario, CANADA....511

WATER-SKIING

Camp Greylock *(Res — Boys Ages 6-16; FAM)* ....Becket, MA....496
Camp Skylemar *(Res — Boys Ages 7-15; FAM)*... Naples, ME....517
Snowy Owl Camp *(Res — Girls Ages 8-15)*... Harmony, ME....517
Brant Lake Camp *(Res — Boys Ages 7-15)*...Brant Lake, NY....487

WATERSPORTS

Big Bear Sports *(Res — Coed Ages 7-17)* ....Big Bear City, CA....486
Malibu Water Polo *(Res & Day — Coed Ages 12-18)* .... Malibu, CA....505
Snowy Owl Camp *(Res — Girls Ages 8-15)*... Harmony, ME....517
Princeton U Sports *(Res — Coed Ages 10-18; Day — Coed 5-18)* .... Princeton, NJ....512
Olympia Sports Camp *(Res — Coed Ages 8-19)* .... Huntsville, Ontario, CANADA....511

WEIGHT TRAINING

Camp Chikopi *(Res — Boys Ages 7-17)* .... Magnetawan, Ontario, CANADA....489

WINTER SPORTS

WRESTLING

Instructional Sports Programs

ALFRED UNIVERSITY SPORTS CAMPS
Res — Coed Ages 12-17; Day — Coed 8-17

Alfred, NY 14802. Office of Summer Prgms, 1 Saxon Dr. Tel: 607-871-2612.
Fax: 607-871-2045.
www.alfred.edu/summer/hs.cfm   E-mail: summerpro@alfred.edu
Melody McLay, Dir.
Grades 7-12. Adm: FCFS. Appl due: Rolling. Enr: 20-40. Enr cap: 25-40. Staff: Admin 5.
Couns 12. Res 12.
Focus: Equestrian Swim.
Fees 2011: Res $425-850 (+$50), 1 wk. Day $275-350, 1 wk.
Housing: Dorms. Avg per room/unit: 2. Swimming: Pool.
Est 1998. Nonprofit. Ses: 2. Wks/ses: 1. Operates July.

Alfred University conducts residential athletic camps for high school students in two sports. The swim camp, for boys and girls entering grades 7-12, addresses stroke development, training techniques and competitive strategies. Residential riders (ages 14-17) may participate in an English equestrian camp, while day riders (ages 8-16) choose from English or Western programs; no prior riding experience is necessary. Each camper is assigned a horse and has the opportunity to ride and care for the horse while refining his or her riding skills.

CAMP ALL-STAR
Res — Coed Ages 8-15

Kents Hill, ME 04349. 1614 Main St, PO Box 217. Tel: 207-685-7242.
Fax: 207-685-4169.
Contact (Aug-June): PO Box 77475, Charlotte, NC 28271. Tel: 704-443-4400.
Fax: 704-443-4334.
Year-round Toll-free: 800-283-3558.
www.campallstar.com   E-mail: info@campallstar.com
Craig H. Rosen & Cammi Rosen, Dirs.
Adm: FCFS. Appl due: Rolling. Enr: 180. Enr cap: 180. Staff: Admin 10. Couns 60.
Focus: Baseball Basketball Ice_Hockey Lacrosse Soccer Tennis. Features: Crafts Fine_
Arts Aquatics Archery Boating Canoe Climbing_Wall Deep-sea Fishing Fishing Hiking
Kayak Mtn_Biking White-water_Raft Woodcraft Equestrian Field_Hockey Golf Softball
Swim Volleyball Water-skiing Watersports Weight_Trng.
Fees 2012: Res $2999-6999, 2-6 wks.
Housing: Dorms. Swimming: Lake.
Est 2001. Inc. Ses: 6. Wks/ses: 2-6. Operates June-Aug. ACA.

Conducted on the 600-acre campus of Kents Hill School, the camp seeks to develop athletic skills in its campers through individualized instruction. Prior to enrollment, boys and girls typically choose two of the following sports for intensive instruction: ice hockey, basketball, soccer, baseball, tennis or flag football. Campers receive instruction in these major sports for up to two periods per day. Boys and girls fill out their daily schedules by choosing from such pursuits as other land sports, watersports and arts activities.

ANDREWS OSBORNE ACADEMY
SUMMER ADVENTURE HORSEBACK RIDING CAMP
Res — Girls Ages 9-15

Willoughby, OH 44094. 38588 Mentor Ave. Tel: 440-942-3600. Fax: 440-942-3660.
www.andrewsosborne.org   E-mail: amay@andrewsosborne.org

Bernie Villeneuve, Coord.
Adm: FCFS. **Appl due:** Rolling. **Enr:** 30. **Enr cap:** 30. **Staff:** Admin 4. Couns 8. Res 6.
Focus: Equestrian. **Features:** Crafts Cooking Swim.
Fees 2012: Res $800, 1 wk.
Housing: Dorms. Avg per room/unit: 2. **Swimming:** Pool.
Est 1988. Nonprofit. **Ses:** 3. **Wks/ses:** 1. Operates June-Aug.

This girls' riding program groups campers according to ability level. Beginning activities include grooming, tacking up and basic riding positions, while more advanced topics are beginning jumping, small-course jumping, and advanced work in equitation and flatwork. Campers ride twice a day and also take part in arts and crafts, sports, swimming and evening activities.

BIG BEAR SPORTS RANCH
Res — Coed Ages 7-17

Big Bear City, CA 92314. 2080 Erwin Ranch Rd, PO Box 767. Tel: 909-585-3133.
   Fax: 909-585-5295.
www.bigbearsportsranch.com   E-mail: info@bigbearsportsranch.com
Bob Durkin, Dir.
Adm: FCFS. **Appl due:** Rolling.
Focus: Basketball Gen_Sports Golf Tennis Volleyball Watersports. **Features:** Swim.
Fees 2011: Res $650-975, 1 wk.
Housing: Cabins. **Swimming:** Pool.
Est 1971. Ses: 7. **Wks/ses:** 1. Operates June-Aug. ACA.

Big Bear offers small-group instruction in various sports for players of all ability levels. Each camper receives a minimum of four hours of daily instruction, with tournaments conducted on weekends.

BLUE DEVIL GOLF SCHOOLS
Res — Boys Ages 11-18

Durham, NC 27705. Karcher-Ingram Golf Ctr, 3001 Cameron Blvd, Ste 1.
   Tel: 919-410-6158.
www.bluedevilgolfschools.com   E-mail: info@bluedevilgolfschools.com
Jamie Green, Dir.
Adm: FCFS. **Appl due:** Rolling. **Staff:** Admin 11. Couns 9.
Focus: Golf.
Fees 2011: Res $1095-2400, ½-1 wk.
Housing: Dorms.
Est 1974. Spons: Duke University. **Ses:** 4. **Wks/ses:** ½-1. Operates June-July.

Open to boys of all ability levels, the traditional camp addresses golf rules and etiquette, practice habits, putting, chipping, pitching, bunker techniques, swing concepts, mental management and course management. Video swing analysis is also part of the program. Boys receive individualized instruction and are grouped by age and ability. Open to boys ages 14-17, an elite camp provides intensive instruction for advanced players over two days.

BLUE STREAK STABLES HORSEMANSHIP CAMPS
Res — Girls Ages 7-15

Seguin, TX 78155. 365 Blackjack Oak Rd. Tel: 830-372-1677. Fax: 830-372-0677.
www.summerhorsecamp.com   E-mail: rideahorse@bluestreakstables.com
Reba Martinez & Larry Martinez, Dirs.
Adm: FCFS. **Appl due:** Rolling.

Focus: Equestrian.
Fees 2010: Res $850-3200, 1-4 wks.
Housing: Cabins.
Est 1995. Ses: 9. **Wks/ses:** 1-4. Operates June-July. ACA.

Blue Streak Stables offers Western riding lessons for beginning through advanced riders, and English instruction for intermediate and advanced riders. Progressive lesson plans address body alignment, balance, leg pressures and seat weight. Campers also work on communication skills and horsemanship safety. Girls also engage in specialty programs and evening activities.

BRANT LAKE CAMP
Res — Boys Ages 7-15

Brant Lake, NY 12815. 7586 State Rte 8. Tel: 518-494-2406. Fax: 518-494-7372.
www.brantlake.com E-mail: info@brantlake.com
Richard B. Gersten, Exec Dir.
Adm: FCFS. **Enr:** 330. **Staff:** Admin 10. Couns 105.
Focus: Baseball Basketball Golf Roller_Hockey Soccer Swim Tennis Water-skiing. **Features:** Crafts Theater Aquatics Archery Boating Canoe Climbing_Wall Hiking Kayak Mountaineering Mtn_Biking Riding Ropes_Crse Sail Equestrian Lacrosse Softball Track Volleyball Watersports.
Fees 2012: Res $10,475 (+$50-675), 7 wks.
Housing: Cabins. **Swimming:** Lake.
Est 1916. Inc. **Ses:** 1. **Wks/ses:** 7. Operates June-Aug. ACA.

This sports-oriented camp, which comprises junior, intermediate and senior divisions, groups boys according to age, skill level, prior experience and maturity. Older boys take a greater responsibility in scheduling their activities, and competition becomes more intense at the intermediate and senior levels. Brant Lake's location in the Adirondack Mountains lends itself to many waterfront and other outdoor activities.

BRITANNIA SOCCER CAMP
Res — Coed Ages 10-18; Day — Coed 4-18

Ojai, CA. Ojai Valley School.
Contact (Year-round): 701 E Santa Clara St, Ste 42, Ventura, CA 93001.
Tel: 319-389-5791.
www.vcfusion.com E-mail: adcsmith63@hotmail.com
Adam Smith, Dir.
Grades K-10. Adm: FCFS. **Appl due:** Rolling. **Enr:** 110. **Staff:** Admin 10. Couns 10.
Focus: Soccer. **Features:** Swim.
Fees 2011: Res $495, 1 wk. Day $125-345, 1 wk.
Housing: Dorms. Avg per room/unit: 2. **Swimming:** Pool.
Est 1981. Ses: 1. **Wks/ses:** 1. Operates Aug.

Hosted by Ojai Valley School, this soccer camp teaches fundamental techniques through drills, videotape reviews and personal evaluations. Instructors supervise advanced and regular sessions and additional recreation. Half-day sessions are available for younger campers.

THE BUDDY TEEVENS FOOTBALL SCHOOL
Res and Day — Boys Ages 12-18

Hanover, NH 03755. PO Box 711. Tel: 603-646-2475. Fax: 603-646-3576.
www.buddyteevensfootballcamp.com E-mail: clinton.cosgrove@dartmouth.edu
Michael Bruno, Dir.
Grades 7-12. Adm: FCFS. **Appl due:** Rolling. **Enr:** 200. **Staff:** Admin 3. Couns 25. Res 25.

Focus: Football.
Fees 2011: Res $425 (+$75), 1 wk. Day $300 (+$75), 1 wk.
Housing: Dorms. Avg per room/unit: 2.
Est 1992. Ses: 1. Wks/ses: 1. Operates June.

The program combines instruction from college coaches with strength training, guest speakers and films. Coaches teach techniques and strategy for both offensive and defensive positions and supervise camp scrimmages and drills.

CARMEL VALLEY TENNIS CAMP
Res — Coed Ages 10-17

Carmel Valley, CA 93924. 20805 Cachagua Rd. Tel: 831-659-2615. Fax: 831-659-2840.
www.carmelvalleytenniscamp.com   E-mail: cvtcss@gmail.com
Susan Reeder & Steve Proulx, Dirs.
Grades 5-12. Adm: FCFS. **Appl due:** Rolling. **Enr:** 52. **Staff:** Admin 2. Couns 14.
Focus: Tennis. **Features:** Crafts Archery Climbing_Wall Ropes_Crse Badminton Basketball Swim Volleyball.
Fees 2010: Res $1025-2050, 1-2 wks.
Housing: Dorms. **Swimming:** Pool.
Est 1969. Inc. Ses: 7. Wks/ses: 1-2. Operates June-Aug. ACA.

CVTC provides three hours of small-group tennis instruction daily, plus additional match play. Other daytime offerings include swimming, a climbing wall and a ropes course, basketball, archery, beach volleyball, Ping-Pong, games, and arts and crafts; evening activities include talent shows, team games, game shows, campfires and dances. The camp schedules weekend field trips.

CARRABASSETT VALLEY ACADEMY SUMMER CAMPS
Res and Day — Coed Ages 9-15

Carrabassett Valley, ME 04947. 3197 Carrabassett Dr. Tel: 207-237-2250.
   Fax: 207-237-2213.
www.gocva.com   E-mail: info@gocva.com
Adm: FCFS. **Appl due:** Rolling. **Enr:** 32. **Enr cap:** 35. **Staff:** Admin 3. Couns 8.
Locations: ME OR.
Focus: Extreme_Sports Skateboarding Winter_Sports. **Features:** Hiking Mtn_Biking Mtn_Trips Swim Tennis Weight_Trng.
Fees 2011: Res $625-4100 (+airfare), 1-2 wks. Day $420, 1 wk.
Housing: Dorms Houses. **Swimming:** Pond River.
Est 1984. Nonprofit. Ses: 4. Wks/ses: 1. Operates June-July.

CVA conducts two distinct summer camps: a snowboarding program in Oregon's Mt. Hood mountains and an on-campus skateboarding and trampolining camp. The snowboarding camp focuses on half-pipe and slope-style techniques and incorporates on-hill coaching, video review and daily dry-land activities, in addition to the full use of on- and off-snow facilities. The skateboarding and trampolining program provides young skiers and snowboarders with an alternate method of training during the summer; older campers receive weight-training instruction during the session.

CAMP CARYSBROOK EQUESTRIAN PROGRAM
Res — Girls Ages 10-16

Riner, VA 24149. 3500 Camp Carysbrook Rd. Tel: 540-382-1670. Fax: 540-382-6134.
www.campcarysbrook.com   E-mail: info@campcarysbrook.com
Rachel Baughman, Dir.

Adm: FCFS. **Appl due:** Rolling. **Enr:** 20. **Staff:** Admin 5.
Focus: Equestrian. **Features:** Hiking Riding Swim Tennis.
Fees 2010: Res $1850, 2 wks.
Housing: Cabins. Avg per room/unit: 5. **Swimming:** Lake.
Est 1923. Inc. **Ses:** 1. **Wks/ses:** 2. Operates July. ACA.

Situated on a 218-acre tract on the Little River in the Blue Ridge Mountains, this equestrian program emphasizes English riding. Enrolling girls of all ability levels, Carysbrook organizes classes by skill level, not age. Daily activities include mounted lessons, trail rides, jumping, swimming on horseback and equine first aid.

CAMP CHIKOPI
Res — Boys Ages 7-17

Magnetawan, P0A 1P0 Ontario, Canada. 373 Chikopi Rd. Tel: 705-387-3811.
Fax: 705-387-4747.
Contact (Sept-May): 2132 NE 17th Ter, Fort Lauderdale, FL 33305. Tel: 954-566-8235.
Fax: 954-566-3951.
www.campchikopi.com   E-mail: campchikopi@aol.com
Bob Duenkel & Colette Duenkel, Dirs.
Grades 2-12. Adm: FCFS. **Appl due:** Rolling. **Enr cap:** 85. **Staff:** Admin 2. Couns 20.
Focus: Badminton Baseball Basketball Cricket Cross-country Field_Hockey Football Golf Lacrosse Rugby Soccer Softball Swim Team_Handball Tennis Track Ultimate_Frisbee Volleyball Weight_Trng Wrestling. **Features:** Aquatics Archery Canoe Climbing_Wall Fishing Hiking Kayak Mtn_Biking Sail Seamanship Survival_Trng Wilderness_Camp Wilderness_Canoe Water_Polo.
Fees 2011: Res $1500-4800 (+$250), 2-7 wks. Aid 2010 (Need): $17,500.
Housing: Cabins. Avg per room/unit: 14. **Swimming:** Lake.
Est 1920. Inc. Nondenom Christian. **Ses:** 5. **Wks/ses:** 2-7. Operates June-Sept.

Offering instruction in more than two dozen sports, Chikopi emphasizes strength, stamina, flexibility and self-confidence. Watersports range from swimming, diving and water polo to kayaking, canoeing and sailing; land sports range from soccer, tennis and baseball to golf, basketball, and track and field. Competition includes sailing and paddling regattas, running races and swim meets. Olympic, national, university and high school coaches constitute the instructional staff.

CHRISTIAN HOCKEY CAMPS INTERNATIONAL
Res and Day — Coed Ages 9-17

Montreal, H3B 2S2 Quebec, Canada. PO Box 7, Windsor Sta, Ste 265, 1100 de la Gauchetiere W. Tel: 514-395-1717. Fax: 514-394-9449.
www.hockeyministries.org   E-mail: camps@hockeyministries.org
Christy Liesemer, Dir.
Adm: FCFS. **Appl due:** Apr.
Locations: AK FL IL MA MI MN MO NC ND PA TX Canada Europe.
Focus: Ice_Hockey.
Fees 2011: Res $500-695 (+$10-20), 1 wk. Day $315-495 (+$10-20), 1 wk.
Housing: Dorms.
Est 1977. Nonprofit. **Spons:** Hockey Ministries International. Nondenom Christian. **Ses:** 28.
Wks/ses: 1. Operates June-Aug.

Boys and girls of all skill levels attend CHCI programs in Canada, the US, Slovakia, Sweden, Switzerland and the Czech Republic. Daily on-ice instruction features sessions involving power skating, hockey drills and scrimmages. Off-ice workouts and recreational sports complete the program.

CLEMSON TIGER TENNIS CAMP
Res — Coed Ages 9-17; Day — Coed 4-17

Clemson, SC 29633. PO Box 1251. Tel: 864-656-1323. Fax: 864-656-6386.
www.clemsontenniscamp.com   E-mail: info@clemsontenniscamp.com
Nancy Harris, Dir.
Grades 4-12. Adm: FCFS. Appl due: Rolling. Enr: 112. Staff: Admin 3. Couns 20.
Focus: Tennis. Features: Swim.
Fees 2012: Res $615 (+$20), 1 wk. Day $225-375, 1 wk.
Housing: Dorms. Avg per room/unit: 4. Swimming: Pool.
Ses: 4. Wks/ses: 1. Operates June-July.

This Clemson University tennis camp divides instruction into four divisions, from beginning to tournament levels. The basic fundamentals of the sport, including grips, strokes and footwork, are taught in half-day sessions at Purple Camp (ages 4-8). White Camp reinforces the fundamentals and prepares players for the next level. Orange Camp is designed for the intermediate to advanced player with some tournament experience, and Orange Crush prepares serious players for college competition. All camps feature daily classroom sessions and match play. Popular evening group activities are games, movies and swimming.

CONTACT FOOTBALL CAMPS
Res and Day — Boys Ages 8-18

San Rafael, CA 94903. c/o US Sports Camps, 750 Lindaro St, Ste 220.
   Tel: 415-479-6060, 800-433-6060. Fax: 415-479-6061.
www.contactfootball.com   E-mail: football@ussportscamps.com
Grades 3-PG. Adm: FCFS. Staff: Admin 10. Couns 30.
Locations: CA IL MA PA TX.
Focus: Football. Features: Swim.
Fees 2011: Res $625-665, 1 wk. Day $395-525, 1 wk.
Housing: Dorms. Swimming: Pool.
Est 1977. Inc. Ses: 8. Wks/ses: 1. Operates June-July.

These camps, which are held on various college campuses in the US, feature live contact and scrimmages. Campers learn current techniques from college coaches and professional players. Instruction three times a day stresses conditioning and the development of proper technique at each position, both individually and as a team. Sessions divide boys by age, weight and ability.

CRAFTSBURY RUNNING CAMPS
Res and Day — Coed Ages 14 and up

Craftsbury Common, VT 05827. c/o Craftsbury Outdoor Ctr, 535 Lost Nation Rd.
   Tel: 802-586-7767. Fax: 802-586-7768.
www.craftsbury.com   E-mail: stay@craftsbury.com
Greg Wenneborg, Dir.
Adm: FCFS. Appl due: Rolling. Enr: 30. Staff: Admin 5. Couns 8.
Focus: Cross-country. Features: Bicycle_Tours Canoe Kayak Mtn_Trips Swim.
Fees 2012: Res $980, 1 wk.
Housing: Cabins Dorms. Swimming: Lake.
Est 1977. Nonprofit. Spons: Craftsbury Outdoor Center. Ses: 2. Wks/ses: 1. Operates July-Aug.

Conducted by experienced coaches, the camps provide customized instruction for runners of varying ability levels. Distinct, weeklong and weekend camps address marathon running, short-distance racing and general aspects of running. Features of the program are daily lectures and discussions relating to training and racing, videotaped form analysis, sports psychology, yoga and stretching, hill running, cross-training and complimentary massages.

CRAFTSBURY SCULLING CENTER
Res and Day — Coed Ages 12 and up

Craftsbury Common, VT 05827. c/o Craftsbury Outdoor Ctr, 535 Lost Nation Rd. Tel: 802-586-7767. Fax: 802-586-7768.
www.craftsbury.com   E-mail: sculling@craftsbury.com
Norm Graf, Dir.
Adm: FCFS. **Appl due:** Rolling. **Enr:** 40. **Staff:** Admin 5. Couns 50.
Focus: Rowing/Sculling. **Features:** Yoga Swim.
Fees 2012: Res $1068-1390, 1 wk.
Housing: Cabins Dorms. Avg per room/unit: 2. **Swimming:** Lake.
Est 1976. Nonprofit. **Spons:** Craftsbury Outdoor Center. **Ses:** 18. **Wks/ses:** 1. Operates May-Sept.

Weeklong programs at the center address all aspects of rowing. Located in Vermont's Northeast Kingdom, Craftsbury serves beginners, recreational rowers and accomplished rowers of various ages. Training on the water combines individual and group instruction in single shells. Off-water programming includes discussions of rigging, training and stretching, as well as reviews of video footage taken on the water. Scullers are also able to row doubles and quads.

CRYSTAL VALLEY RANCH SUMMER RIDING CAMP
Res and Day — Coed Ages 6-16

Romney, WV 26757. Rte 28, HC 65, Box 1350. Tel: 304-822-7444. Fax: 304-822-8888.
www.crystalvalleyranch.com   E-mail: info@crystalvalleyranch.com
LaFaye Massie, Dir.
Adm: FCFS. **Appl due:** Rolling. **Enr:** 20.
Focus: Equestrian.
Fees 2009: Res $900, 1 wk. Day $500, 1 wk.
Ses: 5. **Wks/ses:** 1. Operates June-Aug.

Crystal Valley Ranch operates day and overnight camps that combine horsemanship and riding with leisure activities. Instruction addresses grooming, tacking and untacking, horse care and theory. Group riding lessons are held for two hours each day. Other activities include fishing, archery, swimming, hiking and games.

DAVE MURRAY SUMMER SKI AND SNOWBOARD CAMPS
Res — Coed Ages 7 and up

Whistler, V0N 1B4 British Columbia, Canada. 106-4368 Main St, Ste 981. Tel: 604-932-3238. Fax: 347-521-7530.
www.skiandsnowboard.com   E-mail: camp@skiandsnowboard.com
Greg Daniells, Dir.
Adm: FCFS. **Appl due:** Rolling. **Enr cap:** 150. **Staff:** Admin 2. Couns 5. Res 5.
Focus: Winter_Sports. **Features:** Climbing_Wall Mtn_Biking Paintball Golf Skateboarding Swim.
Fees 2011: Res $2000, 1 wk. Day $225, 1 wk.
Housing: Hotels. **Swimming:** Lake Pool.
Est 1970. Inc. **Ses:** 2. **Wks/ses:** 1. Operates June-July.

Conducted in one of the most renowned North American destinations for year-round winter sports, these eight-day camps accommodate skiers and snowboarders of all ability levels.

Coaches focus on each individual's development progression while assessing specific needs and goals. Enrollment is limited to enable campers to maximize their practice time. Whistler Valley's lakes and parks provide participants with access to such off-hill activities as mountain biking, in-line skating, swimming, canoeing, hiking and land sports.

DAVID W. COWENS BASKETBALL SCHOOL
Res — Coed Ages 12-18

Norton, MA. Wheaton College.
Contact (Year-round): 150 Wood Rd, Ste 304, Braintree, MA 02184. Tel: 781-849-9393.
Fax: 781-849-9595.
www.dcowens.com   E-mail: dwcbasketball@yahoo.com
David W. Cowens, Dir.
Adm: FCFS. **Appl due:** Rolling.
Focus: Basketball. **Features:** Swim.
Fees 2011: Res $699 (+$35-50), 1 wk.
Housing: Dorms. Avg per room/unit: 2. **Swimming:** Pool.
Est 1971. Inc. **Ses:** 3. **Wks/ses:** 1. Operates July-Aug.

Conducted on the campus of Wheaton College, the camp provides daily instruction in fundamental basketball skills. Boys and girls play at least two games per day, with playoff games conducted on Friday. Players undergo a talent evaluation on the first day of camp to ensure proper competitive placement.

DUKE SOCCER CAMP
Res — Boys Ages 13-18; Day — Boys 5-18

Durham, NC 27708. PO Box 99037. Tel: 919-240-5761.
www.dukesoccercamp.com   E-mail: dukesoccercamps@aol.com
John Kerr, Dir.
Grades 8-12. Adm: FCFS. **Appl due:** Rolling. **Enr:** 350. **Enr cap:** 350. **Staff:** Admin 4. Couns 50.
Focus: Soccer. **Features:** Swim.
Fees 2009: Res $625 (+$30-70), 1 wk. Day $295-525 (+$30), 1 wk.
Housing: Dorms. **Swimming:** Pool.
Est 1980. Inc. **Ses:** 3. **Wks/ses:** 1. Operates June-July.

Designed for intermediate and advanced players, this soccer camp employs instructors from around the world. Staff teach boys new skills, while also helping further develop those that the camper already has. A goalkeeper school is available during each camp session.

DUNKLEY'S GYMNASTICS CAMP
Res — Coed Ages 7-17

South Hero, VT 05486. 35 Kibbe Farm Rd. Tel: 802-372-8898. Fax: 802-372-8898.
Contact (Sept-June): 22 Ayers Dr, Jericho, VT 05465. Tel: 802-899-3479.
Fax: 802-899-3479.
www.gymcamp.homestead.com   E-mail: dunkleysgymcamp@aol.com
Ruth Dunkley McGowan, Dir.
Grades 1-12. Adm: FCFS. **Appl due:** Rolling. **Enr:** 35. **Enr cap:** 35. **Staff:** Admin 2. Couns 9.
Focus: Gymnastics. **Features:** Circus_Skills Crafts Dance Fine_Arts Canoe Climbing_ Wall Cooking Fishing Kayak Mtn_Biking Sail Aerobics Martial_Arts Swim Water-skiing Watersports Kickboxing.
Fees 2011: Res $700-1200, 1-2 wks. Aid 2009 (Need): $3000.
Housing: Cabins Lodges. Avg per room/unit: 5. **Swimming:** Lake.

Est 1973. **Inc. Ses:** 8. **Wks/ses:** 1-2. Operates June-Aug.

This small camp on Lake Champlain provides gymnastics training for participants from throughout New England and Canada. In addition to gymnastics, Dunkley's offers a strong waterfront program, dance, martial arts, fine arts, modified team sports and traditional camp activities.

DUNPHY VOLLEYBALL CAMP
Res — Coord Ages 14-18

Malibu, CA. Pepperdine Univ.
Contact (Year-round): 33370 Decker School Rd, Malibu, CA 90265. Tel: 310-457-6889.
www.dunphyvolleyball.com   E-mail: info@dunphyvolleyball.com
Marv Dunphy, Dir.
Grades 8-PG. Adm: FCFS. **Appl due:** Rolling. **Enr:** 200. **Enr cap:** 225. **Staff:** Couns 12.
Focus: Volleyball.
Fees 2012: Res $700 (+$25-40), 1 wk.
Housing: Dorms. Avg per room/unit: 2.
Est 1977. **Ses:** 2. **Wks/ses:** 1. Operates July.

Conducted at Pepperdine University, the camp offers separate setter hitter camp sessions for boys and girls. Each session starts with specific technical position training that addresses all aspects of setting or hitting. Setters and hitters are then brought together for combined training. Beginning, intermediate and advanced players may enroll, as the camp groups boys and girls by age, experience and ability level. Players receive comprehensive training in all volleyball techniques, while also learning tactics and team systems.

DUSTIN PEDROIA SUMMER BASEBALL CAMP
Res — Boys Ages 9-16; Day — Coed 7-16

North Easton, MA. Stonehill College.
Contact (Year-round): c/o RBI Baseball Academy, 97 Green St, Ste 2, Foxboro, MA
02035. Tel: 508-543-9595. Fax: 508-543-9596.
www.rbiacademy.com   E-mail: jbreen@rbiacademy.com
Paul Rappoli, Pres.
Adm: FCFS. Admitted: 100%. **Appl due:** Rolling. **Staff:** Admin 6. Couns 30.
Focus: Baseball.
Fees 2012: Res $849, 1 wk. Day $549, 1 wk.
Housing: Dorms. Avg per room/unit: 2-3.
Est 1995. **Ses:** 1. **Wks/ses:** 1. Operates Aug.

The camp features five days of intensive instruction in the fundamentals of hitting, pitching, fielding, throwing, catching and base running. Players participate in daily games and instructional drills, and current and former professional baseball players make guest appearances during the course of the session. Nightly activities vary by age group.

EAST WEST FIELD HOCKEY CAMPS
Res and Day — Coed Ages 12-19

East Dorset, VT 05253. PO Box 99. Toll-free: 866-342-4042. Fax: 802-362-2743.
www.eastwestfieldhockeycamps.com
E-mail: bill@eastwestfieldhockeycamps.com
Bill Davidson, Dir.
Adm: FCFS. **Appl due:** Rolling. **Enr cap:** 100.
Locations: CA MA NY.
Focus: Field_Hockey.

Fees 2012: Res $480, ½ wk. Day $380, ½ wk.
Housing: Dorms.
Est 1994. Inc. Ses: 3. **Wks/ses:** ½. Operates July-Aug.

East West operates four-day field hockey camps at the Siena College (Loudonville, NY), the University of California-Santa Barbara and Worcester State College (Worcester, MA). Players of all skill levels learn individual and team skills, tactics and strategies through drills, circuits and team play. In addition to attending daily field training sessions, campers address specific skills in small groups or one-on-one sessions with instructors. Morning jogs, relaxation sessions, video analysis and goalkeeping instruction complete the program.

EDUKICK
Res and Day — Coed Ages 10-18

Oakville, L6M 4T1 Ontario, Canada. 2029 Grand Oak Trail. Tel: 905-469-5661, 866-338-5425. Fax: 905-469-5971.
www.edukick.com   E-mail: info@edukick.com
Jon Morgan, General Manager.
Adm: FCFS. Admitted: 100%. **Appl due:** Rolling. **Staff:** Admin 2.
Intl program focus: Lang. **Locations:** Canada Europe. Home stays avail.
Focus: Soccer. **Features:** Lang Swim.
Fees 2012: Res $3500-4500 (+$350-500), 3 wks.
Housing: Hotels Houses. Avg per room/unit: 2. **Swimming:** Pool.
Est 2000. Inc. Ses: 8. **Wks/ses:** 3. Operates July.

EduKick youth summer programs combine language study and cultural immersion with intensive soccer instruction at locations in Brazil, China, Germany, Italy, France, Spain, England and Canada. Players train at professional soccer training facilities under FIFA-licensed international coaches. Daily language lessons focus upon situational and conversational learning. EduKick frequently utilizes home stays to facilitate language acquisition.

EUROSTAR SOCCER CAMPS
Res — Coed Ages 12-17; Day — Coed 10-17

London, N6H 5V2 Ontario, Canada. 740-712 Proudfoot Ln. Toll-free: 800-742-3076. Fax: 800-742-3076.
www.eurostarcamps.com   E-mail: jeni@eurostarcamps.com
Pellumb Luka Shaqiri, Pres.
Adm: FCFS. **Appl due:** Rolling. **Enr:** 160. **Staff:** Admin 12. **Couns** 4.
Focus: Soccer. **Features:** Swim.
Fees 2012: Res Can$750-1730 (+Can$80), 1-2 wks. Day Can$225-450 (+Can$80), 1-2 wks.
Housing: Dorms. **Swimming:** Pool.
Est 1998. Ses: 6. **Wks/ses:** 1-2. Operates July-Aug.

Eurostar campers begin the week by completing a survey that determines their training focus. Athletes attend five sessions daily of tactical, physical, technical and psychological classes, then are assigned to teams for the camp tournament. Evening activities include movie nights, socials and cultural excursions.

FIVE-STAR CROSS COUNTRY CAMP
Res — Coed Ages 12-18

Rock Hill, NY.
Contact (Year-round): 750 Lindaro St, Ste 220, San Rafael, CA 94901. Toll-free: 800-645-3226. Fax: 415-479-6061.

www.5starxc.com   E-mail: ussc-running@ussportscamps.com
Richard Furst, Dir.
Grades 7-12. Adm: FCFS. **Appl due:** Rolling. **Enr:** 115. **Enr cap:** 160. **Staff:** Admin 8. Couns 30.
Focus: Cross-country. **Features:** Drama Aquatics Softball Swim Ultimate_Frisbee Volleyball.
Fees 2011: Res $670 (+$25), 1 wk.
Housing: Cabins. Avg per room/unit: 8-12. **Swimming:** Pool.
Est 1981. Inc. **Ses:** 1. **Wks/ses:** 1. Operates Aug.

Using the facilities of Brookwood Camps, Five-Star groups runners according to ability and conditioning levels. Each running group, with its own counselor and running program, consists of two to five campers. Participants run twice a day.

FORRESTEL FARM CAMP
Res — Coed Ages 7-17

Medina, NY 14103. 4536 S Gravel Rd. Tel: 585-798-2222. Fax: 585-798-0941.
www.forrestel.com   E-mail: summer@forrestel.com
Mary Herbert, Dir.
Adm: FCFS. **Appl due:** Rolling. **Enr:** 72. **Enr cap:** 72. **Staff:** Admin 2. Couns 20.
Focus: Equestrian. **Features:** Crafts Theater Aquatics Archery Bicycle_Tours Canoe Climbing_Wall Cooking Exploration Farm Fishing Hiking Kayak Mtn_Biking Riding Riflery Rock_Climb Ropes_Crse Wilderness_Camp Woodcraft Baseball Basketball Football Golf Lacrosse Soccer Softball Swim Tennis Volleyball Watersports.
Fees 2012: Res $1050-2100 (+$50), 1-2 wks.
Housing: Tents. **Swimming:** Pond.
Est 1978. Ses: 5. **Wks/ses:** 1-2. Operates June-Aug. ACA.

Campers may choose an equestrian program and ride once each day, or an advanced horsemanship program and ride twice each day. Participants also feed and groom the horses, learn basic stable management, and observe the blacksmith and the veterinarian at work. Facilities include an outdoor hunt course and a cross-country jumping course, and advanced lessons in dressage are available. Recreational activities and farm experiences complement the program.

4 STAR TENNIS AND GOLF CAMPS
Res and Day — Coed Ages 10-18

Charlottesville, VA. Univ of Virginia.
Contact (Year-round): PO Box 3387, Falls Church, VA 22043. Tel: 703-866-4900, 800-334-7827. Fax: 703-866-7775.
www.4starcamps.com   E-mail: info@4starcamps.com
Mitch Popple, Exec Dir.
Adm: FCFS. **Appl due:** Rolling. **Enr:** 130. **Staff:** Admin 2. Couns 35.
Focus: Golf Tennis. **Features:** Canoe Hiking White-water_Raft Basketball Soccer Weight_Trng.
Fees 2011: Res $895-1095, 1 wk. Day $595-795, 1 wk.
Housing: Dorms.
Est 1975. Inc. **Ses:** 16. **Wks/ses:** 1. Operates June-Aug.

Tennis players and golfers choose from various session options, with some focusing primarily on tennis, some on golf and one on both sports. Other camps combine professional tennis or golf instruction with various other athletic and recreational activities. As the majority of campers attend for more than one week, 4 Star schedules one-day excursions from the University of Virginia location each Saturday and Sunday.

FRIENDSHIP EQUESTRIAN CAMP
Res — Girls Ages 9-16

Palmyra, VA 22963. 573 Friendship Way, PO Box 145. Tel: 434-589-8950, 800-873-3223. Fax: 434-589-5880.
www.campfriendship.com   E-mail: stables@campfriendship.com
Skye Ackenbom, Dir.
Adm: FCFS. **Appl due:** Rolling.
Focus: Equestrian.
Fees 2012: Res $1200, 1 wk.
Housing: Cabins.
Est 1966. Ses: 7. Wks/ses: 1. Operates June-Aug.

For beginning to advanced riders, the equestrian program at Camp Friendship provides intensive instruction and experience with horses for campers interested in refining their skills in many phases of horsemanship, progressing from fundamentals to the finer points of equitation. The program includes daily mounted lessons and recreational riding, participation in a camp show, lectures and demonstrations, and opportunities for older campers to teach beginning recreational riders from the general camp. A group of accomplished equestrians is selected for a show team that trains, studies, works and lives together.

GEORGIA SOUTHERN UNIVERSITY
EAGLE BASEBALL CAMPS
Res — Boys Ages 10-18; Day — Boys 6-12

Statesboro, GA 30460. PO Box 8095. Tel: 912-478-1350. Fax: 912-478-1366.
www.georgiasoutherneagles.com   E-mail: baseball@georgiasouthern.edu
Rodney Hennon, Dir.
Grades 5-PG. Adm: FCFS. **Appl due:** Rolling. **Enr:** 100. **Staff:** Admin 2. Couns 12.
Focus: Baseball.
Fees 2011: Res $360, 1 wk. Day $130, 1 wk.
Housing: Dorms.
Est 1975. Ses: 2. Wks/ses: 1. Operates July.

High school and college coaches teach the fundamentals and the strategies of baseball to players of all skill levels in a disciplined environment. Defensive instruction emphasizes sound baseball mechanics, strategy, drill work and total team defense, while pitching instruction centers on proper form, as well as arm care and fielding. Each camper has the opportunity to work on his hitting by taking hundreds of swings and receiving videotaped evaluation by members of the coaching staff.

CAMP GREYLOCK
Res — Boys Ages 6-16

Becket, MA 01223. 1525 Main St. Tel: 413-623-8921. Fax: 413-623-5049.
Contact (Sept-Apr): 150 E 75th St, Ste 3B, New York, NY 10022. Tel: 212-582-1042. Fax: 212-765-8177.
www.campgreylock.com   E-mail: info@campgreylock.com
Michael R. Marcus & Lukas T. Horn, Dirs.
Grades 2-10. Adm: FCFS. **Appl due:** Rolling. **Enr:** 400. **Enr cap:** 400. **Staff:** Admin 10. Couns 160.
Focus: Baseball Basketball Football Golf Lacrosse Swim Tennis Water-skiing. **Features:** Crafts Dance Fine_Arts Aquatics Archery Boating Canoe Climbing_Wall Fishing Hiking Mountaineering Mtn_Biking Mtn_Trips Ropes_Crse Sail Wilderness_Camp Wilderness_ Canoe Woodcraft Fencing Roller_Hockey Soccer Watersports Weight_Trng Ping-Pong.
Housing: Cabins Lodges. Avg per room/unit: 8. **Swimming:** Lake.
Est 1916. Inc. Ses: 1. Wks/ses: 7. Operates June-Aug. ACA.

Greylock is a traditional sports camp for boys. The instructional program helps boys improve their athletic skills in most sports. Other programs include canoeing, sailing, watersports, fishing and climbing.

GRIER SUMMER
ALLEGHENY RIDING CAMP
Res — Girls Ages 6-17

Tyrone, PA 16686. PO Box 308. Tel: 814-684-3000. Fax: 814-684-2177.
www.bestcamp.org   E-mail: bestcamp@grier.org
Helen Zientek, Dir.
Adm: FCFS. **Appl due:** Rolling. **Enr:** 70. **Enr cap:** 70. **Staff:** Admin 4. Couns 36.
Focus: Equestrian. **Features:** Crafts Riding Soccer Swim Tennis.
Fees 2012: Res $1000-10,400 (+$75-175), 1-6 wks.
Housing: Dorms. **Swimming:** Pool.
Est 1975. Nonprofit. **Spons:** Grier School. **Ses:** 7. **Wks/ses:** 1-6. Operates June-Aug.
ACA.

Located on the 350-acre Grier School campus in the mountains of central Pennsylvania, the camp features daily instruction in English hunter-jumper horseback riding, equine studies and many traditional recreational activities. Girls of all ability levels may enroll, with a show camper program and riding internships available to advanced riders. Allegheny also offers a three-day mother-daughter session for first-time campers ages 6-10.

HARTWICK COLLEGE SUMMER SPORTS CAMPS
Res — Coed Ages 8-18; Day — Boys 10-16, Girls 8-18

Oneonta, NY 13820. Binder Physical Ed Ctr. Tel: 607-431-4700.
www.hartwick.edu   E-mail: sportscamps@hartwick.edu
Betty Powell, Dir.
Adm: FCFS. **Appl due:** Rolling.
Focus: Basketball Field_Hockey Soccer Swim Volleyball.
Fees 2009: Res $375-940, ½-2 wks. Day $295-565, ½-2 wks.
Swimming: Pool.
Ses: 10. **Wks/ses:** ½-2. Operates June-July.

Hartwick conducts sports camps in boys' and girls' basketball, soccer, and swimming and diving, as well as girls' volleyball and field hockey.

HEARTLAND HOCKEY CAMPS
Res and Day — Coed Ages 4 and up (Coord — 4-18)

Deerwood, MN 56444. 24921 Arena Dr. Tel: 218-534-3298, 800-945-7465.
Fax: 218-534-3297.
www.heartlandhockey.com   E-mail: steve@heartlandhockey.com
Steve Jensen, Dir.
Adm: Somewhat selective. Admitted: 10%. **Appl due:** May. **Enr:** 120. **Enr cap:** 120. **Staff:** Admin 6. Couns 20. Res 30.
Focus: Ice_Hockey. **Features:** Archery Boating Canoe Fishing Hiking Kayak Sail Basketball Golf Roller_Hockey Street_Hockey Swim Tennis Volleyball Water-skiing Watersports Weight_Trng.
Fees 2012: Res $1100-1200 (+$50), 1 wk. Day $950 (+$50), 1 wk. Aid 2009 (Need): $8000.
Housing: Apartments Dorms Lodges. **Swimming:** Lake Stream.
Est 1985. Inc. **Ses:** 30. **Wks/ses:** 1. Operates June-Aug.

Located on a 45-acre tract in the Brainerd Lakes area, HHC offers up to six hours of ice time daily to hockey players of varying ability levels. In addition to focusing on both basic and advanced hockey skills, instructors teach campers the importance of personal fitness, including daily exercise and proper nutrition and diet. Skill development programming addresses skating, shooting, stickhandling, passing and, for older players, body checking. Super Select camps serve advanced players in all age groups.

HIGH CASCADE SNOWBOARD CAMP
Res and Day — Coed Ages 9-20

Government Camp, OR 97028. PO Box 368. Tel: 503-272-0116. Fax: 503-272-3637. Contact (Sept-May): 5014 NE 15th St, Portland, OR 97211. Tel: 503-206-8520. Fax: 503-432-8871. Year-round Toll-free: 800-334-4272. www.highcascade.com E-mail: highcascade@highcascade.com Preston Strout, Dir. Adm: FCFS. **Appl due:** Rolling. **Enr:** 200. **Staff:** Admin 5. Couns 30. **Focus:** Winter_Sports. **Features:** Crafts Filmmaking Music Photog Aquatics Hiking Mtn_ Biking Mtn_Trips Paintball Riding White-water_Raft Basketball Golf Skateboarding Soccer Swim Volleyball Watersports. **Fees 2012: Res $1975-2075 (+$100), 1 wk. Day $1175 (+$100), 1 wk.** Aid (Need). **Housing:** Houses Lodges. Avg per room/unit: 16. **Swimming:** Lake. **Est 1989.** Inc. **Ses:** 6. **Wks/ses:** 1½. Operates June-Aug. ACA.

HCSC's summer program coaches young snowboarders of all ability levels. Instruction includes group coaching, personalized video analysis, and tuning clinics from demo specialists and sponsors. Among afternoon activities are skateboarding, mountain biking, hiking, golf and yoga.

HOCKEY OPPORTUNITY CAMP
Res and Day — Coed Ages 7-16

Sundridge, P0A 1Z0 Ontario, Canada. PO Box 448. Tel: 705-386-7702, 888-576-2752. Fax: 705-386-0179. www.learnhockey.com E-mail: hoc@learnhockey.com Kevin McLaughlin & Sophie McLaughlin, Dirs. Grades 2-11. Adm: FCFS. **Appl due:** Rolling. **Enr cap:** 240. **Staff:** Admin 8. Couns 30. **Focus:** Ice_Hockey. **Features:** Archery Canoe Hiking Mtn_Biking Roller_Hockey Swim Water-skiing. **Fees 2012: Res Can$845-895, 1 wk. Day Can$360-585, 1 wk. Housing:** Cabins Lodges. **Swimming:** Lake. **Est 1966. Ses:** 8. **Wks/ses:** 1. Operates July-Aug.

Ice time at the camp totals two and a half hours daily, with instruction in all phases of hockey. The program also features off-ice lectures and exercises. For goaltenders, a full-time instructor oversees a specialized program that includes video analysis and a detailed written evaluation. Aside from hockey, activities include waterfront activities, field sports and outdoor camping.

HOOFBEAT RIDGE
Res — Girls Ages 7-16; Day — Boys 7-9, Girls 7-12

Mazomanie, WI 53560. 5304 Reeve Rd. Tel: 608-767-2593. Fax: 608-767-2590. www.hoofbeat.org E-mail: hoofbeat@midplains.net Ted Marthe & Mary Bennett-Marthe, Dirs. Adm: FCFS. **Appl due:** Rolling. **Enr:** 65. **Enr cap:** 65. **Staff:** Admin 7. Couns 30. **Focus:** Equestrian. **Features:** Crafts Drama Hiking Riding.

Fees 2012: Res $649-1178 (+$20-45), 1-2 wks. Day $224 (+$10-15), 1 wk.
Housing: Cabins Lodges.
Est 1962. Inc. **Ses:** 12. **Wks/ses:** 1-2. Operates June-Aug. ACA.

The camp emphasizes horsemanship through three daily skill sessions that include English and Western riding, horse science, arts and crafts, pioneer skills and land sports. Hoofbeat Ridge also features trail rides and hayrides.

IMG ACADEMIES
Res and Day — Coed Ages 8-18

Bradenton, FL 34210. 5500 34th St W. Tel: 941-752-2600, 800-872-6425.
  Fax: 941-752-2531.
www.imgacademies.com   E-mail: netsales@imgworld.com
Sam Zussman, Dir.
Adm: FCFS. **Appl due:** Rolling.
Focus: Baseball Basketball Golf Soccer Swim Tennis. **Features:** Weight_Trng.
Fees 2009: Res $1225-1975, 1 wk. Day $975-1725, 1 wk. Aid avail.
Housing: Dorms Hotels. **Swimming:** Pool.
Est 1978. Wks/ses: 1. Operates Year-round.

IMG Academies encompasses the IMG Bollettieri Tennis Academy; the IMG Leadbetter Golf Academy; soccer, baseball and basketball academies; the Wellness Spa; the IMG Performance Institute; and the Evert Tennis Academy in Boca Raton. In addition to its summer camps, IMGA conducts weekly programs throughout the year, as well as full-time semester, adult, family and corporate programs. Individuals of all ability levels may enroll.

INTERNATIONAL RIDING CAMP
Res — Girls Ages 7-17

Greenfield Park, NY 12435. 200 Birchall Rd. Tel: 845-647-3240.
Contact (Nov-Apr): 9655 W Maiden Ct, Vero Beach, FL 32963. Tel: 914-850-9027.
www.horseridingcamp.com   E-mail: arnomares1@mac.com
Arno Mares, Dir.
Adm: FCFS. **Appl due:** May. **Staff:** Admin 4. Couns 20.
Focus: Equestrian. **Features:** Crafts Fine_Arts Music Riding Basketball Swim Tennis Water-skiing Watersports Polo.
Fees 2012: Res $2000-14,700, 1-10 wks.
Housing: Cabins. **Swimming:** Lake Pool.
Est 1978. Inc. **Ses:** 21. **Wks/ses:** 1-10. Operates June-Aug.

Providing three hours of riding daily, the camp offers programs to develop skills in hunt-seat equitation, showing, polo and cross-country jumping. Cross-country trails, a hunt course, a dressage ring, a stadium jumping ring and an indoor arena are among the facilities. Other activities include crafts, tennis, swimming and water-skiing.

INTERNATIONAL SPORTS TRAINING CAMP
Res — Coed Ages 8-17

Stroudsburg, PA 18360. 1100 Twin Lake Rd. Tel: 570-620-2267, 888-879-4782.
  Fax: 570-620-1692.
www.international-sports.com   E-mail: office@international-sports.com
Mark Major & Kara Klaus-Major, Dirs.
Grades 3-12. Adm: FCFS. **Appl due:** Rolling. **Enr:** 250. **Staff:** Admin 5. Couns 85. Res 100.
Focus: Gen_Sports Soccer. **Features:** Crafts Aquatics Archery Boating Climbing_Wall Fishing Hiking Kayak Mtn_Biking Rappelling Rock_Climb Ropes_Crse Baseball Cricket

Field_Hockey Football Gymnastics Lacrosse Rugby Softball Swim Ultimate_Frisbee Volleyball Water-skiing Watersports.
Fees 2012: Res $935-1285, 1 wk.
Housing: Cabins. Avg per room/unit: 20. **Swimming:** Lake.
Est 1991. Inc. **Ses:** 9. **Wks/ses:** 1. Operates June-Aug. ACA.

ISTC provides individualized sports instruction in many land sports and watersports. In addition to a soccer program, the camp conducts a general sports program. This program allows campers to receive training in a wide selection of sports (including less traditional offerings such as mountain biking) instead of focusing on only one. IXTC, a program for campers ages 15-17, combines sports and adventure pursuits.

JENNIFER AVERILL'S WAKE FOREST FIELD HOCKEY CAMP
Res and Day — Girls Ages 10-18

Winston-Salem, NC 27106. 112 Belle Vista Ct. Tel: 336-655-0395. Fax: 336-758-4565.
www.wakeforestfieldhockeycamp.com   E-mail: wfhockey@gmail.com
Jennifer Averill, Dir.
Grades 6-12. Adm: FCFS. Admitted: 100%. **Appl due:** Rolling. **Enr:** 200. **Enr cap:** 200.
Staff: Admin 2. Couns 20. Res 5.
Focus: Field_Hockey.
Fees 2012: Res $490, 1 wk. Day $417, 1 wk.
Housing: Dorms.
Est 1993. Inc. **Ses:** 2. **Wks/ses:** 1. Operates July.

This Wake Forest sports program consists of two camps. The residential and day individual camp serves girls of all experience and ability levels, while the elite camp (for boarders only) is designed specifically for girls interested in playing field hockey at a higher level. In addition to skills instruction, the program includes applied mental and sports psychology techniques, video analysis, sport-specific fitness and conditioning tips, and a discussion of college recruiting issues.

JOE MACHNIK'S NO. 1 SOCCER CAMPS
Res and Day — Coed Ages 8-18

Isle of Palms, SC 29451. 26 Intracoastal Ct. Tel: 843-270-2600.
www.no1soccercamps.com   E-mail: info@no1soccercamps.com
Joseph A. Machnik, Dir.
Grades 3-PG. Adm: FCFS. **Enr:** 200.
Locations: CA CO CT FL GA IL MA MD OH OR PA SC TX VA.
Focus: Soccer. **Features:** Swim.
Fees 2011: Res $400-1389, ½-2 wks. Day $249-350, ½-1 wk.
Housing: Dorms. **Swimming:** Pool.
Est 1977. Inc. **Wks/ses:** ½-1. Operates June-Aug.

Camp sessions throughout the country include separate goalkeeper and striker programs at both regular and advanced levels. Campers are grouped by age, size and ability and are continually reevaluated. Half-week minicamps operate at certain locations.

JOEL ROSS TENNIS & SPORTS CAMP
Res — Coed Ages 8-18

Kent, CT. Kent School. Tel: 860-927-6339. Fax: 860-927-6340.
Contact (Sept-May): PO Box 62H, Scarsdale, NY 10583. Tel: 914-723-2165.
Fax: 914-723-4579.
www.joelrosstennis.com   E-mail: info@joelrosstennis.com

Joel Ross, Dir.
Adm: FCFS. **Appl due:** Rolling. **Enr:** 100. **Staff:** Couns 25.
Focus: Golf Tennis. **Features:** Crafts Archery Canoe Chess Fishing Hiking Kayak Basketball Football Soccer Softball Swim Ultimate_Frisbee Volleyball.
Fees 2012: Res $2790-7770, 2-6 wks.
Housing: Dorms. **Swimming:** Pool.
Est 1991. Inc. **Ses:** 3. **Wks/ses:** 2. Operates June-Aug. ACA.

Joel Ross conducts separate tennis and golf camps. Tennis players, from beginner to advanced, get four to six hours of daily instruction and match play. The camp schedules ladder matches each day and tournaments weekly. Golfers play at least nine holes daily at local courses and practice on the camp's own driving range and 300-yard hole. Various activities and other sports round out the program.

JOHN NEWCOMBE TENNIS RANCH SUMMER ACADEMY
Res and Day — Coed Ages 8-18

New Braunfels, TX 78132. 325 Mission Valley Rd. Tel: 830-625-9105, 800-444-6204.
Fax: 830-625-2004.
www.newktennis.com   E-mail: academy@newktennis.com
Phil Hendrie, Dir.
Adm: FCFS. **Appl due:** Rolling. **Enr:** 200. **Enr cap:** 250. **Staff:** Admin 25. Couns 50.
Focus: Tennis. **Features:** Aquatics Kayak Rappelling Rock_Climb Ropes_Crse Basketball Swim Ultimate_Frisbee Watersports Weight_Trng.
Fees 2012: Res $740, 1 wk. Day $425, 1 wk.
Housing: Cabins Dorms Lodges. **Swimming:** Pool.
Est 1969. Inc. **Ses:** 8. **Wks/ses:** 1. Operates June-Aug.

The Summer Academy instructs players of all ability levels in basic and advanced tennis techniques while developing teamwork and leadership skills. The camp stresses individual attention, and all campers receive a written evaluation during their stay. Tennis instruction combines classroom sessions, drills, match play and team competitions. Among recreational activities are swimming and water park trips.

KEMUR CAMP
Res — Girls Ages 7-14

Cambridge, N1R 5S5 Ontario, Canada. 2130 W River Rd. Tel: 519-621-2109.
Fax: 519-621-4872.
www.kemurcamp.com   E-mail: info@kemurcamp.com
Lee Murray & Erin Murray, Dirs.
Adm: FCFS. **Appl due:** May. **Enr:** 55. **Enr cap:** 55. **Staff:** Couns 20.
Focus: Equestrian. **Features:** Riding Swim.
Fees 2012: Res $950, 1 wk.
Housing: Houses. Avg per room/unit: 26-28. **Swimming:** Pool.
Est 1969. Inc. **Ses:** 9. **Wks/ses:** 1. Operates July-Sept.

Kemur's program, which emphasizes English horsemanship, includes varied levels of instruction, stable management, a cross-country course and weekly horse shows. Other activities are swimming, sports and hayrides.

KINYON/JONES TENNIS CAMP
Res and Day — Coed Ages 10-17

Hanover, NH. Dartmouth College.
Contact (Year-round): 24 College Hill, Hanover, NH 03755. Tel: 603-646-0751.

Fax: 603-646-0757.
www.dartmouth.edu/~mten/camp.html   E-mail: tenniscamp@kjtctennis.com
Chris Drake & Bob Dallis, Dirs.
Adm: FCFS. **Appl due:** Rolling. **Enr:** 56. **Staff:** Couns 11.
Focus: Tennis. **Features:** Soccer Swim.
Fees 2012: Res $750, 1 wk. Day $550, 1 wk.
Housing: Dorms. **Swimming:** Pool.
Est 1988. Inc. **Ses:** 5. **Wks/ses:** 1. Operates June-Aug.

Held at Dartmouth College, KJTC provides one-on-one tennis instruction, drills, games, physical training and lectures. Recreational activities and free time are part of the schedule.

KUTSHER'S SPORTS ACADEMY
Res — Coed Ages 7-17

Great Barrington, MA 01230. PO Box 252. Tel: 413-644-0077, 888-874-5400.
Fax: 413-644-0078.
www.kutsherssportsacademy.com   E-mail: marc@kutsherssportsacademy.com
Marc White, Exec Dir.
Adm: FCFS. **Appl due:** May. **Enr:** 500. **Enr cap:** 500. **Staff:** Admin 10. Couns 120.
Focus: Baseball Basketball Cross-country Equestrian Field_Hockey Football Golf Gymnastics Lacrosse Soccer Softball Swim Tennis Track Volleyball Wrestling. **Features:** Circus_Skills Crafts Aquatics Boating Canoe Climbing_Wall Fishing Kayak Mtn_Biking Paintball Sail White-water_Raft Woodcraft Aerobics Martial_Arts Roller_Hockey Skateboarding Water-skiing Watersports Weight_Trng.
Fees 2012: Res $2800-8600 (+$400), 2-7 wks. Aid avail.
Housing: Cabins Dorms. Avg per room/unit: 6. **Swimming:** Lake Pool.
Est 1968. Inc. **Ses:** 7. **Wks/ses:** 2-7. Operates June-Aug. ACA.

Boys and girls specialize in their favorite sports under the direction of highly regarded coaches and teachers. KSA provides intensive instruction in a wide array of individual and team athletics. Boys and girls design their own camp programs on an elective basis—with assistance from coaches and counselors—according to personal needs and interests.

LAKE OWEN CAMP
Res — Coed Ages 7-17

Cable, WI 54821. 46445 Krafts Point Rd. Tel: 715-798-3785. Fax: 715-798-3898.
www.lakeowencamp.com   E-mail: campoffice@lakeowencamp.com
Ron Lenz, Dir.
Adm: FCFS. **Appl due:** Apr. **Enr:** 300.
Focus: Cheerleading Extreme_Sports Gymnastics Skateboarding. **Features:** Crafts Dance Aquatics Boating Climbing_Wall Ropes_Crse In-line_Skating Swim Water-skiing.
Fees 2012: Res $745-965 (+$20), 1 wk.
Housing: Cabins. **Swimming:** Lake.
Est 1986. Inc. **Ses:** 10. **Wks/ses:** 1. Operates June-Aug.

Lake Owen provides instruction in five areas: gymnastics, cheerleading, skateboarding and freestyle BMX biking. Gymnastics and cheerleading campers engage in five hours of structured class time daily, plus two hours of supervised open workout time; campers in the action sports programs receive three hours of daily instruction and up to seven hours of supervised open practice time. Participants in all sports take part in afternoon recreation.

LAKE PLACID SOCCER CENTRE SUMMER CAMP
Res and Day — Coed Ages 5-18

Lake Placid, NY 12946. PO Box 847. Tel: 518-523-4395, 800-845-9959.
Fax: 518-523-9476.
www.lakeplacidsoccer.com   E-mail: coach@lpsoccer.com
Michael McGlynn, Dir.
Grades K-12. Adm: FCFS. Appl due: Rolling. Enr: 125-350. Enr cap: 400. Staff: Admin
1. Couns 70.
Locations: NY.
Focus: Soccer. Features: Swim.
Fees 2010: Res $665-950, 1 wk. Day $189-325, 1 wk.
Housing: Dorms. Swimming: Pool.
Est 1976. Inc. Ses: 12. Wks/ses: 1. Operates June-Aug.

LPSC conducts regular programs at several private school and college campuses in New York State, as well as elite/advanced, team training and goalkeeper sessions. Boys and girls improve their skills with the aid of internationally known soccer players, as well as noted coaches and trainers. Elite sessions enroll accomplished high school and college-bound players, while team training sessions serve club and high school teams of various ages. Players ages 8-18 may attend the goalkeeping camp.

MADAWASKA VOLLEYBALL AND ALL-SPORT CAMPS
Res — Coed Ages 9-18

Palmer Rapids, K0J 2E0 Ontario, Canada. RR 2, 38483 Hwy 28. Tel: 613-758-2365.
Fax: 613-758-2427.
Contact (Sept-July): 1801 Dundas St E, PO Box 70570, Whitby, L1N 9G3 Ontario,
Canada. Tel: 905-438-8822. Fax: 905-438-8801.
Year-round Toll-free: 866-553-0655.
www.madawaskacamps.com   E-mail: info@madawaskacamps.com
Ian Eibbitt, Dir.
Grades 4-12. Adm: FCFS. Appl due: Rolling. Staff: Admin 1. Couns 130.
Focus: Gen_Sports Volleyball. Features: Archery Canoe Climbing_Wall Kayak Rock_
Climb Ropes_Crse Basketball Roller_Hockey Soccer Street_Hockey Swim Tennis Ulti-
mate_Frisbee Water-skiing Watersports.
Fees 2011: Res Can$791-1396 (+Can$50-120), 1-2 wks.
Housing: Cabins. Avg per room/unit: 12-16. Swimming: Lake.
Est 1973. Inc. Ses: 3. Wks/ses: 1-2. Operates Aug-Sept.

Athletes at these instructional sports camps are grouped by age, ability and gender. Campers enroll in either a general sports program or a volleyball camp or combine the two by attending for two weeks. Boys and girls receive individual attention and also engage in competitive team play. Canoeing, kayaking and climbing, as well as daily recreational swimming, supplement traditional sports instruction.

CAMP MAH-KEE-NAC
Res — Boys Ages 7-15

Lenox, MA 01240. 6 Hawthorne Rd. Tel: 413-637-0781. Fax: 413-637-8245.
Contact (Sept-May): 3 New King St, White Plains, NY 10604. Tel: 914-997-6043.
Fax: 914-997-6063.
Year-round Toll-free: 800-753-9118.
www.campmkn.com   E-mail: info@campmkn.com
Walter Synalovski, Dir.
Grades 2-10. Adm: FCFS. Appl due: Rolling. Enr: 350. Staff: Admin 5. Couns 160.
Travel: CA MA ME NY.

Focus: Gen_Sports. **Features:** Crafts Creative_Writing Filmmaking Music Painting Photog Studio_Art Theater Adventure_Travel Aquatics Archery Bicycle_Tours Boating Canoe Chess Climbing_Wall Community_Serv Cooking Farm Fishing Hiking Kayak Mtn_Biking Outdoor_Ed Rock_Climb Ropes_Crse Sail White-water_Raft Wilderness_Camp Wood-craft Baseball Basketball Cross-country Football Golf Gymnastics Lacrosse Roller_ Hockey Rugby Soccer Softball Street_Hockey Swim Tennis Track Ultimate_Frisbee Volleyball Water-skiing Watersports Weight_Trng Wrestling.
Fees 2012: Res $4750-8800 (+$100-300), 3-7 wks.
Housing: Cabins. Avg per room/unit: 10. **Swimming:** Lake Pool.
Est 1929. Inc. Ses: 5. Wks/ses: 3-7. Operates June-Aug. ACA.

Mah-Kee-Nac maintains a particularly strong athletic program for boys of varying skill levels, with all sports directed by either high school or college coaches. In addition, campers may participate in such nonsporting activities such as art, wood shop, rocketry, camp radio and newspaper. Hiking, overnight camping and nature are other important aspects of camp life. Older campers embark on group trips to sites of interest in Maine, Massachusetts, New York and California.

MAINE GOLF & TENNIS ACADEMY
Res — Coed Ages 8-17

North Belgrade, ME 04917. 35 Golf Academy Dr. Tel: 207-465-3226, 800-465-3226.
Fax: 207-465-2822.
www.golfcamp.com   E-mail: fun@golfcamp.com
Joel Lavenson, Dir.
Adm: FCFS. **Appl due:** Mar. **Enr:** 100. **Staff:** Admin 8. Couns 39.
Focus: Golf Ice_Hockey Tennis. **Features:** ESL Crafts Dance Media Theater Aquatics Bicycle_Tours Boating Canoe Climbing_Wall Fishing Hiking Kayak Mountaineering Mtn_Biking Mtn_Trips Rock_Climb Ropes_Crse Sail White-water_Raft Wilderness_ Camp Baseball Basketball Football Soccer Swim Volleyball Water-skiing Watersports.
Fees 2012: Res $3500-9500 (+$275-325), 2-8 wks.
Housing: Cabins. Avg per room/unit: 7. **Swimming:** Lake.
Est 1996. Ses: 6. Wks/ses: 2-4. Operates June-Aug. ACA.

The academy's golf instruction center and golf school is conducted by PGA professionals, golf instructors and golf coaches. Instruction and play incorporate daily outings throughout Maine to 18-hole golf courses for afternoon play, tournaments, video analysis, club making and sports psychology. The tennis program comprises instruction and afternoon competition, intercamp matches and daily outings throughout Maine. Campers may also enroll in an ice hockey camp, and combination programs of any two of the three target sports are available.

MALIBU SOCCER ACADEMY
Res — Boys Ages 9-13, Girls 9-17; Day — Coed 5-12

Malibu, CA 90264. PO Box 6742. Tel: 310-506-7774.
www.malibusocceracademy.com   E-mail: info@malibusocceracademy.com
Tim Ward & Twila Kaufman, Dirs.
Adm: FCFS. **Appl due:** Rolling. **Enr:** 120. **Staff:** Admin 3.
Focus: Soccer. **Features:** Swim.
Fees 2009: Res $490-575, 1 wk. Day $185-235, 1 wk.
Housing: Dorms. **Swimming:** Ocean Pool.
Est 1995. Inc. Ses: 7. Wks/ses: 1. Operates June-Aug.

Conducted at Pepperdine University, the academy addresses technical training, tactical decision making and positional play as it works with players on skill development. Players are grouped according to age and ability. Most sessions are coeducational, but the camp schedules one all-girls week for residential players of high school age.

MALIBU WATER POLO CAMP
Res and Day — Coed Ages 12-18

Malibu, CA. Pepperdine Univ.
Contact (Year-round): PO Box 3095, Thousand Oaks, CA 91359. Tel: 818-889-8732.
Fax: 818-889-7368.
www.posturepack.net   E-mail: tasdc1@hotmail.com
Terry A. Schroeder, Dir.
Adm: FCFS. **Appl due:** Rolling. **Staff:** Couns 10.
Focus: Watersports. **Features:** Aquatics Swim.
Fees 2011: Res $485-895, ½-1 wk. Day $435-750, ½-1 wk.
Housing: Dorms. **Swimming:** Ocean Pool.
Inc. **Ses:** 5. **Wks/ses:** ½-1. Operates June-July.

Conducted at Pepperdine University, the camp conducts separate programs for advanced water polo players having at least two years experience and for less experienced boys and girls. With an emphasis on higher-level skills, the advanced camp places campers by position into three groups. Instruction addresses both individual and team skills, and demonstrations and lectures are part of the program.

MARMON VALLEY FARM
Res — Coed Ages 7-17

Zanesfield, OH 43360. 7754 State Rte 292. Tel: 937-593-8051. Fax: 937-593-6900.
www.marmonvalley.com   E-mail: info@marmonvalley.com
Kyle Augsburger, Admin.
Adm: FCFS. **Appl due:** Rolling. **Enr:** 115. **Enr cap:** 115. **Staff:** Admin 4. Couns 30.
Focus: Equestrian. **Features:** Crafts Archery Boating Climbing_Wall Farm Fishing Hiking Kayak Pack_Train Riding Rock_Climb Ropes_Crse Swim.
Fees 2012: Res $410-630 (+$10), ½-1 wk. Aid 2009 (Need): $20,000.
Housing: Cabins. Avg per room/unit: 9. **Swimming:** Lake.
Est 1964. Nonprofit. Nondenom Christian. **Ses:** 26. **Wks/ses:** ½-1. Operates June-Aug. ACA.

This Christian horse camp emphasizes four main areas as it enrolls riders of varying ability levels: grooming and saddling, arena riding, trail riding and theory. In all programs, campers ride an assigned horse or pony for the week and learn elements of horse care. Advanced riders ages 12-17 who have upper-level English riding and jumping experience may attend the equestrian camp. A horse packing session features tent camping and cattle roundups.

MAUI SURFER GIRLS
Res — Girls Ages 12-17

Puunene, HI 96784. PO Box 1158. Tel: 808-280-8165. Fax: 808-242-4127.
www.mauisurfergirls.com   E-mail: info@mauisurfergirls.com
Dustin Tester, Dir.
Adm: FCFS. **Appl due:** Rolling. **Enr cap:** 20. **Staff:** Admin 3. Couns 10.
Focus: Surfing. **Features:** Hiking Kayak Swim.
Fees 2012: Res $1900-4450, 1-3 wks.
Housing: Cabins. Avg per room/unit: 5. **Swimming:** Ocean.
Est 2000. Inc. **Ses:** 3. **Wks/ses:** 1-3. Operates July.

MSG provides morning training for beginning and intermediate surfers. Girls devote afternoons to such sign-up activities as Hawaiian bracelet making, snorkeling trips, windsurfing lessons, mountain hiking and visits to the local aquarium.

McCALLIE LACROSSE CAMPS
Res — Boys Ages 11-15; Day — Boys 8-15

Chattanooga, TN 37404. 500 Dodds Ave. Tel: 423-493-5852. Fax: 423-493-5426.
www.msc.mccallie.org   E-mail: wce@mccallie.org
Troy Kemp, Dir.
Adm: FCFS. **Appl due:** Rolling. **Enr:** 90. **Enr cap:** 90.
Focus: Lacrosse.
Fees 2011: Res $550, 1 wk. Day $225-425, 1 wk.
Housing: Dorms.
Nonprofit. **Spons:** McCallie School. **Ses:** 2. **Wks/ses:** 1. Operates June.

Players learn all aspects of team lacrosse play at the camps, with an emphasis placed on the development of fundamental skills and the mechanics of individual offense and defense. Individual and team skill sessions and a team game are part the program each day. Camps serve both beginning and experienced players, with level of expertise helpful in determining the appropriate week of camp.

McCALLIE SOCCER CAMP
Res — Boys Ages 11-15

Chattanooga, TN 37404. 500 Dodds Ave. Tel: 423-493-5852. Fax: 423-493-5426.
www.msc.mccallie.org   E-mail: wce@mccallie.org
Tony Meyers, Dir.
Grades 5-10. Adm: FCFS. **Appl due:** Rolling. **Enr:** 20. **Enr cap:** 20.
Focus: Soccer.
Fees 2011: Res $450, 1 wk.
Housing: Dorms.
Nonprofit. **Spons:** McCallie School. **Ses:** 1. **Wks/ses:** 1. Operates June.

Staffed by experienced high school and college players, the camp seeks to develop the participant's basic technical and tactical skills. Instruction typically involves small-sided games that provide the player with many opportunities to touch the ball and make decisions. Repetition of play facilitates skill development and improves the player's versatility. Boys are grouped by age and ability level.

McCALLIE SPORTS CAMP
Res — Boys Ages 9-15

Chattanooga, TN 37404. 500 Dodds Ave. Tel: 423-493-5528, 800-672-2267.
    Fax: 423-493-5426.
www.msc.mccallie.org   E-mail: sportscamp@mccallie.org
Michael O. Wood, Dir.
Adm: FCFS. **Appl due:** Rolling. **Enr:** 120. **Enr cap:** 140.
Focus: Baseball Basketball Field_Hockey Football Golf Lacrosse Soccer Swim Tennis
    Track. **Features:** Aquatics Climbing_Wall Exploration Hiking Paintball White-water_Raft
    Cross-country Volleyball Watersports Wrestling.
Fees 2012: Res $1950, 2 wks.
Housing: Dorms. **Swimming:** Pool.
Est 1977. Nonprofit. **Ses:** 3. **Wks/ses:** 2. Operates June-July.

Emphasizing fun, sportsmanship and participation, MSC provides sports instruction in baseball, basketball, football, soccer, lacrosse, tennis and golf, as well as in swimming, water polo, wrestling and weight training. White-water rafting and trips to local sporting events and amusement parks are among the camp's other activities.

McCALLIE TENNIS CAMP
Res — Boys Ages 11-16

Chattanooga, TN 37404. 500 Dodds Ave. Tel: 423-493-5852. Fax: 423-493-5426.
www.msc.mccallie.org   E-mail: wce@mccallie.org
Eric Voges, Dir.
Adm: FCFS. **Appl due:** Rolling. **Enr:** 20. **Enr cap:** 20.
Focus: Tennis.
Fees 2011: Res $550, 1 wk.
Housing: Dorms.
Nonprofit. **Spons:** McCallie School. **Ses:** 2. **Wks/ses:** 1. Operates June-July.

The structure of this camp enables boys to hit many tennis balls each day. Instructors address technique, strategy and conditioning during the course of the week. Sessions are divided by skill level and age, and daily activities vary according to the player's skill level.

MERCERSBURG ACADEMY
STORM WRESTLING CAMPS
Res and Day — Boys Ages 6-15

Mercersburg, PA 17236. 300 E Seminary St. Tel: 717-328-6225. Fax: 717-328-9072.
www.mercersburgsummer.com   E-mail: summerprograms@mercersburg.edu
Nate Jacklin, Dir.
Grades 1-10. Adm: FCFS. **Appl due:** Rolling.
Focus: Wrestling. **Features:** Swim.
Fees 2009: Res $215-355, ½-1 wk. Day $160-255, ½-1 wk.
Housing: Dorms. **Swimming:** Pool.
Nonprofit. **Ses:** 2. **Wks/ses:** ½-1. Operates June.

Taking a systematic approach to the sport, Mercersburg teaches wrestling skills at two camps: a half-week junior program for children in grades 1-4, and a weeklong senior session for students in grades 5-10. The programs integrate technique and drilling sessions, live wrestling, mental preparation training and recreational competitions. Guest clinicians join with base staff to provide instruction.

MERESTEAD SPORTS CAMPS
Res and Day — Girls Ages 10-17

Richmond, VA 23227. PO Box 9278. Tel: 804-440-9551. Fax: 804-767-1161.
www.merestead.com   E-mail: info@merestead.com
Missy Ackerman, Dir.
Grades 5-12. Adm: FCFS. **Appl due:** Rolling.
Locations: PA VA VT.
Focus: Field_Hockey Lacrosse. **Features:** Swim.
Fees 2012: Res $575, 1 wk. Day $450, 1 wk.
Swimming: Pool.
Est 1946. Inc. **Ses:** 4. **Wks/ses:** 1. Operates June-July.

Merestead conducts girls' field hockey and lacrosse camps at three locations: Castleton State College, Castleton, VT; Sweet Briar College, Sweet Briar, VA; and Bryn Mawr College, Bryn Mawr, PA. Sessions include stick work and technique instruction, match games, tournaments, video analysis and lectures. Participants are grouped by experience and ability. In addition to the general camps, Merestead offers special goalkeeping and coaching clinics.

MIDDLE STATES SOCCER CAMP
Res and Day — Coed Ages 8-18

Burke, VA 22009. PO Box 11742. Tel: 703-455-5772. Fax: 703-455-5778.
www.middlestatessoccercamp.com
E-mail: pholmes@middlestatessoccercamp.com
Richard Deane Broad, Dir.
Grades 3-12. **Adm:** FCFS. **Appl due:** Rolling. **Enr:** 100. **Enr cap:** 150. **Staff:** Admin 4.
  Couns 5. Res 10.
Locations: DE VA.
Focus: Soccer. **Features:** Swim.
Fees 2011: Res $595-635 (+$50), 1 wk. Day $335-495 (+$50), 1 wk. Aid 2009 (Need):
  $2000.
Housing: Dorms. Avg per room/unit: 2. **Swimming:** Pool.
Est 1974. Inc. **Ses:** 4. **Wks/ses:** 1. Operates July-Aug.

Designed to help serious players develop skills and experience game competition, MSSC's curriculum and schedule are modeled after top youth soccer academies in Europe and South America. Players receive seven hours of daily instruction and compete in both 11-on-11 games and small-sided play. Specialized sessions focus on goal scoring/goalkeeping, skill enhancement, preseason training and advanced player instruction. Camps operate on two campuses: Episcopal High School in Alexandria and St. Andrew's School, Middletown, DE.

MINNESOTA HOCKEY CAMPS
Res — Coed Ages 8 and up; Day — Coed 5-8

Nisswa, MN 56468. 24621 S Clark Lake Rd. Tel: 218-963-2444, 877-423-2447.
  Fax: 218-963-2325.
www.mnhockeycamps.com   E-mail: carrie@mnhockeycamps.com
Carrie Grillo, Dir.
Adm: FCFS. **Appl due:** Rolling. **Enr:** 200. **Enr cap:** 200. **Staff:** Admin 45. Couns 12.
Focus: Ice_Hockey. **Features:** Boating Canoe Fishing Weight_Loss Basketball Roller_
  Hockey Skateboarding Street_Hockey Swim Volleyball Weight_Trng.
Fees 2012: Res $925-6525 (+$75), 1-9 wks. Day $380 (+$75), 1 wk.
Housing: Cabins Dorms Lodges. Avg per room/unit: 3. **Swimming:** Lake.
Est 1979. Inc. **Ses:** 22. **Wks/ses:** 1-9. Operates June-Aug.

MHC operates a summer league and instructional camps for all ability levels. Basic skills camps offer on- and off-ice training to players of all ability levels, and select camps are designed for top players in six different age groups (starting at age 11). Goalie and parent/child camps are part of the annual schedule.

MISS PORTER'S SCHOOL ROWING ACADEMY
Res — Girls Ages 12-15

Farmington, CT 06032. 60 Main St. Tel: 860-409-3692, 800-447-2724.
  Fax: 860-409-3537.
www.porters.org/summerprograms   E-mail: summer_programs@missporters.org
Wes Ng, Dir.
Grades 7-10. **Adm:** FCFS. **Appl due:** Rolling.
Focus: Rowing/Sculling.
Fees 2011: Res $1000, 1 wk. Aid (Merit & Need).
Housing: Dorms. Avg per room/unit: 2.
Nonprofit. **Ses:** 1. **Wks/ses:** 1. Operates July.

Girls enrolled in this program learn from experienced coaches and benefit from Miss Porter's well-developed athletic facilities. Guest speakers and special workshops complement morning, afternoon and early-evening training sessions. Instruction addresses both rowing technique and tactical knowledge.

MT. HOOD SUMMER SKI CAMPS
Res — Coed Ages 9 and up

Government Camp, OR 97028. PO Box 317. Tel: 503-337-2230. Fax: 888-580-4764.
www.mthood.com   E-mail: mike@mthood.com
Mike Annett, Dir.
Adm: FCFS. **Appl due:** Rolling. **Enr cap:** 150. **Staff:** Admin 10. Couns 45.
Focus: Winter_Sports. **Features:** Aquatics Bicycle_Tours Boating Caving Hiking Mtn_ Biking Paintball Rappelling Rock_Climb Ropes_Crse Sail White-water_Raft Baseball Basketball Skateboarding Soccer Softball Swim Volleyball Water-skiing Watersports Weight_Trng.
Fees 2012: Res $1025-1195, 1 wk.
Housing: Cabins Dorms Houses Lodges. Avg per room/unit: 8. **Swimming:** Lake Ocean River Stream.
Est 1979. Inc. Ses: 13. **Wks/ses:** 1. Operates May-Aug.

Winter sports athletes choose from the following summer options at Mt. Hood: ski racing (covering slalom, giant slalom and super G), freestyle skiing and snowboarding. Campers spend Saturdays resting and sightseeing in Oregon, then devote Sundays to light skiing and snowboarding. While mature campers as young as age 9 may enroll, the vast majority of campers are at least 12 years old.

NATIONAL ALPINE SKI CAMP
Res and Day — Coed Ages 8-18

Government Camp, OR 97028. PO Box 418. Tel: 303-579-3562.
Contact (Sept-May): PO Box 652, Ophir, CO 81426. Tel: 970-728-6112.
Year-round Toll-free: 800-453-6272.
www.skicamp.com   E-mail: nasc@skicamp.com
Brad Alire, Dir.
Adm: FCFS. **Appl due:** Rolling. **Enr:** 50. **Staff:** Admin 4. Couns 10.
Focus: Winter_Sports. **Features:** Bicycle_Tours Boating Canoe Climbing_Wall Hiking Mountaineering Mtn_Biking Mtn_Trips Rock_Climb Ropes_Crse Sail White-water_Raft Wilderness_Camp Badminton Basketball Football Roller_Hockey Skateboarding Swim Tennis Ultimate_Frisbee Volleyball.
Fees 2012: Res $1659-4395 (+$50), 1-3 wks. Day $1695-2195, 1-1½ wks.
Housing: Cabins Houses Lodges. Avg per room/unit: 6. **Swimming:** Lake Pond Pool.
Est 1984. Inc. Ses: 5. **Wks/ses:** 1-3. Operates June-Aug.

Located on Mt. Hood, NASC operates a comprehensive program for those ranging in ability from intermediate skiers to top-level racers. During each day of camp, campers receive training in several aspects of ski training: after a free skiing warm-up, the program features skills work and free skiing drills, which are combined with running gate drills and courses. The camp's structure enables skiers to work simultaneously on fundamental skills and racing tactics and strategies. Instructors help skiers work at appropriate levels of difficulty and intensity.

NIKE BIG LEAGUE BASEBALL CAMP
Res and Day — Boys Ages 8-17

Sparta, NJ 07871. PO Box 15. Tel: 973-691-0070, 800-433-6060. Fax: 973-347-5832.
www.psccamps.com   E-mail: sportscamp@aol.com
John Carlesi & Vincent Carlesi, Jr., Dirs.
Adm: FCFS. **Appl due:** Rolling. **Staff:** Admin 3. Couns 15.

Locations: NJ NY.
Focus: Baseball. **Features:** Swim.
Fees 2011: Res $655-699 (+$45), 1 wk. **Day** $295-575 (+$45), 1 wk.
Housing: Dorms. **Swimming:** Pool.
Est 1946. Inc. **Spons:** Professional Sports Camps. **Ses:** 5. **Wks/ses:** 1. Operates June-Aug.

With locations at Lawrenceville Academy (Lawrenceville, NJ), Adelphi University (Garden City, NY) and the State University of New York Maritime College (in Throggs Neck) the camp emphasizes the fundamentals of baseball and strong positional play. A staff consisting of experienced coaches provide lectures, conduct drills and oversee instructional games. Instruction is appropriate for players of all skill levels.

NORTHEAST FIELD HOCKEY CLINICS
Res — Girls Ages 10-18; Day — Girls 8-18

Byfield, MA. The Governor's Academy.
Contact (Year-round): PO Box 839, East Hampstead, NH 03826. Tel: 603-887-4907.
Fax: 603-887-3502.
www.northeastclinics.com   E-mail: northeastclinics@hotmail.com
Shannon LeBlanc Hlebichuk, Dir.
Grades 3-12. Adm: FCFS. **Appl due:** Rolling.
Focus: Field_Hockey.
Fees 2012: Res $515, ½ wk. **Day** $140-445, ½ wk.
Housing: Dorms Houses.
Est 1976. Inc. **Ses:** 1. **Wks/ses:** ½. Operates July.

This instructional field hockey camp welcomes players of all ability levels, from beginning players to varsity athletes. Held on the campus of The Governor's Academy, the program utilizes the school's 10 regulation fields, four indoor synthetic surfaces, a gymnasium, dormitories and dining halls. Morning instruction in individual skills, stick work and defensive techniques is put into practice in afternoon and evening competitions. Young girls entering grades 3 and 4 may attend as day campers only.

NORTHWEST SOCCER CAMP
Res and Day — Coed Ages 7-18

Kenmore, WA 98028. c/o Bastyr Univ, 14500 Juanita Dr NE.
Contact (Sept-May): 15600 NE 8th St, Ste 647, Bellevue, WA 98008.
Year-round Tel: 425-644-0470, Fax: 888-471-1965.
www.nwsoccer.org   E-mail: info@nwsoccer.org
Cliff McCrath & Denise Foreman, Exec Dirs.
Grades 2-12. Adm: FCFS. **Appl due:** Rolling. **Enr cap:** 188. **Staff:** Admin 8. Couns 20.
Focus: Soccer. **Features:** Crafts Hiking Swim.
Fees 2012: Res $355-799, ½-1 wk. **Day** $130-495, ½-1 wk. Aid (Need).
Housing: Cabins Dorms. **Swimming:** Lake.
Est 1973. Nonprofit. **Ses:** 14. **Wks/ses:** ½-1. Operates June-Aug.

Conducted at Bastyr University, Northwest Soccer offers a range of intensive instructional camps for children of different ages and ability levels. Residential campers attend two sessions each day and play league games. Sessions focus on basic skills, technical and tactical play, fitness, training and sportsmanship. Recreational activities include arts and crafts, swimming, trail hikes, volleyball and movies. Day camp sessions address physical and technical skills. All players receive a written evaluation at the end of camp.

OKANAGAN HOCKEY SCHOOL
Res — Coed Ages 10-18; Day — Coed 5 and up

Penticton, V2A 9C4 British Columbia, Canada. 201-851 Eckhardt Ave W.
Tel: 250-493-1408, 888-844-6611. Fax: 250-493-9222.
www.hockeyschools.com   E-mail: ohs@hockeyschools.com
Andy Oakes, Pres.
Adm: FCFS.
Locations: Canada Europe.
Focus: Ice_Hockey.
Fees 2012: Res Can$998-1899, 1 wk. Day Can$299-1500.
Housing: Dorms.
Est 1963. Ses: 19. **Wks/ses:** 1. Operates July-Aug.

Professional instruction includes power skating, passing, puck control and stickhandling, shooting, offensive and defensive play, and checking. Camps operate at five locations in Canada, as well as one in St. Polten, Austria.

OLYMPIA SPORTS CAMP
Res — Coed Ages 8-19

Huntsville, P1H 2J6 Ontario, Canada. RR 4, 2400 Limberlost Rd. Tel: 705-635-2491.
Fax: 705-635-1601.
Contact (Sept-May): 145 Renfrew Dr, Unit 112, Markham, L3R 9R6 Ontario, Canada.
Tel: 905-479-9388. Fax: 905-479-9313.
www.olympiasportscamp.com   E-mail: info@olympiasportscamp.com
Dave Grace, Dir.
Adm: FCFS. **Appl due:** Rolling. **Staff:** Admin 6. Couns 150.
Focus: Baseball Basketball Cheerleading Cross-country Field_Hockey Football Gen_ Sports Golf Gymnastics Ice_Hockey Lacrosse Rowing/Sculling Soccer Softball Swim Tennis Volleyball Watersports Wrestling. **Features:** Circus_Skills Dance Filmmaking Aquatics Canoe Climbing_Wall Conservation Fishing Hiking Kayak Mtn_Biking Rappelling Rock_Climb Ropes_Crse Sail Wilderness_Camp.
Fees 2012: Res Can$730, 1 wk.
Housing: Cabins. Avg per room/unit: 9. **Swimming:** Lake.
Est 1974. Inc. Ses: 9. **Wks/ses:** 1. Operates July-Sept.

Specialty camps provide intensive training in a number of sports, including basketball, volleyball, tennis, football, wrestling and soccer. Each camper receives approximately six hours of daily instruction in his or her sport of choice. Aside from programs for specific sports, Olympia conducts a general sports and adventure camp that enables participants to sample many different sports.

PEAK PERFORMANCE AND DEVELOPMENTAL TENNIS CAMP
Res and Day — Coed Ages 9-18

Williamsburg, VA 23187. PO Box 399. Tel: 757-221-7375. Fax: 757-221-7377.
www.ppanddtenniscamp.com   E-mail: pbdaub@wm.edu
Peter Daub, Dir.
Adm: FCFS. **Appl due:** Rolling. **Staff:** Couns 10.
Focus: Tennis.
Fees 2011: Res $717, 1 wk. Day $278-552, 1 wk.
Housing: Dorms.
Est 1977. Inc. Ses: 2. **Wks/ses:** 1. Operates June-July.

Conducted on the campus of the College of William and Mary, PP&D accommodates beginning and intermediate players. Instruction concentrates on strategy, court zones, target areas, self-correction and mental training. The College Prep Camp, limited to eight players, serves nationally ranked high school juniors and seniors who are planning to play college tennis. Videotape analysis and film study enrich the program.

PINEBROOK FARMS HORSEMANSHIP CAMP
Res and Day — Coed Ages 7-15

Magnolia, TX 77354. 611 Virgie Community Rd. Tel: 281-356-3441. Fax: 281-356-7018.
www.pinebrook-farms.com   E-mail: jorine@pinebrook-farms.com
Jorine Seale, Dir.
Adm: FCFS. **Appl due:** Rolling. **Enr:** 35. **Enr cap:** 35. **Staff:** Admin 3. Couns 19.
Focus: Equestrian. **Features:** Crafts Archery Riding Swim Volleyball.
Fees 2012: Res $850-1600 (+$10), 1-2 wks. Day $550 (+$10), 1 wk. Aid 2007 (Need): $2800.
Housing: Dorms. **Swimming:** Pool.
Est 1975. Inc. **Ses:** 6. **Wks/ses:** 1-2. Operates June-Aug.

Pinebrook Farms offers programs for riders representing all experience levels. Daily activities include English and Western riding lessons, horse shows, horsemanship instruction, vaulting, trail rides and traditional camping pursuits. Experienced riders partake of advanced horsemanship and riding opportunities.

PONY FARM
Res — Girls Ages 8-14

Temple, NH 03084. 13 Pony Farm Ln. Tel: 603-654-6308. Fax: 603-654-4077.
www.touchstone-farm.org
Boo Martin, Dir.
Adm: FCFS. **Appl due:** May. **Enr:** 48. **Staff:** Admin 4. Couns 20.
Focus: Equestrian. **Features:** Farm Swim.
Fees 2012: Res $1550-3100 (+$70), 1-2 wks.
Housing: Houses Lodges. **Swimming:** Pool.
Est 1970. Inc. **Ses:** 5. **Wks/ses:** 1-2. Operates June-Aug. ACA.

Pony Farm is a hunt seat riding camp that features mounted instruction, stable management, trail rides and the opportunity to participate in a horse show. Swimming and arts and crafts are among the camp's other activities.

PRINCETON UNIVERSITY SPORTS CAMPS
Res — Coed Ages 10-18; Day — Coed 5-18

Princeton, NJ 08544. 71 University Pl. Tel: 609-258-3369. Fax: 609-258-4656.
www.princetonsportscamps.com   E-mail: camps@princeton.edu
Andrew S. Dudley, Mgr.
Grades K-12. Adm: FCFS. **Appl due:** Rolling. **Staff:** Admin 1.
Focus: Baseball Basketball Cross-country Fencing Field_Hockey Football Ice_Hockey Lacrosse Rowing/Sculling Soccer Softball Squash Swim Tennis Track Watersports Wrestling.
Housing: Dorms. **Swimming:** Pool.
Ses: 65. **Wks/ses:** 1. Operates June-Aug.

Members of the Princeton varsity coaching staff direct separately run camps in an array of sports. College coaches and players from around the country serve as assistant coaches.

PRO AMBITIONS HOCKEY CAMPS
Res — Coed Ages 10-17; Day — Coed 6-17

Dover, MA 02030. PO Box 565. Tel: 508-497-1089. **Fax:** 508-785-0865.
www.proambitions.com   E-mail: js@proambitions.com
Jeff Serowik, Pres.
Grades 1-12. **Adm:** FCFS. **Appl due:** Rolling. **Staff:** Admin 8. Couns 50.
Locations: AL AZ CA CO CT FL IL IN MA MD ME MI MN NC NH NJ NY OH PA RI TN TX UT VA VT WI Canada.
Focus: Ice_Hockey. **Features:** Canoe Cruises Exploration Kayak Mtn_Biking Paintball Riding Aerobics Lacrosse Street_Hockey Swim Weight_Trng.
Fees 2012: Res $1054-4914, 1-3 wks. Day $215-1254, ½-2 wks. Aid 2006 (Need): $10,000.
Housing: Dorms. **Swimming:** Lake Pond Ocean Pool Stream.
Est 1990. Inc. **Ses:** 300. **Wks/ses:** ½-3. Operates June-Aug.

Pro Ambitions offers intensive day and residential hockey camps throughout the country. Camps are designed for all ages and ability levels, from beginners to serious players. Boarding programs—which operate at Boston University, Kents Hill School (Kents Hill, ME), Stratton Mountain School (Stratton Mountain, VT), the University of Rhode Island, Milton Academy (Milton, MA) and Lake Tahoe, NV—feature five hours of daily ice time and off-ice drills, conditioning and lectures. Day programs operate at more than 90 locations nationwide. Specialty camps offer focused instruction for elite players and defensemen.

PROFESSIONAL SPORTS BASKETBALL CAMP
Res and Day — Coord Ages 10-17

West Caldwell, NJ. Caldwell College.
Contact (Year-round): PO Box 15, Sparta, NJ 07871. Tel: 973-691-0070, 800-433-6060. Fax: 973-347-5832.
www.psccamps.com   E-mail: sportscamp@aol.com
Ken Webb, Dir.
Adm: FCFS. **Appl due:** Rolling.
Focus: Basketball. **Features:** Swim.
Fees 2012: Res $685 (+$30), 1 wk. Day $385 (+$30), 1 wk.
Housing: Dorms. **Swimming:** Pool.
Est 1946. Inc. **Ses:** 6. **Wks/ses:** 1. Operates June-Aug.

Offering boys' and girls' sessions on Caldwell College campus each summer, the camp employs lectures, drills and instructional games to develop campers' skills. Professional coaches work with 10 to 15 campers at a time on specific aspects of basketball, including rebounding, dribbling, shooting, passing and defense. Instruction is appropriate for players of all skill levels.

PROFESSIONAL SPORTS SOCCER CAMP
Res and Day — Coed Ages 7-16

Throgs Neck, NY. State Univ of New York-Maritime.
Contact (Year-round): PO Box 15, Sparta, NJ 07871. Tel: 973-691-0070, 800-433-6060. Fax: 973-347-5832.
www.psccamps.com   E-mail: sportscamp@aol.com
John Harrington, Dir.
Adm: FCFS. **Appl due:** Rolling.
Focus: Soccer. **Features:** Swim.
Fees 2009: Res $575 (+$15), 1 wk. Day $275 (+$15), 1 wk.
Housing: Dorms. **Swimming:** Pool.
Est 1946. Inc. **Ses:** 5. **Wks/ses:** 1. Operates July-Aug.

The camp, conducted at the State University of New York-Maritime, addresses all aspects of soccer during the course of a week. In the morning, coaches teach such individual skills as precision passing and power shooting. Afternoon programming focuses on tactics and the importance of teamwork. Resident campers benefit from an early evening session that emphasizes games and competition.

RAMEY TENNIS AND EQUESTRIAN SCHOOLS
Res — Coed Ages 8 and up; Day — Coed 8-17

Rockport, IN 47635. 2354 S 200 W. Tel: 812-649-2668. Fax: 812-649-2668.
www.rameycamps.com   E-mail: jramey66@yahoo.com
Joan G. Ramey, Dir.
Grades 3-12. Adm: FCFS. **Appl due:** Rolling. **Enr:** 8. **Staff:** Admin 1. Couns 3. Res 2.
Focus: Equestrian Tennis. **Features:** Swim.
Fees 2011: Res $775-1500 (+$25-50), 1-2 wks. Day $300-600, 1 wk.
Housing: Houses Lodges. Avg per room/unit: 5. **Swimming:** Pool.
Est 1962. Inc. Ses: 8. **Wks/ses:** 1-2. Operates June-Aug.

Ramey Tennis School specializes in instruction for beginners and advanced players. Campers receive a minimum of six hours of daily instruction, including drills, competitive play and skill tests. Adult programs and family camps operate as well. The Equestrian School provides instruction in horsemanship and equitation. In addition, campers learn about horse care and stable maintenance. More-advanced riders take part in dressage, jumping and cross-country riding.

RASPBERRY RIDGE FARMS
Res and Day — Girls Ages 6 and up

Newburgh, K0K 2S0 Ontario, Canada. 545 Hunt Rd, RR 1. Tel: 613-378-0321.
Fax: 613-378-0352.
www.raspberryridge.com   E-mail: info@raspberryridge.com
Cheryl Spencer, Dir.
Adm: FCFS. **Appl due:** Rolling.
Focus: Equestrian.
Fees 2009: Res Can$525, 1 wk. Day Can$295, 1 wk.
Inc. **Ses:** 8. **Wks/ses:** 1. Operates July-Aug.

Campers at Raspberry Ridge Farms receive instruction in safe horse-handling techniques, leading and haltering, grooming and feeding the horses, and riding safely and responsibly. Other topics covered include breeds and markings, basic horse anatomy, common illnesses and their treatment, and styles of riding. Riding lessons are held once or twice daily, in addition to trail rides, games and other activities.

RAY REID SOCCER SCHOOL
Res — Boys Ages 9-18; Day — Coed 5-18

Avon, CT 06001. c/o Gold, Orluk & Partners, PO Box 1177. Tel: 860-674-1500.
Fax: 860-674-1704.
www.rayreid.com   E-mail: info@rayreid.com
Ray Reid, Dir.
Adm: FCFS. **Appl due:** Rolling. **Enr:** 200. **Staff:** Admin 8. Couns 25.
Locations: CT NY.
Focus: Soccer. **Features:** Swim.
Fees 2011: Res $589, 1 wk. Day $150-479, 1 wk.
Housing: Dorms. **Swimming:** Pool.
Est 1996. Inc. Ses: 19. **Wks/ses:** 1. Operates June-Aug.

This program for field players and goalkeepers provides eight hours a day of individual skills, small-group competition, soccer games and various competitions, followed by two hours of training and game film. Extended-day and junior sessions—as well as position-specific three-day minicamps—are available. Overnight camps for elite players are conducted on the University of Connecticut campus; day-only sessions are held at various locations in Connecticut and New York.

RIPKEN BASEBALL YOUTH CAMPS
Res — Boys Ages 9-18; Day — Boys 7-18

Aberdeen, MD.
Contact (Year-round): 1427 Clarkview Rd, Ste 100, Baltimore, MD 21209.
 Toll-free: 800-486-0850. Fax: 410-558-6728.
www.ripkencamps.com   E-mail: camps@ripkenbaseball.com
Matt Backert, Dir.
Adm: FCFS. **Appl due:** Rolling. **Enr:** 240.
Focus: Baseball.
Housing: Dorms.
Est 2003. Ses: 11. **Wks/ses:** 1. Operates July-Aug. ACA.

This baseball camp combines age- and ability-specific instruction with structured drills and games. The camp's complex features four youth baseball fields, a synthetic infield and batting cages. Evening activities for overnight campers include movies, games and an excursion to a minor-league baseball game.

ST. OLAF COLLEGE DIVING CAMP
Res — Coed Ages 13-17

Northfield, MN 55057. 1520 St Olaf Ave. Tel: 507-786-3042, 800-726-6523.
 Fax: 507-786-3690.
www.stolaf.edu/camps   E-mail: summer@stolaf.edu
Gabe Kortuem, Dir.
Grades 8-12. Adm: FCFS. **Appl due:** Rolling. **Staff:** Admin 1. Couns 1. Res 3.
Focus: Diving.
Fees 2011: Res $470, 1 wk.
Housing: Dorms. Avg per room/unit: 2-3.
Est 2007. Nonprofit. Ses: 1. **Wks/ses:** 1. Operates June.

Designed for boys and girls who have been diving competitively in an association or a school program for at least one season, the camp conducts a comprehensive diving program that incorporates pool time, dry-land training, dry-board practice, video review and classroom sessions. St. Olaf, whose program addresses all aspects of diving, divides boys and girls into two groups by age and ability. Campers engage in recreational pursuits with participants in St. Olaf Swim Camps (separately listed).

ST. OLAF COLLEGE SWIM CAMPS
Res — Coed Ages 10-18

Northfield, MN 55057. 1520 St Olaf Ave. Tel: 507-786-3042. Fax: 507-786-3690.
www.stolaf.edu/camps   E-mail: summer@stolaf.edu
Bob Hauck & Dave Hauck, Dirs.
Grades 5-12. Adm: FCFS. **Appl due:** Rolling. **Staff:** Admin 1. Couns 2. Res 6.
Focus: Swim.
Fees 2011: Res $440-480, 1 wk.
Housing: Dorms. **Swimming:** Pool.
Est 1980. Ses: 3. **Wks/ses:** 1. Operates June.

St. Olaf's Stroke Technique Camp, which serves competitive swimmers age 10 to grade 12, focuses on proper stroke form and efficient starts and turns. Elements of the program are two daily pool sessions for stroke development, one daily pool session for videotaping, individual videos (with one-on-one review) and written critiques from instructors. Serving experienced swimmers age 10 to grade 12, the High Performance Camp maintains a maximum enrollment of 30 to ensure individualized instruction. Dry-land training promotes strength and flexibility in participants of both programs.

SANS SOUCI RIDING CENTRE
Res — Boys Ages 10-15, Girls 8-17

St Clotilde, J0L 1W0 Quebec, Canada. 1183 Rte 209. Tel: 450-826-3772. Fax: 450-826-1083.
www.sans-souci.qc.ca   E-mail: info@sans-souci.qc.ca
Don Sedgwick & Carolyn Sedgwick, Dirs.
Adm: FCFS. **Enr:** 65. **Staff:** Admin 3. Couns 18.
Focus: Equestrian. **Features:** Riding Swim.
Fees 2012: Res Can$880-5860, 1-8 wks.
Housing: Dorms. **Swimming:** Pool.
Est 1970. Inc. Ses: 8. **Wks/ses:** 1-2. Operates June-Aug.

Sans Souci's primary emphasis is on teaching the fundamentals of handling and riding horses from beginning through advanced levels, with opportunities for exhibitions, stadium jumping, trail rides and field trips. Also available are swimming, excursions and games.

SARAH BEHN BASKETBALL CAMP
Res — Girls Ages 9-17; Day — Girls 6-15

Foxboro, MA 02035. PO Box 349. Tel: 508-549-0997. Fax: 508-549-0998.
www.behncamp.com   E-mail: behncamp@aol.com
Sarah Behn, Pres.
Adm: FCFS. **Appl due:** Rolling. **Enr cap:** 250. **Staff:** Admin 1. Couns 20.
Focus: Basketball.
Fees 2012: Res $699, 1 wk. Day $155-369, 1 wk. Aid 2007 (Need): $20,000.
Housing: Dorms.
Est 1993. Inc. Ses: 20. **Wks/ses:** 1. Operates July-Aug.

Sarah Behn's girls' basketball camps place an emphasis on fundamentals. Day camps operate at schools throughout Massachusetts, while overnight sessions are conducted at both the Governor's Academy in Byfield and Wheaton College in Norton. The camp divides girls into groups according to age and ability. Daily instruction comprises drills, demonstrations and team games.

SIXERS CAMPS
Res — Boys Ages 9-17, Girls 11-17

Wayne, PA.
Contact (Year-round): PO Box 25050, Philadelphia, PA 19147. Tel: 610-668-7676, 800-723-2267. Fax: 215-952-5911.
www.sixerscamps.com   E-mail: director@sixerscamps.com
Todd Landrey, Dir.
Adm: FCFS. **Appl due:** Rolling. **Staff:** Admin 15. Couns 30.
Locations: DE NJ PA.
Focus: Basketball. **Features:** Boating Canoe Swim Volleyball.
Fees 2009: Res $600-1300 (+$30), 1-2 wks. Day $300-350, 1 wk.
Housing: Cabins. Avg per room/unit: 11. **Swimming:** Pool.

Est 1985. Ses: 20. **Wks/ses:** 1-2. Operates June-Aug.

Enrolling for one or two weeks, players work on basketball skills during daily drills. Boys and girls take part in two full-court games each day. Areas of emphasis are ball handling, passing, offensive play with and without the ball, shooting and rebounding. Weeklong day camps operate at 13 locations in Delaware, New Jersey and Pennsylvania.

SJ RANCH
Res — Girls Ages 8-16

**Ellington, CT 06029. 130 Sandy Beach Rd. Tel: 860-872-4742. Fax: 860-870-4914. www.sjridingcamp.com   E-mail: info@sjridingcamp.com
Pat Haines, Dir.**
Grades 3-11. **Adm:** FCFS. **Appl due:** Rolling. **Enr:** 48. **Enr cap:** 48. **Staff:** Admin 2. Couns 12.
Focus: Equestrian. **Features:** Crafts Aquatics Archery Boating Canoe Farm Ranch Badminton Basketball Swim Tennis.
Fees 2012: Res $1185-3200 (+$20-180), 1-3 wks.
Housing: Cabins. Avg per room/unit: 6. **Swimming:** Lake Pond.
Est 1956. Inc. Ses: 4. **Wks/ses:** 1-3. Operates June-Aug. ACA.

Extensive English riding and horse care are the primary areas of emphasis at this equestrian camp. Campers ride twice daily in one of the three large riding rings, on wooded trails or over cross-country jumps. Staff teach proper equitation, jumping basics and dressage, and advanced riders may practice on stadium and cross-country courses.

CAMP SKYLEMAR
Res — Boys Ages 7-15

**Naples, ME 04055. 457 Sebago Rd. Tel: 207-693-6414. Fax: 207-693-3865.
Contact (Sept-May): PO Box 1010, Sparks, MD 21152. Tel: 410-329-5995.
  Fax: 410-329-5095.
www.campskylemar.com   E-mail: info@skylemar.com
Arleen Shepherd & Shep Shepherd, Dirs.**
Grades 1-11. **Adm:** FCFS. Admitted: 100%. **Appl due:** Rolling. **Enr:** 17. **Staff:** Admin 15. Couns 60.
Focus: Baseball Basketball Football Golf Lacrosse Soccer Swim Tennis Water-skiing. **Features:** Crafts Filmmaking Fine_Arts Painting Photog Theater Aquatics Archery Boating Canoe Chess Cooking Deep-sea Fishing Fishing Hiking Kayak Mtn_Trips Outdoor_Ed Ropes_Crse Sail Survival_Trng Wilderness_Camp Woodcraft Cross-country Softball Street_Hockey Track Ultimate_Frisbee Volleyball Watersports Weight_Trng.
Fees 2012: Res $6950-10,750 (+$350), 3-7 wks.
Housing: Cabins. Avg per room/unit: 6. **Swimming:** Lake.
Est 1948. Inc. Ses: 2. **Wks/ses:** 3-7. Operates June-Aug. ACA.

Skylemar provides athletic instruction for campers of all ability levels. Boys receive specialized, intensive training from coaches and college athletes in numerous team and individual sports. Ample indoor and outdoor playing areas, including outdoor education facilities, facilitate instruction in many sports.

SNOWY OWL CAMP FOR GIRLS
Res — Girls Ages 8-15

**Harmony, ME 04942. 74 S Merrill Rd. Tel: 207-683-2032.
Contact (Sept-May): Tel: 305-793-3708.
Year-round Fax: 207-683-2142.
www.snowyowlcamp.com   E-mail: info1@snowyowlcamp.com**

Burt Jordan & Risa Jordan, Dirs.
Adm: FCFS. **Appl due:** Rolling. **Enr:** 30. **Enr cap:** 30. **Staff:** Admin 5. Couns 20.
Focus: Water-skiing Watersports. **Features:** Crafts Dance Filmmaking Music Theater Aquatics Cooking Exploration Hiking Kayak Sail Survival_Trng White-water_Raft Wood-craft Softball Swim Tennis Volleyball.
Fees 2011: Res $875-1150, 1 wk.
Housing: Cabins Lodges. Avg per room/unit: 5. **Swimming:** Lake Pool.
Est 2003. Inc. Ses: 3. **Wks/ses:** 1. Operates May-July.

Snowy Owl focuses its programming on water-skiing and other watersports. In addition to water-skiing, girls may receive instruction in tubing, competitive and noncompetitive swimming, windsurfing, kayaking, sailing and recreational diving, among others. Crafts and theater are among the optional land activities for interested campers.

SPRUCELANDS EQUESTRIAN CENTER SUMMER HORSE CAMP
Res — Coed Ages 6-17

Java Center, NY 14082. 1316 Pit Rd, PO Box 54. Tel: 585-457-4150.
www.sprucelands.com   E-mail: spruceland@gmail.com
Eileen Thompson, Dir.
Grades 1-12. Adm: FCFS. **Appl due:** May. **Enr:** 60. **Enr cap:** 60. **Fac 25. Staff:** Admin 4. Couns 8.
Focus: Equestrian. **Features:** Crafts Canoe Riding Baseball Basketball Swim Tennis.
Fees 2012: Res $1700-6680 (+$30-50), 2-8 wks.
Housing: Cabins Lodges. **Swimming:** Pond.
Est 1935. Inc. Ses: 10. **Wks/ses:** 2-8. Operates June-Aug.

Sprucelands offers three programs for campers: Horsemasters participate in an intensive horse care and riding program and ride for an hour daily; Accelerated Horsemasters may ride two hours a day for an additional fee; and Master-Regs divide their time between riding lessons and regular camp activities. Beginners in the riding program learn basic skills, while intermediate and advanced riders may participate in jumping, dressage, drill team, centered riding techniques and trail riding.

STEVE KNAPMAN BRIT-AM SOCCER ACADEMY RESIDENTIAL SUMMER CAMP
Res and Day — Coed Ages 10-17

Frostburg, MD. Frostburg State Univ.
Contact (Year-round): 12853 Climbing Ivy Dr, Germantown, MD 20874.
Tel: 301-916-9053. Fax: 301-916-1119.
www.brit-am.com   E-mail: stevek@brit-am.com
Steve Knapman, Pres.
Adm: FCFS. **Appl due:** Rolling. **Enr:** 100. **Enr cap:** 100. **Staff:** Admin 10. Couns 2.
Focus: Soccer.
Fees 2011: Res $550, 1 wk. Day $400, 1 wk.
Housing: Dorms.
Est 1999. Inc. Ses: 2. **Wks/ses:** 1. Operates July.

Campers at the academy begin the session by taking part in assessment games designed to gauge skill level. Skill and techniques training, team training and tactical development, and scrimmages are important components of the program.

STONELEIGH-BURNHAM SCHOOL
BONNIE CASTLE RIDING CAMP
Res — Girls Ages 9-16

Greenfield, MA 01301. 574 Bernardston Rd. Tel: 413-774-2711. Fax: 413-772-2602.
www.sbschool.org   E-mail: emarback@sbschool.org
Erica Marback, Dir.
Adm: FCFS. **Appl due:** Rolling. **Enr:** 36. **Enr cap:** 36. **Staff:** Admin 4. Couns 9.
Focus: Equestrian. **Features:** Dance Fine_Arts Theater Aquatics Swim.
Fees 2012: Res $2600 (+$100), 2 wks.
Housing: Dorms. **Swimming:** Pool.
Est 1982. Nonprofit. **Ses:** 3. **Wks/ses:** 2. Operates July-Aug.

The aim of Bonnie Castle's program is to develop and improve skills in riding for girls at all ability levels. The riding program features instruction in hunting, jumping, equitation, dressage, combined training and equine studies. Social and recreational activities round out the program.

STOWE SUMMER SPORTS FESTIVAL
Res — Coed Ages 9-18

Stowe, VT 05672. 39 Edson Hill Rd. Tel: 802-253-7223, 800-344-1546.
Fax: 802-253-2023.
www.roundhearth.com   E-mail: info@roundhearth.com
Grady Vigneau, Exec Dir.
Grades 3-12. Adm: FCFS. **Appl due:** June. **Enr:** 650.
Focus: Cross-country Winter_Sports. **Features:** Canoe Climbing_Wall Hiking Kayak Mtn_ Biking Rock_Climb Ropes_Crse Swim.
Fees 2011: Res $495-945, 1 wk.
Housing: Dorms Lodges. **Swimming:** Lake Pool Stream.
Est 1988. Inc. **Ses:** 2. **Wks/ses:** 1. Operates Aug.

SSSF offers residential cross-country running and dry-land Alpine ski-racing camps. Ski camps incorporate serious training on in-line skates, as well as mountain biking, cross-training, speed and quickness development, aerial and balance drills and equipment workshops.

SURF CAMP
Res — Coed Ages 10-15; Day — Coed 6 and up

Wrightsville Beach, NC 28480. 530 Causeway Dr, Ste B-1. Tel: 910-256-7873, 866-844-7873. Fax: 910-686-9664.
www.wbsurfcamp.com   E-mail: info@wbsurfcamp.com
Rick Civelli, Dir.
Grades 1-12. Adm: FCFS. **Appl due:** Rolling. **Enr cap:** 24. **Staff:** Admin 5. Couns 35.
Locations: FL HI NC Australia/New_Zealand Caribbean Mexico/Central_America.
Focus: Surfing. **Features:** Ecol Environ_Sci Sci Adventure_Travel Aquatics Community_ Serv Conservation Exploration Fishing Kayak Outdoor_Ed Scuba Yoga Skateboarding Swim.
Fees 2012: Res $1595-3495, 1-2 wks. Day $195-450, 1 wk. Aid (Need).
Housing: Dorms Hotels Lodges. **Swimming:** Ocean.
Est 1995. Inc. **Ses:** 19. **Wks/ses:** 1-2. Operates June-Aug. ACA.

Surf Camp operates day and overnight camps at locations in North Carolina, Florida, Hawaii, Australia, Costa Rica, Barbados and the Bahamas. No prior surfing experience is necessary, and most campers are beginners. Instruction focuses on safety, surfing etiquette, board riding and wave selection. Surfers also learn about marine science and coastal ecology through accompanying activities. The camper-instructor ratio does not exceed 3:1.

SURF CAMP HAWAII
Res — Coed Ages 10-17

Kapolei, HI 96709. c/o Camp Timberline, PO Box 700308. Tel: 808-262-4538, 888-345-4374. Fax: 808-672-6293.
www.kamaainakids.com/surf_camp   E-mail: campt@kamaainakids.com
Jolie Moniz, Dir.
Adm: FCFS. **Appl due:** Rolling. **Staff:** Admin 3. Couns 8.
Focus: Surfing. **Features:** Aquatics Archery Bicycle_Tours Boating Caving Climbing_Wall Conservation Exploration Fishing Hiking Kayak Mtn_Trips Ropes_Crse Sail Seamanship Swim.
Housing: Cabins Tents. **Swimming:** Ocean Pool.
Est 1994. Nonprofit. Spons: Kama'aina Kids. **Ses:** 3. **Wks/ses:** 1. Operates June-July.

Participants in Surf Camp learn the fundamentals of surfing on Oahu's beaches. The camp is based at Camp Timberline.

TAMARACK TENNIS CAMP
Res — Coed Ages 10-15

Franconia, NH 03580. 111 Easton Valley Rd. Tel: 603-823-5656.
www.tamarackcamp.com   E-mail: tamaracktenniscamp@gmail.com
Adm: FCFS. **Appl due:** May. **Enr:** 48. **Staff:** Admin 3. Couns 14.
Focus: Tennis. **Features:** Climbing_Wall Hiking Mtn_Biking Mtn_Trips Soccer Swim Volleyball.
Fees 2012: Res $2545-3475 (+$100), 3-4 wks.
Housing: Cabins Dorms. **Swimming:** Lake Pond River Stream.
Est 1962. Inc. Ses: 2. **Wks/ses:** 3-4. Operates July-Aug.

Tamarack conducts a comprehensive tennis program for beginning, intermediate and advanced players. Campers receive a minimum of four hours of daily instruction, six days a week. All players participate in outside matches and tournaments with boys and girls from surrounding camps, as well as in Tamarack tournaments. Swimming, soccer, hiking and volleyball are popular leisure-time activities.

TENNIS: EUROPE
Res — Coed Ages 14-18

Stamford, CT 06903. 73 Rockridge Ln. Tel: 203-322-9803, 800-253-7486.
Fax: 203-322-0089.
www.tenniseurope.com   E-mail: tenniseuro@aol.com
Martin Vinokur & Gary Weiner, Dirs.
Grades 9-PG. Adm: Selective. **Appl due:** Rolling. **Enr:** 180. **Staff:** Admin 2. Couns 23.
Intl program focus: Lang Culture. **Locations:** CA WA Canada Europe. Home stays avail.
Focus: Tennis. **Features:** Lang Bicycle_Tours Hiking Sail Swim Water-skiing Watersports.
Fees 2012: Res $4495-7999 (+$airfare), 2½-4 wks. Aid 2011 (Need): $12,500.
Housing: Apartments Hotels Lodges. Avg per room/unit: 2-3. **Swimming:** Lake Ocean Pool.
Est 1973. Inc. Ses: 12. **Wks/ses:** 2½-4. Operates June-Aug.

Participants (who should be of high school varsity caliber) play a series of international tennis tournaments against juniors from all over the world, with coaches analyzing the matches and conducting instructional practice sessions. In addition to playing tennis, boys and girls socialize with European teenagers, visit historical sights, gain cultural insight and improve foreign language skills. Players wishing to remain in North America may enroll in touring tournament circuits at locations in the US and Canada.

TOP DOG HOCKEY CAMPS
Res and Day — Coed Ages 5-18

Minneapolis, MN 55423. PO Box 23037. Tel: 952-233-0101, 877-466-4596. Fax: 952-513-2034.
www.topdoghockey.com   E-mail: info@topdoghockey.com
John Haglund, Dir.
Adm: FCFS. **Appl due:** Rolling. **Enr:** 100. **Staff:** Admin 9. Couns 9.
Focus: Ice_Hockey. **Features:** Swim.
Fees 2012: Res $549-779 (+$40), 1 wk. Day $90-409 (+$45), ½-1 wk. Aid avail.
Housing: Dorms Lodges. Avg per room/unit: 3. **Swimming:** Lake Pool.
Est 1989. Inc. **Ses:** 12. **Wks/ses:** ½-1. Operates June-Aug.

Top Dog offers hockey instruction to children of all ages and ability levels at four Minnesota locations. Residential and day options are available at each of the following: a developmental camp for beginners, an accelerated camp for above-average players, and a goalie camp. In addition, Top Dog offers a weeklong golf/hockey session that provides combined instruction. Ice sessions, instructional games, videotape analysis, classroom sessions and off-ice training are featured in all programs.

UNIVERSITY OF ILLINOIS SUMMER SPORT CAMPS
Res and Day — Coed Ages 8-18

Champaign, IL 61820. 1700 S 4th St. Tel: 217-244-7278. Fax: 217-265-8122.
www.fightingillini.com/camps   E-mail: sumcamps@illinois.edu
Brian V. Walsh, Dir.
Grades 3-12. Adm: FCFS. **Admitted:** 100%. **Appl due:** Rolling.
Focus: Baseball Basketball Cross-country Football Golf Gymnastics Soccer Softball Swim Tennis Track Volleyball Wrestling.
Housing: Dorms. **Swimming:** Pool.
Est 1974. Nonprofit. Operates June-Aug.

These specialized camps are directed by University of Illinois varsity head coaches. Soccer, cross-country, swimming and tennis camps are coeducational. Boys may enroll in baseball, basketball, football, golf, gymnastics, track and field, and wrestling programs, while girls may take part in basketball, golf, gymnastics, soccer, softball, track and field, and volleyball camps. In addition to the individual camps, the university offers basketball, football, wrestling and volleyball team camps.

UNIVERSITY OF MAINE SUMMER SPORTS CAMPS
Res — Coed Ages 8-18; Day — Coed 6-18

Orono, ME 04469. 5747 Memorial Gym. Tel: 207-581-2267. Fax: 207-581-3987.
www.goblackbears.com/camps   E-mail: sport.camps@umit.maine.edu
Adm: FCFS. **Appl due:** Rolling.
Focus: Baseball Basketball Cross-country Diving Field_Hockey Football Ice_Hockey Soccer Softball Swim Track.
Fees 2009: Res $300-495, 1 wk. Day $150-365, 1 wk.
Housing: Dorms. **Swimming:** Pool.
Est 1975. Nonprofit. **Ses:** 26. **Wks/ses:** 1. Operates June-Aug.

The University of Maine offers instructional camps in a full complement of sports. Under the direction of varsity coaches from the university, sessions emphasize skill development, conditioning and sportsmanship. Certain camps are designed for advanced players, while others focus on specific positions. Athletes have full access to the university's athletic facilities.

UNIVERSITY OF SAN DIEGO SPORTS CAMPS
Res and Day — Coed Ages 6-18

San Diego, CA 92110. 5998 Alcala Park. Tel: 619-260-2999. Fax: 619-260-2213.
www.usdcamps.com   E-mail: sportscamps@sandiego.edu
Ky Snyder, Dir.
Adm: FCFS. **Appl due:** Rolling. **Staff:** Admin 1. Couns 12.
Focus: Baseball Basketball Football Gen_Sports Soccer Softball Swim Tennis Volleyball.
Fees 2011: Res $470-769 (+$20), 1 wk. Day $175-519, 1 wk.
Housing: Dorms. **Swimming:** Pool.
Est 1970. Nonprofit. Roman Catholic. **Wks/ses:** 1. Operates June-Aug.

USD coaches conduct camps in general sports, swimming, soccer, tennis, basketball, volleyball, softball, baseball, football and sports performance. Each camp includes personalized instruction, drills, tournaments and recreational activities.

VAN DER MEER TENNIS CENTER
JUNIOR SUMMER CAMPS
Res — Coed Ages 10-21; Day — Coed 8-21

Hilton Head Island, SC 29938. PO Box 5902. Tel: 843-785-8388, 800-845-6138.
  Fax: 843-785-7032.
www.vandermeertennis.com   E-mail: tennis@vandermeertennis.com
Dennis Van Der Meer & Pat Van Der Meer, Dirs.
Adm: FCFS. **Enr:** 160. **Fac 20. Staff:** Admin 4. Couns 12.
Locations: PA SC VA.
Focus: Tennis. **Features:** Swim.
Fees 2011: Res $940, 1 wk. Day $660-810, 1 wk.
Housing: Dorms. **Swimming:** Lake Pool.
Inc. **Ses:** 18. **Wks/ses:** 1. Operates June-Aug.

The Junior Summer Camps are tailored to the player's learning speed and ability. Professional instructors teach sound strokes, strategy and tactics for every level of play. In addition to the main location at Hilton Head Island, camps operate in Sweet Briar, VA, and Mercersburg, PA.

VERSHIRE RIDING SCHOOL
Res — Boys Ages 8-12, Girls 8-17

Vershire, VT 05079. 336 Vershire Riding School Rd. Tel: 802-685-2239.
  Fax: 802-685-2239.
www.vershireridingschool.com   E-mail: info@vershireridingschool.com
Sarah Wright, Dir.
Adm: FCFS. Admitted: 98%. **Appl due:** Rolling. **Enr:** 35. **Enr cap:** 45. **Staff:** Admin 2. Couns 17. Res 2.
Focus: Equestrian. **Features:** Crafts Fine_Arts Painting Farm Yoga Swim Tennis Volleyball.
Fees 2012: Res $1350-7300 (+$250-500), 1-6 wks. Aid (Need).
Housing: Cabins Dorms. Avg per room/unit: 2. **Swimming:** Pond.
Est 1970. Inc. **Ses:** 12. **Wks/ses:** 1-6. Operates June-Aug.

Each camper enrolled at Vershire is assigned a horse, and participants receive four hours of mounted lessons, stable management and sound equitation skills per day. Staff members have experience in teaching dressage, jumping and cross-country. Among Vershire's leisure-time activities are tennis, swimming, art, sports and music.

VOGELSINGER SOCCER ACADEMY
Res and Day — Coed Ages 9-18

San Rafael, CA 94901. c/o US Sports Camps, 750 Lindaro St, Ste 220.
Tel: 415-451-2202, 888-780-2267. Fax: 415-479-6061.
www.vogelsingersoccer.com   E-mail: vogelsinger@ussportscamps.com
Hubert Vogelsinger, Dir.
Grades 5-12. Adm: FCFS. Appl due: Rolling. Enr: 260.
Locations: CA MA NJ OR.
Focus: Soccer. Features: Swim.
Fees 2010: Res $895-2995, 1-3 wks. Day $275-595, 1 wk.
Housing: Dorms. Swimming: Pool.
Est 1965. Inc. Spons: US Sports Camps. Ses: 23. Wks/ses: 1-3. Operates June-Aug.

Vogelsinger operates instructional soccer camps at high school and university campuses around the country. Most locations feature programs for beginning, intermediate and elite players, as well as sessions for goalkeepers. Positional instruction, team play, preseason preparation and individual skills programs are addresses during weeklong sessions. Two- to three-week soccer academies for serious players feature elite competition, one-on-one attention and visualization exercises. Beach trips, movies, shopping and guest lectures are among the weekend pursuits.

WAKE FOREST UNIVERSITY
JERRY HAAS GOLF CAMP
Res — Coed Ages 11-18; Day — Coed 7-14

Winston-Salem, NC 27109. PO Box 7567. Tel: 336-758-6000. Fax: 336-758-6105.
http://wakeforestsports.cstv.com/camps/wake-camps.html
E-mail: stathals@wfu.edu
Jerry Haas, Dir.
Adm: FCFS. Appl due: Rolling. Enr: 50. Staff: Admin 1. Couns 7.
Focus: Golf.
Fees 2012: Res $1295, 1 wk. Day $395, 1 wk.
Housing: Dorms.
Est 1998. Inc. Ses: 4. Wks/ses: 1. Operates June-Aug.

Held at Wake Forest University, the camp is led by head golf coaches from various universities. Notable features of the program are individualized instruction by age and ability, daily critiques of each camper, evening strategy lectures on different facets of the game, videotape study sessions and tournament play on the session's final day.

WESTCOAST CONNECTION SPORTS PROGRAMS
Res — Coed Ages 13-17

Mamaroneck, NY 10543. 154 E Boston Post Rd. Tel: 914-835-0699, 800-767-0227.
Fax: 914-835-0798.
www.westcoastconnection.com   E-mail: info@westcoastconnection.com
Ira Solomon & Symon Hay, Prgm Dirs.
Grades 8-11. Adm: FCFS. Appl due: Rolling. Enr: 30.
Travel: CA DC FL IL MA MD MI NY OH OR PA WA WI Canada Mexico/Central_America.
Focus: Surfing Winter_Sports. Features: Kayak Sail Scuba Swim.
Fees 2012: Res $4399-8799 (+airfare), 2-5 wks.
Housing: Dorms Lodges. Swimming: Ocean Pool.
Est 1982. Inc. Ses: 5. Wks/ses: 2-5. Operates June-Aug.

Ski & Snowboard Sensation offers professional instruction for boys and girls of intermediate or advanced ability in two settings: Mount Hood, OR, and Whistler-Blackcomb,

British Columbia, Canada. During the session, participants visit Seattle, WA, and Vancouver, British Columbia. A three-week surfing, sailing and SCUBA camp operates in Belize and Costa Rica. Program participants live aboard a sailboat while honing their sailing and diving skills. Although they do not involve athletic instruction, three touring programs enable baseball enthusiasts to attend Major League Baseball games throughout the country.

WILLOW HILL FARM CAMP
Res and Day — Coed Ages 8-17

Keeseville, NY 12944. 75 Cassidy Rd. Tel: 518-834-9746. Fax: 518-834-4670.
www.willowhillfarm.com   E-mail: julie@willowhillfarm.com
Col. Gerald Edwards & Julie Edwards, Dirs.
Grades 3-12. Adm: FCFS. **Appl due:** Rolling. **Enr:** 36. **Enr cap:** 36. **Fac 6. Staff:** Admin 2.
Focus: Equestrian. **Features:** Farm Hiking Riding Swim.
Fees 2011: Res $2400-6600 (+$40-160), 2-8 wks. **Day** $375-400, 1-2 wks.
Housing: Cabins Dorms. Avg per room/unit: 8. **Swimming:** Lake.
Est 1977. Ses: 15. **Wks/ses:** 2-8. Operates June-Aug. ACA.

Campers at Willow Hill live on a 500-acre working farm in the Adirondacks. The equestrian program offers riding twice daily and instruction in dressage, cross-country and stadium jumping. Competitions take place on Sundays. Other activities include swimming, hiking, farm chores, horse care and nature studies.

CAMP WINADU
Res — Boys Ages 7-15

Pittsfield, MA 01201. 700 Churchill St. Tel: 413-447-8900. Fax: 413-447-8905.
Contact (Sept-Apr): 3 New King St, White Plains, NY 10604. Tel: 914-437-7200.
Fax: 914-422-3635.
Year-round Toll-free: 800-494-6238.
www.campwinadu.com   E-mail: info@campwinadu.com
Shelley Weiner, Arleen Weiner, Mark Benerofe, Jared Shapiro & Jill Shapiro, Directors.
Grades 2-10. Adm: FCFS. **Appl due:** Rolling. **Enr:** 400. **Staff:** Admin 20. Couns 175.
Focus: Gen_Sports. **Features:** Crafts Fine_Arts Music Photog Theater Aquatics Archery Bicycle_Tours Boating Canoe Climbing_Wall Exploration Fishing Hiking Kayak Mountaineering Mtn_Biking Mtn_Trips Sail Scuba White-water_Raft Wilderness_Camp Woodcraft Baseball Basketball Cross-country Fencing Football Golf Ice_Hockey Lacrosse Martial_Arts Roller_Hockey Skateboarding Soccer Softball Swim Tennis Track Volleyball Water-skiing Watersports Weight_Trng Wrestling.
Fees 2012: Res $750-9950 (+$600-800), 1-7 wks.
Housing: Cabins Dorms. **Swimming:** Lake Pool.
Est 1927. Inc. Ses: 3. **Wks/ses:** 1-7. Operates June-Aug. ACA.

Located in the Berkshire Mountains, Winadu conducts a traditional camp with a particularly strong instructional sports component. The following optional programs are available for an additional fee: ice hockey, golf and partial golf. Other noteworthy offerings are computers, music instruction, photography, rocketry and woodcraft. While most campers attend for seven weeks, Winadu schedules a weeklong program for first-time campers entering grades 2-5 and a five-week session for first-time boys entering grades 2-6.

CAMP WINAUKEE
Res — Boys Ages 7-15

Moultonboro, NH 03254. 432 Winaukee Rd. Fax: 603-253-8337.

Contact (Sept-May): 3 New King St, White Plains, NY 10604. Fax: 914-422-3635.
Year-round Tel: 603-253-9272, 800-487-9157.
www.winaukee.com   E-mail: info@winaukee.com
Bart Sobel & Jeff Freedman, Dirs.
Grades 1-10. Adm: FCFS. Appl due: Rolling. Enr: 370. Staff: Admin 40. Couns 120.
Focus: Gen_Sports. Features: Astron Crafts Archery Boating Canoe Climbing_Wall
Exploration Fishing Hiking Kayak Mtn_Biking Mtn_Trips Riding Ropes_Crse Sail White-
water_Raft Baseball Basketball Cross-country Equestrian Field_Hockey Football Golf
Ice_Hockey Lacrosse Roller_Hockey Soccer Softball Swim Tennis Volleyball Water-
skiing Watersports.
Fees 2012: Res $5000-10,350 (+$300), 3-7 wks.
Housing: Cabins. Avg per room/unit: 8. Swimming: Lake.
Est 1920. Inc. Ses: 4. Wks/ses: 3-7. Operates June-Aug. ACA.

This general sports and adventure camp is divided into two: the Mainland camp (ages 7-12)
and the Island camp (ages 13-15). Winaukee maintains a particularly strong sports program,
with campers receiving instruction from certified college and high school coaches. Social
events, musical and dramatic productions, and talent shows round out the program. Three-
week sessions serve boys entering grades 1-4 only; all other campers enroll for five or seven
weeks.

WINDELL'S CAMP
Res — Coed Ages 10 and up; Day — Coed 10-17

Sandy, OR.
Contact (Year-round): PO Box 628, Welches, OR 97067. Tel: 503-622-3736,
800-765-7669. Fax: 503-622-4582.
www.windells.com   E-mail: info@windells.com
Tim Windell, Pres.
Adm: FCFS. Appl due: Rolling. Enr cap: 180. Staff: Admin 15. Couns 27. Res 52.
Focus: Extreme_Sports Winter_Sports. Features: Crafts Aquatics Fishing Hiking Mtn_
Biking Mtn_Trips Outdoor_Ed Paintball White-water_Raft Wilderness_Camp Yoga Bas-
ketball Gymnastics Skateboarding Swim Watersports Weight_Trng Trampolining.
Fees 2011: Res $995-1949 (+$100-150), 1 wk. Day $795-1649, 1 wk.
Housing: Apartments Cabins Hotels Houses. Avg per room/unit: 10. Swimming: Lake
River.
Est 1988. Inc. Ses: 8. Wks/ses: 1. Operates June-Aug. ACA.

Windell's operates summer snowboard, freestyle skiing and skateboard camps. Conducted
on Mount Hood at the only year-round ski area in North America, Windell's provides seven
hours of professional freestyle skiing or snowboarding instruction daily for campers of varying
ability levels. Programming combines on-hill instruction with off-hill activities and cross-
training methods. Skateboard camps utilize Windell's 15,000-square-foot indoor skate park
and travel daily to other facilities in Oregon. Boys and girls in all Windell's summer sessions
may receive supplemental skiing, skateboarding and BMX biking instruction.

WINDRIDGE TENNIS & SPORTS CAMPS
Res — Coed Ages 8-15

Roxbury, VT 05669. 1215 Roxbury Rd. Tel: 802-485-5400. Fax: 802-485-8092.
Contact (Sept-May): PO Box 4501, Burlington, VT 05406. Tel: 802-860-2005.
Fax: 802-860-2004.
www.windridgecamps.com   E-mail: info@windridgecamps.com
Norbert Auger, Dir.
Grades 2-10. Adm: FCFS. Appl due: Rolling. Enr: 168. Enr cap: 168. Staff: Admin 10.
Couns 60.

Focus: Equestrian Soccer Tennis. **Features:** Crafts Dance Photog Theater Archery Mtn_ Biking Riding Ropes_Crse Basketball Golf Swim Volleyball.
Fees 2011: Res $1550-5400, 1-4 wks.
Housing: Cabins. Avg per room/unit: 4. **Swimming:** Pool.
Est 1968. Inc. **Ses:** 6. **Wks/ses:** 1-2. Operates June-Aug. ACA.

At two locations in Vermont, the Windridge Camps at Craftsbury Common (P.O. Box 27, 05827; 802-586-9646) and Teela-Wooket in Roxbury provide tennis instruction with a 4:1 instructor-student ratio. Teela-Wooket also offers majors in soccer and (for an additional fee) horseback riding, while Craftsbury features a waterfront program.

WOODWARD CAMP
Res — Coed Ages 7-18

Woodward, PA 16882. 134 Sports Camp Dr, PO Box 93. Tel: 814-349-5633.
Fax: 814-349-5643.
www.woodwardcamp.com   E-mail: office@woodwardcamp.com
Russ Haerer, Mgr.
Adm: FCFS. **Appl due:** Rolling. **Enr:** 800. **Enr cap:** 800. **Staff:** Admin 30. Couns 100.
Locations: CA CO PA WI.
Focus: Cheerleading Extreme_Sports Gymnastics In-line_Skating Skateboarding. **Features:** Crafts Media Music Photog Climbing_Wall Paintball Riding Rock_Climb Ropes_ Crse Basketball Martial_Arts Swim Volleyball Winter_Sports BMX_Biking.
Fees 2010: Res $725-1075 (+$100), 1 wk. Aid 2008 (Need): $200,000.
Housing: Cabins. Avg per room/unit: 14. **Swimming:** Pool.
Est 1970. Inc. **Ses:** 12. **Wks/ses:** 1. Operates June-Aug.

Certified coaches provide gymnastics, cheerleading, in-line skating, skateboarding and action sports instruction at this camp for boys and girls of all ability levels, including beginners. For gymnasts, facilities include three gyms and bungee trampolines to provide assistance with technique. The action sports program utilizes indoor and outdoor ramps, concrete bowls, half pipes, street courses, rails and foam pits. In addition to its Pennsylvania site, Woodward operates camps in Tehachapi, CA; Cable, WI; and Copper Mountain, CO.

SPECIAL-NEEDS PROGRAMS

Special-needs programs are arranged alphabetically by name. The Table of Contents lists the conditions addressed, and an index beginning on page 528 lists the programs under each of those conditions. Programs offering a family session are indicated by "FAM" at the end of the age range in the index. A Key to Conditions Accepted on page 547 presents the abbreviations used in this chapter.

A more complete compilation of schools serving children or young adults with learning disabillities and special needs is available in Porter Sargent's *Guide to Private Special Education.* For details, please visit www.portersargent.com or see page 880.

INDEX BY CONDITION ACCEPTED

DIABETES

Camp ASCCA *(Res — Coed Ages 6+; FAM)* ....Jacksons Gap, AL....550
  Therapies: *Music Rec*

Bearskin Meadow Camp ....Kings Canyon National Park, CA....552
  (Res — Coed Ages 7-17; Day — Coed 7-13; FAM)

Camp Buck *(Res — Coed Ages 8-17; FAM)* ....Portola, CA....555

Camp Conrad-Chinnock *(Res — Coed Ages 7-16; FAM)* ....Angelus Oaks, CA....560

Breckenridge Outdoor *(Res — Coed Ages 8-25)* ....Breckenridge, CO....554
  Therapies: *Art Music Rec Phys Occup*

Camp Colorado *(Res — Coed Ages 8-17)* ....Woodland Park, CO....560

Colorado Lions Camp *(Res — Coed Ages 8+)* ....Woodland Park, CO....560
  Therapies: *Rec Psych*

FL Diabetes Camp *(Res — Coed Ages 6-18; FAM)* ....Gainesville, FL....570

Ridge Creek *(Res — Coed Ages 12-18)* ....Dahlonega, GA....596
  Therapies: *Rec Psych*

Albrecht Acres *(Res — Coed Ages 2+)* .... Sherrill, IA....549

East Seals-Sunnyside *(Res — Coed Ages 4+; Day — Coed 4-17)* ....Des Moines, IA....565

Camp Hertko Hollow *(Res — Coed Ages 6-18; FAM)* ....Boone, IA....576

Camp Fun in the Sun *(Res — Coed Ages 8-18)* ....Rathdrum, ID....572

Camp Granada *(Res — Coed Ages 8-16)* ....Monticello, IL....574

Camp Little Giant *(Res — Coed Ages 8+; Day — Coed 7+)* ....Carbondale, IL....586
  Therapies: *Rec*

Triangle D Camp *(Res — Coed Ages 9-13)* ....Ingleside, IL....603

Jameson Camp *(Res — Coed Ages 7-17)* ....Indianapolis, IN....580

Camp John Warvel *(Res — Coed Ages 7-15)* ....North Webster, IN....580

Barton Ctr Diabetes ....North Oxford, MA....551
  (Res — Coord Ages 6-16; Day — Coed 6-12; FAM)

4-H Camp Howe *(Res — Coed Ages 7-16; Day — Coed 7-13)* ....Goshen, MA....570

Camp Greentop *(Res & Day — Coed Ages 7-21; FAM)* ....Sabillasville, MD....574
  Therapies: *Rec*

Lions Camp Merrick *(Res — Coed Ages 6-16; FAM)* ....Nanjemoy, MD....585

Camp Friendship-MN *(Res & Day — Coed Ages 5+)* ....Annandale, MN....572

EDI-Gloria Hirsch *(Res — Coed Ages 7-17)* ....Fredericktown, MO....568

Camp Hickory Hill *(Res — Coed Ages 7-17)* ....Columbia, MO....576

Camp Carolina Trails *(Res — Coed Ages 7-17)* .... King, NC....556

Easter Seals NE *(Res — Coed Ages 6+; FAM)* ....Fremont, NE....566
  Therapies: *Rec*

Camp Allen *(Res & Day — Coed Ages 6+)* ....Bedford, NH....549

Camp Carefree *(Res — Coed Ages 8-15)* ....Wolfeboro, NH....556

Camp Nejeda *(Res — Coed Ages 7-16; FAM)* ....Stillwater, NJ....590

Clover Patch Camp *(Res — Coed Ages 5+; Day — Coed 5-18)* ....Glenville, NY....559
  Therapies: *Art Music Rec Occup*

EMOTIONAL DISTURBANCES

EMOTIONAL DISTURBANCES *(CONT.)*

HIV/AIDS

INTELLECTUAL DISABILITIES

INTELLECTUAL DISABILITIES *(CONT.)*

LEARNING DISABILITIES

Camp ASCCA *(Res — Coed Ages 6+; FAM)* ....Jacksons Gap, AL....550
Therapies: *Music Rec*

Camp-A-Lot *(Res — Coed Ages 5+)* ....San Diego, CA....556

Easter Seals Harmon *(Res — Coed Ages 8+)*.................................... Boulder Creek, CA....564

Camp Krem *(Res — Coed Ages 5+)* .... Boulder Creek, CA....583

Breckenridge Outdoor *(Res — Coed Ages 8-25)*............................... Breckenridge, CO....554
Therapies: *Art Music Rec Phys Occup*

Colorado Lions Camp *(Res — Coed Ages 8+)*...............................Woodland Park, CO....560
Therapies: *Rec Psych*

Glenholme School *(Res & Day — Coed Ages 10-18)* ....Washington, CT....573
Therapies: *Speech Psych*

Easter Seals Challng *(Res — Coed Ages 6+)* ....Sorrento, FL....564

Ridge Creek *(Res — Coed Ages 12-18)* ....Dahlonega, GA....596
Therapies: *Rec Psych*

Albrecht Acres *(Res — Coed Ages 2+)* .... Sherrill, IA....549

Camp Courageous-Iowa *(Res — Coed Ages 3-21)* .... Monticello, IA....562

East Seals-Sunnyside *(Res — Coed Ages 4+; Day — Coed 4-17)* .... Des Moines, IA....565

Camp Little Giant *(Res — Coed Ages 8+; Day — Coed 7+)*....................Carbondale, IL....586
Therapies: *Rec*

Camp Red Leaf *(Res — Coed Ages 9+)*...Ingleside, IL....596
Therapies: *Music Rec*

Camp Isanogel *(Res & Day — Coed Ages 8+)*...Muncie, IN....579

Jameson Camp *(Res — Coed Ages 7-17)* ....Indianapolis, IN....580

Berkshire Hills *(Res & Day — Coed Ages 16-25)* .... South Hadley, MA....552
Therapies: *Music Rec Psych*

4-H Camp Howe *(Res — Coed Ages 7-16; Day — Coed 7-13)*....................Goshen, MA....570

Camp Mitton *(Res — Coed Ages 7-13)*.. Brewster, MA....588

Camp Fairlee Manor *(Res — Coed Ages 6+)* ....Chestertown, MD....570
Therapies: *Art Rec*

Camp Greentop *(Res & Day — Coed Ages 7-21; FAM)* .... Sabillasville, MD....574
Therapies: *Rec*

Fowler Ctr *(Res — Coed Ages 6-26; Day — Coed 6-20)* ....Mayville, MI....571

Camp Buckskin *(Res — Coed Ages 6-18)* .... Ely, MN....555

Courage Ctr Camps *(Res — Coed Ages 7+; FAM)* ....Maple Lake, MN....561
Therapies: *Speech*

Camp Friendship-MN *(Res & Day — Coed Ages 5+)* ....Annandale, MN....572

Camp New Hope *(Res — Coed Ages 6+)* ....McGregor, MN....591

SOAR Adventures *(Res — Coed Ages 8-25; FAM)*...Balsam, NC....599
Therapies: *Rec*

Talisman Summer Camp *(Res — Coed Ages 8-21; FAM)*.........................Zirconia, NC....602

Easter Seals NE *(Res — Coed Ages 6+; FAM)*.. Fremont, NE....566
Therapies: *Rec*

LEARNING DISABILITIES *(CONT.)*

Camp Allen *(Res & Day — Coed Ages 6+)* .... Bedford, NH....549

Easter Seals Sno-Mo *(Res — Coed Ages 11-21)*................. Gilmanton Iron Works, NH....565

Camp Starfish *(Res — Coed Ages 7-16; Day — Coed 5-10)*..........................Rindge, NH....600

Wediko *(Res — Coed Ages 6-18)*... Windsor, NH....605
    Therapies: *Psych*

Camp Merry Heart *(Res & Day — Coed Ages 5+)*..............................Hackettstown, NJ....588

Camp Nova *(Res — Coed Ages 12-28)* ....Branchville, NJ....593

Clover Patch Camp *(Res — Coed Ages 5+; Day — Coed 5-18)*................ Glenville, NY....559
    Therapies: *Art Music Rec Occup*

Camp HASC *(Res — Coed Ages 3+; Day — Coed 3-21)* .... Parksville, NY....575
    Therapies: *Art Music Rec Phys Speech Psych Occup*

Camp Huntington *(Res — Coed Ages 6-21)*... High Falls, NY....578

Camp Northwood *(Res — Coed Ages 8-18)*...Remsen, NY....592

Camp Ramapo *(Res — Coed Ages 6-16)* ....Rhinebeck, NY....595

Sunshine Camp *(Res — Coed Ages 7-21)* ....Rush, NY....601

Camp Courageous-OH *(Res — Coed Ages 15+; Day — Coed 7-21)*....Whitehouse, OH....562
    Therapies: *Art Rec*

Camp Echoing Hills *(Res — Coed Ages 7+; FAM)* .... Warsaw, OH....567

Camp Nuhop *(Res — Coed Ages 6-18)*...Perrysville, OH....593

Meadowood Springs *(Res — Coed Ages 6-16; Day — Coed 5-11)* ....Weston, OR....587
    Therapies: *Speech*

Upward Bound *(Res & Day — Coed Ages 12+)* ....Stayton, OR....604
    Therapies: *Art Rec*

Beacon Lodge Camp *(Res — Coed Ages 6-18; FAM)* .... Mount Union, PA....551
    Therapies: *Art Music Rec*

Camp Lee Mar *(Res — Coed Ages 5-21)*...Lackawaxen, PA....585

Summit Camp & Travel *(Res — Coed Ages 8-19)*.................................... Honesdale, PA....601

Variety Camp *(Res — Coed Ages 7-17; Day — Coed 5-21)* .... Worcester, PA....604
    Therapies: *Rec Phys Speech Occup*

Easter Seals TN Camp *(Res — Coed Ages 8+)* ....Nashville, TN....567
    Therapies: *Rec*

Mid-South Arc Camp *(Res — Coed Ages 8+)*..Memphis, TN....588

Children's Assoc *(Res — Coed Ages 5-45)* .... Center Point, TX....558

Marbridge *(Res — Coed Ages 16-30)*.. Manchaca, TX....586
    Therapies: *Art Music Rec Phys Occup*

Camp Summit-TX *(Res — Coed Ages 6+)*.. Argyle, TX....600

Camp Kostopulos *(Res — Coed Ages 7+; FAM)* .... Salt Lake City, UT....583
    Therapies: *Rec*

Easter Seals UCP *(Res — Coed Ages 6+; FAM)* ....New Castle, VA....567
    Therapies: *Rec Speech Occup*

Camp Thorpe *(Res — Coed Ages 10-20)* ....Goshen, VT....603

Stand By Me-Vaughn *(Res — Coed Ages 7+; FAM)* .... Vaughn, WA....599

Wawbeek *(Res — Coed Ages 7+)* ....Wisconsin Dells, WI....565
  Therapies: *Rec*
Special Touch *(Res — Coed Ages 10+; FAM)* ....Waupaca, WI....599
  Therapies: *Art Music Rec Phys*
Wisconsin Badger *(Res — Coed Ages 3+)*....................................Prairie du Chien, WI....607
Camp Kodiak *(Res — Coed Ages 6-18)*......................... McKellar, Ontario, CANADA....582
  Therapies: *Art Music Rec*

ORTHOPEDIC/NEUROLOGICAL

Camp ASCCA *(Res — Coed Ages 6+; FAM)*......................................Jacksons Gap, AL....550
  Therapies: *Music Rec*
Camp HONOR *(Res — Coed Ages 8-17)*..Payson, AZ....578
Lions Camp Tatiyee *(Res — Coed Ages 7+)* ....Mesa, AZ....585
Camp-A-Lot *(Res — Coed Ages 5+)* ....San Diego, CA....556
Dream Street Camps *(Res — Coed Ages 4-14)*...................................Beverly Hills, CA....563
Easter Seals Harmon *(Res — Coed Ages 8+)*.............................. Boulder Creek, CA....564
Camp Esperanza *(Res — Coed Ages 8-17)* .... Big Bear Lake, CA....569
Camp Krem *(Res — Coed Ages 5+)* .... Boulder Creek, CA....583
Breckenridge Outdoor *(Res — Coed Ages 8-25)*.............................. Breckenridge, CO....554
  Therapies: *Art Music Rec Phys Occup*
Talking with Tech *(Res — Coed Ages 6-21)* .... Empire, CO....558
  Therapies: *Speech*
Colorado Lions Camp *(Res — Coed Ages 8+)*...............................Woodland Park, CO....560
  Therapies: *Rec Psych*
Rocky Mountain Vill *(Res — Coed Ages 6+)* .... Empire, CO....597
Easter Seals Challng *(Res — Coed Ages 6+)* ....Sorrento, FL....564
Camp Thunderbird *(Res — Coed Ages 8+)* .... Apopka, FL....603
Camp Breathe Easy *(Res — Coed Ages 7-13)* ....Rutledge, GA....554
Camp Independence *(Res — Coed Ages 8-16)* ....Rutledge, GA....579
Albrecht Acres *(Res — Coed Ages 2+)* .... Sherrill, IA....549
Camp Courageous-Iowa *(Res — Coed Ages 3-21)* .... Monticello, IA....562
East Seals-Sunnyside *(Res — Coed Ages 4+; Day — Coed 4-17)* .... Des Moines, IA....565
Camp Little Giant *(Res — Coed Ages 8+; Day — Coed 7+)*...................Carbondale, IL....586
  Therapies: *Rec*
Camp Red Leaf *(Res — Coed Ages 9+)* ....Ingleside, IL....596
  Therapies: *Music Rec*
CHAMP Camp *(Res — Coed Ages 6-18)* ....Martinsville, IN....557
Camp Isanogel *(Res & Day — Coed Ages 8+)*..Muncie, IN....579
Jameson Camp *(Res — Coed Ages 7-17)* ....Indianapolis, IN....580
Camp Freedom *(Res — Coed Ages 6-11)* .... Lebanon Junction, KY....571
Camp Bon Coeur *(Res — Coed Ages 7-16; FAM)*..Eunice, LA....553

ORTHO/NEURO (*CONT.*)

Berkshire Hills *(Res & Day — Coed Ages 16-25)* .... South Hadley, MA 552
    Therapies: *Music Rec Psych*

4-H Camp Howe *(Res — Coed Ages 7-16; Day — Coed 7-13)*.....................Goshen, MA 570

Camp Fairlee Manor *(Res — Coed Ages 6+)* ....Chestertown, MD 570
    Therapies: *Art Rec*

Camp Greentop *(Res & Day — Coed Ages 7-21; FAM)* .... Sabillasville, MD 574
    Therapies: *Rec*

Agassiz Village *(Res — Coed Ages 8-17; FAM)*.. Poland, ME 549

Easter Seals Camping *(Res — Coed Ages 8-14)*...................................West Poland, ME 566

Pine Tree Camp *(Res — Coed Ages 8-18; Day — Coed 5-12)* ....Rome, ME 595

Bay Cliff Health *(Res — Coed Ages 3-17)*...Big Bay, MI 551
    Therapies: *Music Rec Phys Speech Occup*

Camp Bold Eagle *(Res — Coed Ages 6-13)*...Holton, MI 553

Fowler Ctr *(Res — Coed Ages 6-26; Day — Coed 6-20)* ....Mayville, MI 571

Courage Ctr Camps *(Res — Coed Ages 7+; FAM)* ....Maple Lake, MN 561
    Therapies: *Speech*

Camp Eden Wood *(Res — Coed Ages 5+; Day — Coed 5-21)* .... Eden Prairie, MN 568

Camp Friendship-MN *(Res & Day — Coed Ages 5+)* ....Annandale, MN 572

Camp New Hope *(Res — Coed Ages 6+)* ....McGregor, MN 591

Easter Seals NE *(Res — Coed Ages 6+; FAM)*... Fremont, NE 566
    Therapies: *Rec*

Camp Allen *(Res & Day — Coed Ages 6+)* .... Bedford, NH 549

Easter Seals Sno-Mo *(Res — Coed Ages 11-21)*................. Gilmanton Iron Works, NH 565

Camp Starfish *(Res — Coed Ages 7-16; Day — Coed 5-10)*...........................Rindge, NH 600

Camp Merry Heart *(Res & Day — Coed Ages 5+)*.............................Hackettstown, NJ 588

Camp Nova *(Res — Coed Ages 12-28)* ....Branchville, NJ 593

Camp Oakhurst *(Res — Coed Ages 8-21)* ....Oakhurst, NJ 593
    Therapies: *Art Music Rec Phys*

Clover Patch Camp *(Res — Coed Ages 5+; Day — Coed 5-18)*................ Glenville, NY 559
    Therapies: *Art Music Rec Occup*

Double H Ranch *(Res — Coed Ages 6-16)*...Lake Luzerne, NY 563
    Therapies: *Art Music Rec Phys Speech Psych*

Camp Good Days *(Res — Coed Ages 8-17; Day — Coed 4-7; FAM)* ..... Branchport, NY 573
    Therapies: *Art Psych*

Camp HASC *(Res — Coed Ages 3+; Day — Coed 3-21)* .... Parksville, NY 575
    Therapies: *Art Music Rec Phys Speech Psych Occup*

Sunshine Camp *(Res — Coed Ages 7-21)* ....Rush, NY 601

Camp Courageous-OH *(Res — Coed Ages 15+; Day — Coed 7-21)*....Whitehouse, OH 562
    Therapies: *Art Rec*

Camp Echoing Hills *(Res — Coed Ages 7+; FAM)* ....Warsaw, OH 567

Upward Bound *(Res & Day — Coed Ages 12+)* ....Stayton, OR 604
    Therapies: *Art Rec*

PERVASIVE DEVELOPMENTAL DISORDER

PDD *(CONT.)*

SPEECH AND LANGUAGE

SPEECH & LANGUAGE*(CONT.)*

Breckenridge Outdoor *(Res — Coed Ages 8-25)* .... Breckenridge, CO....554
    Therapies: *Art Music Rec Phys Occup*

Talking with Tech *(Res — Coed Ages 6-21)* .... Empire, CO....558
    Therapies: *Speech*

Colorado Lions Camp *(Res — Coed Ages 8+)* .... Woodland Park, CO....560
    Therapies: *Rec Psych*

Easter Seals Challng *(Res — Coed Ages 6+)* .... Sorrento, FL....564

Albrecht Acres *(Res — Coed Ages 2+)* .... Sherrill, IA....549

Camp Courageous-Iowa *(Res — Coed Ages 3-21)* .... Monticello, IA....562

East Seals-Sunnyside *(Res — Coed Ages 4+; Day — Coed 4-17)* .... Des Moines, IA....565

Camp Little Giant *(Res — Coed Ages 8+; Day — Coed 7+)* .... Carbondale, IL....586
    Therapies: *Rec*

Camp Red Leaf *(Res — Coed Ages 9+)* .... Ingleside, IL....596
    Therapies: *Music Rec*

Camp Isanogel *(Res & Day — Coed Ages 8+)* .... Muncie, IN....579

4-H Camp Howe *(Res — Coed Ages 7-16; Day — Coed 7-13)* .... Goshen, MA....570

Camp Fairlee Manor *(Res — Coed Ages 6+)* .... Chestertown, MD....570
    Therapies: *Art Rec*

Bay Cliff Health *(Res — Coed Ages 3-17)* .... Big Bay, MI....551
    Therapies: *Music Rec Phys Speech Occup*

Fowler Ctr *(Res — Coed Ages 6-26; Day — Coed 6-20)* .... Mayville, MI....571

Courage Ctr Camps *(Res — Coed Ages 7+; FAM)* .... Maple Lake, MN....561
    Therapies: *Speech*

Camp Friendship-MN *(Res & Day — Coed Ages 5+)* .... Annandale, MN....572

Easter Seals NE *(Res — Coed Ages 6+; FAM)* .... Fremont, NE....566
    Therapies: *Rec*

Camp Allen *(Res & Day — Coed Ages 6+)* .... Bedford, NH....549

Easter Seals Sno-Mo *(Res — Coed Ages 11-21)* .... Gilmanton Iron Works, NH....565

Camp Nova *(Res — Coed Ages 12-28)* .... Branchville, NJ....593

Clover Patch Camp *(Res — Coed Ages 5+; Day — Coed 5-18)* .... Glenville, NY....559
    Therapies: *Art Music Rec Occup*

Camp HASC *(Res — Coed Ages 3+; Day — Coed 3-21)* .... Parksville, NY....575
    Therapies: *Art Music Rec Phys Speech Psych Occup*

Camp Ramapo *(Res — Coed Ages 6-16)* .... Rhinebeck, NY....595

Sunshine Camp *(Res — Coed Ages 7-21)* .... Rush, NY....601

Camp Echoing Hills *(Res — Coed Ages 7+; FAM)* .... Warsaw, OH....567

Camp Nuhop *(Res — Coed Ages 6-18)* .... Perrysville, OH....593

Meadowood Springs *(Res — Coed Ages 6-16; Day — Coed 5-11)* .... Weston, OR....587
    Therapies: *Speech*

Upward Bound *(Res & Day — Coed Ages 12+)* .... Stayton, OR....604
    Therapies: *Art Rec*

VISUAL IMPAIRMENTS

VISUAL IMPAIRMENTS *(CONT.)*

Camp Red Leaf *(Res — Coed Ages 9+)* ....Ingleside, IL 596
  Therapies: *Music Rec*

Camp Isanogel *(Res & Day — Coed Ages 8+)* ....Muncie, IN 579

KY Lions Youth Camp *(Res — Coed Ages 6-15)* ....Lebanon Junction, KY 581

Berkshire Hills *(Res & Day — Coed Ages 16-25)* .... South Hadley, MA 552
  Therapies: *Music Rec Psych*

Carroll Center Blind *(Res — Coed Ages 15-21)* ....Newton, MA 557

4-H Camp Howe *(Res — Coed Ages 7-16; Day — Coed 7-13)* ....Goshen, MA 570

Camp Fairlee Manor *(Res — Coed Ages 6+)* ....Chestertown, MD 570
  Therapies: *Art Rec*

Camp Greentop *(Res & Day — Coed Ages 7-21; FAM)* .... Sabillasville, MD 574
  Therapies: *Rec*

Lions Camp Merrick *(Res — Coed Ages 6-16; FAM)* ....Nanjemoy, MD 585

Bay Cliff Health *(Res — Coed Ages 3-17)* ....Big Bay, MI 551
  Therapies: *Music Rec Phys Speech Occup*

Fowler Ctr *(Res — Coed Ages 6-26; Day — Coed 6-20)* ....Mayville, MI 571

Courage Ctr Camps *(Res — Coed Ages 7+; FAM)* ....Maple Lake, MN 561
  Therapies: *Speech*

Camp Friendship-MN *(Res & Day — Coed Ages 5+)* ....Annandale, MN 572

Easter Seals NE *(Res — Coed Ages 6+; FAM)* ....Fremont, NE 566
  Therapies: *Rec*

Natl Blind Children *(Res — Coed Ages 9-65)* ....Lincoln, NE 590

Camp Allen *(Res & Day — Coed Ages 6+)* ....Bedford, NH 549

Easter Seals Sno-Mo *(Res — Coed Ages 11-21)* .... Gilmanton Iron Works, NH 565

Camp Nova *(Res — Coed Ages 12-28)* ....Branchville, NJ 593

Clover Patch Camp *(Res — Coed Ages 5+; Day — Coed 5-18)* .... Glenville, NY 559
  Therapies: *Art Music Rec Occup*

Double H Ranch *(Res — Coed Ages 6-16)* ....Lake Luzerne, NY 563
  Therapies: *Art Music Rec Phys Speech Psych*

Sunshine Camp *(Res — Coed Ages 7-21)* ....Rush, NY 601

Highbrook Lodge *(Res — Coed Ages 8-18; FAM)* ....Cleveland, OH 559

Camp Echoing Hills *(Res — Coed Ages 7+; FAM)* ....Warsaw, OH 567

Beacon Lodge Camp *(Res — Coed Ages 6-18; FAM)* ....Mount Union, PA 551
  Therapies: *Art Music Rec*

Variety Camp *(Res — Coed Ages 7-17; Day — Coed 5-21)* .... Worcester, PA 604
  Therapies: *Rec Phys Speech Occup*

Easter Seals TN Camp *(Res — Coed Ages 8+)* ....Nashville, TN 567
  Therapies: *Rec*

Mid-South Arc Camp *(Res — Coed Ages 8+)* ....Memphis, TN 588

Children's Assoc *(Res — Coed Ages 5-45)* .... Center Point, TX 558

Camp Summit-TX *(Res — Coed Ages 6+)* .... Argyle, TX 600

Texas Lions Camp *(Res & Day — Coed Ages 7-16)* ....Kerrville, TX 602

Therapies: *Music Rec*
Camp Kostopulos *(Res — Coed Ages 7+; FAM)* .... Salt Lake City, UT....583
   Therapies: *Rec*
Easter Seals UCP *(Res — Coed Ages 6+; FAM)* .... New Castle, VA....567
   Therapies: *Rec Speech Occup*
Camp Holiday Trails *(Res — Coed Ages 5-17; FAM)* ....Charlottesville, VA....577
Stand By Me-Vaughn *(Res — Coed Ages 7+; FAM)* .... Vaughn, WA....599
Special Touch *(Res — Coed Ages 10+; FAM)* ....Waupaca, WI....599
   Therapies: *Art Music Rec Phys*
Wisconsin Badger *(Res — Coed Ages 3+)*.....................................Prairie du Chien, WI....607
Wisconsin Lions Camp *(Res — Coed Ages 6-17)* ....Rosholt, WI....608

WEIGHT LOSS

Camp La Jolla *(Res — Coed Ages 8-17)*...La Jolla, CA....584
Wellspring-CA *(Res — Coed Ages 12-25)* ....Reedley, CA....605
   Therapies: *Art Rec Psych*
New Image-Vanguard *(Res — Coed Ages 7-19)* ....Lake Wales, FL....591
Camp Kingsmont *(Res — Coed Ages 9-18)* ....Amherst, MA....582
Camp Jump Start *(Res — Coed Ages 9-17)*...Imperial, MO....581
Wellspring Adventure *(Res — Coed Ages 11-18)* ....Black Mountain, NC....606
   Therapies: *Art Rec Psych*
Camp Pennbrook *(Res — Girls Ages 8-21)* .... Pennington, NJ....595
Camp Shane *(Res — Boys Ages 7-19, Girls 7-25)* .... Ferndale, NY....598
Wellspring NY *(Res — Girls Ages 11-24)* ....Paul Smiths, NY....606
New Image-Pocono *(Res — Coed Ages 7-19)* ....Reeders, PA....591
Camp Sweeney *(Res — Coed Ages 5-18; FAM)* .... Gainesville, TX....601
   Therapies: *Art Music Rec Phys Psych Occup*
Camp Holiday Trails *(Res — Coed Ages 5-17; FAM)* ....Charlottesville, VA....577

OTHER CONDITIONS

MDA Summer Camp *(Res — Coed Ages 6-17)*...Tucson, AZ....589
Dream Street Camps *(Res — Coed Ages 4-14)*...................................Beverly Hills, CA....563
Easter Seals Harmon *(Res — Coed Ages 8+)*................................. Boulder Creek, CA....564
Camp Esperanza *(Res — Coed Ages 8-17)* .... Big Bear Lake, CA....569
Colorado Lions Camp *(Res — Coed Ages 8+)*...............................Woodland Park, CO....560
   Therapies: *Rec Psych*
Rocky Mountain Vill *(Res — Coed Ages 6+)* .... Empire, CO....597
Glenholme School *(Res & Day — Coed Ages 10-18)* ....Washington, CT....573
   Therapies: *Speech Psych*
Camp Thunderbird *(Res — Coed Ages 8+)* ....Apopka, FL....603

OTHER CONDITIONS *(CONT.)*

KEY TO CONDITIONS ACCEPTED

ADD	Attention Deficit Disorder	**HI**	Hearing Impairment
ADHD	Attention Deficit Hyperactivity Disorder	**ID**	Intellectual Disabilities
AN	Anorexia Nervosa	**IP**	Infantile Paralysis
Anx	Anxiety Disorders	**LD**	Learning Disabilities
Ap	Aphasia	**Lk**	Leukemia
APD	Auditory Processing Disorders	**MD**	Muscular Dystrophy
Apr	Apraxia	**Mood**	Mood Disorder
Ar	Arthritis	**MS**	Multiple Sclerosis
As	Asthma	**Nf**	Neurofibromatosis
Asp	Asperger's Syndrome	**NLD**	Nonverbal Learning Disabilities
Au	Autism	**OCD**	Obsessive–Compulsive Disorder
Bu	Bulimia	**ODD**	Oppositional Defiant Disorder
B/VI	Blindness/Visual Impairment	**ON**	Orthopedic/Neurological Impairments
C	Cardiac Disorder	**PDD**	Pervasive Developmental Disorder
CD	Conduct Disorder		
CF	Cystic Fibrosis	**Psy**	Psychosis
CLP	Cleft Lip/Cleft Palate	**PTSD**	Posttraumatic Stress Disorder
CP	Cerebral Palsy	**PW**	Prader–Willi Syndrome
D	Deafness	**S**	Speech Impairments
D-B	Deaf-Blindness	**SA**	Sexually Abused
Db	Diabetes	**SB**	Spina Bifida
Dc	Dyscalculia	**SC**	Sickle Cell Anemia
Dg	Dysgraphia	**SO**	Sex Offender
Dlx	Dyslexia	**SP**	School Phobia
Dpx	Dyspraxia	**Subst**	Substance Abuse
DS	Down Syndrome	**Sz**	Schizophrenia
ED	Emotional Disturbances	**TBI**	Traumatic Brain Injury
Ep	Epilepsy	**TS**	Tourette's Syndrome
Hemo	Hemophilia		

Special-Needs Programs

AGASSIZ VILLAGE
Res — Coed Ages 8-17

Poland, ME 04274. 71 Agassiz Village Ln. Tel: 207-998-4340. Fax: 207-998-5043.
Contact (Sept-June): 238 Bedford St, Ste 8, Lexington, MA 02420. Tel: 781-860-0200. Fax: 781-860-0352.
www.agassizvillage.org   E-mail: tsemeta@agassizvillage.org
Thomas Semeta, Dir.
Adm: FCFS. **Appl due:** Rolling. **Enr:** 100.
Conditions accepted: Phys_Impair.
Features: Crafts Dance Drama Music Photog Aquatics Archery Boating Canoe Fishing Hiking Kayak Ropes_Crse Sail Scuba Wilderness_Camp Wilderness_Canoe Baseball Basketball Lacrosse Soccer Softball Swim Tennis Watersports.
Fees 2012: Res $350-700, 1-2 wks. Aid (Need).
Housing: Cabins. **Swimming:** Lake.
Est 1935. Nonprofit. **Wks/ses:** 1-2. Operates July-Aug. ACA.

Serving boys and girls with physical special needs, the Village offers traditional waterfront activities, sports, camp craft, nature studies, arts and crafts, drama and music. A wilderness tripping program for campers ages 13 and 14 seeks to develop leadership skills on hiking and canoeing excursions.

CAMP ALBRECHT ACRES OF THE MIDWEST
Res — Coed Ages 2 and up

Sherrill, IA 52073. 14837 Sherrill Rd, PO Box 50. Tel: 563-552-1771. Fax: 563-552-2732.
www.albrechtacres.org   E-mail: info@albrechtacres.org
Deborah L. Rahe, Exec Dir.
Adm: FCFS. **Appl due:** Rolling. **Enr cap:** 72. **Staff:** Admin 2. Couns 35.
Conditions accepted: ADD ADHD As Asp Au C CP D Diabetes Dx ED Ep ID LD PDD Phys_Impair Speech & Lang TBI Visual_Impair.
Features: Crafts Dance Drama Music Aquatics Fishing Hiking Swim.
Fees 2012: Res $540, 1 wk.
Housing: Cabins Lodges Tepees. Avg per room/unit: 10. **Swimming:** Pool.
Est 1975. Nonprofit. **Ses:** 8. **Wks/ses:** 1. Operates June-Aug. ACA.

This camp for children and adults with mental or physical special needs offers daily classes in art, music and drama, and nature study. Activities include swimming, fishing, camping, sing-alongs and hiking. Special programs serve those with severe or profound disabilities.

CAMP ALLEN
Res and Day — Coed Ages 6 and up

Bedford, NH 03110. 56 Camp Allen Rd. Tel: 603-622-8471. Fax: 603-626-4295.
www.campallennh.org   E-mail: deb@campallennh.org
Michael Constance, Dir.
Adm: FCFS. **Appl due:** Rolling. **Enr:** 65. **Staff:** Admin 3. Couns 40. Special needs 2.
Conditions accepted: ADD ADHD Asp Au CP D Diabetes Ep ID LD Phys_Impair Speech & Lang Visual_Impair.
Features: Crafts Dance Music Theater Aquatics Fishing Hiking Basketball Swim.
Fees 2011: Res $775, 1 wk. Day $400, 1 wk.
Housing: Cabins Dorms Tents Tepees. **Swimming:** Pool.

Est 1931. Nonprofit. **Ses:** 17. **Wks/ses:** 1. Operates June-Aug. ACA.

Accepting children and adults with disabilities, this camp adjusts activities to camper ability. Projects include arts and crafts, nature, aquatics, games, special events, evening programs and field trips.

CAMP ASCCA
Res — Coed Ages 6 and up

Jacksons Gap, AL 36861. 5278 Camp ASCCA Dr, PO Box 21. Tel: 256-825-9226, 800-843-2267. Fax: 256-825-8332.
www.campascca.org   E-mail: info@campascca.org
Matt Rickman, Dir.
Adm: Selective. **Appl due:** Rolling. **Enr cap:** 100. **Staff:** Admin 7. Couns 40. Special needs 3.
Conditions accepted: As Asp Au CP Diabetes Ep ID LD Phys_Impair Speech & Lang TBI Visual_Impair. **Therapy:** Music Rec.
Features: Environ_Sci Crafts Filmmaking Music Aquatics Archery Boating Canoe Climbing_Wall Farm Fishing Outdoor_Ed Rappelling Riding Riflery Ropes_Crse Scuba Badminton Basketball Equestrian Golf Softball Swim Tennis Volleyball Water-skiing Watersports.
Fees 2012: Res $495-695, 1 wk. Aid 2007 (Need): $300,000.
Housing: Cabins Lodges. Avg per room/unit: 10. **Swimming:** Lake Pool.
Est 1976. Nonprofit. **Spons:** Alabama Easter Seal Society. **Ses:** 8. **Wks/ses:** 1. Operates June-Aug. ACA.

This large camp offers traditional camping activities to children and adults with disabilities. Outdoor adventure, aquatics and outdoor education are among more than 20 recreational and educational activities. While campers from out of state pay a set weekly fee, Alabama residents may receive camperships.

AUSTINE GREEN MOUNTAIN LIONS CAMP
Res — Coed Ages 6-18; Day — Coed 3-5

Brattleboro, VT 05301. 209 Austine Dr. Tel: 802-258-9513. TTY: 802-258-9513. Fax: 802-254-3921.
www.vcdhh.org   E-mail: camp@vcdhh.org
Bradley Hammond, Dir.
Grades K-12. Adm: FCFS. **Appl due:** May. **Enr:** 35. **Staff:** Admin 3. Couns 8.
LD Services: Acad_Instruction Tut.
Conditions accepted: D.
Features: Ecol Environ_Sci Crafts Creative_Writing Theater Aquatics Canoe Conservation Fishing Hiking Rappelling Rock_Climb Ropes_Crse Survival_Trng Wilderness_Camp Wilderness_Canoe Swim.
Fees 2011: Res $360-675, 2 wks. Day $360, 1 wk. Aid (Need).
Housing: Cabins Tents. Avg per room/unit: 8. **Swimming:** Lake Pond Pool River.
Est 1992. Nonprofit. **Ses:** 4. **Wks/ses:** 1-2. Operates June-July.

A collaboration between the Vermont Lions Club and Austine School for the Deaf, the camp serves children who are deaf or hard of hearing and their siblings. Counselors teach American Sign Language and other strategies for effective communication. Sessions, which serve children ages 3-5 (commuters only), 6-12 and 13-18, involve various age-appropriate recreational activities, as well as such special events as a fishing contest, hot-air balloon rides and field trips.

THE BARTON CENTER FOR DIABETES EDUCATION
SUMMER CAMPS
Res — Coord Ages 6-16; Day — Coed 6-12

North Oxford, MA 01537. 30 Ennis Rd, PO Box 356. Tel: 508-987-2056. Fax: 508-987-2002.
www.bartoncenter.org   E-mail: info@bartoncenter.org
Mary Ledbetter & Mark Bissell, Dirs.
Adm: FCFS. **Appl due:** Rolling. **Enr:** 100. **Enr cap:** 100. **Staff:** Admin 14. Couns 65. Special needs 3.
LD Services: Acad_Instruction.
Locations: CT MA NY.
Conditions accepted: Diabetes.
Features: Crafts Dance Drama Music Aquatics Archery Boating Canoe Exploration Fishing Hiking Mtn_Trips Outdoor_Ed Ropes_Crse Survival_Trng Wilderness_Camp Wilderness_Canoe Basketball Equestrian Field_Hockey Football Gymnastics Lacrosse Rugby Soccer Softball Swim Tennis Ultimate_Frisbee Volleyball.
Fees 2012: Res $1100-2320 (+$50), 1-2 wks. Day $600 (+$50), 1 wk. Aid 2011 (Need): $443,575.
Housing: Cabins. Avg per room/unit: 9. **Swimming:** Lake Pond Pool.
Est 1932. Nonprofit. **Ses:** 4. **Wks/ses:** 1-2. Operates June-Aug. ACA.

The Barton Center offers various camping options for individuals with insulin-dependent diabetes, all of which provide special education about coping with the disease. Residential camp options for children ages 6-16 include Camp Clara Barton for girls, located in North Oxford, MA; Camp Joslin for boys, located in Charlton, MA; and weeklong, coeducational adventure and wilderness camps. Boys and girls ages 6-12 may attend coed day camps in Connecticut, Massachusetts and New York. A weeklong family camp operates each August.

BAY CLIFF HEALTH CAMP
Res — Coed Ages 3-17

Big Bay, MI 49808. PO Box 310. Tel: 906-345-9314. Fax: 906-345-9890.
www.baycliff.org   E-mail: baycliff@baycliff.org
Tim Bennett, Exec Dir.
Adm: FCFS. **Appl due:** Rolling. **Enr:** 180. **Enr cap:** 180. **Staff:** Admin 8. Couns 60. Res 130. Special needs 30.
Conditions accepted: CP D Ep Phys_Impair Speech & Lang TBI Visual_Impair Ar MD SB.
Therapy: Music Occup Phys Rec Speech.
Features: Astron Crafts Aquatics Canoe Kayak Weight_Loss Swim.
Fees 2011: Res $3500, 7 wks.
Housing: Cabins Dorms. Avg per room/unit: 5. **Swimming:** Lake Pool.
Est 1934. Nonprofit. **Ses:** 1. **Wks/ses:** 7. Operates June-Aug.

Bay Cliff enrolls children with all types of physical disabilities. Staff provide daily therapy in the areas of speech and hearing, physical and occupational therapies, and visual impairment. In addition, the program incorporates arts and crafts, recreation, swimming, nature study, camping and music. All prospective campers must meet eligibility requirements and must obtain a referral from a therapist. Enrollment priority goes to boys and girls from Michigan's Upper Peninsula.

BEACON LODGE CAMP
Res — Coed Ages 6-18

Mount Union, PA 17066. 114 SR 103 S. Tel: 814-542-2511. Fax: 814-542-7437.
www.beaconlodge.com   E-mail: beaconlodgecamp@verizon.net
Hayley Lacombe, Coord.

Adm: FCFS. **Appl due:** Rolling. **Enr:** 6-23. **Enr cap:** 72. **Staff:** Admin 5. Couns 23. Special needs 2.
Conditions accepted: ADD ADHD As Asp Au CP D Diabetes Dx ED Ep ID LD PDD Phys_Impair Speech & Lang TBI Visual_Impair. **Therapy:** Art Music Rec.
Features: Crafts Dance Music Theater Aquatics Archery Canoe Climbing_Wall Community_Serv Cooking Exploration Fishing Hiking Kayak Rappelling Riflery Rock_Climb Ropes_Crse Wilderness_Camp Woodcraft Yoga Aerobics Basketball Swim.
Fees 2012: Res $450-550 (+$75), 1-1½ wks. Aid (Need).
Housing: Cabins Dorms Lodges. Avg per room/unit: 6. **Swimming:** Pond Pool River.
Est 1948. Nonprofit. **Spons:** Pennsylvania Lions. **Ses:** 7. **Wks/ses:** 1-1½. Operates June-Aug.

The summer camping program provides recreation and rehabilitation for children and adults (in separate sessions) with various special needs. Activities include swimming, arts and crafts, bowling, archery/riflery, a climbing wall and a zip line, among other pursuits. Boys and girls also go on an overnight camping trip.

BEARSKIN MEADOW CAMP
Res — Coed Ages 7-17; Day — Coed 7-13

Kings Canyon National Park, CA.
Contact (Year-round): c/o Diabetic Youth Foundation, 5167 Clayton Rd, Ste F, Concord, CA 94521. **Tel:** 925-680-4994. **Fax:** 925-680-4863.
www.dyf.org   **E-mail:** info@dyf.org
Jennifer Goerzen, Dir.
Adm: FCFS. **Appl due:** Rolling. **Staff:** Admin 8. Couns 50. Special needs 48.
Conditions accepted: Diabetes.
Features: Crafts Dance Fine_Arts Music Photog Theater Adventure_Travel Aquatics Archery Conservation Fishing Hiking Mountaineering Mtn_Trips Wilderness_Camp Baseball Basketball Football Soccer Softball Swim.
Fees 2011: Res $875-995, 1-1½ wks. Day $300, 1 wk.
Swimming: Pool.
Est 1938. Nonprofit. **Spons:** Diabetic Youth Foundation. **Ses:** 3. **Wks/ses:** 1-1½. Operates June-July. ACA.

Bearskin Meadow enables young children, adolescents and families affected by diabetes to develop self-reliance and partake of camping experiences, while also receiving support and learning to better manage the disease. Activities include traditional recreational pursuits, backpacking, campfires and dances. Family camps enable a child with diabetes to attend with one or both parents.

BERKSHIRE HILLS MUSIC ACADEMY SUMMER PROGRAM
Res and Day — Coed Ages 16-25

South Hadley, MA 01075. 48 Woodbridge St. Tel: 413-540-9720. Fax: 413-534-3875.
www.berkshirehills.org   **E-mail:** ktillona@berkshirehills.org
Tom Gajewski, Prgm Dir.
Adm: Somewhat selective. Admitted: 98%. **Appl due:** Rolling. **Enr:** 30. **Enr cap:** 30. **Fac 12. Staff:** Admin 4. Couns 7. Res 8. Special needs 7.
Type of instruction: Rem_Eng Rem_Math Rem_Read. **LD Services:** Acad_Instruction. **Avg class size:** 5. **Daily hours for:** Classes 9. Study 1. Rec 2.
Conditions accepted: Asp Au ID LD PDD TBI Visual_Impair CP DS NLD. **Therapy:** Music Psych Rec.
Features: Music Theater Canoe Cooking Hiking Swim.
Fees 2012: Res $5600, 4 wks. Day $4000, 4 wks.
Housing: Dorms. Avg per room/unit: 2. **Swimming:** Lake.
Est 2001. Nonprofit. **Ses:** 2. **Wks/ses:** 2. Operates July-Aug.

BHMA enrolls students with a variety of conditions that may accompany an intellectual disability who have significant interest in exploring music. The Summer Program teaches independent living and vocational skills and also features individual and group music lessons. Enrichment activities include trips to concerts, museums, parks, nature preserves and bike trails. Students work on a research project based on the musical genre that is being studied. Suitable applicants have basic self-care skills, display consistently positive social behavior and exhibit mature group behavior.

CAMP BLOOMFIELD
Res — Coed Ages 3-25

Malibu, CA.
Contact (Year-round): c/o Junior Blind of America, 5300 Angeles Vista Blvd, Los Angeles, CA 90043. **Tel:** 323-295-4555, 800-352-2290. **Fax:** 323-296-0424.
www.juniorblind.org/site/camp-bloomfield   **E-mail:** info@juniorblind.org
Frank Cardenas, Dir.
Adm: FCFS. **Appl due:** Rolling. **Staff:** Admin 4. Couns 40. Special needs 2.
Conditions accepted: Visual_Impair.
Features: Art Crafts Dance Music Theater Aquatics Fishing Hiking Kayak Riding Baseball Basketball Equestrian Football Golf Martial_Arts Swim Track.
Fees 2009: Res $25, 1 wk.
Housing: Cabins Lodges. **Swimming:** Ocean Pool.
Est 1958. Nonprofit. **Spons:** Junior Blind of America. **Ses:** 6. **Wks/ses:** 1-2. Operates June-Aug. ACA.

Serving those with visual impairments, Bloomfield offers specialized sessions for children and young adults. Activities include traditional recreational pursuits, campfires, riding and beach trips.

CAMP BOLD EAGLE
Res — Coed Ages 6-13

Holton, MI.
Contact (Year-round): c/o Hemophilia Foundation of Michigan, 1921 W Michigan Ave, Ypsilanti, MI 48197. **Tel:** 734-544-0015, 800-482-3041. **Fax:** 734-544-0095.
www.hfmich.org   **E-mail:** hfm@hfmich.org
Tim Wicks, Coord.
Grades 1-8. Adm: FCFS. **Appl due:** May. **Enr:** 100.
Conditions accepted: Blood.
Features: Crafts Archery Boating Canoe Fishing Hiking Baseball Basketball Soccer Softball Swim.
Fees 2009: Res $500, 1 wk. Aid (Need).
Housing: Cabins. Avg per room/unit: 6. **Swimming:** Lake.
Est 1969. Nonprofit. **Spons:** Hemophilia Foundation of Michigan. **Ses:** 2. **Wks/ses:** 1. Operates July.

Located on the shores of Big Blue Lake, this camp for young people with hereditary bleeding disorders combines traditional summer recreation with bleeding disorders education. Archery, arts and crafts, water activities and nature exploration are particularly popular. Campers are encouraged to self-infuse their own factor while at camp.

CAMP BON COEUR
Res — Coed Ages 7-16

Eunice, LA 70535. 1202 Academy Rd.
Contact (Aug-June): 405 W Main St, Lafayette, LA 70501.

Year-round Tel: 337-233-8437, Fax: 337-233-4160.
www.heartcamp.com   E-mail: info@heartcamp.com
Susannah Craig, Dir.
Adm: FCFS. **Appl due:** May. **Enr:** 50. **Staff:** Admin 2. Couns 8. Special needs 10.
Conditions accepted: C.
Features: Crafts Drama Fine_Arts Media Music Aquatics Archery Canoe Conservation Outdoor_Ed Riding Baseball Basketball Street_Hockey Swim.
Fees 2012: Res $1500 (+$40-60), 2 wks. Aid 2006 (Need): $40,000.
Housing: Dorms. **Swimming:** Pool.
Est 1985. Nonprofit. **Ses:** 2. **Wks/ses:** 2. Operates July. ACA.

Bon Coeur serves children with heart defects. Campers learn more about their heart conditions in class and participate in typical summer camp activities, among them sports, swimming, canoeing, horseback riding and art.

CAMP BREATHE EASY
Res — Coed Ages 7-13

Rutledge, GA.
Contact (Year-round): c/o Camp Twin Lakes, 600 Means St, Ste 110, Atlanta, GA 30318. Tel: 404-231-9887. Fax: 404-577-8854.
www.campbreatheeasy.net   E-mail: mandy@camptwinlakes.org
Mandy Smith, Coord.
Adm: FCFS. **Appl due:** Apr. **Enr:** 200. **Staff:** Admin 2. Couns 100. Special needs 5.
Conditions accepted: As.
Features: Crafts Music Photog Archery Bicycle_Tours Canoe Climbing_Wall Community_Serv Cooking Fishing Kayak Mtn_Biking Rappelling Ropes_Crse Survival_Trng Wilderness_Camp Baseball Basketball Golf Softball Swim Tennis Volleyball.
Fees 2012: Res $275, 1 wk. Aid (Need).
Housing: Cabins. **Swimming:** Pool.
Nonprofit. **Spons:** American Lung Association—Southeast Region. **Ses:** 1. **Wks/ses:** 1. Operates June-July.

This camp for children with asthma offers such traditional camping activities as survival training, canoeing, biking, tennis, baseball, basketball, volleyball and swimming. Campers learn strategies for best coping with the disease.

BRECKENRIDGE OUTDOOR EDUCATION CENTER SUMMER CAMPS
Res — Coed Ages 8-25

Breckenridge, CO 80424. PO Box 697. Tel: 970-453-6422, 800-383-2632. Fax: 970-453-4676.
www.boec.org   E-mail: boec@boec.org
Bruce Fitch, Exec Dir.
Adm: FCFS. **Appl due:** Rolling. **Enr cap:** 6-10. **Staff:** Admin 10.
Conditions accepted: ADD ADHD Asp Au Cancer CP D Diabetes Dx ED Ep ID LD Phys_Impair Speech & Lang TBI Visual_Impair. **Therapy:** Art Music Occup Phys Rec.
Features: Crafts Adventure_Travel Canoe Climbing_Wall Cooking Exploration Hiking Kayak Mountaineering Rock_Climb Ropes_Crse Survival_Trng White-water_Raft Wilderness_Camp Wilderness_Canoe Equestrian.
Fees 2010: Res $500-900 (+$100), 1 wk. Aid (Merit & Need).
Housing: Cabins Lodges Tepees.
Est 1976. Nonprofit. **Ses:** 4. **Wks/ses:** 1. Operates June-Aug.

BOEC conducts four weeklong summer programs for at-risk groups and individuals with physical or mental disabilities or serious illnesses: Camp Big Tree (for campers ages 12-16 who have sensory processing disorders), Wilderness Camp (ages 16-25; developmental disabilities), Junior Adventures Camp (ages 8-14; developmental and processing disorders) and Visually Impaired Wilderness Camp (ages 15-19). BOEC programs accommodate boys and girls of all ability levels and include such mountain and river activities as canoeing, rafting, rock climbing, teamwork and leadership development, ropes courses, hiking, backpacking and camping.

CAMP BUCK
Res — Coed Ages 8-17

Portola, CA.
Contact (Year-round): 1005 Terminal Way, Ste 170, Reno, NV 89502.
 Tel: 775-856-3839, 800-379-3839. Fax: 775-348-7591.
www.diabetesnv.org   E-mail: camp@diabetesnv.org
Sarah Gleich, Dir.
Adm: FCFS. **Appl due:** Rolling. **Staff:** Admin 4. Couns 30. Special needs 15.
Conditions accepted: Diabetes.
Features: Ecol Environ_Sci Crafts Dance Drama Music Painting Archery Boating Canoe Climbing_Wall Community_Serv Cooking Fishing Hiking Kayak Rock_Climb Ropes_ Crse Yoga Aerobics Baseball Basketball Field_Hockey Football Soccer Softball Street_ Hockey Swim Ultimate_Frisbee Volleyball Watersports.
Fees 2011: Res $499, 1 wk. Aid (Need).
Housing: Cabins. **Swimming:** Lake Pool Stream.
Est 1988. Nonprofit. **Ses:** 1. **Wks/ses:** 1. Operates Aug.

In an outdoor, recreational setting, the camp helps children with Type 1 diabetes better understand and control the condition. Staff promote nutritional awareness as an essential component of diabetes management. Activities include music, art, dance, aquatic sports and riding.

CAMP BUCKSKIN
Res — Coed Ages 6-18

Ely, MN 55731. PO Box 389. Tel: 218-365-2121. Fax: 218-365-2880.
Contact (Sept-May): 4124 Quebec Ave N, Ste 300, Minneapolis, MN 55427.
 Tel: 763-208-4805. Fax: 763-208-8668.
www.campbuckskin.com   E-mail: info@campbuckskin.com
Thomas R. Bauer, Dir.
Grades K-12. Adm: FCFS. **Appl due:** Rolling. **Enr:** 100. **Staff:** Admin 11. Couns 45. Special needs 3.
LD Services: Acad_Instruction Tut.
Conditions accepted: ADD ADHD Asp Dx LD PDD.
Features: Ecol Environ_Sci Expository_Writing Crafts Creative_Writing Music Aquatics Archery Canoe Conservation Fishing Hiking Outdoor_Ed Riflery Wilderness_Camp Wilderness_Canoe Woodcraft Aerobics Basketball Cricket Football Rugby Soccer Softball Swim Ultimate_Frisbee Volleyball Watersports.
Fees 2011: Res $4025-4275 (+$60), 4½ wks.
Housing: Cabins Tents. Avg per room/unit: 9. **Swimming:** Lake.
Est 1959. Inc. **Ses:** 2. **Wks/ses:** 4½. Operates June-Aug. ACA.

The typical camper at Buckskin has an attentional disorder, a learning disability or Asperger's syndrome and, as a result, has experienced social-skill difficulties, diminished academic success and self-esteem issues. Regularly scheduled activities include canoeing, swimming, nature studies, arts and crafts, archery, riflery and reading, in addition to electives and field trips. A formalized social skills program addresses such areas as interpersonal communication, problem solving, initiative and task completion.

CAMP-A-LOT
Res — Coed Ages 5 and up

San Diego, CA 92102. 3030 Market St, Ste B. Tel: 619-685-1178. Fax: 619-234-3759.
www.arc-sd.com   E-mail: pals@arc-sd.com
Lin Taylor, Dir.
Adm: FCFS. Admitted: 95%. Appl due: Rolling. Enr: 60. Enr cap: 60. Staff: Admin 5. Couns 38.
Conditions accepted: ADD ADHD Asp Au CP Ep ID PDD.
Features: Crafts Drama Aquatics Community_Serv Hiking Outdoor_Ed Aerobics Baseball Basketball Softball Swim.
Fees 2011: Res $885 (+$65), 1 wk.
Housing: Cabins. Swimming: Pool.
Est 1964. Nonprofit. Spons: Arc of San Diego. Ses: 5. Wks/ses: 1. Operates July-Aug. ACA.

Camp-A-Lot serves children, teenagers and adults with developmentally disabilities, a limited number of whom have mobility restrictions. Traditional camp activities, including hiking, arts and crafts, swimming, songs and games, nature lore, overnights, campfires and cookouts, are part of each session. Older campers may also take part in drama programs.

CAMP CAREFREE
Res — Coed Ages 8-15

Wolfeboro, NH 03894. PO Box 2118. Tel: 603-859-0410. Fax: 603-859-0410.
Contact (Sept-June): PO Box 342, Newmarket, NH 03857. Tel: 603-659-7061. Fax: 603-659-8891.
www.campcarefreekids.org   E-mail: br4sox@comcast.net
Phyllis Woestemeyer, Dir.
Grades 3-10. Adm: FCFS. Appl due: May. Enr: 120. Enr cap: 120. Staff: Admin 7. Couns 24.
Conditions accepted: Diabetes.
Features: Crafts Drama Photog Aquatics Archery Boating Canoe Fishing Hiking Kayak Outdoor_Ed Ropes_Crse Wilderness_Camp Yoga Aerobics Baseball Basketball Football Soccer Softball Swim Volleyball Watersports.
Fees 2011: Res $1200 (+$30), 2 wks. Aid 2010 (Need): $25,000.
Housing: Cabins Tepees. Avg per room/unit: 15. Swimming: Lake.
Est 1976. Nonprofit. Spons: American Diabetes Association. Ses: 1. Wks/ses: 2. Operates July-Aug. ACA.

Conducted by the American Diabetes Association, Camp Carefree provides an educational environment in which campers learn to live with diabetes. Youth gain an understanding on how to balance exercise, diet and insulin while also developing a renewed sense of independence and confidence. Among the camp's recreational pursuits are field trips, hiking, overnight camp outs, arts and crafts, games, waterfront activities and camper/counselor shows.

CAMP CAROLINA TRAILS
Res — Coed Ages 7-17

King, NC.
Contact (Year-round): 2418 Blue Ridge Rd, Ste 206, Raleigh, NC 27607.
Tel: 919-743-5400, 888-342-2383. Fax: 919-783-7838.
www.diabetes.org   E-mail: jthomas@diabetes.org
Justin Thomas, Dir.
Grades 3-11. Adm: FCFS. Appl due: Rolling. Enr: 160. Enr cap: 160. Staff: Admin 6. Couns 68.
Conditions accepted: Diabetes.

Features: Crafts Archery Canoe Hiking Kayak Riding Riflery Rock_Climb Ropes_Crse Wilderness_Camp Equestrian Swim.
Fees 2012: Res $700, 1 wk. Aid 2011 (Need): $19,000.
Housing: Cabins. Avg per room/unit: 12. **Swimming:** Lake Pool.
Est 1967. Nonprofit. **Spons:** American Diabetes Association. **Ses:** 1. **Wks/ses:** 1. Operates June.

Located in the Sauertown Mountains, this camp for children with diabetes combines instruction on diabetes management with a full recreational camping experience. Activities include sports, arts and crafts, music, drama, dance, aquatics, nature lore and camp craft.

CARROLL CENTER FOR THE BLIND
YOUTH IN TRANSITION PROGRAM
Res — Coed Ages 15-21

Newton, MA 02458. 770 Centre St. Tel: 617-969-6200, 800-852-3131.
Fax: 617-969-6204.
www.carroll.org   E-mail: intake@carroll.org
Karen Ross, Dir.
Adm: FCFS. **Admitted:** 90%. **Appl due:** Rolling. **Enr:** 40. **Staff:** Special needs 12.
LD Services: Acad_Instruction Tut.
Conditions accepted: Visual_Impair.
Features: Crafts Drama Music Photog Canoe Climbing_Wall Cooking Sail Social_Servs Work Fencing Swim.
Fees 2009: Res $7400, 5 wks.
Housing: Dorms. **Swimming:** Pool.
Est 1966. Nonprofit. **Ses:** 2. **Wks/ses:** 5. Operates June-Aug.

Youth in Transition assists teens and young adults who are blind or visually impaired in developing life skills and independence. Tutoring and instruction are available in personal management, mobility and communications. Counseling is also offered individually or in peer groups. Recreational and social activities include field trips, canoeing, sailing and dances. The center also provides academic tutoring and conducts work experience and computer training programs.

CHAMP CAMP
Res — Coed Ages 6-18

Martinsville, IN.
Contact (Year-round): 212 W 10th St, Ste B-210, Indianapolis, IN 46202.
Tel: 317-679-1860. Fax: 317-245-2291.
www.champcamp.org   E-mail: admin@champcamp.org
Jennifer Kobylarz, Exec Dir.
Grades 1-12. Adm: FCFS. **Appl due:** Apr. **Staff:** Couns 100. Special needs 75.
Conditions accepted: As.
Features: Crafts Music Aquatics Boating Canoe Climbing_Wall Conservation Fishing Riding Rock_Climb Wilderness_Camp Woodcraft Equestrian Swim.
Fees 2012: Res $250, 1 wk. Aid (Need).
Housing: Cabins. **Swimming:** Pool.
Est 1991. Nonprofit. **Ses:** 1. **Wks/ses:** 1. Operates June. ACA.

Children and adolescents with tracheostomies and those who require respiratory assistance (including the use of ventilators) may enroll in this program. Crafts, music, climbing, canoeing, boating, fishing and games are among the activities. Most counselors are medical professionals.

CHILDREN'S ASSOCIATION FOR MAXIMUM POTENTIAL CAMP
Res — Coed Ages 5-45

Center Point, TX 78010. PO Box 999. Tel: 830-634-2267. Fax: 210-858-8035.
Contact (Sept-Apr): PO Box 27086, San Antonio, TX 78227. Tel: 210-671-5411.
  Fax: 210-671-5225.
www.campcamp.org   E-mail: campmail@campcamp.org
Brandon G. Briery, Dir.
Adm: FCFS. Appl due: Rolling.
Conditions accepted: Asp C CP D Diabetes Dx ED Ep ID LD Phys_Impair Speech & Lang
  TBI Visual_Impair DS SB.
Features: Crafts Aquatics Archery Canoe Hiking Riflery Equestrian Swim.
Fees 2012: Res $300-1500, 1 wk.
Housing: Cabins. Swimming: Lake Pool.
Est 1988. Nonprofit. Ses: 8. Wks/ses: 1. Operates May-Aug.

The camp serves children with special needs, their siblings and other interested children. Any child, regardless of the severity of his or her condition, may attend. Opportunities for campers include archery, riflery, swimming, canoeing, riding, crafts, nature hikes and specially adapted field sports. Fees are determined along a sliding scale according to family income.

CHILDREN'S HOSPITAL OF DENVER
TALKING WITH TECHNOLOGY CAMP
Res — Coed Ages 6-21

Empire, CO.
Contact (Year-round): 13123 E 16th Ave, Aurora, CO 80045. Tel: 720-777-6024.
  Fax: 720-777-7169.
www.thechildrenshospital.org/conditions/speech/camp
E-mail: lich.kim@tchden.org
Kim Lich, Coord.
Adm: FCFS. Appl due: Apr. Enr: 38. Staff: Admin 3. Couns 25. Res 25. Special needs
  40.
Conditions accepted: Au CP ID Speech & Lang. Therapy: Speech.
Features: Computers Crafts Dance Drama Media Music Photog Aquatics Farm Fishing
  Hiking Riding Ropes_Crse Equestrian Golf Swim.
Housing: Cabins. Avg per room/unit: 20. Swimming: Pool.
Est 1985. Ses: 1. Wks/ses: 1. Operates July.

This intensive, weeklong program serves young people who use augmentative and alternative communication devices as their primary means of expression. TWT provides individualized instruction in system use and also teaches campers new uses of vocabulary. The improvement of social skills is another program goal, as boys and girls learn to interact more effectively with adults and other children. Traditional camp activities round out the program. Scholarship assistance (through the Scottish Rite Foundation) is available to Colorado residents only.

CLARKE SCHOOLS FOR HEARING AND SPEECH
SUMMER ADVENTURE
Res and Day — Coed Ages 9-13

Northampton, MA 01060. 47 Round Hill Rd. Tel: 413-584-3450. TTY: 413-584-3450.
  Fax: 413-584-8273.
www.clarkeschools.org   E-mail: info@clarkeschools.org
Martha A. deHahn, Coord.
Adm: FCFS. Appl due: Rolling. Enr: 30. Enr cap: 30. Staff: Admin 2.
LD Services: Acad_Instruction.
Conditions accepted: D.

Features: Computers Speech Writing/Journ Crafts Music Exploration Hiking Outdoor_Ed Swim.
Fees 2012: Res $1395 (+$75), 2 wks. Day $895 (+$75), 2 wks. Aid (Merit & Need).
Housing: Dorms. Avg per room/unit: 2. **Swimming:** Pool.
Est 1982. Nonprofit. **Ses:** 1. **Wks/ses:** 2. Operates July.

Summer Adventure provides an enriched academic experience for children with hearing loss, as well as an opportunity for boys and girls to interact socially with others who have hearing loss. Masters-level trained teachers of the deaf maintain an auditory/oral environment for the campers. Various enrichment and recreational activities take place during the day, while evenings provide children with the opportunity to relax and get to know one another. A number of off-site field trips augment the program, including a daylong trip during the weekend.

CLEVELAND SIGHT CENTER
HIGHBROOK LODGE
Res — Coed Ages 8-18

Cleveland, OH 44106. 1909 E 101st St, PO Box 1988. Tel: 216-791-8118.
    Fax: 216-791-1101.
www.clevelandsightcenter.org/highbrooklodge.aspx
E-mail: camp@clevelandsightcenter.org
Bob Kochmit, Mgr.
Adm: FCFS. **Appl due:** Rolling. **Enr:** 45. **Enr cap:** 45. **Staff:** Admin 4. Couns 20.
LD Services: Tut.
Conditions accepted: Visual_Impair.
Features: Bus/Fin Computers Ecol Crafts Creative_Writing Dance Music Theater Aquatics Archery Climbing_Wall Exploration Riding Ropes_Crse Sail Social_Servs Wilderness_Camp Baseball Swim Watersports.
Fees 2011: Res $480-540 (+$20), 1 wk. Aid 2006 (Need): $60,000.
Housing: Cabins Lodges Tents. Avg per room/unit: 40. **Swimming:** Pond Pool.
Est 1928. Nonprofit. **Ses:** 4. **Wks/ses:** 1. Operates June-Aug. ACA.

Sponsored by the Cleveland Sight Center, Highbrook Lodge offers academics and recreation for individuals with visual impairments who may also have other disabilities. Camp life includes tutoring, music, art, dance, aquatic sports, trips and riding. Various adult and family programs are available.

CLOVER PATCH CAMP
Res — Coed Ages 5 and up; Day — Coed 5-18

Glenville, NY 12302. 55 Helping Hand Ln. Tel: 518-384-3081. Fax: 518-384-3001.
www.cloverpatchcamp.org   E-mail: cloverpatchcamp@cfdsny.org
Laura Taylor, Dir.
Adm: FCFS. **Appl due:** Rolling. **Enr:** 24. **Enr cap:** 24. **Staff:** Admin 3. Couns 18. Res 23. Special needs 5.
Conditions accepted: ADD ADHD Asp Au CP D Diabetes Dx ED Ep ID LD PDD Phys_Impair Speech & Lang TBI Visual_Impair. **Therapy:** Art Music Occup Rec.
Features: Environ_Sci Sci Crafts Dance Music Painting Theater Aquatics Hiking Baseball Basketball Golf Soccer Softball Swim Volleyball Watersports.
Fees 2011: Res $1250, 1 wk. Day $650, 1 wk. Aid 2009 (Need): $84,000.
Housing: Cabins. Avg per room/unit: 8. **Swimming:** Pool.
Est 1965. Nonprofit. **Spons:** Center for Disability Services. **Ses:** 7. **Wks/ses:** 1. Operates June-July. ACA.

Clover Patch provides a program of swimming, arts and crafts, music, drama and outdoor living skills for children and adults with various special needs, including mental retardation, physical handicaps, cerebral palsy and seizure disorders. Individuals with extreme behavioral disorders are not accepted. Medical approval and screening precedes admittance.

CAMP COLORADO
Res — Coed Ages 8-17

Woodland Park, CO.
Contact (Year-round): c/o American Diabetes Assoc, 2480 W 26th Ave, Ste 120B, Denver, CO 80211. Tel: 720-855-1102, 800-676-4065. Fax: 720-855-1302.
www.diabetes.org/adacampcolorado   E-mail: emfay@diabetes.org
Emily Fay, Dir.
Adm: FCFS. **Appl due:** May. **Enr:** 260. **Enr cap:** 260. **Staff:** Admin 5. Couns 75. Special needs 15.
Conditions accepted: Diabetes.
Features: Crafts Aquatics Archery Canoe Climbing_Wall Fishing Hiking Kayak Mtn_Biking Mtn_Trips Rappelling Riflery Rock_Climb Ropes_Crse White-water_Raft Wilderness_ Camp Basketball Equestrian Swim Volleyball Watersports.
Fees 2012: Res $610-650, 1 wk. Aid 2007 (Need): $25,000.
Housing: Cabins Tents. Avg per room/unit: 7. **Swimming:** Lake.
Nonprofit. **Spons:** American Diabetes Association. **Ses:** 1. **Wks/ses:** 1. Operates June-July.

Children at the camp, which is held at Eagle Lake Camp in the Pike National Forest, participate in a camping program while learning diabetes management. Staff address diabetic lifestyle issues through discussion of nutrition, exercise, emotional well-being and glucose control. Two programs operate each summer: a traditional recreational camp and a teen camp that combines recreational activities with adventure pursuits.

COLORADO LIONS CAMP
Res — Coed Ages 8 and up

Woodland Park, CO 80866. PO Box 9043. Tel: 719-687-2087. Fax: 719-687-7435.
www.coloradolionscamp.org   E-mail: coloradolionscamp@msn.com
James Pierie, Exec Dir.
Adm: FCFS. **Appl due:** Rolling. **Enr:** 40-45. **Staff:** Admin 3. Couns 22. Special needs 2.
Conditions accepted: ADD ADHD Asp Au D Diabetes Dx Ep ID LD Phys_Impair Speech & Lang TBI Visual_Impair DS. **Therapy:** Psych Rec.
Features: Astron Crafts Dance Music Theater Aquatics Fishing Hiking Mtn_Biking Out-door_Ed Ropes_Crse Badminton Baseball Basketball Softball Swim Volleyball.
Fees 2012: Res $500, 1 wk. Aid 2011 (Need): $70,000.
Housing: Dorms Tepees. **Swimming:** Pool.
Est 1969. Nonprofit. **Spons:** Lions Clubs Colorado. **Ses:** 10. **Wks/ses:** 1. Operates June-Aug.

A project of Lions Clubs throughout the state of Colorado, the camp provides mountain camping experiences and outdoor adventures for blind, deaf, mentally limited and physically impaired populations. Campers participate in backpacking, swimming, riding, hiking, fishing, overnight camping, outdoor cooking, hayrides, nature study, and arts and crafts.

CAMP CONRAD-CHINNOCK
Res — Coed Ages 7-16

Angelus Oaks, CA 92305. 4700 Jenks Lake Rd E. Tel: 909-794-6712.
Fax: 909-752-5354.
Contact (Sept-June): c/o Diabetes Camping & Educational Services, 12045 E Water-front Dr, Playa Vista, CA 90094. Tel: 310-751-3057. Fax: 888-800-4010.

Year-round Toll-free: 888-800-4010.
www.campconradchinnock.org   E-mail: rosie@dys.org
Rocky Wilson, Exec Dir.
Adm: FCFS. **Appl due:** Rolling. **Enr:** 95. **Enr cap:** 110. **Staff:** Admin 6. Couns 12. Special needs 20.
Conditions accepted: Diabetes.
Features: Astron Ecol Crafts Drama Aquatics Archery Canoe Caving Climbing_Wall Exploration Fishing Hiking Mountaineering Mtn_Biking Rappelling Riflery Rock_Climb Ropes_Crse Basketball Swim.
Fees 2011: Res $470 (+$30), 1 wk. Aid 2010 (Need): $18,000.
Housing: Cabins. Avg per room/unit: 10. **Swimming:** Pool.
Est 1957. Nonprofit. **Spons:** Diabetes Camping and Educational Services. **Ses:** 6. **Wks/ses:** 1. Operates June-Aug. ACA.

The camp provides recreational, social and educational opportunities for youth with insulin-dependent diabetes. Campers acquire diabetes self-management skills while participating in many traditional camping activities. Programming combines cabin-group activities with free-choice periods. Younger children spend most of their time with cabin mates, while older campers exercise a greater degree of control over their schedules.

COURAGE CENTER CAMPS
Res — Coed Ages 7 and up

Maple Lake, MN 55358. 8046 83rd St NW. Tel: 320-963-3121, 866-520-0504. Fax: 320-963-3698.
www.couragecenter.org/camp   E-mail: camping@couragecenter.org
Tom Fogarty, Dir.
Adm: FCFS. **Appl due:** Rolling. **Enr:** 700. **Staff:** Admin 10. Couns 90. Special needs 11.
Conditions accepted: As Asp Au Blood Cancer CP D Ep LD Phys_Impair Speech & Lang TBI Visual_Impair. **Therapy:** Speech.
Features: Computers Ecol Environ_Sci Crafts Media Photog Aquatics Bicycle_Tours Canoe Farm Riding Sail Wilderness_Camp Swim.
Fees 2012: Res $500-950, ½-1 wk. Aid (Need).
Housing: Cabins. Avg per room/unit: 20. **Swimming:** Lake Pool.
Est 1955. Nonprofit. **Spons:** Courage Center. **Ses:** 19. **Wks/ses:** ½-1. Operates June-Aug. ACA.

Courage Center conducts recreational summer programming for young people with various special needs at the 305-acre Camp Courage site, located approximately 50 miles west of the Twin Cities. A teen session serves boys and girls with a physical disability or a visual impairment, while a leadership week offers intensive leadership and life skills training for teens with a physical disability or a sensory impairment. A specialty week accommodates campers ages 7-14 who have a communication disorder. Also available is a half-week sampler session for first-time overnight campers.

COURAGE NORTH
Res — Coed Ages 7-17

Lake George, MN 56458. PO Box 1626. Tel: 218-266-3658. Fax: 218-266-3458.
Contact (Winter): c/o Courage Ctr, 3915 Golden Valley Rd, Golden Valley, MN 55422. Tel: 763-520-0520. Fax: 763-520-0577.
Year-round Toll-free: 888-276-3631.
www.couragecenter.org/camps   E-mail: couragecamps@couragecenter.org
Jan Malcolm, CEO.
Adm: FCFS. **Appl due:** Rolling.
Conditions accepted: D.

Focus: Basketball. **Features:** Crafts Photog Adventure_Travel Archery Boating Canoe Hiking Kayak Sail Soccer Swim Tennis Watersports.
Fees 2011: Res $750, 1 wk.
Housing: Cabins. **Swimming:** Lake.
Est 1972. Nonprofit. **Spons:** Courage Center. **Ses:** 1. **Wks/ses:** 1. Operates Aug. ACA.

Operated by the Courage Center, Courage North is a traditional summer camp for children and adolescents who are deaf or hard of hearing. A sliding fee scale is available. Popular pursuits include watersports and other water activities, digital photography, and arts and crafts. The camp also seeks to help boys and girls gain independence and develop social and leadership skills. An optional canoeing trip (offered for an additional fee) runs for five days at the conclusion of the regular session.

CAMP COURAGEOUS
Res — Coed Ages 15 and up; Day — Coed 7-21

Whitehouse, OH 43571. 12701 Waterville-Swanton Rd. Tel: 419-875-6828.
www.campcourageous.com   E-mail: camping@campcourageous.com
Steve Kiessling, Dir.
Adm: FCFS. **Appl due:** Rolling. **Enr:** 200. **Staff:** Admin 3. Couns 20.
Conditions accepted: ADD ADHD Asp ID LD Phys_Impair. **Therapy:** Art Rec.
Features: Crafts Dance Music Aquatics Hiking Wilderness_Camp Baseball Basketball Swim.
Fees 2011: Res $743, 1 wk. Day $240, 1 wk.
Housing: Dorms. **Swimming:** Pool.
Est 1963. Nonprofit. **Ses:** 9. **Wks/ses:** 1. Operates June-Aug. ACA.

Courageous provides residential camping for children and adults with mental retardation and developmental disabilities. Core program activities are aquatics, arts and crafts, sports, outdoor recreation and leisure skills, nature and weather studies, drama, cookouts and campfires. The camp's facilities and grounds are wheelchair accessible.

CAMP COURAGEOUS OF IOWA SUMMER YOUTH WEEKS
Res — Coed Ages 3-21

Monticello, IA 52310. 12007 190th St, PO Box 418. Tel: 319-465-5916.
Fax: 319-465-5919.
www.campcourageous.org   E-mail: info@campcourageous.org
Jeanne Muellerleile, Dir.
Adm: FCFS. **Appl due:** Jan. **Enr:** 45-80. **Enr cap:** 80. **Staff:** Admin 4. Couns 40. Res 55.
Conditions accepted: As Asp Au CP Ep ID LD PDD Phys_Impair Speech & Lang TBI Visual_Impair MD MS.
Features: Crafts Fine_Arts Adventure_Travel Aquatics Archery Canoe Caving Climbing_Wall Fishing Hiking Rappelling Rock_Climb Ropes_Crse Basketball Swim.
Fees 2012: Res $450, 1 wk. Aid (Need).
Housing: Cabins Dorms Houses Tents Tepees. Avg per room/unit: 8. **Swimming:** Pool.
Est 1972. Nonprofit. **Ses:** 12. **Wks/ses:** 1. Operates May-Aug. ACA.

This year-round recreational and respite care facility for children and adults with special needs conducts weeklong summer camps for young people. Offerings include traditional outdoor activities, arts and crafts, and adventure pursuits. Persons served range from those with mental, physical or multiple disabilities to those with Asperger's syndrome or brain injury.

DEAF CHILDREN'S CAMP
Res — Coed Ages 4-16

Milford, IN.
Contact (Year-round): 100 W 86th St, Indianapolis, IN 46260. Tel: 317-846-3404.
Fax: 317-844-1034.
www.indeafcamps.org   E-mail: deafcamp@hotmail.com
Phil Harden, Dir.
Adm: FCFS. **Appl due:** Rolling. **Enr cap:** 180. **Staff:** Admin 5. Couns 90. Special needs 3.
Conditions accepted: D.
Features: Ecol Sci Crafts Drama Music Painting Aquatics Archery Boating Canoe Climbing_Wall Fishing Hiking Kayak Outdoor_Ed Riding Ropes_Crse Sail Basketball Golf Swim Ultimate_Frisbee Volleyball Watersports.
Fees 2012: Res $300, 1 wk. Aid 2010 (Need): $29,000.
Housing: Cabins Dorms Lodges Tents. Avg per room/unit: 10. **Swimming:** Lake.
Est 1973. Nonprofit. **Ses:** 1. **Wks/ses:** 1. Operates July.

The camp serves children who are deaf or hard of hearing. Both speaking and signing campers participate in such activities as swimming, canoeing, crafts, hiking, games, fishing and sports. A CIT program serves boys and girls ages 17 and 18.

THE DOUBLE H RANCH
Res — Coed Ages 6-16

Lake Luzerne, NY 12846. 97 Hidden Valley Rd. Tel: 518-696-5676. **Fax:** 518-696-4528.
www.doublehranch.org   E-mail: theranch@doublehranch.org
Jacqueline Royael, Dir.
Adm: FCFS. **Appl due:** Rolling. **Enr:** 105. **Enr cap:** 126. **Staff:** Admin 22. Couns 50. Res 10. Special needs 30.
Conditions accepted: Blood Cancer CP HIV/AIDS Phys_Impair TBI Visual_Impair. **Therapy:** Art Music Phys Psych Rec Speech.
Features: Crafts Creative_Writing Dance Drama Music Aquatics Archery Boating Conservation Exploration Fishing Hiking Riding Ropes_Crse Wilderness_Camp Woodcraft Baseball Basketball Equestrian Football Swim Tennis.
Fees 2012: Free. Res 1 wk.
Housing: Cabins. **Swimming:** Lake Pool.
Est 1993. Nonprofit. **Spons:** Hole in the Wall Gang Association. **Ses:** 8. **Wks/ses:** 1. Operates June-Aug. ACA.

The camp provides recreation and education for children with cancer, serious blood disorders and neuromuscular impairments. The schedule of activities includes swimming, fishing, boating, riding, conservation practices, camping, nature walks, arts and crafts, music and theater. Weekly scheduled trips allow campers to go white-water rafting and to local amusement and water parks.

DREAM STREET FOUNDATION SUMMER CAMPS
Res — Coed Ages 4-14

Beverly Hills, CA 90210. 433 N Camden Dr, Ste 600. Tel: 424-248-0696.
www.dreamstreetfoundation.org   E-mail: dreamstreetca@gmail.com
Patty Grubman, Dir.
Adm: FCFS. **Appl due:** Apr. **Enr:** 140. **Enr cap:** 140. **Staff:** Admin 6. Couns 125. Special needs 18.
Locations: AR AZ CA MI NJ.
Conditions accepted: Blood Cancer C Ep HIV/AIDS CF.

Features: Circus_Skills Crafts Dance Music Aquatics Archery Climbing_Wall Hiking Riding Ropes_Crse Survival_Trng Woodcraft Basketball Gymnastics Swim.
Fees 2012: Free. Res 1 wk.
Housing: Cabins Dorms Lodges. Avg per room/unit: 6. **Swimming:** Pool.
Est 1989. Nonprofit. **Ses:** 3. **Wks/ses:** 1. Operates July-Aug.

Dream Street sponsors cost-free camps across the country for children with such chronic and life-threatening illnesses as cancer, AIDS and blood disorders. At the camps, boys and girls take part in activities from which they would typically be excluded due to their illnesses. Offerings include arts and crafts, sports, dance, drama, music, aquatics and hiking.

EASTER SEALS CAMP CHALLENGE
Res — Coed Ages 6 and up

Sorrento, FL 32776. 31600 Camp Challenge Rd. Tel: 352-383-4711.
Fax: 352-383-0744.
www.fl.easterseals.com   E-mail: camp@fl.easterseals.com
Michael Archbold, Dir.
Adm: FCFS. **Appl due:** Rolling. **Enr cap:** 70. **Staff:** Couns 20.
Conditions accepted: ADD ADHD Asp Au CP D ID LD PDD Phys_Impair Speech & Lang TBI Visual_Impair.
Features: Crafts Dance Drama Music Painting Archery Climbing_Wall Farm Paintball Rappelling Ropes_Crse Baseball Basketball Field_Hockey Football Golf Soccer Softball Swim Ultimate_Frisbee Volleyball.
Fees 2012: Res $900-1800, 1-2 wks. Aid (Need).
Housing: Cabins Dorms. Avg per room/unit: 12-18. **Swimming:** Pool.
Est 1961. Nonprofit. **Spons:** Easter Seals Florida. **Ses:** 4. **Wks/ses:** 1-2. Operates June-July. ACA.

Camp Challenge, Florida's Easter Seal camp, addresses the needs of individuals with physical or cognitive disabilities. The camp provides specific activities for children, adolescents and adults, including aquatic sports, arts and crafts, socials, skits, nature study and a challenge course. Children accepted to the camp must not be aggressive towards themselves or others.

EASTER SEALS CAMP HARMON
Res — Coed Ages 8 and up

Boulder Creek, CA 95006. 16403 Hwy 9. Tel: 831-338-3383.
Contact (Sept-May): c/o Easter Seals Central California, 9010 Soquel Dr, Aptos, CA 95003. Tel: 831-684-2166.
Year-round Fax: 831-684-1018.
www.centralcal.easterseals.com   E-mail: campharmon@es-cc.org
June Stockbridge, Dir.
Adm: FCFS. **Appl due:** Rolling. **Enr:** 75. **Enr cap:** 80. **Staff:** Admin 3. Couns 30. Res 10.
Conditions accepted: ADD ADHD Asp Au CP Ep ID LD Phys_Impair TBI DS.
Features: Crafts Dance Drama Aquatics Archery Hiking Baseball Basketball Equestrian Golf Swim Track Volleyball.
Fees 2012: Res $726, 1 wk. Aid (Need).
Housing: Cabins Lodges. Avg per room/unit: 9. **Swimming:** Pool.
Est 1964. Nonprofit. **Spons:** Easter Seals Central California. **Ses:** 7. **Wks/ses:** 1. Operates June-July. ACA.

Each session at the camp accommodates a specific age group and works with individuals with developmental or physical disabilities or both. Campers engage in a variety of activities, enabling them to explore new interests while also participating in favorite pursuits. Harmon maintains the camper-staff ratio at 2:1.

EASTER SEALS CAMP SNO-MO
Res — Coed Ages 11-21

Gilmanton Iron Works, NH 03837. 260 Griswold Ln. Tel: 603-364-5818.
Fax: 603-364-0230.
Contact (Sept-Apr): 200 Zachary Rd, Bldg B, Manchester, NH 03109.
Tel: 603-206-6733. Fax: 603-669-9413.
www.eastersealsnh.org   E-mail: rkelly@eastersealsnh.org
Robert E. Kelly, Dir.
Adm: FCFS. Admitted: 95%. Appl due: Rolling. Staff: Admin 1. Couns 12.
Conditions accepted: ADHD Asp Au CP D ED Ep ID LD Phys_Impair Speech & Lang TBI
Visual_Impair.
Features: Ecol Crafts Dance Fine_Arts Music Aquatics Archery Boating Canoe Exploration Fishing Kayak Mountaineering Riflery Ropes_Crse Sail Baseball Soccer Swim Volleyball.
Fees 2012: Res $640-1280 (+$150-300), 1-2 wks. Aid (Need).
Housing: Lodges Tents. Avg per room/unit: 15. Swimming: Lake.
Est 1972. Nonprofit. Spons: Easter Seals New Hampshire/New Hampshire Snowmobile Association. Ses: 7. Wks/ses: 1-2. Operates June-Aug.

This coeducational camp integrates campers with disabilities and able-bodied Boy Scouts. Campers are involved in developing their schedules of activities for the week. In addition to the usual recreational activities, the program includes animal shows and woodworking. Sno-Mo is equipped to accommodate campers with special medical and nutritional needs.

EASTER SEALS CAMP SUNNYSIDE
Res — Coed Ages 4 and up; Day — Coed 4-17

Des Moines, IA 50313. 401 NE 66th Ave. Tel: 515-289-1933. TTY: 515-289-4069.
Fax: 515-289-1281.
www.eastersealsia.org   E-mail: kanderson@eastersealsia.org
Adm: FCFS. Appl due: Rolling. Staff: Admin 10. Couns 75.
Conditions accepted: Asp Au Cancer C CP D Diabetes ED Ep HIV/AIDS ID LD Phys_
Impair Speech & Lang TBI Visual_Impair.
Features: Crafts Fine_Arts Music Aquatics Archery Boating Canoe Climbing_Wall Fishing Hiking Riding Social_Servs Weight_Loss Swim.
Fees 2011: Res $575, 1 wk. Aid 2007 (Need): $70,000.
Housing: Cabins Tents. Swimming: Lake Pool.
Est 1961. Nonprofit. Spons: Easter Seals of Iowa. Ses: 8. Wks/ses: 1. Operates June-Aug.
ACA.

Camp Sunnyside offers a full recreational program for children and adults with disabilities. In addition to its summer programming, Easter Seals of Iowa conducts weekend respite camps and winter break and spring break residential programs.

EASTER SEALS CAMP WAWBEEK
Res — Coed Ages 7 and up

Wisconsin Dells, WI.
Contact (Year-round): c/o Easter Seals Wisconsin, 101 Nob Hill Rd, Ste 301,
Madison, WI 53713. Tel: 608-277-8288, 800-422-2324. Fax: 608-277-8333.
www.eastersealswisconsin.com   E-mail: camp@eastersealswisconsin.com
Carissa Miller, Dir.
Adm: FCFS. Appl due: Rolling. Staff: Admin 5. Couns 90. Special needs 3.
Conditions accepted: ADD ADHD As Asp Au CP ED Ep ID LD PDD Phys_Impair Speech
& Lang TBI. Therapy: Rec.

Features: Crafts Drama Music Aquatics Archery Canoe Climbing_Wall Cooking Fishing Hiking Riflery Ropes_Crse Baseball Basketball Soccer Softball Swim.
Fees 2011: Res $720-1440 (+$100), 1-2 wks.
Housing: Cabins. **Swimming:** Pool.
Est 1938. Nonprofit. **Spons:** Easter Seals Wisconsin. **Ses:** 6. **Wks/ses:** 1-2. Operates June-July. ACA.

This recreational program for individuals with physical, cognitive, emotional and behavioral disabilities enables parents and caregivers to receive a break from caring for their loved one. Held on a 400-acre, wooded site, Wawbeek features sports, arts and crafts, trail rides, nature hikes, singing, storytelling, campfires and many other traditional recreational pursuits. A one-to-one camper to counselor ratio enables staff to assist with activities and address the specific needs of the camper. A separate session serves teens and young adults with Asperger's syndrome or high-functioning autism.

EASTER SEALS CAMPING PROGRAM
Res — Coed Ages 8-14

West Poland, ME.
Contact (Year-round): c/o Easter Seals Massachusetts, 484 Main St, 6th Fl, Worcester, MA 01608. Tel: 508-751-6410, 800-244-2756. Fax: 508-751-6444.
www.eastersealsma.org   E-mail: camp@eastersealsma.org
Colleen Flanagan, Mgr.
Adm: FCFS. **Appl due:** Rolling. **Enr:** 30. **Enr cap:** 30.
Locations: CT ME.
Conditions accepted: Au CP Phys_Impair.
Features: Crafts Dance Music Theater Adventure_Travel Aquatics Archery Boating Canoe Farm Fishing Hiking Ropes_Crse Sail Wilderness_Camp Woodcraft Baseball Basketball Gymnastics Softball Swim Tennis Watersports.
Fees 2011: Res $2700-3100, 1-2 wks. Aid (Need).
Housing: Cabins. **Swimming:** Lake Pond Pool.
Est 1965. Nonprofit. **Spons:** Easter Seals Massachusetts. **Ses:** 2. **Wks/ses:** 1-2. Operates Aug.

Held at Agassiz Village in Maine, the program provide traditional camping activities for children with physical disabilities. Significant financial assistance is available, with fees determined along a sliding scale according to family income.

CAMP EASTER SEALS NEBRASKA
Res — Coed Ages 6 and up

Fremont, NE.
Contact (Year-round): c/o Easter Seals Nebraska, 638 N 109th Plz, Omaha, NE 68154. Tel: 402-345-2200, 800-650-9880. Fax: 402-345-2500.
www.campeastersealsne.com   E-mail: tlewis@ne.easterseals.com
Tony Lewis, Coord.
Adm: FCFS. **Appl due:** Apr. **Enr:** 25. **Enr cap:** 28. **Staff:** Admin 2. Couns 20. Special needs 3.
Conditions accepted: ADD ADHD Asp Au C CP D Diabetes Dx ED Ep ID LD PDD Phys_Impair Speech & Lang TBI Visual_Impair. **Therapy:** Rec.
Features: Astron Ecol Crafts Creative_Writing Dance Music Painting Theater Aquatics Archery Boating Canoe Climbing_Wall Cooking Fishing Hiking Kayak Mountaineering Rappelling Riding Riflery Ropes_Crse Wilderness_Camp Woodcraft Work Baseball Basketball Equestrian Football Golf Gymnastics Rugby Soccer Softball Swim Tennis Track Watersports.
Housing: Cabins. Avg per room/unit: 8. **Swimming:** Pool.
Est 1968. Nonprofit. **Ses:** 6. **Wks/ses:** 1. Operates June-July.

This recreational camp serves children and adults with all types of physical and developmental disabilities. Activities include swimming, arts and crafts, music, canoeing, fishing, camp outs, cookouts, nature hikes and a ropes course.

EASTER SEALS TENNESSEE CAMP
Res — Coed Ages 8 and up

Nashville, TN 37204. 3011 Armory Dr, Ste 100. Tel: 615-292-6640. TTY: 615-385-3485.
   Fax: 615-251-0994.
www.eastersealstn.com   E-mail: camp@eastersealstn.com
Gay Bruner, Dir.
Adm: FCFS. Appl due: Rolling. Enr: 12. Enr cap: 30. Staff: Admin 1. Couns 10.
Conditions accepted: ADD ADHD As Asp Au Blood Cancer CP D Diabetes Dx ED Ep ID
   LD PDD Phys_Impair Speech & Lang TBI Visual_Impair. Therapy: Rec.
Features: Crafts Dance Music Painting Theater Aquatics Archery Boating Canoe Climb-
   ing_Wall Fishing Hiking Outdoor_Ed Ropes_Crse Sail Wilderness_Camp Wilderness_
   Canoe Basketball Equestrian Football Golf Soccer Softball Street_Hockey Swim Tennis
   Ultimate_Frisbee Volleyball Water-skiing Watersports.
Fees 2011: Res $850 (+$15), 1 wk. Aid 2011 (Need): $6000.
Housing: Cabins Lodges. Avg per room/unit: 7. Swimming: Pool.
Est 1959. Nonprofit. Spons: Easter Seals Tennessee. Ses: 6. Wks/ses: 1. Operates July-
   Sept.

The camp serves children and adults with physical or cognitive disabilities. It provides a recreational camping experience that includes such activities as games, crafts, aquatics and boating.

CAMP EASTER SEALS UCP
Res — Coed Ages 6 and up

New Castle, VA 24127. 900 Camp Easter Seals Rd. Tel: 540-864-5750.
   Fax: 540-864-6797.
Contact (Sept-May): 201 E Main St, Salem, VA 24153. Tel: 540-777-7325.
   Fax: 540-777-2194.
www.campeastersealsucp.com   E-mail: camp@eastersealsucp.com
Alex Barge, Dir.
Adm: FCFS. Appl due: Rolling. Enr: 63. Staff: Admin 3. Couns 40. Special needs 8.
Conditions accepted: ADD ADHD Asp Au CP Ep ID LD PDD Phys_Impair Speech & Lang
   TBI Visual_Impair. Therapy: Occup Rec Speech.
Features: Crafts Drama Music Aquatics Archery Canoe Climbing_Wall Fishing Hiking
   Peace/Cross-cultural Riding Riflery Basketball Softball Swim.
Fees 2011: Res $750-3575, 1-4 wks. Aid (Need).
Housing: Cabins. Avg per room/unit: 14-20. Swimming: Pool.
Est 1957. Nonprofit. Spons: Easter Seals UCP North Carolina & Virginia. Ses: 6. Wks/ses:
   1-2. Operates June-July. ACA.

Easter Seals UCP provides recreational therapy, activities, sports and nature study for campers with cognitive or physical disabilities. An adventure camp features hiking, exploration and camping.

CAMP ECHOING HILLS
Res — Coed Ages 7 and up

Warsaw, OH 43844. 36272 County Rd 79. Tel: 740-327-2311, 800-419-6513.
   Fax: 740-327-2333.
www.campechoinghills.org   E-mail: info@ehvi.org

Lauren Unger, Admin.
Adm: FCFS. **Appl due:** Apr. **Enr:** 84. **Staff:** Admin 3. Couns 30. Special needs 3.
Conditions accepted: ADD ADHD Au CP D Ep ID LD Phys_Impair Speech & Lang TBI Visual_Impair.
Features: Crafts Aquatics Archery Canoe Fishing Hiking Ropes_Crse Swim.
Fees 2012: Res $650-1000, 1 wk.
Housing: Cabins. Avg per room/unit: 15. **Swimming:** Pool.
Est 1966. Nonprofit. Nondenom Christian. **Ses:** 8. **Wks/ses:** 1. Operates June-Aug. ACA.

A Christian camp for individuals with developmental disabilities, Echoing Hills seeks to bring healthy social, physical and spiritual development to its members. Swimming, hayrides, cookouts, music and art are all part of the summer plan for campers.

CAMP EDEN WOOD
Res — Coed Ages 5 and up; Day — Coed 5-21

Eden Prairie, MN 55346. 6350 Indian Chief Rd.
Contact (Sept-May): 10509 108th St NW, Annandale, MN 55302.
Year-round Tel: 952-852-0101, 800-450-8376. Fax: 952-852-0123.
www.friendshipventures.org   E-mail: info@friendshipventures.org
Laurie Tschetter, Exec Dir.
Adm: FCFS. **Appl due:** Rolling. **Enr:** 35. **Staff:** Admin 2. Couns 15.
Conditions accepted: Asp Au CP ID Phys_Impair.
Features: Crafts Dance Music Aquatics Archery Boating Canoe Climbing_Wall Cooking Fishing Ropes_Crse Basketball Golf Swim Volleyball.
Fees 2009: Res $825-1356, 1 wk. Day $470-674, 1 wk.
Housing: Cabins Dorms. **Swimming:** Lake Pool.
Est 1958. Nonprofit. **Spons:** Friendship Ventures. **Ses:** 24. **Wks/ses:** 1. Operates June-Aug. ACA.

Eden Wood is open to children and adults with developmental disabilities. Traditional and specialty sessions are adapted to the age and ability level of the camper. Eden Wood schedules day and evening excursions out of camp.

CAMP EDI
THE GLORIA HIRSCH CAMP FOR CHILDREN WITH DIABETES
Res — Coed Ages 7-17

Fredericktown, MO.
Contact (Year-round): c/o American Diabetes Association, 425 S Woods Mill Rd, Ste 110, Town and Country, MO 63017. Tel: 314-822-5490, 888-342-2383.
Fax: 314-576-0002.
www.diabetes.org   E-mail: chartmann@diabetes.org
Cathy Hartmann, Dir.
Adm: FCFS. **Appl due:** Rolling. **Enr:** 128. **Enr cap:** 128. **Staff:** Admin 3. Couns 39. Special needs 40.
Conditions accepted: Diabetes.
Features: Ecol Environ_Sci Crafts Aquatics Archery Boating Canoe Conservation Exploration Fishing Hiking Kayak Outdoor_Ed Weight_Loss Woodcraft Basketball Football Soccer Softball Swim Tennis Ultimate_Frisbee Volleyball.
Fees 2012: Res $400-700, 1 wk. Aid 2011 (Merit & Need): $20,000.
Housing: Cabins Dorms. Avg per room/unit: 8. **Swimming:** Lake.
Est 1952. Nonprofit. **Spons:** American Diabetes Association. **Ses:** 2. **Wks/ses:** 1. Operates June.

Camp EDI (Exercise-Diet-Insulin) provides an opportunity for children with diabetes to learn to manage their disease more independently. Camping activities include games, swimming, canoeing, crafts, hiking, sports and wellness classes.

ENCHANTED HILLS CAMP
Res — Coed Ages 5 and up

Napa, CA 94558. 3410 Mt Veeder Rd. Tel: 707-224-4023. Fax: 707-224-5435.
Contact (Sept-May): c/o LightHouse for the Blind, 214 Van Ness Ave, San Francisco, CA 94102. Tel: 415-431-1481. Fax: 415-863-7568.
Year-round TTY: 415-431-4572.
www.lighthouse-sf.org   E-mail: ehc@lighthouse-sf.org
Tony Fletcher, Dir.
Adm: FCFS. Admitted: 90%. **Appl due:** Rolling. **Enr:** 60. **Enr cap:** 60. **Staff:** Admin 4. Couns 21. Res 6. Special needs 3.
Conditions accepted: Visual_Impair.
Features: Environ_Sci Crafts Dance Music Theater Aquatics Cooking Hiking Riding Yoga Swim.
Fees 2010: Res $85-600, ½-1½ wks. Aid 2009 (Need): $150,000.
Housing: Cabins Dorms Houses. **Swimming:** Pool.
Est 1958. Nonprofit. **Spons:** LightHouse for the Blind. **Ses:** 9. **Wks/ses:** ½-1½. Operates June-Aug. ACA.

Enchanted Hills offers a traditional camping experience for children and adult campers with blindness, visual impairments, deafness and blindness, or multiple disabilities. The program includes activities in swimming, sports, horseback riding, hiking, dancing, drama, music and crafts.

CAMP ESPERANZA
Res — Coed Ages 8-17

Big Bear Lake, CA.
Contact (Year-round): c/o Arthritis Foundation, Southern California Chapter, 800 W 6th St, Ste 1250, Los Angeles, CA 90017. Tel: 323-954-5750, 800-954-2873. Fax: 323-954-5790.
www.arthritis.org/chapters/southern-california   E-mail: jziegler@arthritis.org
Jennifer Ziegler, Dir.
Adm: FCFS. Admitted: 98%. **Appl due:** Rolling. **Enr:** 115. **Staff:** Admin 3. Couns 70. Special needs 9.
Conditions accepted: Phys_Impair Ar.
Features: Astron Crafts Music Aquatics Archery Canoe Climbing_Wall Rappelling Riding Rock_Climb Ropes_Crse Basketball Equestrian Swim Volleyball.
Fees 2012: Free (+$25), 1 wk.
Housing: Cabins Lodges. Avg per room/unit: 3-16. **Swimming:** Pool.
Est 1985. Nonprofit. **Spons:** Arthritis Foundation—Southern California Chapter. **Ses:** 2. **Wks/ses:** 1. Operates July-Aug.

Providing a five-day recreational program, the camp serves children with either juvenile arthritis or a rheumatic disease such as lupus or scleroderma. Activities include riding, swimming, arts and crafts, a ropes course and campfires. Families pay a nominal registration fee only.

EXPLORE YOUR FUTURE
Res — Coed Ages 16-18

Rochester, NY 14623. 52 Lomb Memorial Dr. Tel: 585-475-6700. TTY: 585-475-6700. Fax: 585-475-2696.
www.ntid.rit.edu/camps/eyf   E-mail: eyfinfo@rit.edu
Grades 11-12. Adm: Selective. **Appl due:** Apr. **Enr:** 140. **Fac 20. Staff:** Admin 4. Couns 12.
Avg class size: 11.

Conditions accepted: D.
Features: Bus/Fin Comp_S ci Engineering Sci Studio_Art Baseball Swim.
Fees 2012: Res $650, 1 wk. Aid (Need).
Housing: Dorms. **Swimming:** Pool.
Est 1985. Spons: Rochester Institute of Technology/National Technical Institute for the Deaf. **Ses:** 2. **Wks/ses:** 1. Operates July.

This program at Rochester Institute of Technology, conducted in conjunction with the National Technical Institute for the Deaf, enrolls rising high school juniors and seniors who are deaf or hard of hearing. Campers experience college life by participating in various academic and social activities. Career awareness activities are offered in business, computer science, engineering, science and visual communications.

CAMP FAIRLEE MANOR
Res — Coed Ages 6 and up

Chestertown, MD 21620. 22242 Bay Shore Rd. Tel: 410-778-0566. Fax: 410-778-0567.
www.de.easterseals.com   E-mail: contact@esdel.org
Adm: FCFS. **Appl due:** Rolling. **Enr:** 50-75.
Conditions accepted: ADD ADHD Au CP ED Ep ID Phys_Impair Speech & Lang TBI Visual_Impair MS. **Therapy:** Art Rec.
Features: Crafts Drama Adventure_Travel Aquatics Archery Boating Canoe Climbing_Wall Cruises Fishing Hiking Riding Ropes_Crse Basketball Swim Tennis Volleyball.
Fees 2011: Res $1050-2150 (+$50), 1-2 wks.
Housing: Cabins. Avg per room/unit: 10. **Swimming:** Pool.
Est 1954. Nonprofit. **Spons:** Easter Seals Delaware and Maryland's Eastern Shore. **Ses:** 2. **Wks/ses:** 1. Operates June-Aug. ACA.

Fairlee Manor's social and recreational program accommodates individuals with physical disabilities and cognitive impairments. Activities address the interests and ability levels of the campers. Weekend respite camps run throughout the year.

FLORIDA DIABETES CAMP
Res — Coed Ages 6-18

Gainesville, FL 32604. University Sta, PO Box 14136. Tel: 352-334-1321.
    Fax: 352-334-1326.
www.floridadiabetescamp.org   E-mail: fccyd@floridadiabetescamp.org
Gary Cornwell, Dir.
Adm: FCFS. **Appl due:** Rolling. **Enr:** 67. **Staff:** Admin 3. Couns 120. Special needs 50.
Conditions accepted: Diabetes.
Features: Crafts Aquatics Bicycle_Tours Canoe Exploration Hiking Sail Baseball Basketball Football Golf Soccer Swim Tennis Volleyball Watersports.
Fees 2011: Res $425-575, 1 wk.
Housing: Cabins. Avg per room/unit: 12. **Swimming:** Lake Pool.
Est 1962. Nonprofit. **Ses:** 6. **Wks/ses:** 1. Operates June-Aug. ACA.

The camp provides summer programs for insulin-dependent children with Type 1 diabetes. Sessions include family retreats, a teen cycling camp, a teen sports camp and traditional residential programs.

4-H CAMP HOWE
Res — Coed Ages 7-16; Day — Coed 7-13

Goshen, MA 01032. PO Box 326. Tel: 413-549-3969. Fax: 413-577-0760.
www.camphowe.com   E-mail: info@camphowe.com
Heidi Gutekenst, Dir.

Adm: FCFS. Admitted: 95%. **Appl due:** Rolling. **Enr:** 110. **Staff:** Admin 8. Couns 32. Res 40.
Conditions accepted: ADD ADHD As Asp Au CP D Diabetes Dx Ep ID LD Phys_Impair Speech & Lang TBI Visual_Impair.
Features: Ecol Environ_Sci Crafts Dance Theater Aquatics Archery Boating Canoe Climbing_Wall Conservation Cooking Exploration Farm Fishing Hiking Kayak Outdoor_Ed Rappelling Riflery Rock_Climb Ropes_Crse Sail White-water_Raft Basketball Cricket Swim.
Fees 2012: Res $460-875, 1-2 wks. Day $300, 1 wk. Aid (Need).
Housing: Cabins. Avg per room/unit: 9. **Swimming:** Lake.
Est 1928. Nonprofit. **Ses:** 7. **Wks/ses:** 1-2. Operates July-Aug. ACA.

Located on a 52-acre tract of state forestland in the foothills of the Berkshire Mountains, Camp Howe offers an array of traditional recreational pursuits to both nondisabled and special-needs children. Among the camp's activities are a challenge course, wall and rock climbing, skeet shooting, and farm and leadership programs. Campers ages 7-20 with various physical special needs may enroll in the ECHO Program, which promotes a greater degree of independence, encourages social integration within the camp and teaches leisure skills.

THE FOWLER CENTER FOR OUTDOOR LEARNING
RESIDENTIAL SUMMER CAMP
Res — Coed Ages 6-26; Day — Coed 6-20

Mayville, MI 48744. 2315 Harmon Lake Rd. Tel: 989-673-2050. Fax: 989-673-6355.
www.thefowlercenter.org   E-mail: info@thefowlercenter.org
Kyle L. Middleton, Exec Dir.
Adm: FCFS. **Appl due:** Mar. **Enr:** 80-90. **Enr cap:** 90. **Staff:** Admin 8. Couns 40.
Conditions accepted: Asp Au CP ED Ep HIV/AIDS ID LD Phys_Impair Speech & Lang TBI Visual_Impair.
Features: Crafts Adventure_Travel Aquatics Archery Boating Canoe Climbing_Wall Fishing Hiking Rock_Climb Ropes_Crse Wilderness_Camp Baseball Basketball Equestrian Swim Volleyball.
Fees 2012: Res $600, 1 wk. Day $150, 1 wk. Aid 2009 (Need): $20,000.
Housing: Cabins. Avg per room/unit: 16. **Swimming:** Lake.
Est 1957. Nonprofit. **Spons:** Fowler Center. **Ses:** 5. **Wks/ses:** 1. Operates July-Aug.

The camp serves persons with multiple special needs, including intellectual disabilities, autism and emotional disturbances. Those with associated physical disabilities, such as spina bifida, muscular dystrophy, cystic fibrosis, multiple sclerosis, cerebral palsy, Down syndrome, epilepsy and HIV/AIDS, as well as individuals with problems arising from closed head injuries, may also attend. Activities include boating, picnics, dances, nature study, field trips, a challenge course, equestrianism and archery.

CAMP FREEDOM
Res — Coed Ages 6-11

Lebanon Junction, KY 40150. 1480 Pine Tavern Rd, PO Box 607. Tel: 502-833-3554, 888-879-8884. Fax: 502-833-4249.
www.lions-campcrescendo.org   E-mail: bjflannery@lions-campcrescendo.org
Dale Streble, Dir.
Adm: FCFS. **Appl due:** May. **Enr cap:** 100.
Conditions accepted: ED Phys_Impair.
Features: Crafts Dance Archery Boating Canoe Fishing Hiking Riflery Basketball Swim Volleyball.
Fees 2012: Free (in-state residents). Res 1 wk.
Housing: Dorms. **Swimming:** Pool.
Est 2006. Nonprofit. **Ses:** 1. **Wks/ses:** 1. Operates June.

This free camp serves Kentucky children with mild to moderate behavioral, emotional or physical special needs who are either in foster care or in the custody of their grandparents. Campers engage in traditional recreational pursuits during the weeklong session.

CAMP FRIENDSHIP
Res and Day — Coed Ages 5 and up

Annandale, MN 55302. c/o Friendship Ventures, 10509 108th St NW.
Tel: 952-852-0101, 800-450-8376. Fax: 952-852-0123.
www.friendshipventures.org   E-mail: fv@friendshipventures.org
Laurie Tschetter, Exec Dir.
Adm: FCFS. **Appl due:** Rolling. **Enr cap:** 30-135.
Conditions accepted: ADD ADHD Asp Au CP D Diabetes Dx ED Ep ID LD PDD Phys_ Impair Speech & Lang Visual_Impair.
Features: Crafts Dance Music Aquatics Archery Boating Canoe Climbing_Wall Community_Serv Cooking Exploration Farm Hiking Mtn_Biking Mtn_Trips Rock_Climb Ropes_ Crse Equestrian Swim.
Fees 2012: Res $980-1559, 1 wk. Day $540-769, 1 wk. Aid (Need).
Housing: Cabins. Avg per room/unit: 8. **Swimming:** Lake Pool.
Est 1964. Nonprofit. **Spons:** Friendship Ventures. **Ses:** 62. **Wks/ses:** 1. Operates June-Aug. ACA.

The camp serves children and adults who have developmental or physical disabilities or both. Traditional recreational activities are adapted to the age and ability level of the camper, and participants choose either a general session or a special-interest camp.

CAMP FUN IN THE SUN
Res — Coed Ages 8-18

Rathdrum, ID.
Contact (Year-round): c/o Inland Northwest Health Services, PO Box 469, Spokane, WA 99210. Tel: 509-232-8145. Fax: 509-232-8151.
www.campfininthesun.org   E-mail: randalll@cherspokane.org
Lisa L. Randall, Dir.
Grades 3-12. Adm: FCFS. **Appl due:** Rolling. **Enr:** 80. **Enr cap:** 80. **Staff:** Admin 3. Couns 25. Special needs 18.
Conditions accepted: Diabetes.
Features: Crafts Aquatics Canoe Fishing Hiking Swim.
Fees 2012: Res $325, 1 wk. Aid 2011 (Need): $10,275.
Housing: Cabins. Avg per room/unit: 8. **Swimming:** Lake.
Est 1981. Nonprofit. **Spons:** Inland Northwest Health Services. **Ses:** 1. **Wks/ses:** 1. Operates July.

This traditional recreational camp enrolls children with diabetes. Activities include canoeing, arts and crafts, swimming, hiking, fishing, campfires and games.

GALES CREEK CAMP
Res — Coed Ages 8-17

Portland, OR 97223. 6975 SW Sandburg St, Ste 150. Tel: 503-968-2267.
Fax: 503-443-2313.
www.galescreekcamp.org   E-mail: cheryl@galescreekcamp.org
Cheryl Sheppard, Exec Dir.
Grades 3-12. Adm: FCFS. **Appl due:** Rolling. **Staff:** Admin 2. Couns 12.
LD Services: Acad_Instruction.
Conditions accepted: Diabetes.

Features: Crafts Aquatics Conservation Hiking Badminton Baseball Basketball Field_ Hockey Football Soccer Softball Swim Tennis Volleyball Watersports Ping-Pong.
Fees 2011: Res $375 (+$20), 1 wk.
Housing: Dorms. **Swimming:** Pool.
Est 1953. Nonprofit. **Ses:** 8. **Wks/ses:** 1. Operates June-Aug. ACA.

Young people with diabetes receive training and participate in recreational activities suited to their needs. Campers participate in swimming, hiking, fishing, field trips, crafts and games, and various sports.

THE GLENHOLME SCHOOL SUMMER PROGRAM
Res and Day — Coed Ages 10-18

Washington, CT 06793. 81 Sabbaday Ln. Tel: 860-868-7377. Fax: 860-868-7413.
www.glenholmesummerprogram.org   E-mail: info@theglenholmeschool.org
Maryann Campbell, Exec Dir.
Grades 5-12. Adm: Selective. **Appl due:** Rolling. **Enr cap:** 120.
Type of instruction: Enrich Rem_Eng Rem_Math Rem_Read. **LD Services:** Acad_ Instruction Diagnostic_Services Tut.
Conditions accepted: ADHD Asp Au ED LD Anx Mood OCD PDD TS. **Therapy:** Psych Speech.
Features: Eng Math Art Dance Filmmaking Fine_Arts Media Music Painting Photog Theater Aquatics Archery Chess Community_Serv Cooking Fishing Hiking Outdoor_Ed Ranch Ropes_Crse Yoga Aerobics Badminton Baseball Basketball Equestrian Golf Gymnastics Soccer Softball Swim Tennis Ultimate_Frisbee Volleyball Weight_Trng.
Fees 2012: Res $6555-13,800, 3-7 wks. Day $4370-9200, 3-7 wks.
Housing: Houses. **Swimming:** Pool.
Est 1967. Nonprofit. **Ses:** 5. **Wks/ses:** 3-7. Operates July-Aug.

Glenholme uses an evidence-based treatment milieu in a structured therapeutic setting. The program serves boys and girls who are considered fragile and complex, having been diagnosed with Asperger's, ADHD, PDD, OCD, Tourette's, depression and anxiety, as well as learning differences. The program builds competence socially and academically and integrates a learning approach to activities, the arts, an equestrian program, sports and various other interests. While providing a strong academic curriculum, Glenholme utilizes a positive behavior support model to promote relationships among peers, an understanding of boundaries and appropriate social behaviors. Students attend two classes per day and engage in regular activities throughout the week. **See Also Page 28**

CAMP GOOD DAYS AND SPECIAL TIMES
Res — Coed Ages 8-17; Day — Coed 4-7

Branchport, NY 14418. 58 W Lake Rd. Tel: 315-595-2779. Fax: 315-595-6153.
Contact (Oct-May): 1332 Pittsford-Mendon Rd, PO Box 665, Mendon, NY 14506.
Tel: 585-624-5555. Fax: 585-624-5799.
Year-round Toll-free: 800-785-2135.
www.campgooddays.org   E-mail: info@campgooddays.org
Wendy Bleier-Mervis, Exec Dir.
Adm: FCFS. **Appl due:** Rolling. **Staff:** Admin 10. Special needs 10.
Conditions accepted: Blood Cancer HIV/AIDS. **Therapy:** Art Psych.
Features: Crafts Drama Music Aquatics Archery Boating Canoe Climbing_Wall Community_Serv Fishing Hiking Peace/Cross-cultural Rock_Climb Ropes_Crse Scuba Social_ Servs Woodcraft Baseball Basketball Golf Soccer Softball Swim Tennis Volleyball Watersports.
Fees 2012: Free. Res 1 wk. Day 1 wk.
Housing: Cabins Dorms. **Swimming:** Lake Pool.
Est 1979. Nonprofit. **Ses:** 13. **Wks/ses:** 1. Operates June-Sept. ACA.

The camp provides a full recreational program for children and families affected by cancer, AIDS, sickle cell anemia or violence. Activities include crafts, music, drama, canoeing, scuba diving, hiking, swimming and land sports.

CAMP GRANADA
Res — Coed Ages 8-16

Monticello, IL.
Contact (Year-round): c/o American Diabetes Assoc, 2501 Chatham Rd, Ste 210, Springfield, IL 62704. Tel: 217-875-9011, 888-342-2383. Fax: 217-875-6849.
www.diabetes.org/adacampgranada   E-mail: wwallace@diabetes.org
Wendy Wallace, Dir.
Adm: FCFS. **Appl due:** Rolling. **Enr:** 141. **Enr cap:** 141. **Staff:** Admin 4. Couns 57. Special needs 21.
LD Services: Acad_Instruction.
Conditions accepted: Diabetes.
Features: Crafts Aquatics Archery Canoe Climbing_Wall Fishing Hiking Ropes_Crse Softball Swim Volleyball.
Fees 2011: Res $495, 1 wk. Aid 2007 (Need): $36,000.
Housing: Cabins. **Swimming:** Lake.
Est 1979. Nonprofit. **Ses:** 1. **Wks/ses:** 1. Operates July.

At Granada, campers with diabetes learn to better manage their condition in a recreational setting. Volleyball, softball, canoeing, swimming, archery, and arts and crafts are among the camp's activities.

CAMP GREENTOP
Res and Day — Coed Ages 7-21

Sabillasville, MD 21780. 15001 Park Central Rd. Tel: 301-416-0801. Fax: 301-416-0585.
Contact (Sept-May): c/o League for People with Disabilities, 1111 E Cold Spring Ln, Baltimore, MD 21239. Tel: 410-323-0500. Fax: 410-323-3298.
www.campgreentop.org   E-mail: bmorgan@leagueforpeople.org
Bill Morgan, Dir.
Adm: FCFS. **Appl due:** May. **Enr:** 65. **Enr cap:** 65. **Staff:** Admin 10. Couns 55. Special needs 2.
Conditions accepted: ADD ADHD As Asp Au CP Diabetes ED Ep ID LD PDD Phys_ Impair TBI Visual_Impair. **Therapy:** Rec.
Features: Crafts Dance Fine_Arts Music Theater Adventure_Travel Aquatics Archery Canoe Fishing Hiking Mountaineering Riding Wilderness_Camp Baseball Basketball Equestrian Swim Watersports.
Fees 2012: Res $1176-2880 (+$50), 1-2 wks. Day $576-720, 1 wk.
Housing: Cabins. **Swimming:** Pool.
Est 1937. Nonprofit. **Spons:** League for People with Disabilities. **Ses:** 7. **Wks/ses:** 1-2. Operates June-Aug.

One of the nation's oldest residential camps specifically designed for children and adults with physical and multiple disabilities, Greentop occupies a 200-acre tract in the Catoctin Mountain National Park. The camp's age-appropriate recreational activities attempt to foster independence, participation in recreation and enjoyment of the outdoors. Day trips to local attractions, among them Cunningham Falls State Park, Catoctin Mountain Zoological Park and local minor-league baseball games, round out the program.

CAMP HAMWI
Res — Coed Ages 7-17

Danville, OH.
Contact (Year-round): c/o Central Ohio Diabetes Assoc, 1100 Dennison Ave, Columbus, OH 43201. Tel: 614-884-4400, 800-422-7946. Fax: 614-884-4484.
www.diabetesohio.org   E-mail: coda@diabetesohio.org
Darlene Honigford, Dir.
Grades 2-12. Adm: FCFS. **Appl due:** Rolling. **Enr:** 80. **Enr cap:** 80. **Staff:** Admin 6. Couns 72. Special needs 20.
Conditions accepted: Diabetes.
Features: Crafts Theater Aquatics Archery Canoe Fishing Hiking Rappelling Riding Ropes_Crse Wilderness_Camp Baseball Basketball Equestrian Football Soccer Swim Ultimate_Frisbee Volleyball.
Fees 2012: Res $410, 1 wk. Aid 2011 (Need): $28,683.
Housing: Cabins. Avg per room/unit: 8. **Swimming:** Pool.
Est 1967. Nonprofit. **Spons:** Central Ohio Diabetes Association. **Ses:** 2. **Wks/ses:** 1. Operates July-Aug. ACA.

Hamwi offers children and young adults with diabetes a combination of diabetes education and traditional camping activities. Art, dance, watersports, riding, archery, canoeing and rappelling are among the camp's most popular activities.

CAMP HAPPY DAYS
Res — Coed Ages 4-18

Charleston, SC 29407. 1622 Ashley Hall Rd. Tel: 843-571-4336. Fax: 843-571-4394.
www.camphappydays.com   E-mail: teresa@camphappydays.com
Teresa Bishop, Prgm Dir.
Grades K-12. Adm: FCFS. **Appl due:** Rolling. **Enr:** 160. **Enr cap:** 200. **Staff:** Admin 4. Couns 100.
Conditions accepted: Cancer. **Therapy:** Rec.
Features: Circus_Skills Crafts Dance Aquatics Boating Canoe Climbing_Wall Fishing Kayak Rappelling Riding Ropes_Crse Baseball Basketball Football Golf Swim.
Fees 2012: Free. Res 1 wk.
Housing: Lodges. Avg per room/unit: 12. **Swimming:** Lake.
Est 1982. Nonprofit. **Ses:** 1. **Wks/ses:** 1. Operates June-July.

Happy Days offers a traditional camp experience to children diagnosed with cancer and their siblings. The waterfront program features swimming, boating, tubing, fishing and a waterslide. Other popular activities are woodworking, arts and crafts, painting, sewing, baking, ceramics, a climbing wall, a high-ropes adventure course and team-building games.

CAMP HASC
Res — Coed Ages 3 and up; Day — Coed 3-21

Parksville, NY 12768. 361 Parksville Rd. Tel: 845-292-6821. Fax: 845-292-9492.
Contact (Sept-June): 5902 14th Ave, Brooklyn, NY 11219. Tel: 718-686-5930. Fax: 718-686-5935.
www.hasc.net/camp   E-mail: chaya.miller@hasc.net
Ronn Yaish, Prgm Dir.
Adm: FCFS. **Appl due:** Feb. **Enr:** 300. **Staff:** Admin 10. Couns 225. Special needs 35.
LD Services: Acad_Instruction Mainstream.
Conditions accepted: Au CP Ep ID LD Phys_Impair Speech & Lang. **Therapy:** Art Music Occup Phys Psych Rec Speech.
Features: Crafts Dance Drama Music Aquatics Baseball Basketball Gymnastics Softball Swim Volleyball.

Fees 2012: Res $6500-7500 (+$450), 7 wks. Aid 2008 (Need): $130,000.
Housing: Cabins. Avg per room/unit: 12. **Swimming:** Pool.
Est 1972. Nonprofit. **Spons:** Hebrew Academy for Special Children. Jewish. **Ses:** 1. **Wks/ses:** 7. Operates July-Aug.

Serving children and adults with mental retardation, the program provides academic instruction, remedial reading, music, art, dance, aquatic sports and trips. Speech therapy, occupational therapy, physical education and rehabilitation counseling are available.

CAMP HEART TO HEART
Res — Coed Ages 5-12

Lebanon Junction, KY 40150. 1480 Pine Tavern Rd, PO Box 607. Tel: 502-833-3554, 888-879-8884. Fax: 502-833-4249.
www.lions-campcrescendo.org   E-mail: bjflannery@lions-campcrescendo.org
Daniel Coe & Audra Cain-Grogg, Dirs.
Adm: FCFS. **Appl due:** Rolling.
Conditions accepted: HIV/AIDS.
Features: Crafts Archery Boating Canoe Fishing Hiking Riflery Swim.
Fees 2012: Free
Housing: Dorms. **Swimming:** Pool.
Est 1999. Nonprofit. **Ses:** 1. **Wks/ses:** 1. Operates July.

This free camp admits children whose lives have been closely impacted by HIV or AIDS. Eligible boys and girls either have HIV/AIDS or have an immediate family member who is HIV positive or who has died of AIDS. Campers engage in traditional recreational pursuits. A 24-hour nurse is on duty throughout the week.

CAMP HERTKO HOLLOW
Res — Coed Ages 6-18

Boone, IA. Tel: 515-897-9009. Fax: 352-259-4776.
Contact: 101 Locust St, Des Moines, IA 50309. Tel: 515-471-8523. Fax: 515-288-2424.
Year-round Toll-free: 888-437-8652.
www.camphertkohollow.com   E-mail: camphertkohollow@aol.com
Vivian Murray, Dir.
Grades 1-PG. Adm: FCFS. Admitted: 100%. **Appl due:** Rolling. **Enr:** 200. **Enr cap:** 200.
Staff: Admin 3. Couns 35. Res 70. Special needs 30.
Conditions accepted: Diabetes.
Features: Crafts Aquatics Archery Canoe Climbing_Wall Hiking Riding Ropes_Crse Basketball Equestrian Swim.
Fees 2012: Res $750, 1 wk. Aid (Need).
Housing: Cabins. Avg per room/unit: 10. **Swimming:** Pool.
Est 1968. Nonprofit. **Ses:** 2. **Wks/ses:** 1. Operates June-July. ACA.

Activities at this camp for boys and girls with diabetes include horseback riding, swimming, athletics, canoeing, rappelling, crafts, high and low ropes courses, archery, riflery, a zip line and a climbing wall. Healthcare professionals and counselors provide diabetes education and help campers gain independence. Hertko Hollow schedules the following special events: a carnival, a talent contest, a dance and overnight trips.

CAMP HICKORY HILL
Res — Coed Ages 7-17

Columbia, MO 65205. PO Box 1942. Tel: 573-445-9146. Fax: 573-884-4609.
www.camphickoryhill.com   E-mail: camphickoryhill@yahoo.com
Jessica La Mantia Bernhardt, Dir.

Adm: FCFS. **Appl due:** Rolling. **Enr:** 75. **Staff:** Admin 2. Couns 12. Special needs 4.
Conditions accepted: Diabetes.
Features: Crafts Aquatics Archery Boating Canoe Caving Fishing Hiking Rappelling Riflery Ropes_Crse Basketball Soccer Softball Swim Tennis Volleyball.
Fees 2011: Res $1200, 1 wk.
Housing: Cabins. Avg per room/unit: 7. **Swimming:** Pool.
Est 1975. Nonprofit. **Ses:** 3. **Wks/ses:** 1. Operates July. ACA.

Campers at Hickory Hill learn more about diabetes and how to better manage it. The educational program includes one hour of formal classroom training per day in such subjects as insulin administration, insulin reactions, glucose monitoring, diet, complications and the emotional aspects of living with diabetes. In addition to learning more about their disease, campers take part in various recreational pursuits. Camp costs are determined along a sliding scale according to family income.

CAMP HO MITA KODA
Res — Coed Ages 6-15

Newbury, OH 44065. 14040 Auburn Rd. Tel: 440-564-5125.
Contact (Aug-May): c/o Diabetes Partnership of Cleveland, 3601 S Green Rd, Ste 100, Cleveland, OH 44122. Tel: 216-591-0800.
Year-round Fax: 216-591-0320.
www.camphomitakoda.org   E-mail: camp@diabetespartnership.org
Julie Hewitt, Mgr.
Adm: FCFS. **Appl due:** Rolling. **Enr:** 64. **Staff:** Admin 10. Couns 16.
Conditions accepted: Diabetes.
Features: Sci Crafts Dance Music Theater Aquatics Archery Bicycle_Tours Boating Canoe Climbing_Wall Fishing Hiking Riding Ropes_Crse Survival_Trng Weight_Loss Baseball Basketball Equestrian Field_Hockey Football Softball Swim Tennis Volleyball Watersports.
Fees 2012: Res $250-800, ½-2 wks.
Housing: Cabins. Avg per room/unit: 8. **Swimming:** Lake Pool.
Est 1929. Nonprofit. **Spons:** Diabetes Partnership of Cleveland. **Ses:** 5. **Wks/ses:** ½-2. Operates June-July. ACA.

Insulin-dependent children with Type 1 diabetes take part in music, art, and recreational and aquatic sports at Ho Mita Koda. The camp is open to any child with diabetes who is able to function in a normal summer camp setting. In addition to the main residential camp, Ho Mita Koda conducts a one-day mini-camp for children ages 4-10 and their siblings and parents.

CAMP HOLIDAY TRAILS
Res — Coed Ages 5-17

Charlottesville, VA 22903. 400 Holiday Trails Ln. Tel: 434-977-3781.
Fax: 434-977-8814.
www.campholidaytrails.org   E-mail: campisgood@campholidaytrails.org
Tina LaRoche, Exec Dir.
Grades K-12. Adm: FCFS. **Appl due:** Rolling. **Enr:** 60. **Enr cap:** 60. **Staff:** Admin 5. Couns 24. Res 27. Special needs 8.
Conditions accepted: As Blood Cancer C CP D Diabetes Ep HIV/AIDS Visual_Impair.
Focus: Health/Weight_Reduct. **Features:** Environ_Sci Sci Crafts Dance Drama Music Photog Aquatics Archery Canoe Climbing_Wall Community_Serv Conservation Cooking Fishing Hiking Kayak Outdoor_Ed Rappelling Riding Ropes_Crse Basketball Equestrian Football Lacrosse Soccer Swim Tennis Volleyball.
Fees 2011: Res $120, 1-2 wks. Aid 2009 (Need): $89,000.
Housing: Cabins. Avg per room/unit: 6. **Swimming:** Pool.
Est 1973. Nonprofit. **Ses:** 5. **Wks/ses:** 1-2. Operates June-Aug. ACA.

Located in the foothills of the Blue Ridge Mountains, near the University of Virginia and its medical center, the camp brings together children with special medical needs and chronic illnesses. One- and two-week sessions feature a full program of sports and therapeutic and educational activities. Family weekend camps and a weeklong family camp are available.

CAMP HONOR
Res — Coed Ages 8-17

Payson, AZ.
Contact (Year-round): c/o Hemophilia Assoc, 818 E Osborn Rd, Ste 105, Phoenix, AZ 85014. Tel: 602-955-3947. Fax: 602-955-1962.
www.hemophiliaz.org
Andy Blackledge, Dir.
Adm: FCFS. **Appl due:** Rolling. **Enr cap:** 126. **Staff:** Admin 20. Couns 60.
Conditions accepted: Blood HIV/AIDS.
Features: Circus_Skills Crafts Aquatics Archery Canoe Outdoor_Ed Paintball Basketball Skateboarding Swim.
Fees 2012: Res $35, 1 wk. Aid (Need).
Housing: Cabins. **Swimming:** Lake Pool.
Est 1994. Nonprofit. **Spons:** Hemophilia Association. **Ses:** 1. **Wks/ses:** 1. Operates July. ACA.

Camp HONOR (Hemophiliacs Overcoming New Obstacles Resourcefully) provides a traditional summer camp experience for children with such blood disorders as hemophilia, von Willebrand's disease and thrombophilia, as well as boys and girls who have been diagnosed with HIV/AIDS. Activities include swimming, canoeing, sports, archery and arts and crafts. Siblings may also enroll in the camp.

CAMP HORIZONS
Res — Coed Ages 8-39

South Windham, CT 06266. PO Box 323. Tel: 860-456-1032. TTY: 860-456-1032. Fax: 860-456-4721.
www.horizonsct.org   E-mail: cmcnaboe@horizonsct.org
Scott Lambeck, Dir.
Adm: FCFS. **Appl due:** Rolling. **Enr:** 130. **Enr cap:** 130. **Staff:** Admin 16. Couns 75.
Conditions accepted: Au ID PDD.
Features: Crafts Dance Music Theater Aquatics Boating Exploration Fishing Riding Wood-craft Badminton Basketball Equestrian Golf Soccer Swim Tennis Volleyball Weight_ Trng.
Fees 2012: Res $2372-8790, 2-8 wks.
Housing: Cabins. Avg per room/unit: 12. **Swimming:** Pool.
Est 1979. Nonprofit. **Ses:** 4. **Wks/ses:** 2-8. Operates June-Aug. ACA.

Horizons serves children and adults with developmental disabilities. Prominent offerings include horseback riding, aquatics, crafts, fitness activities and nature study. Pottery, boating, language arts, drama and vocational training are also available.

CAMP HUNTINGTON
Res — Coed Ages 6-21

High Falls, NY 12440. 56 Bruceville Rd, PO Box 37. Tel: 845-687-7840, 866-514-5281. Fax: 845-853-1172.
www.camphuntington.com
Michael Bednarz, Exec Dir.
Adm: FCFS. **Appl due:** Rolling.

LD Services: Acad_Instruction.
Conditions accepted: ADD ADHD Asp Au ID LD PDD.
Features: Computers Art Crafts Drama Filmmaking Music Outdoor_Ed Riding Ropes_Crse Badminton Baseball Basketball Soccer Tennis Volleyball Handball Ping-Pong.
Fees 2012: Res $6450, 3 wks.
Housing: Cabins.
Est 1961. Ses: 3. **Wks/ses:** 3. Operates June-Aug. ACA.

Camp Huntington serves children and young adults with learning disabilities, neurological impairments, attentional disorders or mild to moderate developmental disabilities. A comprehensive schedule of recreational and educational activities includes work training for eligible teenagers and young adults.

CAMP INDEPENDENCE
Res — Coed Ages 8-16

Rutledge, GA.
Contact (Year-round): c/o National Kidney Foundation of Georgia, 2951 Flowers Rd S, Ste 211, Atlanta, GA 30341. Tel: 770-452-1539, 800-633-2339. Fax: 770-452-7564.
www.kidneyga.org   E-mail: danielle.hall@kidney.org
Danielle Hall, Prgm Dir.
Adm: FCFS. **Appl due:** May.
Conditions accepted: Phys_Impair.
Features: Crafts Drama Aquatics Archery Bicycle_Tours Boating Canoe Climbing_Wall Fishing Mtn_Biking Riding Ropes_Crse Basketball Softball Swim Tennis.
Fees 2012: Free (in-state residents). Res 1 wk.
Housing: Cabins. **Swimming:** Pool.
Est 1973. Nonprofit. **Spons:** National Kidney Foundation of Georgia. **Ses:** 1. **Wks/ses:** 1. Operates July.

Held at the Camp Twin Lakes facility in Georgia, Camp Independence serves children who have been diagnosed with kidney disease, are on dialysis, or have had a kidney, heart, lung or liver transplant. The program is free for Georgia and Alabama residents. Activities include swimming, music, computers, art, dance and sports.

CAMP ISANOGEL
Res and Day — Coed Ages 8 and up

Muncie, IN 47304. 7601 W Isanogel Rd.
Contact (Sept-May): c/o Hillcroft Services, 114 E Streeter Ave, Muncie, IN 47303.
Year-round Tel: 765-288-1073, Fax: 765-288-3103.
www.hillcroft.org   E-mail: epiazza@hillcroft.org
Elizabeth Piazza, Dir.
Adm: FCFS. **Appl due:** Rolling. **Enr:** 48.
Conditions accepted: ADHD Au CP ED Ep ID LD Phys_Impair Speech & Lang Visual_ Impair.
Features: Ceramics Crafts Aquatics Climbing_Wall Ropes_Crse Swim.
Fees 2011: Res $600-875, 1-2 wks. Day $400, 1 wk.
Swimming: Pool.
Est 1962. Nonprofit. **Spons:** Hillcroft Services. **Ses:** 7. **Wks/ses:** 1-2. Operates June-Aug. ACA.

Isanogel serves children and adults with physical and intellectual disabilities. Program areas include nature pursuits, creative arts, recreation and aquatics.

CAMP ISOLA BELLA
Res — Coed Ages 8-18

Taconic, CT 06079. 410 Twin Lakes Rd. Tel: 860-824-5558. TTY: 860-824-5558. Fax: 860-824-4276.
Contact (Sept-June): c/o American School for the Deaf, 139 N Main St, West Hartford, CT 06107. Tel: 860-570-2300. TTY: 860-570-2222. Fax: 860-570-2253.
www.asd-1817.org/ib   E-mail: steve.borsotti@asd-1817.org
Alyssa Pecorino, Dir.
Grades 4-12. Adm: FCFS. Appl due: Rolling. Enr: 48. Enr cap: 48. Staff: Admin 6. Couns 8.
Conditions accepted: D.
Features: Environ_Sci Sci Crafts Drama Archery Boating Canoe Exploration Fishing Hiking Kayak Mtn_Trips Outdoor_Ed Sail Wilderness_Camp Basketball Softball Swim Ultimate_Frisbee Volleyball Water-skiing.
Fees 2009: Res $500-750, 1-2 wks.
Housing: Cabins Lodges Tents. Avg per room/unit: 12. Swimming: Lake.
Est 1964. Nonprofit. Spons: American School for the Deaf. Ses: 2. Wks/ses: 1-2. Operates June-Aug.

This camp for children with hearing impairments blends educational instruction in communications with recreational activities. The camp staff comprises qualified deaf and hearing staff members with experience in education, childcare and counseling.

JAMESON CAMP
Res — Coed Ages 7-17

Indianapolis, IN 46231. 2001 Bridgeport Rd, PO Box 31156. Tel: 317-241-2661. Fax: 317-241-2760.
www.jamesoncamp.org   E-mail: tim@jamesoncamp.org
Tim Nowak, Prgm Dir.
Grades 1-12. Adm: FCFS. Appl due: Rolling. Enr: 75. Enr cap: 80. Staff: Admin 9. Couns 34. Special needs 1.
Conditions accepted: ADD ADHD As Asp Diabetes ED HIV/AIDS LD.
Features: Writing/Journ Crafts Dance Drama Aquatics Archery Climbing_Wall Community_Serv Cooking Fishing Hiking Ropes_Crse Wilderness_Camp Basketball Football Soccer Swim Ultimate_Frisbee Volleyball.
Fees 2011: Res $75-575, 1 wk.
Housing: Cabins. Avg per room/unit: 8. Swimming: Pool.
Est 1928. Nonprofit. Ses: 7. Wks/ses: 1. Operates June-Aug. ACA.

Serving children who may have minor social, emotional and behavioral challenges, Jameson also enrolls those who have been impacted by HIV or AIDS. Campers choose from a host of traditional summer activities. All fees are determined along a sliding scale according to family income.

CAMP JOHN WARVEL
Res — Coed Ages 7-15

North Webster, IN.
Contact (Year-round): c/o American Diabetes Assoc, 6415 Castleway W Dr, Ste 114, Indianapolis, IN 46250. Tel: 317-352-9226, 888-342-2383. Fax: 317-594-0748.
www.diabetes.org/adacampjohnwarvel   E-mail: cdixon@diabetes.org
Carol Dixon, Dir.
Adm: FCFS. Appl due: Rolling. Enr: 157. Enr cap: 180. Staff: Admin 7. Couns 24.
Conditions accepted: Diabetes.

Features: Crafts Drama Archery Boating Canoe Climbing_Wall Riding Sail Weight_Loss Baseball Basketball Equestrian Swim Tennis Ultimate_Frisbee Volleyball Watersports. **Fees 2011: Res $450, 1 wk.** Aid (Need). **Housing:** Cabins. **Swimming:** Lake. **Est 1955.** Nonprofit. **Spons:** American Diabetes Association. **Ses:** 1. **Wks/ses:** 1. Operates June.

Sponsored by the American Diabetes Association, Camp Warvel provides an educational outdoor experience for children with Type 1 or Type 2 diabetes. Campers acquire new skills in caring for their disease and gain confidence in their self-management of diabetes.

CAMP JUMP START
Res — Coed Ages 9-17

Imperial, MO 63052. 3602 Lions Den Rd. Tel: 636-287-5004.
www.campjumpstart.com E-mail: contact@campjumpstart.com
Jean Huelsing, Dir.
Grades 6-12. Adm: FCFS. **Appl due:** Rolling. **Enr:** 120.
Focus: Health/Weight_Reduct. **Features:** Crafts Dance Drama Aquatics Bicycle_Tours Canoe Caving Conservation Fishing Hiking Mtn_Biking Rappelling Riding Rock_Climb Ropes_Crse Aerobics Baseball Basketball Equestrian Field_Hockey Football Martial_Arts Soccer Softball Swim Volleyball Watersports.
Fees 2012: Res $3695-6895, 4-8 wks.
Housing: Cabins. Avg per room/unit: 10. **Swimming:** Lake Pool.
Est 2003. Ses: 3. **Wks/ses:** 4-8. Operates June-Aug. ACA.

This weight-loss camp emphasizes self-discipline and the development of an improved self-image as part of the camper's lifestyle adjustment. Boys and girls participate in fitness activities, behavior modification and nutrition education while eating balanced, portion-controlled meals. A self-defense program seeks to increase campers' confidence and self-esteem. Other activities include caving, rock climbing, mountain biking and talent shows.

KENTUCKY LIONS YOUTH CAMP
Res — Coed Ages 6-15

Lebanon Junction, KY 40150. 1480 Pine Tavern Rd, PO Box 607. Tel: 502-833-3554, 888-879-8884. Fax: 502-833-4249.
www.lions-campcrescendo.org E-mail: bjflannery@lions-campcrescendo.org
Will Mayer & Christina Turpen, Dirs.
Adm: FCFS. **Appl due:** Rolling.
Conditions accepted: D Visual_Impair.
Features: Crafts Dance Archery Boating Canoe Fishing Hiking Riflery Swim.
Fees 2012: Free (in-state residents). Res 1 wk.
Housing: Dorms. **Swimming:** Pool.
Est 1982. Nonprofit. **Ses:** 1. **Wks/ses:** 1. Operates July.

This free camp serves Kentucky residents who fall into one of two main special-needs populations. One eligible group consists of children who have either been classified as visually impaired, legally blind or totally blind or diagnosed with a declining vision issue. The other comprises boys and girls who either have had a cochlear implant or have been classified as totally or partially deaf or hard of hearing (with a hearing aid). Campers engage in traditional recreational pursuits during the weeklong session.

CAMP KINGSMONT
Res — Coed Ages 9-18

Amherst, MA 01002. 893 West St. Tel: 413-835-5689.
Contact (Sept-May): 1638 1st Pl, McLean, VA 22101. Tel: 703-288-0047.
Year-round Toll-free: 877-348-2267, Fax: 703-288-0075.
www.campkingsmont.com   E-mail: info@campkingsmont.com
Meghan Roman, Dir.
Grades 4-12. Adm: FCFS. Admitted: 95%. **Appl due:** Rolling. **Enr:** 250. **Enr cap:** 350. **Staff:** Admin 4. Couns 55. Res 59. Special needs 6.
LD Services: Tut.
Focus: Health/Weight_Reduct. **Features:** Crafts Music Theater Aquatics Archery Bicycle_ Tours Cooking Hiking Mtn_Biking Mtn_Trips Paintball Riding Ropes_Crse White-water_ Raft Aerobics Badminton Baseball Basketball Field_Hockey Football Golf Lacrosse Soccer Softball Street_Hockey Swim Tennis Track Ultimate_Frisbee Volleyball Water-sports Weight_Trng.
Fees 2012: Res $2495-7995, 2-8 wks. Aid 2009 (Need): $100,000.
Housing: Dorms. Avg per room/unit: 2-3. **Swimming:** Lake Pool.
Est 1971. Nonprofit. **Ses:** 28. **Wks/ses:** 2-8. Operates June-Aug. ACA.

Kingsmont offers campers a specialized health and fitness program designed for weight reduction. Boys and girls take cooking and nutrition classes, and the camp emphasizes behavior modification as a means to improve eating habits and lead a more active lifestyle. A full range of traditional activities includes arts and crafts, individual and team sports, riding, canoeing, hiking and bicycling. Campers with diabetes and other weight-related conditions may enroll.

CAMP KODIAK
Res — Coed Ages 6-18

McKellar, P0G 1C0 Ontario, Canada. Gen Delivery. Tel: 705-389-1910.
Fax: 705-389-1911.
Contact (Sept-June): 4069 Pheasant Run, Mississauga, L5L 2C2 Ontario, Canada.
Tel: 905-569-7595. Fax: 905-569-6045.
Year-round Toll-free: 877-569-7595.
www.campkodiak.com   E-mail: info@campkodiak.com
David Stoch, Dir.
Adm: FCFS. **Appl due:** Rolling. **Enr:** 234. **Enr cap:** 234. **Staff:** Admin 35. Couns 90. Special needs 6.
LD Services: Acad_Instruction Tut.
Conditions accepted: ADD ADHD Asp Dx LD Speech & Lang. **Therapy:** Art Music Rec.
Features: Computers Environ_Sci Expository_Writing Crafts Creative_Writing Dance Drama Filmmaking Fine_Arts Music Painting Photog Pottery Aquatics Archery Boating Canoe Chess Climbing_Wall Conservation Cooking Fishing Hiking Kayak Outdoor_Ed Rappelling Riding Rock_Climb Ropes_Crse Sail Survival_Trng Aerobics Badminton Baseball Basketball Cross-country Equestrian Football Golf Gymnastics Martial_Arts Soccer Softball Swim Tennis Ultimate_Frisbee Volleyball Water-skiing Watersports Weight_Trng Wrestling Rocketry.
Fees 2012: Res $3975-8375, 3-7 wks.
Housing: Cabins. Avg per room/unit: 9. **Swimming:** Lake.
Est 1991. Inc. **Ses:** 3. **Wks/ses:** 3-7. Operates July-Aug.

On a 425-acre site northeast of Parry Sound, Kodiak offers recreational camping activities, a social skills program and academic tutoring for children with learning disabilities, attentional disorders and Asperger's syndrome. Each morning, campers engage in one hour of enrichment course work or receive an hour of individual or small-group academic tutoring. The remainder of the day, boys and girls participate in traditional camping activities.

CAMP KORELITZ
Res — Coed Ages 8-15

Hamilton, OH.
Contact (Year-round): 4555 Lake Forest Dr, Ste 396, Cincinnati, OH 45242.
Tel: 513-759-9330. **Fax:** 513-421-2203.
www.diabetes.org/adacampkorelitz **E-mail:** ecrosby@diabetes.org
Erin Crosby, Dir.
Adm: FCFS. **Appl due:** June. **Enr:** 150. **Enr cap:** 160. **Staff:** Admin 1. Couns 35. Res 75. Special needs 30.
Conditions accepted: Diabetes.
Features: Crafts Dance Aquatics Archery Bicycle_Tours Canoe Climbing_Wall Fishing Hiking Mtn_Biking Outdoor_Ed Rock_Climb Ropes_Crse Wilderness_Camp Woodcraft Baseball Basketball Field_Hockey Football Lacrosse Soccer Softball Street_Hockey Swim Ultimate_Frisbee Volleyball Watersports.
Fees 2011: Res $525-550, 1 wk. Aid 2011 (Need): $30,000.
Housing: Cabins. Avg per room/unit: 10. **Swimming:** Pool.
Est 1978. Nonprofit. **Spons:** American Diabetes Association. **Ses:** 1. **Wks/ses:** 1. Operates Aug.

Korelitz offers diabetes management instruction (for both Type 1 and Type 2 diabetes), as well as nature study and ecology. Other activities include team sports, waterfront games, campfires, arts and crafts, drama and archery.

CAMP KOSTOPULOS
Res — Coed Ages 7 and up

Salt Lake City, UT 84108. 2500 Emigration Canyon. **Tel:** 801-582-0700.
Fax: 801-583-5176.
www.campk.org **E-mail:** information@campk.org
Taryn Roberts, Coord.
Adm: FCFS. Admitted: 100%. **Appl due:** Rolling. **Enr:** 50. **Enr cap:** 50. **Staff:** Admin 6. Couns 30. Special needs 3.
Travel: UT WY.
Conditions accepted: ADD ADHD Asp Au CP D ED Ep ID LD Phys_Impair Speech & Lang TBI Visual_Impair OCD. **Therapy:** Rec.
Features: Crafts Dance Drama Music Adventure_Travel Aquatics Canoe Climbing_Wall Fishing Hiking Mtn_Trips Ropes_Crse Social_Servs Wilderness_Camp Equestrian Swim.
Fees 2011: Res $405, 1 wk. Aid (Need).
Housing: Cabins Lodges Tents Tepees. **Swimming:** Pool.
Est 1958. Nonprofit. **Ses:** 11. **Wks/ses:** 1. Operates June-Aug. ACA.

Kostopulos offers recreational opportunities for special-needs individuals of all ages and all ability levels. Activities include music, riding, nature study, arts and crafts, swimming, fishing, canoeing and hiking. In addition, Kostopulos conducts trips to Jackson Hole, WY, and to Yellowstone, Arches and Zion national parks.

CAMP KREM
Res — Coed Ages 5 and up

Boulder Creek, CA.
Contact (Year-round): 4610 Whitesands Ct, El Sobrante, CA 94803. **Tel:** 510-222-6662.
Fax: 510-223-3046.
www.campingunlimited.com **E-mail:** campkrem@gmail.com
Mary Farfaglia, Exec Dir.

Adm: FCFS. **Appl due:** Rolling. **Enr cap:** 85. **Staff:** Admin 18. Couns 55. Special needs 5.
Conditions accepted: ADD ADHD Asp Au CP ED ID LD Phys_Impair TBI.
Features: Crafts Dance Drama Fine_Arts Music Painting Adventure_Travel Aquatics Canoe Community_Serv Cooking Exploration Hiking Outdoor_Ed Sail White-water_Raft Wilderness_Camp Woodcraft Work Badminton Baseball Basketball Soccer Softball Swim Volleyball Watersports.
Fees 2012: Res $980-1680, 1-2 wks. Aid (Need).
Housing: Cabins Tents. Avg per room/unit: 7. **Swimming:** Pool.
Est 1957. Nonprofit. **Spons:** Camping Unlimited. **Ses:** 6. **Wks/ses:** 1-2. Operates June-Aug. ACA.

Camp Krem offers various free-choice programs for children and adults with disabilities. Activities include daily swimming, hiking, field trips, arts and crafts, music, drama, backpacking, independent living skills, talent shows and theme-based events. Outdoor adventure and travel programs enable campers to experience challenges and develop more independence.

CAMP LA JOLLA
Res — Coed Ages 8-17

La Jolla, CA.
Contact (Year-round): 176 C Ave, Coronado, CA 92118. **Tel:** 619-435-7990, 800-825-8746. **Fax:** 619-435-8188.
www.camplajolla.com   **E-mail:** camp@camplajolla.com
Judith Wood, Exec Dir.
Grades 3-12. **Adm:** FCFS. **Appl due:** Rolling. **Enr:** 250. **Staff:** Admin 10. Couns 60.
Focus: Health/Weight_Reduct. **Features:** Crafts Dance Aquatics Climbing_Wall Cooking Hiking Kayak Mtn_Biking Rock_Climb Yoga Aerobics Basketball Football Martial_Arts Soccer Softball Swim Tennis Ultimate_Frisbee Volleyball Watersports Weight_Trng.
Fees 2012: Res $4495-11,595 (+$200), 2-8 wks.
Housing: Dorms. **Swimming:** Ocean Pool.
Est 1979. Inc. **Ses:** 6. **Wks/ses:** 2-8. Operates June-Aug. ACA.

This weight-loss and fitness camp combines a focus on healthy lifestyle changes with classes in nutrition and behavior modification. La Jolla also provides a 10-month follow-up program for its campers. Separate programs serve preteens, teens, boys and young adults.

CAMP LAUREL
Res and Day — Coed Ages 6-17

Pasadena, CA 91105. 75 S Grand Ave. **Tel:** 626-683-0800. **Fax:** 626-683-0890.
www.camplaurel.org   **E-mail:** info@camplaurel.org
Margot Anderson, Exec Dir.
Adm: FCFS. **Appl due:** Rolling. **Enr:** 90. **Enr cap:** 90. **Staff:** Admin 4. Couns 200. Special needs 10.
Conditions accepted: HIV/AIDS. **Therapy:** Art Psych Rec.
Features: Ecol Environ_Sci Writing/Journ Crafts Creative_Writing Music Photog Theater Adventure_Travel Aquatics Archery Canoe Climbing_Wall Conservation Hiking Kayak Mtn_Biking Outdoor_Ed Riding Rock_Climb Ropes_Crse Survival_Trng Wilderness_ Camp Baseball Basketball Soccer Softball Swim Volleyball Watersports.
Fees 2012: Free. Res 1 wk. Day 1 wk.
Housing: Cabins. **Swimming:** Lake Pool.
Est 1993. Nonprofit. **Ses:** 2. **Wks/ses:** 1. Operates July. ACA.

Children living with HIV or AIDS choose from traditional, adventure and leadership challenge programs at the camp. Neither overnight nor day campers incur a fee for attendance. Activities focus upon the camper's mental, physical, social and spiritual development.

CAMP LEE MAR
Res — Coed Ages 5-21

Lackawaxen, PA 18435. 450 Rte 590. Tel: 570-685-7188. Fax: 570-685-7590.
Contact (Sept-May): 805 Redgate Rd, Dresher, PA 19025. Tel: 215-658-1708.
Fax: 215-658-1710.
www.leemar.com   E-mail: gtour400@aol.com
Lee Morrone, Dir.
Adm: FCFS. **Appl due:** Rolling. **Enr:** 160. **Fac 25. Staff:** Admin 15. Couns 70.
Conditions accepted: ID LD Speech & Lang.
Features: Speech Crafts Dance Music Work Basketball Football Swim Tennis.
Fees 2011: Res $9500, 7 wks.
Housing: Cabins. **Swimming:** Pool.
Est 1953. Inc. Ses: 1. **Wks/ses:** 7. Operates June-Aug. ACA.

Children with mild to moderate developmental disabilities engage in academics, speech and language therapies, vocational training and recreation at Lee Mar. The academic program focuses on skill development in the areas of communication, reading and math. Activities include waterfront activities, tennis, calisthenics and perceptual-motor training.

LIONS CAMP MERRICK
Res — Coed Ages 6-16

Nanjemoy, MD 20662. 3650 Rick Hamilton Pl, PO Box 56. Tel: 301-870-5858.
Fax: 301-246-9108.
Contact (Oct-May): 3050 Crain Hwy, Ste 202, PO Box 375, Waldorf, MD 20604.
Tel: 301-645-5616. Fax: 301-374-2282.
www.lionscampmerrick.org   E-mail: campmerrick@aol.com
Melissa M. Lynch, Admin.
Adm: FCFS. Admitted: 99%. **Appl due:** Rolling. **Enr:** 85. **Enr cap:** 90. **Staff:** Admin 2.
Couns 30. Res 1.
Conditions accepted: D Diabetes Visual_Impair.
Features: Crafts Dance Drama Aquatics Archery Canoe Climbing_Wall Community_Serv Fishing Hiking Ropes_Crse Baseball Basketball Football Soccer Softball Swim Volleyball.
Fees 2010: Res $450-675 (+$5), 1 wk. Aid 2009 (Need): $42,002.
Housing: Cabins Houses. Avg per room/unit: 12. **Swimming:** Pool.
Est 1980. Nonprofit. Ses: 7. **Wks/ses:** 1. Operates June-Sept. ACA.

This recreational camp offers separate programs for children who are deaf or hard-of-hearing, children who are blind and children who have diabetes. A complete waterfront program features swimming and canoeing, and other activities include a climbing wall, a high and low ropes course, sports, arts and crafts, and various outdoor pursuits.

LIONS CAMP TATIYEE
Res — Coed Ages 7 and up

Mesa, AZ 85216. PO Box 6910. Tel: 480-380-4254.
www.arizonalionscamp.com   E-mail: arizonalionscamp@cox.net
Adm: FCFS. **Enr cap:** 600.
Conditions accepted: CP D ID Phys_Impair Visual_Impair.
Features: Crafts.
Fees 2010: Free. Res 1 wk.
Est 1961. Ses: 8. **Wks/ses:** 1. Operates June-Aug. ACA.

Sponsored by the Lions of Arizona, Lions Camp Tatiyee serves children and adults with physical handicaps, including those with cerebral palsy or visual or hearing impairments. Separate sessions serve adults, young adults, children and individuals with hearing impairments. Activities include arts and crafts, swimming, sports, games, camp outs, talent shows and movies.

CAMP LITTLE GIANT
Res — Coed Ages 8 and up; Day — Coed 7 and up

Carbondale, IL 62901. c/o **Touch of Nature Environmental Ctr, Southern Illinois Univ, Mail Code 6888. Tel: 618-453-1121. Fax: 618-453-1188.**
www.ton.siu.edu   E-mail: tonec@siu.edu
Vicki Lang-Mendenhall, Dir.
Adm: FCFS. **Appl due:** Rolling. **Enr:** 80. **Enr cap:** 80. **Staff:** Admin 5. Couns 28. Special needs 1.
Conditions accepted: ADD ADHD Asp Au CP D Diabetes Dx ED Ep ID LD Phys_Impair Speech & Lang TBI Visual_Impair MD. **Therapy:** Rec.
Features: Ecol Environ_Sci Speech Crafts Dance Drama Music Painting Aquatics Boating Fishing Hiking Outdoor_Ed Riding Baseball Basketball Equestrian Softball Swim Volleyball.
Fees 2011: Res $500-2100, 1-2 wks. Aid 2011 (Need): $12,000.
Housing: Cabins. Avg per room/unit: 3-8. **Swimming:** Lake.
Est 1952. Nonprofit. **Spons:** Southern Illinois University. **Ses:** 8. **Wks/ses:** 1-2. Operates June-Aug. ACA.

Little Giant accepts children and adults with physical, developmental, cognitive and social disabilities. Swimming, arts and crafts, hayrides, special events, horseback riding, boating, games and sports are among the activities offered.

CAMP LITTLE RED DOOR
Res — Coed Ages 8-18

Martinsville, IN.
Contact (Year-round): c/o **Little Red Door Cancer Agency, 1801 N Meridian St, Indianapolis, IN 46202. Tel: 317-925-5595. Fax: 317-925-5597.**
www.littlereddoor.org   E-mail: mail@littlereddoor.org
Adm: FCFS. **Appl due:** Rolling. **Enr:** 96. **Enr cap:** 96. **Staff:** Admin 10. Couns 50. Res 10. Special needs 5.
Conditions accepted: Cancer. **Therapy:** Rec.
Features: Crafts Aquatics Archery Canoe Climbing_Wall Community_Serv Conservation Exploration Hiking Outdoor_Ed Rappelling Riding Ropes_Crse Survival_Trng Wilderness_Camp Wilderness_Canoe Equestrian Swim.
Fees 2011: Res $25, 1 wk. Aid (Need).
Housing: Cabins Tents. Avg per room/unit: 10. **Swimming:** Lake Pool.
Est 1981. Nonprofit. **Spons:** Little Red Door Cancer Agency. **Ses:** 1. **Wks/ses:** 1. Operates July.

Camp Little Red Door serves children with cancer and, space permitting, one sibling per camper. All campers must have received or be receiving treatment in the state of Indiana. Older campers participate in the leadership program and mentor younger children. Activities include hiking, swimming, horseback riding, canoeing, archery, challenge course, and arts and crafts.

MARBRIDGE SUMMER CAMP
Res — Coed Ages 16-30

Manchaca, TX 78652. PO Box 2250. Tel: 512-282-1144. Fax: 512-282-3723.
www.marbridge.org/enrichment/summer-camp.php
E-mail: wchoermann@marbridge.org
Melanie Perez, Coord.

Adm: FCFS. **Appl due:** Apr. **Enr cap:** 223. **Staff:** Admin 1. Couns 6. Special needs 3. **LD Services:** Acad_Instruction.
Conditions accepted: Asp Au CP ID LD PDD Speech & Lang TBI DS. **Therapy:** Art Music Occup Phys Rec.
Features: Crafts Dance Music Aquatics Hiking Ranch Riding Baseball Basketball Equestrian Softball Swim.
Fees 2011: Res $605 (+$10-20), 1 wk.
Housing: Cabins Houses. Avg per room/unit: 8. **Swimming:** Pool.
Est 1999. Nonprofit. **Ses:** 9. **Wks/ses:** 1. Operates June-Aug.

Located on a 300-acre ranch near Austin, Marbridge offers a varied recreational program to campers with a developmental disability or a cognitive challenge. Activities are adapted to meet campers' interest, skill and age levels and positively reinforce the progress that each person makes in problem solving, interpersonal communications, self-assurance and independent living tasks. Out-of-camp day trips, horseback riding, swimming and a low ropes course are part of the program. All applicants must be ambulatory.

CAMP MARK SEVEN
Res — Coed Ages 9-16

Old Forge, NY 13420. 144 Mohawk Hotel Rd. Tel: 315-357-6089. TTY: 866-572-9102. Fax: 315-357-6403.
Contact (Sept-May): 8100 Glendale Dr, Frederick, MD 21702. Tel: 240-575-2073. TTY: 240-575-2073. Fax: 301-663-6174.
Year-round Toll-free: 866-572-9102.
www.campmark7.org   E-mail: execdir@campmark7.org
Andrew T. Brinks, Exec Dir.
Adm: FCFS. **Appl due:** Rolling. **Enr:** 72. **Enr cap:** 74. **Staff:** Admin 10. Couns 16. Res 50.
Conditions accepted: D.
Features: Crafts Painting Theater Aquatics Boating Canoe Hiking Mtn_Trips Sail Whitewater_Raft Wilderness_Camp Wilderness_Canoe Basketball Equestrian Soccer Swim Tennis Volleyball Water-skiing Watersports.
Fees 2012: Res $450-1150, 1-2 wks. Aid (Need).
Housing: Lodges. Avg per room/unit: 2-6. **Swimming:** Lake.
Est 1981. Nonprofit. **Spons:** Mark Seven Deaf Foundation. Roman Catholic. **Ses:** 2. **Wks/ses:** 1-2. Operates July-Aug. ACA.

This intensive American Sign Language program facilitates learning with classroom instruction, recreational activities and a deaf culture. Classifiers, discourse, storytelling, pragmatics, semantics, nonmanual grammar and linguistics of ASL are all part of the program. CM7 boys and girls engage in an array of traditional camp activities.

MEADOWOOD SPRINGS SPEECH AND HEARING CAMP
Res — Coed Ages 6-16; Day — Coed 5-11

Weston, OR.
Contact (Year-round): 316 SE Emigrant Ave, PO Box 1025, Pendleton, OR 97801. Tel: 541-276-2752. Fax: 541-276-7227.
www.meadowoodsprings.org   E-mail: info@meadowoodsprings.org
Adm: FCFS. **Appl due:** May. **Enr:** 60. **Staff:** Admin 2. Couns 50.
Conditions accepted: D LD Speech & Lang. **Therapy:** Speech.
Features: Crafts Canoe Soccer Swim Volleyball.
Fees 2012: Res $1500, 1 wk. Day $350, ½ wk.
Housing: Cabins Dorms Lodges. **Swimming:** Pool.
Est 1964. Nonprofit. **Ses:** 3. **Wks/ses:** ½-1. Operates July.

Designed to help young people with diagnosed speech, hearing or language difficulties, Meadowood offers campers a full range of recreational and clinical activities, including swimming, canoeing, fishing, camp outs, nature hikes, and arts and crafts. Boys and girls typically improve their communicational skills during the course of the camp.

CAMP MERRY HEART
Res and Day — Coed Ages 5 and up

Hackettstown, NJ 07840. 21 O'Brien Rd. Tel: 908-852-3896. Fax: 908-852-9263.
www.eastersealsnj.org   E-mail: jmauk@nj.easterseals.com
Jonathan Mauk, Dir.
Adm: FCFS.
Conditions accepted: ID LD Phys_Impair.
Features: Crafts Dance Music Aquatics Canoe Climbing_Wall Fishing Kayak Ropes_Crse Basketball Soccer Swim.
Fees 2011: Res $1100-2150, 1-2 wks. Aid (Need).
Housing: Cabins. **Swimming:** Pool.
Est 1949. Nonprofit. **Spons:** Easter Seals New Jersey. **Wks/ses:** 1-2. Operates Year-round.

New Jersey children and adults with developmental and physical challenges and learning disabilities follow an organized program of music, arts and crafts, a ropes course, swimming, boating and nature study.

MID-SOUTH ARC SUMMER CAMP
Res — Coed Ages 8 and up

Memphis, TN 38111. 3485 Poplar Ave, Ste 210. Tel: 901-327-2473. Fax: 901-327-2687.
www.thearcmidsouth.org   E-mail: info@thearcmidsouth.org
Michelle Alexander, Coord.
Adm: FCFS. **Appl due:** Rolling. **Enr:** 30. **Staff:** Couns 17.
Conditions accepted: As Au CP ED ID LD Phys_Impair Speech & Lang TBI Visual_Impair.
Features: Crafts Dance Fine_Arts Music Baseball Basketball Football Golf Swim Volleyball.
Fees 2011: Res $400, 1 wk. Aid (Need).
Housing: Cabins. **Swimming:** Pool.
Est 1967. Nonprofit. **Ses:** 2. **Wks/ses:** 1. Operates July-Aug.

The camp enables individuals with developmental disabilities to develop socially, physically and emotionally. Activities include arts and crafts, hiking, music, games, dancing, swimming, fishing, socializing, special guests, celebrity entertainment and campfires.

CAMP MITTON
Res — Coed Ages 7-13

Brewster, MA 02631. 46 Featherbed Ln. Tel: 508-385-0951. Fax: 508-385-0953.
Contact (Sept-May): 119 Myrtle St, Duxbury, MA 02332. Tel: 781-834-2700.
Fax: 781-834-2701.
Year-round Toll-free: 888-543-7284.
www.crossroads4kids.org   E-mail: registrar@crossroads4kids.org
Lisa Bower & Michael Clancy, Co-Directors.
Adm: FCFS. **Appl due:** Apr. **Enr:** 192. **Enr cap:** 192. **Staff:** Admin 5. Couns 30. Special needs 1.
Conditions accepted: ADD ADHD ED.
Features: Computers Ecol Environ_Sci Crafts Creative_Writing Dance Drama Fine_Arts Music Aquatics Canoe Exploration Hiking Mtn_Trips Rock_Climb Baseball Basketball Football Soccer Softball Swim Volleyball.

Fees 2009: Res $1285-1840, 2-3 wks.
Housing: Cabins. **Swimming:** Lake.
Est 1936. Nonprofit. **Spons:** Crossroads for Kids. **Ses:** 3. **Wks/ses:** 2-3. Operates June-Aug. ACA.

This Crossroads for Kids program serves children from Cape Cod and Greater Boston who have experienced or are still experiencing crisis situations in the form of homelessness, abuse or neglect. Mitton's small, structured program helps boys and girls better cope with their situations by combining anger and behavior management instruction with noncompetitive camp activities.

MUSCULAR DYSTROPHY ASSOCIATION SUMMER CAMP
Res — Coed Ages 6-17

Tucson, AZ 85718. 3300 E Sunrise Dr. Tel: 520-529-2000, 800-572-1717.
Fax: 520-529-5300.
www.mda.org   E-mail: mda@mdausa.org
Jodi Wolff, Dir.
Adm: FCFS. **Appl due:** Rolling.
Locations: AK AL AR AZ CA CO CT DC DE FL GA HI IO ID IL IN KS KY LA MA MD ME MI MN MO MI MT NC NE NH NJ NM NV NY OH OK OR PA PR RI SC SD TN TX UT VA VT WA WI WV WY.
Conditions accepted: MD.
Features: Crafts Archery Boating Fishing Riding Soccer Softball Swim.
Fees 2012: Free. Res 1 wk.
Swimming: Pool.
Est 1955. Nonprofit. **Ses:** 80. **Wks/ses:** 1. Operates June-Aug.

A nationwide network of approximately 80 MDA-sponsored summer camp sessions offers a wide range of programs for young people with neuromuscular diseases. Activities, designed for children who have limited mobility or who use wheelchairs and geared to the abilities of campers, range from outdoor sports such as swimming, boating, baseball and horseback riding to less physically demanding programs like arts and crafts and talent shows. At most camps, counselors work one-on-one with campers on a 24-hour basis.

NATIONAL ASSOCIATION OF THE DEAF YOUTH LEADERSHIP CAMP
Res — Coed Ages 16-18

Stayton, OR.
Contact (Year-round): c/o National Assoc of the Deaf, 8630 Fenton St, Ste 820, Silver Spring, MD 20910. Tel: 301-587-1788. Fax: 301-587-1791.
www.nad.org/ylc
Allie Rice, Coord.
Adm: FCFS. **Appl due:** Feb. **Enr:** 64. **Enr cap:** 64.
Conditions accepted: D.
Features: Computers Debate Environ_Sci Govt Lang Writing/Journ Creative_Writing Filmmaking Media Photog Theater Canoe Community_Serv Exploration Hiking Mtn_Trips Outdoor_Ed Ropes_Crse Swim.
Fees 2012: Res $1750, 4 wks.
Housing: Cabins. Avg per room/unit: 6. **Swimming:** Lake Pool.
Est 1969. Ses: 1. **Wks/ses:** 4. Operates July-Aug.

Held at Camp Taloali, YLC provides training in leadership and literacy skills, social studies, and programs in deaf history, group dynamics, drama and outdoor education for deaf and hard-of-hearing youth. It also offers opportunities for integration and participation with members of the hearing community. Guest speakers, academic activities and field trips round out the program.

NATIONAL CAMPS FOR BLIND CHILDREN
Res — Coed Ages 9-65

Lincoln, NE 68506. PO Box 6097. Tel: 402-488-0981. Fax: 402-488-7582.
www.blindcamp.org   E-mail: info@christianrecord.org
Peggy Hansen, Dir.
Adm: FCFS. **Appl due:** Rolling.
Locations: AR CA CO FL ID IN MI TN Canada.
Conditions accepted: Visual_Impair.
Features: Marine_Bio/Stud Crafts Archery Bicycle_Tours Canoe Climbing_Wall Hiking
    Rappelling Rock_Climb Ropes_Crse Sail Sea_Cruises Woodcraft Baseball Basketball
    Equestrian Golf Softball Swim Water-skiing Watersports.
Fees 2011: Free. Res 1 wk.
Housing: Cabins Dorms. Avg per room/unit: 4. **Swimming:** Lake Pool.
Est 1967. Nonprofit. **Spons:** Christian Record Services. Seventh-day Adventist. **Ses:** 13.
Wks/ses: 1. Operates June-Aug.

Christian Record Services operates programs throughout the country and in Canada for
legally blind individuals. Activities include archery, beeper baseball, beeper basketball,
watersports, tandem bicycling, crafts, hiking, rock climbing and horseback riding. Attendees
must be able to take care of their personal needs. Campers attend free of charge, although they
pay a nominal processing fee.

CAMP NEEDLEPOINT
Res — Coed Ages 8-16; Day — Coed 5-9

Hudson, WI.
Contact (Year-round): c/o American Diabetes Assoc, 5100 Gamble Dr, Ste 394, St
    Louis Park, MN 55416. Tel: 763-593-5333, 888-342-2383. Fax: 952-582-9000.
www.diabetes.org/adacampneedlepoint   E-mail: rbarnett@diabetes.org
Becky Barnett, Dir.
Adm: FCFS. **Appl due:** Rolling. **Enr:** 425. **Staff:** Admin 2. Couns 60. Special needs 2.
Conditions accepted: Diabetes.
Features: Crafts Archery Boating Canoe Climbing_Wall Kayak Riding Rock_Climb Ropes_
    Crse Sail Wilderness_Camp Wilderness_Canoe Basketball Equestrian Soccer Swim
    Tennis Ultimate_Frisbee Volleyball.
Fees 2011: Res $300-815, ½-1 wk. Day $250, 1 wk. Aid 2007 (Need): $75,000.
Housing: Cabins Tents. Avg per room/unit: 9. **Swimming:** River.
Est 1957. Nonprofit. **Spons:** American Diabetes Association. **Ses:** 3. **Wks/ses:** ½-1. Oper-
ates Aug.

Sponsored by the American Diabetes Association, this camp for children living with diabetes
offers a varied recreational program. Activities include swimming, sailing, rock climbing and
athletics, among others. Needlepoint also schedules two- and three-night wilderness canoeing
trips.

CAMP NEJEDA
Res — Coed Ages 7-16

Stillwater, NJ 07875. 910 Saddleback Rd, PO Box 156. Tel: 973-383-2611.
    Fax: 973-383-9891.
www.campnejeda.org   E-mail: information@campnejeda.org
Jim Daschbach, Dir.
Adm: FCFS. **Appl due:** Rolling. **Enr:** 80. **Enr cap:** 80. **Staff:** Admin 3. Couns 45.
Conditions accepted: Diabetes.
Features: Aquatics Archery Bicycle_Tours Boating Canoe Fishing Hiking Kayak Mtn_Biking
    Ropes_Crse Sail Baseball Basketball Soccer Softball Swim Tennis Volleyball.

Fees 2012: Res $950-1850 (+$25), 1-2 wks. Aid 2009 (Need): $110,000.
Housing: Cabins Tepees. Avg per room/unit: 8. **Swimming:** Pond Pool.
Est 1958. Nonprofit. **Ses:** 4. **Wks/ses:** 1-2. Operates June-Aug. ACA.

Serving children with Type 1 diabetes, Nejeda provides an active and safe camping experience that helps them learn about and understand their disorder. Activities include boating, swimming, fishing, archery, sports, nature lore and crafts, as well as camping skills instruction.

CAMP NEW HOPE
Res — Coed Ages 6 and up

McGregor, MN 55760. 53035 Lake Ave.
Contact (Sept-May): c/o Friendship Ventures, 10509 108th St NW, Annandale, MN 55302.
Year-round Tel: 952-852-0101, 800-450-8376. Fax: 952-852-0123.
www.friendshipventures.org E-mail: info@friendshipventures.org
Laurie Tschetter, Exec Dir.
Adm: FCFS. **Appl due:** Rolling. **Enr:** 30. **Enr cap:** 30. **Staff:** Admin 3. Couns 20.
Conditions accepted: ADD ADHD Au ID Phys_Impair.
Features: Crafts Dance Music Theater Aquatics Canoe Fishing Hiking Social_Servs Wilderness_Camp Basketball Softball Swim Volleyball.
Fees 2012: Res $1299-1559, 1 wk. Aid (Need).
Housing: Cabins. Avg per room/unit: 10. **Swimming:** Lake.
Est 1968. Nonprofit. **Spons:** Friendship Ventures. **Ses:** 6. **Wks/ses:** 1. Operates July-Aug. ACA.

New Hope provides recreational and educational services for youth and adults with developmental and physical disabilities. Activities include arts and crafts, music, swimming, boating, fishing and nature study.

NEW IMAGE CAMP POCONO TRAILS
Res — Coed Ages 7-19

Reeders, PA.
Contact (Year-round): PO Box 417, Norwood, NJ 07648. Tel: 201-750-1557, 800-365-0556. Fax: 201-750-1558.
www.newimagecamp.com E-mail: tsparber@aol.com
Tony Sparber & Dale Sparber, Dirs.
Adm: FCFS. **Appl due:** Rolling.
Focus: Health/Weight_Reduct. **Features:** Dance Drama Aquatics Archery Climbing_Wall Hiking Riding Ropes_Crse Basketball Football Golf Ice_Hockey Soccer Softball Swim Tennis Track Volleyball Water-skiing Weight_Trng.
Fees 2012: Res $2390-8990 (+$200), 1½-7½ wks.
Housing: Cabins. **Swimming:** Lake Pool.
Est 1991. Inc. **Ses:** 11. **Wks/ses:** 1½-7½. Operates June-Aug. ACA.

Combining exercise, recreation and nutrition consultation, the camp helps boys and girls lose two to four pounds per week in a noncompetitive setting. The program does not include pills, drugs or food supplements, instead focusing on healthy eating habits and lifestyle changes. Campers who have vegetarian, Kosher or other special dietary requirements are accommodated. See the separate New Image listing under Lake Wales, FL.

NEW IMAGE CAMP VANGUARD
Res — Coed Ages 7-19

Lake Wales, FL.

Contact (Year-round): PO Box 417, Norwood, NJ 07648. Tel: 201-750-1557,
800-365-0556. Fax: 201-750-1558.
www.newimagecamp.com   E-mail: tsparber@aol.com
Maxine Spadaro, Dir.
Adm: FCFS. Appl due: Rolling.
Focus: Health/Weight_Reduct. Features: Dance Drama Aquatics Hiking Riding Baseball
Basketball Football Golf Soccer Swim Tennis Track Volleyball Watersports.
Fees 2012: Res $3350-7790 (+$200), 2-6 wks.
Housing: Dorms. Swimming: Pool.
Est 1991. Inc. Ses: 8. Wks/ses: 2-6. Operates June-Aug. ACA.

See program description under Reeders, PA.

NEW JERSEY CAMP JAYCEE
Res and Day — Coed Ages 7 and up

Effort, PA 18330. 198 Ziegler Rd. Tel: 570-629-3291. Fax: 570-620-9851.
Contact (Sept-May): 985 Livingston Ave, North Brunswick, NJ 08902.
Tel: 732-246-2525. Fax: 732-214-1834.
www.campjaycee.org   E-mail: info@campjaycee.org
Jason Brakeman, Dir.
Adm: FCFS. Appl due: Rolling. Enr cap: 200. Staff: Admin 2. Couns 80. Res 80.
Conditions accepted: ID.
Features: Environ_Sci Crafts Dance Music Canoe Baseball Basketball Soccer Softball
Swim Tennis Volleyball.
Fees 2012: Res $690, 1 wk. Day $400, 1 wk.
Housing: Cabins. Avg per room/unit: 8. Swimming: Lake Pond.
Est 1975. Nonprofit. Spons: New Jersey Jaycees/Arc of New Jersey. Ses: 8. Wks/ses: 1.
Operates June-Aug. ACA.

This camp for children and adults with mental retardation is a collaborative effort of the
New Jersey Jaycees and the Arc of New Jersey. Activities at the 185-acre Pocono Mountains
camp include arts and crafts, games, sports, music, nature study, camp craft, aquatics, drama,
dance and self-help skills. Prospective campers must be toilet trained and self-feeding, and
they must not be severely emotionally disturbed.

CAMP NORTHWOOD
Res — Coed Ages 8-18

Remsen, NY 13438. 132 State Rte 365. Tel: 315-831-3621. Fax: 315-831-5867.
www.nwood.com   E-mail: northwoodprograms@hotmail.com
Gordon W. Felt, Dir.
Grades 5-12. Adm: Somewhat selective. Appl due: Rolling. Enr: 140. Staff: Admin 18.
Couns 82. Special needs 12.
Type of instruction: Rem_Math Rem_Read Rev. LD Services: Acad_Instruction.
Conditions accepted: ADD ADHD Asp Dx LD PDD.
Features: Crafts Creative_Writing Dance Theater Aquatics Archery Canoe Chess Cooking
Hiking Sail Wilderness_Camp Badminton Basketball Soccer Softball Swim Tennis Vol-
leyball Water-skiing Watersports.
Fees 2012: Res $9600, 7 wks.
Housing: Cabins. Avg per room/unit: 6. Swimming: Lake.
Est 1976. Inc. Ses: 1. Wks/ses: 7. Operates July-Aug. ACA.

Northwood's special-needs program serves learning-challenged and high-functioning
autistic children. Campers take part in traditional camping activities while receiving the extra
support and structure they require. Children develop self-esteem and social skills through
participation in daily academics and an array of activities, and staff also provide formalized
social skills instruction.

CAMP NOVA
Res — Coed Ages 12-28

Branchville, NJ.
Contact (Year-round): c/o Epilepsy Foundation of New Jersey, 1 AAA Dr, Ste 203, Trenton, NJ 08691. **Toll-free:** 800-336-5843. **Fax:** 609-392-5621.
www.efnj.com/content/services/camp_nova.html
E-mail: vtrathen@familyresourcenetwork.org
Veronica Trathen, Prgm Dir.
Adm: FCFS. **Appl due:** Mar. **Enr:** 50. **Staff:** Admin 2. Couns 30.
Conditions accepted: ADD ADHD Asp Au CP D Ep ID LD PDD Phys_Impair Speech & Lang Visual_Impair.
Features: Acting Crafts Dance Archery Boating Fishing Yoga Basketball Martial_Arts Swim.
Housing: Cabins Lodges. **Swimming:** Lake Pool.
Est 1989. Nonprofit. **Spons:** Epilepsy Foundation of New Jersey. **Ses:** 1. **Wks/ses:** 1. Operates Aug.

Nova serves boys and girls with epilepsy and other developmental disabilities. Activities range from swimming to yoga. The camp cannot accept medically fragile individuals or those with severe behavioral problems.

CAMP NUHOP
Res — Coed Ages 6-18

Perrysville, OH 44864. 1077 Hanover Twp Rd 2916. Tel: 419-938-7151.
Fax: 419-938-7151.
Contact (Sept-May): 404 Hillcrest Dr, Ashland, OH 44805. **Tel:** 419-289-2227.
Fax: 419-289-2227.
www.campnuhop.org **E-mail:** info@campnuhop.org
Trevor Dunlap, Exec Dir.
Grades 1-12. Adm: FCFS. **Appl due:** Rolling. **Enr:** 80. **Staff:** Admin 6. Couns 30.
Conditions accepted: ADD ADHD Au ED LD Speech & Lang.
Features: Adventure_Travel Aquatics Archery Bicycle_Tours Canoe Climbing_Wall Exploration Hiking Rock_Climb Ropes_Crse Sail Wilderness_Camp Swim.
Fees 2011: Res $745-2000, 1-2 wks. Aid (Need).
Housing: Cabins. **Swimming:** Lake Pool.
Est 1974. Nonprofit. **Ses:** 6. **Wks/ses:** 1-2. Operates June-Aug.

Serving children with learning, behavioral and attentional disorders, Nuhop offers 20 camps, from which a camper may choose exploration, wilderness, acclimatization, bicycling, backpacking, athletic skills, leadership, canoeing, discovery, arts, science or adventure. Daily activities incorporate basic academic concepts, problem solving and socialization skills, and the camp focuses on self-esteem building and behavior management techniques.

CAMP OAKHURST
Res — Coed Ages 8-21

Oakhurst, NJ 07755. 111 Monmouth Rd. Tel: 732-531-0215. **Fax:** 732-531-0292.
Contact (Sept-May): 1140 Broadway, Ste 903, New York, NY 10001. **Tel:** 212-533-4020.
Fax: 212-533-4023.
www.campoakhurst.com **E-mail:** info@campoakhurst.com
Charles Sutherland, Dir.
Adm: FCFS. **Appl due:** Rolling. **Enr:** 90. **Staff:** Admin 7. Couns 45. Special needs 2.
LD Services: Acad_Instruction.
Conditions accepted: CP Phys_Impair TBI MD ON SB. **Therapy:** Art Music Phys Rec.

Features: Writing/Journ Crafts Creative_Writing Media Music Theater Aquatics Cooking Baseball Basketball Football Soccer Swim Volleyball. **Fees 2009: Res $750, 1 wk.** Aid (Need).
Housing: Cabins. Avg per room/unit: 12. **Swimming:** Pool.
Est 1906. Nonprofit. **Ses:** 4. **Wks/ses:** 2. Operates June-Aug. ACA.

Oakhurst accepts children and young adults who have physical special needs. The daily program includes activities such as swimming, adaptive sports, arts, crafts, drama, music, dance, cooking, photography and nature programs. Special events and social outings to beaches, boardwalks and other areas of interest supplement the program.

CAMP OKIZU
Res — Coed Ages 6-17

Berry Creek, CA.
Contact (Year-round): c/o Okizu Foundation, 16 Digital Dr, Ste 130, Novato, CA 94949. Tel: 415-382-9083. Fax: 415-382-8384.
www.okizu.org   E-mail: info@okizu.org
Suzanne B. Randall, Dir.
Adm: FCFS. **Appl due:** Rolling. **Staff:** Admin 15. Couns 40.
Conditions accepted: Cancer.
Features: Crafts Archery Fishing Hiking Ropes_Crse Social_Servs Basketball Swim Volleyball Watersports.
Fees 2012: Free. Res 1 wk.
Housing: Cabins Lodges. **Swimming:** Lake.
Est 1982. Nonprofit. **Spons:** Okizu Foundation. **Ses:** 3. **Wks/ses:** 1. Operates June-Aug. ACA.

Affiliated with the American Cancer Society, Okizu serves children who have or who once had cancer and their siblings. Activities include swimming, boating, fishing, archery, arts and crafts, and nature study.

ONE STEP AT A TIME CAMP
Res — Coed Ages 7-19

Williams Bay, WI. Aurora Univ.
Contact (Year-round): c/o Children's Oncology Services, 213 W Institute Pl, Ste 511, Chicago, IL 60610. Tel: 312-924-4220. Fax: 312-440-8897.
www.onestepcamp.org   E-mail: mtbernal@aol.com
Maria T. Bernal, Dir.
Grades 2-12. Adm: FCFS. **Appl due:** Rolling. **Enr:** 250. **Enr cap:** 250. **Staff:** Admin 20. Couns 100. Special needs 23.
Conditions accepted: Cancer.
Features: Crafts Drama Filmmaking Riding Rock_Climb Sail Scuba Equestrian Golf Swim Volleyball Watersports.
Fees 2012: Res $100, 1 wk.
Housing: Cabins Dorms Tents. **Swimming:** Lake.
Est 1978. Nonprofit. **Spons:** Children's Oncology Services. **Ses:** 2. **Wks/ses:** 1. Operates July.

The camp serves boys and girls from Illinois, northern Indiana and Wisconsin who have cancer or leukemia. Any child well enough to enjoy the camp experience may attend, whether or not he or she is currently undergoing therapy. Programs progress from traditional recreational sessions for young children to more specialized sessions for older campers.

CAMP PENNBROOK
Res — Girls Ages 8-21

Pennington, NJ. Pennington School.
Contact (Year-round): PO Box 5, Leonia, NJ 07605. Tel: 212-354-2267, 800-442-7366.
www.camppennbrook.com   E-mail: info@camppennbrook.com
Flip Shulman, Exec Dir.
Adm: FCFS. **Appl due:** Rolling. **Staff:** Admin 8. Couns 20. Special needs 1.
Focus: Health/Weight_Reduct. **Features:** Crafts Dance Drama Aquatics Hiking Riding Basketball Soccer Swim Tennis Track Volleyball Watersports.
Fees 2012: Res $1990-8190 (+$25-250), 2-8 wks.
Housing: Dorms. **Swimming:** Pool.
Est 1993. Inc. **Ses:** 6. **Wks/ses:** 2-8. Operates June-Aug. ACA.

Campers at Pennbrook focus on the fundamentals of healthy eating. By combining proper nutrition with recreational activities, the program promotes a healthy approach to weight loss that parents can easily reinforce. Each camper meets with a food advisor upon arrival to review her goals and objectives. She has another private session before going home to review a personalized menu planner and discuss issues and concerns about maintaining weight loss after camp. A combination of recreational activities, specialty programs, events and trips completes the program.

PINE TREE CAMP
Res — Coed Ages 8-18; Day — Coed 5-12

Rome, ME 04963. 114 Pine Tree Camp Rd. Tel: 207-397-2141. Fax: 207-397-5324.
Contact (Oct-Apr): c/o Pine Tree Society, 149 Front St, PO Box 518, Bath, ME 04530.
Tel: 207-443-3341. Fax: 207-443-1070.
www.pinetreesociety.org/camp.asp   E-mail: ptcamp@pinetreesociety.org
Dawn Willard-Robinson, Prgm Dir.
Adm: FCFS. **Appl due:** Rolling. **Enr:** 100. **Fac 70.**
Conditions accepted: CP Ep ID Phys_Impair TBI.
Features: Crafts Drama Drawing Music Painting Photog Pottery Woodworking Aquatics Archery Boating Canoe Fishing Kayak Mtn_Trips Wilderness_Camp Woodcraft Basketball Equestrian Football Golf Soccer Street_Hockey Swim Volleyball Watersports.
Fees 2011: Res $1600, 1 wk. Day $150, 1 wk. Aid (Need).
Swimming: Pond.
Est 1945. Nonprofit. **Spons:** Pine Tree Society. **Ses:** 3. **Wks/ses:** 1. Operates July-Aug. ACA.

Pine Tree accepts children with physical and developmental disabilities. Campers take part in activities such as swimming, basketball, crafts, music, drama, theater, canoeing and equestrian. No camper is denied acceptance due to an inability to pay, and fees may be determined along a sliding scale according to family income. Pine Tree operates a separate summer program for special-needs adults.

CAMP RAMAPO
Res — Coed Ages 6-16

Rhinebeck, NY 12572. Rte 52, PO Box 266. Tel: 845-876-8403. Fax: 845-876-8414.
www.ramapoforchildren.org   E-mail: office@ramapoforchildren.org
Michael Kunin, Dir.
Adm: FCFS. **Appl due:** Rolling. **Enr:** 175. **Enr cap:** 175. **Staff:** Admin 35. Couns 200. Special needs 9.
Conditions accepted: ADD ADHD Asp Au Dx ED LD PDD Speech & Lang.
Features: Crafts Music Theater Aquatics Boating Canoe Climbing_Wall Hiking Mtn_Trips

Ropes_Crse Wilderness_Camp Woodcraft Baseball Basketball Soccer Swim Volleyball.
Fees 2012: Res $1600-11,400, 1-8 wks. Aid (Need).
Housing: Cabins. **Swimming:** Lake Pool.
Est 1922. Nonprofit. **Spons:** Ramapo for Children. **Ses:** 8. **Wks/ses:** 1-8. Operates June-Aug. ACA.

Serving children with social and emotional special needs, learning disabilities, and speech and language impairments, Camp Ramapo conducts a varied recreational program that includes swimming, boating, athletics, crafts, music and special events. The camp operates two distinct programs: Summer Adventure (ages 6-14) and Teen Leadership (ages 14-16).

CAMP RED LEAF
Res — Coed Ages 9 and up

Ingleside, IL 60041. 26710 W Nippersink Rd. Tel: 847-740-5010. Fax: 847-740-5014.
www.jcys.org   E-mail: enewport@jcys.org
Erin Newport, Dir.
Adm: FCFS. **Appl due:** Rolling. **Staff:** Admin 2. Couns 27. Special needs 1.
Conditions accepted: ADD ADHD Asp Au CP D Dx Ep ID LD PDD Phys_Impair Speech & Lang TBI Visual_Impair. **Therapy:** Music Rec.
Features: Crafts Music Theater Adventure_Travel Aquatics Archery Boating Canoe Climbing_Wall Fishing Hiking Ropes_Crse Sail Baseball Basketball Soccer Softball Swim Tennis Volleyball Watersports.
Housing: Lodges. Avg per room/unit: 35. **Swimming:** Lake Pool.
Est 1911. Nonprofit. **Spons:** Jewish Council for Youth Services. Jewish. **Ses:** 8. **Wks/ses:** 1. Operates June-Sept.

Affiliated with the Jewish Council for Youth Services, Red Leaf provides camping and training programs for young people and adults with mild to moderate developmental disabilities. Activities include crafts, music, boating and canoeing, fishing, hiking, nature study and sports.

RIDGE CREEK
Res — Coed Ages 12-18

Dahlonega, GA 30533. 830 Hidden Lake Rd. Tel: 706-867-1720. Fax: 706-864-5826.
www.ridgecreek.org   E-mail: information@ridgecreek.org
Chris Grimwood, Admin.
Grades 7-12. Adm: Somewhat selective. Admitted: 98%. **Appl due:** Rolling. **Enr:** 18. **Enr cap:** 24. **Staff:** Admin 2. Couns 2. Res 9. Special needs 18.
LD Services: Acad_Instruction Tut.
Conditions accepted: ADD ADHD Asp Diabetes ED LD ODD. **Therapy:** Psych Rec.
Features: Environ_Sci Govt Lang Sci Writing/Journ Creative_Writing Adventure_Travel Canoe Caving Climbing_Wall Community_Serv Fishing Hiking Mountaineering Mtn_Trips Outdoor_Ed Rappelling Rock_Climb Ropes_Crse Survival_Trng Wilderness_Camp Wilderness_Canoe Aerobics Swim Weight_Trng.
Fees 2012: Res $8150 (+$800), 4 wks.
Housing: Dorms. **Swimming:** Pool River.
Est 2001. Inc. **Ses:** 12. **Wks/ses:** 4. Operates Year-round.

Ridge Creek's clinically integrated outdoor leadership program combines cognitive-based therapeutic work with wilderness training and adventure. Adolescents enrolled in the program, which operates throughout the year, range from those simply needing to refocus to those experiencing significant behavioral difficulties. Most students exhibit behaviors consistent with oppositional defiant disorder, and boys and girls may struggle with adolescent adjustment and authority issues. The 28-day program seeks to address misbehavior that typically leads to impaired social, academic or occupational functioning. Applicants must not be suffering from hallucinations or delusions, nor can they be actively suicidal or homicidal.

ROCKY MOUNTAIN VILLAGE
Res — Coed Ages 6 and up

Empire, CO 80438. PO Box 115. Tel: 303-569-2333. Fax: 303-569-3857.
www.co.easterseals.com   E-mail: campinfo@eastersealscolorado.org
Adm: FCFS. **Appl due:** Apr.
Conditions accepted: Au Blood ID Phys_Impair TBI MD.
Features: Media Climbing_Wall Fishing Riding Basketball Softball Swim Tennis Gardening.
Fees 2011: Res $800-1050, 1 wk. Aid (Need).
Swimming: Pool.
Est 1951. Spons: Colorado Easter Seal Society. **Ses:** 16. **Wks/ses:** 1. Operates May-Aug.

Operated by the Colorado Easter Seal Society, the camp conducts sessions for children and adults with developmental and physical disabilities, as well as specialty programs for those with hemophilia and autism. Activities include horseback riding, swimming, fishing and hiking, as well as wilderness camping and outdoor education.

CAMP RONALD McDONALD FOR GOOD TIMES
Res — Coed Ages 9-18

Mountain Center, CA 92561. 56400 Apple Canyon Rd, PO Box 35. Tel: 951-659-4609.
Fax: 951-659-4710.
Contact (Winter): 1954 Cotner Ave, Los Angeles, CA 90025. Tel: 310-268-8488.
Fax: 310-473-3338.
Year-round Toll-free: 800-625-7295.
www.campronaldmcdonald.org   E-mail: dot@campronaldmcdonald.org
Jennifer Mains, Dir.
Adm: FCFS. **Appl due:** Rolling. **Enr:** 100. **Staff:** Admin 3. Couns 50. Special needs 3.
Conditions accepted: Cancer.
Features: Crafts Dance Media Music Photog Theater Archery Cooking Fishing Hiking Riding Ropes_Crse Swim.
Fees 2012: Free. Res 1 wk.
Housing: Cabins. **Swimming:** Pool.
Est 1982. Nonprofit. **Ses:** 5. **Wks/ses:** 1. Operates June-Aug. ACA.

The camp serves children who have (or who once had) cancer and their families. Distinct sessions serve patients ages 9-15 and their siblings and patients ages 16-18 and their siblings. Activities include swimming, riding, nature study, hiking, sports, drama, dancing, photography, arts and crafts, a ropes course and a radio station.

SERTOMA CAMP ENDEAVOR
Res — Coed Ages 6-17

Dundee, FL 33838. 1221 Camp Endeavor Blvd, PO Box 910. Tel: 863-439-1300.
www.sertomacampendeavor.org   E-mail: campendeavor@verizon.net
George Boyd, Dir.
Adm: FCFS. **Appl due:** Rolling. **Enr:** 60. **Enr cap:** 96. **Staff:** Admin 1. Couns 8. Special needs 16.
Conditions accepted: D.
Features: Crafts Drama Archery Boating Canoe Climbing_Wall Fishing Hiking Mtn_Biking

Outdoor_Ed Rappelling Riding Ropes_Crse Baseball Basketball Football Golf Swim Team_Handball Volleyball Watersports. **Housing:** Cabins. Avg per room/unit: 16. **Swimming:** Lake. **Est 1976.** Nonprofit. **Ses:** 2. **Wks/ses:** 1. Operates July.

Camp Endeavor provides a traditional camp experience for children who are deaf or hard of hearing. Wilderness education includes nature hikes and wildlife identification, while the performing arts program features dance, drama, storytelling, songs, and arts and crafts. Swimming, canoeing, water skiing and tubing are some of the pursuits in the aquatics program. Many counselors at Endeavor have hearing impairments.

CAMP SETEBAID
Res — Coed Ages 8-17

Shickshinny, PA.
Contact (Year-round): c/o Setebaid Services, PO Box 196, Winfield, PA 17889.
 Tel: 570-524-9090, 866-738-3224. Fax: 570-523-0769.
www.setebaidservices.org   E-mail: info@setebaidservices.org
Mark Moyer, Exec Dir.
Adm: FCFS. **Appl due:** Rolling. **Enr cap:** 100. **Staff:** Admin 10. Couns 70. Special needs 10.
Conditions accepted: Diabetes.
Features: Environ_Sci Writing/Journ Crafts Dance Music Photog Theater Aquatics Archery Bicycle_Tours Boating Canoe Climbing_Wall Hiking Ropes_Crse Wilderness_Camp Baseball Basketball Martial_Arts Soccer Softball Street_Hockey Swim Volleyball.
Fees 2010: Res $880, 1 wk. Aid 2009 (Need): $80,000.
Housing: Cabins Tents. Avg per room/unit: 4-12. **Swimming:** Pool.
Est 1978. Nonprofit. **Spons:** Setebaid Services. **Ses:** 5. **Wks/ses:** 1. Operates July-Aug. ACA.

This recreational camping experience serves children with diabetes. Setebaid Services provides campers with professional assistance in developing diabetes management skills. Healthcare professionals, including physicians, nurses and dieticians, are on site at all times.

CAMP SHANE
Res — Boys Ages 7-19, Girls 7-25

Ferndale, NY 12734. 302 Harris Rd. Tel: 845-292-4644. Fax: 845-292-8636.
Contact (Sept-May): 134 Teatown Rd, Croton-on-Hudson, NY 10520.
 Tel: 914-271-4141. Fax: 914-271-2103.
www.campshane.com   E-mail: office@campshane.com
David Ettenberg, Dir.
Grades 3-12. Adm: FCFS. **Appl due:** Rolling. **Enr:** 797.
Focus: Health/Weight_Reduct. **Features:** Crafts Dance Fine_Arts Music Theater Bicycle_Tours Boating Canoe Climbing_Wall Cooking Mtn_Biking Riding Ropes_Crse Scuba Wilderness_Camp Woodcraft Aerobics Baseball Basketball Equestrian Soccer Softball Swim Tennis Volleyball Water-skiing Weight_Trng.
Fees 2012: Res $3700-8600, 3-9 wks.
Housing: Cabins. **Swimming:** Lake Pool.
Est 1968. Ses: 5. **Wks/ses:** 3-9. Operates June-Aug.

This weight-reduction camp places particular emphasis on diet and nutrition. Classes in basic nutrition show boys and girls how to enjoy meals while losing weight through portion control and food substitutions. The traditional camp setting includes sports and creative activities. In addition to the regular camp, Shane offers a separate program for young women ages 18-25.

SOAR SUMMER ADVENTURES
Res — Coed Ages 8-25

Balsam, NC 28707. PO Box 388. Tel: 828-456-3435. Fax: 828-456-3449.
www.soarnc.org   E-mail: admissions@soarnc.org
John Willson, Dir.
Adm: FCFS. **Appl due:** Rolling. **Enr cap:** 10-21. **Staff:** Admin 10. Couns 60.
LD Services: Acad_Instruction.
Intl program focus: Culture. **Locations:** CA FL NC WY Mexico/Central_America South_ America.
Conditions accepted: ADD ADHD Asp Dx LD. **Therapy:** Rec.
Features: Adventure_Travel Canoe Caving Climbing_Wall Fishing Hiking Kayak Mountaineering Mtn_Biking Mtn_Trips Pack_Train Rappelling Riding Riflery Rock_Climb Ropes_Crse Scuba Sea_Cruises Survival_Trng White-water_Raft Wilderness_Camp Wilderness_Canoe Swim.
Fees 2012: Res $2800-4400 (+$40-115), 2-3½ wks. Aid 2010 (Need): $40,000.
Housing: Cabins Tents. Avg per room/unit: 7. **Swimming:** Ocean Pool River Stream.
Est 1975. Nonprofit. **Ses:** 23. **Wks/ses:** 2-3½. Operates June-Aug.

Success Oriented Achievement Realized schedules a full range of summer expeditions for students diagnosed with learning disabilities or attentional disorders. Adventure activities include wilderness backpacking and llama trekking, horse packing, rock climbing, whitewater rafting, mountain biking, snorkeling and caving. Staff place emphasis on developing self-confidence, social skills, problem-solving techniques, and organizational and time management strategies. Programs operate in the Appalachian Mountains of North Carolina, the Florida Keys, Wyoming, Belize, Costa Rica and Peru. SOAR also provides a one-month academic remediation program that incorporates wilderness-based adventures.

SPECIAL TOUCH MINISTRY SUMMER GET AWAY
Res — Coed Ages 10 and up

Waupaca, WI 54981. PO Box 25. Tel: 715-258-2713. Fax: 715-258-2777.
www.specialtouch.org   E-mail: summergetaway@specialtouch.org
Debbie Chivers, Coord.
Adm: FCFS. **Appl due:** Rolling.
Locations: AR AZ CT FL IL KY MN OK VA WI.
Conditions accepted: Asp Au CP D Ep ID LD Phys_Impair Speech & Lang TBI Visual_ Impair. **Therapy:** Art Music Phys Rec.
Features: Relig_Stud Crafts Music Painting Theater Aquatics Archery Boating Climbing_ Wall Fishing Hiking Outdoor_Ed Paintball Rappelling Ropes_Crse Aerobics Baseball Basketball Equestrian Soccer Softball Swim Volleyball Watersports.
Fees 2011: Res $380-695, 1 wk. Aid (Need).
Housing: Cabins Dorms Houses Lodges. Avg per room/unit: 4. **Swimming:** Lake Pool.
Est 1982. Nonprofit. Nondenom Christian. **Ses:** 9. **Wks/ses:** 1. Operates May-Sept.

Special Touch provides Christian camping experiences nationwide for people with intellectual or physical special needs and their families. Individuals with intellectual disabilities enter a program geared to their understanding and participation levels. Participants with physical special needs take part in a separate program that provides Bible teaching, tailored to the spiritual issues they face, as well as recreation, entertainment and fellowship. Activities vary by location.

CAMP STAND BY ME
Res — Coed Ages 7 and up

Vaughn, WA 98394. 17809 S Vaughn Rd KPN, PO Box 289. Tel: 253-884-2722.
Fax: 253-884-0200.

www.wa.easterseals.com   E-mail: camp@wa.easterseals.com
Ellen Stone, Dir.
Adm: FCFS. **Enr:** 288.
Conditions accepted: ADD ADHD Au CP D Diabetes Dx Ep ID LD Phys_Impair Speech & Lang TBI Visual_Impair.
Features: Crafts Aquatics Archery Boating Fishing Hiking Riding Swim.
Fees 2012: Res $690-910, 1 wk.
Housing: Cabins. Avg per room/unit: 8. **Swimming:** Pool.
Est 1975. Nonprofit. **Spons:** Easter Seals Washington. **Ses:** 9. **Wks/ses:** 1. Operates June-Aug. ACA.

Aquatics, arts and crafts, and riding are among the activities available at this camp for those with physical, mental, sensory or developmental special needs.

CAMP STARFISH
Res — Coed Ages 7-16; Day — Coed 5-10

Rindge, NH.
Contact (Year-round): 1121 Main St, Lancaster, MA 01523. Tel: 978-368-6580.
Fax: 978-368-6578.
www.campstarfish.org   E-mail: campers@campstarfish.org
Emily Golinsky, Exec Dir.
Adm: FCFS. **Appl due:** Rolling. **Enr:** 48. **Staff:** Admin 15. Couns 40.
LD Services: Acad_Instruction.
Conditions accepted: ADD ADHD Asp ED LD Phys_Impair.
Features: Computers Environ_Sci Expository_Writing Lang Crafts Dance Music Theater Aquatics Boating Canoe Community_Serv Fishing Hiking Kayak Basketball Football Swim Tennis Volleyball Watersports.
Fees 2012: Res $1375-5000, 1-2½ wks. Day $255-315, 1 wk. Aid (Need).
Housing: Cabins. Avg per room/unit: 4-5. **Swimming:** Lake.
Est 1998. Nonprofit. **Ses:** 8. **Wks/ses:** 1-2½. Operates June-Aug.

Starfish assigns boys and girls to bunks according to camper age, ability level and specific needs. Each bunk of four or five campers is supervised by five counselors and engages as a group in traditional recreational activities. A learning center enables boys and girls to take part in basic science experiments, creative writing activities and educational board games.

CAMP SUMMIT
Res — Coed Ages 6 and up

Argyle, TX 76226. 921 Copper Canyon Rd.
Contact (Sept-Apr): 17210 Campbell Rd, Ste 180-W, Dallas, TX 75252.
Year-round Tel: 972-484-8900, Fax: 972-620-1945.
www.campsummittx.org   E-mail: camp@campsummittx.org
Lisa J. Braziel, Dir.
Adm: FCFS. **Appl due:** Rolling. **Enr:** 80. **Staff:** Admin 10. Couns 60.
Conditions accepted: Asp Au CP D Ep ID LD Phys_Impair TBI Visual_Impair.
Features: Crafts Dance Music Theater Aquatics Hiking Riding Ropes_Crse Swim.
Fees 2011: Res $1300, 1 wk. Aid (Need).
Housing: Cabins. Avg per room/unit: 8. **Swimming:** Pool.
Est 1993. Nonprofit. **Ses:** 11. **Wks/ses:** 1. Operates May-Aug. ACA.

Various outdoor programs, including swimming, horseback riding, camp outs, a ropes course and handicrafts, are available for individuals with physical disabilities, developmental delays, or visual or hearing impairments.

SUMMIT CAMP & TRAVEL
Res — Coed Ages 8-19

Honesdale, PA 18431. 168 Duck Harbor Rd. Tel: 570-253-4381. Fax: 570-253-2937.
Contact (Sept-June): 322 Rte 46 W, Ste 210, Parsippany, NJ 07054. Tel: 973-732-3230.
Fax: 973-732-3226.
Year-round Toll-free: 800-323-9908.
www.summitcamp.com E-mail: info@summitcamp.com
Eugene Bell, Dir.
Adm: FCFS. **Appl due:** Rolling. **Enr:** 300. **Enr cap:** 300.
LD Services: Acad_Instruction.
Travel: AZ HI Canada Mexico/Central_America Middle_East.
Conditions accepted: ADD ADHD Asp Dx ED LD PDD Speech & Lang Mood NLD OCD TS.
Features: Computers Sci Crafts Dance Drama Music Adventure_Travel Aquatics Bicycle_Tours Canoe Climbing_Wall Hiking Kayak Mtn_Biking Ropes_Crse Sail Woodcraft Baseball Basketball Field_Hockey Gymnastics Martial_Arts Soccer Softball Swim Tennis Volleyball.
Fees 2012: Res $4100-7950, 2-3 wks.
Housing: Cabins. Avg per room/unit: 9. **Swimming:** Lake Pool.
Est 1969. Inc. **Ses:** 7. **Wks/ses:** 2-3. Operates June-Aug. ACA.

This therapeutic camp for boys and girls with various special needs provides waterfront and land sports; enrichment programs in nature study, overnight hiking, arts and crafts, dramatics, music, shop, home economics, creative movement and ceramics; academic remediation; videography; computers; and social programs. Older teens may take part in a work camp program that integrates young adult education with work experience while stressing life and social skills. A travel program offers campers ages 15-19 travel tours to the following destinations: Arizona and Hawaii, Israel, Canada and Costa Rica.

SUNSHINE CAMP
Res — Coed Ages 7-21

Rush, NY. Tel: 585-533-2080.
Contact (Year-round): c/o Rochester Rotary Club, 180 Linden Oaks, Ste 200,
Rochester, NY 14625. Tel: 585-546-7435.
Year-round Fax: 585-546-8675.
www.sunshinecampus.org E-mail: kelly@rochesterrotary.org
Tracy Dreisbach, Exec Dir.
Adm: FCFS. **Appl due:** May. **Enr:** 120. **Enr cap:** 130. **Staff:** Admin 6. Couns 75.
Conditions accepted: ADD ADHD As Asp Au Blood C CP D Diabetes Ep HIV/AIDS PDD Phys_Impair Speech & Lang TBI Visual_Impair.
Features: Ecol Crafts Music Theater Aquatics Archery Boating Canoe Climbing_Wall Fishing Outdoor_Ed Rock_Climb Ropes_Crse Wilderness_Camp Yoga Baseball Basketball Football Soccer Softball Swim Volleyball.
Fees 2012: Free (in-state residents). Res 1 wk.
Housing: Cabins. Avg per room/unit: 20. **Swimming:** Pool.
Est 1922. Nonprofit. **Spons:** Rochester Rotary Club. **Ses:** 2. **Wks/ses:** 1. Operates July.

The camp serves children and young adults with physical disabilities from the Greater Rochester area in a residential camping program. The cost-free program features a variety of traditional camp activities and sports.

CAMP SWEENEY
Res — Coed Ages 5-18

Gainesville, TX 76241. PO Box 918. Tel: 940-665-2011. Fax: 940-665-9467.

www.campsweeney.org   E-mail: info@campsweeney.org
Ernie M. Fernandez, Dir.
Grades K-12. Adm: FCFS. **Appl due:** Rolling. **Enr:** 245. **Enr cap:** 245. **Staff:** Admin 10. Couns 48. Special needs 16.
Conditions accepted: Diabetes. **Therapy:** Art Music Occup Phys Psych Rec.
Focus: Health/Weight_Reduct. **Features:** Computers Writing/Journ Crafts Dance Filmmaking Media Music Painting Photog Theater Aquatics Archery Boating Canoe Climbing_Wall Exploration Fishing Hiking Kayak Paintball Rappelling Riflery Rock_Climb Ropes_Crse Aerobics Baseball Basketball Cross-country Field_Hockey Football Golf Gymnastics Lacrosse Roller_Hockey Skateboarding Soccer Softball Swim Tennis Ultimate_Frisbee Volleyball Water-skiing Watersports Weight_Trng.
Fees 2012: Res $2900, 3 wks. Aid 2008 (Need): $750,000.
Housing: Cabins Lodges. **Swimming:** Lake Pool.
Est 1950. Nonprofit. **Spons:** Southwestern Diabetic Foundation. **Ses:** 3. **Wks/ses:** 3. Operates June-Aug.

The only camp in Texas designed specifically to teach diabetes management skills to children with Type 1 or Type 2 diabetes, Camp Sweeney helps children with the disease learn how to live a near-normal lifestyle and to avoid the debilitating effects of their endocrine disorder. Lifestyle modification (appropriate dietary choices and regular exercise) is at the heart of the program. Campers learn how and when to give themselves insulin injections.

TALISMAN SUMMER CAMP
Res — Coed Ages 8-21

Zirconia, NC 28790. 64 Gap Creek Rd. Tel: 828-697-6313, 888-458-8226.
   Fax: 828-697-6249.
www.talismancamps.com   E-mail: summer@talismancamps.com
Linda Tatsapaugh, Exec Dir.
Adm: FCFS. **Appl due:** Rolling. **Enr:** 85. **Enr cap:** 100. **Staff:** Admin 7. Couns 45. Special needs 2.
LD Services: Acad_Instruction.
Conditions accepted: ADD ADHD Asp Au ED LD.
Features: Crafts Adventure_Travel Canoe Hiking Kayak Mountaineering Mtn_Trips Rock_Climb Ropes_Crse Sail White-water_Raft Wilderness_Camp Wilderness_Canoe Swim.
Fees 2012: Res $2665-3895, 2-3 wks.
Housing: Cabins Tents. Avg per room/unit: 8. **Swimming:** Lake Pond Pool Stream.
Est 1980. Spons: Aspen Education Group. **Ses:** 6. **Wks/ses:** 2-3. Operates June-Aug. ACA.

Talisman offers an adventure program of hiking, camping, white-water rafting, rock climbing and canoeing for young people with attentional disorders, learning disabilities, autism and Asperger's syndrome. Focused on social skills development, personal regulation and self-esteem, the camp is open to physically nonaggressive children with an IQ of 85 or above.

TEXAS LIONS CAMP
Res and Day — Coed Ages 7-16

Kerrville, TX 78029. PO Box 290247. Tel: 830-896-8500. TTY: 830-896-8500.
   Fax: 830-896-3666.
www.lionscamp.com   E-mail: tlc@lionscamp.com
Stephen S. Mabry, Exec Dir.
Adm: FCFS. **Appl due:** Rolling. **Staff:** Admin 18. Couns 140.
Conditions accepted: As C CP D Diabetes Ep Phys_Impair Visual_Impair. **Therapy:** Music Rec.
Features: Crafts Dance Drama Fine_Arts Music Photog Aquatics Archery Fishing Hiking Ropes_Crse Wilderness_Camp Baseball Equestrian Golf Softball Swim Volleyball.

Fees 2012: Free. Res 1 wk. **Day** ½ wk.
Housing: Cabins. **Swimming:** Pond Pool.
Est 1949. Nonprofit. Ses: 8. **Wks/ses:** ½-1. Operates June-Aug. ACA.

TLC conducts distinct recreational camp sessions for Texas children with either physical disabilities or diabetes. Swimming, boating, music, sports, ropes courses, horseback riding, photography, arts and crafts, archery and nature studies are among the available activities. The half-week day camp serves children with physical disabilities only.

CAMP THORPE
Res — Coed Ages 10-20

Goshen, VT 05733. 680 Capen Hill Rd. Tel: 802-247-6611.
www.campthorpe.org   E-mail: cthorpe@sover.net
Lyle P. Jepson, Dir.
Adm: FCFS. **Appl due:** Rolling. **Enr:** 180. **Staff:** Admin 2. Couns 18.
Conditions accepted: Au CP Ep ID LD Phys_Impair Speech & Lang.
Features: Crafts Music Theater Boating Fishing Hiking Basketball Swim Tennis.
Fees 2012: Res $600, 1-2 wks. Aid (Need).
Housing: Cabins. **Swimming:** Pool.
Est 1927. Nonprofit. Ses: 4. **Wks/ses:** 1-2. Operates June-Aug.

The camp serves campers with such physical and mental challenges as cerebral palsy, intellectual disabilities, spina bifida, epilepsy, muscular dystrophy, emotional difficulties and abuse histories. Activities include swimming, boating, fishing, farm animal care, art, music, theater, dances, games and sports.

CAMP THUNDERBIRD
Res — Coed Ages 8 and up

Apopka, FL 32712. 909 E Welch Rd.
Contact (Winter): c/o Quest, PO Box 531125, Orlando, FL 32853.
Year-round Tel: 407-889-8088, Fax: 407-889-8072.
www.questinc.org   E-mail: campthunderbird@questinc.org
Rob Cage, Dir.
Adm: FCFS. **Appl due:** Rolling. **Enr:** 500.
Conditions accepted: Au CP ID DS.
Features: Art Crafts Theater Canoe Fishing Ropes_Crse Swim.
Fees 2012: Res $675-1300, 1-2 wks.
Housing: Cabins. **Swimming:** Pool.
Est 1969. Nonprofit. Spons: Quest. **Ses:** 8. **Wks/ses:** 1-2. Operates June-Aug. ACA.

This camp for children and adults with physical and behavioral challenges offers a traditional camping experience that emphasizes daily living and social skills. Campers, who must be ambulatory, choose from six- and 12-day sessions. Activities include swimming, canoeing, nature study, drama, arts and crafts, sports, games and a ropes course.

TRIANGLE D CAMP FOR CHILDREN WITH DIABETES
Res — Coed Ages 9-13

Ingleside, IL.
Contact (Year-round): c/o American Diabetes Assoc, 55 E Monroe St, Ste 3420,
**   Chicago, IL 60603. Tel: 312-346-1805. Fax: 312-346-5342.**
www.diabetes.org/living-with-diabetes/parents-and-kids/ada-camps
E-mail: jross@diabetes.org
Grades 3-8. Adm: FCFS. **Appl due:** Rolling. **Enr:** 140. **Staff:** Admin 2. Special needs 40.
Conditions accepted: Diabetes.

Features: Crafts Aquatics Archery Canoe Climbing_Wall Basketball Soccer Softball Swim Volleyball.
Fees 2011: Res $795-895, 1 wk. Aid 2006 (Need): $10,000.
Housing: Cabins. **Swimming:** Pool.
Est 1944. Nonprofit. **Spons:** American Diabetes Association. **Ses:** 1. **Wks/ses:** 1. Operates July.

Triangle D's program for children with diabetes combines self-care education and recreation. Campers learn to be responsible for their diabetes management. Many traditional summer camp activities are available.

UPWARD BOUND SUMMER CAMP
Res and Day — Coed Ages 12 and up

Stayton, OR 97383. PO Box C. Tel: 503-897-2447. Fax: 503-897-4116.
www.upwardboundcamp.org   E-mail: upward.bound.camp@gmail.com
Jerry Pierce & Laura Pierce, Dirs.
Adm: FCFS. Admitted: 100%. **Appl due:** Rolling. **Enr:** 35. **Enr cap:** 35. **Staff:** Admin 4. Couns 16. Res 4. Special needs 4.
Conditions accepted: Asp Au CP ED ID LD PDD Phys_Impair Speech & Lang. **Therapy:** Art Rec.
Features: Crafts Dance Fine_Arts Music Painting Photog Theater Aquatics Archery Boating Canoe Cooking Fishing Hiking Outdoor_Ed Wilderness_Camp Swim Volleyball Billiards Horseshoes.
Fees 2012: Res $695, 1 wk. Day $125, 1 wk. Aid 2011 (Need): $3800.
Housing: Cabins Dorms Lodges Tents. **Swimming:** River Stream.
Est 1978. Nonprofit. Nondenom Christian. **Ses:** 7. **Wks/ses:** 1. Operates June-Sept. ACA.

Located on Evans Creek, this Christian camp serves special populations with cognitive impairments. Campers may have secondary special needs such as brain injury, deafness, and visual or physical impairments. Campers may participate in a variety of activities, including fishing, swimming, crafts, hiking, nature study, music, drama and archery.

VARIETY CAMP
Res — Coed Ages 7-17; Day — Coed 5-21

Worcester, PA 19490. 2950 Potshop Rd, PO Box 609. Tel: 610-584-4366.
Fax: 610-584-5586.
www.varietyphila.org   E-mail: angusmurray@varietyphila.org
Angus Murray, Managing Dir.
Adm: FCFS. **Appl due:** Rolling. **Enr:** 230. **Staff:** Admin 10. Couns 120. Res 40. Special needs 4.
LD Services: Acad_Instruction.
Conditions accepted: ADD ADHD As Asp Au C CP D Dx Ep ID LD PDD Phys_Impair Speech & Lang TBI Visual_Impair. **Therapy:** Occup Phys Rec Speech.
Features: Computers Ecol Environ_Sci Sci Ceramics Crafts Dance Music Theater Aquatics Canoe Cooking Farm Fishing Hiking Outdoor_Ed Scuba Baseball Basketball Golf Soccer Swim Tennis.
Fees 2011: Res $600 (+$20), 1 wk. Day $325 (+$25), 1 wk. Aid 2010 (Need): $11,000.
Housing: Cabins. Avg per room/unit: 10. **Swimming:** Pool.
Est 1949. Nonprofit. **Spons:** Variety: The Children's Charity. **Ses:** 8. **Wks/ses:** 1. Operates June-Aug.

Variety conducts traditional camping sessions for children with physical or developmental disabilities. The overnight camp serves boys and girls with physical disabilities, while the day camp enrolls campers with developmental disabilities. Specialty programs focus upon adapted aquatics, wheelchair basketball, dance, music and scuba diving.

CAMP VIRGINIA JAYCEE
Res — Coed Ages 7 and up; Day — Coed 5 and up

Blue Ridge, VA 24064. 2494 Camp Jaycee Rd, PO Box 648. Tel: 540-947-2972, 800-865-0092.
www.campvajc.org   E-mail: info@campvajc.org
Dana Zyrowski, Dir.
Adm: FCFS. **Appl due:** Rolling. **Staff:** Admin 7. Couns 50.
Conditions accepted: Au CP Ep ID TBI DS PW.
Features: Crafts Dance Drama Music Aquatics Boating Climbing_Wall Fishing Hiking Baseball Basketball Equestrian Golf Soccer Softball Swim Tennis Volleyball.
Fees 2012: Res $650-700 (+$150), 1 wk. **Day** $240, 1 wk. Aid (Need).
Housing: Cabins. Avg per room/unit: 16. **Swimming:** Pool.
Est 1971. Nonprofit. **Ses:** 9. **Wks/ses:** 1. Operates June-July. ACA.

Virginia Jaycee provides outdoor education and traditional camping experiences for children and adults with mental retardation and, in some cases, other special needs. Campers engage in an array of traditional recreational pursuits during the day, then take part in such activities as dances, hayrides, vespers, talent shows, scavenger hunts, puppet shows, singing and campfires in the evening.

WEDIKO SUMMER PROGRAM
Res — Coed Ages 6-18

Windsor, NH 03244. 11 Bobcat Blvd. Tel: 603-478-5236. Fax: 603-478-2049.
Contact (Sept-June): 72-74 E Dedham St, Boston, MA 02118. Tel: 617-292-9200. Fax: 617-292-9275.
www.wediko.org   E-mail: wediko@wediko.org
Harry W. Parad, Exec Dir.
Adm: Selective. **Appl due:** Rolling. **Enr:** 155. **Enr cap:** 160. **Staff:** Admin 6. Res 78. Special needs 16.
Type of instruction: Dev_Read Tut. **LD Services:** Acad_Instruction.
Conditions accepted: ADD ADHD Asp Dx ED LD PDD Anx Mood NLD PTSD. **Therapy:** Psych.
Features: Crafts Dance Fine_Arts Music Painting Theater Aquatics Archery Canoe Chess Cooking Exploration Fishing Hiking Kayak Mtn_Biking Social_Servs Work Yoga Baseball Basketball Football Soccer Swim Tennis Volleyball Weight_Trng.
Fees 2011: Res $12,825, 6½ wks.
Housing: Cabins. Avg per room/unit: 10. **Swimming:** Lake.
Est 1934. Nonprofit. **Spons:** Wediko Children's Services. **Ses:** 1. **Wks/ses:** 6½. Operates July-Aug.

This therapeutic program serves children and adolescents who have a range of emotional, behavioral and learning issues. Boys and girls develop new skills and learn to better manage their behavior through a variety of group and individual supports, academic programming and recreational activities. Psychotherapy, daily group therapy, milieu therapy and family therapy are important aspects of the program.

WELLSPRING ACADEMY OF CALIFORNIA SUMMER SESSION
Res — Coed Ages 12-25

Reedley, CA 93654. 42675 Rd 44. Toll-free: 866-364-0808.
www.wellspringacademies.com/summer_weight_loss_programs.html
David Melear, Exec Dir.
Adm: FCFS. **Appl due:** Rolling. **Enr:** 120. **Enr cap:** 120. **Fac 10. Staff:** Admin 15. Couns 30.
Type of instruction: Rem_Eng Rem_Math Rem_Read Study_Skills Tut. **LD Services:**

Acad_Instruction Tut. **Avg class size:** 8. **Daily hours for:** Classes 5. Study 1. Rec 6. High school credit.
Therapy: Art Psych Rec.
Focus: Health/Weight_Reduct. **Features:** Bus/Fin Expository_Writing Govt Lang Crafts Creative_Writing Photog Theater Aquatics Bicycle_Tours Canoe Cooking Hiking Kayak Mountaineering Mtn_Biking Mtn_Trips Paintball Riding Rock_Climb Social_Servs White-water_Raft Wilderness_Camp Baseball Basketball Cross-country Equestrian Field_Hockey Football Golf Soccer Softball Swim Tennis Volleyball Watersports.
Fees 2012: Res $13,450-18,500, 10-13 wks.
Housing: Dorms. **Swimming:** Pool River.
Est 2004. Inc. **Spons:** Wellspring Academies. **Ses:** 2. **Wks/ses:** 10-13. Operates June-Aug. ACA.

Wellspring, which enrolls boys and girls who have had weight problems for two years or more and who are at least 30 pounds overweight, combines intensive diet and activity management with an emphasis on behavioral change. Instructors attempt to permanently change thinking and behavior regarding diet and physical activity. A classroom component includes compulsory nutrition and culinary arts course work and traditional academics; all students select two core classes that lead to transferable high school credit.

WELLSPRING ADVENTURE CAMP NORTH CAROLINA
Res — Coed Ages 11-18

Black Mountain, NC.
Contact (Year-round): c/o Wellspring Camps, 42675 Road 44, Reedley, CA 93654.
Tel: 559-638-4570, 866-364-0808. Fax: 559-638-2685.
www.wellspringadventurecamp.com
Jessie Dean, Dir.
Grades 6-11. Adm: FCFS. **Appl due:** Rolling. **Enr:** 60. **Staff:** Admin 5. Couns 20.
LD Services: Acad_Instruction.
Therapy: Art Psych Rec.
Focus: Health/Weight_Reduct. **Features:** Crafts Adventure_Travel Bicycle_Tours Boating Canoe Caving Climbing_Wall Cooking Exploration Hiking Kayak Mountaineering Mtn_Biking Mtn_Trips Rappelling Rock_Climb Ropes_Crse Survival_Trng White-water_Raft Wilderness_Camp Wilderness_Canoe Baseball Field_Hockey Soccer Softball Swim Volleyball Watersports.
Fees 2012: Res $5345-12,495 (+$500), 3-12 wks.
Housing: Cabins Tents. Avg per room/unit: 10. **Swimming:** Pool Stream.
Est 2004. Inc. **Spons:** Wellspring Weight Loss Programs. **Ses:** 25. **Wks/ses:** 3-12. Operates June-Aug.

Wellspring Adventure Camp is designed to help boys and girls lose weight, develop healthy habits and improve self-esteem. Located in the Blue Ridge mountains of North Carolina, the camp offers beginning instruction in white-water rafting, rock climbing and rappelling. Wellspring's clinical program combines cognitive behavioral therapy, dietary changes and physical activity. Writing exercises and educational seminars complete the program. Applicants must be at least 20 pounds overweight and must have been attempting to lose weight for at least a year.

WELLSPRING NEW YORK
Res — Girls Ages 11-24

Paul Smiths, NY. Paul Smith's College.
Contact (Year-round): c/o Wellspring Camps, 42675 Road 44, Reedley, CA 93654.
Tel: 559-638-4570, 866-364-0808. Fax: 559-638-2685.
www.wellspringny.com   **E-mail:** ksomma@wellspringcamps.com
Kimberly Mueller, Dir.

Grades 9-Col. Adm: FCFS. **Appl due:** Rolling. **Enr:** 100. **Staff:** Admin 7. Couns 30. **Focus:** Health/Weight_Reduct. **Features:** Crafts Dance Drama Fine_Arts Photog Aquatics Archery Bicycle_Tours Boating Canoe Climbing_Wall Exploration Fishing Hiking Mountaineering Mtn_Biking Mtn_Trips Rappelling Rock_Climb Ropes_Crse White-water_Raft Baseball Basketball Cross-country Field_Hockey Football Golf Lacrosse Soccer Softball Swim Tennis Volleyball Watersports Wrestling.
Fees 2012: Res $4995-9995 (+$300), 3-8 wks.
Housing: Dorms. **Swimming:** Lake Pool.
Est 2004. Inc. **Spons:** Wellspring Weight Loss Programs. **Ses:** 6. **Wks/ses:** 3-8. Operates June-Aug.

Wellspring New York's clinical weight-loss program focuses on behavioral change as a way of sustaining healthy living. Sessions use methods such as stimulus control, decision counseling, rational emotive therapy, relapse prevention training, positive focusing and stress management. Educational seminars and poetry workshops are also featured. Professional chefs conduct sessions on healthy foods preparation. Applicants must be at least 20 pounds overweight and must have been attempting to lose weight for at least a year.

CAMP WING/DUXBURY STOCKADE
Res — Coed Ages 7-14

Duxbury, MA 02332. 742 Keene St. Tel: 781-837-4279. Fax: 781-837-3892.
Contact (Sept-May): c/o Crossroads for Kids, 119 Myrtle St, Duxbury, MA 02332.
   Tel: 781-834-2700. Fax: 781-834-2701.
Year-round Toll-free: 888-543-7284.
www.crossroads4kids.org   E-mail: info@crossroads4kids.org
Pat Cleary, Dir.
Adm: FCFS. **Appl due:** Apr. **Enr:** 320. **Staff:** Admin 8. Couns 87. Special needs 1.
Conditions accepted: ED. **Therapy:** Art Music.
Features: Computers Crafts Creative_Writing Dance Drama Fine_Arts Aquatics Archery Boating Canoe Exploration Farm Hiking Sail Baseball Basketball Football Soccer Swim Volleyball Watersports.
Fees 2009: Res $1160-1655, 2-3 wks.
Housing: Cabins. **Swimming:** Lake Pool.
Est 1936. Nonprofit. **Ses:** 3. **Wks/ses:** 2-3. Operates June-Aug. ACA.

The camp offers a variety of activities designed to help emotionally and behaviorally at-risk youth build their self-esteem. Boys and girls engage in a wide range of traditional summer recreational pursuits.

WISCONSIN BADGER CAMP
Res — Coed Ages 3 and up

Prairie du Chien, WI 53821. 11815 Munz Ln. Tel: 608-988-4558. Fax: 608-988-4586.
Contact (Sept-May): PO Box 723, Platteville, WI 53818. Tel: 608-348-9689.
   Fax: 608-348-9737.
www.badgercamp.org   E-mail: wiscbadgercamp@centurytel.net
Brent Bowers, Exec Dir.
Adm: FCFS. **Appl due:** Rolling. **Enr:** 104. **Enr cap:** 104. **Staff:** Admin 5. Couns 40. Special needs 3.
Conditions accepted: ADD ADHD Asp Au CP D ED Ep ID LD Phys_Impair Speech & Lang TBI Visual_Impair.
Features: Crafts Drama Music Aquatics Archery Canoe Fishing Hiking Riding Woodcraft Baseball Basketball Equestrian Soccer Softball Swim Volleyball.
Fees 2012: Res $600-1200, 1-2 wks. Aid 2010 (Need): $273,125.
Housing: Cabins Dorms Lodges. **Swimming:** Pool.
Est 1966. Nonprofit. **Ses:** 10. **Wks/ses:** 1-2. Operates June-Aug. ACA.

This camp for children and adults with developmental disabilities offers creative programs and a host of activities: swimming, camping, hiking, fishing, nature studies, arts and crafts, an animal farm, dances, a talent show, Olympic-style games, cookouts, campfires and theme weeks. A tripping program features horseback riding and a trek down the Mississippi River, among other options.

WISCONSIN LIONS CAMP
Res — Coed Ages 6-17

Rosholt, WI 54473. 3834 County Rd A. Tel: 715-677-4761. TTY: 715-677-6999. Fax: 715-677-3297.
www.wisconsinlionscamp.com   E-mail: info@wisconsinlionscamp.com
Adm: FCFS. **Appl due:** Mar. **Enr:** 150. **Enr cap:** 150. **Staff:** Admin 7. Couns 28. Res 55. Special needs 1.
Conditions accepted: D Diabetes ID Visual_Impair.
Features: Crafts Aquatics Archery Boating Canoe Climbing_Wall Fishing Hiking Kayak Ropes_Crse Sail Basketball Field_Hockey Soccer Swim Volleyball.
Fees 2012: Free. Res 1 wk.
Housing: Cabins. Avg per room/unit: 7. **Swimming:** Lake.
Est 1956. Nonprofit. **Ses:** 12. **Wks/ses:** 1. Operates June-Aug. ACA.

WLC offers separate camping sessions for children with visual, hearing or mild cognitive disabilities, and children with diabetes. All programs are offered free of charge to Wisconsin residents; nonresidents are admitted on a space-available basis after the deadline and pay a minimal fee. Typical camp activities include swimming, canoeing, sailing, boating, kayaking, fishing, archery, crafts, nature programs, sports and games. Older campers take canoeing and backpacking trips.

CAMPS WITH A
RELIGIOUS FOCUS

These recreational programs are arranged in alphabetical state order, and within each state, programs are arranged alphabetically first by town and then name. An index beginning on page 610 lists programs by religion, as shown in the Table of Contents. Programs offering a family session are indicated by "FAM" at the end of the age range in the index.

Although similar in many ways to traditional recreational camps, these programs place a primary emphasis on religious activities and values. While many camps in this chapter identify themselves as nondenominational Christian, others affiliate themselves with a specific religion.

INDEX BY RELIGION

LUTHERAN

LUTHERAN *(CONT.)*

LUTHERAN-MISSOURI SYNOD

MENNONITE

NONDENOM CHRISTIAN

ORTHODOX JEWISH

PRESBYTERIAN

PRESBYTERIAN *(CONT.)*

Camps with a Religious Focus

ALABAMA

CAMP ALAMISCO
Res — Coed Ages 7-17

Dadeville, AL 36853. 1771 Camp Alamisco Rd. Tel: 256-825-9482. Fax: 256-825-5484.
Contact (Aug-May): 6450 Atlanta Hwy, Montgomery, AL 36124. Tel: 334-272-7493.
Fax: 334-272-7987.
www.alamisco.org   E-mail: alamisco@gscsda.org
James Mangum, Dir.
Grades 1-12. Adm: FCFS.
Features: Crafts Archery Canoe Mtn_Biking Riding Rock_Climb Basketball Gymnastics Swim Water-skiing Watersports.
Fees 2010: Res $250-300 (+$25), 1 wk.
Swimming: Lake.
Est 1967. Nonprofit. Seventh-day Adventist. Ses: 4. Wks/ses: 1. Operates June-July. ACA.

Operated by the Seventh-day Adventist Church, Alamisco schedules morning and evening all-camp worship, as well as counselor-planned cabin worship and a Friday night Bible pageant. Recreational activities include rock climbing, camping, mountain biking, horsemanship, canoeing, swimming, water-skiing, nature study, sports and crafts.

CAMP SKYLINE
Res — Girls Ages 6-16

Mentone, AL 35984. 4888 Alabama Hwy 117, PO Box 287. Tel: 256-634-4001, 800-448-9279. Fax: 256-634-3018.
www.campskyline.com   E-mail: info@campskyline.com
Sally C. Johnson & Alisa Harrison Gillis, Dirs.
Grades 1-10. Adm: FCFS. Appl due: Rolling. Enr: 300. Enr cap: 300. Staff: Admin 10. Couns 90.
Features: Circus_Skills Crafts Dance Music Painting Theater Aquatics Archery Canoe Climbing_Wall Cooking Mtn_Biking Riding Riflery Ropes_Crse White-water_Raft Basketball Equestrian Golf Gymnastics Lacrosse Soccer Softball Swim Tennis Volleyball.
Fees 2012: Res $1520-2835, 1-2 wks. Aid avail.
Housing: Cabins. Avg per room/unit: 15. Swimming: Pool River.
Est 1947. Inc. Nondenom Christian. Ses: 7. Wks/ses: 1-2. Operates June-Aug. ACA.

Located atop Lookout Mountain, this Christian camp maintains a spiritual emphasis, with horseback riding, circus skills, ropes courses, mountain biking, canoeing and archery among its activities. Campers also choose from an array of traditional recreational pursuits. A well-regarded horsemanship program, set on three large riding rings, focuses upon English riding. In addition to its standard two-week sessions, Skyline schedules weeklong programs for children ages 6-8.

ARKANSAS

CAMP BEAR TRACK
Res — Coed Ages 7-15

Drasco, AR 72530. 295 Prim Rd, PO Box 125. Tel: 501-825-8222. Fax: 501-825-8255.
www.campbeartrack.com   E-mail: info@campbeartrack.com
Jack Dowell & Olivia Dowell, Dirs.
Grades 2-10. Adm: FCFS. Appl due: Rolling. Enr: 110. Enr cap: 120. Staff: Admin 7. Couns 40.
Travel: NC TN.
Features: Crafts Adventure_Travel Aquatics Canoe Climbing_Wall Cooking Hiking Mountaineering Mtn_Biking Outdoor_Ed Rappelling Riding Riflery Rock_Climb Ropes_Crse White-water_Raft Wilderness_Camp Basketball Cheerleading Equestrian Extreme_ Sports Golf Lacrosse Soccer Swim Tennis Ultimate_Frisbee Volleyball Water-skiing Watersports.
Fees 2010: Res $850-1800, 1-2 wks. Aid 2007 (Need): $4000.
Housing: Cabins. Avg per room/unit: 10. Swimming: Lake Pool.
Est 1994. Inc. Nondenom Christian. Ses: 6. Wks/ses: 1-2. Operates June-Aug. ACA.

Located on a 200-acre site on Greers Ferry Lake in the Ozark Mountains, Bear Track offers most traditional camping activities. In addition, the program includes cheerleading, model railroad construction and extreme sports. An adventure tripping camp features backpacking, camping and white-water rafting through Tennessee and North Carolina.

CALIFORNIA

CAMP ALONIM
Res — Coed Ages 5-17

Brandeis, CA 93064. 1101 Peppertree Ln.
Contact (Sept-Apr): 1101 Peppertree Ln, Brandeis, CA 93064.
Year-round Tel: 310-440-1234, 877-225-6646. Fax: 877-856-3250.
www.alonim.com   E-mail: alonim@ajula.edu
Josh Levine, Dir.
Adm: FCFS. Appl due: Rolling.
Fees 2010: Res $980-2440, 1-3 wks.
Est 1941. Jewish. Ses: 4. Wks/ses: 1-3. Operates June-Aug. ACA.

Alonim's program combines recreational camping and Jewish cultural programming. Activities include sports, riding, swimming, crafts, drama, music and folk dancing. Jewish heritage and culture are emphasized, and kashrut is observed.

WILSHIRE BOULEVARD TEMPLE CAMPS
Res — Coed Ages 8-15

Malibu, CA 90265. 11495 E Pacific Coast Hwy. Tel: 310-457-7861. Fax: 310-457-4614.
Contact (Sept-May): 3663 Wilshire Blvd, Los Angeles, CA 90010. Tel: 213-388-2401. Fax: 213-388-2595.
www.wbtcamps.org   E-mail: info@wbtcamps.org
Douglas Lynn, Dir.
Grades 3-10. Adm: FCFS.
Features: Crafts Dance Music Theater Aquatics Archery Climbing_Wall Hiking Mtn_Biking

Rappelling Ropes_Crse Scuba Baseball Basketball Equestrian Golf Soccer Softball Swim Tennis Volleyball Watersports.
Fees 2012: Res $1440-4260, 1-3½ wks.
Swimming: Ocean Pool.
Est 1952. Jewish. Ses: 5. **Wks/ses:** 1-3½. Operates June-Aug. ACA.

Situated on adjoining sites, Camp Hess Kramer and Gindling Hilltop Camp provide a balance of recreational, religious and cultural programming through sports, music, drama, arts and crafts, nature, and daily and Shabbat worship. Special teen programs focus on self-esteem, peer pressure, substance abuse and social responsibility, in addition to the regular camp activities. Teens may take part in mitzvah and leadership programs.

CAMP WAWONA
Res — Coed Ages 7-17

Wawona, CA 95389. PO Box 2055. Tel: 209-375-6231. Fax: 209-375-1527.
www.campwawona.org   E-mail: office@campwawona.org
Elden Ramirez, Dir.
Adm: FCFS. **Appl due:** Rolling.
Features: Astron Ecol Sci Ceramics Crafts Filmmaking Fine_Arts Media Music Photog Aquatics Archery Bicycle_Tours Boating Climbing_Wall Conservation Hiking Mountaineering Mtn_Trips Pack_Train Rappelling Rock_Climb Ropes_Crse Survival_Trng Whitewater_Raft Wilderness_Camp Basketball Equestrian Gymnastics Softball Swim Volleyball Water-skiing Watersports.
Fees 2011: Res $275-725, 1 wk.
Housing: Cabins Dorms Lodges Tents Tepees. Avg per room/unit: 7. **Swimming:** Pool River.
Est 1929. Nonprofit. Seventh-day Adventist. Ses: 6. **Wks/ses:** 1-6. Operates June-Aug. ACA.

Located in Yosemite National Park, this Seventh-day Adventist camp offers various weeklong programs. Special sessions emphasize wakeboarding, water-skiing, rock climbing, backpacking, wilderness survival skills, drama, digital photography, videography, guitar and equestrianism.

COLORADO

EAGLE LAKE RESIDENT CAMPS
Res — Coed Ages 8-18

Colorado Springs, CO 80934. PO Box 6819. Tel: 719-472-1260, 800-873-2453.
Fax: 719-623-0148.
www.eaglelake.org   E-mail: registrar.el@navigators.org
Mark Heffentrager, Dir.
Grades 3-12. Adm: FCFS. **Enr:** 200. **Staff:** Admin 12. Couns 85.
Features: Crafts Music Archery Canoe Fishing Hiking Mtn_Biking Mtn_Trips Ranch Rappelling Rock_Climb Ropes_Crse Sail Survival_Trng Wilderness_Camp Work Equestrian Swim Volleyball.
Fees 2011: Res $375-735, 1-2 wks. Day $199.
Housing: Cabins Tents Tepees. **Swimming:** Lake.
Est 1957. Nonprofit. Spons: Navigators Ministry. Nondenom Christian. **Ses:** 10. **Wks/ses:** 1-2. Operates June-Aug. ACA.

Consisting of beginning (ages 8-11), junior high (ages 12-14) and senior high (ages 15-18) programs, the camps maintain a wide selection of recreational activities that revolve around an annual theme. In the morning, campers undertake such group-oriented activities as hikes, problem-solving initiatives and games; in the afternoon, boys and girls have free time; an in the evening the focus turns to campfires and concerts. All attendees study the Bible and learn tenets of Christianity.

J-CC RANCH CAMP
Res — Coed Ages 7-16

Elbert, CO 80106. 21441 N Elbert Rd. Tel: 303-648-3800. Fax: 800-630-8469.
Contact (Winter): c/o Robert E Loup Jewish Community Ctr, 350 S Dahlia St, Denver, CO 80246. Tel: 303-316-6384. Fax: 303-320-0042.
www.ranchcamp.org   E-mail: miriams@jccdenver.org
Miriam Shwartz & Gilad Shwartz, Dirs.
Grades 2-10. Adm: FCFS. **Appl due:** Rolling. **Enr:** 200. **Enr cap:** 200. **Staff:** Admin 2. Couns 80.
Features: Crafts Drama Music Adventure_Travel Aquatics Archery Bicycle_Tours Canoe Climbing_Wall Conservation Exploration Hiking Mountaineering Mtn_Biking Mtn_Trips Ranch Riding Rock_Climb Ropes_Crse Wilderness_Camp Equestrian Soccer Swim Watersports.
Fees 2012: Res $1190-4325 (+$156), 1-4 wks. Aid avail.
Housing: Cabins. Avg per room/unit: 12. **Swimming:** Pool.
Est 1953. Nonprofit. **Spons:** Robert E. Loup Jewish Community Center. Jewish. **Ses:** 4. **Wks/ses:** 1-4. Operates June-Aug.

Situated on 400 acres in Colorado's Black Forest, J-CC Ranch Camp provides a varied camping experience that integrates Jewish values, traditions and services. In addition to its flagship ranch program, J-CC conducts an equestrian program featuring Western riding, feeding and grooming, and horse show performances. Mountain biking adventures, a travel program and other specialty programs are available to teens.

SKY RANCH
Res — Coed Ages 7-14

Fort Collins, CO 80521. 805 S Shields St. Tel: 970-493-5258. Fax: 970-493-7960.
www.fortnet.org/skyranch   E-mail: info@ldoubler.org
Rod Pearce, Exec Dir.
Grades 2-9. Adm: FCFS. **Appl due:** Rolling.
Features: Environ_Sci Crafts Hiking Peace/Cross-cultural Ropes_Crse.
Fees 2009: Res $199-475, ½-1 wk.
Est 1963. Nondenom Christian. **Ses:** 7. **Wks/ses:** ½-1. Operates June-Aug. ACA.

Sky Ranch's program features Bible study, peace and justice issues, and environmental education.

MAURICE B. SHWAYDER CAMP
OF CONGREGRATION EMANUEL
Res — Coed Ages 7-15

Idaho Springs, CO 80452. 9118 State Hwy 103. Tel: 303-567-2722. Fax: 303-567-0172.
Contact (Sept-May): 51 Grape St, Denver, CO 80220. Tel: 303-388-4013.
Fax: 303-388-6328.
www.shwayder.com   E-mail: info@shwayder.com
Zim S. A. Zimmerman, Dir.
Grades 2-10. Adm: FCFS. **Appl due:** Rolling. **Enr:** 120. **Enr cap:** 120. **Staff:** Admin 5. Couns 30.
Features: Lang Crafts Dance Drama Filmmaking Fine_Arts Media Music Painting Photog

Studio_Art Adventure_Travel Archery Conservation Exploration Hiking Mountaineering Mtn_Trips Outdoor_Ed Riding Ropes_Crse Wilderness_Camp Baseball Basketball Equestrian Soccer Softball Ultimate_Frisbee Volleyball.
Fees 2009: Res $870-1725 (+$25), 1-2 wks. Aid 2006 (Need): $30,000.
Housing: Cabins Tents. Avg per room/unit: 12.
Est 1948. Nonprofit. Jewish. **Ses:** 6. **Wks/ses:** 1-2. Operates June-Aug. ACA.

Situated on a 240-acre site at an elevation of 10,200 feet in the Rocky Mountains, Shwayder is one of the country's oldest Reform Jewish camps. Campers may go hiking, backpacking and overnight camping in the Arapaho National Forest. Among other popular activities are riding, sports and the creative arts. The program revolves around Judaism, and boys and girls attend weekly Shabbat celebrations. One-week sessions serve children entering grades 2-4 only; all other campers attend for two weeks.

CONNECTICUT

CAMP LAURELWOOD
Res — Coed Ages 7-16

Madison, CT 06443. 463 Summer Hill Rd. Tel: 203-421-3736. Fax: 203-421-3570.
www.camplaurelwood.org   E-mail: info@camplaurelwood.org
Ruth Ann Ornstein, Exec Dir.
Adm: FCFS. **Appl due:** May.
Features: Crafts Dance Archery Hiking Mtn_Biking Ropes_Crse Baseball Basketball Golf Gymnastics Soccer Softball Swim Tennis.
Fees 2012: Res $2975-6500 (+$25-100), 2-7 wks. Day $350-2250, 1-7 wks.
Housing: Cabins. **Swimming:** Lake Pool.
Est 1936. Jewish. **Ses:** 13. **Wks/ses:** 1-7. Operates June-Aug. ACA.

Emphasizing Jewish traditions and culture, Laurelwood offers a complete sports program, as well as instruction in music, dance, drama, arts and crafts, photography, pioneering, boating, sailing and gymnastics.

FLORIDA

CAMP WORLDLIGHT
Res — Girls Ages 8-18

Jacksonville, FL 32207. 1230 Hendricks Ave. Tel: 904-596-3141, 800-226-8584.
Fax: 904-596-4472.
www.campworldlight.org   E-mail: campworldlight@flbaptist.org
Anne M. Wilson, Dir.
Grades 3-12. Adm: FCFS. **Appl due:** Rolling. **Enr:** 120. **Enr cap:** 150. **Staff:** Admin 8. Couns 25.
Features: Crafts Dance Music Theater Aquatics Canoe Climbing_Wall Peace/Cross-cultural Ropes_Crse Gymnastics Swim.
Fees 2012: Res $230 (+$60), 1 wk.
Housing: Cabins. **Swimming:** Lake Pool.
Est 1946. Nonprofit. Baptist. **Ses:** 5. **Wks/ses:** 1. Operates June-July. ACA.

The Women's Missions and Ministries Department of the Florida Baptist Convention runs girls' camps at two locations. Campers in both programs take part in boating, cultural experiences and Bible study and also choose from such activities as cheerleading, gymnastics, crafts, and fitness and music classes.

CAMP DOVEWOOD
Res — Girls Ages 7-14

O'Brien, FL 32071. 23221 101st Rd. Tel: 386-935-0863. Fax: 386-935-0863.
www.campdovewood.org   E-mail: campdovewood@windstream.net
Roberta Richmond, Dir.
Grades 2-9. Adm: FCFS. Admitted: 98%. **Appl due:** Rolling. **Enr:** 83. **Enr cap:** 83. **Staff:** Admin 14. Couns 12. Res 2.
Features: Computers Crafts Dance Drama Music Photog Aquatics Archery Riding Basketball Equestrian Gymnastics Martial_Arts Soccer Softball Swim Tennis Volleyball Watersports.
Fees 2009: Res $499-860 (+$75), 1-2 wks.
Housing: Cabins. Avg per room/unit: 8-14. **Swimming:** Pool.
Est 1977. Nonprofit. Nondenom Christian. **Ses:** 4. **Wks/ses:** 1-2. Operates June-July. ACA.

With its staff consisting exclusively of born-again Christians, Dovewood offers a variety of recreational programs in a Christian setting. A horsemanship program addresses English and Western riding, as well as grooming, feeding, veterinary care and general horse care; a ballet program teaches basic fundamentals and choreography; and a gymnastics program focuses upon technique and exercises, culminating in a day of competition. Other activities include tennis and various other sports, overnight trail riding, river rafting and opportunities in the arts.

DOGWOOD ACRES
Res — Coed Ages 7-17

Vernon, FL 32462. PO Box 369. Tel: 850-535-2695. Fax: 850-535-7414.
Contact (Aug-May): PO Box 7, Chipley, FL 32428. Tel: 850-638-2322.
Fax: 850-638-2373.
www.dogwoodacres.org   E-mail: dogwoodacres@presbyteryofflorida.com
Kevin Veldhuisen, Dir.
Grades 2-12. Adm: FCFS. **Appl due:** Rolling. **Enr:** 65. **Enr cap:** 100. **Staff:** Admin 1. Couns 15.
Features: Crafts Dance Drama Music Aquatics Archery Canoe Fishing Hiking Ropes_Crse Basketball Swim Ultimate_Frisbee.
Fees 2010: Res $175-300, ½-1 wk. Aid 2007 (Need): $3700.
Housing: Cabins Tents. Avg per room/unit: 6. **Swimming:** Lake Pond Pool.
Est 1966. Nonprofit. Presbyterian. **Ses:** 8. **Wks/ses:** ½-1. Operates June-Aug.

Camp life at Dogwood Acres revolves around such Christian practices as Bible study, devotions and worship. Boys and girls take part in recreational activities as part of a small group that typically consists of six boys, six girls, a male counselor and a female counselor. Camp structure varies according to age.

GEORGIA

CAMP BARNEY MEDINTZ
Res — Coed Ages 8-16

Cleveland, GA 30528. 4165 Hwy 129 N. Tel: 706-865-2715. Fax: 706-865-1495.
Contact (Sept-May): c/o Marcus Jewish Community Ctr of Atlanta, 5342 Tilly Mill Rd, Dunwoody, GA 30338. Tel: 678-812-3844. Fax: 770-481-0101.
www.campbarney.org   E-mail: summer@campbarney.org
Jim Mittenthal, Dir.
Grades 3-11. Adm: FCFS. Staff: Admin 6.
Features: Writing/Journ Crafts Dance Music Theater Adventure_Travel Aquatics Archery Boating Canoe Climbing_Wall Conservation Farm Fishing Hiking Kayak Mtn_Biking Mtn_Trips Riding Rock_Climb Ropes_Crse Sail Scuba Survival_Trng White-water_Raft Wilderness_Camp Basketball Equestrian Football Martial_Arts Soccer Softball Swim Tennis Volleyball Water-skiing Watersports.
Fees 2012: Res $2850-4950 (+$75), 2-4 wks.
Housing: Cabins Tents. **Swimming:** Lake Pool.
Est 1963. Nonprofit. **Spons:** Atlanta Jewish Community Center. Jewish. **Ses:** 3. **Wks/ses:** 2-4. Operates June-Aug. ACA.

Children experience their Jewish heritage at the camp through exposure to traditional Jewish values, culture and history. Camp Barney holds Shabbat services and maintains a kosher kitchen. Activities include a full waterfront program, individual and team sports, horseback riding and adventure pursuits. The camps also holds a four-week session for campers with special needs.

CALVIN CENTER
Res — Coed Ages 12-14

Hampton, GA 30228. 13550 Woolsey Rd. Tel: 770-946-4276. Fax: 770-946-4191.
www.calvincenter.org
Paul Fogg, Exec Dir.
Adm: FCFS.
Features: Riding Sail Watersports.
Fees 2009: Res $160-630, 1-1½ wks.
Est 1959. Presbyterian. **Ses:** 3. **Wks/ses:** 1-1½. Operates June-July. ACA.

Operated for the member churches of the Presbytery, Calvin Center offers traditional activities such as canoeing and kayaking, creative arts, swimming, Bible study, fishing, hiking and nature study.

WINSHAPE CAMPS
Res — Coord Ages 7-17

Mount Berry, GA 30149. PO Box 490009. Tel: 706-238-7717, 800-448-6955.
Fax: 706-238-7742.
www.winshapecamps.org   E-mail: info@winshapecamps.org
David Trejo & Trudy Cathy White, Dirs.
Grades 2-12. Adm: FCFS. Admitted: 95%. Appl due: Rolling. **Enr:** 500. **Enr cap:** 500.
Staff: Admin 9. Couns 200.
Features: Crafts Dance Photog Theater Adventure_Travel Aquatics Archery Caving Climbing_Wall Hiking Mtn_Biking Mtn_Trips Riding Rock_Climb Ropes_Crse White-water_Raft Wilderness_Camp Yoga Basketball Football Soccer Softball Swim Tennis Ultimate_Frisbee Volleyball Water-skiing Weight_Trng Wrestling.
Fees 2009: Res $1395, 2 wks. Aid (Need).

Housing: Cabins Dorms. Avg per room/unit: 4-6. **Swimming:** Pool.
Est 1985. Nonprofit. Nondenom Christian. **Ses:** 4. **Wks/ses:** 2. Operates June-July. ACA.

Divided into boys and girls divisions, WinShape offers many traditional camping activities. In addition to the regular in-camp pursuits, both divisions offer programs that allow campers to experience more of the outdoors. The boys' Sioux and the girls' Creek sessions offer adventures for those in grades 11 and 12 in rock climbing, white-water rafting and extended overnight camping. All programs have a strong Christian focus.

IDAHO

CAMP PERKINS
Res — Coed Ages 10-17

Ketchum, ID 83340. HC 64, Box 9384.
Contact (Oct-May): PO Box 1965, Hailey, ID 83333.
Year-round Tel: 208-788-0897.
www.campperkins.org   E-mail: info@campperkins.org
Signe White, Exec Dir.
Grades 5-12. Adm: FCFS. **Appl due:** Rolling. **Staff:** Admin 3. Couns 35.
Features: Crafts Music Photog Aquatics Boating Canoe Climbing_Wall Fishing Hiking Kayak Mtn_Biking Mtn_Trips Ropes_Crse Sail White-water_Raft Wilderness_Camp Swim.
Fees 2011: Res $275-355, 1 wk. Aid (Need).
Housing: Cabins. Avg per room/unit: 12. **Swimming:** Lake River.
Est 1955. Nonprofit. Lutheran-Missouri Synod. **Ses:** 34. **Wks/ses:** 1. Operates June-Aug.

Perkins provides a Christian camping experience in the Sawtooth Mountains National Forest. In addition to its general youth sessions, the camp conducts specialty sessions emphasizing horseback riding, white-water rafting, fly-fishing, photography, sailing, backpacking and guitar.

ILLINOIS

WALCAMP
Res — Coed Ages 6-17

Kingston, IL 60145. 32653 Five Points Rd. Tel: 815-784-5141. Fax: 815-784-4085.
www.walcamp.org   E-mail: registrar@walcamp.org
Deon Hull, Exec Dir.
Grades 1-12. Adm: FCFS. **Staff:** Admin 3. Couns 23.
Features: Astron Ecol Environ_Sci Crafts Creative_Writing Drama Adventure_Travel Aquatics Canoe Climbing_Wall Community_Serv Fishing Hiking Outdoor_Ed Riding Ropes_Crse Survival_Trng Wilderness_Camp Wilderness_Canoe Equestrian Swim.
Fees 2011: Res $430-555, 1 wk.
Housing: Cabins Lodges Tents. **Swimming:** Lake River.
Est 1963. Nonprofit. Lutheran. **Ses:** 58. **Wks/ses:** 1. Operates June-Aug. ACA.

Provided in a Christian setting, Walcamp offers recreational activities, Bible studies, devotions, campfires, canoeing, swimming, and arts and crafts. Other offerings are special-interest and trip camps and adventure camping. A special program serves children and adults with cognitive disabilities.

JENSEN WOODS CAMP
Res — Coed Ages 7-17

Timewell, IL 62375. RR 1, Box 150. Tel: 217-773-2491. Fax: 217-773-3001.
www.jensenwoods.com E-mail: jensenwoods@igrcamp.org
Grades 2-12. Adm: FCFS. **Appl due:** Rolling. **Enr:** 90. **Staff:** Admin 3. Couns 15.
Features: Photog Aquatics Archery Boating Cooking Exploration Fishing Hiking Riding Swim.
Fees 2009: Res $145-455, ½-1 wk.
Housing: Tents. Avg per room/unit: 8. **Swimming:** Lake Stream.
Est 1963. Nonprofit. United Methodist. **Ses:** 26. **Wks/ses:** ½-1. Operates June-Aug.

Located on 550 wooded acres, Jensen Woods is a faith-based camp that combines recreation with Bible study and campfire worship. Archery, horseback riding, mountain biking and craft specialty camps allow campers to focus on an area of interest. Family horse camps accommodate children of all ages and their families.

INDIANA

CAMP LIVINGSTON
Res — Coed Ages 8-17

Bennington, IN 47011. 4998 Nell Lee Rd. Tel: 812-427-2202. Fax: 812-427-3699.
Contact (Sept-May): 8401 Montgomery Rd, Cincinnati, OH 45236. Tel: 513-793-5554.
Fax: 513-793-5004.
Year-round Toll-free: 888-564-2267.
www.camplivingston.com E-mail: info@camplivingston.com
Ben Davis, Exec Dir.
Grades 3-12. Adm: FCFS. **Appl due:** Rolling. **Enr:** 200. **Enr cap:** 225. **Staff:** Admin 20. Couns 55.
Features: Ecol Crafts Dance Drama Music Painting Photog Adventure_Travel Aquatics Archery Boating Canoe Caving Climbing_Wall Community_Serv Conservation Exploration Fishing Hiking Kayak Mtn_Biking Outdoor_Ed Peace/Cross-cultural Rappelling Riding Rock_Climb Ropes_Crse Social_Servs White-water_Raft Wilderness_Camp Wilderness_Canoe Yoga Baseball Basketball Equestrian Football Golf Gymnastics Lacrosse Roller_Hockey Soccer Softball Street_Hockey Swim Team_Handball Tennis Ultimate_Frisbee Volleyball Watersports.
Fees 2012: Res $1995-3880 (+$50), 2-4 wks. Aid 2011 (Merit & Need): $48,000.
Housing: Cabins Tents. Avg per room/unit: 10. **Swimming:** Lake Pool.
Est 1920. Nonprofit. **Spons:** Jewish Community Center Association. Jewish. **Ses:** 5. **Wks/ses:** 2-4. Operates June-Aug. ACA.

This Jewish camp provides a range of traditional recreational options. The equestrian program addresses all aspects of horsemanship, including grooming, saddling and trail riding. An adventure program for campers entering grade 1o teaches outdoor living skills as campers embark on hiking, caving and rafting trips. Bar and Bat Mitzvah tutoring is available at no additional fee. A trip to Israel is available to 15- to 17-year-olds.

CAMP PYOCA
Res — Coed Ages 6-17

Brownstown, IN 47220. 886 E County Rd 100 S. Tel: 812-358-3413, 866-251-2267.
Fax: 812-358-5501.
www.pyoca.org E-mail: pyoca@pyoca.org
Maggie Platt, Prgm Dir.

Grades 1-12. Adm: FCFS. Admitted: 99%. **Appl due:** Rolling. **Enr:** 100. **Staff:** Admin 3. Couns 15.
Features: Ecol Environ_Sci Crafts Dance Music Theater Adventure_Travel Aquatics Boating Canoe Climbing_Wall Fishing Hiking Kayak Outdoor_Ed Ropes_Crse White-water_Raft Wilderness_Camp Basketball Soccer Swim Ultimate_Frisbee Volleyball.
Fees 2010: Res $163-408, ½-1 wk. Aid 2007 (Need): $4000.
Housing: Cabins Tents Tepees. Avg per room/unit: 20. **Swimming:** Lake.
Est 1952. Nonprofit. Presbyterian. **Ses:** 12. **Wks/ses:** ½-1. Operates June-Aug. ACA.

Pyoca offers a selection of traditional recreational programs. Specialty programs include an explorers' camp (grades 2-3); a discovery camp (grades 4-6); junior high (grades 7-9) and senior high camps (grades 10-12); and work and adventure camps.

CAMP ALEXANDER MACK
Res — Coed Ages 7-18

Milford, IN 46542. PO Box 158. Tel: 574-658-4831.
www.campmack.org   E-mail: info@campmack.org
Rex M. Miller, Exec Dir.
Grades 2-PG. Adm: FCFS. **Appl due:** Mar. **Enr:** 150. **Enr cap:** 180. **Staff:** Admin 6. Couns 100. Res 3.
Features: Environ_Sci Crafts Music Adventure_Travel Aquatics Bicycle_Tours Canoe Caving Climbing_Wall Cooking Field_Ecol Hiking Kayak Ropes_Crse Sail Wilderness_Camp Baseball Basketball Soccer Softball Swim Volleyball.
Fees 2011: Res $283-451, ½-1 wk. Aid 2009 (Need): $10,250.
Housing: Cabins Dorms Tents. Avg per room/unit: 6. **Swimming:** Lake.
Est 1925. Nonprofit. Church of the Brethren. **Ses:** 19. **Wks/ses:** ½-1. Operates June-Aug. ACA.

Owned and operated by the Church of the Brethren in Indiana, Camp Mack offers swimming, crafts, hiking, a low ropes course, sailing, Bible study and worship, nature, boating, Brethren heritage, singing, kayaking, canoeing and cookouts. Sessions that focus on adventure and the environment are also offered.

IOWA

CAMP SHALOM
Res — Coed Ages 7-18

Maquoketa, IA 52060. 6262 Caves Rd. Tel: 563-652-3311.
Contact (Sept-May): 2136 Brady St, Davenport, IA 52803. Tel: 563-323-2790.
Year-round Fax: 563-326-1422.
www.campshalomia.org   E-mail: office@campshalomia.org
Rev. Eric Elkin, Exec Dir.
Grades 2-12. Adm: FCFS. **Appl due:** Rolling. **Staff:** Admin 3. Couns 15.
Features: Crafts Music Canoe Mtn_Trips Wilderness_Camp Swim.
Fees 2011: Res $150-500, ½-1 wk.
Housing: Cabins Lodges. **Swimming:** Pool River.
Est 1976. Nonprofit. Ecumenical. **Ses:** 8. **Wks/ses:** ½-1. Operates June-Aug. ACA.

Crafts, music, canoeing and mountain trips are some of this ecumenical Christian camp's recreational pursuits.

LUTHERAN LAKESIDE CAMP
Res — Coed Ages 7-18

Spirit Lake, IA 51360. 2491 170th St. Tel: 712-336-2109. Fax: 712-336-0638.
www.lutheranlakeside.com   E-mail: carolyn@lutheranlakeside.com
Carolyn Fritsch & Jerry Fritsch, Exec Dirs.
Grades 2-PG. Adm: FCFS. **Appl due:** Rolling. **Staff:** Admin 3. Couns 30.
Features: Music Aquatics Archery Canoe Fishing Kayak Sail Scuba Soccer Swim.
Fees 2010: Res $100-380 (+$40), ½-1 wk.
Housing: Cabins. **Swimming:** Pool.
Est 1960. Nonprofit. Lutheran. **Ses:** 9. **Wks/ses:** ½-1. Operates June-Aug.

Located on the shores of Lake Okoboji, Lakeside offers many waterfront activities, most notably sailing, canoeing, kayaking, boating and fishing. On-site activities include swimming, an adventure course, archery, crafts, hiking, volleyball and basketball.

CAMP WYOMING
Res — Coed Ages 7-17

Wyoming, IA 52362. 9106 42nd Ave. Tel: 563-488-3893. Fax: 563-488-3895.
www.campwyoming.net   E-mail: campwyo@netins.net
Kevin Cullum, Dir.
Grades 2-12. Adm: FCFS. **Appl due:** Rolling. **Staff:** Admin 6. Couns 24.
Conditions accepted: ID Phys_Impair.
Features: Crafts Drama Music Canoe Ropes_Crse Equestrian Swim.
Fees 2011: Res $190-370 (+$10), ½-1 wk.
Housing: Cabins. **Swimming:** Pool.
Est 1960. Nonprofit. Presbyterian. **Ses:** 44. **Wks/ses:** 1. Operates June-Aug. ACA.

This Christian camp combines traditional summer recreation with Bible studies and religious activities. Crafts, music, drama, canoeing, equestrian, a ropes course and swimming are among the camp's popular pursuits. A special-needs week serves individuals age 16 and older who have mild or moderate mental or physical disabilities.

MAINE

NEW ENGLAND CAMP CEDARBROOK
Res — Girls Ages 8-17

Alfred, ME 04002. PO Box 154. Tel: 207-247-5251. Fax: 866-389-6322.
www.newenglandcampcedarbrook.org   E-mail: info@cedarbrookne.org
Becky Riley, Dir.
Grades 3-12. Adm: FCFS. **Appl due:** Rolling. **Enr:** 150. **Staff:** Admin 15. Couns 30.
Features: Crafts Drama Aquatics Archery Boating Canoe Hiking Kayak Mountaineering Riding Riflery Sail White-water_Raft Wilderness_Camp Wilderness_Canoe Basketball Swim Water-skiing.
Fees 2011: Res $480 (+$150), 1 wk. Aid (Need).
Housing: Cabins. Avg per room/unit: 10. **Swimming:** Lake.
Est 1945. Nonprofit. Nondenom Christian. **Ses:** 8. **Wks/ses:** 1. Operates June-Aug. ACA.

Each of Camp Cedarbrook's weekly sessions revolves around a central theme. Traditional recreational pursuits complement the special thematic activities. Certified instructors take older campers backpacking through the White Mountains and canoeing and white-water rafting on the Kennebec River in northern Maine.

CAMP MODIN
Res — Coed Ages 7-16

Belgrade, ME 04917. 51 Modin Way. Tel: 207-465-4444. Fax: 207-465-4447.
Contact (Sept-May): 401 E 80th St, Ste 28EF, New York, NY 10075. Tel: 212-570-1600.
Fax: 212-570-1677.
www.modin.com   E-mail: modin@modin.com
Howard Salzberg & Lisa Wulkan, Dirs.
Adm: FCFS. Appl due: Jan. Enr: 375. Enr cap: 375. Staff: Admin 20. Couns 140.
Travel: Canada.
Features: Crafts Dance Filmmaking Fine_Arts Media Painting Photog Theater Aquatics Archery Boating Canoe Climbing_Wall Community_Serv Fishing Hiking Kayak Mountaineering Mtn_Trips Rappelling Riflery Rock_Climb Ropes_Crse Sail White-water_ Raft Wilderness_Camp Wilderness_Canoe Baseball Basketball Gymnastics Lacrosse Soccer Softball Swim Tennis Volleyball Water-skiing Watersports Weight_Trng.
Fees 2012: Res $6300-10,200 (+$250-500), 3½-7 wks.
Housing: Cabins. Avg per room/unit: 12. Swimming: Lake.
Est 1922. Inc. Jewish. Ses: 3. Wks/ses: 3½-7. Operates June-Aug. ACA.

Located in the Belgrade Lakes region, New England's oldest Jewish summer camp provides professional instruction in various land sports, watersports, the creative and performing arts, and wilderness adventures. Specialized programs for teenagers include cycling tours, whitewater rafting, Canadian excursions and leadership training.

CAMP MICAH
Res — Coed Ages 7-15

Bridgton, ME 04009. 156 Moose Cove Lodge Rd. Tel: 207-647-8999.
Fax: 207-647-4145.
Contact (Sept-May): PO Box 67414, Chestnut Hill, MA 02467. Tel: 617-244-6540.
Fax: 617-277-7108.
www.campmicah.com   E-mail: markl@campmicah.com
Mark Lipof, Dir.
Grades 2-10. Adm: FCFS. Appl due: Rolling. Enr: 270. Staff: Admin 6. Couns 110.
Features: Crafts Dance Filmmaking Media Music Painting Photog Theater Aquatics Archery Bicycle_Tours Boating Canoe Climbing_Wall Fishing Hiking Kayak Mtn_Biking Mtn_Trips Outdoor_Ed Rappelling Riding Riflery Rock_Climb Ropes_Crse Sail Survival_Trng White-water_Raft Wilderness_Camp Yoga Baseball Basketball Field_Hockey Football Golf Gymnastics Lacrosse Martial_Arts Roller_Hockey Rugby Skateboarding Soccer Softball Street_Hockey Swim Tennis Ultimate_Frisbee Volleyball Water-skiing Watersports Weight_Trng Wrestling BMX_Biking.
Fees 2012: Res $3800-9600 (+$200), 2-7 wks.
Housing: Cabins. Swimming: Lake Pool.
Est 2001. Jewish. Ses: 4. Wks/ses: 2-7. Operates June-Aug. ACA.

Jewish traditions and values play an important role at this recreational camp. Micah has six activity periods daily; boys and girls choose their activities within a structured format. Friday evenings feature a Shabbat dinner followed by Shabbat services and a special evening program. Saturdays include optional Shabbat study, guided meditations, Israeli dancing, afternoon all-camp activities, dinner and Havdallah, the service that separates Shabbat from the rest of the week.

CAMP NEWFOUND
CAMP OWATONNA
Res — Coord Ages 7-16

Harrison, ME 04040. 4 Camp Newfound Rd. Tel: 207-583-6711. Fax: 207-583-6710.

www.newfound-owatonna.com   E-mail: info@newfound-owatonna.com
Jamie Bollinger, Exec Dir.
Grades 2-11. Adm: FCFS. **Appl due:** Rolling. **Enr:** 100. **Enr cap:** 100. **Staff:** Admin 2. Couns 70.
Features: Crafts Dance Drama Painting Aquatics Archery Boating Canoe Climbing_Wall Hiking Kayak Mountaineering Rock_Climb Ropes_Crse Sail Wilderness_Camp Wilderness_Canoe Woodcraft Baseball Basketball Field_Hockey Lacrosse Soccer Street_ Hockey Swim Tennis Ultimate_Frisbee Volleyball Water-skiing Watersports.
Fees 2012: Res $1630-4725 (+$80), 2-7 wks. Aid 2006 (Need): $95,000.
Housing: Cabins. Avg per room/unit: 8. **Swimming:** Lake.
Est 1919. Nonprofit. Christian Science. **Ses:** 4. **Wks/ses:** 2-7. Operates June-Aug.

Located on Long Lake, brother and sister camps Newfound for girls and Owatonna for boys conduct an array of traditional camping activities in a Christian Science environment. In addition to a variety of land sports and watersports, the camps offer three-day hiking, canoeing, kayaking, sailing and rock climbing trips. A special two-week session serves first-time campers under age 11.

CAMP BISHOPSWOOD
Res — Coed Ages 7-15

Hope, ME 04847. 98 Bishopswood Rd. Tel: 207-763-3148.
Contact (Sept-June): 143 State St, Portland, ME 04101. Tel: 207-772-1953.
Year-round Toll-free: 800-244-6062, Fax: 207-773-0095.
www.bishopswood.org   E-mail: georgia@bishopswood.org
Georgia L. Koch, Dir.
Grades 2-10. Adm: FCFS. **Appl due:** Rolling. **Enr:** 95. **Enr cap:** 95. **Staff:** Admin 1. Couns 30.
Features: Crafts Drama Music Canoe Cooking Exploration Soccer Softball Swim.
Fees 2011: Res $405, 1 wk.
Housing: Cabins. Avg per room/unit: 10. **Swimming:** Lake.
Est 1962. Nonprofit. Episcopal. **Ses:** 7. **Wks/ses:** 1. Operates June-Aug. ACA.

This Episcopal church camp offers such activities as crafts, swimming, boating, sports, worship opportunities and faith development exercises. Bishopswood encourages campers to attend multiple sessions.

CAMP MECHUWANA
Res — Coed Ages 12-18

Winthrop, ME 04364. PO Box 277. Tel: 207-377-2924. **Fax:** 207-377-4388.
www.mechuwana.org   E-mail: mechuwana@fairpoint.net
Norman Thombs, Dir.
Adm: FCFS. **Appl due:** Rolling. **Enr:** 100-150. **Enr cap:** 100-150.
Features: Crafts Creative_Writing Dance Drama Fine_Arts Photog Aquatics Boating Canoe Hiking Mtn_Trips Outdoor_Ed Wilderness_Camp Wilderness_Canoe Basketball Soccer Swim.
Fees 2010: Res $210-365, 1 wk. Aid avail.
Housing: Cabins. **Swimming:** Lake.
Est 1948. Nonprofit. United Methodist. **Ses:** 8. **Wks/ses:** 1. Operates July-Aug. ACA.

This Methodist camp offers travel tours in addition to on-site programs. In-camp sessions focus on the following: sports, outdoor skills, musical theater and creative arts. Hiking, canoeing and backpacking trips make use of Mechuwana's 240-acre campsite and two lakes.

MARYLAND

CAMP PECOMETH
Res — Coed Ages 8-17; Day — Coed 5-10

Centreville, MD 21617. 136 Bookers Wharf Rd. Tel: 410-556-6900. Fax: 410-556-6901.
www.pecometh.org   E-mail: campinfo@pecometh.org
Richelle Darrell, Dir.
Grades 1-12. Adm: FCFS. **Appl due:** Rolling. **Enr cap:** 200. **Staff:** Admin 5. Couns 75.
Features: Crafts Adventure_Travel Aquatics Archery Canoe Climbing_Wall Hiking Kayak Riding Rock_Climb Ropes_Crse Sail White-water_Raft Wilderness_Camp Basketball Equestrian Soccer Swim Volleyball Watersports.
Fees 2011: Res $249-699, ½-1 wk. **Day** $195, 1 wk. Aid 2010 (Need): $32,000.
Housing: Cabins Dorms Tents. Avg per room/unit: 10. **Swimming:** Pool River.
Est 1946. Nonprofit. United Methodist. **Ses:** 14. **Wks/ses:** ½-1. Operates June-Aug. ACA.

Pecometh conducts riverside programs for young people of all ages. Special programs include adventure camps, aquatics programs, specialty camps and, for an additional fee, a special-needs session. Tripping programs that emphasize rock climbing, white-water rafting and sailing are also available.

CAMP WABANNA
Res — Coed Ages 7-17; Day — Coed 4-13

Edgewater, MD 21037. 101 Likes Rd. Tel: 410-798-0455. Fax: 410-798-1214.
www.campwabanna.org   E-mail: info@campwabanna.org
Tara Peddicord, Dir.
Adm: FCFS. **Appl due:** Rolling. **Staff:** Admin 20. Couns 22.
Features: Marine_Bio/Stud Crafts Dance Photog Aquatics Archery Boating Canoe Climbing_Wall Fishing Kayak Outdoor_Ed Rock_Climb Ropes_Crse Sail Basketball Field_Hockey Football Lacrosse Soccer Street_Hockey Swim Tennis Ultimate_Frisbee Volleyball Watersports.
Fees 2011: Res $385-420, 1 wk. **Day** $255, 1 wk. Aid (Need).
Housing: Cabins. Avg per room/unit: 40. **Swimming:** Pool.
Est 1941. Nonprofit. Nondenom Christian. **Ses:** 8. **Wks/ses:** 1. Operates June-Aug.

This nondenominational Christian camp is located on Chesapeake Bay. Daily Bible study, chapel and individual reflection are integral to the program. Canoeing, crabbing, swimming, rock climbing, games and sailing are popular recreational pursuits.

MAR-LU-RIDGE
Res — Coed Ages 6-17; Day — Coed 6-10

Jefferson, MD 21755. 3200 Mar-Lu-Ridge Rd. Tel: 301-874-5544, 800-238-9974.
Fax: 301-874-5545.
www.mar-lu-ridge.org   E-mail: mlr@mar-lu-ridge.org
Andrew Rickel, Dir.
Grades 1-12. Adm: FCFS. Admitted: 100%. **Appl due:** Rolling. **Enr:** 88. **Enr cap:** 200.
Staff: Admin 4. Couns 24.
Features: Crafts Fine_Arts Music Aquatics Archery Bicycle_Tours Canoe Fishing Hiking Mountaineering Mtn_Trips Rappelling Riding Rock_Climb Ropes_Crse White-water_Raft Basketball Equestrian Swim Volleyball.
Fees 2010: Res $272-780, ½-1 wk. **Day** $175, 1 wk. Aid (Need).
Housing: Cabins Lodges. **Swimming:** Pool.
Est 1959. Nonprofit. Lutheran. **Ses:** 40. **Wks/ses:** ½-1. Operates June-Aug.

A Lutheran camp, Mar-Lu-Ridge stresses worship and Bible study in a traditional recreational environment. Specialty camps address horseback riding, fishing, golf, art, animal studies, biking and canoeing.

RIVER VALLEY RANCH
Res — Coed Ages 7-17; Day — Coed 4-10

Manchester, MD 21102. 4443 Grave Run Rd. Tel: 443-712-1010. Fax: 443-712-1015. www.rivervalleyranch.com   E-mail: info@rivervalleyranch.com
Jon Bisset, Exec Dir.
Grades PS-12. Adm: FCFS. Appl due: Rolling. Enr: 310. Staff: Admin 12. Couns 45. Travel: WV.
Features: Crafts Drama Music Adventure_Travel Archery Climbing_Wall Community_Serv Exploration Hiking Mtn_Biking Paintball Ranch Riding Riflery Rock_Climb Ropes_Crse Survival_Trng Wilderness_Camp Basketball Equestrian Football Skateboarding Soccer Swim Volleyball.
Fees 2011: Res $295-685 (+$25-100), ½-1 wk. Day $250, 1 wk. Aid (Need).
Housing: Cabins Tents Tepees. Swimming: Pool River Stream.
Est 1952. Nonprofit. Nondenom Christian. Ses: 8. Wks/ses: ½-1. Operates June-Aug.

River Valley offers a series of outdoor recreational camps with a strong emphasis on Christian principles. Campers in three age groups choose either classic wilderness camps or specialty programs in trail riding, scouting, horsemanship, rodeo or extreme sports. Swimming, hiking, games, survival and first aid training are featured in most camps.

CAMP ST. CHARLES
Res — Coed Ages 6-13

Newburg, MD 20664. 15375 Stella Maris Dr. Tel: 301-259-2645. Fax: 301-523-9437.
Contact (Sept-May): 9692 Meadowview Dr, Newburg, MD 20664. Tel: 240-233-3106. Fax: 301-576-5944.
www.campstcharles.com   E-mail: csclaurahall@gmail.com
Laura Hall, Dir.
Adm: FCFS. Appl due: Rolling. Enr: 155. Enr cap: 155. Staff: Admin 5. Couns 26.
Features: Environ_Sci Crafts Aquatics Archery Boating Canoe Fishing Riflery Ropes_Crse Wilderness_Camp Basketball Equestrian Football Soccer Softball Swim Volleyball.
Fees 2012: Res $1275 (+$70), 2 wks. Aid (Need).
Housing: Cabins. Avg per room/unit: 23. Swimming: Pool.
Est 1952. Nonprofit. Roman Catholic. Ses: 4. Wks/ses: 2. Operates June-Aug. ACA.

Owned and operated by the Society of the Divine Savior, the camp offers land sports and watersports, trail riding, boating, arts and crafts, archery and riflery ranges, and environmental education.

CAMP WRIGHT
Res — Coed Ages 7-14; Day — Coed 6-14

Stevensville, MD 21666. 400 Camp Wright Ln. Tel: 410-643-4171. Fax: 410-643-8421.
www.campwright.com   E-mail: director@campwright.com
Dee Zeller, Exec Dir.
Grades 1-10. Adm: FCFS. Admitted: 95%. Appl due: Rolling. Enr: 144. Enr cap: 144. Staff: Admin 10. Couns 50.
Features: Writing/Journ Crafts Dance Music Theater Adventure_Travel Aquatics Archery Boating Canoe Community_Serv Conservation Kayak Sail White-water_Raft Wilderness_Camp Basketball Martial_Arts Soccer Swim Tennis Volleyball.
Fees 2010: Res $525-945, 1-1½ wks. Day $185-270, 1 wk. Aid 2009 (Need): $17,000.
Housing: Cabins. Avg per room/unit: 8. Swimming: Pool.

Est 1930. Nonprofit. Episcopal. **Ses:** 7. **Wks/ses:** ½-1½. Operates June-Aug.

The camp combines Christian education with such traditional pursuits as archery, arts and crafts, outdoor living, canoeing, ropes courses, hiking, leadership development, nature studies, sailing and land sports. Biking, kayaking, rafting and wilderness trips round out the program.

MASSACHUSETTS

CAMP BAUERCREST
Res — Boys Ages 7-16

Amesbury, MA 01913. 17 Old County Rd. Tel: 978-388-4732. Fax: 978-388-0303.
Contact (Sept-June): 20 Normandy Dr, Sudbury, MA 01776. Tel: 978-443-0582.
Fax: 978-443-0540.
www.bauercrest.org   E-mail: rob@bauercrest.org
Rob Brockman, Exec Dir.
Grades 2-11. Adm: FCFS. **Appl due:** Rolling. **Enr:** 285. **Staff:** Admin 10. Couns 80.
Features: Crafts Music Photog Theater Aquatics Archery Canoe Hiking Kayak Sail Wilderness_Camp Basketball Golf Soccer Softball Swim Tennis Track Volleyball Water-skiing Watersports Weight_Trng.
Fees 2012: Res $2650-6800, 2-8 wks.
Housing: Cabins. **Swimming:** Lake.
Est 1931. Nonprofit. Jewish. **Ses:** 6. **Wks/ses:** 2-8. Operates June-Aug. ACA.

This Jewish recreational camp's program centers around three general activities: sports, waterfront activities and arts pursuits. A complete program of athletic activities includes land sports, swimming and waterfront sports. Among other features are drama, arts and crafts, photography and trips. Two-week sessions are open to first-time campers only.

EISNER CAMP
Res — Coed Ages 7-15

Great Barrington, MA 01230. PO Box 569. Tel: 413-528-1652. Fax: 413-644-9524.
Contact (Sept-May): 301 Rte 17 N, Rutherford, NJ 07070. Tel: 201-804-9700.
Fax: 201-804-9785.
www.urjnecamps.org   E-mail: necampinstitute@urj.org
Louis Bordman, Dir.
Grades 2-10. Adm: FCFS. **Appl due:** Rolling. **Enr:** 500. **Staff:** Admin 5. Couns 150.
Features: Crafts Creative_Writing Dance Filmmaking Fine_Arts Media Music Photog Theater Aquatics Boating Canoe Climbing_Wall Conservation Cooking Farm Fishing Hiking Kayak Mtn_Biking Rock_Climb Ropes_Crse Basketball Football Martial_Arts Roller_Hockey Soccer Softball Swim Tennis Volleyball.
Fees 2009: Res $1995-7980, 2-8 wks. Aid (Need).
Housing: Cabins. Avg per room/unit: 15. **Swimming:** Lake Pool.
Est 1958. Nonprofit. **Spons:** Union for Reform Judaism. Jewish. **Ses:** 5. **Wks/ses:** 2-8. Operates June-Aug. ACA.

Campers at this camp, which follows the tenets of Reform Judaism, participate in traditional outdoor activities in the Berkshire Mountains while building a religious identity. Creative expression is emphasized through indoor and outdoor theaters, an art center, a photo lab, camp newspaper and an FM radio station. Among group and individual outdoor activities are mountain biking, climbing and hiking.

CAMP RAMAH
Res — Coed Ages 8-16

Palmer, MA 01069. 39 Bennett St. Tel: 413-283-9771. Fax: 413-283-6661.
Contact (Winter): 2 Commerce Way, Norwood, MA 02062. Tel: 781-702-5290.
Fax: 781-702-5239.
www.campramahne.org   E-mail: edg@campramahne.org
Rabbi Ed Gelb, Dir.
Grades 3-10. Adm: FCFS. Appl due: Dec. Enr: 500. Staff: Admin 35. Couns 100.
Features: Lang Crafts Dance Music Photog Theater Aquatics Bicycle_Tours Boating Canoe
Hiking Kayak Mtn_Biking Ropes_Crse Sail Woodcraft Baseball Basketball Gymnastics
Soccer Softball Swim Tennis Volleyball Watersports.
Fees 2012: Res $1840-7520 (+$300-1010), 2-7½ wks.
Housing: Cabins. **Swimming:** Lake.
Est 1953. Nonprofit. **Spons:** Jewish Theological Seminary. Jewish. **Ses:** 5. **Wks/ses:** 2-7½.
Operates June-Aug.

Operated under the auspices of the Jewish Theological Seminary, Ramah places considerable emphasis on Jewish studies and worship. Each day, campers spend two hours in creative programs pertaining to the Hebrew language, Jewish history, religion, law and ethics. Activities include a full waterfront program, sports, trips, music, dance, drama, and arts and crafts.

CAMP PEMBROKE
Res — Girls Ages 8-16

Pembroke, MA 02359. Lake Oldham, 306 Oldham St. Tel: 781-294-8006.
Fax: 781-294-4659.
Contact (Winter): 30 Main St, Ashland, MA 01721. Tel: 508-881-1002.
Fax: 508-881-1006.
www.camppembroke.org   E-mail: pembroke@cohencamps.org
Ellen Felcher, Dir.
Adm: FCFS. Appl due: Rolling.
Features: Art Ceramics Crafts Dance Music Painting Theater Archery Boating Canoe
Riding Ropes_Crse Sail Aerobics Basketball Cheerleading Cross-country Field_Hockey
Figure_Skating Golf Gymnastics Lacrosse Martial_Arts Soccer Softball Swim Tennis
Volleyball Water-skiing.
Fees 2012: Res $4000-7000, 3½-7 wks. Aid (Need).
Housing: Cabins. **Swimming:** Lake Pool.
Est 1935. Jewish. **Ses:** 3. **Wks/ses:** 3½-7. Operates June-Aug. ACA.

Athletics, horseback riding and waterfront sports complement a Judaic program. Shabbath services, Israeli dancing and song, arts and crafts, and dramatics are among the activities.

CRANE LAKE CAMP
Res — Coed Ages 8-15

West Stockbridge, MA 01266. 46 State Line Rd. Tel: 413-232-4257. Fax: 413-232-0290.
Contact (Winter): 56 Ridgewood Rd, Washington Township, NJ 07676.
Tel: 201-722-0400. Fax: 201-722-0444.
www.cranelake.urjcamps.org   E-mail: dshriber@urj.org
Debby Shriber, Dir.
Grades 3-10. Adm: FCFS. Appl due: Rolling. Enr: 350. Staff: Admin 15. Couns 135.
Features: Crafts Dance Fine_Arts Music Theater Aquatics Archery Boating Canoe Climb-
ing_Wall Conservation Farm Fishing Hiking Kayak Mtn_Trips Riding Ropes_Crse Sail
White-water_Raft Aerobics Baseball Basketball Football Golf Gymnastics Lacrosse

Martial_Arts Soccer Softball Street_Hockey Swim Team_Handball Tennis Track Volleyball Water-skiing Watersports.
Fees 2012: Res $2370-9130, 1½-7½ wks. Aid (Need).
Housing: Cabins. **Swimming:** Lake Pool.
Est 1922. Spons: Union for Reform Judaism. Jewish. **Ses:** 5. **Wks/ses:** 1½-7½. Operates June-Aug. ACA.

Crane Lake offers waterfront activities, individual and team sports, and art instruction. Judaic study, services and cultural evening activities are integral to the program. Tutoring is also available.

MICHIGAN

BEECHPOINT CHRISTIAN CAMP
Res — Coed Ages 8-14; Day — Coed 6-13

Allegan, MI 49010. 3212 125th Ave. Tel: 269-673-6155, 800-991-2267.
Fax: 269-673-6775.
www.beechpoint.com   E-mail: beechpoint@beechpoint.com
Mark Davidhizar, Dir.
Adm: FCFS. **Appl due:** Rolling. **Enr:** 240.
Features: Crafts Music Archery Boating Canoe Climbing_Wall Fishing Hiking Riding Riflery Rock_Climb Ropes_Crse Basketball Soccer Swim Volleyball Watersports.
Fees 2011: Res $300, 1 wk. Day $130, 1 wk. Aid (Need).
Housing: Cabins Lodges Tents. **Swimming:** Lake.
Est 1978. Nonprofit. Evangelical. **Ses:** 7. **Wks/ses:** 1. Operates June-Aug.

This Christian camp offers recreational camping activities to disadvantaged youth from Detroit, western Michigan and Chicago, IL.

GREENWOOD PRESBYTERIAN CAMP
Res — Coed Ages 5-17

Gowen, MI 49326. 13564 MacClain Rd. Tel: 616-754-7258.
www.campgreenwood.org   E-mail: office@campgreenwood.org
Greg Hoekman, Dir.
Grades K-12. Adm: FCFS. **Appl due:** Rolling. **Staff:** Admin 2. Couns 12.
Features: Crafts Drama Music Photog Archery Boating Canoe Fishing Hiking Kayak Riding Wilderness_Camp Baseball Basketball Field_Hockey Football Soccer Softball Swim Volleyball.
Fees 2012: Res $125-625, ½-2 wks. Aid (Need).
Housing: Cabins Houses Lodges. Avg per room/unit: 10. **Swimming:** Lake.
Est 1975. Nonprofit. Presbyterian. **Ses:** 15. **Wks/ses:** ½-2. Operates June-Aug. ACA.

Greenwood's summer program combines traditional camping activities with Christian education and worship. Sessions typically include swimming, arts and crafts, canoeing, hiking, archery, outdoor cooking and off-site trips. A One-week horseback riding session is also available.

WARNER CAMP
Res — Coed Ages 9-18

Grand Junction, MI 49056. 60 55th St. Tel: 269-434-6844. Fax: 269-434-6451.
www.warnercamp.com   E-mail: warnercamp@ymail.com

R. Doc Stevens, Admin.
Adm: FCFS. Admitted: 100%. **Appl due:** Rolling. **Enr:** 125. **Staff:** Admin 6. Couns 18. Res 10.
Features: Crafts Drama Music Photog Adventure_Travel Aquatics Archery Boating Canoe Climbing_Wall Community_Serv Conservation Fishing Hiking Kayak Mtn_Biking Outdoor_Ed Paintball Riding Rock_Climb Ropes_Crse Wilderness_Camp Badminton Basketball Cross-country Football Soccer Softball Swim Ultimate_Frisbee Volleyball Waterskiing Watersports.
Housing: Cabins Houses Lodges Tents. Avg per room/unit: 9. **Swimming:** Lake.
Est 1952. Nonprofit. Nondenom Christian. **Ses:** 8. **Wks/ses:** 1-2. Operates June-Aug.

Sponsored by the Church of God, this camp and retreat center offers youth and family opportunities over the summer. Parent-child weekend sessions supplement the weeklong camps for boys and girls. All counselors must be born again.

LAKE ANN CAMP
Res — Coed Ages 9-18

Lake Ann, MI 49650. PO Box 109. Tel: 231-275-7329, 800-223-7329.
Fax: 231-275-5174.
www.lakeanncamp.com   E-mail: info@lakeanncamp.com
Ken Riley, Exec Dir.
Grades 4-PG. Adm: FCFS. **Appl due:** Rolling. **Staff:** Admin 2. Couns 60. Res 9.
Features: Crafts Aquatics Archery Canoe Climbing_Wall Paintball Rappelling Rock_Climb Ropes_Crse White-water_Raft Wilderness_Camp Basketball Roller_Hockey Swim Volleyball.
Fees 2012: Res $349-429 (+$20-30), 1 wk.
Housing: Cabins Lodges Tepees. **Swimming:** Lake.
Est 1948. Nonprofit. Nondenom Christian. **Ses:** 8. **Wks/ses:** 1. Operates June-Aug. ACA.

In a Christian environment, Lake Ann conducts different programs that are organized by camper interest and age. Camp comprises six groups, ranging from grade 4 through high school. Activities include Bible study, a ropes course, nature study, watersports and land sports, swimming and canoeing.

CAMP LEELANAU
CAMP KOHAHNA
Res — Coord Ages 6-18

Maple City, MI 49664. 1653 Port Oneida Rd. Tel: 231-334-3808. Fax: 231-334-6238.
www.leelanau-kohahna.org   E-mail: office@leelanau-kohahna.org
Glenn C. Johnson & Sue Pierce, Dirs.
Adm: FCFS. **Appl due:** Rolling.
Features: Ceramics Crafts Dance Drama Silversmithing Canoe Hiking Kayak Riding Sail Wilderness_Camp Baseball Basketball Football Roller_Hockey Soccer Swim Tennis Volleyball Water-skiing Watersports.
Housing: Cabins. **Swimming:** Lake.
Est 1921. Nonprofit. Christian Science. **Ses:** 3. **Wks/ses:** 3-7. Operates June-Aug. ACA.

These single-gender camps are located on Pyramid Point, a 300-foot bluff overlooking Lake Michigan. Leelanau and Kohahna draw campers from catechism programs of Christian Science branch churches. Boys and girls choose from a traditional selection of recreational camping activities, all offered at beginning through advanced skill levels. An extensive tripping program focuses on wilderness camping in minimally populated and well-protected areas. In all pursuits, campers and staff apply Christian Science principles.

CAMP HENRY
Res — Coed Ages 7-17; Day — Coed 5-8

Newaygo, MI 49337. 5575 Gordon Rd. Tel: 231-652-6472.
Contact (Sept-May): Tel: 616-459-2267.
Year-round Fax: 231-652-9460.
www.camphenry.org   E-mail: info@camphenry.org
Jake Jacobs, Dir.
Adm: FCFS. **Appl due:** Rolling. **Staff:** Admin 6. Couns 33.
Travel: AK.
Features: Astron Ecol Environ_Sci Crafts Music Adventure_Travel Aquatics Archery Boating Canoe Climbing_Wall Conservation Exploration Fishing Hiking Kayak Outdoor_Ed Riding Rock_Climb Ropes_Crse Sail White-water_Raft Wilderness_Camp Equestrian Field_Hockey Soccer Swim Water-skiing Watersports.
Fees 2012: Res $255-495, ½-1 wk. **Day** $185, 1 wk. Aid (Need).
Housing: Cabins Lodges Tepees. **Swimming:** Lake.
Est 1937. Nonprofit. Presbyterian. **Ses:** 10. **Wks/ses:** ½-1. Operates June-Aug. ACA.

The regular session at this Christian camp offers land sports and watersports, nature study, conservation, ecology, art and horseback riding. Specialty camps are available in horseback riding, water-skiing, kayaking, hiking and white-water rafting. Each day begins with chapel and ends with vespers.

CAMP MAAS
Res — Coed Ages 7-14

Ortonville, MI 48462. 4361 Perryville Rd. Tel: 248-627-2821. Fax: 248-627-4576.
Contact (Sept-May): 6735 Telegraph Rd, Ste 380, Bloomfield Hills, MI 48301.
Tel: 248-647-1100. Fax: 248-647-1493.
www.tamarackcamps.com   E-mail: tamarack@tamarackcamps.com
Lee Trepeck, Dir.
Grades 2-9. Adm: FCFS. **Appl due:** Apr. **Staff:** Admin 25.
Features: Aquatics Bicycle_Tours Canoe Hiking Mtn_Trips Riding Sail Scuba Wilderness_Camp Wilderness_Canoe Woodcraft Baseball Basketball Cross-country Equestrian Football Golf Gymnastics Soccer Swim Tennis Track Volleyball Water-skiing Watersports.
Housing: Cabins Lodges. **Swimming:** Lake Pool.
Est 1902. Nonprofit. **Spons:** Fresh Air Society. Jewish. **Ses:** 5. **Wks/ses:** 1½-7. Operates June-Aug.

Located on a 1500-acre site that includes two lakes, the camp combines traditional camping pursuits with outdoor adventure and Jewish cultural activities. Recreational activities include softball, basketball, tennis, floor hockey, riding, video, photography, a ropes course, water-skiing, sailing, kayaking, canoeing and gymnastics.

CAMP ROGER
Res — Coed Ages 6-18

Rockford, MI 49341. 8356 Belding Rd. Tel: 616-874-7286. Fax: 616-874-5734.
www.camproger.org   E-mail: office@camproger.org
Douglas Vanderwell, Exec Dir.
Adm: FCFS. **Appl due:** Rolling. **Staff:** Admin 4. Couns 20.
Features: Ecol Environ_Sci Dance Drama Aquatics Canoe Climbing_Wall Hiking Ropes_Crse Wilderness_Camp Wilderness_Canoe Swim.
Fees 2009: Res $160-550, ½-1½ wks. Aid (Need).
Housing: Cabins. **Swimming:** Lake.

Est 1941. Nonprofit. Nondenom Christian. **Ses:** 23. **Wks/ses:** ½-1½. Operates June-Aug. ACA.

Though not a church organization, this Christian camp maintains close associations with the Christian Reformed communities of Michigan, Illinois, Indiana and Ohio. Campers of all faiths engage in such activities as canoeing, swimming, crafts, a ropes course, a climbing tower, nature lore, and campwide games and events. Several specialty camps complement the traditional recreational program.

CAMP AMIGO
Res — Coed Ages 8-15

Sturgis, MI 49091. 26455 Banker Rd. Tel: 269-651-2811. Fax: 269-659-0084.
www.amigocentre.org   E-mail: info@amigocentre.org
Cliff Brubaker, Exec Dir.
Grades 3-9. Adm: FCFS. **Appl due:** Rolling. **Enr:** 500. **Staff:** Admin 14. Couns 16.
Features: Astron Environ_Sci Sci Crafts Drama Music Photog Aquatics Archery Boating Canoe Conservation Exploration Fishing Hiking Outdoor_Ed Ropes_Crse Wilderness_Camp Wilderness_Canoe Woodcraft Basketball Equestrian Soccer Swim Tennis Volleyball.
Fees 2009: Res $245-355, 1 wk. Day $75, 1 wk. Aid avail.
Housing: Cabins Lodges Tents. **Swimming:** Lake.
Est 1957. Nonprofit. **Spons:** Amigo Centre. Mennonite. **Ses:** 11. **Wks/ses:** 1. Operates June-Aug.

A Mennonite camp, Amigo runs weeklong traditional programs for children that vary by age and focus. Regular activities include swimming, cookouts, fishing, camp outs, sports, nature hikes and Bible study. Among specialized options are sports, horse and teen adventure camps.

MINNESOTA

NORTH CENTRAL CAMP CHERITH
Res — Coord Ages 7-18

Frazee, MN 56544. 32884 Camp Cherith Rd. Tel: 218-334-8454.
Contact (Sept-May): 10039 James Cir S, Bloomington, MN 55431. Tel: 952-884-1451.
www.camp-cherith.com   E-mail: info@camp-cherith.com
Becky Nelson, Exec Dir.
Grades 2-12. Adm: FCFS. **Appl due:** Rolling.
Features: Crafts Drama Aquatics Archery Canoe Fishing Hiking Kayak Riflery Sail Equestrian Swim Water-skiing Watersports.
Fees 2009: Res $285 (+$15), 1 wk.
Housing: Cabins Lodges. Avg per room/unit: 7. **Swimming:** Lake.
Est 1947. Nonprofit. Nondenom Christian. **Ses:** 7. **Wks/ses:** 1. Operates June-Aug. ACA.

Camp Cherith provides interdenominational Christian programs that include a variety of traditional outdoor, athletic and artistic activities. Boys and girls attend separate sessions. Specialized programs emphasizing horsemanship, waterfront pursuits and lifeguard training are available as alternatives to the standard camp.

CATHOLIC YOUTH CAMP
Res — Coed Ages 7-18

McGregor, MN 55760. 19590 520th Ln. Tel: 218-426-3383.
Contact (Sept-May): 2131 Fairview Ave N, Ste 200, Roseville, MN 55113.
Tel: 651-636-1645.
Year-round Fax: 651-628-9323.
www.cycamp.org   E-mail: office@cycamp.org
Natalie King, Exec Dir.
Grades 2-PG. Adm: FCFS. **Appl due:** Rolling. **Enr:** 70. **Enr cap:** 144. **Staff:** Admin 2. Couns 20. Res 1.
Features: Ecol Environ_Sci Crafts Dance Drama Music Aquatics Archery Boating Canoe Community_Serv Fishing Kayak Outdoor_Ed Wilderness_Camp Basketball Football Soccer Softball Swim Volleyball Watersports.
Fees 2011: Res $285-470 (+$70), ½-1½ wks. Aid 2010 (Need): $7000.
Housing: Cabins. Avg per room/unit: 12. **Swimming:** Lake.
Est 1947. Nonprofit. Roman Catholic. **Ses:** 9. **Wks/ses:** ½-1½. Operates June-Aug. ACA.

Traditional camping activities at CYC include swimming, field games, arts and crafts, music, drama, hiking, boating, sports, tomahawk throwing and a slingshot range. Enrolling children of all faiths, the camp holds morning and evening praise and worship sessions daily, in addition to Mass once per session.

GRINDSTONE LAKE BIBLE CAMP
Res — Coed Ages 6-18

Sandstone, MN 55072. 13222 Grindstone Lake Rd. Tel: 320-245-2777.
www.grindstonecamp.com   E-mail: glbc@grindstonecamp.com
Grades 1-12. Adm: FCFS. **Appl due:** Rolling. **Enr cap:** 154. **Staff:** Admin 6. Couns 20.
Features: Crafts Theater Canoe Basketball Soccer Street_Hockey Swim Volleyball.
Fees 2011: Res $110-165, 1 wk.
Housing: Cabins. **Swimming:** Lake.
Est 1932. Nonprofit. Evangelical. **Ses:** 8. **Wks/ses:** 1. Operates June-Aug.

GLBC provides a camping program designed to help children grow spiritually and socially, and to create interest in missions, evangelism and spiritual growth through Bible teaching and Christian music. Recreational activities complement Bible instruction.

CAMP LEBANON SUMMER YOUTH CAMPS
Res — Coed Ages 6-18

Upsala, MN 56384. PO Box 370. Tel: 320-573-2125, 800-816-1502. Fax: 320-573-2116.
www.camplebanon.org   E-mail: babeler@camplebanon.org
Bill Abeler, Exec Dir.
Grades 1-PG. Adm: FCFS. **Appl due:** Rolling. **Enr:** 190. **Staff:** Admin 9. Couns 30.
Features: Crafts Music Archery Boating Canoe Fishing Hiking Outdoor_Ed Sail Basketball Soccer Softball Swim Ultimate_Frisbee Watersports.
Fees 2009: Res $115-295 (+$20), ½-1 wk. Aid 2006 (Need): $8000.
Housing: Cabins Dorms Lodges. **Swimming:** Lake.
Est 1947. Nonprofit. Nondenom Christian. **Ses:** 10. **Wks/ses:** ½-1. Operates June-Aug.

Located on the northern side of Cedar Lake, this Christian camp offers an array of traditional recreational pursuits. Camp Lebanon schedules four family events each summer.

MISSOURI

CAMP SABRA
Res — Coed Ages 8-15

Rocky Mount, MO 65072. 30750 Camp Sabra Rd. Tel: 573-365-1591.
Contact (Sept-May): 2 Millstone Campus Dr, St Louis, MO 63146. Tel: 314-442-3151.
Year-round Toll-free: 800-526-8097, Fax: 573-365-0577.
www.campsabra.com   E-mail: tgrossman@jccstl.org
Terri Grossman, Dir.
Grades 3-10. Adm: FCFS. Appl due: Rolling. Enr: 350. Staff: Admin 5. Couns 125.
Features: Crafts Drama Fine_Arts Photog Aquatics Archery Canoe Climbing_Wall Fishing
Hiking Mtn_Biking Ropes_Crse Sail Wilderness_Camp Basketball Equestrian Football
Lacrosse Soccer Softball Swim Tennis Volleyball Water-skiing.
Fees 2012: Res $1195-7825, 1-8 wks.
Housing: Cabins Tents. Swimming: Lake.
Est 1970. Nonprofit. Spons: Jewish Community Center of St. Louis. Jewish. Ses: 15. Wks/
ses: 1-8. Operates June-Aug. ACA.

Among the activities at this Jewish camp are arts and crafts, drama, canoeing, swimming,
hiking, fishing, mountain biking, and individual and team sports. Rising juniors may embark
on a three-week trip to Israel. Campers attend religious services on the Sabbath.

CAMP TABLE ROCK
Res — Coed Ages 11-19

Shell Knob, MO 65747. 2079 Peninsula Dr. Tel: 417-858-9222. Fax: 417-858-0311.
www.camptablerock.com   E-mail: camp@camptablerock.com
Rev. Rick Pearson, Dir.
Grades 7-12. Adm: FCFS. Appl due: Rolling. Enr: 250. Enr cap: 250. Staff: Admin 2.
Couns 15. Res 4.
Features: Boating Community_Serv Fishing Hiking Work Basketball Football Golf Soccer
Swim Ultimate_Frisbee Volleyball Water-skiing Watersports.
Fees 2012: Res $195, 1 wk.
Housing: Cabins. Avg per room/unit: 20. Swimming: Lake.
Est 1997. Nonprofit. Spons: Fun in the Son Ministries. Nondenom Christian. Ses: 1. Wks/
ses: 1. Operates June.

Points of emphasis at this Christian camp are discipleship, evangelism and leadership
training. Campers spend mornings engaged in training seminars and worship services. Lake
activities and land sports fill the afternoon hours.

MONTANA

CHRISTIKON
Res — Coed Ages 10-18

McLeod, MT 59052. 4661 Boulder Rd. Tel: 406-932-6300. Fax: 406-932-6300.
Contact (Oct-May): 1108 24th St W, Billings, MT 59102. Tel: 406-656-1969.
Fax: 406-656-1969.
www.christikon.org   E-mail: christikon@aol.com
Rev. Robert L. Quam, Dir.
Grades 6-PG. Adm: FCFS. Appl due: Rolling. Enr: 40-80. Enr cap: 40-80. Staff: Admin
6. Couns 15. Res 22.

Features: Crafts Dance Hiking Mtn_Trips Wilderness_Camp.
Fees 2012: Res $375-395, 1 wk. Aid 2010 (Need): $17,000.
Housing: Cabins. Avg per room/unit: 7.
Est 1951. Nonprofit. Lutheran. **Ses:** 7. **Wks/ses:** ½-1. Operates June-Aug. ACA.

Affiliated with the Evangelical Lutheran Church in America, Christikon offers both on-site and trail-based programs. The residential camps offer hiking and camping, in addition to Bible study, service projects and recreational activities. The backpacking programs include hiking through mountain terrain, participation in worship and Bible study, and the option of helping to build and repair trails and damaged wilderness areas.

NEW HAMPSHIRE

BROOKWOODS
DEER RUN
Res — Coord Ages 8-16

Alton, NH 03809. 34 Camp Brookwoods Rd. Tel: 603-875-3600. Fax: 603-875-4606.
www.christiancamps.net   E-mail: info@christiancamps.net
Bob Strodel, Exec Dir.
Adm: FCFS. **Appl due:** Rolling. **Enr:** 430. **Staff:** Couns 50. Res 10.
Features: Crafts Drama Music Photog Aquatics Archery Bicycle_Tours Boating Canoe Climbing_Wall Cooking Fishing Hiking Mountaineering Mtn_Biking Mtn_Trips Outdoor_ Ed Paintball Riding Riflery Ropes_Crse Sail Scuba White-water_Raft Wilderness_Camp Wilderness_Canoe Woodcraft Badminton Baseball Basketball Equestrian Field_Hockey Football Golf Lacrosse Soccer Softball Swim Tennis Ultimate_Frisbee Volleyball Water-skiing Watersports.
Fees 2012: Res $1695-2825, 2-4 wks. Aid 2009 (Need): $130,000.
Housing: Cabins Dorms. Avg per room/unit: 12. **Swimming:** Lake.
Est 1944. Nonprofit. **Spons:** Christian Camps and Conferences. Nondenom Christian. **Ses:** 6. **Wks/ses:** 2-4. Operates June-Aug. ACA.

Brookwoods and Deer Run, its sister camp, offer crafts; an array of sports and outdoor activities; and short (usually overnight) canoe, sailing and hiking trips. Boys and girls participate in various coeducational activities.

CAMP YOUNG JUDAEA
Res — Coed Ages 8-15

Amherst, NH 03031. 9 Camp Rd. Tel: 603-673-3710. Fax: 603-672-4486.
Contact (Sept-May): 22 Priscilla Cir, Wellesley Hills, MA 02481. Tel: 781-237-9410.
Fax: 781-431-7336.
www.cyj.org   E-mail: cyjnh@aol.com
Ken Kornreich, Exec Dir.
Grades 3-10. Adm: FCFS. **Appl due:** Dec. **Enr:** 350. **Enr cap:** 350. **Staff:** Admin 25. Couns 90.
Features: Ecol Crafts Dance Drama Music Painting Photog Aquatics Archery Boating Canoe Chess Climbing_Wall Fishing Hiking Kayak Riflery Ropes_Crse Sail White-water_Raft Wilderness_Camp Woodcraft Aerobics Basketball Lacrosse Martial_Arts Soccer Softball Swim Tennis Track Ultimate_Frisbee Volleyball Water-skiing Watersports Wrestling.
Fees 2012: Res $3300-6295 (+$250-500), 3½-7 wks. Aid (Need).
Housing: Cabins. Avg per room/unit: 10-14. **Swimming:** Lake Pool.
Est 1939. Nonprofit. **Spons:** Friends of Young Judaea. Jewish. **Ses:** 3. **Wks/ses:** 3½-7. Operates June-Aug. ACA.

Activities at this kosher, Zionist Jewish camp include individual and team sports, performing arts, waterfront and pool pursuits, arts and crafts, riflery, archery and camp craft. Campers from various Jewish backgrounds attend Sabbath services and engage in Judaic studies programs. Boys and girls may receive one-on-one Bar or Bat Mitzvah tutoring for an additional fee.

CAMP TEVYA
Res — Coed Ages 8-16

Brookline, NH 03033. Lake Potanipo, 1 Mason Rd. Tel: 603-673-4010.
Fax: 603-673-0571.
Contact (Winter): 30 Main St, Ashland, MA 01721. Tel: 508-881-1002.
Fax: 508-881-1006.
www.camptevya.org   E-mail: tevya@cohencamps.org
Mindee Meltzer, Dir.
Adm: FCFS. **Appl due:** Apr. **Enr cap:** 335. **Staff:** Couns 125.
Features: Ceramics Dance Music Painting Photog Theater Woodworking Archery Boating Canoe Fishing Outdoor_Ed Ropes_Crse Sail Aerobics Basketball Cross-country Lacrosse Martial_Arts Soccer Softball Swim Tennis Ultimate_Frisbee Volleyball Waterskiing Watersports Gardening.
Fees 2012: Res $4600-7800, 3½-7 wks.
Housing: Cabins. **Swimming:** Lake.
Est 1940. Jewish. Ses: 3. **Wks/ses:** 3½-7. Operates June-Aug. ACA.

Emphasis at Tevya is on Jewish heritage, with Shabbath services, Israeli dance, music and culture sessions. Drama, arts and crafts, land sports and watersports are integral parts of the program.

CAMP SENTINEL
Res — Coed Ages 5-15

Center Tuftonboro, NH 03816. 29 Sentinel Lodge Rd. Tel: 603-539-4839.
www.campsentinel.org   E-mail: kevin@campsentinel.org
Rev. Kevin Van Brunt, Pres.
Adm: FCFS. **Appl due:** Rolling. **Enr:** 50. **Enr cap:** 100. **Staff:** Admin 2. Couns 25.
Features: Environ_Sci Crafts Music Theater Aquatics Archery Boating Canoe Hiking Kayak Sail Wilderness_Camp Baseball Basketball Football Soccer Softball Swim Watersports.
Fees 2011: Res $430-599 (+$30), 1 wk. Day $185, 1 wk. Aid avail.
Housing: Cabins. Avg per room/unit: 8. **Swimming:** Lake Pond.
Est 1949. Nonprofit. Nondenom Christian. Ses: 8. **Wks/ses:** 1. Operates June-Aug.

Located on 645 acres in the foothills of the Ossipee Mountains, this nondenominational camp offers separate sessions for different age groups. Special sessions include a junior high outpost offering a primitive setting, hiking, boating and outdoor cooking, in addition to a spiritual development camp. Sentinel maintains an affiliation with Gove Hill in Norwich, VT.

CAMP MARIST
Res — Coed Ages 6-16

Effingham, NH 03882. 22 Abel Blvd. Tel: 603-539-4552. Fax: 603-539-8318.
www.campmarist.org   E-mail: office@campmarist.org
Vinny Gschlecht, Dir.
Grades 1-10. Adm: FCFS. **Appl due:** Rolling. **Enr:** 250. **Enr cap:** 250. **Staff:** Admin 5. Couns 70.
Features: ESL Crafts Dance Theater Aquatics Archery Bicycle_Tours Boating Canoe Deep-sea Fishing Exploration Fishing Hiking Kayak Mtn_Biking Mtn_Trips Riding Riflery Rock_Climb Ropes_Crse Sail White-water_Raft Baseball Basketball Equestrian Field_

Hockey Football Golf Lacrosse Martial_Arts Roller_Hockey Rugby Soccer Softball Swim Tennis Track Volleyball Water-skiing Watersports Weight_Trng Wrestling.
Fees 2012: Res $1700-5250 (+$175), 2-7 wks. Aid (Need).
Housing: Cabins. **Swimming:** Lake.
Est 1949. Nonprofit. Roman Catholic. **Ses:** 6. **Wks/ses:** 2-7. Operates June-Aug. ACA.

Located on a 300-acre tract on Ossipee Lake in the White Mountains, this Catholic camp offers a strong waterfront program, individual and team sports, arts and crafts, and a ropes course, among other pursuits. Marist schedules several off-campus trips for interested campers. English as a Second Language and remedial tutoring is available for boys and girls who require it.

CAMP FATIMA
CAMP BERNADETTE
Res — Coord Ages 6-15

Gilmanton Iron Works, NH 03837. 32 Fatima Rd, PO Box 206. Tel: 603-364-5851.
Fax: 603-364-5038.
www.campsfatimabernadette.org   E-mail: info@campsfatimabernadette.org
Michael Drumm & Susan Marcoux, Dirs.
Adm: FCFS. **Enr:** 270-310. **Staff:** Admin 10.
Features: Crafts Dance Drama Aquatics Canoe Climbing_Wall Kayak Ropes_Crse Sail Baseball Basketball Lacrosse Soccer Softball Swim Tennis Volleyball.
Fees 2012: Res $475-3440, 1-8 wks.
Housing: Cabins. **Swimming:** Lake.
Est 1949. Nonprofit. Roman Catholic. **Ses:** 5. **Wks/ses:** 1-8. Operates June-Aug. ACA.

Owned and operated by the Roman Catholic Diocese of Manchester, these brother and sister camps complement programs in sports, aquatics and radio with specialty activities such as archery, arts and crafts, horseback trail riding, riflery, drama, dance and an obstacle course. Camp Bernadette is located at 83 Richards Rd., Wolfeboro 03894 (603-569-1692).

CAMP TEL NOAR
Res — Coed Ages 8-16

Hampstead, NH 03841. Sunset Lake, Main St. Tel: 603-329-6931. Fax: 603-329-4967.
Contact (Winter): 30 Main St, Ashland, MA 01721. Tel: 508-881-1002.
Fax: 508-881-1006.
www.camptelnoar.org   E-mail: telnoar@cohencamps.org
Molly Lourie Butter, Dir.
Adm: FCFS. **Enr cap:** 265. **Staff:** Couns 90.
Features: Art Ceramics Crafts Dance Music Painting Photog Theater Woodworking Archery Boating Outdoor_Ed Ropes_Crse Sail Aerobics Basketball Lacrosse Martial_Arts Soccer Softball Street_Hockey Swim Tennis Ultimate_Frisbee Volleyball Water-skiing Watersports Gardening.
Fees 2012: Res $2400-7800, 2-7 wks.
Housing: Cabins. **Swimming:** Lake Pond.
Est 1945. Jewish. **Ses:** 4. **Wks/ses:** 2-7. Operates June-Aug. ACA.

A Judaic program incorporates culture sessions as well as Israeli songs and dances. Campers engage in waterfront activities and other traditional camping pursuits.

CAMP BEREA
Res — Coed Ages 8-18

Hebron, NH 03241. 68 Berea Rd. Tel: 603-744-6344. Fax: 603-744-6346.

www.berea.org
Ron Ward, Exec Dir.
Grades 3-PG. Adm: FCFS. **Appl due:** Rolling. **Staff:** Admin 10. Couns 40.
Features: Crafts Aquatics Archery Canoe Climbing_Wall Kayak Mountaineering Paintball Riflery Rock_Climb Ropes_Crse Sail Baseball Basketball Football Swim Tennis Volleyball Water-skiing.
Fees 2011: Res $350-700, 1-2 wks.
Housing: Cabins. Avg per room/unit: 9. **Swimming:** Lake.
Est 1945. Nonprofit. Nondenom Christian. **Ses:** 9. **Wks/ses:** 1-2. Operates June-Aug.

Riflery, sports, archery, mountain climbing and a waterfront program are elements of this Christian camp. Separate programs (grouped by age) include single-gender and coed camps.

WANAKEE UNITED METHODIST CENTER SUMMER CAMP
Res — Coed Ages 4-18; Day — Coed 4-12

Meredith, NH 03253. 75 Upper New Hampton Rd. Tel: 603-279-7950.
Fax: 603-279-4499.
www.wanakee.org   **E-mail: mail@wanakee.org**
Michael Moore & Jean Moore, Dirs.
Grades K-PG. Adm: FCFS. Admitted: 100%. **Appl due:** Rolling. **Staff:** Admin 4. Couns 19.
Features: Astron Ecol Environ_Sci Crafts Dance Media Music Theater Adventure_Travel Aquatics Bicycle_Tours Boating Canoe Climbing_Wall Cooking Hiking Mtn_Biking Mtn_Trips Rock_Climb Ropes_Crse White-water_Raft Wilderness_Camp Swim.
Fees 2011: Res $295-510, 1 wk. Day $165, 1 wk. Aid 2008 (Need): $3700.
Housing: Cabins. Avg per room/unit: 8. **Swimming:** Lake.
Est 1962. Nonprofit. United Methodist. **Ses:** 8. **Wks/ses:** 1. Operates July-Aug.

Recreational sessions at this United Methodist camp offer arts, games, hiking, swimming, canoeing and other adventure activities. Minicamps are available for younger children, while those entering grades 4-12 participate in specialty camps featuring one of the following: swimming, a ropes course, hiking, music, arts and crafts, drama, pioneering, mountain biking, or clowning and mime.

CAMP YAVNEH
Res — Coed Ages 8-16

Northwood, NH 03261. 18 Lucas Pond Rd. Tel: 603-942-5593. Fax: 603-942-7805.
Contact (Winter): 160 Herrick Rd, Newton, MA 02459. Tel: 617-559-8860.
Fax: 617-559-8861.
www.campyavneh.org   **E-mail: debbie@campyavneh.org**
Deborah Sussman, Dir.
Grades 3-11. Adm: FCFS.
Features: Crafts Dance Drama Music Aquatics Archery Boating Climbing_Wall Basketball Softball Swim Tennis Volleyball.
Fees 2012: Res $1975-7100, 2-7 wks.
Housing: Cabins. **Swimming:** Lake.
Est 1944. Nonprofit. Jewish. **Ses:** 5. **Wks/ses:** 2-7. Operates June-Aug. ACA.

Yavneh combines its traditional camping pursuits with a strong Judaic component. Individual and team sports, waterfront activities, performing arts and a wide range of electives constitute the program. First-time campers entering grades 3-5 may enroll in a two-week session.

CAMP CALUMET LUTHERAN
Res — Coed Ages 8-16; Day — Coed 6-12

**West Ossipee, NH 03890. 1090 Ossipee Lake Rd, PO Box 236. Tel: 603-539-4773.
Fax: 603-539-5343.**
www.calumet.org   E-mail: boomchickaboom@calumet.org
Karl Ogren, Exec Dir.
Grades 1-12. Adm: FCFS. **Appl due:** Rolling. **Enr:** 290. **Staff:** Admin 35. Couns 100.
Features: Crafts Dance Music Photog Theater Aquatics Archery Bicycle_Tours Boating
Canoe Hiking Kayak Mountaineering Mtn_Biking Mtn_Trips Rock_Climb Ropes_Crse
Sail Wilderness_Camp Wilderness_Canoe Basketball Softball Swim Tennis Volleyball.
Fees 2012: Res $555, 1 wk. Day $190, 1 wk.
Housing: Cabins Tents. Avg per room/unit: 8. **Swimming:** Lake.
Est 1960. Nonprofit. Lutheran. **Ses:** 12. **Wks/ses:** 1. Operates June-Aug. ACA.

Situated in the foothills of the White Mountains, Calumet offers a variety of arts, team
and individual sports, and waterfront activities. Outdoor adventures for teenagers include
weeklong backpacking, canoeing and mountain biking trips.

CAMP WILMOT
Res — Coed Ages 8-18

Wilmot, NH 03287. 5 Whites Pond Rd. Tel: 603-768-3350.
www.campwilmot.org   E-mail: campwilmot@hotmail.com
Rev. Rob Mark, Dir.
Grades 3-12. Adm: FCFS. **Appl due:** Rolling. **Staff:** Admin 10. Couns 20.
Travel: ME Canada.
Features: Ecol Environ_Sci Geol Writing/Journ Crafts Creative_Writing Dance Drama
Fine_Arts Music Photog Adventure_Travel Aquatics Archery Boating Canoe Com-
munity_Serv Conservation Cooking Exploration Farm Hiking Kayak Mountaineering
Mtn_Trips Peace/Cross-cultural Ropes_Crse Wilderness_Camp Woodcraft Basketball
Football Soccer Swim Ultimate_Frisbee Volleyball.
Fees 2011: Res $450-500, 1 wk. Aid avail.
Housing: Cabins Houses Lodges. Avg per room/unit: 8. **Swimming:** Pond.
Est 1961. Nonprofit. Presbyterian. **Ses:** 7. **Wks/ses:** 1. Operates July-Aug.

This Presbyterian camp offers intensive Christian education, as well as camping and
recreational activities. Offerings include Bible study, crafts, swimming and nature exploration.
Junior camps (grades 3-8), adventure camps (grades 6-12) and advanced adventure camps
(grades 8-12) emphasize outdoor skills, ecology, arts and crafts, waterfront activities and
spiritual development.

NEW MEXICO

FORT LONE TREE CAMP
Res — Coed Ages 8-12

Capitan, NM 83316. PO Box 547. Tel: 575-354-3322, 888-854-4801. Fax: 575-354-4266.
www.lonetree.org   E-mail: nmfort@lonetree.org
Eric McNamara & Jenn McNamara, Dirs.
Adm: FCFS. **Appl due:** Rolling. **Enr:** 135. **Staff:** Admin 2. Couns 20.
Features: Crafts Drama Music Archery Caving Climbing_Wall Hiking Rappelling Riding
Riflery Ropes_Crse Basketball Swim Volleyball Watersports.
Fees 2011: Res $344, 1 wk.
Housing: Cabins Lodges. **Swimming:** Stream.

Est 1991. Nonprofit. Nondenom Christian. **Ses:** 9. **Wks/ses:** 1. Operates June-Aug. ACA.

This Christian camp offers an array of traditional recreational activities, with an emphasis on adventure pursuits. Bible study is a prominent part of the program.

LONE TREE RANCH
Res — Coed Ages 12-18

Capitan, NM 88316. PO Box 523. Tel: 575-354-2523. Fax: 575-354-2961.
www.lonetree.org   E-mail: nmranch@lonetree.org
Steve Dirks, Dir.
Adm: FCFS. **Appl due:** Rolling. **Enr cap:** 140. **Staff:** Admin 3. Couns 15.
Features: Climbing_Wall Hiking Mountaineering Mtn_Biking Mtn_Trips Rappelling Riflery Rock_Climb Ropes_Crse Wilderness_Camp Basketball Equestrian Volleyball.
Fees 2011: Res $324 (+$40), 1 wk.
Housing: Cabins Dorms Lodges.
Est 1980. Nonprofit. Nondenom Christian. **Ses:** 11. **Wks/ses:** 1. Operates June-Aug. ACA.

Activities at this Christian camp include horseback riding, mountain biking, riflery, a high ropes course, climbing wall, hiking and Bible study. An extensive challenge course emphasizes teamwork, goal setting and communication.

CAMP STONEY
Res — Coed Ages 8-18

Santa Fe, NM 87505. 7855 Old Santa Fe Trail. Tel: 505-983-5610. Fax: 505-216-0706.
www.campstoney.org   E-mail: info@campstoney.org
Grades 3-12. Adm: FCFS. **Appl due:** Rolling. **Enr:** 72. **Enr cap:** 72. **Staff:** Admin 4. Couns 14. Res 2.
Features: Crafts Drama Music Pottery Archery Community_Serv Hiking Mtn_Trips Outdoor_Ed Rock_Climb Ropes_Crse White-water_Raft Wilderness_Camp Soccer Softball Swim Volleyball.
Fees 2012: Res $400-500 (+$50-100), 1 wk. Aid 2011 (Need): $350.
Housing: Cabins Tepees. Avg per room/unit: 12. **Swimming:** Pool.
Est 1965. Nonprofit. Episcopal. **Ses:** 11. **Wks/ses:** 1. Operates June-July. ACA.

Stoney's programs combine Bible study and worship with summer recreational activities. Separate adventure camps serve junior high and high school students, and other specialty options address opera and outreach ministry, among other topics. A family camp over Memorial Day weekend is also available.

NEW YORK

HABONIM DROR CAMP NA'ALEH
Res — Coed Ages 8-16

Bainbridge, NY 13733. 368 County Hwy 1. Tel: 607-563-8900. Fax: 607-563-9804.
Contact (Sept-May): 114 W 26th St, 10th Fl, New York, NY 10001. Tel: 212-229-2700. Fax: 212-229-2711.
www.naaleh.org   E-mail: info@naaleh.org
Adam Benmoise, Exec Dir.
Grades 2-12. Adm: FCFS. **Enr:** 100. **Staff:** Admin 5. Couns 20.
Features: Ecol Environ_Sci Govt Lang Crafts Dance Music Photog Theater Aquatics Boating Canoe Community_Serv Hiking Kayak Peace/Cross-cultural Ropes_Crse Social_

Servs Survival_Trng Wilderness_Camp Work Baseball Basketball Soccer Softball Swim Tennis Volleyball. **Fees 2011: Res $2195-6,835 (+$75), 2-7 wks.** Aid 2009 (Need): $5000. **Housing:** Cabins Tents. Avg per room/unit: 10. **Swimming:** Lake. **Est 1998.** Nonprofit. Jewish. **Ses:** 2. **Wks/ses:** 2-4. Operates June-Aug.

Na'aleh offers a traditional program including waterfront activities, arts and crafts, photography, drama, media, sports and hiking. Based on the values of the Israeli kibbutz, the program offers an experience in communal and cooperative living in a progressive atmosphere designed to appeal to culturally Jewish youth.

SURPRISE LAKE CAMP
Res — Coed Ages 7-15

Cold Spring, NY 10516. 382 Lake Surprise Rd. Tel: 845-265-3616. Fax: 845-265-3646. Contact (Sept-May): 307 7th Ave, Ste 900, New York, NY 10001. Tel: 212-924-3131. Fax: 212-924-5112.
www.surpriselake.org   E-mail: info@surpriselake.org
Jordan Dale, Exec Dir.
Grades 2-10. Adm: FCFS. **Appl due:** Rolling. **Enr:** 960. **Staff:** Admin 40. Couns 100.
Features: Crafts Dance Drama Music Photog Aquatics Archery Boating Canoe Climbing_Wall Conservation Cooking Fishing Hiking Kayak Outdoor_Ed Ropes_Crse Sail Wilderness_Camp Work Yoga Baseball Basketball Field_Hockey Golf Gymnastics Soccer Softball Street_Hockey Swim Tennis Ultimate_Frisbee Volleyball Watersports.
Fees 2012: Res $500-7450 (+$25-130), 1-8 wks. Aid (Need).
Housing: Cabins. Avg per room/unit: 8-13. **Swimming:** Lake.
Est 1902. Nonprofit. Jewish. **Ses:** 7. **Wks/ses:** 1-8. Operates June-Aug. ACA.

Serving the Jewish community of Greater New York, Surprise Lake offers various athletics and waterfront activities, as well as dance and drama opportunities. Teens select a special interest and spend the morning hours developing their skills in one of the following areas: sports, tennis, waterfront, camping and hiking, performing arts, arts and crafts, guitar, photography, physical fitness or Jewish leadership. Weeklong sessions are open to young campers entering grades 2-6.

BERKSHIRE HILLS EMANUEL CAMPS
Res — Coed Ages 7-15

Copake, NY 12516. PO Box 16. Tel: 518-329-3303. Fax: 518-329-4778. Contact (Sept-May): 547 Saw Mill River Rd, Ste 3D, Ardsley, NY 10502. Tel: 914-693-8952. Fax: 914-674-8952.
Year-round Toll-free: 877-543-4333.
www.bhecamps.com   E-mail: info@bhecamps.com
Seth Adelsberg, Dir.
Adm: FCFS. **Appl due:** Rolling. **Enr:** 210. **Staff:** Admin 20. Couns 70.
Features: Crafts Dance Drama Aquatics Archery Canoe Climbing_Wall Fishing Mtn_Biking Riding Ropes_Crse Basketball Equestrian Golf Lacrosse Martial_Arts Roller_Hockey Soccer Softball Swim Tennis Volleyball Water-skiing Watersports.
Fees 2012: Res $800-5700 (+$50), 1-7 wks. Aid (Need).
Housing: Cabins. Avg per room/unit: 13. **Swimming:** Lake Pool.
Est 1930. Nonprofit. **Spons:** UJA Federation of New York. Jewish. **Ses:** 3. **Wks/ses:** 1-7. Operates June-Aug. ACA.

The daily program at BHEC includes waterfront and pool activities, field sports, and special interest electives such as arts and crafts, dance, music, drama, cooking, riding, weight training and archery. Campers take weekly trips to area events and attractions. For an additional fee, a limited number of campers may receive Bar or Bat Mitzvah lessons.

WOODSMOKE CAMP
Res — Coed Ages 10-17

Hancock, NY 13783. 1500 Hathaway Pond Rd. Tel: 607-637-5401.
Contact (Sept-June): 560 W 218th St, Apt 4C, New York, NY 10034. Tel: 212-569-1599.
Year-round Fax: 212-569-6897.
www.kingswoodcampsite.org   E-mail: jcwityk@aol.com
Cynthia Price, Dir.
Grades 5-12. Adm: FCFS. Appl due: Rolling. Enr: 38. Enr cap: 38. Staff: Admin 3. Couns 8. Res 17.
Features: Debate Ecol Crafts Aquatics Boating Canoe Community_Serv Cooking Exploration Hiking Outdoor_Ed Swim Volleyball.
Fees 2011: Res $500 (+$10), 1 wk. Aid 2010 (Need): $4500.
Housing: Tents. Avg per room/unit: 5. Swimming: Lake.
Est 1983. Nonprofit. United Methodist. Ses: 2. Wks/ses: 1. Operates July. ACA.

Operated by the New York Annual Conference of the United Methodist Church, Woodsmoke occupies a 766-acre site in the Catskill Mountains. Boys and girls engage in a variety of traditional, age-appropriate recreational and camping activities. In keeping with the spiritual focus of the program, campers at each grade level also take part in a service project.

CAMP KINDER RING
Res — Coed Ages 8-15

Hopewell Junction, NY 12533. 335 Sylvan Lake Rd. Tel: 845-221-2771.
Fax: 845-227-7881.
Contact (Winter): 574 E Meadow Ave, East Meadow, NY 11554. Tel: 516-280-3157.
Fax: 516-280-3158.
www.campkr.com   E-mail: info@campkr.com
Irene Drantch, Dir.
Grades 3-10. Adm: FCFS. Appl due: Rolling. Enr: 450. Staff: Admin 20. Couns 75.
Travel: DC FL MA.
Features: Computers Crafts Dance Drama Fine_Arts Music Aquatics Archery Boating Canoe Climbing_Wall Community_Serv Fishing Hiking Kayak Mtn_Biking Riding Ropes_Crse Sail White-water_Raft Woodcraft Baseball Golf Gymnastics Roller_Hockey Soccer Softball Swim Tennis Track Volleyball Water-skiing Watersports.
Fees 2012: Res $5100-9950 (+$275-1300), 3-7 wks.
Housing: Cabins. Swimming: Lake Pool.
Est 1927. Nonprofit. Spons: Workmen's Circle. Jewish. Ses: 3. Wks/ses: 3-7. Operates June-Aug. ACA.

Kinder Ring provides a traditional recreational camp experience in a Jewish cultural atmosphere. Handball, folk dancing, chess, broadcasting, lifesaving and snorkeling are some of the camp's activities. Special events include a Fourth of July carnival and a camp Olympics. Beginning at age 12, campers embark on trips that vary according to age group; destinations are Lake George; Boston, MA, and Philadelphia, PA; Hershey Park, PA, and Washington, DC; and Canada.

CAMP VICTORY LAKE
Res — Coed Ages 8-15

Hyde Park, NY 12538. 277 Crum Elbow Rd, PO Box 482. Tel: 845-229-8851.
www.campvictorylake.org   E-mail: janedoe@mysitemyway.com
Philip Wesley II, Dir.
Adm: FCFS. Appl due: Rolling. Staff: Admin 7. Couns 20.
Features: Computers Debate Crafts Creative_Writing Drama Archery Canoe Hiking Baseball Basketball Soccer Swim Volleyball.

Fees 2011: Res $650-1275, 2-4 wks. Day $550-1075.
Housing: Cabins Dorms Houses. **Swimming:** Pool.
Est 1955. Nonprofit. Seventh-day Adventist. **Ses:** 3. **Wks/ses:** 2-4. Operates July-Aug. ACA.

Victory Lake offers structured programming for children who wish to partake of recreational camping in a Christian environment. Programs incorporate the outdoors, the arts, swimming, cooking, sewing, archery, canoeing, mountaineering, hiking and sports. One-on-one instruction is available in most areas.

CAMP SHOMRIA
Res — Coed Ages 8-15

Liberty, NY 12754. 52 Lake Marie Rd.
Contact (Sept-June): 114 W 26th St, Ste 1001, New York, NY 10001.
Year-round Tel: 212-627-2830, 877-746-6742. Fax: 212-989-9840.
www.campshomria.com E-mail: info@campshomria.org
Shaked Angel, Dir.
Adm: FCFS. **Appl due:** Rolling. **Enr:** 150. **Staff:** Admin 3. Couns 30.
Features: Ecol Environ_Sci Govt Lang Crafts Creative_Writing Dance Music Theater Aquatics Boating Canoe Community_Serv Hiking Peace/Cross-cultural Work Baseball Basketball In-line_Skating Soccer Softball Swim Volleyball.
Fees 2011: Res $850-3995, 1-6 wks.
Housing: Cabins Tents. Avg per room/unit: 15. **Swimming:** Pool.
Est 1923. Nonprofit. **Spons:** Hashomer Hatzair. Jewish. **Ses:** 6. **Wks/ses:** 1-6. Operates June-Aug.

In a kibbutz-style setting, Shomria emphasizes a commitment to Israel, Jewish continuity and social justice. Religious and cultural programming incorporates Israeli dancing and singing. Outdoor activities include camping, hiking, sports and scouting. Some Israeli children enroll each year, and the camp organizes a trip to Israel for children entering 11th grade.

CAMP WHITMAN ON SENECA LAKE
Res — Coed Ages 8-17

Penn Yan, NY 14527. 150 Whitman Rd. Tel: 315-536-7753. Fax: 315-536-2128.
www.campwhitman.org E-mail: camp@campwhitman.org
Idelle Dillon, Dir.
Grades 3-12. Adm: FCFS. **Appl due:** Rolling. **Enr:** 100. **Staff:** Admin 6. Couns 12.
Features: Crafts Drama Fine_Arts Music Aquatics Bicycle_Tours Boating Canoe Hiking Kayak Ropes_Crse Sail Wilderness_Camp Wilderness_Canoe Soccer Softball Swim.
Fees 2011: Res $235-315, ½-1 wk. Aid (Need).
Housing: Cabins. **Swimming:** Lake Pool.
Est 1953. Nonprofit. Presbyterian. **Ses:** 28. **Wks/ses:** ½-1. Operates June-Aug.

Sailing, canoeing, hiking, swimming, crafts, sports and Bible study are among Camp Whitman's morning and afternoon scheduled activities. Evenings consist of all-camp activities, games and campfires. Specialty sessions focus on kayaking, canoeing, music and drama, sailing and music. Adventure canoeing and biking trips accommodate campers in grades 8-12. A camp for children with developmental disabilities is also available.

CAMP LI-LO-LI
Res — Coed Ages 8-17

Randolph, NY 14772. 8811 Sunfish Run Rd.
Contact (Aug-June): 55 Kernwood Dr, Rochester, NY 14624.

Year-round Tel: 716-945-4900, 877-518-1704. Fax: 716-945-0423.
www.campli-lo-li.com   E-mail: registrar@campli-lo-li.com
Allan McIntee, Admin.
Adm: FCFS. Appl due: Rolling. Enr: 150. Staff: Admin 4. Couns 30.
Features: Astron Crafts Aquatics Archery Canoe Climbing_Wall Fishing Hiking Mtn_Biking Riding Riflery Ropes_Crse Wilderness_Camp Wilderness_Canoe Baseball Basketball Equestrian Football Swim Tennis Volleyball.
Fees 2011: Res $230-460 (+$38-76), 1-2 wks.
Housing: Cabins Lodges Tepees. Avg per room/unit: 10. Swimming: Pond Pool.
Est 1953. Nonprofit. Nondenom Christian. Ses: 7. Wks/ses: 1-2. Operates July-Sept.

This Christian camp comprises a preteen camp for children ages 8-13, a teen camp for those ages 13-17 and a family camp. Li-Lo-Li features waterfront pursuits, sports, crafts, horseback riding and a ropes course. In addition, the program includes a lifeguard training course and a Roundup week that includes horsemanship, archery, music, art in nature, mountain biking, backpacking, volleyball and other specialty areas. Daily cabin devotions, special studies, Bible memorization exercises and prayer times are among Li-Lo-Li's religious activities.

CAMP TURNER
Res — Coed Ages 7-16

Salamanca, NY 14779. Allegany State Park, PO Box 264. Tel: 716-354-4555.
Fax: 716-354-2055.
www.campturner.com   E-mail: campturner@gmail.com
John Mann, Dir.
Adm: FCFS. Appl due: Rolling. Enr: 110. Enr cap: 110. Staff: Admin 5. Couns 38. Res 10.
Features: Ecol Crafts Dance Drama Music Aquatics Archery Chess Cooking Fishing Hiking Riding Ropes_Crse Wilderness_Camp Yoga Basketball Equestrian Soccer Softball Street_Hockey Swim.
Fees 2009: Res $305-345 (+$15), 1 wk.
Housing: Cabins. Avg per room/unit: 10. Swimming: Lake.
Est 1923. Nonprofit. Roman Catholic. Ses: 6. Wks/ses: 1. Operates July-Aug.

Operated by the Catholic Youth Department of the Diocese of Buffalo, Turner offers recreational activities in a Christian setting. Scheduled activities include horseback riding, athletics, outdoor living skills, arts and crafts, nature study, swimming and Native American lore. Campfires, hikes, picnics and camp outs are also popular.

CAMP QUINIPET
Res — Coed Ages 6-17

Shelter Island Heights, NY 11965. 99 Shore Rd, PO Box 549. Tel: 631-749-0430.
Fax: 631-749-3403.
www.quinipet.org   E-mail: info@quinipet.org
Greg Nissen, Dir.
Grades 1-12. Adm: FCFS. Appl due: Rolling. Enr: 107.
Features: Crafts Music Hiking Sail Swim.
Fees 2012: Res $550-600, 1 wk. Day $500, 1 wk.
Housing: Cabins. Swimming: Lake.
Est 1947. Nonprofit. Nondenom Christian. Ses: 6. Wks/ses: 1. Operates July-Aug. ACA.

Traditional sessions at Quinipet provide opportunities for hiking, swimming, and arts and crafts, while specialty camps emphasize sailing, bicycling, choir, ecology and athletics.

DEERFOOT LODGE
Res — Boys Ages 9-16

Speculator, NY 12164. PO Box 228. Tel: 518-548-5277. Fax: 518-548-6333.
Contact (Sept-May): Tel: 518-256-0106, Fax: 518-207-0434.
www.deerfoot.org   E-mail: deerfoot@deerfoot.org
Ronald W. Mackey, Dir.
Adm: FCFS. **Appl due:** Rolling. **Enr:** 150. **Staff:** Admin 30. Couns 45. Res 75.
Features: Crafts Aquatics Archery Canoe Fishing Hiking Mountaineering Mtn_Trips Outdoor_Ed Riflery Ropes_Crse Sail Survival_Trng Wilderness_Camp Wilderness_Canoe Woodcraft Swim.
Fees 2012: Res $1100 (+$50), 2 wks. Aid (Need).
Housing: Cabins Tents Tepees. **Swimming:** Lake.
Est 1930. Nonprofit. Nondenom Christian. **Ses:** 4. **Wks/ses:** 2. Operates June-Aug. ACA.

At this Christian camp, boys are divided into three sections: Woodsmen (ages 8-11) and Pioneers (ages 12 and 13) are housed in cabins, while Indians (ages 14-16) live in teepees. All boys participate in two- or three-day hiking or canoeing trips, while experienced campers may embark on 12-day treks. Campers are immersed in a Christ-centered environment that includes fellowship, prayer and worship.

CAMP TAPAWINGO
Res — Girls Ages 9-15

Speculator, NY 12164. 106 Downey Ave, PO Box 250. Tel: 518-548-4311.
Fax: 518-548-4324.
www.camp-of-the-woods.org   E-mail: tapawingo@camp-of-the-woods.org
Joy Huseland, Dir.
Adm: FCFS. **Appl due:** Rolling. **Enr:** 72. **Enr cap:** 72. **Staff:** Admin 8. Couns 20.
Features: Drama Music Archery Canoe Climbing_Wall Hiking Riding Ropes_Crse Sail Survival_Trng Wilderness_Camp Swim Tennis Water-skiing.
Fees 2012: Res $515 (+$20-30), 1 wk. Aid 2009 (Need): $10,000.
Housing: Cabins Tents. Avg per room/unit: 8. **Swimming:** Lake.
Est 1959. Nonprofit. **Spons:** Gospel Volunteers. Nondenom Christian. **Ses:** 8. **Wks/ses:** 1. Operates June-Aug. ACA.

Located on an island in Lake Pleasant, this Christian camp offers Bible study, land sports and watersports, hiking, woodcraft, music, and arts and crafts. Tapawingo conducts a CIT program for 16- and 17-year-old girls.

CAMP YOUNG JUDAEA SPROUT LAKE
Res — Coed Ages 7-13

Verbank, NY 12585. 6 Sprout Lake Camp Rd. Tel: 845-677-3411. Fax: 845-677-6912.
Contact (Winter): 50 W 58th St, 8th Fl, New York, NY 10019. Tel: 212-451-6233.
Fax: 212-451-6222.
www.cyjsl.org   E-mail: campsproutlake@youngjudaea.org
Helene Drobenare, Dir.
Grades 2-8. Adm: FCFS. **Fac 3. Staff:** Admin 4. Couns 100. Special needs 5.
Features: Crafts Dance Music Theater Aquatics Canoe Hiking Mtn_Trips Social_Servs Wilderness_Camp Baseball Basketball Soccer Swim Tennis.
Fees 2012: Res $1190-3950, 1-4 wks.
Housing: Cabins Houses. **Swimming:** Pool.
Est 1976. Nonprofit. Jewish. **Ses:** 2. **Wks/ses:** 1-4. Operates June-Aug. ACA.

Activities at this Jewish camp include aquatics, sports, arts and crafts, music, dance, drama, nature and camp craft. Older campers spend three days on a special trip, while younger children may enroll in a two-week session.

NORTH CAROLINA

CAMP ROCKMONT
Res — Boys Ages 7-16; Day — Coed 6-10

Black Mountain, NC 28711. 375 Lake Eden Rd. Tel: 828-686-3885. Fax: 828-686-7332.
www.rockmont.com   E-mail: info@rockmont.com
Dan Davis, Dir.
Adm: FCFS. **Enr:** 405. **Staff:** Admin 10. Couns 100.
Features: Crafts Aquatics Archery Canoe Caving Climbing_Wall Farm Fishing Hiking Kayak Mtn_Biking Rappelling Riding Riflery Rock_Climb Sail White-water_Raft Wilderness_Camp Basketball Cross-country Equestrian Football Golf Lacrosse Soccer Softball Swim Tennis Volleyball Water-skiing Watersports.
Fees 2012: Res $1115-4725 (+$90-215), 1-4 wks. Day $295, 1 wk.
Housing: Cabins Lodges. Avg per room/unit: 8. **Swimming:** Lake.
Est 1956. Inc. Nondenom Christian. **Ses:** 8. **Wks/ses:** 1-4. Operates June-Aug.

With a varied program featuring land sports and watersports, riflery, trips, hiking, riding and crafts, this Christian camp operates in a mountain setting near Asheville. In 2009, Rockmont established a coeducational day program for young campers.

CAMP JUDAEA
Res — Coed Ages 8-16

Hendersonville, NC 28792. 48 Camp Judaea Ln. Tel: 828-685-8841.
Fax: 828-685-8840.
Contact (Sept-May): 2700 Northeast Expy, Ste C500, Atlanta, GA 30345.
Tel: 404-634-7883. Fax: 404-325-2743.
Year-round Toll-free: 800-788-1567.
www.campjudaea.org   E-mail: info@campjudaea.org
Tom Rosenberg, Dir.
Grades 3-11. Adm: FCFS. Admitted: 99%. **Appl due:** Rolling. **Enr:** 250. **Enr cap:** 250.
Staff: Admin 5. Couns 40.
Travel: DC NY.
Features: Crafts Dance Drama Fine_Arts Music Photog Aquatics Archery Canoe Climbing_Wall Community_Serv Fishing Hiking Outdoor_Ed Rappelling Riding Rock_Climb Ropes_Crse Wilderness_Camp Baseball Basketball Equestrian Roller_Hockey Soccer Softball Swim Tennis Ultimate_Frisbee Volleyball.
Fees 2012: Res $4000-4575, 3½ wks. Aid (Need).
Housing: Cabins. **Swimming:** Lake Pool.
Est 1961. Nonprofit. Jewish. **Ses:** 2. **Wks/ses:** 3½. Operates June-Aug. ACA.

Campers enrich their Jewish identity through music, dance and crafts relevant to Judaism, and also take part in traditional camp activities. Programming also emphasizes the importance of environmentalism. Offerings include land sports and watersports, riding, fine arts and hiking. A weeklong trip to Washington, DC, is available for campers in grade 9. CJ is a kosher camp that observes Shabbat and kashrut.

CAMP WILLOW RUN
Res — Coed Ages 8-17

Littleton, NC 27850. 190 Mangum Ln. Tel: 252-586-4665. Fax: 252-586-4909.
www.campwillowrun.org   E-mail: info@campwillowrun.org
Robbie Harris, Dir.
Grades 3-12. Adm: FCFS. **Fac 45. Staff:** Admin 5. Couns 20.

Features: Crafts Music Aquatics Archery Canoe Climbing_Wall Riflery Ropes_Crse Sail Basketball Swim Water-skiing.
Fees 2011: Res $420, 1 wk.
Housing: Cabins. **Swimming:** Lake.
Est 1968. Nonprofit. **Spons:** Youth Camps for Christ. Nondenom Christian. **Ses:** 8. **Wks/ses:** 1. Operates June-Aug. ACA.

CWR offers swimming, canoeing, sailing, a ropes course, archery, riflery, basketball, crafts and model rocketry. Campers sleep in boxcars that have been converted into dorms. In addition to recreational activities, boys and girls participate in Bible study, Christian music and devotions.

CAMP RIDGECREST FOR BOYS
CAMP CRESTRIDGE FOR GIRLS
Res — Coord Ages 7-16

Ridgecrest, NC 28770. PO Box 279. Tel: 828-669-8051, 800-968-1630. Fax: 828-669-5512.
www.ridgecrestcamps.com   E-mail: rscamps@ridgecrestcamps.com
Ron Springs, Dir.
Grades 2-11. Adm: FCFS. **Appl due:** Rolling. **Enr:** 250. **Enr cap:** 250. **Staff:** Couns 40.
Features: Environ_Sci Crafts Aquatics Archery Canoe Climbing_Wall Hiking Mountaineering Mtn_Biking Mtn_Trips Outdoor_Ed Paintball Riding Riflery Rock_Climb Ropes_Crse White-water_Raft Wilderness_Camp Woodcraft Baseball Basketball Cross-country Equestrian Football Gymnastics Lacrosse Soccer Swim Tennis Ultimate_Frisbee Volleyball Weight_Trng Rocketry.
Fees 2012: Res $650-5800 (+$30), 1-8 wks.
Housing: Cabins. Avg per room/unit: 8. **Swimming:** Lake.
Est 1929. Nonprofit. **Spons:** Lifeway Christian Resources. Nondenom Christian. **Ses:** 11. **Wks/ses:** 1-8. Operates June-Aug. ACA.

Owned and operated by Lifeway Christian Resources, these Christian brother and sister camps offer a traditional recreational program. Activities include horseback riding, archery, riflery, and a variety of sports and aquatics. A six-day session is available only to first-time campers who are preparing for grades 2-6; traditional sessions run for two to eight weeks.

HIGHER GROUND SUMMER CAMP
Res — Coed Ages 8-18

Swannanoa, NC 28778. 170 Woodland Dr. Tel: 919-656-5042.
Contact (Aug-June): 3809 Sparrow Pond Ln, Raleigh, NC 27606. Tel: 919-859-2226.
www.carolinacamp.com   E-mail: shanebazer@gmail.com
Paul David Kurts, Dir.
Adm: FCFS. **Appl due:** Rolling. **Enr:** 136. **Enr cap:** 136. **Staff:** Couns 32.
Features: Crafts Dance Drama Aquatics Archery Boating Canoe Climbing_Wall Fishing Paintball Riflery Ropes_Crse Basketball Football Soccer Softball Swim Tennis Volleyball Watersports.
Fees 2012: Res $365, 1 wk. Aid (Need).
Housing: Cabins. Avg per room/unit: 15. **Swimming:** Lake.
Est 1960. Nonprofit. Nondenom Christian. **Ses:** 1. **Wks/ses:** 1. Operates July.

Located 10 miles east of Asheville on a 100-acre site in the Blue Ridge Mountains, Higher Ground combines group activities such as paintball, sports, archery and dance with supervised optional pursuits such as swimming, paddle boating, fishing and wall climbing. Christian activities include worship, chapel services and interactive small-group discussions.

OHIO

CAMP WANAKE
Res — Coed Ages 6-18; Day — Coed 6-11

Beach City, OH 44608. 9463 Manchester Ave SW. Tel: 330-756-2333, 800-831-3972. Fax: 330-756-2300.
www.campwanake.org   E-mail: info@campwanake.org
Julie Lautt, Dir.
Grades 1-12. Adm: FCFS. **Appl due:** Rolling. **Enr:** 125. **Enr cap:** 175. **Staff:** Admin 13. Couns 25. Res 45.
Features: Environ_Sci Crafts Creative_Writing Drama Fine_Arts Music Aquatics Archery Canoe Caving Climbing_Wall Community_Serv Farm Fishing Hiking Mtn_Biking Outdoor_Ed Rappelling Riding Rock_Climb Ropes_Crse White-water_Raft Wilderness_Camp Baseball Equestrian Soccer Swim.
Fees 2012: Res $299-1099, 1 wk. Day $159-179, 1 wk. Aid 2010 (Need): $6400.
Housing: Cabins Dorms Lodges. Avg per room/unit: 6-18. **Swimming:** Pool.
Est 1946. Nonprofit. United Methodist. **Ses:** 7. **Wks/ses:** 1. Operates June-Aug.

Wanake's sessions for young campers (entering grades 1-3) concentrate on such traditional pursuits as games, crafts, horseback riding and swimming, while programs for those entering grades 4-8 focus on hiking, riding, climbing, drama or music, among others activities. High schoolers may engage in more challenging activities, such as wilderness camping, white-water rafting and leadership development.

CAMP BURTON
Res — Coed Ages 6-18; Day — Coed 4-8

Burton, OH 44021. 14282 Butternut Rd. Tel: 440-834-8984, 877-793-4766. Fax: 440-834-0525.
www.campburton.org   E-mail: mail@campburton.org
Dave Scull, Dir.
Grades PS-12. Adm: FCFS. **Appl due:** Rolling. **Enr:** 170. **Staff:** Admin 5. Couns 18.
Features: Crafts Drama Music Adventure_Travel Aquatics Archery Canoe Climbing_Wall Hiking Paintball Rappelling Riflery Rock_Climb Ropes_Crse Wilderness_Camp Baseball Basketball Softball Swim Volleyball Watersports.
Fees 2010: Res $190-275 (+$30), ½-1 wk. Day $150, 1 wk.
Housing: Cabins Tepees. Avg per room/unit: 7. **Swimming:** Pool.
Est 1956. Nonprofit. Baptist. **Ses:** 12. **Wks/ses:** ½-1. Operates June-Aug.

This Christian camp offers aquatics, canoeing, sports, campfires, Bible study, ropes courses and a climbing wall. Day camp sessions accommodate children from age 4 through grade 3.

CAMP WISE
Res — Coed Ages 7-15

Chardon, OH 44024. 13164 Taylor Wells Rd. Tel: 440-635-5444. Fax: 440-635-0201.
Contact (Winter): c/o Jewish Community Center of Cleveland, 26001 S Woodland Rd, Beachwood, OH 44122. Tel: 216-593-6250. Fax: 216-831-7796.
www.campwise.org   E-mail: wisekids@mandeljcc.org
Sean Morgan, Dir.
Grades 2-10. Adm: FCFS. **Appl due:** Jan.
Features: Crafts Drama Media Archery Canoe Hiking Kayak Mtn_Biking Riding Ropes_Crse Basketball Football Golf Soccer Softball Swim Tennis Tubing.
Fees 2012: Res $1290-8200, 1-7 wks. Aid (Need).
Housing: Cabins. Avg per room/unit: 8-12. **Swimming:** Lake.

Est 1907. **Spons:** Jewish Community Center of Cleveland. Jewish. **Ses:** 16. **Wks/ses:** 1-7. Operates June-Aug. ACA.

Situated on a rustic, 300-acre site, the camp conducts a full recreational program in a Jewish setting. Many programs feature Jewish themes, and campers and staff celebrate each Shabbat. In addition, Bar and Bat Mitzvah training is offered once a week. Each camper selects and participates in five activities during the session.

EAST OHIO CAMPS
Res — Coed Ages 5 and up

North Canton, OH 44720. 8800 Cleveland Ave NW, PO Box 2800. Tel: 330-499-3972. Fax: 330-499-8336.
www.eastohiocamps.org   E-mail: camp@eocumc.com
Eric Dingler, William Graham & Julie Lautt, Dirs.
Grades K-12. Adm: FCFS. Admitted: 100%. **Appl due:** Rolling.
Features: Astron Computers Environ_Sci Sci Crafts Creative_Writing Dance Filmmaking Fine_Arts Media Music Photog Theater Adventure_Travel Aquatics Archery Bicycle_ Tours Boating Canoe Caving Climbing_Wall Cooking Farm Fishing Hiking Kayak Mtn_ Biking Ranch Rappelling Riding Rock_Climb Ropes_Crse Sail Scuba White-water_Raft Wilderness_Camp Wilderness_Canoe Basketball Equestrian Golf Soccer Swim Ultimate_Frisbee Volleyball Water-skiing Watersports.
Fees 2010: Res $279-499, 1 wk. Aid 2009 (Need): $30,000.
Housing: Cabins Dorms Lodges Tents Tepees. **Swimming:** Lake Pool.
Nonprofit. United Methodist. **Ses:** 9. **Wks/ses:** 1. Operates June-Aug.

Operating in Carrollton, Hiram and Beach City, these three Methodist camps offer Bible study, worship, swimming, hiking, canoeing and other traditional activities. Specialty-camp selections include horseback riding, canoeing, pioneering, water-skiing and scuba diving. Older teens may enroll in backpacking and canoeing, bicycling or white-water canoeing trip camps. EOC also conducts separate sessions for children and adults with mental special needs.

BEULAH BEACH CAMP
Res — Coed Ages 7-18; Day — Coed 5-11

Vermilion, OH 44089. 6101 W Lake Rd. Tel: 440-967-4861. Fax: 440-967-4783.
www.beulahbeach.org   E-mail: rtrainer@beulahbeach.org
Ralph Trainer, Exec Dir.
Grades K-PG. Adm: FCFS. **Appl due:** Mar. **Enr:** 375.
Features: Crafts Dance Drama Aquatics Archery Bicycle_Tours Boating Canoe Climbing_Wall Fishing Hiking Paintball Rappelling Riding Ropes_Crse Sail Survival_Trng Wilderness_Camp Wilderness_Canoe Work Baseball Basketball Field_Hockey Football Soccer Softball Swim Watersports.
Fees 2010: Res $290-330, ½-1 wk. Day $115, 1 wk.
Housing: Cabins Dorms Houses Lodges. **Swimming:** Lake Pool.
Nonprofit. Nondenom Christian. **Ses:** 23. **Wks/ses:** ½-1. Operates June-Aug.

Beulah Beach balances music, sports, swimming, crafts and other pursuits with Christian education. Specialty residential camps enable boys and girls to focus on an area such as watersports, adventure, creative arts or performing arts. Although they are less specialized than sleepover programs, day camps also revolve around a theme.

LUTHERAN OUTDOOR MINISTRIES IN OHIO SUMMER CAMPS
Res — Coed Ages 5-17

Westerville, OH 43081. 863 Eastwind Dr. Tel: 614-890-2267, 800-431-5666.
Fax: 614-890-8210.
www.lomocamps.org   E-mail: info@lomocamps.org
Penny R. Christensen, Exec Dir.
Grades K-12. Adm: FCFS.
Features: Environ_Sci Crafts Music Theater Canoe Climbing_Wall Hiking Rappelling Riding Ropes_Crse White-water_Raft Basketball Equestrian Soccer Swim Volleyball.
Fees 2010: Res $175-515, ½-1 wk.
Housing: Cabins Lodges Tents. **Swimming:** Pool.
Nonprofit. Lutheran. **Ses:** 11. **Wks/ses:** ½-1. Operates June-Aug.

LOMO offers Bible study, worship, hiking, swimming and crafts at five Ohio locations. In addition to traditional recreational camps, the program offers specialty camps pertaining to soccer, music, adventure, leadership training, international adventure and faith building. Travel and adventure offerings include white-water rafting, and bicycle and canoe trips. Campers with special needs are mainstreamed into the activities of the appropriate age group.

OKLAHOMA

NEW LIFE RANCH
Res — Coed Ages 8-18

Colcord, OK 74338. 160 New Life Ranch Dr. Tel: 918-422-5506. Fax: 918-422-5644.
www.newliferanch.com   E-mail: info@newliferanch.com
David Jaquess, Exec Dir.
Grades 3-12. Adm: FCFS. **Appl due:** Rolling. **Enr:** 240. **Enr cap:** 250. **Staff:** Admin 30. Couns 50. Res 30.
Features: Crafts Creative_Writing Dance Drama Photog Adventure_Travel Aquatics Archery Bicycle_Tours Canoe Caving Climbing_Wall Fishing Hiking Kayak Mountaineering Mtn_Biking Mtn_Trips Outdoor_Ed Paintball Ranch Rappelling Riding Riflery Rock_Climb Ropes_Crse Basketball Equestrian Football Soccer Swim Tennis Ultimate_ Frisbee Volleyball Weight_Trng.
Fees 2012: Res $48-585 (+$50-100), 1 wk. Aid 2009 (Merit & Need): $100,000.
Housing: Cabins. Avg per room/unit: 10. **Swimming:** Pool Stream.
Est 1958. Nonprofit. Nondenom Christian. **Ses:** 8. **Wks/ses:** 1. Operates June-Aug. ACA.

This Christian camp provides Bible study and chapel each day. In addition, campers choose two classes daily from the following options: horsemanship, archery, riflery, tennis, swimming, canoeing, crafts, sports and a ropes course. Campers participate in other recreational activities during their free time.

OREGON

CAMP HOWARD
Res — Coed Ages 6-14; Day — Coed 6-9

Corbett, OR 97019. 11010 SE Camp Howard Rd.
Contact (Sept-May): c/o Catholic Youth Organization, 825 NE 20th Ave, Ste 120, Portland, OR 97232.

Year-round Tel: 503-231-9484, Fax: 503-231-9531.
www.cyocamphoward.org   E-mail: allyh@cyocamphoward.org
Slater Swan, Dir.
Adm: FCFS. **Appl due:** Rolling. **Enr:** 150. **Staff:** Admin 6. Couns 34.
Features: Crafts Aquatics Archery Canoe Hiking Paintball Riflery Basketball Football Swim Volleyball.
Fees 2012: Res $175-550 (+$50), ½-1 wk. Day $250 (+$50), 1 wk.
Housing: Cabins. Avg per room/unit: 8. **Swimming:** Pool.
Est 1942. Nonprofit. **Spons:** Catholic Youth Organization. Roman Catholic. **Ses:** 8. **Wks/ses:** ½-1. Operates July-Aug. ACA.

A member agency of Catholic Charities, the camp accepts boys and girls of all faiths. Programming places a particular emphasis on athletic instruction, which is provided by certified coaches. A number of specialty camps are available.

B'NAI B'RITH CAMP
Res — Coed Ages 7-16; Day — Coed 3-13

Neotsu, OR 97219.
Contact (Winter): 9400 Beaverton-Hillsdale Hwy, Ste 147, Beaverton, OR 97005.
Year-round Tel: 503-452-3443, Fax: 503-452-0750.
www.bbcamp.org   E-mail: dzimmerman@bbcamp.org
Michelle Koplan, Exec Dir.
Grades PS-11. Adm: FCFS. **Appl due:** Rolling. **Enr:** 150-175. **Enr cap:** 175. **Staff:** Admin 12. Couns 40.
Features: Ecol Environ_Sci Geol Lang Marine_Bio/Stud Sci Writing/Journ Crafts Creative_ Writing Dance Drama Fine_Arts Music Painting Studio_Art Adventure_Travel Aquatics Archery Bicycle_Tours Boating Canoe Community_Serv Conservation Cooking Exploration Fishing Hiking Kayak Mtn_Trips Outdoor_Ed Rock_Climb Ropes_Crse Sail Survival_Trng White-water_Raft Wilderness_Camp Yoga Aerobics Baseball Basketball Football Golf Gymnastics Lacrosse Martial_Arts Rugby Soccer Softball Swim Tennis Ultimate_Frisbee Volleyball Water-skiing Watersports.
Fees 2012: Res $1000-3365 (+$100-150), 1-4 wks. Day $120 (+$10-30), 1 wk. Aid 2011 (Need): $36,000.
Housing: Cabins Houses Lodges. Avg per room/unit: 17. **Swimming:** Lake Ocean Pool.
Est 1921. Nonprofit. Jewish. **Ses:** 10. **Wks/ses:** 1-4. Operates June-Aug. ACA.

In a lakeside setting on the Oregon coast, B'nai B'rith conducts a wide-ranging program of Jewish enrichment activities (including Shabbat celebrations), aquatics, athletics, arts and crafts, leadership opportunities, creative arts, high and low ropes courses, and nature study. Campers of all ages go on overnight camp outs, while older boys and girls embark on white-water rafting trips.

CAMP MAGRUDER
Res — Coed Ages 6-19; Day — Coed 6-12

Rockaway Beach, OR 97136. 17450 Old Pacific Hwy. Tel: 503-355-2310.
Fax: 503-355-8701.
www.campmagruder.org   E-mail: office@campmagruder.org
James Ralston, Prgm Dir.
Adm: FCFS. Admitted: 99%. **Appl due:** Rolling. **Enr:** 190. **Enr cap:** 250. **Staff:** Admin 3. Couns 85. Res 3.
Features: Ecol Environ_Sci Marine_Bio/Stud Sci Crafts Dance Drama Music Aquatics Archery Boating Canoe Community_Serv Conservation Exploration Fishing Hiking Kayak Outdoor_Ed Riding Ropes_Crse Sail Social_Servs Badminton Baseball Basketball Swim Ultimate_Frisbee Volleyball Watersports.
Fees 2010: Res $265-500 (+$25), 1 wk. Day $90, 1 wk. Aid (Need).

Housing: Cabins Dorms Lodges. **Swimming:** Lake Ocean.
Est 1945. Nonprofit. United Methodist. **Ses:** 15. **Wks/ses:** 1. Operates Year-round. ACA.

Magruder offers an ocean beach, boating, archery, a low ropes challenge course and various other activities. Ecology learning, team building and leadership are special programs.

CANYONVIEW CAMP
Res — Coed Ages 8-18; Day — Coed 6-12

Silverton, OR 97381. PO Box 128. Tel: 971-239-1347, 888-516-5655.
  Fax: 503-873-8369.
www.canyonviewcamp.org   E-mail: info@canyonview.us
Rick Saffeels, Prgm Dir.
Adm: FCFS. Admitted: 95%. **Appl due:** Rolling. **Enr cap:** 35-150. **Staff:** Admin 5. Couns 40. Res 12.
Features: Crafts Music Painting Aquatics Archery Boating Canoe Rock_Climb Wilderness_Camp Equestrian Swim.
Fees 2009: Res $215-380, 1 wk. Day $100, 1 wk. Aid 2009 (Merit & Need): $150.
Housing: Cabins Tepees. Avg per room/unit: 6. **Swimming:** Lake.
Est 1970. Nonprofit. **Spons:** Bible Teaching Inc. Nondenom Christian. **Ses:** 10. **Wks/ses:** 1. Operates June-Sept.

Canyonview offers horseback riding and wilderness adventure camps with a Christian focus. Beach trips, games and Bible lessons are some of the featured activities.

BIG LAKE YOUTH CAMP
Res — Coed Ages 7-17

Sisters, OR 97759. 13100 Hwy 20.
Contact (Sept-May): 19800 Oatfield Rd, Gladstone, OR 97027.
Year-round Tel: 503-850-3583, Fax: 503-850-3483.
www.biglake.org   E-mail: jillany@biglake.org
Monte Torkelsen, Dir.
Adm: FCFS. **Appl due:** Rolling. **Enr:** 250. **Enr cap:** 250. **Staff:** Admin 8. Couns 30.
Features: Crafts Drama Music Photog Aquatics Archery Bicycle_Tours Canoe Mtn_Biking Riding Rock_Climb Sail Survival_Trng White-water_Raft Wilderness_Camp Basketball Equestrian Golf Gymnastics Skateboarding Swim Volleyball Water-skiing.
Fees 2009: Res $365-450, 1 wk.
Housing: Cabins. **Swimming:** Lake.
Est 1962. Nonprofit. Seventh-day Adventist. **Ses:** 9. **Wks/ses:** 1. Operates June-Aug. ACA.

Campers participating in this traditional program rotate among activities according to their interests. Boys and girls wishing to focus on rock climbing, skateboarding, mountaineering, watersports, mountain biking or one of several land sports may enroll in a specialty program.

PENNSYLVANIA

SEQUANOTA
Res — Coed Ages 6-18; Day — Coed 6-11

Boswell, PA 15531. 368 Sequanota Rd.
Contact (Winter): PO Box 245, Jennerstown, PA 15547.
Year-round Tel: 814-629-6627, Fax: 814-629-0128.
www.sequanota.com   E-mail: contact@sequanota.com

Rev. George Mason, Exec Dir.
Adm: FCFS. **Appl due:** Rolling. **Enr:** 600. **Staff:** Admin 5. Couns 24.
Features: Crafts Music Photog Bicycle_Tours Canoe Climbing_Wall Fishing Hiking Mtn_ Trips Rappelling Riding Rock_Climb Ropes_Crse White-water_Raft Wilderness_Camp Basketball Soccer Swim Volleyball.
Fees 2011: Res $195-465, ½-1 wk. Day $70, 1 wk. Aid 2009 (Need): $295.
Housing: Cabins Dorms. **Swimming:** Pool.
Est 1947. Nonprofit. Lutheran. **Ses:** 6. **Wks/ses:** ½-1. Operates June-Aug. ACA.

At this Evangelical Lutheran camp, children may enroll in guitar, sports, photography, horseback riding, fishing and wilderness skills specialty camps. Popular activities include swimming, hiking, nature activities, Bible study, campfires and crafts. Sequanota conducts special half- and full-week sessions for families, younger campers and individuals with special needs.

SPRUCE LAKE WILDERNESS CAMP
Res — Coed Ages 7-18

Canadensis, PA 18325. 5389 Rte 447. Tel: 570-595-7505, 800-822-7505.
Fax: 570-595-0328.
www.wildernesscamp.org   E-mail: erick@sprucelake.org
Eric Kauffman, Dir.
Adm: FCFS. **Appl due:** Rolling. **Enr:** 135. **Enr cap:** 154. **Staff:** Admin 8. Couns 18. Res 24.
Features: Environ_Sci Sci Crafts Creative_Writing Dance Drama Photog Adventure_Travel Aquatics Archery Boating Canoe Caving Climbing_Wall Community_Serv Cooking Hiking Kayak Mountaineering Mtn_Biking Mtn_Trips Outdoor_Ed Pack_Train Rappelling Rock_Climb Ropes_Crse White-water_Raft Wilderness_Camp Wilderness_Canoe Baseball Basketball Football Soccer Softball Street_Hockey Swim Ultimate_Frisbee Volleyball.
Fees 2012: Res $172-345 (+$25), ½-1 wk. Aid 2010 (Need): $32,500.
Housing: Tents. Avg per room/unit: 8. **Swimming:** Pool.
Est 1963. Nonprofit. Mennonite. **Ses:** 9. **Wks/ses:** ½-1. Operates June-Aug. ACA.

Located on an 370 acres in the Pocono Mountains, Spruce Lake combines swimming, adventure programming, outdoor education and recreation with daily evening worship and devotionals. Children ages 7-10 may attend either with a (same-gender) parent or alone for a partial or full week. Campers ages 11-18 enroll in either an on-site resident session or an off-site expedition. Expeditions often involve out-of-state travel.

CAMP KIRCHENWALD
Res — Coed Ages 7-17; Day — Coed 6-8

Colebrook, PA 17042. 1 Cut Off Rd. Tel: 717-964-3121. Fax: 717-677-7597.
Contact (Sept-May): c/o Lutheran Camping Corp of Central Pennsylvania, PO Box 459, Arendtsville, PA 17303. Tel: 717-677-8211. Fax: 717-677-8211.
www.lutherancamping.org   E-mail: kirchenwald@lutherancamping.org
Michael Youse, Dir.
Grades 1-12. Adm: FCFS. **Appl due:** Rolling. **Enr:** 85. **Enr cap:** 85. **Staff:** Admin 3. Couns 16. Res 33.
Features: Crafts Aquatics Archery Canoe Caving Climbing_Wall Conservation Hiking Kayak Mtn_Biking Rock_Climb Ropes_Crse Survival_Trng Wilderness_Camp Wilderness_Canoe Badminton Soccer Swim Ultimate_Frisbee Volleyball Watersports.
Fees 2012: Res $205-495, ½-1 wk. Day $135, 1 wk. Aid 2011 (Need): $11,000.
Housing: Cabins Dorms. Avg per room/unit: 7. **Swimming:** Pool.
Est 1969. Nonprofit. **Spons:** Lutheran Camping Corporation of Central Pennsylvania. Lutheran. **Ses:** 8. **Wks/ses:** ½-1. Operates June-Aug.

Located on 340 acres of undeveloped timberland, this Lutheran camp integrates daily worship and Bible study into a traditional outdoor program. General camps allow children to sample a range of activities, and special sessions focus on horsemanship, survival training, soccer, kayaking, and arts and crafts. Weeklong canoeing and hiking trips to the Adirondack Mountains are also available.

CAMP DORA GOLDING
Res — Boys Ages 7-14

East Stroudsburg, PA 18301. 550 Craigs Meadow Rd. Tel: 570-223-0417. Fax: 570-223-0701.
Contact (Sept-June): 5515 New Utrecht Ave, Brooklyn, NY 11219. Tel: 718-437-7117. Fax: 718-437-7644.
www.campdoragolding.com   E-mail: info@campdoragolding.com
Alexander Z. Gold, Dir.
Grades 2-9. Adm: FCFS. **Appl due:** Rolling. **Enr:** 325. **Enr cap:** 325.
Features: Media Aquatics Archery Boating Canoe Climbing_Wall Fishing Hiking Kayak Mountaineering Rock_Climb Ropes_Crse Wilderness_Camp Baseball Basketball Field_Hockey Football Soccer Softball Swim Tennis Volleyball Watersports.
Fees 2011: Res $2095-3795 (+$95-190), 4-8 wks.
Housing: Cabins Houses. **Swimming:** Lake Pool.
Est 1925. Nonprofit. Orthodox Jewish. **Ses:** 2. **Wks/ses:** 4. Operates June-Aug.

This Orthodox Jewish camp combines Torah study with conventional camp activities. CDG's specialty sessions address archery, rock climbing, miniature golf and boating.

WLD RANCH SUMMER CAMP
Res — Coed Ages 5-18

Girard, PA 16417. 7351 Woolsey Rd. Tel: 814-474-3414. Fax: 562-286-5505.
www.wldranch.com   E-mail: info@wldranch.com
Malcolm Beall, Exec Dir.
Grades K-12. Adm: FCFS. Admitted: 98%. **Appl due:** Rolling. **Enr cap:** 40-90. **Staff:** Admin 4. Couns 16.
Features: Crafts Adventure_Travel Archery Canoe Climbing_Wall Fishing Hiking Rappelling Riding Riflery Ropes_Crse Wilderness_Camp Wilderness_Canoe Equestrian Swim.
Fees 2010: Res $160-350 (+$15-75), ½-1 wk. Aid 2009 (Need): $4000.
Housing: Cabins. Avg per room/unit: 15. **Swimming:** Pool.
Est 1963. Nonprofit. Evangelical. **Ses:** 10. **Wks/ses:** ½-1. Operates June-Aug.

WLD Ranch offers adventure-oriented programs that incorporate Bible classes and Christian activities. Three-day sessions serve as an introduction to camping for young boys and girls, while the standard six-day sessions provide a general recreational experience. Specialty camp options enable boys and girls to focus on horseback riding, adventure, canoeing or target sports.

CRYSTAL LAKE CAMPS
Res — Coed Ages 7-16

Hughesville, PA 17737. 1676 Crystal Lake Rd. Tel: 570-584-5608, 877-252-5437. Fax: 570-584-0169.
www.crystallakecamps.org   E-mail: camp@crystallakecamps.org
Elizabeth Hall, Exec Dir.
Adm: FCFS. **Enr:** 100. **Enr cap:** 100.
Features: Ecol Lang Crafts Creative_Writing Dance Filmmaking Music Photog Theater

Aquatics Archery Boating Canoe Climbing_Wall Cooking Fishing Hiking Kayak Mountaineering Mtn_Biking Mtn_Trips Riding Rock_Climb Ropes_Crse Sail Survival_Trng Wilderness_Camp Basketball Cross-country Equestrian Field_Hockey Soccer Swim Tennis Volleyball Watersports.
Fees 2012: Res $650-3249 (+$75), 1-6 wks.
Housing: Cabins. Avg per room/unit: 10. **Swimming:** Lake.
Est 1949. Nonprofit. Christian Science. **Ses:** 5. **Wks/ses:** 1-6. Operates June-Aug. ACA.

Crystal Lake offers aquatics and the usual land sports, as well as instruction in outdoor skills, music, drama and crafts. Applicants must regularly attend Christian Science Sunday school to gain admittance, and Christian Science is integral to daily activities for campers and staff.

HAYCOCK CAMPING MINISTRIES
Res — Coord Ages 7-12, Boys 13-16

Kintnersville, PA 18930. 3100 School Rd. Tel: 610-346-7155. Fax: 610-346-8927.
www.haycock.org   E-mail: info@haycock.org
Chris Hendrickson, Exec Dir.
Adm: FCFS. **Appl due:** Rolling. **Staff:** Admin 4. Couns 40. Res 4.
Features: Crafts Music Painting Aquatics Archery Aviation/Aero Boating Canoe Fishing Hiking Kayak Mtn_Trips Outdoor_Ed Paintball Rappelling Riding Riflery Rock_Climb Ropes_Crse Sail White-water_Raft Wilderness_Camp Woodcraft Basketball Equestrian Soccer Swim Ultimate_Frisbee Volleyball Water-skiing.
Fees 2011: Res $30-600, 1 wk. Aid (Need).
Housing: Cabins Lodges Tents Tepees. Avg per room/unit: 8. **Swimming:** Pool.
Est 1963. Nonprofit. Nondenom Christian. **Ses:** 7. **Wks/ses:** 1. Operates June-Aug. ACA.

Activities at this Christian camp include riflery, archery, canoeing, camp craft, horsemanship and swimming, in addition to a ropes course and adventure games. Specialty camps address horsemanship, riflery, music, kayaking, sports, aviation and paintball. While Haycock serves primarily boys, it conducts one girls' week each summer.

B'NAI B'RITH PERLMAN CAMP
Res — Coed Ages 8-16

Lake Como, PA 18437. 661 Rose Hill Rd. Tel: 570-635-9200. Fax: 570-635-9201.
Contact (Sept-May): 4 Professional Dr, Ste 122, Gaithersburg, MD 20879.
Tel: 301-977-0050. Fax: 301-977-0051.
www.perlmancamp.org   E-mail: info@perlmancamp.org
Lewis Sohinki, Dir.
Grades 3-11. Adm: FCFS. **Appl due:** Rolling. **Enr:** 375. **Staff:** Admin 10. Couns 100.
Features: Crafts Dance Drama Fine_Arts Media Music Photog Aquatics Archery Boating Canoe Climbing_Wall Conservation Cooking Fishing Hiking Kayak Mtn_Biking Rappelling Riding Rock_Climb Ropes_Crse Sail White-water_Raft Wilderness_Camp Woodcraft Baseball Basketball Field_Hockey Football Golf Gymnastics Lacrosse Martial_Arts Roller_Hockey Soccer Softball Swim Tennis Volleyball Watersports.
Fees 2012: Res $2430-8820 (+$135-185), 2-7 wks. Aid (Need).
Housing: Cabins. **Swimming:** Lake Pool.
Est 1954. Nonprofit. Jewish. **Ses:** 6. **Wks/ses:** 2-7. Operates June-Aug. ACA.

On a 400-acre site in the Pocono Mountains, this Jewish camp offers waterfront pursuits, outdoor living, athletics, arts, media and communications options, and two- to eight-day off-site trips. Boys and girls participate in six daily cabin activities, a general selection of their choosing and an evening activity that typically involves the entire camp. Color wars, camp carnivals and Israel day are among Perlman's special events.

CAMP RAMAH IN THE POCONOS
Res — Coed Ages 9-16

Lakewood, PA 19103. 2618 Upper Woods Rd. Tel: 570-798-2504. Fax: 215-798-2049.
Contact (Winter): 2100 Arch St, Philadelphia, PA 19103. Tel: 215-885-8556.
Fax: 215-885-8905.
www.ramahpoconos.org   E-mail: info@ramahpoconos.org
Rabbi Todd Zeff, Dir.
Grades 5-11. Adm: FCFS. **Appl due:** Rolling. **Enr:** 300. **Staff:** Couns 60.
Features: Lang Crafts Dance Drama Fine_Arts Music Photog Aquatics Archery Boating Canoe Climbing_Wall Cooking Fishing Hiking Kayak Mtn_Biking Mtn_Trips Ropes_Crse Sail Survival_Trng White-water_Raft Wilderness_Camp Woodcraft Baseball Basketball Soccer Softball Street_Hockey Swim Tennis Volleyball Watersports.
Fees 2012: Res $4300-7850 (+$475), 4-8 wks.
Housing: Cabins. Avg per room/unit: 12. **Swimming:** Lake Pool.
Est 1948. Nonprofit. Jewish. **Ses:** 3. **Wks/ses:** 4-8. Operates June-Aug. ACA.

Ramah conducts a particularly strong sports program that includes basketball, baseball, street hockey, soccer, volleyball, gymnastics and tennis. Boys and girls also gain exposure to the cultural arts: photography, woodworking, radio, dance and drama. Backpacking and canoe trips, as well as overnight hikes, teach basic outdoor living skills. Study of the Hebrew language and Jewish texts are part of the daily schedule, and the camp observes Shabbat.

CAMP MOUNT LUTHER
Res — Coed Ages 6-16; Day — Coed 5-11

Mifflinburg, PA 17844. 355 Mt Luther Ln. Tel: 570-922-1587. Fax: 570-922-1118.
www.campmountluther.org   E-mail: cml@campmountluther.org
Chad Hershberger, Dir.
Grades 2-12. Adm: FCFS. **Staff:** Admin 10. Couns 14.
Features: Crafts Music Photog Theater Archery Canoe Caving Fishing Hiking Mtn_Biking Rock_Climb Survival_Trng Wilderness_Camp Swim Watersports.
Fees 2011: Res $315-560, 1-2 wks. Day $197, 1 wk.
Housing: Cabins. Avg per room/unit: 8. **Swimming:** Pool.
Est 1963. Nonprofit. Lutheran. **Ses:** 7. **Wks/ses:** 1-2. Operates June-Aug. ACA.

Activities at this Evangelical Lutheran camp include swimming, crafts, Bible study, worship, campfires, camp outs, backpacking and canoeing. Specialty camps allow boys and girls to concentrate on fishing, theater arts, bicycling, outdoor exploration and survival, sports, archery or photography. Campers age 14 and above may go on extended canoeing or backpacking and white-water rafting trips, or they may participate in a service project and leadership program.

LUTHERLYN
Res — Coed Ages 7-18; Day — Coed 7-10

Prospect, PA 16052. PO Box 355. Tel: 724-865-2161. Fax: 724-865-9794.
www.lutherlyn.com   E-mail: registrar@lutherlyn.com
Rev. Randal K. Gullickson, Exec Dir.
Grades 2-12. Adm: FCFS. Admitted: 99%. **Appl due:** Rolling. **Enr:** 170. **Staff:** Admin 4. Couns 41.
Features: Archaeol Astron Ecol Environ_Sci Geol Crafts Music Theater Adventure_Travel Aquatics Archery Aviation/Aero Canoe Caving Climbing_Wall Community_Serv Conservation Fishing Hiking Kayak Mtn_Biking Outdoor_Ed Rappelling Riding Rock_Climb Ropes_Crse Survival_Trng White-water_Raft Wilderness_Camp Baseball Basketball Equestrian Soccer Softball Swim Ultimate_Frisbee Volleyball.
Fees 2009: Res $425-600, 1 wk. Day $130, 1 wk. Aid 2008 (Need): $30,000.
Housing: Cabins. Avg per room/unit: 9. **Swimming:** Lake Pool.

Est 1948. Nonprofit. Lutheran. **Ses:** 8. **Wks/ses:** 1. Operates June-Aug. ACA.

Swimming, campfires, arts and crafts, canoeing, hiking and sports are among the traditional activities at this Lutheran camp. Specialty programs cover such areas as nature, archaeology, Western and English riding, art, model rocketry, aviation, sports and adventure tripping. All programs include morning and evening devotions, Bible study and worship.

CAMP MEN-O-LAN
Res — Coed Ages 7-18; Day — Coed 6-11

Quakertown, PA 18951. 1415 Doerr Rd. Tel: 215-679-5144. Fax: 215-679-0226.
www.menolan.org   E-mail: bsmith.menolan@gmail.com
James Hite, Prgm Dir.
Grades 1-12. Adm: FCFS. **Appl due:** Rolling. **Enr:** 130. **Staff:** Admin 7. Couns 30.
Features: Crafts Aquatics Archery Boating Canoe Climbing_Wall Fishing Rappelling Riding Ropes_Crse Wilderness_Camp Baseball Basketball Equestrian Soccer Softball Swim Tennis Volleyball Watersports.
Fees 2009: Res $300, 1 wk. Day $165-210, 1 wk.
Housing: Cabins Tents. Avg per room/unit: 12. **Swimming:** Pool.
Est 1941. Nonprofit. Mennonite. **Ses:** 16. **Wks/ses:** 1. Operates June-Sept.

Men-O-Lan's recreational program places strong emphasis on Christian activities and Bible study. In addition to the regular sessions, the camp conducts a horsemanship session and a four-day, three-night canoeing trek down the Delaware River. Men-O-Lan occupies 174 wooded acres in Upper Bucks County.

KIRKWOOD CAMP
Res — Coed Ages 7-18; Day — Coed 3-11

Stroudsburg, PA 18360. RR 14, Box 7507. Tel: 570-421-8625. Fax: 570-421-3064.
www.kirkwoodcamp.org   E-mail: kirkwood@presbyphl.org
Judy Trigg, Dir.
Grades PS-12. Adm: FCFS. **Appl due:** Rolling. **Enr:** 100. **Staff:** Admin 3. Couns 16. Res 25.
Features: Crafts Music Hiking Mtn_Trips Ropes_Crse Basketball Equestrian Soccer Softball Swim.
Fees 2012: Res $250-495, ½-1 wk. Day $150, 1 wk. Aid 2011 (Need): $33,000.
Housing: Cabins Lodges Tents. Avg per room/unit: 12. **Swimming:** Pond Stream.
Est 1964. Nonprofit. Presbyterian. **Ses:** 15. **Wks/ses:** ½-1. Operates June-Aug. ACA.

Bible study, worship, games, swimming, crafts, archery and singing are some of Kirkwood's most popular activities. Special events, which occur throughout the week, include talent shows, campfires, cookouts and nature hikes. Older campers also engage in adventure pursuits and scheduled evening activities.

PINEMERE CAMP
Res — Coed Ages 6-14

Stroudsburg, PA 18360. 8100 Bartonsville Woods Rd. Tel: 570-629-0266.
Fax: 570-620-9053.
Contact (Sept-May): 4100 Main St, Ste 301, Philadelphia, PA 19127.
Tel: 215-487-2267. Fax: 215-487-2265.
www.pinemere.com   E-mail: camp@pinemere.com
Toby Ayash, Exec Dir.
Grades 2-9. Adm: FCFS. **Appl due:** Rolling. **Enr:** 250. **Enr cap:** 250. **Staff:** Admin 20. Couns 75.
Features: Crafts Dance Fine_Arts Music Theater Aquatics Archery Bicycle_Tours Canoe

Climbing_Wall Cooking Fishing Hiking Mtn_Biking Outdoor_Ed Riflery Ropes_Crse Wilderness_Camp Woodcraft Baseball Basketball Field_Hockey Football Lacrosse Soccer Softball Street_Hockey Swim Tennis Ultimate_Frisbee Volleyball.
Fees 2012: Res $3990-7420 (+$150), 3-7 wks. Aid (Need).
Housing: Cabins Tents. **Swimming:** Lake Pool.
Est 1942. Nonprofit. **Spons:** Jewish Community Center Association. Jewish. **Ses: 3. Wks/ses:** 3-7. Operates June-Aug. ACA.

Situated on a 180-acre campus in the Pocono Mountains, this Jewish camp offers such group-oriented activities as team sports, boating and canoeing, pioneering, archery, tennis and riflery. Drama and arts and crafts are also part of the program. Campers select and attend activities as both bunk mates and individuals. In addition to its regular sessions (which last for a minimum of three weeks), Pinemere conducts the three-day SPARK Program for children entering grades 1-4. The camp observes Shabbat and kashrut.

STREAMSIDE CAMP
Res — Coed Ages 8-16
(Coord — Res 12-16)

Stroudsburg, PA 18360. 303 Possinger Dr. Tel: 570-629-1902. Fax: 570-629-9650.
www.streamside.org   E-mail: summercamp@streamside.org
Matt Brown, Dir.
Adm: FCFS. **Appl due:** Rolling. **Enr:** 130. **Staff:** Admin 6. Couns 22.
Features: Environ_Sci Crafts Dance Drama Music Photog Aquatics Archery Canoe Conservation Exploration Fishing Hiking Mtn_Trips Ropes_Crse Wilderness_Camp Wilderness_Canoe Basketball Soccer Swim Volleyball.
Fees 2012: Res $249, 1 wk.
Housing: Cabins Lodges. Avg per room/unit: 8. **Swimming:** Pond Pool Stream.
Est 1942. Nonprofit. Nondenom Christian. **Ses:** 8. **Wks/ses:** 1. Operates June-July.

This Christian camp focuses on the needs of inner-city children. Recreational activities include swimming, boating, canoeing, sports, arts and crafts, hiking, nature study, archery, drama, choir, mountain climbing and horseback riding. An eight-day wilderness adventure camp is open to campers ages 13-16. The program for children ages 8-12 is coeducational; single-gender camps operate for boys and girls ages 12-16.

CAMP SUSQUE
Res — Coord Ages 6-16

Trout Run, PA 17771. 47 Susque Camp Rd. Tel: 570-998-2151.
www.susque.org   E-mail: susque@susque.org
Mike Miosi, Dir.
Grades 1-11. Adm: FCFS. **Enr:** 168. **Staff:** Admin 3. Couns 15.
Features: Astron Photog Archery Canoe Hiking Mtn_Biking Riflery Ropes_Crse Wilderness_Camp Wilderness_Canoe Swim.
Fees 2011: Res $399-1117 (+$20), 1-3 wks.
Housing: Cabins Tents Tepees. Avg per room/unit: 7. **Swimming:** Pool Stream.
Est 1947. Nonprofit. Nondenom Christian. **Ses:** 7. **Wks/ses:** 1-3. Operates June-Aug. ACA.

This Christian camp offers a variety of traditional camp activities. In addition to its single-gender programs, Susque operates a coed wilderness adventure camp for ages 14-18, two family camps and a three-day coeducational camp for six- to eight-year-olds.

PENN-YORK CAMP
Res — Coed Ages 6-18; Day — Coed 6-9

Ulysses, PA 16948. 266 Northern Potter Rd. Tel: 814-848-9811. Fax: 814-848-7471.
www.pennyork.com　E-mail: pennyork@pennyork.com
Joshua Lehman, Dir.
Adm: FCFS. **Appl due:** Rolling. **Enr:** 90. **Staff:** Admin 2. Couns 14.
Features: Crafts Dance Drama Music Adventure_Travel Aquatics Archery Canoe Climbing_Wall Fishing Hiking Mtn_Biking Mtn_Trips Rappelling Rock_Climb Ropes_Crse Wilderness_Camp Wilderness_Canoe Work Badminton Baseball Basketball Football Soccer Softball Swim Ultimate_Frisbee Volleyball.
Fees 2012: Res $140-275, ½-1 wk. Day $140, 1 wk. Aid (Need).
Housing: Cabins Tents. **Swimming:** Pool.
Est 1970. Nonprofit. Nondenom Christian. **Ses:** 12. **Wks/ses:** ½-1. Operates July-Aug.

Penn-York offers traditional camps promoting outdoor education and spiritual growth. Mountain boarding, hiking, rafting and rock climbing are offered in the nearby Tioga State Forest. Music instruction or overnight camping trips are available during certain sessions. Special-needs campers may enroll and are mainstreamed into most activities.

CAPITAL CAMPS
Res — Coed Ages 8-15

Waynesboro, PA 17268. 12750 Buchanan Trail E. Tel: 717-794-2177.
Fax: 717-794-5789.
Contact (Sept-June): 12230 Wilkins Ave, Rockville, MD 20852. Tel: 301-468-2267.
Fax: 301-468-1719.
Year-round Toll-free: 866-430-2267.
www.capitalcamps.org　E-mail: info@capitalcamps.org
Jon Shapiro, Dir.
Grades 3-10. Adm: FCFS. **Appl due:** Mar. **Enr:** 330. **Enr cap:** 330. **Staff:** Admin 25. Couns 110.
Features: Environ_Sci Writing/Journ Crafts Dance Drama Music Photog Adventure_Travel Aquatics Archery Bicycle_Tours Boating Canoe Caving Climbing_Wall Conservation Fishing Hiking Kayak Mtn_Biking Mtn_Trips Rappelling Rock_Climb Ropes_Crse Whitewater_Raft Wilderness_Camp Woodcraft Baseball Basketball Field_Hockey Football Golf Gymnastics Lacrosse Martial_Arts Roller_Hockey Soccer Softball Swim Tennis Volleyball Water-skiing Watersports.
Fees 2010: Res $2550-4675, 2-4 wks. Aid (Need).
Housing: Cabins Dorms Lodges. **Swimming:** Lake Pool Stream.
Est 1987. Nonprofit. Jewish. **Ses:** 6. **Wks/ses:** 2-4. Operates June-Aug. ACA.

The daily schedule followed at these Jewish camps balances camper choice, cabin activities and campwide programs, with special attention paid to the needs of the various age groups. Boys and girls participate in individual and team sports, arts and crafts, the performing arts, aquatics and outdoor education. Older campers take a three-day adventure hiking trip on the Appalachian Trail.

SOUTH CAROLINA

CAMP GRAVATT
Res — Coed Ages 6-17

Aiken, SC 29805. 1006 Camp Gravatt Rd. Tel: 803-648-1817. Fax: 803-648-7453.
www.bishopgravatt.org　E-mail: camp@bishopgravatt.org

Scott McNeeley, Dir.
Grades 1-12. Adm: FCFS. **Appl due:** Rolling. **Enr:** 120. **Enr cap:** 120. **Staff:** Admin 8. Couns 24. Res 32.
Features: Crafts Music Aquatics Archery Canoe Climbing_Wall Conservation Fishing Hiking Outdoor_Ed Ropes_Crse Basketball Soccer Swim.
Fees 2012: Res $250-650, ½-2 wks. Aid 2011 (Need): $28,000.
Housing: Cabins Tents. Avg per room/unit: 8. **Swimming:** Lake.
Est 1949. Nonprofit. Episcopal. **Ses:** 8. **Wks/ses:** ½-2. Operates June-Aug. ACA.

This Episcopal camp offers high and low ropes courses, swimming, fishing, music, art, canoeing and hiking. The 250-acre setting on Lake Sylvia in rural Aiken County is conducive to many other outdoor activities as well. Elementary (grades 1-6), junior high (grades 7-9) and senior high (grades 10-12) campers attend separate sessions, and Gravatt also conducts a CIT program for rising sophomores.

CAMP ST. CHRISTOPHER
Res — Coed Ages 6-18

Johns Island, SC 29455. 2810 Seabrook Island Rd. Tel: 843-768-1337.
Fax: 843-768-4729.
www.stchristopher.org   E-mail: summercamp@stchristopher.org
Joe Gibson, Dir.
Grades 1-12. Adm: FCFS. Admitted: 90%. **Appl due:** Rolling. **Enr:** 128. **Enr cap:** 128. **Staff:** Admin 2. Couns 80. Res 30.
Features: Environ_Sci Marine_Bio/Stud Crafts Dance Drama Painting Aquatics Archery Hiking Kayak Ropes_Crse Sail Survival_Trng Basketball Swim Tennis Ultimate_Frisbee Volleyball.
Fees 2012: Res $369-495, ½-1 wk. Aid (Need).
Housing: Cabins. Avg per room/unit: 8. **Swimming:** Ocean.
Est 1936. Nonprofit. Episcopal. **Ses:** 9. **Wks/ses:** ½-1. Operates June-Aug.

Owned and operated by the Episcopal Diocese of South Carolina, Saint Christopher offers both Christian education and traditional camp activities. Offerings include swimming, sailing, crabbing, canoeing and land sports. Archery, hiking, arts and crafts, singing, dancing and drama are also available.

CAMP CHERITH IN THE CAROLINAS
Res — Coord Ages 7-18

Pendleton, SC.
Contact (Year-round): 1276 Pine Creek Dr, Woodstock, GA 30188. Tel: 770-924-8436.
www.carolinacherith.com   E-mail: duck@carolinacherith.com
Rich Butela, Dir.
Grades 2-11. Adm: FCFS. **Appl due:** Rolling. **Enr:** 150. **Staff:** Admin 3. Couns 40.
Features: Crafts Drama Archery Canoe Fishing Hiking Riding Ropes_Crse Sail Equestrian Swim Water-skiing.
Fees 2011: Res $395 (+$10-100), 1 wk.
Housing: Cabins. **Swimming:** Lake Pool.
Est 1984. Nonprofit. Nondenom Christian. **Ses:** 1. **Wks/ses:** 1. Operates Aug. ACA.

Boys and girls at this Christian camp attend separate sessions. Activities include archery, arts and crafts, ceramics, ropes courses, drama, riflery, sailing, swimming, canoeing and Bible study. Participation in horsemanship and water-skiing programs incurs an additional fee.

SOUTH DAKOTA

BYRON BIBLE CAMP
Res — Coed Ages 8-19; Day — Coed 6-13

**Huron, SD 57350. 40546 S Shore Rd, PO Box 211. Tel: 605-352-7267.
Fax: 605-352-2041.
www.byronbiblecamp.com   E-mail: campbyron@yahoo.com
Jon M. Duba, Exec Dir.
Adm:** FCFS. **Appl due:** Rolling. **Enr:** 100. **Enr cap:** 100. **Staff:** Admin 5. Couns 20. Res 1. **Travel:** MN WY.
Features: Environ_Sci Crafts Painting Archery Boating Canoe Climbing_Wall Community_Serv Fishing Hiking Kayak Mtn_Trips Outdoor_Ed Riding Riflery Ropes_Crse Wilderness_Camp Wilderness_Canoe Work Baseball Basketball Equestrian Golf Soccer Softball Swim Volleyball Water-skiing Watersports.
Fees 2011: Res $200-300 (+$20), 1 wk. **Day** $30-100, ½-1 wk. Aid (Need).
Housing: Cabins Dorms Lodges Tents Tepees. Avg per room/unit: 10. **Swimming:** Lake.
Est 1937. Nonprofit. Nondenom Christian. **Ses:** 12. **Wks/ses:** ½-1. Operates May-Aug.

In addition to standard recreational overnight and day sessions, this Christian camp conducts weeklong canoe tripping (in the northern Minnesota waters) and backpacking and white-water rafting programs (in Wyoming's Bighorn Mountains). A weekend family camp is also available.

TENNESSEE

INDIAN CREEK CAMP
Res — Coed Ages 7-17

**Liberty, TN 37095. 150 Cabin Circle Dr. Tel: 615-548-4411. Fax: 615-548-4029.
Contact (Sept-May):** c/o Kentucky-Tennessee Conference of Seventh-day Adventists, PO Box 1088, Goodlettsville, TN 37070. **Tel:** 615-859-1391. **Fax:** 615-850-1931.
**www.indiancreekcamp.com   E-mail: youth@kytn.net
Wendy Eberhardt, Dir.
Adm:** FCFS. **Appl due:** Rolling. **Enr:** 200. **Staff:** Admin 8. Couns 20.
Features: Crafts Drama Aquatics Bicycle_Tours Canoe Caving Conservation Mtn_Biking Rappelling Rock_Climb White-water_Raft Wilderness_Camp Basketball Equestrian Football Swim Water-skiing Watersports.
Fees 2009: Res $252-395 (+$20-30), 1 wk.
Housing: Cabins. **Swimming:** Lake Pool.
Est 1959. Nonprofit. Seventh-day Adventist. **Ses:** 7. **Wks/ses:** 1. Operates June-Aug. ACA.

Affiliated with the Seventh-day Adventists, Indian Creek conducts several camps for young people each summer. These recreational programs serve campers separately at the following age divisions: ages 7-9, ages 10-12 and ages 13-17. Program features include canoeing, caving, a horse pack trip, mountain biking, rock climbing and rappelling and water-skiing. Two family camps are also available.

TEXAS

HIS HILL RANCH CAMP
Res — Coed Ages 8-18; Day — Coed 6-10

Comfort, TX 78013. 102 Mill Dam Rd, PO Box 9. Tel: 830-995-3388. Fax: 830-995-2050.
www.hishill.org   E-mail: camp@hishill.org
Charlie McCall, Dir.
Adm: FCFS. **Appl due:** Rolling. **Enr:** 120. **Staff:** Admin 3. Couns 25.
Features: Crafts Archery Canoe Climbing_Wall Hiking Ranch Rappelling Riding Riflery
Basketball Equestrian Swim Tennis Volleyball.
Fees 2012: Res $475-495 (+$20), 1 wk. Day $250 (+$20), 1 wk.
Housing: Cabins. Avg per room/unit: 7. **Swimming:** Pool River.
Est 1975. Nonprofit. Nondenom Christian. **Ses:** 10. **Wks/ses:** 1. Operates June-Aug.

Activities offered at this Christian camp include archery, a low ropes course, tennis, crafts, wall climbing and zip line, riding, rappelling, canoeing and riflery. Bible study and chapel sessions are integral to the program.

JOHN KNOX RANCH
Res — Coed Ages 8-18; Day — Coed 3-10

Fischer, TX 78623. 1661 John Knox Rd. Tel: 830-935-4568. Fax: 830-935-4189.
www.johnknoxranch.com   E-mail: info@johnknoxranch.com
Kathy Anderson, Exec Dir.
Adm: FCFS. **Appl due:** Rolling. **Enr:** 100. **Staff:** Admin 15. Couns 24.
Features: Crafts Adventure_Travel Aquatics Archery Boating Canoe Fishing Hiking Mtn_
Trips Rappelling Rock_Climb Ropes_Crse Sail Wilderness_Camp Woodcraft Basketball
Soccer Swim Watersports.
Fees 2012: Res $430-750, 1-2 wks. Day $190, 1 wk.
Housing: Cabins. Avg per room/unit: 5-8. **Swimming:** Pool River.
Est 1963. Nonprofit. Presbyterian. **Ses:** 10. **Wks/ses:** 1-1½. Operates June-Aug. ACA.

A Presbyterian camp located on a 300-acre site, JKR conducts several summer programs. Both the resident camp and the day camp offer the typical range of recreational activities. In addition to the general camps, John Knox Ranch conducts specialty backpacking, sailing and beach camps. Christian faith-based activities are integral to all programs.

FRONTIER CAMP
Res — Coed Ages 8-16

Grapeland, TX 75844. 131 Frontier Camp Rd. Tel: 936-544-3206. Fax: 936-546-0341.
www.frontiercamp.org   E-mail: info@frontiercamp.org
Matt Raines, Exec Dir.
Grades 3-11. Adm: FCFS. **Appl due:** Rolling. **Enr:** 168. **Enr cap:** 182. **Staff:** Admin 6.
Couns 26. Res 12.
Features: Ecol Geol Sci Crafts Dance Aquatics Archery Bicycle_Tours Boating Canoe
Climbing_Wall Fishing Hiking Kayak Mtn_Biking Outdoor_Ed Riding Riflery Ropes_Crse
Sail Survival_Trng Woodcraft Baseball Basketball Equestrian Skateboarding Soccer
Softball Swim Ultimate_Frisbee Volleyball Water-skiing Watersports.
Fees 2011: Res $610-645 (+$30), 1 wk. Aid (Need).
Housing: Cabins Lodges. Avg per room/unit: 4-13. **Swimming:** Lake Stream.
Est 1969. Nonprofit. Nondenom Christian. **Ses:** 11. **Wks/ses:** 1. Operates May-Aug. ACA.

This Christian camp offers a variety of traditional recreational activities that includes water-skiing, horseback riding, swimming, canoeing, crafts and sports. Morning Bible studies and evening campfires focus on relevant religious topics.

CAMP STEWART FOR BOYS
HEART O' THE HILLS
Res — Coord Ages 6-16

Hunt, TX 78024. 612 FM 1340. Tel: 830-238-4670, 800-724-7325. Fax: 830-238-4737.
www.campstewart.com; www.hohcamp.com
E-mail: jeeper@campstewart.com; jane@hohcamp.com
Jeeper Ragsdale, Meredith Ragsdale & Jane Ragsdale, Dirs.
Adm: FCFS. **Appl due:** Rolling. **Enr cap:** 150-275. **Staff:** Admin 5. Couns 90.
Features: Crafts Dance Fine_Arts Music Theater Aquatics Archery Canoe Climbing_Wall Conservation Cooking Farm Fishing Hiking Kayak Ranch Rappelling Riding Riflery Rock_Climb Wilderness_Camp Wilderness_Canoe Baseball Basketball Equestrian Field_Hockey Football Golf Gymnastics Martial_Arts Soccer Softball Swim Tennis Track Volleyball Water-skiing Watersports.
Fees 2012: Res $1550-4200 (+$300), 2-4 wks.
Housing: Cabins Tepees. **Swimming:** River.
Est 1924. Inc. Nondenom Christian. Ses: 7. Wks/ses: 1-4. Operates June-Aug. ACA.

These nondenominational, Christian-oriented brother and sister camps offer English and Western horsemanship, riflery, water-skiing, land sports, crafts, drama and camping. Each boy and girl chooses nine activities from 50 offerings. Older campers have a choice of specialized programs. The girls' camp, Heart o' the Hills, is located at 2430 Hwy. 39 (830-238-4650). The nine-day short term serves younger campers ages 6-11 only.

CAMP GOOD NEWS
Res — Coed Ages 7-16

Huntsville, TX 77340. 34 Forest Glen. Tel: 936-295-7641. Fax: 936-295-8479.
www.forestglen.org   E-mail: fgcc@forestglen.org
Kevin Edney, Dir.
Adm: FCFS. **Appl due:** Rolling. **Enr:** 160. **Enr cap:** 160. **Staff:** Admin 6. Couns 30.
Features: Crafts Drama Aquatics Archery Bicycle_Tours Canoe Climbing_Wall Exploration Fishing Hiking Rappelling Riding Riflery Rock_Climb Ropes_Crse Survival_Trng Basketball Field_Hockey Football Golf Soccer Swim Volleyball Watersports.
Fees 2009: Res $550 (+$15), 1 wk. Aid 2006 (Need): $50,000.
Housing: Cabins Lodges Tents. Avg per room/unit: 10. **Swimming:** Lake Pool.
Est 1965. Nonprofit. Nondenom Christian. Ses: 5. Wks/ses: 1. Operates June-July. ACA.

This Christian camp provides the usual selection of recreational choices. Among adventure options are a climbing wall and a ropes course, and Bible studies are also part of each session. A CIT program serves campers about to enter grades 8-11.

LUTHERHILL MINISTRIES SUMMER CAMP PROGRAMS
Res — Coed Ages 6-18

La Grange, TX 78945. 3782 Lutherhill Rd, PO Box 99. Tel: 979-249-3232,
888-266-4613. Fax: 979-249-4032.
www.lutherhill.org   E-mail: office@lutherhill.org
Matt Kindsvatter, Dir.
Grades 1-12. Adm: FCFS. **Appl due:** Rolling. **Enr:** 140. **Enr cap:** 200. **Staff:** Admin 15. Couns 60. Res 3.
Travel: CO LA.
Features: Crafts Adventure_Travel Aquatics Archery Canoe Climbing_Wall Community_

Serv Hiking Outdoor_Ed Ropes_Crse Basketball Soccer Swim Ultimate_Frisbee Volleyball.
Fees 2009: Res $200-425 (+$20), 1-2 wks.
Housing: Cabins. Avg per room/unit: 10. **Swimming:** Pond Pool.
Est 1954. Nonprofit. Lutheran. **Ses:** 9. **Wks/ses:** 1-2. Operates June-Aug. ACA.

Programs offered at Lutherhill include camps for young children and high school students and families, a leadership experience, a beach camp, an adventure trek to Colorado and a service trip to New Orleans, LA.

CHO-YEH CAMP
Res — Coed Ages 6-16

Livingston, TX 77351. 2200 S Washington Ave. Tel: 936-328-3200, 888-455-8326.
Fax: 936-328-3231.
www.cho-yeh.org   E-mail: info@cho-yeh.org
Garret Larsen, Dir.
Grades 1-11. Adm: FCFS. **Appl due:** Rolling. **Enr:** 300. **Enr cap:** 325. **Staff:** Admin 20. Couns 200.
Features: Crafts Dance Drama Adventure_Travel Aquatics Archery Canoe Climbing_Wall Fishing Hiking Kayak Mtn_Biking Outdoor_Ed Paintball Riding Riflery Ropes_Crse Baseball Basketball Football Golf Martial_Arts Soccer Softball Swim Tennis Ultimate_Frisbee Volleyball Water-skiing Watersports Weight_Trng.
Fees 2012: Res $775-1425 (+$120), 1-2 wks. Aid (Need).
Housing: Cabins Lodges. Avg per room/unit: 15. **Swimming:** Lake Pool.
Est 1947. Nonprofit. Presbyterian. **Ses:** 12. **Wks/ses:** 1-2. Operates June-Aug. ACA.

This Presbyterian camp combines ecumenical Bible study with such recreational activities as arts and crafts, a ropes course, sports, nature study and swimming. Older campers may take advantage of adventure travel opportunities.

CAMP HUAWNI
Res — Boys Ages 7-15, Girls 7-16

Timpson, TX 75975. 954 County Rd 4235. Tel: 936-254-3223.
Contact (Aug-May): 103 S Main St, Ste C, Henderson, TX 75654. Tel: 903-657-7723.
Year-round Fax: 903-657-1642.
www.camphuawni.com   E-mail: fun@camphuawni.com
Mike Adams, Dir.
Adm: FCFS. **Appl due:** Rolling. **Enr:** 135. **Staff:** Admin 3. Couns 60.
Features: Crafts Dance Aquatics Archery Bicycle_Tours Canoe Fishing Hiking Riding Baseball Basketball Soccer Swim Volleyball Watersports Parasailing.
Fees 2009: Res $925-1775, 1-2 wks.
Housing: Cabins. Avg per room/unit: 11. **Swimming:** Pond Pool Stream.
Est 1965. Inc. Nondenom Christian. **Ses:** 4. **Wks/ses:** 1-2. Operates June-July. ACA.

This Christian camp in the eastern part of the state offers outdoor pursuits, team sports, watersports, horseback riding, and traditional events such as sing-alongs and talent shows. Most days consist of six activity periods—three in the morning and three in the afternoon—followed by a campwide evening event.

SKY RANCH SUMMER CAMP
Res — Coed Ages 6-16; Day — Coed 5-11

Van, TX 75790. 24657 County Rd 448. Tel: 903-266-3300, 800-962-2267.
Fax: 903-569-6357.
www.skyranchcamps.com   E-mail: guestregistrations@skyranch.org

Chris Witt, Exec Dir.
Adm: FCFS. **Appl due:** Rolling. **Enr:** 610. **Enr cap:** 700. **Staff:** Admin 15. Couns 350.
Features: Crafts Drama Filmmaking Photog Adventure_Travel Aquatics Archery Canoe Climbing_Wall Community_Serv Exploration Fishing Hiking Kayak Mountaineering Mtn_Biking Mtn_Trips Outdoor_Ed Paintball Rappelling Riding Riflery Rock_Climb Ropes_Crse Sail Survival_Trng White-water_Raft Wilderness_Camp Wilderness_Canoe Work Basketball Equestrian Golf Soccer Softball Swim Volleyball Water-skiing Watersports.
Fees 2012: Res $715-1898 (+$50-100), 1-2 wks. Day $225 (+$35), 1 wk. Aid avail.
Housing: Cabins. Avg per room/unit: 20. **Swimming:** Lake Pond Pool.
Est 1955. Nonprofit. Nondenom Christian. **Ses:** 12. **Wks/ses:** 1-2. Operates May-Aug. ACA.

This Christian camp offers an array of traditional recreational activities. All boys and girls participate in a rodeo at the end of each session. Older campers may take part in Rocky Mountain Adventures, which features backpacking and kayaking/rafting trips.

CAMP YOUNG JUDAEA
Res — Coed Ages 7-14

Wimberley, TX 78676. 121 Camp Young Judaea Dr. Tel: 512-847-9564.
   Fax: 512-847-5086.
Contact (Sept-May): 9647 Hillcroft St, Houston, TX 77096. Tel: 713-723-8354.
   Fax: 713-728-5061.
Year-round Toll-free: 800-226-7295.
www.cyjtexas.org   E-mail: info@cyjtexas.org
Frank Silberlicht, Dir.
Grades 2-9. Adm: FCFS. **Appl due:** Rolling. **Enr:** 280. **Enr cap:** 280. **Staff:** Couns 85.
Travel: AZ NM NV TX UT.
Features: Crafts Dance Drama Filmmaking Music Photog Adventure_Travel Aquatics Archery Bicycle_Tours Boating Canoe Caving Climbing_Wall Conservation Cooking Deep-sea Fishing Exploration Fishing Hiking Mtn_Biking Outdoor_Ed Rappelling Ropes_Crse Survival_Trng White-water_Raft Basketball Football Soccer Softball Swim Tennis Ultimate_Frisbee Volleyball Watersports.
Fees 2009: Res $1300-3800 (+$10-150), 1-3 wks. Aid (Need).
Housing: Cabins Lodges. Avg per room/unit: 12-14. **Swimming:** Lake Pool River.
Est 1952. Nonprofit. Jewish. **Ses:** 7. **Wks/ses:** 1-3. Operates June-Aug. ACA.

Located in the Texas hills, Young Judaea offers outdoor education and such traditional Jewish activities as Hebrew, singing and dancing. Campers learn teamwork, communication and problem-solving skills. A ropes course, athletics, canoeing, cooking, mountain biking, tennis and ceramics are among the camp's activities.

VERMONT

BETHANY BIRCHES CAMP
Res — Coed Ages 6-18

Plymouth, VT 05056. 2610 Lynds Hill Rd. Tel: 802-672-5220. Fax: 802-672-5220.
www.bethanybirches.org   E-mail: bbc@vermontel.net
Amber Bergey, Dir.
Grades 2-12. Adm: FCFS. Admitted: 99%. **Appl due:** Rolling. **Enr:** 70. **Enr cap:** 70. **Staff:** Admin 4. Couns 10. Res 7.
Features: Environ_Sci Geol Marine_Bio/Stud Sci Writing/Journ Crafts Creative_Writing Music Painting Theater Aquatics Archery Canoe Cooking Exploration Fishing Hiking Kayak Mountaineering Mtn_Biking Mtn_Trips Peace/Cross-cultural Rock_Climb Ropes_

Crse Social_Servs White-water_Raft Wilderness_Camp Woodcraft Work Baseball Basketball Field_Hockey Soccer Softball Swim Ultimate_Frisbee Volleyball Watersports. **Fees 2010: Res $240 (+$7-55), 1 wk.** Aid (Need). **Housing:** Cabins Tepees. Avg per room/unit: 6. **Swimming:** Pond Stream. **Est 1965.** Nonprofit. Mennonite. **Ses:** 18. **Wks/ses:** 1. Operates June-Aug.

Located on 100 acres of woodland at an 1800-foot elevation, Bethany Birches offers a wilderness camp in a Christian environment. Spiritual components of the program include Bible lessons, prayer and fireside discussions. Campers share daily responsibilities (such as gathering firewood and cooking meals) and participate in nature hikes, group games, and arts and crafts. Outpost camps for older campers feature one- and two-night rock climbing, whitewater rafting and backpacking trips.

VIRGINIA

MAKEMIE WOODS
Res — Coed Ages 6-17

Barhamsville, VA 23011. PO Box 39. Tel: 757-566-1496, 800-566-1496. Fax: 757-566-8803.
www.makwoods.org   E-mail: makwoods@makwoods.org
Rev. Michelle D. Burcher, Dir.
Grades 1-12. Adm: FCFS. **Appl due:** Rolling. **Enr:** 60. **Enr cap:** 70. **Staff:** Admin 4. Couns 28.
Conditions accepted: Diabetes.
Features: Circus_Skills Crafts Dance Fine_Arts Music Photog Theater Adventure_Travel Archery Boating Canoe Caving Climbing_Wall Community_Serv Cruises Exploration Hiking Outdoor_Ed Riding Rock_Climb Ropes_Crse Sail Scuba Survival_Trng Whitewater_Raft Wilderness_Camp Equestrian Swim Watersports.
Fees 2009: Res $110-799 (+$15-20), ½-2 wks. Aid 2007: $12,000.
Housing: Cabins Lodges Tents. **Swimming:** Pond.
Est 1964. Nonprofit. Presbyterian. **Ses:** 37. **Wks/ses:** ½-2. Operates June-Aug. ACA.

This Presbyterian camp features Bible study, swimming, boating, crafts and recreation. In addition, specialized camps address music and drama, canoeing, sailing, a high ropes course, swimming, tent camping and nature study. Campers may also embark on trips that include rock climbing, hang-gliding, scuba diving or horseback riding. A 10-day program serves children with diabetes.

CAMP BETHEL
Res — Coed Ages 6-17; Day — Coed 5-12

Fincastle, VA 24090. 328 Bethel Rd. Tel: 540-992-2940. Fax: 540-992-6498.
www.campbethelvirginia.org   E-mail: campbetheloffice@gmail.com
Barry LeNoir, Dir.
Grades K-12. Adm: FCFS. **Appl due:** Rolling. **Staff:** Admin 2. Couns 20.
Features: Crafts Drama Fine_Arts Music Adventure_Travel Canoe Caving Conservation Hiking Mtn_Biking Ropes_Crse White-water_Raft Wilderness_Camp Wilderness_Canoe Swim.
Fees 2010: Res $120-425, 1 wk. Day $110, 1 wk.
Housing: Cabins Tents. Avg per room/unit: 10. **Swimming:** Pool Stream.
Est 1927. Nonprofit. Church of the Brethren. **Ses:** 8. **Wks/ses:** 1. Operates June-Aug. ACA.

Bethel conducts small-enrollment camps in a Christian environment. Among the activities available are swimming, hiking, nature study, crafts, singing, Bible study and low-impact camping. For boys and girls entering grades 7-12, adventure camps enable campers to engage in river canoeing, white-water rafting, backpacking, horseback riding, caving and mountain biking.

CAROLINE FURNACE LUTHERAN CAMP
Res — Coed Ages 6-17

Fort Valley, VA 22652. 2239 Camp Roosevelt Rd. Tel: 540-933-6266. Fax: 540-933-6971.
www.carolinefurnace.org   E-mail: info@carolinefurnace.org
Rev. Wayne R. Shelor, Exec Dir.
Grades 1-12. Adm: FCFS. Admitted: 98%. **Appl due:** Rolling. **Enr:** 60. **Enr cap:** 100. **Staff:** Admin 3. Couns 20. Res 3.
Features: Archaeol Astron Ecol Environ_Sci Geol Sci Crafts Music Theater Adventure_ Travel Aquatics Archery Canoe Caving Community_Serv Conservation Exploration Fishing Hiking Mountaineering Mtn_Biking Mtn_Trips Outdoor_Ed Rappelling Riding Rock_Climb Ropes_Crse Social_Servs White-water_Raft Wilderness_Camp Wilderness_Canoe Woodcraft Equestrian Swim Ultimate_Frisbee Volleyball.
Fees 2012: Res $385-505, 1 wk. Aid (Need).
Housing: Cabins Lodges Tents. Avg per room/unit: 8-12. **Swimming:** Lake.
Est 1957. Nonprofit. Lutheran. **Ses:** 8. **Wks/ses:** 1. Operates June-Aug.

Traditional programs at Caroline Furnace include a pioneering camp, with such activities as swimming, arts and crafts, and canoeing, and a more rustic adventure camp, which offers overnight backpacking and canoeing trips. Fishing, music, horse and environmental camps allow children to concentrate on one activity, while backpacking and canoeing camp participants have weeklong wilderness experiences. Quest Camp offers white-water rafting and rock climbing. All programs feature theme-based daily worship and Bible study.

CAMP HANOVER
Res — Coed Ages 7-17

Mechanicsville, VA 23111. 3163 Parsleys Mill Rd. Tel: 804-779-2811, 877-687-2267. Fax: 804-779-3056.
www.camphanover.org   E-mail: info@camphanover.org
Bob Pryor, Dir.
Grades 2-12. Adm: FCFS. **Appl due:** Rolling. **Enr:** 162. **Enr cap:** 162. **Staff:** Admin 7. Couns 32.
Features: Archaeol Ecol Crafts Dance Drama Aquatics Canoe Caving Climbing_Wall Community_Serv Conservation Cooking Hiking Mtn_Trips Rappelling Riding Rock_Climb Ropes_Crse Sail Scuba White-water_Raft Wilderness_Camp Woodcraft Soccer Softball Swim Ultimate_Frisbee Volleyball.
Fees 2011: Res $180-775 (+$10), ½-2 wks. Aid 2008 (Need): $14,000.
Housing: Cabins Dorms Tents. Avg per room/unit: 6. **Swimming:** Lake Pool.
Est 1957. Nonprofit. Presbyterian. **Ses:** 5. **Wks/ses:** ½-2. Operates June-Aug. ACA.

Hanover offers structured and camper-designed recreational programs, including one that combines community service with sailing instruction. Adventure sessions featuring rappelling and rock climbing, white-water canoeing and hiking are available for those in grades 9-12. All programming maintains a Christian focus.

CAMP CHANCO
Res — Coed Ages 8-18

Surry, VA 23883. PO Box 378. Tel: 757-294-3012. Fax: 757-294-0727.

www.chanco.org/camp-chanco   E-mail: director@chanco.org
Jim Sitzler, Dir.
Adm: FCFS. **Appl due:** Rolling. **Enr:** 144. **Staff:** Admin 6. Couns 40.
Features: Environ_Sci Crafts Photog Adventure_Travel Aquatics Archery Boating Canoe Caving Climbing_Wall Cooking Hiking Kayak Mountaineering Mtn_Biking Mtn_Trips Rappelling Rock_Climb Ropes_Crse Sail Scuba Wilderness_Camp Wilderness_Canoe Basketball Golf Soccer Swim Volleyball.
Fees 2012: Res $410-925 (+$15), 1-2 wks.
Housing: Cabins. Avg per room/unit: 18. **Swimming:** Pool River.
Est 1968. Nonprofit. Episcopal. **Ses:** 9. **Wks/ses:** 1-2. Operates June-Aug. ACA.

Activities at this Christian camp include canoeing, sailing, swimming, arts and crafts, music, drama and nature studies. Chanco features specialty camps in sailing and scuba diving, and campers may also go on canoeing, sailing, hiking, rock climbing, caving and biking adventure trips.

WASHINGTON

CAMP BERACHAH
Res — Coed Ages 7-18; Day — Coed 5-12

Auburn, WA 98092. 19830 SE 328th Pl. Tel: 253-939-0488, 800-859-2267.
Fax: 253-833-7027.
www.campberachah.org   E-mail: register@campberachah.org
Steve Altick, Exec Dir.
Adm: FCFS. **Appl due:** Rolling. **Staff:** Admin 22. Couns 90.
Features: Crafts Drama Music Aquatics Archery Bicycle_Tours Boating Canoe Climbing_ Wall Hiking Mountaineering Mtn_Biking Mtn_Trips Paintball Riding Riflery Rock_Climb Ropes_Crse Equestrian Soccer Swim Water-skiing.
Fees 2011: Res $139-368 (+$10), ½-1 wk. Day $146 (+$43), 1 wk. Aid 2009 (Need): $45,000.
Housing: Cabins Dorms Houses Lodges Tents. **Swimming:** Lake Pool.
Est 1973. Nonprofit. Nondenom Christian. **Ses:** 42. **Wks/ses:** ½-1. Operates June-Aug.

Berachah conducts a variety of camping programs in a Christian setting. Day camp sessions include games and activities, Bible lessons, devotions and daily chapel. Overnight campers may enroll in specialty games that address soccer, adventure, mountain biking and equestrianism. In addition, leadership programs serve boys and girls ages 13-17.

CAMP FIRWOOD
Res — Coed Ages 8-17; Day — Coed 6-11

Bellingham, WA 98229. 4605 Cable St. Tel: 360-733-6840, 800-765-3477.
Fax: 360-733-6926.
www.thefirs.org   E-mail: info@thefirs.org
Rob Lee, Dir.
Grades 3-12. Adm: FCFS. **Appl due:** June. **Enr:** 230. **Staff:** Admin 20. Couns 29.
Features: Crafts Dance Fine_Arts Theater Aquatics Archery Canoe Hiking Kayak Mtn_ Trips Paintball Riflery Rock_Climb Ropes_Crse Sail Wilderness_Camp Basketball Swim Volleyball Water-skiing Watersports.
Housing: Cabins. **Swimming:** Lake.
Est 1955. Nonprofit. **Spons:** Firs Bible and Missionary Conference. Nondenom Christian. **Ses:** 10. **Wks/ses:** 1. Operates June-Aug. ACA.

Firwood offers three Christian-oriented traditional camping programs for children and adolescents: junior (grades 3-6); junior high (grades 7-8); and high school (grades 9-12) sessions. All programs offer water-skiing, sailing, kayaking, climbing, paintball, outdoor challenges and games.

CAMP HUSTON
Res — Coed Ages 6-17

Gold Bar, WA 98251. 14725 Ley Rd, PO Box 140. Tel: 360-793-0441.
Fax: 360-793-3822.
www.huston.org   E-mail: info@huston.org
Bill Tubbs, Dir.
Grades 1-12. Adm: FCFS. **Appl due:** Rolling. **Enr cap:** 85. **Staff:** Admin 2. Couns 25.
Features: Crafts Theater Hiking Kayak Ropes_Crse Wilderness_Camp Swim.
Fees 2011: Res $270-615, ½-1 wk.
Housing: Cabins Dorms. Avg per room/unit: 7. **Swimming:** Pool.
Est 1928. Nonprofit. Episcopal. **Ses:** 6. **Wks/ses:** ½-1. Operates July-Aug.

At this Christian camp, children participate in games, hikes, worship, swimming, camp outs, singing and crafts. A four-day session serves younger campers. Horse and theater camps are also available. High school students may attend as CITs.

MIRACLE RANCH
Res — Coed Ages 8-17; Day — Coed 6-12

Port Orchard, WA 98367. 15999 Sidney Rd SW. Tel: 253-851-4410, 877-723-4373.
Fax: 253-857-4128.
www.cristacamps.com   E-mail: information@cristacamps.com
Steve Fisher, Dir.
Grades 3-12. Adm: FCFS. Admitted: 100%. **Appl due:** Rolling. **Enr:** 180. **Staff:** Admin 29. Couns 21.
Features: Crafts Aquatics Archery Boating Canoe Paintball Riding Ropes_Crse Basketball Equestrian Skateboarding Soccer Swim Ultimate_Frisbee Volleyball Watersports.
Fees 2009: Res $415-474 (+$45-104), 1 wk. Day $191 (+$78-104), 1 wk. Aid 2008 (Need): $12,000.
Housing: Cabins. **Swimming:** Lake.
Est 1960. Nonprofit. **Spons:** CRISTA Ministries. Nondenom Christian. **Ses:** 10. **Wks/ses:** 1. Operates June-Aug.

Within a strong Christian environment, the camp offers such activities as golf, archery, marksmanship, canoeing, boating, rocketry, arts and crafts, and sports. Particularly strong horsemanship programs (including one consisting of four hours of riding each day) feature trail rides and Western and English instruction; these programs incur an additional fee.

ISLAND LAKE CAMP
Res — Coed Ages 9-17

Poulsbo, WA 98370. 12500 Camp Ct NW. Tel: 360-697-1212, 877-723-4373.
Fax: 360-697-1709.
www.cristacamps.com   E-mail: information@cristacamps.com
Shane Carlson, Dir.
Grades 4-12. Adm: FCFS. **Appl due:** Rolling. **Enr:** 200. **Staff:** Admin 41. Couns 25.
Features: Crafts Archery Canoe Mtn_Biking Paintball Riding Riflery Ropes_Crse Basketball Skateboarding Swim Volleyball Water-skiing Watersports.
Fees 2009: Res $415-489, 1 wk.
Housing: Cabins Dorms. **Swimming:** Lake.

Est 1974. Nonprofit. **Spons:** CRISTA Ministries. Nondenom Christian. **Ses:** 4. **Wks/ses:** 1. Operates June-Aug.

This nondenominational Christian camp offers such activities as skateboarding, paintball, motorcycling, archery, rocketry, and arts and crafts. Programming places strong emphasis on Christian values.

WEST VIRGINIA

CAMP SANDY COVE
Res — Coed Ages 7-15

High View, WV 26808. Rte 1, Box 471. Tel: 304-856-2959. Fax: 304-856-1683.
Contact (Oct-Apr): 60 Sandy Cove Rd, North East, MD 21901. Tel: 410-287-5433.
  Fax: 410-287-3196.
Year-round Toll-free: 800-234-2683.
www.campsandycove.org   E-mail: campinfo@sandycove.org
Tim Nielsen, Dir.
Grades 2-10. Adm: FCFS. **Appl due:** Rolling. **Enr:** 150. **Staff:** Admin 10. Couns 40.
Features: Circus_Skills Crafts Drama Filmmaking Photog Adventure_Travel Aquatics Archery Bicycle_Tours Canoe Caving Climbing_Wall Fishing Hiking Kayak Mountaineering Mtn_Biking Mtn_Trips Rappelling Riding Riflery Rock_Climb Ropes_Crse Sail Survival_Trng White-water_Raft Wilderness_Camp Wilderness_Canoe Baseball Basketball Equestrian Field_Hockey Football Gymnastics Lacrosse Martial_Arts Roller_Hockey Soccer Softball Swim Tennis Volleyball Water-skiing.
Fees 2012: Res $665 (+$20-110), 1 wk. Day $225. Aid (Need).
Housing: Cabins. Avg per room/unit: 10. **Swimming:** Pool.
Est 1950. Nonprofit. Nondenom Christian. **Ses:** 7. **Wks/ses:** 1. Operates June-Aug. ACA.

Activities at this Christian camp include archery, crafts, drama, sports, nature studies, outdoor living skills, cooking and swimming. Campers age 12 and up participate in a leadership program and may also take self-defense or video journalism classes. Each week, campers participate in a day trip in the Blue Ridge Mountains that may involve hiking, fishing, canoeing, mountain boarding, horseback riding, white-water-rafting or rock climbing.

WISCONSIN

CAMP CHETEK
Res — Coed Ages 8-17

Chetek, WI 54728. PO Box 26. Tel: 715-924-3236. Fax: 715-924-3234.
www.campchetek.org   E-mail: office@campchetek.org
Randy Tanis, Dir.
Grades 3-12. Adm: FCFS. **Appl due:** Rolling. **Staff:** Admin 4. Couns 25.
Features: Archery Boating Canoe Climbing_Wall Community_Serv Fishing Hiking Riflery Baseball Basketball Soccer Softball Swim Volleyball Water-skiing Watersports.
Fees 2010: Res $215, 1 wk.
Housing: Cabins Dorms Lodges. Avg per room/unit: 8. **Swimming:** Lake.
Est 1944. Nonprofit. Baptist. **Wks/ses:** 1. Operates June-Aug.

This highly structured Bible camp accepts boys and girls of all faiths, including those without a religious identity. Popular activities at Chetek include riding, water-skiing and tubing, the obstacle course, crafts and archery. Biblical preaching is an important element of camp life.

CAMP INTERLAKEN
Res — Coed Ages 8-16

Eagle River, WI 54521. 7050 Old Hwy 70. Tel: 715-479-8030. Fax: 715-479-8527.
Contact (Sept-May): c/o Harry & Rose Samson Family JCC, 6255 N Santa Monica Blvd, Milwaukee, WI 53217. Tel: 414-967-8240. Fax: 414-964-0922.
www.campinterlaken.org   E-mail: info@campinterlaken.org
Toni Davison Levenberg, Dir.
Grades 3-11. Adm: FCFS. Admitted: 100%. **Appl due:** Rolling. **Enr:** 250. **Enr cap:** 275. **Staff:** Admin 15. Couns 44.
Features: Crafts Dance Drama Fine_Arts Photog Adventure_Travel Aquatics Archery Boating Canoe Climbing_Wall Hiking Rock_Climb Ropes_Crse Sail Basketball Gymnastics Soccer Softball Swim Tennis Volleyball Water-skiing.
Fees 2010: Res $2250-6740, 2-8 wks.
Housing: Cabins Houses Tents. Avg per room/unit: 10. **Swimming:** Lake.
Est 1966. Nonprofit. **Spons:** Harry & Rose Samson Family JCC. Jewish. **Ses:** 6. **Wks/ses:** 2-8. Operates June-Aug. ACA.

Pursuits at this Jewish camp include athletics, waterfront activities, cultural and creative arts, and nature/tripping. Academic tutoring and Bar and Bat Mitzvah preparation courses are also available. Campers learn about Jewish values and traditions by participating in various activities, among them Shabbat services and singing and dancing.

B'NAI B'RITH BEBER CAMP
Res — Coed Ages 7-17

Mukwonago, WI 53149. W 1741 Hwy J. Tel: 262-363-6800. Fax: 262-363-6804.
Contact (Sept-June): 4930 Oakton St, Ste 405, Skokie, IL 60077. Tel: 847-677-7130. Fax: 847-677-7132.
Year-round Toll-free: 800-803-2267.
www.bebercamp.com   E-mail: info@bebercamp.com
Stefan Teodosic, Exec Dir.
Grades 2-11. Adm: FCFS. **Appl due:** Rolling. **Enr:** 260. **Enr cap:** 275. **Staff:** Admin 30. Couns 75.
Features: Crafts Dance Fine_Arts Music Photog Theater Aquatics Archery Boating Canoe Climbing_Wall Community_Serv Cooking Farm Fishing Hiking Mtn_Biking Rappelling Riding Rock_Climb Ropes_Crse Sail Social_Servs Wilderness_Camp Wilderness_ Canoe Aerobics Baseball Basketball Cross-country Equestrian Football Golf Martial_ Arts Roller_Hockey Soccer Softball Street_Hockey Swim Tennis Ultimate_Frisbee Volleyball Water-skiing Watersports.
Fees 2010: Res $1975-7900 (+$30), 2-8 wks. Aid (Need).
Housing: Cabins. **Swimming:** Lake Pool.
Est 1976. Nonprofit. Jewish. **Ses:** 5. **Wks/ses:** 2-8. Operates June-Aug. ACA.

Situated on Lake Beulah, Beber blends traditional camping activities with Jewish customs and cultural pursuits. Younger campers gain exposure to all program areas to develop new skills and interests, while teens plan their own activities, programs and trips.

OLIN SANG RUBY UNION INSTITUTE SUMMER CAMP
Res — Coed Ages 7-17

Oconomowoc, WI 53066. 600 Lac La Belle Dr. Tel: 262-567-6277. Fax: 262-567-8885.
Contact (Sept-May): 555 Skokie Blvd, Ste 333, Northbrook, IL 60062.

Tel: 847-509-0990. Fax: 847-509-0970.
www.osrui.org   E-mail: osrui@urj.org
Gerard W. Kaye, Dir.
Grades 2-12. Adm: FCFS. Admitted: 98%. Appl due: Rolling. Staff: Admin 6. Couns 115.
Features: Ecol Environ_Sci Lang Crafts Dance Filmmaking Fine_Arts Media Music Paint-
ing Photog Theater Adventure_Travel Aquatics Archery Bicycle_Tours Boating Canoe
Climbing_Wall Cooking Farm Hiking Mtn_Trips Outdoor_Ed Riding Rock_Climb Ropes_
Crse Sail Wilderness_Camp Baseball Basketball Equestrian Fencing Golf Martial_Arts
Soccer Softball Swim Tennis Volleyball Water-skiing.
Fees 2010: Res $680-4915, 1-7 wks. Aid 2009 (Need): $150,000.
Housing: Cabins Tents. Avg per room/unit: 13. Swimming: Lake Pool.
Est 1952. Nonprofit. Spons: Union for Reform Judaism. Jewish. Ses: 12. Wks/ses: 1-7.
Operates June-Aug. ACA.

This Jewish camp offers various traditional camping programs. Offerings include arts
options, land sports, watersports, sailing, canoeing, climbing and Hebrew. Horseback riding
incurs an additional fee.

CAMP WAKONDA
Res — Coed Ages 8-16

Oxford, WI 53952. W8368 County Rd E.
Contact (Sept-May): PO Box 100, Fall River, WI 53932.
Year-round Tel: 608-296-2126, Fax: 608-296-4329.
www.wakonda.org   E-mail: akking@wi.adventist.org
Greg Taylor, Dir.
Adm: FCFS. Appl due: Rolling. Enr: 80. Staff: Admin 3. Couns 11.
Features: Crafts Archery Canoe Climbing_Wall Riding Wilderness_Camp Basketball Swim
Water-skiing Watersports.
Fees 2011: Res $225, 1 wk.
Housing: Tents. Avg per room/unit: 6. Swimming: Lake.
Est 1978. Nonprofit. Seventh-day Adventist. Ses: 3. Wks/ses: 1. Operates July.

Activities at Wakonda include wakeboarding, water-skiing, horseback riding, archery,
swimming, a climbing wall, crafts and games.

WISCONSIN UNITED METHODIST CAMPS
Res — Coed Ages 6-17

Sun Prairie, WI 53590. 750 Windsor St, PO Box 620. Tel: 608-837-3388, 877-947-2267.
Fax: 608-837-8547.
www.wiumcamps.org   E-mail: camping@wisconsinumc.org
Laura Hutler, Prgm Dir.
Grades 2-12. Adm: FCFS. Appl due: Rolling.
Features: Crafts Drama Music Studio_Art Adventure_Travel Aquatics Archery Bicycle_
Tours Boating Canoe Fishing Hiking Outdoor_Ed Peace/Cross-cultural Riding Rock_
Climb Ropes_Crse Sail Wilderness_Canoe Basketball Equestrian Soccer Swim Water-
sports.
Fees 2009: Res $130-470, ½-1 wk.
Housing: Cabins Tents. Swimming: Lake.
Nonprofit. United Methodist. Wks/ses: ½-1. Operates June-Aug.

This organization provides Christian camping opportunities at two Wisconsin sites: Pine
Lake Camp and Lake Lucerne. Separate sessions have different emphases and include a
program for special needs; horse camps; and general youth camps. Weekend family camps
also operate.

HONEY ROCK CAMP
Res — Coed Ages 9-17

Three Lakes, WI 54562. 8660 HoneyRock Rd. Tel: 715-479-7474. Fax: 715-479-7475.
www.honeyrockcamp.org   E-mail: info@honeyrockcamp.org
Rob Ribbe, Dir.
Adm: FCFS. **Fac 19. Staff:** Admin 7. Couns 90. Special needs 4.
Features: Crafts Archery Canoe Hiking Kayak Mountaineering Mtn_Biking Riding Riflery Sail Survival_Trng Wilderness_Camp Wilderness_Canoe Equestrian Swim Water-skiing.
Fees 2012: Res $565-1975 (+$95), 1-7 wks. Aid (Merit & Need).
Housing: Cabins Tents. **Swimming:** Lake.
Est 1948. Nonprofit. **Spons:** Wheaton College (IL). Nondenom Christian. **Ses:** 8. **Wks/ses:** 1-7. Operates June-Aug.

At this Christian residential camp (grades 4-8), campers sign up daily for the activities of their choice, which may include swimming, sailing, water-skiing, archery, riflery, crafts and nature. Cabins share in a wilderness trip and Bible studies. Those in grades 9-11 combine the residential camp with tripping and wilderness skills. Skill focus choices are horsemanship, canoeing, kayaking, backpacking, mountain biking and climbing. High Road wilderness programs (grades 9-12) are small-group wilderness expeditions emphasizing skill instruction in backpacking, canoeing, biking and climbing, and relevant scripture studies.

CAMP YOUNG JUDAEA MIDWEST
Res — Coed Ages 8-14

Waupaca, WI 54981. E989 Stratton Lake Rd. Tel: 715-258-2288. Fax: 715-258-2830.
Contact (Sept-May): 4711 Golf Rd, Ste 600, Skokie, IL 60076. Tel: 847-675-6790.
    Fax: 847-679-5286.
www.cyjmid.org   E-mail: info@cyjmid.org
Noah Gallagher, Dir.
Grades 3-9. Adm: FCFS. **Appl due:** Rolling. **Enr:** 150. **Staff:** Admin 2. Couns 35.
Features: Crafts Dance Media Music Photog Theater Aquatics Boating Canoe Climbing_Wall Cooking Fishing Hiking Mtn_Biking Outdoor_Ed Riding Ropes_Crse Sail Baseball Basketball Equestrian Soccer Softball Swim Tennis Ultimate_Frisbee Volleyball Water-skiing.
Fees 2012: Res $2100-3300, 2-3½ wks. Aid (Need).
Housing: Cabins. Avg per room/unit: 10. **Swimming:** Lake.
Est 1969. Nonprofit. Jewish. **Ses:** 4. **Wks/ses:** 2-3. Operates June-Aug. ACA.

CYJ structures its programming toward Jewish and Zionist content. Campers adhere to Jewish values and follow Jewish traditions: The camp observes kashrut and Shabbat. Popular activities include dance, drama, creative arts, waterfront activities and land sports, in addition to overnight trips and horseback riding.

HERZL CAMP
Res — Coed Ages 8-16

Webster, WI 54893. 7260 Mickey Smith Hwy. Tel: 715-866-8177.
Contact (Sept-May): 7204 W 27th St, Ste 226, St Louis Park, MN 55426.
    Tel: 952-927-4002.
Year-round Fax: 866-235-8764.
www.herzlcamp.org   E-mail: info@herzlcamp.org
Anne Hope, Dir.
Grades 3-11. Adm: FCFS. **Appl due:** Rolling. **Staff:** Admin 4. Couns 100.
Features: Crafts Dance Drama Fine_Arts Music Photog Adventure_Travel Aquatics Archery Bicycle_Tours Boating Canoe Climbing_Wall Conservation Fishing Hiking Rock_Climb

Ropes_Crse Sail White-water_Raft Wilderness_Camp Wilderness_Canoe Basketball Field_Hockey Football Golf Gymnastics Lacrosse Soccer Softball Swim Tennis Volleyball Watersports.
Fees 2012: Res $825-4025, 1-6 wks. Aid (Need).
Housing: Cabins Dorms Houses Lodges Tents. **Swimming:** Lake.
Est 1946. Nonprofit. Jewish. **Ses:** 12. **Wks/ses:** 1-6. Operates June-Aug. ACA.

Activities at this Jewish camp include swimming, canoeing, outdoor skills, climbing wall, sports, crafts and the performing arts. Older campers have wilderness adventure options. Boys and girls learn about Judaism, observe Shabbat and eat kosher meals.

Canada

ALBERTA

BIRCH BAY RANCH
Res — Coed Ages 8-16

Sherwood Park, T8E 1H1 Alberta, Canada. 51505 Range Rd 215. Tel: 780-922-2883.
   Fax: 780-922-3944.
www.birchbayranch.com   E-mail: office@birchbayranch.com
Darryl Fraess, Dir.
Adm: FCFS. **Appl due:** Rolling. **Enr:** 100. **Enr cap:** 100. **Staff:** Admin 2. Couns 20. Res 5.
Features: Archery Climbing_Wall Outdoor_Ed Rappelling Riding Ropes_Crse Equestrian
   Swim.
Fees 2011: Res Can$350 (+Can$18), 1 wk. Aid (Need).
Housing: Cabins. Avg per room/unit: 14. **Swimming:** Lake.
Est 1966. Nonprofit. Nondenom Christian. **Ses:** 8. **Wks/ses:** 1. Operates July-Aug.

Located on 104 acres of lakeside property, this Christian-oriented camp offers an array of activities that includes horseback riding, a high ropes course, archery, a climbing wall and a low obstacle course. The horsemanship program enables campers to develop Western riding skills while also learning to care for a horse and its equipment.

ONTARIO

CAMP GESHER
Res — Coed Ages 7-16

Cloyne, K0H 1K0 Ontario, Canada. General Delivery. Tel: 613-336-2583.
   Fax: 613-336-1719.
Contact (Sept-May): 272 Codsell Ave, Toronto, M3H 3X2 Ontario, Canada.
   Tel: 416-633-2511. Fax: 416-636-5248.
www.campgesher.com   E-mail: info@campgesher.com
Shaul Zobary, Admin Dir.
Grades 2-11. Adm: FCFS. **Appl due:** Rolling. **Enr:** 220. **Staff:** Admin 5. Couns 40.
Features: Debate Environ_Sci Crafts Music Theater Aquatics Canoe Cooking Hiking
   Kayak Wilderness_Camp Wilderness_Canoe Work Baseball Basketball Football Soccer
   Softball Swim Volleyball Watersports.
Fees 2012: Res Can$1241-5259, 2-7 wks.
Housing: Cabins. **Swimming:** Lake.
Est 1963. Nonprofit. **Spons:** Habonim Dror. Jewish. **Ses:** 7. **Wks/ses:** 2-7. Operates June-
   Aug.

Sponsored by Habonim Dror, the Labour Zionist Youth Movement, Gesher offers sports and waterfront activities, work projects, interest clubs, scouting, Hebrew and a full Judaic program.

CAMP IAWAH
Res — Coord Ages 7-17; Day — Coord 6-12

Godfrey, K0H 1T0 Ontario, Canada. 304 Iawah Rd, RR 2. Tel: 613-273-5621.
Fax: 613-273-3487.
www.iawah.com   E-mail: info@iawah.com
Jeff Friesen, Dir.
Grades 1-12. Adm: FCFS. **Appl due:** Rolling. **Enr cap:** 120. **Staff:** Admin 12. Couns 30.
Features: Ecol Geol Sci Crafts Media Music Photog Theater Archery Canoe Climbing_Wall
Fishing Hiking Outdoor_Ed Rock_Climb Ropes_Crse Sail Survival_Trng Wilderness_
Canoe Baseball Basketball Golf Soccer Swim Volleyball Water-skiing Watersports.
Fees 2011: Res Can$525-1100 (+$30-50), 1-3 wks.
Housing: Cabins Lodges. **Swimming:** Lake.
Est 1956. Nonprofit. Nondenom Christian. **Ses:** 13. **Wks/ses:** 1. Operates July-Aug.

This Christian camp provides such recreational activities as swimming, canoeing, water-skiing, windsurfing, climbing, a challenge course, crafts and Bible study for young people. IAWAH conducts both single-gender and coeducational programs, as well as adult and family camps.

CAMP FRENDA
Res — Coed Ages 8-16

Port Carling, P0B 1J0 Ontario, Canada. 1231 Morinus Rd. Tel: 705-765-5597.
Fax: 705-765-7310.
Contact (Sept-May): 1110 King St E, Oshawa, L1H 1H8 Ontario, Canada.
Tel: 905-571-4211. Fax: 905-571-4781.
www.campfrenda.com   E-mail: loliveira@adventistontario.org
Glenn DeSilva, Dir.
Adm: FCFS. **Appl due:** Rolling. **Enr:** 110. **Staff:** Admin 4. Couns 50.
Features: Crafts Theater Aquatics Archery Canoe Kayak Mtn_Biking Ropes_Crse Equestrian Gymnastics Swim Water-skiing Watersports.
Fees 2011: Res Can$510-585 (+Can$40-60), 1 wk.
Housing: Cabins. Avg per room/unit: 8. **Swimming:** Lake.
Est 1953. Nonprofit. Seventh-day Adventist. **Ses:** 6. **Wks/ses:** 1. Operates June-Aug.

Operated by the Seventh-day Adventist Church, Frenda offers sports, nature study, drama, horseback riding, arts and crafts, canoeing and waterfront activities. Specialty camps address water-skiing and wakeboarding.

ONTARIO PIONEER CAMP
Res — Coed Ages 5-18
(Coord — Res 11-16)

Port Sydney, P0B 1L0 Ontario, Canada. 942 Clearwater Lake Rd. Tel: 705-385-2370,
800-361-2267. Fax: 705-385-3649.
www.pioneercamp.ca   E-mail: info@pioneercamp.com
Calvin Bennett, Exec Dir.
Grades K-11. Adm: FCFS. **Appl due:** Rolling. **Enr:** 595. **Enr cap:** 625. **Staff:** Admin 20.
Couns 200.
Features: Crafts Dance Drama Filmmaking Painting Photog Aquatics Archery Aviation/
Aero Bicycle_Tours Boating Canoe Hiking Kayak Mtn_Biking Ropes_Crse Sail Survival_Trng Wilderness_Camp Wilderness_Canoe Baseball Basketball Cross-country
Soccer Softball Swim Ultimate_Frisbee Volleyball Watersports Weight_Trng.
Fees 2012: Res Can$685-1370 (+Can$100), 1-2 wks. Aid 2009 (Need): $130,000.
Housing: Cabins Lodges Tents. Avg per room/unit: 5. **Swimming:** Lake.
Est 1929. Nonprofit. Nondenom Christian. **Ses:** 18. **Wks/ses:** 1-2. Operates June-Sept.

Pioneer operates at three different campsites. Programs include single-gender boys' and girls' sessions (ages 11-16), a white-water canoe tripping program, a CIT program and a coeducational camp for younger children (ages 5-10). In addition, an integrated program allows a limited number of special-needs children to take part in traditional recreational pursuits.

CAMP RAMAH
Res — Coed Ages 8-16

Utterson, P0B 1M0 Ontario, Canada. 1104 Fish Hatchery Rd. Fax: 705-769-2167.
Contact (Sept-May): 491 Lawrence Ave W, Ste 400, Toronto, M5M 1C7 Ontario, Canada. Fax: 416-789-3970.
Year-round Tel: 416-789-2193.
www.campramah.com   E-mail: info@campramah.com
Michael Wolf, Dir.
Adm: FCFS. **Appl due:** Rolling. **Enr:** 380-450. **Enr cap:** 450. **Staff:** Admin 6. Couns 180.
Features: Lang Crafts Dance Media Music Photog Theater Aquatics Bicycle_Tours Boating Canoe Climbing_Wall Community_Serv Cooking Fishing Kayak Sail Wilderness_Camp Wilderness_Canoe Woodcraft Yoga Aerobics Basketball Field_Hockey Football Golf Martial_Arts Soccer Softball Street_Hockey Swim Tennis Ultimate_Frisbee Volleyball Water-skiing.
Fees 2012: Res $1900-7500, 2-7½ wks. Aid (Merit & Need).
Housing: Cabins. Avg per room/unit: 12. **Swimming:** Lake.
Est 1960. Nonprofit. Jewish. **Ses:** 4. **Wks/ses:** 2-7½. Operates June-Aug.

Ramah provides a full range of land sports and watersports and arts activities in a Jewish milieu. The program fully integrates experiential Jewish living and learning. A two-week session enrolls rising third and fourth graders only.

QUEBEC

CAMP KINNERET AND BILUIM
Res and Day — Coed Ages 7-16

Mont Tremblant, Quebec, Canada. 184 Rue Harisson. Tel: 819-425-3332.
Contact (Year-round): 5555 Westminster Ave, Ste 300, Cote Saint-Luc, H4W 2J2 Quebec, Canada. Tel: 514-735-3167.
Year-round Toll-free: 800-426-5108, Fax: 514-735-3833.
www.campkinneret-biluim.com   E-mail: guy@ckb.ca
Guy Korngold, Dir.
Adm: FCFS. **Appl due:** Rolling. **Staff:** Admin 2. Couns 55.
Features: Lang Writing/Journ Crafts Dance Fine_Arts Media Music Theater Aquatics Canoe Exploration Hiking Wilderness_Camp Baseball Basketball Football Swim Volleyball.
Fees 2012: Res Can$2100-5933 (+Can$230), 2½-6 wks.
Housing: Cabins Tents. **Swimming:** Lake.
Est 1948. Nonprofit. **Spons:** Canadian Young Judaea. Jewish. **Ses:** 2. **Wks/ses:** 2½-3½. Operates July-Aug.

Located in the Laurentian Mountains, Kinneret offers a Jewish and Zionist summer camping experience complemented by recreational activities. The program includes sports, drama, dance, canoeing, riding, aquatics, crafts, nature and hiking. Sixteen-year-olds take part in a program focusing upon leadership enrichment. The camp conducts Shabbat services each Friday evening, as well as optional Saturday morning services.

RECREATIONAL CAMPS

Recreational camps are arranged in alphabetical state order, and within each state, programs are arranged alphabetically first by town and then name. Canadian camps appear after US camps. Boys', girls', coeducational, and coordinate (operating concurrently) single-gender boys' and girls' camps appear in one large chapter. The program type is indicated in the age range following the camp name. An index of camps offering family sessions begins on page 682.

INDEX OF RECREATIONAL CAMPS
OFFERING FAMILY SESSIONS

Recreational Camps

ALABAMA

RIVERVIEW CAMP FOR GIRLS
Res — Girls Ages 6-16

Mentone, AL 35984. 757 County Rd 614, PO Box 299. Tel: 256-634-4043, 800-882-0722. Fax: 256-634-3601.
www.riverviewcamp.com   E-mail: info@riverviewcamp.com
Susan C. Hooks & Larry Hooks, Dirs.
Adm: FCFS. **Appl due:** Rolling. **Enr cap:** 248. **Staff:** Couns 50.
Features: Crafts Dance Music Theater Aquatics Archery Canoe Climbing_Wall Hiking Rappelling Riding Riflery Rock_Climb Ropes_Crse Basketball Equestrian Golf Gymnastics Swim Tennis Volleyball.
Fees 2012: Res $1275-2375 (+$75-250), 1-2 wks. Aid 2009 (Need): $49,410.
Housing: Cabins. Avg per room/unit: 16. **Swimming:** Pool River.
Est 1987. Inc. Nondenom Christian. **Ses:** 11. **Wks/ses:** 1-2. Operates June-July. ACA.

A nondenominational Christian camp, Riverview offers riding, watersports, land sports, a ropes course and activities in the arts, among other traditional camping pursuits. White-water rafting trips are also available. A particularly strong horsemanship program features certified instruction in English riding and supervised trail rides.

ARIZONA

ORME WESTERN CAMP
Res — Coed Ages 7-16

Mayer, AZ 86333. HC 63, Box 3040. Tel: 928-632-7601. Fax: 928-632-7605.
www.ormewesterncamp.org   E-mail: pteskey@ormeschool.org
Pamela Teskey, Dir.
Adm: FCFS. **Enr:** 113. **Enr cap:** 150. **Staff:** Admin 1. Couns 33.
Features: ESL Lang Crafts Dance Drama Adventure_Travel Aquatics Archery Hiking Mountaineering Mtn_Biking Mtn_Trips Outdoor_Ed Riding Riflery Rock_Climb Survival_Trng Working_Cattle_Ranch Equestrian Soccer Swim Tennis Volleyball.
Fees 2011: Res $1200-2000, 2-6 wks.
Housing: Cabins Dorms. **Swimming:** Pool.
Est 1929. Nonprofit. **Spons:** Orme School. **Ses:** 3. **Wks/ses:** 2. Operates June-Aug. ACA.

Using the facilities of Orme School, the camp has strong programs in Western and English riding, rodeo and related ranch activities, the creative arts, sports, swimming, outdoor survival and mountain biking. Four- to 10-day treks are also available.

FRIENDLY PINES CAMP
Res — Coed Ages 6-13

Prescott, AZ 86303. 933 Friendly Pines Rd. Tel: 928-445-2128, 888-281-2267. Fax: 928-445-6065.
www.friendlypines.com   E-mail: info@friendlypines.com
Kevin Nissen, Dir.
Adm: FCFS. **Appl due:** Rolling. **Enr:** 210. **Staff:** Couns 50.

Features: Circus_Skills Crafts Dance Drama Photog Aquatics Archery Canoe Climbing_ Wall Farm Fishing Hiking Rappelling Riding Riflery Rock_Climb Ropes_Crse Equestrian Gymnastics Martial_Arts Soccer Swim Tennis Water-skiing Watersports Sewing.
Fees 2012: Res $1275-5670 (+$30), 1½-6½ wks. Day $500-900, 1-2 wks.
Housing: Cabins. Avg per room/unit: 6. **Swimming:** Pool.
Est 1941. Inc. **Ses:** 5. **Wks/ses:** 1½-6½. Operates June-Aug. ACA.

While horseback riding and pony driving are featured at Friendly Pines, the roster of activities includes water-skiing, a ropes course, tennis, swimming, nature study, and rock and mountain climbing. Camping trips range from overnights to multi-day mountaineering trips.

ARKANSAS

CAMP WINNAMOCKA
Res — Coed Ages 7-15

Arkadelphia, AR 71923. 68 Fort Jackson Rd. Tel: 870-246-4599, 888-687-5387.
   Fax: 870-246-6345.
www.winnamocka.com   E-mail: camp@winnamocka.com
Niki Jackson & Brent Jackson, Dirs.
Adm: FCFS. **Appl due:** Rolling. **Enr:** 105. **Enr cap:** 105. **Staff:** Admin 2. Couns 35.
Features: Crafts Dance Canoe Climbing_Wall Exploration Ropes_Crse Basketball Swim.
Fees 2010: Res $925-1650, 1-2 wks. Aid 2007 (Need): $1450.
Housing: Cabins Lodges. Avg per room/unit: 12. **Swimming:** Pond Pool River.
Est 1986. Inc. **Ses:** 7. **Wks/ses:** 1-2. Operates May-Aug.

Winnamocka offers traditional recreational camping in a noncompetitive setting. Most sessions last one week, but a pair of two-week programs are available.

JOSEPH PFEIFER KIWANIS CAMP
Res — Coed Ages 9-14

Little Rock, AR 72223. 5512 Ferndale Cutoff. Tel: 501-821-3714. Fax: 501-821-2629.
www.pfeifercamp.com   E-mail: info@pfeifercamp.com
Sanford Tollette, Exec Dir.
Adm: FCFS. **Appl due:** Rolling. **Enr cap:** 72. **Staff:** Admin 10. Couns 8.
Features: Crafts Aquatics Canoe Hiking Wilderness_Camp Wilderness_Canoe Swim.
Fees 2010: Free. Res 1 wk.
Housing: Cabins. Avg per room/unit: 12. **Swimming:** Pool.
Est 1929. Nonprofit. **Spons:** Downtown Kiwanis Club of Little Rock. **Ses:** 5. **Wks/ses:** 1. Operates June-July. ACA.

This Kiwanis camp provides cost-free residential camping opportunities for economically disadvantaged young people in central Arkansas. Among Pfeifer Camp's activities are swimming instruction, hiking, canoeing, camping, environmental education, arts and crafts, and sports. Campers age 15 and older may attend as counselors-in-training.

CALIFORNIA

CRAZZY'S WASEWAGAN CAMP AND RETREAT
Res — Coed Ages 5-16

Angelus Oaks, CA 92305. 42121 Seven Oaks Rd. Tel: 909-794-2910.
   Fax: 909-794-8453.
www.campwasewagan.com   E-mail: crazzycraig@earthlink.net
Craig Johnson, Dir.
Adm: FCFS. **Appl due:** Rolling. **Enr:** 100. **Enr cap:** 100. **Staff:** Admin 3. Couns 8.
Features: Crafts Aquatics Archery Canoe Climbing_Wall Exploration Fishing Hiking Mtn_
   Biking Paintball Riding Riflery Ropes_Crse White-water_Raft Basketball Equestrian
   Fencing Swim Volleyball Watersports.
Fees 2012: Res $800-1750 (+$270), 1-2 wks.
Housing: Cabins Lodges. Avg per room/unit: 10. **Swimming:** Lake Pool River Stream.
Est 1936. Inc. **Ses:** 4. **Wks/ses:** 1-2. Operates June-Aug. ACA.

Situated in the San Bernardino Mountains, the camp offers a range of traditional recreational activities. Among the special events are white-water rafting trips, movie night, scavenger hunt, junior Olympics and stunt day.

WOODCRAFT RANGERS SUMMER CAMP
Res — Coed Ages 7-11

Big Bear City, CA.
Contact (Year-round): 1625 W Olympic Blvd, Ste 800, Los Angeles, CA 90015.
   Tel: 213-249-9293. Fax: 213-388-7088.
www.woodcraftrangers.org   E-mail: camp@woodcraftrangers.org
Sergio Medrano, Dir.
Grades 2-6. Adm: FCFS. **Appl due:** Rolling. **Enr:** 100. **Staff:** Admin 3. Couns 30.
Features: Geol Crafts Drama Aquatics Archery Climbing_Wall Hiking Woodcraft Baseball
   Basketball Soccer Swim.
Fees 2009: Res $370, 1 wk. Aid (Need).
Housing: Cabins Tents. **Swimming:** Lake Pool.
Est 1922. Nonprofit. **Ses:** 3. **Wks/ses:** 1. Operates Aug. ACA.

Activities at the camp include archery, a climbing wall and ropes course, arts and crafts, hiking, team sports, nature exploration and out-of-camp trips. In addition to its traditional sessions, Woodcraft Rangers conducts specialized camping programs in such areas as outdoor education, leadership and peer mentoring.

ACADEMY BY THE SEA
CAMP PACIFIC
Res — Coed Ages 7-17

Carlsbad, CA 92018. 2605 Carlsbad Blvd. Tel: 760-434-7564. Fax: 760-729-1574.
www.abts.com   E-mail: summer@abts.com
Candace Heidenrich, Dir.
Adm: FCFS. **Appl due:** Rolling. **Enr cap:** 250. **Staff:** Admin 10. Couns 60.
Features: Crafts Creative_Writing Dance Drama Media Music Painting Photog Aquatics
   Kayak Paintball Riflery Baseball Basketball Football Lacrosse Martial_Arts Soccer Soft-
   ball Swim Tennis Volleyball Watersports Weight_Trng.
Fees 2011: Res $895-4495 (+$200-450), 1-5 wks.
Housing: Cabins Dorms. Avg per room/unit: 3. **Swimming:** Ocean Pool.
Est 1943. Nonprofit. **Spons:** Army and Navy Academy. **Ses:** 2. **Wks/ses:** 3. Operates June-
   Aug. ACA.

688   *Guide to Summer Programs*

Camp Pacific, owned and operated by the Army and Navy Academy, provides various recreational activities for boys and girls. In the morning, campers take part in weekly skill classes, then participate in recreational activities or sports in the afternoon. Evening activities include talent shows, scavenger hunts, folk dancing and camp fires. In addition to the traditional three-week session, the camp offers two weeklong surfing and bodyboarding sessions and a five-week leadership challenge camp.

DOUGLAS RANCH CAMPS
Res — Coed Ages 7-16; Day — Coed 5-16

Carmel Valley, CA 93924. 33200 E Carmel Valley Rd. Tel: 831-659-2761.
Fax: 831-659-5690.
www.douglascamp.com   E-mail: director@douglascamp.com
Steve Ehrhardt, Dir.
Adm: FCFS. **Appl due:** Rolling. **Staff:** Admin 5. Couns 30.
Features: Crafts Theater Aquatics Archery Hiking Ranch Riding Riflery Basketball Equestrian Soccer Swim Tennis Volleyball.
Fees 2012: Res $1475-4650 (+$75-150), 1-4 wks. Day $800, 2 wks.
Housing: Cabins. **Swimming:** Pool.
Est 1925. Inc. Ses: 5. **Wks/ses:** 1-4. Operates June-Aug.

This traditional, coeducational recreational camp conducts separate daytime activities for boys and girls. All campers participate in a structured program with six core activities: Western horseback riding, swimming, arts and crafts, tennis, riflery and archery. Other offerings include hiking, drama, overnight sleep outs and folk dancing.

CAMP COTTONTAIL
Res — Coed Ages 6-16

Castaic, CA 91384. 30910 S Sloan Canyon Rd.
Contact (Winter): 26500 W Agoura Rd, Ste 102-229, Calabasas, CA 91302.
Year-round Toll-free: 888-982-3222, Fax: 818-688-0168.
www.campcottontail.com   E-mail: info@campcottontail.com
Lynn Pedroza, Dir.
Adm: FCFS. **Appl due:** Rolling. **Enr:** 200.
Features: Crafts Dance Drama Boating Climbing_Wall Deep-sea Fishing Fishing Hiking Rappelling Rock_Climb Ropes_Crse Baseball Basketball Equestrian Football Softball Swim Tennis Volleyball Water-skiing Watersports.
Fees 2011: Res $1480-5100, 1-4 wks.
Housing: Cabins Dorms. **Swimming:** Lake Ocean Pool.
Est 1958. Inc. Ses: 4. **Wks/ses:** 1-4. Operates June-Aug. ACA.

Cottontail offers such activities as horseback riding, watersports, land sports, archery, riflery, minibikes, and arts and crafts. For an additional fee, campers may go on trips to Disneyland, Universal Studios and Magic Mountain. Weeklong sessions serve children ages 6-8.

CATALINA SEA CAMP
Res — Coed Ages 8-17

Catalina Island, CA. Toyon Bay.
Contact (Year-round): c/o Guided Discoveries, PO Box 1360, Claremont, CA 91711.
Tel: 909-625-6194, 800-645-1423. Fax: 909-625-7305.
www.catalinaseacamp.org   E-mail: info@guideddiscoveries.org
Paul Kupferman, Dir.
Grades 3-12. Adm: FCFS. **Appl due:** Rolling. **Enr:** 200. **Enr cap:** 200. **Staff:** Admin 10. Couns 60.

Features: Environ_Sci Marine_Bio/Stud Photog Climbing_Wall Cooking Kayak Mtn_Biking Ropes_Crse Sail Scuba Swim.
Fees 2012: Res $1395-3800 (+$200), 1-3 wks.
Housing: Dorms. **Swimming:** Ocean.
Est 1978. Nonprofit. **Ses:** 5. **Wks/ses:** 1-3. Operates June-Aug. ACA.

A full range of camp activities on Catalina Island includes scuba diving, snorkeling, sailing, windsurfing, underwater photography and video, marine biology, oceanography, ecology, hiking and fishing. Weeklong Junior Sea Camp sessions enroll campers ages 8-12.

See Also Page 26

PLANTATION FARM CAMP
Res — Coed Ages 8-17

Cazadero, CA 95421. 34285 Kruse Ranch Rd. Tel: 707-847-3494.
Contact (Sept-May): 1708 Eola St, Berkeley, CA 94703. Tel: 510-849-1084.
www.plantationcamp.com   E-mail: tracy@plantationcamp.com
John Chakan & Kelly Marston, Dirs.
Adm: FCFS. **Appl due:** Rolling. **Enr cap:** 100. **Staff:** Admin 5. Couns 30.
Focus: Wildlife_Stud. **Features:** Crafts Dance Drama Music Aquatics Archery Canoe Cooking Farm Fishing Hiking Kayak Ranch Riding Wilderness_Camp Woodcraft Basketball Equestrian Football Soccer Swim Volleyball.
Fees 2012: Res $1200-4400 (+$150), 1-3½ wks.
Housing: Tents. Avg per room/unit: 13. **Swimming:** Lake Pool River.
Est 1952. Inc. **Ses:** 3. **Wks/ses:** 1-3½. Operates June-Aug. ACA.

Campers choose from such activities as horseback riding, hiking, drama, arts and crafts, capture the flag, field sports, song and dance, swimming, fishing and boating, watersports, archery and photography. Farm and animal projects, as well as an overnight canoeing and kayaking trip, are also available.

CAMP OLIVER
Res — Coed Ages 6-16

Descanso, CA 91916. 8761 Riverside Dr, PO Box 206. Tel: 619-445-5945.
Fax: 619-445-3326.
www.campoliver.com   E-mail: director@campoliver.com
Lia Morales, Exec Dir.
Adm: FCFS. **Appl due:** Rolling. **Enr:** 60. **Enr cap:** 72. **Staff:** Admin 5. Couns 20. Res 2.
Features: Ecol Environ_Sci Crafts Dance Drama Aquatics Archery Conservation Cooking Hiking Outdoor_Ed Peace/Cross-cultural Ropes_Crse Wilderness_Camp Yoga Baseball Basketball Football Soccer Swim Volleyball.
Fees 2011: Res $350-450, 1 wk. Aid (Need).
Housing: Cabins. Avg per room/unit: 16. **Swimming:** Pool.
Est 1949. Nonprofit. Roman Catholic. **Ses:** 5. **Wks/ses:** 1. Operates June-Aug. ACA.

Campers at Oliver take part in archery, drama, sports, swimming, hiking, music, nature, arts and crafts, singing and campfires. Talent shows, outdoor cooking, stargazing and nighttime pool parties are special features.

COPPERCREEK CAMP
Res — Coed Ages 7-15

Greenville, CA 95947. PO Box 749. Tel: 530-284-7617, 800-350-0006.
Fax: 530-284-7497.
www.coppercreek.com   E-mail: becky@coppercreek.com
Lauren Lindskog Allen, John Lindskog, Becky Hogland & Craig Hogland, Dirs.

Grades 3-10. Adm: FCFS. **Appl due:** Rolling. **Enr:** 110. **Staff:** Admin 5. Couns 35.
Features: Crafts Dance Music Theater Aquatics Archery Canoe Caving Climbing_Wall Exploration Hiking Kayak Mountaineering Mtn_Biking Mtn_Trips Riding Riflery Rock_Climb Ropes_Crse White-water_Raft Wilderness_Camp Equestrian Golf Swim Volley-ball Water-skiing Watersports.
Fees 2012: Res $1425-6625 (+$40), 1-6 wks.
Housing: Cabins Lodges. Avg per room/unit: 7. **Swimming:** Lake Pond Pool.
Est 1965. Inc. **Ses:** 4. **Wks/ses:** 1-6. Operates June-Aug. ACA.

Located in the Sierra Nevada Mountains, Coppercreek features English riding, jumping, overnights, backpacking into wilderness areas, and trail riding. Other activities include wakeboarding, kayaking, mountain biking, drama, rock climbing and crafts.

CAMP TAWONGA
Res — Coed Ages 7-15

Groveland, CA.
Contact (Year-round): 131 Steuart St, Ste 460, San Francisco, CA 94105.
Tel: 415-543-2267. Fax: 415-543-5417.
www.tawonga.org   E-mail: info@tawonga.org
Jamie Simon, Dir.
Grades 2-10. Adm: FCFS. **Appl due:** Rolling. **Staff:** Admin 11. Couns 160.
Features: Crafts Dance Drama Fine_Arts Media Music Adventure_Travel Aquatics Archery Bicycle_Tours Boating Canoe Farm Hiking Kayak Mountaineering Mtn_Biking Mtn_Trips Peace/Cross-cultural Rappelling Rock_Climb Wilderness_Camp Baseball Basketball Football Martial_Arts Soccer Softball Swim Volleyball.
Fees 2012: Res $925-3555 (+$40), 1-3 wks. Aid (Need).
Housing: Cabins. **Swimming:** Lake Pool River.
Est 1925. Nonprofit. Jewish. **Ses:** 6. **Wks/ses:** 1-3. Operates June-Aug. ACA.

Tawonga's weeklong session (for children entering grades 2-7) consists of arts and crafts, swimming, boating, sports, nature activities, visits to the animal farm and a day trip to Yosemite National Park. Two-week sessions (grades 3-9) feature a backpacking overnight in Yosemite or the Stanislaus National Forest and a day on the ropes course. Three-week programs (grades 5-10) include backpacking, a ropes course, dances, sports, drama, and arts and crafts. In addition, older campers choose from advanced offerings in arts and crafts, drama, self-defense, a cappella singing and dance. Jewish traditions and learning opportunities are part of the program.

PALI OVERNIGHT ADVENTURES
Res — Coed Ages 9-16

Lake Arrowhead, CA.
Contact (Year-round): PO Box 2237, Running Springs, CA 92382. Tel: 909-867-5743, 888-678-6637. Fax: 909-867-7643.
www.paliadventures.com   E-mail: info@paliadventures.com
Ian Brassett, Dir.
Adm: FCFS. **Appl due:** Rolling. **Enr:** 250. **Staff:** Admin 15. Couns 56. Res 15.
Features: Writing/Journ Crafts Creative_Writing Dance Filmmaking Media Music Photog Theater Aquatics Archery Boating Climbing_Wall Cooking Hiking Kayak Mtn_Biking Paintball Riding Riflery Rock_Climb Ropes_Crse Scuba Yoga Basketball Equestrian Martial_Arts Skateboarding Swim Water-skiing Watersports.
Fees 2009: Res $1535-5750 (+$50-200), 1-4 wks.
Housing: Cabins. Avg per room/unit: 10. **Swimming:** Lake Pond Pool.
Est 1997. Inc. **Ses:** 14. **Wks/ses:** 1-2. Operates June-Aug. ACA.

Pali offers both traditional and specialty camp programs. Campers in the traditional program participate in four daily activity periods, chosen from swimming, watersports, horseback riding, a climbing wall, paintball and karaoke. The specialty program combines emphasis on a specific activity with limited time for two electives. Options include stunt camp, cooking, acting, scuba diving, equestrianism, film and leadership, among others.

GOLD ARROW
Res — Coed Ages 6-14

Lakeshore, CA 93634. PO Box 155. Fax: 559-893-6201.
Contact (Sept-May): 644 Pollasky Ave, Ste 100, Clovis, CA 93612. Fax: 559-664-3875.
Year-round Tel: 559-893-6641, 800-554-2267.
www.goldarrowcamp.com   E-mail: mail@goldarrowcamp.com
Audrey K. Monke & Steve Monke, Dirs.
Adm: FCFS. **Appl due:** Rolling. **Enr:** 260. **Enr cap:** 260. **Staff:** Admin 25. Couns 85.
Features: Crafts Painting Photog Theater Aquatics Archery Canoe Climbing_Wall Fishing Hiking Kayak Mountaineering Mtn_Biking Rappelling Riding Riflery Rock_Climb Ropes_ Crse Sail Wilderness_Camp Equestrian Swim Water-skiing Watersports.
Fees 2012: Res $1750-4355 (+$50), 1-4 wks.
Housing: Cabins Tents. Avg per room/unit: 10. **Swimming:** Lake.
Est 1933. Inc. **Ses:** 10. **Wks/ses:** 1-4. Operates June-Aug. ACA.

Boys and girls at Gold Arrow take part in various watersports, wilderness pursuits and traditional camp activities. One-week specialty camps focus upon rock climbing, water-skiing, horseback riding and wilderness backpacking. One-week sessions for first-time 6- and 7-year-old campers are also offered.

SANTA CATALINA SCHOOL
SUMMER AT SANTA CATALINA
Res and Day — Girls Ages 8-14

Monterey, CA 93940. 1500 Mark Thomas Dr. Tel: 831-655-9386. Fax: 831-649-3056.
www.santacatalina.org   E-mail: summercamp@santacatalina.org
Julie Forrest, Dir.
Grades 3-9. Adm: FCFS. **Appl due:** Rolling. **Enr:** 140. **Enr cap:** 140. **Staff:** Admin 5. Couns 16. Res 22.
Type of instruction: Enrich.
Features: Marine_Bio/Stud Crafts Creative_Writing Dance Drama Drawing Fine_Arts Music Painting Photog Musical_Theater Aquatics Cooking Outdoor_Ed Yoga Basketball Equestrian Golf Soccer Swim Tennis Volleyball Winter_Sports.
Fees 2011: Res $2250-5100, 2-5 wks. Day $1200-2900, 2-5 wks.
Housing: Dorms. Avg per room/unit: 2. **Swimming:** Pool.
Est 1953. Nonprofit. Roman Catholic. **Ses:** 3. **Wks/ses:** 2-5. Operates June-July.

Santa Catalina campers fill six daily activity periods with offerings including drama, dance, digital photography, theater arts, musical theater, soccer, basketball, water polo, tennis, cooking and others. Horseback riding and golf instruction are available for an additional fee.

CYO CAMP
Res — Coed Ages 9-16; Day — Coed 8-13

Occidental, CA 95465. 2136 Bohemian Hwy, PO Box 188. Tel: 707-874-0200.
Fax: 707-874-0230.
www.cyocamp.org   E-mail: summercamp@cccyo.org
Rick Garcia, Dir.
Grades 2-11. Adm: FCFS. **Appl due:** Rolling. **Enr:** 150. **Enr cap:** 200. **Staff:** Admin 2. Couns 45. Res 12.
Features: Environ_Sci Crafts Dance Drama Aquatics Archery Canoe Hiking Basketball Swim Ultimate_Frisbee Volleyball.
Fees 2009: Res $650, 1 wk. Day $185, 1 wk. Aid 2009 (Need): $80,000.

Housing: Cabins Lodges. **Swimming:** Pool.
Est 1946. Nonprofit. **Spons:** Catholic Charities CYO. Roman Catholic. **Ses:** 5. **Wks/ses:** 1. Operates June-Aug. ACA.

Located near the coast on a 216-acre site in a redwood forest, the camp provides a traditional recreational program that maintains a Catholic emphasis. Traditional day camps enroll children entering grades 2-9, while a teen adventure and leadership session serves campers ages 13-16. Rising high school juniors may take part in the camp's counselor-in-training program.

MOUNTAIN CAMP
Res — Coed Ages 7-15

Pollock Pines, CA 95726. PO Box 1348.
Contact (Sept-May): 3717 Buchanan St, Ste 300, San Francisco, CA 94123.
Year-round Tel: 415-351-2267, Fax: 415-351-3939.
www.mountaincamp.com E-mail: info@mountaincamp.com
Scott Whipple & Sally Whipple, Dirs.
Grades 2-10. Adm: FCFS. **Appl due:** Mar. **Enr:** 180. **Enr cap:** 180. **Staff:** Admin 2. Couns 70.
Features: Crafts Dance Drama Filmmaking Fine_Arts Music Aquatics Archery Boating Canoe Climbing_Wall Conservation Fishing Kayak Mountaineering Mtn_Biking Ropes_Crse Sail Survival_Trng Wilderness_Camp Badminton Baseball Basketball Football Gymnastics Lacrosse Martial_Arts Soccer Swim Ultimate_Frisbee Volleyball Water-skiing Watersports.
Fees 2009: Res $1300-4400 (+$50), 1-4 wks.
Housing: Cabins Lodges. Avg per room/unit: 10. **Swimming:** Lake Stream.
Est 1986. Inc. **Ses:** 13. **Wks/ses:** 1-4. Operates June-Aug. ACA.

Each day, campers spend one and a half hours participating in all three of the following instructional areas: waterfront, outdoor and lodge activities. Program choices include guitar, video production, camp newspaper, mountain biking, karate, outdoor cooking, fencing, watersports and a radio station.

WALTON'S GRIZZLY LODGE
Res — Coed Ages 7-14

Portola, CA 96122. PO Box 519. Tel: 530-832-4834. Fax: 530-832-4195.
Contact (Sept-May): 510 W Main St, Grass Valley, CA 95945. Tel: 530-274-9577. Fax: 530-274-9677.
www.grizzlylodge.com E-mail: waltons@grizzlylodge.com
Adam Stein, Julie Stein, Jared Stein & Erica Stein, Dirs.
Adm: FCFS. **Appl due:** Rolling. **Enr:** 175. **Enr cap:** 175. **Staff:** Admin 15. Couns 30. Res 45.
Features: Crafts Dance Music Photog Theater Aquatics Archery Boating Canoe Climbing_Wall Fishing Hiking Mtn_Trips Outdoor_Ed Rappelling Riding Riflery Ropes_Crse Sail Woodcraft Basketball Equestrian Golf Lacrosse Skateboarding Soccer Street_Hockey Swim Tennis Ultimate_Frisbee Volleyball Water-skiing Watersports Wrestling.
Fees 2012: Res $1500-2975 (+$50), 1-2 wks.
Housing: Cabins. Avg per room/unit: 16. **Swimming:** Lake.
Est 1926. Inc. **Ses:** 6. **Wks/ses:** 1-2. Operates June-Aug. ACA.

The varied program of recreational activities at Walton's includes swimming, windsurfing, skateboarding, crafts, a high and low ropes course, sports, hiking, woodcraft and horseback trail riding.

MOUNTAIN CAMP WOODSIDE
Res — Coed Ages 7-14; Day — Coed 5-14

Portola Valley, CA 94028. 302 Portola Rd. Tel: 650-851-8225.
Contact (Sept-May): 3717 Buchanan St, Ste 300, San Francisco, CA 94123.
  Tel: 650-576-2267.
Year-round Fax: 415-351-3939.
www.mountaincampwoodside.com   E-mail: info@mountaincampwoodside.com
Jim Politis, Dir.
Adm: FCFS. **Appl due:** Rolling. **Staff:** Admin 4. Couns 16.
Features: Crafts Dance Drama Archery Mtn_Biking Outdoor_Ed Riding Wilderness_Camp Baseball Basketball Equestrian Football Martial_Arts Soccer Swim Tennis Ultimate_ Frisbee Volleyball.
Fees 2012: Res $995, 1 wk. Day $545, 1 wk.
Housing: Dorms. **Swimming:** Pool Stream.
Est 1979. Inc. **Ses:** 8. **Wks/ses:** 1. Operates June-Aug. ACA.

Located on the campus of Woodside Priory School, the camp offers yoga, mountain biking, survival skills, arts and crafts, drama and jazz dance. Also available are horseback riding, archery, and various individual and team sports. Resident campers may participate in beach trips to Half Moon Bay and water-skiing and wakeboarding outings at a nearby lake.

RIVER WAY RANCH CAMP
Res — Coed Ages 7-16

Sanger, CA 93657. 6450 Elwood Rd. Tel: 559-787-2551, 800-821-2801.
  Fax: 559-787-3851.
www.riverwayranchcamp.com   E-mail: inquiry@riverwayranchcamp.com
Jerry Reid, Dir.
Grades 2-10. Adm: FCFS. **Admitted:** 100%. **Appl due:** Rolling. **Enr cap:** 300. **Staff:** Admin 20. Couns 85. Res 125.
Features: Computers Writing/Journ Crafts Dance Filmmaking Music Painting Photog Theater Aquatics Archery Boating Canoe Climbing_Wall Fishing Hiking Kayak Mtn_Biking Mtn_Trips Outdoor_Ed Paintball Riding Riflery Ropes_Crse Sail White-water_Raft Wilderness_Camp Yoga Baseball Basketball Equestrian Football Golf Gymnastics Martial_ Arts Roller_Hockey Rugby Skateboarding Soccer Softball Swim Tennis Ultimate_Frisbee Volleyball Water-skiing Watersports Wrestling.
Fees 2012: Res $1595-3450 (+$178-208), 1-2 wks.
Housing: Cabins. Avg per room/unit: 8. **Swimming:** Lake Pool River.
Est 1967. Inc. **Ses:** 4. **Wks/ses:** 1-2. Operates June-Aug. ACA.

River Way divides campers into three divisions according to age and grade level. Various watersports and land sports are among more than 75 camp activities. In addition to the regular program, boys and girls choose from specialty camps pertaining to water-skiing and horseback riding.

SIERRA ADVENTURE CAMPS
Res — Coed Ages 8-17; Day — Coed 7-17

Santa Monica, CA 90405. 2633 Lincoln Blvd, Ste 604. Tel: 310-392-3100.
  Fax: 310-392-4362.
www.sierraadventurecamps.com   E-mail: amy@sierraadventurecamps.com
Heather Hibbeler, Dir.
Grades 2-12. Adm: FCFS. **Appl due:** Rolling. **Enr:** 72. **Enr cap:** 72. **Staff:** Admin 3. Couns 12. Res 17.
Features: Crafts Aquatics Boating Canoe Community_Serv Hiking Kayak Mtn_Trips Sail Swim Water-skiing Watersports.

Fees 2009: Res $1550 (+$50), 2 wks. Day $954 (+$50), 3 wks. Aid 2009 (Merit & Need): $1000.
Housing: Tents. Avg per room/unit: 5. **Swimming:** Lake Ocean River Stream.
Est 1965. Nonprofit. **Ses:** 9. **Wks/ses:** 1-2. Operates June-Aug. ACA.

Sierra offers a traditional residential program and a day-only watersports camp. At Sierra Sleep-Away, campers sleep in tents and participate in day trips to Yosemite, canoeing, sports and scavenger hunts. Sailing, swimming, surfing and canoeing are featured in the aquatic sports program.

CLOVERLEAF RANCH
Res — Coed Ages 7-15; Day — Coed 5-12

Santa Rosa, CA 95403. 3892 Old Redwood Hwy. Tel: 707-545-5906.
Fax: 707-545-5908.
www.cloverleafranch.com   **E-mail: cloverleafranch@hotmail.com**
Shawna DeGrange, Dir.
Grades K-9. Adm: FCFS. **Appl due:** Rolling. **Enr:** 50. **Enr cap:** 80. **Staff:** Admin 2. Couns 30.
Features: Crafts Creative_Writing Dance Music Painting Photog Theater Aquatics Archery Chess Community_Serv Conservation Cooking Hiking Kayak Mtn_Biking Outdoor_Ed Ranch Riding Riflery Ropes_Crse Wilderness_Camp Yoga Baseball Basketball Equestrian Football Gymnastics Rugby Soccer Softball Swim Tennis Ultimate_Frisbee Volleyball Watersports.
Fees 2011: Res $995-1990, 1-2 wks. Day $425, 1 wk. Aid (Merit & Need).
Housing: Cabins Tents. Avg per room/unit: 10. **Swimming:** Pond Pool.
Est 1947. Inc. **Ses:** 7. **Wks/ses:** 1. Operates June-Aug. ACA.

On this year-round working horse ranch, campers live in a reproduction of a frontier Western town. Campers may participate in an equestrian program and also have access to a ropes course, team and individual sports, waterfront activities and camp outs. In addition, staff provide swimming instruction.

KENNOLYN CAMPS
Res — Coed Ages 6-14; Day — Coed 5-13

Soquel, CA 95073. 8205 Glen Haven Rd. Tel: 831-479-6714. Fax: 831-479-6718.
www.kennolyncamps.com   **E-mail: camps@kennolyn.com**
Andrew Townsend, Dir.
Grades 1-9. Adm: FCFS. **Appl due:** Rolling. **Enr:** 244. **Staff:** Admin 15. Couns 65.
Features: Crafts Dance Drama Music Photog Adventure_Travel Aquatics Archery Climbing_Wall Cooking Exploration Hiking Mtn_Biking Outdoor_Ed Riding Riflery Ropes_Crse Baseball Basketball Equestrian Fencing Golf Martial_Arts Swim Tennis Volleyball.
Fees 2011: Res $1475-2975 (+$40), 1-2 wks. Day $475-875 (+$15), 1-2 wks.
Housing: Cabins. **Swimming:** Ocean Pool.
Est 1946. Inc. **Ses:** 8. **Wks/ses:** 1-2. Operates June-Aug. ACA.

Campers at Kennolyn learn riding and vaulting, take trail rides and overnight treks, and take part in three-day backpacking and climbing trips. Sports, traditional outdoor activities, ceramics and photography are some of the program options. Among specialty camps are the following: an equestrian program (ages 11-16) and an adventure camp that introduces boys and girls entering grades 8-10 to backpacking, rock climbing and river rafting in the High Sierra Mountains.

CAMP CONCORD
Res — Coord Ages 8-14

South Lake Tahoe, CA 96158. Mt Tallac Trailhead Rd, PO Box 8406. Tel: 530-541-1203. Fax: 530-542-2433.
Contact (Sept-May): c/o Concord Parks & Recreation, 1950 Parkside Dr, Mail Stop 11, Concord, CA 94519. Tel: 925-671-3273. Fax: 925-671-3449.
www.cityofconcord.org/recreation/camp   E-mail: camp@ci.concord.ca.us
Grades 3-9. Adm: FCFS. **Appl due:** Rolling. **Enr:** 110. **Enr cap:** 110. **Staff:** Admin 9. Couns 29.
Features: Astron Ecol Crafts Dance Photog Aquatics Archery Canoe Exploration Fishing Hiking Riding Ropes_Crse White-water_Raft Basketball Equestrian Swim Volleyball.
Fees 2009: Res $492-517 (+$50), 1 wk. Aid 2006 (Need): $43,278.
Housing: Cabins. Avg per room/unit: 5-6. **Swimming:** Lake.
Est 1967. Nonprofit. **Ses:** 12. **Wks/ses:** 1. Operates June-Aug. ACA.

Located high in the Sierra Mountains near the shores of Lake Tahoe and Fallen Leaf Lake, this traditional youth camp features such activities as archery, arts and crafts, hiking, environmental games, crawdad fishing, swimming and camp fires. The Leaders in Training program (ages 14 and 15) combines standard camping activities with involvement with and supervision of the younger campers, while the CIT program enables mature teens (ages 16 and 17) to learn about camp counseling.

MOUNTAIN MEADOW RANCH
Res — Coed Ages 8-16

Susanville, CA 96130. PO Box 610. Tel: 530-257-4419. Fax: 530-257-7155.
www.mountainmeadow.com   E-mail: fun@mountainmeadow.com
Jack Ellena, Jr., Dir.
Adm: FCFS. **Enr cap:** 120.
Fees 2010: Res $1200-3300, 1-3 wks.
Est 1956. Ses: 4. **Wks/ses:** 1-3. Operates June-Aug. ACA.

A full program of recreational activities includes horsemanship, water-skiing, boating, fishing, swimming and hiking. Campers may also participate in riflery, archery, tennis, backpacking, ceramics and photography. Excursions and camp outs are part of the program.

CATALINA ISLAND CAMPS
Res — Coed Ages 7-16

Two Harbors, CA.
Contact (Year-round): PO Box 94146, Pasadena, CA 91109. Tel: 626-296-4040, 800-696-2267. Fax: 626-794-1401.
www.catalinaislandcamps.com   E-mail: info@catalinaislandcamps.com
Maria Horner & Tom Horner, Exec Dirs.
Grades 2-11. Adm: FCFS. **Appl due:** Rolling. **Enr:** 190. **Staff:** Admin 15. Couns 50.
Features: Ecol Environ_Sci Marine_Bio/Stud Crafts Photog Aquatics Archery Boating Climbing_Wall Conservation Hiking Kayak Riflery Ropes_Crse Sail Sea_Cruises Basketball Soccer Swim Tennis Volleyball Water-skiing Watersports.
Fees 2010: Res $1550-4900 (+$50), 1-4 wks.
Housing: Cabins. **Swimming:** Ocean.
Est 1922. Inc. **Ses:** 8. **Wks/ses:** 1-4. Operates June-Aug. ACA.

During a camper's first week at CIC, activities are scheduled by cabin group to provide an introduction to each activity. There are four activity periods each day, with boys and girls also participating in an evening activity. Campers begin their second week by focusing on a specific skill area. Older boys and girls depart in groups of three to five cabins for an overnight camping trip.

SKYLAKE YOSEMITE CAMP
Res — Coed Ages 7-16

Wishon, CA 93669. 37976 Rd 222. Tel: 559-642-3720. Fax: 559-642-3395.
www.skylake.com   E-mail: natalie@skylake.com
Jeff Portnoy, Dir.
Grades 2-10. Adm: FCFS. **Appl due:** Rolling. **Enr:** 210. **Staff:** Admin 7. Couns 62.
Features: Crafts Drama Painting Photog Aquatics Archery Canoe Climbing_Wall Hiking Kayak Mtn_Biking Mtn_Trips Riding Ropes_Crse Wilderness_Camp Basketball Equestrian Soccer Softball Swim Tennis Ultimate_Frisbee Volleyball Water-skiing.
Fees 2012: Res $2800-5000, 2-4 wks.
Housing: Cabins Lodges. Avg per room/unit: 6. **Swimming:** Lake.
Est 1945. Inc. Ses: 7. **Wks/ses:** 2-4. Operates June-Aug. ACA.

At Skylake Yosemite Camp, boys and girls participate in team and individual sports, horsemanship, hiking, backpacking and mountain climbing. Day and overnight trips are available, as are lake activities, watersports, mountain biking, archery and a ropes course.

COLORADO

COLVIG SILVER CAMPS
Res — Coed Ages 7-17
(Coord — Res 11-13)

Durango, CO 81301. 9665 Florida Rd. Tel: 970-247-2564, 800-858-2850.
Fax: 970-247-2547.
www.colvigsilvercamps.com   E-mail: office@colvigsilvercamps.com
Clay Colvig, Dir.
Grades 3-12. Adm: FCFS. **Appl due:** Rolling. **Enr:** 125. **Staff:** Admin 6. Couns 50.
Features: Archaeol Astron Ecol Environ_Sci Geol Writing/Journ Crafts Creative_Writing Dance Drama Music Photog Adventure_Travel Aquatics Archery Boating Canoe Climbing_Wall Conservation Cooking Exploration Farm Fishing Hiking Mountaineering Mtn_Biking Mtn_Trips Peace/Cross-cultural Ranch Riding Riflery Rock_Climb Ropes_Crse Survival_Trng White-water_Raft Wilderness_Camp Wilderness_Canoe Woodcraft Work Basketball Equestrian Swim Tennis Volleyball.
Fees 2010: Res $2110-4760 (+$200), 2-4 wks.
Housing: Cabins. Avg per room/unit: 5. **Swimming:** Pond Stream.
Est 1970. Inc. Ses: 4. **Wks/ses:** 2. Operates June-Aug. ACA.

Colvig operates five distinct programs to meet the needs of campers of various ages: Homestead (entering grades 3-5), featuring the only two-week sessions; Silver Saddle and Silver Spruce (grades 6-8), separate girls' and boys' programs that share some coed activities; Outpost (grades 9 and 10), in which campers spend three-quarters of their stay on wilderness trips; and Pathfinding, a wilderness adventure for campers entering grades 10-12. Each emphasizes outdoor living and skills in a noncompetitive environment. Expedition trips include visits to Utah, New Mexico and Colorado for river rafting, canoeing, archaeology, ghost town exploration, backpacking and rock climbing. Colvig offers a two-week session option for seven- to 10-year-olds only; older campers must enroll for four weeks.

SANBORN WESTERN CAMPS
Res — Coord Ages 7-16

Florissant, CO 80816. 2000 Old Stage Rd, PO Box 167. Tel: 719-748-3341.
Fax: 719-748-3259.
www.sanbornwesterncamps.com   E-mail: info@sanbornwesterncamps.com

Mike MacDonald & Julie Richardson, Dirs.
Adm: FCFS. **Appl due:** Rolling. **Enr:** 220. **Staff:** Admin 20. Couns 80.
Features: Astron Ecol Environ_Sci Geol Crafts Creative_Writing Dance Music Photog Theater Adventure_Travel Aquatics Archery Canoe Caving Climbing_Wall Conservation Exploration Fishing Hiking Mountaineering Mtn_Biking Mtn_Trips Ranch Rappelling Riding Rock_Climb Ropes_Crse Wilderness_Camp Woodcraft Basketball Soccer Softball Swim Tennis Watersports.
Fees 2012: Res $2150-4300 (+$200), 2-4 wks.
Housing: Cabins Lodges Tents Tepees. Avg per room/unit: 10. **Swimming:** Pool.
Est 1948. Nonprofit. **Spons:** Sanborn Western Camps. **Ses:** 4. **Wks/ses:** 2-4. Operates June-Aug. ACA.

High Trails Ranch for Girls and Big Spring Ranch for Boys, which constitute Sanborn Western Camps, provide a traditional camping experience with a strong emphasis on outdoor adventures. With the assistance of staff, campers select daily activities from the following areas: watersports, land sports, creative arts, astronomy, nature/geology, Western riding and Western history. Tripping is integral to the program, with two- to five-day excursions to dozens of destinations designed for both novice and experienced hikers, riders, backpackers and climbers.

GENEVA GLEN
Res — Coed Ages 6-16

Indian Hills, CO 80454. Box 248. **Tel:** 303-697-4621. **Fax:** 303-697-9429.
www.genevaglen.org **E-mail: ggcamp@genevaglen.org**
Ken Atkinson & Nancy Atkinson, Dirs.
Adm: FCFS.
Est 1922. Ses: 5. **Wks/ses:** 1-2. Operates June-Aug. ACA.

Geneva Glen Camps provide opportunities to develop new skills in archery, crafts, riflery, music, drama, pageantry, hiking, wilderness exploration, swimming, horseback riding, backpacking, overnights and leadership training.

CONNECTICUT

CAMP AWOSTING
CAMP CHINQUEKA
Res — Coord Ages 6-16

Bantam, CT 06750. c/o Ebner Camps, PO Box 355. **Tel:** 860-567-4924, 800-662-2677.
Fax: 860-626-8301.
www.mysummerfamily.com **E-mail: info@awosting.com; info@chinqueka.com**
Pauline Jepson, Steven Jepson & Kristin Ebner, Dirs.
Grades K-10. Adm: FCFS. **Appl due:** Rolling. **Enr:** 120-160. **Staff:** Admin 12. Couns 100.
Features: Sci Writing/Journ Crafts Creative_Writing Dance Drama Filmmaking Media Music Photog Adventure_Travel Aquatics Archery Boating Canoe Climbing_Wall Deep-sea Fishing Fishing Hiking Kayak Mtn_Biking Mtn_Trips Outdoor_Ed Rappelling Riding Rock_Climb Ropes_Crse Sail Wilderness_Camp Woodcraft Aerobics Basketball Extreme_Sports Fencing Field_Hockey Golf Gymnastics Martial_Arts Soccer Softball Swim Tennis Volleyball Water-skiing Watersports.
Fees 2012: Res $2600-8000 (+$50-200), 2-8 wks.
Housing: Cabins. Avg per room/unit: 11. **Swimming:** Lake.
Est 1900. Inc. **Spons:** Ebner Camps. **Ses:** 10. **Wks/ses:** 2-8. Operates June-Aug. ACA.

Awosting for boys and Chinqueka for girls offer a full program that includes land sports and watersports, riding and crafts. Water-skiing, gymnastics and go-kart riding are popular activities. Morning sessions are structured, while afternoon programs are elective. Daily instruction by sports specialists is designed to improve athletic skills and stimulate camper interest. Camp Awosting is located on Bantam Lake in Morris, while Camp Chinqueka operates five miles away on Mount Tom Pond in Litchfield.

INCARNATION CAMP
Res — Coed Ages 7-15; Day — Coed 6-12

Ivoryton, CT 06442. 253 Bushy Hill Rd, PO Box 577. Tel: 860-767-0848. Fax: 860-767-8432.
www.incarnationcamp.org   E-mail: info@incarnationcamp.org
Nancy Nygard Pilon, Exec Dir.
Adm: FCFS. **Staff:** Admin 10. Couns 100.
Focus: Religion. **Features:** Crafts Dance Fine_Arts Music Theater Aquatics Archery Bicycle_Tours Boating Canoe Conservation Exploration Hiking Kayak Peace/Cross-cultural Sail Wilderness_Camp Wilderness_Canoe Baseball Basketball Cross-country Equestrian Football Gymnastics Soccer Softball Street_Hockey Swim Tennis Volleyball.
Fees 2012: Res $1375-4595, 2-8 wks.
Housing: Lodges Tents Tepees. **Swimming:** Lake.
Est 1886. Nonprofit. Episcopal. **Ses:** 6. **Wks/ses:** 2-8. Operates June-Aug. ACA.

Located on a 700-acre, wooded site, Incarnation Camp is the nation's oldest coeducational camp. Pequot for Boys and Sherwood for Girls provide traditional camp programming for children ages 7-13. Pioneer Village, an adventure camp for older boys and girls (ages 14 and 15), teaches advanced wilderness camping skills. Canoeing, biking and hiking trips highlight the adventure program.

KENMONT FOR BOYS
KENWOOD FOR GIRLS
Res — Coord Ages 8-14

Kent, CT 06757. 65 Kenmont Rd, PO Box 548. Tel: 860-927-3042. Fax: 860-927-4487. Contact (Sept-May): PO Box 398596, Miami Beach, FL 33239. Tel: 305-673-3310. Fax: 305-673-4131.
www.kmkwcamp.com   E-mail: david@kencamp.com
David Miskit, Sharon Miskit & Tom Troche, Dirs.
Adm: FCFS. **Appl due:** Rolling. **Enr:** 450. **Enr cap:** 450.
Features: Astron Animation Art Ceramics Crafts Dance Music Photog Theater Woodworking Archery Canoe Climbing_Wall Fishing Hiking Kayak Outdoor_Ed Riding Ropes_Crse Sail Baseball Basketball Extreme_Sports Golf Gymnastics Lacrosse Roller_Hockey Soccer Softball Street_Hockey Swim Tennis Volleyball Water-skiing Watersports.
Housing: Cabins. **Swimming:** Lake Pool.
Est 1924. Ses: 2. **Wks/ses:** 4. Operates June-Aug. ACA.

Conducted a hilly, 200-acre site with pine forests and lakefront, these brother and sister camps offers campers freedom of choice within a structured program. Campers of both genders may engage in either competitive or noncompetitive sports; athletics instruction emphasizes enjoyment and skill development. Each four-week session includes one out-of-camp day trip to engage in outdoor adventure or to visit a music festival or a water park.

CAMP CLAIRE
Res — Coed Ages 8-14; Day — Coed 7-14

Lyme, CT 06371. PO Box 702. Tel: 203-235-5705, 888-582-2622. Fax: 203-235-8044.
www.campclaire.org   E-mail: campclaire@yahoo.com

Beth Owen-Mishou, Dir.
Grades 2-9. Adm: FCFS. **Staff:** Admin 2. Couns 14. Special needs 1.
Features: Writing/Journ Crafts Creative_Writing Fine_Arts Theater Aquatics Canoe Hiking Kayak Wilderness_Canoe Baseball Basketball Soccer Swim.
Fees 2011: Res $445-900 (+$25), 1-2 wks. Day $325 (+$25), 1 wk.
Housing: Cabins Houses Lodges. **Swimming:** Pool.
Est 1916. Nonprofit. Congregational. **Ses:** 12. **Wks/ses:** 1-2. Operates June-Aug.

Operated by the First Congregational Church, this camp offers classes in the following five areas: water activities, crafts, outdoor living skills, creative arts and land sports. Campers ages 12-16 may take an advanced program such as canoeing or overnight hiking. Nightly vesper services take place at the camp's outdoor chapel.

WINDHAM-TOLLAND 4-H CAMP
Res — Coed Ages 9-15; Day — Coed 6-15

Pomfret Center, CT 06259. 326 Taft Pond Rd. Tel: 860-974-3379. Fax: 860-974-3327.
www.4hcampct.org   E-mail: windham4h@earthlink.net
Heather Logee, Dir.
Grades 2-12. Adm: FCFS. **Appl due:** Rolling. **Enr:** 129. **Staff:** Admin 3. Couns 40.
Features: Ecol Environ_Sci Writing/Journ Crafts Dance Drama Fine_Arts Music Aquatics Archery Canoe Climbing_Wall Conservation Exploration Fishing Hiking Kayak Mtn_Biking Riding Ropes_Crse Wilderness_Camp Baseball Basketball Cricket Crosscountry Equestrian Football Golf Gymnastics Martial_Arts Rugby Soccer Softball Swim Volleyball Watersports Rocketry.
Fees 2011: Res $390-400 (+$140), 1 wk. Day $200-205 (+$15-115), 1 wk. Aid avail.
Housing: Cabins. Avg per room/unit: 7. **Swimming:** Lake.
Est 1954. Nonprofit. **Ses:** 7. **Wks/ses:** 1. Operates June-Aug. ACA.

Windham-Tolland offers both general outdoor and special sessions on a 207-acre site. Theme camps feature instruction in archery, horseback riding, drama, sports, fishing and canoeing. Campers in all programs compete on a low ropes course and take part in hiking, swimming, arts and crafts, nature and gymnastics.

CAMP WAH-NEE
Res — Coed Ages 8-16

Torrington, CT 06790. 128 Wah-Nee Rd. Tel: 860-379-2273. Fax: 860-379-2249.
Contact (Sept-May): 61 Bogart Ave, Port Washington, NY 11050. Tel: 516-883-1285.
Fax: 516-883-9070.
www.wahnee.com   E-mail: wahnee1042@aol.com
Harvey Mandell & Hal Rosen, Dirs.
Adm: FCFS. **Enr:** 400. **Staff:** Couns 140.
Features: Circus_Skills Crafts Dance Theater Boating Canoe Climbing_Wall Ropes_Crse Sail Scuba Woodcraft Baseball Basketball Gymnastics Roller_Hockey Soccer Softball Swim Tennis Volleyball Watersports.
Fees 2012: Res $8200 (+$550), 7 wks.
Housing: Cabins. Avg per room/unit: 10. **Swimming:** Lake Pool.
Est 1925. Inc. **Ses:** 1. **Wks/ses:** 7. Operates June-Aug.

Located on Shadow Lake in the Berkshires, Wah-Nee offers diversified sports and waterfront programs. Activities include crafts, dance, dramatics, weight training, circus trapeze, a ropes course and mountain boarding.

FLORIDA

PINE TREE CAMPS
Res — Coed Ages 6-13; Day — Coed 3-14

Boca Raton, FL 33431. 3601 N Military Trail. Tel: 561-237-7310. Fax: 561-237-7962.
www.pinetreecamp.com   E-mail: lwallace@lynn.edu
Diane DiCerbo, Dir.
Grades PS-9. Adm: FCFS. Appl due: Rolling. Enr: 900. Enr cap: 1000. Staff: Admin 10. Couns 150.
Features: Archaeol Astron Computers Sci Circus_Skills Crafts Dance Filmmaking Fine_ Arts Media Music Photog Theater Archery Boating Canoe Fishing Baseball Basketball Football Golf Martial_Arts Roller_Hockey Soccer Softball Swim Tennis Ultimate_Frisbee Volleyball.
Fees 2011: Res $2130, 3 wks. Day $590-1045, 3 wks. Aid 2006 (Need): $10,000.
Housing: Dorms. Swimming: Pool.
Est 1978. Nonprofit. Spons: Lynn University. Ses: 3. Wks/ses: 3. Operates June-Aug. ACA.

Conducted on the campus of Lynn University, this traditional recreation camp offers crafts, music, dance, drama, canoeing, tennis, golf, basketball and swimming. Specialty programs addressing sports, computers, music, circus skills, creative arts, magic, space and rocket study, science and multimedia are also available.

GEORGIA

CAMP JULIETTE LOW
Res — Girls Ages 7-17

Cloudland, GA 30731. 321 Camp Juliette Low Rd. Tel: 706-862-2169.
    Fax: 706-862-6525.
Contact (Aug-May): PO Box 5113, Marietta, GA 30061. Tel: 770-428-1062.
    Fax: 770-428-1302.
www.cjl.org   E-mail: info@cjl.org
Nancy Brim & Kappy Kelly, Dirs.
Grades 2-12. Adm: FCFS. Appl due: Rolling. Enr: 460. Staff: Admin 4. Couns 30.
Features: Environ_Sci Crafts Dance Drama Music Aquatics Archery Canoe Climbing_Wall Exploration Hiking Riding Rock_Climb Ropes_Crse Sail Survival_Trng Wilderness_ Camp Wilderness_Canoe Woodcraft Equestrian Swim Tennis.
Fees 2012: Res $730-1425 (+$40), 1-2 wks.
Housing: Cabins Tents. Swimming: Lake Pool River.
Est 1922. Nonprofit. Ses: 6. Wks/ses: 1-2. Operates June-July. ACA.

Situated on a mountaintop in northwest Georgia, the camp conducts a program featuring such activities as camp craft, watersports, tennis, riding, trail hiking, botanical studies, music, dramatics and handicrafts. Advanced swimmers may take part in sailing and canoeing.

CAMP WOODMONT
Res — Coed Ages 6-14

Cloudland, GA 30731. 381 Moonlight Dr. Tel: 706-398-0833.
Contact (Sept-May): 551 Chatata Valley Rd, Cleveland, TN 37323. Tel: 423-472-6070.
www.campwoodmont.com   E-mail: alyson@campwoodmont.com
Tyran Bennett & Alyson Gondek, Dirs.

Adm: FCFS. **Appl due:** Rolling. **Enr:** 80-90. **Enr cap:** 110. **Staff:** Admin 5. Couns 18.
Features: Crafts Dance Music Theater Aquatics Archery Canoe Climbing_Wall Conservation Fishing Hiking Riding Rock_Climb Ropes_Crse Wilderness_Camp Basketball Equestrian Gymnastics Soccer Softball Swim Volleyball Watersports.
Fees 2012: Res $795-1250 (+$80-160), 1-2 wks. Aid avail.
Housing: Cabins. Avg per room/unit: 7. **Swimming:** Lake Pond Pool.
Est 1981. Inc. Nondenom Christian. **Ses:** 12. **Wks/ses:** 1-2. Operates June-Aug. ACA.

A nondenominational program set in a strong Christian atmosphere, Camp Woodmont conducts a traditional recreational camp on Lookout Mountain, in the northwest corner of Georgia. The program, which features an array of traditional camping activities, places particular emphasis on nature and environmental stewardship, outdoor adventure, horseback riding and noncompetitive sports.

CAMP BLUE RIDGE
Res — Coed Ages 6-16

Mountain City, GA 30562. Hwy 441 & Playhouse St, PO Box R. Tel: 706-746-5491.
Fax: 706-746-2774.
Contact (Sept-May): PO Box 2888, Miami Beach, FL 33140. Tel: 954-450-4252.
Fax: 305-532-3152.
Year-round Toll-free: 800-878-2267.
www.blueridgecamp.com   E-mail: campcbr@aol.com
Joey Waldman, Dir.
Grades 2-11. Adm: FCFS. Admitted: 100%. **Appl due:** Rolling. **Enr:** 250. **Enr cap:** 250.
Staff: Admin 9. Couns 75. Res 1.
Features: Ecol Environ_Sci Writing/Journ Crafts Dance Fine_Arts Music Painting Photog Theater Aquatics Archery Boating Canoe Caving Chess Climbing_Wall Exploration Fishing Hiking Kayak Mountaineering Mtn_Trips Outdoor_Ed Paintball Rappelling Riding Riflery Rock_Climb Ropes_Crse Survival_Trng White-water_Raft Wilderness_Camp Wilderness_Canoe Woodcraft Yoga Aerobics Baseball Basketball Cross-country Equestrian Field_Hockey Football Golf Gymnastics Lacrosse Martial_Arts Roller_Hockey Rugby Skateboarding Soccer Softball Street_Hockey Swim Tennis Track Ultimate_Frisbee Volleyball Water-skiing Watersports Weight_Trng Wrestling Rocketry.
Fees 2012: Res $4000-7850 (+$275), 4-8 wks. Aid (Need).
Housing: Cabins. Avg per room/unit: 12. **Swimming:** Lake Pool.
Est 1969. Inc. **Ses:** 5. **Wks/ses:** 4-8. Operates June-Aug.

Blue Ridge's elective program emphasizes aquatics, the arts, outdoor adventure and athletics. Staff schedule various recreational events as a complement to traditional camp activities. While standard sessions run for four, six and eight weeks, campers may arrange one- or two-week sessions.

IDAHO

CAMP CROSS
Res — Coed Ages 7-18

Coeur d'Alene, ID 83814. 42353 W Coeur d'Alene Lake SHR. Tel: 208-667-9695.
Contact (Oct-May): 245 E 13th Ave, Spokane, WA 99202. Tel: 509-624-3191.
Year-round Fax: 509-747-0049.
www.campcross.org   E-mail: campcross@spokanediocese.org
Maureen Cosgrove, Exec Dir.
Grades 2-PG. Adm: FCFS. **Appl due:** Rolling. **Enr:** 60. **Staff:** Admin 2. Couns 10.

Features: Crafts Music Aquatics Boating Canoe Fishing Hiking Sail Basketball Soccer Softball Swim Volleyball Water-skiing Watersports.
Fees 2012: Res $249-270 (+$20), 1 wk.
Housing: Cabins. **Swimming:** Lake.
Est 1923. Nonprofit. Episcopal. **Ses:** 5. **Wks/ses:** 1. Operates June-Aug.

This Christian camp conducts traditional recreational programs. In addition to its youth sessions, Camp Cross also offers family camps, men's and women's weeks, and religious retreats.

ILLINOIS

CAMP SHAW-WAW-NAS-SEE
Res — Coed Ages 7-16

Manteno, IL 60950. 6641 N 6000W Rd. Tel: 815-933-3011. Fax: 815-933-3028.
www.campshaw.org   E-mail: ewever@campshaw.org
Emily Wever, Dir.
Adm: FCFS. **Appl due:** Rolling. **Enr:** 140. **Enr cap:** 250. **Staff:** Admin 3. Couns 36. Res 7.
Features: Ecol Environ_Sci Geol Sci Crafts Creative_Writing Dance Fine_Arts Music Painting Theater Adventure_Travel Aquatics Archery Canoe Community_Serv Conservation Cooking Farm Hiking Outdoor_Ed Riding Ropes_Crse Scuba Survival_Trng Wilderness_Camp Wilderness_Canoe Yoga Baseball Basketball Football Lacrosse Soccer Softball Swim Ultimate_Frisbee Volleyball.
Fees 2011: Res $300-800, 1-1½ wks.
Housing: Cabins. Avg per room/unit: 10. **Swimming:** Pool Stream.
Est 1946. Nonprofit. **Spons:** Northern Illinois 4-H Camp Association. **Ses:** 7. **Wks/ses:** 1-1½. Operates June-July.

Boys and girls at Shaw-Waw-Nas-See engage in a range of land sports and watersports, artistic activities, games, nature pursuits and team-building exercises. Specialized options include Extreme Camp, which features canoe trips, horseback trail rides and rock climbing, and, for older campers (ages 14-16), Outdoor Teen Leadership Camp. The latter combines team challenges, first aid and CPR certification training, and a canoeing trip down the Kankakee and Wisconsin rivers.

WHITE PINES RANCH
Res — Coed Ages 8-15

Oregon, IL 61061. 3581 Pines Rd. Tel: 815-732-7923. Fax: 815-732-7924.
www.whitepinesranch.com   E-mail: info@whitepinesranch.com
Andrea Brehm, Dir.
Adm: FCFS. **Appl due:** May. **Enr:** 125. **Enr cap:** 125. **Staff:** Admin 3. Couns 25.
Features: Crafts Archery Farm Hiking Outdoor_Ed Ranch Riding Wilderness_Camp Equestrian Swim.
Fees 2011: Res $550 (+$20-25), 1 wk.
Housing: Dorms. **Swimming:** Pool.
Est 1958. Inc. **Ses:** 7. **Wks/ses:** 1. Operates July-Aug.

This working ranch has a particularly strong horseback riding component. Other summertime activities include swimming, hayrides, hiking, volleyball, country line dancing and crafts. Boys are girls may also help care for the animals.

CAMP TUCKABATCHEE
Res — Coed Ages 6-15; Day — Coed 5-10

Ottawa, IL 61350. 1973 N 35th Rd. Tel: 815-433-2984, 800-524-8825.
Fax: 815-433-3493.
www.camptuckabatchee.org   E-mail: tuckabatchee@ivnet.com
Kelly Bunnell, Exec Dir.
Adm: FCFS. **Appl due:** Rolling. **Enr:** 100. **Enr cap:** 100. **Staff:** Admin 5. Couns 28. Res 18.
Features: Crafts Aquatics Archery Bicycle_Tours Canoe Fishing Hiking Riding Scuba Woodcraft Equestrian Swim Volleyball.
Fees 2012: Res $415-455, 1 wk. Day $175, 1 wk.
Housing: Cabins Tents. Avg per room/unit: 8. **Swimming:** Pool Stream.
Est 1927. Nonprofit. **Ses:** 12. **Wks/ses:** 1. Operates June-July. ACA.

Each camper selects one of the following as his or her morning program for the entire session: water adventure; Native American handicrafts; horsemanship; outdoor adventure, which comprises archery, hiking, canoeing, outdoor cooking and trail riding; or backwoods biking. Boys and girls have a choice of traditional camp activities in the afternoon. Operated at a separate site, Teen Travel is a program for campers ages 13-15 that offers tenting, camp craft, swimming, canoeing, scuba diving and riding.

CAMP ONDESSONK
Res — Coed Ages 8-15

Ozark, IL 62972. 3760 Ondessonk Rd. Tel: 618-695-2489. Fax: 618-695-3593.
www.ondessonk.com   E-mail: camp@ondessonk.com
Dan King, Exec Dir.
Adm: FCFS. **Appl due:** Rolling. **Enr:** 250-350. **Enr cap:** 360. **Staff:** Admin 11. Couns 90.
Features: Crafts Aquatics Archery Canoe Climbing_Wall Conservation Exploration Fishing Hiking Kayak Pack_Train Riflery Rock_Climb Ropes_Crse Wilderness_Camp Wilderness_Canoe Equestrian Swim.
Fees 2010: Res $255-499, ½-1 wk. Aid avail.
Housing: Cabins Dorms Lodges Tents. **Swimming:** Lake Stream.
Est 1959. Nonprofit. Roman Catholic. **Ses:** 9. **Wks/ses:** ½-1. Operates June-Aug. ACA.

This recreational camp offers girls-only, boys-only or coeducational sessions. Four-day minicamps serve younger campers ages 8 and 9. Ondessonk also conducts specialty sessions relating to horseback riding, backpacking and adventure, as well as a family camp.

INDIANA

CULVER SUMMER SCHOOLS & CAMPS
Res — Coed Ages 7-17

Culver, IN 46511. 1300 Academy Rd, Box 138. Tel: 574-842-8300, 800-221-2020.
Fax: 574-842-8462.
www.culver.org/summer   E-mail: summer@culver.org
Anthony Mayfield, Dir.
Adm: FCFS. **Appl due:** Rolling. **Enr:** 1375. **Enr cap:** 1375. **Staff:** Admin 5. Couns 375.
Features: Astron Computers Ecol Environ_Sci ESL Lang Marine_Bio/Stud Relig_Stud Sci Speech Writing/Journ Crafts Creative_Writing Dance Fine_Arts Music Painting Photog Theater Aquatics Archery Aviation/Aero Canoe Chess Climbing_Wall Fishing Kayak Milit_Trng Riding Riflery Ropes_Crse Sail Scuba Seamanship Yoga Aerobics Badminton Baseball Basketball Cross-country Equestrian Fencing Football Golf Ice_Hockey

Lacrosse Martial_Arts Rugby Soccer Softball Swim Tennis Track Volleyball Water-skiing Watersports Weight_Trng Wrestling.
Fees 2011: Res $5100 (+$550-1300), 6 wks. Aid (Merit & Need).
Housing: Cabins Dorms. Avg per room/unit: 2-12. **Swimming:** Lake Pool.
Est 1902. Nonprofit. **Spons:** Culver Academies. **Ses:** 8. **Wks/ses:** 6. Operates June-Aug. ACA.

Located on a 1800-acre site on Lake Maxinkuckee, Culver combines traditional recreational camping experiences with various specialty programs. Campers have access to an equestrian center, sailboats and an aviation school, and Culver also offers an extensive Indian lore program. Family and friends may visit on weekends.

CAMP LAWRENCE
Res — Coed Ages 7-14

Valparaiso, IN.
Contact (Year-round): c/o Northwest Indiana CYO, 7725 Broadway, Ste C, Merrillville, IN 46410. Tel: 219-736-8931. Fax: 219-736-9457.
www.nwicyo.org   E-mail: nwicyo@comcast.net
Paul B. Wengel, Exec Dir.
Grades 2-8. Adm: FCFS. **Appl due:** Rolling. **Enr:** 100-150. **Enr cap:** 160. **Staff:** Admin 6. Couns 16.
Features: Ecol Crafts Exploration Hiking Basketball Football Soccer Softball Swim Volleyball Watersports.
Fees 2011: Res $225 (+$17), 1 wk. Aid 2011 (Need): $14,040.
Housing: Cabins. **Swimming:** Lake.
Est 1959. Nonprofit. **Spons:** Northwest Indiana CYO. Roman Catholic. **Ses:** 5. **Wks/ses:** 1. Operates June-Aug.

The camp offers most traditional camping activities, including swimming and water activities, nature hiking, campfires and stories of Indian lore, softball, soccer, volleyball, basketball, movies, crafts and a talent show. Each day begins with morning liturgy.

MAINE

PINE ISLAND CAMP
Res — Boys Ages 9-15

Belgrade Lakes, ME 04918. Tel: 207-465-3031.
Contact (Sept-June): PO Box 242, Brunswick, ME 04011. Tel: 207-729-7714.
www.pineisland.org   E-mail: benswan@pineisland.org
Benjamin Swan, Dir.
Adm: FCFS. **Appl due:** Rolling. **Enr:** 85. **Enr cap:** 85. **Staff:** Couns 25.
Features: Archery Boating Canoe Fishing Hiking Kayak Mountaineering Mtn_Trips Riflery Sail Wilderness_Camp Wilderness_Canoe Woodcraft Swim Tennis.
Fees 2012: Res $7300 (+$150), 6 wks.
Housing: Cabins Tents. **Swimming:** Lake Ocean.
Est 1902. Nonprofit. **Ses:** 1. **Wks/ses:** 6. Operates June-Aug.

All campers at Pine Island participate in the full six-week session, thus providing time for an array of traditional in-camp activities and out-of-camp canoeing, kayaking and hiking trips. The camp schedules easier trips early in the summer, with boys choosing their own excursions. Each boy spends time aboard a small craft during his session.

CAMP RUNOIA
Res — Girls Ages 8-15

Belgrade Lakes, ME 04918. PO Box 450. Tel: 207-495-2228. **Fax:** 207-495-2287.
www.runoia.com E-mail: info@runoia.com
Pamela Cobb Heuberger, Alex Jackson & Lani Toscano, Dirs.
Adm: FCFS. **Appl due:** Rolling. **Enr:** 100. **Staff:** Admin 4. Couns 35.
Features: Ecol Environ_Sci Writing/Journ Crafts Creative_Writing Drama Photog Aquatics Archery Boating Canoe Conservation Hiking Kayak Mtn_Trips Riding Riflery Ropes_ Crse Sail Survival_Trng Wilderness_Camp Wilderness_Canoe Cross-country Equestrian Golf Soccer Softball Swim Tennis Volleyball Watersports.
Fees 2012: Res $5100-7950 (+$800), 3-7 wks.
Housing: Cabins. Avg per room/unit: 10-14. **Swimming:** Lake.
Est 1907. Inc. **Ses:** 3. **Wks/ses:** 3-7. Operates June-Aug. ACA.

The camp offers extensive waterfront activities and sailing. Sports include tennis, golf and softball. Riflery, photography, arts and crafts, riding and a ropes course are other offerings. Runoia also schedules coeducational canoeing and wilderness trips that last for two to three weeks.

JCC MACCABI CAMP KINGSWOOD
Res — Coed Ages 8-16

Bridgton, ME 04009. 104 Wildwood Rd. Tel: 207-647-3969. **Fax:** 207-647-3828.
Contact (Sept-May): 333 Nahanton St, Newton, MA 02459. Tel: 617-558-6528.
Fax: 617-244-1289.
www.kingswood.org E-mail: info@kingswood.org
Stuart Silverman, Dir.
Grades 3-11. Adm: FCFS. Admitted: 100%. **Appl due:** Rolling. **Enr:** 200. **Enr cap:** 200.
Staff: Admin 10. Couns 50.
Travel: ME NH.
Features: Crafts Creative_Writing Dance Music Painting Photog Theater Aquatics Archery Boating Canoe Climbing_Wall Community_Serv Cooking Fishing Hiking Kayak Mountaineering Mtn_Biking Mtn_Trips Outdoor_Ed Rappelling Riding Rock_Climb Ropes_ Crse Sail Wilderness_Camp Wilderness_Canoe Yoga Aerobics Baseball Basketball Cross-country Football Gymnastics Lacrosse Roller_Hockey Rugby Soccer Softball Street_Hockey Swim Tennis Ultimate_Frisbee Volleyball Water-skiing Watersports.
Fees 2009: Res $1890-5945, 2-7 wks. Aid (Need).
Housing: Cabins. Avg per room/unit: 8. **Swimming:** Lake.
Est 1948. Nonprofit. **Spons:** Jewish Community Center of Greater Boston. Jewish. **Ses:** 6.
Wks/ses: 2-7. Operates July-Aug. ACA.

Known for three generations simply as Camp Kingswood, the camp offers a diverse selection of traditional recreational activities. Each week, campers choose three electives from a group that includes arts and crafts, photography, dance, radio, newspaper, theater, waterfront activities and athletics. Bar and Bat Mitzvah tutoring is a element of this Jewish camp's programming.

CAMP WILDWOOD
Res — Boys Ages 7-15

Bridgton, ME 04009. 318 Wildwood Rd. Tel: 207-647-8864. **Fax:** 207-647-5656.
www.campwildwood.com E-mail: campwildwood@campwildwood.com
Mark Meyer & Peter Meyer, Dirs.
Adm: FCFS. **Appl due:** Rolling.
Features: Computers Crafts Archery Canoe Climbing_Wall Fishing Ropes_Crse Sail Baseball Basketball Golf Lacrosse Roller_Hockey Soccer Street_Hockey Swim Tennis Track Volleyball Water-skiing Watersports Wrestling.

Housing: Cabins. Avg per room/unit: 6-7. **Swimming:** Pond.
Est 1953. Ses: 1. **Wks/ses:** 7. Operates June-Aug. ACA.

Wildwood offers boys a wide array of competitive and noncompetitive sports options, with instruction available in baseball, basketball, roller and street hockey, soccer, lacrosse and tennis. Other popular activities include waterfront pursuits, arts and crafts, and the camp newspaper.

WINONA CAMPS
Res — Boys Ages 7-16

Bridgton, ME 04009. 35 Winona Rd. Tel: 207-647-3721. Fax: 207-647-2750.
www.winonacamps.com E-mail: information@winonacamps.com
Alan B. Ordway & Michelle S. Ordway, Dirs.
Adm: FCFS. **Appl due:** Rolling. **Enr:** 250. **Enr cap:** 250. **Staff:** Admin 5. Couns 110.
Features: Crafts Aquatics Archery Canoe Climbing_Wall Fishing Hiking Kayak Mountaineering Mtn_Biking Mtn_Trips Riding Riflery Rock_Climb Sail Wilderness_Camp Wilderness_Canoe Woodcraft Baseball Basketball Equestrian Lacrosse Soccer Softball Swim Tennis Watersports.
Fees 2012: Res $5150-7850 (+$200), 3½-7 wks. Aid (Merit & Need).
Housing: Cabins Tents. Avg per room/unit: 5. **Swimming:** Lake Pond.
Est 1908. Inc. Ses: 3. **Wks/ses:** 3½-7. Operates June-Aug. ACA.

The diversified program places special emphasis on canoe and mountain tripping, the Junior Maine Guide Program, kayaking, riding, tennis and sailing. There are four units, each with separate facilities, programs and encampments. Winona maintains an affiliation with Wyonegonic Camps for girls.

CAMP ROBIN HOOD
Res — Coed Ages 7-17

Brooksville, ME 04617. Herrick Rd, PO Box 189. Tel: 207-359-8313.
Fax: 207-359-8538.
Contact (Sept-May): 13750 Center St, Carmel Valley, CA 93924. Tel: 831-659-9143.
Fax: 831-659-9148.
www.robinhoodcamp.com E-mail: robinhood@robinhoodcamp.com
Frederic S. Littlefield, Dir.
Adm: FCFS. **Appl due:** Apr. **Staff:** Admin 8. Couns 100.
Features: Astron Environ_Sci Marine_Bio/Stud Crafts Dance Music Photog Theater Aquatics Bicycle_Tours Canoe Conservation Cruises Exploration Hiking Mountaineering Mtn_Trips Pack_Train Riding Sail Scuba Sea_Cruises Seamanship Survival_Trng Wilderness_Camp Wilderness_Canoe Woodcraft Baseball Basketball Cross-country Equestrian Football Golf Gymnastics Swim Tennis Track Water-skiing.
Fees 2012: Res $4400-8500 (+$400), 3-7 wks.
Housing: Cabins. Avg per room/unit: 10. **Swimming:** Lake Ocean.
Est 1928. Ses: 7. **Wks/ses:** 3-7. Operates June-Aug.

Activities at Robin Hood include arts and crafts, waterfront pursuits, gymnastics, martial arts, fishing, white-water canoeing and yacht cruises. Also available are island excursions, horseback riding, mountain biking, scuba diving, nature and environmental study, and a tripping program.

CAMP ARCADIA
Res — Girls Ages 8-18

Casco, ME 04015. PO Box 158. Tel: 207-627-4605. Fax: 207-627-7162.
Contact (Sept-May): 42 Goodwives River Rd, Darien, CT 06820. Tel: 203-956-0939.

Fax: 203-655-2267.
www.camparcadia.com **E-mail:** louise.johnson@camparcadia.com
Louise Fritts Johnson, Dir.
Grades 2-11. **Adm:** FCFS. **Appl due:** Rolling. **Enr:** 175. **Enr cap:** 175. **Staff:** Admin 5.
Couns 75. Res 65.
Features: Astron Ecol Environ_Sci Crafts Creative_Writing Dance Fine_Arts Music Photog
Theater Aquatics Canoe Conservation Exploration Hiking Kayak Mountaineering Mtn_
Trips Riding Sail Survival_Trng Wilderness_Camp Wilderness_Canoe Equestrian Gymnastics Swim Tennis.
Fees 2012: Res $700-7000 (+$400), 1-7 wks. Aid (Need).
Housing: Cabins. Avg per room/unit: 6. **Swimming:** Lake.
Est 1916. Inc. **Ses:** 5. **Wks/ses:** 1-7. Operates June-Aug. ACA.

Each camper selects her own program from a wide variety of offerings that includes the arts, gymnastics, photography, tennis, swimming, sailing and seamanship. Horseback riding is optional. Experienced campers may go on overnight canoeing, camping and wilderness trips, as well as one- to five-day canoeing and hiking wilderness excursions.

CAMP CEDAR
Res — Boys Ages 8-15

Casco, ME 04015. 112 Camp Cedar Rd, PO Box 240. Tel: 207-627-4266.
Fax: 207-627-4152.
Contact (Sept-May): 1758 Beacon St, Brookline, MA 02445. Tel: 617-277-8080.
Fax: 617-277-1488.
www.campcedar.com **E-mail:** info@campcedar.com
Jeff Hacker & Sue Hacker-Wolf, Dirs.
Grades 3-9. **Adm:** FCFS. **Appl due:** Rolling. **Enr:** 300. **Staff:** Admin 25. Couns 100.
Features: Crafts Drama Photog Aquatics Archery Bicycle_Tours Boating Canoe Climbing_Wall Cooking Fishing Hiking Mountaineering Mtn_Biking Mtn_Trips Rappelling
Rock_Climb Ropes_Crse Sail Wilderness_Camp Baseball Basketball Football Golf
Lacrosse Roller_Hockey Soccer Softball Swim Tennis Volleyball Water-skiing Watersports Wrestling.
Fees 2012: Res $10,450, 7 wks.
Housing: Cabins. Avg per room/unit: 10-16. **Swimming:** Lake.
Est 1954. Inc. **Ses:** 1. **Wks/ses:** 7. Operates June-Aug. ACA.

Located in the Sebago Lake area, Cedar offers a wide selection of land sports, in addition to adventure and waterfront activities. Campers may embark upon one- to four-night canoeing and backpacking trips.

CAMP WALDEN
Res — Girls Ages 9-15

Denmark, ME 04022. 93 Walden Dr. Tel: 207-452-2901. Fax: 207-452-2902.
www.campwalden.com **E-mail:** walden@campwalden.com
Kathy Jonas, Dir.
Grades 2-10. **Adm:** FCFS. **Appl due:** Rolling. **Enr:** 150. **Enr cap:** 150. **Staff:** Admin 3.
Couns 60.
Features: Crafts Dance Drawing Fine_Arts Painting Studio_Art Theater Pottery Archery
Canoe Climbing_Wall Hiking Kayak Mountaineering Mtn_Trips Riding Ropes_Crse Sail
Wilderness_Camp Wilderness_Canoe Basketball Equestrian Gymnastics Lacrosse
Soccer Softball Swim Tennis Volleyball Water-skiing Watersports.
Fees 2012: Res $9500 (+$400), 7 wks.
Housing: Cabins. Avg per room/unit: 8. **Swimming:** Lake.
Est 1916. Inc. **Ses:** 1. **Wks/ses:** 7. Operates June-Aug. ACA.

Walden's individualized programming balances camper interests with the need for growth and challenge. Optional intensive programs serves girls wishing to specialize in tennis, riding and certain land sports. An extensive tripping program features mountain hiking and canoeing treks. Campers in all age groups learn to support one another through Walden's council system. A four-week option is open to first-time campers only.

WYONEGONIC CAMPS
Res — Girls Ages 8-18

Denmark, ME 04022. 215 Wyonegonic Rd. Tel: 207-452-2051. Fax: 207-452-2611.
www.wyonegonic.com   E-mail: info@wyonegonic.com
Carol S. Sudduth & Steve Sudduth, Dirs.
Adm: FCFS. **Appl due:** Rolling. **Enr:** 200. **Staff:** Admin 6. Couns 80.
Features: Ecol Crafts Dance Theater Aquatics Archery Canoe Hiking Mtn_Trips Riding Riflery Ropes_Crse Sail Wilderness_Camp Wilderness_Canoe Equestrian Swim Track Water-skiing.
Fees 2012: Res $5150-7850 (+$125), 3½-7 wks.
Housing: Cabins. Avg per room/unit: 3-6. **Swimming:** Lake.
Est 1902. Inc. Ses: 3. **Wks/ses:** 3½-7. Operates June-Aug. ACA.

Wyonegonic comprises three separate camps, each with its own staff, program and facilities. While structured, the noncompetitive program is diversified and flexible enough to meet the specific needs of campers. Activities include watersports, land sports, creative arts, and three- to five-day canoe and hiking trips. Teenagers coordinate some activities with the affiliated Camp Winona for boys.

FLYING MOOSE LODGE
Res — Boys Ages 10-16

East Orland, ME 04431. 157 Craig Pond Trail. Tel: 207-941-9202.
Contact (Sept-May): 15 Waldron Rd, Bar Harbor, ME 04609. Tel: 207-288-3088.
Year-round Toll-free: 877-766-0131, Fax: 207-288-0239.
www.flyingmooselodge.com   E-mail: prices@flyingmooselodge.com
Christopher Price & Shelly Price, Dirs.
Adm: FCFS. **Appl due:** Rolling. **Enr cap:** 50. **Staff:** Admin 6. Couns 14.
Features: Canoe Fishing Hiking Mountaineering Mtn_Trips Wilderness_Camp Wilderness_Canoe Swim.
Fees 2011: Res $3500-6700 (+$50-100), 2½-7 wks. Aid 2009 (Need): $14,000.
Housing: Tents. Avg per room/unit: 5-6. **Swimming:** Pond.
Est 1921. Inc. Ses: 7. **Wks/ses:** 2½-7. Operates June-Aug.

Flying Moose teaches camping skills by means of canoe, hiking and mountain climbing trips. Beginners go on easy climbs, while advanced climbers take extended backpacking trips along the Appalachian Trail and two-week wilderness trips down the Allagash, St. Croix or Moose rivers. Traditional land and water activities take place at base camp.

CAMP VEGA
Res — Girls Ages 7-15

Fayette, ME 04349. 317 Echo Lake Rd. Tel: 207-685-3707, 800-838-8342.
Fax: 207-685-5520.
www.campvega.com   E-mail: info@campvega.com
Linda Courtiss, Kyle Courtiss & Emily Courtiss, Dirs.
Grades 2-9. Adm: FCFS. **Appl due:** Apr. **Enr cap:** 300. **Staff:** Admin 12. Couns 162.
Features: Lang Writing/Journ Crafts Dance Drama Fine_Arts Music Painting Studio_Art Aquatics Archery Boating Canoe Climbing_Wall Community_Serv Conservation Fishing Hiking Kayak Mtn_Trips Outdoor_Ed Riding Rock_Climb Ropes_Crse Sail Social_Servs White-water_Raft Wilderness_Camp Aerobics Basketball Cross-country Equestrian

Field_Hockey Golf Gymnastics Lacrosse Soccer Softball Swim Tennis Track Volleyball Water-skiing Watersports Weight_Trng.
Fees 2012: Res $10,600 (+$575-775), 7 wks.
Housing: Cabins. Avg per room/unit: 10. **Swimming:** Lake.
Est 1936. Inc. Ses: 1. **Wks/ses:** 7. Operates June-Aug. ACA.

Vega offers an extensive waterfront program, riding, tennis, gymnastics, dance, crafts, team sports and drama. The pioneering program includes a ropes course, canoe trips, mountain climbing and camp craft instruction.

CAMP WINNEBAGO
Res — Boys Ages 8-15

Fayette, ME 04349. 19 Echo Lake Rd. Tel: 207-685-4918. Fax: 207-685-9190.
Contact (Sept-May): 131 Ocean St, South Portland, ME 04106. Tel: 207-767-1019.
   Fax: 207-767-1018.
Year-round Toll-free: 800-932-1646.
www.campwinnebago.com   E-mail: unkandycw@aol.com
Andy Lilienthal, Dir.
Adm: FCFS. **Appl due:** Rolling. **Enr:** 160. **Enr cap:** 160. **Staff:** Admin 8. Couns 60.
Features: Fine_Arts Photog Theater Aquatics Archery Canoe Community_Serv Conservation Cooking Hiking Kayak Mountaineering Mtn_Trips Outdoor_Ed Sail Seamanship Wilderness_Camp Wilderness_Canoe Woodcraft Baseball Basketball Football Lacrosse Soccer Softball Swim Team_Handball Tennis Ultimate_Frisbee Volleyball Water-skiing.
Fees 2012: Res $7050-11,150 (+$100), 3½-7½ wks.
Housing: Cabins. **Swimming:** Lake.
Est 1919. Inc. Ses: 3. **Wks/ses:** 3½-7½. Operates June-Aug. ACA.

Each camper at Winnebago participates daily in athletics, swimming and two instructional activities of his selection. The program also includes two- to nine-day mountain, lake and river trips, intercamp athletics and special activities.

HIDDEN VALLEY CAMP
Res — Coed Ages 8-14

Freedom, ME 04941. 161 Hidden Valley Rd. Tel: 207-342-5177, 800-922-6737.
   Fax: 207-342-5685.
www.hiddenvalleycamp.com   E-mail: summer@hiddenvalleycamp.com
Peter Kassen & Meg Kassen, Dirs.
Grades 3-9. Adm: FCFS. **Appl due:** Mar. **Enr:** 280. **Enr cap:** 280. **Staff:** Admin 7. Couns 100.
Features: ESL Crafts Creative_Writing Dance Music Photog Theater Adventure_Travel Aquatics Canoe Climbing_Wall Cooking Farm Hiking Mtn_Biking Riding Ropes_Crse Woodcraft Baseball Basketball Equestrian Gymnastics Soccer Swim Tennis.
Fees 2012: Res $3200-8700, 2-8 wks.
Housing: Cabins Tepees. **Swimming:** Lake Pool.
Est 1946. Inc. Ses: 5. **Wks/ses:** 2-8. Operates June-Aug. ACA.

This unregimented program features stained glass, ceramics, dance, theater, gymnastics and photography. Many land sports and watersports are included, as are llama and animal care, a ropes course, a Native American village for tepee living and a specialty riding group.

INDIAN ACRES CAMP FOR BOYS
FOREST ACRES CAMP FOR GIRLS
Res — Coord Ages 7-16, Girls 6

Fryeburg, ME 04037. 1712 Main St. Tel: 207-935-2300.

Contact (Sept-May): 1307 Forest Trails Dr, Castle Pines, CO 80108. **Tel:** 720-389-4912. **Year-round Fax:** 720-763-9518.
www.forestacres.com E-mail: geoff@indianacres.com
Lisa Newman & Geoff Newman, Dirs.
Adm: FCFS. **Appl due:** Rolling. **Enr:** 150. **Fac 10. Staff:** Admin 4. Couns 50.
Features: Writing/Journ Ceramics Crafts Dance Drama Drawing Music Painting Photog Sculpt Archery Canoe Cooking Fishing Kayak Mtn_Biking Sail Aerobics Baseball Basketball Field_Hockey Golf Gymnastics Lacrosse Softball Street_Hockey Swim Tennis Volleyball Water-skiing Watersports.
Fees 2012: Res $6500-10,700 (+$300), 4-7 wks.
Housing: Cabins. **Swimming:** Lake Pool River.
Est 1924. Inc. Ses: 2. **Wks/ses:** 4-7. Operates June-Aug. ACA.

Located two miles apart along the Saco River, these brother and sister camps feature traditional land sports and watersports, weekly mountain and canoe trips, horseback riding and arts offerings. Campers engage in such coeducational activities as dances and choral and musical productions. In addition, counselors arrange weekly visits between siblings at the two camps. Tutoring is available in mathematics, music, reading and English.

CAMP FERNWOOD COVE
Res — Girls Ages 8-15

Harrison, ME 04040. 350 Island Pond Rd. **Tel:** 207-583-2381. **Fax:** 207-583-6016.
www.fernwoodcove.com E-mail: cove@fernwoodcove.com
Jim M. Gill & Beigette Gill, Dirs.
Adm: FCFS. **Appl due:** Feb. **Enr:** 170. **Staff:** Admin 5. Couns 70.
Features: Crafts Creative_Writing Dance Drama Fine_Arts Music Photog Archery Bicycle_Tours Canoe Climbing_Wall Exploration Hiking Kayak Mountaineering Mtn_Biking Mtn_Trips Riding Riflery Rock_Climb Ropes_Crse Sail Wilderness_Camp Basketball Equestrian Field_Hockey Gymnastics Lacrosse Martial_Arts Soccer Softball Swim Tennis Volleyball Water-skiing.
Fees 2012: Res $6000 (+$100-125), 3½ wks.
Housing: Cabins. Avg per room/unit: 10. **Swimming:** Lake.
Est 1998. Inc. Ses: 2. **Wks/ses:** 3½. Operates June-Aug. ACA.

This traditional girls' camp offers many activities, among them water-skiing, kayaking and sailing on a private lake, in addition to horseback riding through 220 acres of nature trails. Campers select weekly focus activities for specialized instruction, and the Cove schedules daily periods for additional instruction or exploration of new pursuits. The program also includes weekly out-of-camp trips or overnights, as well as intercamp sporting events.

CAMP PINECLIFFE
Res — Girls Ages 7-15

Harrison, ME 04040. 64 Camp Pinecliffe Rd. **Tel:** 207-583-2201.
Contact (Sept-May): 277 S Cassingham Rd, Columbus, OH 43209. **Tel:** 614-236-5698. **Year-round Fax:** 614-235-2267.
www.pinecliffe.com E-mail: pinecliffe@msn.com
Susan R. Lifter & Patricia S. Lifter, Dirs.
Adm: FCFS. **Enr:** 215. **Staff:** Admin 5. Couns 85.
Features: Crafts Drama Fine_Arts Photog Aquatics Archery Canoe Conservation Hiking Mountaineering Mtn_Trips Riding Ropes_Crse Sail Wilderness_Camp Field_Hockey Golf Gymnastics Lacrosse Martial_Arts Soccer Softball Swim Tennis Water-skiing.
Housing: Cabins. Avg per room/unit: 8. **Swimming:** Lake.
Est 1917. Inc. Ses: 1. **Wks/ses:** 7. Operates June-Aug. ACA.

Ecology, riding, overnight mountain and canoe trips, sailing and other aquatics, individual sports, tennis, music and crafts are major focuses of Pinecliffe's program. Younger campers gain exposure to all major activities at the camp, while older girls take more responsibility for formulating their schedules.

CAMP WEKEELA
Res — Coed Ages 6-16

Hartford, ME 04220. 1750 Bear Pond Rd. Tel: 207-224-7878. Fax: 207-224-7999.
Contact (Sept-May): 979 Allison Ct, Ridgewood, NJ 07450. Tel: 201-612-5125.
   Fax: 201-612-9927.
www.campwekeela.com   E-mail: ephram@campwekeela.com
Ephram A. Caflun & Lori Caflun, Dirs.
Grades 1-10. Adm: FCFS. **Appl due:** Rolling. **Enr:** 290. **Enr cap:** 290. **Staff:** Admin 15.
   Couns 85. Res 100.
Travel: NH Canada.
Features: Astron Crafts Creative_Writing Dance Drama Fine_Arts Media Music Painting Photog Studio_Art Aquatics Archery Aviation/Aero Bicycle_Tours Boating Canoe Climbing_Wall Community_Serv Cooking Exploration Fishing Hiking Kayak Mountaineering Mtn_Biking Mtn_Trips Outdoor_Ed Rappelling Riding Rock_Climb Ropes_Crse Sail Scuba White-water_Raft Wilderness_Camp Wilderness_Canoe Woodcraft Aerobics Baseball Basketball Cross-country Equestrian Field_Hockey Football Golf Gymnastics Lacrosse Skateboarding Soccer Softball Street_Hockey Swim Tennis Track Ultimate_Frisbee Volleyball Water-skiing Watersports Weight_Trng.
Fees 2012: Res $3700-9100 (+$200-450), 2-7 wks.
Housing: Cabins. **Swimming:** Lake.
Est 1922. Inc. Ses: 5. **Wks/ses:** 2-7. Operates June-Aug. ACA.

Wekeela offers more than 70 activities, including Red Cross swimming, sailing, windsurfing, scuba, water-skiing, canoeing, wilderness camping, a radio station, creative and performing arts, culinary arts, sports and a ropes course. National sports figures participate in visiting coach programs. Trips take campers to Maine's rivers and coastline, New Hampshire and Montreal, Canada.

ALFORD LAKE CAMP
Res — Boys Ages 14-16, Girls 8-16

Hope, ME 04847. 258 Alford Lake Rd. Tel: 207-785-2400. Fax: 207-785-5290.
Contact (Winter): 5 Salt Marsh Way, Cape Elizabeth, ME 04107. Tel: 207-799-3005.
   Fax: 207-799-5044.
www.alfordlakecamp.com   E-mail: explore@alfordlakecamp.com
Sue McMullan, Dir.
Grades 3-11. Adm: FCFS. **Appl due:** Rolling. **Enr:** 175. **Fac 60. Staff:** Admin 15.
Travel: Canada Europe.
Features: Dance Drama Canoe Hiking Riding Sail Wilderness_Camp Field_Hockey Gymnastics Lacrosse Swim Tennis.
Fees 2012: Res $5300-8900, 3½-7 wks.
Housing: Tents. **Swimming:** Lake Ocean.
Est 1907. Inc. Ses: 7. **Wks/ses:** 3½-7. Operates June-Aug. ACA.

Activities at Alford Lake include swimming, sailing, riding, tennis, canoeing, gymnastics, archery, a challenge course, creative arts, dramatics and outdoor living skills. Also offered are a coed hiking trip on the Appalachian Trail; a tour of several sites in Great Britain; and wilderness excursions to Nova Scotia and through the Alps.

CAMP NEOFA
Res and Day — Coed Ages 8-14

Liberty, ME 04949. PO Box 101. Tel: 207-589-4133.

Contact (Sept-June): 35 Hillside Ave, Keene, NH 03431. Tel: 603-352-0061.
www.campneofa.org   E-mail: cmesser@ne.rr.com
Carla Messer, Dir.
Grades 3-8. Adm: FCFS. Appl due: Rolling. Enr: 94. Enr cap: 94. Staff: Admin 2. Couns 25.
Features: Environ_Sci Crafts Dance Drama Aquatics Archery Boating Canoe Conservation Fishing Hiking Kayak Baseball Basketball Soccer Softball Swim Tennis Volleyball.
Fees 2012: Res $285 (+$10), 1 wk. Day $135 (+$10), 1 wk.
Housing: Cabins. Avg per room/unit: 8. Swimming: Lake.
Est 1957. Nonprofit. Spons: Northeast Odd Fellows Association. Ses: 4. Wks/ses: 1. Operates July-Aug. ACA.

This traditional camping program is sponsored by the Odd Fellows and Rebekahs of the Northeast Odd Fellows Association. Among NEOFA's activities are organized swimming instruction, crafts, forestry and nature study, and various sports.

CAMP COBBOSSEE
Res — Boys Ages 6-16

Monmouth, ME 04259. PO Box 299. Tel: 207-933-4503, 800-473-6104.
Fax: 207-933-4560.
www.campcobbossee.com   E-mail: directors@campcobbossee.com
Josh Cohen & Jill Cohen, Dirs.
Adm: FCFS. Enr: 150. Enr cap: 150.
Features: Crafts Photog Woodworking Archery Canoe Climbing_Wall Fishing Hiking Kayak Mtn_Biking Ropes_Crse Sail Baseball Basketball Cross-country Golf Lacrosse Roller_Hockey Soccer Street_Hockey Swim Team_Handball Tennis Watersports.
Fees 2011: Res $5900, 4 wks.
Housing: Cabins. Avg per room/unit: 8-12. Swimming: Lake.
Est 1902. Ses: 2. Wks/ses: 4. Operates June-Aug. ACA.

Cobbossee's program includes various team sports, canoe tripping, tennis, sailing, waterfront activities, and arts and crafts.

CAMP KIPPEWA
Res — Girls Ages 6½-15

Monmouth, ME 04259. 1 Kippewa Dr.
Contact (Sept-May): 15 Myrtle Ave, Westford, MA 01886.
Year-round Tel: 207-933-2993, 800-547-7392. Fax: 207-933-2996.
www.kippewa.com   E-mail: info@kippewa.com
Ginger Clare & Stephen Clare, Dirs.
Grades 2-10. Adm: FCFS. Appl due: Rolling. Enr: 140. Staff: Admin 3. Couns 50. Res 1.
Features: Crafts Creative_Writing Dance Fine_Arts Painting Photog Theater Aquatics Archery Boating Canoe Climbing_Wall Fishing Hiking Kayak Mtn_Trips Riding Ropes_Crse Sail Sea_Cruises White-water_Raft Wilderness_Camp Wilderness_Canoe Woodcraft Aerobics Baseball Basketball Equestrian Gymnastics Soccer Softball Swim Tennis Volleyball Water-skiing Watersports.
Fees 2012: Res $6050, 4 wks. Aid 2009 (Need): $100,000.
Housing: Cabins. Avg per room/unit: 6. Swimming: Lake.
Est 1957. Inc. Ses: 2. Wks/ses: 4. Operates June-Aug. ACA.

Kippewa's wide-ranging program includes arts and crafts, dance, drama, theater, canoeing, sailing, water-skiing, hiking and most traditional sports. The camp offers an equestrian program for an additional fee.

CAMP MATAPONI
Res — Girls Ages 7-15

Naples, ME 04055. 838 Sebago Rd. Tel: 207-787-3221. Fax: 207-787-3222.
Contact (Sept-May): PO Box 1882, Jupiter, FL 33468. Tel: 561-748-3684.
Fax: 561-748-5125.
www.campmataponi.com   E-mail: info@campmataponi.com
Dan Isdaner & Marcy Isdaner, Dirs.
Adm: FCFS. **Appl due:** Apr. **Enr:** 320.
Features: Ceramics Crafts Dance Drama Canoe Kayak Outdoor_Ed Ropes_Crse Sail Basketball Cross-country Field_Hockey Gymnastics Lacrosse Soccer Softball Tennis Volleyball Water-skiing.
Fees 2012: Res $10,450, 7 wks.
Housing: Cabins.
Est 1910. Ses: 1. **Wks/ses:** 7. Operates June-Aug. ACA.

Mataponi's full range of programs seeks to develop basic skills. The schedule includes water-skiing, boating, swimming, riding, tennis, team sports, sailing and gymnastics. Campers also participate in dance, drama and crafts.

CAMP TAKAJO
Res — Boys Ages 7-15

Naples, ME. Tel: 207-693-6675. Fax: 207-693-6654.
Contact (Sept-May): 34 Maple Ave, Armonk, NY 10504. Tel: 914-273-5020.
Fax: 914-273-5352.
www.takajo.com
Jeffrey A. Konigsberg, Dir.
Grades 2-10. Adm: FCFS. **Appl due:** Rolling. **Enr:** 390.
Features: Ceramics Crafts Drama Drawing Music Painting Photog Archery Canoe Hiking Mountaineering Rock_Climb Ropes_Crse Sail Baseball Basketball Lacrosse Soccer Street_Hockey Swim Tennis Water-skiing Weight_Trng.
Housing: Cabins. **Swimming:** Lake.
Est 1947. Ses: 1. **Wks/ses:** 7. Operates June-Aug. ACA.

The program includes all waterfront and small-craft activities; team and individual sports; extensive backpacking, canoe tripping and rock climbing; and nature study, music, drama, art and science.

KIEVE CAMP FOR BOYS
WAVUS CAMP FOR GIRLS
Res — Coord Ages 8-16

Nobleboro, ME 04555. 42 Kieve Rd, PO Box 169. Tel: 207-563-5172.
Fax: 207-563-5215.
www.kieve.org   E-mail: boyscamp@kieve.org; wavus@kieve.org
Henry R. Kennedy, Exec Dir.
Adm: FCFS. **Appl due:** Rolling. **Enr:** 150-225. **Staff:** Admin 12. Couns 60-80.
Features: Crafts Music Photog Theater Adventure_Travel Aquatics Archery Boating Canoe Climbing_Wall Community_Serv Conservation Cooking Exploration Fishing Hiking Kayak Mountaineering Mtn_Trips Outdoor_Ed Rappelling Riflery Rock_Climb Ropes_ Crse Sail Sea_Cruises White-water_Raft Wilderness_Camp Wilderness_Canoe Woodcraft Baseball Basketball Football Lacrosse Soccer Swim Tennis Ultimate_Frisbee Volleyball Watersports.
Fees 2012: Res $2550-5300, 1½-3½ wks. Aid 2011 (Need): $230,000.
Housing: Cabins. Avg per room/unit: 13. **Swimming:** Lake Ocean.
Est 1926. Nonprofit. Ses: 2. **Wks/ses:** 1½-3½. Operates June-Aug. ACA.

Located 60 miles northeast of Portland on a peninsula in Damariscotta Lake, these traditional brother and sister camps offer noncompetitive sports, waterfront activities, arts and crafts, nature activities and a ropes course. In addition, all boys and girls take part in wilderness trips around New England that range from two days to three weeks. A separate program, Kieve West, is a 23-day coeducational wilderness trek in Colorado for older campers ages 16-18.

CAMP MANITOU
Res — Boys Ages 7-16

Oakland, ME 04963. 47 Camp Manitou Cove. Fax: 207-465-9877.
Contact (Sept-May): PO Box 5099, Westport, CT 06881. Fax: 203-286-2555.
Year-round Tel: 207-465-2271, 800-326-1916.
www.campmanitou.com   E-mail: mailbox@campmanitou.com
Jon Deren & Sarah Deren, Dirs.
Grades 2-10. Adm: FCFS. **Enr:** 300. **Staff:** Admin 25. Couns 100.
Features: Astron Writing/Journ Crafts Drama Media Photog Pottery Aquatics Archery Boating Canoe Climbing_Wall Cooking Fishing Hiking Kayak Mtn_Biking Mtn_Trips Riflery Rock_Climb Ropes_Crse Sail Scuba White-water_Raft Wilderness_Camp Woodcraft Baseball Basketball Football Golf Ice_Hockey Lacrosse Martial_Arts Roller_Hockey Soccer Softball Street_Hockey Swim Team_Handball Tennis Track Volleyball Waterskiing Watersports Wrestling.
Fees 2012: Res $6550-10,650 (+$150), 3½-7 wks.
Housing: Cabins. Avg per room/unit: 10. **Swimming:** Lake.
Est 1947. Inc. Ses: 3. **Wks/ses:** 3½-7. Operates June-Aug. ACA.

Manitou offers instruction in land, water and creative activities. Pursuits include waterskiing, crafts, computer, scuba, photography, drama, land sports and a tripping program.

KAMP KOHUT
Res — Coed Ages 7-16

Oxford, ME 04270. 151 Kohut Rd. Tel: 207-539-0966. Fax: 207-539-4701.
Contact (Sept-May): 2 Tall Pine Rd, Cape Elizabeth, ME 04107. Tel: 207-767-2406.
    Fax: 207-767-0604.
Year-round Toll-free: 888-465-6488.
www.kampkohut.com   E-mail: info@kampkohut.com
Lisa M. Tripler & Daniel Rapaport, Dirs.
Grades 3-10. Adm: FCFS. **Appl due:** Rolling. **Enr:** 200. **Enr cap:** 200. **Staff:** Admin 4. Couns 85. Res 31.
Features: Computers ESL Writing/Journ Crafts Creative_Writing Dance Drama Fine_Arts Media Music Painting Photog Studio_Art Aquatics Archery Bicycle_Tours Boating Canoe Caving Climbing_Wall Community_Serv Conservation Exploration Fishing Hiking Kayak Mountaineering Mtn_Biking Outdoor_Ed Rappelling Riding Rock_Climb Ropes_Crse Rowing/Sculling Sail Survival_Trng Wilderness_Camp Wilderness_Canoe Woodcraft Yoga Aerobics Baseball Basketball Cricket Cross-country Equestrian Fencing Field_Hockey Football Golf Gymnastics Lacrosse Roller_Hockey Rugby Soccer Softball Street_Hockey Swim Tennis Track Ultimate_Frisbee Volleyball Water-skiing Watersports.
Fees 2012: Res $3300-5800 (+$100), 2-4 wks.
Housing: Cabins. Avg per room/unit: 10. **Swimming:** Lake.
Est 1907. Inc. Ses: 4. **Wks/ses:** 2-4. Operates June-Aug. ACA.

Emphasizing camaraderie and the acquisition of new skills, Kohut's program comprises land sports, waterfront activities, and arts, media and adventure offerings. Each day consists of eight elective activity periods, including one that allows campers to further explore an area of particular interest. Weekly events include campfires, theatrical performances, and nature-oriented day and overnight trips. Two-week sessions are open to rising third and fourth graders only.

CAMP FERNWOOD
Res — Girls Ages 8-15

Poland, ME 04274. 48 Camp Fernwood Ln. Tel: 207-998-4346. Fax: 207-998-4852.
Contact (Sept-May): 6035 Goshen Rd, Newtown Square, PA 19073. Tel: 610-356-7602.
  Fax: 484-441-1306.
www.campfernwood.com   E-mail: fernwood@campfernwood.com
Fritz Seving & Christine Seving, Dirs.
Grades 4-10. Adm: FCFS. **Enr:** 210. **Enr cap:** 210. **Staff:** Admin 3. Couns 120.
Features: Crafts Dance Fine_Arts Music Photog Theater Aquatics Archery Canoe Climb-
  ing_Wall Fishing Hiking Kayak Mountaineering Mtn_Biking Mtn_Trips Rappelling Riding
  Riflery Rock_Climb Ropes_Crse Sail Wilderness_Canoe Woodcraft Basketball Eques-
  trian Field_Hockey Gymnastics Lacrosse Soccer Softball Swim Tennis Volleyball Water-
  skiing Watersports.
Fees 2011: Res $9900 (+$150-700), 7 wks. Aid 2009 (Need): $50,000.
Housing: Cabins. Avg per room/unit: 10. **Swimming:** Lake.
Est 1921. Inc. Ses: 1. Wks/ses: 7. Operates June-Aug. ACA.

Located on Lake Thompson, Fernwood conducts a structured program that allows girls
to select their own program of activities with the guidance of camp staff. Various outdoor
pursuits are available, and girls may also engage in many different arts activities. The tripping
program includes both day excursions and extended treks that involve white-water canoeing
and kayaking, biking, hiking and rock climbing.

TRIPP LAKE CAMP
Res — Girls Ages 8-16

Poland, ME 04274. PO Box 99. Tel: 207-998-4347. Fax: 207-998-2073.
Contact (Winter): 34 Maple Ave, Armonk, NY 10504. Tel: 914-273-4065.
  Fax: 914-273-5963.
www.tripplakecamp.com   E-mail: leslie@tripplakecamp.com
Leslie Konigsberg Levy, Dir.
Grades 3-11. Adm: FCFS. **Appl due:** Rolling. **Enr:** 350. **Staff:** Admin 7. Couns 160.
Features: Crafts Dance Fine_Arts Photog Theater Aquatics Archery Bicycle_Tours Boat-
  ing Canoe Climbing_Wall Hiking Kayak Mountaineering Mtn_Trips Rappelling Riding
  Rock_Climb Ropes_Crse Sail White-water_Raft Wilderness_Camp Wilderness_Canoe
  Basketball Field_Hockey Golf Gymnastics Lacrosse Soccer Softball Swim Tennis Vol-
  leyball Water-skiing.
Housing: Cabins. **Swimming:** Lake.
Est 1911. Inc. Ses: 1. Wks/ses: 7. Operates June-Aug. ACA.

Situated on a 260-acre tract, the camp is structured yet affords flexibility and room for self-
expression. Tripp Lake divides girls into seven groups based upon age and school grade, with
activities scheduled by age group. Campers take part in particularly strong waterfront, riding,
tennis, team sports, and performing and visual arts programs. Weekly day trips and three-day
excursions enable girls to explore the region and develop their hiking, canoeing, sailing, biking
or photography skills.

CAMP NORTH STAR
Res — Coed Ages 7-16

Poland Spring, ME 04274. 200 Verrill Rd. Tel: 207-998-4777. Fax: 207-998-4722.
www.campnorthstarmaine.com   E-mail: office@campnorthstarmaine.com
Susan Goldberg & Jason Goldberg, Dirs.
Grades 2-11. Adm: FCFS. **Appl due:** Rolling. **Enr cap:** 225. **Staff:** Admin 6. Couns 65.
Features: Computers Ecol Environ_Sci ESL Writing/Journ Crafts Creative_Writing Dance
  Filmmaking Fine_Arts Media Music Painting Photog Theater Aquatics Archery Avia-
  tion/Aero Canoe Climbing_Wall Community_Serv Cooking Cruises Farm Fishing Hiking

Kayak Mountaineering Mtn_Biking Mtn_Trips Rappelling Riding Rock_Climb Ropes_ Crse Sail White-water_Raft Wilderness_Camp Wilderness_Canoe Woodcraft Baseball Basketball Cricket Cross-country Equestrian Field_Hockey Golf Gymnastics Lacrosse Martial_Arts Rugby Soccer Softball Street_Hockey Swim Tennis Ultimate_Frisbee Volleyball Water-skiing Watersports.
Fees 2010: Res $3200-9000 (+$100), 2-8 wks.
Housing: Cabins Lodges Tepees. Avg per room/unit: 11. **Swimming:** Lake.
Est 1989. Inc. **Ses:** 10. **Wks/ses:** 2-8. Operates June-Aug.

North Star combines the arts, music and theater with outdoor adventure trips, waterfront activities and sports. Among the arts offerings are stained glass, pottery, photography, video, computer graphics, drama, music and dance. Weekly backpacking and canoeing trips, horseback riding instruction and rock climbing are other noteworthy aspects of the program. Campers choose their own activities on a weekly basis.

MAINE TEEN CAMP
Res — Coed Ages 13-17

Porter, ME 04068. 481 Brownfield Rd.
Contact (Sept-May): 170 W Valentine St, Westbrook, ME 04092.
Year-round Tel: 207-625-8581, 800-752-2267. Fax: 207-625-8738.
www.teencamp.com   E-mail: mtc@teencamp.com
Monique Pines & Matthew Pines, Dirs.
Adm: FCFS. **Appl due:** Rolling. **Enr:** 225. **Staff:** Admin 30. Couns 70.
Features: ESL Lang Creative_Writing Dance Filmmaking Music Painting Photog Theater Adventure_Travel Aquatics Bicycle_Tours Canoe Climbing_Wall Community_Serv Cooking Fishing Hiking Kayak Mtn_Biking Ropes_Crse Sail White-water_Raft Yoga Aerobics Basketball Football Golf Soccer Softball Swim Tennis Ultimate_Frisbee Volleyball Water-skiing Watersports Weight_Trng.
Fees 2012: Res $3000-7200, 2-8 wks. Aid 2011 (Need): $75,000.
Housing: Cabins. Avg per room/unit: 15. **Swimming:** Lake.
Est 1984. Inc. **Ses:** 6. **Wks/ses:** 2-8. Operates June-Aug. ACA.

Located on a 55-acre site on Stanley Lake, MTC conducts a varied program that features professional tennis instruction, a rock music program and wakeboarding. Other popular activities are land sports, watersports, creative and performing arts pursuits, community service opportunities and off-site trips. An array of evening activities completes the program.

CAMP AGAWAM
Res — Boys Ages 8-15

Raymond, ME 04071. 54 Agawam Rd. Tel: 207-627-4780. Fax: 207-627-8003.
Contact (Oct-May): Tel: 207-892-1200, Fax: 207-892-1220.
www.campagawam.org   E-mail: chiefc@campagawam.org
Erik Calhoun, Dir.
Adm: FCFS. **Appl due:** Rolling. **Enr:** 134. **Enr cap:** 134. **Staff:** Admin 4. Couns 45.
Features: Astron Environ_Sci Crafts Drama Music Photog Aquatics Archery Boating Canoe Fishing Hiking Mountaineering Mtn_Trips Riflery Ropes_Crse Sail Wilderness_Camp Wilderness_Canoe Woodcraft Baseball Basketball Cross-country Lacrosse Soccer Swim Tennis Track.
Fees 2012: Res $8600 (+$300), 7 wks. Aid 2007: $108,000.
Housing: Cabins Tents. Avg per room/unit: 4-8. **Swimming:** Lake.
Est 1919. Nonprofit. **Ses:** 1. **Wks/ses:** 7. Operates June-Aug. ACA.

Agawam combines waterfront activities, land sports, creative arts opportunities, and an outdoor living skills program that includes one- to five-day backpacking and canoeing trips. Boys receive guidance in selecting their activities, and an award system tracks progress and serves as a source of motivation. Tennis and sailing are particularly strong elements of the program. Although Agawam is essentially a seven-week camp, a very limited three-and-a-half-week session is open to certain new campers.

KINGSLEY PINES CAMP
Res — Coed Ages 8-15

Raymond, ME 04071. 51 Coughlan Cove Rd. Tel: 207-655-7181, 800-480-1533.
Fax: 207-655-4121.
www.kingsleypines.com   E-mail: info@kingsleypines.com
Alan Kissack, Dir.
Grades 3-10. Adm: FCFS. **Appl due:** Rolling. **Enr:** 200. **Staff:** Admin 10. Couns 70.
Features: Crafts Fine_Arts Music Theater Aquatics Archery Canoe Hiking Mtn_Biking Rock_Climb Sail Wilderness_Camp Woodcraft Baseball Basketball Golf Soccer Swim Tennis Water-skiing.
Fees 2012: Res $1845-6995, 2-6 wks.
Housing: Cabins. **Swimming:** Lake.
Est 1983. Inc. **Ses:** 7. **Wks/ses:** 2-6. Operates June-Aug. ACA.

Kingsley Pines offers a full waterfront program that includes swimming, sailing, canoeing and water-skiing. Tennis, arts and crafts, ecology, dance, music, drama, computers and archery are additional activities.

CAMP NASHOBA NORTH
Res — Coed Ages 7-15

Raymond, ME 04071. 198 Raymond Hill Rd. Tel: 207-655-7170. Fax: 207-655-4063.
Contact (Sept-May): 140 Nashoba Rd, Littleton, MA 01460. Tel: 978-486-8236.
Fax: 978-952-2442.
www.campnashoba.com   E-mail: info@campnashoba.com
Sarah Seaward & Janet Seaward, Dirs.
Grades 2-10. Adm: FCFS. **Appl due:** Rolling. **Enr:** 190. **Enr cap:** 190. **Staff:** Admin 4. Couns 80.
Travel: NH.
Features: Crafts Dance Fine_Arts Music Painting Photog Theater Aquatics Archery Canoe Climbing_Wall Community_Serv Cooking Farm Fishing Hiking Kayak Mountaineering Mtn_Trips Riding Rock_Climb Sail Seamanship White-water_Raft Wilderness_Camp Wilderness_Canoe Woodcraft Badminton Baseball Basketball Cricket Cross-country Equestrian Field_Hockey Golf Lacrosse Rugby Soccer Softball Swim Tennis Ultimate_ Frisbee Volleyball Water-skiing Watersports.
Fees 2012: Res $3300-8800 (+$600), 2-8 wks.
Housing: Cabins. Avg per room/unit: 9. **Swimming:** Lake.
Est 1928. Inc. **Ses:** 6. **Wks/ses:** 2-8. Operates June-Aug. ACA.

An elective program at Nashoba North offers land and waterfront activities, with specialties in hunt-seat equitation, horsemanship, theater arts, tennis, field sports and watersports. Some boys and girls embark on trips lasting up to three days and two nights in Maine and New Hampshire. The camp conducts a pair of 15-day sessions for young first-time campers; all others attend for at least four weeks.

CAMP PINEHURST
Res — Coed Ages 6-14

Raymond, ME 04071. 23 Curtis Rd. Tel: 207-627-4670. Fax: 207-627-4793.
Contact (Sept-May): 12 Cider Ln, Nashua, NH 03063. Tel: 603-880-6287.
Fax: 603-880-6287.
www.camppinehurst.com   E-mail: director@camppinehurst.com
John Curtis, Jean Curtis, Jack Curtis & Elizabeth Curtis, Dirs.

Grades 1-8. Adm: FCFS. **Appl due:** Rolling. **Enr:** 50. **Enr cap:** 80. **Staff:** Admin 4. Couns 25. Res 25.
Features: Dance Aquatics Archery Boating Canoe Climbing_Wall Fishing Hiking Kayak Mtn_Biking Mtn_Trips Riflery Sail White-water_Raft Wilderness_Camp Yoga Baseball Basketball Soccer Softball Swim Tennis Ultimate_Frisbee Water-skiing Watersports.
Fees 2012: Res $2250-5475, 2-6 wks.
Housing: Cabins. Avg per room/unit: 8. **Swimming:** Lake.
Est 1946. **Inc. Ses:** 6. **Wks/ses:** 2-6. Operates July-Aug.

This traditional camp features an individualized daily schedule and skill instruction at all ability levels. The wide-ranging program includes swimming, sailing, team and individual sports, riflery, nature, archery, and canoeing and hiking trips.

CAMP TIMANOUS
Res — Boys Ages 7-15

Raymond, ME 04071. 85 Plains Rd. Tel: 207-655-4569.
Contact (Sept-May): c/o St Mark's School, 25 Marlborough Rd, Southborough, MA 01772. Tel: 508-485-8020.
Year-round Fax: 508-449-3989.
www.campt.com   E-mail: info@campt.com
David Suitor & Linda Suitor, Dirs.
Adm: FCFS. **Appl due:** Rolling. **Enr:** 125. **Enr cap:** 125. **Staff:** Admin 3. Couns 45.
Features: Crafts Drama Aquatics Archery Bicycle_Tours Boating Canoe Climbing_Wall Fishing Hiking Kayak Mountaineering Mtn_Trips Riflery Sail Wilderness_Camp Woodcraft Baseball Basketball Soccer Softball Swim Tennis Volleyball Water-skiing Watersports.
Fees 2012: Res $5350-8500 (+$120), 3½-7 wks. Aid (Need).
Housing: Cabins. Avg per room/unit: 11. **Swimming:** Lake.
Est 1917. **Inc. Ses:** 3. **Wks/ses:** 3½-7. Operates June-Aug. ACA.

Timanous' program is largely elective and is broad enough to include dramatics, camp craft, tennis, sailing and competitive athletics. The camp's flexible schedule incorporates daily periods of free time. Timanous draws campers from a wide geographical area that encompasses many states and more than a half-dozen foreign countries.

CAMP WAWENOCK
Res — Girls Ages 8-17

Raymond, ME 04071. 33 Wawenock Rd. Tel: 207-655-4657. Fax: 207-655-4662.
www.campwawenock.com   E-mail: wawenock@campwawenock.com
June W. Gray, Patricia A. Smith, Andy Sangster & Catriona Logan Sangster, Directors.
Adm: FCFS. **Appl due:** Rolling. **Enr:** 110. **Enr cap:** 110. **Staff:** Admin 4. Couns 50.
Features: Crafts Dance Drama Fine_Arts Music Painting Aquatics Archery Boating Canoe Community_Serv Leadership Outdoor_Ed Riding Riflery Sail Woodcraft Equestrian Swim Tennis.
Fees 2012: Res $7500 (+$150), 7 wks.
Housing: Cabins. Avg per room/unit: 6. **Swimming:** Lake.
Est 1910. **Inc. Ses:** 1. **Wks/ses:** 7. Operates June-Aug. ACA.

Wawenock enables each girl to select her own program of activities for the season. Campers make their selections from an array of traditional camp activities. All girls engage in camp service projects, and leadership opportunities available to campers increase with age.

CAMP WOHELO
Res — Girls Ages 6-16

Raymond, ME 04071. 25 Gulick Rd. Tel: 207-655-4739. Fax: 207-655-2292.
www.wohelo.com   E-mail: wohelo@wohelo.com
Quincy Van Winkle, Heidi Gorton & Mark Van Winkle, Dirs.
Grades 1-9. Adm: FCFS. **Appl due:** Rolling. **Enr:** 200. **Enr cap:** 200. **Staff:** Admin 4.
Couns 75.
Features: Ecol Crafts Dance Drama Fine_Arts Music Painting Pottery Weaving Aquatics
Archery Boating Canoe Conservation Hiking Kayak Mtn_Trips Outdoor_Ed Sail Swim
Tennis Water-skiing Watersports.
Fees 2012: Res $1600-8400 (+$300), 1-7 wks.
Housing: Cabins. Avg per room/unit: 6. **Swimming:** Lake.
Est 1907. Inc. Ses: 4. **Wks/ses:** 1-7. Operates June-Aug. ACA.

Little Wohelo, the camp for younger girls (ages 6-12), and Sebago Wohelo, for older girls,
are separate camps situated half a mile apart. Little Wohelo girls attend activities on a regularly
scheduled basis, with frequent chances for choosing their own activities, while the program at
Sebago Wohelo is entirely elective. A weeklong session enrolls girls ages 6-8 only.

CAMP LAUREL
Res — Coed Ages 7-15

Readfield, ME 04355. PO Box 327. Tel: 207-685-4945. Fax: 207-685-9812.
Contact (Sept-May): PO Box 508, Westport, CT 06881. Tel: 203-227-8866.
Fax: 203-227-8864.
Year-round Toll-free: 800-327-3509.
www.camplaurel.com   E-mail: summer@camplaurel.com
Keith Klein, Debbie Sollinger & Jeremy Sollinger, Dirs.
Grades 2-10. Adm: FCFS. **Appl due:** Rolling. **Enr:** 480. **Enr cap:** 480.
Features: Crafts Dance Theater Riding Sail Baseball Basketball Football Gymnastics Ice_
Hockey Swim Tennis Water-skiing.
Fees 2012: Res $10,800 (+$1050-2400), 7 wks.
Housing: Cabins. **Swimming:** Lake.
Est 1950. Inc. Ses: 1. **Wks/ses:** 7. Operates June-Aug. ACA.

Laurel offers a variety of waterfront activities, sports, creative and performing arts,
horseback riding, tennis, adventure and tripping, and special interests. The camp is divided
into six campuses, three for boys and three for girls; campuses are further divided by camper
age.

CAMP O-AT-KA
Res — Boys Ages 8-16

Sebago, ME 04029. PO Box 239. Tel: 207-787-3401, 800-818-8455. Fax: 207-787-3930.
www.campoatka.com   E-mail: info@campoatka.com
Ron Hall, Exec Dir.
Adm: FCFS. **Appl due:** Rolling. **Enr:** 150. **Enr cap:** 150. **Staff:** Admin 25. Couns 45.
Features: ESL Crafts Photog Theater Aquatics Archery Bicycle_Tours Boating Canoe
Climbing_Wall Conservation Fishing Hiking Kayak Mountaineering Mtn_Biking Mtn_
Trips Riflery Rock_Climb Sail Seamanship White-water_Raft Wilderness_Camp Wilder-
ness_Canoe Woodcraft Baseball Basketball Cross-country Football Lacrosse Soccer
Swim Tennis Track Water-skiing Watersports.
Fees 2012: Res $3100-8800, 2-7½ wks.
Housing: Cabins Lodges. Avg per room/unit: 8. **Swimming:** Lake.
Est 1906. Nonprofit. Nondenom Christian. Ses: 4. **Wks/ses:** 2-7½. Operates June-Aug.
ACA.

Daily offerings at O-AT-KA include swimming and diving, sailing, water-skiing, team and individual sports, camp craft, riflery and crafts. Boys ages 12½-15 may participate in three- to five-day hiking, biking, canoeing or kayaking wilderness trips. Although campers of all faiths are accepted, campers must attend Sunday chapel services.

CAMP MATOAKA
Res — Girls Ages 8-15

Smithfield, ME 04978. 1 Great Pl. Tel: 207-362-2500. Fax: 207-362-2525.
Contact (Sept-May): 15 Canavan Cir, Needham, MA 02492. Tel: 781-449-0222.
Fax: 781-449-0322.
www.matoaka.com E-mail: matoaka@matoaka.com
Jason Silberman & Leslie Silberman, Dirs.
Grades 3-10. Adm: FCFS. **Appl due:** Rolling. **Enr:** 280. **Enr cap:** 280. **Staff:** Admin 12. Couns 120.
LD Services: Tut.
Features: Computers Crafts Dance Fine_Arts Music Photog Theater Aquatics Archery Bicycle_Tours Canoe Climbing_Wall Fishing Kayak Mtn_Biking Riding Ropes_Crse Sail Basketball Equestrian Field_Hockey Golf Gymnastics Lacrosse Soccer Softball Swim Tennis Volleyball Water-skiing Watersports.
Fees 2012: Res $6250-10,400 (+$275-500), 3½-7 wks.
Housing: Cabins. Avg per room/unit: 10-20. **Swimming:** Lake Pool.
Est 1951. Inc. **Ses:** 3. **Wks/ses:** 3½-7. Operates June-Aug. ACA.

Girls select activities from an elective program offering individual and team sports, riding, aquatics, dramatics, and arts and crafts. Accelerated instruction is available in the latter four, as well as in gymnastics, dance, tennis and computer. Campers may receive tutoring for an additional fee.

FRIENDS CAMP
Res — Coed Ages 7-17

South China, ME 04358. 729 Lakeview Dr. Tel: 207-445-2361.
Contact (Sept-May): 25 Burleigh St, Waterville, ME 04901. Tel: 207-873-3499.
Year-round Fax: 207-445-5451.
www.friendscamp.org E-mail: director@friendscamp.org
Nat Shed, Dir.
Grades 3-12. Adm: FCFS. **Appl due:** Apr. **Staff:** Admin 1. Couns 22.
Features: Astron Debate Ecol Writing/Journ Crafts Creative_Writing Dance Fine_Arts Music Photog Theater Aquatics Canoe Conservation Fishing Hiking Peace/Cross-cultural Sail Wilderness_Camp Woodcraft Baseball Basketball Soccer Swim Volleyball Watersports.
Fees 2011: Res $420-890, 1-2 wks.
Housing: Cabins. Avg per room/unit: 7. **Swimming:** Lake Pond.
Est 1953. Nonprofit. Religious Society of Friends. **Ses:** 6. **Wks/ses:** 1-2. Operates June-Aug.

Located on China Lake, this Quaker camp offers a traditional program that includes sailing, water activities, crafts, noncompetitive sports, drama, photography and pottery. Campers select their own programs. While most boys and girls attend for two weeks, younger children may enroll for one week. The camp holds Meeting for Worship daily.

CAMP SUSAN CURTIS
Res — Coed Ages 8-16

Stoneham, ME 04231. 236 Allen Rd. Tel: 207-928-2955.
Contact (Sept-May): c/o Susan L Curtis Foundation, 1321 Washington Ave, Ste 104, Portland, ME 04103. Tel: 207-774-1552.

Year-round Fax: 207-774-4240.
www.susancurtisfoundation.org **E-mail:** info@susancurtisfoundation.org
Terri Mulks, Dir.
Adm: FCFS. **Appl due:** Apr. **Enr:** 650. **Staff:** Admin 7. Couns 28.
Features: Astron Ecol Environ_Sci Geol Sci Crafts Creative_Writing Dance Drama Fine_ Arts Music Adventure_Travel Aquatics Archery Boating Canoe Climbing_Wall Exploration Fishing Hiking Mountaineering Mtn_Trips Rock_Climb Seamanship White-water_ Raft Wilderness_Camp Wilderness_Canoe Baseball Basketball Equestrian Football Martial_Arts Roller_Hockey Soccer Softball Swim Watersports.
Fees 2010: Free (in-state residents). Res 2 wks.
Housing: Cabins Lodges. **Swimming:** Lake.
Est 1974. Nonprofit. **Spons:** Susan L. Curtis Foundation. **Ses:** 4. **Wks/ses:** 2. Operates June-Aug. ACA.

This cost-free camp for economically underprivileged children from Maine provides performing and creative arts opportunities, adventure challenges, environmental education and traditional recreational pursuits. Leadership opportunities for older campers (ages 13 and 14) combine camper activities with special-interest programs and trips.

CAMP TAPAWINGO
Res — Girls Ages 8-16

Sweden, ME 04040. 166 Tapawingo Rd. Tel: 207-647-3351. **Fax:** 207-647-2232.
Contact (Sept-May): PO Box 248, Maplewood, NJ 07040. **Tel:** 973-275-1139.
Fax: 973-275-1182.
www.camptapawingo.com **E-mail:** info@camptapawingo.com
Jane Lichtman, Dir.
Grades 3-11. **Adm:** FCFS. **Appl due:** Rolling. **Enr:** 175. **Enr cap:** 175. **Staff:** Admin 6. Couns 58. Res 70.
Features: Crafts Dance Fine_Arts Music Painting Photog Theater Adventure_Travel Aquatics Archery Boating Canoe Hiking Kayak Mountaineering Mtn_Biking Mtn_Trips Riding Ropes_Crse Sail Social_Servs White-water_Raft Wilderness_Camp Wilderness_Canoe Aerobics Basketball Equestrian Field_Hockey Gymnastics Lacrosse Soccer Softball Swim Tennis Volleyball Water-skiing Watersports.
Fees 2012: Res $5000-10,200 (+$250-350), 3-7 wks.
Housing: Cabins. Avg per room/unit: 8. **Swimming:** Lake.
Est 1919. Inc. **Ses:** 3. **Wks/ses:** 3-7. Operates June-Aug. ACA.

Riding, sailing, waterfront activities, land sports, arts and crafts, tennis and a ropes course are among Tapawingo's activities. Two- to six-day wilderness backpacking and canoeing excursions traverse the Allagash, Saco, Androscoggin, Kennebec and Penobscot rivers, as well as various area lakes. The camp's 200 acres of woods, fields and beaches are within view of Mount Washington and the White Mountains of New Hampshire to the west.

MED-O-LARK CAMP
Res — Coed Ages 8-16

Washington, ME 04574. 82 Med-O-Lark Rd. Tel: 207-845-2555.
Contact (Sept-May): 10 Prospect Ct, Madison, CT 06443. **Tel:** 203-927-8688.
Year-round Toll-free: 800-292-7757, **Fax:** 207-845-2332.
www.medolark.com **E-mail:** info@medolark.com
Scott Weinstein & Dana Weinstein, Dirs.
Adm: FCFS. **Appl due:** Rolling. **Enr:** 300. **Staff:** Admin 6. Couns 70.
Features: Circus_Skills Crafts Dance Fine_Arts Music Photog Theater Aquatics Archery Boating Canoe Climbing_Wall Cooking Fishing Kayak Mtn_Biking Riding Ropes_Crse Sail White-water_Raft Yoga Equestrian Fencing Martial_Arts Roller_Hockey Skateboarding Soccer Softball Swim Tennis Volleyball Water-skiing Watersports Weight_Trng.
Fees 2012: Res $3300-8800 (+$200-800), 2-8 wks.

Housing: Cabins. **Swimming:** Lake.
Est 1967. Inc. Ses: 8. **Wks/ses:** 2-8. Operates June-Aug. ACA.

This noncompetitive, minimally structured camp features electives in land sports and watersports, in addition to a particularly strong creative arts program. Campers of all ages embark on excursions that range from shopping trips to white-water rafting and kayaking treks. Two-week sessions are open to new campers only.

BIRCH ROCK CAMP
Res — Boys Ages 7-15

Waterford, ME 04088. PO Box 148. Tel: 207-583-4478.
Contact (Sept-May): 30 Bellevue Ave, South Portland, ME 04106. **Tel:** 207-741-2930.
Year-round Fax: 207-741-2920.
www.birchrock.org   E-mail: brc@birchrock.org
Michael A. Mattson, Dir.
Adm: FCFS. **Appl due:** Rolling. **Enr:** 80. **Enr cap:** 80. **Staff:** Couns 35.
Features: Studio_Art Woodworking Canoe Kayak Sail Basketball Swim.
Fees 2012: Res $3300-6500, 2-7 wks.
Housing: Cabins. **Swimming:** Lake.
Est 1926. Ses: 7. **Wks/ses:** 2-7. Operates June-Aug. ACA.

Birch Rock offers mountain and canoe trips, as well as in-camp activities such as waterfront pursuits, land sports and nature study. Two- to three-day hiking, biking and rafting trips are other options. Academic tutoring is available.

CAMP WAZIYATAH
Res — Coed Ages 7-15

Waterford, ME 04088. 530 Mill Hill Rd.
Contact (Sept-May): 45 Joy St, Apt PH, Boston, MA 02114.
Year-round Tel: 207-583-2267, **Fax:** 509-357-2267.
www.wazi.com   E-mail: info@wazi.com
Gregg Parker & Mitch Parker, Dirs.
Grades 2-10. **Adm:** FCFS. **Appl due:** Rolling. **Enr:** 200. **Enr cap:** 200. **Staff:** Admin 7. Couns 93.
Features: Ecol Environ_Sci Circus_Skills Crafts Creative_Writing Dance Fine_Arts Music Painting Photog Theater Adventure_Travel Aquatics Archery Boating Canoe Climbing_Wall Conservation Exploration Fishing Hiking Kayak Mountaineering Mtn_Trips Outdoor_Ed Rappelling Riding Riflery Rock_Climb Sail White-water_Raft Wilderness_Camp Wilderness_Canoe Baseball Basketball Cross-country Equestrian Field_Hockey Football Gymnastics Lacrosse Martial_Arts Skateboarding Soccer Softball Swim Tennis Volleyball Water-skiing Watersports Weight_Trng.
Fees 2012: Res $2950-8950 (+$175-375), 2-8 wks. Aid (Need).
Housing: Cabins. Avg per room/unit: 6-12. **Swimming:** Lake.
Est 1922. Inc. Ses: 6. **Wks/ses:** 2-8. Operates June-Aug. ACA.

Teen and junior camps at Wazi provide team and individual sports, waterfront activities, theater, arts and crafts, tennis, English riding, wilderness trips and water-skiing. Two-week sessions are open to boys and girls entering grades 2-6 only.

CAMP WIGWAM
Res — Boys Ages 7-15

Waterford, ME 04088. 57 Wigwam Pass. Tel: 207-583-2300. **Fax:** 207-583-6242.
www.campwigwam.com   E-mail: wigwam@maine.com
Robert W. Strauss, Dir.

Adm: FCFS. **Appl due:** Rolling. **Enr:** 165. **Staff:** Admin 10. Couns 45.
Features: Computers Writing/Journ Ceramics Crafts Drama Music Photog Woodworking Aquatics Archery Boating Canoe Climbing_Wall Cooking Fishing Hiking Kayak Mountaineering Mtn_Biking Mtn_Trips Rock_Climb Sail Baseball Basketball Football Golf Lacrosse Roller_Hockey Soccer Softball Swim Tennis Water-skiing.
Fees 2010: Res $7400-8400 (+$250), 5-7 wks.
Housing: Cabins. Avg per room/unit: 4. **Swimming:** Lake.
Est 1910. **Inc. Ses:** 2. **Wks/ses:** 5-7. Operates June-Aug. ACA.

Wigwam places emphasis on waterfront skills, tennis, golf and water-skiing, in addition to rustic camping in the area's wilderness. Other popular activities are crafts, music, photography, canoeing, sailing and team sports.

CAMP ANDROSCOGGIN
Res — Boys Ages 8-15

Wayne, ME 04284. 126 Leadbetter Rd. Tel: 207-685-4441. Fax: 207-685-4391.
Contact (Sept-May): 601 West St, Harrison, NY 10528. Tel: 914-835-5800.
Fax: 914-777-2718.
www.campandro.com   E-mail: directors@campandro.com
Peter K. Hirsch & Roberta Hirsch, Dirs.
Adm: FCFS. **Appl due:** Rolling. **Enr:** 270. **Enr cap:** 270.
Features: Animation Ceramics Drama Music Photog Video_Production Archery Canoe Climbing_Wall Fishing Kayak Riflery Ropes_Crse Sail Baseball Basketball Golf Lacrosse Soccer Street_Hockey Swim Tennis Volleyball Water-skiing Watersports.
Fees 2012: Res $6700-10,700, 4-7 wks.
Housing: Cabins. Avg per room/unit: 6. **Swimming:** Lake.
Est 1907. **Ses:** 2. **Wks/ses:** 4-7. Operates June-Aug.

This 125-acre lakeside camp features a full range of land and water activities, including team and individual sports, arts and crafts, nature study, swimming, water-skiing and sailing. Although primarily a seven-week camp, Androscoggin offers a four-week option for first-time campers.

CAMP KAWANHEE
Res — Boys Ages 7-15

Weld, ME 04285. 58 Kawanhee Ln. Tel: 207-585-2210. Fax: 207-585-2620.
Contact (Sept-May): PO Box 789, Yarmouth, ME 04096. Tel: 207-846-7741.
Fax: 207-846-7731.
www.kawanhee.com   E-mail: kawanhee@kawanhee.com
Dan Webster, Dir.
Adm: FCFS.
Features: Music Studio_Art Archery Boating Canoe Climbing_Wall Fishing Hiking Kayak Mtn_Biking Riflery Ropes_Crse Sail Baseball Basketball Football Lacrosse Soccer Softball Swim Tennis Volleyball Water-skiing.
Fees 2012: Res $2850-7300, 2-7 wks.
Housing: Cabins. Avg per room/unit: 10. **Swimming:** Lake.
Est 1920. **Ses:** 4. **Wks/ses:** 2-7. Operates June-Aug. ACA.

Kawanhee offers land sports and watersports, among them tennis, soccer, wrestling, riflery, sailing, swimming and water-skiing, as well as fishing and canoe and mountain tripping. Industrial arts, camp craft and nature study are other features.

CAMP CARIBOU
Res — Boys Ages 7-15

Winslow, ME 04901. 1 Caribou Way. Tel: 207-872-9313. Fax: 207-872-8637.
Contact (Sept-May): 26 Hickory Hill Rd, Box 129, Wayland, MA 01778.
  Tel: 508-358-5050. Fax: 508-358-5876.
www.campcaribou.com E-mail: info@campcaribou.com
Bill Lerman & Martha Lerman, Dirs.
Adm: FCFS. **Appl due:** Rolling.
Features: Crafts Theater Aquatics Archery Boating Canoe Climbing_Wall Exploration Fishing Hiking Kayak Mtn_Trips Rappelling Riflery Ropes_Crse Sail White-water_Raft Wilderness_Camp Wilderness_Canoe Woodcraft Baseball Basketball Football Golf Lacrosse Martial_Arts Roller_Hockey Soccer Street_Hockey Swim Team_Handball Tennis Ultimate_Frisbee Volleyball Water-skiing Watersports Boxing.
Fees 2012: Res $6150-10,000, 3½-7 wks.
Housing: Cabins. Avg per room/unit: 10. **Swimming:** Lake.
Est 1923. Inc. **Ses:** 3. **Wks/ses:** 3½-7. Operates June-Aug. ACA.

The camp's program combines scheduled and elective activities. Caribou offers professional instruction in various land sports, watersports and crafts. Wednesdays are noninstructional days: Boys engage in campwide activities and, on occasion, out-of-camp excursions.

CAMP CHEWONKI FOR BOYS
CAMP CHEWONKI FOR GIRLS
Res — Coord Ages 8-15, Girls 16

Wiscasset, ME 04578. c/o Chewonki Foundation, 485 Chewonki Neck Rd.
  Tel: 207-882-7323. Fax: 207-882-4074.
www.chewonki.org E-mail: camp@chewonki.org
Garth Altenburg & Abby Burbank, Dirs.
Adm: FCFS. **Appl due:** Rolling. **Staff:** Admin 5. Couns 60.
Features: Ecol Environ_Sci Marine_Bio/Stud Crafts Drama Photog Archery Canoe Conservation Exploration Hiking Kayak Mountaineering Mtn_Trips Ropes_Crse Sail Wilderness_Camp Wilderness_Canoe Woodcraft Baseball Basketball Soccer Softball Swim Tennis.
Fees 2012: Res $1200-8000, 1-7 wks.
Housing: Cabins Lodges Tents. Avg per room/unit: 8. **Swimming:** River.
Est 1915. Nonprofit. **Spons:** Chewonki Foundation. **Ses:** 7. **Wks/ses:** 1-7. Operates June-Aug. ACA.

Chewonki's single-gender camps for boys and girls offer formalized instruction in the following areas: nature, camp craft, canoeing, sailing, kayaking, art, swimming, tennis, field sports, archery, farming and organic gardening, woodworking and photography. Programming emphasizes natural history and ecology, as well as wilderness canoeing, mountain and sailing trips.

CHOP POINT CAMP
Res — Coed Ages 12-18

Woolwich, ME 04579. 420 Chop Point Rd. Tel: 207-443-5860. Fax: 207-443-6760.
www.choppoint.org E-mail: camp@choppoint.org
David Wilkinson, Dir.
Grades 6-12. Adm: FCFS. **Appl due:** Rolling. **Enr:** 80. **Enr cap:** 80. **Staff:** Admin 6. Couns 18.
Type of instruction: Enrich Tut.
Travel: Canada.
Features: Computers ESL Crafts Dance Music Painting Photog Theater Aquatics Bicycle_Tours Boating Canoe Community_Serv Cruises Deep-sea Fishing Fishing Hiking

Kayak Mountaineering Mtn_Biking Mtn_Trips Ropes_Crse Sail Sea_Cruises Seamanship Social_Servs White-water_Raft Wilderness_Camp Wilderness_Canoe Work Baseball Basketball Soccer Softball Surfing Swim Tennis Ultimate_Frisbee Volleyball Waterskiing Watersports Weight_Trng.
Fees 2011: Res $1750-3200 (+$200), 3-6 wks.
Housing: Cabins. Avg per room/unit: 10. **Swimming:** Lake River.
Est 1966. Nonprofit. **Ses:** 3. **Wks/ses:** 3-6. Operates June-Aug. ACA.

Chop Point offers sailing, windsurfing, tennis, computer, crafts, music, gardening, conservation, canoeing, deep-sea fishing and video in a Christian setting. All campers attend an interdenominational chapel service on Sunday mornings. Campers may embark on three- to five-day wilderness cycling, canoeing or hiking trips in Maine or Canada.

MARYLAND

CAMP AIRY
CAMP LOUISE
Res — Coord Ages 7-17

Baltimore, MD 21215. 5750 Park Heights Ave. Tel: 410-466-9010. Fax: 410-466-0560.
www.airylouise.org   E-mail: airlou@airylouise.org
Rick Frankle & Alicia Berlin, Dirs.
Grades 2-11. Adm: FCFS. **Appl due:** Rolling. **Enr:** 410. **Enr cap:** 410. **Staff:** Admin 25. Couns 166.
Features: Writing/Journ Robotics Crafts Creative_Writing Dance Filmmaking Fine_Arts Media Music Photog Theater Aquatics Archery Canoe Caving Climbing_Wall Cooking Fishing Hiking Kayak Mountaineering Mtn_Biking Mtn_Trips Paintball Rock_Climb Ropes_Crse Scuba Survival_Trng White-water_Raft Wilderness_Camp Woodcraft Baseball Basketball Cross-country Field_Hockey Football Golf Gymnastics Lacrosse Martial_Arts Skateboarding Soccer Softball Swim Tennis Volleyball Watersports Weight_ Trng Wrestling Rocketry.
Fees 2009: Res $1700-6800 (+$50-200), 2-8 wks.
Housing: Cabins. Avg per room/unit: 13. **Swimming:** Pool.
Est 1922. Nonprofit. Jewish. **Ses:** 9. **Wks/ses:** 2-8. Operates June-Aug. ACA.

These camps for Jewish children—Airy for boys (in Thurmont) and Louise for girls (in Cascade)—combine offerings in athletics, the arts, nature studies, swimming and outdoor living with Jewish traditions and Shabbat services. Counselors and specialists provide instruction in a particularly varied selection of fine and performing arts activities. Trips, special events, and theme days and evenings are part of the program, and activities between the camps are regularly scheduled.

CAMP PUH'TOK
Res — Coed Ages 7-16; Day — Coed 5-9

Monkton, MD 21111. 17433 Big Falls Rd. Tel: 410-329-6590. Fax: 410-329-6034.
www.camppuhtok.com   E-mail: info@camppuhtok.com
Alexi Kousouris, Dir.
Adm: FCFS. **Appl due:** Rolling. **Enr:** 140. **Staff:** Admin 3. Couns 55.
Features: Archaeol Astron Ecol Environ_Sci Writing/Journ Crafts Dance Music Aquatics Archery Bicycle_Tours Boating Canoe Conservation Cooking Farm Fishing Hiking Mtn_Biking Mtn_Trips Ranch Riding Riflery Ropes_Crse Sail Survival_Trng Whitewater_Raft Wilderness_Camp Wilderness_Canoe Woodcraft Equestrian Field_Hockey Golf Lacrosse Soccer Softball Swim Tennis Volleyball Watersports.
Fees 2011: Res $560-1250 (+$25), 1-2 wks. Day $300, 1 wk.

Housing: Cabins Lodges Tents Tepees. Avg per room/unit: 9. **Swimming:** Pool River. **Est 1942.** Nonprofit. **Ses:** 12. **Wks/ses:** 1-2. Operates June-Aug. ACA.

Puh'tok provides younger campers with basic camping skills and an appreciation for nature. Older campers participate in additional activities, including Native American dance and crafts, cycling, lacrosse, archery and canoeing. The most experienced campers take mountain hikes, sail, ride horses and learn black powder shooting. The Tipi Encampment, a special program for boys and girls ages 13-16, teaches campers about Native American culture; campers learn to set up their own tepees and cook outdoors, while also studying songs, dances, customs, history, sign language and survival skills.

ECHO HILL CAMP
Res — Coed Ages 7-16

Worton, MD 21678. 13655 Bloomingneck Rd. Tel: 410-348-5303. Fax: 410-348-2010. www.echohillcamp.com   E-mail: info@echohillcamp.com
Peter P. Rice, Jr., Dir.
Adm: FCFS. **Enr:** 145. **Staff:** Admin 6. Couns 50.
Type of instruction: Tut.
Features: Environ_Sci Crafts Creative_Writing Dance Music Theater Aquatics Archery Canoe Climbing_Wall Exploration Fishing Hiking Kayak Riding Ropes_Crse Sail Survival_Trng Wilderness_Camp Basketball Equestrian Lacrosse Soccer Softball Swim Tennis Volleyball Water-skiing Watersports.
Fees 2011: Res $2360-6170, 2-8 wks.
Housing: Cabins Tents. **Swimming:** Ocean.
Est 1948. Nonprofit. **Ses:** 4. **Wks/ses:** 2-8. Operates June-Aug. ACA.

Echo Hill, located on Chesapeake Bay, offers a flexible program designed to meet individual needs and abilities. Swimming, sailing, water-skiing, fishing and crabbing, sports, creative arts, horseback riding and nature are among the activities.

MASSACHUSETTS

CAMP WINNEKEAG
Res — Coed Ages 8-16

Ashburnham, MA.
Contact (Year-round): 34 Sawyer St, PO Box 1169, South Lancaster, MA 01561.
Tel: 978-365-4551. Fax: 978-365-3838.
www.campwinnekeag.com
Josue Feliciano, Dir.
Adm: FCFS. Admitted: 99%. **Appl due:** Rolling. **Enr:** 80. **Enr cap:** 96. **Staff:** Admin 5. Couns 18. Res 30.
Features: Crafts Drama Music Photog Aquatics Archery Bicycle_Tours Boating Canoe Climbing_Wall Hiking Kayak Mtn_Biking Mtn_Trips Rappelling Riding Rock_Climb Ropes_Crse Sail White-water_Raft Wilderness_Camp Baseball Basketball Equestrian Football Gymnastics Soccer Softball Swim Volleyball Water-skiing Watersports BMX_Biking.
Fees 2011: Res $390-420, 1 wk. Aid 2009 (Need): $500.
Housing: Cabins Lodges Tents Tepees. Avg per room/unit: 9. **Swimming:** Lake.
Est 1951. Nonprofit. Seventh-day Adventist. **Ses:** 4. **Wks/ses:** 1. Operates June-Aug. ACA.

Located on Lake Winnekeag, this Seventh-day Adventist camp offers land sports, horseback riding, boating and a range of other water activities, arts and crafts, nature study and swimming. Specialty programs allow campers to develop new skills or pursue specific interests.

4-H CAMP MIDDLESEX
Res — Coed Ages 8-15; Day — Coed 6-12

Ashby, MA 01431. 1031 Erickson Rd, PO Box 185. Tel: 978-386-7704.
Fax: 978-386-7046.
www.campmiddlesex.com   E-mail: info@campmiddlesex.com
Steven LaFountain, Dir.
Adm: FCFS. **Appl due:** Rolling. **Enr:** 125. **Enr cap:** 150. **Staff:** Admin 4. Couns 22.
Features: Environ_Sci Sci Dance Theater Aquatics Archery Boating Canoe Conservation Farm Fishing Hiking Kayak Riding Ropes_Crse Survival_Trng Woodcraft Equestrian Soccer Swim Rocketry.
Fees 2010: Res $430-915, 1-2 wks. Day $255, 1 wk. Aid 2008 (Need): $2000.
Housing: Cabins. **Swimming:** Pool.
Est 1941. Nonprofit. **Ses:** 7. **Wks/ses:** 1. Operates June-Aug. ACA.

Camp Middlesex offers a variety of traditional activities, among them canoeing, hiking, soccer and a ropes course. Horse riding and rocketry are available for an additional weekly fee. Evening events such as band concerts and dances are also part of the program.

CAMP WATITOH
Res — Coed Ages 7-16

Becket, MA 01223. Center Lake. Tel: 413-623-8951. Fax: 413-623-8955.
Contact (Sept-May): 28 Sammis Ln, White Plains, NY 10605. Tel: 914-428-1894.
Fax: 914-428-1648.
www.campwatitoh.com   E-mail: info@campwatitoh.com
William Hoch, Dir.
Grades 2-10. Adm: FCFS. **Appl due:** Rolling. **Enr:** 200. **Staff:** Couns 55.
Features: Astron Ecol Environ_Sci Writing/Journ Crafts Fine_Arts Media Music Painting Photog Studio_Art Theater Aquatics Archery Boating Canoe Chess Conservation Farm Fishing Hiking Kayak Outdoor_Ed Riding Ropes_Crse Sail Badminton Baseball Basketball Equestrian Field_Hockey Football Golf Gymnastics Lacrosse Roller_Hockey Soccer Softball Swim Team_Handball Tennis Track Ultimate_Frisbee Volleyball Waterskiing Watersports.
Fees 2012: Res $5100-8100 (+$205-330), 4-7 wks.
Housing: Cabins. Avg per room/unit: 8. **Swimming:** Lake.
Est 1937. Inc. **Ses:** 2. **Wks/ses:** 4-7. Operates June-Aug.

Watitoh, located on 85 acres in the Berkshires, conducts a wide array of land sports and waterfront activities. Other offerings include creative and performing arts, as well as outdoor living skills instruction.

CAMP ROTARY
Res — Coed Ages 7-15

Boxford, MA 01921. 372 Ipswich Rd, PO Box 270. Tel: 978-352-9952.
Contact (Sept-May): Tel: 978-595-5323.
www.camprotary.org   E-mail: camprotaryma@aol.com
Richard Cowdell, Dir.
Adm: FCFS. **Appl due:** Mar. **Enr:** 200. **Staff:** Admin 7. Couns 30.
Features: Crafts Dance Drama Photog Aquatics Archery Boating Canoe Fishing Hiking Kayak Riflery Ropes_Crse Sail Baseball Basketball Cross-country Soccer Softball Swim Tennis Track Volleyball Watersports BMX_Biking.
Fees 2012: Res $620-1240 (+$60-120), 1-2 wks.
Housing: Cabins. **Swimming:** Lake.
Est 1921. Nonprofit. **Spons:** Greater Lynn Rotary Club. **Ses:** 7. **Wks/ses:** 1-2. Operates June-Aug. ACA.

Traditional camping activities at the camp include arts and crafts, drama, canoeing, sailing, fishing, hiking and sports. A ropes challenge course and a zip line are both on Rotary's grounds, as is a competitive BMX bike racing track. The camp's one annual two-week session enrolls boys and girls ages 13-15 only.

CAPE COD SEA CAMPS
Res — Coed Ages 8-14; Day — Coed 4-17

Brewster, MA 02631. 3057 Main St, PO Box 1880. Tel: 508-896-3451. Fax: 508-896-8272.
www.capecodseacamps.com　　E-mail: info@capecodseacamps.com
Nancy W. Garran, Exec Dir.
Adm: FCFS. **Appl due:** Apr. **Enr:** 300-375. **Staff:** Admin 12. Couns 160.
Features: Crafts Dance Fine_Arts Photog Theater Aquatics Archery Boating Canoe Kayak Mtn_Biking Riflery Ropes_Crse Sail Woodcraft Baseball Basketball Field_Hockey Lacrosse Soccer Swim Tennis Water-skiing Watersports.
Fees 2012: Res $2610-9615 (+$300), 1½-7 wks. Day $650-4200, 1-7 wks.
Housing: Cabins. Avg per room/unit: 10-14. **Swimming:** Lake Ocean Pool.
Est 1922. Inc. **Ses:** 14. **Wks/ses:** 1-7. Operates June-Aug. ACA.

Although emphasizing instruction in a variety of traditional camp activities, Cape Cod Sea Camps, Monomoy and Wono, also feature an extensive waterfront program. Sailing is offered on both a recreational and a competitive basis. The sports program includes a strong tennis component. The camp also provides woodworking, arts and crafts, archery, riflery, theater and cycling.

SHIRE VILLAGE CAMP
Res — Coed Ages 8-14

Cummington, MA 01026. Mellor Rd. Tel: 413-634-2281.
Contact (Winter): 175 Eastern Pky, Apt 6J, Brooklyn, NY 11238. Tel: 718-622-8204.
www.shirevillage.org　　E-mail: beths@mmfsnyc.org
Stephanie Rabins, Dir.
Adm: FCFS. **Enr:** 100.
Features: Art Ceramics Crafts Creative_Writing Dance Drawing Music Photog Sculpt Theater Woodworking Archery Canoe Cooking Farm Hiking Riding Yoga Basketball Soccer Softball Swim Tennis Volleyball Gardening.
Fees 2011: Res $2000-5200, 2-7 wks. Aid (Need).
Housing: Cabins. **Swimming:** Pool River.
Est 1972. **Ses:** 5. **Wks/ses:** 2-7. Operates July-Aug. ACA.

Shire Village stresses individualized programming, with campers choosing activities from a variety of specialized areas. Offerings include farming, outdoor living, animal care, arts and crafts, theater, film and photography, woodworking, horseback riding, swimming, canoeing and other individual, noncompetitive sports. First-time campers ages 7-11 may enroll in a two-week introductory session; other boys and girls attend for at least three weeks.

CAMP HALF MOON
Res — Coed Ages 6-16; Day — Coed 3-15

Great Barrington, MA 01230. PO Box 188. Tel: 413-528-0940. Fax: 413-528-0941.
www.camphalfmoon.com　　E-mail: info@camphalfmoon.com
Ric Fritch & Gretchen Mann-Fritch, Dirs.
Adm: FCFS. **Appl due:** May. **Staff:** Admin 30. Couns 80.
Features: ESL Writing/Journ Crafts Creative_Writing Dance Drama Painting Aquatics Archery Boating Canoe Climbing_Wall Fishing Hiking Kayak Mtn_Biking Riding Ropes_Crse Sail Aerobics Badminton Baseball Basketball Equestrian Football Golf Gymnastics

Martial_Arts Rugby Skateboarding Soccer Softball Street_Hockey Swim Tennis Volleyball Water-skiing Winter_Sports Wrestling.
Fees 2012: Res $1400-8120 (+$65-455), 1-7 wks. Day $290-500, 1 wk.
Housing: Cabins. Avg per room/unit: 7. **Swimming:** Lake Pool.
Est 1922. Inc. **Ses:** 14. **Wks/ses:** 1-7. Operates June-Aug.

Half Moon offers extensive waterfront activities and tutoring, as well as team sports and creative arts and crafts.

CAMP DANBEE
Res — Girls Ages 6-15

Hinsdale, MA 01235. Rte 143. Tel: 413-655-8115. Fax: 413-655-2956.
Contact (Sept-May): 24 Woodshire Ter, Towaco, NJ 07082. Tel: 973-402-0606.
 Fax: 973-402-1771.
www.campdanbee.com   E-mail: danbee@campdanbee.com
Jay Toporoff, Dir.
Grades 1-10. Adm: FCFS. **Staff:** Admin 20. Couns 150.
Features: Crafts Dance Music Photog Theater Aquatics Archery Bicycle_Tours Boating Canoe Climbing_Wall Community_Serv Fishing Hiking Kayak Riding Ropes_Crse Sail Basketball Equestrian Field_Hockey Golf Gymnastics Ice_Hockey Lacrosse Soccer Softball Swim Tennis Track Volleyball Water-skiing Watersports.
Fees 2010: Res $9950 (+$150-750), 7 wks.
Housing: Cabins. **Swimming:** Lake Pool.
Est 1950. Inc. **Ses:** 1. **Wks/ses:** 7. Operates June-Aug. ACA.

Daily activities at Danbee focus on aquatics and sports instruction. Dance, arts and crafts, theater, photography and horseback riding are among the specialty options offered.

CAMP EMERSON
Res — Coed Ages 8-15

Hinsdale, MA 01235. 212 Longview Ave, PO Box 808. Tel: 413-655-8123.
 Fax: 413-655-2571.
Contact (Sept-May): 91 Minuteman Rd, Ridgefield, CT 06877. Tel: 203-894-9663.
 Fax: 203-894-9673.
Year-round Toll-free: 800-782-3395.
www.campemerson.com   E-mail: directors@campemerson.com
Marvin Lein, Addie Lein, Sue Lein & Kevin McDonough, Dirs.
Adm: FCFS. **Appl due:** Rolling. **Enr:** 200. **Staff:** Admin 20. Couns 60.
Features: Computers Sci Robotics Circus_Skills Crafts Dance Filmmaking Fine_Arts Media Music Photog Theater Cartooning Aquatics Archery Boating Climbing_Wall Cooking Fishing Ropes_Crse Sail Woodcraft Baseball Basketball Golf Gymnastics Martial_Arts Roller_Hockey Soccer Softball Swim Tennis Volleyball Water-skiing Watersports Rocketry.
Fees 2011: Res $2990-8490 (+$175-375), 2-6 wks.
Housing: Cabins. Avg per room/unit: 8. **Swimming:** Lake Pond Pool.
Est 1966. Inc. **Ses:** 3. **Wks/ses:** 2-6. Operates June-Aug. ACA.

Boys and girls participate in sports, trips, music, dance, gymnastics, drama, science, crafts and other camp activities in an noncompetitive atmosphere. Emerson's Step Beyond program features advanced classes in robotics, rocketry and Web design.

CAMP TACONIC
Res — Coed Ages 7-15

Hinsdale, MA 02135. 770 New Windsor Rd. Tel: 413-655-2717. Fax: 413-655-2707.
Contact (Sept-May): 20 Glenwood Ct, Tenafly, NJ 07670. Tel: 201-871-2086.

Fax: 201-871-2088.
www.camptaconic.com   E-mail: info@camptaconic.com
Loren Kleinman & Jill Kleinman, Dirs.
Adm: FCFS. Enr: 400. Staff: Admin 20. Couns 100.
Features: Computers Environ_Sci Writing/Journ Crafts Dance Fine_Arts Media Music
    Photog Theater Aquatics Archery Canoe Climbing_Wall Fishing Hiking Mtn_Trips Riding
    Sail Wilderness_Camp Woodcraft Baseball Basketball Equestrian Golf Gymnastics
    Lacrosse Roller_Hockey Soccer Softball Swim Tennis Volleyball Water-skiing.
Fees 2012: Res $6295-9949 (+$350-595), 4-7 wks.
Housing: Cabins. Avg per room/unit: 10. Swimming: Lake Pool.
Est 1932. Inc. Ses: 2. Wks/ses: 4-7. Operates June-Aug. ACA.

Located on Lake Ashmere in the Berkshires, Taconic offers a selection of land sports and
watersports, in addition to mountain trips, nature, hiking, activities in the arts, riding and
computer training. The camp also features deep-sea fishing trips and visits to the Tanglewood
Music Festival, the Berkshire Theatre Festival and other events. A four-week session is open
to first-time campers only.

CAMP LENOX
Res — Coed Ages 7-16

Lee, MA 01238. 2042 N Main Rd. Tel: 413-243-2223. Fax: 413-243-3446.
Contact (Sept-May): PO Box 75-9900, Coral Springs, FL 33075. Tel: 954-340-6634.
    Fax: 954-340-8282.
www.camplenox.com   E-mail: info@camplenox.com
Rich Moss & Stephanie Moss, Dirs.
Adm: FCFS. Appl due: Rolling. Enr: 300. Staff: Admin 20. Couns 100.
Features: Expository_Writing Crafts Creative_Writing Dance Drama Fine_Arts Media
    Music Aquatics Canoe Hiking Mtn_Trips Paintball Riding Sail Scuba White-water_Raft
    Baseball Basketball Cross-country Football Golf Ice_Hockey Roller_Hockey Soccer
    Swim Tennis Volleyball Water-skiing Watersports.
Fees 2012: Res $6150-9900, 3½-7 wks.
Housing: Cabins. Swimming: Lake.
Est 1918. Ses: 3. Wks/ses: 3½-7. Operates June-Aug. ACA.

Campers create their own programs by choosing two major offerings per day. At the end
of each week, campers may repeat their choices or choose two new activities. Lenox offers
instruction in an array of land sports and watersports. Among other pursuits are horseback
riding, dance, a climbing wall, a ropes course, hiking, canoeing and swimming. Younger
campers (grade 5 and below) enroll in a half session, while older boys and girls attend for
seven weeks.

TABOR ACADEMY SUMMER PROGRAM
Res — Coed Ages 9-15; Day — Coed 6-15

Marion, MA 02738. 66 Spring St. Tel: 508-291-8342. Fax: 508-291-8392.
www.taboracademy.org/summer   E-mail: summer@taboracademy.org
Noel Pardo, Dir.
Grades 4-9. Adm: FCFS. Appl due: Rolling. Enr: 140-200. Enr cap: 160-200. Staff: Admin
    5. Couns 70.
Type of instruction: Dev_Read Enrich Preview Rev Study_Skills.
Features: Computers ESL Lang Marine_Bio/Stud Oceanog Sci Crafts Creative_Writing
    Photog Studio_Art Theater Sail Baseball Basketball Field_Hockey Lacrosse Soccer
    Softball Squash Swim Tennis Ultimate_Frisbee Volleyball.
Fees 2012: Res $1700-8000 (+$200), 1-6 wks. Day $495-2575, 1-6 wks.
Housing: Dorms. Swimming: Ocean.
Est 1917. Nonprofit. Ses: 11. Wks/ses: 1-6. Operates June-Aug. ACA.

Tabor offers instruction in a full range of athletic areas, with an emphasis on waterfront activities. An optional academic curriculum complements recreational opportunities with elective course work, available in most disciplines for review, preview or enrichment.

CAMP FARLEY
Res — Coed Ages 8-15; Day — Coed 6-12

Mashpee, MA 02649. 615 Rte 130. Tel: 508-477-0181. Fax: 508-539-0080.
www.campfarley.com   E-mail: office@campfarley.com
Joyce Oberthal, Dir.
Grades 1-10. Adm: FCFS. **Appl due:** Rolling. **Enr:** 173. **Staff:** Admin 6. Couns 32.
Features: Crafts Music Theater Aquatics Archery Canoe Climbing_Wall Cooking Fishing Kayak Riding Ropes_Crse Soccer Swim Volleyball.
Fees 2009: Res $425, 1 wk. Day $275, 1 wk. Aid 2006 (Need): $20,000.
Housing: Cabins. Avg per room/unit: 100. **Swimming:** Lake.
Est 1934. Nonprofit. **Ses:** 8. **Wks/ses:** 1. Operates July-Aug. ACA.

Situated on a 32-acre site on Mashpee-Wakeby Lake, Farley offers various traditional recreational activities, among them arts and crafts, swimming, canoeing, archery, animal care, performing arts and adventure skills. The daily program consists of five activities, the first three selected by camp counselors and the other two chosen by the camper. An optional horseback riding camp is available for an additional fee.

CAMP AVODA
Res — Boys Ages 7-15

Middleboro, MA 02346. 23 Gibbs Rd. Tel: 508-947-3800.
Contact (Sept-May): 11 Essex St, Lynnfield, MA 01940. Tel: 781-433-0131.
Year-round Fax: 781-334-4779.
www.campavoda.org   E-mail: info@campavoda.org
Ken Shifman, Dir.
Grades 2-10. Adm: FCFS. **Appl due:** Rolling. **Enr:** 150. **Enr cap:** 150. **Staff:** Admin 7. Couns 35.
Features: Crafts Filmmaking Music Photog Aquatics Archery Boating Canoe Climbing_Wall Deep-sea Fishing Fishing Hiking Kayak Mtn_Trips Ropes_Crse Sail White-water_Raft Wilderness_Canoe Woodcraft Basketball Cross-country Football Golf Lacrosse Roller_ Hockey Soccer Softball Street_Hockey Swim Tennis Track Ultimate_Frisbee Volleyball Water-skiing Watersports Weight_Trng Wrestling.
Fees 2012: Res $2525-6850 (+$150-875), 2-7½ wks. Aid 2009 (Need): $31,000.
Housing: Cabins. Avg per room/unit: 8. **Swimming:** Lake.
Est 1927. Nonprofit. Jewish. **Ses:** 5. **Wks/ses:** 2-7½. Operates June-Aug. ACA.

Team and individual sports, aquatics, arts and crafts, camping and field trips are among the activities available at this Jewish camp. The camp also features a 55-foot climbing wall and a ropes/challenge course. Avoda holds religious services each Friday evening and Saturday morning, and kosher meals are served.

CAMP ATWATER
Res — Coord Ages 8-15

North Brookfield, MA 01535. 20 Shore Rd. Tel: 508-867-6916.
Contact (Sept-June): c/o Urban League of Springfield, 765 State St, Springfield, MA 01109. Tel: 413-739-7211.
Year-round Fax: 413-732-9364.
www.campatwater.org   E-mail: info@campatwater.org
Shadae Thomas, Dir.

Adm: FCFS. **Appl due:** Rolling. **Enr:** 100. **Enr cap:** 160. **Staff:** Admin 10. Couns 30.
Features: Bus/Fin Computers Debate Expository_Writing Govt Speech Writing/Journ Crafts Creative_Writing Dance Fine_Arts Media Music Theater Aquatics Archery Boating Canoe Chess Fishing Hiking Riding Sail Aerobics Baseball Basketball Cross-country Football Golf Gymnastics Lacrosse Martial_Arts Soccer Softball Swim Tennis Track Volleyball Watersports.
Fees 2011: Res $1750-3500 (+$250), 2-4 wks. Aid (Need).
Housing: Cabins. Avg per room/unit: 10. **Swimming:** Lake.
Est 1921. Nonprofit. **Spons:** Urban League of Springfield. **Ses:** 6. **Wks/ses:** 2-4. Operates June-Aug. ACA.

Primarily serving the African-American community, Atwater offers boating, arts and crafts, individual and team sports, horseback riding, African-American history and leadership development, among other recreational activities. Various cultural and recreational field trips is also available. Separate boys' and girls' sessions operate during different weeks.

CAMP BOURNEDALE
Res — Boys Ages 6-16

Plymouth, MA 02360. 110 Valley Rd. Tel: 508-888-2634. Fax: 508-833-5187.
www.campbournedale.com   E-mail: information@campbournedale.com
Arnie Gerson, Dir.
Adm: FCFS. **Appl due:** Rolling. **Enr:** 140.
Features: Canoe Kayak Sail Scuba Baseball Basketball Golf Ice_Hockey Soccer Swim Tennis Water-skiing Watersports.
Fees 2012: Res $4900-7800, 3½-7 wks.
Housing: Cabins. **Swimming:** Lake.
Est 1939. Ses: 3. **Wks/ses:** 3½-7. Operates June-Aug.

In addition to a full program of waterfront activities, Bournedale offers many land sports, including golf, tennis and team sports. Computer instruction is also available.

ROWE CENTER SUMMER CAMPS
Res — Coed Ages 8-19

Rowe, MA 01367. 22 King's Highway Rd, PO Box 273. Tel: 413-339-4954.
Fax: 413-339-5728.
www.rowecenter.org   E-mail: info@rowecenter.org
Felicity Pickett, Dir.
Grades 4-PG. Adm: FCFS. **Appl due:** Jan. **Enr:** 72. **Enr cap:** 72. **Staff:** Admin 15. Couns 20.
Features: Crafts Canoe Rock_Climb Ropes_Crse Basketball Swim Ultimate_Frisbee Volleyball.
Fees 2011: Res $650-2130, 1-3 wks. Aid 2010 (Need): $50,000.
Housing: Cabins Lodges Tents. Avg per room/unit: 10. **Swimming:** Lake.
Est 1924. Nonprofit. Unitarian Universalist. **Ses:** 5. **Wks/ses:** 1-3. Operates June-Aug.

Rowe Center, affiliated with the Unitarian Universalist Association, runs elementary, junior high and senior high camps. Camp fees are determined along a sliding scale according to family income.

CAMP MARSHALL
Res — Coed Ages 8-15; Day — Coed 5-14

Spencer, MA 01562. c/o Worcester County 4-H Ctr, 92 McCormick Rd.
Tel: 508-885-4891. Fax: 508-885-0119.
www.campmarshall.org   E-mail: campmarshall4h@yahoo.com

Jeanne, Dir.
Adm: FCFS. **Appl due:** May. **Enr:** 300. **Staff:** Admin 2. Couns 31.
Features: Ecol Environ_Sci Lang Crafts Dance Drama Fine_Arts Music Photog Archery Boating Canoe Conservation Cooking Farm Fishing Hiking Kayak Riding Riflery Ropes_ Crse Baseball Basketball Equestrian Softball Swim Watersports.
Fees 2011: Res $450-655, 1 wk. Day $285-465, 1 wk.
Housing: Cabins Tepees. **Swimming:** Lake.
Nonprofit. **Spons:** Worcester County 4-H Center. **Ses:** 6. **Wks/ses:** 1. Operates July-Aug.

Marshall's recreational program provides most traditional camping activities, including arts and crafts, drama, boating, canoeing, hiking and sports. The Cloverleaf day program (ages 6-8) offers daily activities, an animal farm and mandatory swimming lessons. Older campers may enroll in one of three specialty horseback riding programs.

CAMP WINGATE KIRKLAND
Res — Coed Ages 8-15

Yarmouth Port, MA 02675. 79 White Rock Rd. Tel: 508-362-3798. Fax: 508-362-1614.
www.campwk.com   E-mail: heycamp@campwk.com
Sandy Rubenstein & Will Rubenstein, Dirs.
Grades 3-10. Adm: FCFS. **Appl due:** Mar. **Enr:** 185. **Enr cap:** 185. **Staff:** Admin 4. Couns 50.
Features: Crafts Creative_Writing Dance Music Painting Photog Theater Aquatics Archery Bicycle_Tours Boating Canoe Chess Climbing_Wall Community_Serv Conservation Deep-sea Fishing Fishing Hiking Kayak Mtn_Biking Ropes_Crse Sail Yoga Badminton Baseball Basketball Fencing Golf Gymnastics Lacrosse Martial_Arts Soccer Softball Street_Hockey Swim Tennis Track Ultimate_Frisbee Volleyball Watersports Wrestling.
Fees 2012: Res $3750-9775, 2-7 wks.
Housing: Cabins. Avg per room/unit: 12. **Swimming:** Pond Ocean.
Est 1957. Inc. **Ses:** 4. **Wks/ses:** 2-7. Operates June-Aug. ACA.

This traditional camp features team and individual sports, aquatics, performing arts, community service and horseback riding. Boys and girls make selections for four instructional periods each day. Campers explore Cape Cod through field trips to local sites of interest and recreational areas, and WK also schedules longer excursions to such destinations as Provincetown, Boston's Museum of Science, water parks and professional baseball games. Rising third, fourth and fifth graders only may attend the two-week session, while rising high school sophomores must enroll for the full season.

MICHIGAN

CAMP KIDWELL
Res — Coed Ages 7-16; Day — Coed 4-16

Allegan, MI.
Contact (Year-round): 39000 1st Ave, Bloomingdale, MI 49026. Tel: 269-521-3559.
Fax: 269-521-3623.
www.campkidwell.org   E-mail: campkidwell@btc-bci.com
K. J. Kelly, Dir.
Adm: FCFS. **Appl due:** Rolling. **Enr:** 65. **Enr cap:** 80. **Staff:** Admin 3. Couns 16. Res 25.
Features: Astron Crafts Creative_Writing Dance Drama Aquatics Archery Boating Canoe Climbing_Wall Community_Serv Cooking Hiking Kayak Outdoor_Ed Rappelling Riding Riflery Ropes_Crse Wilderness_Camp Baseball Basketball Equestrian Football Soccer Softball Swim Volleyball Watersports.

Fees 2010: Res $300 (+$15-30), 1 wk. **Day** $200 (+$15-30), 1 wk. Aid 2009 (Need): $30,000.
Housing: Cabins Tents. Avg per room/unit: 12. **Swimming:** Lake.
Est 1949. Nonprofit. **Spons:** Allegan County 4-H Clubs. **Ses:** 6. **Wks/ses:** 1. Operates June-Aug. ACA.

This 4-H camp occupies 150 acres near Eagle Lake. Kidwell offers traditional camp activities in both small groups and campwide sessions. During certain weeks, campers may choose a focus area to extend the session of their favorite activity. Facilities include a ropes course, horse corral, sports fields, fishing dock and water trampoline. While the camp is not specifically designed for special-needs children, boys and girls with attentional disorders are considered on a case-by-case basis.

CAMP WALDEN
Res — Coed Ages 7-17

Cheboygan, MI 49721. 5607 S River Rd. Tel: 231-625-2050. Fax: 231-625-2600.
Contact (Sept-May): 2335 Mistletoe Ave, Fort Worth, TX 76110. Tel: 817-923-9536.
  Fax: 817-923-7992.
www.campwaldenmi.com   E-mail: summer@campwaldenmi.com
Larry Stevens, Ina Stevens, Liz Stephens & Scott Ruthart, Dirs.
Grades 2-12. Adm: FCFS. Admitted: 100%. **Appl due:** Rolling. **Enr:** 200. **Enr cap:** 250.
  Staff: Admin 11. Couns 100.
Travel: MI Canada.
Features: Astron Environ_Sci Writing/Journ Crafts Dance Fine_Arts Media Music Photog Theater Aquatics Archery Canoe Farm Fishing Hiking Kayak Mtn_Biking Outdoor_Ed Riding Sail Wilderness_Camp Yoga Aerobics Basketball Cross-country Equestrian Fencing Football Golf Gymnastics Lacrosse Rugby Soccer Softball Swim Tennis Ultimate_Frisbee Volleyball Water-skiing Watersports.
Fees 2012: Res $2700-7200 (+$250), 2-7 wks.
Housing: Cabins. Avg per room/unit: 11-14. **Swimming:** Lake.
Est 1959. Inc. **Ses:** 6. **Wks/ses:** 2-7. Operates June-Aug. ACA.

Walden's extensive activity program incorporates the arts, English riding, and many traditional land and water pursuits. The camp also offers one- to three-night hiking trips to locations in northern Michigan, as well as day trips to the nearby Mackinac Island. Among the camp's special events are carnivals, color competitions, counselor hunts, scavenger hunts and campfires.

LAKE OF THE WOODS CAMP
GREENWOODS CAMP
Res — Coord Ages 7-15

Decatur, MI 49045. 84600 47½ St. Tel: 269-423-3091. Fax: 269-423-8889.
Contact (Sept-May): 650 Vernon Ave, Apt 202, Glencoe, IL 60022. Tel: 847-242-0009.
  Fax: 847-242-0008.
Year-round Toll-free: 888-459-2492.
www.lakeofthewoodscamp.com   E-mail: info@lwcgwc.com
Dayna Glasson Hardin, Dir.
Adm: FCFS. **Appl due:** Rolling. **Enr:** 165-200. **Staff:** Admin 5. Couns 150.
Features: Computers Crafts Dance Fine_Arts Painting Theater Archery Canoe Climbing_Wall Fishing Kayak Outdoor_Ed Riding Riflery Sail Wilderness_Camp Yoga Aerobics Baseball Basketball Equestrian Football Golf Gymnastics Lacrosse Roller_Hockey Soccer Softball Swim Tennis Volleyball Water-skiing Wrestling.
Fees 2012: Res $2550-8000 (+$90), 2-8 wks.
Housing: Cabins. Avg per room/unit: 14. **Swimming:** Lake Pool.
Est 1935. Inc. **Ses:** 7. **Wks/ses:** 2-8. Operates June-Aug. ACA.

Lake of the Woods for girls and Greenwoods for boys provide individualized programming for each camper that includes camp craft, swimming, archery, canoeing, golf, guitar, riflery, sailing, rowing, team sports, tennis, horseback riding, water-skiing, arts and crafts, computer instruction and tutoring.

SPRINGHILL CAMPS
Res — Coed Ages 7-18

Evart, MI 49631. PO Box 100. Tel: 231-734-2616. Fax: 866-332-5572.
www.springhillcamps.com E-mail: register@springhillcamps.com
Michael Perry, Pres.
Grades 2-PG. Adm: FCFS. **Appl due:** Rolling. **Staff:** Admin 80. Couns 700.
Features: Computers Crafts Drama Aquatics Archery Bicycle_Tours Canoe Climbing_Wall Hiking Mtn_Trips Paintball Rappelling Riding Riflery Rock_Climb Ropes_Crse White-water_Raft Wilderness_Camp Wilderness_Canoe Basketball Equestrian Golf Gymnastics Lacrosse Roller_Hockey Soccer Swim Tennis Volleyball Water-skiing Watersports.
Fees 2012: Res $335-1115 (+$30), ½-2 wks. Aid avail.
Housing: Cabins Tents Tepees. Avg per room/unit: 12. **Swimming:** Lake Pool.
Est 1969. Nonprofit. **Ses:** 10. **Wks/ses:** ½ -2. Operates June-Aug. ACA.

Each session at SpringHill features both a major in which campers receive daily instruction and several minors. Majors include aquatics, BMX biking, Western horsemanship and rock climbing, sports and fine arts. Campers with mental or physical special needs may participate fully in all camp programs.

CRYSTALAIRE ADVENTURES & CAMP LOOKOUT
Res — Coed Ages 8-17; Day — Coed 5-9

Frankfort, MI 49635. PO Box 1129. Tel: 231-352-7589.
www.crystalaireadventures.com; www.lookoutsummer.com
E-mail: info@crystalaireadventures.com; info@lookoutsummer.com
David P. Reid & Kathi Houston, Dirs.
Adm: FCFS. **Appl due:** Rolling. **Enr:** 65. **Enr cap:** 65. **Staff:** Admin 4. Couns 10.
Features: Ecol Environ_Sci Crafts Creative_Writing Dance Fine_Arts Music Painting Studio_Art Theater Adventure_Travel Aquatics Bicycle_Tours Boating Canoe Caving Chess Community_Serv Conservation Cooking Exploration Farm Fishing Hiking Kayak Mtn_Biking Outdoor_Ed Peace/Cross-cultural Sail Social_Servs Survival_Trng Wilderness_Camp Wilderness_Canoe Yoga Baseball Basketball Cricket Cross-country Equestrian Football Rugby Soccer Softball Swim Team_Handball Tennis Ultimate_Frisbee Volleyball Water-skiing Watersports.
Fees 2009: Res $550-1600 (+$10-30), 1-3 wks. Day $180-300, 1-2 wks. Aid 2009 (Need): $1000.
Housing: Cabins. Avg per room/unit: 6. **Swimming:** Lake.
Est 1917. Inc. **Ses:** 8. **Wks/ses:** 1-3. Operates June-Aug.

The individualized, noncompetitive programs at Lookout include swimming, sailing, windsurfing, tennis, creative arts, farm animal care, riding, and frequent overnight backpacking, canoeing and biking trips. In addition to the traditional programs, Crystalaire conducts specialized adventure treks focusing on canoeing, kayaking, caving and backpacking.

CAMP TANUGA
Res — Coed Ages 6-15

Kalkaska, MI 49646. 6874 Camp Tanuga Rd NE. Tel: 231-258-9150. Fax: 231-258-9182.
Contact (Oct-May): 139 W Maple Rd, Ste E, Birmingham, MI 48009. Tel: 248-258-9150.
Fax: 248-258-9467.
www.camptanuga.com E-mail: info@camptanuga.com

Mark Coden & Sid Friedman, Dirs.
Grades 1-9. Adm: FCFS. **Appl due:** Rolling. **Enr:** 180. **Staff:** Admin 6. Couns 65. Res 100.
Features: Astron Expository_Writing Circus_Skills Crafts Creative_Writing Dance Filmmaking Fine_Arts Music Painting Photog Theater Adventure_Travel Aquatics Archery Boating Canoe Climbing_Wall Fishing Hiking Kayak Mtn_Biking Outdoor_Ed Riding Rock_Climb Ropes_Crse Sail Survival_Trng Wilderness_Camp Wilderness_Canoe Woodcraft Yoga Aerobics Badminton Basketball Equestrian Field_Hockey Football Golf Gymnastics Lacrosse Martial_Arts Roller_Hockey Soccer Softball Street_Hockey Swim Tennis Ultimate_Frisbee Volleyball Water-skiing Watersports Weight_Trng.
Fees 2009: Res $3350-7500 (+$200), 3-7 wks.
Housing: Cabins. Avg per room/unit: 12. **Swimming:** Lake.
Est 1952. Inc. Ses: 3. **Wks/ses:** 3-7. Operates June-Aug.

To accommodate differences among camper abilities and interests, Tanuga allows boys and girls to select up to six instructional activities on two occasions during the session. Programming includes special days at least once a week; these days involve a break from the usual camp structure and may include off-camp excursions or in-camp activities or competitions. Overnight tripping is integral to Tanuga's program, with trips increasing in length and difficulty as campers age.

CAMP MAPLEHURST
Res — Coed Ages 7-17

Kewadin, MI 49648. 12055 Waring Rd. Tel: 231-264-9675. Fax: 231-264-5041.
Contact (Sept-May): 1455 Quarton Rd, Birmingham, MI 48009. Tel: 248-647-2646.
    Fax: 248-647-6716.
www.campmaplehurst.com   E-mail: info@campmaplehurst.com
Laurence Cohn & Brenda Cohn, Dirs.
Grades 2-12. Adm: FCFS. **Appl due:** June. **Enr:** 120. **Enr cap:** 125. **Staff:** Admin 6. Couns 27.
Features: Crafts Creative_Writing Dance Filmmaking Fine_Arts Music Photog Theater Aquatics Archery Canoe Conservation Fishing Kayak Mtn_Biking Riding Riflery Sail Scuba Basketball Equestrian Football Golf Gymnastics Martial_Arts Skateboarding Soccer Softball Swim Tennis Volleyball Water-skiing.
Fees 2011: Res $2595-6295, 2-5 wks.
Housing: Cabins Houses Lodges. Avg per room/unit: 10. **Swimming:** Lake.
Est 1955. Inc. Ses: 6. **Wks/ses:** 2-5. Operates June-Aug.

Maplehurst offers tutoring, astronomy, swimming, sailing, water-skiing, scuba diving, fishing, professional tennis instruction, golf, soccer, and English and Western riding. Arts and crafts offerings include silk-screening, printing, drawing and painting, ceramics, lapidary work and photography.

CEDAR LODGE
Res — Coed Ages 8-16

Lawrence, MI 49064. 47000 52nd St, PO Box 218. Tel: 269-674-8071.
    Fax: 269-674-8071.
www.cedarlodge.com   E-mail: campcedarlodge@gmail.com
Amy Edwards, Dir.
Grades 3-10. Adm: FCFS. **Appl due:** Rolling. **Enr:** 60. **Staff:** Admin 3. Couns 12.
Features: Crafts Dance Drama Music Aquatics Archery Bicycle_Tours Boating Canoe Conservation Fishing Hiking Kayak Mtn_Biking Riding Sail Wilderness_Camp Work Baseball Basketball Equestrian Gymnastics Soccer Softball Swim Ultimate_Frisbee Volleyball Watersports.
Fees 2010: Res $654-4620 (+$110-880), 1-8 wks. Day $380, 1 wk.
Housing: Cabins Lodges. **Swimming:** Lake.

Est 1980. Inc. **Ses:** 8. **Wks/ses:** 1-8. Operates June-Aug. ACA.

In addition to its traditional summer program, the camp offers a complete riding program featuring daily classes and instruction in vaulting, jumping and basic horsemanship. Other scheduled activities are sports, biking, swimming, canoeing, and arts and crafts. Show Team is a program for advanced riders who spend a week in concentrated lessons, demonstrations and preparation for weekend shows.

CAMP NEWAYGO
Res — Girls Ages 7-17; Day — Coed 5-9

Newaygo, MI 49337. 5333 Centerline Rd, PO Box 610. Tel: 231-924-0641.
Fax: 231-652-2542.
www.campnewaygo.org   E-mail: campnewaygo@ncats.net
Jane Vitek, Dir.
Adm: FCFS. **Appl due:** Rolling. **Enr:** 125. **Staff:** Admin 5. Couns 40.
Features: Astron Ecol Environ_Sci Geol Sci Circus_Skills Crafts Creative_Writing Dance Fine_Arts Music Painting Photog Studio_Art Theater Adventure_Travel Aquatics Archery Boating Canoe Climbing_Wall Community_Serv Conservation Cooking Exploration Farm Fishing Hiking Kayak Mtn_Biking Outdoor_Ed Riding Ropes_Crse Sail Survival_Trng Wilderness_Camp Wilderness_Canoe Woodcraft Yoga Aerobics Basketball Equestrian Fencing Swim Tennis Ultimate_Frisbee Volleyball Water-skiing Watersports.
Fees 2009: Res $312-838, ½-2 wks. Day $150, 1 wk. Aid (Need).
Housing: Cabins Dorms Lodges Tents. **Swimming:** Lake.
Est 1926. Nonprofit. **Spons:** Newaygo County Community Services. **Ses:** 6. **Wks/ses:** ½-2. Operates June-Aug.

Situated on an 101-acre wooded ridge in the Manistee National Forest region, the camp offers traditional recreational programming for girls from all over the world. Newaygo schedules three instructional periods per day, as well as a fourth noninstructional activity period featuring open waterfront offerings and crafts. Cookouts, evening activities and overnight camping opportunities complete the program. In addition to its girls' residential camp, Newaygo operates six weeklong day camps each summer for young boys and girls.

CAMP WESTMINSTER
Res — Coed Ages 7-17; Day — Coed 7-12

Roscommon, MI 48653. 116 Westminster Dr. Tel: 989-821-9474. Fax: 989-821-7462.
Contact (Sept-May): 17567 Hubbell Ave, Detroit, MI 48235. Tel: 313-341-8969.
Fax: 313-341-8616.
www.campwestminster.com   E-mail: info@campwestminster.com
Suzanne Getz Bates, Exec Dir.
Grades 2-12. **Adm:** FCFS. **Appl due:** Rolling. **Enr:** 100. **Enr cap:** 100. **Staff:** Admin 5. Couns 20.
Features: Crafts Dance Music Theater Adventure_Travel Aquatics Archery Canoe Climbing_Wall Exploration Fishing Hiking Kayak Outdoor_Ed Rock_Climb Ropes_Crse Sail Seamanship Survival_Trng Wilderness_Camp Wilderness_Canoe Baseball Basketball Soccer Swim Tennis Volleyball Watersports.
Fees 2009: Res $235-795 (+$10-50), ½-2 wks. Day $235 (+$10), 1 wk. Aid (Need).
Housing: Cabins Tents. Avg per room/unit: 7. **Swimming:** Lake River.
Est 1925. Nonprofit. Presbyterian. **Ses:** 26. **Wks/ses:** ½-2. Operates June-Aug. ACA.

Westminster's programs for children in grades 2-5 include a session for first-time campers; a music, art and drama camp; a pioneer adventure camp; and fishing and swimming programs. Middle school campers (grades 6-8) may focus on sailing, climbing, backpacking, fishing, art or swimming. Programs for boys and girls in grades 9-12 emphasize leadership development, sailing, backpacking, canoe tripping or climbing.

MINIWANCA
Res — Coord Ages 8-17; Day — Coord 6-12

Shelby, MI 49455. c/o American Youth Foundation, 8845 W Garfield Rd.
   Tel: 231-861-2262. Fax: 231-861-5244.
www.ayf.com   E-mail: miniwancacamps@ayf.com
Tom Moore, Dir.
Grades 1-12. Adm: FCFS. **Appl due:** Apr. **Enr:** 300. **Staff:** Couns 80.
Features: Crafts Dance Music Theater Aquatics Archery Bicycle_Tours Boating Canoe
   Climbing_Wall Fishing Hiking Kayak Mtn_Biking Rappelling Riding Ropes_Crse Sail
   Wilderness_Camp Wilderness_Canoe Woodcraft Baseball Basketball Soccer Softball
   Swim Tennis Volleyball Watersports.
Fees 2012: Res $840-5355, 1-6 wks. Day $160, 1 wk.
Housing: Cabins Houses. **Swimming:** Lake Stream.
Est 1925. Nonprofit. **Spons:** American Youth Foundation. Ecumenical. **Ses:** 3. **Wks/ses:**
   2-6. Operates June-Aug.

Separate but concurrent camps serve boys and girls at this traditional camp. An array of recreational and artistic activities appeals to boys and girls with varying interests. Older campers may embark on five- to 25-day sailing or wilderness adventure trips. Weeklong day-only sessions serve children entering grades 1-6.

WOLVERINE CAMPS
Res — Coed Ages 10-17

Wolverine, MI 49799. PO Box 217. Tel: 231-525-8211. Fax: 231-525-6112.
www.wolverinecamps.com   E-mail: camps@wolverinecamps.com
John Zimmerle & Erik Schupbach, Dirs.
Grades 5-12. Adm: FCFS. **Appl due:** Rolling. **Staff:** Admin 3. Couns 12.
Features: Creative_Writing Music Studio_Art Theater Outdoor_Ed Rock_Climb Ropes_
   Crse Basketball Cross-country Soccer Swim.
Fees 2011: Res $195-395 (+$25), ½-1 wk.
Housing: Dorms Lodges. **Swimming:** Lake River.
Est 1968. Inc. **Ses:** 22. **Wks/ses:** ½-1. Operates June-Aug.

Wolverine conducts a variety of specialty camps in athletics and the arts. Boys and girls choose from separately conducted theater arts, creative writing, art, basketball, soccer, vocal music, adventure, volleyball, orchestra, cross-country, instrumental band, marching band, and (for school groups) outdoor education and adventure camps.

MINNESOTA

CAMP THUNDERBIRD FOR BOYS
CAMP THUNDERBIRD FOR GIRLS
Res — Coord Ages 8-16

Bemidji, MN 56601. 20758 County 9. Tel: 218-751-5171. Fax: 314-596-4228.
Contact (Sept-May): 802 De Mun Ave, St Louis, MO 63105. Tel: 314-647-3168.
   Fax: 314-647-7218.
www.camptbird.com   E-mail: mail@camptbird.com
Shari Sigoloff & Roger Bristowe, Dirs.
Grades 2-10. Adm: FCFS. **Appl due:** Apr. **Enr:** 350. **Staff:** Admin 12. Couns 160.
Features: Crafts Music Photog Theater Adventure_Travel Aquatics Archery Bicycle_Tours
   Canoe Climbing_Wall Conservation Fishing Hiking Kayak Mountaineering Mtn_Biking
   Riding Riflery Rock_Climb Sail Seamanship Wilderness_Camp Wilderness_Canoe

Woodcraft Baseball Basketball Equestrian Football Golf Gymnastics Soccer Softball Swim Tennis Water-skiing Watersports.
Fees 2012: Res $4800-8750, 3-8 wks.
Housing: Cabins. Avg per room/unit: 8. **Swimming:** Lake.
Est 1946. Inc. **Ses:** 7. **Wks/ses:** 3-8. Operates June-Aug. ACA.

Located on a 450-acre tract that includes four and a half miles of beach, Thunderbird for Boys features both English and Western riding, extended backpacking trips for older campers, aquatics and crafts. Thunderbird for Girls, which occupies an adjacent 250-acre tract of deciduous and pine forest with a mile of sand beach, features both English and Western riding, extended backpacking trips for older campers, aquatics and crafts. Other activities include music, dramatics, ecology, sports, sailing, fishing, bicycling, water-skiing and sailboarding. Qualified campers may embark on a 21-day canoeing trip.

CAMP CHIPPEWA
Res — Boys Ages 7-17

Cass Lake, MN 56633. 22767 Cap Endres Rd. Tel: 218-335-8807. Fax: 218-335-7742.
Contact (Sept-May): 15 E 5th St, Ste 4022, Tulsa, OK 74103. Tel: 918-599-7968.
  Fax: 918-582-7896.
Year-round Toll-free: 800-262-1544.
www.campchippewa.com   E-mail: mike@campchippewa.com
Michael K. Thompson & Natalie Thompson, Dirs.
Grades 3-12. Adm: FCFS. **Appl due:** Rolling. **Enr:** 68. **Enr cap:** 68. **Staff:** Admin 3. Couns 24.
Features: Aquatics Archery Canoe Conservation Exploration Kayak Riflery Sail Wilderness_Camp Wilderness_Canoe Basketball Fencing Soccer Swim Tennis Water-skiing.
Fees 2012: Res $2850-8300 (+$50), 2-8 wks.
Housing: Cabins. Avg per room/unit: 6. **Swimming:** Lake.
Est 1935. Nonprofit. **Ses:** 5. **Wks/ses:** 2-8. Operates June-Aug. ACA.

Chippewa's in-camp program includes tennis, archery, riflery, sailing, swimming, fencing, soccer and canoe tripping. One- to 21-day Canadian wilderness canoe trips and four-day fishing expeditions are available to qualified campers. Two-week sessions are open to boys entering grades 3-6 only; other campers enroll for four or eight weeks.

CAMP VOYAGEUR
Res — Boys Ages 9-18

Ely, MN 55731. PO Box 420. Tel: 218-365-6042, 800-950-7291.
www.campvoyageur.com   E-mail: cvspirit@campvoyageur.com
John C. Erdmann & Deb Erdmann, Dirs.
Adm: FCFS. **Staff:** Admin 4. Couns 13.
Features: Crafts Canoe Fishing Hiking Sail Wilderness_Camp Wilderness_Canoe Baseball Basketball Football Swim Tennis.
Fees 2012: Res $3400-6800 (+$150), 4-8 wks.
Housing: Cabins. **Swimming:** Lake.
Est 1951. Inc. **Ses:** 2. **Wks/ses:** 4. Operates June-Aug. ACA.

At Voyageur, campers receive training in canoeing and minimum-impact camping and are assigned to trips according to their interests and abilities. While experienced campers may spend up to half their time on the trail, those remaining at the base camp may participate in team and individual sports, water-skiing, swimming, fishing, sailing, arts and crafts, and other traditional activities.

CAMP MISHAWAKA FOR BOYS
CAMP MISHAWAKA FOR GIRLS
Res — Coord Ages 8-15

Grand Rapids, MN 55744. Mishawaka Rd, PO Box 368. Tel: 218-326-5011, 800-308-5011. Fax: 218-326-9228.
www.campmishawaka.com   E-mail: info@campmishawaka.com
Steve Purdum & Julie Purdum, Dirs.
Grades 3-10. Adm: FCFS. **Appl due:** Rolling. **Enr:** 140. **Enr cap:** 160. **Staff:** Admin 10.
Features: Drama Aquatics Archery Boating Canoe Climbing_Wall Fishing Hiking Kayak Mtn_Biking Riding Ropes_Crse Sail Wilderness_Camp Wilderness_Canoe Baseball Basketball Equestrian Soccer Softball Swim Tennis Volleyball Water-skiing.
Fees 2012: Res $2450-7300 (+$100-400), 2-8 wks.
Swimming: Lake.
Est 1910. Inc. Ses: 6. **Wks/ses:** 2-8. Operates June-Aug. ACA.

Located on Lake Pokegama, these brother and sister camps conduct a rotating schedule of activities. Morning pursuits follow a two-week rotation, while afternoons are planned on a daily basis. Options include swimming, sailing, canoeing, boating, windsurfing, fishing, land sports, riflery, soccer, archery and tennis. Campwide games, camping trips and special events take place in the evening. The two camps share many facilities and traditions, and certain activities are coeducational.

CAMP LINCOLN FOR BOYS
CAMP LAKE HUBERT FOR GIRLS
Res — Coord Ages 8-17

Lake Hubert, MN 56459. PO Box 1308. Tel: 218-963-2339. Fax: 218-963-2447.
Contact (Sept-May): 10179 Crosstown Cir, Eden Prairie, MN 55344.
**   Tel: 952-922-2545. Fax: 952-922-7149.**
Year-round Toll-free: 800-242-1909.
www.lincoln-lakehubert.com   E-mail: home@lincoln-lakehubert.com
Sam Cote & Bill Jones, Dirs.
Grades 3-11. Adm: FCFS. **Appl due:** Rolling. **Enr:** 200. **Enr cap:** 200. **Staff:** Admin 20. Couns 120.
Features: Crafts Dance Media Theater Aquatics Archery Canoe Chess Climbing_Wall Fishing Hiking Kayak Mtn_Biking Paintball Riding Riflery Ropes_Crse Sail Social_Servs Wilderness_Camp Wilderness_Canoe Yoga Aerobics Baseball Basketball Cricket Football Golf Gymnastics Lacrosse Martial_Arts Soccer Softball Street_Hockey Swim Tennis Ultimate_Frisbee Volleyball Watersports Weight_Trng.
Fees 2012: Res $650-7300 (+$150-300), 1-8 wks. Aid 2011 (Need): $50,000.
Housing: Cabins. Avg per room/unit: 18. **Swimming:** Lake.
Est 1909. Inc. Ses: 10. **Wks/ses:** 1-8. Operates June-Aug. ACA.

Camp Lincoln and its sister camp, Lake Hubert, feature riding, canoeing trips, sailing, riflery, arts and crafts, nature study and wilderness experiences in two-, three- and four-week traditional sessions. Weeklong sessions consisting of professional golf and tennis instruction are also available, as is a 10-day coeducational session in August for campers who have completed grades 3-9.

CAMP BIRCHWOOD
Res — Girls Ages 7-17

LaPorte, MN 56461. 6983 N Steamboat Lake Dr NW. Tel: 218-335-6706.
**   Fax: 218-335-7866.**
Contact (Sept-May): 1035 Vermont St, Ste B, Lawrence, KS 66044. Tel: 785-865-1557.
**   Fax: 785-865-4313.**

Year-round Toll-free: 800-451-5270.
www.campbirchwood.com   E-mail: cbgwc@aol.com
Terry Bredemus & Rachel Bredemus, Dirs.
Grades 2-12. Adm: FCFS. **Appl due:** Rolling.
Features: Crafts Archery Canoe Fishing Kayak Mtn_Biking Riding Riflery Sail Wilderness_ Camp Swim Tennis Water-skiing.
Fees 2011: Res $1450-4280, 1-4 wks.
Housing: Cabins. **Swimming:** Lake.
Est 1959. Ses: 8. **Wks/ses:** 1-4. Operates June-Aug. ACA.

The camp, which emphasizes seamanship and riding, also offers a range of watersports and land sports. Wilderness canoe trips last for up to two weeks.

CAMP FOLEY
Res — Coed Ages 8-16

Pine River, MN 56474. 9303 Father Foley Dr. Tel: 218-543-6161. Fax: 218-543-4269.
www.campfoley.com   E-mail: fun@campfoley.com
Marie Schmid, Dir.
Adm: FCFS. **Appl due:** Rolling. **Enr:** 165. **Staff:** Admin 6. Couns 44.
Features: Crafts Aquatics Archery Boating Canoe Climbing_Wall Fishing Hiking Mtn_Biking Outdoor_Ed Paintball Riflery Sail Wilderness_Canoe Woodcraft Basketball Cross-country Fencing Soccer Swim Tennis Weight_Trng.
Fees 2012: Res $1100-4100, 1-4 wks.
Housing: Cabins. Avg per room/unit: 10. **Swimming:** Lake.
Est 1924. Ses: 4. **Wks/ses:** 1-4. Operates June-Aug. ACA.

The camp places emphasis on such water activities as swimming, water-skiing, wilderness canoe tripping and a specialized sailing program. An array of traditional recreational pursuits completes the program.

MISSOURI

SHERWOOD FOREST CAMP
Res — Coed Ages 7-16

Lesterville, MO 63654. PO Box 210. Tel: 573-637-2476. Fax: 573-637-2478.
Contact (Winter): 2708 Sutton Blvd, St Louis, MO 63143. Tel: 314-644-3322.
   Fax: 314-644-3330.
www.sherwoodforestcamp.com   E-mail: office@sherwoodforestcamp.com
Michael Castulik, Dir.
Adm: FCFS. **Appl due:** Rolling. **Enr cap:** 450. **Staff:** Admin 7. Couns 50.
Features: Astron Ecol Writing/Journ Crafts Adventure_Travel Aquatics Archery Canoe Hiking Ropes_Crse Wilderness_Camp Swim.
Fees 2012: Res $50, 1-7½ wks.
Housing: Cabins. **Swimming:** Pool.
Est 1937. Nonprofit. **Ses:** 4. **Wks/ses:** 1-4. Operates June-Aug. ACA.

Serving economically disadvantaged children primarily from Greater St. Louis, Sherwood Forest operates three distinct summer programs. Children ages 7-8 take part in a structured, six-day minicamp designed to introduce them to summer camping. The program for 9- to 10-year-olds helps children develop new skills, enhance interpersonal relationships and learn about various program options. A third program assists adolescents ages 11-16 with leadership skills development by exposing them to various wilderness camping and team-building experiences.

CAMP TAUM SAUK
Res — Coed Ages 8-15

Lesterville, MO 63654. 499 County Rd 368. Tel: 573-637-2489.
Contact (Sept-May): 14 Rio Vista Dr, St Louis, MO 63124. Tel: 314-993-1655.
Year-round Fax: 314-993-1655.
www.taumsauk.com   E-mail: nsmithcts@aol.com
Nick Smith, Dir.
Adm: FCFS. **Admitted:** 100%. **Appl due:** Rolling. **Enr:** 120. **Enr cap:** 120. **Staff:** Admin 6. Couns 20. Res 65.
Features: Crafts Drama Aquatics Archery Bicycle_Tours Canoe Caving Climbing_Wall Conservation Fishing Hiking Kayak Mtn_Biking Outdoor_Ed Rappelling Riding Riflery Rock_Climb Ropes_Crse Sail Scuba Wilderness_Camp Wilderness_Canoe Badminton Basketball Equestrian Field_Hockey Soccer Softball Street_Hockey Swim Tennis Ultimate_Frisbee Volleyball Watersports.
Fees 2011: Res $825-4150, 1-6 wks. Aid (Merit & Need).
Housing: Cabins Houses Lodges. Avg per room/unit: 10. **Swimming:** Pool River.
Est 1946. Inc. Ses: 5. **Wks/ses:** 1-8. Operates June-Aug. ACA.

Occupying a 145-acre tract along the Black River in the Ozark Mountains, Taum Sauk offers an array of traditional camping activities. The region's varied geology lends itself to caving, rock climbing and exploration, while a high ropes course provides additional challenge for campers.

WENTWORTH MILITARY ACADEMY CAMP LEAD
Res — Coed Ages 12-18

Lexington, MO 64067. 1880 Washington Ave. Tel: 660-259-2221, 800-962-7682.
Fax: 660-259-2677.
www.wma1880.org   E-mail: pratliff@wma.edu
Col. Rick Cotrell, Dir.
Grades 8-12. Adm: FCFS. **Appl due:** Rolling. **Enr:** 100. **Staff:** Admin 30. Couns 9. Res 9.
Features: Computers Eng ESL Lang Marine_Bio/Stud Math Sci Aquatics Canoe Fishing Hiking Milit_Trng Paintball Rappelling Ropes_Crse Survival_Trng Baseball Basketball Golf Soccer Softball Swim Tennis Volleyball Watersports.
Fees 2012: Res $2700-4495 (+$50-350), 3-6 wks.
Housing: Dorms. **Swimming:** Pool.
Est 1940. Nonprofit. Ses: 2. **Wks/ses:** 3-6. Operates June-July.

Conducted on the campus of Wentworth Military Academy, LEAD makes full use of the school's facilities and playing fields. Military training and daily remedial academic instruction are important elements of the program. Activities are planned to meet the campers' interests and needs and include tennis, golf, swimming, team sports and canoeing. Special sessions focus on English as a Second Language and marine biology.

MONTANA

TRAIL'S END RANCH
Res — Coed Ages 8-17; Day — Coed 5-11

Ekalaka, MT 59324. Box 460. Tel: 406-775-6401. Fax: 406-775-6441.
www.ter.org   E-mail: ter@midrivers.com
Bob Anderson, Exec Dir.
Grades 3-12. Adm: FCFS. **Appl due:** Rolling. **Enr:** 127. **Enr cap:** 160. **Staff:** Admin 24. Couns 24. Res 60.

Focus: Religion. **Features:** Relig_Stud Crafts Drama Music Aquatics Archery Climbing_ Wall Hiking Mtn_Biking Outdoor_Ed Paintball Ranch Rappelling Riding Riflery Ropes_ Crse Survival_Trng Wilderness_Camp Woodcraft Working_Cattle_Ranch Baseball Basketball Equestrian Field_Hockey Soccer Softball Swim Ultimate_Frisbee Volleyball.
Fees 2011: Res $299, 1 wk. Day $125, 1 wk. Aid 2007 (Need): $20,000.
Housing: Cabins Tepees. Avg per room/unit: 7. **Swimming:** Pool.
Est 1978. Nonprofit. **Spons:** New Life Fellowship of Montana. Nondenom Christian. **Ses:** 8.
Wks/ses: 1. Operates June-Aug. ACA.

This interdenominational Christian camp, which emphasizes sports and adventure, offers crafts, music, drama, BMX and mountain biking, and other recreational activities. An equestrian program features trail rides, vaulting and roping, while the high adventure program features rappelling, ropes courses, a zip line and a climbing tower.

NEW HAMPSHIRE

KABEYUN
Res — Boys Ages 7-15

Alton Bay, NH 03810. PO Box 325. Tel: 603-875-3060. Fax: 603-875-3060.
www.kabeyun.org
Ken Robbins, Dir.
Adm: FCFS. **Appl due:** Rolling. **Staff:** Admin 2. Couns 40.
Features: Crafts Music Photog Theater Aquatics Archery Canoe Fishing Hiking Kayak Mountaineering Mtn_Trips Ropes_Crse Sail Wilderness_Camp Wilderness_Canoe Woodcraft Badminton Baseball Basketball Soccer Street_Hockey Swim Tennis Waterskiing.
Fees 2012: Res $3750-7900 (+$25), 3-8 wks.
Housing: Cabins. **Swimming:** Lake.
Est 1924. Nonprofit. **Ses:** 4. **Wks/ses:** 3-8. Operates June-Aug.

Kabeyun allows boys to choose their own activities from such options as music, drama, rock climbing, canoeing, sailing, water-skiing, windsurfing, hiking, swimming and noncompetitive athletics. One- to six-day backpacking, canoeing, rock climbing and white-water rafting trips are also available. A three-week introductory session enrolls children ages 7-9 only.

CAMP QUINEBARGE
Res and Day — Coed Ages 7-15

Center Harbor, NH 03226. PO Box 608. Tel: 603-253-6029, 800-869-8497.
Fax: 603-253-6027.
www.campquinebarge.com   E-mail: adventures@campquinebarge.com
Thomas H. Hannaford, Dir.
Grades 2-10. Adm: FCFS. **Appl due:** Rolling. **Enr:** 70. **Enr cap:** 100. **Staff:** Admin 4. Couns 24.
Features: Crafts Fine_Arts Photog Aquatics Archery Bicycle_Tours Boating Canoe Climbing_Wall Conservation Exploration Fishing Hiking Kayak Mountaineering Mtn_Biking Mtn_Trips Outdoor_Ed Riding Rock_Climb Ropes_Crse Sail White-water_Raft Wilderness_Camp Wilderness_Canoe Woodcraft Baseball Basketball Equestrian Fencing Gymnastics Lacrosse Soccer Softball Swim Tennis Volleyball Watersports.
Fees 2012: Res $1750-5250 (+$25), 2-7 wks. Day $350-1875, 1-7 wks. Aid 2009 (Need): $18,000.
Housing: Cabins. Avg per room/unit: 6-8. **Swimming:** Lake.
Est 1936. Inc. **Ses:** 7. **Wks/ses:** 1-7. Operates June-Aug.

Located on Lake Kanasatka, Quinebarge features land sports, nature activities, watersports, crafts and horseback riding. Day and overnight trips enable boys and girls to further develop their canoeing, hiking, camping, fishing, backpacking, mountain biking and white-water rafting skills. Campers attend from throughout the US and from such countries as France, Estonia, Latvia, Russia, Mexico, Spain and Germany.

CAMP MERROWVISTA
Res — Coed Ages 8-17; Day — Coed 5-8

Center Tuftonboro, NH 03816. 147 Canaan Rd. Tel: 603-539-6607. Fax: 603-539-7504.
www.ayf.com   E-mail: merrowvistacamps@ayf.com
Kris Light, Dir.
Grades K-12. Adm: FCFS. **Appl due:** Rolling. **Enr:** 221-287. **Enr cap:** 300.
Travel: ME Canada.
Features: Crafts Dance Painting Theater Woodworking Adventure_Travel Aquatics Archery Bicycle_Tours Canoe Climbing_Wall Community_Serv Exploration Fishing Hiking Kayak Mtn_Trips Outdoor_Ed Ropes_Crse Sail Survival_Trng Wilderness_Camp Wilderness_ Canoe Yoga Baseball Basketball Field_Hockey Football Lacrosse Rugby Soccer Softball Swim Ultimate_Frisbee Volleyball.
Fees 2012: Res $815-3995 **(+$40-80), 1-4 wks. Day** $175, 1 wk. Aid (Need).
Housing: Cabins. Avg per room/unit: 6. **Swimming:** Lake.
Est 1924. Nonprofit. **Spons:** American Youth Foundation. **Ses:** 20. **Wks/ses:** 1-4. Operates June-Aug. ACA.

Merrowvista's program comprises a progression of age-appropriate activities and experiences. Campers ages 8-13 engage in a range of pursuits that includes sports, windsurfing, sailing, woodworking, nature and the arts. Boys and girls ages 14-17 take part in a series of four- to 21-day wilderness adventure trips in New England and Canada that includes bicycle tours, canoeing and backpacking. Weeklong introductory camps enroll children entering grades 3-7.

WILLIAM LAWRENCE CAMP
Res — Boys Ages 8-15

Center Tuftonboro, NH 03816. 139 Federal Corner Rd. Tel: 603-569-3698.
Fax: 603-569-5468.
www.wlcamp.org   E-mail: knoll@wlcamp.org
Nat Crane, Dir.
Grades 3-10. Adm: FCFS. **Appl due:** Rolling. **Enr:** 112. **Staff:** Admin 10. Couns 35.
Features: Crafts Aquatics Archery Boating Canoe Climbing_Wall Fishing Hiking Kayak Mountaineering Mtn_Trips Outdoor_Ed Riflery Rock_Climb Ropes_Crse Sail Survival_ Trng Wilderness_Camp Wilderness_Canoe Woodcraft Baseball Basketball Cricket Lacrosse Soccer Street_Hockey Swim Tennis Volleyball Water-skiing.
Fees 2012: Res $1975-4900 **(+$100-200), 2-7 wks.** Aid (Need).
Housing: Cabins. Avg per room/unit: 8. **Swimming:** Lake.
Est 1913. Nonprofit. **Ses:** 6. **Wks/ses:** 2-7. Operates June-Aug. ACA.

William Lawrence's program includes team sports, tripping, watersports, tennis, archery, art, riflery, sailing, canoeing and a ropes course. The camp organizes two- to four-day backpacking and canoeing trips for interested campers. Two-week sessions are available to boys entering grades 3-8. Sixteen-year-olds may enroll in a leader-in-training program.

CAMP TOHKOMEUPOG
Res — Boys Ages 8-16

East Madison, NH 03849. 2151 E Madison Rd. Tel: 603-367-8362, 800-414-2267.
Fax: 603-367-8664.

www.tohko.com   E-mail: tohko@tohko.com
Andrew Mahoney, Dir.
Grades 3-11. Adm: FCFS. **Appl due:** Rolling. **Enr:** 110. **Staff:** Admin 7. Couns 22.
Features: Crafts Aquatics Archery Boating Canoe Climbing_Wall Field_Ecol Fishing Hiking Kayak Mountaineering Mtn_Biking Mtn_Trips Rappelling Riflery Rock_Climb Ropes_Crse Sail Wilderness_Camp Baseball Basketball Football Golf Lacrosse Soccer Street_Hockey Swim Tennis Track Volleyball Water-skiing Watersports.
Fees 2012: Res $2390-5895 (+$10-70), 2-7 wks.
Housing: Cabins Lodges Tepees. **Swimming:** Lake.
Est 1932. Inc. **Ses:** 7. **Wks/ses:** 2-7. Operates June-Aug. ACA.

Tohkomeupog's location on 1000 acres of woodland and lakes offers opportunities for outdoor living, numerous climbing excursions to the nearby White Mountains, waterfront activities, sports and hobbies. Tutoring is available.

CAMP WAUKEELA
Res — Girls Ages 8-15

Eaton Center, NH 03832. PO Box 265. Tel: 603-447-2260. Fax: 603-447-1387.
Contact (Winter): 22 Clifford St, Portland, ME 04102. Tel: 207-774-7777.
   Fax: 207-774-1311.
Year-round Toll-free: 800-626-0207.
www.waukeela.com   E-mail: phil@waukeela.com
Phil Steele, Dir.
Grades 3-10. Adm: FCFS. **Appl due:** Rolling. **Enr:** 130. **Staff:** Couns 55.
Features: Art Crafts Dance Drama Music Photog Pottery Archery Canoe Kayak Riding Riflery Sail Swim Tennis Watersports.
Fees 2012: Res $3050-7150, 2-8 wks.
Housing: Cabins. **Swimming:** Lake.
Est 1922. Ses: 5. **Wks/ses:** 2-8. Operates June-Aug.

Located in the White Mountains of New Hampshire, Waukeela offers activities in seven departments: creative arts, performing arts, land sports, swimming, boating, outdoor adventure and horseback riding.

FLEUR DE LIS CAMP
Res — Girls Ages 8-15

Fitzwilliam, NH 03447. 120 Howeville Rd. Tel: 603-585-7751. Fax: 603-585-7751.
www.fleurdeliscamp.org   E-mail: carrie@fleurdeliscamp.org
Carrie Kashawlic, Exec Dir.
Grades 3-10. Adm: FCFS. **Appl due:** Apr. **Enr:** 100. **Staff:** Admin 7. Couns 26.
Features: Writing/Journ Crafts Dance Drama Filmmaking Photog Aquatics Archery Boating Canoe Hiking Kayak Riding Riflery Sail Basketball Equestrian Soccer Softball Swim Tennis Volleyball Water-skiing Watersports.
Fees 2011: Res $2500-6500 (+$75-140), 2-7 wks. Aid (Need).
Housing: Cabins Tents. **Swimming:** Lake.
Est 1929. Nonprofit. **Ses:** 7. **Wks/ses:** 2-7. Operates June-Aug. ACA.

Fleur de Lis offers such land sports and watersports as sailing, swimming, water-skiing, windsurfing, riding, tennis, riflery, crafts and theater arts. Girls may take part in a riding program for an additional fee.

CODY CAMPS
Res — Coed Ages 7-15

Freedom, NH 03836. 9 Cody Rd. Tel: 603-539-4997, 800-399-4436. Fax: 603-539-5840.

www.cody.org   E-mail: info@cody.org
Nick Robbins, Dir.
Adm: FCFS. **Appl due:** Rolling. **Enr:** 200. **Staff:** Admin 5. Couns 75. Res 80.
Features: Geol Crafts Dance Music Photog Theater Adventure_Travel Aquatics Archery Bicycle_Tours Boating Canoe Cooking Deep-sea Fishing Fishing Hiking Kayak Mtn_ Biking Mtn_Trips Outdoor_Ed Riflery Sail Scuba White-water_Raft Wilderness_Camp Baseball Basketball Football Lacrosse Soccer Softball Street_Hockey Swim Tennis Volleyball Water-skiing Watersports.
Fees 2010: Res $1295-6295 (+$200-400), 2-6 wks.
Housing: Cabins. Avg per room/unit: 10. **Swimming:** Lake.
Est 1926. Inc. Ses: 9. **Wks/ses:** 2-6. Operates June-Aug.

Operating distinct programs for boys and girls, Cody allows campers to select more of their activities as they mature. The youngest campers follow a highly structured program that results in their sampling as many different activities as possible. By age 13, boys and girls choose all six of their daily activities, enabling them to receive in-depth instruction in their favorite activities. Two daily activities are specialty clinics of a week's duration that permit especially high levels of instruction.

CRAGGED MOUNTAIN FARM
Res — Coed Ages 5-13

Freedom, NH 03836. 239 Cold Brook Rd. Tel: 603-539-4070.
Contact (Sept-June): 330 Washington St, Apt 3, Brookline, MA 02445.
   Tel: 617-739-6147.
Year-round Fax: 603-669-9330.
www.craggedmountainfarm.com   E-mail: kathy7@aol.com
Katherine Utter, Dir.
Grades K-8. Adm: FCFS. **Appl due:** Rolling. **Enr:** 70. **Enr cap:** 70. **Staff:** Admin 3. Couns 16. Res 35.
Features: Crafts Music Photog Studio_Art Aquatics Canoe Climbing_Wall Hiking Mountaineering Mtn_Trips Wilderness_Camp Wilderness_Canoe Yoga Soccer Swim Ultimate_Frisbee.
Fees 2012: Res $2000-3200, 2-4 wks. Aid 2010 (Need): $5000.
Housing: Cabins. Avg per room/unit: 7. **Swimming:** Lake River Stream.
Est 1927. Inc. Ses: 5. **Wks/ses:** 2-4. Operates June-Aug.

This nonregimented camp features day and overnight canoe and hiking trips, as well as swimming, arts and crafts, photography, nature, sports, games and music. Adventure options include a climbing wall and a month-long tripping program for 14-year-olds.

CAMP ROBIN HOOD
Res — Coed Ages 8-16

Freedom, NH 03836. 65 Robin Hood Ln. Tel: 603-539-4500. Fax: 603-539-4599.
Contact (Sept-May): 18001 Shaker Blvd, Shaker Heights, OH 44120.
   Tel: 216-491-2267. Fax: 216-491-2268.
www.camprobinhood.com   E-mail: dc@camprobinhood.com
Jamie Cole, David Cole & Richard Woodstein, Dirs.
Adm: FCFS. **Appl due:** May. **Enr:** 290. **Staff:** Admin 8. Couns 110.
Features: Ceramics Crafts Dance Fine_Arts Photog Theater Woodworking Aquatics Archery Canoe Hiking Kayak Mtn_Trips Riding Riflery Sail Wilderness_Camp Woodcraft Baseball Basketball Equestrian Field_Hockey Football Golf Gymnastics Lacrosse Soccer Softball Street_Hockey Swim Team_Handball Tennis Track Volleyball Water-skiing Watersports.
Fees 2012: Res $3600-9500 (+$75-350), 2-7 wks.
Housing: Cabins. Avg per room/unit: 5-8. **Swimming:** Lake.
Est 1927. Inc. Ses: 4. **Wks/ses:** 2-7. Operates June-Aug. ACA.

Located on 200 level acres along the White Mountain National Forest, Robin Hood features many land sports, including horseback riding, tennis, gymnastics, archery and riflery, as well as the traditional watersports. Campers may participate in drama, crafts, wood shop, ceramics, photography, and one- to four-day mountain, canoe and sailing trips.

CAMP ONAWAY
Res — Girls Ages 9-15

Hebron, NH 03241. 27 Camp Onaway Dr. Tel: 603-744-2180. Fax: 603-744-2180.
Contact (Sept-May): PO Box 4064, Albany, NY 12204. Tel: 518-443-0004.
   Fax: 518-443-0004.
www.camponaway.org   E-mail: aconolly@camponaway.org
Anne Peterson Conolly, Dir.
Adm: FCFS. **Appl due:** Rolling. **Enr:** 90. **Enr cap:** 90. **Staff:** Couns 26.
Features: Ceramics Crafts Creative_Writing Dance Drama Music Photog Woodworking Boating Canoe Hiking Rowing/Sculling Sail Wilderness_Camp Swim Tennis.
Fees 2012: Res $6100 (+$155-205), 7 wks. Aid (Need).
Housing: Cabins. **Swimming:** Lake.
Est 1911. Nonprofit. **Ses:** 1. **Wks/ses:** 7. Operates June-Aug.

Onaway conducts a structured program that combines traditional camp activities with strong arts offerings. Scheduled morning instruction time leads into free choice periods each afternoon. Girls receive two hours a week of morning instruction in tennis, arts and crafts, woodworking, sewing, classical dance, boating or canoeing, and sailing or crew. Counselors allot an hour per week to nature study, camp craft and drama, as well as extra time for trips, rehearsals and practical experience. The daily schedule also features two swimming periods: one for lessons and the other for free swimming. Optional creative pursuits and an active tripping program round out Onaway's offerings.

CAMP PASQUANEY
Res — Boys Ages 12-16

Hebron, NH 03241. 19 Pasquaney Ln. Tel: 603-744-8043.
Contact (Sept-May): 5 S State St, Concord, NH 03301. Tel: 603-225-4065.
Year-round Fax: 603-225-4015.
www.pasquaney.org   E-mail: office@pasquaney.org
Vincent J. Broderick, Dir.
Adm: FCFS. **Appl due:** Rolling. **Enr:** 95. **Staff:** Admin 3. Couns 30.
Features: Music Theater Canoe Conservation Fishing Hiking Mtn_Trips Rowing/Sculling Sail Wilderness_Camp Wilderness_Canoe Woodcraft Baseball Swim Tennis Watersports.
Fees 2012: Res $5900 (+$100), 7 wks. Aid 2009 (Need): $70,000.
Housing: Cabins. **Swimming:** Lake.
Est 1895. Nonprofit. **Ses:** 1. **Wks/ses:** 7. Operates June-Aug.

Pasquaney places emphasis on individual development and community responsibility. All campers participate in a broad range of activities that includes crew, tennis, baseball, sailing, drama, natural history and woodworking. An extensive hiking and camping program is centered on an outpost in Crawford Notch, from which campers and counselors maintain the Nancy Pond and other Pemigewasset Wilderness trails.

CAMP WICOSUTA
Res — Girls Ages 7-15

Hebron, NH 03241. 21 Wicosuta Dr. Tel: 603-744-3301. Fax: 603-744-5570.
Contact (Sept-May): 3 New King St, White Plains, NY 10604. Tel: 914-946-0927.

Fax: 781-455-1486.
Year-round Toll-free: 800-846-9426.
www.campwicosuta.com   **E-mail:** campwicosuta@campwicosuta.com
Justin Dockswell & Corey Dockswell, Dirs.
Grades 2-10. Adm: FCFS. **Appl due:** Rolling. **Enr cap:** 275. **Staff:** Admin 15. Couns 110. Res 130.
Features: Crafts Dance Fine_Arts Music Painting Photog Theater Aquatics Archery Boating Canoe Climbing_Wall Cooking Fishing Hiking Kayak Mtn_Trips Outdoor_Ed Rappelling Riding Rock_Climb Ropes_Crse Sail Wilderness_Camp Wilderness_Canoe Yoga Aerobics Basketball Equestrian Golf Gymnastics Lacrosse Soccer Softball Swim Team_Handball Tennis Volleyball Water-skiing Watersports Pilates.
Fees 2012: Res $3650-6195, 2-4 wks.
Housing: Cabins. Avg per room/unit: 8. **Swimming:** Lake Pool.
Est 1920. Inc. **Ses:** 4. **Wks/ses:** 2-4. Operates June-Aug. ACA.

Wicosuta's program includes individual and team sports, dance, drama, hiking, fishing and outdoor cooking. Out-of-camp trips include river rafting and canoeing expeditions and visits to nearby nature attractions. For an additional fee, girls may receive riding or golf instruction. While most campers attend for four weeks, Wicosuta schedules a pair of two-week introductory sessions for girls entering grades 2-6.

CAMP DEERWOOD
Res — Boys Ages 8-15

Holderness, NH 03245. Rte 3, PO Box 188. Tel: 603-279-4237.
Contact (Sept-May): PO Box 307, Waterbury Center, VT 05677. **Tel:** 802-244-1203.
www.campdeerwood.com   **E-mail:** info@campdeerwood.com
Lorne Thomsen & Peter Thomsen, Dirs.
Grades 3-10. Adm: FCFS. **Appl due:** Rolling. **Enr:** 130. **Enr cap:** 130. **Staff:** Admin 2. Couns 45.
Features: Crafts Filmmaking Music Photog Theater Aquatics Archery Canoe Climbing_Wall Fishing Hiking Kayak Mtn_Biking Mtn_Trips Rappelling Riflery Rock_Climb Ropes_Crse Sail Survival_Trng Wilderness_Camp Wilderness_Canoe Woodcraft Badminton Basketball Lacrosse Soccer Swim Tennis Water-skiing Watersports.
Fees 2010: Res $3875-6600 (+$20-40), 3½-7 wks. Aid (Need).
Housing: Cabins. Avg per room/unit: 14. **Swimming:** Lake.
Est 1945. Inc. **Ses:** 3. **Wks/ses:** 3½-7. Operates June-Aug.

Located on Squam Lake in the White Mountains, Deerwood presents boys with a diversified program of activities and day and overnight canoe and mountain trips. In addition to the camp's traditional pursuits, Deerwood offers mountain biking, a ropes course and blacksmithing.

CAMP WA-KLO
Res — Girls Ages 6-17

Jaffrey, NH 03452. PO Box 570. Tel: 603-563-8531. **Fax:** 603-563-8129.
Contact (Sept-May): 36 Franklin Ct, Garden City, NY 11530. **Tel:** 516-747-1326. **Fax:** 516-747-1328.
Year-round Toll-free: 800-352-9102.
www.campwaklo.com   **E-mail:** info@campwaklo.com
Virginia E. Maurer, Dir.
Grades 1-12. Adm: FCFS. **Appl due:** Rolling. **Enr:** 150. **Enr cap:** 170. **Staff:** Admin 5. Couns 40.
Features: Crafts Dance Drama Fine_Arts Painting Aquatics Archery Boating Canoe Community_Serv Hiking Kayak Mtn_Biking Mtn_Trips Riding Ropes_Crse Sail White-water_Raft Wilderness_Camp Aerobics Basketball Cross-country Equestrian Field_Hockey Gymnastics Lacrosse Soccer Softball Swim Tennis Ultimate_Frisbee Volleyball Water-skiing Watersports Weight_Trng Gardening.

Fees 2012: Res $3200-8875, 2-7 wks.
Housing: Cabins Houses. Avg per room/unit: 8. **Swimming:** Lake.
Est 1938. Inc. Ses: 5. **Wks/ses:** 2-7. Operates June-Aug. ACA.

Wa-Klo offers a traditional selection of waterfront activities and sports. Creative activities include dramatic and musical productions, dance lessons, painting and drawing classes and arts and crafts. Community service opportunities are also available. Overnight trips may include white-water rafting, kayaking, city visits or college tours.

CAMP GLEN BROOK
Res — Coed Ages 8-13

Marlborough, NH 03455. 35 Glenbrook Rd. Tel: 603-876-3342. Fax: 603-876-3763.
www.glenbrook.org   E-mail: glenbrook@glenbrook.org
Twain Braden, Dir.
Adm: FCFS. **Appl due:** Rolling. **Enr:** 65. **Enr cap:** 65. **Staff:** Admin 7. Couns 25.
Features: Crafts Dance Drama Fine_Arts Music Painting Aquatics Archery Bicycle_Tours Boating Canoe Caving Climbing_Wall Community_Serv Exploration Hiking Kayak Mtn_ Biking Mtn_Trips Outdoor_Ed Rappelling Rock_Climb Ropes_Crse Wilderness_Camp Wilderness_Canoe Woodcraft Baseball Basketball Soccer Softball.
Fees 2011: Res $2940-5145 (+$50), 3-6 wks. Aid 2007 (Need): $15,000.
Housing: Cabins Dorms Houses. Avg per room/unit: 7.
Est 1946. Ses: 3. **Wks/ses:** 3-6. Operates June-Aug. ACA.

Team and individual sports, waterfront activities, crafts, music, dramatics, gardening, and canoeing and hiking trips are offered at Glen Brook.

CAMP ROBINDEL
Res — Girls Ages 7-15

Moultonboro, NH 03254. 81 Geneva Point Rd. Tel: 603-253-9271. Fax: 603-253-7866.
Contact (Sept-May): 1271 Mill Rd, Meadowbrook, PA 19046. Tel: 215-884-3326.
Fax: 215-887-2325.
Year-round Toll-free: 800-325-3396.
www.robindel.com   E-mail: natman@comcast.net
Ann Greenfield & Nat Greenfield, Dirs.
Grades 2-10. Adm: FCFS. **Appl due:** May. **Enr:** 220. **Enr cap:** 230. **Staff:** Admin 6. Couns 80. Res 80.
Features: Crafts Dance Fine_Arts Painting Theater Aquatics Boating Canoe Climbing_ Wall Hiking Kayak Mtn_Trips Outdoor_Ed Rappelling Riding Ropes_Crse Sail White-water_Raft Wilderness_Camp Yoga Aerobics Basketball Equestrian Golf Lacrosse Soccer Softball Swim Tennis Track Volleyball Water-skiing Watersports.
Fees 2012: Res $10,775 (+$200), 7 wks.
Housing: Cabins. Avg per room/unit: 12. **Swimming:** Lake.
Est 1951. Ses: 2. **Wks/ses:** 5-7. Operates June-Aug. ACA.

Major features at Robindel are a ropes course, tennis, gymnastics, water-skiing, sailing, windsurfing, swimming and tripping. Campers may also engage in arts and crafts, drama, canoeing and various field sports. A five-week option is open to a limited number of international and first-year campers.

CAMP TECUMSEH
Res — Boys Ages 8-16

Moultonboro, NH 03254. 975 Moultonboro Neck Rd. Tel: 603-253-4010.
Contact (Sept-May): 1906 Johnson Rd, Plymouth Meeting, PA 19462.
Tel: 610-275-6634.

Year-round Fax: 610-275-6635.
www.camptecumseh.net   E-mail: camptecumseh@comcast.net
Jim Talbot, Dir.
Adm: FCFS. **Appl due:** Rolling. **Enr:** 170. **Staff:** Admin 3. Couns 50.
Travel: ME NY VT.
Features: Drama Archery Bicycle_Tours Boating Exploration Fishing Hiking Mountaineering Mtn_Biking Riding Sail Woodcraft Baseball Basketball Cross-country Football Golf Martial_Arts Roller_Hockey Soccer Softball Swim Track Volleyball Water-skiing Watersports Weight_Trng Wrestling.
Fees 2012: Res $4800-6900 (+$250), 3½-7 wks.
Housing: Cabins Tents. **Swimming:** Lake.
Est 1903. Nonprofit. **Ses:** 3. **Wks/ses:** 3½-7. Operates June-Aug. ACA.

On Lake Winnipesaukee, Tecumseh offers a program that centers around athletic competition, dramatics, waterfront activities and mountain hiking. Sports clinics, which take place the last two weeks of camp, allow campers to specialize in a sport. The drama program features musicals and well-rehearsed short plays and acts. Campers of all ages regularly embark on mountain hiking trips, while experienced older boys hike mountain ranges in New York, Vermont, Maine and New Hampshire.

CAMP MERRIWOOD
Res — Girls Ages 8-15

Orford, NH 03777. 11 Camp Rd. Tel: 603-353-9882. Fax: 603-353-4821.
Contact (Sept-May): 51 Forest Ave, Ste 107, Old Greenwich, CT 06870.
    Tel: 203-637-4674. Fax: 203-637-5132.
www.merriwood.com   E-mail: info@merriwood.com
Gary Miller & Judy Miller, Dirs.
Adm: FCFS.
Travel: Canada.
Features: Canoe Fishing Mountaineering Swim.
Fees 2010: Res $3625-7725, 3-7 wks.
Swimming: Lake.
Est 1949. Ses: 2. **Wks/ses:** 3-4. Operates June-Aug. ACA.

This full instructional program of sports and the arts includes watersports, swimming and special events. Merriwood schedules weekly trips that may include mountain climbing, canoeing, trips to the White Mountains, overnights, deep-sea fishing and an excursion to Quebec, Canada.

CAMP MOOSILAUKE
Res — Boys Ages 8-15

Orford, NH 03777. 35 Camp Rd. Tel: 603-353-4545, 800-353-4546. Fax: 603-353-9103.
www.moosilauke.com   E-mail: info@moosilauke.com
Bill McMahon, Dir.
Adm: FCFS. **Appl due:** Apr. **Enr:** 130. **Enr cap:** 130. **Staff:** Admin 10. Couns 50.
Features: Art Crafts Woodworking Archery Bicycle_Tours Canoe Exploration Fishing Hiking Kayak Mountaineering Mtn_Biking Mtn_Trips Sail Wilderness_Camp Wilderness_Canoe Woodcraft Baseball Basketball Golf Lacrosse Soccer Street_Hockey Swim Tennis Ultimate_Frisbee Water-skiing Watersports.
Fees 2012: Res $3500-6150 (+$150), 2½-4½ wks. Aid avail.
Housing: Cabins. Avg per room/unit: 7. **Swimming:** Lake.
Est 1904. Inc. **Ses:** 2. **Wks/ses:** 2½-4½. Operates June-Aug. ACA.

Situated on a 300-acre tract in the White Mountains, Moosilauke combines sports, waterfront and outdoor adventure activities. One- to four-night backpacking, canoeing and biking trips are part of the program.

BRANTWOOD
Res — Coed Ages 11-14

Peterborough, NH 03458. PO Box 3350. Tel: 603-924-3542. Fax: 603-924-9307.
www.brantwood.org   E-mail: info@brantwood.org
Amy E. Willey, Exec Dir.
Adm: FCFS. **Enr:** 120. **Enr cap:** 120. **Staff:** Couns 55.
Fees 2009: Res $250, 2 wks.
Est 1904. Ses: 3. **Wks/ses:** 2. Operates June-Aug. ACA.

Serving underprivileged children from the Northeast, Brantwood offers separate facilities for boys and girls in Peterborough and Rindge, respectively. Competition between cabins is based on athletics, daily inspection and outdoor challenges. Most campers are referred to Brantwood by social agencies and churches, but some apply independently.

KINGSWOOD CAMP
Res — Boys Ages 7-15

Piermont, NH 03779. 949 Rte 25C. Tel: 603-989-5556. Fax: 603-989-3114.
Contact (Sept-May): 7101 Clarden Rd, Bethesda, MD 20814. Tel: 301-656-8406.
   Fax: 301-656-8406.
www.kingswoodcamp.com   E-mail: bob@kingswoodcamp.com
Robert Wipfler, Dir.
Adm: FCFS. **Appl due:** Rolling. **Enr:** 150.
Features: Astron Ecol Environ_Sci Crafts Music Aquatics Archery Boating Canoe Conservation Exploration Fishing Hiking Kayak Mtn_Trips Riflery Sail Wilderness_Camp Woodcraft Baseball Basketball Cross-country Football Golf Lacrosse Soccer Softball Swim Tennis Track Volleyball Water-skiing Watersports Wrestling.
Fees 2012: Res $4400-8000, 3-7 wks.
Housing: Cabins. Avg per room/unit: 10. **Swimming:** Lake.
Est 1984. Inc. Ses: 3. **Wks/ses:** 3-7. Operates June-Aug. ACA.

Kingswood's traditional program features instructional activities, intercamp competition and overnight trips. Boys choose their activities on a daily basis. Options include archery, boating, crafts, land sports and water-skiing.

CAMP WALT WHITMAN
Res — Coed Ages 8-15

Piermont, NH 03779. 1000 Cape Moonshine Rd. Tel: 603-764-5521.
   Fax: 603-764-9146.
Contact (Sept-May): 3 New King St, White Plains, NY 10604. Tel: 914-948-9151.
   Fax: 914-948-9155.
Year-round Toll-free: 800-657-8282.
www.campwalt.com   E-mail: cww@campwalt.com
Carolyn Dorfman & Jed Dorfman, Dirs.
Grades 3-10. Adm: FCFS. **Appl due:** Jan. **Enr:** 390. **Staff:** Admin 20. Couns 200. Res 100.
Features: Crafts Creative_Writing Dance Painting Photog Studio_Art Theater Aquatics Archery Bicycle_Tours Boating Canoe Chess Climbing_Wall Community_Serv Cooking Fishing Hiking Kayak Mountaineering Mtn_Trips Rappelling Riding Rock_Climb Ropes_Crse Sail Wilderness_Camp Baseball Basketball Equestrian Field_Hockey Football Golf Gymnastics Lacrosse Soccer Softball Street_Hockey Swim Tennis Ultimate_Frisbee Volleyball Water-skiing Watersports Weight_Trng.
Fees 2012: Res $5250-10,350 (+$50), 3-7 wks.
Housing: Cabins. Avg per room/unit: 10. **Swimming:** Lake Pool River.
Est 1948. Inc. Ses: 3. **Wks/ses:** 3-7. Operates June-Aug. ACA.

Required activities at Walt Whitman include tennis, soccer, swimming, sailing, dance, art, hiking and camping. The afternoon elective program allows campers to specialize in areas of their choice. Intensive sports instruction, outdoor adventure, music and photography are among the electives offered.

CAMP SPOFFORD
Res and Day — Coed Ages 8-16

Spofford, NH 03462. 24 Rte 9A, PO Box 162. Tel: 603-363-4788. Fax: 603-363-8969.
www.campspofford.org   E-mail: info@campspofford.org
Peter M. Olson, Admin.
Grades 3-10. Adm: FCFS. **Staff:** Admin 20. Couns 16.
Features: Crafts Boating Canoe Basketball Soccer Swim Volleyball Water-skiing Watersports.
Fees 2012: Res $340-400 (+$30), 1 wk. Day $240-300, 1 wk.
Housing: Cabins. **Swimming:** Lake.
Est 1963. Nonprofit. Evangelical. **Ses:** 7. **Wks/ses:** 1. Operates June-Aug.

Campers at Spofford take part in an array of sports, games, and small- and large-group activities. Camp life has a distinctly spiritual dimension, as boys and girls devote time each day to morning chapel and evening cabin reflection. Specialty weeks serve campers with a strong interest in water-skiing, basketball or soccer.

CAMP PEMIGEWASSETT
Res — Boys Ages 8-15

Wentworth, NH 03282. PO Box 222. Tel: 603-764-5833.
Contact (Oct-May): 35 Felt Rd, Keene, NH 03431. Tel: 603-903-0735.
Year-round Fax: 603-764-9601.
www.camppemi.com   E-mail: camppemi@camppemi.com
Thomas L. Reed, Jr. & Daniel R. Kerr, Dirs.
Adm: FCFS. **Appl due:** May. **Enr:** 168. **Enr cap:** 168. **Staff:** Admin 10. Couns 45. Res 70.
Features: Astron Ecol Environ_Sci Geol Sci Crafts Creative_Writing Fine_Arts Music Photog Theater Aquatics Archery Boating Canoe Caving Conservation Hiking Kayak Mtn_Trips Outdoor_Ed Sail Wilderness_Camp Wilderness_Canoe Woodcraft Baseball Basketball Lacrosse Soccer Swim Tennis Track Ultimate_Frisbee Volleyball Waterskiing.
Fees 2012: Res $5000-7600 (+$100-150), 3½-7 wks. Aid 2009 (Need): $150,000.
Housing: Cabins Tents. **Swimming:** Pond.
Est 1908. Inc. **Ses:** 3. **Wks/ses:** 3½-7. Operates June-Aug. ACA.

Pemi divides campers into four groups, according to age. Afternoons are free for individually selected activities, while mornings are devoted to instruction in each boy's choice of the following: nature study, music, woodworking, arts and crafts, camp craft, sailing, rugby, canoeing, archery, tennis, baseball, soccer, track, lacrosse, basketball, swimming, windsurfing and water-skiing. Every camper participates in roughly one hiking, backpacking or canoeing trip per week.

CAMP KENWOOD
CAMP EVERGREEN
Res — Coord Ages 7-15

Wilmot, NH 03287. 114 Eagle Pond Rd. Tel: 603-735-5189. Fax: 603-735-5780.
Contact (Sept-May): 239 Moose Hill St, Sharon, MA 02067. Tel: 781-793-0091.
**   Fax: 781-793-0606.**
www.kenwood-evergreen.com   E-mail: info@kenwood-evergreen.com
Scott Brody & Phyllis Dank, Dirs.

Adm: FCFS. **Enr:** 320. **Enr cap:** 320. **Staff:** Admin 11. Couns 150.
Features: Crafts Dance Music Photog Theater Aquatics Archery Canoe Mountaineering Mtn_Trips Riding Ropes_Crse Sail Wilderness_Camp Woodcraft Baseball Basketball Football Golf Gymnastics Soccer Swim Tennis Volleyball Water-skiing.
Fees 2012: Res $7500-10,950 (+$200), 4-7 wks.
Swimming: Pond.
Est 1930. Inc. Jewish. **Ses:** 2. **Wks/ses:** 4-7. Operates June-Aug.

Kenwood for boys and Evergreen for girls feature a wide variety of sports, arts, theater, adventure trips and aquatic activities. Administrators schedule weekend events between the two camps. While most boys and girls attend for seven weeks, the camps operate a four-week session for a limited number of young first-time campers.

WINDSOR MOUNTAIN INTERNATIONAL SUMMER CAMP
Res — Coed Ages 8-14

Windsor, NH 03244. 1 World Way. Tel: 603-478-3166, 800-862-7760. Fax: 603-478-5260.
www.windsormountain.org E-mail: mail@windsormountain.org
Jake Labovitz, Dir.
Grades 3-9. Adm: FCFS. **Appl due:** Rolling. **Enr:** 200. **Enr cap:** 200. **Staff:** Admin 10. Couns 60.
Features: ESL Crafts Dance Filmmaking Fine_Arts Music Painting Theater Adventure_ Travel Aquatics Archery Bicycle_Tours Boating Canoe Climbing_Wall Community_Serv Conservation Exploration Farm Fishing Hiking Kayak Mountaineering Mtn_Biking Mtn_ Trips Outdoor_Ed Peace/Cross-cultural Rappelling Rock_Climb Ropes_Crse Sail Survival_Trng Wilderness_Camp Wilderness_Canoe Woodcraft Basketball Cricket Crosscountry Football Rugby Soccer Softball Swim Tennis Ultimate_Frisbee.
Fees 2012: Res $2795-7295 (+$100), 2-7½ wks. Aid (Need).
Housing: Cabins Dorms Tents. Avg per room/unit: 6. **Swimming:** Lake.
Est 1961. Inc. **Ses:** 6. **Wks/ses:** 2-7½. Operates June-Aug. ACA.

This international camp focuses on cross-cultural understanding. Campers take an active part in choosing, shaping and carrying out their own activity programs, sharing their summer with campers from a multitude of backgrounds. Activities include music, theater, wilderness and adventure, applied arts and sports. While Windsor Mountain's main sessions last for at least three and a half weeks, the camp also offers several two-week introductory programs for boys and girls who cannot attend a full-length session.

PIERCE CAMP BIRCHMONT
Res — Coed Ages 7-15

Wolfeboro, NH 03894. 693 Governor John Wentworth Way. Tel: 603-569-1337.
Fax: 603-569-5813.
Contact (Winter): Mineola Ave, Roslyn, NY 11576. Tel: 516-621-5035.
Fax: 516-621-0489.
www.campbirchmont.com E-mail: mail@campbirchmont.com
Gregory C. Pierce & Laura Pierce, Dirs.
Adm: FCFS. **Appl due:** Rolling.
Features: Art Crafts Drama Music Woodworking Archery Canoe Fishing Kayak Mtn_Biking Riflery Sail Yoga Baseball Basketball Golf Gymnastics Soccer Softball Street_Hockey Swim Tennis Volleyball Water-skiing Watersports Weight_Trng Wrestling.
Fees 2012: Res $5100-9800 (+$225), 4-7 wks.
Housing: Dorms. **Swimming:** Lake.
Est 1951. Ses: 3. **Wks/ses:** 4-7. Operates June-Aug.

All children in the recreational camp play tennis and enjoy waterfront activities every day. Other activities include field sports, boating and canoeing, archery, crafts, golf, English riding, riflery, gymnastics and fine arts.

NEW JERSEY

LINDLEY G. COOK 4-H CAMP
Res — Coed Ages 9-16

Branchville, NJ 07826. 100 Struble Rd. Tel: 973-948-3550. Fax: 973-948-0735.
www.nj4hcamp.rutgers.edu   E-mail: 4hcamp@njaes.rutgers.edu
James Tavares, Dir.
Grades 4-11. Adm: FCFS. **Appl due:** Rolling. **Enr:** 150. **Enr cap:** 150. **Staff:** Admin 3.
Couns 36.
Features: Crafts Theater Aquatics Archery Boating Canoe Fishing Hiking Kayak Outdoor_
Ed Riflery Survival_Trng Wilderness_Camp Swim.
Fees 2012: Res $500, 1 wk. Aid (Need).
Housing: Cabins. Avg per room/unit: 15. **Swimming:** Lake.
Est 1951. Nonprofit. **Ses:** 6. **Wks/ses:** 1. Operates July-Aug.

Each afternoon, campers at Lindley Cook choose their own activities from a selection that
varies day to day. Dances and other campwide evening activities facilitate further interaction
among the campers.

CAMP DARK WATERS
Res — Coed Ages 7-14

Medford, NJ 08055. 26 New Freedom Rd, PO Box 263. Tel: 609-654-8846.
Fax: 609-654-2022.
www.campdarkwaters.org   E-mail: info@campdarkwaters.net
Travis W. Simmons, Dir.
Adm: FCFS. **Appl due:** Rolling. **Enr:** 96. **Enr cap:** 96. **Staff:** Admin 5. Couns 20. Res 30.
Features: Ecol Environ_Sci Crafts Creative_Writing Dance Music Painting Adventure_
Travel Aquatics Archery Canoe Climbing_Wall Conservation Fishing Hiking Kayak Out-
door_Ed Riding Ropes_Crse Wilderness_Camp Wilderness_Canoe Basketball Eques-
trian Soccer Softball Swim Ultimate_Frisbee Volleyball.
Fees 2012: Res $630-1120 (+$10-35), 1-2 wks. Aid 2011 (Need): $20,000.
Housing: Cabins. Avg per room/unit: 8. **Swimming:** Pool River.
Est 1928. Nonprofit. Religious Society of Friends. **Ses:** 5. **Wks/ses:** 1-2. Operates June-
Aug. ACA.

Founded on Quaker principles, Dark Waters offers a comprehensive outdoors program that
includes swimming and diving, pioneering, riding, fishing, a ropes course, camp craft, music
and nature. The program also features one- to three-day camping and canoeing trips.

CAMP VACAMAS
Res — Coed Ages 7-17; Day — Coed 5-14

West Milford, NJ 07480. 256 Macopin Rd. Tel: 973-838-1394, 877-428-8222.
Fax: 973-838-7534.
www.vacamas.org   E-mail: info@vacamas.org
Elly Newberry, Dir.
Grades K-12. Adm: FCFS. **Appl due:** Rolling. **Enr:** 400. **Staff:** Admin 25. Couns 150.
Features: Ecol Environ_Sci Writing/Journ Crafts Creative_Writing Dance Drama Fine_Arts
Music Aquatics Archery Bicycle_Tours Boating Canoe Climbing_Wall Conservation
Cooking Exploration Farm Fishing Hiking Mountaineering Mtn_Biking Mtn_Trips Out-
door_Ed Rock_Climb Ropes_Crse Survival_Trng Weight_Loss Wilderness_Camp Wil-
derness_Canoe Woodcraft Baseball Basketball Soccer Softball Swim Volleyball.
Fees: Day $250-2000, 1-8 wks. Aid (Need).
Housing: Cabins Dorms Lodges Tents. Avg per room/unit: 8. **Swimming:** Lake.

Est 1924. Nonprofit. **Spons:** Vacamas Programs for Youth. **Ses:** 3. **Wks/ses:** 3. Operates June-Aug.

With its residential programs divided into junior (ages 7-13) and teen (ages 14-16) sessions, Vacamas offers a broad range of activities that includes canoeing, backpacking, camping, music, dance, theater and leadership training. A 50-acre private lake provides ample opportunities for waterfront pursuits. Residential camp fees are determined along a sliding scale.

NEW YORK

CAMP MA-HE-TU
Res — Girls Ages 7-15

Bear Mountain, NY. Tel: 845-351-4508.
Contact (Year-round): 6 Soundview Dr N, Huntington, NY 11743. Tel: 631-351-1657.
Year-round Fax: 845-351-4508.
www.campmahetu.org   E-mail: registrar@mahetu.jorg
Janet Paddack, Dir.
Adm: FCFS. **Appl due:** Rolling. **Enr:** 100. **Enr cap:** 100. **Staff:** Admin 6. Couns 30.
Features: Astron Crafts Dance Music Photog Theater Aquatics Archery Boating Canoe Climbing_Wall Conservation Fishing Hiking Kayak Mountaineering Mtn_Trips Ropes_ Crse Sail Woodcraft Baseball Basketball Gymnastics Soccer Softball Swim Tennis Volleyball.
Fees 2011: Res $895 (+$35), 2 wks. Aid avail.
Housing: Cabins Tents. Avg per room/unit: 6. **Swimming:** Lake.
Est 1937. Nonprofit. Lutheran. **Ses:** 3. **Wks/ses:** 2. Operates July-Aug. ACA.

Situated on Lake Kanawauke, this girls' camp offers such traditional camp activities as swimming, boating, canoeing, sailing, windsurfing, hiking, and arts and crafts. Other offerings include land sports and various artistic pursuits. Ma-He-Tu also conducts optional overnight hiking and canoe trips.

POINT O' PINES CAMP FOR GIRLS
Res — Girls Ages 6-13

Brant Lake, NY 12815. 7201 State Rte 8. Tel: 518-494-3213. Fax: 518-494-3489.
www.pointopines.com   E-mail: info@pointopines.com
Sue Himoff & Jim Himoff, Dirs.
Adm: FCFS. **Appl due:** Apr. **Enr:** 320. **Enr cap:** 325. **Staff:** Admin 8. Couns 170. Res 170.
Features: Ecol Environ_Sci Lang Crafts Dance Filmmaking Fine_Arts Music Painting Photog Theater Adventure_Travel Aquatics Archery Boating Canoe Conservation Cooking Fishing Hiking Kayak Mtn_Trips Outdoor_Ed Riding Ropes_Crse Sail White-water_ Raft Wilderness_Camp Yoga Aerobics Baseball Basketball Equestrian Field_Hockey Golf Gymnastics Lacrosse Soccer Softball Swim Tennis Track Volleyball Water-skiing Watersports Gardening.
Fees 2012: Res $10,750 (+$300), 8 wks.
Housing: Cabins. Avg per room/unit: 8. **Swimming:** Lake.
Est 1956. Inc. **Ses:** 1. **Wks/ses:** 8. Operates June-Aug. ACA.

This traditional camp features tennis, golf, team sports, aquatics and horseback riding. An extensive arts program includes fine arts, media, drama and dance. Point O' Pines schedules hiking and canoeing trips, and girls engage in organic gardening and explore environmental issues.

FOREST LAKE CAMP
Res — Coord Ages 8-16

Chestertown, NY 12817. 261 Forest Lake Rd. Tel: 518-623-4771. Fax: 518-557-8891.
www.forestlakecamp.com   E-mail: info@forestlakecamp.com
Gene Devlin, Dir.
Grades 2-11. Adm: FCFS. Appl due: May. **Enr:** 140. **Enr cap:** 160. **Staff:** Admin 10. Couns 30. Res 10.
Features: Astron Crafts Dance Music Painting Studio_Art Theater Aquatics Archery Boating Canoe Climbing_Wall Exploration Fishing Hiking Kayak Mtn_Biking Mtn_Trips Outdoor_Ed Riding Riflery Sail White-water_Raft Wilderness_Camp Wilderness_Canoe Woodcraft Yoga Baseball Basketball Cross-country Equestrian Fencing Field_Hockey Golf Lacrosse Rugby Soccer Softball Street_Hockey Swim Tennis Ultimate_Frisbee Volleyball Water-skiing Watersports Weight_Trng.
Fees 2012: Res $2990-6790, 2-7 wks. Aid (Need).
Housing: Cabins. Avg per room/unit: 10. **Swimming:** Lake.
Est 1926. Inc. Ses: 6. **Wks/ses:** 2-7. Operates June-Aug. ACA.

In addition to regular land sports and watersports, this brother and sister camp offers physical fitness, ecology and astronomy. Of the four daily activity periods, one is a time for general swimming, a second is devoted to team sports and the other two are reserved for individual pursuits. For an additional fee, campers of all ability levels may receive riding and water-skiing instruction, and English-language immersion and one-on-one tutoring programs are also available at an extra charge. Forest Lake conducts one- to three-day canoeing, fishing and backpacking trips in the Adirondacks.

CAMP PONTIAC
Res — Coed Ages 6-17

Copake, NY 12516. PO Box 100. Tel: 518-329-6555. Fax: 518-329-2302.
Contact (Winter): 10 Brook Ln, Brookville, NY 11545. Tel: 516-626-7668.
Fax: 516-626-8943.
www.camppontiac.com   E-mail: camppontiac@hotmail.com
Ricky Etra, Susan Etra, Kenny Etra & Karen Etra, Dirs.
Grades 2-10. Adm: FCFS. **Enr cap:** 600. **Staff:** Couns 185.
Features: Crafts Dance Fine_Arts Music Theater Adventure_Travel Aquatics Canoe Climbing_Wall Conservation Exploration Fishing Hiking Mountaineering Sail Wilderness_Camp Woodcraft Baseball Basketball Cross-country Football Golf Gymnastics Ice_Hockey Lacrosse Roller_Hockey Soccer Swim Tennis Track Water-skiing Weight_Trng.
Fees 2012: Res $1500, 7 wks.
Housing: Cabins Dorms Houses Lodges Tents Tepees. **Swimming:** Lake Pool.
Est 1922. Inc. Ses: 1. **Wks/ses:** 7. Operates June-Aug. ACA.

This traditional camp's structured program combines athletic instruction with fine arts activities. Options include tennis, golf, all team sports and watersports, waterfront activities, drama, art and outdoor adventure. Younger campers also engage in a daily hobby period. Although many evening activities and special events are coeducational, daily programs are run separately.

CAMP WALDEN
Res — Coed Ages 7-16

Diamond Point, NY 12824. 429 Trout Lake Rd. Tel: 518-644-9441. Fax: 518-644-2929.
Contact (Sept-June): 36 Feather Ln, Old Tappan, NJ 07675. Tel: 201-750-6767.
Fax: 201-750-2226.
www.campwalden-ny.com   E-mail: info@campwalden-ny.com
Lauren Pine Bernstein & Mark Bernstein, Dirs.

Grades 2-10. **Adm:** FCFS. **Appl due:** Rolling. **Enr:** 325. **Enr cap:** 325. **Staff:** Admin 15. Couns 130.
Features: Crafts Dance Music Painting Theater Adventure_Travel Aquatics Archery Bicycle_Tours Boating Canoe Climbing_Wall Cooking Fishing Hiking Kayak Mtn_Biking Mtn_Trips Outdoor_Ed Riding Rock_Climb Ropes_Crse Sail White-water_Raft Wilderness_Camp Woodcraft Yoga Baseball Basketball Equestrian Fencing Field_Hockey Football Golf Gymnastics Lacrosse Martial_Arts Roller_Hockey Soccer Softball Street_Hockey Swim Tennis Ultimate_Frisbee Volleyball Water-skiing Watersports.
Fees 2012: Res $3900-8990 (+$100), 2-7 wks.
Housing: Cabins. Avg per room/unit: 9. **Swimming:** Lake Pool.
Est 1931. Inc. **Ses:** 4. **Wks/ses:** 2-7. Operates June-Aug. ACA.

Located on more than 100 acres in the Adirondack Mountains, Walden offers a full program of traditional waterfront and land activities. Theater, arts and crafts, and hiking complement the sports program. A tw0-week session is available to first-time Walden campers only.

CAMP SCATICO
Res — Coord Ages 8-15

Elizaville, NY 12523. 1558 Rte 19, PO Box 6. Tel: 845-756-4040. Fax: 845-756-2298.
www.scatico.com   E-mail: info@scatico.com
David Fleischner, Dir.
Grades 3-10. **Adm:** FCFS. **Enr:** 260. **Enr cap:** 260. **Staff:** Admin 20. Couns 80.
Features: Crafts Dance Fine_Arts Music Photog Theater Aquatics Archery Canoe Climbing_Wall Conservation Hiking Kayak Riflery Sail Wilderness_Camp Woodcraft Baseball Basketball Cross-country Field_Hockey Football Golf Gymnastics Soccer Softball Swim Tennis Track.
Fees 2012: Res $1000-9100, 1-7 wks.
Housing: Cabins. **Swimming:** Lake.
Est 1921. Inc. **Ses:** 3. **Wks/ses:** 1-7. Operates June-Aug. ACA.

Scatico is a traditional brother and sister camp with separate campuses for boys and girls at opposite ends of the 250-acre property. Younger campers (ages 7-11) take part in a structured program designed to encourage them to try many activities and learn new skills. Older campers (ages 12-15) choose about half of their programming, thus allowing them to pursue areas of interest.

BROOKWOOD CAMPS
Res — Coed Ages 6-15

Glen Spey, NY 12737. Rte 32. Tel: 845-557-6661. Fax: 845-557-6907.
Contact (Sept-May): 3242 Judith Ln, Oceanside, NY 11572. Tel: 516-764-2112.
    Fax: 516-536-7725.
www.brookwoodcamps.com   E-mail: info@brookwoodcamps.com
Ken Fiedler, Donna Fiedler & Scott Fiedler, Dirs.
Grades 1-10. **Adm:** FCFS. **Appl due:** Rolling. **Enr:** 300. **Enr cap:** 300. **Staff:** Admin 12. Couns 115. Res 4.
Features: ESL Crafts Dance Drama Fine_Arts Music Photog Aquatics Archery Boating Canoe Chess Cooking Fishing Kayak Mtn_Biking Riding Sail Woodcraft Aerobics Baseball Basketball Cross-country Equestrian Field_Hockey Football Golf Gymnastics Lacrosse Martial_Arts Roller_Hockey Soccer Softball Street_Hockey Swim Tennis Track Ultimate_Frisbee Volleyball Water-skiing Watersports Weight_Trng Wrestling.
Fees 2012: Res $5150-8600 (+$650), 4-7 wks.
Housing: Cabins Dorms. **Swimming:** Lake Pool.
Est 1938. Inc. **Ses:** 3. **Wks/ses:** 4-7. Operates June-Aug.

Brookwood combines a strong instructional sports program with arts and crafts, theater and nature studies. The camp organizes leagues and conducts tournaments in basketball, baseball, softball, volleyball, football, lacrosse, field hockey and other team sports. Private tennis and golf lessons are available at no extra charge. Boys and girls may also develop their skills in dance, cheerleading, yoga, computers, fishing, music and rocketry. First-time campers only may enroll in Brookwood's four- and five week sessions.

CAMP EMUNAH
Res — Girls Ages 9-15

Greenfield Park, NY 12435. PO Box 266. Tel: 845-647-8742. Fax: 845-647-2248.
Contact (Sept-June): 824 Eastern Pky, Brooklyn, NY 11213. Tel: 718-735-0225.
   Fax: 718-735-1202.
www.campemunah.com   E-mail: campemunahbjj@gmail.com
Chave Hecht, Dir.
Grades 3-10. Adm: FCFS. **Appl due:** Apr. **Enr:** 550. **Enr cap:** 600. **Staff:** Admin 5. Couns
   40.
Features: Crafts Dance Music Photog Theater Aquatics Boating Climbing_Wall Cooking
   Aerobics Baseball Basketball Softball Swim Team_Handball Tennis Volleyball.
Fees 2011: Res $1750 (+$200), 4 wks. Aid 2009 (Merit & Need): $5090.
Housing: Cabins. Avg per room/unit: 10. **Swimming:** Lake Pool.
Est 1953. Nonprofit. Jewish. **Ses:** 2. **Wks/ses:** 4. Operates June-Aug.

Within a traditional Jewish context, girls enjoy recreation in the form of computer and educational programs, field days, carnivals, vocational arts and watersports. The junior and senior divisions occupy separate campuses.

CAMP HILLTOP
Res — Coed Ages 7-15

Hancock, NY 13783. 7825 County Hwy 67. Tel: 607-637-5201, 800-782-5319.
   Fax: 607-637-2389.
www.camphilltop.com   E-mail: hilltop@hancock.net
Bill Young & Kathy Young, Dirs.
Adm: FCFS. **Enr:** 240. **Staff:** Admin 5. Couns 70.
Features: Crafts Dance Music Theater Farm Hiking Riding Ropes_Crse Sail Basketball
   Equestrian Golf Gymnastics Lacrosse Soccer Softball Swim Tennis Water-skiing.
Fees 2012: Res $1700-7110, 2-8 wks.
Housing: Cabins. **Swimming:** Lake Pool.
Est 1924. Inc. **Ses:** 10. **Wks/ses:** 2-8. Operates June-Aug. ACA.

Boys and girls at Hilltop may participate in individually scheduled sports, arts and crafts, sailing, riding and equestrian, water-skiing, hiking, and high and low ropes courses.

CAMP LINCOLN
CAMP WHIPPOORWILL
Res — Coord Ages 8-15

Keeseville, NY 12944. 395 Frontage Rd. Tel: 518-834-5152.
Contact (Sept-May): PO Box 1246, Middletown Springs, VT 05757. Tel: 802-235-2908.
www.northcountrycamps.com   E-mail: nancy@northcountrycamps.com
Nancy Gucker Birdsall, Exec Dir.
Adm: FCFS. **Appl due:** Rolling. **Enr:** 190. **Enr cap:** 190. **Staff:** Admin 4. Couns 70.
Features: Art Crafts Dance Drama Drawing Painting Photog Pottery Woodworking Archery
   Canoe Climbing_Wall Fishing Hiking Kayak Mountaineering Mtn_Biking Riding Rock_
   Climb Sail Wilderness_Camp Yoga Aerobics Baseball Basketball Equestrian Lacrosse
   Soccer Softball Swim Tennis Ultimate_Frisbee Volleyball Watersports Gardening.
Fees 2012: Res $6200-7200, 5-7 wks. Aid (Need).
Housing: Cabins. Avg per room/unit: 4-7. **Swimming:** Lake.

Est 1920. Spons: North Country Camps. **Ses:** 3. **Wks/ses:** 5-7. Operates June-Aug.

The single-gender Camp Lincoln for boys and Camp Whippoorwill for girls (which together constitute North Country Camps), occupy 150 wooded acres on Augur Lake, between the Adirondacks and Lake Champlain. These small camps, located about a half-mile apart, join together for a variety of activities. Although team sports are available, they do not dominate the program. Girls and boys select two morning instructional activities for a week's participation, then choose afternoon and evening pursuits daily.

CAMP TREETOPS
Res — Coed Ages 8-14

Lake Placid, NY 12946. 4382 Cascade Rd. Tel: 518-523-9329. Fax: 518-523-4858.
www.camptreetops.org   E-mail: karen@camptreetops.org
Karen Culpepper, Dir.
Grades 2-9. Adm: FCFS. **Enr:** 165. **Staff:** Admin 7. Couns 70.
Features: Ecol Environ_Sci Crafts Dance Fine_Arts Music Photog Theater Adventure_
Travel Aquatics Boating Canoe Climbing_Wall Conservation Farm Fishing Hiking Kayak
Mountaineering Mtn_Trips Riding Rock_Climb Sail Wilderness_Camp Wilderness_
Canoe Woodcraft Work Baseball Basketball Equestrian Soccer Swim Tennis.
Fees 2012: Res $5900-8300 (+$30), 4-7 wks. Aid (Need).
Housing: Tents. Avg per room/unit: 4. **Swimming:** Lake Pond.
Est 1921. Nonprofit. **Spons:** North Country School. **Ses:** 2. **Wks/ses:** 4-7. Operates June-Aug. ACA.

Affiliated with North Country School and located on an organic farm in the Adirondack Mountains, Treetops maintains both junior (ages 8-11) and senior (ages 12-14) divisions. In a noncompetitive environment, the camp offers swimming, canoeing, sailing, horseback riding, music, creative arts, camp craft, athletics, nature study, and farm work on an operating farm with gardens and animals. Children take day and overnight camping trips by foot, horse and canoe. All boys and girls participate in a work program that addresses community needs.

CAMP STELLA MARIS
Res — Coed Ages 7-15; Day — Coed 5-12

Livonia, NY 14487. 4395 E Lake Rd. Tel: 585-346-2243. Fax: 585-346-6921.
www.campstellamaris.org   E-mail: info@campstellamaris.org
John Quinlivan, Exec Dir.
Adm: FCFS. **Appl due:** Rolling. **Staff:** Admin 20. Couns 52.
Features: Crafts Dance Pottery Aquatics Archery Canoe Fishing Kayak Ropes_Crse Sail
Basketball Football Soccer Softball Swim Tennis Volleyball Water-skiing.
Fees 2012: Res $552-1238, 1-2 wks. Day $175-191, 1 wk.
Housing: Cabins. **Swimming:** Lake.
Est 1926. Nonprofit. Roman Catholic. **Ses:** 9. **Wks/ses:** 1-2. Operates June-Aug. ACA.

This Catholic camp offers many recreational options, including canoeing, archery, pottery, dance, fishing and swimming. Water-skiing and sailing programs accommodate boys and girls of varying ability levels.

CAMP CHATEAUGAY
Res — Coed Ages 7-16

Merrill, NY 12955. 233 Gadway Rd. Tel: 518-425-6888. Fax: 860-425-3487.
Contact (Sept-May): PO Box 202, Roxbury, CT 06783. Tel: 860-350-8822.
Fax: 888-431-5267.
Year-round Toll-free: 800-431-1184.
www.chateaugay.com   E-mail: hallyons@chateaugay.com

Hal Lyons & Dov Shapiro, Dirs.
Grades 2-10. Adm: FCFS. **Enr:** 270. **Staff:** Admin 30. Couns 70.
Features: Crafts Dance Fine_Arts Photog Theater Aquatics Archery Bicycle_Tours Canoe Hiking Mountaineering Mtn_Biking Mtn_Trips Riding Rock_Climb Sail Seamanship White-water_Raft Wilderness_Camp Wilderness_Canoe Woodcraft Baseball Basketball Equestrian Football Golf Gymnastics Lacrosse Martial_Arts Roller_Hockey Soccer Softball Swim Tennis Volleyball Water-skiing.
Fees 2012: Res $5700-9275 (+$150), 3½-7 wks.
Housing: Cabins. Avg per room/unit: 10. **Swimming:** Lake Pool.
Est 1946. Inc. **Ses:** 2. **Wks/ses:** 3½. Operates June-Aug. ACA.

Chateaugay offers land sports and watersports, theater, dance, nature, arts and crafts, and trips. Campers ages 14-16 may participate in a wilderness program, living apart from the rest of the children and taking weeklong bicycling, canoeing and backpacking trips.

CAMP JEANNE D'ARC
Res — Girls Ages 7-16

Merrill, NY 12955. 154 Gadway Rd. Tel: 518-425-3311. **Fax:** 518-425-6673.
Contact (Sept-May): 1213 Balfour Dr, Arnold, MD 21012. Tel: 410-647-7733.
   Fax: 410-295-7254.
www.campjeannedarc.com   E-mail: jehanne@campjeannedarc.com
Jehanne McIntyre Edwards, Dir.
Grades 2-11. Adm: FCFS. **Appl due:** May. **Enr:** 125. **Enr cap:** 125. **Staff:** Admin 10. Couns 35.
Features: ESL Lang Crafts Creative_Writing Dance Drama Filmmaking Music Painting Studio_Art Aquatics Archery Boating Canoe Fishing Hiking Kayak Mountaineering Mtn_Trips Outdoor_Ed Riding Riflery Sail Wilderness_Camp Aerobics Badminton Basketball Cross-country Equestrian Field_Hockey Golf Lacrosse Soccer Softball Swim Tennis Volleyball Water-skiing Watersports.
Fees 2011: Res $3000-8000 (+$20-150), 2-7 wks. Aid 2008 (Need): $50,000.
Housing: Cabins. Avg per room/unit: 11. **Swimming:** Lake.
Est 1922. Inc. Roman Catholic. **Ses:** 6. **Wks/ses:** 2-7. Operates June-Aug.

Located on Lake Chateaugay, Jeanne d'Arc is the oldest girls' camp in the Adirondack Mountains. The camp complements a full waterfront and watersports program with land sports and clinics in soccer, field hockey and lacrosse. Optional horseback riding is available (for an additional fee) three or six times per week at beginning through advanced levels. Also available are arts and crafts, boating trips and overnight camping opportunities. Jeanne d'Arc conducts both Catholic and nondenominational religious services. Two-week sessions accommodates first-time campers.

CAMP BACO
CHE-NA-WAH
Res — Coord Ages 7-16

Minerva, NY 12851. 2723 State Rte 28N. Tel: 518-251-2919.
Contact (Sept-May): 484 S Wood Rd, Rockville Centre, NY 11570. Tel: 516-867-3895.
Year-round Fax: 516-868-3819.
www.campbaco.com   E-mail: info@campbaco.com; info@campchenawah.com
Robert Wortman & Barbara Wortman, Dirs.
Grades 2-11. Adm: FCFS. **Appl due:** Rolling. **Enr:** 150-200.
Features: Ceramics Crafts Dance Drama Music Archery Canoe Climbing_Wall Fishing Hiking Kayak Ropes_Crse Sail White-water_Raft Wilderness_Camp Yoga Basketball Field_Hockey Golf Gymnastics Lacrosse Roller_Hockey Soccer Softball Swim Tennis Ultimate_Frisbee Volleyball Water-skiing Watersports Weight_Trng.
Fees 2012: Res $8250-8975.

Housing: Cabins. **Swimming:** Lake.
Est 1923. Ses: 1. **Wks/ses:** 7. Operates June-Aug.

Situated in the Adirondack Mountains, these brother and sister camps lie a half-mile apart on Lake Balfour. The camps offer a traditional combination of land sports, waterfront activities and creative pursuits. Making full use of Baco and Che-Na-Wah's mountain setting, specially trained counselors take boys and girls on age-appropriate hikes.

CAMP MONROE
Res — Coed Ages 6-16

Monroe, NY 10949. PO Box 475. Tel: 845-782-8695. Fax: 845-782-2247.
www.campmonroe.com   E-mail: office@campmonroe.com
Stanley Felsinger, Dir.
Adm: FCFS. **Appl due:** Rolling.
Features: Computers Writing/Journ Crafts Dance Photog Theater Archery Boating Climbing_Wall Fishing Riding Basketball Gymnastics Soccer Softball Street_Hockey Swim Tennis Volleyball.
Fees 2009: Res $3900-7900 (+$250-825), 3½-7½ wks.
Housing: Cabins. **Swimming:** Pool.
Est 1941. Jewish. **Ses:** 3. **Wks/ses:** 3½-7½. Operates June-Aug. ACA.

Located on a 200-acre tract in the Catskill Mountains, this Jewish camp offers a structured, traditional program. Programming comprises various athletic, social and artistic activities, with instruction provided in basic and advanced skill areas. The camp's menu is strictly kosher, and Monroe conducts Sabbath morning services for those who wish to attend.

CAMP KENNYBROOK
Res — Coed Ages 7-16

Monticello, NY 12701. 73 Camp Rd, PO Box 5014. Tel: 845-794-5320.
    Fax: 845-791-4738.
Contact (Sept-June): 633 Saw Mill River Rd, Ardsley, NY 10502. Tel: 914-693-3037.
    Fax: 914-693-7678.
www.kennybrook.com   E-mail: kennybrook@aol.com
Howard Landman & Stacey Landman, Dirs.
Grades 2-9. **Adm:** FCFS. **Enr:** 300.
Travel: CA NV OR WA Canada.
Features: Ceramics Crafts Dance Drama Fine_Arts Photog Woodworking Aquatics Archery Bicycle_Tours Boating Canoe Chess Climbing_Wall Cooking Fishing Hiking Kayak Mtn_Biking Rappelling Riding Rock_Climb Ropes_Crse White-water_Raft Aerobics Badminton Baseball Basketball Field_Hockey Football Golf Gymnastics Lacrosse Roller_Hockey Soccer Softball Street_Hockey Swim Tennis Volleyball Water-skiing Watersports Weight_Trng.
Fees 2012: Res $5500-8550 (+$500), 3½-7½ wks.
Housing: Cabins. Avg per room/unit: 9. **Swimming:** Lake Pool.
Est 1941. Inc. **Ses:** 3. **Wks/ses:** 3½-7. Operates June-Aug. ACA.

Among Kennybrook's offerings are such athletic, creative and cultural activities as drama, photography, crafts, water-skiing, mountain biking, team sports, swimming and cooking. Campers follow a structured activity schedule in which they choose two electives daily. A special program (available for an additional fee), the Teen Travel Experience, enables rising ninth and tenth graders to combine six weeks at Kennybrook with two weeks of travel throughout the West Coast and into western Canada.

CAMP SCHODACK
Res — Coed Ages 7-15

Nassau, NY 12123. 40 Krouner Rd. Tel: 518-766-3100. Fax: 518-766-3035.
Contact (Sept-May): 400 Hillside Ave, Ste 11, Needham, MA 02494. Tel: 781-444-5520.
    Fax: 781-444-5589.
www.schodack.com   E-mail: camp@schodack.com
Paul Krouner & Linda Krouner, Dirs.
Adm: FCFS. Enr: 270. Staff: Couns 130.
Fees 2010: Res $5500-8750, 3½-7 wks.
Est 1957. Ses: 2. Wks/ses: 3½. Operates June-Aug.

Schodack's program includes most land and water activities. The camp conducts hiking, canoeing and white-water rafting trips.

ADIRONDACK WOODCRAFT CAMPS
Res — Coed Ages 6-15

Old Forge, NY 13420. 285 Woodcraft Rd, PO Box 219. Tel: 315-369-6031,
    800-374-4840. Fax: 315-369-6032.
www.woodcraftcamps.com   E-mail: tim@awc1.com
David R. Leach, John Leach & Tim Leach, Dirs.
Grades 1-11. Adm: FCFS. Appl due: Rolling. Enr: 120. Enr cap: 120. Staff: Admin 3.
    Couns 30.
Features: Astron Ecol Environ_Sci Sci Crafts Painting Photog Aquatics Archery Boating
    Canoe Climbing_Wall Conservation Exploration Fishing Hiking Kayak Mountaineering
    Mtn_Biking Mtn_Trips Rappelling Riding Riflery Rock_Climb Sail Survival_Trng White-
    water_Raft Wilderness_Camp Wilderness_Canoe Woodcraft Basketball Equestrian
    Soccer Softball Swim Tennis Ultimate_Frisbee Volleyball Watersports.
Fees 2011: Res $3993-6389 (+$100), 3-7 wks. Aid 2010 (Need): $7500.
Housing: Cabins. Avg per room/unit: 5. Swimming: Lake.
Est 1925. Inc. Ses: 3. Wks/ses: 3-7. Operates June-Aug.

Featuring 300 acres of woodland, two large lakes and nearly two miles of wilderness river, Woodcraft has eight divisional camps, with programs for each age group structured to allow campers to expand their abilities. While AWC offers a diverse program, wilderness living skills are emphasized. Activities include photography, crafts, natural science, forestry, land sports and watersports, wilderness and mountain climbing trips, technical rock climbing, rappelling, zip lines, survival techniques and mountain biking.

CAMP REGIS-APPLEJACK
Res — Coed Ages 6-16

Paul Smiths, NY 12970. PO Box 245. Tel: 518-327-3117. Fax: 518-327-3193.
Contact (Winter): 60 Lafayette Rd W, Princeton, NJ 08540. Tel: 609-688-0368.
    Fax: 609-688-0369.
www.campregis-applejack.com   E-mail: campregis@aol.com
Michael S. Humes, Dir.
Grades 1-10. Adm: FCFS. Appl due: Rolling. Enr: 240. Staff: Admin 10. Couns 50.
Features: Lang Crafts Dance Fine_Arts Music Theater Aquatics Archery Bicycle_Tours
    Boating Canoe Fishing Hiking Mountaineering Mtn_Biking Riding Sail Wilderness_Camp
    Wilderness_Canoe Baseball Basketball Field_Hockey Football Gymnastics Lacrosse
    Soccer Softball Swim Tennis Volleyball Water-skiing Watersports.
Fees 2012: Res $3950-7350 (+$100), 4-8 wks.
Housing: Cabins Lodges. Swimming: Lake.
Est 1946. Inc. Ses: 3. Wks/ses: 4-8. Operates June-Aug. ACA.

In a multicultural setting in the Adirondack Mountains, Camp Regis-AJ conducts an elective program that features sailing, windsurfing, water-skiing, swimming, canoeing, tennis, athletics, arts and crafts, dramatics, mountain climbing and wilderness camping. Applejack, the teen division, schedules weeklong trips to sites in the Northeast and eastern Canada.

CAMPUS KIDS
MINISINK
Res — Coed Ages 7-16

Port Jervis, NY 12771. PO Box 3160. Tel: 845-856-6433. Fax: 845-856-5103.
Contact (Sept-May): PO Box 224, Bethel, CT 06801. Tel: 203-743-6395.
  Fax: 203-743-6973.
Year-round Toll-free: 888-621-2267.
www.campuskids.com/CKMinisinkPage.htm
E-mail: ckminisink@campuskids.com
Jani Brokaw, Dir.
Grades 2-11. Adm: FCFS. **Appl due:** Rolling. **Enr:** 250. **Enr cap:** 250. **Staff:** Admin 14.
  Couns 80. Res 115.
Features: Ecol Environ_Sci Writing/Journ Crafts Creative_Writing Dance Drama Fine_Arts Music Photog Aquatics Archery Boating Canoe Chess Climbing_Wall Community_Serv Conservation Cooking Fishing Hiking Kayak Mtn_Biking Outdoor_Ed Riding Ropes_ Crse Sail Yoga Aerobics Badminton Baseball Basketball Cricket Equestrian Fencing Field_Hockey Football Golf Gymnastics Lacrosse Martial_Arts Soccer Softball Swim Tennis Ultimate_Frisbee Volleyball.
Fees 2012: Res $2105-8030 (+$300), 2-8 wks.
Housing: Cabins. Avg per room/unit: 8. **Swimming:** Lake.
Est 1991. Inc. **Ses:** 4. **Wks/ses:** 2-8. Operates June-Aug. ACA.

Enrolling campers from New Jersey, New York, Connecticut and Pennsylvania, Minisink combines sports, aquatics, performing and creative arts, outdoor adventure, hiking, high ropes training and special events. Boys and girls select their own activities each day. Campers spend weekdays at camp, then return home on weekends; transportation is provided.

ADIRONDACK CAMP
Res — Coed Ages 7-16

Putnam Station, NY 12861. PO Box 97. Tel: 518-547-8261. Fax: 518-547-8973.
www.adirondackcamp.com   E-mail: info@adirondackcamp.com
Matthew Basinet, Dir.
Adm: FCFS. **Appl due:** Rolling. **Enr:** 185. **Staff:** Admin 3. Couns 80.
Features: Crafts Dance Drama Fine_Arts Music Studio_Art Aquatics Archery Boating Canoe Caving Climbing_Wall Cooking Exploration Fishing Hiking Kayak Mountaineering Mtn_Trips Rappelling Rock_Climb Ropes_Crse Sail White-water_Raft Wilderness_ Camp Basketball Fencing Field_Hockey Golf Lacrosse Soccer Softball Swim Tennis Volleyball Water-skiing Watersports.
Fees 2009: Res $3000-8000 (+$20-390), 2-8 wks. Aid 2009: $20,000.
Housing: Cabins. **Swimming:** Lake.
Est 1904. Inc. **Ses:** 6. **Wks/ses:** 2-8. Operates June-Aug.

Adirondack offers a wide range of waterfront activities, sports, outdoor adventures and trips. Creative pursuits include arts and crafts, culinary courses, drama, music and publishing. Older campers embark on mountain biking, rock climbing and white-water rafting excursions. Dances, magic shows and camp Olympics are some of the special events.

RAQUETTE LAKE BOYS CAMP
RAQUETTE LAKE GIRLS CAMP
Res — Coord Ages 6-15

Raquette Lake, NY 13436. HC 2, Box 203. Tel: 315-354-4382. Fax: 315-354-4317.
Contact (Sept-May): 444 Old Post Rd, Ste A, Bedford, NY 10506. Tel: 914-764-1500.
Fax: 914-764-1600.
Year-round Toll-free: 800-786-8373.
www.raquettelake.com   E-mail: director@raquettelake.com
Ed Lapidus, Kathy Lapidus & Steven Norman, Dirs.
Adm: Selective. Appl due: Rolling. Enr: 340.
Features: Ceramics Crafts Dance Painting Photog Theater Woodworking Aquatics Archery
Canoe Climbing_Wall Fishing Hiking Kayak Mountaineering Mtn_Biking Mtn_Trips
Riding Ropes_Crse Sail Survival_Trng White-water_Raft Wilderness_Camp Wilderness_Canoe Woodcraft Aerobics Baseball Basketball Equestrian Football Golf Gymnastics Ice_Hockey Lacrosse Roller_Hockey Soccer Softball Street_Hockey Swim
Tennis Volleyball Water-skiing Watersports Weight_Trng.
Fees 2010: Res $10,250 (+$305-500), 7 wks.
Housing: Cabins. Avg per room/unit: 6-8. Swimming: Lake.
Est 1916. Inc. Ses: 1. Wks/ses: 7. Operates June-Aug. ACA.

These brother and sister camps occupy opposite sides of Raquette Lake in the Adirondack
Mountains. The boys' camp emphasizes athletics: Each week, the camp offers concentration
in nine sports, and older campers with particular interest in a specific sport may engage in a
specialty program to promote further mastery. Girls choose from arts and crafts, ceramics, team
and individual sports, canoeing, swimming, sailing, hiking, rock climbing and an equestrian
program, among other pursuits. The camp plans canoeing, sailing, rafting and mountain
climbing day trips, as well as recreational excursions to the Olympic Training Center in Lake
Placid, the Adirondack Museum, the Baseball Hall of Fame in Cooperstown and a local water
park.

IROQUOIS SPRINGS
Res — Coed Ages 7-16

Rock Hill, NY 12775. PO Box 487. Tel: 845-434-6500. Fax: 845-434-6508.
Contact (Sept-May): PO Box 20126, Dix Hills, NY 11746. Tel: 631-462-2550.
Fax: 631-462-0779.
www.iroquoissprings.com   E-mail: summers@iroquoissprings.com
Mark Newfield & Laura Newfield, Dirs.
Grades 2-11. Adm: FCFS. Appl due: Rolling. Enr: 400. Staff: Admin 25. Couns 180.
Features: Crafts Dance Photog Theater Aquatics Archery Bicycle_Tours Boating Canoe
Climbing_Wall Cooking Exploration Fishing Hiking Mtn_Biking Riding Rock_Climb
Ropes_Crse White-water_Raft Baseball Basketball Equestrian Golf Gymnastics
Lacrosse Roller_Hockey Soccer Softball Swim Tennis Ultimate_Frisbee Volleyball
Water-skiing.
Fees 2010: Res $4950-8150, 3-6 wks.
Housing: Cabins. Avg per room/unit: 11. Swimming: Lake Pool.
Est 2000. Inc. Ses: 3. Wks/ses: 3-6. Operates June-Aug. ACA.

Located on a 180-acre site in a mountainous region of the state, Iroquois Springs offers
a traditional camping experience in a noncompetitive setting. Programming comprises land
sports, arts offerings, extensive outdoor adventure pursuits and water sports. Although most
boys and girls enroll from the Northeast, all regions of the country are represented at the
camp.

TIMBER LAKE WEST
Res — Coed Ages 8-16

Roscoe, NY 12776. 76 Timber Lake Rd. Tel: 845-439-4440. Fax: 845-439-3165.
Contact (Sept-June): 85 Crescent Beach Rd, Glen Cove, NY 11542.
Tel: 516-656-4210. Fax: 516-656-4215.
Year-round Toll-free: 800-828-2267.
www.timberlakewest.com   E-mail: info@timberlakewest.com
Justin Mayer & Jennifer DeSpagna, Dirs.
Grades 3-11. Adm: FCFS. **Appl due:** Rolling. **Enr:** 300. **Enr cap:** 300. **Staff:** Admin 30.
Couns 110. Res 185.
Features: Crafts Dance Fine_Arts Painting Theater Aquatics Archery Bicycle_Tours Boat-
ing Canoe Climbing_Wall Farm Hiking Kayak Mtn_Biking Ropes_Crse Wilderness_
Camp Woodcraft Basketball Football Lacrosse Martial_Arts Roller_Hockey Skateboard-
ing Soccer Softball Swim Tennis Volleyball Water-skiing Watersports.
Fees 2011: Res $6450 (+$150), 4 wks.
Housing: Cabins. **Swimming:** Lake Pool.
Est 1987. Inc. Ses: 2. **Wks/ses:** 4. Operates July-Aug. ACA.

TLW offers extensive athletic and waterfront offerings and an elective program that
provides individualized instruction in camper-selected fields. Campers engage in two athletic,
two waterfront and two free-choice periods per day. Athletics include both individual and
team sports. The camp schedules age-appropriate day trips to nearby sites of interest each
Wednesday.

LOURDES CAMP
Res — Coed Ages 7-14; Day — Coed 7-11

Skaneateles, NY 13152. Ten Mile Pt. Tel: 315-673-2888.
Contact (Winter): 1653 W Onondaga St, Syracuse, NY 13204. Tel: 315-424-1812.
www.lourdescamp.com   E-mail: lourdes4me@aol.com
Michael Preston, Dir.
Adm: FCFS.
Fees 2009: Res $325-335 (+$10), 1 wk. Day $185 (+$10), 1 wk.
Housing: Cabins.
Est 1942. Ses: 6. **Wks/ses:** 1. Operates July-Aug. ACA.

Lourdes' selection of activities includes arts and crafts, photography, swimming, canoeing,
archery, basketball, soccer and riding. Campers also participate in overnight hikes, cookouts
and other special events.

CAMP CHIPINAW
Res — Coed Ages 7-17

Swan Lake, NY 12783. 85 Silver Lake Rd. Tel: 845-583-5600. Fax: 845-583-5454.
Contact (Sept-May): 11939 NW 37th St, Coral Springs, FL 33065. Tel: 954-227-7700.
Fax: 954-227-0481.
Year-round Toll-free: 800-244-7462.
www.chipinaw.com   E-mail: info@chipinaw.com
Michael Baer, Dir.
Grades 2-10. Adm: FCFS. **Appl due:** Rolling. **Enr:** 250-500. **Staff:** Admin 12. Couns 200.
Features: Computers Circus_Skills Crafts Dance Fine_Arts Painting Photog Studio_Art
Theater Aquatics Archery Boating Canoe Climbing_Wall Cooking Fishing Kayak Moun-
taineering Mtn_Biking Riding Rock_Climb Ropes_Crse Sail Scuba Woodcraft Aero-
bics Baseball Basketball Equestrian Fencing Field_Hockey Football Golf Gymnastics
Lacrosse Martial_Arts Roller_Hockey Skateboarding Soccer Softball Street_Hockey
Swim Tennis Volleyball Water-skiing Watersports Weight_Trng.
Fees 2012: Res $5550-9150 (+$300), 4-8 wks.

Housing: Cabins. Avg per room/unit: 8. **Swimming:** Lake Pool.
Est 1926. Inc. Ses: 3. **Wks/ses:** 4-8. Operates June-Aug. ACA.

Located in the Catskill Mountains, Chipinaw offers a diverse program of sports, arts and adventure within an eight-week session. Campers looking for a shorter program may attend Chipinaw @ Silver Lake, which runs for four weeks and is located adjacent to Chipinaw. In both programs, activities include arts and crafts, land sports, watersports, adventure programming, riding and circus skills, among others.

CAMP REDWOOD
Res — Coed Ages 5-16
(Coord — Res 5-12)

Walden, NY 12586. 576 Rock Cut Rd. Tel: 845-564-1180, 888-600-6655.
 Fax: 845-564-1128.
www.camp-redwood.com E-mail: info@campredwood.net
Adm: FCFS. **Appl due:** Rolling.
Type of instruction: Rem_Math Rem_Read.
Features: ESL Crafts Dance Music Archery Canoe Fishing Kayak Riding Riflery Woodcraft Basketball Field_Hockey In-line_Skating Lacrosse Soccer Softball Street_Hockey Swim Volleyball Water-skiing Watersports Bowling.
Housing: Cabins. **Swimming:** Lake.
Est 1961. Ses: 1. **Wks/ses:** 8. Operates June-Aug.

Located on a 40-acre site in the foothills of the Shawangunk Mountains, Redwood provides instruction in a wide variety of land sports and aquatic activities. Boys and girls ages 5-12 attend single-gender sessions, while older campers engage in coeducational programming. The camp schedules an array of trips and tours during its eight-week session to such destinations as a nearby lake, a water park, New York City landmarks and West Point. ESL instruction and remedial math and reading are available. Offered to teenagers for an additional fee, a flight training program enables boys and girls to receive 10 hours of flight instruction, while also accruing 20 hours of cockpit observation.

CAMP POK-O-MOONSHINE
CAMP MACCREADY
Res — Coord Ages 6-16; Day — Coord 6-12

Willsboro, NY 12996. PO Box 397. Tel: 518-963-7656, 800-982-3538.
 Fax: 518-963-4165.
www.pokomac.com E-mail: info@pokomac.com
Sharp Swan, Exec Dir.
Grades 1-10. Adm: FCFS. **Appl due:** Rolling. **Enr:** 215. **Enr cap:** 245. **Staff:** Admin 15. Couns 50.
Type of instruction: Rem_Eng Rem_Math Rem_Read.
Features: ESL Writing/Journ Crafts Creative_Writing Dance Music Painting Photog Theater Aquatics Archery Boating Canoe Climbing_Wall Conservation Exploration Farm Fishing Hiking Kayak Mountaineering Mtn_Biking Mtn_Trips Riding Riflery Rock_Climb Ropes_Crse Sail Wilderness_Camp Wilderness_Canoe Woodcraft Baseball Basketball Equestrian Lacrosse Soccer Softball Street_Hockey Swim Tennis Ultimate_Frisbee Volleyball Watersports.
Fees 2011: Res $3300-6250 (+$150), 3-7 wks. Day $1650-1850 (+$50), 3 wks. Aid 2010 (Need): $45,000.
Housing: Cabins Lodges. Avg per room/unit: 6. **Swimming:** Lake.
Est 1905. Inc. Ses: 3. **Wks/ses:** 3-7. Operates June-Aug. ACA.

Activities at Pok-O-MacCready (Camp Pok-O-Moonshine for boys and Camp MacCready for girls) include team and individual sports, camp craft, rock climbing, blacksmithing, Indian lore, extensive horseback riding, farming, mountain biking, ecology and nature study, as well as one- to three-day wilderness trips in the Adirondacks. Tutoring is available to campers in grades 1-8.

TRADE WINDS LAKE CAMP
Res — Coord Ages 7-16

Windsor, NY 13865. 2276 Old Rte 17. Tel: 607-467-3356.
Contact (Sept-June): 256 Macopin Rd, West Milford, NJ 07480. Tel: 973-838-1394.
Year-round Fax: 607-467-2793.
www.tradewindslakecamp.org   E-mail: registrar@vacamas.org
Riel Peerbooms, Exec Dir.
Grades 2-11. Adm: FCFS. **Enr:** 160. **Staff:** Admin 6. Couns 40.
Features: Environ_Sci Crafts Dance Fine_Arts Music Photog Theater Aquatics Archery Boating Canoe Fishing Hiking Basketball Gymnastics Martial_Arts Soccer Softball Swim Tennis Volleyball.
Housing: Cabins. **Swimming:** Lake.
Est 1989. Inc. **Ses:** 2. **Wks/ses:** 4. Operates July-Aug. ACA.

This academically enriched, traditional camp caters to inner-city minority children and features a structured program. Activities are geared primarily toward athletics, waterfront activities, dramatics, arts and crafts, literacy and earth science. Fees are determined along a sliding scale according to family income.

CAMP LAKOTA
Res — Coed Ages 6-16

Wurtsboro, NY 12790. 56 Park Rd. Tel: 845-888-5611. Fax: 845-888-5230.
Contact (Sept-May): 1 Balint Dr, Ste 265, Yonkers, NY 10710. Tel: 914-779-8668.
Fax: 914-274-8311.
Year-round Toll-free: 866-752-5682.
www.camplakota.com   E-mail: info@camplakota.com
Carol Hager & Doug Katz, Dirs.
Grades 2-10. Adm: FCFS. **Appl due:** May. **Enr:** 380. **Enr cap:** 380. **Staff:** Admin 20. Couns 150.
Features: Computers Ecol Environ_Sci Crafts Dance Filmmaking Media Music Painting Photog Theater Aquatics Archery Bicycle_Tours Boating Canoe Climbing_Wall Community_Serv Cooking Fishing Hiking Kayak Mountaineering Mtn_Biking Outdoor_Ed Rappelling Rock_Climb Ropes_Crse Sail Scuba Aerobics Baseball Basketball Equestrian Football Golf Gymnastics Lacrosse Martial_Arts Roller_Hockey Soccer Softball Street_Hockey Swim Tennis Track Ultimate_Frisbee Volleyball Water-skiing Watersports Weight_Trng.
Fees 2012: Res $3800-8000 (+$200), 3-7 wks.
Housing: Cabins Dorms Lodges. Avg per room/unit: 8. **Swimming:** Lake Pool.
Est 1924. Ses: 3. **Wks/ses:** 3-7. Operates June-Aug. ACA.

Situated on a 200-acre site atop the Wurtsboro Hills, Lakota offers a full range of traditional camping activities. Programming combines athletic and nonathletic options. Campers in grades 9 and 10 embark on a three-day sightseeing trip.

CAMP SCULLY
Res — Coed Ages 7-14

Wynantskill, NY 12198. 24 Camp Scully Way. Tel: 518-283-1617.
Contact (Sept-May): 40 N Main Ave, Albany, NY 12203. Tel: 518-453-6613.
Year-round Fax: 518-453-6792.
http://campscully.squarespace.com   E-mail: campscully@rcda.org
Colin Stewart, Dir.

Adm: FCFS. Admitted: 100%. **Appl due:** Rolling. **Enr:** 60. **Enr cap:** 60. **Staff:** Admin 8. Couns 20.
Features: Astron Ecol Environ_Sci Writing/Journ Crafts Dance Drama Music Painting Aquatics Archery Boating Canoe Conservation Cooking Fishing Hiking Kayak Outdoor_ Ed Ropes_Crse Social_Servs Wilderness_Camp Baseball Basketball Field_Hockey Football Soccer Softball Swim Ultimate_Frisbee Volleyball.
Fees 2012: Res $325, 1 wk. Day $165, 1 wk. Aid 2008 (Need): $58,200.
Housing: Cabins. Avg per room/unit: 10. **Swimming:** Lake.
Est 1920. Nonprofit. **Ses:** 9. **Wks/ses:** 1. Operates June-Aug. ACA.

Scully provides an educational recreation program that fosters social skill development in a natural environment. Offerings include arts and crafts, hiking, archery, boating, ropes courses, field sports and swimming. While the camp serves all children, it facilitates the enrollment of boys and girls from low-income families through an expansive scholarship program.

NORTH CAROLINA

CAMP HOLLYMONT
Res — Girls Ages 6-15

Asheville, NC 28806. c/o Asheville School, 360 Asheville School Rd.
   Tel: 828-252-2123. Fax: 828-252-2451.
Contact (Sept-May): 475 Lake Eden Rd, Black Mountain, NC 28711.
   Tel: 828-686-5343. Fax: 828-686-7206.
www.hollymont.com   E-mail: 4info@hollymont.com
Lauren G. Glass, Dir.
Adm: FCFS. **Appl due:** Rolling. **Enr:** 110. **Staff:** Admin 6. Couns 40.
Focus: Religion. **Features:** Crafts Creative_Writing Dance Music Photog Theater Aquatics Archery Cooking Riding Rock_Climb White-water_Raft Aerobics Basketball Equestrian Golf Gymnastics Soccer Softball Swim Tennis Volleyball Water-skiing Sewing.
Fees 2012: Res $1520-5600 (+$240), 1-4 wks.
Housing: Dorms. **Swimming:** Pool.
Est 1983. Inc. Nondenom Christian. **Ses:** 11. **Wks/ses:** 1-4. Operates June-Aug. ACA.

Located on the campus of the Asheville School, this Christian camp offers land sports, watersports, artistic endeavors, cooking, camping and hiking. The daily schedule enables girls to develop their abilities in six skill areas. Talent shows, campfire nights and scavenger hunts are among the evening activities.

CAMP MERRI-MAC
CAMP TIMBERLAKE
Res — Coord Ages 7-16, Girls 6

Black Mountain, NC 28711. 1123 Montreat Rd. Tel: 828-669-8766. Fax: 828-669-6822.
www.merri-mac.com; www.camptimberlake.com
E-mail: mail@merri-mac.com; email@camptimberlake.com
Adam Boyd, Ann Boyd & Dan Singletary, Dirs.
Adm: FCFS. **Appl due:** Rolling. **Enr cap:** 100-200. **Staff:** Admin 8. Couns 80.
Features: Crafts Dance Fine_Arts Music Theater Adventure_Travel Aquatics Archery Canoe Climbing_Wall Fishing Hiking Kayak Mountaineering Mtn_Biking Mtn_Trips Paintball Rappelling Riding Riflery Rock_Climb Ropes_Crse White-water_Raft Wilderness_Camp Wilderness_Canoe Basketball Equestrian Fencing Gymnastics Soccer Swim Tennis Volleyball Water-skiing Watersports Weight_Trng Wrestling.
Fees 2012: Res $1200-5300 (+$50), 1-5 wks.
Housing: Cabins. **Swimming:** Lake.

Est 1945. Inc. Nondenom Christian. **Ses:** 9. **Wks/ses:** 1-5. Operates June-Aug. ACA.

Various land sports and watersports, horseback riding, white-water canoeing, archery, backpacking, kayaking, crafts, drama and dance constitute the program at Merri-Mac for girls and Timberlake for boys. The town of Black Mountain is surrounded by the Blue Ridge Mountains.

CAMP CAROLINA
Res — Boys Ages 7-18

Brevard, NC 28712. Lambs Creek Rd, PO Box 919. Tel: 828-884-2414, 800-551-9136. Fax: 828-884-2454.
www.campcarolina.com   E-mail: info@campcarolina.com
Alfred Thompson, Dir.
Grades 2-PG. Adm: FCFS. **Appl due:** Apr. **Enr cap:** 281. **Staff:** Admin 15. Couns 110.
Features: Crafts Creative_Writing Filmmaking Media Music Adventure_Travel Aquatics Archery Bicycle_Tours Boating Canoe Caving Climbing_Wall Community_Serv Cooking Exploration Fishing Hiking Kayak Mountaineering Mtn_Biking Mtn_Trips Pack_Train Paintball Peace/Cross-cultural Rappelling Riding Riflery Rock_Climb Ropes_Crse Sail Scuba White-water_Raft Wilderness_Camp Yoga Baseball Basketball Equestrian Fencing Field_Hockey Football Golf Lacrosse Skateboarding Soccer Softball Surfing Swim Tennis Volleyball Water-skiing Watersports.
Fees 2012: Res $2750-9950 (+$70-350), 2-10 wks.
Housing: Cabins Lodges. Avg per room/unit: 7. **Swimming:** Lake River Stream.
Est 1924. Inc. Ses: 10. **Wks/ses:** 2-10. Operates June-Aug. ACA.

Carolina provides instruction and adventure opportunities in such activities as watersports, white-water kayaking and rafting, mountain trips, tennis, golf, riding, team sports, mountain biking and hiking. Facilities include a hang-gliding flight trainer, tennis courts, a gym, two skate parks, a low ropes course and a zip line. Two-week sessions are open to children entering grades 2-6 only.

GWYNN VALLEY CAMP
Res — Coed Ages 6-14; Day — Coed 6-10

Brevard, NC 28712. 301 Gwynn Valley Trail. Tel: 828-885-2900. Fax: 828-885-2413.
www.gwynnvalley.com   E-mail: mail@gwynnvalley.com
Anne Bullard & Grant Bullard, Dirs.
Grades 1-9. Adm: FCFS. **Appl due:** Rolling. **Enr:** 210. **Enr cap:** 210. **Staff:** Admin 10. Couns 120. Res 90.
Features: Ecol Crafts Creative_Writing Dance Fine_Arts Music Theater Archery Canoe Climbing_Wall Conservation Cooking Exploration Farm Fishing Hiking Kayak Mountaineering Mtn_Biking Mtn_Trips Riding Rock_Climb Wilderness_Camp Wilderness_Canoe Woodcraft Basketball Equestrian Lacrosse Rugby Soccer Swim Ultimate_Frisbee Volleyball.
Fees 2011: Res $1375-3600, 1-3 wks. **Day** $390, 1 wk. Aid (Need).
Housing: Cabins. Avg per room/unit: 8. **Swimming:** Lake Pool River Stream.
Est 1935. Inc. Ses: 7. **Wks/ses:** 1-3. Operates June-Aug. ACA.

Situated on 320 acres in the Blue Ridge Mountains, Gwynn Valley offers a noncompetitive program that emphasizes individual achievement in swimming, canoeing, arts, crafts, music, sports, nature study and riding for the younger child. Campers feed animals, garden, milk cows and goats, and harvest fruits and vegetables on the camp's working farm. Dating back to the 1890s, a grist mill provides opportunities for grinding, fishing, cornbread baking and ice cream making.

CAMP ILLAHEE
Res — Girls Ages 7-16

Brevard, NC 28712. 500 Illahee Rd. Tel: 828-883-2181. Fax: 828-883-8738.
www.campillahee.com   E-mail: mail@campillahee.com
Laurie Strayhorn & Gordon Strayhorn, Dirs.
Grades 2-10. **Adm:** FCFS. **Appl due:** Rolling. **Enr:** 250. **Staff:** Admin 5. Couns 80.
Features: Crafts Dance Drama Painting Archery Canoe Climbing_Wall Cooking Hiking Kayak Mountaineering Rappelling Riding Riflery Rock_Climb Ropes_Crse White-water_Raft Wilderness_Canoe Woodcraft Aerobics Basketball Equestrian Field_Hockey Golf Gymnastics Lacrosse Soccer Softball Swim Tennis Volleyball Watersports.
Fees 2012: Res $1275-4850 (+$40-80), 2-4 wks.
Housing: Cabins. Avg per room/unit: 6-8. **Swimming:** Lake.
Est 1921. Inc. Nondenom Christian. **Ses:** 6. **Wks/ses:** 2-4. Operates June-Aug. ACA.

Illahee's activity program features riding, swimming, tennis, riflery, canoeing, creative arts, crafts, dance, archery, dramatics and gymnastics. White-water kayaking and rock climbing are part of a tripping program for older girls. The camp conducts a Christian worship service each Sunday.

CAMP KAHDALEA FOR GIRLS
CAMP CHOSATONGA FOR BOYS
Res — Coord Ages 8-18, Girls 7

Brevard, NC 28712. 2500 Morgan Mill Rd. Tel: 828-884-6834. Fax: 828-884-6834.
www.kahdalea.com   E-mail: office@kahdalea.com
Anne Trufant & David Trufant, Dirs.
Grades 1-12. **Adm:** FCFS. **Appl due:** Rolling. **Enr:** 80-150. **Enr cap:** 80-150. **Staff:** Admin 6. Couns 130.
Features: Crafts Dance Music Theater Aquatics Archery Canoe Caving Chess Climbing_Wall Community_Serv Hiking Kayak Mountaineering Mtn_Biking Mtn_Trips Outdoor_Ed Rappelling Riding Riflery Rock_Climb Ropes_Crse White-water_Raft Wilderness_Camp Basketball Equestrian Football Gymnastics Soccer Swim Tennis Volleyball.
Fees 2010: Res $2275-6680 (+$70-315), 2-8½ wks.
Housing: Cabins. Avg per room/unit: 6. **Swimming:** Lake.
Est 1964. Inc. Nondenom Christian. **Ses:** 4. **Wks/ses:** 2-8½. Operates June-Aug.

Located approximately a mile apart at an altitude of about 3000 feet within the Pisgah National Forest, Kahdalea and Chosatonga are traditional camps with a wilderness emphasis. Instruction in each activity spans from the simplest and most basic principles to advanced techniques. Two-week sessions are open to young campers only (girls ages 7-12, boys ages 8-12).

KEYSTONE CAMP
Res — Girls Ages 6-14

Brevard, NC 28712. 101 Keystone Camp Rd, PO Box 829. Tel: 828-884-9125.
Fax: 828-883-8234.
www.keystonecamp.com   E-mail: office@keystonecamp.com
Page Ives Lemel, Dir.
Grades 1-9. **Adm:** FCFS. **Appl due:** Rolling. **Enr:** 125. **Staff:** Admin 4. Couns 40.
Features: Crafts Dance Drama Painting Aquatics Archery Canoe Climbing_Wall Hiking Mountaineering Outdoor_Ed Rappelling Riding Riflery Rock_Climb Ropes_Crse Wilderness_Camp Wilderness_Canoe Aerobics Badminton Baseball Basketball Equestrian Football Golf Gymnastics Soccer Softball Swim Tennis Volleyball.
Fees 2012: Res $1250-4825 (+$45), 1-4 wks.
Housing: Cabins. Avg per room/unit: 8. **Swimming:** Lake Stream.
Est 1916. Inc. **Ses:** 6. **Wks/ses:** 1-4. Operates June-Aug. ACA.

Keystone's offerings include daily riding lessons, horsemanship, land sports, canoeing, rock climbing, and overnight camping and hiking trips. Girls may also participate in dance, dramatics, and an extensive arts and crafts program.

ROCKBROOK CAMP
Res — Girls Ages 6-16

Brevard, NC 28712. PO Box 792. Tel: 828-884-6151. Fax: 828-884-6459.
www.rockbrookcamp.com   E-mail: office@rockbrookcamp.com
Sarah Carter & Jeff Carter, Dirs.
Adm: FCFS. **Appl due:** Rolling. **Enr:** 192. **Enr cap:** 192. **Staff:** Admin 7. Couns 60.
Features: Crafts Creative_Writing Dance Drama Music Photog Aquatics Archery Canoe Climbing_Wall Conservation Exploration Fishing Hiking Kayak Mtn_Biking Riding Riflery Rock_Climb Ropes_Crse White-water_Raft Wilderness_Camp Wilderness_Canoe Basketball Equestrian Golf Gymnastics Soccer Swim Tennis Volleyball.
Fees 2012: Res $2500-4700 (+$75), 1½-3½ wks.
Housing: Cabins. **Swimming:** Pond.
Est 1921. Inc. Ses: 7. **Wks/ses:** 1½-3½. Operates June-Aug. ACA.

Located in a mountain setting at an elevation of 2250 feet, Rockbrook administers its program according to the age, ability level and interests of the camper. Twice weekly, each girl selects her own daily activities. Girls may participate in horseback riding, land sports, watersports and various arts offerings.

SKYLAND CAMP
Res — Girls Ages 6-15; Day — Girls 6-9

Clyde, NC 28721. 317 Spencer St, PO Box 128. Tel: 828-627-2470. Fax: 828-627-2071.
www.skylandcamp.com   E-mail: sherry@skylandcamp.com
Sherry Brown, Dir.
Grades 1-9. Adm: FCFS. **Appl due:** Rolling. **Enr:** 75. **Enr cap:** 75. **Staff:** Admin 10. Couns 26.
Features: Crafts Dance Music Theater Archery Canoe Hiking Mtn_Trips Riding Ropes_Crse White-water_Raft Wilderness_Camp Baseball Basketball Equestrian Gymnastics Softball Swim Tennis Volleyball.
Fees 2012: Res $2650-4900 (+$150-250), 2½-5 wks. Day $300, 1 wk.
Housing: Cabins Lodges. **Swimming:** Pond.
Est 1917. Inc. Ses: 4. **Wks/ses:** 1-5. Operates June-July.

Skyland offers many outdoor activities, including archery, swimming, arts and crafts, and nature study. The program emphasizes riding, tennis, sports, drama and camping trips.

CAMP PINNACLE
Res — Coed Ages 8-14

Flat Rock, NC 28731. PO Box 1321. Tel: 828-692-2677, 855-378-1928.
Fax: 828-698-0339.
www.camppinnacle.com   E-mail: info@camppinnacle.com
Ben Lea, Dir.
Grades 3-8. Adm: FCFS. **Appl due:** Rolling. **Enr cap:** 160. **Staff:** Admin 5. Couns 55. Res 3.
Features: Crafts Painting Adventure_Travel Aquatics Archery Boating Canoe Caving Climbing_Wall Exploration Farm Fishing Hiking Kayak Mtn_Biking Mtn_Trips Outdoor_Ed Rappelling Riflery Rock_Climb White-water_Raft Wilderness_Camp Wilderness_Canoe Woodcraft Basketball Lacrosse Soccer Softball Swim Tennis Ultimate_Frisbee Volleyball Watersports.
Fees 2012: Res $2695-4995, 2-4 wks. Aid (Need).

Housing: Cabins Tents. Avg per room/unit: 8. **Swimming:** Lake River Stream. **Est 1928.** Inc. **Ses:** 3. **Wks/ses:** 2-4. Operates July-Aug.

Located in the Blue Ridge Mountains on Wolfe Lake, Pinnacle engages campers in such diverse offerings as land sports, riding, crafts, swimming, archery, riflery, tennis, lake and white-water canoeing, backpacking, mountaineering and rock climbing. The program emphasizes outdoor exploration and adventure.

BLUE STAR CAMPS
Res — Coed Ages 6-16

Hendersonville, NC 28793. PO Box 1029. Tel: 828-692-3591. Fax: 828-692-7030.
Contact (Sept-May): 3595 Sheridan St, Ste 107, Hollywood, FL 33021.
  Tel: 954-963-4494. Fax: 954-963-2145.
www.bluestarcamps.com   E-mail: fun@bluestarcamps.com
Lauren Poplin-Herschthal & Seth Herschthal, Dirs.
Grades 1-11. Adm: FCFS. **Admitted:** 95%. **Appl due:** May. **Enr:** 600. **Enr cap:** 700. **Staff:** Admin 45. Couns 175.
Features: Environ_Sci Lang Crafts Filmmaking Fine_Arts Media Music Painting Studio_ Art Theater Pottery Aquatics Archery Canoe Chess Climbing_Wall Community_Serv Exploration Farm Fishing Hiking Kayak Mountaineering Mtn_Biking Outdoor_Ed Riding Riflery Rock_Climb Ropes_Crse White-water_Raft Wilderness_Camp Wilderness_ Canoe Yoga Basketball Equestrian Football Soccer Softball Street_Hockey Swim Tennis Ultimate_Frisbee Volleyball Water-skiing Watersports Weight_Trng.
Fees 2012: Res $5075-8000 (+$100), 4-8 wks.
Housing: Cabins. Avg per room/unit: 9. **Swimming:** Lake Pool.
Est 1948. Inc. Jewish. **Ses:** 4. **Wks/ses:** 4-8. Operates June-Aug. ACA.

The camp conducts separate programs for each age and grade group. Activities include riding, land sports and watersports, tripping and camp craft, extensive arts and tennis programs, a ropes challenge course, mountain biking, kayaking and rock climbing. Blue Star espouses Jewish cultural and religious values.

CAMP KANUGA
Res — Coed Ages 7-16

Hendersonville, NC 28793. PO Box 250. Tel: 828-692-9136. Fax: 828-696-3589.
www.campkanuga.org   E-mail: info@kanuga.org
Adm: FCFS. **Enr:** 618. **Staff:** Admin 6. Couns 26.
Features: Crafts Dance Music Theater Aquatics Archery Canoe Climbing_Wall Fishing Hiking Rappelling Rock_Climb Ropes_Crse White-water_Raft Wilderness_Camp Basketball Soccer Swim Volleyball.
Fees 2012: Res $935-1675, 1½-2 wks. Aid avail.
Housing: Cabins. Avg per room/unit: 10. **Swimming:** Lake.
Est 1928. Episcopal. **Ses:** 5. **Wks/ses:** 1½-2. Operates June-Aug. ACA.

Kanuga, an Episcopal-affiliated camp open to children of all denominations, offers an adventure program, aquatics, environmental awareness/outdoor living skills, performing arts, and team and individual sports.

CAMP TON-A-WANDAH
Res — Girls Ages 5-16

Hendersonville, NC 28739. 300 W Ton-A-Wandah Rd. Tel: 828-692-4251,
  800-322-0178. Fax: 828-692-9780.
www.camptonawandah.com   E-mail: info@camptonawandah.com
Billy Haynes & Judy Haynes, Executive Directors.

Adm: FCFS. **Appl due:** Rolling. **Enr:** 225. **Enr cap:** 225. **Staff:** Admin 6. Couns 80.
Features: Aquatics Archery Canoe Climbing_Wall Community_Serv Hiking Kayak Mountaineering Mtn_Trips Rappelling Riding Riflery Rock_Climb Ropes_Crse White-water_Raft Wilderness_Camp Wilderness_Canoe Woodcraft Aerobics Baseball Basketball Equestrian Golf Gymnastics Soccer Softball Swim Tennis Volleyball.
Fees 2012: Res $1150-3300 (+$95-150), 1-3 wks.
Housing: Cabins Lodges. Avg per room/unit: 12. **Swimming:** Lake.
Est 1933. Inc. Nondenom Christian. **Ses:** 7. **Wks/ses:** 1-3. Operates June-Aug. ACA.

Situated alongside a 10-acre lake in the Blue Ridge Mountains, Ton-A-Wandah offers land sports and watersports, music, dance, dramatics, computers, soccer and crafts. Daily horse riding, available for an additional fee, is an important aspect of camp life. The camp organizes trips to Pisgah National Forest and the Biltmore House. Ton-A-Wandah's weeklong starter session is open to first-time campers ages 5-8 only; enrollment in other sessions begins at age 6.

CAMP HIGHLANDER
Res — Coed Ages 5-16

Horse Shoe, NC 28742. 42 Dalton Rd. Tel: 828-891-7721. Fax: 828-891-1960.
www.camphighlander.com   E-mail: email@camphighlander.com
Gaynell Tinsley, Jr., Dir.
Grades K-10. Adm: FCFS. **Appl due:** Rolling. **Enr:** 330. **Staff:** Admin 11. Couns 70. Res 150.
Features: Crafts Dance Fine_Arts Music Painting Photog Theater Aquatics Archery Bicycle_Tours Canoe Climbing_Wall Cooking Exploration Hiking Kayak Mountaineering Mtn_Biking Mtn_Trips Riding Riflery Rock_Climb Ropes_Crse Survival_Trng White-water_Raft Wilderness_Camp Wilderness_Canoe Woodcraft Yoga Basketball Equestrian Fencing Soccer Softball Swim Tennis Water-skiing Watersports.
Fees 2012: Res $1100-3700, 1-3 wks.
Housing: Cabins Tents. Avg per room/unit: 10. **Swimming:** Lake Pool River Stream.
Est 1957. Inc. **Ses:** 3. **Wks/ses:** 1-3. Operates June-Aug. ACA.

Highlander offers many land sports and watersports, including tubing, kayaking and rafting. Day trips, backpacking and wilderness activities are main camp features. Campers may take part in extensive programs in wilderness camping, rock climbing, canoeing and horseback riding. In addition to its regular programs, the camp schedules two special weeklong sessions for campers ages 5-10 only.

EAGLE'S NEST CAMP
Res — Coed Ages 6-17

Pisgah Forest, NC 28768. 43 Hart Rd. Tel: 828-877-4349. Fax: 828-884-2788.
Contact (Aug-May): PO Box 5127, Winston-Salem, NC 27113. Tel: 336-761-1040.
Fax: 336-727-0030.
www.enf.org   E-mail: contactus@enf.org
Paige Lester-Niles, Dir.
Grades 1-12. Adm: FCFS. **Appl due:** Rolling. **Enr:** 158. **Enr cap:** 158. **Staff:** Admin 15. Couns 70.
Features: Ecol Environ_Sci Crafts Creative_Writing Dance Music Photog Theater Blacksmithing Woodworking Adventure_Travel Aquatics Archery Bicycle_Tours Canoe Caving Climbing_Wall Community_Serv Exploration Fishing Hiking Kayak Mtn_Biking Mtn_Trips Outdoor_Ed Peace/Cross-cultural Riding Rock_Climb Wilderness_Camp Wilderness_Canoe Woodcraft Yoga Baseball Basketball Cricket Rugby Soccer Swim Tennis Ultimate_Frisbee Volleyball Watersports.
Fees 2012: Res $1350-3700, 1-3 wks. Aid (Need).
Housing: Cabins. Avg per room/unit: 12. **Swimming:** Lake River Stream.

Est 1927. Nonprofit. **Spons:** Eagle's Nest Foundation. **Ses:** 4. **Wks/ses:** 1-3. Operates June-Aug. ACA.

Eagle's Nest offers many activities at all age levels, including English-style trail riding, land sports, swimming and canoeing, music, crafts, nature and mountaineering. Hante Adventures, accepting children ages 13-17, offers nine off-camp programs in survival and mountaineering. Components of this program are extensive treks, bicycle hikes, climbing and canoeing trips in locations across the US and in Australia.

CAMP MERRIE-WOODE
Res — Girls Ages 7-17

Sapphire, NC 28774. 100 Merrie-Woode Rd. Tel: 828-743-3300. Fax: 828-743-5846. www.merriewoode.com E-mail: phyllis@merriewoode.com
Denice Dunn & James Dunn, Exec Dirs.
Adm: FCFS. **Appl due:** Oct. **Enr:** 200. **Enr cap:** 200. **Staff:** Admin 6. Couns 80.
Features: Crafts Dance Fine_Arts Music Painting Photog Theater Aquatics Archery Canoe Caving Climbing_Wall Conservation Hiking Kayak Mountaineering Mtn_Trips Riding Rock_Climb Ropes_Crse Sail Wilderness_Camp Woodcraft Equestrian Gymnastics Lacrosse Soccer Swim Tennis Volleyball.
Fees 2010: Res $2100-4750 (+$150-250), 1½-5 wks. Aid (Need).
Housing: Cabins. **Swimming:** Lake.
Est 1919. Nonprofit. Nondenom Christian. **Ses:** 3. **Wks/ses:** 1½-5. Operates June-Aug. ACA.

Based on nondenominational Christian principles, Merrie-Woode operates a structured program in which girls sign up for as many as eight activities and attend classes in the morning and the afternoon (except when on trips or engaged in special projects). Campers make selections from an array of artistic and outdoor pursuits. Hiking, backpacking, camping, trail riding, rock climbing, and white-water canoeing and kayaking excursions are integral to the program.

CAMP ARROWHEAD
Res — Boys Ages 6-16; Day — Boys 6-10

Tuxedo, NC 28784. PO Box 248. Tel: 828-692-1123. Fax: 828-692-3789.
www.camparrowhead.org E-mail: info@camparrowhead.org
Sam Pollina, Exec Dir.
Adm: FCFS. Admitted: 100%. **Appl due:** Rolling. **Enr cap:** 130. **Staff:** Admin 4. Couns 30.
Features: Ecol Environ_Sci Circus_Skills Crafts Music Painting Photog Studio_Art Adventure_Travel Aquatics Archery Bicycle_Tours Boating Canoe Caving Chess Climbing_Wall Community_Serv Cooking Fishing Hiking Kayak Mountaineering Mtn_Biking Mtn_Trips Outdoor_Ed Paintball Rappelling Riding Riflery Rock_Climb Ropes_Crse Sail Survival_Trng Wilderness_Camp Woodcraft Basketball Equestrian Football Lacrosse Martial_Arts Soccer Swim Ultimate_Frisbee Water-skiing.
Fees 2012: Res $1200-6700 (+$50-100), 1-6 wks. **Day** $275, 1 wk. Aid 2011 (Need): $30,000.
Housing: Cabins Lodges. Avg per room/unit: 10. **Swimming:** Lake Stream.
Est 1937. Nonprofit. Nondenom Christian. **Ses:** 7. **Wks/ses:** 1-6. Operates June-Aug.

Arrowhead's 217-acre tract provides the setting for traditional land sports and watersports, including climbing and white-water kayaking. Emphasis is on wilderness adventure.

FALLING CREEK CAMP FOR BOYS
Res — Boys Ages 6-16

Tuxedo, NC 28784. PO Box 98. Tel: 828-692-0262. Fax: 828-696-1616.

www.fallingcreek.com   E-mail: mail@fallingcreek.com
Yates Pharr & Marisa Pharr, Dirs.
Adm: FCFS. **Appl due:** Rolling. **Enr:** 200-280. **Enr cap:** 200-280. **Staff:** Admin 6. Couns 70.
Features: Crafts Aquatics Archery Canoe Climbing_Wall Fishing Hiking Kayak Mtn_Biking Riding Riflery Rock_Climb Ropes_Crse Sail Scuba Wilderness_Camp Wilderness_ Canoe Woodcraft Basketball Equestrian Lacrosse Soccer Swim Tennis Track Volleyball.
Fees 2012: Res $1225-4850, 1-4 wks.
Housing: Cabins. Avg per room/unit: 7. **Swimming:** Lake.
Est 1969. Inc. **Ses:** 4. **Wks/ses:** 1-4. Operates June-Aug. ACA.

Falling Creek's program features a variety of waterfront, forest and in-camp activities, including riding, swimming, sailing, tennis, and woodcraft. Two- to seven-day backpacking, rock climbing and white-water canoeing trips are important aspects of camp life.

CAMP GLEN ARDEN
Res — Girls Ages 6-16

Tuxedo, NC 28784. PO Box 7. Tel: 828-692-8362. Fax: 828-692-6259.
www.campglenarden.com   E-mail: tajarden@aol.com
Casey Thurman, Dir.
Grades 1-11. Adm: FCFS. **Appl due:** Rolling. **Enr:** 162. **Enr cap:** 162. **Staff:** Admin 5. Couns 40.
Features: Ecol Crafts Dance Drama Music Adventure_Travel Aquatics Archery Canoe Hiking Kayak Mountaineering Mtn_Trips Riding Riflery Rock_Climb Wilderness_Camp Wilderness_Canoe Basketball Equestrian Gymnastics Soccer Softball Swim Tennis Volleyball.
Fees 2012: Res $2500-4750, 2-4 wks.
Housing: Cabins Lodges. Avg per room/unit: 5. **Swimming:** Lake Pool Stream.
Est 1951. Inc. Ecumenical. **Ses:** 5. **Wks/ses:** 2-4. Operates June-Aug.

Riding, performing arts offerings, wilderness camping, rock climbing, white-water canoeing and kayaking, and the usual land sports and watersports are among the featured activities at Glen Arden for girls. Tajar Time is a special two-week session that introduces girls entering grades 1-4 to overnight camping.

CAMP MONDAMIN
CAMP GREEN COVE
Res — Coord Ages 6-17

Tuxedo, NC 28784. PO Box 8. Tel: 828-693-7446, 800-688-5789. Fax: 828-696-8895.
www.mondamin.com; www.greencove.com
E-mail: mondamin@mondamin.com; greencove@greencove.com
Frank D. Bell, Jr. & Nancy Bell, Dirs.
Adm: FCFS. **Appl due:** Rolling. **Enr cap:** 190. **Staff:** Admin 20. Couns 120.
Features: Crafts Photog Aquatics Archery Boating Canoe Climbing_Wall Conservation Fishing Hiking Kayak Mountaineering Mtn_Biking Mtn_Trips Riding Riflery Rock_Climb Ropes_Crse Sail White-water_Raft Wilderness_Camp Wilderness_Canoe Woodcraft Equestrian Swim Tennis Watersports.
Fees 2012: Res $1040-5800, 1-5 wks.
Housing: Cabins. Avg per room/unit: 6. **Swimming:** Lake.
Est 1922. Inc. **Ses:** 4. **Wks/ses:** 1-5. Operates June-Aug.

Mondamin and its sister camp, Green Cove, conduct a nonregimented, noncompetitive program that includes swimming; sailing; one- to six-day backpacking, kayaking and wilderness trips; rock climbing; and tennis. Boys and girls who take part in the longer main session may reach advanced levels of a major activity. The camps schedule dances or other coeducational activities on each Saturday.

OHIO

CAMP ROOSEVELT FOR BOYS
CAMP FIREBIRD FOR GIRLS
Res — Coord Ages 7-16

Bowerston, OH 44695. 4141 Dublin Rd SW. Tel: 740-269-7891, 866-404-2020.
Fax: 740-269-9900.
www.camproosevelt.net; www.campfirebird.net   E-mail: info@rooseybird.net
Andrew Schwartz & Debbie Collins, Dirs.
Grades 2-10. Adm: FCFS. Appl due: Rolling. Enr: 125. Staff: Admin 7. Couns 30.
Features: Debate Environ_Sci Crafts Dance Filmmaking Fine_Arts Media Theater Adventure_Travel Aquatics Archery Boating Canoe Conservation Exploration Fishing Hiking Mountaineering Paintball Riding Riflery Ropes_Crse Sail Survival_Trng White-water_Raft Wilderness_Camp Wilderness_Canoe Work Baseball Basketball Equestrian Golf Gymnastics Lacrosse Soccer Softball Swim Tennis Volleyball Water-skiing Watersports.
Fees 2011: Res $1000-4800 (+$60-90), 1-6 wks.
Housing: Cabins Lodges. Avg per room/unit: 8. Swimming: Lake.
Est 1918. Inc. Ses: 6. Wks/ses: 1-6. Operates June-Aug. ACA.

Roosevelt and Firebird feature English riding and watersports, among other traditional activities. Other activities include team sports, individual sports and arts and crafts. A special horsemanship group rides daily, learns more about horses and training, and studies horsemanship. Campers take part in certain coeducational activities.

FALCON CAMP
Res — Coord Ages 6-16

Carrollton, OH 44615. 4251 Delta Rd SW. Tel: 330-627-4269.
Contact (Sept-May): 22232 Rye Rd, Shaker Heights, OH 44122. Tel: 216-991-2489.
Year-round Toll-free: 800-837-2267, Fax: 330-627-2220.
www.falconcamp.com   E-mail: info@falconcamp.com
David Devey & Emily Devey, Dirs.
Grades 1-10. Adm: FCFS. Appl due: Rolling. Enr: 110. Enr cap: 110. Staff: Admin 5. Couns 35.
Features: Ecol Environ_Sci ESL Crafts Creative_Writing Drama Media Photog Aquatics Archery Boating Canoe Fishing Hiking Outdoor_Ed Riding Riflery Sail Survival_Trng Woodcraft Basketball Equestrian Lacrosse Soccer Softball Street_Hockey Swim Tennis Ultimate_Frisbee Volleyball Watersports.
Fees 2012: Res $2150-6675 (+$75-150), 2-8 wks. Aid 2011 (Merit & Need): $25,000.
Housing: Cabins. Avg per room/unit: 8. Swimming: Lake.
Est 1959. Inc. Ses: 9. Wks/ses: 2-8. Operates June-Aug. ACA.

The camp conducts separate boys' and girls' programming, although campers come together for certain coeducational events. In addition to its traditional camp, Falcon maintains a separate program for girls that features Western and English riding and lake sports. Each August, younger campers may participate in a weeklong introductory session.

LUTHERAN MEMORIAL CAMP
Res — Coed Ages 6-18

Fulton, OH 43321. 2790 State Rte 61, PO Box 8. Tel: 419-864-8030. Fax: 419-864-1582.
www.lomocamps.org/summer   E-mail: lmc@lomocamps.org
Becky Stabler, Dir.
Grades 1-PG. Adm: FCFS. Appl due: Rolling. Enr: 75. Staff: Admin 6. Couns 24.
Focus: Riding. Features: Astron Ecol Crafts Drama Fine_Arts Music Aquatics Climbing_

Wall Conservation Exploration Farm Fishing Hiking Ropes_Crse Survival_Trng Basketball Soccer Swim.
Fees 2009: Res $344-354, 1 wk. Aid (Need).
Housing: Cabins Tents. Avg per room/unit: 7. **Swimming:** Pool.
Est 1948. Nonprofit. **Spons:** Lutheran Outdoor Ministries in Ohio. Lutheran. **Ses:** 9. **Wks/ses:** 1. Operates June-Aug. ACA.

Primary campers at LMC (entering grades 1-3) sample swimming, crafts, nature, campfires and other traditional activities. Junior campers (grades 4-6) engage in outdoor skills such as fishing and hiking, while Intermediate boys and girls (grades 7-9) navigate challenge courses and learn pioneering skills. High schoolers enhance their skills in art, music and drama while exploring the backwoods trails on the 400-acre site. Bible study and worship are integral to all programs.

WHITEWOOD CAMP
Res — Coed Ages 8-14; Day — Coed 6-12

Windsor, OH 44099. 7983 S Wiswell Rd. Tel: 440-272-5275, 800-967-2267. Fax: 440-272-5276.
www.4hcampwhitewood.com E-mail: campwhitewood@cfaes.osu.edu
Eliza Porter, Prgm Dir.
Adm: FCFS. **Appl due:** Rolling. **Enr:** 180. **Enr cap:** 180. **Staff:** Admin 3.
Features: Ecol Environ_Sci Sci Crafts Aquatics Archery Boating Canoe Conservation Hiking Riflery Ropes_Crse Wilderness_Camp Basketball Swim Ultimate_Frisbee.
Fees 2009: Res $225-250, 1 wk. Day $100-125, 1 wk.
Housing: Cabins Lodges. Avg per room/unit: 12. **Swimming:** Lake.
Est 1940. Nonprofit. **Spons:** Northeast Ohio 4-H Camps. **Ses:** 8. **Wks/ses:** 1. Operates June-Aug.

Daily activities at Whitewood include arts and crafts, environmental education, swimming, watercraft, archery and riflery, and outdoor living skills. Dancing, night hikes, carnivals, talent shows, campfires and guest appearances are among the evening programs.

OREGON

CAMP TAMARACK
Res — Coed Ages 7-16
(Coord — Res 8-16)

Sisters, OR 97759. PO Box 97. Tel: 541-595-1006, 800-595-7720. Fax: 541-595-6665.
www.camptamarack.com E-mail: info@camptamarack.com
Ashton Ryan, Dir.
Grades 3-10. Adm: FCFS. **Appl due:** Rolling. **Enr:** 200. **Staff:** Admin 4. Couns 20.
Features: Crafts Dance Drama Aquatics Archery Boating Canoe Hiking Mtn_Biking Mtn_Trips Riding Ropes_Crse Wilderness_Camp Wilderness_Canoe Woodcraft Equestrian Swim Tennis Watersports.
Fees 2010: Res $1280-3970, 1-3 wks. Aid (Need).
Housing: Cabins Lodges. **Swimming:** Lake.
Est 1935. Nonprofit. **Ses:** 5. **Wks/ses:** 1-3. Operates June-Sept.

In separate sessions for girls and boys, campers take part in such activities as waterfront offerings, arts and crafts, tennis, archery, outdoor living skills training, a ropes course and mountain biking. A horsemanship program provides both Western and English riding. Campers choosing the traditional camping program are assigned a horse for daily riding. A separate trail riding program places less emphasis on arena riding, while a ground school experience teaches campers horse care. A backpacking session for older campers is also available.

PENNSYLVANIA

TRAIL'S END CAMP
Res — Coed Ages 7-16

Beach Lake, PA 18405. PO Box 9. Tel: 570-729-7111. Fax: 570-729-8130.
Contact (Sept-May): 1714 Wantagh Ave, Wantagh, NY 11793. Tel: 516-781-5200.
   Fax: 516-781-5021.
Year-round Toll-free: 800-408-1404.
www.trailsendcamp.com   E-mail: contact@trailsendcamp.com
Rona Honigfeld, Marc Honigfeld, Starr Goldberg & Stan Goldberg, Dirs.
Grades 2-11. Adm: FCFS. Admitted: 99%. **Appl due:** Rolling. **Enr:** 540. **Enr cap:** 540.
   Staff: Couns 150.
Features: Ecol Environ_Sci Crafts Dance Filmmaking Fine_Arts Music Painting Theater
   Aquatics Archery Boating Canoe Climbing_Wall Hiking Kayak Mountaineering Mtn_
   Biking Outdoor_Ed Rappelling Rock_Climb Ropes_Crse Sail Wilderness_Camp Wood-
   craft Yoga Aerobics Baseball Basketball Football Golf Gymnastics Lacrosse Martial_Arts
   Roller_Hockey Soccer Softball Street_Hockey Swim Team_Handball Tennis Volleyball
   Water-skiing Watersports Weight_Trng.
Fees 2010: Res $9500 (+$100-300), 7 wks.
Housing: Cabins Dorms. **Swimming:** Lake Pool.
Est 1947. Inc. Ses: 1. **Wks/ses:** 7. Operates June-Aug. ACA.

Programs at this traditional camp include athletics, waterfront pursuits, special day and evening activities, and tournaments. An outdoor adventure program, for boys and girls in grade 5 and up, includes various wilderness trips.

CAMP SUSQUEHANNOCK FOR BOYS
CAMP SUSQUEHANNOCK FOR GIRLS
Res — Coord Ages 7-16

Brackney, PA 18812. 2308 Tripp Lake Rd. Tel: 570-967-2323, 866-482-2677.
www.susquehannock.com   E-mail: info@susquehannock.com
Edwin Shafer, Jr., Cannie Shafer, Andrew Hano & Tricia Pearson, Dirs.
Adm: FCFS. **Appl due:** Rolling. **Staff:** Admin 3. Couns 25.
Features: ESL Lang Crafts Dance Theater Aquatics Archery Boating Canoe Climbing_Wall
   Fishing Hiking Mtn_Biking Paintball Riding Sail Scuba Wilderness_Canoe Woodcraft
   Work Baseball Basketball Equestrian Field_Hockey Golf Lacrosse Martial_Arts Soccer
   Softball Swim Tennis Volleyball Watersports Weight_Trng.
Fees 2012: Res $2600-6750, 2-7 wks.
Housing: Cabins Lodges. Avg per room/unit: 9. **Swimming:** Lake.
Est 1905. Nonprofit. Ses: 5. **Wks/ses:** 2-7. Operates June-Aug. ACA.

Susquehannock's camps emphasize team and individual sports and lakefront activities. Horseback riding, as well as individual academic tutoring, is available for an additional fee. Other offerings include camp traditions, arts and crafts, camping and coeducational activities.

CAMP CANADENSIS
Res — Coed Ages 7-16

Canadensis, PA 18325. 199 Camp Canadensis Rd. Tel: 570-595-7461.
Fax: 570-595-9290.
Contact (Sept-May): 1250 Germantown Pike, Ste 110, Plymouth Meeting, PA 19462.
Tel: 484-674-1941. Fax: 484-674-1942.
www.canadensis.com   E-mail: info@canadensis.com
Brian Krug, Dir.
Grades 2-10. Adm: FCFS. Enr: 450. Staff: Admin 13. Couns 175.
Features: Astron Crafts Dance Fine_Arts Music Photog Theater Aquatics Archery Bicycle_
Tours Boating Canoe Caving Climbing_Wall Cooking Fishing Hiking Kayak Mtn_Biking
Riding Rock_Climb Ropes_Crse Sail Scuba Woodcraft Aerobics Baseball Basketball
Equestrian Football Golf Gymnastics Lacrosse Martial_Arts Roller_Hockey Soccer Soft-
ball Street_Hockey Swim Tennis Track Volleyball Water-skiing Watersports Weight_Trng
Wrestling.
Fees 2012: Res $9450 (+$400-800), 7 wks.
Housing: Cabins. Avg per room/unit: 10. Swimming: Pool.
Est 1941. Inc. Jewish. Ses: 1. Wks/ses: 7. Operates June-Aug. ACA.

Located in the Pocono Mountains, Canadensis offers all general athletics, waterfront activities, swimming, outdoor programs (including climbing walls and ropes), mountain biking, drama, and arts and crafts.

POCONO PLATEAU CAMP
Res — Coed Ages 7-17

Cresco, PA 18326. RR 2, Box 2747. Tel: 570-676-3665, 877-862-2267.
Fax: 570-676-9388.
www.poconoplateau.org/summer   E-mail: camp@poconoplateau.org
Rev. Ronald Schane, Dir.
Grades 2-12. Adm: FCFS. Appl due: Rolling. Enr cap: 24-70. Staff: Admin 6. Couns 20.
Features: Crafts Adventure_Travel Aquatics Archery Boating Canoe Climbing_Wall Explo-
ration Fishing Hiking Rock_Climb Ropes_Crse Wilderness_Camp Basketball Soccer
Swim.
Fees 2011: Res $275-465, ½-1 wk.
Housing: Cabins Lodges Tents. Swimming: Lake.
Est 1946. Nonprofit. United Methodist. Ses: 8. Wks/ses: ½-1. Operates June-Aug. ACA.

At this Christian camp, main site campers sleep in lodges and eat at the dining hall, while adventure site campers sleep in platform tents and cook one or two of their own meals daily. Activities include Bible study, swimming, boating, fishing, singing, archery, and team and individual sports. Some sessions focus on special interests such as pioneer life, ecology, music and adventure challenges, while off-site camps include backpack trips, rock climbing and canoe trips.

POCONO RIDGE
Res — Boys Ages 9-15, Girls 8-15

Dimock, PA 18816. PO Box 167, Dimock Rd. Tel: 570-278-3798.
Contact (Winter): 392 Spotswood Gravel Hill Rd, Monroe Township, NJ 08831.
Tel: 732-521-4796.
Year-round Fax: 732-400-9144.
www.poconoridge.com   E-mail: info@poconoridge.com
Shellie Santay, Dir.
Grades 3-10. Adm: FCFS. Appl due: Rolling. Enr: 250. Staff: Admin 25. Couns 75.
Features: Ecol Sci Writing/Journ Circus_Skills Crafts Dance Fine_Arts Media Music
Photog Theater Aquatics Archery Bicycle_Tours Canoe Climbing_Wall Cooking Explo-

ration Fishing Hiking Mountaineering Mtn_Biking Mtn_Trips Rappelling Riding Riflery Rock_Climb Ropes_Crse Sail Scuba Wilderness_Camp Wilderness_Canoe Woodcraft Basketball Equestrian Golf Gymnastics Martial_Arts Roller_Hockey Soccer Softball Swim Tennis Volleyball Water-skiing Watersports.
Fees 2011: Res $1750-3500, 2-4 wks.
Housing: Cabins Dorms. **Swimming:** Lake Pool Stream.
Est 1958. Inc. Ses: 3. **Wks/ses:** 2-4. Operates June-Aug. ACA.

Located in the Pocono Mountains approximately 90 miles from Philadelphia and New York City, Pocono Ridge divides its daily schedule into two bunk electives, three individual electives, a rest hour, two free periods, a night activity and canteen, and a general swimming period in the pool.

CAMP EQUINUNK
CAMP BLUE RIDGE
Res — Coord Ages 7-16

Equinunk, PA 18417. PO Box 365. Tel: 570-224-4121. Fax: 570-224-7583.
Contact (Winter): PO Box 808, East Hampton, NY 11937. Tel: 631-329-3239.
  Fax: 631-329-3023.
www.campequinunk.com E-mail: info@cecbr.com
Richard F. Kamen & Sheryl Kamen, Dirs.
Grades 2-11. Adm: FCFS. **Enr:** 500.
Features: Crafts Dance Fine_Arts Music Photog Theater Aquatics Archery Boating Canoe Caving Climbing_Wall Cooking Fishing Hiking Kayak Rappelling Rock_Climb Ropes_Crse Sail White-water_Raft Woodcraft Baseball Basketball Golf Lacrosse Roller_Hockey Soccer Softball Swim Tennis Track Volleyball Water-skiing Watersports.
Fees 2012: Res $10,250, 7 wks.
Housing: Cabins. **Swimming:** Lake.
Est 1920. Inc. Ses: 1. **Wks/ses:** 7. Operates June-Aug.

Located on opposite sides of a private, spring-fed lake, Equinunk for boys and Blue Ridge for girls offer waterfront activities, sports, drama, nature, and arts and crafts. Pursuits in the camp's hobby center include rocketry, sculpture, computers, radio, cooking, photography, video and wood shop. Special programs are conducted jointly between the two camps.

LAKE GREELEY CAMP
Res — Coed Ages 6-15

Greeley, PA 18425. 222 Greeley Lake Rd. Tel: 570-685-7196. Fax: 570-685-2660.
Contact (Winter): PO Box 219, Moscow, PA 18444. Tel: 570-842-3739.
  Fax: 570-842-0410.
www.lakegreeley.com   E-mail: info@lakegreeley.com
Matt Buynak & Rose Buynak, Dirs.
Grades 1-10. Adm: FCFS. **Appl due:** Rolling. **Enr cap:** 275. **Staff:** Admin 35. Couns 85.
Features: Astron Circus_Skills Crafts Dance Music Photog Theater Aquatics Archery Bicycle_Tours Boating Canoe Climbing_Wall Fishing Hiking Kayak Mtn_Biking Riding Riflery Rock_Climb Ropes_Crse Sail Scuba White-water_Raft Wilderness_Camp Wilderness_Canoe Woodcraft Badminton Baseball Basketball Equestrian Field_Hockey Football Golf Gymnastics Lacrosse Martial_Arts Roller_Hockey Skateboarding Soccer Softball Swim Tennis Volleyball Ping-Pong Trampolining.
Fees 2012: Res $2200-7600, 2-8 wks.
Housing: Cabins. **Swimming:** Lake Pool.
Est 1963. Ses: 10. **Wks/ses:** 2-8. Operates June-Aug. ACA.

With an emphasis on first-time campers, the camp offers more than 60 daily activities, including land sports and watersports, an extensive arts program, flying trapeze and a skateboard park. Campers entering grade 6 and above select a full daily elective program. Lake

Greeley offers special evening events and also schedules daily trips and rafting and canoeing excursions.

LAKE OWEGO CAMP
CAMP TIMBER TOPS
Res — Coord Ages 7-17

Greeley, PA 18425. 1687 Rte 6. Tel: 570-226-3636. Fax: 570-226-1401.
Contact (Sept-May): 1528 Walnut St, Ste 1900, Philadelphia, PA 19102.
 Tel: 267-639-2488. Fax: 267-687-2785.
www.lakeowego.com; www.timbertops.com
E-mail: info@lakeowego.com; info@timbertops.com
Sheldon Silver & David Schreiber, Dirs.
Grades 2-11. Adm: FCFS. Appl due: Rolling. Staff: Couns 70.
Features: Computers Circus_Skills Crafts Dance Filmmaking Fine_Arts Media Music
 Photog Theater Adventure_Travel Aquatics Archery Bicycle_Tours Boating Canoe
 Climbing_Wall Conservation Cooking Exploration Fishing Hiking Kayak Mountaineer-
 ing Mtn_Biking Mtn_Trips Ranch Rappelling Riding Riflery Rock_Climb Ropes_Crse
 Sail Survival_Trng White-water_Raft Wilderness_Camp Wilderness_Canoe Woodcraft
 Baseball Basketball Cross-country Equestrian Field_Hockey Football Golf Gymnas-
 tics Lacrosse Martial_Arts Roller_Hockey Soccer Softball Swim Tennis Track Volleyball
 Water-skiing Watersports.
Fees 2012: Res $2950-9950, 2-7 wks.
Housing: Cabins Tents. Avg per room/unit: 10. Swimming: Lake Pool.
Est 1961. Ses: 7. Wks/ses: 2-7. Operates June-Aug. ACA.

Lake Owego for boys and Timber Tops for girls conduct extensive programs that include many traditional recreational activities. The camps also plan special events and trips. Two-week sessions are open to Lake Owego boys entering grades 2-4 at only; all other campers attend for at least three and a half weeks.

PINE FOREST CAMP
Res — Coed Ages 7-16

Greeley, PA 18425. 185 Pine Forest Rd. Tel: 570-685-7141. Fax: 570-685-7165.
Contact (Sept-June): 1528 Walnut St, Ste 1900, Philadelphia, PA 19102.
 Tel: 267-639-2488. Fax: 267-687-2785.
www.pineforestcamp.com E-mail: info@pineforestcamp.com
Mickey Black, Dir.
Grades 2-11. Adm: FCFS. Appl due: Rolling. Enr: 400.
Features: Computers Crafts Dance Filmmaking Fine_Arts Music Photog Theater Aquat-
 ics Archery Bicycle_Tours Boating Canoe Climbing_Wall Conservation Cooking Explo-
 ration Fishing Hiking Kayak Mountaineering Mtn_Biking Mtn_Trips Ranch Rappelling
 Riding Riflery Rock_Climb Ropes_Crse Sail Survival_Trng White-water_Raft Wilder-
 ness_Camp Baseball Basketball Cross-country Equestrian Field_Hockey Football Golf
 Gymnastics Lacrosse Martial_Arts Roller_Hockey Soccer Softball Swim Tennis Track
 Volleyball Water-skiing Watersports.
Fees 2012: Res $9950, 7 wks.
Housing: Cabins. Avg per room/unit: 10. Swimming: Lake Pool.
Est 1931. Inc. Ses: 1. Wks/ses: 7½. Operates June-Aug. ACA.

Pine Forest provides an well-rounded program with activities and specialized activities designed to develop individual talents.

CAMP SHOHOLA
CAMP NETIMUS
Res — Coord Ages 7-15, Girls 16

Greeley, PA 18425. 105 Weber Rd. Tel: 570-371-4760. Fax: 570-504-1702.
Contact (Sept-June): 11218 Hunters Landing Dr, Charlotte, NC 28273.
Tel: 570-371-4760. Fax: 570-504-1702.
www.shohola.com; www.netimus.com
E-mail: office@shohola.com; info@netimus.com
Duncan Barger, Holly Barger, Darlene Calton, Tabz Taber & Donna Kistler, Dirs.
Adm: FCFS. **Appl due:** Rolling. **Enr:** 145-155. **Staff:** Admin 5. Couns 75.
Features: Computers Crafts Filmmaking Photog Adventure_Travel Aquatics Archery Bicycle_Tours Boating Canoe Climbing_Wall Exploration Fishing Hiking Kayak Mtn_Biking Rappelling Riding Riflery Rock_Climb Ropes_Crse Sail White-water_Raft Wilderness_Camp Wilderness_Canoe Woodcraft Baseball Basketball Equestrian Football Golf Lacrosse Martial_Arts Roller_Hockey Soccer Softball Swim Tennis Volleyball Waterskiing Watersports Wrestling.
Fees 2011: Res $2600-6800 (+$150), 2-7 wks.
Housing: Cabins. **Swimming:** Lake.
Est 1930. Inc. Ses: 6. **Wks/ses:** 2-7. Operates June-Aug. ACA.

Shohola for boys, on Lake Greeley, and Netimus for girls (570-296-6131), located in Milford on 400 acres of woodland in the Pocono Mountains, offer more than 40 activities, among them canoeing, sailing, swimming, equitation, English-style riding, electronics, and individual and team sports. The camps operate their own AM and shortwave radio station. Among shared activities between Shohola and Netimus are dances, trips and games.

CAMP GREEN LANE
Res — Coed Ages 6-18

Green Lane, PA 18054. 249 Camp Green Lane Rd. Tel: 215-234-8666.
Fax: 215-234-0430.
www.greenlane.com   E-mail: melcgl@aol.com
Mel Brodsky & Jon Weston, Dirs.
Grades 2-11. Adm: FCFS. **Appl due:** Rolling. **Enr:** 325. **Enr cap:** 350. **Staff:** Admin 12. Couns 110.
Features: Crafts Dance Drama Filmmaking Fine_Arts Media Music Photog Aquatics Archery Canoe Climbing_Wall Cooking Fishing Hiking Kayak Mtn_Biking Outdoor_Ed Rappelling Riding Rock_Climb Ropes_Crse Scuba White-water_Raft Woodcraft Yoga Aerobics Baseball Basketball Cross-country Football Golf Gymnastics Lacrosse Roller_Hockey Rugby Skateboarding Soccer Softball Street_Hockey Swim Tennis Track Ultimate_Frisbee Volleyball Watersports Weight_Trng.
Fees 2012: Res $4675-7295 (+$300-400), 3½-7 wks.
Housing: Cabins. Avg per room/unit: 12. **Swimming:** Lake Pool.
Est 1926. Jewish. Ses: 2. **Wks/ses:** 3½-7. Operates June-Aug. ACA.

Located on hundreds of acres in a rural section of eastern Pennsylvania, Green Lane is a traditional Jewish recreational camp. The daily program consists of six activity periods, with swimming instruction every other day and free swim every afternoon. Programming balances active and passive activities. Campers choose an area of specialization to engage in every other day; at the end of each week, boys and girls can either continue with the same elective or choose another one for the coming week. Green Lane schedules occasional trips and special-event days.

CAMP LINDENMERE
Res — Coed Ages 7-17

Henryville, PA 18332. RR 1, Box 1765. Tel: 570-629-0240. Fax: 208-723-3288.
Contact (Sept-May): 6901 SW 18th St, Ste E202, Boca Raton, FL 33433.
Tel: 561-361-3590. Fax: 561-353-1957.
Year-round Toll-free: 888-220-4773.
www.camplindenmere.com E-mail: fun@camplindenmere.com
Mitch Garfinkel, Charles Maltzman & Craig Odiorne, Dirs.
Adm: FCFS. Admitted: 95%. **Appl due:** Rolling. **Enr:** 300. **Enr cap:** 300. **Staff:** Admin 18. Couns 130.
Features: Circus_Skills Crafts Dance Filmmaking Fine_Arts Media Music Painting Photog Studio_Art Theater Aquatics Archery Canoe Climbing_Wall Cooking Fishing Hiking Kayak Mtn_Biking Mtn_Trips Rappelling Riding Rock_Climb Ropes_Crse Survival_Trng Woodcraft Yoga Baseball Basketball Equestrian Football Golf Gymnastics Ice_Hockey Lacrosse Martial_Arts Roller_Hockey Skateboarding Soccer Softball Street_Hockey Swim Tennis Ultimate_Frisbee Volleyball Watersports Weight_Trng.
Fees 2010: Res $3450-6950, 3-6 wks.
Housing: Cabins. Avg per room/unit: 8-12. **Swimming:** Pool.
Est 1935. Inc. Ses: 2. **Wks/ses:** 3. Operates June-Aug. ACA.

Located on approximately 175 acres in the Pocono Mountains, Lindenmere combines offerings in the arts with athletics and recreational pursuits. Each camper selects three major activities with the program director at the start of the three-week session, then chooses three minor activities each morning. The camp conducts programs in the visual and fine arts, the performing arts, horseback riding, team sports, extreme sports, circus skills and waterfront pursuits.

CAMP CAYUGA
Res — Coed Ages 5-15

Honesdale, PA 18431. 321 Niles Pond Rd. Tel: 570-253-3133. Fax: 570-253-3194.
Contact (Sept-May): PO Box 151, Peapack, NJ 07977. Tel: 908-470-1224.
Fax: 908-470-1228.
Year-round Toll-free: 800-422-9842.
www.campcayuga.com E-mail: info@campcayuga.com
Brian B. Buynak, Dir.
Grades K-10. Adm: FCFS. **Appl due:** Rolling. **Enr:** 390. **Staff:** Admin 8. Couns 100.
Travel: NY Canada.
Features: ESL Circus_Skills Crafts Dance Fine_Arts Media Music Photog Theater Aquatics Archery Boating Canoe Chess Climbing_Wall Fishing Hiking Kayak Mtn_Biking Paintball Rappelling Riding Riflery Rock_Climb Ropes_Crse Sail Scuba Wilderness_ Camp Wilderness_Canoe Yoga Aerobics Badminton Baseball Basketball Equestrian Field_Hockey Football Golf Gymnastics Lacrosse Martial_Arts Roller_Hockey Rugby Skateboarding Soccer Softball Street_Hockey Swim Tennis Track Ultimate_Frisbee Volleyball Watersports Weight_Trng Wrestling.
Fees 2012: Res $2400-7800, 2-8 wks.
Housing: Cabins. **Swimming:** Lake Pool.
Est 1957. Ses: 9. **Wks/ses:** 2-8. Operates June-Aug. ACA.

Cayuga offers more than 60 daily activities, including horseback riding, flying trapeze and circus acts, creative and performing arts, land sports and watersports. The camp maintains a separate teen campus and conducts a special Junior Campus Program for children ages 5-12. Various special events and regularly scheduled trips are important aspects of camp life.

INDIAN HEAD CAMP
Res — Coed Ages 7-15

Honesdale, PA 18431. PO Box 2005. Tel: 570-224-4111. Fax: 570-224-4067.
Contact (Sept-May): PO Box 1199, Scarsdale, NY 10583. Tel: 914-345-2155.
Fax: 914-345-2479.
www.indianhead.com   E-mail: ihcisfun@indianhead.com
Shelley Tager & David Tager, Dirs.
Grades 2-10. Adm: FCFS. **Appl due:** Rolling. **Enr:** 500. **Staff:** Admin 16.
Travel: AZ CA CO NV UT.
Features: Crafts Dance Drama Fine_Arts Photog Adventure_Travel Aquatics Archery
Boating Canoe Caving Climbing_Wall Fishing Hiking Kayak Mountaineering Mtn_Biking
Mtn_Trips Rappelling Wilderness_Camp Wilderness_Canoe Woodcraft Aerobics
Baseball Basketball Football Golf Gymnastics Lacrosse Martial_Arts Roller_Hockey
Skateboarding Soccer Softball Swim Tennis Track Volleyball Water-skiing Watersports
Weight_Trng.
Fees 2012: Res $10,100 (+$185-375), 7 wks.
Housing: Cabins. Avg per room/unit: 10. **Swimming:** Lake Pool.
Est 1940. Inc. **Ses:** 1. **Wks/ses:** 7. Operates June-Aug. ACA.

Indian Head offers instruction in land sports, watersports, and the creative and performing arts. Outdoor programs include hiking, rock climbing, caving, a ropes course, canoe tripping and mountain biking. Tribe West, IHC's adventure travel program for rising high school sophomores, features white-water rafting treks, rock-climbing expeditions and camping visits to such sites as the Grand Canyon.

LAKE BRYN MAWR CAMP
Res — Girls Ages 7-15

Honesdale, PA 18431. 593 Bryn Mawr Rd. Tel: 570-253-2488. Fax: 570-253-1342.
Contact (Winter): PO Box 612, Short Hills, NJ 07078. Tel: 973-467-3518.
Fax: 973-467-3750.
www.campbrynmawr.com   E-mail: dan@campbrynmawr.com
Jane Kagan & Dan Kagan, Dirs.
Grades 2-10. Adm: FCFS. **Appl due:** Apr.
Features: Art Ceramics Crafts Dance Drama Music Archery Boating Climbing_Wall Cook-
ing Fishing Hiking Kayak Mtn_Biking Outdoor_Ed Riding Ropes_Crse Aerobics Basket-
ball Golf Gymnastics Soccer Softball Swim Tennis Volleyball Water-skiing.
Fees 2012: Res $10,400 (+$400), 7 wks.
Housing: Cabins. Avg per room/unit: 8-14. **Swimming:** Lake Pool.
Est 1921. Ses: 1. **Wks/ses:** 7. Operates June-Aug.

Program specialties include tennis, English and show riding, arts and crafts, sailing, swimming, gymnastics, drama, dance, water-skiing, music and land sports.

CAMP TOWANDA
Res — Coed Ages 6-17

Honesdale, PA 18431. 700 Niles Pond Rd. Tel: 570-253-3266. Fax: 570-253-6334.
Tel: 845-639-4582, Fax: 845-638-2194.
www.camptowanda.com   E-mail: info@camptowanda.com
Mitch Reiter & Stephanie Reiter, Dirs.
Adm: FCFS.
Features: Astron Crafts Dance Fine_Arts Media Theater Adventure_Travel Aquatics Bicy-
cle_Tours Canoe Farm Hiking Mtn_Trips Riding Sail Scuba Wilderness_Camp Wood-
craft Baseball Basketball Cross-country Football Golf Gymnastics Swim Tennis Track
Water-skiing.
Fees 2012: Res $10,105 (+$275), 7 wks.

Housing: Cabins. **Swimming:** Lake Pool. **Est 1923.** Inc. Jewish. **Ses:** 1. **Wks/ses:** 7. Operates June-Aug. ACA.

Located on a 200-acre site, Towanda provides a traditional program that emphasizes skill development in land sports and watersports and includes activities pertaining to outdoor adventure, the arts and life skills.

STONE MOUNTAIN ADVENTURES
Res — Coed Ages 12-16

Huntingdon, PA 16652. 9803 Old Hawn Rd. Tel: 814-667-3874. Fax: 814-667-2498.
www.sma-summers.com   E-mail: info@sma-summers.com
Judson Millar, Dir.
Adm: FCFS. **Enr:** 56. **Staff:** Admin 3. Couns 14.
Features: Crafts Theater Bicycle_Tours Canoe Farm Hiking Mtn_Trips Riding Sail Scuba Wilderness_Camp Wilderness_Canoe Basketball Equestrian Football Rugby Soccer Swim Tennis Volleyball Water-skiing.
Fees 2012: Res $2475-7000 (+$100), 2-7 wks.
Housing: Cabins. **Swimming:** Lake River Stream.
Est 1983. Ses: 6. **Wks/ses:** 2-7. Operates June-Aug.

Campers at SMA choose adventure activities daily. Riding, sailing, caving, rafting, tennis, water-skiing, rock climbing, service projects, mountain biking, canoeing and rugby are among the camp's offerings.

CAMP LOHIKAN
Res — Coed Ages 6-15

Lake Como, PA 18437. 343 Wallerville Rd. Tel: 570-798-2707. Fax: 570-798-0255.
Contact (Sept-May): PO Box 189, Gladstone, NJ 07934. Tel: 908-470-9317.
Fax: 908-470-9319.
Year-round Toll-free: 800-488-4321.
www.lohikan.com   E-mail: info@lohikan.com
Mark Buynak, Dir.
Grades 1-10. Adm: FCFS. **Appl due:** Rolling. **Enr:** 380. **Staff:** Admin 5. Couns 140. Res 200.
Features: Bus/Fin ESL Writing/Journ Circus_Skills Crafts Creative_Writing Dance Film-making Fine_Arts Media Music Painting Photog Studio_Art Theater Aquatics Archery Bicycle_Tours Boating Canoe Chess Climbing_Wall Conservation Exploration Fishing Hiking Kayak Mountaineering Mtn_Biking Mtn_Trips Paintball Rappelling Riding Riflery Rock_Climb Ropes_Crse Sail Scuba Survival_Trng White-water_Raft Wilderness_Camp Wilderness_Canoe Woodcraft Aerobics Baseball Basketball Cross-country Equestrian Field_Hockey Football Golf Gymnastics Lacrosse Martial_Arts Roller_Hockey Skateboarding Soccer Softball Street_Hockey Swim Tennis Track Volleyball Water-skiing Watersports Weight_Trng Wrestling.
Fees 2012: Res $800-8000 (+$200), 1-8 wks.
Housing: Cabins Lodges. Avg per room/unit: 10. **Swimming:** Lake Pool.
Est 1957. Inc. **Ses:** 10. **Wks/ses:** 1-8. Operates June-Aug. ACA.

Lohikan occupies a wooded, 1200-acre site in the northeast Pocono Mountains. Younger campers follow a structured program, while older boys and girls entering grade 6 or above may select their activities. Campers participate in an array of noncompetitive team and individual sports, aquatics, outdoor pursuits and arts offerings. A seven-day minicamp is available to first-time attendees.

INDEPENDENT LAKE CAMP
Res — Coed Ages 6-17

Lakewood, PA 18439. PO Box 29.
Contact (Sept-May): PO Box 86, Newberry, FL 32669.
Year-round Toll-free: 800-399-2267.
www.independentlake.com   E-mail: ilcnigel@aol.com
Nigel G. Watson, Dan Gould & Anne Gould, Dirs.
Adm: FCFS. **Appl due:** Rolling. **Staff:** Admin 30. Couns 220.
Features: ESL Writing/Journ Circus_Skills Crafts Creative_Writing Dance Fine_Arts Media Music Painting Photog Theater Aquatics Archery Boating Canoe Climbing_Wall Fishing Kayak Mtn_Biking Rock_Climb Ropes_Crse Sail Basketball Cross-country Equestrian Field_Hockey Golf Gymnastics Ice_Hockey Lacrosse Martial_Arts Roller_Hockey Skateboarding Soccer Softball Swim Tennis Volleyball Water-skiing Watersports.
Fees 2012: Res $1100-3225, 1-3 wks. Aid (Need).
Housing: Cabins. **Swimming:** Lake Pool.
Est 1992. **Inc. Ses:** 5. **Wks/ses:** 1-3. Operates June-Aug.

Located on a 300-acre site in the Pocono Mountains, the camp offers a varied program that includes dance, writing, team and individual sports, science and waterfront activities. Campers may also take classes in magic, art, ESL and computers and circus arts. In addition, ILC conducts a particularly strong circus program.

CAMP WEEQUAHIC
Res — Coed Ages 6-16

Lakewood, PA 18439. 210 Woods Rd.
Contact (Sept-June): PO Box 32669, Palm Beach Gardens, FL 33420.
Year-round Toll-free: 877-899-9695, Fax: 570-798-2999.
www.weequahic.com   E-mail: info@weequahic.com
Cole Kelly & Kate Kelly, Dirs.
Adm: FCFS. **Appl due:** Rolling. **Enr cap:** 300. **Staff:** Admin 25. Couns 100.
Features: Crafts Dance Drama Aquatics Archery Boating Canoe Climbing_Wall Cooking Fishing Hiking Kayak Mountaineering Mtn_Biking Rappelling Riding Rock_Climb Ropes_Crse Sail White-water_Raft Woodcraft Aerobics Badminton Baseball Basketball Field_Hockey Football Golf Gymnastics Lacrosse Roller_Hockey Rugby Soccer Softball Street_Hockey Swim Team_Handball Tennis Track Ultimate_Frisbee Volleyball Water-skiing Watersports Weight_Trng Wrestling.
Fees 2012: Res $4400-8250 (+$100-150), 3-6 wks. Aid avail.
Housing: Cabins. Avg per room/unit: 9. **Swimming:** Lake Pool.
Est 1953. **Inc. Ses:** 2. **Wks/ses:** 3. Operates June-Aug. ACA.

Weequahic provides a program of team activities, tripping and pioneering, and creative opportunities. Instruction is offered in various waterfront activities. Overnight canoeing trips are part of the program.

LIGONIER CAMP
Res — Coed Ages 6-17

Ligonier, PA 15658. 188 Macartney Ln. Tel: 724-238-6428. Fax: 724-238-6971.
www.ligoniercamp.org   E-mail: ligcamp@ligoniercamp.org
Stef Walker, Dir.
Grades 3-12. Adm: FCFS. **Appl due:** Rolling. **Enr:** 216. **Staff:** Admin 4. Couns 40.
Features: Crafts Theater Aquatics Archery Canoe Caving Climbing_Wall Fishing Hiking Mtn_Biking Riding Riflery Rock_Climb Ropes_Crse White-water_Raft Wilderness_Camp Badminton Basketball Lacrosse Soccer Swim Tennis Ultimate_Frisbee Volleyball.
Fees 2012: Res $415-685, 1-2 wks. Aid avail.
Housing: Cabins Lodges. Avg per room/unit: 9. **Swimming:** Pool.

Est 1914. Nonprofit. Presbyterian. **Ses:** 8. **Wks/ses:** 1-2. Operates June-Aug. ACA.

This Presbyterian camp features Bible study and offers a ropes course, caving, rock climbing, canoeing, sports and crafts. Campers may attend an adventure camp instead of the traditional recreational program. A three-day minicamp enrolls children ages 6-8.

MERCERSBURG ADVENTURE CAMPS
Res — Coed Ages 7-16

Mercersburg, PA 17236. 300 E Seminary St. Tel: 717-328-6225. Fax: 717-328-9072.
www.mercersburgsummer.com   E-mail: summerprograms@mercersburg.edu
Quentin McDowell, Dir.
Adm: FCFS. **Appl due:** Rolling. **Enr cap:** 26-75.
Features: Computers Ecol Crafts Creative_Writing Dance Drama Fine_Arts Canoe Hiking Riding Basketball Golf Soccer Swim Tennis Volleyball Watersports.
Fees 2009: Res $800-5250, 1-6 wks.
Swimming: Pool.
Nonprofit. **Spons:** Mercersburg Academy. **Ses:** 6. **Wks/ses:** 1-2. Operates June-Aug.

Mercersburg Academy conducts three similar adventure programs: Junior Adventure Camp (for children ages 7 and 8); Mercersburg Adventure Camp (ages 8-14); and Teen Adventures (ages 14-17). Campers participate in sports and games, outdoor activities, and enrichment activities in academic areas and the arts. Excursions to local sites of interest—including day trips to Hershey Park and to a minor-league baseball game—are also available.

CAMP ONAS
Res — Coed Ages 8-13

Ottsville, PA 18942. 609 Geigel Hill Rd. Tel: 610-847-5858.
www.camponas.org   E-mail: friends@camponas.org
Suzan Neiger Gould, Dir.
Adm: FCFS. **Appl due:** Rolling. **Enr:** 141. **Staff:** Admin 3. Couns 60.
Features: Crafts Drama Filmmaking Music Photog Adventure_Travel Aquatics Archery Canoe Climbing_Wall Community_Serv Conservation Cooking Farm Fishing Hiking Mtn_Trips Peace/Cross-cultural Rock_Climb Ropes_Crse Wilderness_Camp Wilderness_Canoe Woodcraft Basketball Field_Hockey Football Soccer Softball Swim Volleyball Watersports Wrestling.
Fees 2011: Res $1058-2238 (+$25), 2-4 wks.
Housing: Tents. Avg per room/unit: 8. **Swimming:** Pool Stream.
Est 1922. Nonprofit. Religious Society of Friends. **Ses:** 4. **Wks/ses:** 2. Operates June-Aug. ACA.

This Friends camp emphasizes sharing, cooperation, understanding and simplicity. Campers sleep in tents and covered pavilions and unite for family-style meals in the camp dining hall. Boys and girls select their activities from a variety of sports, arts, drama, aquatics and outdoor skills. Meeting for Worship convenes twice a week.

CAMP SAGINAW
Res — Coed Ages 6-16

Oxford, PA 19363. 740 Saginaw Rd. Tel: 610-932-8467. Fax: 610-932-3313.
Contact (Sept-May): 125 N Burnt Mill Rd, Ste 200, Cherry Hill, NJ 08003.
    Tel: 856-428-6256. Fax: 856-428-6289.
Year-round Toll-free: 888-477-2267.
www.campsaginaw.com   E-mail: askus@campsaginaw.com
Mike Petkov, Dir.
Grades 1-11. **Adm:** FCFS. **Enr:** 400.

Travel: Caribbean.
Features: Crafts Dance Photog Theater Aquatics Archery Boating Canoe Climbing_Wall Cooking Fishing Kayak Rappelling Riflery Rock_Climb Ropes_Crse Scuba Woodcraft Badminton Baseball Basketball Football Golf Gymnastics Skateboarding Soccer Softball Street_Hockey Swim Tennis Volleyball Water-skiing.
Fees 2012: Res $2750-8150, 2-8 wks.
Housing: Cabins. Avg per room/unit: 9. **Swimming:** Lake Pool Stream.
Est 1929. Inc. **Ses:** 7. **Wks/ses:** 2-8. Operates June-Aug. ACA.

Daily activities offered at this camp are team and individual sports, water-skiing, go-karting, fishing, canoeing, kayaking, photography and an adventure course. Special events include campwide Olympics, water carnivals, campfires and dance nights. All campers take out-of-camp day trips, while high school juniors may embark on a weeklong trip to the Bahamas for an additional fee.

CAMP POYNTELLE LEWIS VILLAGE
Res — Coed Ages 7-16

Poyntelle, PA 18454. PO Box 66. Tel: 570-448-2161. Fax: 570-448-2117.
Contact (Sept-May): 212-00 23rd Ave, Bayside, NY 11360. Tel: 718-279-0690.
Fax: 718-224-4676.
www.poyntelle.com   E-mail: summers@poyntelle.com
Sarah Raful Whinston, Exec Dir.
Grades 2-11. Adm: FCFS. **Appl due:** Rolling. **Enr:** 350. **Staff:** Admin 3. Couns 100.
Features: Crafts Dance Theater Aquatics Boating Canoe Climbing_Wall Fishing Hiking Kayak Mtn_Trips Rappelling Rock_Climb Ropes_Crse Sail White-water_Raft Baseball Basketball Golf Martial_Arts Roller_Hockey Soccer Softball Swim Tennis Volleyball Water-skiing Watersports.
Fees 2010: Res $4000-6800 (+$50), 3-7 wks. Aid (Need).
Housing: Cabins. Avg per room/unit: 12. **Swimming:** Lake Pool.
Est 1949. Nonprofit. Jewish. **Ses:** 3. **Wks/ses:** 3-7. Operates June-Aug. ACA.

Campers at Poyntelle (entering grades 2-7) and Lewis Village (entering grades 8-11) participate in many traditional activities, among them land sports, boating, canoeing, crafts, drama, music, swimming and water-skiing. A strong outdoor adventure program features high and low ropes courses, hiking, camping and a climbing tower.

CAMP WESTMONT
Res — Coed Ages 7-15

Poyntelle, PA 18454. 81 Spruce Lake Rd. Tel: 570-448-2500. Fax: 570-448-2063.
Contact (Sept-May): 2116 Merrick Ave, Ste 3005, Merrick, NY 11566.
Tel: 516-771-3660. Fax: 516-771-2654.
Year-round Toll-free: 888-570-2267.
www.campwestmont.com   E-mail: info@campwestmont.com
Minna Moskowitz, Fred Moskowitz & Ross Moskowitz, Dirs.
Grades 2-10. Adm: FCFS. **Appl due:** Rolling. **Enr:** 450. **Enr cap:** 450. **Staff:** Admin 30. Couns 120. Res 5.
Features: Computers Circus_Skills Crafts Dance Drama Fine_Arts Music Woodworking Aquatics Archery Bicycle_Tours Boating Canoe Climbing_Wall Cooking Hiking Mtn_Biking Rappelling Riding Ropes_Crse Sail White-water_Raft Baseball Basketball Equestrian Football Golf Gymnastics In-line_Skating Lacrosse Roller_Hockey Soccer Softball Swim Tennis Track Volleyball Water-skiing Watersports Weight_Trng Rocketry.
Fees 2011: Res $8350 (+$375), 7 wks.
Housing: Cabins. **Swimming:** Lake Pool.
Est 1981. Inc. **Ses:** 1. **Wks/ses:** 7. Operates June-Aug. ACA.

Westmont's recreational program features one-on-one instruction, team participation, and a combination of self-selected and assigned activities. Waterfront activities include boating, canoeing, sailing, water-skiing, windsurfing, kayaking, tubing, peddle boating and swimming. An array of land sports, trapeze, arts and crafts, dance, drama and hiking are among the other camp offerings.

CAMP WAYNE FOR GIRLS
CAMP WAYNE FOR BOYS
Res — Coord Ages 7-15, Boys 6

Preston Park, PA 18455. 56 Nice People Pl. Tel: 570-798-2591.
Contact (Sept-May): 9 Hansel Rd, Newtown, PA 18940. Tel: 215-944-3069.
www.campwaynegirls.com; www.campwayne.com
E-mail: info@campwaynegirls.com; info@campwayne.com
Noel Corpuel & Georgeann Corpuel, Dirs.
Grades 2-10. Adm: FCFS. **Appl due:** Oct. **Enr:** 250-350. **Staff:** Admin 20. Couns 140.
Features: Crafts Dance Fine_Arts Music Painting Photog Studio_Art Theater Aquatics Archery Bicycle_Tours Boating Canoe Climbing_Wall Conservation Cooking Exploration Fishing Hiking Kayak Mountaineering Mtn_Biking Mtn_Trips Rappelling Rock_Climb Ropes_Crse Sail White-water_Raft Woodcraft Yoga Aerobics Badminton Baseball Basketball Cross-country Field_Hockey Football Golf Gymnastics Lacrosse Martial_Arts Roller_Hockey Soccer Softball Swim Tennis Track Volleyball Water-skiing Watersports.
Fees 2012: Res $10,200 (+$500), 7 wks.
Housing: Cabins. Avg per room/unit: 12. **Swimming:** Lake Pool.
Est 1921. Inc. **Ses:** 1. **Wks/ses:** 7. Operates June-Aug. ACA.

Camp Wayne for Girls features a full waterfront program, tennis, team sports, drama, nature, gymnastics, and performing and fine arts, while its brother camp (516-883-3067) offers a traditional program that emphasizes sports instruction and the acquisition of basic athletic skills. Dance and cheerleading instruction is part of the girls' program. Special events, creative evening activities and off-camp adventure trips complete the program.

CAMP STARLIGHT
Res — Coord Ages 7-15

Starlight, PA 18461. 151 Starlight Lake Rd.
Contact (Sept-May): PO Box 33389, Palm Beach Gardens, FL 33420.
Year-round Tel: 570-798-2525, 877-875-3971.
www.campstarlight.com   E-mail: info@campstarlight.com
David Miller & Allison Miller, Dirs.
Adm: FCFS. **Appl due:** Rolling. **Enr:** 440. **Staff:** Admin 12. Couns 120.
Features: Crafts Dance Drama Fine_Arts Music Aquatics Bicycle_Tours Canoe Hiking Mtn_Trips Sail Woodcraft Baseball Basketball Golf Gymnastics Swim Tennis Volleyball Water-skiing Watersports.
Fees 2012: Res $10,100 (+$250), 7 wks.
Housing: Cabins. **Swimming:** Lake Pool.
Est 1947. Inc. **Ses:** 1. **Wks/ses:** 7. Operates June-Aug. ACA.

Offerings at this coordinate recreational camp include athletic specialty camps, performing arts pursuits, tournaments and intercamp games. Starlight schedules canoeing, hiking and golfing trips, as well as excursions to the Baseball Hall of Fame, a petting zoo, Hershey Park and Niagara Falls. Special events such as beach and pool parties, campfires, talent shows, karaoke and a masquerade party complete the camp's program.

SPORTS AND ARTS CENTER AT ISLAND LAKE
Res — Coed Ages 7-17

Starrucca, PA 18462. 50 Island Lake Rd. Tel: 570-798-2550. Fax: 570-798-2346.
Contact (Sept-May): 175 Tompkins Ave, Pleasantville, NY 10570. Tel: 914-769-6060.
Fax: 914-769-6161.
Year-round Toll-free: 800-869-6083.
www.islandlake.com   E-mail: info@islandlake.com
Beverly Stoltz, Mike Stoltz & Matthew Stoltz, Dirs.
Grades 3-12. Adm: FCFS. Appl due: Rolling. Staff: Admin 25. Couns 150.
Features: Astron Computers Ecol Environ_Sci Geol Sci Circus_Skills Crafts Dance Film-
    making Fine_Arts Media Music Painting Photog Studio_Art Theater Aquatics Archery
    Bicycle_Tours Boating Canoe Climbing_Wall Fishing Hiking Kayak Mountaineering
    Mtn_Biking Outdoor_Ed Rappelling Riding Rock_Climb Ropes_Crse Sail Survival_Trng
    Wilderness_Camp Woodcraft Aerobics Baseball Basketball Cross-country Equestrian
    Field_Hockey Football Golf Gymnastics Lacrosse Martial_Arts Roller_Hockey Rugby
    Skateboarding Soccer Softball Street_Hockey Swim Tennis Volleyball Water-skiing
    Watersports Weight_Trng Wrestling.
Fees 2012: Res $3150-10,250, 2-8 wks.
Housing: Cabins. Avg per room/unit: 12. Swimming: Lake Pool.
Est 1986. Inc. Ses: 3. Wks/ses: 2-3. Operates June-Aug. ACA.

Each camper selects his or her own schedule from a variety of activities, including circus arts, team and individual sports, tennis, gymnastics, mountain biking, ropes, climbing, English and Western horseback riding, theater, technical theater, dance and magic. Island Lake also offers music, pioneering, waterfront activities, science, and arts and crafts.

JOURNEY'S END FARM CAMP
Res — Coed Ages 7-12

Sterling, PA 18463. PO Box 23. Tel: 570-689-3911.
www.journeysendfarm.org   E-mail: camp@journeysendfarm.org
Tim Curtis, Dir.
Grades 2-7. Adm: FCFS. Admitted: 90%. Appl due: Jan. Enr: 35. Enr cap: 35. Staff:
    Admin 4. Couns 10. Res 22.
Features: Crafts Dance Drama Music Aquatics Conservation Exploration Farm Fish-
    ing Hiking Mtn_Trips Outdoor_Ed Peace/Cross-cultural Wilderness_Camp Woodcraft
    Soccer Swim Ultimate_Frisbee.
Fees 2011: Res $1830-2520, 2-3 wks. Aid 2009 (Need): $7200.
Housing: Cabins Tents. Swimming: Pond.
Est 1939. Inc. Religious Society of Friends. Ses: 3. Wks/ses: 2-3. Operates July-Aug.

Activities at this working farm/home include outdoor games, nature study, cookouts, ceramics, wood shop, swimming, campfires, folk singing, creative dramatics, berry picking, gardening and caring for farm animals. Motivated campers may embark on a three-day trip during their session. Camp pursuits commonly combine work and play.

CAMP ONEKA
Res — Girls Ages 7-16

Tafton, PA 18464. 325 Rte 390. Tel: 570-226-4049. Fax: 570-226-4522.
Contact (Sept-May): 10 Oakford Rd, Wayne, PA 19087. Tel: 610-687-6260.
Fax: 610-687-6260.
www.oneka.com   E-mail: info@oneka.com
Dale H. Dohner & Barbara Dohner, Dirs.
Grades 2-11. Adm: FCFS. Appl due: Rolling. Enr: 125. Enr cap: 130. Staff: Admin 5.
    Couns 35.
Features: Ecol Crafts Fine_Arts Music Theater Aquatics Archery Boating Canoe Climb-

ing_Wall Community_Serv Conservation Cooking Hiking Kayak Mtn_Biking Outdoor_ Ed Riding Sail Wilderness_Camp Wilderness_Canoe Woodcraft Baseball Field_Hockey Soccer Softball Swim Tennis Volleyball Water-skiing Watersports.
Fees 2012: Res $2500-6400 (+$50-380), 2-7 wks. Aid 2009 (Need): $24,000.
Housing: Cabins Tents. Avg per room/unit: 3-6. **Swimming:** Lake.
Est 1908. Ses: 4. **Wks/ses:** 2-7. Operates June-Aug. ACA.

The camp provides opportunities to develop and expand responsibility, independence and awareness. Oneka offers many activities, among them water-skiing, sailing, canoeing, tennis, archery, team sports and crafts. A two-week session is open to first-time campers only; other girls attend for at least three and a half weeks.

CAMP CHEN-A-WANDA
Res — Coed Ages 6-16

Thompson, PA 18465. 355 Camp Rd. Tel: 570-756-2016.
Contact (Sept-June): 1 Ellis Ct, Woodcliff Lake, NJ 07677. Tel: 201-391-2294.
Year-round Fax: 570-756-2086.
www.campchen-a-wanda.com   E-mail: jon@campcaw.com
Jon Grabow & Elissa Grabow, Dirs.
Adm: FCFS. **Enr:** 400. **Staff:** Admin 40. Couns 125.
Travel: MA VA Canada.
Features: Crafts Dance Fine_Arts Theater Aquatics Archery Boating Canoe Climbing_Wall Fishing Kayak Mtn_Biking Riding Rock_Climb Ropes_Crse Sail White-water_Raft Baseball Basketball Golf Gymnastics Lacrosse Roller_Hockey Rugby Soccer Softball Swim Tennis Track Volleyball Water-skiing.
Fees 2012: Res $5650-9100 (+$450), 4-7 wks.
Housing: Cabins. Avg per room/unit: 11. **Swimming:** Pool.
Est 1939. Inc. Ses: 1. **Wks/ses:** 7. Operates June-Aug. ACA.

Chen-a-Wanda offers land sports and watersports, as well as ceramics, gymnastics, boating, theater, and high and low ropes courses. Special events include movies, roller skating, carnivals and out-of-camp day trips. Older campers may take a three-day trip to Virginia; Boston, MA; or Toronto, Canada.

VALLEY FORGE MILITARY ACADEMY SUMMER CAMP
Res — Coed Ages 9-17; Day — Coed 6-17

Wayne, PA 19087. 1001 Eagle Rd. Tel: 610-989-1262. Fax: 610-989-1485.
www.vfmac.edu/camp   E-mail: summercamp@vfmac.edu
Joe Haughey, Dir.
Adm: FCFS. **Appl due:** Rolling. **Enr:** 360. **Staff:** Admin 5. Couns 80.
Avg class size: 10.
Features: Crafts Fine_Arts Theater Aquatics Archery Canoe Climbing_Wall Community_ Serv Farm Hiking Leadership Paintball Rappelling Riding Riflery Rock_Climb Ropes_ Crse Sail Scuba Social_Servs Baseball Basketball Equestrian Field_Hockey Football Ice_Hockey Martial_Arts Rugby Soccer Softball Street_Hockey Swim Tennis Volleyball Weight_Trng.
Fees 2011: Res $2300-3900 (+$275), 2-4 wks. Day $430, 1 wk.
Housing: Dorms. Avg per room/unit: 2. **Swimming:** Pool.
Est 1945. Nonprofit. Ses: 3. **Wks/ses:** 2-4. Operates June-July.

In a structured environment, Valley Forge offers a traditional recreational camping experience that includes many of the traditional summer pursuits. Campers may supplement their recreational activities with academic work or engagement in an area of special interest. Leadership training and outdoor adventure activities are particularly strong elements of the program.

RHODE ISLAND

CANONICUS CAMP
Res — Coed Ages 6-18; Day — Coed 4-12

Exeter, RI 02822. 54 Exeter Rd, PO Box 330. Tel: 401-294-6318, 800-294-6318.
Fax: 401-294-7780.
www.canonicus.org   E-mail: camp@canonicus.org
Melanie Towle & Rebekah Malone, Dirs.
Grades PS-12. Adm: FCFS. **Appl due:** Rolling. **Staff:** Admin 8. Couns 21.
Features: Astron Environ_Sci Crafts Dance Drama Media Music Painting Aquatics Archery Aviation/Aero Bicycle_Tours Boating Canoe Community_Serv Cooking Fishing Hiking Kayak Mtn_Trips Outdoor_Ed Rappelling Rock_Climb Ropes_Crse White-water_Raft Wilderness_Camp Baseball Basketball Equestrian Soccer Softball Swim Ultimate_Frisbee Volleyball Watersports.
Fees 2009: Res $300-475, 1 wk. Day $200-230, 1 wk. Aid 2008 (Need): $20,000.
Housing: Cabins Lodges Tents. Avg per room/unit: 12. **Swimming:** Lake.
Est 1948. Nonprofit. Baptist. **Ses:** 8. **Wks/ses:** 1. Operates June-Aug. ACA.

At Canonicus, children explore the outdoors through hiking, swimming, boating, sports and games. Specialty programs focus upon fishing, horsemanship, skateboarding, cooking and outdoor adventure.

SOUTH CAROLINA

NOSOCA PINES RANCH SUMMER CAMP
Res — Coed Ages 7-17

Liberty Hill, SC 29074. 2990 Singleton Creek Rd, PO Box 200. Tel: 803-273-8200.
Fax: 803-273-9196.
www.nosoca.org   E-mail: npr@carolinasda.com
Rick Faber, Dir.
Adm: FCFS. **Appl due:** Rolling. **Staff:** Admin 10. Couns 21. Res 6.
Features: Crafts Drama Aquatics Archery Boating Canoe Climbing_Wall Hiking Mtn_Biking Rock_Climb Sail White-water_Raft Baseball Basketball Equestrian Golf Gymnastics Soccer Softball Swim Tennis Volleyball Water-skiing Watersports.
Fees 2011: Res $375-460, 1 wk.
Housing: Cabins Lodges. **Swimming:** Pool.
Est 1972. Nonprofit. Seventh-day Adventist. **Ses:** 15. **Wks/ses:** 1. Operates June-July. ACA.

This Seventh-day Adventist camp offers land sports, water sports, horseback riding, canoeing, nature study and rock climbing. Campers may attend specialty camps that focus upon riding, waterfront activities, rock climbing and white-water rafting, or basketball.

CAMP CHATUGA
Res — Coed Ages 6-16

Mountain Rest, SC 29664. 291 Camp Chatuga Rd. Tel: 864-638-3728.
Fax: 864-638-0898.
www.campchatuga.com   E-mail: mail@campchatuga.com
Angela Gordon Sullivan, Lucy Gordon Barnett & Rick Moxley, Dirs.
Grades 1-11. Adm: FCFS. **Appl due:** Rolling. **Enr cap:** 150. **Staff:** Admin 8. Couns 30.
Features: Crafts Creative_Writing Dance Drama Aquatics Archery Canoe Cooking Fish-

ing Hiking Mtn_Biking Outdoor_Ed Riding Riflery Basketball Cricket Equestrian Football Soccer Swim Tennis Ultimate_Frisbee Volleyball Water-skiing Watersports.
Fees 2012: Res $635-2940, 1-4 wks.
Housing: Cabins. Avg per room/unit: 6. **Swimming:** Lake.
Est 1956. Inc. **Ses:** 9. **Wks/ses:** 1-4. Operates June-Aug. ACA.

Chatuga features more than 30 activity choices, among them horseback riding, water-skiing, swimming, canoeing, crafts, drama, guitar, creative writing, sports and nature. Each camper spends the first day sampling the most popular activities, then chooses a personalized daily schedule according to his or her interests. Chatuga schedules frequent evening and special activities, and boys and girls who spend more than a week at camp participate in a daylong excursion. A horseback specialty week for girls is available.

SOUTH DAKOTA

LUTHERANS OUTDOORS IN SOUTH DAKOTA
SUMMER CAMPS
Res and Day — Coed Ages 5-17

Sioux Falls, SD 57197. c/o Augustana College, 2001 S Summit Ave.
Tel: 605-274-5326, 800-888-1464. Fax: 605-274-5024.
www.losd.org   E-mail: info@losd.org
Layne D. Nelson, Exec Dir.
Grades K-12. Adm: FCFS. **Appl due:** Rolling. **Staff:** Admin 15.
Features: Environ_Sci Relig_Stud Crafts Music Adventure_Travel Bicycle_Tours Canoe Caving Community_Serv Fishing Hiking Kayak Mtn_Biking Mtn_Trips Ranch Riding Rock_Climb Ropes_Crse Wilderness_Camp Equestrian Swim.
Fees 2012: Res $360-405, 1 wk. Day $85, 1 wk.
Housing: Cabins Lodges Tents Tepees. **Swimming:** Lake.
Est 1968. Nonprofit. Evangelical. **Ses:** 9. **Wks/ses:** 1. Operates June-Aug.

LOSD operates Christian summer programs for young people at five campsites: NeSoDak, Klein Ranch, Joy Ranch, Outlaw Ranch and Atlantic Mountain Ranch. Boys and girls choose from Bible, leadership, music and confirmation programs at NeSoDak in Waubay. Camps at Atlantic Mountain Ranch and Outlaw Ranch, both situated outside Custer in the Black Hills, combine worship with such outdoor pursuits as hiking, riding, backpacking and canoeing. Located in Isabel, Klein Ranch provides ranching and equestrian experiences on an authentic Western horse ranch. Joy Ranch is a barrier-free camp and retreat center on the shores of Lyle Lake.

TENNESSEE

CAMP NAKANAWA
Res — Girls Ages 8-17

Crossville, TN 38571. 1084 Camp Nakanawa Rd. Tel: 931-277-3711.
Fax: 931-277-5552.
www.campnakanawa.com   E-mail: campnak@frontiernet.net
Ann Perron & Pepe Perron, Dirs.
Grades 3-12. Adm: FCFS. **Appl due:** Rolling. **Enr:** 250. **Staff:** Admin 3. Couns 100.
Features: Crafts Dance Music Painting Theater Aquatics Archery Boating Canoe Caving

Climbing_Wall Fishing Hiking Rappelling Riding Riflery Ropes_Crse Sail White-water_ Raft Equestrian Fencing Golf Soccer Softball Swim Tennis Volleyball.
Fees 2011: Res $1750-2900 (+$20-40), 2-4 wks.
Housing: Cabins. Avg per room/unit: 8. **Swimming:** Lake.
Est 1920. Inc. Ses: 2. **Wks/ses:** 2-4. Operates June-July.

Nakanawa, which is located at an elevation of 2000 feet on the Cumberland Plateau, divides its traditional girls' camps into junior, intermediate and senior sections, depending upon age. Staff encourage girls at the junior camp to try every activity in order to gain experience and to develop fundamental skills. Campers in the intermediate and senior camps engage in only four required activities (swimming, tennis, canoeing and glee club), thus providing them with the opportunity to set their own schedules. A free day each week allows girls to take part in a planned trip off site or receive additional instruction in an activity.

CAMP MARYMOUNT
Res — Coord Ages 6-16

Fairview, TN 37062. 1318 Fairview Blvd. Tel: 615-799-0410. Fax: 615-799-2261.
www.campmarymount.com   E-mail: info@campmarymount.com
Tommy Hagey, Dir.
Grades 1-11. Adm: FCFS. **Enr:** 200. **Staff:** Admin 8. Couns 60.
Features: Crafts Theater Archery Canoe Fishing Riding Riflery Ropes_Crse Equestrian Swim Wrestling.
Fees 2011: Res $780-1010, 2-3 wks.
Housing: Cabins. Avg per room/unit: 10. **Swimming:** Lake.
Est 1939. Nonprofit. Roman Catholic. **Ses:** 3. **Wks/ses:** 2-3. Operates May-July. ACA.

A Catholic camp serving campers of all faiths, Marymount offers swimming, arts and crafts, riflery and archery, nature activities, riding, athletics and wagon rides in separate programs for boys and girls. Horsemanship is a particularly popular offering, with interested campers learning safety techniques, riding skills, and saddling and horse care.

CIRCLE Y I RANCH
Res — Coed Ages 7-14; Day — Coed 7-10

LaVergne, TN 37086. 599 Jones Mill Rd. Tel: 615-459-3971.
Contact (Winter): c/o Youth Inc, 1160 Gallatin Rd S, Ste 121, Madison, TN 37115.
Tel: 615-865-0003.
Year-round Fax: 615-865-0094.
www.campyi.org   E-mail: campyidirector@gmail.com
Kim Hutchison, Dir.
Adm: FCFS. **Appl due:** Rolling. **Enr:** 400. **Staff:** Admin 4. Couns 35.
Features: Aquatics Boating Canoe Climbing_Wall Conservation Fishing Hiking Rappelling Riding Ropes_Crse Sail Wilderness_Camp Equestrian Field_Hockey Swim Water-skiing.
Fees 2011: Res $375-675 (+$20), 1-2 wks. Day $185, 1 wk.
Housing: Cabins Houses Lodges. Avg per room/unit: 8. **Swimming:** Lake Pool.
Est 1945. Nonprofit. **Ses:** 7. **Wks/ses:** 1-2. Operates June-July. ACA.

For boys and girls of Nashville and middle Tennessee, this camp provides daily activities consisting of swimming, canoeing, arts and crafts, sailing, fishing, horseback riding, high and low ropes courses, an alpine climbing tower and water-skiing, in addition to overnight trips, hiking and cooking.

TEXAS

PRUDE RANCH SUMMER CAMP
Res — Coed Ages 7-16

Fort Davis, TX 79734. PO Box 1907. Tel: 432-426-4406, 800-458-6232.
Fax: 432-426-3502.
www.prude-ranch.com   E-mail: info@prude-ranch.com
Kelly Prude Boultinghouse, Dir.
Grades 2-10. Adm: FCFS. Appl due: Rolling. Enr: 100. Enr cap: 120. Staff: Admin 8. Couns 30.
Features: Crafts Dance Drama Aquatics Archery Climbing_Wall Hiking Mountaineering Outdoor_Ed Paintball Rappelling Riding Riflery Rock_Climb Ropes_Crse Working_ Cattle_Ranch Yoga Badminton Baseball Basketball Equestrian Football Golf Gymnastics Soccer Softball Swim Tennis Ultimate_Frisbee Volleyball.
Fees 2011: Res $650-1500 (+$100), 1-2 wks. Aid 2007 (Need): $2000.
Housing: Cabins Lodges. Avg per room/unit: 10. Swimming: Pool.
Est 1951. Inc. Ses: 6. Wks/ses: 1-2. Operates June-Aug. ACA.

Campers ages 7-11 learn basic riding skills and participate in both rodeo activities and instructional activity classes. Those ages 12 and 13 spend more time with horses and are offered geology, advanced camp lore and environmental awareness activities. Boys and girls ages 14 to 16 participate in ranch life by taking long mountain trail rides, working cattle, learning horse care, and engaging in orienteering, skeet shooting, rappelling and two-night camp outs.

CAMP LA JUNTA
Res — Boys Ages 7-14

Hunt, TX 78024. PO Box 139. Tel: 830-238-4621. Fax: 830-238-4888.
www.lajunta.com   E-mail: info@lajunta.com
Blake W. Smith, Dir.
Grades 2-9. Adm: FCFS. Appl due: Rolling. Enr: 270. Enr cap: 270. Staff: Admin 8. Couns 50.
Features: Filmmaking Photog Aquatics Archery Aviation/Aero Bicycle_Tours Canoe Climbing_Wall Hiking Kayak Mtn_Biking Rappelling Riding Riflery Ropes_Crse Sail Scuba Survival_Trng Wilderness_Camp Woodcraft Basketball Equestrian Golf Soccer Softball Swim Tennis Volleyball Water-skiing Watersports.
Fees 2012: Res $2150-3900, 2-4 wks.
Housing: Cabins. Swimming: Pond River.
Est 1928. Inc. Ses: 6. Wks/ses: 2-4. Operates June-July.

Activities at this camp include swimming, horseback riding, canoeing, water-skiing, sailing, scuba diving, camp outs, riflery and archery. An award system recognizes achievement in camp activities by rewarding boys with patches, special trips and honors.

CAMP RIO VISTA
CAMP SIERRA VISTA
Res — Coord Ages 6-16

Ingram, TX 78025. 175 Rio Vista Rd. Tel: 830-367-5353, 800-545-3233.
Fax: 830-367-4044.
www.vistacamps.com   E-mail: info@vistacamps.com
John Hawkins, Dir.
Grades 1-10. Adm: FCFS. Appl due: Rolling. Enr: 150-250. Enr cap: 250. Staff: Admin 10. Couns 68. Res 5.
Features: Writing/Journ Crafts Dance Drama Aquatics Archery Canoe Climbing_Wall

Fishing Hiking Kayak Rappelling Riding Riflery Ropes_Crse Sail Woodcraft Aerobics Basketball Football Golf Lacrosse Martial_Arts Soccer Softball Swim Tennis Track Volleyball Water-skiing Watersports Weight_Trng Wrestling.
Fees 2012: Res $1400-3750 (+$50), 1-4 wks.
Housing: Cabins. Avg per room/unit: 8-16. **Swimming:** River.
Est 1921. Inc. **Ses:** 9. **Wks/ses:** 1-4. Operates June-Aug.

Campers at Rio Vista for boys and Sierra Vista for girls choose from more than 30 activities. The program offers land sports, aquatic activities, archery, sailing and horseback riding.

CAMP CHAMPIONS
Res — Coed Ages 6-18

Marble Falls, TX 78654. 775 Camp Rd. Tel: 830-598-2571. Fax: 830-598-1095.
www.campchampions.com   E-mail: info@campchampions.com
Steve Baskin & Susie Baskin, Dirs.
Adm: FCFS. **Appl due:** Rolling.
Features: Crafts Dance Aquatics Canoe Riding Riflery Sail Baseball Basketball Football Soccer Swim Tennis Volleyball Water-skiing.
Fees 2012: Res $1395-3550 (+$40), 1-3 wks.
Housing: Cabins. **Swimming:** Lake.
Est 1967. Ses: 3. **Wks/ses:** 1-3. Operates June-Aug. ACA.

CC emphasizes watersports and land sports. Other programming includes sailing, horseback riding, riflery, dance and cheerleading.

CAMP FERN
Res — Coed Ages 6-16

Marshall, TX 75672. 1046 Camp Rd. Tel: 903-935-5420. Fax: 903-935-6372.
www.campfern.com   E-mail: info@campfern.com
Margaret R. Lee, Dir.
Grades 1-9. Adm: FCFS. **Appl due:** Rolling. **Staff:** Admin 4. Couns 75.
Features: Crafts Dance Drama Music Aquatics Archery Boating Canoe Climbing_Wall Fishing Hiking Mountaineering Rappelling Riding Riflery Ropes_Crse Sail Survival_Trng Basketball Equestrian Soccer Swim Tennis Volleyball Water-skiing Watersports.
Fees 2012: Res $1200-3475 (+$50-100), 1-4 wks.
Housing: Cabins. Avg per room/unit: 9. **Swimming:** Lake.
Est 1934. Inc. Nondenom Christian. **Ses:** 9. **Wks/ses:** 1-4. Operates May-Aug.

The camp offers a two-week coed session as its basic camping experience, and more advanced activities and special trips and programs in separate four-week boys' and girls' sessions. In addition to traditional summer pursuits, the program includes daily swimming and English horseback riding and jumping courses. Overnight horseback rides and four-day mountain climbing and river trips complete the program.

CAMP LANGSTON
Res — Coed Ages 6-16

Mount Pleasant, TX 75455. 50 County Rd 3227. Tel: 903-572-5935.
www.camplangston.net   E-mail: info@camplangston.net
Melody Paul & Phil Paul, Dirs.
Adm: FCFS. **Staff:** Admin 4. Couns 26.
Features: Crafts Dance Archery Boating Canoe Deep-sea Fishing Exploration Hiking Ranch Riding Riflery Baseball Basketball Football Gymnastics Soccer Softball Swim Volleyball Watersports.
Fees 2010: Res $450-550 (+$30), 1 wk.
Housing: Cabins. **Swimming:** Lake Pond Pool Stream.

Est 1951. Ses: 5. **Wks/ses:** 1. Operates June-July.

Located on the hundreds of acres of pastures, fields, wooded hills and valleys of Jack Langston Ranch, Langston offers swimming, lifesaving, boating, horseback riding, hiking, nature study and archery. Other activities include crafts, trampolining, first aid and safety, riflery, leather craft and woodworking. On a picture-taking tour of the ranch, campers photograph the freely roaming deer, elk and buffalo.

CAMP OLYMPIA
Res — Coed Ages 7-16

Trinity, TX 75862. 723 Olympia Dr. Tel: 936-594-2541, 800-735-6190. Fax: 936-594-8143.
www.campolympia.com   E-mail: campinfo@campolympia.com
Tommy D. Ferguson, Dir.
Adm: FCFS. **Appl due:** Rolling.
Features: Crafts Dance Drama Filmmaking Photog Archery Canoe Climbing_Wall Fishing Kayak Mtn_Biking Outdoor_Ed Rappelling Riding Riflery Ropes_Crse Sail Scuba Aerobics Baseball Basketball Equestrian Football Golf Gymnastics Lacrosse Soccer Softball Swim Tennis Track Volleyball Water-skiing Watersports Weight_Trng.
Fees 2010: Res $2735-3685 (+$75), 2-3 wks.
Housing: Cabins. Avg per room/unit: 12. **Swimming:** Lake Pool.
Est 1968. Inc. Nondenom Christian. **Ses:** 4. **Wks/ses:** 2-3. Operates May-Aug. ACA.

Located on a 500-acre peninsula in Lake Livingston, Olympia conducts a full program of aquatics, athletics and outdoor activities. Offerings include both individual and team sports, riding, nature study, ecology, hiking and sailing.

ROCKY RIVER RANCH
Res — Girls Ages 7-14

Wimberley, TX 78676. 100 Flite Acres Rd, PO Box 109. Tel: 512-847-2513, 800-863-2267. Fax: 512-847-9067.
www.rockyriverranch.com   E-mail: info@rockyriverranch.com
Rue Hatfield, Exec Dir.
Grades 2-11. Adm: FCFS. **Enr:** 100. **Staff:** Admin 3. Couns 24.
Features: Crafts Creative_Writing Dance Photog Theater Aquatics Archery Canoe Climbing_Wall Cooking Fishing Rappelling Riding Riflery Basketball Equestrian Swim Tennis Volleyball Watersports.
Fees 2012: Res $815-1630 (+$50-80), 1-2 wks.
Housing: Cabins. Avg per room/unit: 18. **Swimming:** Pool River.
Est 1953. Inc. **Ses:** 6. **Wks/ses:** 1-2. Operates June-Aug. ACA.

In addition to a particularly strong equestrian program, RRR offers sports, recreation, dramatics, aquatics, canoeing, crafts and nature studies.

VERMONT

BROWN LEDGE CAMP
Res — Girls Ages 10-18

Colchester, VT 05446. 71 Brown Ledge Rd.
Contact (Sept-May): 25 Wilson St, Burlington, VT 05401.
Year-round Tel: 802-862-2442, 800-246-1958. Fax: 802-658-1614.
www.brownledge.org   E-mail: info@brownledge.org

William Neilsen & Katharine Neilsen, Dirs.
Adm: FCFS. **Appl due:** Rolling. **Enr:** 180. **Staff:** Couns 65.
Features: Crafts Fine_Arts Theater Archery Canoe Kayak Riding Riflery Sail Equestrian Swim Tennis Water-skiing Watersports.
Fees 2012: Res $4900-6950 (+$740-980), 4-8 wks.
Housing: Cabins. **Swimming:** Lake.
Est 1926. Nonprofit. **Ses:** 3. **Wks/ses:** 4-8. Operates June-Aug. ACA.

Horsemanship, water-skiing, swimming, sailing, theater arts and tennis are featured at Brown Ledge, which is located on Lake Champlain. Inclusive tuition covers all activities, overnight trips, and recognized horse shows and events.

NIGHT EAGLE WILDERNESS ADVENTURES
Res — Boys Ages 10-14

Cuttingsville, VT 05738. PO Box 374. Tel: 802-773-7866.
www.nighteaglewilderness.com   E-mail: nightegl@sover.net
Bruce Moreton, Dir.
Grades 5-9. Adm: FCFS. **Appl due:** Rolling. **Enr:** 40. **Enr cap:** 40. **Staff:** Admin 2. Couns 15. Res 15.
Features: Crafts Aquatics Archery Canoe Conservation Cooking Hiking Outdoor_Ed Survival_Trng Wilderness_Camp Swim.
Fees 2010: Res $1725-4050, 2-6 wks.
Housing: Tepees. Avg per room/unit: 4. **Swimming:** Lake.
Est 1999. Inc. **Ses:** 6. **Wks/ses:** 2-6. Operates July-Aug. ACA.

Night Eagle places particular emphasis on maintaining a simple lifestyle and instilling in campers a respect for nature. Boys learn about the culture of the American Indian while taking part in a noncompetitive program with a strong outdoor component. The nature-based program features crafts, canoeing, hiking and wilderness skills, among other pursuits.

ALOHA CAMP
Res — Girls Ages 12-17

Fairlee, VT 05045. 2039 Lake Morey Rd. Tel: 802-333-3410. Fax: 802-333-3404.
www.alohafoundation.org   E-mail: ellen_bagley@alohafoundation.org
Marijean L. Parry, Dir.
Grades 6-11. Adm: FCFS. **Appl due:** Rolling. **Enr:** 140. **Enr cap:** 140.
Features: Crafts Creative_Writing Dance Drama Fine_Arts Music Painting Photog Studio_Art Aquatics Archery Bicycle_Tours Boating Canoe Hiking Kayak Mtn_Biking Mtn_Trips Riding Riflery Ropes_Crse Sail Wilderness_Camp Wilderness_Canoe Woodcraft Badminton Basketball Cross-country Equestrian Field_Hockey Lacrosse Soccer Softball Swim Tennis Volleyball.
Fees 2012: Res $5450-8375 (+$500), 3½-7 wks.
Housing: Cabins Tents. Avg per room/unit: 3. **Swimming:** Lake.
Est 1905. Nonprofit. **Spons:** Aloha Foundation. **Ses:** 3. **Wks/ses:** 3½-7. Operates June-Aug. ACA.

Overnight camping, one- to five-day mountain climbing trips, canoe tripping, swimming, boating and tennis are important elements of the program. Music, dramatics, dance, crafts, riding, photography and reading are among the camp's other activities. Two affiliated camps, Aloha Hive for younger girls and Lanakila for boys (see separate listings), are located nearby.

CAMP ALOHA HIVE
Res — Girls Ages 7-12

Fairlee, VT 05045. 846 State Rte 244. Tel: 802-333-3420. Fax: 802-333-3404.

www.alohafoundation.org   E-mail: ellen_bagley@alohafoundation.org
Kathryn K. Plunkett, Dir.
Grades 2-6. Adm: FCFS. **Appl due:** Rolling. **Enr:** 155. **Enr cap:** 155. **Staff:** Admin 4. Couns 80.
Features: Environ_Sci Crafts Dance Drama Fine_Arts Music Photog Archery Canoe Conservation Exploration Hiking Kayak Riding Rock_Climb Ropes_Crse Sail Wilderness_ Camp Basketball Equestrian Gymnastics Lacrosse Soccer Softball Swim Tennis.
Fees 2012: Res $2700-8375, 1½-7 wks.
Housing: Tents. Avg per room/unit: 3. **Swimming:** Lake.
Est 1915. Nonprofit. **Spons:** Aloha Foundation. **Ses:** 4. **Wks/ses:** 3½-7. Operates June-Aug. ACA.

Nine miles from two affiliated camps, Camp Lanakila for boys and Aloha Camp for older girls (see separate listings), this camp provides a program specially designed for young girls. Waterfront activities are emphasized, as are riding, gymnastics, dramatics, music, dance and crafts. Aloha Hive conducts one- to three-day mountain and canoe trips for interested campers. The Elfin Program provides a 10-day introduction to camp for students entering grades 2-4.

CAMP LANAKILA
Res — Boys Ages 8-14

Fairlee, VT 05045. c/o The Aloha Foundation, 2968 Lake Morey Rd. Tel: 802-333-3430. Fax: 802-333-3404.
www.alohafoundation.org   E-mail: ellen_bagley@alohafoundation.org
D. Barnes Boffey, Dir.
Grades 3-8. Adm: FCFS. **Appl due:** Rolling. **Enr:** 155. **Enr cap:** 155. **Staff:** Admin 4. Couns 85.
Features: Crafts Music Photog Theater Archery Boating Canoe Exploration Hiking Kayak Mtn_Biking Mtn_Trips Riflery Ropes_Crse Sail Woodcraft Baseball Basketball Soccer Street_Hockey Swim Tennis Ultimate_Frisbee Watersports.
Fees 2012: Res $5450-8375 (+$500), 3½-7 wks. Aid 2006 (Need): $80,000.
Housing: Cabins Tents. Avg per room/unit: 3. **Swimming:** Lake.
Est 1922. Nonprofit. **Spons:** Aloha Foundation. **Ses:** 3. **Wks/ses:** 3½-7. Operates June-Aug. ACA.

A camp of the Aloha Foundation, Lanakila offers a full in-camp program, as well as extensive river and white-water trips and day- to weeklong hiking and mountain climbing trips. Two affiliated girls' camps, Aloha and Aloha Hive (see separate listings), operate nearby.

CAMP KILLOOLEET
Res — Coed Ages 9-14

Hancock, VT 05748. Tel: 802-767-3152. Fax: 802-767-3111.
Contact (Sept-May): 70 Trull St, Somerville, MA 02145. Tel: 617-666-1484. Fax: 617-666-0378.
www.killooleet.com   E-mail: kseeger@killooleet.com
Katherine Seeger & Dean Spencer, Dirs.
Adm: FCFS. **Appl due:** Rolling. **Enr:** 100. **Enr cap:** 100. **Staff:** Admin 5. Couns 30. Res 45.
Features: Crafts Dance Filmmaking Fine_Arts Music Studio_Art Theater Aquatics Archery Bicycle_Tours Boating Canoe Community_Serv Conservation Cooking Exploration Hiking Kayak Mountaineering Mtn_Biking Mtn_Trips Riding Rock_Climb Wilderness_ Camp Woodcraft Yoga Basketball Equestrian Martial_Arts Soccer Softball Swim Tennis Ultimate_Frisbee Volleyball Watersports.
Fees 2011: Res $7800 (+$60), 8 wks. Aid 2008 (Need): $55,000.
Housing: Cabins. Avg per room/unit: 8-12. **Swimming:** Lake Stream.
Est 1927. Inc. **Ses:** 1. **Wks/ses:** 8. Operates June-Aug. ACA.

Killooleet's program incorporates the performing and visual arts, the outdoors, and team and individual sports. Days consist of four hour-long activity periods, with half-hour blocks of free time between periods. Campers plan their daily schedules. New campers have the option of attending the first four weeks of camp before committing to the full session.

CAMP FARWELL
Res — Girls Ages 6-16

Newbury, VT 05051. PO Box 300. Tel: 802-429-2244. Fax: 802-429-2037.
www.farwell.com   E-mail: mailfordirectors@farwell.com
Charyl Hanson, Bob Hanson & Marley Hanson, Dirs.
Grades 1-11. Adm: FCFS. **Appl due:** Rolling. **Enr:** 125. **Enr cap:** 125. **Staff:** Admin 10. Couns 50. Res 60.
Features: Lang Crafts Dance Drama Fine_Arts Music Painting Photog Aquatics Archery Canoe Fishing Hiking Kayak Outdoor_Ed Riding Sail White-water_Raft Equestrian Field_Hockey Gymnastics Lacrosse Soccer Softball Swim Tennis Volleyball Water-skiing Watersports Windsurfing.
Fees 2011: Res $3070-8165 (+$260-910), 2-7 wks. Aid (Need).
Housing: Cabins. Avg per room/unit: 6. **Swimming:** Lake.
Est 1906. Inc. Ses: 5. **Wks/ses:** 2-7. Operates July-Aug. ACA.

Located on Halls Lake, Farwell offers its campers a well-rounded, traditional camping experience that includes a specialized riding program for girls of all ability levels. Other activities include individual and team sports, performing arts, a diverse waterfront program, arts and crafts, and photography.

CAMP SANGAMON
CAMP BETSEY COX
Res — Coord Ages 9-15

Pittsford, VT 05763. 382 Camp Ln.
Contact (Jan-Apr): PO Box 886, Key Largo, FL 33037.
Year-round Tel: 802-483-2862, 888-345-9193.
www.campsangamon.com; www.campbetseycox.com
E-mail: sangamonvt@aol.com
Mike Byrom & Lorrie Byrom, Dirs.
Grades 4-10. Adm: FCFS. **Appl due:** Rolling. **Enr:** 90. **Staff:** Admin 3. Couns 60.
Features: Crafts Photog Pottery Weaving Archery Canoe Caving Farm Fishing Hiking Kayak Mtn_Biking Riding Rock_Climb Sail Basketball Soccer Swim Tennis.
Fees 2012: Res $2090-8360, 2-8 wks.
Housing: Cabins. **Swimming:** Lake.
Est 1922. Ses: 8. **Wks/ses:** 2-8. Operates June-Aug. ACA.

Each camper at the adjacently situated Sangamon for boys and Betsey Cox for girls (866-213-4717) prepares a daily schedule. Among the offerings are a waterfront program, riding, weaving, athletics, farming, artistic pursuits, tripping and special events. The two camps operate some programs jointly.

INDIAN BROOK
Res — Girls Ages 9-14

Plymouth, VT 05056. c/o Farm & Wilderness Foundation, 263 Farm & Wilderness Rd.
Tel: 802-422-3761. Fax: 802-422-8660.
www.farmandwilderness.org   E-mail: info@farmandwilderness.org
Amy Bowen, Dir.
Adm: FCFS. **Appl due:** Rolling. **Enr:** 120.
Features: Crafts Dance Drama Music Studio_Art Canoe Climbing_Wall Community_Serv

Conservation Cooking Exploration Farm Hiking Mtn_Trips Outdoor_Ed Peace/Cross-cultural Rappelling Rock_Climb Ropes_Crse Social_Servs Wilderness_Camp Wilderness_Canoe Woodcraft Work Soccer Swim Ultimate_Frisbee.
Fees 2011: Res $2375-7100, 2-7 wks. Aid (Merit & Need).
Housing: Cabins. Avg per room/unit: 8. **Swimming:** Lake.
Est 1941. Nonprofit. **Spons:** Farm and Wilderness Foundation. **Ses:** 3. **Wks/ses:** 2-7. Operates July-Aug. ACA.

Adhering to Quaker values, Indian Brook involves girls in such morning activities as feeding the pigs, milking the cows and gathering eggs. Many of the camp's pursuits relate to practical outdoor living skills or the creative arts. Campers utilize these living skills during two- to eight-day outdoor adventures involving canoeing, rock climbing and backpacking. Girls attend Meeting for Worship daily.

TIMBERLAKE
Res — Boys Ages 9-14

Plymouth, VT 05056. c/o Farm & Wilderness Foundation, 263 Farm & Wilderness Rd. Tel: 802-422-3761. Fax: 802-422-8660.
www.farmandwilderness.org   E-mail: info@farmandwilderness.org
Tulio Browning, Dir.
Adm: FCFS. **Appl due:** Rolling. **Enr:** 110. **Enr cap:** 110.
Features: Crafts Dance Music Studio_Art Canoe Climbing_Wall Community_Serv Conservation Cooking Exploration Farm Hiking Mountaineering Mtn_Trips Outdoor_Ed Peace/Cross-cultural Rock_Climb Ropes_Crse Wilderness_Camp Wilderness_Canoe Woodcraft Swim Ultimate_Frisbee.
Fees 2011: Res $2375-7100, 2-7 wks. Aid (Merit & Need).
Housing: Cabins. Avg per room/unit: 8. **Swimming:** Lake.
Est 1939. Nonprofit. **Spons:** Farm and Wilderness Foundation. **Ses:** 3. **Wks/ses:** 2-7. Operates July-Aug. ACA.

Timberlake's natural surroundings provide the foundation for pursuits involving outdoor living skills, the farm and gardens, and the waterfront. Work projects, arts and crafts, and games are prominent aspects of the program. Boys also embark on one- to five-night canoeing, rock climbing and service trips.

LOCHEARN CAMP FOR GIRLS
Res — Girls Ages 7-16

Post Mills, VT 05058. 1061 Robinson Hill Rd, PO Box 44. Tel: 802-333-4211, 877-649-4151. Fax: 802-333-4856.
www.lochearncamp.com   E-mail: info@lochearncamp.com
Rich Maxson & Ginny Maxson, Dirs.
Grades 2-10. Adm: FCFS. **Appl due:** Rolling. **Enr:** 172. **Enr cap:** 172. **Staff:** Admin 15. Couns 60.
Features: Writing/Journ Crafts Creative_Writing Dance Fine_Arts Painting Studio_Art Theater Aquatics Archery Canoe Community_Serv Cooking Hiking Mtn_Trips Riding Sail Yoga Aerobics Baseball Basketball Cross-country Equestrian Field_Hockey Gymnastics Lacrosse Soccer Softball Swim Tennis Volleyball Water-skiing Watersports.
Fees 2012: Res $1300-10,650 (+$20-200), 1-8 wks. Aid 2009 (Need): $60,000.
Housing: Cabins. Avg per room/unit: 7. **Swimming:** Lake.
Est 1916. Inc. **Ses:** 8. **Wks/ses:** 1-8. Operates June-Aug. ACA.

The camp offers comprehensive programs in watersports, riding, land sports, outdoor adventure and the creative arts. Campers design their schedules with guidance from staff members. One of the oldest private girls' camps in the US, Lochearn maintains three divisions: a junior camp for children ages 7-10, a subsenior camp for girls ages 11 and 12, and a senior camp for campers ages 13-15. Fifteen- and 16-year-olds may participate in a four- or eight-week leadership training program, and a one-week minicamp option provides an introduction to camp life.

KEEWAYDIN DUNMORE
SONGADEEWIN OF KEEWAYDIN
Res — Coord Ages 8-16

Salisbury, VT 05769. 10 Keewaydin Rd. Tel: 802-352-4770. Fax: 802-352-4772.
www.keewaydin.org   E-mail: pete@keewaydin.org; ellen@keewaydin.org
Peter C. Hare & Ellen M. Flight, Dirs.
Grades 2-9. Adm: FCFS. **Appl due:** Rolling. **Enr:** 316. **Staff:** Couns 110.
Features: Crafts Dance Photog Theater Aquatics Canoe Climbing_Wall Conservation Exploration Hiking Kayak Mountaineering Mtn_Trips Riflery Rock_Climb Sail Wilderness_Camp Wilderness_Canoe Woodcraft Baseball Basketball Soccer Swim Tennis Ultimate_Frisbee Volleyball Watersports Wrestling.
Fees 2012: Res $3800-7950 (+$100), 2-8 wks.
Housing: Cabins Tents. **Swimming:** Lake.
Est 1910. Nonprofit. **Ses:** 6. **Wks/ses:** 2-8. Operates June-Aug. ACA.

Located on Lake Dunmore in the Green Mountains, Keewaydin Dunmore for boys and Songadeewin for girls (500 Rustic Ln.; 802-352-9860) offer a general program with an emphasis on canoeing and tripping. Traditional activities include swimming, boating, tennis, baseball, arts and crafts, sailing, soccer and dramatics. Each camper takes a monthly three- to 17-day canoeing or hiking trip, with the duration varying according to age.

VIRGINIA

CAMP HORIZONS
Res — Coed Ages 6-16

Harrisonburg, VA 22802. 3586 Horizons Way. Tel: 540-896-7600. Fax: 540-896-5455.
www.camphorizonsva.com   E-mail: camp@horizonsva.com
John Hall, Dir.
Grades 1-11. Adm: FCFS. **Appl due:** Rolling. **Enr:** 175-250. **Enr cap:** 250. **Staff:** Admin 12. Couns 60.
Features: Ecol Environ_Sci Writing/Journ Crafts Creative_Writing Dance Filmmaking Music Photog Theater Aquatics Archery Canoe Caving Climbing_Wall Exploration Hiking Kayak Mountaineering Mtn_Biking Mtn_Trips Outdoor_Ed Riding Rock_Climb Ropes Crse Scuba White-water Raft Wilderness_Camp Basketball Equestrian Golf Lacrosse Roller_Hockey Soccer Softball Street_Hockey Swim Tennis Ultimate_Frisbee Volleyball.
Fees 2012: Res $1050-1850 (+$95-275), 1-2 wks.
Housing: Cabins Tepees. Avg per room/unit: 10. **Swimming:** Lake Pond Pool.
Est 1982. Inc. **Ses:** 4. **Wks/ses:** 1-2. Operates June-Aug. ACA.

Children from around the world participate in a varied program that includes a range of land and water activities. Campers ages 15-17 may participate in the Adventure Program, which includes high and low ropes courses, caving, rock climbing and rappelling, hiking, mountain biking, overnight backpacking, white-water rafting and a canoe trip. The Explorer Program (ages 12-16) combines traditional camping pursuits with some adventure and performing arts activities, among them caving, hiking, mountain biking, rock climbing, a ropes course, tubing, drama, dance and music.

CAMP MONT SHENANDOAH
Res — Girls Ages 7-16

Millboro Springs, VA 24460. 218 Mont Shenandoah Ln. Tel: 540-997-5994. Fax: 540-997-0678.
www.campmontshenandoah.com E-mail: info@campmontshenandoah.com
Jay Batley & Ann Batley, Dirs.
Adm: FCFS.
Features: Crafts Drama Music Aquatics Archery Canoe Hiking Riding Equestrian Field_ Hockey Lacrosse Soccer Softball Swim Tennis.
Fees 2012: Res $1075-4995 (+$100), 1-6 wks. Aid (Need).
Housing: Cabins. **Swimming:** River.
Est 1927. Inc. **Ses:** 4. **Wks/ses:** 1-6. Operates June-Aug. ACA.

Daily activities at CMS include swimming, canoeing, arts and crafts, drama, music, sports and other traditional camp activities. On weekends, the camp holds athletic competitions and offers river canoe trips. An English-style equestrian program is available for an additional fee.

CAMP FRIENDSHIP
Res — Coed Ages 6-16

Palmyra, VA 22963. PO Box 145. Tel: 434-589-8950, 800-873-3223. Fax: 434-589-5880.
www.campfriendship.com E-mail: info@campfriendship.com
Samantha Leonard, Dir.
Adm: FCFS. **Appl due:** Rolling. **Enr:** 450. **Enr cap:** 450. **Staff:** Admin 10. Couns 100.
Features: ESL Crafts Dance Filmmaking Fine_Arts Music Photog Theater Adventure_Travel Aquatics Archery Bicycle_Tours Canoe Caving Climbing_Wall Fishing Hiking Kayak Mountaineering Mtn_Biking Mtn_Trips Rappelling Riding Riflery Rock_Climb Ropes_ Crse White-water_Raft Wilderness_Camp Wilderness_Canoe Basketball Cross-country Equestrian Fencing Field_Hockey Golf Gymnastics Lacrosse Soccer Swim Tennis Track Volleyball Water-skiing Watersports.
Fees 2012: Res $1000-1200 (+$40), 1 wk. Aid (Need).
Housing: Cabins. Avg room/unit: 10. **Swimming:** Lake Pool River Stream.
Est 1966. Nonprofit. **Ses:** 9. **Wks/ses:** 1-2. Operates June-Aug. ACA.

Junior campers live in separate boys' and girls' villages apart from the senior village. Boys and girls individually select a weekly schedule of activities from the following: watersports, canoeing, tennis, team sports, gymnastics, riding, creative and performing arts, photography, archery, riflery and fishing. Challenge trips for older campers begin with a ropes course and offer canoeing, river rafting, caving, kayaking, trail riding, mountain biking and rock climbing.

CAMP CARYSBROOK
Res — Girls Ages 6-16; Day — Girls 6-12

Riner, VA 24149. 3500 Camp Carysbrook Rd. Tel: 540-382-1670. Fax: 540-382-6134.
www.campcarysbrook.com E-mail: info@campcarysbrook.com
Kathy Baker, Dir.
Grades K-10. Adm: FCFS. **Appl due:** Rolling. **Enr:** 100. **Enr cap:** 100. **Staff:** Admin 4. Couns 25.
Features: Crafts Dance Drama Fine_Arts Music Aquatics Archery Canoe Caving Climbing_Wall Hiking Mountaineering Mtn_Trips Rappelling Riding Riflery Rock_Climb Wilderness_Camp Equestrian Fencing Swim Tennis.
Fees 2012: Res $865-4600 (+$25-200), 1-8 wks. Day $220, 1 wk.
Housing: Cabins. Avg per room/unit: 5. **Swimming:** Lake.
Est 1923. Inc. **Ses:** 6. **Wks/ses:** 1-8. Operates June-Aug. ACA.

Located on a 200-acre tract in the Blue Ridge Mountains, Carysbrook offers a program of group, individual, organized and informal activities that includes riding, fencing, gymnastics, crafts, hiking, canoeing, swimming, tennis, archery, dance, dramatics and music. Carysbrook provides instruction at five skill levels, from beginning through advanced, for each pursuit. The camper chooses her activities each day.

SIDWELL FRIENDS SCHOOL
RIVERVIEW
Res — Coed Ages 10-14

Tappahannock, VA.
Contact (Year-round): 3825 Wisconsin Ave NW, Washington, DC 20016.
Tel: 202-537-8133. Fax: 202-537-2483.
www.sidwell.edu/summer   E-mail: summer@sidwell.edu
Lauren Brownlee, Dir.
Grades 5-9. Adm: FCFS. **Appl due:** Rolling.
Features: Crafts Dance Drama Drawing Canoe Cooking Kayak Ropes_Crse Sail Yoga Basketball Lacrosse Swim Water-skiing.
Fees 2012: Res $975-1950, 1-2 wks.
Swimming: River.
Est 1996. Nonprofit. Religious Society of Friends. **Ses:** 2. **Wks/ses:** 1. Operates June-July.

Taking place on the campus of St. Margaret's School, the camp enables young campers to acquire new outdoor skills in a Quaker setting. Boys and girls participate in such beachfront activities as tubing, canoeing and kayaking. A variety of academic enrichment, athletic and artistic courses are also offered.

JAMESTOWN 4-H EDUCATIONAL CENTER SUMMER CAMP
Res — Coed Ages 9-13

Williamsburg, VA 23185. 3751 4-H Club Rd. Tel: 757-253-4931. Fax: 757-253-7231.
www.jamestown4hcenter.org   E-mail: smithm06@vt.edu
Marlie Smith, Prgm Dir.
Adm: FCFS. **Appl due:** Rolling. **Enr:** 212. **Enr cap:** 220. **Staff:** Admin 6. Couns 12.
Features: Environ_Sci Marine_Bio/Stud Writing/Journ Crafts Dance Media Painting Theater Aquatics Archery Canoe Community_Serv Cooking Farm Fishing Kayak Outdoor_Ed Riflery Ropes_Crse Sail Wilderness_Camp Woodcraft Basketball Football Lacrosse Soccer Softball Swim Volleyball.
Fees 2009: Res $175-200 (+$30-50), 1 wk.
Housing: Cabins Lodges. Avg per room/unit: 35. **Swimming:** Pool.
Est 1928. Nonprofit. **Spons:** Virginia Cooperative Extension. **Ses:** 9. **Wks/ses:** 1. Operates June-Aug. ACA.

The center provides traditional recreational camping, with hands-on learning sessions devoted to canoeing, marine science, kayaking and swimming, among other areas. Younger boys and girls (ages 5-8) may enroll in an introductory weekend camping program.

WASHINGTON

FOUR WINDS*WESTWARD HO
Res — Coed Ages 7-18

Deer Harbor, WA 98243. 286 Four Winds Ln, PO Box 140. Tel: 360-376-2277.
Fax: 360-376-5741.

www.fourwindscamp.org   E-mail: info@fourwindscamp.org
Paul Sheridan, Dir.
Grades 2-10. Adm: FCFS. **Appl due:** Rolling. **Enr:** 170. **Enr cap:** 170. **Staff:** Admin 10. Couns 90. Res 90.
Features: Crafts Creative_Writing Dance Fine_Arts Music Photog Theater Adventure_ Travel Archery Boating Canoe Kayak Riding Sail Wilderness_Camp Woodcraft Basketball Equestrian Lacrosse Soccer Swim Tennis Ultimate_Frisbee Volleyball Gardening.
Fees 2012: Res $975-4250, 1-4 wks. Aid (Merit & Need).
Housing: Cabins Tents. Avg per room/unit: 6. **Swimming:** Ocean.
Est 1927. Nonprofit. **Ses:** 2. **Wks/ses:** 1-4. Operates June-Aug. ACA.

Campers select activities from programs in sailing, canoeing, gardening, archery, riding, tennis and team sports, and the creative arts also play a prominent role in camp life. Boys and girls help plan their one- to six-day hiking, canoeing, sailing and kayaking trips. A junior session enrolls children ages 7-10; the regular four-week program enrolls campers ages 9-18.

HIDDEN VALLEY
Res — Coed Ages 7-15

Granite Falls, WA 98252. 24314 Hidden Valley Rd. Tel: 425-334-1040.
Fax: 425-397-0497.
Contact (Winter): 14314 274th Pl NE, Duvall, WA 98019. Tel: 425-844-8896.
Fax: 425-844-8302.
www.hvc-wa.com   E-mail: hiddenvalleycamp@earthlink.net
Todd McKinlay, Dir.
Adm: FCFS. **Enr cap:** 117. **Staff:** Couns 53.
Fees 2010: Res $1250-1760, 2-3 wks.
Est 1947. Ses: 3. **Wks/ses:** 2-3½. Operates June-Aug. ACA.

Hidden Valley features horseback riding, swimming, sailing, tennis, boating, canoeing, archery, arts and crafts, drama and mountain backpacking trips.

CAMP NOR'WESTER
Res — Coed Ages 9-16

Roche Harbor, WA 98250. PO Box 4395.
Contact (Sept-May): PO Box 668, Lopez Island, WA 98261.
Year-round Tel: 360-468-2225, Fax: 360-468-2472.
www.norwester.org   E-mail: norwester@rockisland.com
Sheila Tallman, Dir.
Adm: FCFS. **Appl due:** Rolling. **Staff:** Admin 3. Couns 80.
Features: Crafts Dance Music Theater Archery Bicycle_Tours Canoe Conservation Hiking Kayak Mountaineering Mtn_Trips Ropes_Crse Sail Wilderness_Camp Woodcraft Swim.
Fees 2012: Res $1975-4075, 2-4 wks. Aid 2009 (Need): $50,000.
Housing: Tents Tepees. Avg per room/unit: 4. **Swimming:** Ocean.
Est 1935. Nonprofit. **Ses:** 2. **Wks/ses:** 2-4. Operates June-Aug.

Nor'wester offers instruction in crafts, sailing, canoeing, kayaking, archery, mountaineering, bicycling, nature, Indian lore, drama and music. Other activities include sports, high and low ropes courses, backpacking, and four- or five-day trips for campers ages 13-16 that include a mountain climb and hiking, biking, sailing and canoeing to outlying islands.

WEST VIRGINIA

CAMP GREENBRIER FOR BOYS
Res — Boys Ages 7-18; Day — Boys 7-15

Alderson, WV 24910. Rte 2, Box 5A. Tel: 304-445-7168. Fax: 304-445-7168.
Contact (Sept-May): PO Box 585, Exmore, VA 23350. Tel: 757-789-3477.
Fax: 757-789-3477.
Year-round Toll-free: 888-226-7427.
www.campgreenbrier.com   E-mail: woofus@juno.com
William J. Harvie, Dir.
Grades 2-12. Adm: FCFS. Appl due: Rolling. Enr: 145. Enr cap: 145. Staff: Admin 6.
Couns 45. Res 60.
Type of instruction: Rem_Eng Rem_Math Tut.
Features: Crafts Creative_Writing Drama Fine_Arts Painting Aquatics Archery Canoe
Caving Climbing_Wall Fishing Hiking Kayak Mountaineering Outdoor_Ed Rappel-
ling Riflery Rock_Climb Survival_Trng White-water_Raft Wilderness_Camp Woodcraft
Baseball Basketball Cross-country Golf Lacrosse Soccer Swim Tennis Track Ultimate_
Frisbee Volleyball Watersports Wrestling.
Fees 2012: Res $2675-4625 (+$75-150), 3-6 wks. Day $1000-2000 (+$50), 3-6 wks. Aid
(Need).
Housing: Tents. Avg per room/unit: 3. Swimming: River.
Est 1898. Nonprofit. Ses: 3. Wks/ses: 3-6. Operates June-Aug. ACA.

The program includes team and individual activities, white-water canoeing, crafts, music,
conservation, woodcraft and hiking. A semistructured plan stresses an individual approach,
with the camper selecting his own activities. Boys who have completed grade 10 or 11 enroll
in a separate program, the Leadership Academy, that focuses upon leadership development
through outdoor activities. Greenbrier schedules hourlong daily tutoring sessions in math and
English for interested campers.

CAMP TALL TIMBERS
Res — Coed Ages 7-16

High View, WV 26808. Rte 1, Box 472. Tel: 304-856-3722. Fax: 304-856-3765.
Contact (Sept-May): 3735 Spicebush Dr, Urbana, MD 21704. Tel: 301-874-0111.
Fax: 301-874-0113.
Year-round Toll-free: 800-862-2678.
www.camptalltimbers.com   E-mail: funcamp@aol.com
Glenn Smith, Dir.
Grades 2-11. Adm: FCFS. Appl due: Rolling. Enr: 150-175. Enr cap: 200. Staff: Admin
6. Couns 40.
Features: Ecol Crafts Creative_Writing Dance Fine_Arts Music Painting Photog Theater
Aquatics Archery Bicycle_Tours Canoe Climbing_Wall Farm Fishing Hiking Kayak
Mountaineering Mtn_Biking Pack_Train Riding Riflery Rock_Climb Ropes_Crse Sur-
vival_Trng White-water_Raft Wilderness_Camp Badminton Baseball Basketball Cross-
country Equestrian Field_Hockey Football Golf Gymnastics Lacrosse Martial_Arts
Roller_Hockey Soccer Softball Street_Hockey Swim Tennis Track Ultimate_Frisbee Vol-
leyball Water-skiing Watersports Wrestling.
Fees 2012: Res $1100-8100 (+$160), 1-8 wks. Aid 2010 (Need): $10,000.
Housing: Cabins Tents. Avg per room/unit: 8. Swimming: Lake Pool.
Est 1970. Inc. Ses: 7. Wks/ses: 1-8. Operates June-Aug. ACA.

The camp provides boys and girls with individualized schedules. Campers engage in a
broad range of traditional camping pursuits. Tall Timbers schedules frequent trips to parks and
other local destinations.

TIMBER RIDGE CAMPS
Res — Coed Ages 6-15

High View, WV 26808. Rte 1, Box 470. Tel: 304-856-2630. Fax: 304-856-2325.
Contact (Sept-May): 301 Main St, Ste 2C, Reisterstown, MD 21136. Tel: 410-833-4080.
 Fax: 410-833-4083.
Year-round Toll-free: 800-258-2267.
www.trcamps.com   E-mail: trcamps@aol.com
Fred Greenberg, Pres.
Grades 1-10. Adm: FCFS. Appl due: Apr. Enr: 250. Enr cap: 250. Staff: Admin 20. Couns 100.
Features: ESL Lang Circus_Skills Crafts Dance Fine_Arts Music Photog Theater Aquatics Archery Bicycle_Tours Canoe Climbing_Wall Conservation Fishing Hiking Mountaineering Mtn_Biking Mtn_Trips Paintball Rappelling Riding Riflery Rock_Climb Ropes_Crse White-water_Raft Wilderness_Camp Wilderness_Canoe Woodcraft Baseball Basketball Cross-country Equestrian Field_Hockey Football Golf Gymnastics Lacrosse Martial_ Arts Roller_Hockey Skateboarding Soccer Softball Street_Hockey Swim Tennis Track Ultimate_Frisbee Volleyball Water-skiing Watersports Weight_Trng Wrestling.
Fees 2012: Res $2600-8400, 2-8 wks.
Housing: Cabins Lodges. Avg per room/unit: 12. Swimming: Lake Pond Pool River.
Est 1955. Ses: 5. Wks/ses: 2-8. Operates June-Aug. ACA.

Timber Ridge conducts complete athletic, performing arts, pioneering and waterfront programs. Campers may participate in gymnastics, riding, mountain climbing and rafting, and one- and two-night trips to Shenandoah National Park are scheduled by age group. A CIT program serves boys and girls entering grade 10.

CAMP ALLEGHANY
Res — Girls Ages 8-16

Lewisburg, WV 24901. PO Box 86. Tel: 304-645-1316. Fax: 304-645-1387.
Contact (Sept-May): PO Box 664, Fredericksburg, VA 22404. Tel: 540-898-4782.
 Fax: 540-898-5475.
www.campalleghany.com   E-mail: campghany@gmail.com
Bonnie E. Dawson & Samuel C. Dawson III, Dirs.
Adm: FCFS. Appl due: Rolling. Enr: 200. Staff: Admin 7. Couns 75.
Features: Crafts Dance Drama Aquatics Archery Canoe Caving Hiking Riflery Ropes_Crse Basketball Field_Hockey Lacrosse Soccer Swim Tennis Volleyball.
Fees 2012: Res $1166-4800, 1-6 wks.
Housing: Tents. Avg per room/unit: 4. Swimming: River.
Est 1922. Inc. Ses: 4. Wks/ses: 1-6. Operates June-Aug. ACA.

This traditional camp, the oldest girls' camp in the Virginias, is located in the Alleghany Mountains. Girls are divided into two main groups: junior camp (ages 8-12) and senior camp (ages 13-16). Campers select four focus activities per term. In addition to its regular sessions, Alleghany holds a family week and a weeklong minicamp for girls ages 7-11.

CAMP TWIN CREEKS
Res — Coed Ages 7-16

Marlinton, WV 24954. HC 82, Box 132. Tel: 304-799-6156. Fax: 304-799-4949.
Contact (Sept-May): PO Box 219, Elmsford, NY 10523. Tel: 914-345-0707.
 Fax: 914-345-2120.
Year-round Toll-free: 800-451-8806.
www.camptwincreeks.com   E-mail: info@camptwincreeks.com
Gordon Josey & Fran Josey, Dirs.
Adm: FCFS. Appl due: Rolling. Enr: 200. Staff: Admin 6. Couns 70.
Features: Computers ESL Crafts Dance Drama Media Archery Canoe Chess Climbing_

Wall Fishing Hiking Kayak Mtn_Biking Outdoor_Ed Riding Rock_Climb Ropes_Crse Sail Seamanship White-water_Raft Wilderness_Camp Woodcraft Aerobics Baseball Basketball Equestrian Field_Hockey Golf Lacrosse Roller_Hockey Soccer Softball Swim Tennis Volleyball Water-skiing Watersports.
Fees 2012: Res $2495 (+$145), 2 wks. Aid (Need).
Housing: Cabins. Avg per room/unit: 12. **Swimming:** Lake Pool River.
Est 1943. Inc. Ses: 4. **Wks/ses:** 2. Operates June-Aug. ACA.

The program has campers travel by cabins to different activity areas throughout the day, exposing boys and girls to all available activities. Older campers select their own programming.

CAMP RIM ROCK
Res — Girls Ages 7-16

Yellow Spring, WV 26865. 343 Camp Rim Rock Rd. Tel: 304-856-2869.
Fax: 304-856-3201.
www.camprimrock.com   E-mail: info@camprimrock.com
Joe Greitzer, Dir.
Grades 2-11. Adm: FCFS. **Appl due:** Rolling. **Enr:** 280. **Staff:** Admin 10. Couns 70.
Features: Crafts Dance Drama Drawing Fine_Arts Music Pottery Aquatics Archery Canoe Hiking Riding Basketball Equestrian Field_Hockey Lacrosse Soccer Softball Swim Tennis Volleyball Watersports.
Fees 2012: Res $1300-4200 (+$80), 1-4 wks.
Housing: Cabins. Avg per room/unit: 10-40. **Swimming:** Pond Pool River.
Est 1952. Inc. Ses: 12. **Wks/ses:** 1-4. Operates June-Aug. ACA.

Campers participate in small-group activities such as canoeing, swimming, archery, arts and crafts, tennis, drama and dance. Divisions are by age, grade level and experience. Although Rim Rock is a traditional camp, girls at all ability levels may take part in a complete equestrian program that features ring lessons, trail and river rides, dressage and jumping, and stable management.

WISCONSIN

CAMP MARIMETA FOR GIRLS
Res — Girls Ages 7-15

Eagle River, WI 54521. 3782 Gaffney Dr. Tel: 715-479-9990. Fax: 715-479-7290.
Contact (Sept-May): 501 Lakeview Dr, Mundelein, IL 60060. Tel: 847-970-4386.
Fax: 847-970-9766.
www.marimeta.com   E-mail: info@marimeta.com
Sandy Cohen & Terry Cohen, Dirs.
Adm: FCFS. **Enr:** 165-185. **Staff:** Admin 7. Couns 45.
Features: Crafts Dance Photog Theater Aquatics Archery Canoe Climbing_Wall Fishing Riding Riflery Sail Baseball Basketball Golf Gymnastics Martial_Arts Soccer Softball Swim Tennis Volleyball Water-skiing Watersports.
Housing: Cabins. Avg per room/unit: 14. **Swimming:** Lake.
Est 1947. Inc. Ses: 3. **Wks/ses:** 4-8. Operates June-Aug. ACA.

Located on Lake Meta, Marimeta offers an array of land sports and watersports, with particular emphasis placed on swimming, water-skiing, tennis and sailing.

CAMP MENOMINEE
Res — Boys Ages 7-16

Eagle River, WI 54521. 4985 County Rd D. Tel: 715-479-2267. Fax: 715-479-5512.
Contact (Sept-May): 1262 Arbor Vitae Rd, Deerfield, IL 60015. Tel: 847-914-0992.
Fax: 847-914-0994.
Year-round Toll-free: 800-236-2267.
www.campmenominee.com   E-mail: fun@campmenominee.com
Steve Kanefsky & Bari Kanefsky, Dirs.
Grades 2-9. Adm: FCFS. Appl due: Rolling. Enr: 180. Staff: Admin 5. Couns 45.
Features: Crafts Photog Archery Boating Canoe Climbing_Wall Fishing Kayak Riflery Sail Woodcraft Baseball Basketball Cross-country Football Golf Roller_Hockey Soccer Softball Swim Tennis Track Volleyball Water-skiing Watersports Wrestling.
Fees 2012: Res $2400-7595 (+$200), 2-8 wks. Aid 2010 (Need): $15,000.
Housing: Cabins. Swimming: Lake.
Est 1928. Inc. Ses: 5. Wks/ses: 2-8. Operates June-Aug. ACA.

Activities offered at this sports-oriented camp include land sports, swimming, water-skiing and canoeing. Campers may also participate in arts and crafts, woodworking and rocketry. For boys interested in photography, Menominee maintains a darkroom and a processing lab.

CAMP NICOLET
Res — Girls Ages 8-15

Eagle River, WI 54521. PO Box 1359. Tel: 715-545-2522.
www.campnicolet.com   E-mail: campnicolet@gmail.com
Georgianna S. Starz, Exec Dir.
Grades 2-11. Adm: FCFS. Appl due: Rolling. Enr: 100. Enr cap: 100. Staff: Admin 3. Couns 40. Res 2.
Features: Ecol Writing/Journ Crafts Creative_Writing Music Theater Aquatics Archery Bicycle_Tours Boating Canoe Climbing_Wall Community_Serv Conservation Exploration Hiking Kayak Mtn_Biking Riding Ropes_Crse Sail Scuba White-water_Raft Wilderness_Camp Wilderness_Canoe Yoga Baseball Basketball Equestrian Martial_Arts Soccer Softball Swim Tennis Ultimate_Frisbee Volleyball Water-skiing Watersports.
Fees 2012: Res $2200-8600 (+$150-350), 2-8 wks. Aid 2010 (Merit & Need): $75,000.
Housing: Cabins. Avg per room/unit: 10. Swimming: Lake.
Est 1944. Inc. Ses: 3. Wks/ses: 2-8. Operates June-Aug. ACA.

Located in Wisconsin's North Woods, Nicolet offers swimming, sailing, riding, tennis, crafts, water-skiing, various land sports, canoeing, kayaking, stand-up paddling and wilderness trips. Campers and staff represent approximately 20 states and countries.

TOWERING PINES
CAMP WOODLAND
Res — Coord Ages 7-14

Eagle River, WI 54521. 5586 County Rd D. Tel: 715-479-4540. Fax: 715-479-1119.
Contact (Sept-June): 242 Bristol St, Northfield, IL 60093. Tel: 847-446-7311.
Fax: 847-446-7710.
Year-round Toll-free: 800-882-7034.
www.toweringpinescamp.com; www.campwoodland.com
E-mail: info@toweringpinescamp.com; info@campwoodland.com
John M. Jordan & JoAnne Jordan Trimpe, Dirs.
Adm: FCFS. Appl due: Rolling. Enr: 70-100. Enr cap: 100. Staff: Admin 5. Couns 60.
Features: Computers Ecol Environ_Sci Crafts Dance Music Theater Aquatics Archery Canoe Cruises Hiking Riding Riflery Ropes_Crse Sail Seamanship Wilderness_Camp Wilderness_Canoe Basketball Fencing Gymnastics Lacrosse Soccer Swim Tennis Water-skiing Watersports.

Fees 2012: Res $2195-5395 (+$100), 2-6 wks. Aid 2009 (Need): $20,000.
Housing: Cabins. Avg per room/unit: 10. **Swimming:** Lake.
Est 1946. Inc. **Ses:** 4. **Wks/ses:** 2-6. Operates June-Aug. ACA.

Located a mile apart in the heart of the American Legion State Forest, Towering Pines for boys and Woodland for girls offer a full recreational and camping experience for campers ages 7-14, as well as a leadership training program for campers ages 15 and 16. Major features are horsemanship, tennis, sailing and seamanship, aquatics, team and individual sports, and the arts. A two-week introductory session serves children ages 7-9 only.

CAMP NORTH STAR
Res — Boys Ages 8-15

Hayward, WI 54843. 10970 W Boys Camp Rd. Tel: 715-462-3254.
Contact (Sept-May): 6101 E Paseo Cimarron, Tucson, AZ 85750. Tel: 520-577-7925.
Year-round Fax: 866-875-2442.
www.northstarcamp.com   E-mail: andy@northstarcamp.com
Robert Lebby, Susan Lebby & Andy Shlensky, Dirs.
Grades 3-10. Adm: FCFS. **Appl due:** Rolling. **Enr:** 150. **Enr cap:** 150. **Staff:** Admin 8. Couns 85.
Features: Ecol Environ_Sci Crafts Creative_Writing Filmmaking Music Painting Photog Theater Adventure_Travel Aquatics Archery Bicycle_Tours Boating Canoe Climbing_ Wall Conservation Cooking Exploration Fishing Hiking Kayak Mtn_Biking Mtn_Trips Outdoor_Ed Rappelling Riding Riflery Rock_Climb Ropes_Crse Sail Seamanship Survival_Trng Wilderness_Camp Wilderness_Canoe Woodcraft Baseball Basketball Cross-country Equestrian Field_Hockey Football Golf Gymnastics Lacrosse Martial_Arts Soccer Softball Swim Tennis Track Ultimate_Frisbee Volleyball Water-skiing Watersports Weight_Trng.
Fees 2012: Res $4875-8200 (+$150-300), 4-8 wks.
Housing: Cabins. Avg per room/unit: 8. **Swimming:** Lake.
Est 1945. Inc. **Ses:** 3. **Wks/ses:** 4-8. Operates June-Aug. ACA.

North Star conducts a highly individualized program of adventure, athletics, creative arts and watersports. An extensive wilderness tripping program is also available. Programming combines camper choice with the structure of a balanced and coordinated schedule.

CAMP NEBAGAMON
Res — Boys Ages 9-15

Lake Nebagamon, WI 54849. PO Box 429. Tel: 715-374-2275. Fax: 715-374-3310.
Contact (Sept-May): 877 Chardie Rd, Boise, ID 83702. Tel: 208-345-5544.
Fax: 208-345-5454.
www.campnebagamon.com   E-mail: info@campnebagamon.com
Adam Kaplan & Stephanie Hanson, Dirs.
Grades 4-10. Adm: FCFS. **Appl due:** Rolling. **Enr:** 240. **Staff:** Admin 12. Couns 100.
Features: Ecol Crafts Photog Archery Bicycle_Tours Boating Canoe Fishing Hiking Riflery Sail Wilderness_Camp Wilderness_Canoe Baseball Basketball Soccer Softball Swim Tennis Watersports.
Fees 2012: Res $4800-8100, 4-8 wks.
Housing: Cabins. Avg per room/unit: 10. **Swimming:** Lake.
Est 1929. Inc. **Ses:** 3. **Wks/ses:** 4-8. Operates June-Aug. ACA.

The camp features a program of recreational activities, leadership development, canoeing, hiking and wilderness trips. Nebagamon provides individualized instruction in such areas as swimming, team sports, crafts, photography, tennis and sailing.

CLEARWATER CAMP FOR GIRLS
Res — Girls Ages 8-16

Minocqua, WI 54548. 7490 E Clearwater Rd. Tel: 715-356-5030, 800-399-5030.
Fax: 715-356-3124.
www.clearwatercamp.com   E-mail: clearwatercamp@newnorth.net
Laurie Smith & Perry Smith, Dirs.
Grades 3-11. Adm: FCFS. Appl due: Rolling. Enr: 120. Enr cap: 120. Staff: Admin 3.
Couns 40. Res 50.
Travel: Canada.
Features: Art Crafts Creative_Writing Drama Photog Aquatics Archery Canoe Fishing
Hiking Kayak Mtn_Biking Outdoor_Ed Riding Sail Wilderness_Camp Wilderness_Canoe
Equestrian Swim Tennis Water-skiing Watersports.
Fees 2010: Res $3500-6400 (+$400), 3½-7 wks.
Housing: Cabins. Avg per room/unit: 5. Swimming: Lake.
Est 1933. Nonprofit. Ses: 3. Wks/ses: 3½-7. Operates June-Aug. ACA.

Clearwater offers a broad range of activities, with emphasis placed on sailing, aquatics, canoeing, riding and primitive camping. An extensive tripping program ranges from overnights for the younger campers to an extended hiking trip or a Canadian canoeing trip for older campers.

CAMP KAWAGA
Res — Boys Ages 6-15

Minocqua, WI 54548. 10000 Kawaga Rd, PO Box 90. Tel: 715-356-6262.
Fax: 715-356-5484.
Contact (Sept-May): 1415 Larchmont Dr, Buffalo Grove, IL 60089. Tel: 847-383-5643.
Fax: 847-383-5643.
www.kawaga.com   E-mail: braves@kawaga.com
Matt Abrams & Karen Abrams, Dirs.
Adm: FCFS. Appl due: Rolling. Enr: 185-200. Enr cap: 185-200. Staff: Admin 4. Couns
55.
Features: Writing/Journ Crafts Drama Music Aquatics Archery Boating Canoe Climbing_
Wall Fishing Hiking Mtn_Biking Outdoor_Ed Paintball Riflery Sail Wilderness_Camp
Wilderness_Canoe Woodcraft Baseball Basketball Football Golf Ice_Hockey Lacrosse
Roller_Hockey Rugby Soccer Softball Street_Hockey Swim Tennis Track Ultimate_Fris-
bee Volleyball Water-skiing Watersports Weight_Trng Wrestling.
Fees 2012: Res $1000-7500 (+$150-200), 1-8 wks. Aid (Need).
Housing: Cabins. Avg per room/unit: 5-10. Swimming: Lake.
Est 1915. Inc. Ses: 4. Wks/ses: 1-8. Operates June-Aug. ACA.

Kawaga offers a comprehensive program of land sports and waterfront activities. Other features include wilderness trips, archery, arts and crafts, and Native American lore. The weeklong rookie camp accommodates boys ages 6-10; older campers attend for four or eight weeks.

RED PINE CAMP FOR GIRLS
Res — Girls Ages 7-16

Minocqua, WI 54548. PO Box 69.
Contact (Winter): 5233 Balmoral Ln, Bloomington, MN 55437.
Year-round Tel: 715-356-6231, Fax: 715-356-1077.
www.redpinecamp.com   E-mail: rpc@q.com
Constance H. Scholfield, Exec Dir.
Grades 2-11. Adm: FCFS. Appl due: Apr. Enr: 120. Enr cap: 120. Staff: Admin 10. Couns
35.
Features: Crafts Dance Music Theater Aquatics Archery Bicycle_Tours Boating Canoe

Conservation Hiking Kayak Mtn_Biking Riding Sail Survival_Trng Wilderness_Camp Wilderness_Canoe Basketball Field_Hockey Gymnastics Martial_Arts Soccer Softball Swim Tennis Volleyball Water-skiing Watersports.
Fees 2012: Res $4000-7800 (+$150), 4-8 wks.
Housing: Cabins. Avg per room/unit: 8. **Swimming:** Lake.
Est 1937. Inc. Ses: 5. **Wks/ses:** 2-8. Operates June-Aug. ACA.

This deep-woods camp provides an individually planned program that includes watersports, daily equitation, tennis, gymnastics, archery, and arts and crafts. Three- to eight-day canoeing trips, as well as kayaking expeditions around the Apostle Islands, enable girls to develop proper techniques while learning safety precautions and how to use equipment correctly. Interested girls may take part in a horseback riding program for an additional fee. Red Pine conducts a two-week session for first-time campers entering grades 2-5.

BIRCH TRAIL CAMP FOR GIRLS
Res — Girls Ages 8-15

Minong, WI 54859. PO Box 527. Tel: 715-466-2216. Fax: 715-466-2217.
Contact (Sept-Apr): 10523 N Pine Tree Cir, Mequon, WI 53092. Tel: 262-238-1263.
 Fax: 262-238-1269.
www.birchtrail.com   E-mail: info@birchtrail.com
Barbara Chernov & Gabe Chernov, Dirs.
Grades 3-10. Adm: FCFS. **Appl due:** Mar. **Enr:** 200. **Enr cap:** 200. **Staff:** Admin 4. Couns 80.
Features: Ecol Environ_Sci Writing/Journ Crafts Creative_Writing Dance Fine_Arts Music Theater Aquatics Archery Bicycle_Tours Canoe Climbing_Wall Conservation Exploration Fishing Hiking Kayak Mtn_Biking Rappelling Riding Rock_Climb Ropes_Crse Sail Seamanship Survival_Trng Wilderness_Camp Wilderness_Canoe Baseball Basketball Equestrian Football Golf Gymnastics Soccer Swim Tennis Volleyball Water-skiing Watersports.
Fees 2011: Res $4800-8200, 4-8 wks.
Housing: Cabins. Avg per room/unit: 6-12. **Swimming:** Lake.
Est 1959. Inc. Ses: 3. **Wks/ses:** 4-8. Operates June-Aug.

Located on a 430-acre site, Birch Trail combines freedom of activity choice with a balanced and coordinated schedule. An extensive wilderness tripping program is also available. Lesson plans vary according to camper age and skill level. Wilderness trips are an important element of the program.

CAMP BIRCH KNOLL
Res — Girls Ages 8-16

Phelps, WI 54554. 3500 Dam Ln, PO Box 67. Tel: 715-545-2556. Fax: 715-545-2137.
Contact (Sept-May): PO Box 13, Stevens Point, WI 54481. Tel: 715-252-3825.
 Fax: 715-341-4261.
www.birchknoll.com   E-mail: cbkfun@aol.com
Gary Baier, Dir.
Adm: FCFS. **Appl due:** Apr. **Enr:** 150. **Enr cap:** 150.
Features: Art Archery Canoe Riding Basketball Cheerleading Gymnastics Soccer Softball Swim Tennis Volleyball Water-skiing.
Fees 2012: Res $595-8800, 1-8 wks.
Housing: Cabins. **Swimming:** Lake.
Est 1945. Ses: 9. **Wks/ses:** 1-8. Operates June-Aug. ACA.

Girls at Birch Knoll choose from a variety of session lengths and activities. The daily schedule includes five instructed activity periods, with options including team and individual sports, arts, and horseback riding. The waterfront program provides opportunities for swimming, canoeing, sailing, water skiing and wakeboarding. Parties, games, movie nights and trips to local amusement parks are also featured.

CAMP ANOKIJIG
Res — Coed Ages 7-16

Plymouth, WI 53073. W5639 Anokijig Ln. Tel: 920-893-0782, 800-741-6931.
  Fax: 920-893-0873.
www.anokijig.com   E-mail: anokijig@excel.net
Darin Holden, Prgm Dir.
Grades 2-10. Adm: FCFS. **Appl due:** Rolling. **Enr:** 315. **Enr cap:** 315. **Staff:** Admin 9.
  Couns 80.
Features: Geol Crafts Dance Drama Music Photog Adventure_Travel Aquatics Archery Boating Canoe Caving Climbing_Wall Community_Serv Conservation Farm Fishing Hiking Kayak Outdoor_Ed Paintball Ranch Rappelling Riding Riflery Rock_Climb Ropes_Crse Sail Survival_Trng White-water_Raft Wilderness_Camp Wilderness_Canoe Woodcraft Baseball Basketball Equestrian Golf Swim Volleyball Watersports.
Fees 2009: Res $515-595 (+$40), 1 wk. Aid (Need).
Housing: Cabins Dorms Lodges Tents. **Swimming:** Lake.
Est 1926. Nonprofit. **Ses:** 9. **Wks/ses:** 1. Operates June-Aug. ACA.

Anokijig's overnight camp features four types of programming: skill periods, campwide activities, sectional activities and directed free time. Individualized instruction is available during skill periods, while all-camp activities include group games, beach parties, cookouts, campfires, dances and so on. Sectional activities provide campers with an opportunity to join in group activities with boys and girls who live nearby. During directed free time, staff supervise all program areas; campers may either choose one pursuit for the entire week or divide their time among several.

CAMP HORSESHOE
Res — Boys Ages 8-16

Rhinelander, WI 54501. PO Box 458. Tel: 715-362-2000. Fax: 715-362-2001.
Contact (Sept-May): PO Box 1938, Highland Park, IL 60035. Tel: 847-433-9140.
  Fax: 847-433-9145.
www.camphorseshoe.com   E-mail: fun@camphorseshoe.com
Fran Shiner & Jordan Shiner, Dirs.
Grades 3-11. Adm: FCFS. **Appl due:** Rolling. **Enr:** 200. **Enr cap:** 200. **Staff:** Admin 10.
  Couns 70.
Features: Aquatics Archery Boating Canoe Climbing_Wall Fishing Hiking Kayak Mtn_Biking Riflery Ropes_Crse Sail Baseball Basketball Field_Hockey Football Golf Ice_Hockey Lacrosse Roller_Hockey Soccer Softball Swim Tennis Track Volleyball Water-skiing.
Fees 2009: Res $4550-7350 (+$350), 4-8 wks.
Housing: Cabins. Avg per room/unit: 8. **Swimming:** Lake.
Est 2003. Inc. **Ses:** 3. **Wks/ses:** 4-8. Operates June-Aug. ACA.

Located in the midst of Wisconsin's Northwoods region, Horseshoe offers a traditional program that allows boys to pursue individual interests while also taking part in group activities and team sports. Each week, campers choose two main activities, which are then alternated day to day. During the afternoon, boys engage in league play in various team sports. Evenings provide time for campwide events, while trip days feature either an excursion from camp or a special day at camp.

CAMP HIGHLANDS FOR BOYS
Res — Boys Ages 8-16

Sayner, WI 54560. 8450 Camp Highlands Rd. Tel: 715-542-3443. Fax: 715-542-3868.
Contact (Sept-May): 4146 Lawn Ave, Western Springs, IL 60558. Tel: 708-246-1238.
   Fax: 708-246-3216.
Year-round Toll-free: 800-868-3398.
www.camphighlands.com   E-mail: chmike@aol.com
Mike Bachmann & Andy Bachmann, Dirs.
Grades 2-10. Adm: FCFS. Appl due: Rolling. Enr: 120. Enr cap: 120. Staff: Admin 5.
   Couns 60. Res 80.
Features: Crafts Music Theater Aquatics Archery Boating Canoe Climbing_Wall Conserva-
   tion Exploration Fishing Hiking Kayak Rappelling Riflery Ropes_Crse Sail Wilderness_
   Camp Wilderness_Canoe Woodcraft Baseball Basketball Cross-country Football Golf
   Lacrosse Soccer Softball Swim Tennis Track Volleyball Water-skiing Watersports.
Fees 2012: Res $3000-6000 (+$75), 3-7 wks.
Housing: Cabins. Avg per room/unit: 6. Swimming: Lake.
Est 1904. Inc. Ses: 3. Wks/ses: 3-7. Operates June-Aug.

Located in the Northern Highlands State Forest, this camp offers waterfront sports such as
swimming, water-skiing, skin diving, sailing, windsurfing, canoeing and fishing. Land sports,
interest clubs, hiking, and canoeing and sailing trips are also featured.

CAMP FOREST SPRINGS
Res — Coed Ages 8-17

Westboro, WI 54490. N8890 Forest Ln. Tel: 715-427-5241. Fax: 715-427-5211.
www.campforestsprings.org   E-mail: youthregistration@campforestsprings.org
Brad Eidsen & Ruth Eidsen, Dirs.
Grades 3-12. Adm: FCFS. Appl due: Rolling. Enr: 185. Staff: Admin 5. Couns 24.
Features: Crafts Drama Fine_Arts Photog Archery Boating Canoe Farm Fishing Hiking
   Kayak Mountaineering Mtn_Biking Rappelling Riflery Rock_Climb Ropes_Crse Sail
   Wilderness_Camp Wilderness_Canoe Cross-country Soccer Softball Swim Tennis Ulti-
   mate_Frisbee Volleyball Watersports Ping-Pong.
Housing: Cabins. Avg per room/unit: 8. Swimming: Lake.
Est 1958. Nonprofit. Nondenom Christian. Ses: 9. Wks/ses: 1. Operates June-July.

Forest Springs offers various recreational pursuits on both land and water. Campers may
also earn ranks and awards in air riflery and archery. The camp schedules off-site kayaking,
canoeing, rock climbing and rappelling, and backpacking wilderness trips.

CAMP WEHAKEE
Res — Girls Ages 7-17

Winter, WI 54896. N8104 Barker Lake Rd. Tel: 715-266-3263. Fax: 715-266-2267.
Contact (Sept-May): 715 28th St S, La Crosse, WI 54601. Tel: 608-787-8304.
   Fax: 608-787-8257.
Year-round Toll-free: 800-582-2267.
www.wehakeecampforgirls.com   E-mail: info@wehakeecampforgirls.com
Bob Braun & Maggie Braun, Dirs.
Grades 2-12. Adm: FCFS. Appl due: Rolling. Enr: 100. Enr cap: 112. Staff: Admin 6.
   Couns 30.
Features: Crafts Creative_Writing Dance Drama Music Painting Photog Aquatics Archery
   Bicycle_Tours Boating Canoe Cooking Fishing Hiking Kayak Mtn_Biking Riding Sail
   Aerobics Badminton Basketball Cricket Equestrian Field_Hockey Gymnastics Lacrosse
   Soccer Softball Swim Tennis Volleyball Water-skiing.
Fees 2012: Res $1995-5995 (+$35-250), 2-6 wks. Aid (Need).
Housing: Cabins. Avg per room/unit: 8. Swimming: Lake Pool.

Est 1923. Nonprofit. Roman Catholic. **Ses:** 6. **Wks/ses:** 2-6. Operates June-Aug. ACA.

WeHaKee features horseback riding, swimming, watersports, land sports, arts and crafts, music and dramatics. Academic tutoring, overnight camping and canoeing trips, and a leadership academy for teens are also available.

CAMP TIMBERLANE FOR BOYS
Res — Boys Ages 8-15

Woodruff, WI 54568. PO Box 1188. Tel: 715-356-6022. Fax: 715-356-7599.
Contact (Sept-May): 6202 N Camino Almonte, Tucson, AZ 85718. Tel: 520-615-7770.
Fax: 520-615-7771.
www.camptimberlane.com   E-mail: mike@camptimberlane.com
Mike Cohen & Leslie Cohen, Dirs.
Grades 3-10. Adm: FCFS. **Appl due:** Rolling. **Enr:** 160. **Enr cap:** 160. **Staff:** Admin 6. Couns 50. Res 80.
Features: Crafts Fine_Arts Media Music Photog Aquatics Archery Canoe Climbing_Wall Fishing Hiking Kayak Mtn_Biking Mtn_Trips Riding Riflery Rock_Climb Ropes_Crse Sail Scuba Wilderness_Camp Wilderness_Canoe Yoga Baseball Basketball Equestrian Golf Gymnastics Soccer Swim Tennis Volleyball Water-skiing Weight_Trng.
Fees 2012: Res $4800-8150 (+$200), 4-8 wks.
Housing: Cabins. Avg per room/unit: 12. **Swimming:** Lake.
Est 1960. Inc. **Ses:** 3. **Wks/ses:** 4-8. Operates June-Aug. ACA.

Timberlane offers water-skiing, athletics, tennis, golf, gymnastics, scuba, riflery and archery. A camp radio station and instruction in pottery, rocketry, photography, and arts and crafts are also available. Three- to 12-day canoe, backpacking, sea kayaking and rock climbing trips vary in length and difficulty according to age and experience level.

Canada

BRITISH COLUMBIA

TAMWOOD INTERNATIONAL CAMPS
Res — Coed Ages 7-17

Whistler, British Columbia, Canada. 301-4204 Village Sq. Tel: 604-932-3611.
Fax: 604-938-9864.
Contact (Sept-May): 909 Burrard St, 3rd Fl, Vancouver, V6Z 2N2 British Columbia,
Canada.
Tel: 604-899-4480. Fax: 604-899-4481.
Year-round Toll-free: 866-533-0113.
www.tamwood.com   E-mail: home@tamwood.com
Marnee Tull, Prgm Mgr.
Adm: FCFS. Appl due: Rolling. Enr: 1100.
Features: Ecol ESL Canoe Kayak Outdoor_Ed Riding Rock_Climb Sail White-water_Raft
Golf Soccer Swim Tennis Ultimate_Frisbee Volleyball Watersports.
Fees 2012: Res Can$1979-8499, 1-6 wks.
Housing: Dorms. Swimming: Lake.
Est 1993. Ses: 6. Wks/ses: 1-6. Operates July-Aug.

Tamwood conducts a traditional camp for Canadian, American and international boys and
girls each summer. Specialized programs include English and French language camps, an
adventure camp, a tennis camp and a golf camp. All programs feature lessons in sports and
creative areas, cultural events, camping trips and sightseeing excursions to Vancouver.

ONTARIO

CAMP AK-O-MAK
Res — Girls Ages 7-16

Ahmic Harbor, P0A 1A0 Ontario, Canada. 240 Ak-O-Mak Rd. Tel: 705-387-3810.
Fax: 705-387-0077.
Contact (Sept-May): 14-441 Stonehenge Dr, Ancaster, L9K 0B1 Ontario, Canada.
Tel: 416-427-3171. Fax: 905-304-2982.
www.campakomak.com   E-mail: info@campakomak.com
Dianne Young, Exec Dir.
Grades 2-11. Adm: FCFS. Appl due: Rolling. Enr: 100. Enr cap: 100. Staff: Admin 5.
Couns 20.
Features: Aquatics Archery Canoe Climbing_Wall Conservation Fishing Hiking Kayak
Mtn_Biking Riding Ropes_Crse Sail Survival_Trng Wilderness_Camp Wilderness_
Canoe Baseball Basketball Cross-country Field_Hockey Football Golf Lacrosse Soccer
Softball Swim Tennis Track Volleyball Watersports.
Fees 2012: Res Can$1908-5763 (+Can$300), 2-7 wks.
Housing: Cabins. Avg per room/unit: 13. Swimming: Lake.
Est 1928. Inc. Ses: 4. Wks/ses: 2-7. Operates June-Aug.

Founded as a competitive swimming camp, Ak-O-Mak now offers a combination of
athletic instruction and traditional summer camping activities. Special sports sessions address
competitive flat-water canoeing and kayaking, as well as competitive swimming. Campers

may swim up to three times daily, individually and in groups, with instruction focusing on stroke enhancement, race planning and strategy, and mental preparation.

CAMP NORTHWAY
CAMP WENDIGO
Res — Coord Ages 12-16, Girls 7-11

Algonquin Park, P1H 2G7 Ontario, Canada. Cache Lake, Lock Box 10003.
Tel: 705-633-5595.
Contact (Sept-May): 294 Regent St, Box 1184, Niagara-on-the-Lake, L0S 1J0 Ontario, Canada. Tel: 905-468-4455.
www.campnorthway.com   E-mail: info@campnorthway.com
Brookes Prewitt & Joan Prewitt, Dirs.
Adm: FCFS. **Appl due:** Rolling. **Enr:** 7-51. **Enr cap:** 7-51. **Staff:** Admin 4. Couns 20. Res 24.
Features: Crafts Drama Aquatics Canoe Hiking Kayak Mtn_Biking Sail Wilderness_Camp Wilderness_Canoe Swim.
Fees 2011: Res Can$1482-4700 (+Can$38-152), 2-7 wks.
Housing: Tents. Avg per room/unit: 3. **Swimming:** Lake.
Est 1906. Ses: 7. **Wks/ses:** 2-7. Operates July-Aug.

In a wilderness setting, Northway offers swimming, sailing, canoeing, kayaking, arts and crafts, and dramatics. Northway's strong canoeing program, which serves campers of varying proficiency levels, is an integral element of camp life. Wendigo emphasizes canoeing trips of three to 10 days in length.

CAMP TAMARACK
Res — Coed Ages 7-16

Bracebridge, P1L 1W9 Ontario, Canada. 1391 Stoneleigh Rd, RR 2.
Tel: 705-645-4881. Fax: 705-645-3996.
Contact (Sept-May): 160 Steeprock Dr, Toronto, M3J 2T4 Ontario, Canada.
Tel: 416-782-0736. Fax: 416-789-5525.
www.camptamarack.info   E-mail: info@camptamarack.info
Rick Howard, Ellen Howard & Marc Cooper, Dirs.
Adm: FCFS. **Appl due:** Rolling.
Features: Ceramics Dance Film Music Theater Woodworking Archery Canoe Climbing_Wall Cooking Kayak Mtn_Biking Rock_Climb Baseball Basketball Football Golf Gymnastics In-line_Skating Martial_Arts Roller_Hockey Skateboarding Soccer Street_Hockey Swim Tennis Volleyball Water-skiing Watersports.
Fees 2009: Res Can$1200-5975, 1-7 wks.
Housing: Cabins. **Swimming:** Lake.
Est 1980. Ses: 5. **Wks/ses:** 1-7. Operates June-Aug.

This structured but flexible program, offered at a 1000-acre, lakefront location, features a wide array of waterfront activities, land sports and arts offerings. Programming combines group-oriented cabin activities with individual choice periods that enable campers to pursue areas of interest. All boys and girls receive daily swimming instruction, and Tamarack's direct connection with Zodiac Swim School results in a particular emphasis on this skill.

CAMP WENONAH
Res — Coed Ages 5-17

Bracebridge, P1L 1X1 Ontario, Canada. 1324 Bird Lake Rd, RR 3. Tel: 705-645-6163.
Fax: 705-645-5760.
Contact (Sept-June): 3584 Commerce Ct, Burlington, L7N 3L7 Ontario, Canada.

Tel: 905-631-2849. Fax: 905-631-2850.
www.campwenonah.com   E-mail: info@campwenonah.com
Mike Stewart & Jeff Bradshaw, Dirs.
Adm: FCFS. Appl due: Rolling. Enr: 200. Enr cap: 200. Staff: Res 80.
Features: Crafts Music Theater Aquatics Archery Canoe Climbing_Wall Fishing Kayak Leadership Outdoor_Ed Ropes_Crse Sail Wilderness_Camp Wilderness_Canoe Swim Tennis.
Fees 2010: Res Can$190-3080, ½-4 wks.
Housing: Cabins Tents. Swimming: Lake.
Est 1996. Inc. Ses: 10. Wks/ses: ½-4. Operates July-Sept.

The traditional recreational program at Wenonah follows a one-month session model, with two-week programs also available. First-time campers ages 5-7 also have a half-week option at the end of the summer. Boys and girls chooses three activities for morning participation from the following categories: water, creative, land, paddle sports and sailing. Afternoons provide the opportunity for each camper to engage in a selected activity for an hour. In addition, Wenonah conducts various cabin-based, section-based and campwide programs.

THE HOLLOWS CAMP
Res — Coed Ages 7-15

Bradford, L3Z 2A5 Ontario, Canada. 3155 13th Line, RR 2. Tel: 905-775-2694.
Fax: 905-775-2694.
www.hollowscamp.com   E-mail: info@hollowscamp.com
Stephen Fine & Janet Fine, Dirs.
Adm: FCFS. Appl due: Rolling. Enr cap: 60.
Features: Crafts Music Adventure_Travel Aquatics Archery Canoe Kayak Mtn_Biking Paintball Riding Ropes_Crse Equestrian Swim Tennis Watersports.
Fees 2012: Res Can$750-1800, 1-2 wks. Day Can$300, 1 wk.
Housing: Cabins. Swimming: Lake.
Est 1982. Inc. Ses: 6. Wks/ses: 1-2. Operates July-Aug.

Offerings at The Hollows include English riding, kayaking, canoeing, a ropes course, archery, drama, and arts and crafts. Tennis and swimming are integral parts of the program.

CAMP CAN-AQUA
Res — Coed Ages 7-15; Day — Coed 6-10

Cardiff, K0L 1M0 Ontario, Canada. 503 Beaver Lake Dr, PO Box 70. Tel: 613-339-2969.
Fax: 613-339-3207.
www.canaqua.ca   E-mail: info@canaqua.ca
Brett Moore, Dir.
Adm: FCFS. Appl due: Rolling. Enr: 130. Enr cap: 130. Staff: Admin 3. Couns 60.
Features: Crafts Photog Aquatics Archery Canoe Conservation Hiking Kayak Outdoor_Ed Sail Wilderness_Camp Wilderness_Canoe Woodcraft Soccer Swim Volleyball Water-skiing Watersports.
Fees 2012: Res Can$820-3050 (+Can$40), 1-4 wks. Day Can$185, 1 wk.
Housing: Cabins. Swimming: Lake.
Est 1981. Inc. Ses: 9. Wks/ses: 1-4. Operates July-Aug.

Offering more than 20 major land and water activities, Can-Aqua seeks to improve campers' social, activity and personal skills. Offerings are tailored to the age and ability of the participant. A program counselor structures the day for the youngest children, while all other campers choose their daily activities. Three- to six-day canoeing trips are available.

CIRCLE R RANCH
Res — Coed Ages 8-14; Day — Coed 6-14

Delaware, N0L 1E0 Ontario, Canada. 3017 Carriage Rd. Tel: 519-471-3799, 877-844-8738.
www.circlerranch.ca   E-mail: info@circlerranch.ca
Nigel Tracy, Dir.
Grades 1-11. Adm: FCFS. **Appl due:** Rolling.
Features: Crafts Archery Boating Canoe Farm Fishing Kayak Mtn_Biking Riding Ropes_ Crse Swim.
Fees 2009: Res Can$705-1340, 1-2 wks. Day Can$350, 1 wk.
Housing: Tents. Avg per room/unit: 4. **Swimming:** Pond.
Est 1966. Ses: 14. Wks/ses: 1-2. Operates June-Aug.

Circle R Ranch's main program, Western horseback riding, includes daily trail rides and horsemanship sessions. Campers may also participate in swimming, canoeing, field games, arts and crafts, hiking, kayaking and camp craft. The camp occupies 220 acres in the Dingman Creek Valley.

CAMP MI-A-KON-DA
Res — Girls Ages 7-16

Dunchurch, P0A 1G0 Ontario, Canada. RR 2.
Contact (Sept-June): 756 Mineral Springs Rd, Dundas, L9H 5E3 Ontario, Canada.
Year-round Tel: 905-648-9382, 877-642-5663. Fax: 905-648-1305.
www.miakonda.com   E-mail: plamont@miakonda.com
Pam Lamont & David Smith, Dirs.
Adm: FCFS. **Appl due:** Rolling. **Enr:** 98. **Staff:** Admin 1. Couns 30. Res 65.
Features: Ecol Crafts Dance Drama Music Aquatics Archery Canoe Climbing_Wall Conservation Hiking Kayak Mtn_Biking Outdoor_Ed Rock_Climb Ropes_Crse Sail Wilderness_Camp Wilderness_Canoe Woodcraft Swim.
Fees 2011: Res Can$1660-3145 (+Can$60), 2-4 wks.
Housing: Cabins Tents. Avg per room/unit: 4. **Swimming:** Lake.
Est 1955. Inc. Ses: 6. Wks/ses: 2-4. Operates July-Aug.

At Mi-A-Kon-Da, located on Birch Island in Lake Wah Wash Kesh (near Parry Sound), staff place emphasis on such outdoor activities as swimming, sailing, hiking, canoeing and kayaking. Girls formulate their own instruction programs. The camp schedules canoe trips of two to six days.   **See Also Page 36**

CAMP PONACKA
Res — Boys Ages 8-15

Highland Grove, K0L 2A0 Ontario, Canada. 376 Ponacka Rd. Tel: 613-332-4125.
Contact (Sept-June): 1674 Killoran Rd, RR 4, Peterborough, K9J 6X5 Ontario, Canada. Tel: 705-748-9470.
Year-round Toll-free: 866-766-2252, Fax: 705-748-3880.
www.ponacka.com   E-mail: info@ponacka.com
Anne Morawetz & Don Bocking, Dirs.
Grades 3-10. Adm: FCFS. **Appl due:** Apr. **Enr:** 155. **Staff:** Admin 15. Couns 40. Res 65.
Features: Crafts Drama Aquatics Archery Bicycle_Tours Canoe Climbing_Wall Fishing Hiking Kayak Mtn_Biking Riding Rock_Climb Ropes_Crse Sail Scuba Wilderness_Camp Wilderness_Canoe Woodcraft Basketball Equestrian Field_Hockey Soccer Street_Hockey Swim Water-skiing Watersports.
Fees 2012: Res Can$1850-3400 (+Can$100), 2-4 wks.
Housing: Cabins Tents. **Swimming:** Lake.
Est 1947. Inc. Ses: 6. Wks/ses: 2-4. Operates June-Aug.

Situated on a peninsula in Lake Baptiste, Ponacka offers swimming, canoeing, sailing, riding, water-skiing, crafts, nature lore, camp craft and land sports, among other activities. The program also includes one- to seven-day hiking and canoeing trips. Although sessions typically run for four weeks, boys ages 8 and 9 may attend for two weeks. All counselors are former campers.

CAMP AHMEK
CAMP WAPOMEO
Res — Coord Ages 7-16

Huntsville, P1H 2H2 Ontario, Canada. Canoe Lake, Algonquin Park, PO Box 10007.
Tel: 705-633-5573. Fax: 705-633-5574.
Contact (Sept-May): 59 Hoyle Ave, Toronto, M4S 2X5 Ontario, Canada.
Tel: 416-486-6959. Fax: 416-486-1837.
www.taylorstattencamps.com   E-mail: info@taylorstattencamps.com
Jason Kennedy & Jackie Pye, Dirs.
Adm: FCFS. **Appl due:** June. **Staff:** Admin 10. Couns 75.
Features: Crafts Theater Canoe Riding Sail Wilderness_Camp Wilderness_Canoe Basketball Swim Tennis.
Fees 2012: Res Can$2000-7550, 1-8 wks.
Housing: Cabins. **Swimming:** Lake.
Est 1921. Inc. **Ses:** 4. **Wks/ses:** 1-8. Operates June-Aug.

Located on two islands in Algonguin Park's Canoe Lake, these brother and sister camps provide a varied recreational program that is adaptable to individual needs. The camps are sufficiently distant from each other to function as independent units, but they are also near enough to facilitate intercamp interaction each Thursday. Tennis, archery, windsurfing, music, sailing, swimming, horseback riding, drama, and arts and crafts are among the daily activities. In addition, boys and girls may embark on canoeing trips of 20, 30, 40 or 50 days.

CAMP AROWHON
Res — Coed Ages 7-16

Huntsville, P1H 2G6 Ontario, Canada. Box 10002. Tel: 705-633-5651.
Fax: 705-633-5663.
Contact (Sept-June): 555 Eglinton Ave W, Toronto, M5N 1B5 Ontario, Canada.
Tel: 416-975-9060. Fax: 416-975-0130.
www.camparowhon.com   E-mail: info@camparowhon.com
Joanne Kates, Dir.
Adm: FCFS. **Appl due:** Rolling. **Enr:** 300. **Enr cap:** 300. **Staff:** Admin 15. Couns 125.
Features: Ecol Crafts Music Theater Aquatics Archery Canoe Climbing_Wall Conservation Fishing Hiking Kayak Outdoor_Ed Rappelling Riding Rock_Climb Ropes_Crse Sail Wilderness_Camp Wilderness_Canoe Woodcraft Baseball Basketball Equestrian Soccer Softball Swim Tennis Ultimate_Frisbee Volleyball Watersports Gardening Windsurfing.
Fees 2012: Res Can$2370-8225 (+Can$300), 2-8 wks.
Housing: Cabins. Avg per room/unit: 9. **Swimming:** Lake.
Est 1934. Inc. **Ses:** 5. **Wks/ses:** 2-8. Operates June-Aug.

Arowhon's flexible program incorporates waterfront pursuits, horseback riding, three- to 10-day canoe trips, nature lore, sports, drama, crafts and other traditional camp activities. Each day, boys and girls select their own programming for six activity periods. Skill development is an important aspect of the noncompetitive program.

SWALLOWDALE CAMP
Res — Coed Ages 7-15

Huntsville, P1H 2J6 Ontario, Canada. 635 Swallowdale Rd, RR 4.

Contact (Sept-June): c/o CISS, 439 University Ave, Ste 2110, Toronto, M5G 1Y8 Ontario, Canada.
Year-round Tel: 416-646-5400, 866-258-4303. Fax: 416-646-5403.
www.swallowdalecamp.com   E-mail: camps@cisscanada.com
Deanna Hoenselaar, Dir.
Adm: FCFS. Appl due: Rolling. Enr cap: 150. Fac 6. Staff: Admin 4.
Type of instruction: Enrich. Avg class size: 15. Daily hours for: Classes 2. Rec 3.
Intl program focus: Lang.
Features: ESL Art Crafts Dance Woodworking Archery Canoe Fishing Kayak Mtn_Biking Outdoor_Ed Sail Aerobics Baseball Basketball Soccer Swim Tennis Volleyball Watersports.
Housing: Cabins. Avg per room/unit: 10. Swimming: Lake.
Est 1943. Inc. Spons: Canadian International Student Services. Ses: 12. Wks/ses: 2-4. Operates July-Aug.

Swallowdale's program features five one-hour instructional periods daily. Nonnative English speakers may receive oral and written English as a Second Language instruction for two of the daily activity periods (for a total of 10 hours each week), then spend the other three periods engaging in traditional land and water offerings. Campers not requiring ESL instruction develop their skills in land- or water-based activities of their choosing. Evening activities, weekly campfires and overnight trips complete the program.

CAMP TANAMAKOON
Res — Girls Ages 7-16

Huntsville, P1H 2H5 Ontario, Canada. PO Box 10010. Tel: 705-633-5541.
Contact (Oct-Apr): 297 Lakeshore Rd E, Ste 2, Oakville, L6J 1J3 Ontario, Canada.
Tel: 905-338-9464.
Year-round Fax: 905-338-3039.
www.tanamakoon.com   E-mail: info@tanamakoon.com
Kim Smith, Marilyn Smith & Patti Thom, Dirs.
Adm: FCFS. Appl due: May. Enr: 200. Staff: Admin 1. Couns 80.
Features: Ecol Environ_Sci Crafts Photog Theater Fishing Kayak Mtn_Biking Ropes_Crse Sail Wilderness_Camp Wilderness_Canoe Woodcraft Swim Tennis Volleyball.
Fees 2012: Res Can$1905-3505, 2-4 wks.
Housing: Cabins Tents. Swimming: Lake.
Est 1925. Ses: 6. Wks/ses: 2-4. Operates June-Aug.

Located on Tanamakoon Lake, surrounded by lakes, rivers and forests, this deepwoods camp provides latitude for individual choice. Activities include kayaking, canoeing, sailing, woodcraft, tennis, archery, crafts, music, sketching and dramatics. Younger girls go on overnight and two-day canoe trips, older campers on longer canoe trips and three-day backpacking trips.

CAMP TAWINGO
Res — Coed Ages 7-16; Day — Coed 7-12

Huntsville, P1H 2N2 Ontario, Canada. 1844 Ravenscliffe Rd. Tel: 705-789-5612.
Fax: 705-789-6624.
www.tawingo.net   E-mail: camp@tawingo.net
Michael Pearse & Tia Pearse, Dirs.
Grades 2-11. Adm: FCFS. Admitted: 99%. Appl due: Rolling. Enr: 400. Enr cap: 400.
Staff: Admin 25. Couns 125. Res 25.
Features: Astron Ecol Environ_Sci Geol Sci Crafts Dance Fine_Arts Music Theater Aquatics Archery Boating Canoe Fishing Hiking Kayak Outdoor_Ed Peace/Cross-cultural Ropes_Crse Sail Survival_Trng Wilderness_Camp Wilderness_Canoe Woodcraft Badminton Baseball Basketball Cross-country Field_Hockey Football Golf Lacrosse Rugby Soccer Softball Street_Hockey Swim Tennis Ultimate_Frisbee Volleyball Watersports.

Fees 2010: Res Can$767-2294 (+Can$200), 1-3 wks. Day Can$235, 1 wk. Aid (Merit & Need).
Housing: Cabins. Avg per room/unit: 8. **Swimming:** Lake.
Est 1961. Inc. Ses: 7. Wks/ses: 1-3. Operates June-Aug.

Conducted on a 220-acre site on the shores of Lake Vernon, Tawingo's daily program includes an interest group period, afternoon recreational options and allotments of free time. Interest groups emphasize skill acquisition in the areas of nature, camp craft, swimming, canoeing and tripping. In the evening, campers participate in various recreational activities that are either campwide or organized by cabin group, age group or gender. Among these evening pursuits are campfires, musical productions, pioneer activities and crafts, night hikes and sporting events.

LAKEFIELD CAMP INTERNATIONAL
Res — Coed Ages 9-16

Lakefield, K0L 2H0 Ontario, Canada. c/o Lakefield College School.
Fax: 416-646-5403.
Contact (Sept-June): c/o CISS, 439 University Ave, Ste 2110, Toronto, M5G 1Y8 Ontario, Canada. Fax: 416-646-5403.
Year-round Tel: 416-646-5400, 866-258-4303.
www.lakefieldcamp.com   E-mail: camps@cisscanada.com
Tim French, Dir.
Adm: FCFS. **Appl due:** Rolling. **Enr cap:** 175. **Fac 7. Staff:** Admin 4. Couns 25.
Type of instruction: Enrich. **Avg class size:** 15. **Daily hours for:** Classes 2. Rec 3.
Intl program focus: Lang.
Features: ESL Crafts Dance Theater Archery Canoe Kayak Ropes_Crse Sail Baseball Basketball Soccer Swim Tennis Volleyball Watersports.
Housing: Dorms. **Swimming:** Lake.
Est 1985. Inc. Spons: Canadian International Student Services. **Ses:** 14. **Wks/ses:** 2-4. Operates July-Aug.

Lakefield combines a full recreational program with optional English as a Second Language course work for campers who require it. ESL students may receive between 10 to 15 hours of weekly instruction. All boys and girls participate in traditional activities that encompass the arts, waterfront pursuits and land sports. Wilderness education and leadership programming are available to those fluent in English.

CAMP OTTERDALE
Res — Coed Ages 7-15

Lombardy, K0G 1L0 Ontario, Canada. 30 Frayn Rd, RR 1, Box 309. Tel: 613-284-2700.
www.campotterdale.com   E-mail: campotterdale@sympatico.ca
Jeff Brown & Sue Brown, Dirs.
Grades 2-10. Adm: FCFS. Admitted: 100%. **Appl due:** Rolling. **Enr:** 160. **Enr cap:** 160.
Staff: Admin 1. Couns 60.
Features: Sci Crafts Drama Aquatics Archery Canoe Climbing_Wall Farm Kayak Mtn_ Biking Rock_Climb Sail Survival_Trng Woodcraft Basketball Golf Street_Hockey Swim Tennis Water-skiing Watersports.
Fees 2011: Res Can$900-3560 (+Can$125), 1-4 wks.
Housing: Cabins. Avg per room/unit: 10. **Swimming:** Lake.
Est 1955. Inc. Ses: 4. Wks/ses: 1-4. Operates July-Aug.

Otterdale provides instruction in a wide range of activities that includes sailing, canoeing, kayaking, tennis, archery, water-skiing, windsurfing, climbing, golfing and drama. Campers engage in six activity periods daily, with one reserved for swimming. Special activities, games, campfires, skits and regattas represent some of the popular evening pursuits.

HURONTARIO
Res — Boys Ages 5-16

MacTier, P0C 1H0 Ontario, Canada. Tel: 705-375-5306.
Contact (Sept-May): 1 Ridge Dr Park, Toronto, M4T 2E4 Ontario, Canada.
Tel: 416-488-2077.
Year-round Fax: 416-486-0865.
www.camphurontario.com   E-mail: hurontario@sympatico.ca
Pauline Hodgetts & Donald Marston, Dirs.
Adm: FCFS. Appl due: Rolling. Enr: 195. Enr cap: 195.
Features: Environ_Sci Sci Art Music Woodworking Archery Canoe Fishing Kayak Rock_
Climb Ropes_Crse Sail Swim Watersports.
Fees 2011: Res Can$845-3999, 1-7 wks.
Housing: Cabins. Swimming: Lake.
Est 1946. Ses: 10. Wks/ses: 1-3½. Operates July-Aug.

Hurontario takes advantage of its 300-acre tract in the Thirty Thousand Islands of Georgian Bay by conducting a varied selection of outdoor pursuits. Small groups of six to eight boys, together with a counselor and a CIT, stay together all day long throughout the summer, allowing for program flexibility. As part of Hurontario's tripping program, novice campers embark on three- to five-day trips within the nearby Massassauga Provincial Park, while more experienced boys strike out on successively longer excursions to more remote destinations.

KILCOO CAMP
Res — Boys Ages 7-15

Minden, K0M 2K0 Ontario, Canada. 10735-10737 Hwy 35. Tel: 705-286-1091.
Fax: 705-286-1206.
Contact (Sept-June): 150 Eglinton Ave E, Ste 204, Toronto, M4P 1E8 Ontario,
Canada. Tel: 416-486-5264. Fax: 416-486-3854.
www.kilcoo.com   E-mail: info@kilcoo.com
David Latimer, Dir.
Grades 2-10. Adm: FCFS. Appl due: Rolling. Enr: 224. Enr cap: 224. Staff: Admin 3.
Couns 100.
Features: Crafts Drama Music Aquatics Archery Boating Canoe Climbing_Wall Hiking
Kayak Mountaineering Mtn_Biking Rock_Climb Ropes_Crse Sail White-water_Raft
Wilderness_Camp Wilderness_Canoe Woodcraft Baseball Basketball Football Soccer
Softball Street_Hockey Swim Tennis Ultimate_Frisbee Volleyball Watersports.
Fees 2012: Res $1950-3600 (+$150), 2-4 wks.
Housing: Cabins. Avg per room/unit: 8. Swimming: Lake.
Est 1932. Ses: 6. Wks/ses: 2-4. Operates June-Aug.

Located on 165 acres, with over half a mile of shoreline on a protected bay in Gull Lake, Kilcoo provides ample opportunity for canoeing, sailing, kayaking, windsurfing, tennis, archery, nature lore, arts and crafts, music and athletics. The camp schedules three- to 14-day canoe trips.

ONONDAGA CAMP
Res — Coed Ages 6-16

Minden, K0M 2K0 Ontario, Canada. 1120 Rackety Trail, RR 3. Tel: 705-286-1030.
Fax: 705-286-6098.
Contact (Sept-June): 544 Eglinton Ave E, Ste 100, Toronto, M4P 1N9 Ontario,
Canada. Tel: 416-482-0782. Fax: 416-482-6237.
www.onondagacamp.com   E-mail: camp@onondagacamp.com
Duncan Robertson, Dir.
Adm: FCFS. Enr: 300. Staff: Admin 10. Couns 70.
Features: Crafts Dance Drama Aquatics Archery Canoe Climbing_Wall Fishing Kayak

Riding Rock_Climb Sail Woodcraft Basketball Equestrian Golf Soccer Swim Tennis Water-skiing Watersports.
Fees 2012: Res $1410-4444, 1-4 wks.
Housing: Cabins Tents. Avg per room/unit: 7. **Swimming:** Lake.
Est 1918. Inc. **Ses:** 8. **Wks/ses:** 1-4. Operates June-Sept.

Younger children at Onondaga follow a preset activity rotation that enables them to sample many pursuits, while older campers take part in a daily sign-up session in which they choose activities for the following day. Each day consists of five 50-minute periods. A weeklong wakeboarding and water-skiing camp is available.

CAMP WALDEN
Res — Coed Ages 7-16

Palmer Rapids, K0J 2E0 Ontario, Canada. RR 2. Tel: 613-758-2365.
Fax: 416-736-9971.
Contact (Winter): 158 Limestone Crescent, Toronto, M3J 2S4 Ontario, Canada.
Tel: 416-736-4443. **Fax:** 613-758-2427.
Year-round Toll-free: 888-254-4274.
www.campwalden.ca   E-mail: office@campwalden.ca
Sol Birenbaum, Dir.
Grades 2-11. **Adm:** FCFS.
Fees 2010: Res $2400-7100, 2-7 wks.
Est 1970. Ses: 4. **Wks/ses:** 2-7. Operates June-Aug.

Walden offers a comprehensive program of land sports and watersports, as well as visual arts, musical theater and outdoor camping.

CAMP MANITOU
Res — Coed Ages 7-16

Parry Sound, P2A 2W7 Ontario, Canada. 10 Camp Rd, RR 1. Tel: 705-389-2410.
Fax: 705-389-3079.
Contact (Sept-June): 2478 Yonge St, Toronto, M4P 2H5 Ontario, Canada.
Tel: 416-322-5888. **Fax:** 416-322-3635.
www.manitoucamp.com   E-mail: mark@manitoucamp.com
Jeff Wilson & Mark Diamond, Dirs.
Grades 2-11. **Adm:** FCFS. **Appl due:** Rolling. **Enr:** 400. **Enr cap:** 400. **Staff:** Admin 10. Couns 160.
Features: Ecol Writing/Journ Crafts Creative_Writing Dance Filmmaking Fine_Arts Media Music Painting Photog Studio_Art Theater Guitar Video Aquatics Archery Boating Canoe Climbing_Wall Community_Serv Fishing Hiking Kayak Outdoor_Ed Rappelling Riding Rock_Climb Ropes_Crse Sail Wilderness_Camp Wilderness_Canoe Woodcraft Yoga Baseball Basketball Equestrian Field_Hockey Football Golf Lacrosse Martial_Arts Roller_Hockey Soccer Softball Street_Hockey Swim Tennis Volleyball Water-skiing Watersports.
Fees 2012: Res Can$2475-8115 (+Can$300), 2-7 wks.
Housing: Cabins. Avg per room/unit: 10. **Swimming:** Lake River.
Est 1958. Inc. **Ses:** 5. **Wks/ses:** 2-7. Operates June-Aug.

Manitou offers approximately 35 activities in the following areas: land sports, watersports, visual and theater arts, and outdoor adventure. Campers of all ability levels receive instruction and support in their chosen activities. Each day consists of five programming periods (and one open period). Boys and girls may choose to pursue an activity every day, every other day or, on occasion, twice daily, thereby enabling campers to take part in as many as 10 activities at a time.

MUSKOKA WOODS SUMMER CAMP
Res — Coed Ages 7-17

Rosseau, P0C 1J0 Ontario, Canada. 4585 Hwy 141, PO Box 130. Tel: 705-732-4373.
Fax: 705-732-6430.
Contact (Sept-June): 20 Bamburgh Cir, Ste 200, Scarborough, M1W 3Y5 Ontario,
Canada. Tel: 416-495-6960. Fax: 416-495-1300.
www.muskokawoods.com   E-mail: info@muskokawoods.com
John McAuley, Pres.
Adm: FCFS. Enr: 500.
Features: Crafts Dance Drama Media Music Photog Adventure_Travel Archery Canoe
Climbing_Wall Fishing Kayak Mtn_Biking Paintball Riding Rock_Climb Ropes_Crse
Sail Wilderness_Camp Wilderness_Canoe Badminton Basketball Golf Gymnastics Ice_
Hockey Lacrosse Soccer Swim Tennis Volleyball Water-skiing Watersports.
Fees 2011: Res Can$929-1749, 1 wk.
Housing: Cabins Lodges. Avg per room/unit: 8. **Swimming:** Lake.
Est 1979. Nonprofit. Nondenom Christian. **Ses:** 9. **Wks/ses:** 1. Operates June-Aug.

This nondenominational Christian camp, located on 760 acres of woodland on Lake Rosseau, offers an array of sports and other activities. While the youngest boys and girls (ages 7 and 8) participate in a structured program, older campers may engage in a specialized session.

GLEN BERNARD CAMP
Res — Girls Ages 6-16

Sundridge, P0A 1Z0 Ontario, Canada. 2066 S Lake Bernard Rd. Tel: 705-384-7062.
Fax: 705-384-0155.
Contact (Oct-May): 206 Lord Seaton Rd, Toronto, M2P 1K9 Ontario, Canada.
Tel: 416-225-4166. Fax: 416-225-6036.
www.gbcamp.com   E-mail: info@gbcamp.com
Jocelyn Palm, Dir.
Grades 1-11. Adm: FCFS. Appl due: Apr. Enr: 250. Staff: Res 110.
Features: Astron Ecol Environ_Sci Art Crafts Photog Theater Aquatics Archery Canoe
Climbing_Wall Conservation Hiking Kayak Mtn_Biking Outdoor_Ed Riding Rock_Climb
Ropes_Crse Sail Wilderness_Camp Wilderness_Canoe Woodcraft Basketball Eques-
trian Golf Swim Tennis Volleyball Watersports.
Fees 2012: Res Can$915-2750, 1-3 wks.
Housing: Cabins. Avg per room/unit: 9. **Swimming:** Lake.
Est 1922. Inc. **Ses:** 7. **Wks/ses:** 1-3. Operates June-Aug.

Glen Bernard combines aquatic activities, outdoor pursuits and artistic offerings. Environmental education is an important aspect of the program. Special opportunities include theater and leadership programs and a 12-day wilderness canoe trip.

CANADIAN ADVENTURE CAMP
Res — Coed Ages 5½-17

Temagami, Ontario, Canada. Group Box 18, Adventure Island.
Contact (Year-round): 15 Idleswift Dr, Thornhill, L4J 1K9 Ontario, Canada.
Tel: 905-886-1406, 800-966-1406. Fax: 905-889-8983.
www.canadianadventurecamp.com   E-mail: info@canadianadventurecamp.com
Skip Connett, Dir.
Adm: FCFS. Appl due: Rolling. Enr: 130. Staff: Admin 2. Couns 23.
Features: Astron Ecol Crafts Dance Theater Archery Canoe Climbing_Wall Fishing Hiking
Kayak Rock_Climb Sail Basketball Gymnastics Soccer Swim Volleyball Water-skiing
Watersports Trampolining.
Fees 2012: Res Can$2090-7100 (+Can$400), 2-8 wks.
Housing: Cabins. Avg per room/unit: 8. **Swimming:** Lake.

Est 1975. Inc. Ses: 9. **Wks/ses:** 2-8. Operates June-Aug.

CAC offers a main choice between gymnastics, trampolining, water-skiing and general camping. An international staff guides campers in a wide variety of activities, among them canoe tripping, swimming, sailing, kayaking, giant water slides, theater, music and rock climbing.

CAMP WABIKON
Res — Coed Ages 6-17

Temagami, P0H 2H0 Ontario, Canada. Temagami Island. Tel: 705-237-8940.
   Fax: 705-237-8940.
Contact (Sept-May): 48 Delhi Ave, Toronto, M5M 3B7 Ontario, Canada.
   Tel: 416-483-3172. Fax: 416-483-4345.
www.wabikon.com   E-mail: info@wabikon.com
Marcello Bernardo & Margaret Bernardo, Dirs.
Adm: FCFS. **Appl due:** Rolling. **Enr:** 150. **Enr cap:** 150. **Staff:** Admin 6. Couns 60. Res 2.
Features: Crafts Dance Music Theater Aquatics Archery Canoe Conservation Exploration Fishing Hiking Kayak Mtn_Biking Ropes_Crse Sail Wilderness_Camp Wilderness_ Canoe Woodcraft Aerobics Badminton Baseball Basketball Football Lacrosse Soccer Softball Swim Tennis Ultimate_Frisbee Volleyball Watersports.
Fees 2012: Res Can$1365-2575, 1½-3 wks.
Housing: Cabins. Avg per room/unit: 8. **Swimming:** Lake.
Est 1944. Inc. Ses: 3. **Wks/ses:** 1½-3. Operates July-Aug.

Serving an international clientele representing approximately 30 nations, Wabikon offers a complete recreational program in a large-island setting. Boys and girls make program selections for three morning periods and two afternoon ones, and the schedule includes free time for additional choices twice daily. Out-of-town campers may take advantage of escorted transportation from Toronto, Ontario.

CAMP OCONTO
Res — Girls Ages 4-15

Tichborne, K0H 2V0 Ontario, Canada. Tel: 613-375-6678.
Contact (Sept-May): 49 Rosemead Close, Unionville, L3R 3Z4 Ontario, Canada.
   Tel: 905-470-2030.
Year-round Toll-free: 877-292-0630, Fax: 613-375-6216.
www.campoconto.com   E-mail: lisa@campoconto.com
Lisa L. Wilson & Bruce Wilson, Dirs.
Adm: FCFS. **Appl due:** Rolling. **Enr:** 220. **Enr cap:** 220. **Staff:** Admin 4. Couns 60. Res 64.
Features: Astron Ecol Crafts Dance Drama Fine_Arts Music Painting Aquatics Archery Boating Canoe Conservation Fishing Hiking Kayak Outdoor_Ed Riding Ropes_Crse Sail Wilderness_Camp Wilderness_Canoe Woodcraft Baseball Basketball Equestrian Football Soccer Swim Tennis Volleyball Watersports.
Fees 2011: Res Can$1490-3475, 1½-4 wks.
Housing: Cabins. Avg per room/unit: 4. **Swimming:** Lake.
Est 1924. Ses: 6. **Wks/ses:** 1½-4. Operates July-Aug.

At Oconto, the program provides opportunities for swimming, boating, canoeing, sailing, riding, tennis, land sports, crafts, music and dramatics. Horseback riding and canoeing trips are featured.

MEDEBA SUMMER CAMP
Res — Coed Ages 6-17; Day — Coed 6-15

West Guildford, K0M 2S0 Ontario, Canada. 1270 Kennisis Lake Rd, PO Box 138.
Tel: 705-754-2444, 800-461-6253. Fax: 705-754-1530.
www.medeba.com   E-mail: info@medeba.com
Steve Archibald, Dir.
Grades 1-11. Adm: FCFS. **Appl due:** Rolling. **Enr:** 132.
Features: Crafts Archery Canoe Caving Climbing_Wall Fishing Hiking Kayak Mtn_Biking Rappelling Riflery Rock_Climb Ropes_Crse Woodcraft Baseball Swim Volleyball.
Fees 2010: Res Can$275-659 (+Can$100), ½-1 wk. Day Can$189, 1 wk.
Housing: Cabins Lodges. Avg per room/unit: 8. **Swimming:** Lake Pond.
Est 1952. Nonprofit. Nondenom Christian. **Ses:** 10. **Wks/ses:** ½-1. Operates July-Aug.

This Christian camp conducts five outdoor adventure sessions for children of varying ages and interests. Campers choose among such instructional and recreational activities as juggling, rowing, woodworking, rocketry, drama, archery and frog catching. Medeba also has mountain biking trails, climbing towers, ropes courses and zip lines on site.

QUEBEC

WILVAKEN
Res — Coed Ages 6-15

Magog, J1X 3W2 Quebec, Canada. 241 chemin Willis. Tel: 819-843-5353.
Fax: 819-843-3024.
Contact (Sept-May): PO Box 741, Hudson Heights, J0P 1J0 Quebec, Canada.
Tel: 450-458-5051. Fax: 450-458-2581.
www.wilvaken.com   E-mail: wilvaken@wilvaken.com
Maya Willis & Dave Willis, Dirs.
Grades 1-10. Adm: FCFS. **Appl due:** Rolling. **Enr:** 100. **Enr cap:** 100. **Staff:** Admin 2. Couns 28.
Features: Ecol ESL Lang Crafts Drama Music Aquatics Archery Boating Canoe Conservation Hiking Kayak Riding Riflery Sail Wilderness_Camp Wilderness_Canoe Badminton Basketball Equestrian Soccer Swim Tennis Volleyball Water-skiing Watersports.
Fees 2012: Res Can$1800-6450, 2-8 wks.
Housing: Cabins. Avg per room/unit: 8. **Swimming:** Lake.
Est 1958. Inc. **Ses:** 9. **Wks/ses:** 2-8. Operates June-Aug.

Located southeast of Montreal, Wilvaken offers a traditional recreational program in a bilingual setting. French as a Second Language and English as a Second Language instruction aids those interested in improving their French or English. Boys and girls have the autonomy to choose their own activities, as the daily schedule is not overly structured. Campers may embark on three- to four-day canoeing or hiking trips. An English-style riding program is available for an additional fee.

CAMP NOMININGUE
Res — Boys Ages 7-16

Nominingue, J0W 1R0 Quebec, Canada. 1889 chemin des Mesanges.
Tel: 819-278-3383. Fax: 819-278-3107.
Contact (Sept-June): 112 rue Lippee, Les Coteaux, J7X 1J4 Quebec, Canada.
Tel: 450-458-1551. Fax: 450-458-1271.
Year-round Toll-free: 866-910-1551.
www.nominingue.com   E-mail: info@nominingue.com

Grant McKenna, Dir.
Adm: FCFS. **Appl due:** Rolling. **Enr:** 220. **Enr cap:** 220. **Staff:** Admin 3. Couns 80. Res 1.
Features: ESL Crafts Music Theater Aquatics Archery Canoe Climbing_Wall Kayak Mtn_ Biking Riflery Sail Wilderness_Camp Wilderness_Canoe Woodcraft Basketball Lacrosse Soccer Swim Tennis Volleyball Watersports.
Fees 2012: Res Can$850-4525 (+Can$175), 1-7 wks.
Housing: Tents. Avg per room/unit: 5. **Swimming:** Lake.
Est 1925. Inc. Ses: 13. **Wks/ses:** 1-7. Operates July-Aug.

Campers are divided into seven age groups, with programs planned to suit their needs and interests. Boys receive instruction in two areas of their choice each day. Nominingue features wilderness canoe trips ranging in duration from two to 10 days, depending on age. A nine-day family camp closes the summer season.

PRIPSTEIN'S CAMP MISHMAR
Res — Coed Ages 7-16

**St Adolphe d'Howard, J0T 2B0 Quebec, Canada. 1580 chemin Lac des Trois Freres.
Tel: 819-327-2260. Fax: 819-327-2441.**
Contact (Sept-June): 4999 Ste Catherine St W, Ste 220, Westmount, H3Z 1T3 Quebec, Canada. Tel: 514-481-1875. Fax: 514-481-7863.
Year-round Toll-free: 866-481-1875.
www.mishmar.com   E-mail: camp@mishmar.com
Avi Satov & Emerson Thomas, Dirs.
Grades 2-11. Adm: FCFS. **Appl due:** Apr. **Enr:** 225. **Enr cap:** 225. **Staff:** Admin 10. Couns 90. Res 100.
Features: Crafts Dance Fine_Arts Music Painting Aquatics Archery Boating Canoe Climbing_Wall Kayak Rock_Climb Sail Baseball Basketball Field_Hockey Football Golf Ice_ Hockey Soccer Softball Swim Tennis Volleyball Water-skiing Watersports.
Fees 2012: Res Can$2500-7990 (+Can$100), 2-7 wks.
Housing: Cabins. Avg per room/unit: 10. **Swimming:** Lake Pool.
Est 1941. Inc. Ses: 6. **Wks/ses:** 2-7. Operates June-Aug.

Located in Quebec's Laurentian Mountains, Pripstein's offers combination of watersports and athletic and creative activities. The waterfront program is especially strong, with instruction available in many boating pursuits. Land sports combine instructional activities with house leagues, in-camp tournaments and occasional intercamp competitions. The in-line skate park is particularly popular, and Pripstein's also maintains an on-site indoor ice arena for ice hockey and skating. The camp's arts program consists of arts and crafts, bead and jewelry making, pottery, music recording and jazz dance. Two-week sessions enroll campers entering grades 2-5 only.

CAMP OUAREAU
Res — Girls Ages 6-16

St Donat, J0T 2C0 Quebec, Canada. PO Box 1090. Tel: 819-424-2662.
Fax: 819-424-4145.
www.ouareau.com   E-mail: info@ouareau.com
Jacqui Raill, Dir.
Adm: FCFS. **Appl due:** Rolling. **Enr cap:** 134.
Features: Lang Crafts Dance Music Theater Aquatics Archery Canoe Climbing_Wall Hiking Kayak Mountaineering Mtn_Trips Rock_Climb Ropes_Crse Sail Wilderness_Camp Wilderness_Canoe Swim Tennis Watersports.
Fees 2011: Res Can$530-3315 (+Can$150), 1-4 wks.
Housing: Cabins Tents. Avg per room/unit: 4-6. **Swimming:** Lake.
Est 1922. Inc. Ses: 14. **Wks/ses:** 1-4. Operates June-Aug.

Located in the Laurentian Mountains, this bilingual camp emphasizes swimming, sailing and canoeing, with three- to six-day canoe trips featured. Other activities include tennis, archery, boardsailing, drama and crafts. The program provides a multicultural living experience for French- and English-speaking children. Six- and seven-year-olds attend for one week, while girls ages 8-16 enroll for at least two weeks.

CAMP EDPHY INTERNATIONAL
Res — Coed Ages 4-17

Val Morin, J0T 2R0 Quebec, Canada. 1200 14th Ave.
Contact (Sept-May): 203-920 Cure-Labelle Blvd, Blainville, J7C 2L2 Quebec, Canada.
Year-round Tel: 450-435-6668, 888-463-3749. Fax: 450-435-5851.
www.edphy-international.com   E-mail: info@edphy-international.com
Luc Dubois, Pres.
Adm: FCFS. **Appl due:** Rolling. **Staff:** Admin 8. Couns 150.
Features: Lang Circus_Skills Crafts Dance Aquatics Archery Bicycle_Tours Canoe Climbing_Wall Hiking Kayak Mountaineering Mtn_Biking Paintball Riding Rock_Climb Ropes_ Crse Sail Scuba Survival_Trng White-water_Raft Wilderness_Camp Wilderness_Canoe Baseball Basketball Equestrian Football Golf Gymnastics Martial_Arts Soccer Softball Swim Team_Handball Tennis Track Volleyball Watersports.
Fees 2012: Res Can$365-915, 1-2 wks.
Housing: Lodges. Avg per room/unit: 6. **Swimming:** Lake Pool.
Est 1965. Nonprofit. **Wks/ses:** 1-2. Operates June-Aug.

Edphy offers horseback riding, a circus workshop, canoeing, archery, tennis, swimming and sailing. Expeditions, biking, mountain climbing, tours, and courses in French and English are among the camp's other activities.

ASSOCIATIONS AND ORGANIZATIONS

ACCREDITING ASSOCIATIONS

ALBERTA CAMPING ASSOCIATION
11759 Groat Rd NW, Edmonton, Alberta, T5M 3K6 Canada.
Tel: 780-427-6605. Fax: 780-427-6695. E-mail: info@albertacamping.com.
www.albertacamping.com.

AMERICAN CAMP ASSOCIATION
5000 State Rd 67 N, Martinsville, IN 46151. Tel: 765-342-8456.
Fax: 765-342-2065. E-mail: psmith@acacamps.org. www.acacamps.org.

ASSOCIATION DES CAMPS DU QUEBEC
4545 Pierre-de-Coubertin Ave, PO Box 1000, Station M, Montreal, Quebec,
H1V 3R4 Canada. Tel: 514-252-3113. Fax: 514-252-1650.
E-mail: info@camps.qc.ca. www.camps.qc.ca.

BRITISH COLUMBIA CAMPING ASSOCIATION
c/o Sasamat Outdoor Centre, 3302 Senkler Rd, Belcarra, British Columbia,
V3H 4S3 Canada. Fax: 604-939-8522. E-mail: info@bccamping.org.
www.bccamping.org.

MANITOBA CAMPING ASSOCIATION
302-960 Portage Ave, Winnipeg, Manitoba, R3G 0R4 Canada.
Tel: 204-784-1134. Fax: 204-784-1133. E-mail: info@mbcamping.ca.
www.mbcamping.ca.

NEW BRUNSWICK CAMPING ASSOCIATION
440 Wilsey Rd, Ste 105, Frederickton, New Brunswick, E3B 7G5 Canada.
Tel: 506-853-3507. Fax: 506-450-6066. www.nbcamping.ca.

ONTARIO CAMPING ASSOCIATION
250 Merton St, Ste 301, Toronto, Ontario, M4S 1B1 Canada.
Tel: 416-485-0425. Fax: 416-485-0422. E-mail: info@ontariocamps.ca.
www.ontariocamps.ca.

SASKATCHEWAN CAMPING ASSOCIATION
3590 Castle Rd, Regina, Saskatchewan, S4S 6A4 Canada.
Tel: 306-586-4026. Fax: 306-790-8634. E-mail: info@saskcamping.ca.
www.saskcamping.ca.

ADVOCACY ORGANIZATIONS

AMERICAN HIKING SOCIETY
1422 Fenwick Ln, Silver Spring, MD 20910. Tel: 301-565-6704.
Fax: 301-565-6714. E-mail: info@americanhiking.org.
www.americanhiking.org.

APPALACHIAN MOUNTAIN CLUB
5 Joy St, Boston, MA 02108. Tel: 617-523-0636. Fax: 617-523-0722.
E-mail: information@outdoors.org. www.outdoors.org.

ASSOCIATION FOR EXPERIENTIAL EDUCATION
3775 Iris Ave, Ste 4, Boulder, CO 80301. Tel: 303-440-8844.
Fax: 303-440-9581. E-mail: admin@aee.org. www.aee.org.

EASTER SEALS
233 S Wacker Dr, Ste 2400, Chicago, IL 60606. Tel: 312-726-6200.
Fax: 312-726-1494. E-mail: info@easter-seals.org. www.easter-seals.org.

EPILEPSY FOUNDATION OF AMERICA
8301 Professional Pl, Landover, MD 20785. Tel: 301-459-3700.
Fax: 301-731-8733. E-mail: info@efa.org. www.epilepsyfoundation.org.

NATIONAL EDUCATION ASSOCIATION
1201 16th St NW, Washington, DC 20036. Tel: 202-833-4000.
Fax: 202-822-7974. www.nea.org.

WILDERNESS EDUCATION ASSOCIATION
PO Box 4554, Burlington, VT 05406. Tel: 802-448-1191. www.weainfo.org.

PROFESSIONAL ASSOCIATIONS

**AMERICAN ASSOCIATION FOR PHYSICAL ACTIVITY
AND RECREATION**
1900 Association Dr, Reston, VA 20191. Tel: 703-476-3430.
Fax: 703-476-9527. E-mail: aapar@aahperd.org. www.aapar.org.

ASSOCIATION OF CAMP NURSES
8630 Thorsonveien Rd NE, Bemidji, MN 8630. Tel: 218-586-2633.
Fax: 218-586-8770. E-mail: acn@acn.org. www.acn.org.

ASSOCIATION OF INDEPENDENT CAMPS
5000 State Rd 67 N, Martinsville, IN 46151. Tel: 765-342-8456.
Fax: 765-342-2065. E-mail: info@aiccamps.org. www.aiccamps.org.

CERTIFIED HORSEMANSHIP ASSOCIATION
4307 Iron Works Pky, Ste 180, Lexington, KY 40511. Tel: 859-259-3399.
Fax: 859-255-0726. E-mail: office@cha-ahse.org. www.cha-ahse.org;
www.chainstructors.com.

NEW YORK STATE CAMP DIRECTORS ASSOCIATION
c/o Pierce Country Day Camp, 37 Mineola Ave, Roslyn, NY 11576.
Tel: 516-621-0275. E-mail: info@nyscda.org. www.nyscda.org.

STUDENT YOUTH TRAVEL ASSOCIATION
8400 Westpark Dr, 2nd Floor, McLean, VA 22102. Tel: 703-610-1263.
Fax: 703-610-0270. E-mail: info@syta.org. www.syta.org.

RECREATION

AMERICAN CANOE ASSOCIATION
108 Hanover St, Fredericksburg, VA 22401. Tel: 540-907-4460.
Fax: 888-229-3792. E-mail: aca@americancanoe.org.
www.americancanoe.org.

BOY SCOUTS OF AMERICA
1325 W Walnut Hill Ln, PO Box 152079, Irving, TX 75015.
Tel: 972-580-2000. Fax: 972-580-2502. www.scouting.org.

CAMP FIRE USA
1100 Walnut St, Ste 1900, Kansas City, MO 64106. Tel: 816-285-2010.
Fax: 816-285-9444. E-mail: info@campfireusa.org. www.campfireusa.org.

CANADIAN CAMPING ASSOCIATION
2494 Rte 125 S, St-Donat, Quebec, JOT 2CO Canada. Tel: 819-424-2662.
Fax: 819-424-4145. E-mail: jeff@campwenonah.com. www.ccamping.org.

FOUNDATION FOR JEWISH CAMP
15 W 36th St, 13th Fl, New York, NY 10018. Tel: 646-278-4500.
 E-mail: questions@jewishcamp.org. www.jewishcamp.org.

GIRL SCOUTS OF THE USA
420 5th Ave, New York, NY 10018. Tel: 212-852-8000. Fax: 212-852-6517.
E-mail: mevans@girlscouts.org. www.girlscouts.org.

HOSTELLING INTERNATIONAL USA
8401 Colesville Rd, Ste 600, Silver Spring, MD 20910. Tel: 301-495-1240.
Fax: 301-495-6697. E-mail: hostels@hiusa.org. www.hiayh.org.

NATIONAL ARCHERY ASSOCIATION
711 N Tejon St, Colorado Springs, CO 80906. Tel: 719-578-4576.
Fax: 719-632-4733. E-mail: info@usarchery.org. www.usarchery.org.

NATIONAL FIELD ARCHERY ASSOCIATION
800 Archery Ln, Yankton, SD 57078. Tel: 605-260-9279. Fax: 605-260-9280.
E-mail: archery@iw.net. www.fieldarchery.com.

US SAILING ASSOCIATION
15 Maritime Dr, PO Box 1260, Portsmouth, RI 02871. Tel: 401-683-0800.
Fax: 401-683-0840. E-mail: info@ussailing.org. www.ussailing.org.

YMCA OF THE USA
101 N Wacker Dr, Chicago, IL 60606. Tel: 312-977-0031. Fax: 312-977-4809.
E-mail: fulfillment@ymca.net. www.ymca.net.

PROGRAM NAME INDEX

PROGRAM NAME INDEX

Program names are referenced by page number. Note that program names beginning with "Camp" are alphabetized under the next significant word in the Index.

Boldface page numbers refer to the optional Featured Programs of summer programs that subscribe for space. To facilitate the use of this section, refer to the separate index preceding that section. Featured Program cross-references also appear at the end of the free editorial listings of subscribing programs.

Yes, send me the most recent editions of:

Title	Price	Qty	Total
The Handbook of Private Schools	$99.00		
Guide to Private Special Education	$32.00		
Guide to Summer Camps and Summer Schools	$27.00		
Schools Abroad of Interest to Americans	$45.00		

Order Amount	Shipping	
$1-$50	$6.95	
$51-$200	$15.95	
$201-$300	$19.95	
$300+	6% of total	

Subtotal

US shipping (*see rates at left*)

TOTAL

☐ Check or money order enclosed (payable on a US bank)

☐ Bill me (organizations only)

☐ Visa ☐ MasterCard

Card # _____ Exp. Date _____

3-digit Security Code _____

Card Holder_____

Signature _____

Charge on your statement will read "ALY*ALLOYEDUCATION"

First Name   Last Name

Company Name

Street Address (no P.O. Boxes, please)

City   State   Zip

Country   Postal Code

E-mail _____

Daytime phone _____

GPS12

PORTER SARGENT HANDBOOKS
A division of Alloy Education
2 LAN Dr   Ste 100   Westford, MA 01886   USA
Tel: 978-842-2812   Fax: 978-692-2304
info@portersargent.com   www.portersargent.com

Follow @SummerPgmSearch on Twitter!